GW01057515

Employment Law in Europe

Employment Law in Europe

General Editors

Susan Mayne
Solicitor, CMS Cameron McKenna

Susan Malyon
Solicitor, CMS Cameron McKenna

With contributions from European practitioners

Butterworths
London, Dublin and Edinburgh
2001

United Kingdom	Butterworths, a Division of Reed Elsevier (UK) Ltd, Halsbury House, 35 Chancery Lane, London WC2A 1EL and 4 Hill Street, Edinburgh EH2 3JZ
Australia	Butterworths, a Division of Reed International Books Australia Pty Ltd, CHATSWOOD, New South Wales
Canada	Butterworths Canada Ltd, MARKHAM, Ontario
Hong Kong	Butterworths Hong Kong, a division of Reed Elsevier (Greater China) Ltd, HONG KONG
India	Butterworths India, NEW DELHI
Ireland	Butterworth (Ireland) Ltd, DUBLIN
Malaysia	Malayan Law Journal Sdn Bhd, KUALA LUMPUR
New Zealand	Butterworths of New Zealand Ltd, WELLINGTON
Singapore	Butterworths Asia, SINGAPORE
South Africa	Butterworths Publishers (Pty) Ltd, DURBAN
USA	Lexis Law Publishing, CHARLOTTESVILLE, Virginia

© Reed Elsevier (UK) Ltd 2001

A CIP Catalogue record for this book is available from the British Library.

ISBN 0 406 923 604

Typeset by Phoenix Photosetting, Chatham, Kent
Printed and bound in Great Britain by The Cromwell Press, Trowbridge, Wiltshire
Visit Butterworths LEXIS *direct* at www.butterworths.com

Foreword

Lawyers tend to be insular, and they tend to be conservative. They would prefer to shelter from the winds of change rather than to weather them – particularly when they blow from abroad. But there is now something approaching a gale embracing the country. The laws of the European Community as well as the decisions of the European Court of Human Rights are whistling through the dusty corners of English law. Labour lawyers are particularly affected – witness the considerable number of references to the European Court in discrimination and related issues.

This trend reflects and reinforces the truth that the countries of Europe are growing ever closer. Businesses cross frontiers, and so do their staff. A basic knowledge of the laws of these European countries – or at least ready access to that knowledge – is becoming increasingly important. This is especially relevant for the practical lawyer, advising companies or employees about the laws of a foreign state. But it is not only of interest to those in practice. It is also challenging for the more academically or theoretically minded, who like to reflect upon how different countries find different solutions to essentially common problems.

This book provides an ideal introduction to the employment regimes of 18 European countries. Each chapter discusses how a particular country deals with common employment problems, such as redundancy, unfair dismissal, holiday and sickness rights and so forth. This common structure greatly aids comparison of different regimes. The chapters are written by experts in the country concerned, all brought together under the guiding hand of the two editors, Susan Mayne and Susan Malyon. They are lawyers in CMS Cameron McKenna, one of the leading employment law firms in the country, where they have gained a wide experience in the field of labour relations.

The editors can be proud of a book which will be of real value to anyone involved in the field of comparative employment law. I warmly recommend it.

Patrick Elias
The Honourable Mr Justice Elias

Preface

This work is aimed at practitioners and others with an interest in employment law who wish to obtain a practical understanding of this subject throughout Europe. Increasing numbers of organisations have operations in various European jurisdictions and we, as lawyers, are frequently asked for advice as to how a particular employment issue would be dealt with in a different jurisdiction, not only from a legal perspective but also in terms of custom and practice. All too often, clients have remarked that although there would appear to be academic works on the subject of comparative employment law, there is little in the way of practical guidance.

This book is aimed at those with an interest in employment law within our own profession, in industry, and indeed within all areas of business, although we think it will have particular appeal for human resource professionals who manage transnational businesses concentrated in Europe. It will give those with an interest in the subject a sound and practical grasp of the legal systems in each European jurisdiction which is covered in the book together with a good understanding of the principles which apply. We have aimed throughout to provide straightforward answers to the most commonly-asked questions, and, where appropriate, we have provided checklists for those readers who may need to assimilate the information quickly. Where we believe it will assist the reader's understanding of a particular issue, we provide practical examples. For the reader who needs further information and who may wish to research a particular issue in greater depth, we have provided cross references and footnotes so that important references can be obtained where necessary. We have also reproduced a number of important European Community measures in the Appendices to this work for ease of reference.

Although we intend this work to be easily readable and digestible it aims to state more than the basic principles. We intend to make this a guide which enables our readers to have a real grasp of the nature of employment law in the various jurisdictions. Inevitably, the legal principles underlying modern employment law change rapidly. The practitioner who has an understanding of custom and practice has a far greater chance of remaining up to date than the practitioner who relies solely on being made aware of changes in the law.

Inevitably, there will be certain aspects of employment law which it is not feasible to deal with in this format. However, we hope that our readers will agree that we have concentrated on the most important and relevant matters to those who are required to advise on employment matters in practice. Some of our readers may require information in relation to the movement of workers throughout Europe, and to that end we have also included a section in this book in relation to UK immigration, produced by Julia Onslow-Cole. In addition, we have included consideration of social security implications in certain jurisdictions, where the relevant contributor believes this is of primary importance.

We would like to thank the following for their help and support: first and foremost, Caroline Humphries whose assistance and critical eye have been truly invaluable; our secretaries Terri Samuel, Glenda Goodwin (and other excellent secretaries in the group) for their hard work, patience and good humour, our CMS Cameron McKenna employment partners, Simon Jeffreys and Anthony Fincham, Marc Meryon for his help in particular on the UK collective rights section and support in general, Mark Gardner for his helpful comments and suggestions on the text, our colleagues at CMS Cameron McKenna (from trainees to partners) for their forbearance and encouragement and last and most certainly not least our families – our spouses (Marc and Mark), parents (Kenneth and Raquel Mayne and Jack and Pamela Malyon) and children (Rory and Elsa) who have all had to make sacrifices for this book to be written.

The law is stated as at 1 March 2001. Where possible, we have sought to highlight any possible changes in employment law or practice which are thought to be forthcoming at the time of publication.

Susan Mayne and Susan Malyon

CMS Cameron McKenna

Contents

Contents

Contents

Appendix 869

Index 987

List of Contributors

AUSTRIA
Dr Bernhard Hainz
CMS Strommer Reich-Rohrwig
Karasek Hainz
Phone: +43 1 40 4430
Fax: +43 1 405 92 00
Email: bernhard.hainz@cmslegal.at
Website: www.cmslegal.at

Dr Martin E Risak
Phone: +43 1 4277 35604
Fax: +43 1 4277 9356
Email: martin.risak@univie.ac.at
Website: www.univie.ac.at/juridicum

BELGIUM
Stanislas van Wassenhove and Michaël
de Leersnyder
CMS Derks Star Busmann Hanotiau,
Brussels
Phone: +32 2 626 22 00
Fax: +32 2 626 22 55
Email: svanwassenhove@cmslegal.be;
mdeleersnyder@cmslegal.be
Website: www.cmslegal.be

DENMARK
Klaus Ewald Madsen
Bech-Bruun Dragsted, Copenhagen
Phone: +45 33 143 333
Fax: +45 33 324 333
Email:
klaus.ewald.madsen@bechbruundragste
d.com
Website: www.bechbruundragsted.com

ENGLAND AND WALES
Susan Mayne, Susan Malyon and Julia
Onslow-Cole
CMS Cameron McKenna
Phone: +44 (0)20 7367 3000
Fax: +44 (0)20 7367 2000
Email: susan,mayne@cmck.com;
susan.malyon@cmck.com;
julia.onslowcole@cmck.com;
Website: www.cmck.com

NORTHERN IRELAND
Chris Ritchie
Kennedy's, Belfast
Phone: +44(0)28 9024 0067
Fax: +44 (0)28 9031 5557
Email: chris.ritchie@kennedys-law.com
Website: www.kennedys-law.com

FINLAND
Jan Kuhlefelt
Castrén & Snellman, Helsinki
Phone: +358-9-228 58 338
Fax: +358 9 228 58 371
Email: jan.kuhlefelt@castren.fi
Website: www.castren.fi

FRANCE
Pascale Lagesse
Freshfields Bruckhaus Deringer, Paris
Phone: +33 1 44 56 44 56
Fax: +33 1 44 56 44 00/01/02/03
Email: pascale.lagesse@freshfields.com
Website: www.freshfields.com

Hubert Flichy
Flichy & Associés
Phone: +33 1 56 62 30 00
Fax: +33 1 56 62 30 01
Email: hubertflichy@flichy-associes.com

GERMANY
Marion Keunster, Dr Ante-Kathrin Uhl
and Astrid Wellhöner
CMS Hasche Sigle Eschenlohr Peltzer
Shäfer, Berlin
Phone: +(49-30) 203 600
Fax: +(49-30) 201 60 290
E-mail: marion.kuenster@cmslegal.de
CMS Hasche Sigle Eschenlohr Peltzer
Shäfer, Stuttgart
Phone: +(49-0)711/9764-0
Fax: +(49-0)711/9764-900
E-mail: Kathrin.uhl@cmslegal.de;
Astrid.wellhoener@cmslegal.de
Website: www.cmslegal.de

IRELAND
James Trueick and Jennifer Cashman
A & L Goodbody, Dublin
Phone: +353 1 649 2000
Fax: +353 1 649 2649
Email: jtrueick@algoodbody.ie;
jcashman@algoodbody.ie
Website: www.algoodbody.ie

ITALY
Franco Toffoletto
Toffoletto & Soci
Phone: +39 02 541.641
Fax: +39 02 541 64 500
Email: f.toffoletto@toffoletto.it
Website: www.toffoletto.it

LUXEMBOURG
Guy Arendt and Anne Morel
Bonn & Schmitt & Steichen
Phone: +352 45 58 58-1
Fax: +352 45 58 59
Email: garendt@bss.law.lu;
amorel@bsslaw.lu

THE NETHERLANDS
Jos W M Pothof
CMS Derks Star Busmann Hanotiau,
Utrecht
Phone: +31 30 212 1645
Fax: +31 30 212 1165
Email: j.pothof@cmsderks.nl
Website: www.derks.nl

NORWAY
Jan Tormod Dege and Erik Aas
Brækhus Dege, Oslo
Phone: +47 23 23 90 90
Fax: +47 22 83 60 60
Email: dege@brakhusdege.no;
aas@brakhusdege.no
Website: www.brakhusdege.no

PORTUGAL
Carlos Costa e Silva
Barrocas & Alves Pereira, Lisbon
Phone: +351 21 384 33 00
Fax: +351 21 387 02 65
Email: Bap-
lis@mail.telepac.pt;costaesilva@bap.pt

SCOTLAND
Alexander M S Green
CMS Cameron McKenna, Aberdeen
Phone: +44(0)1224 622 002
Fax: +44(0)1224 622 066
Email: asg@cmck.com
Website: www.cmck.com

SPAIN
Lourdes Martin, Marina Mengotti and
Juan Reyes Herreros
Uria & Menéndez, Madrid
Phone: + 34 91 586 03 34
Fax: + 34 915 860 403
Email: Lourdes at lmf@uria.com;
Marina at mme@uria.com;Juan at
jrh@uria.com
Website: www.uria.com

SWEDEN
Sven Erfors
Lindh Stabell Horten KB, Stockholm
Phone: +46 8 701 7800
Fax: +46 8 796 8223
Email: Sven.Efors@lindhs.se
Website: www.lsh-law.com

SWITZERLAND
Dr Rudolf von Erlach and Cyrill
P Rigamonti
CMS von Erlach Klainguti Stettler
Wille, Zürich, Switzerland
Phone: +41 1 285 11 11
Fax: +41 1 285 11 22
Email: office@vonerlach.ch;
r.vonerlach@vonerlach.ch
Website: www.vonerlach.ch

Table of Statutes

Table of Statutory Instruments

Table of EU Legislation

Cases

J

Jenkins v Kingsgate (Clothing Productions) Ltd: 96/80 [1981] 1 WLR 972, [1981] ECR 911, [1981] 2 CMLR 24, [1981] ICR 592, [1981] IRLR 228, 125 Sol Jo 442, ECJ B5.2.2; E5.5.14

Jones v Associated Tunnelling Co Ltd [1981] IRLR 477, EAT E1.2.3, E1.2.26

Jones v Governing Body of Burdett Coutts School [1997] ICR 390, 571 IRLB 9, EAT; revsd [1999] ICR 38, [1998] IRLR 521, [1998] 18 LS Gaz R 32, 142 Sol Jo LB 142, CA E6.5.15

Jones v Tower Boot Co Ltd [1997] 2 All ER 406, [1997] ICR 254, [1997] IRLR 168, [1997] NLJR 60, CA E5.2.23

Jowett (Angus) & Co Ltd v National Union of Tailors and Garment Workers [1985] ICR 646, [1985] IRLR 326, EAT E9.7.5

Judgment 1994/317 of 28 November 1994 . . . . Q5.2.3

Judgment of the Superior Court of Justice of Basque Country 16 June 1993 . . . . Q5.2.2

K

Kaempf v Schmit CSJ July 1 1981 . . . . L9.1.13

Kenny v Hampshire Constabulary [1999] ICR 27, [1999] IRLR 76, EAT E5.3.14

Kerry Foods Ltd v Creber [2000] ICR 556, [2000] IRLR 10, EAT E9.7.5

Khanum v Mid-Glamorgan Area Health Authority [1979] ICR 40, [1978] IRLR 215, 13 ITR 303, EAT E6.3.17

King v Great Britain-China Centre [1992] ICR 516, [1991] IRLR 513, CA E5.2.7

L

Labour Judge of Milano, February 4 1994, reported in Lav. Giur Review 1994 . . . . K4.2.6

Lassman v Secretary of State for Trade and Industry [1999] ICR 416, [1999] IRLR 413, EAT; revsd [2000] ICR 1109, sub nom Secretary of State for Trade and Industry v Lassman (Pan Graphics Industries Ltd, in receivership) [2000] IRLR 411, CA E6.5.17

Laws v London Chronicle (Indicator Newspapers) Ltd [1959] 2 All ER 285, [1959] 1 WLR 698, 103 Sol Jo 470, CA E1.2.12

Ledernes Hovedorganisation (acting for Rygard) v Dansk Arbejdsgiverforening (acting for Stø Mølle Akustik A/S): C-48/94 [1995] ECR I-2745, [1996] 3 CMLR 45, [1996] ICR 333, [1996] IRLR 51, ECJ E9.2.1; L9.1.8

Leonard (Cyril) & Co v Simo Securities Trust Ltd [1971] 3 All ER 1313, [1972] 1 WLR 80, 115 Sol Jo 911, CA E1.4.5

Leverton v Clwyd County Council [1989] AC 706, [1989] 2 WLR 47, [1988] 2 CMLR 811, 87 LGR 269, [1989] ICR 33, [1988] IRLR 239, CA; affd [1989] AC 706, [1989] 1 All ER 78, [1989] 2 WLR 47, 87 LGR 269, [1989] ICR 33, [1989] IRLR 28, 133 Sol Jo 45, [1989] 19 LS Gaz R 41, HL E5.5.11

Levez v TH Jennings (Harlow Pools) Ltd: C-326/96 [1998] ECR I-7835, [1999] All ER (EC) 1, [1999] 2 CMLR 363, [1999] ICR 521, [1999] IRLR 36, 608 IRLB 3, ECJ; apld sub nom Levez and Hicking v TH Jennings (Harlow Pools) Ltd and Basford Group Ltd (in receivership) [1999] 3 CMLR 715, sub nom Levez v TH Jennings (Harlow Pools) Ltd [2000] ICR 58, sub nom Levez v TH Jennings (Harlow Pools) Ltd (No 2) [1999] IRLR 764, 629 IRLB 7, EAT E5.5.16

Lock v Cardiff Railway Co Ltd [1998] IRLR 358, 599 IRLB 6, EAT E1.2.7, E6.3.18

Longden v Ferrari Ltd [1994] ICR 443, [1994] BCC 250, sub nom Longden and Paisley v Ferrari Ltd and Kennedy International Ltd [1994] IRLR 157, EAT E9.2.7

Lunt v Merseyside TEC Ltd [1999] ICR 17, [1999] IRLR 458, EAT E11.3.2

Lustig-Prean and Beckett v United Kingdom (1999) 29 EHRR 548, ECtHR E13.1.6

M

MSF v GEC Ferranti (Defence Systems) Ltd (No 2) [1994] IRLR 113, EAT E6.6.4

MacDonald v Ministry of Defence [2001] 1 All ER 620, [2001] ICR 1, [2000] IRLR 748, EAT E5.2.37

Malik v Bank of Credit and Commerce International SA (in liquidation) [1998] AC 20, [1997] 3 All ER 1, [1997] 3 WLR 95, [1997] ICR 606, [1997] IRLR 462, [1997] 94 LS Gaz R 33, [1997] NLJR 917, HL E1.4.3; J6.2.1

N

O

P

Decisions of the European Court of Justice are listed below numerically. These decisions are also included in the preceding alphabetical list.

A   European Community Law – an Overview

1.1   Background

A1.1.1   The impact of European Community or EC law on employment in the member states cannot be underestimated. Employment is one of the key areas of involvement of the EC in member states' affairs, being a matter of social policy as well as an economic factor.

A1.1.2   Article 2 of the Treaty of Rome[1] establishing the EC (the EC Treaty) makes specific reference to the objectives of achieving a high level of employment and social protection as well as equality between men and women.

[1]   This Treaty was amended by the Treaty of Amsterdam, which came into force on 1 May 1999, and its provisions renumbered.

A1.1.3   EC employment law is in itself a vast subject, and it is not the intention of this overview to explain every aspect, but rather to provide an explanation of key terms and concepts that the reader will encounter in this book.

1.2   The Member States

A1.2.1   The member states of the EC are France, Germany, the Netherlands, Belgium, Luxembourg, Italy, the UK, Ireland, Spain, Portugal, Greece, Denmark, Austria, Finland and Sweden.

1.3   EC Institutions

A1.3.1   The four main institutions of the European Community are set out below.

THE COUNCIL OF MINISTERS

A1.3.2   The Council of Ministers is made up of Ministers from the government of each member state. It acts as the decision-making body of the EC, voting on proposals put forward by the Commission. A President heads the Council, and each member state has the opportunity to hold the presidency in turn. Where matters of employment policy are to be discussed, the relevant Ministers would be the employment Ministers of each respective member state.

THE COMMISSION

A1.3.3   The Commission implements the decisions made by the Council of Ministers. It is composed of 20 members, or Commissioners, who are nationals of the member states. France, Germany, Italy, Spain and the UK have two Commissioners; the other member states have one each.

A1.3.4 Each Commissioner has a specific area of responsibility for formulating EC policy. The Commissioners must act in the interests of the EC as a whole, not in the national interests of their respective member states. The member states appoint their Commissioners for fixed five-year terms, which may be renewed.

A1.3.5 The Commission is required to ensure that the treaty provisions are applied, make recommendations and deliver opinions as to Treaty matters, take decisions as to the measures to be taken by the Council and the European Parliament, and implement the rules made by the Council. The Commission could therefore, for example, take action against a member state for its failure to implement a provision of EC law as part of its national law.

THE EUROPEAN PARLIAMENT

A1.3.6 The Parliament is composed of members from each member state, directly elected at national level. There are currently 626 members, or MEPs. The Parliament is responsible for exercising democratic control over the EC institutions. It may suggest amendments to certain legislative measures proposed by the Council, and under the co-decision procedure may even veto legislation in a number of areas, particularly measures intended to develop the single market. The Treaty of Amsterdam has extended the areas in which the co-decision procedure may be used.

THE EUROPEAN COURT OF JUSTICE

A1.3.7 The European Court of Justice or ECJ is comprised of 15 Judges and 8 Advocates General, and is headed by a President. Its responsibility is to ensure the correct interpretation and application of EC law by the member states and by the other EC institutions.

A1.3.8 The Advocates General act as independent assessors of claims and actions brought before the ECJ, and assist the ECJ in reaching an opinion. Although the Advocate General will reach a conclusion on each case brought before the ECJ, the ECJ is not required to follow the opinion and may reach an entirely different conclusion (as happened for example in the *Grant* case).[1]

[1] See para **E5.2.35**.

A1.3.9 An action may be brought before the ECJ against a member state that is alleged to have failed to fulfil a Treaty obligation. Such an action could be commenced either by the Commission or by another member state.

A1.3.10 Alternatively, the ECJ has the power to review any act of an EC institution (such as the Council or Commission) that is alleged to be contrary to EC law. Any act that is found to be contrary to EC law may be annulled by the ECJ.

A1.3.11 The national courts of member states may also refer the interpretation of a point of EC law to the ECJ for a ruling. This is an important function. Once the ECJ has given its decision on interpretation, the matter is returned to the national court that then applies the given interpretation to the facts and makes its decision.

A1.3.12   Finally, the ECJ may hear cases brought against the EC by individuals or by member states alleging loss suffered as a result of EC actions.

1.4   Sources of EC Law

A1.4.1   EC law is based on the following sources: treaties, regulations, directives, ECJ decisions, and recommendations and opinions.

A1.4.2   Treaties are the foundation and primary source of EC law. The EC Treaty is of particular importance in employment law, stating for example the right of male and female workers to receive equal pay for equal work.[1]

[1]   Article 141 EC Treaty, formerly art 119.

A1.4.3   Regulations are binding in their entirety and directly applicable in all member states. There is therefore no need for member states to implement regulations by introducing any legislation of their own to bring them into effect.

A1.4.4   Directives are binding on member states as to the result to be achieved. However, it is left to each member state to decide the form and method by which this is to be achieved.

A1.4.5   A decision of the ECJ is binding on the party to whom it is addressed. Recommendations and opinions have no binding force.

A1.4.6   Certain EC rights may be enforced by individuals despite the fact that the rights in question have not been transposed into national law. This is described as the principle of direct applicability, or 'direct effect'. Regulations are, as stated above, directly applicable and therefore enforceable in this way. Other rights will only have direct effect if the provision is sufficiently clear and precise, unconditional, and not dependent on further action by the EC or national authorities to bring it into effect.

A1.4.7   Where a national authority has failed to transpose an EC right as contained in a directive into national law, the national authority must compensate an individual who suffers loss as a result.[1]

[1]   *Francovich v Italy* [1991] ECR I-5357.

A1.4.8   In addition, it should be noted that national law must always be interpreted in such a way as to give effect to EC law and objectives, a principle sometimes referred to as the purposive effect. This principle applies irrespective of whether the provision of national law in question pre-dates or post-dates the provision of EC law.

THE AGREEMENT ON SOCIAL POLICY (OR SOCIAL CHAPTER)

A1.4.9   A summit of EC leaders at Maastricht in 1991 led to the conclusion of an Agreement on Social Policy by the then member states excluding the UK. As the measures agreed were originally intended to form part of the Maastricht Treaty, the Agreement is sometimes referred to as the 'Social Chapter'.

A1.4.10   The Agreement aimed to promote a dialogue between management and labour in matters of social policy and provided that the

EC Commission should consult such parties before submitting proposals in the social policy field. It also provided for the extension of qualified majority voting in certain areas of social policy. Following the change of government in the UK in 1997, the UK confirmed that it wished to 'opt-in' to the provisions of the Agreement. Further to the Treaty of Amsterdam, the Agreement's provisions were incorporated into a new Social Chapter of the Treaty of Rome (new arts 136–145).

A1.4.11   The UK has now accepted that it is bound by the directives adopted by the other member states between 1994 and 1998, for example the directives on parental leave, European works councils, and part-time workers.

1.5   Key Provisions of European Employment Law

A1.5.1   The following are important provisions of EC law that the reader is likely to encounter in the following chapters.

EQUAL PAY

A1.5.2   The principle of equal pay for equal work was established by the EC Treaty, art 119 (now art 141). The principle was enhanced by the Equal Pay Directive 75/117/EEC (equal pay for work of equal value).

EQUAL TREATMENT

A1.5.3   The Equal Treatment Directive 76/207/EEC establishes the principle of equal treatment for men and women in relation to access to employment, vocational training and promotion, and working conditions. The Directive also explicitly outlaws discrimination based on marital or family status.

A1.5.4   Other directives extend the principle of equal treatment to social security matters and occupational social security schemes.

ACQUIRED RIGHTS

A1.5.5   The Acquired Rights Directive 77/187/EEC aims to safeguard employees' rights where there is a transfer of their employer's business and the business retains its identity following the transfer, and to set standards for informing and consulting with employees (see also Directive 98/50).

INSOLVENCY

A1.5.6   Directive 80/987/EEC is aimed at the protection of employees in the event of their employer becoming insolvent.

PREGNANT WORKERS

A1.5.7   The Pregnant Workers Directive 92/85/EEC is aimed at the protection of the health and safety of pregnant workers, those who have recently given birth, and breastfeeding workers.

WORKING TIME

A1.5.8   The Working Time Directive 93/104/EC aims to impose minimum rest periods and annual leave provisions in order to protect the health and safety of workers.

YOUNG WORKERS

A1.5.9   The Young Workers Directive 94/33/EC is aimed at the protection of the health and safety of young workers by imposing restrictions on their hours and the types of work which they are allowed to perform.

EUROPEAN WORKS COUNCILS

A1.5.10   The European Works Councils Directive 94/45/EC promotes the establishment of European Works Councils for Community-wide businesses for the purpose of informing and consulting with employees on Community-wide issues (see also Directive 97/74/EC).

DATA PROTECTION

A1.5.11   The Data Protection Directive 95/46/EC is aimed to protect the interests of individuals in relation to the processing of personal data.

PARENTAL LEAVE

A1.5.12   The Parental Leave Directive 96/34 introduced the concept of parental leave for men and women on the birth or the adoption of a child (see also Directive 97/75/EC).

POSTED WORKERS

A1.5.13   The Posted Workers Directive 96/71/EC aims to protect the position of workers who are required to perform some of their duties in a different member state to the state in which they normally work, and to ensure that they are able to take advantage of the minimum standards guaranteed to other workers in that member state (namely protective employment provisions).

BURDEN OF PROOF – SEX DISCRIMINATION CASES

A1.5.14   Directive 97/80/EC aims to ensure that where a complainant presents facts on which a complaint of discrimination may be presumed, it will be for the respondent to prove that there has been no breach of the principle of equal treatment (see also Directive 98/52/EC extending this Directive to the UK).

COLLECTIVE REDUNDANCIES

A1.5.15   The Collective Redundancies Directive 98/59/EC aims to set standards for information and consultation with employee representatives, and procedures to be followed by the employer, where collective redundancies are proposed.

PART-TIME WORKERS

A1.5.16   The Part-time Workers Directive 97/81/EC aims to ensure that part-time workers are not treated less favourably than full-time workers.

FIXED-TERM WORK

A1.5.17   The Fixed-term Work Directive 99/70/EC is aimed at the prevention of less favourable treatment of fixed-term contract workers as compared with permanent workers.

EQUAL TREATMENT BASED ON RACE AND ETHNIC ORIGIN

A1.5.18   This Directive (2000/43/EC) is aimed at the promotion of equal treatment based on race and ethnic origin. It refers to both direct and indirect discrimination, as well as harassment and victimisation. In addition, the Directive requires that it shall be for the respondent to prove that there has been no breach of the equal treatment principle, rather than it being for the complainant to prove that there has. The Directive must be implemented into national law by 19 July 2003.

EQUAL TREATMENT (FRAMEWORK) DIRECTIVE

A1.5.19   This new Directive (2000/78/EC) has recently been agreed, and is aimed at preventing discrimination on the grounds of religion or belief, disability, age or sexual orientation. The new Directive addresses both direct and indirect discrimination on these grounds. Measures relating to grounds save for age and disability must be implemented into national law by 2 December 2003. Measures relating to age and disability must be implemented into national law by 2 December 2006 at the latest.

1.6   The EC Charter of Fundamental Rights of the European Union

A1.6.1   Readers should be aware that an EC Charter has recently been agreed which expresses a number of fundamental rights and freedoms, and in particular a number of social and economic rights. The draft of the Charter was agreed by a special European Council Convention on 2 October 2000. The Charter is similar in terms of areas of protection to other measures such as the European Convention on Human Rights, and protects areas such as private and family life, personal data, the right to equality, the right to collective bargaining and action, and the right to protection in the event of unjustified dismissal.

A1.6.2   In the event of a discrepancy between national law and the provisions of the Charter, it is envisaged that the complainant would be able to assert his rights under the Charter before the national court, and if necessary could request an interpretation of the law from the European Court of Justice. It is not however necessary for the member states to amend the provisions of their own national law to implement the Charter provisions. The effect of the Charter remains to be seen, but it is of course an important indication of the growing trend towards political and social integration.

1.7   Implementation of EC law

A1.7.1   As stated above, it is for the member states to decide the manner and form of legislation which implements EC directives, provided of course that the objectives of EC law as set out in the directives are honoured. The following chapters illustrate the differences in approach that the various member states have taken in each area of employment law.

BIBLIOGRAPHY

Bercusson *European Labour Law*
Barnard *EC Employment Law* (2nd edn)
Deakin and Morris *Labour Law* (2nd edn)
Butterworths Expert Guide to the European Union
Horspool *Butterworths Core Text: European Union Law* (2nd edn)

USEFUL WEBSITES

The European Commission's website on employment and social affairs can be found at:

*   http://europa.eu.int/comm/employment_social/index_en.htm

The website of the Employment and Social Affairs Directorate-General can be found at:

*   http//europa.eu.int/comm/dgs/employment_social/index_en.htm

B   Austria

Dr Bernhard Hainz and Dr Martin E Risak

Dr Hainz is a Partner at CMS Strommer Reich-Rohrwig Karasek Hainz, Vienna. He is also an assistant at the Institute for Labour Law, University of Vienna and a lecturer at the University of Vienna. He is an author of numerous articles on Labour Law.

CMS Strommer Reich-Rohrwig Karasek Hainz
Phone: +43 1 40 4430
Fax: +43 1 405 92 00
Email: bernhard.hainz@cmslegal.at
Website: www.cmslegal.at

Dr Risak is Assistant and Lecturer at the Institute for Labour Law and Law of Social Security at the University of Vienna and a former associate with CMS Strommer Reich-Rohrwig Karasek Hainz, Vienna.

Email: martin.risak@univie.ac.at
Phone: +43 1 4277 35604
Fax: +43 1 4277 9356
Website: www.univie.ac.at/juridicum

AUSTRIA

Rights	Yes/No	Explanatory notes
CONTRACTS OF EMPLOYMENT		
Minimum notice	YES	White-collar employees: statutory notice of six weeks to five months; blue-collar employees: notice set by collective bargaining agreement
Terms:		
Express	YES	
Implied	YES	But rarely seen or required
Incorporated by statute	YES	By statute/collective bargaining or work agreement
REMUNERATION		
Minimum wage regulation	YES	By collective bargaining agreement
Further rights and obligations:		
Right to paid holiday	YES	Set by statute: usually 25–30 days per year
Right to sick pay	YES	Period depends on blue/white-collar status, reason for absence, and length of service
WORKING TIME		
Regulation of hours per day/ working week	YES	Maximum hours: 10 per day/50 per week (subject to exceptions)
Regulation of night work	YES	Different rules apply to night work as between male / female workers
Right to paid holiday	YES	25–30 days per year
Right to rest periods	YES	Compulsory daily/weekly rest breaks
EQUAL OPPORTUNITIES		
Discrimination protection:		
Sex	YES	Protection from direct and indirect discrimination, and harassment
Race/other grounds for discrimination	NO	No specific statutory protection, although the courts apply a general principle of 'equal treatment'
Disability	YES	Equal pay principle set out in statute: the 'equal treatment' principle otherwise applies (see above)
Equal pay legislation	YES	
TERMINATION OF EMPLOYMENT		
Right not to be dismissed in breach of contract	YES	Employee entitled to compensation for breach
Statutory rights on termination	YES	Employee can challenge either unfair summary dismissal, or unjust/unlawful dismissal, and claim compensation

Right to severance payment	YES	Statutory payment made to employees having three or more years' service on dismissal

COLLECTIVE DISMISSALS

Statutory protection	YES	Applies to dismissal of five or more employees in a period of 30 days
Right to additional severance pay	NO	Payment as for individual dismissal
Right to collective consultation	YES	30-day notification period Negotiations required with the local Labour Exchange office, works council, and Chambers of Labour and Commerce

YOUNG WORKERS

Protection of children and young persons at work	YES	Restrictions on working hours, and compulsory time off for schooling

MATERNITY RIGHTS

Right to maternity leave	YES	Eight weeks prior to, plus eight after the birth
Notice period	YES	Employee must notify employer of pregnancy and expected date of confinement as soon as possible
Maternity pay (during leave)	YES	Full salary payment made by Public Health Insurance, not employer
Protection from dismissal	YES	Notice may not be given during pregnancy, within four months of childbirth, or for up to four weeks following maternity leave or part-time work without consent of the Employment Court
Health and safety protection	YES	Extends to pregnant and breastfeeding women
Right to parental leave	YES	Right to parental leave and/or part-time work
Right to time off for dependants	YES	One week per year for care of a close relative living in the same household, one additional week per year for care of a child younger than 12 years of age

BUSINESS TRANSFERS

Right to protection on transfer	YES	Employment contracts transferred by operation of law
Protection of existing terms and conditions	YES	Work agreements remain in force Salaries may not be reduced
Right to information and consultation	YES	Works council must be consulted in advance
Right not to be dismissed	YES	Termination by transferor is null and void if not justified by reasons not relating to the transfer

COLLECTIVE RIGHTS AND BARGAINING

Conclusion of collective bargaining agreements	YES	Commonly concluded at industry level; work agreements usually concluded between employer and works council
Works councils	YES	Works councils must be elected in every business which employs at least five employee
Consultation rights	YES	Works councils must be consulted on the economic situation of the enterprise and any substantial changes proposed

EMPLOYMENT DISPUTES

Special court jurisdiction	YES	All employment disputes are referred to the employment court

WHISTLEBLOWING

Protection from dismissal/ detriment	NO	No specific statutory protection

DATA PROTECTION

Protection	YES	Use and processing of personal data regulated

HUMAN RIGHTS

Statutory protection of human rights:

Public authority	YES	European Convention on Human Rights directly applicable in Austria
Private organisations	NO	

1   THE EMPLOYMENT RELATIONSHIP

1.1   Background

B1.1.1   Like any other contract, the contract of employment is concluded by consensus of the parties involved.

B1.1.2   An employment contract (*Arbeitsvertrag, Dienstvertrag*) is deemed to exist if a person (the employee) undertakes to provide services to another person (the employer) for a period of time.[1] However, it is only if the employee is obliged to render services in 'personal dependence' that an employment contract under Austrian law is properly established. Personal dependence fundamentally means that the employee cannot do what he likes during his working hours. Therefore, a contract which does not oblige an individual to render his services in person, or which provides that a substitute may be deployed, cannot be qualified an employment contract. Another characteristic feature of an employment contract is the employee's integration into an employer's organisation. The employee has to comply with the (personal) instructions given to him by the employer, and he is also subject to supervision and disciplinary measures by his employer.

[1]   Civil Code (*Allgemeines Buergerliches Gesetzbuch*), s 1551.

B1.1.3   Not all of these features have to exist at the same time in a particular case. An overall assessment determines whether a contractual relationship can be considered an employment contract or not. If the features characteristic for an employment contract outweigh the uncharacteristic ones such a contract exists.

B1.1.4   Under a 'free service contract' (*freier Dienstvertrag*) a person undertakes to provide services for a certain period of time. However, the individual worker is not personally dependent. Typically the 'free service contractor' is not integrated into the corporate organisation, can organise his own working time himself and uses his own resources.

B1.1.5   In contrast to the employment contract and the free service contract where services have to be provided, under a contract for work and services (*Werkvertrag*) a particular result has to be delivered and a specific successful performance must be guaranteed.[1] The contractor (*Werkunternehmer*) is not integrated into the principal's (*Werkbesteller*) organisation, has no obligation to do the work personally and usually uses his own resources. The contractor will also bear the entrepreneurial risk.

[1]   Civil Code, s 1551.

1.2   Contract of Service

A   CONTRACT AND ITS WRITTEN PARTICULARS

B1.2.1   Under Austrian law there is generally no specific form or requirements for an employment contract. This means that such a contract can be concluded orally or in writing as well as through performance.

13

B1.2.2 As an exception to this general rule, an apprenticeship contract must be drawn up in writing.[1] Some specific provisions in contracts of employment must also be in writing eg the making of a deposit as security for damage claims of the employer against the employee or the granting of future service inventions to the employer.[2]

[1] Apprenticeship Act (*Berufsausbildungsgesetz*), s 12.
[2] Act on the Protection of Deposits (*Kautionsschutzgesetz*), s 1; Patent Act (*Patentgesetz*), s 7.

B1.2.3 After the commencement of employment, the employer has to provide the employee, without undue delay, with a written record outlining the essential rights and obligations arising from the contract of service. In Austria this statement is referred to as *Dienstzettel*. The written record must contain the following information:

(a) name and address of employer;
(b) name and address of employee;
(c) starting date of employment;
(d) where the employment is for a fixed period, the end date of employment;
(e) period of notice and termination date (ie the date on which the employment relationship may end);[1]
(f) usual place of work (indication of changes in places of work where applicable);
(g) if a salary scheme under collective bargaining agreement exists, the employee's classification in such a salary scheme;
(h) types of services to be performed;
(i) initial salary and other compensation as well as due dates of the salary;
(j) holiday entitlement;
(k) agreed daily or weekly normal working hours;
(l) reference to applicable collective bargaining agreements and work agreements.

[1] See para **B6.3.2**.

B1.2.4 In addition, if an employee will have to work for more than a month abroad, the written record must contain the following additional information:

(m) expected period of work abroad;
(n) if the employee is not paid in Austrian Schillings (ATS) the currency in which payment will be made;
(o) if applicable, conditions for a return to Austria;
(p) if applicable, additional remuneration for service abroad.

B1.2.5 The information in items (e), (f), (i)–(l) and (n)–(p) (see paras **B1.2.3**–**B1.2.4**) does not have to be specifically indicated; the written record may instead refer to a specific legislative act, collective bargaining agreement or work agreement. In such a case there is no requirement to update the written record if such conditions change.

B1.2.6 The employer does not need to provide such a written record if the employment is for a fixed period of not more than one month or if a written employment contract exists that covers all necessary issues.

B1.2.7   If any of the above-mentioned terms and conditions included in the written record change, the employee must be informed of the changes in writing or be given an updated written record within one month.

B1.2.8   The employer has to provide the employee with the written record without undue delay after the commencement of the employment relationship. If the employer fails to provide this, the employee may sue the employer to issue the written record before the employment court. The decision of the court states that the employee has the right to a written record but the court itself cannot provide the employee with such a written record. However, failure to comply with this decision of the employment court will make the employer subject to sanctions for contempt of court.

Terms of the contract

B1.2.9   The employment contract is made up of terms and conditions that are not necessarily set out in the written record or the written contract of service. They may be in writing, oral or be implied or incorporated.

Express terms

B1.2.10   The express terms which may be oral and/or in writing constitute the basis for the employment relationship. If a term is unclear or ambiguous it is interpreted in a way that is disadvantageous to the party who relies on it.[1] This is usually the employer (who drafts the written contract of service). Examples of express terms follow in paras **B1.2.11–B1.2.20**.

[1]   Civil Code, s 915.

Service inventions

B1.2.11   In general, if the employee has made an invention that is covered by the provisions of the Patent Act, the employee is entitled to a patent for the inventions he has made during his employment. An agreement under which future inventions belong to and can only be exploited by the employer is admissible only for service inventions (*Diensterfindungen*) and must be recorded in writing. A service invention is defined as an invention of an employee:

- if it falls within the line of business of the enterprise where the employee works; and
- if either the activities that have led to the invention were part of his normal duties; or
- if the invention was considerably facilitated through the use of the company's resources; or
- if the employee's invention was inspired by his work in the company.[1]

[1]   Patent Act (*Patentgesetz*), s 7.

B1.2.12   Under the Austrian Patent Act, the employee is also entitled to special compensation in consideration for making a service invention available to his employer.[1]

[1]   Patent Act, s 8.

15

Restrictive covenants

B1.2.13 A duty of non-competition extends beyond termination of employment only if this has been explicitly agreed upon in the contract of service. The law places several restrictions on such restrictive covenants. The clause is invalid if the employee was a minor when the agreement was entered into.[1] Otherwise, the restrictive covenant is only valid as far as the restriction on the activities:

- refers to the employers' lines of business; and
- does not exceed one year.

Additionally the restrictive covenant must not constitute an undue hardship on the employee's career in relation to the business interests of the employer.

[1] Act on White Collar Workers (*Angestelltengesetz*), s 36.

B1.2.14 The employer is restricted from enforcing a restrictive covenant if the circumstances leading to the immediate or ordinary termination of the employment were caused by the employer (eg delay in paying remuneration) or if he has terminated employment without just cause. In the latter case the employer may still invoke the restrictive covenant if he is willing to continue full payment to the former employee for the period of the restrictive covenant.

Penalty clause

B1.2.15 Frequently restrictive covenants as well as other obligations of the employee are secured by a penalty clause. If such a clause has been agreed upon, the employee infringing the employment contract has to pay the agreed sum of money. The main advantage for the employer is that the actual damage does not have to be estimated.

B1.2.16 Such a clause is subject to equitable review and reduction by the court.[1] In case of the use of a penalty clause in connection with a restrictive covenant, the existence of a penalty clause prevents the employer from enforcing the restrictive covenant by any means other than the penalty (eg cease-and-desist orders or additional damages).[2]

[1] Act on White Collar Workers (*Angestelltengesetz*), s 38.
[2] Act on White Collar Workers, s 37.

Forfeiture clause

B1.2.17 Generally the employee may raise claims based on the employment contract within three years after the due date.[1] It is possible to shorten this period down to three months by express agreement.

[1] Civil Code (*Allgemeines Buergerliches Gesetzbuch*), s 1486.

Choice of law

B1.2.18 Austrian conflict of law rules[1] provide for the direct application of the European Convention on the Law Applicable to Contractual Obligations. According to art 6 of this Convention, employment contracts are subject to the law of the country in which the employee will regularly perform the contracted work. The law of that country will govern, even if the employee is temporarily assigned to work in another country. If the employee regularly performs work in more than one country or if there is no place where the work is regularly performed, the law of the country where the place of business for which he was engaged is situated applies. Any other choice of law will be valid only if there is an agreement (which does not have to be explicit)[2] and only to the extent that this choice must not deprive the employee of the protection granted to him by the mandatory rules of the law which would apply in the absence of the choice of law agreement.

[1]   International Private Law Act (*Internationales Privatrechtsgesetz*), s 50.

[2]   European Convention on the Law Applicable to Contractual Obligations, art 3.

B1.2.19   If the employee's regular place of work is in Austria, the employment relationship will therefore be governed by Austrian law. A contractual choice of law will then only be possible with respect to optional statutory provisions, ie provisions which may be changed by mutual agreement.

B1.2.20   It is not possible to exclude the jurisdiction of the employment court in advance. An arbitration agreement is only possible for an existing dispute.[1]

[1]   Act on the Procedure in Labour Law and Social Law Matters (*Arbeits- und Sozialgerichtsgesetz*), s 9.

Implied terms

B1.2.21   If the meaning of an employment contract is not clear, it has to be ascertained by way of interpretation in accordance with the respective rules of the Civil Code.[1] The first step of interpretation takes the wording in its common meaning into account. On this basis the intention of the parties has to be reconstructed. In Austria the intentions of the declaring party as seen by an objective receiving party are relevant. If a clear meaning cannot be determined on the basis of the parties' intentions, the meaning will be taken to comply with common custom and practice.

[1]   Civil Code (*Allgemeines Buergerliches Gesetzbuch*), s 914 f.

B1.2.22   If, after the conclusion of the contract, conflicts arise which were not foreseen by the parties and therefore were not settled in the contract, the issue has to be solved in the light of the other provisions in the contract. The aim is to find a solution that honest parties after due consideration would have agreed upon. In many cases additional contractual obligations are determined by further interpretation of the contract (eg confidentiality).

B1.2.23   With regard to the contract of employment, numerous provisions of statutory law and collective bargaining agreements exist. Therefore, there is usually not much need for supplementary interpretation of contracts of employment.

Incorporated terms

B1.2.24   The parties to the employment contract may incorporate into the contract, terms from other sources. It is not uncommon to incorporate internal regulations set out by the employer (eg for the use of a company car or the reimbursement of business travel expenses).

B1.2.25 Collective bargaining agreements and work agreements do not have to be incorporated into the employment contract because these two sources of law have the same force as a statute, although usually they cannot alter statutory provisions to the disadvantage of the employee. Like statutory rights, rights arising under collective bargaining agreements and work agreements can be enforced by every individual covered by the agreement – not just the parties to the agreement.

B   STATUTE

B1.2.26 In Austria there is no single Labour Code. The legal provisions concerning labour law are spread throughout different acts (eg Act on White Collar Workers, Working Hours Act). This is complicated by the distinction between white-collar and blue-collar employees. The acts concerning health and safety regulations and the Labour Relations Act (*Arbeitsverfassungsgesetz*) as well as the Vacation Act (*Urlaubsgesetz*) apply to both groups.

B1.2.27 Austrian labour law still recognises the distinction between blue-collar and white-collar workers (*Arbeiter* and *Angestellte*).

In order to qualify as a white-collar worker, an employee must perform one of the following activities:

- activity of a 'commercial' character, which basically includes activity connected with sales, marketing, accounting or finance, the performance of which requires some commercial training and/or ability;
- more complex activities of a non-commercial nature, which require particular training and which an employee performs independently with a high degree of trust by the employer;
- office work which does not include the most simple forms of clerical work.[1]

All other employees are considered blue-collar workers.

[1]   Act on White-Collar Workers (*Angestelltengesetz*), s 2.

B1.2.28 The distinction between white-collar and blue-collar employees has lost much of its significance, but still has some consequences. In collective labour law, separate works councils exist to represent blue and white-collar employees. The union organisation is based on the distinction of the two groups of employees. Accordingly, different collective bargaining agreements apply. In individual labour law the rules for continued remuneration in the event of sickness differ; regulations for periods and dates of notice are also less favourable for blue-collar workers.

B1.2.29 The most important legislation for white-collar workers is the Act on White-Collar Workers (*Angestelltengesetz*). For blue-collar workers the parts of the Civil Code regulating the employment contract apply. Provisions for the termination of the contract of employment of blue-collar workers are found in the Industrial Code (*Gewerbeordnung*).

> **White-collar employees**
> * 'commercial' activity *or*
>   more complex activities of a non-commercial nature *or* office work
> * separate works councils from blue-collar employees
> * different rules on notice, sick pay
> * different collective bargaining agreements

C   COLLECTIVE AGREEMENTS

B1.2.30   In addition to statutory regulation, major areas of labour law provisions (especially those on pay, flexible work time, wage supplements etc) are collectively bargained and defined by employees' and employers' representatives. In Austria around 85% of employees are subject to collectively agreed labour regulations, the remainder being mostly civil servants who are subject to statutory regulations.

B1.2.31   Work agreements may cover employment issues for a particular business of an undertaking or for the entire undertaking. A work agreement is a written contract, concluded between the employer and the works council. It may only deal with those matters reserved to work agreements by statute law or collective bargaining agreement.

B1.2.32   Individual contracts of service may only deviate from collective bargaining agreements and work agreements in favour of the employee.[1]

[1]   Labour Relations Act (*Arbeitsverfassungsgesetz*), ss 3, 31.

D   LAW BASED ON SUPREME COURT (OGH) DECISIONS

B1.2.33   Although Austrian law is statute-based and not case-law-based, the decisions of the Supreme Court (*Oberster Gerichtshof – OGH*) are of major importance. For example, the equal treatment principle, ie that an employer may not without good cause treat a minority of employees worse than other employees with regard to working conditions, is a creation of the Austrian Courts.[1]

[1]   Eg Supreme Court (*Oberster Gerichtshof – OGH*) ZAS 1996, 167 = DRdA 1996, 315; RdW 1995, 432; DRdA 1996, 24; DRdA 1996, 246; Arb 10. 301.

1.3   Variation of Contract

B1.3.1   The employment contract cannot be altered unilaterally. Amendment can be achieved only by mutual consent of employer and employee. This can be done explicitly or by way of implied consent. For example: a change may be introduced by the employer and although the employee does not expressively consent to the change he continues to work without objection. This can be interpreted as an implied consent to the change of working conditions.

B1.3.2   Numerous decisions of the Austrian Supreme Court have held that employees may have implicit contractual entitlements in the light of long standing employment practices (*Betriebsuebung*).[1] Thus, employers who repeatedly grant benefits to employees without a contractual or statutory basis become obliged to continue granting such benefits on the basis of an implicit contractual agreement. To prevent such an implicit agreement, the employer must explicitly state the discretionary character of the benefit granted, or reserve the right to cease granting such benefits.

[1] Eg Supreme Court (*Oberster Gerichtshof – OGH*) ZAS 1997, 102; ZAS 1980, 99; ZAS 1980, 178, ZAS 1982, 10; ZAS 1987, 84.

B1.3.3 If the employer wishes to introduce a change to the contract in the future, he may include a right of variation in the contract. For example, it is not unusual for the employer to move an employee from one place or position to another and he would therefore wish to include a contractual mobility clause.

B1.3.4 In the absence of an express right to alter the employment contract, the employer can terminate the existing contract by serving notice, and then offering the employee a new contract or withdrawing termination if the employee agrees to alter the existing contract (dismissal with the option of altered conditions of employment, or *Aenderungskuendigung*). It is possible for an employee employed in a business with more than four workers to challenge such a termination in court, if substantial interests of the employee are affected and the employer cannot prove that circumstances relating to the employee or operational requirements are the reasons for the termination: see para **B1.4.4**.[1]

[1] Labour Relations Act (*Arbeitsverfassungsgesetz*), s 105: see paras **B6.6.1– B6.6.14**.

1.4 Remedies

A   EMPLOYEE'S REMEDIES

Damages

B1.4.1 Every contract of employment can be terminated by either side when one party cannot reasonably be expected to continue employment (constructive/summary dismissal, *Austritt/Entlassung*). If an employer terminates the employment contract by summary dismissal, even though the requirement of good cause is not met, the employment will normally nevertheless end immediately.[1] The employee will be entitled to 'compensation for notice' (*Kuendigungsentschaedigung*).[2] This remedy originates from the law of damages and compensates the employee for the damage he has suffered because of the premature termination of his employment. He is therefore put into the same financial situation as if proper notice had been given to him. The compensation for notice payable to the employee therefore consists of the remuneration that would have been paid during the notice period if due notice had been given. The same principle applies to inadequate notice.

[1] Established practice of the Supreme Court (*Oberster Gerichtshof – OGH*) since 1967 (Arb 8470).
[2] Act on White-Collar Workers, s 29; Civil Code, s 1162b.

B1.4.2 The employee is entitled to full compensation for notice of up to three months' salary. If, however, the period for which compensation is due exceeds three months, everything the employee has saved by not working, has earned, or has intentionally failed to earn, will be set off against any compensation which would be due to him.[1]

[1] § 31 Act on White Collar Workers (*Angestelltengesetz*), § 1162b Civil Code (*Allgemeines Buergerliches Gesetzbuch*).

Declaration

B1.4.3 If the employment contract of an employee who enjoys special protection against termination of his contract[1] is terminated without the necessary permission of the court or relevant administrative body, the employee can seek a declaratory judgment declaring that his employment contract is still in force.

[1] See paras **B6.5.1– B6.5.3** for further details.

Challenge of termination and dismissal

B1.4.4 All employees working in a business with more than four employees may challenge the termination of their contract, if they have been employed in that business or enterprise for more than six months. In the event of summary dismissal the employer has to prove that good cause (eg disloyalty, inability or refusal to perform services) exists. In the event of termination by giving due notice, the employee has to prove that the termination of the employment contract affects his substantial interests. The employer then has to justify termination either by circumstances relating to the employee or by operational requirements. If the employer fails to do so, the court will render the notice or dismissal ineffective.[1]

[1] Labour Relations Act (*Arbeitsverfassungsgesetz*), s 105: see **B6.6.1–B6.6.14**.

B   EMPLOYER'S REMEDIES

Damages

B1.4.5 An employer can sue an employee for damages for breach of contract (eg if the employee resigns without a reason justifying him to do so). In Austria this happens very rarely mainly because the employer's loss is hard to quantify.

B1.4.6 Damages can also be claimed if the employee breaches a contractual restrictive covenant clause or other provisions of the contract which may be additionally covered by a penalty clause (eg confidentiality, return of employer's property).

Withholding wages

B1.4.7 The employee is entitled to remuneration only in consideration for work for the employer, unless he cannot work for reasons arising from matters that are usually the employer's responsibility eg computer breakdown.[1] Other exceptions are continued payment during the employee's annual leave[2] and the employee's right to continued payment during sick leave.[3]

[1] Civil Code, s 1155.

² See paras **B3.1.1–B3.1.14** for further information.
³ Act on White-Collar Workers, s 8: for blue-collar workers: Continuation of Payment Act (*Entgeltfortzahlungsgesetz*): see paras **B3.2.1–B3.2.4**.

Summary dismissal

B1.4.8   If the employer has good cause, making it unreasonable for him to continue the employment relationship, he has the right to terminate with immediate effect. This applies to any employment relationship whether it has been concluded for a definite or an indefinite period of time.

Injunctive relief

B1.4.9   An employer may also apply for an interlocutory injunction to restrain the disclosure of confidential information or enforce a restrictive covenant. In the case of a restrictive covenant this is not possible if a penalty clause has been agreed.[1]

¹ Act on White-Collar Workers (*Angestelltengesetz*), s 37.

2   REMUNERATION

2.1   Background

B2.1.1   Statute provides almost no regulation on the issue of wage determination, which is mainly left to collective bargaining agreements and beyond that to individual contracts of employment. As a general rule, parties to the employment contract are unrestricted as to how they calculate compensation, as long as any minimum wage set by the collective bargaining agreement is complied with.

2.2   Legal Regulation of Remuneration

B2.2.1   The amount of remuneration depends primarily on the terms of the individual contract of service or the relevant collective bargaining agreement. In Austria, statute does not provide for any minimum wage, but all collective agreements provide for fixed minimum remuneration which the employer must pay in all circumstances.

B2.2.2   Remuneration can be computed either on the basis of intervals (hours, days, weeks or months) or be based on the performance of the employee. Performance-related pay (eg piece-work pay) may only be introduced either by a collective bargaining agreement or, if such provisions do not exist in collective bargaining agreements, by a work agreement.[1] This rule applies to systems of piece-work pay as well as to most other forms of pay based directly on performance. If there is no provision in any collective bargaining agreement or work agreement, the employer is not permitted to introduce such a system of pay.

¹ Labour Relations Act, s 96.

B2.2.3   The employer may also introduce profit sharing plans by way of individual agreement or work agreement.[1]

¹ Labour Relations Act, s 97.

B2.2.4 Usually Austrian contracts of service do not contain increase of salary clauses. Annual pay rises are effected by collective bargaining agreements, which include provisions for minimum wage increase as well as the increase of actual wages. Some collective bargaining agreements (especially for the industrial sector) provide for additional biannual actual wage increases.

B2.2.5 Collective bargaining agreements in Austria state that salaries are paid 14 times a year. The 13th salary is usually called 'vacation benefit' (*Urlaubszuschuss*) and the 14th 'Christmas-pay' (*Weihnachtsremuneration*). 14 monthly salaries are usually standard even for those employees not covered by collective bargaining agreements, as Austrian income tax law applies a very low flat rate of taxation to the 13th and 14th monthly salary.

B2.2.6 The remuneration fixed in the employment contract or the collective bargaining agreement is the basic remuneration. In addition to this basic remuneration, collective bargaining agreements usually provide for premium payments for particular types of work performed, eg night work or particular heavy work. If an employee works for the employer beyond regular work hours, he is entitled to be paid for overtime.

Remuneration
Regulation of remuneration:
- by collective bargaining agreements, not statute;
- '13th month' (holiday pay) and '14th month' (Christmas pay) are standard.

2.3 Deduction from Wages

B2.3.1 An employer may only make deductions from the employee's wages if:
- the deduction is required or authorised by statutory provision (eg for tax and social security contributions or membership fees to Trade Unions); or
- the deduction is based on a judgment or administrative decision (limited by the amount exempted from execution – 'subsistence minimum' as provided in the Execution Code); or
- the deduction is by way of compensation for claims of the employer (limited by the subsistence minimum except for claims in a legal context, salary advance or damages for deliberate acts); or
- the employee has consented to it.

B2.3.2 It has been established by the Austrian Supreme Court that the renunciation of inalienable rights (eg minimum wage as established by collective bargaining agreements) is void during the employment relationship because it is assumed that the employee did not decide freely but under duress.[1]

[1]   Supreme Court (*Oberster Gerichtshof* – OGH) Arb 3725.

2.4   Itemised Pay Statement

B2.4.1   The employer must provide the employee with a written itemised pay statement with the payment of wages at the latest which must set out the gross pay and any deductions (especially any tax and social security contributions).[1]

[1]   Income Tax Act (*Einkommensteuergesetz*), s 78.

3   FURTHER RIGHTS AND OBLIGATIONS

3.1   Holiday Entitlement

B3.1.1   Mandatory provisions of the Vacation Act (*Urlaubsgesetz*) which apply to virtually all employees in the private sector, provide that both blue-collar and white-collar workers are entitled to paid holiday for each year of service, the length of which is prescribed by law. In every year of employment the employee is entitled to a holiday of 30 business days if his period of service is less than 25 years. After more than 25 years of service, the annual holiday is 36 business days.[1] This means, that the employee has five weeks or six weeks vacation respectively per year, Saturday being counted as a 'business day'. In practice vacation for employees working five-day weeks (Monday to Friday) is counted on the basis of 'working days', ie the days the employee actually has to work (Monday to Friday). Therefore, the employee is entitled to 25 working days' holiday per year (30 working days after 25 years' service).

[1]   Vacation Act, s 2.

B3.1.2   In the first year of employment, the full holiday entitlement becomes due only after six months' service. However, during the first six months, the holiday entitlement will increase in proportion to the time served with the employer. From the second year of employment onwards, the holiday entitlement arises at the beginning of the year.[1]

[1]   Vacation Act, s 2.

B3.1.3   The holiday year corresponds with the working year, ie it starts on the day the employee commenced his employment. It can be agreed that the annual leave shall be calculated on the basis of the calendar year rather than the working year if either a collective bargaining agreement or work agreement provides this option or if such calculation will not put the employee in a less favourable position.[1]

[1]   Vacation Act, s 2.

B3.1.4   The timing of holiday must be agreed upon between the employer and employee taking into consideration both the business needs and practical considerations of the enterprise as well as the employee's personal plans. This means that the employee cannot necessarily take his holiday when he pleases, but neither can the employer force the employee to take holiday without the employee's consent.[1]

[1]   Vacation Act, s 4.

B3.1.5   If agreement on holiday is not reached, the employee can take his holiday when he pleases:
- if the company has a works council;
- if the proposed date on which the employee wants to take his holiday was notified to the employer with at least three months prior notice;
- if the requested leave has a minimum duration of 12 business days; and
- if an agreement cannot be reached despite consultation with the works council.

B3.1.6   If, however, the employer has filed legal action with the Employment Court within six to eight weeks before the disputed holiday date, the employee must await the decision of the Employment Court and may not take his holiday.[1]

[1]   Vacation Act, s 4.

B3.1.7   Theoretically, holiday must either be taken in one portion or may be divided into two parts, of which one part must consist of at least six business days.[1] This rule is frequently not followed in practice, as shorter periods of holiday are generally in the interest of both employers and employees alike.

[1]   Vacation Act, s 4.

B3.1.8   If the employer and the employee have reached an agreement on proposed holiday this agreement may only be revoked in particularly serious cases. In these cases, it is necessary to weigh the interests of the employee against those of the employer. Should the agreed leave be cancelled for justified reasons, the employer will have to compensate the employee for any financial loss he might have suffered.

B3.1.9   In practice (particularly at larger companies) employers have 'company shut-down days' during which all employees have to take their vacation. It is not uncommon for there to be an obligation on the employee in his contract of employment to use part of his holiday entitlement during these company shut-down days. These days must not exceed a certain amount and must allow the employee to select a date for at least part of his annual holiday.

B3.1.10   If the employee becomes ill during his holiday and did not cause the illness intentionally or by gross negligence, the days during which the employee is incapable of working do not count as holiday if the incapacity lasts longer than three calendar days. The employee is obliged to notify the employer in a timely manner and prove his incapability to work.[1]

[1]   Vacation Act, s 5.

B3.1.11   The Vacation Act forbids payment in lieu of leave.[1]

[1]   Vacation Act, s 7.

B3.1.12   During his holiday the employee is entitled to remuneration. The Vacation Act provides that the employee is paid the same remuneration during his holiday that he would have been entitled to if he had worked and had not taken a holiday. Accordingly, any overtime worked regularly must be taken into account for the purpose of calculating holiday pay.[1] The 'holiday allowance' constitutes an additional element of remuneration (13th monthly payment, see para **B2.2.5**) and should not be confused with 'holiday pay' as mentioned above.

[1]   Vacation Act, s 6.

B3.1.13   When the employment relationship ends, if the employee has not used up all of his holiday he is entitled to pro rata holiday pay.[1]

[1]   See paras **6.8.1–6.8.3**.

B3.1.14   Generally speaking the entire holiday entitlement for one holiday year should be taken within that year, but entitlements are not forfeited if they are not taken in full. The law provides that holiday entitlement is lost two years after the end of the holiday year in which it arose.[1]

[1]   Vacation Act, s 4.

Vacation Act
- Applies to blue and white-collar employees
- Holiday accrues only proportionally during the first six months of employment and arises fully afterwards
- Holiday year is based on the working year unless agreed otherwise
- Entitlement *less than 25 years' service*: 30 business days (including Saturdays) *more than 25 years' service*: 36 business days (including Saturdays)
- Payment in lieu of holiday not permitted

3.2   Sick Pay

B3.2.1   As a general rule, the employee is entitled to remuneration only if he works. One of the exceptions to this rule is the employee's right to continued payment in the event of sick leave governed by the Continuation of Payment Act (*Entgeltfortzahlungsgesetz*) for blue-collar workers or the Act on White-Collar Workers (*Angestelltengesetz*).

B3.2.2   In the event of illness or injury employees are entitled to receive their full (or reduced) regular remuneration for a specific period of time unless they made themselves unable to work intentionally or through gross negligence. The maximum period of sick pay depends on years of service with the employer and on the cause of the inability to work. In the event of an industrial accident or industrial disease the employee usually has the right to sick pay for a longer period.

B3.2.3   In order to be entitled to sick pay, the employee must notify the employer immediately. If the employer so requests, the employee must present a doctor's confirmation of his inability to work (sick note); this request may be repeated after a certain time.[1] Although failure by the employee to do so does not constitute grounds for summary dismissal, the employee will lose his claim to sick pay for the duration of the delay.

[1] Act on White Collar Workers, s 8; Continuation of Payment Act, s 4.

B3.2.4 The law treats white-collar and blue-collar workers differently:

- A blue-collar worker who is unable to work is entitled to sick pay for a yearly period of six weeks. After five years of employment this period is raised to eight weeks, after 15 years to ten weeks, and after 25 years to 12 weeks. For another four weeks the blue-collar worker has the right to sick pay at one half of salary. If inability to work is caused by an industrial accident or industrial disease, a blue-collar worker is entitled to sick pay for up to eight weeks.[1]
- A white-collar worker is entitled to six weeks' full compensation (eight weeks in the event of an industrial accident or industrial disease) and four weeks at one half of the salary. After five years' service the period of full compensation is eight weeks, after 15 years' service it is ten weeks, and after 25 years' service, twelve weeks; compensation at one half of salary stays at four weeks. If the white-collar employee is unable to work due to illness or accident within six months after recommencing work following an earlier illness, the periods of continuation of payment are the same, but the employee only has to pay half the amount ie 50% and 25% respectively of salary. If the white-collar employee has been in good health for six months, sick pay has to be paid in the full amount.[2]

[1] Continuation of Payment Act, s 2.
[2] Act on White-Collar Workers, s 8.

4 WORKING TIME

4.1 Background

B4.1.1 The regulation of working time in Austria is laid down in the Working Hours Act (*Arbeitszeitgesetz*). In addition, collective bargaining agreements frequently lower weekly working hours and/or increase remuneration for a certain period of working time, in particular for overtime or work at nights or weekends. On particular issues, the Working Hours Act permits collective bargaining agreements to provide for more flexible rules. Provisions concerning hours of rest (daily rest period, weekly/weekend rest period) are governed by the Hours of Rest Act (*Arbeitsruhegesetz*). The Act on Heavy Night Work (*Nachtschwerarbeitsgesetz*) provides rules for employees engaged in night work under difficult circumstances. Restrictions on night work for women are set out in the Act on Women's Night Work (*Frauennachtarbeitsgesetz*).

B4.1.2 All of these national statutes have to be interpreted in the light of European legislation, especially the Working Time Directive (93/104/EC).

4.2 Legislative Control

B4.2.1 As a general rule, all employees in the private sector are protected under the Working Hours Act or the Hours of Rest Act. In practice, the most important exception from the scope of these statutes concerns executives ie persons who carry out decisive management functions under their own responsibility (decision-makers on commercial or technical levels).[1]

[1] Working Hours Act, s 1; Hours of Rest Act, s 1.

B4.2.2 Employers are under a duty to establish and maintain records that show that they comply with the statutory obligations. Labour inspectors have the right to inspect those records, and employers who are not able to produce them are subject to fines.

B4.2.3 As a matter of general principle standard working hours are:
- up to 8 hours per day; and
- up to 40 hours per week.[1]

[1] Working Hours Act, s 3.

B4.2.4 In many businesses the standard weekly working hours have been reduced to 38.5 or 38 hours by way of collective bargaining agreement. Any extra work up to 40 hours per week must be paid as extra work but is calculated without overtime premium at the regular hourly rate if not provided for differently in the collective bargaining agreement.

B4.2.5 The maximum number of the working hours must not exceed:
- 10 hours per day; and
- 50 hours per week.[1]

[1] Working Hours Act, s 9.

B4.2.6 Longer hours may be worked only by way of exception, for example, by shift workers or in public transportation companies.

B4.2.7 There are numerous exceptions allowing the increase of daily and weekly standard working hours. For the purpose of creating longer periods of free time – especially in connection with weekends – daily working hours may be extended to nine hours. For the purpose of creating longer periods of free time in connection with statutory holidays, standard working time may be extended up to ten hours. In this case, the additional time may be allocated to the working days of seven consecutive weeks including the particular holiday (eg working ten extra minutes per day for a month or two extra hours for four days to gain one day off).[1] The principle is, that employees work longer and get compensated with time off (but no overtime premium is payable).

[1] Working Hours Act, s 4.

B4.2.8 Flexible working hours, where allocation of working time is partly left to the employee (*Gleitzeit*), may be established by work agreement or if no works council exists, by written agreement with the employee. In such a case, standard working hours may be extended up to nine hours per day or ten hours per day if the applicable collective bargaining agreement so permits.[1]

[1]   Working Hours Act, s 4b.

B4.2.9   Another form of flexible working hours is only possible if the collective bargaining agreement so permits: working hours during which no overtime premium is paid can generally cover up to 48 hours per week. However, the average weekly working time during the calculation period must correspond to the weekly working hours as set out in the Act on Working Hours Act (40 hours per week) or the respective collective bargaining agreement. This is achieved through compensating extra work with time off.[1]

[1]   Working Hours Act, s 4.

B4.2.10   Hours exceeding the (daily or weekly) statutory standard working time constitute overtime. The employer can request the employee to work overtime if there is a heavier workload or for preparing and finalising work. The employee is obliged to work overtime only if this obligation is laid down by law, collective bargaining agreement, work agreement or individual contract of service, and if the interests of the employee deserving consideration (eg taking care of children) are not an obstacle to it.[1]

The Working Hours Act permits only:
- five hours of overtime work per week (extensions by collective bargaining agreement are permissible); and
- additionally up to 60 hours overtime per year.

---

[1]   Working Hours Act, s 6.

B4.2.11   If overtime work exceeds a statutory maximum amount the employer will be subject to an administrative fine.[1]

[1]   Working Hours Act, s 28.

B4.2.12   If an employee performs overtime work, in addition to regular hourly compensation he is entitled to an overtime premium of 50% of his regular salary per hour of overtime.[1] Collective bargaining agreements often provide for a higher premium for overtime work performed in certain periods (eg at night, over the weekend).

[1]   Working Hours Act, s 10.

B4.2.13   Overtime may also be compensated with time off if this is provided for in the applicable collective bargaining agreement/work agreement or if so agreed between the employer and employee. If payment for overtime is 150% of the salary (including the premium), time off for overtime must also be granted in the same ratio eg a 1 to 1.5 (one-and-a-half hour) ratio.[1]

[1]   Working Hours Act, s 10.

4.3 Opting Out

B4.3.1 It is not possible for employees to opt out of the protection of the Working Hours Act and the Hours of Rest Act.

4.4 Night Workers

B4.4.1 The Act on Heavy Night Work (*Nachtschwerarbeitsgesetz*) provides special legal provisions for the prevention, compensation or alleviation of complications connected with this kind of work. The special provisions concern the amount of annual holiday, rest periods, the law concerning severance pay and protection against dismissal. This Act applies to workers who work between 22:00 and 6:00 and perform the work under difficult circumstances mentioned in the Act.

B4.4.2 The Act on Women's Night Work generally restricts night work for women, who may not work for a period of 11 consecutive hours during the time between 20:00 and 6:00. Several groups of female employees are not subject to the statute (eg doctors, managers) and there are many other exceptions to the rule, permitting night work for women until 22:00, 23:00 or 24:00 or starting from 5:00 (eg for particular types of shift work). It is expected that the night work legislation will be modified soon to provide equal treatment for men and women and implement EC law.

4.5 Rest Period

B4.5.1 The Hours of Rest Act (*Arbeitsruhegesetz*) provides that all employees are entitled to 11 hours' consecutive rest each day. For each calendar week they are entitled to 36 hours' uninterrupted rest, which has to include a full day, normally Sunday.[1]

[1] Hours of Rest Act, 3, 4.

B4.5.2 The Act on Working Hours (*Arbeitszeitgesetz*) provides that an employee working more than six hours a day is entitled to an (unpaid) rest break of at least 30 minutes.[1]

[1] Act on Working Hours, s 11; these daily rest breaks need not be paid.

4.6 Paid Annual Leave

B4.6.1 Employees are entitled to 30 business days' holiday each year (as Saturday is a business day, this generally equates to 25 days for an employee who works Monday to Friday). Part-timers are entitled to pro rata holiday. Holiday entitlement arises at the beginning of the year except in the first year of employment, where the full holiday entitlement only becomes due after six months' service. Before this date the employee is entitled to a proportionate amount of holiday.[1] If the employee has not used up all of his holiday before the end of the employment relationship he is entitled to pro rata holiday pay.[2] It is illegal to pay in lieu of leave save on termination of employment.

[1] See paras **B3.1.1–B3.1.4**.
[2] See paras **B6.8.1–B6.8.3**.

4.7   Remedies

B4.7.1   To supervise and, if necessary, to enforce compliance with health and safety regulations (including legal provisions concerning working time), the labour inspectorates (administrative authorities represented by labour inspectors) have been set up. Among other duties, the labour inspectors are responsible for enforcing record keeping. If they notice infringements of the legal provisions concerning working time they may file a report with the competent criminal administrative authority. The employer may be fined as a result.

B4.7.2   Employees may also bring claims to Employment Courts based on infringements of their rights concerning working time regulations, especially unpaid overtime pay and overtime premiums. Employees will also be protected against termination of the contract if this is in connection with a claim of lawful overtime pay, refusing to work over the working time limits or if they lawfully refuse to perform overtime.[1]

[1]   Labour Relations Act, s 105.

Summary: working hours

	Per day	*Per week*	*Per year*
Standard	8	40	–
Maximum	10	50	–
Permitted overtime	–	5	plus 60
Night work	Act on Heavy Night Work/ Act on Women's Night Work		
Rest periods	11 (plus break of 30 minutes if worked more than six hours)	36	–

---

5   EQUAL OPPORTUNITIES

5.1   Background

B5.1.1   Austrian law contains different sets of rules in different levels of legislation that provide general protection against discrimination by an employer. The constitutional principle of equal treatment[1] outlaws different treatment without good cause. The rulings of the Austrian Constitutional Court hold that differences are only justified if they adhere to objective characteristics.[2] The constitutional principle of equal treatment binds only the legislative and executive powers and provides only Austrian citizens and Austrian legal entities with a subjective right. Austrian courts have established that the constitutional equal treatment principle is also applicable to collective bargaining agreements[3] and work agreements;[4] however, the parties to an employment contract are not bound by this constitutional principle.

[1]   Especially the Constitutional Act of 1867, art 2 (*Staatsgrundgesetz* 1867) and the Austrian Federal Constitution, art 7 (*Bundesverfassungsgesetz*).

[2] Constitutional Court (*Verfassungsgerichtshof*) VfSlg 10.492, 3.778 and others.
[3] Supreme Court (*Oberster Gerichtshof* – OGH) DRdA 1993, 310 and others.
[4] Supreme Court (*Oberster Gerichtshof* – OGH) DRdA 2000, 235 and others.

B5.1.2 European legislation also prohibits discrimination. The Treaty of Amsterdam, art 141, provides that all parties to the Treaty are bound to apply the 'principle, that men and women should receive equal pay for equal work'. In Austria, national legal provisions are found in the Equal Treatment Act (*Gleichbehandlungsgesetz*) which implements the European anti-discrimination provisions. Due to the structure of European law only the European Court of Justice has the right to interpret European law. Therefore the jurisprudence of this court is of fundamental importance in connection with the prevention of discrimination based on sex.

B5.1.3 Legal provisions concerning equal opportunities are found in certain other acts eg for members of the works council,[1] foreign employees,[2] part-time workers,[3] in connection with company pensions,[4] or employees performing tasks in connection with work security.[5]

[1] Labour Relations Act (*Arbeitsverfassungsgesetz*), s 115.
[2] Act on the Employment of Foreigners (*Auslaenderbeschaeftigungsgesetz*), s 8, 14c.
[3] Working Hours Act (*Arbeitszeitgesetz*), s 19d.
[4] Company Pension Act (*Betriebspensionsgesetz*), s 18.
[5] Employment Law Harmonisation Act (*Arbeitsvertragsrechtsanpassungsgesetz*), s 9.

5.2 Unlawful Discrimination

A   DIRECT AND INDIRECT SEX DISCRIMINATION

B5.2.1 The Austrian Equal Treatment Act (*Gleichbehandlungsgesetz*) deals with equal opportunities for men and women concerning working conditions ie the prevention of discrimination based on sex. It covers employers, the parties to collective bargaining agreements (ie unions and chambers of commerce) and work agreements (ie the works council). The core provision of the Equal Treatment Act[1] prohibits all direct and indirect discrimination on the basis of sex in connection with the employment relationship.

[1] Equal Treatment Act (*Gleichbehandlungsgesetz*), s 2.

B5.2.2 Discrimination is defined by the Equal Treatment Act as any detrimental differentiation in treatment without good cause. Direct discrimination occurs where an employer treats one employee less favourably than another because of his sex. The Equal Treatment Act provides that indirect discrimination is also unlawful. This form of discrimination occurs if the differentiation is based on criteria different from the sex of the employee, but which has a disproportionate impact on members of one sex eg special provisions for part-time employees (eg lower hourly wages).[1] In this case the criteria is neutral concerning the employee's sex, but in effect (indirectly) discriminates against women, as they constitute the majority of part-time workers.

[1]   *Jenkins* [1981] ECR 911; see also *Freers and Speckmann* [1996] ECR I–1165.

B5.2.3   Under the Equal Treatment Act, direct and indirect discrimination are treated in the same way.

B5.2.4   The Act prohibits discrimination in connection with:

- the conclusion of the contract of employment;
- determination of remuneration;
- granting of fringe benefits, which do not constitute remuneration;
- training measures;
- promotion;
- all other working conditions; and
- the termination of the employment relationship.

B5.2.5   Less favourable differentiation is only discrimination if it is done without good reason. It may be possible for the employer to justify the differentiation by objective factors which do not have anything to do with discrimination based on sex.[1]

[1]   *Bilka-Kaufhaus GmbH* [1986] ECR 1607; *Nimz* [1991] ECR I–297.

B   HARASSMENT

B5.2.6   The Equal Treatment Act deals with sexual harassment as a form of discrimination based on sex. The employer must not commit actions of harassment himself, nor fail to reasonably prevent sexual harassment by a third party (eg colleague or customer).

B5.2.7   The Equal Treatment Act defines sexual harassment as any sexually-related conduct affecting a person's dignity which is unwanted, inappropriate or indecent for the employee concerned. It also has to create either an intimidating or humiliating working environment or subsequently result in disadvantages in the job because of the victim's reaction (rejection or toleration).[1]

[1]   Equal Treatment Act (*Gleichbehandlungsgesetz*), s 2.

5.3   Disability Discrimination

B5.3.1   The Act on the Employment of Disabled Persons (*Behinderteneinstellungsgesetz*) provides that the remuneration of a disabled person may not be reduced because of his disability ie there must be equal pay for disabled and non-disabled employees.[1] The Act does not otherwise contain an explicit prohibition on disability discrimination, but in the light of the equal treatment principle, a differentiation based on disability will constitute a differentiation based on an illegal criteria and is therefore prohibited.

[1]   Act on the Employment of Disabled Persons, s 7.

	Summary: equal opportunities
Sex	Equal Treatment Act
Race/other	Equal treatment principle in relation to remuneration/ terms and conditions
Disability	Act on Employment of Disabled Persons/equal treatment principle in relation to remuneration/terms and conditions

5.4   Enforcement and Remedies in Discrimination Cases

B5.4.1   An employee who has suffered discrimination may make a claim against the discriminating employer through the Employment Court and claim certain remedies.

B5.4.2   If the discrimination is (directly or indirectly) based on sex, the Equal Treatment Act provides different remedies and time limits for raising a claim depending on the different forms of discrimination:[1]

- if the employment relationship was not finalised for a discriminatory reason, the employee may claim damages of up to two months' pay. The claim must be made within six months;
- if the employee did not get the same wage or fringe benefits as other employees because of his/her sex, he/she has the right to be paid the difference. This claim must be made within three years, if collective bargaining agreements do not provide for other time limits;
- if an employee does not get promoted because of a breach of the Equal Treatment Act, the employee is entitled to damages, which are limited to the wage difference for four months between the remuneration the employee would have earned after the promotion and his actual remuneration. This claim must be made within six months;
- if an employee has been sexually harassed, he/she may file a suit against the harasser and the employer if the employer has negligently failed to put an end to the harassment (eg knowing of the harassment and not taking disciplinary measures against the harassing employee). If the damage is not a financial loss, the employee is entitled to compensation for the injury to his dignity (minimum ATS 5,000 (365)). The claim must be made within six months;
- if the employment of an employee is terminated because of discrimination based on sex, termination can be challenged in court within fourteen days.

[1]   Equal Treatment Act (*Gleichbehandlungsgesetz*), ss 2a, 10b.

B5.4.3   An employee who claims direct or indirect discrimination based on sex has to furnish prima facie evidence for the existence of his claim. The complaint is dismissed if there is evidence that the differentiation results from lawful factors.

B5.4.4   Statistical evidence will be used in cases where an employee claims indirect discrimination to establish whether a measure taken by the employer has a disproportionate impact on the members of one sex.

B5.4.5   If an employee claims to have been treated unfairly in breach of the equal treatment principle he may make a claim at the Employment Court to be put in the same position as comparable employees. This claim must be made within three years if the employment contract or the applicable collective bargaining agreement does not provide for shorter time limits.

B5.4.6   The Equal Treatment Act has also established a special commission, the Equal Opportunities Commission, to deal with all matters of discrimination based on sex. The Equal Opportunities Commission is part of the Federal Chancellery and consists of eleven members, who are nominated by party employer and partly employee organisations. The Commission in particular has to give opinions on questions concerning the violation of the Equal Treatment Act and consider the individual cases brought before it.

B5.4.7   If the Commission finds a breach of the Equal Treatment Act, it will make a written proposal to the employer on how to achieve equal treatment, requesting him to discontinue the discriminatory conduct. Should the employer fail to comply with this request within one month, the case may be brought before the Employment Court for the purpose of declaring a breach of the Equal Treatment Act.

B5.4.8   The Equal Treatment Act created the role of the Equal Opportunities Officer. She and her deputy advise and support those employees who feel that they have been discriminated against because of their sex. She may request the employer to make a written statement and obtain further information within the company. If the Equal Opportunities Officer is convinced that the Equal Treatment Act has been breached, she may refer the case to the Equal Opportunities Commission.

B5.4.9   Apart from the Equal Opportunities Officer, any employee, any employer, the works council or interest groups of employers or employees can file an application for an opinion on a case by the Equal Opportunities Commission. In addition, the Commission can also act in officio.

5.5   Equal Pay and the Equal Treatment Principle

B5.5.1   It is a long established legal principle that an employer may not without good cause treat a single employee (or a small group of employees) worse than other comparable employees with regard to working conditions.[1] This equal treatment principle in practice mainly applies to remuneration, fringe benefits, the granting of company pensions and the employer's use of his/her rights to give orders.

[1]   Supreme Court (*Oberster Gerichtshof* – OGH) ZAS 1996, 167; RdW 1995, 432; DRdA 1996, 24; DRdA 1996, 246 and others.

B5.5.2   The equal treatment principle exists to protect minorities, so the unfairly treated employees must be in a significant minority position.

Therefore the preferential treatment of single employees cannot provide the basis for an equal treatment claim.[1] Only in cases of illegal criteria for differentiation is the number of the employees concerned irrelevant (eg unfavourable treatment based on the works constitution or discrimination because of race or disability).

[1] Supreme Court DRdA 1992, 369; DRdA 1994, 496 and others.

B5.5.3 Because the equal treatment principle only forbids discrimination which is arbitrary or without good reason, objective justification must be considered. A reason is only objective if it is based on the employment relationship. Personal circumstances can only be considered if they have an effect on the employment relationship. The reason also has to be based on a principle which can be generalised.

B5.5.4 It is also established by case law that the application of a deadline is possible,[1] therefore the employer may, for example, refuse to extend a fringe benefit (which has been granted up to a deadline) to new employees as well.

[1] Supreme Court DRdA 1989, 105; ZAS 1986, 167 and others.

6 TERMINATION OF EMPLOYMENT

6.1 Background

B6.1.1 An employment contract is terminated by the expiry of a fixed term contract, the death of the employee, a termination agreement or unilaterally by the employee or the employer with or without notice.

B6.1.2 As a general principle, the termination of an employment contract by giving notice only has to observe statutory notice periods and does not have to be based on good cause. If the employee works in a business with more than four employees, termination can be contested in court if it is unjust on social grounds or based on unlawful criteria. Termination without notice, on the other hand, has to be based on good cause (as provided for in the applicable acts) and terminates the employment relationship immediately.

A TERMINATION BY AGREEMENT

B6.1.3 An employment relationship can be terminated by mutual consent at any time. In the absence of any specific statutory provisions governing the position, the general provisions on the cancellation of contracts apply. A special form is only required in the case of consensual termination of a person who enjoys special protection eg apprentices, expectant mothers etc.

B EXPIRY OF A FIXED TERM CONTRACT

B6.1.4 Fixed term employment contracts do not need to be terminated by giving notice because the nature of fixed term employment suggests that it ends at a fixed date (expiry of term). Even fixed-term contracts can be prematurely terminated by either party for good cause. If the employee continues to work beyond the date on which the contract is to end, with the employer's consent, and a new term is not agreed, the contract of employment will continue for an indefinite period.

C   NOTICE OF TERMINATION

B6.1.5   The most significant distinction in practice is whether there exists a premature termination of employment (constructive dismissal by the employee or summary dismissal by the employer) or whether the employment shall end at a specific date subject to a notice period (termination by either employee or employer).

6.2   Termination with Notice

B6.2.1   Termination with notice does not usually require a reason to be specified and is subject to statutory notice periods that depend on length of employment. Occasionally periods of employment with previous or associated employers are taken into account by agreement.

6.3   Notice Periods

B6.3.1   According to the Act on White-Collar Workers (*Angestelltengesetz*) the employer must respect the following notice periods for the termination of white-collar employees:[1]

Years of service	Notice period
0–2	6 weeks
2–15	2 months
15–25	4 months
more than 25	5 months

[1]   Act on White-Collar Workers, s 20.

B6.3.2   Employment can end only at the end of each calendar quarter (31 March, 30 June, 30 September, 31 December). This rule can be changed by individual agreement so that employment can also end on the 15th or at the end of each month.[1]

[1]   Act on White-Collar Workers, s 20/3.

B6.3.3   For blue-collar workers the applicable notice periods are established in the relevant collective bargaining agreement and are usually not less than two weeks.

B6.3.4   A white-collar employee may terminate employment at the end of every month, but must respect a notice period of one month. This notice period can contractually be extended up to six months, provided the employer's notice period is at least as long.

B6.3.5   A specific form of notice is not normally required, but notice in writing is recommended in case there is any dispute.

B6.3.6   If a works council is established, the employer must notify the works council prior to giving notice to an employee. Within five working days the works council can either object to, not comment on or approve the

37

proposed termination (see paras **B6.6.1–B6.6.14**). If notice is given without notification to the works council or within the time limit granted for comment, it is ineffective.[1]

[1]   Labour Relations Act, s 105.

B6.3.7   It is frequent practice for employers to issue a statement of ordinary termination and, at the same time, to release the employee from work for the duration of the notice period. In such a case the employee will remain on the payroll and will be entitled to his full salary until the notice period has expired. It should be noted that an employee's entitlement to any severance payment is independent of payment for the notice period. An employer may of course insist on the employee continuing to work during the notice period.

B6.3.8   Non-compliance by the terminating party with the prescribed or agreed period or date of notice constitutes untimely notice. Although the employment will effectively terminate prematurely at the incorrect date, the employee is entitled to claim compensation for the period between the actual termination of employment and the date of termination prescribed by law or the employment contract. The party to whom notice was given must be put into the financial situation he would have been in had notice been given in accordance with the agreed or prescribed period or date of notice.[1]

[1]   Act on White-Collar Workers, s 31/1; Civil Code, s 1162b; see paras **B6.7.1–B6.7.2**.

B6.3.9   Employment can be terminated by either party without cause and without observing any special periods or dates of notice, during any probationary period, which must not exceed one month.[1]

[1]   Act on White-Collar Workers, s 19/1; Civil Code, s 1158.

6.4   Termination without Notice

B6.4.1   Employment can be terminated at any time with immediate effect regardless of any notice period, either by employer or employee, for important reasons. Premature termination must always be based on a ground which would make it unreasonable for the employee/employer to continue the employment relationship even with a notice period or until the end of the fixed term.

A   TERMINATION WITHOUT NOTICE BY THE EMPLOYEE (CONSTRUCTIVE DISMISSAL)

B6.4.2   Termination of the employment relationship without notice by the employee (constructive dismissal – *Austritt*) can only be for good cause, and terminates the employment immediately.

B6.4.3   The reasons allowing employees to resign prematurely are stated in the applicable Acts:[1]

- if the employee is unable to continue work; or
- cannot continue work without harm to health or morality; or
- if the employer does not pay his salary properly; or

- ignores other essential obligations of the employment contract; or
- if the employer refuses to respect his statutory duties to protect the employee's life, health or morals.

[1] Act on White-Collar Workers, s 26; Trade Act (*Gewerbeordnung*), s 82a for blue-collar workers.

B6.4.4 After the employee has handed in a justified resignation, he will be entitled to all those claims he would otherwise have been entitled to had the employment relationship been terminated by the employer. Claims for severance pay, holiday compensation and compensation for notice of termination must therefore be satisfied in the event of a justified resignation.[1]

[1] Act on White-Collar Workers, s 29/1; Civil Code, s 1162b.

B6.4.5 If an employee prematurely resigns without good cause, the employment relationship will be terminated immediately. The employee may be held liable to pay damages and cannot assert any of the claims that he would have been entitled to had he resigned for good cause.[1] A good cause entitling the employee to premature termination must be promptly notified to the employer as soon as the cause occurs, otherwise the right to constructive dismissal is forfeited.

[1] Act on White-Collar Workers, s 28; Civil Code, s 1162a.

B   TERMINATION WITHOUT NOTICE BY THE EMPLOYER (SUMMARY DISMISSAL)

B6.4.6 If the employer has a good reason which would make it unreasonable for him to continue to employ the employee, this type of termination is referred to as summary dismissal (*Entlassung*).

B6.4.7 The reasons for summary dismissal according to the Act on White-Collar Workers are eg:
- if the employee is disloyal to the employer; or
- if the employee is unable to perform the promised or appropriate (reasonable) services;
- any breach of the prohibition on competition;
- if the employee disobeys orders;
- if the employee refuses to work for a period deemed reasonable under the circumstances without any legitimate excuse; or
- if he attempts to induce others to disobey the employer's orders.[1]

[1] Act on White-Collar Workers, s 27.

B6.4.8 The grounds for summary dismissal of blue-collar workers are similar and listed exhaustively in the Trade Act (*Gewerbeordnung*).[1]

[1] Trade Act, s 82.

B6.4.9 As a matter of general principle, grounds for dismissal must be asserted immediately. The works council has to be immediately informed of the summary dismissal.[1]

[1] Labour Relations Act, s 106.

B6.4.10   In the case of fair summary dismissal, the employee receives his salary until the date of dismissal, together with any pro rata share of special payments.

B6.4.11   In case of unfair summary dismissal, the employee is entitled to compensation for notice (*Kuendigungsentschaedigung*) ie the remuncration paid for the period which would have had to elapse until the proper date of termination had the employer properly given notice.[1] Other payments that have to be made in case of unfair dismissal are holiday compensation, the pro rata share of special payments and severance pay, if any.

[1]   Act on White-Collar Workers, s 29; Civil Code, s 1162b.

6.5   Protected Employees

B6.5.1   Several groups of employees enjoy special protection against termination with or without notice. The exact scope of protection varies.

B6.5.2   Persons enjoying special protection are in particular:

- apprentices;
- pregnant women;
- mothers or fathers on parental leave;
- persons doing military service or community service in lieu of military service;
- members of the works council; and
- disabled persons.

B6.5.3   The contracts of employment of these employees may not be terminated without prior approval of the Employment Court or other institutions competent in the specific matter. Even ordinary termination requires good cause, and immediate termination is restricted to a few specific reasons.

6.6   Challenge to Notice of Termination (Protection against Termination)

B6.6.1   In all businesses which regularly employ at least five employees, all employees are entitled to protection against termination.

B6.6.2   In general, the employee (or the works council) may contest termination by way of filing a complaint with the Employment Court.

B6.6.3   The employer must notify the works council of the intended termination. The works council may then approve, object to or refrain from comment on the termination within five working days. After that period the employer may proceed with termination.

B6.6.4   In relation to summary dismissal, the works council must be notified without delay after the dismissal, and must comment on the dismissal within three working days.

B6.6.5   Notice of termination can be challenged if:

- it is unjust on social grounds; or
- it is based on an unlawful ground.[1]

[1]   Labour Relations Act, s 105.

B6.6.6   Summary dismissal can be challenged if:

- no good cause exists; *and*
- it is unjust on social grounds; or
- it is based on an unlawful ground.[1]

[1]   Labour Relations Act, s 106.

B6.6.7   In the event of approval of termination by the works council, the employee can contest termination only if it was based on unlawful grounds.

B6.6.8   If the works council objects, the employee concerned can ask the works council to contest termination within one week from the termination date. If the works council refuses to do so or the works council approved or refrained from comment, the employee may contest termination himself. If no works council is established, the employee may contest termination within one week as from termination by filing a complaint with the Employment Court.

B6.6.9   If termination is challenged because it is socially 'unjustified', the employee must prove that:

- termination infringes substantially upon his interests (eg long unemployment); and
- that the terminated employment has lasted at least six months.

B6.6.10   If this requirement is met, the employer may justify termination by proving that:

- termination is based on grounds regarding personal characteristics of the employee that are adverse to the interests of the enterprise (eg frequent absences due to illness,[1] lack of capability to perform contractual duties);[2] or
- that there are economic reasons preventing continuation of employment (eg reduction of workforce, closure of a business).

[1]   Supreme Court (*Oberster Gerichtshof* – OGH) DRdA 1992, 353.
[2]   Supreme Court (*Oberster Gerichtshof* – OGH) DRdA 1988, 229.

B6.6.11   In the event of objection by the works council and if termination is justified according to economic reasons, the employee may still argue that the termination of a comparable employee would have caused less disruption and that the employer should have terminated that employee's contract of employment instead.

B6.6.12   Unlawful termination grounds would include, for example, membership of or working for a trade union, preparing for the election of a works council, running as candidate for the works council or by reason of obviously justified claims by the employee concerning the employment relationship (eg overtime pay). An employee may take legal action against any notice given on unlawful grounds, even if the works council has agreed to termination.

B6.6.13   Both notice of termination and dismissal are challenged by making claims in the Employment Court. If the court dismisses the action, employment will end after the notice period has expired. If the court grants the action, termination (dismissal) is ineffective, the employer must pay arrears of remuneration, and the employee, in turn, must return to work.

B6.6.14   Directors, ie managing directors of limited liability companies and senior executives who have decisive influence on the management of the business, are excluded from the protection procedure.

6.7   Remedies for Dismissal

A   COMPENSATION

B6.7.1   If the employee:
- was subject to summary dismissal without sufficient cause; or
- if he prematurely resigns as a result of good cause acknowledged by law,

he is entitled to compensation for notice.

B6.7.2   The employee who has suffered loss due to premature termination of his employment must be put into the financial situation he would have been in if proper notice had been given to him. Compensation for notice payable to the employee therefore consists of the remuneration that would have been paid had the proper notice period been observed].[1] The employee is also entitled to compensation where insufficient notice is given, ie the notice period was not complied with.

[1]   Act on White Collar Workers (*Angestelltengesetz*), 29.

B6.7.3   If the employee terminates the contract of employment summarily without good cause, he is liable to compensate the employer for any loss he suffers by reason of non-performance of the contractually agreed work, although the employer is obliged to mitigate his loss.[1]

[1]   See para **B6.4.5** for further details.

B   SEVERANCE PAYMENT (ABFERTIGUNG)

B6.7.4   If employment has lasted for three or more years, an employee is entitled to receive severance payment (*abfertigung*) in the event of termination with notice by the employer or in the event of termination by the employee with cause or by termination agreement.[1] If employment is terminated because of the death of the employee, his statutory heirs are, under certain circumstances, entitled to half of the amount of severance pay to which the employee would have been entitled. Severance pay is also due if employment is terminated because the employee has reached retirement age.

[1]   Act on White-Collar Workers, s 23; Act on the Severance Payment for Blue-Collar Workers (*Arbeiterabfertigungsgesetz*).

B6.7.5   The amount due to the employee depends on the length of time the employee has been employed by the employer and is calculated as a multiple of the salary of the last month of employment, increased pro rata by any other payments the employee regularly received eg 13th and 14th monthly salary, regular commission or bonus payments, regularly paid overtime work.

Length of service (years)	Severance payment (months)
3–5	2
5–10	3
10–15	4
15–20	6
20–25	9
over 25	12

B6.7.6   As a matter of general principle, severance pay is not due if:
- the employee gives notice himself; or
- prematurely resigns without cause; or
- is dismissed by the employer for reasons attributable to the employee.

6.8   Other Termination Payments

B6.8.1   If an employment contract is terminated before the employee has taken all of his holiday, he is entitled to a pro rata holiday indemnity payment.[1]

[1]   Vacation Act (*Urlaubsgesetz*), s 9.

B6.8.2   The employee does not have to pay back holiday pay for leave already used in excess of his pro rata holiday entitlement unless the contract of employment is terminated:
- by constructive dismissal without good cause; or
- by summary dismissal for reasons attributable to the employee.

B6.8.3   A pro rata holiday indemnity payment is not due if the employee prematurely resigns without good cause.

6.9   Collective Redundancy

B6.9.1   If the employer intends to substantially reduce staff within a 30-day period, he has to notify the local Labour Exchange office 30 calendar days before giving notice to the first employee (the so-called 'early warning system'). This applies if it is intended to terminate the employment of at least:
- five employees in businesses with 21–100 regularly employed employees; or
- five percent of the workforce in businesses with 100 to 600 employees; or
- 30 employees in businesses with more than 600 regularly employed employees; or
- five employees older than 50 years of age irrespective of the number of employees.[1]

[1]   Act on the Advancement of the Labour Market (*Arbeitsmarkt-foerderungsgesetz*), s 45a.

B6.9.2   The notification must show that the works council has been informed of the mass redundancies. Following this notification, negotiations with the local Labour Exchange office and the works council as well as with the competent chambers of commerce and labour regarding the dismissal of the employees must take place.

B6.9.3   Any dismissal (or giving of notice) expressed prior to the end of the 30-day 'waiting period' is null and void.

B6.9.4   The local employment office can, however, approve the termination prior to the end of the 30-day waiting period if a social plan (see para **B10.3.23**) is filed together with notification of the intended dismissals.

7   YOUNG WORKERS

7.1   General Obligations

B7.1.1   The provisions governing child and youth labour are laid down in the Act on the Employment of Children and Young Persons (*Kinder- und Jugendlichen Beschaeftigungsgesetz*).

B7.1.2   Generally, children (aged 15 or less) must not be employed for any kind of work. This general prohibition does not apply to children who are at least 12 years old and who do a few easy household chores or who work in family businesses or run errands, provided that this work does not pose a risk to their health and development and does not prevent the child from going to school. Children are not allowed to do any work on Sundays or public holidays, and between 20:00 and 8:00 (the night rest period).[1]

[1]   Act of the Employment of Children and Young Persons (*Kinder- und Jugendlichen Beschaeftigungsgesetz*) , s 5a.

B7.1.3   Young persons are individuals who are not children but are not yet 18 years of age. Some protective provisions of the Act of the Employment of Children and Young Persons apply also to apprentices who have already reached age 18.

B7.1.4   Working hours for young persons must not exceed:
- 40 hours a week; and
- eight hours a day.

B7.1.5   The young person must be given time off to attend compulsory vocational school. Remuneration is paid during this time and the classes are credited to weekly working hours.[1]

[1]   Act on the Employment of Children and Young Persons, s 11.

B7.1.6   Young persons are entitled to an uninterrupted half-hour break if their working time exceeds 4.5 hours. They must have an uninterrupted rest period of at least 12 hours at the end of their daily working time.[1] They are not allowed to work between 20:00 and 6:00.[2]

[1]   Act on the Employment of Children and Young Persons, s 15.
[2]   Act on the Employment of Children and Young Persons, s 17.

B7.1.7 Breaches of the provisions governing the employment of children and young persons carry sanctions in the form of administrative fines or prison terms. In the event of repeated breaches, the employer may be prohibited from employing young persons.

7.2 Apprentices

B7.2.1 The provisions governing apprenticeships are laid down in the Vocational Training Act (*Berufsausbildungsgesetz*).

B7.2.2 Apprentices who are under 18 years of age must obtain the consent of their legal representative both for entering into and terminating an apprenticeship contract. The apprenticeship contract must be made in writing.

B7.2.3 The employer is responsible for the on-the-job training of the apprentice. The apprentice may only be assigned to jobs which are compatible with the nature of his training. He must not be assigned to perform any work which exceeds his strength.[1]

[1] Vocational Training Act (*Berufsausbildungsgesetz*), s 9.

B7.2.4 The apprentice is entitled to apprenticeship pay for the term of apprenticeship. If the amount of apprenticeship pay is not governed by any collective bargaining agreement, it will be set out in the apprenticeship contract and must correspond to apprenticeship pay awarded for the same or similar apprenticeship trades.[1]

[1] Vocational Training Act, s 17.

B7.2.5 The apprenticeship always ends upon expiration of the term of apprenticeship agreed in the contract. It may end before expiration of the apprenticeship term for certain reasons laid down by law eg death of the apprentice, death of the apprentice master, lack of authority to train apprentices or the passing of final examinations.[1]

[1] Vocational Training Act, s 14.

B7.2.6 Consensual premature termination of the apprenticeship must be in writing together with a document confirming that the apprentice has been informed about his special protection against termination by the Employment Court or the Chamber of Employees.

B7.2.7 Unilateral termination of apprenticeship by the employer must also be in writing and is possible only on the grounds laid down by law eg criminal conduct of the apprentice, any physical or substantial verbal insult against the employer or persons close to him, neglect or breach of statutory or contractual duties despite repeated warnings.[1]

[1] Vocational Training Act, s 15.

B7.2.8 The apprentice can also only terminate the apprenticeship contract in writing and, if he is under 18, only with the consent of his legal representative. Termination is possible only on the bases laid down by law, such as if the apprenticeship poses a risk to the apprentice's health, or if the employer neglects or is incapable of fulfilling his duties.[1]

[1] Vocational Training Act, s 15/4.

B7.2.9 Upon termination of the apprenticeship by reason of the apprentice passing his final examinations, the employer is obliged to let the apprentice work in the job for which he was trained for another four months.[1]

[1] Vocational Training Act, s 18.

B7.2.10 Breaches of the Vocational Training Act can result in administrative fines or prison terms or a ban on the employment of apprentices.[1]

[1] Vocational Training Act, s 32.

8   MATERNITY AND PARENTAL RIGHTS

8.1   Background

B8.1.1   The provisions concerning expectant mothers are laid down in the Act of Maternity Protection (*Mutterschutzgesetz*), and the rights of the father in the Act on Parental Leave (*Eltern – Karenzurlaubsgesetz).*

B8.1.2   Pregnant women are obliged to notify their employer as soon as they know that they are pregnant, indicating the expected date of confinement. The employer is obliged to notify the pregnancy to the Labour Inspectorate and must make sure that the employee does not perform heavy physical work or engage in any activities that would pose a risk to her own health or the health of her child.

8.2   General Rights

B8.2.1   A female employee must be released from her duty to work, eight weeks prior to the expected date of birth until eight weeks after the birth ('the protection period'). The protection period is prolonged if a medical officer states that the woman's occupation poses a risk to her health or the health of the child.

8.3   Protection from Dismissal

B8.3.1   As a matter of general principle, lawful notice of termination cannot be given to an employee during her pregnancy and for a term of four months after the birth, without the consent of the Employment Court. The employer must either be aware of the pregnancy, or the employee concerned must disclose her pregnancy within five working days after notice was given.[1]

[1] Act of Maternity Protection (*Mutterschutzgesetz*), s 10.

B8.3.2   If the mother takes her maternity leave or works part-time, the period during which she is protected against termination will be extended accordingly. The period of protection against termination ends four weeks after the end of parental leave or part-time work. The same time limits apply in the event of summary dismissal.[1]

[1]   Act of Maternity Protection, s 10/4.

B8.3.3   The employer may obtain the consent of a court for notice or summary dismissal of a person who enjoys special protection against termination. Consent may be granted only for specific reasons set out by law. Notice of termination is generally lawful only if the employer proves that he cannot continue the employment relationship without incurring loss because the scope of its business will either be restricted or shut-down.[1]

[1]   Act of Maternity Protection, s 10.

B8.3.4   The provisions giving protection against termination and dismissal do not apply to fixed-term employment contracts. If the fixed term is not justified by objective reasons or prescribed by law (eg seasonal work as ski instructor or foreigners with temporary work permits), the expiration of a contract will be suspended from the date of notification of pregnancy until the beginning of the protection period (ie eight weeks prior the birth).[1]

Maternity protection from dismissal
Pregnancy   •   four months: after birth
            •   four weeks after the end of parental leave or part-time work

---

[1]   Act of Maternity Protection, s 10a.

8.4   Health and Safety

B8.4.1   The employer must ensure that the expectant mother does not perform heavy physical work or engage in any activities that would pose a risk to her own health or the health of her child.

B8.4.2   Pregnant women and women who are breastfeeding, except in the cases specified by the law:[1]
- must not work overtime;
- must not work on Sundays and public holidays;
- must not work at night;
- must not exceed nine hours daily working time; and
- must not exceed 40 hours weekly working time.

[1]   Act of Maternity Protection, s 3–11.

8.5   Maternity Pay

B8.5.1   During the protection period (eight weeks prior and eight weeks after the birth) public health insurance will pay the expectant mother her full salary.

8.6 Additional Rights to Time Off

B8.6.1   A female employee is entitled to parental leave until two years following the birth of the child. The Act on Parental Leave (*Eltern – Karenzurlaubsgesetz*) also allows fathers to take parental leave if they live in the same household and care predominantly for the child.

B8.6.2   During this period the employee will usually receive parental allowance (*Karenzgeld*) if he/she has paid unemployment insurance contributions for a certain period of time (usually 52 weeks in the last 24 months). Parental allowance is a daily lump sum and does not depend on the previous income of the mother/father.

B8.6.3   A mother/father is also entitled to work part-time up to the child's fourth birthday if neither parent takes parental leave. This period is reduced if parental leave is partly taken.[1]

[1]   Act of Maternity Protection, s 15c.

B8.6.4   Employees are entitled to half the usual statutory severance pay, provided the employment has lasted for an uninterrupted period of five years (but not exceeding three times their monthly remuneration) if they prematurely resign within eight weeks after having given birth to a child (ie within the post-natal protection period). If parental leave is taken, resignation must be handed in no later than three months before the end of this period of parental leave.

B8.6.5   An employee is also entitled to paid leave if his incapacity to work results from his obligation to care for a close relative, especially his children (ie care leave – *Pflegefreistellung*). Each employee is entitled to care leave in an amount not exceeding his regular weekly working hours per year of service, if he proves that his incapacity to work is caused by the fact that he has to take care of a close relative living in the same household who is ill or has had an accident. In relation to children who are younger than 12 years of age, the entitlement for care leave increases by another week. Similar provisions apply to the care of the employee's child if the person who is regularly in charge of caring for the child is prevented from doing so.[1]

[1]   Vacation Act (*Urlaubsgesetz*), s 16.

9   BUSINESS TRANSFERS

9.1   Background

B9.1.1   Pursuant to Directive 77/187/EC (the Acquired Rights Directive),[1] the rights and duties of a transferor of a business resulting from an employment contract are passed to the transferee of the business upon transfer.

[1]   OJ 061 05.03.77 p 26 amended by Directive 98/50/EC (OJ L 201 17.07.98 p 88) and Directive 2001/23/EC (OJ L 082 22.03.01 p 16).

B9.1.2   In addition, Directive 77/187/EC states that the conditions of employment deriving from a collective agreement applicable to the transferor are the same after the transfer until termination of the collective agreement or application of a different collective agreement.

B9.1.3   The Directive also provides that the transfer of a business does not constitute a fair reason for the termination of an employment contract. Termination as a result of economic, technical or organisational reasons is however potentially fair.

B9.1.4   Furthermore, the transferor and transferee are obliged to inform employee representatives about the transfer and must engage in consultation about the transfer upon request.

B9.1.5   The Austrian Employment Law Harmonisation Act (*Arbeitsvertragsrechtsanpassungsgesetz*) was passed in order to implement Council Directive 77/187/EC and applies when a transfer of a business or parts of a business takes place.

B9.1.6   The main points of the Employment Law Harmonisation Act are:
- employment contracts are transferred to the transferee by operation of law;[1]
- collective bargaining agreements remain effective as long as no other collective bargaining agreement applies;[2]
- salaries cannot be reduced even if the new collective bargaining agreement states lower minimum wages;[3]
- a one year cushion applies to worsening of other employment conditions in certain cases;
- work agreements remain valid after the transfer of the business;[4]
- the power of the works council may not be diminished;[5]
- joint and several liability of transferor and transferee applies for obligations of the employment contract,[6] which is particularly important with respect to entitlements for pension payments and severance pay.

[1]   Employment Law Harmonisation Act (*Arbeitsvertragsrechtsanpassungsgesetz*), s 3.
[2]   Employment Law Harmonisation Act, s 4/1.
[3]   Employment Law Harmonisation Act, s 4/2.
[4]   Labour Relations Act (*Arbeitsverfassungsgesetz*), s 31/5–8.
[5]   Labour Relations Act, s 62c.
[6]   Employment Law Harmonisation Act, s 6.

9.2   Identifying a Relevant Transfer

B9.2.1   The term 'part of a business' was introduced by the Employment Law Harmonisation Act (*Arbeitsvertragsrechtsanpassungsesetz*). Difficulties of interpretation arise because this legal term was based on foreign law. However, since the legislature's intention is to fulfil the obligations resulting from Austria's participation in the EU, the interpretation must take the EC Directive 77/187/EC and the cases decided by the European Court of Justice into account.

B9.2.2   The concept of transfer relates to cases in which an economic entity (ie an organised group of persons and assets facilitating the exercise of an economic activity which pursues an objective specific to it) retains its identity following the transaction in question.

49

> In order to determine whether the conditions for the transfer of an entity are met, it is necessary to consider all of the facts characterising the transaction in question, including, in particular:
> - the type of undertaking or business;
> - whether or not its tangible assets, such as buildings and moveable property, are transferred;
> - whether or not its intangible assets are transferred and their value at the time of the transfer;
> - whether or not the majority of its employees are taken over by the new employer;
> - whether or not its customers are transferred;
> - the degree of similarity between the activities pursued before and after the transfer; and
> - the period, if any, for which those activities were suspended.

However, these are single factors in the overall assessment and should not therefore be considered out of the overall context.[1]

[1] *Spijkers* [1986] ECR 1119; *Redmond Stichting* [1992] ECR I–3189.

B9.2.3 In certain labour intensive sectors, a group of workers engaged in activities which they carry on together on a permanent basis may constitute an economic entity. Such an entity is capable of maintaining its identity after it has been transferred, where the new employer does not merely pursue the activity in question but also takes over a significant proportion of the employees, in terms of their numbers and skills, specifically assigned by his predecessor to that task. In those circumstances, the new employer takes over a body of assets enabling him to carry on the activities or certain activities of the transferor undertaking on a regular basis.[1]

[1] *Süzen* [1997] ECR I–1259; see also *Schmidt* [1994] ECR I–1311.

9.3 Affected Employees

B9.3.1 The provisions of the Employment Law Harmonisation Act (*Arbeitsvertragsrechtsanpassungsgesetz*) protect persons who render services in 'personal dependence' ie under a contract of service.[1]

[1] See para **B1.1.2**.

B9.3.2 The employee must be employed by the transferor and be part of the organisation of the business that is subject to the transfer.

B9.3.3 Problems may arise if an employee works in more than one business and only one of those businesses concerned is transferred. In such a case it is decisive in which business the employee predominantly works. For establishing this, the amount of time spent in the respective businesses will be taken into account.

9.4   Effects of the Transfer

B9.4.1   As a matter of general principle a transfer of the business to another owner will not affect the employment relationship. The transferee takes over, by operation of law, all employment relationships together with all rights and obligations existing on the date of transfer.[1] Accordingly, the substance of individual contracts of employment will remain the same and they will not be terminated. This is not applicable in the event of the acquisition of a business that went bankrupt.[2] In this case, the consent of all three parties is needed to take over the employment relationship.

[1]   Employment Law Harmonisation Act (*Arbeitsvertragsrechtsanpassungsgesetz*), s 3/1.
[2]   Employment Law Harmonisation Act, s 3/2.

B9.4.2   The existing employment conditions must remain the same, unless the provisions dealing with collective bargaining agreements, corporate pension promises or the validity of work agreements state differently.[1] The term 'employment conditions' means the complete range of terms that affect employment relations regardless of the source of law, therefore including collective bargaining agreements, work agreements or employment contracts. It also includes conditions that became part of the employment contract by long standing employment practice.[2]

[1]   Employment Law Harmonisation Act, s 3/3.
[2]   See para **B1.3.2.**

B9.4.3   Provisions of collective bargaining agreements can be changed if the transferee belongs to a different collective bargaining agreement that contains different rules, although such a change of applicable collective bargaining agreements may not reduce the salary for standard working hours. If the new collective bargaining agreement provides for lower wages, the more favourable conditions of the old one apply.[1] It should be noted that this rule is only applicable to minimum wages and therefore not applicable to wages higher than those in the collective bargaining agreement.

[1]   Employment Law Harmonisation Act, s 4/2.

B9.4.4   An employee has the right to object to the transfer of his employment within the first month after the transfer of the business, but only if the transferee does not take over the provisions of protection against termination of the collective bargaining agreement or the corporate pension funds.[1] Where the employee does not enjoy this protection or a corporate pension promise, he has no right of objection. Therefore the employment relationship transfers to the transferee even if the employee does not want to work for the transferee. In this case the employee's sole option is resignation.

[1]   Employment Law Harmonisation Act, s 3/4.

9.5   Dismissal of Employees

B9.5.1   The Austrian Supreme Court[1] has held that the Employment Law Harmonisation Act (*Arbeitsvertragsrechtsanpassungsgesetz*) does not contain an express prohibition on termination, but that its provisions are based on the view that a prohibition on termination is necessary to achieve the goal of the Directive. The aim of the Act is the automatic transfer of contracts. Any circumvention of the statute is therefore null and void. In this case – as in other cases of special prohibition against termination – the invalidity principle applies, because damages would not grant enough protection for the employee. Termination of contracts of employment prior to the transfer is therefore void, the consequence being that the employment contracts of the respective employees are transferred to the transferee by operation of law.[2] However, the transferor may prove that the termination was based on grounds not relating to the transfer (ie operational requirements or reasons regarding the personal characteristics of the employee).

[1] Supreme Court (*Oberster Gerichtshof* – OGH) ecolex 1996, 697.
[2] Supreme Court ecolex 1996, 191.

B9.5.2   However, it is unclear how termination by the transferee *after* the transfer of the business is to be treated in this context. There are no relevant cases decided upon by the Supreme Court.

B9.5.3   In our opinion, termination by the transferee cannot be null and void on the basis that it constitutes a circumvention of the provisions of the Employment Law Harmonisation Act (*Arbeitsvertragsrechtsanpassungsgesetz*), because the employment contracts were transferred to the transferee. In the case of termination by the transferor, nullity can be based on the argument that the termination prevents the intended transfer of employment relationships by operation of law. Employees whose contracts have been terminated by the transferee can therefore only rely on general protection against termination.

Dismissal

- *Before the transfer:* dismissal ineffective if employer cannot prove that termination was not based on reasons not relating to the transfer
- *After the transfer:* dismissal likely to be effective but subject to employee's general rights on termination

---

9.6   Variation of Contract

B9.6.1   If the new collective bargaining agreement or the new work agreements would lead to a substantial deterioration of working conditions (eg changes in remuneration), the employee is granted the right to terminate the employment relationship within one month using the periods of notice as set out by statute or by collective bargaining agreements, starting from the time that the employee realised or should have realised the deterioration. To avoid legal uncertainties about the substance of the deterioration, the Employment Law Harmonisation Act (*Arbeitsvertragsrechtsanpassungsgesetz*) enables employees to file an action for a declaratory judgment.[1] It is essential that in this case, the employee is granted the same rights as he is granted in the event of termination by the employer (especially severance pay).

[1]   Employment Law Harmonisation Act, s 3/6.

B9.6.2   The transferee of a business or part of a business can refuse the acceptance of contractual corporate pension promises by giving a proviso. The proviso is on time if made within a deadline to be set by the employee. If the transferee denies the acceptance of a pension promise and the employee did not object to the transfer of his employment, the employee has the right to compensation in the amount of his acquired entitlement.[1] This rule is valid for all cases of cancellation of corporate pension promises as a result of transfers of businesses, in particular as a result of a change or cancellation of collective bargaining agreements and work agreements as well.

[1]   Employment Law Harmonisation Act, s 5.

9.7   Duty of Information and Consultation

B9.7.1   The transferor is obliged to inform the works council about a transfer of business in advance and in due time. This information must include the reasons for the transfer, the legal, economic and social effects on the employees and the measures considered concerning the employees. If the works council so requests, the employer must consult with it.[1]

[1]   Labour Relations Act (*Arbeitsverfassungsgesetz*), s 108/2a.

B9.7.2   After the transfer of the business, the transferee must inform the transferred employees of the change of the employer in writing, within one month.[1]

[1]   Employment Law Harmonisation Act , s 2/6.

9.8   The Effect of the Transfer of Businesses on Collective Bargaining Agreements and Work Agreements

A   COLLECTIVE BARGAINING AGREEMENTS

B9.8.1   Employment conditions that are based on collective bargaining agreements are treated as follows:

*   If the transferee of a business is a member of the same collective bargaining agreement party, there is no change with respect to the governing collective bargaining agreement.
*   If the transferee is not covered by any collective bargaining agreement, the transferee will become a party to the collective bargaining agreement the transferor was a party to.[1] In the event that this provision is not applicable, in particular because the transferor himself only became party to the collective bargaining agreement through a transfer of the business, the transferee must uphold the employment conditions of the transferor's collective bargaining agreement for at least a year.[2]
*   If the transferee is party to another collective bargaining agreement, this agreement applies in relation to the transferred employment

relationships as well. In this case, the Employment Law Harmonisation Act provides that the salary an employee was entitled to for his regular work performance pursuant to a collective bargaining agreement may not be reduced by the transfer of the business.[3]

[1]   Labour Relations Act (*Arbeitsverfassungsgesetz*), s 8/2.
[2]   Employment Law Harmonisation Act , s 4/1.
[3]   Employment Law Harmonisation Act, s 4/2.

B9.8.2   If after the transfer of a business, a newly applicable collective bargaining agreement leads to a substantial deterioration in working conditions , the employees concerned have the right to terminate the employment relationship with the consequences of an employer's termination.[1]

[1]   Employment Law Harmonisation Act, s 3/5: see para **B9.6.1**.

B   WORK AGREEMENTS

B9.8.3   Generally, the continuing validity of any work agreement is assumed. This is the case even where the business does not retain its identity (eg the sale of a business),[1] but rather gets a new identity (by legal independence).[2]

[1]   Labour Relations Act (*Arbeitsverfassungsgesetz*), s 31/4.
[2]   Labour Relations Act, s 31/5.

B9.8.4   Where a business or part of a business is merged with another business, resulting in the establishment of a new business, the work agreement remains valid for those employees that were previously covered by it.[1]

[1]   Labour Relations Act (*Arbeitsverfassungsgesetz*), s 31/6.

B9.8.5   If a business or part of a business does not maintain its identity, because it has been acquired by another business or part of a business, the work agreements of the acquiring corporation are also valid in relation to the acquired business. The work agreements for the acquired business remain valid insofar as the newly applicable agreement does not cover issues that it covers.[1] If all issues are covered by a work agreement of the acquiring business, it is applied to all employment relationships even if this is less favourable for the transferred employees.

[1]   Labour Relations Act, s 31/7.

B9.8.6   In the event that this leads to a substantial deterioration of working conditions, the employees concerned have the right to terminate the employment relationship with the same consequences as if the employer had terminated.[1]

[1]   Employment Law Harmonisation Act, s 3/5: see para **B9.6.1**.

B9.8.7   A special rule was established for work agreements containing pension promises; work agreements of this kind can be terminated by the transferor.[1]

[1]   Labour Relations Act, ss 97/1/18 and 18a, 31/7, 32.

B9.8.8   In the event of a continuing work agreement, both the owner of the business and the newly elected works council enter into the work agreement, meaning that they are subject to all rights and obligations arising from this agreement (eg termination or amendment of the agreement). The termination of work agreements is governed by statutory or contractual provisions.[1]

[1]   Labour Relations Act, ss 32/1, 96/2 and 97/2.

B9.8.9   Terminated work agreements remain valid in relation to previously covered employment relationships, as long as those relationships are not governed by a new work agreement or by a new contract with the employer. Such a contract may not be concluded to the detriment of the employee within one year after the transfer of the business or part of the business.[1]

[1]   Labour Relations Act, s 32/3.

10   COLLECTIVE RIGHTS

10.1 Background

B10.1.1   Industrial relations in Austria are shaped by an institution which is usually called 'social partnership' (*Sozialpartnerschaft*). As a result of the commonly experienced suppression during the Nazi regime and the need to build up a wasted country after the Second World War, employees' and employers' representatives aimed for co-operation rather than opposition. From 1945 onwards a great number of institutions, laws and regulations were introduced as a compromise between the trade unions, which were dominated by the Social Democratic Party, and the predominantly conservative organisations of employers. The conclusion of wage and price agreements characterises these early years of social partnership, being institutionalised by establishing the Wage and Price Parity Commission (*Paritaetische Kommission fuer Lohn und Preisfragen*), chaired by the Federal Chancellor. Relevant Ministers as well as the main interest groups ('the Social Partners' – *Sozialpartner*) take part.

B10.1.2   The Social Partners are:
- the Austrian Chamber of Commerce (*Wirtschaftskammer Oesterreich*);
- the Federal Chamber of Employees (*Bundeskammer fuer Arbeiter und Angestellte);*
- the Association of the Presidents of the Chambers of Agriculture (*Praesidentenkonferenz der Landwirtschaftskammern*);
- the Austrian Trade Union Federation (*Oesterreichischer Gewerkschaftsbund*).

B10.1.3   The two sides of industry have come to terms with each other, maintaining a dialogue and being deeply opposed to social conflict. The spirit of 'social partnership' is therefore best described as co-operation and compromise in industrial relations as well as a high level of centralised problem-solving. One of the obvious effects of this general attitude is that there are almost no strikes and lockouts in Austria, as both employer and employee associations are opposed to industrial action.

B10.1.4   The legal basis for collective rights is to be found in the Labour Relations Act (*Arbeitsverfassungsgesetz*). This Act regulates collective rights at industry level with the conclusion of collective bargaining agreements, or at company level with the establishment of works councils and the conclusion of work agreements.

10.2 Collective Bargaining Agreements

A   BACKGROUND

B10.2.1   The legal framework for collective bargaining is contained in the Labour Relations Act (*Arbeitsverfassungsgesetz*). This includes rules concerning which organisations are permitted to conclude collective bargaining agreements and the permissible content and legal effects of these agreements, as well as conflict rules in the event that more than one collective bargaining agreement is applied to an employment relationship.

B10.2.2   However, the Labour Relations Act does not contain rules on the procedure for adopting collective bargaining agreements. There is no duty to negotiate and there are no provisions for compulsory mediation or similar processes.

B   PARTIES TO COLLECTIVE BARGAINING AGREEMENTS

B10.2.3   The main players in collective bargaining in Austria are the Federal Chamber of Commerce of Austria and its sub-organisations on the one hand, and the Austrian Trade Union Federation and its constituent unions on the other hand. Although the Austrian Chamber of Employees is also permitted to negotiate collective agreements, they do not exercise this right but leave it to the trade unions instead.

C   THE APPLICATION OF A COLLECTIVE BARGAINING
    AGREEMENT AND ITS EFFECT

B10.2.4   The scope of a collective bargaining agreement extends to all employers who are members of the employer organisation that concluded the agreement and to all of their employees regardless of whether or not they are union members. It is illegal to exclude non-union employees from a collective bargaining agreement.[1]

[1]   Labour Relations Act, s 12.

B10.2.5   The provisions included in collective bargaining agreements have a direct impact on individual contracts of employment and may neither be reduced nor abrogated at enterprise or individual level to the disadvantage of workers.[1] However, more favourable regulations for employees are usually possible, provided that the collective bargaining agreement does not exclude any deviation from its provisions. On the other hand, collective bargaining agreements cannot usually alter statutory provisions to the disadvantage of the employee. Rights arising under collective bargaining agreements can be enforced by each and every individual covered by the agreement.

[1]   Labour Relations Act, s 3.

D   MODES AND CONTENTS OF COLLECTIVE BARGAINING AGREEMENTS

B10.2.6   The Labour Relations Act (*Arbeitsverfassungsgesetz*) provides that the following subjects can be regulated by collective bargaining agreements:[1]

- the relations between the parties to the collective bargaining agreement;
- the rights and obligations arising from the employment relationship between employer and employee;
- the change of rights derived from collective bargaining agreements concerning non-active employees (especially provisions concerning pensions);
- social plans ie measures to prevent, remove or mitigate the adverse effects of substantial changes in the business;
- rights of the works council to participate in certain very limited matters (eg social plans);
- common institutions of the parties to the collective bargaining agreement;
- other provisions whose regulation was transferred by law to the parties to the collective bargaining agreement (eg by the Working Hours Act).

[1]   Labour Relations Act , s 2.

B10.2.7   In practice, the most important provisions of collective bargaining agreements concern the limitation of the standard weekly working hours from 40 to 38.5 or 38 hours. As there is no statutory minimum wage in Austria, the minimum wages provided for in collective bargaining agreements are of major importance. Minimum wages are raised every year, and most collective bargaining agreements also provide for annual raises of actual wages. It is very common for collective bargaining agreements to also include provisions concerning the length of paid leave for personal reasons (eg marriage or funerals of relatives). Collective bargaining agreements are also very important for the notice periods for blue-collar workers, because the legal provisions provide for very short periods. It is therefore necessary to establish which collective bargaining agreement applies to an employment relationship and to take its provisions into account in each individual case.

10.3 The Works Council and its Rights

A   WORKS COUNCIL

B10.3.1   Since 1919, Austria has had a statutory system of employee participation at company level in the form of 'works councils' (*Betriebsrat*). The primary task of the works council is to represent the interests of the employees in the company vis-à-vis the employer.[1] The works council aims to facilitate compromise and a balance of interest between employees and employers. If disputes arise under the provisions of the Labour Relations Act dealing with the works council and its rights, they are decided by the Employment Court.

[1]   Labour Relations Act, s 38.

B10.3.2 Works councils must be elected in every business (*Betrieb*), meaning the work place which forms an organisational unit that is largely independent from other parts of the undertaking. Accordingly, a business must have a minimum level of independence, particularly in technical terms concerning its day-to-day business.[1] Several businesses and therefore works councils may exist within the undertaking of one employer.[2]

[1] Labour Relations Act, s 34.
[2] See para **B10.3.10**.

B10.3.3 If a business permanently employs at least five employees older than 18 years of age, a works council must be established. Certain employees, such as members of management or the board of a legal entity, as well as executives who have a decisive influence on the management of the business, do not qualify as employees for this purpose according to the Labour Relations Act.[1]

[1] Labour Relations Act, s 36.

B10.3.4 If any given business employs more than five white-collar workers and more than five blue-collar workers, the Labour Relations Act provides for separate work councils for blue-collar and white-collar workers. For matters concerning both groups of employees in one business, the works councils for blue-collar workers and white-collar workers will together form a joint works committee (*Betriebsausschuss*).[1] However, the two groups of employees may opt for a common works council.

[1] Labour Relations Act, ss 40, 76.

B10.3.5 The number of members to be elected to the works council rises in proportion to the number of employees.[1]

[1] Labour Relations Act, s 50.

B10.3.6 It is calculated as follows:

Number of employees	Members of the works council
5–9	1
10–19	2
20–50	3
51–100	4
over 100 (one hundred)	4 plus 1 additional member for each additional hundred employees (or fraction thereof)
over 1,000 (one thousand)	13 plus 1 additional member for each additional 400 employees (or fraction thereof)

B10.3.7 The works council is elected by all of the employees in the business being older than 18 years of age. To be elected as a member of a works council, a person must in general be employed in the business and be an Austrian citizen or citizen of an EEA member state. In larger businesses, a certain number of members of the works council may be union officials.[1]

[1] Labour Relations Act, s 52.

B10.3.8   In small and medium scale companies, works councils are frequently not established even where many more than the required number of employees are employed.

B10.3.9   The works councils' members are elected for a term of four years. The entire works council may be dismissed before the end of the term by the employees with a two-third majority vote.[1]

[1]   Labour Relations Act, s 62.

B10.3.10   If one employer operates several businesses with different works councils, they may elect a central works council (*Zentralbetriebsrat*) representing the employees' interests in matters concerning employees of more than one business.[1] In affiliated companies eg where legally independent undertakings are merged to form a group under uniform economic management, all works councils or central works councils may form a group wide representation (*Konzernvertretung*).[2] This body of representation, however, has only limited rights unless the works councils decide to delegate power to the group-wide level, which is rarely done.

[1]   Labour Relations Act, ss 80 ff.
[2]   Labour Relations Act, ss 88a ff.

B10.3.11   Undertakings and groups of undertakings with at least 150 employees, in each of at least two different EU or EEA member states, but with no fewer than 1,000 employees in total, and whose central management is located in Austria, must set up a European Works Council on the basis of an agreement between central management and a special negotiating body of the staff.[1] This provision in the Labour Relations Act enacts EC Directive 94/45,[2] concerning European works councils, into Austrian law.

[1]   Labour Relations Act, ss 171 ff.
[2]   OJ L254 30.09.94 p 64.

B   RIGHTS OF THE WORKS COUNCIL

B10.3.12   The Labour Relations Act provides works council participation rights in three different subjects:

- personal;
- social; and
- economic matters.

Rights of participation may be of different intensity:

- to demand information;
- to be actively notified by the employer;
- to supervise certain issues (the employer must then allow such supervision);
- to intervene or to consult in other matters;
- veto rights/rights of approval.

B10.3.13   The most important general rights of the works council include for example:

- The right to supervise the employer's compliance with statutory law safeguarding the interests of the employees. Therefore, the works council may review all payroll records and all documents kept for the purpose of salary computation, check compliance with collective bargaining agreements and work agreements, ensure that occupational safety and health provisions are complied with and inspect personnel files if the employee concerned has agreed.

- The works council may intervene with the employer and with other competent authorities or institutions in all matters relating to the interests of the employees. This includes the right to propose improvements of working conditions, as well as the right to be heard in all such matters.
- The employer must inform the works council, upon the latter's request, of all matters relating to the economic, social, health or cultural interests of the employees.
- The employer is obliged to consult with the works council regularly on current issues and management policies.
- Particularly extensive participation rights exist in the area of occupational health and safety regulations. The works council must be consulted on all relevant decisions and must be given access to health and safety documents and records.

B10.3.14   In personnel matters, the works council has the following rights:

- The works council must be informed if the employer plans to hire new employees. Before hiring, the works council may ask for consultation. After hiring, the works council must be informed of the employment.
- The works council must be informed and, upon request, must be consulted in the case of promotion of an employee.
- Any long term (more than 13 weeks) or permanent assignment of an employee to another position requires the approval of the works council if the assignment will have a disadvantageous impact on the employee's working conditions (especially salary). This approval may be substituted by approval from the Employment Court.
- The works council has (very strong) participation rights concerning the termination of contracts of employment.[1]
- Employee disciplinary measures (other than termination) are only valid if they are regulated in a work agreement and if the works council has participated in the decision-making process or has approved the measure.

[1]   See para **B6.6.1–B6.6.14**.

B10.3.15   Austrian corporate law provides that all joint stock corporations (*Aktiengesellschaft*) and certain limited liability companies (*Gesellschaft mit beschraenkter Haftung*) as well as certain other types of corporate entities must establish a supervisory board (*Aufsichtsrat*). The works council is entitled to nominate one-third of the members of the supervisory board.[1]

[1]   Labour Relations Act, s 110.

B10.3.16   The employee representatives of the supervisory board have the same rights as the other members, except that in order to protect the interests of the shareholders, appointments and recall of the members of the managing board or the chairman and deputy chairman of the supervisory board require a 'double majority'. This means that the majority of the supervisory board as a whole as well as the majority of the capital representatives is necessary.

C   WORK AGREEMENTS

B10.3.17   One of the most important participation rights of the works council is the conclusion of a 'work agreement' (*Betriebsvereinbarung*). This is a collective agreement concluded between the works council and the employer, on issues permitted by the Labour Relations Act or applicable collective bargaining agreements. The Act provides for different types of work agreements, depending on the issue covered.

B10.3.18   For the great majority of issues that may be regulated by work agreement, there is no obligation on either party to conclude such an agreement. In relation to a few matters, however, the law provides for compulsory conciliation. In such cases, if one party (usually the works council) asks for the conclusion of such an agreement and negotiations fail, any party can call upon the Conciliation Board (*Schlichtungsstelle*) to decide the matter, and the work agreement will be substituted by the decision of the Conciliation Board. These work agreements concern eg general working hours, a social plan (measures for the prevention, elimination or mitigation of detrimental consequences of a substantial change in the business) or general rules of conduct in the business.

Works agreements
* between works council and the employer
* relate to some terms and conditions (eg hours), social matters, and general rules of conduct

---

B10.3.19   On issues not regulated by a work agreement, the employer may in general decide matters unilaterally. However, certain measures may not be introduced by the employer without a work agreement permitting such measures, which in effect gives the works council a veto. This is the case, for instance, with technical systems and other means of supervising employees, if such measures have an impact on human dignity (eg certain telephone monitoring or video surveillance systems).[1] On other matters where the employer needs the works council's consent in form of a work agreement, such consent may be substituted by a decision of the Conciliation Board.[2]

[1]   Labour Relations Act, s 96.
[2]   Labour Relations Act, 96a.

B10.3.20   A work agreement has the same legal force as statute, granting individual rights to employees. If the parties to the work agreement exceed their limits, especially if the work agreement covers an issue that cannot be included in such an agreement, the work agreement is invalid and the individual employee cannot derive any rights from it. However, it has been held by rulings of the Austrian Supreme Court, that if such an invalid work

agreement is in fact followed for some time – which is common practice –
an individual employee may be entitled to the benefits provided in the
(invalid) work agreement. This would be on the grounds that there has been
an implicit amendment to the individual contract of service.[1]

[1] Supreme Court (*Oberster Gerichtshof* – OGH) Arb 8802/1970, 8826/1970, 9832/1979 and others.

D   SPECIAL RIGHTS WHERE THERE IS A CHANGE IN OPERATIONS

B10.3.21   The employer must inform the works council of all issues
concerning the economic situation of the enterprise, such as orders booked,
investment projects or the sales situation.[1]

[1] Labour Relations Act, s 108.

B10.3.22   In addition, the employer must notify and consult the works
council before implementing substantial changes in the business, which
include amongst other matters:

- the closure or relocation of the entire business or parts of the business;
- changes in the legal structure or its ownership;
- introduction of important measures to increase productivity; or
- any measure which will cause mass redundancy.[1]

[1] See para **B6.9.1–B6.9.4**.

B10.3.23   In relation to such issues, the works council has the right to
submit proposals to prevent, eliminate or mitigate any negative effects on
the employees. If more than 20 employees are employed and the measure
will result in considerable disadvantages to all or the majority of the
workforce, the works council may request the conclusion of a Social Plan
(*Sozialplan*) ie a work agreement the purpose of which is to prevent,
eliminate or mitigate the anticipated disadvantages. If the Social Plan is not
concluded, a decision by the Conciliation Board may be sought. In practice,
a Social Plan usually provides for additional severance payments (in cases of
dismissal) or other (financial) compensation for employees' disadvantages.

11   EMPLOYMENT DISPUTES

11.1 Jurisdiction

B11.1.1   Labour law matters ie:

- all disputes arising between employers and employees in connection
  with the employment relationship, and its commencement and
  termination (eg unfair dismissal, back pay);
- all disputes between employer or employees and members of the works
  council in connection with their activities; and
- disputes between employees concerning their common activities (eg
  claims for damages); as well as
- disputes concerning collective rights at company level,

must to be transferred to the Employment Court regardless of the value in
dispute. The court is covered by the provisions of the Act on the Procedure
in Labour Law and Social Law Matters (*Arbeits- und Sozialgerichtsgesetz*)
which provides that first instance employment law matters and social

security matters must be referred to the regional courts, acting as employment and social security courts. In Vienna, a special Employment and Social Security Court has been established.

B11.1.2   An appeal from the Employment Court may be made to the Regional Court of Appeals (*Oberlandesgericht*). By way of exception, an appeal can made to the Supreme Court (*Oberster Gerichtshof*) against a judgment given on appeal by the Regional Court of Appeals.

B11.1.3   The local jurisdiction of the Employment Court depends, as a rule, on the place where the employee resides during the employment relationship and (optionally) also on the registered office of an undertaking or the place where at least part of the job was regularly performed or the remuneration was paid.

11.2 Employment Courts

B11.2.1   Employment Courts comprise a panel of three: a legally qualified chairperson, who is a professional judge, and two lay judges with no legal training representing the side of the employee and the employer respectively. The appeal courts and the Supreme Court rule in panels of five: three professional judges and two lay members representing both sides of industry.

12   WHISTLEBLOWING/DATA PROTECTION

12.1 Whistleblowing

B12.1.1   It is a common principle in Austrian employment law that employees are under an obligation not to disclose confidential information or business secrets obtained in the course of their employment relationship even after its termination. Such a disclosure may constitute the basis for summary dismissal[1] and the employer or a third party can sue for damages caused by the employee's behaviour. If such information is revealed for reasons of competition, the employee is also liable to penalties.[2]

[1]   Eg Trade Act (*Gewerbeordnung*), s 82 lit e.
[2]   Unfair Competition Act (*Gesetz gegen den unlauteren Wettbewerb*), s 11.

B12.1.2   Although no specialised legislation exists, jurisprudence has established that an employee who knows that his employer breaks the law (eg tax evasion) may give information against his employer to the competent authority without breaching his obligation of confidentiality.[1] On the other hand, the employee may not threaten disclosure to gain a personal advantage or reveal this information to business partners or the public.[2]

[1]   Supreme Court (*Oberster Gerichtshof* – OGH) DRdA 1997, 389.
[2]   Supreme Court Arb 7622; Administrative Court (*Verwaltungsgerichtshof*) Arb 7431.

12.2 Data Protection

B12.2.1   The Data Protection Act 2000 implements Directive 95/46/EC,[1] on the protection of individuals with regard to the processing of personal data and on the free movement of such data, into Austrian law. This Act, which also applies to the employment relationship, regulates the use of personal data ie data about persons whose identity is determinable. The data covered by the Act is not only electronic data but also hard copies eg personnel files.

[1]   OJ L 281 23.11.95 pp 0031–0050.

B12.2.2   The Data Protection Act 2000 establishes an individual's right to be informed as to who processes what data about an individual, where the data comes from and for what purpose it is used and especially to whom it is transferred. A person also has the right to correction and, if illegally processed, to destruction of the data concerned.

B12.2.3   Provisions restricting the processing of sensitive data (eg data concerning an individual's health or sex life) and the transfer of data, as well as provisions establishing an obligation to notify the relevant authorities of data processing, are also included in the Data Protection Act.

B12.2.4   If the employer wants to establish an electronic data processing system for personal employee data, ranging beyond data the employer is required to process by law (eg for tax or social security reasons), he needs the consent of the works council in the form of a work agreement that may be substituted by a ruling of the Conciliation Board.[1]

[1]   See para **B10.3.18**.

13   HUMAN RIGHTS

13.1 Background

B13.1.1   The European Convention on Human Rights (ECHR) and most of its protocols are directly applicable in Austria and establish individual constitutional rights. It is therefore unlawful to pass legislation and administrative acts which are not in accordance with the provisions of the ECHR. Legislation must be interpreted to be compatible with ECHR rights, or it is subject to annulment by the Constitutional Court. In labour law, freedom of association, particularly concerning trade union membership (art 11) is of relevance.

B13.1.2   The Supreme Court has held in several rulings that the parties to collective bargaining agreements and work agreements are bound by constitutional rights (eg equal treatment) because of the character of these agreements as generally applicable provisions.[1]

[1]   Supreme Court (*Oberster Gerichtshof* – OGH) DRdA 1993, 369; DRdA 1999, 273.

13.2 Private Employers

B13.2.1   Because the rights established by the ECHR are only effective against the state, employees of private entities do not have any rights under the ECHR in relation to their employer.

B13.2.2   Constitutional rights are taken into account when establishing the meaning of public policy. This is called the 'indirect effect of constitutional rights between private parties'.

B13.2.3   This indirect effect is especially important because the Civil Code refers to public policy when providing that a transaction contrary to public policy void. In employment law this, for example, limits the right of the employer to give orders or to discriminate based on race.

B13.2.4   Another area where human rights are considered (especially art 8 ECHR – respect for private and family life) is in dealing with the issue of when technical systems or other means of monitoring employees (eg telephone calls) have an impact on human dignity, in which case they may only be introduced with the consent of the works council.

13.3 Public Employers
B13.3.1   It is clear that the state is obliged to observe constitutional rights when exercising its jurisdiction (eg with regard to civil servants) but opinion is divided as to whether such rights are also directly applicable if the state acts on a private enterprise basis (eg hiring employees on a contractual basis).

13.4 Enforcement
B13.4.1   If constitutional rights are infringed by legislation or administrative acts, the person concerned may institute proceedings against the state with the administrative tribunal or the Employment Court.

B13.4.2   The indirect effect of constitutional rights is claimed in civil courts, especially employment courts eg in cases of compensation for notice because the employee was dismissed on the basis of neglecting an order concerning his private conduct (such conduct has no effect on the employment relationship because an obligation to follow such an order would contravene public policy).

BIBLIOGRAPHY
In English:
- Strasser *Labour law and industrial relations in Austria* (1992)

In German:
- Brodil, Risak and Wolf *Arbeitsrecht in Grundzuegen* (2001)
- Tomandl and Schrammel Arbeitsrecht (1999–2000)
- Schwarz and Löschnigg Arbeitsrecht (2000)

USEFUL WEBSITES
Ministry for Labour and Economic Affairs:
- http://www.bmwa.gv.at

Austrian Federal Economic Chamber:
- http://www.wk.or.at

Austrian legislation (in German) – Legal Information Service of the Federal Chancellery:
- http://www.ris.bka.gv.at

C   Belgium

Stanislas van Wassenhove and Michaël de Leersnyder

Stanislas van Wassenhove is a Partner at CMS Derks Star Busmann
Hanotiau (Belgium). He was admitted in 1984, Brussels and in 1990, Paris.
He was awarded a Dr Jur, 1981; Dr Jr in International Public Affairs, 1982
from the University of Louvain. He is a Lecturer in Social Law at the
Brussels Bar Trainee School; a contributor to *Trends-Tendances*, Belgium's
leading business magazine; Head of the Association of Social Law
Practitioners (AJPDS); President of the CMS Practice Group Employment
and Pensions; member of the European Employment Lawyers Association.

Michaël de Leersnyder is a Senior Associate at CMS Derks Star Busmann
Hanotiau (Belgium). He was admitted in1994, Brussels, He studied at
University of Brussels ULB (Dr Jr, 1994; Special degree in Economic Law,
1995), and the University of Aberdeen, (Certificate of Legal Studies, 1994).
He is a Secretary of the Association of Social Law Practitioners (AJPDS);
contributor to *Guide des Sociétés* (social) published by Kluwer.

CMS Derks Star Busmann Hanotiau, Brussels

Tel: +32 2 626 22 00
Fax: +32 2 626 22 55
Email: svanwassenhove@cmslegal.be; mdeleersnyder@cmslegal.be
Website: www.cmslegal.be

BELGIUM

Rights	Yes/No	Explanatory Notes
THE EMPLOYMENT RELATIONSHIP		
Minimum notice:	YES	Period depends on blue or white-collar status of employee
Express	YES	Certain express terms must be set down in writing (eg probationary period)
Implied	YES	But rare in Belgian law
Incorporated	YES	Very common; incorporated by statute and collective bargaining agreements
REMUNERATION		
Minimum wage regulation	NO	'Wage restraint' measures are indicative, not compulsory
Further rights and obligations:		
Right to paid holiday	YES	Based on days worked during previous years; employees receive additional pay for holiday period
Right to sick pay	YES	Amount and period of payment depends on blue or white-collar status
WORKING TIME		
Regulation of hours per day/ working week	YES	Depends on whether a fixed or variable work schedule applies
Regulation of night work	YES	Night-work generally forbidden, subject to limited exceptions
Right to rest periods	YES	11 hours per 24 hours, plus weekly and daily rest
EQUAL OPPORTUNITIES		
Discrimination protection:		
Sex	YES	Statutory protection; equal treatment principle in relation to sex, pregnancy or maternity, and harassment
Race	YES	Statutory protection
Marital status	NO	Not expressly covered
Disability	YES	
Religion	NO	But may be unlawful if religious characteristic is also a racial characteristic
Age	YES	
Sexual orientation	NO	
Transsexuals/gender reassignment	NO	
Equal pay legislation	YES	Covered by the equal treatment statute, which guarantees equal remuneration for men and women

TERMINATION OF EMPLOYMENT

Right not to be dismissed in breach of contract	YES	
Statutory rights on termination	YES	Right to challenge reasons for dismissal usually only applies to blue-collar employees

REDUNDANCY/ COLLECTIVE DISMISSALS

Statutory definition	YES	Dismissal of at least 10 in a company employing a least 20 employees
Right to payment on collective dismissal	YES	Special compensation payable where the employer dismisses at least six employees
Right to collective consultation	YES	With works council, trade union, European Works Council. Dismissals cannot be implemented for one month after notification to state employment agency

YOUNG WORKERS

Protection of children and young persons at work	YES	

MATERNITY RIGHTS

Right to maternity leave	YES	15 weeks
Maternity pay (during leave)	YES	Maternity allowance paid by state, not employer
Protection from dismissal	YES	Protection runs from notification of pregnancy to one month after the end of maternity leave
Health and safety protection	YES	Whilst pregnant or breastfeeding
Right to parental leave	YES	Three months for both parents
Right to time off for dependants	YES	Right to ten days per annum for urgent reasons (eg sickness of relatives)

BUSINESS TRANSFERS

Right to protection on transfer	YES	Applies to all employees
Transfer of employment obligations	YES	All terms and conditions and collective bargaining agreements transferred
Right to information and consultation	YES	Consultation required if 'measures' are to be taken
Right not to be dismissed	YES	But no additional penalty other than severance pay due for 'normal' dismissal

COLLECTIVE RIGHTS AND BARGAINING

Staff representation	YES	Employees represented by joint committees, unions, and employee representatives. Health and safety committee required where there are 50 or more employees. Works council required where there are 100 or more employees

EMPLOYMENT DISPUTES

WHISTLEBLOWING

Protection from dismissal/ detriment	NO	

DATA PROTECTION

Protection	YES	'Personal data' on employees is controlled

HUMAN RIGHTS

Statutory protection of human rights	YES	European Convention on Human Rights implemented in domestic law

1   THE EMPLOYMENT RELATIONSHIP

1.1   Background

C1.1.1   In Belgium, labour relations are strictly regulated and the parties' freedom of contract is limited by a large number of complex statutory rules, regulations, and legally enforceable collective agreements from which no contractual derogation is permissible.

C1.1.2   The main feature of Belgian employment law is a specific source of law: the collective bargaining agreement concluded by employees and employers' representatives going from national to company level.

C1.1.3   Most of these rules are deemed to be matters of public policy and will apply to any employment relationship in Belgium, irrespective of any choice of foreign law and regardless of the fact that the employees and/or the employer may be foreign nationals or entities.

C1.1.4   Belgian law provides many minimum conditions of employment which the parties may not exclude by agreement (eg conditions as to minimum wage, holiday, and maximum overtime), although it is of course always possible to adopt standards or conditions of employment which are more favourable to the employee.

C1.1.5   The Belgian Civil Code also applies in relation to basic principles of contract law, and will regulate those relations between the employer and the employee which are not regulated by any other source of labour law.

1.2   Contract of Service

C1.2.1   The expression 'contract of service' would be understood in Belgium to refer to a contract or arrangement dealing with the relationship between a company or an individual on the one part and a self-employed person on the other, as opposed to an employment contract. This chapter will only examine the latter, since different rules apply to each type of contract.

C1.2.2   There is a general distinction in Belgian employment law between manual (or 'blue-collar') employees and 'intellectual' (or 'white-collar') employees. In Belgium, the term 'travailleur', which would normally be translated as 'worker', would usually be used to refer to both categories. Nevertheless, taking into account the particular meaning of the term 'worker' to English readers, we will use the term 'employee' throughout, where necessary.

C1.2.3   An employment contract between an employer and an employee is a contract by which the employee commits himself to provide work under the authority of an employer in exchange for remuneration.[1]

[1]   Statute on Contracts of Employment (3 July 1978), arts 2, 3.

C1.2.4 Based on this definition, there are three essential elements in any employment contract: work, remuneration and the authority of the employer over the employee.

Elements of the employment contract between employer and employee
- work
- remuneration
- authority of the employer

C1.2.5 Belgian employment law is founded upon numerous sources of obligations. These obligations are set out in order of priority by the Statute on Collective Bargaining Agreements (5 December 1968), art 51:
- mandatory statutory provisions (both of Belgian and international law);
- Collective Bargaining Agreements (CBAs);
- the employment contract, work regulations, non-mandatory statutory provisions, oral agreements, and finally custom and practice.

A   CONTRACT AND ITS WRITTEN PARTICULARS

C1.2.6 An employment contract can either be oral or written. Certain contracts, for example fixed-term contracts, student contracts (ie contracts with students), and replacement contracts (ie contracts by which the employer is permitted to replace an absent employee for a specified period) must be in writing, otherwise they will be considered to be for an indefinite period.

C1.2.7 Oral employment contracts are possible, because all essential provisions are laid down by Belgian law ie in the Statute on Contracts of Employment (3 July 1978) or in other regulations. For instance, the Statute relating to the Implementation of Work Regulations (8 April 1965) requires that every company must have work regulations, including work schedules, disciplinary sanctions, intervals at which remuneration is paid, and other similar matters. Most contracts in Belgium will be in writing in any event because certain provisions must be set out in a written contract (such as any probationary or trial period, or terms relating to part-time work). If the contract is not in writing, it will be considered to be for an indefinite period.

C1.2.8 If the parties decide to have a written contract they must ensure that all terms are in accordance with the provisions of Belgian law.

B   TERMS OF THE CONTRACT

C1.2.9 The relationship between employer and employee is regulated by Statutes, CBAs, work regulations and, in certain instances, written contractual provisions (see para **C1.2.7**).

C1.2.10 However, companies will frequently have specific rules that are not necessarily contained in one of the above-mentioned documents;

eg there might be specific terms covering group insurance, meal vouchers, reimbursement of expenses and company cars. These terms will also form part of the employment contract.

Regulation of the employment relationship
- statute
- Collective Bargaining Agreements
- work regulations
- contractual provisions

Express terms

C1.2.11   Express terms will normally be in writing. They set out the agreement reached between the employer and the employee. Such terms will only be valid if they are not contrary to statutory provisions or another superior source of law (see the hierarchy set out at para **C1.2.5**).

C1.2.12   Certain express terms can only be laid down in a written contract; eg the notice period for workers earning more than 1,912,000 BEF gross per year (see paras **C6.2.3–C6.2.4**) or any probationary period.

Implied terms

C1.2.13   Implied terms are rare under Belgian law, because of the importance and the extent of statutory provisions (as referred to at paras **C1.3.1–C1.3.4**) namely national and international law, and CBAs. So, for example, the duties of employees and employers are laid down by the Statute on Contracts of Employment (3 July 1978), art 17 (employees' duties) and arts 20–21 (employers' duties).

C1.2.14   Terms contained in a CBA are incorporated in the employment contract unless the contrary is stipulated. Even when a CBA expires, its provisions will continue to apply by reference to the employment contract.

Incorporated terms

C1.2.15   The parties may incorporate terms from other sources or documents, such as particular terms regarding company cars, disciplinary codes, work rules, stock option schemes, or pension schemes, into their relationship. Normally, for such terms to be enforceable, the employer will have to prove that the employees have knowledge of these terms, normally by sending them a copy of the terms and requiring the employees to acknowledge receipt.

Statutory provisions

C1.2.16   As already noted, statutory provisions are the foundation of the relationship between the parties. If the parties have not concluded a written contract, the statutory provisions will apply. If the parties have concluded a written contract, the provisions contained in the contract will only be valid insofar as they are not contrary to mandatory statutory provisions (in Belgium most of the statutory provisions are mandatory since they are for the protection of the weaker party, namely the employee).

C1.2.17   Statutory provisions cover important issues such as the length of the notice period, the parties' obligations, maximum and minimum hours of work, and minimum wage.

1.3   Variation of Contract

C1.3.1   Based on the Civil Code[1] an employment contract has the same force as a statute, which is the highest source of obligations between the parties and cannot therefore be altered unilaterally.

[1]   Civil Code, art 1134.

C1.3.2   Belgian law does not permit the employer to unilaterally alter essential elements of the contract, such as the employee's job description or duties, remuneration, contractual hours and place of work, unless the modifications are minor and the contract allows for the possibility of variation.

C1.3.3   Moreover, the Statute on Contracts of Employment (3 July 1978), art 25, provides that any clause by which the employer reserves the right to unilaterally alter terms of the employment contract is void. Recent case law has, however, made it clear that this provision applies only to important modifications.

C1.3.4   Where the employer proposes to change non-essential terms of the contract, case law states that if the contract expressly mentions that a certain term is non-essential to the main purpose of the contract (and that it is effectively non-essential), the employer should be permitted to modify it without the consent or agreement of the employee.

Variation of contract

Contract cannot be varied unless:
- contract permits unilateral variation; AND
- term to be varied is non-essential

1.4   Remedies

A   EMPLOYEES' REMEDIES

C1.4.1   If the employer does not fulfil his/her obligations, the employee can ask the court to enforce the terms of the contract.

C1.4.2   The employee can also bring an action to rescind the contract, and sue the employer in damages for breach.

C1.4.3 Finally, the employee can invoke the existence of an act which amounts to a breach of the contract (the *'acte équipollent à rupture'*) and ask for an indemnity payment equal to the notice period to which he/she is entitled. The employee must act before too long a period has elapsed; failure to do so means that the employee will be taken in law as having given consent to the modification of his/her working conditions.

C1.4.4 On dismissal by an employer, an employee is entitled to a notice period or a payment in lieu of notice (except where the employee is dismissed for a serious breach of the contract – see para **C6.1.9**). The employee may be entitled to specific damages if there has been an unfair dismissal.

C1.4.5 The Belgian courts are not normally empowered to order the continued performance of an employment contract once it has been breached by one of the parties. In some particular situations, trades unions or employees must request reinstatement of the employees before seeking damages for breach. This is mainly the case with protected workers such as candidates and elected employees of the works council and the committee for prevention and protection (a health and safety committee that must be in place in every company which has more than 50 employees).

Remedies: employee

- action to enforce contract terms
- action to rescind contract
- damages for unfair dismissal
- right to notice or pay in lieu of notice

B   EMPLOYERS' REMEDIES

C1.4.6 If the employee terminates the contract, he must normally serve a notice period. If the employee fails to do so, he will have to make a payment in lieu of notice to the employer.

C1.4.7 If an employee refuses to work normally (other than by reason of a strike), the employer may 'punish' the employee with specific sanctions if those sanctions are laid down in the work regulations (see paras **C11.1.1–C11.3.1**). However, in doing so, the employer runs the risk that such disciplinary provisions may be contrary to the Statute on Contracts of Employment (3 July 1978), art 25, which provides that any clause by which the employer reserves the right to unilaterally alter terms of the employment contract is void.

C1.4.8 If the employee's breach is sufficiently serious, the employer may terminate the contract without notice or pay in lieu of notice, and eventually seek damages if he can prove that the employee's actions have caused him damage. However, this is subject to the limits of the exclusion of liability contained in the Statute on Contracts of Employment (3 July 1978), art 18.

This states that in case of damage caused by the employee to the employer or to a third party, the employee will only be liable for his '*dolus malus*' or wilful fraud and his fault. The employee may be liable for quite minor faults if these are habitual in character.

C1.4.9 Under Belgian law, an employee may work for a competitor after the end of his employment (as long as there is no non-compete clause and if the competition is 'loyal'), and the employer cannot therefore claim for damages on that basis alone. The meaning of the term 'loyal' is very complex and the issue will be determined by a judge taking all the circumstances into consideration.

Remedies: employer
- summary dismissal/damages
- withholding wages
- disciplinary sanctions as set out in the work regulations

---

2   REMUNERATION

2.1   Background

C2.1.1   Remuneration is one of the key elements necessary for the existence of an employment contract. The meaning of remuneration is mainly determined by the Statute concerning the Protection of Employee Remuneration (12 April 1965), but is also dealt with in art 141 (formerly 119) of the EC Treaty, in the Statute on Contracts of Employment (3 July 1978), art 39 (as to payments in lieu of notice) and in the Statute concerning employee social security (28 June 1969), art 14.

2.2   Legal Regulation of Remuneration

C2.2.1   Until recently in Belgium, it was traditional for minimum wage levels to be determined not by the state but by CBAs between employers and employee representative committees, or at an inter-professional level (regulated by Collective Bargaining Agreement 43). From the 1980s onwards, the national legislator made special decrees on this issue, because it became increasingly difficult for the employer and employee representative committees to control excessive remuneration costs (which in turn made competition with other countries difficult).

C2.2.2   At the beginning of the 1990s, the national legislator was forced to intervene once again, and introduced a system whereby every two years a benchmark is fixed within which remuneration can evolve ie a wage inflation figure. This benchmark (contained in the Statute of 7 July 1996) was determined by considering the remuneration cost in Belgium's three neighbouring countries (France, Luxembourg and the Netherlands). These measures were known as the 'wage restraint' measures.

C2.2.3 Since 1 January 1999, the wage restraint measure (5.9%) has been considered as being only indicative rather than compulsory (for the period 1999–2000).

Amount and type of remuneration

C2.2.4 The amount of remuneration payable to the employee is fixed in the employment contract (if there is a written contract).

C2.2.5 Remuneration may vary in accordance with salary scales (minimum wage levels) which vary from joint committee to joint committee (divided by theoretical divisions of different branches of the economy), or, if no decision is made at joint committee level, CBA 43 will apply.

C2.2.6 To calculate whether the minimum wage has been observed, one must take into account not only the employee's normal remuneration, but also any benefits in kind and tips. The value of the benefits in kind in question must be determined, according to case law, by their real value and not their value as agreed between the parties.

C2.2.7 The following are classed as remuneration according to the Statute concerning the Protection of Employee Remuneration (12 April 1965), art 2:

- the monetary remuneration to which the employee is entitled by reason of his employment;
- any tips and service money to which the employee is entitled by reason of his employment or by custom;
- any benefits in kind to which the employee is entitled by reason of his employment.

C2.2.8 Salary is normally index-linked and salary scales are revised as provided by the relevant CBAs (at joint committee or at an inter-professional level).

2.3 Deductions from Wages

C2.3.1 An employer is not normally permitted to withhold the employee's wages or make any deduction from the employee's wages without express approval. Approval is only valid when given after the reason why the employer wants to withhold or make a deduction has been made clear.[1]

[1] Statute on the Protection of Employee Remuneration (12 April 1965), art 23.

2.4 Itemised Pay Statement

C2.4.1 The employee will receive an itemised pay statement at least once a month (sometimes once a fortnight).

3   FURTHER RIGHTS AND OBLIGATIONS

3.1   Holiday Entitlement

C3.1.1   Belgium has special rules regarding holiday entitlement, which are contained primarily in the Statute of 4 January 1974. Each employee is entitled to annual holiday leave based on days worked during the previous year. An employee employed on a five-day week who has worked for 12 months during the previous year would be entitled to 20 days' holiday. The employee's salary during this holiday period is equal to 190% of the employee's usual salary, and is paid by the employer.

C3.1.2   In addition, there are ten official public holidays in Belgium (1 January, Easter Monday, 1 May, Ascension Day, Whit Monday, 21 July, 15 August, 1 and 11 November, 25 December). Employees are entitled to their full normal pay in respect of these days, plus an additional day off in lieu if the public holiday falls on a day which is not normally worked in the company (eg because the public holiday falls on a Saturday or Sunday).

C3.1.3   Employees are also entitled to ten days' leave for urgent reasons (eg sickness of relatives) and other additional leave for special occurrences (eg marriage, birth, or death of a relative). The amount of leave allowed is set by law.

Rights to leave

- holiday
- public holidays
- urgent leave (ten days)
- special leave (set by law)

3.2   Sick Pay

C3.2.1   Employees are entitled to receive pay during periods of sickness or invalidity. Their medical expenses are partially reimbursed by the Invalidity Institute, which is a state body. It is not unusual for employees and employers in Belgium to pay for private healthcare to cover expenses that are not covered by the social security system.

C3.2.2   The employer has to pay the employee's remuneration at the start of his incapacity, for a limited duration with the level of guaranteed remuneration varying as between blue-collar and white-collar employees. If the origin of the incapacity is work-related, the employer will be reimbursed, either by private insurance or by the state. After the period covered by the employer's remuneration has elapsed, the social security branches intervene eg payments may be made from a fund held to compensate for work-related accidents.

3.3   Additional Rights

A   SOCIAL SECURITY PROVISIONS

C3.3.1   Belgium has a highly developed social security system providing employees with welfare benefits in the form of a state pension, sickness benefits, family allowances and unemployment benefits. The system is funded by contributions from both the employer and employees, calculated as a percentage of, and withheld from, monthly salary. The contribution currently represents 13.07% of gross salary for employees and about 34% (40% for manual workers of the gross salary multiplied by 108%) of the gross salary for the employer.

Employee contributions:

- 13.07% gross salary

Employer contributions:

- blue-collar employees: (gross salary x 40%) x 108%
- white-collar employees: gross salary x 34%
- unemployment compensation

C3.3.2   A person who involuntarily becomes unemployed and who is also able to demonstrate that he has worked during a certain predefined period prior to being unemployed, is entitled to unemployment benefits. In 1999 this amounted to a maximum of 30,966 BEF per month.

Family allowances

C3.3.3   Employees who have dependent children under the age of 26 are entitled to family allowances.

Retirement

State retirement benefits

C3.3.4   The legal pensionable age in Belgium is 65 years. However, from 2005, all employees are entitled to a state retirement pension upon reaching the age of 60 with a minimum of 35 years' career.

C3.3.5   On the death of the retired employee, a survivor's pension equal to 80% of the normal pension amount is payable to the surviving spouse if he or she is at least 45 years old.

Early retirement

C3.3.6   To qualify for an early retirement pension ('pre-pension'), an employee must be at least 60 years old and must have been dismissed by the employer (the system of pre-pension has to be laid down in a joint committee's CBA; the CBA may reduce the eligibility age to 58). The pension is paid by the employer in addition to unemployment benefits paid by the social security authorities until the employee reaches 65 years of age. The employer is obliged to replace the pre-pensioned employee with an unemployed person.

C3.3.7   In certain circumstances, the pre-pension age may be reduced to 52 by the Minister of Employment (in respect of enterprises recognised as being in economic difficulties or which are restructuring).

Pension scheme

C3.3.8   Employers may subscribe to a collective insurance policy for their employees under different conditions to insure them with extra pension benefits with defined contributions or defined benefits. The Statute of 6 April 1995 protects employees against discrimination on the basis of sex, and lays down specific provisions relating to information, participation and transfer.

4   WORKING TIME

4.1   Background

C4.1.1   The Statute on Employment (16 March 1971) regulates working hours and is applicable to almost all private (ie non-public) employees and employers.[1]

[1]   The Statute on Employment (16 March 1971), art 1.

C4.1.2   The most important exclusion from this measure is laid down by Royal Decree of 10 February 1965, which excludes persons with leading positions or who have a '*poste de confiance*'. The Royal Decree gives a limited description of persons included within this definition, for example, directors, deputy directors, private secretaries, and individuals who can represent the company vis-à-vis third parties.

C4.1.3   Working hours are the hours during which the employee is at the disposal of the company, as defined by case law.

C4.1.4   The regulations in respect of working hours are very complex and difficult to summarise. The following is a summary of only the most important rules.

4.2   Legislative Control

C4.2.1   There is an important distinction between a fixed work schedule and a variable work schedule.

C4.2.2   In a system with a fixed work schedule, according to the Statute on Employment (16 March 1971), working hours are limited to a maximum of 8 hours a day and 39 hours a week. It is possible to reduce the weekly limit to less than 39 hours by CBA (but this must be without loss of remuneration for the employees).

C4.2.3 Under certain circumstances, the daily limit of eight hours can be increased to nine hours if during the same week the employee receives at least half a day's compensatory rest excluding Sunday. The daily limit can even be increased to ten hours for employees who cannot return home every day, for example because they must perform duties abroad.

C4.2.4 The absolute maximum limit on hours is 12 hours a day and 50 hours a week (in relation to continuous work) or 8 hours a day and 56 hours a week (in relation to work necessary to prevent or remedy an accident, or work necessary on machines or material. By way of an example, employees on a building site may be required to work more than the usual limit on hours because they have prepared concrete for use on the site and need to finish their work before the concrete becomes useless.

C4.2.5 In a system with a *variable* work schedule, maximum working hours can be fixed on an annual basis. Either a CBA or work regulation fixes the average weekly work schedule within determined limits, provided this is in compliance with specific rules provided by the Statute on Employment (16 March 1971), in order to introduce a flexible schedule.

C4.2.6 Very stringent and specific provisions apply where an employee works on a part-time basis. Civil and criminal sanctions may be imposed where limits are exceeded. The minimum working hours are at least three consecutive hours and one-third of the full-time working week, unless a CBA between the employer and the employee representatives specifies a shorter period.

C4.2.7 The work schedule of part-time employees must be publicised. In addition, the schedule and number of working hours per week must be set out in writing in the employment contract.

Fixed work schedule	Variable work schedule
• 8 hours a day/39 hours a week	• hours fixed on an annual basis or by CBA
• 9 hours a day (entitlement to a half-day's compensatory rest excluding Sunday), or	
• 10 hours a day (employee unable to return home), or	
• 12 hours a day/50 hours a week (continuous work), or	
• 8 hours a day/56 hours a week (prevention/remedy of an accident or work with machines or materials).	

4.3 Opting Out/Additional Hours

C4.3.1 In principle, an employee is not permitted to work in excess of the time determined in the work schedule. This general rule applies to full and part-time employees, whether on a fixed or variable work schedule. Nevertheless, under certain circumstances specified in the law, overtime is permitted. In some cases special formalities must be met.[1] If overtime is worked, additional remuneration must be paid; in principle, this will be an additional 50% of usual pay, plus the employee must take compensatory holiday for the period of overtime worked within a certain time limit.

[1]   See Statute on Employment (16 March 1971), art 22.

C4.3.2 It is not possible for the parties to agree that the schedules will not apply. The parties can agree to change the schedule, but only if this has been envisaged by the work regulation.

4.4 Night Work

C4.4.1 In Belgium, the general rule is that night work (ie between 20:00 and 6:00) is forbidden.

C4.4.2 There are three exceptions to this prohibition: firstly, where night work is unavoidable because of the nature of the work[1] (eg work for hotels or for travel agencies); secondly, where night work is justified because of economic imperatives[2] (eg in the building sector, or international commerce); thirdly, where a Royal Decree recognises a special exception to the rules.[3]

[1]   Statute on Employment (16 March 1971), art 36.
[2]   Statute on Employment (16 March 1971), art 37.
[3]   Statute on Employment (16 March 1971), art 37(1).

C4.4.3 If night work is to be introduced into a company ie where the employer wishes to take advantage of one of the exceptions set out in para C4.4.2, special rules and procedures must be respected.[1]

[1]   Statute on Employment (16 March 1971), art 38.

4.5 Rest Periods

C4.5.1 Employees must be permitted to rest for 11 hours before resuming work in any 24-hour period. This period is additional to the Sunday break (or the break replacing the Sunday break if the employees work on Sunday) where the total period of rest would therefore amount to 35 hours (24 plus 11 hours).

C4.5.2 The Statute on Employment (16 March 1971) lays down some very limited exceptions to the above.[1]

[1]   Statute on Employment (16 March 1971), art 38.

C4.5.3 The law also provides that an employee may not normally work more than six consecutive hours without a 15-minute break.

4.6   Paid Annual Leave

C4.6.1   This issue is dealt with at paras **C3.1.1–C3.1.3**.

4.7   Remedies

C4.7.1   Limits on working hours, payment of extra pay and compensatory breaks are supervised by the Work Inspector, a public body responsible for these regulations.

C4.7.2   Employees may also file claims with the tribunals in the event of breach of these provisions.

C4.7.3   If employers do not respect these provisions they are liable to be fined or even imprisoned, in addition to having to account for extra pay to the affected employees.

5   EQUAL OPPORTUNITIES

5.1   Background

C5.1.1   Until recently in Belgium, in contrast to many other European countries, equal opportunities was not subject to significant legislation. There is therefore only limited Belgian case law in relation to equal opportunities. The European Convention that presumes equal pay for equal work, forbids only wage differences which have their source in discrimination based on the sex of the person.

A   RELIGIOUS DISCRIMINATION

C5.1.2   The legislation makes no express reference to discrimination on the grounds of religion. Nevertheless, a claim may be brought where the complainant's religious characteristics are also racial characteristics and he suffers discrimination on those grounds.

B   POSITIVE DISCRIMINATION

C5.1.3   Positive discrimination in favour of certain sexual or racial groups is generally unlawful.

C   AGE DISCRIMINATION

C5.1.4   Age discrimination may constitute unlawful discrimination even if, for certain jobs, the law provides an interdiction for certain age categories (eg work at night).

5.2 Unlawful Discrimination

A SEX DISCRIMINATION AND DISCRIMINATION DUE TO MARITAL STATUS

Principles

C5.2.1 The Belgian legislature recently introduced the Statute of 7 May 1999, which implements the Equal Treatment Directive 76/207/EC.

C5.2.2 The Belgian Constitution, arts 10–11, also reiterate the general principle of non-discrimination, stating that all Belgians are equal in law and that the exercise of the rights and liberties granted to Belgians should be granted without any discrimination.

C5.2.3 The Statute of 7 May 1999 covers access to employment, opportunities for promotion, training, access to independent work, conditions of employment and redundancy, and access to private social security schemes.

C5.2.4 The principle of equal treatment applies to any form of discrimination, either direct or indirect by reference to the sex of the employee, or pregnancy or maternity.[1] Marital status is not expressly covered.

[1]   Statute of 7 May 1999, art 4.

C5.2.5 Special provisions relating to maternity protection are not discriminatory despite the difference in treatment as between men and women. No specific legislation exists regarding transsexuals and sexual orientation.

B HARASSMENT

C5.2.6 There are specific provisions dealing with sexual harassment, which is an act of discrimination under Belgian law.[1]

[1]   Royal Decree of 18 September 1992 regarding the protection of employees against unwanted sexual behaviour at work.

C ENFORCEMENT AND REMEDIES IN DISCRIMINATION CASES

C5.2.7 Provisions of the employment contract or other documents that are contrary to the principle of non-discrimination are void. The consequence of this principle is that employees who have suffered discrimination will be treated in the same way as other employees ie they receive the same advantages as those who have been treated more favourably.

C5.2.8 Any employee who considers that he is being discriminated against can commence proceedings in order to eliminate the discrimination, either through special procedures which should be laid down within the company, or by filing a complaint with the competent administration ie the Inspectorate of Social Legislation. The Inspectorate is a state body designed to ensure compliance with social legislation.

C5.2.9 The labour court can force the employer to terminate the discrimination within a certain period. If the employer does not comply with the court's order, the employee may terminate the contract and claim damages.

C5.2.10 However, if an employment contract is terminated by the employer on discriminatory grounds, the court will not have the power to force the employer to reinstate the employee whose employment contract was terminated. Instead, the court may grant damages to the employee.

C5.2.11 Once an employee has commenced proceedings against the employer for discrimination, he benefits from special protection against termination or modification of the employment conditions. The employer will not be permitted to terminate the employment contract, except for reasons that are unconnected with the complaint or legal action. If the employer seeks to rely on such a reason, he will have to provide proof where termination or modification takes place within the period of 12 months following the complaint. If termination or modification takes place within the period of 3 months from the end of the employee's court case, the employer must also prove that the reasons are unconnected with the complaint or legal action.

C5.2.12 Normally, if the employer does not comply, the employee or his delegate will ask the employer, by registered letter sent within 30 days of the modification or termination, to reinstate the employee or to abandon any modifications. The employer has 30 days to provide an answer to that request.

C5.2.13 If the employer decides to respond to this request in a positive manner, he will have to pay the employee the remuneration lost since the modification or the termination.

C5.2.14 If the employer does not want to reinstate the employee with the original working conditions, the employee may choose between a payment equal to six months' salary or a payment equal to the real damage suffered by the employee. In the latter case, the employee will have to prove the extent of damage claimed.

C5.2.15 Adherence to regulations governing non-discrimination is monitored by the Social Inspectorate. If an employer does not comply with these provisions he may be sentenced to pay statutory fines and may eventually face a prison sentence.[1]

[1]   Statute of 7 May 1999, art 25.

C5.2.16 There is no special protection under the legislation for part-time employees.

Sex discrimination	
• Access to employment	
• Opportunities for promotion	
• Training	
• Access to independent work	
• Conditions of employment	
• Redundancy	
• Social security matters	
• SEX	YES
• MARITAL STATUS	NOT EXPRESSLY COVERED
• PREGNANCY/MATERNITY	YES
• HARASSMENT	YES
• PART-TIMERS	NOT EXPRESSLY COVERED

D   RACE DISCRIMINATION

Principles

C5.2.17   The problem of racial discrimination is regulated in Belgium by the Statute on the punishment of certain acts based on racism and xenophobia (30 July 1981). Racial discrimination is considered to be any form of distinction, exclusion, limitation or preference which tends to, has, or could have as a consequence that the recognition, the benefit or the exercise based on equality of rights of a human being and the fundamental freedom of political, economical, social or cultural area or other social areas are limited or violated.

C5.2.18   The term 'race' is not defined by law, but has been interpreted broadly in case law and could also cover nationality and religion.

Enforcement and remedies in race discrimination cases

C5.2.19   The Statute on the punishment of certain acts based on racism and xenophobia (30 July 1981) provides for criminal sanctions for discrimination eg fines and imprisonment. The employer will be liable to pay fines for which the director or another person within the employer's organisation is liable.

E   VICARIOUS LIABILITY

C5.2.20   There are no specific rules under Belgian labour law regarding vicarious liability for acts of discrimination carried out by an employee. However, general rules apply which state that the employer will be held responsible for any fines and indemnity payments due by the employee who has committed acts of discrimination. In certain cases, the employer may be able to claim the money back from the employee at fault.

F   VICTIMISATION AND HARASSMENT

C5.2.21   When under Belgian law the problem of harassment is examined, it is mainly under the form of sexual harassment. In cases of sexual harassment at work, a specific procedure exists in order to protect the victim.

G   TRANSSEXUALS AND SEXUAL ORIENTATION

C5.2.22   There are no specific rules under Belgian labour law regarding transsexuals and sexual orientation.

H   DISCRIMINATION AND PRIVATE SOCIAL SECURITY SCHEMES

C5.2.23   Where an employer provides benefits that are complementary to the state social security scheme (eg company pension scheme, unemployment benefits, sick pay etc) the employer may not discriminate between employees on unlawful grounds. Such benefits should be granted to all employees belonging to the same category.

5.3   Disability Discrimination

C5.3.1   Since disabled persons often experience difficulties in finding work, Belgian law has introduced specific rules in order to facilitate their introduction into the workplace. For instance, in public entities the state is obliged to engage disabled persons once they have hired more than 20 employees.

C5.3.2   Specific workplaces exist for disabled persons who cannot work under normal conditions.

C5.3.3   Disabled persons enjoy various rights and privileges.

5.4   Enforcement and Remedies

C5.4.1   See paras **C5.2.7–C5.2.16** and **C5.2.19** in relation to remedies for sex and race discrimination.

5.5   Equal Pay

A   REQUIREMENTS

C5.5.1   As stated in paras **C5.2.1–C5.2.5**, the Statute on equal treatment between men and women (7 May 1999) expressly prohibits discrimination, whether direct or indirect, by reference to the sex of the employee. It implies that working conditions must be identical, and so equal treatment also applies to remuneration according to the Statute on equal treatment between men and women (7 May 1999), art 13. Equal pay must therefore be guaranteed as between men and women.

B   REMEDIES

C5.5.2   See paras **C5.2.7–C5.2.16** and **C5.2.19**.

6 TERMINATION OF EMPLOYMENT

6.1 Background

A   MODES OF TERMINATION

Fixed-term employment

C6.1.1   Fixed-term employment agreements end automatically when the duration of the fixed term has expired.

C6.1.2   If the employer terminates the agreement prior to the expiry date, the employee is entitled to a termination payment equal to the remuneration which he would have earned for the period until the expiry date, to a maximum of twice the payment to which he would have been entitled if the agreement had been executed for an unlimited duration (as to which see paras **C6.1.5** ff).

Purpose contracts

C6.1.3   Employment agreements related to a specific purpose end automatically when the purpose has been accomplished.

C6.1.4   Under Belgian law there are no specific rules for early termination of an employment agreement for a specific purpose, although we are of the opinion that the rules for termination of a fixed-term employment agreement would apply.

Unlimited duration contracts

C6.1.5   Employment agreements for an unlimited duration can be terminated by either party at any time (except for protected employees; see para **C6.2.1–C6.2.2**) by serving a written notice in the appropriate language (French or Dutch, as the case may be – see paras **C14.1.1** ff). If the employer does not give adequate notice, a payment equal to the salary and benefits (including holiday pay, bonus, thirteenth month payment etc) which the employee would have earned during the adequate period of notice, based on his last monthly salary, is due from the employer.[1]

[1]   The thirteenth month payment is an amount equal to a month's pay which is paid to all employees employed as at 31 December each year. If the employee has worked for the employer for a full calendar year he receives the full month's pay. If he leaves or joins part-way through the year he receives a pro-rata amount.

C6.1.6   In relation to every type of employment agreement, the parties can agree at any time to terminate their agreement by mutual consent. In this case it is advisable for the parties to conclude a written agreement, that affects the employee's rights to unemployment benefits (the employee will lose his unemployment allowance for a certain period of time).

C6.1.7   There is an important exception to the rules for termination set out in paras **C6.1.1–C6.1.7**: either party can terminate the employment agreement immediately, without notice or payment in lieu of notice, for 'serious cause'. Serious cause is defined as 'any act of behaviour (either by action or by omission) which immediately and permanently precludes any continuation of the working relationship between the employer and the employee'.[1] In this case, the party concerned must terminate the employment agreement by giving notice of dismissal within a period of three days after becoming fully aware of the 'serious cause'. In addition, the nature of the serious cause must be notified to the employer or employee within a period of three days following the date of dismissal.

[1]   Statute on Contracts of Employment (3 July 1978), art 38.

C6.1.8   The means of notification of 'serious cause' is strictly limited in the Statute on Contracts of Employment (3 July 1978) and may only be effected by registered letter or a bailiff's writ. The 'serious cause' must also be described with sufficient precision and clarity.

C6.1.9   Finally, it is also possible that if one of the parties does not respect its obligations, the contract could be terminated, either by commencing legal action to rescind the contract and claim damages, or by an act which amounts to a fundamental breach of contract (the *acte équipollent à rupture*), eg where there is a substantial change in the employee's function, or in the event of non-payment of remuneration.

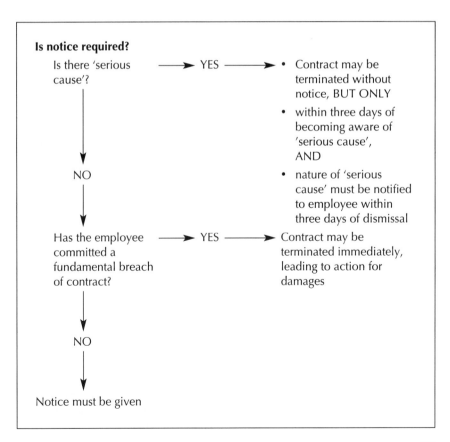

Is notice required?

Is there 'serious cause'? ———➤ YES ———➤ • Contract may be terminated without notice, BUT ONLY

• within three days of becoming aware of 'serious cause', AND

NO

• nature of 'serious cause' must be notified to employee within three days of dismissal

Has the employee committed a fundamental breach of contract? ———➤ YES ———➤ Contract may be terminated immediately, leading to action for damages

NO

Notice must be given

B NOTICE

C6.1.10 The following terms of notice should be observed when notice is served by the employer and the contract is for an indefinite period. Special rules apply when notice is served by the employee, which will not be discussed.

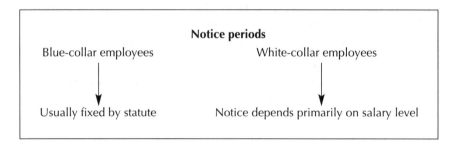

Notice periods

Blue-collar employees   White-collar employees

Usually fixed by statute   Notice depends primarily on salary level

Blue-collar (manual) employees

C6.1.11 The following notice provisions apply:

- between 6 months' and 5 years' seniority: 35 calendar days' notice required.
- between 5 years' and 10 years' seniority: 42 calendar days' notice required.
- between 10 years' and 15 years' seniority: 56 calendar days' notice required.
- between 15 years' and 20 years' seniority: 84 calendar days' notice required.
- more than 20 years' seniority: 112 calendar days' notice required.

6.1.12 A joint committee's bargaining agreement(s) (BA(s)) may provide for a different notice period. The parties can always agree *after* notice has been served (but not before, save in the circumstances set out at para **C6.1.16**) that notice will be shorter.

White-collar (intellectual) employees

C6.1.13 The following periods of notice apply.

Employees earning less than BEF 956,000 a year (as of 1 January 2000)
C6.1.14 Three months' notice are required for every five years' continuous service, eg if the employee has seven years' service, he will be entitled to six months' notice.

Employees earning BEF 956,000 or more a year
C6.1.15 The term of notice is fixed pursuant to mutual agreement and cannot be decided until the time of termination. In the absence of agreement by the parties, the notice period is decided by the Labour Court. There are no general rules provided by law for the determination of the duration of

the notice period, but the main criteria which are taken into account by the courts are the following: age, seniority, position and salary of the employee. Frequently, calculation formulae are used by the courts, the most common being the 'Claeys' formula which takes account of the factors mentioned in paras **C6.1.1–C6.1.12**.

Employees earning over BEF 1,912,000 (as of 1 January 2000) a year and employed after 1 April 1994

C6.1.16 The parties may fix in advance the notice period that must be observed in the event of termination by the employer. The duration of the notice period cannot in this instance be shorter than the notice period for employees earning less than BEF 956,000 a year (as of 1 January, 2000), ie three months' notice for every five years' service, as stated at para **C6.1.14**. In order to be enforceable, an agreement of this nature as to the notice period must be set out in writing before the employment contract is performed.

Notice period (white-collar employees) – relevant factors

- remuneration
- seniority

PLUS If the employee earns more than BEF 956,000 gross per year as at 1 January 2000

- function
- age

Procedure

C6.1.17 Notice given by the employer can only be validly served by means of a registered letter or a bailiff's writ, stating the duration of the notice period and the day from which such period starts to run.

C6.1.18 Where notice is served by means of a registered letter, it will have effect from the third working day after the day of sending. Therefore, in order to be effective from the first day of the month following the month during which the notice has been served, the letter will have to be sent at the latest three working days before the end of the month. If served by a bailiff it is effective immediately.

C6.1.19 In general, a notice which has been properly served runs from the Monday of the week following the week in which notice has been served (for a blue-collar employee), or as from the first day of the month following the month in which notice has been validly served (for a white-collar employee).

Example – notice of termination

An employer wishes to terminate the employment contract of a white-collar employee who earns less than BEF 956,000 per year and who has worked for the company for 12 years. The employee is entitled to nine months' notice. If the employer sends the termination letter on Monday 3 July 2000, notice will be effective as from Thursday 6 July, but the notice period will only start to run as from 1 August.

6.2 Nature of Claims

A   PROTECTED EMPLOYEES

C6.2.1   Employees who are pregnant, have been called up for military service, have filed a complaint of discrimination on sexual grounds, are candidates for political office, have opted for long-term leave as permitted by law, have opted for parental leave or are entitled to time off for training, as well as company doctors, are entitled to special protection against dismissal. If the employer wants to terminate the contract, he must follow a set procedure (which depends on the grounds for protection of the employee). If the employer fails to follow the correct procedure, he must pay an indemnity payment to the employee (this may amount to up to four years' salary).

C6.2.2   Special rules also apply with regard to employee representatives (CBA 5), members of works councils, members of the health and safety committee and unsuccessful candidates for any such posts.[1] These rules require, inter alia, that the dismissal must have been approved by the joint committee (see para or by the court prior to any termination of the employment agreement. If these rules are contravened, significant indemnity payments must be paid by the employer. In some cases, trades union delegates are protected from dismissal.

[1]   Act of 19 March 1991.

B   SALES REPRESENTATIVES

C6.2.3   A 'special clientele' indemnity payment must also be paid by an employer who terminates an employment agreement with a sales representative. The indemnity payment is only due if the terminated employment was the sales representative's main activity and if the sales representative has at least one year's seniority. The payment amounts to three months' salary where the employee's seniority is less than five years. Where the employee's seniority exceeds five years, the indemnity payment increases by one month's salary for each additional period of five years' seniority.

C6.2.4   The indemnity payment is only due if the sales representative can establish that he introduced clients (although such clients need not necessarily be significant or important). There is a presumption that clients have been introduced where the employment contract contains a non-competition clause.

C   ANNUAL BONUSES, HOLIDAY ALLOWANCES AND THIRTEENTH MONTH PAYMENTS

C6.2.5   An employer who terminates an employment agreement has to pay annual bonuses, holiday allowances and in certain cases a thirteenth month payment in proportion to the termination date: see para **C6.1.5**.

C6.2.6   In some sectors of industry and commerce, the same rule applies even where it is the employee who has terminated the employment agreement.

D   BLUE-COLLAR EMPLOYEES – REASONS FOR DISMISSAL

C6.2.7   Where an employer wants to terminate the employment contract of a blue-collar employee, he must substantiate his reasons for termination when the employee requests it. If termination is not related to the performance or conduct of the employee, or to the needs of the company, an additional indemnity payment equivalent to six months' remuneration is payable by the employer.[1]

[1]   Article 63 of the 1978 Statute.

E   TRIAL PERIOD

C6.2.8   Any employment contract, whether for a blue-collar or white-collar employee, may contain a trial period clause allowing either party to terminate the contract during the trial period with a reduced period of notice. To be enforceable, the trial period clause must be in writing and signed before the employee starts his employment.

C6.2.9   For blue-collar employees, the permissible trial period is a minimum of seven days and a maximum of 14 days. The contract may not, however, be terminated by either party during the first seven days except where 'serious cause' is shown. Thereafter, it may be terminated at the end of any working day during the trial period without notice or compensation in lieu thereof.

C6.2.10   For white-collar employees and sales representatives, the trial period is a maximum of six months, or 12 months if the employee's annual remuneration exceeds BEF 1,147,000 (as from 1 January 2000). During the trial period, the contract may be terminated at any time by giving seven days' notice. However, notice given during the first month of employment will be considered as given only at the end of that month. Notice must be given in accordance with various formal requirements (see paras **C6.1.13–C6.1.19**).

6.3   Fairness of Dismissal

A   BACKGROUND

C6.3.1   Under Belgian employment law, the employer does not normally have to justify the termination of the employment contract of a white-collar employee. A white-collar employee cannot therefore claim that his dismissal was unfair, unless he can prove that he has suffered specific damage over and above the damage caused by the termination itself (for example, where termination is combined with insults or threats). The white-collar employee will have to prove that the employer is at fault, that he has suffered damage, and will also have to prove the link between the employer's fault and the damage suffered. Such proof is very difficult to establish, and the amounts allocated by way of compensation are not very high compared to the termination indemnity payment. They generally range from BEF 50,000 up to BEF 500,000, but may be more.

C6.3.2   Where an employer wants to terminate the contract of a blue-collar employee, he will have to substantiate termination.[1]

[1]   Article 63 of the 1978 Statute.

B   REASONS FOR DISMISSAL (BLUE-COLLAR EMPLOYEES)

C6.3.3   Termination must be linked to the performance or conduct of the employee, or to company needs.

C6.3.4   The performance or conduct of the employee may constitute unacceptable conduct (normally a certain degree of seriousness is expected) such as verbal abuse (insults to the employer), or insubordination. There need not necessarily be any misconduct on the part of the employee – the employer may rely, for example, on the employee's sickness absence if such absence is of such a duration that it creates problems within the company, or where the employee's performance does not meet the employer's needs.

C6.3.5   Company needs are determined by the employer and relate to economic grounds or the company's organisation.

C6.3.6   The employer is the sole person competent to evaluate the employee's performance or conduct; tribunals and courts will only examine whether the motive for the dismissal is substantiated. Provided that the sanction is not thought to be excessive, examination of the employer's reasons will be limited.

Written reasons for dismissal

C6.3.7   The employer is not required to provide reasons for dismissal at the time he terminates the contract, but can explain his position for the first time in court. Reasons will normally be provided at an earlier stage, because social documents (eg redundancy form C4)[1] must state the reason for termination of the contract in order to determine whether the employee is entitled to unemployment benefits (ie to confirm that he has become involuntarily unemployed).

[1]   Form C4 is a document which the employer must give to the employee on termination of the contract. The employee needs form C4 in order to claim unemployment allowances.

C6.3.8   If the employer fails to substantiate the termination of a blue-collar employee's employment, he may be required to pay the employee an indemnity payment of up to six months' salary.

6.4 Remedies

C6.4.1 The remedies available to an employee whose employment is terminated unfairly or according to the incorrect procedure are set out in the text above.

REDUNDANCY AND COLLECTIVE DISMISSALS

6.5 Background

C6.5.1 Awareness of the issues surrounding collective dismissals has been raised since the major collective dismissal involving the Renault company in Belgium. Since that incident, the Belgian legislator has become very conscious of the problems linked to collective dismissals.

C6.5.2 The legislation relating to collective dismissals does not apply to companies which employ fewer than 20 employees.

C6.5.3 A collective dismissal is a dismissal for economic or technical reasons resulting, over a period of 60 days:

- in a reduction of 10% of the number of employees employed, subject to a minimum of 10 dismissals;
- in the dismissal of a minimum of 10 employees where the employer employs fewer than 100 employees;
- in the dismissal of a minimum of 30 employees where the employer employs more than 299 employees.

C6.5.4 In the event of collective dismissals, the employer has specific information obligations to meet in addition to the payment of termination indemnities and supplementary indemnities. These requirements are summarised in paras **C6.6.1** ff.

C6.5.5 Furthermore, the employer must respect a minimum period of one month from the notification that collective dismissals are to take place before he can proceed with notification of the termination of the employment contract.

Collective dismissal – definition

The dismissal of at least 10 employees in a company employing at least 20 employees

---

Contractual rights

C6.5.6 Normally there are no specific contractual rights in relation to collective dismissals, because the parties' rights are determined by legislation. It is, however, possible that in the individual employment contract or bargaining agreement (also discussed during the consultation period), the parties may agree that where collective dismissals occur the employees will be entitled to special damages on top of those laid down by legislation.

Statutory rights

C6.5.7 Further to BA 10 of 8 May 1973, employees who are collectively dismissed receive special compensation in addition to normal termination payments. Special compensation is granted for a short period (four months or less, depending on the length of the notice period), and is not very high (normally half of the difference between unemployment benefits and the remuneration previously earned, but with a maximum limit). Special compensation applies not only where there are collective dismissals as legally defined in para **C6.5.5**, but wherever the employer dismisses at least six employees.

6.6   Consultation

A   GENERAL OBLIGATIONS

C6.6.1 Collective Bargaining Agreement 24 of 2 October 1975 contains specific information and consultation procedures. Normally, consultation will cover the possibility of avoiding or limiting dismissals as well as the possibility of mitigating their consequences.

C6.6.2 The Act of 13 February 1998 defines that any such consultation comprises four steps:
- drafting of an information report;
- presentation of the information report;
- organisation of question sessions with employees' representatives (where comments and suggestions can be put forward);
- provision of responses by the employer.

C6.6.3 Collective Bargaining Agreement 9 of 9 March 1972 envisages the provision to the works council of information relating to measures concerning amongst others modification of work conditions and collective dismissals. The information must be given prior to the final decision being taken by the employer. In the absence of a works council, the trade union delegation has the same competence, provided that this competence was granted by a BA.

C6.6.4 The employer may be required to inform and consult with any European Works Council.

B   CLOSING – NOTIFICATION AND CONSULTATION

C6.6.5 In addition to the measures described above, the Royal Decree of 24 May 1976 provides that an employer who envisages collective dismissals is obliged to send a copy of the information provided to the employee representatives to the director of the regional office of the state employment agency.

C6.6.6   Once consultation with employee representatives has been completed, the employer must notify the planned collective dismissals to the same authority. The employer is prohibited from implementing any dismissals or giving notice until one month has elapsed from the date of this notification (the period may be extended to two months in certain circumstances).

C   REMEDIES

Reinstatement/rehiring

C6.6.7   If the special regulations and procedures referred to above are not adhered to and disputed by the employees or their representatives within 30 days, the notice of dismissal given will be void until the procedure has been complied with.

Compensation – redundancy payments

C6.6.8   See para **C6.5.7** in relation to special compensation.

7   YOUNG WORKERS

7.1   General Obligations

C7.1.1   The expression 'young workers' refers to workers who are under the age of 15 years or who are over 15 but still in full-time education.

C7.1.2   Children who are under 15 or who are undergoing compulsory full-time education are not permitted to work under the terms of an employment contract, save in specific cases such as actors, models, singers, dancers, and performers. Even in these cases very specific rules and procedures are applicable (such as express approval of the parents). In addition, in all cases the law restricts the periods during which the child is allowed to work. Certain activities such as underground work, or heavy or unhealthy work are strictly forbidden in any event and no exceptions are allowed.

C7.1.3   The maximum working time for such children is 8 hours a day and 39 hours a week.[1]

[1]   Article 2 of the Statute of 1971.

C7.1.4   Overtime is only possible in case of force majeure,[1] in which case the employer must inform the social inspectorate of this within three days.

[1]   Articles 32(1) and 33(1) of the Statute of 1971.

C7.1.5   Where overtime is worked, a compensatory break equal to the period of overtime worked will have to be taken within the week following the week during which the overtime took place.

C7.1.6   Young workers may not work more than 4½ hours consecutively.

C7.1.7   Where the work lasts longer than 4½ hours the employee is entitled to take a half hour break. If the work amounts to more than 6 hours, the total break is 1 hour, including one break of at least half an hour.

C7.1.8 The period between the end of the working day and the beginning of the following one must be at least 12 consecutive hours.[1]

[1] Articles 34 of the Statute of 1971.

C7.1.9 There are also specific rules concerning night work (normally forbidden), working on Sundays, bank holidays and normal holidays and an obligation applying to companies with more than 50 employees to engage young people.

8 MATERNITY AND PARENTAL RIGHTS

8.1 Background

C8.1.1 The Statute of 16 March 1971 regulates the position as to maternity leave and parental rights.

8.2 General Rights

C8.2.1 A pregnant woman benefits from maternity leave, and from protective provisions relating to redundancy and work conditions due to her status.

A COMMENCEMENT AND END OF LEAVE

C8.2.2 A pregnant woman has the right to leave as from the seventh week before the expected date of childbirth. She must provide a medical certificate as evidence of this date at least eight weeks before the expected date of childbirth.

C8.2.3 The law prohibits expectant mothers from working after the seventh day before the expected date of childbirth.

C8.2.4 After the birth, the employee has the right to eight weeks' leave. This period may be extended on request by the employee to take account of her having not taken leave due before the birth, ie up to seven weeks. The maximum period of leave which may be taken, counting both before and after the birth, is therefore 15 weeks.

C8.2.5 If the baby is required to stay in hospital for more than eight weeks after the birth, the employee may ask that her weeks of leave after the birth should be postponed until such time as the baby returns home (on which basis the employee therefore obtains additional leave).

8.3 Protection from Dismissal

C8.3.1 A pregnant employee's contract may not be terminated save for reasons which are not related to her pregnancy or childbirth.

C8.3.2   The employer will be required to prove that he has terminated the employment contract for reasons independent of the employee's condition (such as her conduct, or economic or technical reasons).

C8.3.3   If the employer cannot prove such independent reasons, he will be held liable to pay an indemnity payment on top of the notice period or the notice indemnity payment amounting to six months' salary.

C8.3.4   The period during which the employee benefits from protection runs from the day the employer is informed of her pregnancy and ends one month after the employee has returned from her maternity leave.

8.4   Health and Safety

C8.4.1   There is a special Royal Decree which protects a woman during her pregnancy and the period she breast-feeds (Royal Decree of 2 May 1995). The Statute of 16 March 1971 also applies.

C8.4.2   An employer is obliged to evaluate any risk to the woman's health and safety, together with a doctor nominated by the employer.

C8.4.3   If they discover any risks, the employer must introduce temporary measures for the woman's protection, such as alternative work or the same work but under different conditions.

C8.4.4   Night work, ie between 20:00 and 6:00, is forbidden from eight weeks before the expected date of childbirth, and for the period of up to four weeks after maternity leave if the employee's doctor so requires.

C8.4.5   Where night work is not possible, the employer must organise day-time work; if this is not possible, the contract will be suspended. In the latter case, if the work cannot be performed during the period of seven weeks before the expected date of childbirth, the employee must begin her maternity leave.

C8.4.6   Overtime is prohibited for pregnant women.

8.5   Maternity pay

A   MATERNITY ALLOWANCES

C8.5.1   Since 1 January 1990, the employer has not been required to pay any maternity allowances. All allowances are paid by the invalidity and sickness insurance cover provided by the state.

C8.5.2   The employee receives 82% of her salary from the social security system during the first 30 days of her maternity leave and 75% thereafter for the remainder of her leave.

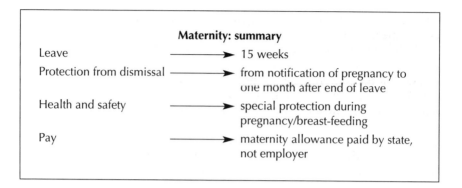

8.6 **Additional Rights to Time Off**

A   PARENTAL LEAVE

C8.6.1 In cases of parental leave (of maximum three months) both parents (mother and father) benefit from protection against termination. The protection of the father is limited to the period during which he is absent; if unfairly dismissed, the indemnity payment amounts to three months' salary.

B   PATERNITY LEAVE

C8.6.2 In certain circumstances, such as hospitalisation or death of the mother, maternity leave can be taken by the father as paternity leave.

C8.6.3 Where the mother is hospitalised, the father has the right to paternity leave if the child is at least seven days old and has left hospital and the mother remains in hospital for longer than seven days.

C8.6.4 Paternity leave ends when the mother leaves hospital and in any event when maternity leave comes to an end.

C8.6.5 Since 1998, all workers have right to career interruption, which can be part-time or full-time and can last a maximum 12 months (or even longer – up to 60 months – under certain specific circumstances).

9   **BUSINESS TRANSFERS**

9.1 **Background**

C9.1.1 Collective Bargaining Agreement 32bis of 7 June 1985 was concluded by the National Labour Council – a public body comprising a maximum of 12 elected members of the representative organisation of the employers and 12 elected members of the representative organisation of the workers. It sets out rules regarding the retention of acquired rights of workers in the event of a change of employer resulting from the transfer of undertakings effected pursuant to a deed or a contract.

C9.1.2   CBA 32bis implements the EC Acquired Rights Directive.[1]

[1]   Directive 77/187/EEC.

9.2   Identifying a relevant transfer

A   BELGIAN LEGISLATION ON TRANSFERS

C9.2.1   CBA 32bis is applicable to '... a change of employer resulting from the transfer of undertakings effected pursuant to a deed or a contract'.

C9.2.2   The following conditions must be fulfilled:
- a change of employer;
- a legal transfer;
- a transfer of an undertaking or a part of undertaking.

C9.2.3   The case law of the European Court of Justice is of importance in interpreting whether these conditions are satisfied.

C9.2.4   The criteria identified by the Court for determining whether there has been a transfer within the meaning of art 1(1) of Directive 77/187/EEC are:
- *an economic entity*, defined as an organised grouping of persons and assets for the exercise of an economic activity which pursues a specific objective, must be concerned in the operation;
- *that entity must be organised in a stable manner* and not limited to performing one specific work contract;
- there must be a *change*, in terms of contractual relations, *in the* legal or natural *person* who is responsible for carrying on the business and *who incurs the obligations of an employer* towards employees of the entity;
- the economic entity must *retain its identity*, which is demonstrated both by the continuation by the new employer of the same activities and by the continuity of its workforce, its management staff, the way its work is organised, its operating methods or the operational resources available to it.

C9.2.5   CBA 32bis does not apply where the employer changes by reason of death. An enterprise (undertaking) means either a legal entity or a technical work/production unit, or a department of the same.

C9.2.6   According to certain Belgian authorities, the requirement that there must be a change of employer means that there must be a change in the legal identity of the employer. Therefore, the selling of shares does not fall within the ambit of CBA 32bis, because a transfer of shares does not modify the relationship between employer and employees within the company. However, it should be noted that a transfer of shares is often followed by other operations of reorganisation involving mergers, or acquisitions, which may in themselves amount to a transfer to which the collective agreement applies.

C9.2.7   There is also some controversy arising in Belgian case law as to whether CBA 32bis applies to companies which employ on average fewer than 20 workers. According to the official comments contained in the preamble to the CBA, there would not be a relevant transfer where the employer employed fewer than 20 employees.

C9.2.8–10 Some legal writers therefore believe that the CBA is very clear on this issue, and that there is consequently no need to refer to the European Directive in interpreting the position.

C9.2.11 The labour courts have yet to publish any judgment relating to this issue. However, it seems to the authors that another interpretation could be argued before the labour courts.

C9.2.12 The general objective of both the European and Belgian legislation on this issue is to protect employees' rights, and to exclude companies with fewer than 20 employees arguably does not comply with these objectives. Furthermore, European legislation takes precedence over domestic legislation, and an action could therefore be brought against Belgium for not having correctly implemented the European Directive. There is also a risk that a Belgian judge may decide to apply the European Directive to a legal transfer without taking into account the number of employees, which after all is not mentioned in the Directive.

9.3 Affected Employees

C9.3.1 CBA 32bis applies to persons who perform their work under an employment contract (both white- and blue-collar employees). It does not apply to the self-employed.

C9.3.2 The CBA covers all employees of the transferred company or part of the company.

C9.3.3 In the event of an employee deciding not to transfer his employment contract or employment relationship to the transferee, under European Community law it is for each member state to determine what the fate of the contract of employment or employment relationship should be.

C9.3.4 The member state may provide, in particular, that in such a case the contract of employment or employment relationship must be regarded as terminated either by the employee or by the employer. According to Belgian law, if an employee refuses to be transferred, he will be considered as having terminated his contract.

C9.3.5 This also means that employees are not required to give their consent to the change of employer and may not consider that such a change amounts to a breach of their employment contract.

9.4 Effects of the Transfer

C9.4.1 The European Court has confirmed that the purpose of the Directive is to ensure that the rights of employees are safeguarded in the event of a change of employer, by enabling them to remain in employment with the new employer on the terms and conditions initially agreed with the transferor.

C9.4.2   The rights and obligations existing at the time of the transfer, and those originating from the transfer or from the employment contract, are transferred to the transferee. In other words, the contract itself is transferred to the new employer.

C9.4.3   The most important consequence of the automatic transfer of the employment contract is the maintenance of the employee's working conditions: seniority, salary, responsibilities, working time, and, unless agreed otherwise, the place of work.

C9.4.4   Article 20 of the 1968 Act on CBAs expressly provides that the CBA which applies within the transferor's business continues to apply notwithstanding the transfer. This has important consequences, because many work conditions (remuneration, working hours, thirteenth month, etc) are governed by such CBAs. After the expiry of a CBA, the same work conditions will continue to apply within the employment contracts unless the employment contracts expressly state otherwise.

C9.4.5   The automatic transfer of rights and obligations does not, however, apply to old-age, invalidity, and survivor's benefits payable under schemes supplementing the official social security system, unless the scheme is contained in a Collective Bargaining Agreement, in which case it must be maintained by the transferee.

C9.4.6   The transferee is not bound by the transferor's obligations relating to early retirement.

C9.4.7   All work conditions which are set out in the transferor's work regulations should also be maintained, because they are deemed to be part of the employment contract.

C9.4.8   The transferor is liable for any debts existing at the time of the transfer, and the transferee is liable for any debts existing at the time of the transfer and subsequent to the transfer (art 8 of the CBA). The CBA therefore prescribes joint liability for debts relating to the employment contracts which occurred before the legal transfer.

C9.4.9   In relation to debts created subsequent to the transfer, the point is considered to be rather controversial under Belgian law. Although most recent case law seems to be unanimous in considering that the transferor may not be deemed liable for such debts, the Supreme Court has not decided the point and it is therefore recommended to have a discharge from the employees for debts arising subsequent to the legal transfer, which should be achieved by all three parties (employee, transferor and transferee) signing an agreement to that effect.

C9.4.10   The transferee should also ensure that the transfer agreement specifies that the transferor will be held liable for debts incurred prior to the transfer date.

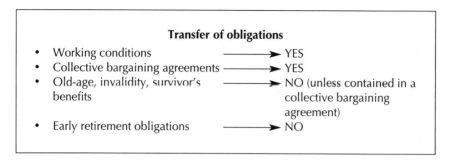

Transfer of obligations

- Working conditions   ⟶ YES
- Collective bargaining agreements ⟶ YES
- Old-age, invalidity, survivor's   ⟶ NO (unless contained in a
  benefits   collective bargaining
                                                        agreement)
- Early retirement obligations   ⟶ NO

9.5   Dismissal

C9.5.1   The change of employer does not in itself constitute grounds for dismissing employees, either on the part of the transferor or the transferee.

C9.5.2   Article 9 of the CBA protects the rights of employees against dismissal (whether by the transferor or transferee) where the sole justification for dismissal is the transfer. The rules of Directive 77/187/EEC and the CBA, in particular those concerning the protection of employees against dismissal by reason of the transfer, are mandatory, and so it is not possible to derogate from them in a manner which is unfavourable to employees.

C9.5.3   Employees who are transferred to a new employer can, however, be dismissed for just cause (eg misconduct) or for economic, technical or organisational reasons which involve changes in the enterprise's employment structure.

C9.5.4   The contract of employment of an employee who is unlawfully dismissed shortly before the transfer is regarded as still existing in relation to the transferee, even if the transferee did not take on the dismissed employee after the undertaking was transferred.

C9.5.5   However, neither Belgian nor European Community legislation provides for specific sanctions if this prohibition is violated. Moreover, recent Belgian case law considers that on that basis alone, the unlawfully dismissed employee is not entitled to any indemnity payment in addition to that due for dismissal in the usual course of events.

C9.5.6   However, this may prove to be controversial since the issue has not been challenged or considered by the labour courts yet.

C9.5.7   The protection of the works council, of the committee for the prevention and protection and of union representatives against dismissal is maintained in case of legal transfer; therefore if the transferee wishes to dismiss such a person he will be required to follow the special procedures previously outlined.

C9.5.8   Committees for special rules apply to protect union representatives, members of the works council or of the committees for prevention and protection, as well as to those who are union representatives against dismissal (Statute of 3 March 1991 and CBA 5). These rules require prior approval by the joint committee (and in certain cases by the court) before dismissal, and the payment of high indemnities in case of violation.

C9.5.9 Employee representation is organised within works councils and committees for prevention and protection. These bodies will be maintained within the transferee or joined with the one already functioning within the transferee in application of specific provisions of the Statute of 20 September 1948 (for the works council) and of the Statute of 4 August 1996 (for the prevention and protection committee).

C9.5.10 Specific rules also apply to union delegations in order to ensure their continuance or re-forming on transfer, depending on the maintaining of the autonomy of the transferred entity (CBA 5).

9.6   Variation of Contract

C9.6.1 Where the employee terminates the contract in protest because the transfer has resulted in a significant change in the employee's terms and conditions of employment and this is to the employee's disadvantage, termination of the employment relationship is deemed to have taken place by reason of the employer's – normally the transferee's – actions.

C9.6.2 Further, it should be noted that art 10 of CBA 32bis provides that if the employment contract or the employment relationship is terminated because the transfer involves a substantial change in working conditions to the detriment of the employee, the employer is regarded as having been responsible for the termination. The employee is entitled to claim damages for such termination.

9.7   Duty to Inform and Consult

C9.7.1 Article 6 of Directive 77/187/EEC states that both companies involved in the transfer must inform the representatives of their respective employees who will be affected by the transfer, in relation to the following points.

- reason for the transfer;
- legal, economic and social consequences of the transfer for the employees;
- measures proposed in respect of the employees.

C9.7.2 The transferor must communicate this information to the employee representatives in good time before the transfer takes place. The transferee must inform the employee representatives in due time and in any case before the employees' working conditions are directly affected by the transfer. If the transferor or the transferee consider taking 'measures' in relation to their respective employees, they will have to confer in due time with the representatives of their respective employees in order to come to an agreement.

C9.7.3 In short, Directive 77/187/EEC establishes a distinction between preliminary information in relation to a transfer, and preliminary consultation in relation to measures (related to redundancy or reorganisation) which will have an influence on employees.

No measures to be taken: information only

Measures proposed: information and consultation required

C9.7.4 Notification and consultation must take place, before publication of any decision, within the transferor and the transferee organisations. Article 11 of the CBA of 9 March 1972 on works councils states that in the case of structural changes in the company due to concentration of the parties' respective businesses (take-overs, mergers, closures, etc), the works council must be informed as to the economic, financial or technical reasons which cause and justify the structural change; as well as in relation to the economic, financial and social consequences of these changes.

C9.7.5 The works council must also be consulted about measures which must be taken to avoid dismissals and changes which downgrade an employee's job and social position, programmes of collective dismissals, transfers and changes and the social measures to be taken.

C9.7.6 If there is no works council in the company, the union delegation is competent to exercise the powers and rights which the works council would be entitled to exercise in conformity with the CBA of 9 March 1972.

C9.7.7 Where there is no works council and no union delegation, Belgian law does not provide for any specific notification or consultation obligations to be met by the company.

C9.7.8 However, where there is no formal representation of the employees within a company, the employer is recommended to inform the employees themselves as to the general outlook and changes in structure which may alter their employment situation. The transferor and the transferee may provide such information together.

C9.7.9 In the event of non-compliance with the CBA of 9 March 1972, which has been made compulsory by Royal Decree, the employer exposes himself to criminal sanctions.[1]

[1] Article 56 of the Act of 5 December 1968 on the CBA.

9.8 Transfer following Insolvency or Judicial Agreement with Creditors

C9.8.1 The third chapter of CBA 32bis determines the rights of employees in the event of a change of employer as a result of a take-over of assets following insolvency or judicial agreement with transfer of assets (a court order relating to insolvency). In particular, it provides that the CBA applies only if the take-over occurs within six months of the date of insolvency or judicial agreement: if it does not, the employees are not covered by the Collective Bargaining Agreement. Thus employee rights are not protected to the same extent in this particular situation; for example, there is no obligation to take over all of the employees, working conditions may be renegotiated, and a trial period may be incorporated.

10   COLLECTIVE RIGHTS AND BARGAINING

10.1 Background

C10.1.1   In Belgium, there is a long tradition of collective rights.[1]

[1]   Law of 24 May 1921; Law of 7 September 1951.

C10.1.2   Joint management/labour comittees (*commissions paritaires*) are in place in many sectors of industry and commerce. Such bodies have an independent chairman and equal numbers of employers' representatives and employees in the relevant sector. They are responsible for promoting good labour relations in their sector and they are entitled to promulgate collective agreements, which are then enforced by royal decree.

C10.1.3   Matters dealt with by joint management/labour committees are varied and include minimum wages, indexation of salary, end-of-year bonus, reduction of working time etc.

10.2 Trade Unions

C10.2.1   Labour unions play a significant role in labour relations, mainly by participating in the negotiations of collective agreements, in the management of some public institutions, in presenting candidates for elections of the works councils or for nominations of labour judges representing employees.

10.3 Collective Bargaining and Collective Representation

C10.3.1   Medium-sized and large companies must elect employee representatives.

C10.3.2   Employee representatives do not participate in the company's management. Employee representation is organised within works councils and prevention and protection committees. These bodies have a limited executive power but extensive rights of consultation and investigation.

C10.3.3   A health and safety committee must be set up in companies employing 50 or more employees. Representatives are elected. The committee has wide-ranging rights to be consulted on health and safety issues at work.

10.4 Works Council

C10.4.1 Works councils are required in companies employing 100 or more employees. They are composed of elected representatives. There are provisions to prevent companies from avoiding their obligations through corporate re-organisations. Works councils exercise an influence mainly on matters relating to the introduction of work regulations, and the provision of financial information, and play a consultative role in cases of work re-organisation.

C10.4.2 Every four years, companies must organise social elections to elect representatives for the works council and the health and safety committee. Middle management has specific representation in the works council.

11 EMPLOYMENT DISPUTES

11.1 Background

C11.1.1 Since there is a relationship of authority between the employer and the employee, Belgian labour law doctrine allows the employer to exert disciplinary powers within his company.

C11.1.2 This disciplinary power must, however, respect general principles of labour law and may not be abused.

C11.1.3 Labour legislation accepts that disciplinary sanctions may be imposed by an employer in specific circumstances.

C11.1.4 However, sanctions such as suspension without remuneration or even fines[1] may be deemed illegal because they violate art 25 of the Statute on Contracts of Employment (3 July 1978).

[1] Up to 1/5 of the daily remuneration – arts 18 and 19 of the Statute of 8 April 1965 relating to the implementation of work regulations.

C11.1.5 All sanctions must be laid down in the work regulations.[1]

[1] Article 16 of the Statute of 8 April 1965 relating to the implementation of work regulations.

C11.1.6 If the employer wants to apply a sanction he must follow a specific procedure.[1]

[1] Article 17 of the Statute of 8 April 1965 relating to the implementation of work regulations.

C11.1.7 Not all sanctions are accepted by the courts, which have the power to check that the sanction, assuming that it is legal, is not used in an abusive way.

11.2 Labour Courts/Tribunals

C11.2.1   Disputes relating to labour relationships (and to the operation of the social security system) which are not settled by the parties, are settled by specially constituted labour courts – at first instance they are called tribunals; on appeal, courts. The tribunals/courts are divided by geographical location.

C11.2.2   Most courts have different chambers, each of which specialises in a different area (blue-collar employees, white-collar employees, social security problems, etc).

C11.2.3   Each chamber is presided over by a career (ie professional) judge (the President) and there is also in most cases one 'employer' judge and one 'employee' judge, appointed on the recommendation of representative organisations of employers and employees.

C11.2.4   The President may sometimes hear the case alone (in *'référé'*), if there is some urgency and his judgment is only provisional.

C11.2.5   If the case deals with problems of public order, the public ministry will also take part in the hearings.

C11.2.6   Specific rules exist concerning the territorial competence of the tribunal and courts.

C11.2.7   Tribunals are known for their expertise in employment disputes.

11.3 Settlements

C11.3   The parties will often settle their dispute privately. There is no special process or form for such settlement.

12   WHISTLEBLOWING/DATA PROTECTION

12.1 Whistleblowing

C12.1.1   There is a general obligation for the employee not to disclose any confidential information both during and after the employment contract.[1] Moreover are criminal sanctions against any person who gives confidential information to third parties.[2]

[1]   Article 17 of the Statute on Contracts of Employment (3 July 1978).
[2]   Article 309 of the Criminal Code.

C12.1.2   Any employer suffering from an employee's breach of his obligations can commence a legal action against the employee to stop the breach and to claim damages.

C12.1.3   The breach of confidentiality can be a ground for a dismissal without notice or indemnity.

12.2 Data Protection

C12.2.1   The provisions of the Data Protection Act of 8 December 1992 should be noted where employers hold 'personal data' in relation to employees. 'Personal data' is defined under the Act as any data from which a living individual is identifiable, whether contained on computer or in a filing system; hard copies of personal data such as personnel files kept in relation to employees are therefore covered by the Act. The general aim of the Act is to ensure that information held in relation to employees is adequate, relevant, and not excessive and that employees are able to review the contents of any files held on them.

13   HUMAN RIGHTS

13.1 Rights and Obligations

C13.1.1   The European Convention on Human Rights has been implemented in Belgian by the Statute of 13 May 1955 and foresees in some obligations related to labour law such as:

- the prohibition of compulsory work (art 4.2);
- the right to constitute trade unions (art 11.2);
- the right to privacy (art 8.1);
- the prohibition of any discrimination (art 14).

14   MISCELLANEOUS DOMESTIC RIGHTS AND OBLIGATIONS

14.1. Use of language

C14.1.1   Belgium has very stringent rules applicable to the language used in labour and social relationships.

C14.1.2   All documents between the employer and the employee must be written in the following languages:

- Dutch for companies located in Flanders and for Dutch-speaking employees if the employer is located in Brussels;
- French for companies registered in Wallonia and for French-speaking employees if the employer is located in Brussels.

C14.1.3   If these rules are not adhered to, the document in question may be ruled void.

USEFUL WEBSITES

Belgian Government site:
- http://www.fgov.be

Major payroll office:
- http://www.partena.be

Official Gazette:
- http://www.moniteur.be

D   Denmark

Klaus Ewald Madsen

Klaus Ewald Madsen is a Partner at Bech-Bruun Dragsted, Copenhagen. He qualified in 1989 and has a Right of Audience before the Supreme Court of Denmark.

Bech-Bruun Dragsted, Copenhagen

Phone: +45 33 143 333
Fax: +45 33 324 333
Email: klaus.ewald.madsen@bechbruundragsted.com
Website: www.bechbruundragsted.com

DENMARK

Rights	Yes/No	Explanatory notes
THE EMPLOYMENT RELATIONSHIP		
Minimum notice	YES	Salaried employees: set by statute (one–six months); other employees: set by collective bargaining agreements
Terms:		
Express	YES	Written particulars of specific terms must be provided within one month of commencement of service
Incorporated	YES	Terms are commonly incorporated by statute or by collective bargaining agreements
REMUNERATION		
Minimum wage regulation	YES	Regulated by collective bargaining agreement only – no statutory regulation
Further rights and obligations:		
Right to paid holiday	YES	Five weeks' statutory holiday per year, or more if agreed under collective bargaining agreement or individual contract
Right to sick pay	YES	Either full salary (salaried employees) or sickness benefit (non-salaried employees)
WORKING TIME		
Regulation of hours per day/ working week	NO	No statutory regulation, although generally regulated by collective bargaining agreement
Regulation of night work	NO	No regulation
Right to paid holiday	YES	See above
Right to rest periods	YES	11 hours per day/24 hours per week
EQUAL OPPORTUNITIES		
Discrimination protection:		
Sex	YES	
Race/nationality	YES	
Marital status	YES	
Disability	NO	
Religion	YES	
Age	NO	
Sexual orientation	YES	
Equal pay legislation	YES	

TERMINATION OF EMPLOYMENT

Right not to be dismissed in breach of contract	YES	Minimum notice period set by statute (salaried employees) or collective bargaining agreements (other employees)
Statutory rights on termination	YES	Termination of employment must be on 'fair and reasonable grounds'
Severance pay	YES	Likely to be agreed by statute (salaried employees), by prior agreement (CEOs) or by collective bargaining agreements (other employees)

REDUNDANCY

Right to payment on redundancy	YES	Redundancy may be a 'fair and reasonable' reason for dismissal. Usual severance pay may be payable
Right to consultation: Individual	NO	No specific rules unless prescribed by collective bargaining agreement/individual contract
Collective	YES	Negotiations required with employee representatives and notification to Labour Council necessary (dismissals ineffective for 30 days)

YOUNG WORKERS

Protection of children and young persons at work	YES	Statutory protection for young workers under the age of 18

MATERNITY RIGHTS

Right to time off for ante-natal care	YES	
Right to maternity leave	YES	Mother: 4 weeks before and 24 weeks after birth. Father: may use some of mother's leave after birth, plus specific paternity leave
Notice requirements	YES	
Maternity pay (during leave)	YES	Salaried employees: 50% salary, then maternity allowance. Non-salaried employees: maternity allowance
Protection from dismissal	YES	During maternity/parental leave
Health and safety protection	YES	
Right to parental leave	YES	Applies to both parents

113

BUSINESS TRANSFERS

Right to protection on transfer	YES	Employment contracts transfer with continuity and terms maintained
Transfer of employment obligations	YES	Transferee inherits all employment rights and liabilities on transfer including terms of collective bargaining agreements
Right to information and consultation	YES	In relation to legal, financial and social implications, and any measures to be taken
Right not to be dismissed	YES	Dismissal by reason of transfer may constitute an unfair dismissal

COLLECTIVE RIGHTS AND BARGAINING

Collective bargaining	YES	Collective bargaining agreements very common, dealing with pay, hours, and other terms and conditions
European works councils	YES	Directive 94/95 implemented
Right to take industrial action	YES	In certain limited circumstances, such forms of action may be lawful

EMPLOYMENT DISPUTES

Civil court jurisdiction/ statutory body	YES YES	Jurisdiction depends on whether employment relationship is governed by collective bargaining agreements

WHISTLEBLOWING

Protection from dismissal/ detriment	NO	No specific statutory provision

DATA PROTECTION

Protection	YES	Directive 95/96 implemented

HUMAN RIGHTS

Statutory protection of human rights	YES	ECHR incorporated in Danish law

1 THE EMPLOYMENT RELATIONSHIP

1.1 Background

D1.1.1 In Denmark union membership is very high – more than 50% of employees are trade union members and in certain industries the percentage is much higher. Consequently, industrial relations are to a large extent regulated by collective bargaining agreements in both the private and the public labour market.

D1.1.2 However, the Danish legislature has become increasingly interested in labour market relations and over the last decade legislation has been introduced in a large number of areas – in particular for the purpose of implementing European Directives.

> On this basis, the sources of law within the Danish industrial relations system are:
>
> - constitution
> - legislation
> - collective agreements
> - individual agreements
> - customs
> - case law including cases decided by arbitration tribunals.

Constitution

D1.1.3 The present Danish Constitution was adopted in 1953. It establishes the fundamental separation of legislature, judiciary and executive powers, and forms the overall basis of the legal system.

D1.1.4 Legislation is passed by Parliament (*Folketinget*) in accordance with the Constitution.

Legislation

D1.1.5 The role of legislation is becoming increasingly dominant, largely because of European Community law.

D1.1.6 Danish legislation can be divided into three general areas:
(i) statutes applying to specific groups of employees;
(ii) statutes governing employment relationships in general;
(iii) rules concerning settlement of industrial disputes.
Details are given below.

D1.1.7 First, various statutes apply to specific groups of employees, eg the Salaried Employees Act (SEA), the Civil Servants Act and the Seamen Act. These acts apply only to those employees within their specific scope.

D1.1.8   Other statutes govern all types of employment relationships, including the Act on Employees' Guarantee Fund, the Act on Sickness Benefits, the Holiday Act, the Equal Treatment Act, the Act on Transfers of Undertakings, the Act on Posted Workers, the Freedom of Association Act and the Act on Employment Contracts.

D1.1.9   Finally, a third group of statutory rules lays down provisions for the settlement of industrial relations disputes, including the Industrial Tribunal Act and the Act on Conciliators.

D1.1.10   Like collective agreements, Danish legislation on industrial relations have the overall objective of protecting the weak party to the agreement, ie the employee. Danish legislation on industrial relations is generally mandatory.

Collective agreements

D1.1.11   The two main organisations of the Danish labour market are the Danish Employers Confederation and the Danish Confederation of Trade Unions, representing employers and employees respectively. They have entered into an agreement (the so-called Main Agreement), which establishes the general legal framework as well as the overall rights and obligations between the main organisations and their member organisations.

D1.1.12   Below the Main Agreement, numerous collective agreements (on specific pay and working conditions) are entered into between trade unions and employers' associations or individual employers.

D1.1.13   Neither legislation nor the Main Agreement include provisions on the substance and form of collective agreements. Such an agreement may therefore be oral or implied. A collective agreement primarily governs the conditions at the workplace such as pay, working hours, notice of termination, shop steward rules etc. Collective agreements also regulate the relations between the parties to the agreement with respect to the resolution of industrial disputes, termination of the collective agreements etc.

Collective agreements
- conditions, eg pay, working hours, notice of termination, shop steward rules
- industrial disputes
- termination of the collective agreement

D1.1.14   Closed shop agreements (ie agreements which require employers to employ only employees who are members of a particular union) are recognised only within the private sector. The legality of closed shop agreements has most recently been recognised by the Supreme Court.

[1]   In a decision of 12 May 2000.

D1.1.15   One of the central elements of collective bargaining is the principle of the employer's managerial right and the no-strike agreement. It follows from the managerial right that the employer is generally free to employ and dismiss staff. However, the right to dismiss staff is restricted in many ways by collective agreements and by statute.

D1.1.16   Further, the employer's managerial right implies that the employer has a privilege of interpretation in the event of disagreements on the interpretation of the collective agreement or uncertainty as to the legality or legitimacy of a claim under a collective agreement.

D1.1.17   Another fundamental rule in the collective bargaining system is that the organisations and their members are subject to an obligation to keep the industrial peace after the conclusion of a collective agreement. As a result, work stoppage/strike, blockade or lock-out constitutes a breach of the collective agreement. If employers or employees take these measures, they are in breach of the collective agreement and may be ordered to pay a penalty by an industrial tribunal.

D1.1.18   However, employers and employees who are not covered by a collective agreement are free to take industrial action for the purpose of concluding a collective agreement.

D1.1.19   If the undertaking is subject to a collective agreement, the employer is obliged to observe the provisions of that collective agreement, for instance on pay and working hours, in all individual employment contracts. This may be done by referring to the collective agreement in the contract. This duty also applies towards non-unionised employees. In the event of the employer's failure to meet this duty, the trade union may bring a claim before the industrial tribunal and be awarded a penalty.

D1.1.20   Conciliation is the usual method of settling disputes between the parties during the term of the collective agreement with industrial arbitration as a last resort.

Individual employment contracts

D1.1.21   Individual employment contracts are entered into between employers and the individual employees. They set out the terms and conditions which apply to the employment relationship, including terms of pay and other working conditions.

D1.1.22   Under Danish law, there is in principle freedom of contract. However, freedom of contract is in some respects restricted by an objectivity requirement and a prohibition against discrimination. In addition, most industrial relations statutes are mandatory, eg the Holiday Act and the SEA, but in certain areas, collective agreements take precedence over legislation on industrial relations.

D1.1.23   Denmark has implemented Directive 91/533 on the employer's obligation to inform employees of the terms and conditions applicable to their employment. In consequence, the employer is obliged to give a written record to his employees of the conditions applicable to the employment relationship, although a service agreement will still be valid even if it is not made in writing.

D1.1.24 If an agreement contains terms which are particularly onerous on the employee, it may be – depending on the circumstances – set aside due to invalidity and possibly due to breach of s 36 of the Contracts Act. The courts will then weigh the parties' assumptions, in particular whether or not the employee was able to fully understand the consequences of the agreement at the time of its conclusion. The validity of the agreement is subject to a case-by-case overall assessment of whether there is a reasonable balance between the benefits to the parties.

Custom

D1.1.25 'Custom' refers to the standard practices at the workplace, ie practices which have been applied without exception and for a long period of time thereby imposing legal obligations on the parties.

D1.1.26 Custom is an important source of law, in particular in relation to the filling of gaps in collective agreements.

'Employee'

D1.1.27 Most rights and obligations under collective agreements and labour law only apply to 'employees'.

D1.1.28 Consequently, the concept of an 'employee' plays a vital role in industrial relations law as well as in legislation on social welfare. The reason is that most rules and regulations include only persons in the labour market who are considered 'employees', as opposed to other workers such as agents, executives, and self-employed traders.

D1.1.29 An 'employee' is not defined by statute, but the concept has been determined by case law. The concept is broad and is interpreted in accordance with the objective of the relevant statute.

D1.1.30 In general, an 'employee' is a person who has an obligation under an employment contract to carry out work personally according to the instructions of his employer, at the employer's risk and expense, under the employer's supervision and in the employer's name. In consideration of this duty, the 'employee' receives pay, usually based on time spent.

D1.1.31 Managers and senior executives, as well as self-employed traders and agents, usually fall outside the concept of an 'employee'. Danish law also distinguishes in some instances between salaried and other employees.

D1.1.32 In 1989, Denmark liberalised the rules and regulations on temping agencies, and it is now lawful to set up temping agencies within all industries. If work is carried out by employees from a temping agency, the temping agency enters into an agreement on pay and working conditions etc with the temp. The temp is not an employee of the undertaking for which the work is performed, and, in general, the temp will not be entitled to claim protection under the general laws of employment.

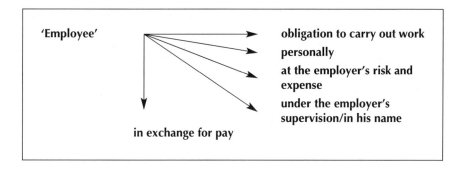

Case law

D1.1.33   The case law of the ordinary courts as well as that of the Labour Court are vital components in the development of individual employment law and collective labour law.

D1.1.34   However, the majority of cases brought before the ordinary courts, the Labour Court and industrial arbitrations are specific disputes based on individual facts and evidence, and do not involve issues of general importance. Accordingly, the value of case law as precedent is often limited.

1.2   Contract of Service

D1.2.1   Under Danish law there is a statutory obligation for the employer to provide written particulars of the terms and conditions applicable to the employment. The information must be provided to the employee no later than one month following commencement of service.

The following information must be included:
- name and address of the employer and the employee;
- place where the work should be performed;
- description of the work to be performed or statement of position or job category;
- when the employment commences;
- the expected duration of the employment (if it is not for an indefinite period of time);
- the employee's right as regard paid holiday;
- termination notices;
- the wage including fringe benefits and other allowances such as pension contributions and the payment dates;
- the usual working hours per day or per week;
- specification of any collective agreements covering the employment.

D1.2.2   Any subsequent amendments or arrangements should also be notified to the employee in writing no later than one month following the amendment/arrangement.

D1.2.3   If an employee has not been provided with the information listed above, he will be entitled to compensation. According to case law, compensation amounts to DKK 5–15,000 depending on the individual circumstances, including whether the missing information has caused or otherwise influenced a dispute between the parties. This amount is tax-free for the employee and is not tax deductible for the employer.

1.3   Variation of Contract

D1.3.1   The employment contract is binding on both parties with regard to the terms and conditions set out therein and any material alterations are subject to agreement between the parties.

D1.3.2   The employer may impose minor changes of terms and conditions and minor changes to the day-to-day performance of the work in accordance with the managerial right. However, material changes in the rights and obligations of the employee – ie changes outside the managerial right – can only be introduced by giving the notice period applicable to the individual employee if the employee in question has not accepted the new terms. In other words, the existing employment contract is terminated and the employee is offered re-employment on new terms and conditions. The employee is free to reject the new terms and conditions and may then have the right to claim severance pay due to unfair dismissal.

D1.3.3   If no notice is given, a material breach of contract will have arisen and the employee can refuse to continue work.

Variation of terms	
Minor changes	*Major changes*
Employer can introduce without difficulty	can only be introduced (i) by agreement; or (ii) by employer giving notice and offering new terms and conditions Employee may reject new. terms and claim severance pay/unfair dismissal

Non-competition and customer clauses

D1.3.4   Under Danish law there is a distinction between non-competition clauses and customer clauses (non-solicitation clauses).

D1.3.5   A non-competition clause is an agreement between an employer and an employee providing that the employee may not for an agreed period of time (following termination of the employment) carry out business or activities of a certain nature or take employment in such a business.

D1.3.6   A customer clause is an agreement between an employer and an employee providing that the employee may not, directly or indirectly, for an agreed period of time have any business relations or take employment with any business which or person who has been a customer or supplier of the employer within a specified period before the date when the employee leaves his position.

Non-competition clauses

D1.3.7   According to the SEA, non-competition clauses may only be entered into if the employee holds a fiduciary position, and furthermore, it is a condition that the employee is paid compensation for the duration of the obligation. The non-competition restriction and the compensation amount must be laid down in a written contract.

D1.3.8   The monthly compensation for a non-competition clause must amount to at least 50% of the employee's salary, including pension contributions, bonus etc, as at the date when the employment terminates. For the first three months, compensation is to be paid as a lump sum on the date when the employee terminates his employment. For the remaining period of the non-competition clause, compensation is payable monthly in arrears.

D1.3.9   If the salaried employee is offered an appropriate new job during the currency of the non-competition clause, ie employment within a professional field that matches his qualifications, the agreed compensation is reduced by the salary paid by his new employer. However, the employee will always be entitled to a minimum compensation payment equivalent to the lump sum paid for the first three months.

D1.3.10   Where the employer dismissed the employee for gross misconduct, or the employee materially violates his obligations under the non-competition clause, there is no right to compensation, but the covenant will remain in force.

D1.3.11   If an employee has been employed for less than three months, a non-competition clause will be ineffective. If the employee has been employed for more than three months, but not more than six months, the duration of the non-competition clause cannot exceed six months. Likewise, a non-competition clause may not be relied upon in the event of unfair dismissal or if the employee's termination of his employment was due to breach on the part of the employer.

D1.3.12   The employer may terminate the non-competition clause by one month's notice during as well as after termination of the employment. However, if the employee leaves his position within a period of six months after the employer has terminated the non-competition clause and if his resignation is due to circumstances which would have entitled the employer to rely on the non-competition clause, the employer is entitled to a minimum compensation payment equivalent to three months' salary.

D1.3.13   The above provisions do not apply if a collective agreement provides different rules on the content and terms of non-competition clauses.

Customer clauses

D1.3.14   Unlike non-competition clauses, customer clauses may be concluded with all types of salaried employees and not just employees who hold fiduciary positions.

D1.3.15   Customer clauses may cover customers and other business relations which the salaried employee has had within a period of 18 months before the date of termination or customer etc relations covered by a customer clause set out in a separate written notice provided to the employee before termination.

D1.3.16   A customer clause requires payment of compensation to the employee for the duration of the obligation and is subject to written agreement. The monthly compensation payment must amount to at least 50% of the salary paid at the time when the employee leaves his position and is payable monthly in arrears. Where the employee is offered a suitable alternative job within this period, the salary paid by his new employer is set off against the employee's claim for compensation.

D1.3.17   The right to compensation is forfeited if the employer dismisses the employee due to gross misconduct.

D1.3.18   A customer clause may be relied upon in any case of termination of the employment, even if the employee is unfairly dismissed.

D1.3.19   If a salaried employee has been employed for less than three months, a customer clause may not be relied upon. If the employee has been employed for more than three months, but not more than six months, the duration of the customer clause may not exceed six months.

D1.3.20   A customer clause may be terminated at any time by the employer by one month's notice to expire at the end of a month.

D1.3.21   The above provisions are not applicable if a collective agreement provides different rules on the contents and terms of customer clauses.

D1.3.22   If an employment contract contains a non-competition clause as well as a customer clause and if the employer pays compensation for the non-competition clause, the employer is not obliged to pay compensation for the customer clause for the period in which the employee receives compensation for the non-competition clause.

Non-competition and customer clauses entered into before 15 June 1999

D1.3.23   Non-competition and customer clauses concluded before 15 June 1999 are valid and enforceable even if they do not contain any provisions concerning compensation.

The Danish Contracts Act

D1.3.24   In addition to the SEA, agreements in restraint of competition are governed by ss 36 and 38 of the Contracts Act.

D1.3.25   Section 38(1) of the Contracts Act provides that a non-competition clause is not binding if it extends further than is reasonably required to protect against competition or if it unreasonably restricts the employee's right to work within the relevant field. For this reason non-competition clauses are unlikely to be enforceable against non-salaried employees.

D1.3.26   Section 38(2) of the Contracts Act stipulates that agreements in restraint of competition may not be relied upon by the employer if an employee is unfairly dismissed or the employee terminates his employment due to a material breach on the part of the employer. Section 38(2) applies to non-competition clauses, but not to customer clauses.

D1.3.27   The general provision of the Contracts Act, s 36, providing that an agreement may be set aside if it is deemed to be unreasonably onerous on one of the parties, may also be applied to provisions concerning payment of liquidated damages in the event of the employee's breach of a non-competition clause or a customer clause.

Chief Executive Officers

D1.3.28   As regards employees who are not covered by the SEA, such as CEOs, it is possible to agree on non-competition and customer clauses which are not subject to the above compensation provisions. However, sections 36 and 38 of the Contracts Act still apply.

2   REMUNERATION

2.1   Background

D2.1.1   There is no mandatory minimum wage under Danish law. However, collective agreements usually stipulate minimum wages within certain areas, and individual employment contracts must always contain provisions concerning wages.

D2.1.2   According to the Equal Remuneration Act (implementing Directive 75/117/EEC), there must be no discrimination in wages based on gender.

D2.1.3   Collective agreements include different concepts regarding wages:
(i)   minimum wages;
(ii)   framework wages;
(iii) normal wages;
(iv)   piecework wages; and
(v)   bonus wages.

D2.1.4   Workers are generally paid per hour or at piece rates, whereas salaried employees are generally paid a fixed salary weekly, every fortnight or on a monthly basis. Salaried employees are usually paid at the end of the month.

D2.1.5 Most collective agreements contain provisions concerning payment for overtime. Individual employment contracts for salaried employees usually imply an obligation to work overtime without any requirement for additional payment or time off in lieu.

2.2 Legal Regulation of Remuneration
D2.2.1 There is no legal regulation of remuneration under Danish law.

2.3 Deductions from Wages
D2.3.1 There is a general prohibition on any deduction from a worker's wages unless:
* the deduction is required or authorised by virtue of a statutory provision (such as the deduction of tax and public charges etc) or a relevant provision of the worker's contract (such as subscription fees to unions, pension contributions etc); or
* the worker has *previously* signified in writing his agreement to the making of the deduction.

D2.3.2 'Wages' means any sum payable to the worker in connection with his employment including any fee, bonus, commission, holiday pay or other emolument referable to his employment whether payable under the contract of employment or otherwise, pensions, fringe benefits (such as company car, free telephone and newspaper etc), statutory sick pay and maternity pay. The term 'wages' excludes, however, advances of wages by way of a loan, expenses, allowances or gratuities in connection with retirement or compensation for loss of office, redundancy payments and any payment to the worker otherwise than in his capacity as a worker.

2.4 Itemised Pay Statement
D2.4.1 An employee is entitled to a written itemised pay statement at or before the time at which any payment of wages is made to him.

3 FURTHER RIGHTS AND OBLIGATIONS

3.1 Holiday Entitlement
D3.1.1 According to the Holiday Act most employees are entitled to five weeks' holiday per year. The Act is mandatory and employees are not only entitled but in fact even obliged to take five weeks' holiday a year. Both collective agreements and individual employment contracts may, however, agree on longer vacation periods and today six weeks' holiday seems to be the rule rather than the exception.

D3.1.2 The right to paid holiday is 'earned' in each calendar year in respect of the following holiday year (2 May–1 May), during which the employee is then entitled to paid holiday (or 12% holiday pay if he prefers). Thus, in the first year of employment the employee will not receive any salary during his holiday (but usually can usually draw on the holiday pay earned during his former employment).

D3.1.3 The employee's summer holiday (usually three weeks) must be notified by the employer no less than three months in advance, whereas remaining holiday must be notified at least one month in advance.

D3.1.4 'Earned' holiday may not be carried over from one year to another. However, the introduction of a more flexible holiday system (enabling employees to transfer part of their holiday from one holiday year to another) is currently being considered.

3.2 Sick Pay

D3.2.1 Salaried employees covered by the SEA are entitled to receive their normal salary during sickness. Other workers – unless otherwise stipulated in a collective agreement – are entitled to sickness benefit.

D3.2.2 Sickness benefit is borne initially by the employer. After a two-week period the employer will be reimbursed by the local authorities as provided by the Sickness Benefits Act.

D3.2.3 A maximum of DKK 2,846 per week will be reimbursed by the local authorities, for a period of up to 52 weeks within the preceding 18 months.

Sick pay	
'Salaried' employees (under the SEA)	Full salary paid by employer
Other	Sickness benefit for 52 weeks out of 18 months; up to DKK 2,846 per month

3.3 Additional Rights and Obligations

Private pension schemes

D3.3.1 In Denmark it is quite common to establish private pension schemes – either individual schemes or collective schemes administered by the employer – and a considerable number of collective agreements contain specific provisions concerning such pension schemes. Pension contributions are often paid partly by the employer (usually a percentage of salary) and partly by the employee. In general, pension contributions are tax deductible.

Working environment

D3.3.2 The Working Environment Act requires a safe and healthy environment to be established at the workplace, and the employer is obliged to ensure that the work is planned and performed in a safe and healthy way.

D3.3.3   In addition, all employers must take out an industrial injury insurance covering employees who are injured during their work.

D3.3.4   If the working environment is not satisfactory, the Working Environment Service may demand that appropriate improvements are undertaken and, if necessary, suspend the work.

D3.3.5   If the employer employs more than 10 persons, a safety steward must be elected. If there are more than 20 employees a safety committee must be established.

D3.3.6   Violation of the Act may result in fines and imprisonment of up to one year. Both the employer and those who manage the work may be responsible pursuant to the Act.

Tax and social costs

D3.3.7   Under Danish tax law everybody with a permanent or temporary residence in Denmark is liable to pay income tax to the Danish state.

D3.3.8   Income tax in Denmark is progressive and ranges between 45 to 63% (year 2000), including an 8% social contribution to the Labour Market Funds and a 1% Labour Market Supplementary Pension contribution (ATP). The personal tax allowance is approximately DKK 33,000. The maximum tax rate applies to income in excess of approximately DKK 250,000 per year.

D3.3.9   All kinds of income in the form of cash or benefits in kind are subject to income tax. Thus, in addition to monthly salary, benefits such as a company car, free accommodation etc are therefore taxable. Interest expenses and certain other expenses including membership fees to unions and unemployment funds are deductible.

D3.3.10   If a person moves to Denmark for the purpose of carrying out work in Denmark, he will be liable to pay tax in Denmark during the entire stay. Accordingly, employees from abroad, who are posted in Denmark for the purpose of carrying out work with a Danish company, must pay tax in Denmark.

D3.3.11   When certain conditions are fulfilled, employees from abroad who are employed by a Danish employer may be subject to a flat tax rate of only 25% excluding the 9% labour market contribution. No annual tax allowance and no deductions are allowed.

The most important conditions are:

- there must be a written contract of employment of a total duration of a minimum of six and a maximum of 36 months (which may be divided into several shorter periods). The employment may be extended for up to 48 months following the 36-month period. During the 48 month period the employee will be subject to general Danish tax rates. The employee must leave Denmark before expiration of the 48-month period;
- the employee will be subject to full tax liability relating to other income in Denmark;
- the employee must not be subject to full tax liability in Denmark before the employment commences;
- if the employee has previously been subject to full tax liability in Denmark, this full tax liability must not be terminated in order to be eligible for the 25% tax rate;
- the employee's monthly salary must be at least (approximately) DKK 53,000, including the 9% labour market contribution; and
- the employee may not take any direct or indirect part in the management, control or capital of the company, nor may he have done so during the past five years prior to the commencement of his employment.

D3.3.12   If the employee is also liable to pay tax on the Danish income in his home country, double taxation arises. To avoid double taxation, Denmark has entered into a number of tax treaties with most other countries. Tax treaties often solve double taxation via the so-called 'credit method', which means that tax paid on the relevant income in one jurisdiction – typically the country of residence – is set off against the tax of the other jurisdiction, meaning that the employee only pays tax in the country with the highest taxation rate of the two countries involved.

Residence and work permits

D3.3.13   The Northern Passport Control Agreement enables citizens of Finland, Iceland, Norway and Sweden to enter and stay in Denmark without a residence permit.

D3.3.14   Citizens from countries which are members of the EU and EFTA may enter and stay in Denmark without a residence permit for a period of three months from their arrival (six months from arrival if they are seeking a job). If EU and EFTA citizens stay in Denmark for a longer period, they must apply for a residence permit, but the authorities will issue such a permit upon request.

D3.3.15   As a general rule, citizens from other countries must obtain a residence permit (visa) in order to enter and stay in Denmark. However, citizens from certain countries (including USA) are allowed to enter and stay in Denmark as tourists for a period of three months without a residence permit.

D3.3.16 Subject to the Aliens Act citizens from Nordic countries (ie Finland, Iceland, Norway and Sweden) do not need a work permit. Neither do persons who have got an unlimited residence permit. EU and EFTA citizens must apply for a work permit and the authorities are obliged to issue such a permit upon request.

D3.3.17 Citizens from other countries must file an application for a residence and work permit with the Danish Embassy/Consulate in their own country. The Embassy/Consulate will arrange for the application to be attended to by the Danish Immigration Service, who will consult the local Labour Market Council in order to ascertain whether any Danish labour is capable of performing the job. Generally, permits will not be issued if this is the case. If the applicant is being expatriated to a Danish subsidiary or branch, no specialisation is necessary. The applicant may also choose to enter Denmark and file an application with the Danish authorities in accordance with the above-mentioned rules concerning visas.

Health insurance

D3.3.18 The Public Health Insurance Act entitles everybody with a permanent residence in Denmark to medical treatment etc. This also includes citizens from abroad if they have an established residence in Denmark and are therefore registered with the National Registration Office, always provided that they were covered by a public health insurance system in their home country.

D3.3.19 Normally there is a six-week waiting period before newcomers can be registered. However, this restriction does not apply to EU citizens by reason of EU Regulation 1408/71 on social security. European Union citizens and their accompanying family members who are normally employed in another state, but who are temporarily (normally not beyond 12 months) posted to work in Denmark, are entitled to medical care, including hospital treatment, dental treatment, medicine etc to the extent required during the stay in Denmark. The 12-month period may be extended upon request.

Posted workers

D3.3.20 On 17 December 1999, Denmark implemented Directive 71/96/EC concerning the posting of workers in the framework of the provision of services. The Danish Act ensures that employees who usually work in a country other than Denmark but work temporarily in Denmark are protected by eg the Health and Safety at Work Act, the Equal Treatment Act, the Act on Equal Pay and the Act on Prohibition against Discrimination on the Labour Market. The Act does not provide for payment of any minimum pay, as Denmark does not have any statutory provisions in this respect. Pay is fixed exclusively by individual or collective agreement.

D3.3.21 In Denmark, the National Labour Market Authority under the auspices of the Danish Ministry of Labour is the office which provides information services to foreign employers and employees concerning the rules applicable to posting in Denmark. An employee who is or has been posted in Denmark may take legal action in Denmark concerning his statutory rights in the jurisdiction where he has carried out work.

Unemployment allowances, public pension and social security

D3.3.22   Employees are entitled to a large number of social benefits in Denmark, including eg national insurance, unemployment insurance and industrial injury insurance.

Unemployment allowances

D3.3.23   Employers must give notice of available jobs to the Public Employment Agency, which allocates the jobs and handles the labour market measures available for the unemployed.

D3.3.24   Members of an Unemployment Fund who are available to the labour market are supported financially during periods of unemployment provided that certain conditions are fulfilled. The unemployed person must have been a member of an Unemployment Fund for at least one year prior to his unemployment, and in addition he must have been employed for at least 52 weeks during the previous three years. The allowance amounts to 90% of his former salary (to a maximum of DKK 2,846 per week – year 2000) and is granted for a maximum of 12 months within a period of 24 months. Subsequently, the unemployed person may receive allowances for a further period of a maximum of 36 months within a 48-month period, provided that the unemployed person does not refuse to take a job offered to him. Self-inflicted unemployment is subject to a five-week period without any allowances.

D3.3.25   Unemployed persons who are not members of an Unemployment Fund or do not fulfil the conditions mentioned are supported by the State, however, at a lower level (see para **D3.3.30**).

Public pension

D3.3.26   All persons who reach the age of 65 are entitled to an old-age pension. From 1 January 2000 the basic pension amounts to approximately DKK 4,000 per month. However, additional pension allowances may be granted provided that certain economic conditions are met.

D3.3.27   Employees are further entitled to the Labour Market Supplementary Pension (ATP), when they reach the age of 65. Contributions to ATP are made by both employers and employees.

D3.3.28   Persons between the age of 60–65 years who wish to retire early can apply for early retirement pay (presently approximately DKK 12,000 per month) when certain conditions are fulfilled, ie 25 years' membership of an Unemployment Fund within the last 30 years. The individual may work during this early retirement period, but the salary from this occupation will be deducted from the early retirement pay.

D3.3.29   Employees between the age of 18 and 60 years who are unable to work in any occupation due to disability are entitled to a 'pre-pension'. The disability must be of a permanent nature.

Social security

D3.3.30 Persons who are not a member of an Unemployment Fund or who do not meet the conditions mentioned above will be entitled to welfare payments to the extent that they are unable to support themselves.

Board representation of employees

D3.3.31 Board representation of employees is mainly governed by the Danish Companies Acts and executive orders concerning the election of employees' representatives to company boards. The rules regarding limited companies (A/S) and private companies (ApS) are similar with respect to board representation of employees.

D3.3.32 Employees of companies with an average staff of at least 35 employees or more in the preceding three years are entitled to elect among themselves a number of members to the board of directors and an equal number of substitutes to act in their place. The number of such directors may equal up to half of the number of other members of the board of directors elected by the general meeting, provided that this is not less than two directors. Thus, the employee representatives always remain a minority.

D3.3.33 There is no obligation for the company to arrange – on its own initiative – an election of employee representatives to the board of directors. However, if the employees request representation on the board of directors, the company must comply with such a request: it cannot veto such a request.

D3.3.34 Detailed rules regarding the election procedures are laid down in the executive orders issued pursuant to the Companies Act.

D3.3.35 If an employee representative of the board of directors is no longer employed by the company, he automatically resigns from the board of directors. An employee who has been given notice will probably keep his mandate until he leaves the company. Members of the board of directors elected by the employees are, however, protected from being dismissed in the same way as a shop steward.

D3.3.36 Members of the board of directors elected by the employees have the same rights and obligations as any other member of the board of directors. However, a member of the board of directors elected by the employees can be disqualified eg in matters concerning labour disputes, negotiations or wage agreements etc. However, it is the opinion of the Danish Ministry of Industry that members of the board of directors elected by the employees are subsequently entitled to read the minute book and have knowledge of matters discussed during meetings from which they have been excluded due to disqualification.

D3.3.37 The members of the board of directors elected by the employees are liable for damages to the same extent as other members of the board of directors, should they intentionally or through negligence cause damage to the company or to the shareholders, creditors or any third party by violation of company legislation or the Articles of Association.

4   WORKING TIME

4.1   Background

D4.1.1   Article 6 of Directive 93/104, which stipulates a maximum of 48 hours of work per week, has not been implemented in Danish law. However, most collective agreements and individual employment contracts usually provide that normal working hours are 37 hours per week. Individual employment contracts may, however, stipulate shorter or longer working hours.

D4.1.2   In addition, the Working Environment Act secures the employee a minimum of 11 hours consecutive rest within every 24-hour period and such other rest periods as are set out in Directive 93/104.

4.2   Legislative Control/Opting Out

D4.2.1   There is no working time regulation under Danish law.

4.3   Night Workers

D4.3.1   No special rules apply.

4.4   Rest Periods

D4.4.1   All workers are entitled to 11 hours' consecutive rest each day; 24 hours' uninterrupted rest each seven-day period.

4.5   Paid Annual Holiday

D4.5.1   See paras D3.1.1–D3.1.4.

5   EQUAL OPPORTUNITIES

5.1   Unlawful Discrimination

D5.1.1   According to Danish legislation and the European Convention on Human Rights forbid discrimination on the basis of sex, race, religion, national origin, and sexual orientation. Harassment by an employer or a fellow employee may constitute unlawful discrimination.

5.2   Disability Discrimination

D5.2.1   Under Danish law there are no rules concerning disability discrimination.

5.3   Enforcement and Remedies in Discrimination Cases

D5.3.1   Violation of the non-discrimination principle may entitle the employee (or an unsuccessful applicant for employment) to compensation, and may also be penalised by fines and imprisonment.

D5.3.2   The Equal Treatment Act implements Directive 76/207/EEC concerning the principles on equal treatment of men and women.

5.4   Equal Pay

D5.4.1   According to the Equal Remuneration Act (implementing Directive 75/117/EEC), there must be no discrimination in wages based on gender where employees perform work of equivalent value.

6   TERMINATION OF EMPLOYMENT

6.1   Background

Contracts for an indefinite period

D6.1.1   If not otherwise agreed, employment continues until terminated by either party. Persons who are employed for an indefinite period are entitled to notice of termination, and during the notice period the employee receives his normal salary. In general, employees may be dismissed at any time provided that the applicable notice of termination is complied with. The employee whose employment is terminated may, however, be entitled to severance pay (see paras **D6.3.9–D6.3.19**).

Contracts for a limited period

D6.1.2   Contracts for a limited period may be entered into under certain circumstances. As a general rule, contracts for a limited period expire without further notice at the end of the contract period or upon the completion of the work contracted for.

Unless otherwise agreed, employment for a limited period is normally considered to be governed by the general rules on termination, which means that the employment may also be terminated within the limited period.

D6.1.3   There are three types of limited period contracts:
- It is possible to agree that the first three months of the employment period will be considered a trial period. During the trial period the employment contract may generally be terminated by the employer with two weeks' notice and by the employee without any notice. If the employment contract is not terminated during the trial period, the employment will continue for an indefinite period.
- It is possible to deviate from the general rules of termination in the case of temporary employment, for instance employment during the summer or Christmas period. However, ifthe employment lasts for more than three months, the general rules of termination will apply.
- It is possible to agree that the employment is limited to a certain period of time, for instance that a person shall only be employed during the absence of another employee due to maternity leave etc. Furthermore, it is possible to agree that the employment only relates to a specific task and consequently that the employment will terminate upon completion of such task. However, it is not possible to circumvent the general rules of termination, for instance by entering into several fixed-term employment contracts in succession. Several consecutive fixed-term

employment contracts will not be accepted by the Danish courts. If an employee continues his employment after the agreed expiry date of the contract or after completion of a specific task, the rules concerning notice apply, and the seniority of the employee will be calculated from the initial date of employment.

6.2   Grounds for Termination

D6.2.1   As already mentioned, employees may in general be dismissed at any time provided that the employer complies with the required notice of termination. However, dismissals which are not considered fair and reasonable will under certain circumstances entitle the employee to severance pay.

D6.2.2   The grounds for termination may either be due to circumstances related to the employer (or his business), or grounds relating to the employee himself. In general, the burden of proof lies with the employer.

D6.2.3   Dismissals based on financial difficulties, lack of work, restructuring etc would usually be considered reasonable, as will dismissals due to the employee's failure to perform, co-operation problems etc. Where the dismissal is related to the employee it is generally required that the employee has received a written warning prior to the dismissal stating that he must expect to be dismissed if he does not improve.

D6.2.4   It may also be agreed that employment terminates by the end of a month during which the employee reaches a certain age.

D6.2.5   Some collective agreements contain provisions that prevent termination during a period of sickness. In general, Danish legislation does not prohibit termination during sickness, although it is commonly recognised that a short absence due to sickness alone will not be considered a fair reason for dismissal. On the other hand, termination due to absence that is frequent or prolonged may be deemed fair and reasonable, and in fact it may be specifically agreed that employees who are absent for more than 120 days (during any 12-month period) due to sickness may be dismissed with one month's notice regardless of seniority.

D6.2.6   Shop and safety stewards enjoy a greater protection against dismissal than other employees.

D6.2.7   `The transfer of an undertaking does not constitute a fair and reasonable ground for dismissal (either by the transferor or the transferee). Dismissal of an employee who demands that the employer comply with the Acts on Sex Discrimination, Equal Salary, Leave etc will never be deemed fair and reasonable. Furthermore a dismissal may not be based on racial grounds or the employee's membership of any particular association.

> **Protection from dismissal**
>
> *Examples*
>
> Unlawful grounds   • Sex, race, equal pay, union membership
> Under collective agreements   eg sickness
> Trade union/health and safety   • Special protection
> representatives
> Transfer-related dismissal   • Special protection

D6.2.8   The employer is entitled to terminate employment without notice (summary dismissal) in the event that the employee materially breaches the employment contract, eg unlawful absence from work or theft from the employer.

D6.2.9   The employer is not required to state the reason(s) for termination in the letter of termination. However, upon request, the employer must inform the employee of his reason(s) in order for the employee to determine whether the termination is unfair and wrongful, and accordingly whether to claim severance pay in this respect.

6.3   Notice Periods

CHIEF EXECUTIVE OFFICERS

D6.3.1   CEOs are not covered by the SEA and therefore the notice period must be agreed between the parties, such as 12 months' notice to be given by the employer and 6 months' notice by the CEO. If there is no agreed notice period, the employment may be terminated on reasonable notice taking into consideration, for example, the responsibilities and the seniority of the CEO.

SALARIED EMPLOYEES

D6.3.2   In relation to salaried employees, notice must be given in writing prior to dismissal.

D6.3.3   According to the SEA, notices must be given (to the end of a month) as follows:

Termination: salaried employees	Notice
Up to five months' service	one month
Between five months and two years nine months' service	three months
Between seven years nine months and five years eight months' service	four months
Between five years eight months and eight years seven months' service	five months
More than eight years seven months' service (maximum)	six months

D6.3.4 Salaried employees may terminate their employment by one month's notice to the end of a month.

D6.3.5 Salary during the notice period includes base salary and all other benefits, eg company car, free telephone, pension and bonus.

D6.3.6 These notice periods cannot be changed (even by agreement) to the detriment of the employee, although it is possible to agree on a mutual increase in the notice periods.

D6.3.7 During the notice period the employee must continue to carry out his duties under the employment contract unless otherwise decided by the employer.

OTHER (NON-SALARIED) EMPLOYEES

D6.3.8 The notice periods for other non-salaried employees are normally stipulated in a collective agreement. In general, within the first six months the parties may terminate the employment without notice, and thereafter the employer may terminate the employment with notice of between 14 and 120 days depending on the employee's seniority. Notice to be given by the employee normally ranges between 7 and 28 days, also dependent on seniority.

Severance pay – seniority

Chief Executive Officers

D6.3.9 Whether the CEO is entitled to severance pay due to seniority depends solely on the agreement between the parties. However, it is quite common that CEOs of listed and major privately-owned companies are entitled to severance payments in the event that they are dismissed by the company.

Salaried employees

D6.3.10 Under the SEA, salaried employees may be entitled to severance pay upon termination of their employment.

D6.3.11 Employees who have been employed for more than 12 years are entitled to severance pay provided that the employment is terminated by the employer and the employee is not entitled to an immediate old-age pension. Employees who have been employed for more than 12 years but less than 15 years are entitled to severance pay corresponding to one month's salary, while employees who have been employed for more than 15 years but less than 18 years are entitled to severance pay corresponding to two months' salary. Employees who have been employed for more than 18 years are entitled to severance pay corresponding to three months' salary, this being the maximum.

D6.3.12 Severance pay is calculated on the basis of salary including all benefits.

Non-salaried employees

D6.3.13   Agreements concerning severance pay based on seniority may be agreed individually or stipulated in a collective agreement.

Severance pay – termination by employer

CEOs	• As agreed between the parties
Salaried employees	
• Less than 12 years' service	• No severance pay
• 12-15 years' service	• 1 month's pay
• 15-18 years' service	• 2 months' pay
• More than 18 years' service	• 3 months' pay
Non-salaried employees	• As per individual or collective agreement

---

Severance pay – unfair dismissal

Chief Executive Officers

D6.3.14   The employer will not be obliged to pay severance pay in the event of unfair dismissal unless the parties have entered into an agreement to that effect.

Salaried employees

D6.3.15   If employment is terminated by the employer, the employee is entitled to (additional) severance pay provided that the termination is not considered fair and reasonable and the employee has been employed for at least one year. The maximum severance pay for employees who have been employed for less than 10 years is an amount corresponding to three months' salary. If the employee has been employed for more than 10 years but less than 15 years the maximum severance pay is an amount corresponding to four months' salary, and if the employee has been employed for more than 15 years, the maximum severance pay is an amount corresponding to six months' salary.

D6.3.16   Severance pay includes base salary and all benefits.

D6.3.17   According to case law, such severance pay does not usually exceed two thirds of the applicable maximum.

D6.3.18   It is difficult to say when a dismissal will be considered fair and reasonable by the courts, cf paras **D6.2.1–D6.2.9**, but in general the employee is given the benefit of the doubt.

Non-salaried employees

D6.3.19   According to the Main Agreement between the Danish Employers' Confederation and the Danish Confederation of Trade Unions, an employee may be entitled to severance pay corresponding to a maximum of 52 weeks' salary if the dismissal is not considered fair and reasonable.

Severance pay – unfair dismissal

CEOs   •   As agreed between the parties

Salaried employees

• Less than 1 year's service	• No severance pay
• 1-10 years' service	• 3 months' pay (max)
• 10-15 years' service	• 4 months' pay (max)
• More than 15 years' service	• 6 months' pay (max)

Non-salaried employees   •   52 weeks' pay (max)

6.4   Damages

D6.4.1   In the event of a material breach of contract on the part of the employee, the employer may claim damages corresponding to actual loss. As a basic rule the employer can claim damages corresponding to half a month's salary due to the salaried employee's unlawful absence.

D6.4.2   If an employee is dismissed without notice (summary dismissal) and the dismissal is subsequently deemed to be unfair, the employee is entitled to claim damages corresponding to salary during the notice period, less any salary which the employee receives if he enters into new employment during the notice period. Salaried employees, however, are always entitled to so-called minimum damages corresponding to three months' salary provided that the notice period is at least three months.

Re-employment

D6.4.3   Employees do not normally enjoy any right to re-employment under Danish law. However, the Main Agreement between the Danish Employers' Confederation and the Danish Confederation of Trade Unions stipulates that the Arbitral Tribunal on Dismissals can decide that the employee should be re-employed unless the relationship between the parties has been substantially damaged.

Bankruptcy

D6.4.4   In the event of the employer's bankruptcy, employment does not automatically terminate, but the liquidator may give notice to terminate the employment relationship. If, because of bankruptcy, the employee (Chief Executive Officers not included) does not receive his normal salary etc, he will be reimbursed by the Employees' Guarantee Fund up to a net limit (excluding tax) of DKK 90,000 plus holiday allowances. The fund subrogates in the employee's rights against the bankrupt debtor with respect to the amount paid. Applications for such reimbursement must be filed on the appropriate forms within four weeks following the employer's bankruptcy.

6.5   Collective Redundancies

D6.5.1   In 1994 Denmark introduced rules based on Directive 75/129/EEC on the employer's duty to follow special procedures with respect to collective redundancies. The purpose of these rules is to avoid dismissals or at least to mitigate the consequences of dismissals to the extent possible.

The 1994 Act applies where an undertaking dismisses, within a period of 30 days:

- 10 or more employees in an undertaking having more than 20 but fewer than 100 employees;
- 10% or more of the employees in an undertaking having at least 100 but fewer than 300 employees; and
- 30 or more employees in an undertaking having at least 300 employees.

D6.5.2   The Act lays down rules on the employer's negotiations with employee representatives, and notification to the Labour Council on the contemplated dismissals. It also provides that dismissals on which the undertaking insists, after the completion of the negotiation procedure, may not be effective until 30 days after the Labour Council has been given written notice.

D6.5.3   If the employer does not comply with the negotiation procedure – ie if the employer does not negotiate with the employees or their representatives or notify the Labour Council – the employer must pay compensation to all affected employees. The compensation payable to the affected employees is the equivalent of 30 days' pay from the date of the notice provided, with a deduction representing any pay which the employee has received during his individual notice period. However, if the company employs more than 100 employees and not less than 50% of the employees are dismissed, the compensation payable to each employee to each employee amounts to eight weeks' pay from the date of the notice, less any pay received during the notice period.

7   YOUNG WORKERS

7.1   General Obligations

D7.1.1   The regulation of work involving children and young persons is covered by the Working Environment Act (implementing Directive 94/33) which contains specific provisions concerning employees under the age of 18.

D7.1.2   Work must be planned and performed with due regard to the age and education, as well as the development and health, of the young employee.

D7.1.3 Certain types of work must not be performed by persons under the age of 18. Working hours are limited in relation to those between the age of 13 and 18, and children below 13 are not allowed to work at all.

8   MATERNITY AND PARENTAL RIGHTS

8.1   Background

D8.1.1 Danish law recognises various types of leave: educational leave, sabbatical leave, maternity/paternal leave and childcare leave.

D8.1.2 Educational leave and sabbatical leave are only available if there is specific agreement between the employer and the employee concerning such leave.

D8.1.3 Maternity/paternal leave and childcare leave are mandatory.

8.2   General Rights

D8.2.1 According to the Equal Treatment Act a mother has the right to four weeks' leave before the expected date of birth and 24 weeks' leave after the actual date of birth. The father may use the last 10 weeks of the 24 weeks' leave (instead of the mother). In addition, the father is entitled to 2 weeks of leave twice within the first six months following the birth.

D8.2.2 After expiry of maternity/paternal leave, the mother or the father may take childcare leave for another period of 13 weeks, though it is possible to be granted 26 weeks' leave, if the childcare leave is commenced before the child's first birthday.

Maternity/parental leave

Before birth:
Mother   • 4 weeks

After birth:
Mother/father
Mother   • 24 weeks
Father   • 10 weeks (to be taken weeks 14–24 after birth instead of mother's leave)

Plus
2 × 2 weeks' leave within 6 months after birth

Parental leave:
Mother/father   13/26 weeks

8.3   Protection from Dismissal

D8.3.1 In order to protect a pregnant employee or an employee on maternity or parental leave, it is not lawful to dismiss an employee due to the fact that he or she is on leave. The employer must prove that the dismissal was not due to the employee's pregnancy or maternity/paternity leave, and if the employer is not able to meet this burden of proof – which is very difficult – the employer may be liable to pay compensation of up to 18 months' salary (according to case law, usual compensation corresponds to six to nine months' salary).

8.4 Maternity Pay

D8.4.1 Salaried employees on leave are entitled to 50% salary during the four weeks before and 14 weeks after the birth, unless better terms are provided for by an individual employment contract or by collective agreement. The employer will be reimbursed an amount corresponding to the maximum public allowance (DKK 2,846 per week).

D8.4.2 For the remaining 10 weeks of the maternity leave period, the employee will receive a public allowance (maximum DKK 2,846 per week).

D8.4.3 Non-salaried employees are entitled to public allowances (maximum DKK 2,846 per week), unless better terms are provided for by collective agreement. The allowances are paid by the national insurance system.

8.5 Health and Safety

D8.5.1 Directive 92/85/EC (regarding pregnant workers) has been implemented in Denmark. The Directive contains provisions regarding protection of the health and safety of the pregnant worker, prohibition against night work, right to absence due to examinations and tests during the pregnancy period, and the right to maternity leave and maternity pay.

D8.5.2 The employer should decide what measures should be taken to avoid exposing a pregnant employee to risk and should consider adjusting working hours and conditions or giving the employee leave. The Pregnant Workers Directive sets out a non-exhaustive list of places and working conditions which are regarded as being potential risks.

9   BUSINESS TRANSFERS

9.1   Background

D9.1.1 The Act on the Legal Position of Employees in connection with the Transfer of Undertakings (ATU) applies when undertakings are transferred in whole or in part. In this context, 'transfer' means the sale, transfer by way of gift, merger, leasing or letting of an undertaking under circumstances comparable to the sale of an undertaking.

D9.1.2 The ATU does not apply when single assets are transferred and they do not constitute an operationally and financially viable unit.

9.2   Effects of the Transfer

D9.2.1 The ATU provides that the transferee immediately takes over the employment rights and obligations existing at the time of transfer. Thus, the transferee automatically takes over all individual agreements on the existing terms. At the same time, the transferor is discharged from his obligations and forfeits his rights towards the employees.

D9.2.2   The transferee does not become a party to collective agreements entered into by the undertaking before the transfer, but is obliged to maintain pay and working conditions under such collective agreements in relation to the employees transferred. However, this obligation does not apply to new employees who were not employed within the undertaking at the time of transfer.

9.3   Dismissal of Employees

D9.3.1   Dismissal due to change of ownership will not be deemed to be reasonable merely because of the transfer of the undertaking, unless the dismissal is due to financial, technical or organisational circumstances causing changes in the employment relationship.

D9.3.2   Change of ownership is not in itself a reasonable ground for dismissal, and the employee may claim compensation for unfair dismissal to the extent that special statutory provisions or any collective agreement authorise payment of such compensation, eg s 2b of the SEA and cl 4(3) of the Main Agreement.

D9.3.3   The Act on the Transfer of Undertakings does not require the employee to continue the employment relationship if the transfer entails material changes to his working conditions, as the employee may object to these changes under the general rules on breach of contract.

9.4   Duty to Inform and Consult

D9.4.1   The ATU also imposes a duty on the transferor as well as the transferee to inform the employees or elected employee representatives of the reason for the transfer, its legal, financial and social implications and any measures proposed with regard to the employees. If it is likely that there will be measures with regard to the employees in connection with the transfer, negotiations must be conducted with the employees or elected employee representatives. Any collective redundancies must be handled in accordance with the prescribed procedure.

D9.4.2   Finally, the ATU provides that the elected employee representatives, including shop stewards and health and safety representatives, must keep their existing positions and functions after the transfer.

10   COLLECTIVE RIGHTS

10.1 Legal Status of Collective Agreements
D10.1.1   See paras **D1.1.11–D1.1.20**.

10.2 Industrial Action

D10.2.1   Under Danish collective labour law the conclusion of a collective agreement has the effect that collective industrial actions are illegal during the term of the agreement. However, the so-called 'peace obligation' is not an absolute one.

D10.2.2   In s 5 of the Standard Rules for Handling Industrial Disputes it is stated that employees are entitled to stop work without notice if wages are not paid by the employer in due time. This rule expresses the basic legal principle that there is no obligation to work if the individual is not paid as agreed between the parties.

D10.2.3   It is further stated in s 5 of the Standard Rules that employees have the right to hold a stoppage of work without notice if matters concerning their honour, or danger to their lives or welfare, are compelling reasons for such action. This general basic principle of law is valid for all labour relationships.

D10.2.4   It is also a basic principle of Danish labour law that an employee can legally refuse to perform work which is considered to be strike work, ie work affected by a strike. According to case law, strike work exists when the work in question should have been performed by employees taking part in a legal strike or by wage employees who are legally locked out.

D10.2.5   Various forms of collective industrial action exist. Stoppage of work has four variants: strikes, lock-outs, boycotts by the employees and boycotts by the employer. Strikes and boycotts are weapons of the employees, whereas lock-outs and boycotts are weapons of the employers.

D10.2.6   In addition to the above, there are other types of industrial action which cannot legally be used. One of the most frequent options is obstruction of work, which includes sit-down strikes, go-slow strikes, and work-to-rule actions. The normal option in Denmark is the go-slow strike, where the employees work at a slower speed than usual.

D10.2.7   See para **D11.2.1** for information on the resolution of disputes.

10.3 European Works Councils

D10.3.1   Directive 94/45 has been implemented in Denmark. Thus, multinational organisations in Denmark must set up European Works Councils if they employ at least 1,000 employees with at least 150 employees in at least two member states.

11 EMPLOYMENT DISPUTES

11.1 Background

> Disputes between an employer and an employee are resolved:
> - in the ordinary courts – Country Court as the first instance (High Court if the claim exceeds DKK 1,000,000) with a right of appeal to the High Court within four weeks of delivery of the judgment (within eight weeks to the Supreme Court if the High Court is the court of first instance) – if the employment relationship is not governed by a collective agreement; and
> - either by conciliation or industrial arbitration if the employment is governed by a collective agreement. The decisions of an industrial tribunal may not be appealed.

D11.1.1 Whereas an employee may institute proceedings before the ordinary courts at his own initiative, actions before an industrial tribunal may only be conducted by the union of which the employee is a member.

D11.1.2 In industrial disputes concerning the interpretation of collective agreements, the trade union is a party to the collective agreement on behalf of the individual members, and handles the case.

D11.1.3 The parties to the collective agreement are obliged to take part in mediation proceedings to solve the dispute. Refusal to participate in mediation will be considered a serious breach of the collective agreement. If a dispute about interpretation of the collective agreement is not resolved by mediation or by negotiation between the parties, each party is entitled to have the dispute brought before a board or Court of Arbitration for a final decision. The ordinary courts are not competent to hear cases concerning the interpretation of collective agreements.

11.2 Labour Courts/Tribunals

D11.2.1 All cases concerning the interpretation of the Main Agreement, breach of collective agreements and cases concerning the legality of industrial action are subject to the jurisdiction of the Labour Court. The Labour Court may fine the organisation as well as individual members if they participate in an illegal strike or otherwise breach the collective agreement. The Labour Court can also fine the employer if the employer breaches the collective agreement. The fines may be considerable (up to DKK 500,000). If a union or an employer does not comply with the decision made by the Labour Court the party may be sued again and will be heavily fined by the Labour Court. The highest fine so far imposed by the Labour Court is DKK 20,000,000. Decisions of the Labour Court and agreements made during its proceedings can be enforced by the Bailiff. The decisions of the Labour Court cannot be appealed.

11.3 Venue and Governing Law

D11.3.1   Employment contracts may be connected with more than one country at the same time. It is important to establish the governing law of the employment relationship, as the rules for termination of employment etc may vary substantially from jurisdiction to jurisdiction.

D11.3.2   Denmark has ratified the EC Civil Jurisdiction and Judgment Convention (the Brussels/San Sebastian Convention), including its provisions on jurisdiction applicable to individual employment contracts. According to the Convention, a jurisdiction agreement is valid in relation to individual employment contracts only if the agreement is entered into after the dispute begins or if the employer relies on the agreement for the purpose of bringing legal action before a court other than the court at the place where the employer is domiciled.

D11.3.3   In general, it is recommended that the employer and the employee should make a choice of law in order to avoid doubt as to what law will govern the contract of employment. The parties are free to do so, but must be aware of the provision in art 6(1) of the Convention on the Law Applicable to Contractual Obligations (the Rome Convention), from which it appears that a choice of law clause will not deprive the employee of the protection afforded to him by mandatory rules in the country where the work is performed.

D11.3.4   In the absence of any choice of law in the employment contract, art 6(2) of the Rome Convention states that a contract of employment is governed by the law of the country in which the employee habitually carries out his work (or the majority of his work) under the employment contract, even if he is temporarily employed in another country.

D11.3.5   Under the Administration of Justice Act, the employee may in individual civil law disputes between the employer and the employee bring legal action in the jurisdiction where the employer has his home court. The home court of a company, association or other society generally lies in the jurisdiction where its principal office is situated. However, the employee may choose to bring an action against the employer before the district court in the jurisdiction from which the commercial activities are carried out if the employee is employed with eg a branch.

12   WHISTLEBLOWING/DATA PROTECTION/ CONFIDENTIALITY

12.1 Whistleblowing

D12.1.1   There is no legislation in Denmark concerning whistleblowing.

D12.1.2   Whether information can be revealed is determined on a case-by-case basis taking into consideration both the employer's interest in maintaining confidentiality and the public's interest in learning about the matter in question.

D12.1.3   As the employee must always act in accordance with his duty of loyalty towards the employer, there may be situations where the right course of action will be for the employee to initially approach the employer and – provided the employer does not take action – subsequently to approach the relevant public authorities.

12.2 Data Protection

D12.2.1   New legislation implementing the Data Protection Directive, Directive 95/46/EC, was passed in the Danish Parliament in May 2000 and came into effect on 1 July 2000.

D12.2.2   The new legislation reflects the general rules on lawfulness and fairness of the processing of data which are found in the Directive. Thus, processing must only take place in accordance with good data processing practice (ie only for specified, explicit, and legitimate purposes, it must be adequate, relevant and not excessive in relation to the purposes for which it is collected, and the data must kept only for as long as necessary). In addition there are specific provisions regarding employees' right of access to the data and their right to object. The employer has a duty to inform the employee about the collection of data, and the employer must obtain explicit consent to transfer data to countries outside the European Economic Area except where an adequate level of protection has been established or the employer warrants 'safe harbour'. There are special provisions concerning the processing of sensitive data ie data relating to racial or ethnic origin, political opinions, religious or philosophical beliefs, trade union membership, and data concerning health and sex life.

12.3 Confidentiality

D12.3.1   During employment an employee is obliged to act loyally towards the employer, and accordingly he is not entitled to disclose to third parties any trade secrets and other confidential information belonging to the employer. If the employee discloses confidential information he will be in breach of his duties to the employer and the employer may dismiss or otherwise discipline the employee, or sue for damages.

D12.3.2   The general non-disclosure obligation is often further strengthened by means of a confidentiality clause. Such confidentiality clauses are often valid even after termination of the employment.

D12.3.3   In addition, s 10(2) of the Marketing Practices Act prohibits unauthorised use or disclosure of trade secrets of which the employee has gained knowledge or which have been put at his disposal in the course of his employment. This prohibition is valid during the employment and for a period of three years following termination of the employment.

13   HUMAN RIGHTS

13.1 Rights and Obligations

D13.1.1   The operative parts of the European Convention on Human Rights (ECHR) has been incorporated in Danish law by means of a reference act. Therefore, it is unlawful to act in any way which is incompatible with the ECHR, and when applying Danish legislation the courts must interpret it as far as possible as being compatible with the ECHR.

BIBLIOGRAPHY

Ole Hasselbalch and Per Jacobsen *Labour Law in Denmark* (1999).
Bent Iversen, Jørgen Nørgaard, Morten Wegner and Niels Ørgaard *Danish Business Law* Chapter 23 (1998).

USEFUL WEBSITES

Danish Ministry of Labour:
• www.am.dk
Danish Parliament:
• www.folketinget.dk
Danish Labour Court:
• www.arbejdsretten.dk
Danish Employers' Confederation:
• www.da.dk
Danish Confederation of Trade Unions:
• www.lo.dk
Confederation of Danish Industries:
• www.di.dk
Union of Commercial and Clerical Employees in Denmark:
• www.hk.dk
Danish Federation of Semi-Skilled Workers:
• www.sid.dk
Association of Danish Lawyers and Economists:
• www.djoef.dk
Danish Bar and Law Society:
• www.advokatsamfundet.dk
law database:
• www.schultz-online.dk
Court of Justice of the European Communities:
• www.curia.eu.int

E   England and Wales

Susan Mayne, Susan Malyon and Julia Onslow-Cole

Susan Mayne is a solicitor in Employment Law at CMS Cameron McKenna, London. Since qualifying in 1988, Susan has concentrated on all aspects of employment law including the employment of directors and senior executives, and the resolution of employment disputes in Employment Tribunals. She is particularly interested in discrimination and TUPE issues. She is a contributor to Tolleys Employment Law, Tolleys Employment Precedents and Procedures, Tolleys CD Rom on Employment Law. She has written several articles (including some for *The Independent*) and has spoken at a number of seminars.

Susan Malyon is a solicitor in Employment Law at CMS Cameron McKenna, London. Susan has specialised in employment law since 1994. She has particular experience in contentious matters conducting cases for clients in the Employment Tribunal, Employment Appeal Tribunal, County Court, High Court and Court of Appeal. Her experience ranges from unfair dismissal claims to enforcing restrictive covenants. Susan's non contentious experience includes drafting employment documentation, directors' service contracts and severance agreements, advising on individual disciplinary and dismissal issues, and mass redundancy programmes. She has also advised on sex, race and disability discrimination and on employee aspects of mergers and acquisitions, outsourcing and public/private partnerships.

Julia Onslow-Cole is a partner and head of the Global Immigration Group of CMS Cameron McKenna and has practised solely in the area of immigration and nationality law for the last 16 years. She is immediate past chair of the International Bar Association's Immigration and Nationality Committee, Council member of the Section for Legal Practice of the International Bar Association, member of the Immigration Law Sub-Committee of the Law Society, Secretary of the Immigration Law Practitioners Association and co-convenor of Employment and Business Sub-Committee.

CMS Cameron McKenna, London

Phone: +44 (0)20 7367 3000
Fax: +44 (0)20 7367 2000
Email: susan.mayne@cmck.com; susan.malyon@cmck.com; julia.onslowcole@cmck.com
Website: www.cmck.com

ENGLAND AND WALES

Rights	Yes/No	Explanatory Notes
THE EMPLOYMENT RELATIONSHIP		
Minimum notice	YES	Minimum notice period set by statute, depending on length of service
Terms:		
Express	YES	Terms commonly implied (eg duty of mutual trust and confidence) and incorporated (eg from collective agreements/company handbook)
Implied	YES	Terms commonly implied (eg duty of mutual trust and confidence) and incorporated (eg from collective agreements/company handbook)
Incorporated by statute	YES	Terms commonly implied (eg duty of mutual trust and confidence) and incorporated (eg from collective agreements/company handbook)
REMUNERATION		
Minimum wage regulation	YES	Applies to workers, not just employees: £3.70 per hour for most workers.
Further rights and obligations:		
Right to paid holiday	YES	20 days per annum for most workers
Right to sick pay	YES	Statutory sick pay may be payable
WORKING TIME		
Regulation of hours per day/ working week	YES	48 hours per week over 17 week reference period
Regulation of night work	YES	Eight hours per night
Right to paid holiday	YES	See above
Right to rest periods	YES	Right to daily/weekly rest
EQUAL OPPORTUNITIES		
Discrimination protection:		
Sex	YES	Includes protection against harassment and victimisation
Race	YES	Includes protection against harassment and victimisation
Marital status	YES	Unlawful to discriminate on the grounds that a person is married
Disability	YES	Employer must not discriminate, and has a duty to make reasonable adjustments
Religion	NO	Not expressly, but religion may also be a racial characteristic

Age	NO	
Sexual orientation	NO	But sexual orientation may be protected under the Sex Discrimination Act 1975 (see text)
Gender reassignment	YES	Expressly protected by statute
Part-time workers	YES	Protected from less favourable treatment
Equal pay legislation	YES	Equal pay for work of equal value

TERMINATION OF EMPLOYMENT

Right not to be dismissed in breach of contract	YES	Claim for damages in civil courts or employment tribunal
Statutory rights on termination	YES	Unfair dismissal claim: qualifying period of service usually required

REDUNDANCY

Statutory definition	YES	
Right to payment on redundancy	YES	Statutory payment and/or additional contractual payment, depending on qualifying period of service
Right to consultation:		
Individual	YES	Failure could lead to unfair dismissal claim
Collective	YES	Where employer proposes to dismiss 20 or more employees at the same establishment within 90 days. Notification also required to Department of Trade and Industry

YOUNG WORKERS

Protection of children and young persons at work	YES	

MATERNITY RIGHTS

Right to time off – antenatal care	YES	Right not to be unreasonably refused time off
Right to maternity leave	YES	All women entitled to ordinary leave of 18 weeks; additional leave for additional service
Notice requirements	YES	
Maternity pay (during leave)	YES	Statutory maternity pay or maternity allowance
Protection from dismissal	YES	Statutory protection: unfair dismissal/sex discrimination
Health and safety protection	YES	Pregnant/breastfeeding women who have given birth within six months are protected

149

Right to parental leave	YES	Up to 13 weeks' leave (unpaid) where child born on or after 15 December 1999, but employee must have one years' qualifying service
Right to time off for dependants	YES	Reasonable amount of unpaid leave to care for dependants

BUSINESS TRANSFERS

Right to protection on transfer	YES	Employees protected if they are employed in the part of the business to be transferred
Transfer of employment obligations	YES	All rights transfer with current exception of pensions
Right to information and consultation	YES	Obligation to inform and/or consult with trade unions or elected employee representatives
Right not to be dismissed	YES	Dismissal for a reason connected with the transfer is automatically unfair

COLLECTIVE RIGHTS

Compulsory recognition of trade union	YES	Trade Union can apply for compulsory recognition on certain conditions
European Works Councils	YES	But no system of compulsory national works councils or employee representation
Right to take industrial action	NO	No positive right, although some acts will be protected industrial action

EMPLOYMENT DISPUTES

Civil Court jurisdiction	YES	Contractual issue
Statutory body	YES	Employment tribunals deal with statutory employment claims, plus some contractual issues

WHISTLEBLOWING

Protection from dismissal/ detriment	YES	Workers protected in the event of making a 'qualifying disclosure'

DATA PROTECTION

Protection	YES	Data Protection Act protects personal data and processing of sensitive data

HUMAN RIGHTS ACT

Statutory protection of human rights:

Public authority	YES	Human Rights Act 1998 implements European convention of human rights
Private organisations	NO	Not covered by the Human Rights Act 1998

1 THE EMPLOYMENT RELATIONSHIP

1.1 Background

E1.1.1 Although it appears that the modern employment relationship between employer and employee is governed increasingly by statute, the essence of the relationship is contractual.

E1.1.2 Under English[1] law, the contract between employer and employee delineates the nature of the relationship and the consequences that flow from it. General contractual principles (see below) set the framework for the rights and obligations of the parties.

[1] For the purposes of this chapter 'English' law shall refer to the law of England and Wales.

E1.1.3 A contract can be oral and/or in writing and consists, in essence, of an offer, acceptance and consideration – there must be an intention to create legal relations, and terms must be certain. If both parties are in agreement on terms, any such agreement (oral and/or written[1]) is enforceable by either party.

[1] *Hawker Siddeley Power Engineering Ltd v Rump* [1979] IRLR 425.

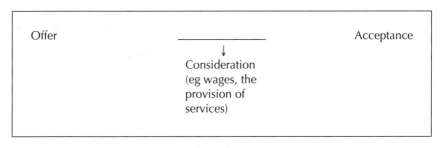

Offer ———————— Acceptance

↓

Consideration
(eg wages, the
provision of
services)

E1.1.4 Although both are governed by general contractual rules, English law distinguishes between employer and employee (a contract of service) and employer and self-employed consultant/freelancer etc (a contract for services) *and arguably an intermediate category of employer and worker.*

1.2 Contract of Service

E1.2.1 There is a statutory obligation to provide written particulars of employment (see below). It is in any event preferable to confirm terms of agreement (and any subsequent amendments or arrangements) in writing. Companies often use staff manuals, handbooks or supplementary documents containing details of standard terms and conditions applicable to all employees, which will form part of the contract if expressly or impliedly incorporated. There are further obligations to keep information in relation to company directors[1] which will not be detailed here.

[1] Companies Act 1985, ss 318, 741; Listing Rules of the London Stock Exchange (The Yellow Book).

> EMPLOYED → governed by statute and contract law
> SELF EMPLOYED → governed largely by contract

A   CONTRACT AND ITS WRITTEN PARTICULARS

E1.2.2

> Employment conditions contained in → letter of engagement
> → principal statement
> → employee handbook
> → policy documents/schemes
> → collective agreements

The Employment Rights Act 1996 (ERA 1996) specifies that certain particulars[1] of an employee's terms and conditions of employment must be supplied in writing, to an employee who has been employed for more than one month, not later than two months from the date of commencement of employment. Certain particulars (marked with an asterisk* below) must be contained in a single document, referred to as the 'principal statement':

(a) the name of the employer;*
(b) the name of the employee;*
(c) the date on which the employment began;*
(d) the date on which the employee's period of continuous employment began, taking into account any employment with a previous employer that counts towards that period eg with an associated company;*
(e) the scale or rate of remuneration or the method of calculating remuneration;*
(f) the intervals at which remuneration is paid;*
(g) hours of work, including any terms or conditions relating to normal working hours;*
(h) holiday entitlement;*
(i) terms and conditions relating to incapacity for work due to sickness or injury, including any provision for sick pay;
(j) pensions and pension schemes;
(k) whether or not a contracting out certificate is in force for the employment in respect of which the statement is given;
(l) length of notice to be given by the employee to terminate the contract of employment;
(m) length of notice to be given by the employer to terminate the contract of employment.

The periods referred to at (l) and (m) above are always subject to statutory minima.[2] The statutory minima do not apply where the employer is entitled to dismiss the employee summarily (or the employee is entitled to claim constructive dismissal because of the employer's fundamental breach). The contract often provides for a longer notice period.

The minimum notice periods under statute are:

To be given by the employer:

Length of service	Notice period
Less than one month's continuous employment:	No minimum period
Between one month and two years' continuous employment:	One week
More than two and up to twelve years' continuous employment:	One week for each complete year of continuous service.
More than twelve years' continuous employment:	12 weeks

To be given by the employee:

Length of service	Notice period
One month or more continuous employment:	One week

(n) where the employment is not intended to be permanent, the period for which it is expected to continue or, if the employment is for a fixed term,[3] the date on which that term will expire;

(o) the employee's job title or a written description of the work which the employee is recruited to carry out;*

(p) the employee's place of work, or where the employee is required to work at various places, an indication that this is the case and details of the main address of the employer;*

(q) any collective agreements which directly affect the terms and conditions of the employment including, where the employer is not a party, the persons by whom they were made;

(r) where the employee is required to work outside the United Kingdom for a period of more than one month, the employer must provide certain specified details:
- the period of work outside the UK;
- the currency in which payment will be made, while working outside the UK;
- any additional pay and benefits to be provided by reason of the work being carried out outside the UK; and
- any terms and conditions relating to the employee's return to the UK.

[1] ERA 1996, ss 1–6.
[2] ERA 1996, s 86.
[3] Note that contracts can be fixed-term or terminable on notice. The Fixed-Term Contracts Directive applies to fixed-term contracts – this Directive came into force on 10 July 1999 and member states have been given two years to comply with the minimum standards of employment protection. The United Kingdom has until 10 July 2001 to implement the Directive into national legislation. The

Directive introduces two principles for fixed-term workers: (1) Member states must ensure that fixed-term contract workers are not treated less favourably than permanent staff unless that treatment can be objectively justified; and (2) Member states must prevent the abuse of fixed-term contracts.

The Government has published the draft Fixed Term Employees (Prevention of Less Favourable Treatment) Regulations 2001 which are under consultation until 31 May 2001. Specifically, there will be a maximum number of renewals of fixed-term contracts, after which the contract will become of indefinite term. Fixed-term employees will be entitled to receive the same terms and conditions as similar permanent employees unless there is an objective reason to justify the less favourable treatment.

E1.2.3   A principal statement can refer the employee to another document, provided that the employee has a reasonable opportunity of reading that document or such document is made reasonably accessible. Whilst the principal statement is evidence of terms of the contract, it is not conclusive[1] – other terms may be set out in other documents, or orally.

[1]   *Jones v Associated Tunnelling Co Ltd* [1981] IRLR 477, EAT.

Disciplinary and grievance procedure

E1.2.4   The principal statement should include a note specifying any disciplinary rules applicable to the employee and identify the person to whom the employee can appeal disciplinary decisions. This does not apply to an employer who employs less than 20.

E1.2.5   The disciplinary procedure (as opposed to disciplinary rules) should generally not be contractual. The failure of an employer to follow the procedure could result, in addition to any statutory claim of unfair dismissal, in a claim for breach of contract.

E1.2.6   The statement should also include the details of the person to whom the employee can apply to redress an employment grievance.

E1.2.7   There is no requirement to specify any rules, disciplinary decisions, grievances or procedures relating to health or safety at work. The Health and Safety at Work etc Act 1974 obliges employers to prepare a written statement for employees of their health and safety policy and the arrangements for its implementation.

ACAS[1] disciplinary procedure
Tribunals considering unfair dismissal complaints will look to see if employers have an acceptable disciplinary procedure – and have followed it. Many companies adopt the standard ACAS[2] procedure.

---

[1]   The Advisory Conciliation and Arbitration Service, established in 1975 to promote settlement of disputes and good industrial relations. Conciliation officers have powers to conciliate between the disputing parties and facilitate an agreement which is binding.

[2]   *Lock v Cardiff Railway Co Ltd* [1998] IRLR 358 (the Employment Appeals Tribunal found that the lower tribunal had failed to pay proper regard to ACAS Code of Practice on disciplinary practice and procedures).

Change of terms

E1.2.8 The employer must inform the employee in writing of changes to any particulars as soon as possible and, in any event, no later than one month after the change.

Failure to provide a written statement

E1.2.9 *An employee employed more than two months* may apply[1] to an employment tribunal if he is not provided with a written statement (or if the statement is incomplete or inaccurate). A tribunal can determine what particulars should have been included in the statement (but it cannot invent a term). These particulars are deemed to have been given by the employer to the employee. The tribunal may not make a monetary award nor can it enforce the contract of employment or interpret the agreement.

[1] ERA 1996, s 1; *Eagland v British Telecommunications plc* [1992] IRLR 323, CA.

B   TERMS OF THE CONTRACT

E1.2.10 Contract terms may be in writing, oral, or be implied or incorporated.

Sources of contract terms

Express terms	• Oral
	• Written
Implied terms	• Central
	• Officious bystander
	• Business efficacy
	• Conduct
	• Custom and practice
Incorporated terms	
Statute	

Express terms

E1.2.11 Express terms (oral and/or written) will only be overridden if they are contrary to statute or public policy. Each term must be clear and unambiguous. In the event of ambiguity, extrinsic evidence may be admissible to assist in interpretation.

Examples of express terms

Summary dismissal

E1.2.12 Employers often set out a non-exhaustive list indicating the types of behaviour considered by the company to be gross misconduct eg being under the influence of alcohol or drugs whilst at work, fighting on the premises, insubordination, behaviour outside the office likely to bring the company into disrepute. Such behaviour entitles the employer to terminate the contract immediately without the need to give notice (or pay in lieu).

155

Without express provision, an employer may still terminate the contract summarily in the event of the employee's fundamental breach, although there may be dispute as to whether the employee's behaviour constitutes gross misconduct.[1]

[1] Whether a single act of carelessness or negligence justifies summary dismissal, see *Laws v London Chronicle (Indicator Newspapers) Ltd* [1959] 1 WLR 698; *Henry v Mount Gay Distilleries Ltd* (21 July 1999, unreported), PC.

Intellectual property protection

E1.2.13   There are certain implied rights in relation to the works produced by an employee in the course of his employment. This is further governed by statute.[1] An express clause can detail an employee's obligations more completely and set out contractual and administrative matters.

[1] Patents Act 1977; Copyright, Designs and Patents Act 1988.

Confidentiality

E1.2.14   It is an implied term that an employee must not breach the confidentiality of his employer, but an express clause can set out examples of what the employer considers to be confidential information (this list should be non-exhaustive). If the employer seeks to impose an obligation of confidentiality after termination of employment, an express clause should cover this position fully.[1]

[1] *Faccenda Chicken Ltd v Fowler* [1986] IRLR 69, CA. See also *FSS Travel and Leisure Systems Ltd v Johnson* [1998] IRLR 382, CA; *SBJ Stephenson Ltd v Mandy* [2000] IRLR 233.

Restrictive covenants

E1.2.15   General contractual rules apply to post-termination restrictive covenants limiting competition after termination of employment.[1] These must be expressly included where appropriate. There is a presumption that such covenants are void as a restraint of trade and therefore unenforceable, except insofar as they are reasonably necessary to protect the legitimate business interests of the employer. In order to enforce such restrictive covenants, two conditions must be met:

* the covenant must be reasonable in the interests of the contracting parties, and
* it must be reasonable in the interests of the public.[2]

[1] For a summary of the law see *Rock Refrigeration Ltd v Jones* [1997] 1 All ER 1, CA.
[2] *Nordenfelt v Maxim Nordenfelt Guns & Ammunitions Co Ltd* [1894] AC 535, HL; *Herbert Morris Ltd v Saxelby* [1916] 1 AC 688, HL.

E1.2.16   The employer's interests that may be capable of protection are customer connections and trade secrets. If a post-termination restraint is found to be unreasonable, it is unenforceable and the court will not re-write its terms to make it enforceable. Covenants usually fall into the following categories:

* non-competition;
* non-solicitation of customers;

- non-dealing *with customers*;
- non-solicitation of employees.

E1.2.17   In considering the enforceability of any covenant, the court will have regard to the status of the employee and the nature of his work, the length of the restriction, how widely the class of protected customers/information is defined, and the geographical area of restraint.

E1.2.18   Where an employer breaches the contract of employment (eg by terminating the contract on short or no notice, or paying in lieu where there is no contractual right to do so) the restrictive covenants cannot be enforced by him.[1]

[1]   *General Billposting Co Ltd v Atkinson* [1909] AC 118, HL; *Rock Refrigeration Ltd v Jones* [1997] 1 All ER 1, CA.

E1.2.19   A restrictive covenant entered into for a payment as part of a severance agreement may also be enforceable if the covenant is reasonable.[1]

[1]   *Turner v Commonwealth & British Minerals Ltd* [2000] IRLR 114, CA.

Payment in lieu of notice

E1.2.20   A payment in lieu of notice clause (entitling the employer to pay for the period of notice instead of expecting the employee to work it out) enables an employer to terminate employment immediately without being in breach of contract (therefore he is not prevented from relying on any appropriate restrictive covenants – see paras **E1.2.15** ff). The disadvantage for the employee is that any such payment in lieu will be subject to deductions for PAYE and National Insurance contributions.

E1.2.21   Some payment in lieu clauses may constitute liquidated damages clauses or debts payable pursuant to the employment contract,[1] thereby payable in full and not subject to the usual duty of an employee to mitigate his loss (see para **E1.4.4**).

[1]   *Abrahams v Performing Rights Society* [1995] IRLR 486, CA; *Cerberus Software Ltd v Rowley* [2001] IRLR 160, CA.

E1.2.22   During some or all of the period of notice, an employer may require the employee to remain at home on full pay and benefits, thereby preventing him from working for anyone else and ensuring that he complies with his general duties of fidelity etc as an employee. Such clauses (known as garden leave clauses)[1] usually tie in with restrictive covenants and may effectively reduce the risk of competition but are unlikely to be enforced for long periods of time. There should always be an express clause, but even where there is, an employer must justify it on similar grounds to those for enforcing a post-termination restrictive covenant.

[1]   *Provident Financial Group plc v Hayward* [1989] IRLR 84, CA; *William Hill Organisation Ltd v Tucker* [1998] IRLR 313, CA; *SBJ Stephenson Ltd v Mandy* [2000] IRLR 233.

Choice of law

E1.2.23 Whatever law the parties select as the proper law governing the contract of employment, the provisions of statute will have effect if employment is in the UK and the necessary conditions are satisfied. The Contracts (Applicable Law) Act 1990 limits the freedom of the parties to choose the law applicable to a contract of employment, although they may agree to include a choice of law provision. A choice of law clause must not deprive the employee of the protection afforded to him by the mandatory rules of the law that would apply in the absence of choice. In the absence of an express choice the contract of employment will be governed by:

- the law of the country in which the employee habitually carried out his work in performance of the contract, even if he temporarily works in another country; or
- if the employee does not habitually carry out his work in any one country, by the law of the country in which the place of business through which he was engaged is situated.

E1.2.24 However, if from the circumstances as a whole it appears that the contract is more closely connected with another country, the law of that country may apply.

E1.2.25 So far as statutory employment rights are concerned, any clause attempting to exclude the jurisdiction of employment tribunals will be void. Attempts to exclude the applicability of contractual rights will be governed by the Civil Jurisdiction and Judgments Act 1982[1] within the EC.

[1]   Incorporating the principles in the 1968 Brussels Convention on Jurisdiction and Enforcement of Judgments in Civil and Commercial Matters.

Implied terms

E1.2.26 A term will not be implied merely because it is reasonable or fair, but only if the parties would have intended to include it in the agreement. Where the contract is silent the question of whether or not a term is to be implied is a question of law. There are various classifications of implied terms:

- *central terms*: eg nature of employee's work and duty to pay etc. The relationship of employer and employee is based on trust and confidence;
- *the 'officious bystander' test*:[1] ie if, while the parties were negotiating, an officious bystander were to suggest an additional express term, both parties would say 'oh of course';
- *business efficacy*: ie terms implied to make the contract workable;[2]
- *conduct*: how the parties have operated the contract in practice;[3]
- *custom and practice*: where a term is regularly adopted in a particular trade industry or locality (and is reasonable, notorious and certain). It is necessary to establish the custom and to show that the individual employee knew or should have known of it. A single incident will not establish an implied term.

Examples of implied terms

Employee's duties
- service ie the employee agrees to be ready and willing to work
- reasonable skill ie an employee should possess and exercise reasonable competence in his particular field
- obedience
- reasonable care in performing duties
- fidelity, loyalty and good faith[4]
- confidentiality
- reasonable notice

Employer's duties
- pay
- to provide work[5]
- health and safety[6]
- trust, good faith and reasonableness
- reasonable notice[7]

---

[1]   *Shirlaw v Southern Foundries (1926) Ltd* [1939] 2 KB 206, CA.
[2]   *Scally v Southern Health and Social Services Board* [1991] IRLR 522, HL; *Jones v Associated Tunnelling Co Ltd* [1981] IRLR 477, EAT.
[3]   *Mears v Safecar Security Ltd* [1982] IRLR 183, CA.
[4]   *Robb v Green* [1895] 2 QB 315, CA; *A-G v Blake* [1998] 1 All ER 833, CA.
[5]   It may sometimes be argued that there is no obligation to provide work – however, there may be such an implied right where, for example, an employee's earnings are based on the work he does (eg commission based).
[6]   Health and Safety at Work etc Act 1974; EC obligations; Common law duty to take reasonable care of employees safety; *Walker v Northumberland County Council* [1995] IRLR 35.
[7]   In the absence of an express provision, common law requires that reasonable notice is given (subject to the statutory minima). The factors which are taken into account in determining the length of notice are the nature of the job, the status of the individual, intervals of pay and whether there is any present custom and practice in the industry. See *Clark v Farenheit 451 (Communications) Ltd* EAT 591/99.

Incorporated terms

E1.2.27   The parties can incorporate into a contract of employment terms from other sources eg disciplinary codes, staff handbooks, works rules or collective agreements. Incorporation can be express or implied. Even when a document is incorporated, some of the terms may be unsuitable eg a collective agreement may contain details governing the relationship between the union and employer.

Examples of incorporated terms
- handbooks and works rules
- collective agreements
- share option schemes[1]
- occupational pension schemes and other benefits[2]

---

1 In most cases the contract of employment is silent on share option rights which may be dealt with separately. However, as share option rights are related to the employment, it is arguable that these form part of a collateral contract: see *Micklefield v SAC Technology Ltd* [1990] IRLR 218; *Chapman and Elkin v CPS Computer Group plc* [1987] IRLR 462.

2 An employer must be careful to ensure that the rules of an occupational pension scheme are not inadvertently incorporated into the contract. The employee may be given the right to join the company pension scheme, but any entitlement must always be made subject to the rules of that scheme which may vary from time to time and to the availability of funds under that scheme for payment. This issue also extends to other benefits provided for in the contract, especially benefits of private medical insurance, life insurance and permanent health insurance, ie any benefits payable under such a policy should be subject always to the insurer's rules applicable to any such scheme.

Statutory provisions

E1.2.28 Statute will sometimes imply a term into a contract of employment (irrespective of what the parties stated or intended) or will sometimes provide that an agreed term is void and unenforceable.

Examples of terms implied by statute	
Equal pay[1]	The contract shall be deemed to include a clause providing for equal pay for men and women for equal work.
Patents[2]	An invention created by an employee shall be taken to belong to his employer if it was made in the normal course of his duties or in the course of duties specially assigned to him.
Copyright and design[3]	Where a literary, dramatic, musical or artistic work or design is created by an employee in the course of his employment, the employer is the first owner of any copyright or any design right in the work, subject to contrary intention.
Working time[4]	48-hour maximum working week is implied by statute.

Examples of terms rendered unenforceable by statute	
Sex, race, and disability discrimination	Any term in the contract which is contrary to the provisions of the Sex Discrimination Act 1975 (SDA 1975), Race Relations Act 1976 (RRA 1976) or Disability Discrimination Act 1995 (DDA 1995) is void and unenforceable against the person discriminated against.
Working time	Any term which attempts to exclude the Working Time Regulations 1998 (as amended) in an impermissible way is void and unenforceable.
Contracting out	Any contractual term attempting to exclude or limit any provision of the Employment Rights Act 1996 (ERA 1996), SDA 1975, RRA 1976 or DDA 1995 or to preclude any person from presenting a complaint to an employment tribunal is void unless contained in a compromise agreement in the required form.[5]

1   Equal Pay Act 1970, s 1.
2   Patents Act 1977, s 39.
3   Copyright Design and Patents Act 1988, s 11.
4   *Barber v RJB Mining (UK) Ltd* [1999] IRLR 308; Working Time Regulations 1998 (as amended).
5   ERA 1996, s 203; SDA 1975, s 77; RRA 1976, s 72; DDA 1995, s 9.

1.3   Variation of Contract

E1.3.1   A contract is legally binding and cannot be altered unilaterally. Throughout the course of an employment relationship, terms will of course change eg salary. Other employment terms may need to alter, which can usually be achieved by mutual consent. If the employer wishes to introduce a change that the employee does not accept, the employer must rely on other means of variation. The contract may include a right to vary either expressly or by implication eg a contractual mobility clause may allow an employer to move an employee from one workplace to another, subject to workability (ie reasonable notice of the move must be given).[1] Individual contracts may also be varied by union agreement which is binding on individual employees. In the absence of an express right to vary a trade union agreement, the employer may terminate the existing contract by serving notice and on expiry of notice immediately re-employ the employees on fresh terms and conditions. Whilst this deals with contractual notice, it may still entitle a qualifying employee to bring a claim for unfair dismissal.

1   *United Bank Ltd v Akhtar* [1989] IRLR 507; *Prestwick Circuits Ltd v McAndrew* [1990] IRLR 191, Ct of Sess; *White v Reflecting Roadstuds Ltd* [1991] IRLR 331, EAT.

E1.3.2   Variation by agreement may be implied or express. If a change is introduced without an employee's express consent and he continues working without objection, it is arguable that he has waived his right to object.

Variation of contract

- By consent
  - Express
  - Implied

- Contractual right to vary
- Union agreement
- Unilateral variation
  - Impose and wait and see
  - Terminate and re-employ

1.4   Remedies

A   EMPLOYEE'S REMEDIES

E1.4.1   On dismissal by an employer, an employee potentially has rights under statute as well as contractual remedies.

Damages

E1.4.2 An employee may elect to keep the contract alive and sue for damages for breach of contract by the employer. Often, an employee will accept his employer's repudiatory breach[1] and will claim constructive dismissal and damages in respect of losses during the notice period. An employee dismissed in breach of contract is entitled to claim damages to put him in the position that he would have been in had the contract been terminated lawfully. Account must therefore be taken of all contractual benefits, such as the following:

- salary, including any contractual entitlement to an increase in salary during the notice period;
- contractual commission or bonus payments falling due during the notice period;
- fringe benefits provided for under the contract eg the provision of a car and private mileage expenses, health, life or dental insurances, school fees, payment of private telephone bills, and subsidised meals. These benefits must be valued at the cost to the employee of replacing them;
- loss of pension rights;
- pay in respect of accrued but untaken holiday;
- any other benefit accruing according to the terms of the contract, possibly including loss of share option rights. This will depend on the terms of the contract and particularly whether the contract excludes the employee's right to compensation in the event of dismissal.[2]

[1] *Cantor Fitzgerald International v Callaghan* [1999] 2 ALL ER 411, CA – failure by employer to pay part of remuneration amounts to a repudiatory breach, regardless of the amount.

[2] *Micklefield v SAC Technology Ltd* [1990] IRLR 218.

E1.4.3 As a general principle, damages will not be recoverable for the manner of dismissal, for example to compensate an employee for injury to feelings or distress. The House of Lords has stated that damages may be recoverable for continuing financial losses where the employer, without reasonable and proper cause, conducts the dismissal in a manner calculated and likely to destroy or seriously damage the relationship of confidence and trust between employer and employee (sometimes described as 'stigma' damages).[1] The House of Lords went on to say, however, that it would be rare for an employee to show all the necessary elements of such a claim.

[1] *Malik v Bank of Credit and Commerce International SA* [1997] IRLR 462, HL.

E1.4.4 For the purposes of assessing damages in a wrongful dismissal context, the reasonableness or otherwise of an employer's actions are irrelevant. Damages are subject to reduction in respect of the employee's duty to mitigate his loss (ie look for/find another job). Where the contract provides that in the event of a dismissal in breach of contract the employer will pay a specific sum (ie liquidated damages) to the employee, there will be no duty on the part of the employee to mitigate. Payment in lieu clauses need to be carefully drafted to avoid this risk.[1] Reductions may also be made in respect of double recovery and accelerated receipt (ie receiving the money early). There are also various tax considerations to be taken into account.

Example

Mr Jones has a twelve month fixed-term contract at a salary of £20,000 pa. After three months, his employer decides he is not the right man for the job. He is called in and dismissed immediately. Mr Jones manages to find a job within three months, paying £10,000 pa.

He is entitled to compensation of three months' full salary (when he was out of work) and six months at half-rate (ie taking into account his new salary).

---

[1] *Abrahams v Performing Rights Society* [1995] IRLR 486, CA; *Cerberus Software Ltd v Rowley* [2001] IRLR 160, CA.

E1.4.5 Note, however, that if an employee's actions constituting gross misconduct come to light after the dismissal, the employer may be able to rely on this and not pay the employee his notice pay.[1]

[1] *Boston Deep Sea Fishing and Ice Co v Ansell* (1888) 39 Ch D 339, CA; *Cyril Leonard & Co v Simo Securities Trust Ltd* [1972] 1 WLR 80.

Declaration

E1.4.6 The courts are able to grant declaratory relief with respect to the status of the contract, rights thereunder and the effect of any terms and conditions. This relief is discretionary and is only granted exceptionally.

Interim relief

E1.4.7 Generally, a court will not enforce a contract of employment once it has been breached. This means an employee is unlikely to get his or her old job back by applying for an injunction. However, in rare circumstances the courts will grant an employee an injunction to restrain the employer from taking action in breach of contract eg to prevent an employer dismissing him until all stages of a contractual disciplinary procedure are fully complied with and where mutual trust and confidence still exist.

Public law remedies

E1.4.8 The most important public law remedy for wrongful dismissal is judicial review. It concerns the decision making process of a public body and can only be used by employees of such a body.

B   EMPLOYER'S REMEDIES

Damages

E1.4.9 An employer can sue an employee in damages for breach of contract (eg where an employee leaves without working his full notice period). This happens very rarely – an employer's loss is usually harder to quantify and the judgment hard to enforce. A claim for damages may be useful where an employee has set up in business or is employed by a competitor in breach of restrictive covenants.

Withholding wages

E1.4.10 Withholding of wages is a possible remedy where an employee is refusing to work normally. However, an employer must ensure that any such action is not in breach of the ERA 1996 ie there should be a clause in the contract specifically providing the right to withhold payment.

Summary dismissal

E1.4.11 If an employee's breach is sufficiently serious, the employer may accept that breach and terminate the contract with immediate effect.

Interim relief

E1.4.12 An employer may apply for an interim injunction to restrain the disclosure of confidential information or to enforce a restrictive covenant. The same principles relating to interim injunctions apply as set out above.

2 REMUNERATION

2.1 Background

E2.1.1 Employers are subject to minimum wage controls under the National Minimum Wage Act 1998 (NMWA 1998). The National Minimum Wage Regulations 1999, SI 1999/584 (the NMW Regulations) implement the NMWA 1998. There are also further statutory provisions limiting the power of an employer to make deductions from monies due to an employee by way of salary, wages or other remuneration.

2.2 Legal Regulation of Remuneration

E2.2.1 The NMW Regulations are drafted to cover a wide variety of working arrangements and circumstances, including:

- time workers – workers employed either on a time basis, or partly on a time basis and partly on a piecework/commission basis;
- output workers – those employed wholly on a piecework or commission basis;
- salaried hours workers – those paid under contract for a set number of basic hours each year; and
- unmeasured workers – workers who do not fall into either of the previous categories, such as those who live on the employer's premises and/or who need to be available 24 hours a day such as care workers.

The term 'workers' is broader than 'employees', and will exclude only those who are genuinely self-employed.

E2.2.2 The NMW Regulations provide that the national minimum wage will exclude consideration of benefits in kind (except for accommodation) and vouchers, such as loans, pension payments, awards made by a court or tribunal, redundancy payments or awards under suggestion schemes. Incentive pay and bonus payments are included but overtime and shift premiums are not.

E2.2.3 The NMW Regulations set out a number of levels to the national minimum wage which depend largely on age. All figures are gross, not net.

E2.2.4 For workers aged under 18, there is no minimum wage.

E2.2.5 Workers aged under 26 who work under an apprenticeship contract, and who are within the first 12 months of the apprenticeship or are 18: no minimum wage.

E2.2.6 Workers aged 18 to 21: £3.20 per hour.

E2.2.7 Workers aged 22 and over who are starting a new job with the employer and are doing *accredited* training (as specifically defined by the NMW Regulations): £3.20 per hour (this is available for the first six months of employment only; thereafter the worker must be paid the standard national minimum wage).

E2.2.8 Other workers: £3.70 per hour.[1]

[1] On 1 October 2001, the minimum wage will be increased to £4.10 per hour. This rate will rise to £4.20 from 1 October 2002 'subject to economic conditions prevailing at the time'. These rates will apply across the board to part-time and full-time workers, agency staff and those who work from home.

E2.2.9 The period to be used in calculating whether a worker has been paid the national minimum wage is one calendar month. The NMW Regulations give further guidance as to how employers must determine whether the national minimum wage has been paid.

E2.2.10 The NMW Regulations also provide that an employer is obliged to keep certain detailed records in relation to remuneration and hours worked.

2.3 Deductions from Wages

E2.3.1 There is a general prohibition on any deduction from a worker's wages unless:

- the deduction is required or authorised by virtue of a statutory provision (such as the deduction of tax and National Insurance contributions) or a relevant provision of the worker's contract; or
- the worker has *previously* signified in writing his agreement to the making of the deduction.[1]

[1] ERA 1996, s 13.

E2.3.2 'Wages' means 'any sums payable to the worker in connection with his employment, including . . . any fee, bonus, commission, holiday pay or other emolument referable to his employment, whether payable under his contract or otherwise', as well as statutory sick pay, statutory maternity pay, a guarantee payment and other payments made by order of an Employment Tribunal.[1] The term 'wages' excludes, however, advances of wages by way of a loan, expenses, pensions, allowances or gratuities in connection with retirement or compensation for loss of office, redundancy payments and any payment to the worker otherwise than in his capacity as a worker. The definition of what constitutes wages has caused some difficulty, particularly in the context of whether a payment in lieu of notice constitutes wages or alternatively damages for breach of contract.

[1]   ERA 1996, s 27(1).

E2.3.3   An employer can lawfully make a deduction from wages in the following circumstances:

- any deduction to recoup an overpayment of wages or expenses;
- any deduction made in consequence of a statutory disciplinary procedure;
- sums payable to a public authority pursuant to any requirement of a statutory provision;
- where the employee has previously agreed that such sums should be paid over to a third party;
- any deduction by reason of the worker's participation in a strike or other industrial action;
- payments in satisfaction of a court or tribunal order.

E2.3.4   Particular rules relate to deductions from the salaries of retail employees to account for cash shortages and stock deficiencies. Deductions may however only be made within a period of 12 months from the date the employer discovered the shortage or deficiency or the date when he ought reasonably to have done so.

E2.3.5   A complete failure on the part of the employer to pay a sum due to any worker is also a 'deduction'. Where a worker complains that an unlawful deduction from his wages has been made, he has the right to bring a claim before the Employment Tribunal within three months of the relevant deduction. The Employment Tribunal can make a declaration to the effect that the deduction was unlawful and order repayment of any deducted amount.

2.4   Itemised Pay Statement

E2.4.1   An employee is entitled to a written itemised pay statement at or before the time at which any payment of wages or salary is made to him, which must set out certain particulars such as gross pay and any deductions.[1]

[1]   ERA 1996, s 8.

3   FURTHER RIGHTS AND OBLIGATIONS

3.1   Holiday Entitlement

E3.1.1   This subject is covered at para E4.6.1.

3.2   Sick Pay

E3.2.1   There is no general obligation requiring an employer to make provision for paying an employee whilst the employee is away from work by reason of sickness. If, however, the relevant statutory requirements are met, an employer will be obliged to pay an employee Statutory Sick Pay, or 'SSP'.

The current rate of SSP is £60.20. SSP is only payable to employees who are not employed on a fixed-term contract of three months or less and whose normal weekly wages are not below the lower earnings level for National Insurance contribution purposes. SSP is paid as a fixed amount each week (irrespective of the employee's usual earnings) and is only payable for a maximum period of 28 weeks in any three-year period. There are specific and fairly complex provisions dealing with the calculation of which periods of absence may count as 'qualifying days' for the purposes of deciding whether SSP is payable for any particular period of absence.[1]

[1]   Social Security Contributions and Benefits Act 1992.

E3.2.2   If an employer agrees to pay an employee compensation during sickness absence over and above SSP, it is important that this agreement is expressed clearly and unambiguously in the contract of employment. Any preconditions to payment, such as notification requirements or the exercise of the employer's discretion, should be made clear.

3.3   Additional Entitlements

E3.3.1   It is common for large corporate employers, or those employing senior or professional employees, to provide additional benefits such as company pension scheme, private healthcare, company car, and other miscellaneous benefits.

E3.3.2   Consideration of social security issues is outside the scope of this book.

4   WORKING TIME

4.1   Background

E4.1.1   The Working Time Regulations 1998 (the WT Regulations 1998) were introduced to put into effect the Working Time Directive 93/104/EC (the WT Directive) and the Young Workers Directive 94/33/EC. UK courts and tribunals will be required to interpret the WT Regulations 1998 'purposively' to give effect to the WT Directive. New proposals to extend the WT Directive to workers in transport, offshore oil and gas workers and junior doctors are presently before the European Parliament. The obligations under the WT Regulations 1998 are aimed at safeguarding the health and safety of workers.

Summary of obligations:

*   to take reasonable steps to ensure working time does not exceed 48 hours per week;
*   to take reasonable steps to ensure night workers' normal hours do not exceed 8 hours per day;
*   to give additional rights to night workers, including free health assessments and a right to transfer to day work;
*   to keep and maintain records;
*   to give workers 4 weeks' paid holiday each year;
*   to give workers 11 hours uninterrupted rest per day, 24 hours uninterrupted rest per week and a rest break of 20 minutes when working 6 hours or more per day.

4.2 Legislative Control

E4.2.1 The WT Regulations 1998 protect 'workers', ie employees and other individuals who personally undertake work for others (eg agency workers and temporary workers). They do not cover self-employed contractors who are genuinely pursuing a business activity on their own account.

E4.2.2 Certain sectors of workers (eg transport, doctors in training, armed forces) were excluded from the Working Time Directive when it came into force because the European Commission and member states agreed that these sectors would require their own special rules. Five measures to extend working time to meet these sectors have so far been proposed. Four have been formally adopted and the Road Transport Directive is likely to be adopted shortly.[1] Workers who exercise absolute control[2] over the hours they work and whose time is not determined by their employer and workers who have some part of their working time set in advance (eg under contract of employment) but who choose to work longer hours (see para **4.2.4**) are not subject to:

*   the limitation on working time;
*   the limitation on night-time working;
*   health assessments;
*   daily/weekly rest breaks;
*   record keeping.

[1] The Horizontal Amending Directive, Seafarer's Directive, Seafarer's Enforcement Directive and Road Transport Directive.

[2] 'On account of the specific characteristics of the activity in which he is engaged the duration of his working time is not measured or predetermined or can be determined by the worker himself . . .': see WT Regulations 1998, reg 20(1).

E4.2.3 There are other specified categories of workers eg travelling salesmen) to whom the limits on night work and entitlements to rest breaks/daily and weekly rest periods do not apply on the grounds that their daily working routine makes it impractical to apply rigid measures governing working time.

E4.2.4 The WT Regulations 1998 were amended with effect from December 1999 to introduce a new category of 'partly exempt' workers.[1] A partly exempt worker is one who, in addition to his usual 'measured' hours, voluntarily undertakes additional hours which are not required by his employer and which are determined by the worker himself. These additional hours are then ignored for the purposes of assessing whether the worker has worked more than 48 hours per week. Furthermore, the employer is only required to keep records in respect of the worker's 'measured' hours. All other workers are automatically protected under the WT Regulations 1998.

[1] The Working Time Regulations 1999 introduced a new Regulation 20 (2) into the WT Regulations 1998 to this effect.

E4.2.5 Unpaid overtime, voluntarily performed by workers in addition to their contractual hours, will not be taken into account in determining the total number of hours worked in a particular week.

Working time

This means any period when the worker is:

- working;
  and
- at the employer's disposal;
  and
- carrying out his duties;
  or
- receiving relevant training;
  or
- additional periods agreed under a 'relevant agreement'.

Calculation of working time

Reference period = rolling period of 17 weeks prior to the date on which calculation is made.

Average working hours $= \dfrac{A + B}{C}$

Where

A   is hours actually worked in the reference period;

B   is hours actually worked in a number of days immediately after the reference period equivalent to the number of 'excluded days';[1] and

C   is the number of weeks in the original reference period.

---

[1]   See the WT Regulations 1998, regs 4(6) and (7).

4.3   Opting Out

E4.3.1   Employers in the excluded sectors such as transport are completely exempt from the effect of the WT Regulations 1998 apart from the provisions applying to young workers. All other employers are affected to some extent. Employers are under a duty to establish and maintain records which show that they are complying with the obligations under the WT Regulations 1998 or to reflect the fact that certain employees have opted-out of protection under the Regulations.[1] They will need to assess workers' average weekly working time[2] and ensure that it does not exceed 48 hours or, if it does, that an opt-out agreement is obtained. Employers should be considering whether they are liable under the WT Regulations 1998 to other 'workers' eg agency staff, and should ensure that they afford such staff the same protections as other employees.

[1]   See the Working Time Regulations 1999 (SI 1999/3372), reg 3(i)(6).
[2]   This includes time working for third parties.

E4.3.2   Employers may secure the agreement of individual employees to opt out of the 48-hour week. The employer will still need to maintain records identifying those workers who have opted out and the terms of agreement. There are specific rules relating to the way in which any opt-out must be agreed and concerning the revocation of any such agreement.

E4.3.3 Employers may also secure agreements with workers or their representative on what constitutes working time and the period over which it should be measured.

4.4   Night Work

E4.4.1 Night workers are further protected by the WT Regulations 1998. Employers must take all reasonable steps to ensure that their *normal* hours of work do not exceed an average of eight hours a day over the rolling 17-week reference period.

E4.4.2 Night-time is a period of seven hours which must include the core hours between midnight and 5:00 (eg 23:00–6:00 or 24:00–7:00). A night worker for the purposes of the WT Regulations 1998 is one who works at least three hours a day during night time hours regularly/on most of his working days. Workers on rotating shifts of early and late nights are night workers for these purposes.

Calculation of average normal hours of night work

$$\frac{A + B}{C}$$

Where:

A   is total number of hours during the reference period that are normal working hours;

B   is total number of days during reference period;

C   is total number of hours during weekly rest days.

E4.4.3 Night workers must be given access to free health checks to assess whether they are fit to work at night.

4.5   Rest Period

E4.5.1 All workers are entitled to 11 hours consecutive rest each day, 24 hours uninterrupted rest in each seven-day period, a rest break of at least 20 minutes[1] away from the work station (if the worker works in excess of six hours) and 'adequate rest breaks' if health and safety may be put at risk.

[1]   Rest breaks of 20 minutes need not be paid.

4.6   Paid Annual Leave

E4.6.1 Workers who qualify[1] are entitled to at least four weeks *paid* leave each leave year. Part-timers are entitled to pro rata holiday. Workers joining or leaving part way through a leave year are entitled to a proportionate amount of leave. A worker is entitled to pay at the rate of a week's pay in respect of each week of annual leave. An employer cannot pay in lieu save on termination of employment.

1   Ie workers who are continuously employed by the employer for 13 weeks – this includes temporary staff, 'bank' staff and agency staff.

Payment in lieu of holiday
(on termination)

$(A \times B) - C$
Where:
A   is the period of leave that the worker is entitled to;
B   is the proportion of the worker's leave year that expired before termination of employment (ie if the worker leaves after six months the figure would be 0.5);
C   is the period of leave taken by the worker in the leave year.

4.7   Remedies

E4.7.1   *The Health and Safety Executive or Local Authority Environmental Health Departments are the bodies responsible for enforcing record-keeping. They have the standard powers under the Health and Safety at Work Act 1974. Criminal sanctions can be applied.*

E4.7.2   A worker can also bring a claim to a tribunal for infringement of his rights under the WT Regulations 1998. He will be protected if he is subjected to a detriment or dismissed[1] in connection with those rights (eg refusing to work longer than the prescribed limits).[2]

Penalties for employers
*   unlimited fines
*   automatically unfair dismissal – compensation
*   compensation for employees who have been subjected to a detriment/ dismissed
*   two years imprisonment for directors
*   civil claim for breach of statutory duty

---

1   Unfair dismissal rights will not apply to *all* workers.
2   See also *Barber v RJB Mining (UK) Ltd* [1999] IRLR 308 – declaration that employees could not be required to continue working in excess of 48-hour limit.

5   EQUAL OPPORTUNITIES

5.1   Background

E5.1.1   English law at present[1] prohibits discrimination based on grounds of sex, race, marital status and disability. The main statutory provisions are the Sex Discrimination Act 1975 (SDA 1975 – sex and marital status), the

171

Equal Pay Act 1970 (EPA 1970), the Race Relations Act 1976 (RRA 1976 – discrimination on racial grounds) and the Disability Discrimination Act 1995 (DDA 1995 – discrimination against disabled persons).

[1]   See, however, Directive 2000/78/EC.

EQUAL TREATMENT (FRAMEWORK) DIRECTIVE

E5.1.2   A new EC Directive (Directive 78/2000) has recently been agreed and is aimed at preventing discrimination on the grounds of religion or belief, disability, age or sexual orientation. The new Directive addresses both direct and indirect discrimination on these grounds. Measures relating to grounds save for age and disability must be implemented into national law by 2 December 2003. Measures relating to age and disability must be implemented into national law by 2 December 2006 at the latest. Discrimination based on the following grounds is not presently unlawful, but the new Directive will change the position significantly over the next few years.

Religious discrimination

E5.1.3   The legislation makes no express reference to discrimination on the grounds of religion, although a claim may be brought where the complainant's religious characteristics are also racial characteristics (eg Sikhism) and he/she suffers discrimination on those grounds.

Positive discrimination

E5.1.4   Positive discrimination in favour of certain sexual or racial groups is generally unlawful.[1] There are a number of very limited statutory exceptions to this rule, that relate solely to training of under-represented persons.

[1]   See the Commission for Racial Equality's Code of Practice for the Elimination of Racial Discrimination and the Promotion of Equality of Opportunity in Employment (1983); and the Equal Opportunities Commission's Code of Practice for the Elimination of Discrimination on the grounds of Sex and Marriage and the Promotion of Equality and Opportunity in Employment (1985).

Age discrimination

E5.1.5   There is currently no legislation outlawing age discrimination in England and Wales,[1] although what appears as discrimination on the basis of age may constitute indirect discrimination on the grounds of sex, race or disability.

[1]   See, however, Code of Practice 'Age Diversity in Employment' which sets out best practice but has no legal force.

5.2   Unlawful Discrimination

E5.2.1   Discrimination on the grounds of sex, marital status or race may be direct or indirect (in relation to disability see paras **5.3.1–5.3.19**). The complainant may also suffer victimisation on unlawful grounds. The Commission for Racial Equality and the Equal Opportunities Commission promote equal opportunities and may provide assistance to complainants.

A   DIRECT DISCRIMINATION

E5.2.2 Direct discrimination occurs where the employer treats the complainant *less favourably* than another employee (the comparator). For the purposes of sex discrimination, the comparator is a person of the opposite sex, either male or female. For the purposes of marital discrimination, the comparator is an unmarried person of the same sex.[1] For the purposes of the RRA 1976, the comparator is someone from another racial group: less favourable treatment must be based on 'racial grounds'.[2]

The SDA 1975, s 6, provides that it is unlawful for a person, in relation to employment by him *at an establishment in Great Britain*, to discriminate against a person:

(i)   in the arrangements he makes for the purposes of determining who should be offered that employment; or

(ii) in the terms on which he offers that employment; or

(iii) by refusing or deliberately omitting to offer that employment.

It is also unlawful for a person, again in the case of a person employed by him *at an establishment in Great Britain*, to discriminate against that employee:

(i)   in the way he affords him access to opportunities for promotion, transfer or training, or to any other benefits, facilities or services, or by refusing or deliberately omitting to afford him access to them; or

(ii) by dismissing him or subjecting him to any other detriment.

---

[1]   It is not unlawful to discriminate against *un*married persons.

[2]   RRA 1976, s 3(1) defines 'racial group' as 'a group of persons defined by reference to colour, race, nationality or ethnic or national origins, and references to a person's racial group refer to any racial group into which he falls'. There is no reference to religion. See *Mandla v Dowell Lee* [1983] 2 AC 548, HL. For broad interpretation of racial grounds, see *Showboat Entertainment Centre Ltd v Owens* [1984] IRLR 7, EAT.

E5.2.3 There are equivalent provisions under the RRA 1976. The employer's motive or intention is irrelevant when determining whether there has been discrimination, although it must be shown that the complainant's treatment was caused by his sex, marital status or race.

Example

An employer has to make a choice on redundancy between dismissing a man or a woman, both of whom are married with children. He decides to dismiss the woman, on the basis of an assumption that her husband is likely to be the family's main source of income. Although he may have had no conscious desire to discriminate against the woman on the basis of her sex, his assumption has directly caused her to suffer less favourable treatment on unlawful grounds.

Comparing treatment

E5.2.4 The complainant must find an appropriate person with whom to compare the employer's treatment of him.[1] The relevant circumstances of the complainant and the comparator must be the same or not materially different. In some cases, a hypothetical comparator may be adopted.

¹ *Webb v EMO Air Cargo Ltd* [1995] IRLR 645, HL; SDA 1975, s 5(3).

Genuine occupational qualifications

E5.2.5 There are a number of limited statutory exceptions to the prohibition on direct discrimination. There are, in addition, certain 'genuine occupational qualifications' (GOQs) under both the SDA 1975 and the RRA 1976, that may, for example, allow an employer to choose a person of a particular sex or racial group (eg for reasons of authenticity in a dramatic performance or at a restaurant where waiters of a particular race would be required to make the atmosphere authentic). The GOQs are listed exhaustively by statute and will apply in only limited circumstances.

E5.2.6 It is not possible for an employer to justify direct discrimination in any circumstances falling outside the statutory exceptions (contrast the defence of justification available in relation to indirect discrimination).

Proving direct discrimination

E5.2.7 Direct discrimination can be proved by inference. Therefore, although the burden currently rests on the complainant to show that he has suffered less favourable treatment on the specified grounds, a tribunal or court will look to the absence of any other, legitimate explanation for the different treatment in question and may draw an inference of unlawful discrimination.[1]

¹ *King v Great Britain-China Centre* [1991] IRLR 513.

E5.2.8 Statistical evidence may also be used by a complainant to draw attention to imbalances in the workforce which may then persuade the tribunal to draw an inference of unlawful discrimination.

Example
A female employee who applies unsuccessfully for a particular position may seek to persuade a tribunal that she was discriminated against on the ground of her sex by producing statistical evidence that, while men and women applied for positions with the employer in equal numbers, very few women were appointed. She would be assisted by use of a sex discrimination questionnaire as this would allow her to probe the employer's workforce information.

B   INDIRECT DISCRIMINATION

E5.2.9   Indirect discrimination occurs where an employer applies a requirement or condition to all employees which has a disproportionate impact on members of one sex or racial group, or married persons.

E5.2.10   The provisions of the SDA 1975 and RRA 1976 are similar.

The SDA 1975, s 1(1)(b), provides that a person discriminates against a woman where 'he applies to her a requirement or condition which he applies or would apply equally to a man but:

(i)   which is such that the proportion of women who can comply with it is considerably smaller than the proportion of men who can comply with it; and

(ii)   which he cannot show to be justifiable irrespective of the sex of the person to whom it is applied; and

(iii)   which is to her detriment because she cannot comply with it.'

There are four elements to consider in cases of indirect discrimination –

* requirement or condition;
* adverse impact;
* detriment suffered; and
* absence of justification.

Requirement or condition

E5.2.11   To establish *indirect* discrimination, a complainant must establish that a requirement or condition was imposed which he/she was obliged to comply with. It is not enough to show that a particular factor weighed particularly heavily against the complainant.

Example

In *Perera v Civil Service Commission (No 2),*[1] the complainant alleged that a factor taken into account by his prospective employer, use of the English language, had disadvantaged him because of his race. The Court of Appeal refused to accept that this was a complete bar to his appointment. There was no single 'requirement or condition' which had to be met, and Mr Perera's claim of indirect discrimination therefore failed.

---

[1]   [1983] IRLR 166, CA.

Disproportionate impact

E5.2.12   The complainant must show that although the requirement or condition is applied equally to the complainant and the comparator, proportionately fewer members of the complainant's group are able to comply with that requirement or condition than those of the comparator group who can comply.

E5.2.13   If the requirement or condition is not applied equally to members of all groups, there cannot be indirect discrimination (although there may be direct discrimination).

E5.2.14   Identification of the comparator group in indirect discrimination cases is often extremely difficult, particularly in indirect race discrimination cases.

E5.2.15   The complainant must next show that a considerably smaller proportion of the relevant group can comply with the requirement as compared to the comparator group. The question of what constitutes a 'considerably smaller' proportion is a question of fact for a tribunal to decide.

Detriment

E5.2.16   The complainant must suffer a detriment because he cannot comply with the relevant requirement or condition. The issue is whether the complainant can comply with the requirement or condition in practice, not whether he could theoretically do so.[1]

[1]   *Mandla v Dowell Lee* [1983] ICR 385, HL.

Justification

E5.2.17   Both the SDA 1975 and the RRA 1976 allow the defence of justification.

E5.2.18   In order to prove justification, the employer must show not only that the requirement is justifiable irrespective of sex or race, but also that the means chosen correspond to a *real need* and are *appropriate and necessary* to that end. This will be a question of fact for the tribunal.

E5.2.19   Justification may be based on the particular circumstances of the employer or on broader social policy reasons.[1]

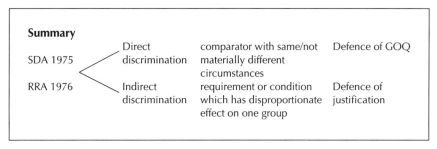

Summary

	Direct discrimination	comparator with same/not materially different circumstances	Defence of GOQ
SDA 1975			
RRA 1976	Indirect discrimination	requirement or condition which has disproportionate effect on one group	Defence of justification

[1]   *R v Secretary of State for Employment, ex p Equal Opportunities Commission* [1994] IRLR 176.

C   HARASSMENT

E5.2.20   Harassment by an employer or a fellow employee may constitute unlawful direct discrimination. The employee must have been less favourably treated on the ground of sex, marital status or race than a person of the opposite sex, marital status or different racial group.[1] The intentions of the harasser are not relevant to the determination of whether a detriment has been suffered – the complainant determines what he finds offensive. A single incident of racial or sexual harassment may constitute an act of discrimination.

[1]   *Porcelli v Strathclyde Regional Council* [1986] ICR 564, EAT.

E5.2.21   The provisions of the Criminal Justice and Public Order Act 1994 (CJPOA 1994), which make intentional harassment a criminal offence, should also be noted.[1] An offence under this provision is punishable by fine or imprisonment (the penalty may be increased where the offence was racially aggravated). A person who pursues a course of conduct which amounts to harassment or which he knows or ought to know amounts to harassment of another, commits an offence under the Protection from Harassment Act 1997 (which is again punishable by fine or imprisonment). The victim of such conduct is also entitled to seek injunctive relief and/or pursue a civil claim for damages against the perpetrator.

[1]   CJPOA 1994, s 154 inserts this offence into the Public Order Act 1986, ss 4A(1), (5).

D   VICARIOUS LIABILITY

E5.2.22   An employer may be vicariously liable for an act of discrimination carried out by an employee acting in the course of his employment. It is possible for a complainant to bring a claim for discrimination against both the employee who carried out the discriminatory act and against his employer.

E5.2.23   If the discriminatory act is found to have taken place during the course of employment, it makes no difference that the employer did not know of the act and had not approved it.

Example

J suffered physical and verbal racial abuse committed by his colleagues at his place of work. The Court of Appeal held that the employer was liable for the acts in question, and referred to the purpose of the legislation as being to deter harassment in the work place through 'a widening of the net of responsibility beyond the guilty employees themselves'.[1]

---

[1] *Jones v Tower Boot Co Ltd* [1997] IRLR 168, CA.

E5.2.24 Courts and tribunals generally take a broad and purposive approach when considering whether a discriminatory act has been committed in the course of employment.

E5.2.25 Difficult questions of liability may arise where an act is committed by an employee outside the workplace or outside working hours. The issue of whether the particular act occurred 'in the course of employment' will be a question of fact for the tribunal to determine. Discriminatory acts that occur whilst employees are preparing to start or finish work, or during breaks, or during the course of work-related social events, are likely to be treated as having been committed in the course of employment.

E5.2.26 An employer may escape vicarious liability if it can show that it took such steps as were reasonably practicable[1] to prevent the employee from doing that particular act, or from doing acts of that description in the course of his employment.

[1] *Balgobin v Tower Hamlets London Borough Council* [1987] ICR 829, EAT.

E5.2.27 The burden is on the employer to make out the defence. An equal opportunities policy alone will not be sufficient. An appropriate policy must be understood, implemented and observed by all of its employees. A complaints procedure must be available to employees.

E5.2.28 An employer may also be primarily liable for discrimination against a fellow employee, for example by failing to address a complaint of discrimination properly and seriously.

E5.2.29 It is also unlawful for an employer to instruct another person to discriminate[1] or to induce or attempt to induce a person to carry out a discriminatory act.[2] If the person asked refuses to carry out the discriminatory act and suffers a detriment as a result, he/she will be able to claim that he has been discriminated against.

> **Example**
> J, who is white, worked for a car hire agency. On her first day she is told by her employer not to hire cars to black people. She refuses to obey the instruction and is dismissed. Her employer has discriminated against her on racial grounds.

[1]   RRA 1976, s 30; SDA 1975, s 39.
[2]   RRA 1976, s 31; SDA 1975, s 40.

E   VICTIMISATION

E5.2.30   Both the SDA 1975 and the RRA 1976 protect those who complain of unlawful discrimination. An employer victimises[1] a person if he treats that person less favourably than he treats or would treat other persons, and does so because the person victimised has:

- brought discrimination proceedings against the employer;
- given evidence or information in connection with any such proceedings;
- otherwise done anything under or by reference to the discrimination legislation in relation to the employer or any other person; or
- alleged that the employer or any other person has committed an act which would amount to a contravention of the discrimination legislation.

[1]   RRA 1976, s 2; SDA 1975, s 4; see *Aziz v Trinity Street Taxis Ltd* [1988] ICR 534, CA.

E5.2.31   The victimisation must be linked to the actions or intended actions of the person victimised. The employer has a defence if the employee's allegations of discrimination are both false *and* not made in good faith.

E5.2.32   A former employer may be liable for victimisation in connection with discrimination proceedings previously brought against it by an individual.[1]

[1]   *Coote v Granada Hospitality Ltd* [1998] IRLR 656, ECJ – victimisation where employer refused to give a reference to a former employee who had brought sex discrimination proceedings against it.

F   TRANSSEXUALS/SEXUAL ORIENTATION

E5.2.33   In the case of *P v S and Cornwall County Council*,[1] P had been dismissed from his post following gender-reassignment surgery. He claimed sex discrimination. The European Court of Justice found that such discrimination was on the grounds of his sex under the Equal Treatment Directive. The rights of a person who intends to undergo, is undergoing, or has undergone gender reassignment, are now protected under the Sex Discrimination (Gender Reassignment) Regulations 1999, adding a new section to the SDA 1975 (s 2A) making less favourable treatment of such persons unlawful. The SDA 1975, ss 7A, 7B, add a number of additional 'genuine occupational qualification' defences and supplementary defences to a claim of discrimination on such grounds.

[1]   [1996] IRLR 347, ECJ.

E5.2.34 However, the courts have taken a much narrower approach in relation to discrimination against men and women on the grounds of sexual orientation. In *Smith v Gardner Merchant Ltd*,[1] Mr Smith suffered harassment from a female colleague on the grounds of his homosexuality. The Court said that to be successful, Mr Smith would have to show that he was treated less favourably as a homosexual man than a homosexual woman (ie not because of his sexual orientation which is not at present covered by the SDA 1975).

[1] [1998] IRLR 510, CA.

E5.2.35 In *Grant v South-West Trains Ltd*,[1] Ms Grant, a lesbian, worked for South-West Trains. Company policy allowed concessionary travel permits to spouses and common law partners of employees, but not to same-sex partners. The European Court of Justice ruled that Ms Grant had not been discriminated against on the grounds of her sex; a male employee with a male partner would not be entitled to a concessionary travel pass for his partner either. The fact of her sexual orientation was not protectable under EC or domestic law.

[1] [1998] IRLR 206, ECJ.

E5.2.36 In the case of *Smith and Grady v United Kingdom*[1] the applicants, both homosexual army service personnel, successfully brought claims before the European Court of Human Rights under the European Convention on Human Rights (ECHR). Ms Smith and Mr Grady had been dismissed for being homosexual, in accordance with army procedure. This was held to be a breach of arts 8 (right to a private life) and 13 (right to an effective remedy) of the ECHR.

[1] [1999] IRLR 734.

MacDonald v Ministry of Defence

E5.2.37 In the case of *MacDonald v Ministry of Defence*,[1] the Employment Appeal Tribunal in Scotland decided that the word 'sex' in the context of the SDA 1975 is ambiguous and that it should therefore be construed in a way which is consistent with the European Convention on Human Rights. The appropriate comparator in a case involving a male homosexual complainant should therefore be a heterosexual woman, not a homosexual woman, as had been suggested in the *Grant* case referred to above. It remains to be seen whether this approach will enable individuals to pursue claims of discrimination on the grounds of sexual orientation under the SDA 1975. It should also be noted in any event that under the EC Framework Directive on Equal Treatment 78/2000/EC (referred to at para 5.1.1) the UK has until 2003 to introduce legislation which specifically outlaws discrimination on the grounds of sexual orientation.

[1] [2001] ICR 1, EAT.

G   JURISDICTION

E5.2.38 Both the SDA 1975 and the RRA 1976 apply to protect both employees and workers under ' ... a contract personally to execute any work or labour' ie independent contractors (see definition of 'employment' under the SDA 1975, s 82 and the RRA 1976, s 78). Contract workers ie workers employed by an agency to work for a client, are also specifically protected (see the SDA 1975, s 9 and the RRA 1976, s 7). The legislation ensures that such workers are able to claim redress in the event of discrimination perpetrated by the client organisation.

H   TERRITORIAL JURISDICTION

E5.2.39 The legislation applies in relation to employment at an establishment in *Great Britain* (ie England, Scotland and Wales). Unless the employee performs his work wholly outside Great Britain, this requirement will be met.

I   PART-TIME WORKERS

E5.2.40   The UK has recently implemented the Part-time Work Directive by introducing the Part-time Workers (Prevention of Less Favourable Treatment) Regulations 2000 (the Regulations) which came into force on 1 July 2000.

E5.2.41   The Regulations apply to workers as well as to employees, and therefore only the genuinely self-employed will be excluded. The Regulations provide that a part-time worker must be treated no less favourably than a full-time worker, unless the treatment can be objectively justified.

E5.2.42   The Regulations also provide that women who return to work part-time after maternity leave are entitled to pro rata terms and conditions as compared to their former full-time package.

E5.2.43   Examples of less favourable treatment could include paying a part-time worker a lower hourly rate than a full-time worker, or excluding a part-time worker from benefits, such as training or company sick pay, or treating part-timers differently on redundancy.

E5.2.44   A part-time worker has the right to demand a written statement of reasons for less favourable treatment, which must be provided within 21 days of the request. Rights under the Regulations are enforceable by employment tribunals.

5.3   Disability Discrimination

A   BACKGROUND

E5.3.1   The framework of the DDA 1995 is fundamentally different to that of previous discrimination legislation. There is no distinction between direct and indirect discrimination for the purposes of disability discrimination. There are however two fundamental concepts – less favourable treatment, and the duty to make reasonable adjustments.

E5.3.2   The Disability Rights Commission (DRC) has recently been introduced to assist disabled persons.

The DRC duplicates functions of the EOC and CRE,[1] eg it has power to:

- provide assistance to applicants;
- issue non-discrimination notices;
- conduct formal investigations; and also
- reach agreement with a person who is committing/has committed an offence under the DDA 1995.

---

[1]   Equal Opportunities Commission for complainants under the SDA 1975; Commission for Racial Equality for complainants under the RRA 1976.

E5.3.3   The DDA 1995 applies to any employer having 15 or more employees. This threshold is likely to be reviewed in the future.

E5.3.4   A person has a disability for the purposes of the DDA 1995[1] if he has a physical or mental impairment that has a substantial and long term adverse effect on his ability to carry out normal day-to-day activities. This includes any person who has had a disability.

[1]   DDA 1995, s 2.

E5.3.5   There is no definition in the DDA 1995 of physical impairment, although, as with many key terms, assistance may be found in Guidance published by the Secretary of State for Education and Employment. Mental impairment may include a mental illness only if the illness is clinically well-recognised.[1] There are a number of specific exclusions: addiction to or dependency on alcohol, nicotine or any other substance (other than in consequence of the substance being medically prescribed), hayfever, pyromania, kleptomania, a tendency to physical or sexual abuse of other persons, exhibitionism, and voyeurism.

[1]   Eg depression.

E5.3.6   The Guidance suggests that in considering whether an adverse effect is substantial,[1] the following should be considered:

- the time taken to carry out an activity;
- the way in which an activity is carried out;
- the cumulative effect of an impairment;
- the effects of the person's behaviour;
- the effects of environment, such as temperature, humidity, time of day or night, tiredness or stress.

[1]   See *Goodwin v Patent Office* [1999] IRLR 4.

E5.3.7   The effect of treatment or correction must be disregarded. The DDA 1995 also recognises that certain progressive conditions – examples given include cancer, multiple sclerosis, muscular dystrophy, and HIV infection – must be treated as an impairment having a substantial adverse effect from the moment any impairment resulting from that condition first has some effect on ability to carry out normal day-to-day activities. Severe disfigurements are also deemed to have an adverse and substantial effect;

examples given in the Guidance are scars, birthmarks, a limp or postural deformation or skin diseases. Tattoos and body piercing are specifically excluded.

E5.3.8   The long-term effect of an impairment is one which has lasted at least 12 months, or is likely to last for at least 12 months or for the rest of the life of the person affected. Recurring conditions will be included as long as the effects are likely to recur beyond 12 months after the first occurrence.

E5.3.9   An impairment affects the ability to carry out normal day-to-day activities[1] if it affects one of the following:

- mobility;
- manual dexterity;
- physical co-ordination;
- continence;
- ability to lift, carry or otherwise move everyday objects;
- speech, hearing or eyesight;
- memory or ability to concentrate, learn or understand; or
- perception of the risk of physical danger.

[1]   DDA 1995, Sch 1.

E5.3.10   The issue is whether the sufferer's ability to carry out one of the activities listed above is affected. Medical advice, and the fact that carrying out the activity may cause pain or fatigue, should be taken into account. A person will not be disabled under the DDA 1995 if they can easily carry out day-to-day activities but encounter problems performing work-related activities.

B   DISCRIMINATION – LESS FAVOURABLE TREATMENT

E5.3.11   An employer discriminates against a disabled person if, for a reason which relates to the disabled person's disability, he treats him less favourably[1] than he treats or would treat others to whom that reason does not or would not apply, and he cannot show that the treatment in question is justified.[2]

[1]   See *Clark v Novacold* [1999] IRLR 318, CA, for appropriate 'comparator'.
[2]   DDA 1995, s 5.

E5.3.12   Unlike direct discrimination based on sex, marital status or race, an employer can justify direct discrimination on the grounds of disability (see below). An employer may discriminate unlawfully against a disabled applicant or employee in the same ways as under the SDA 1975 and the RRA 1976 eg as to recruitment, terms and conditions, promotion or training, and dismissal or any other detriment.

C   THE DUTY TO MAKE REASONABLE ADJUSTMENTS

E5.3.13   An employer may also discriminate against a disabled person under the DDA 1995 where arrangements made for or on behalf of an employer, or any physical feature of premises occupied by the employer, places the disabled person at a substantial disadvantage in comparison with persons who are not disabled, and the employer fails to take such steps as are reasonable to prevent that disadvantage.

E5.3.14   The failure to make an adjustment[1] will be treated as an act of direct discrimination by the employer unless he is able to show that his failure to comply with the duty is justified.

[1]   See *Kenny v Hampshire Constabulary* [1999] IRLR 76, EAT.

E5.3.15   Adjustments may include adjusting the premises or equipment used by the disabled person, or changing arrangements in place for the performance of his duties – such as altering working hours, assigning some of his duties to another person, assigning him to a different place of work, giving training or providing supervision. Reasonableness will depend on the facts of the case.[1]

Reasonableness: factors to be assessed
- effectiveness of preventing the disadvantage
- practicability of the step
- financial and other costs of the adjustment
- extent of the employer's financial or other resources
- availability of financial or other assistance

---

[1]   Guidance is provided by the Code of Practice for the Elimination of Discrimination in the Field of Employment against Disabled Persons or Persons who have had a Disability (1996).

D   JUSTIFICATION

E5.3.16   Justification is relevant both to discrimination on the basis of less favourable treatment and to the duty to make reasonable adjustments. The burden is on the employer to show that either the treatment in question, or his failure to comply with the duty to make reasonable adjustments, is justified. In order to succeed, the employer must show that the reason for his treatment of the disabled person or his failure to adjust, is both material to the circumstances of the particular case and substantial.[1]

Example
An applicant for a typing job is not the best applicant because her typing speed is slow due to arthritis in her hands. If a reasonable adjustment – perhaps an adapted keyboard – would overcome this, her typing speed would not in itself be a substantial reason for not employing her. The employer would be unlawfully discriminating if on account of her typing speed he did not employ her and provide the adjustment.

---

[1]   See the Code of Practice on Disability Discrimination.

E   VICTIMISATION

E5.3.17   The DDA 1995, as with sex, marital status and race discrimination legislation, protects those who complain of unlawful discrimination. It is unlawful for a person to treat another person less favourably than he would treat other people in the same circumstances because that person has brought or given evidence or information in connection with DDA 1995 proceedings, done anything else under the DDA, or alleged that someone has contravened the DDA 1995. As with sex and race discrimination, there is a defence where the discrimination allegation made was false *and* was not made in good faith.

F   HARASSMENT

E5.3.18   There is no separate reference in the DDA 1995 to harassment on the grounds of an individual's disability, although harassing a disabled person on such grounds would amount to a detriment.[1] As with sex and race discrimination, an employer may be liable for a discriminatory act committed by one of his employees, regardless of the fact that it was done without his knowledge or approval. The employer has a defence of having taken such steps as were reasonably practicable to prevent the employee from engaging in discriminatory behaviour in the course of his employment.[2]

1   DDA 1995, s 4(2)(d).
2   DDA 1995, s 58.

G   TERRITORIAL JURISDICTION

E5.3.19   The DDA 1995 applies to employment at an establishment in Great Britain (ie England, Scotland and Wales). Unless the employee performs his work wholly outside Great Britain, this requirement will be met.

5.4   Enforcement and Remedies

E5.4.1   Employment tribunals have jurisdiction to hear complaints of discrimination on the grounds of sex, race, marital status and disability.[1] An application must be made within three months of the act complained of, although where an act of discrimination is continuing (eg where the discriminatory act takes the form of some policy, rule or practice) or where there is a series of discriminatory acts, a tribunal may permit a claim to be made within three months of the most recent act of discrimination.

1   For guidelines in disability cases, see *Goodwin v Patent Office* [1999] IRLR 4, EAT.

E5.4.2   An employee may claim that failure to resolve a grievance or disciplinary procedure to his satisfaction constitutes a fresh act of discrimination, thus extending the period of time available to the employee for a tribunal complaint to be made.[1]

1   *Cast v Croydon College* [1998] IRLR 318, CA.

E5.4.3   An employee may issue proceedings both against the employer (either as the primary discriminator or on the basis of vicarious liability for the actions of other employees) and/or against individual employees alleged to have carried out discriminatory acts. An employee may serve a questionnaire[1] upon his employer or any other respondent to a claim of discrimination within three months of the act of discrimination, or if proceedings have already been issued before a tribunal, within 21 days of presentation of that complaint. Standard forms of questionnaires are available for use by complainants.

[1] The Sex Discrimination (Questions and Replies) Order 1975, the Race Relations (Questions and Replies) Order 1977 and the Disability Discrimination (Questions and Replies) Order 1996.

E5.4.4 Although an employer is not obliged to answer a questionnaire, his failure to do so without reasonable excuse, or the fact that he gives evasive or unhelpful answers, may lead the tribunal to draw an adverse inference from that failure.

A tribunal, on finding that there has been an act of discrimination, may:
- give a declaration of the rights of the parties;
- recommend that the employer should take certain steps eg introduce an equal opportunities policy and appropriate training;
- order payment of compensation by the employer.

E5.4.5 Compensation will be awarded to compensate the complainant for losses already suffered (ie loss of earnings to the date of the tribunal hearing), losses which are likely to be suffered (such as loss of future earnings, including loss of value of benefits associated with the complainant's employment), and for injury to feelings. The amount of an award for injury to feelings is at the tribunal's discretion.[1]

[1] *ARG Armitage, Marsden and HM Prison Service v Johnson* [1997] IRLR 162, EAT.

E5.4.6 The evidence of the complainant as to the particular injury suffered to his feelings is important. In rare cases, a tribunal may award aggravated damages. These will be available only where the employer's conduct was particularly high-handed or oppressive.[1]

[1] *ARG Armitage, Marsden and HM Prison Service v Johnson* [1997] IRLR 162, EAT.

E5.4.7 If an employer is able to show in a case of indirect race discrimination that the discrimination was unintentional, no compensation will be awarded. In relation to unintended indirect discrimination on the grounds of sex or marital status, the tribunal may still award compensation where it has given a declaration or made a recommendation and considers it just and equitable to make an award of compensation as well.[1]

[1] Sex Discrimination and Equal Pay (Miscellaneous Amendments) Regulations 1996 (SI 1996/438).

E5.4.8 There is no maximum limit on the amount of compensation that can be awarded for discrimination. Interest may be awarded on compensation awards.

5.5   Equal Pay

E5.5.1   The Equal Pay Act 1970 aims to implement Directive 75/117/EC (the Equal Pay Directive) and the Treaty of Amsterdam, art 141 (formerly art 119 of The Treaty of Rome). By way of background, on 1 May 1999 the Amsterdam Treaty came into force. This renumbers the provisions of the Maastricht Treaty and the Treaty of Rome. Article 141 provides that:

'. . . each Member State shall . . . ensure and subsequently maintain the application of the principle that men and women should receive equal pay for equal work.'[1]

[1] The meaning of 'equal work' was considered in *Angestelltenbetriebsrat der Wiener Gebietskrankenkasse v Wiener Gebietskrankenkasse* C–309/97 [1999] ECR I–2865, [1999] IRLR 804, ECJ.

E5.5.2   Pay is defined as:

'the ordinary, basic or minimum wage or salary or any other consideration whether in cash or in kind, which the worker receives, directly or indirectly, in respect of his employment from his employer.'

E5.5.3   The Equal Pay Directive provides that the principle of equal pay in art 141 means 'for the same work or for work to which equal value has been attributed, the elimination of all discrimination on grounds of sex with regard to all aspects and conditions of remuneration'.

E5.5.4   The EPA 1970 and the SDA 1975 together attempt to eliminate discrimination in employment between the sexes.[1] They are mutually exclusive: the SDA 1975 deals with non-contractual issues such as access to benefits, promotion, less favourable treatment and dismissal. The EPA 1970 deals with all contractual terms (not just pay). The Equal Opportunities Commission has published a Code of Practice on Equal Pay (26 March 1997) which provides employers with guidance on good practice and a process for resolving pay differentials.

[1] *Strathclyde Regional Council v Wallace* [1998] ICR 205, HL.

E5.5.5   The EPA 1970, like the SDA 1975, protects both men and women and permits comparison between employees of the same or associated employer. It covers a wide definition of 'employee' (including anyone who personally executes any work or labour).

E5.5.6   Any term in a contract that purports to exclude or limit any provision of the EPA 1970 is void and unenforceable.[1]

[1] SDA 1975, s 77(3).

E5.5.7   The Sex Discrimination (Gender Reassignment) Regulations 1999 (SI 1999/1102) confer a right to equal pay on employees who intend to undergo, are undergoing or have undergone a gender reassignment.

A   EQUALITY CLAUSE

E5.5.8   The EPA 1970 implies an 'equality clause' into all contracts of employment.[1] This varies the woman's contract where she can show that she is employed on like or broadly similar work; or her job has been rated as equivalent under a job evaluation scheme (JES); or is of equal value.[2] The contract is modified to the extent needed to ensure that no term is less favourable than the comparable term in the man's contract.[3]

[1]   EPA 1970, s 1(1).
[2]   See *Enderby v Frenchay Health Authority and Secretary of State for Health (No 2)* [2000] ICR 612, CA.
[3]   Or includes a term where that term is absent.

E5.5.9   The contract is not looked at as a whole but rather each term is compared with the equivalent term in the man's contract.[1]

[1]   *Hayward v Cammell Laird Shipbuilders Ltd* [1988] ICR 464, CA.

E5.5.10   The EPA 1970 applies equally to direct and indirect discrimination. Whilst intentional indirect discrimination is always unlawful, unintentional indirect discrimination may not be unlawful if it is justified.

B   COMPARATOR

E5.5.11   The employee must choose her comparator and she may choose more than one.[1] She cannot choose a hypothetical comparator (contrast under the SDA 1975). The comparator must be employed by the woman's employer or an associated employer at the same establishment or with common terms and conditions.

[1]   *Leverton v Clwyd County Council* [1989] ICR 33

E5.5.12   Once a woman has decided who her comparator will be, she next has to show that that comparator is employed on like/broadly similar work;[1] work rated as equivalent[2] or on work of equal value.[3]

[1]   EPA 1970, s 1(4); *Capper Pass Ltd v Lawton* [1977] ICR 83, EAT.
[2]   EPA 1970, s 1(2)(b); *Bromley v H & J Quick Ltd* [1988] ICR 623, CA.
[3]   Equal Pay (Amendment) Regulations 1983; *Pickstone v Freemans plc* [1988] IRLR 357, HL.

C   'MATERIAL FACTOR' DEFENCE

E5.5.13   An employer may be able to make out a defence if he can show that the difference between the term in the woman's contract and that in the man's contract is genuinely due to a material factor which is not the difference of sex.[1] If equality is based on a claim of like/broadly similar work[2] or work rated as equivalent, the factor 'must be' a material difference between the woman's circumstances and the man's. For an equal value claim, the factor 'may be' a material difference between the circumstances. An employer must establish his defence on the balance of probabilities.

[1]   EPA 1970, s 1(3).
[2]   *Rainey v Greater Glasgow Health Board* [1987] ICR 129, HL.

E5.5.14   There is no clear distinction between direct and indirect discrimination as there is under the SDA 1975. The House of Lords[1] has indicated that an employer would not be able to hide behind the defence of 'objective justification' in a case of indirect discrimination. There may, however, be circumstances where objective justification may apply.[2]

1   *Ratcliffe v North Yorkshire County Council* [1995] IRLR 439, HL; see also *Danfoss* C–109/88 [1989] IRLR 532, ECJ.

2   In *Rainey v Greater Glasgow Health Board* [1987] ICR 129, the House of Lords said an employer must show the comparator's more favourable term and the woman's less favourable term arise out of a real need and are appropriate and necessary. The difference must be proportionate. See also *Jenkins v Kingsgate (Clothing Productions) Ltd* [1981] ICR 592, ECJ *and Strathclyde Regional Council v Wallace* [1998] ICR 205, HL.

D   REMEDIES

E5.5.15   A claim under the EPA 1970 is brought before an employment tribunal. An applicant cannot bring a claim if 'she has not been employed in the employment within six months preceding the date of the reference'.[1]

1   EPA 1970, s 2(4).

E5.5.16   If the applicant is successful, the tribunal will award the difference in pay between the woman and her comparator (which includes arrears of pay for up to two years[1]). There is no limit on the amount of compensation that may be awarded.

1   However see *Levez v TH Jennings (Harlow Pools) Ltd* C–326/96 [1999] IRLR 36, ECJ and *Levez v TH Jennings (Harlow Pools) Ltd (No 2)* [1999] IRLR 764, EAT where, following a reference to the ECJ, the two year restriction was held to be incompatible with EC law in that it breached the principle of equivalence. (The point is also the subject of test cases in relation to retrospective claims of occupational pension scheme benefits).

E5.5.17   The tribunal may also make a declaration in respect of the employer's and employee's rights in relation to an equality clause.

E5.5.18   The procedure for cases brought under the EPA 1970 is very complicated. There are various hurdles and stages and, if the case proceeds, it will be referred to an independent expert. The parties may make separate representations to that expert.

6   TERMINATION OF EMPLOYMENT

6.1   Background

E6.1.1   The right of an employee not to be unfairly dismissed is statutory and should always be distinguished from the common law right of an employee not to be dismissed in breach of contract. The fact that an employer may be entitled to terminate the contract of employment by giving the employee his contractual notice is irrelevant to the statutory concept of fairness.

E6.1.2   The right of an employee not to be unfairly dismissed is stated in the ERA 1996, s 94; that right is however subject to qualifying conditions and certain exceptions.

E6.1.3   No claim may be brought by an employee where, under the contract of employment, he ordinarily works outside Great Britain.[1] Certain employees are specifically excluded from bringing a claim eg police officers and master and crew members of fishing vessels.

[1] ERA 1996, s 196; regard should be had to the terms of the contract and all factual circumstances.

E6.1.4 Employees over normal retirement age (either contractual retirement age, or one established by custom and practice, or 65) at the effective date of termination (EDT) may not bring an unfair dismissal claim.[1]

[1] See, however, the case of *Nash v Mash/Roe Group Ltd* [1998] IRLR 168 in which an employment tribunal held that the statutory upper age limit of 65 was indirectly discriminatory against men, in that the number of male employees disqualified from bringing unfair dismissal claims or claims for redundancy payment was considerably larger than the number of female employees.

E6.1.5 An employee with less than one year's continuous employment at the EDT may not bring a claim of unfair dismissal, except where the employee has been dismissed for an automatically unfair reason that does not require a qualifying period.

Examples of reasons constituting automatically unfair dismissals:

- trade union membership/activity;
- pregnancy, childbirth, maternity-related reasons, parental leave and time off to deal with domestic incidents;
- assertion of a statutory right;
- health and safety activities;
- whistleblowing;
- shop workers/betting workers who refuse to work on Sundays or to opt out of the Working Time Regulations;
- employees who refuse to work in excess of 48 hours a week or to opt out;
- employee trustees of occupational pension schemes;
- employee representatives carrying out their official duties in a collective redundancy/transfer situation and participating in an election for employee representatives;
- an employee seeking to rely on the right to be accompanied to a disciplinary or grievance hearing by a trade union official or work colleague.

6.2 Nature of Claims

E6.2.1 The employee must first prove that he has been dismissed[1]. This can occur in three ways:

- termination by the employer with or without notice;
- on expiry of a fixed-term contract without renewal; or
- where the employee terminates the contract, either with or without notice, in circumstances in which he is entitled to do so without notice by reason of his employer's conduct (ie where he claims to have been constructively dismissed).

| **Summary: qualifying conditions** |
| • employee |
| • one year's service |
| • ordinarily employed in Great Britain |
| • has been 'dismissed'[2] |
| • is not in an excluded class |

[1]   ERA 1996, s 95(1).
[2]   ERA 1996, s 95(1).

A   TERMINATION BY THE EMPLOYER

E6.2.2   Termination arises where the employer makes it clear[1] (in writing, orally or by his actions) that he wishes the employment relationship to end. In assessing the employer's intention, regard may be had to the way in which a reasonable employee would view the employer's actions.

[1]   The words terminating the contract must be clear and communicated to the employee.

E6.2.3   Where an employee is told that he is no longer required and is expressly invited to resign, a court or tribunal may find that the employee was dismissed.[1]

[1]   Ie constructively dismissed; see however *International Computers Ltd v Kennedy* [1981] IRLR 28 (where employer warns of impending redundancy and advises employee to look for other work – not a dismissal).

E6.2.4   Where the employer gives notice to terminate the contract and, within that period of notice, the employee gives notice to the employer to terminate the employment contract at an earlier date, the employee is still considered to have been dismissed for the original reason given by the employer.[1]

[1]   ERA 1996, s 95(2).

B   EXPIRY OF A FIXED-TERM CONTRACT

E6.2.5   An employee is dismissed where his fixed-term contract (ie where the maximum length of the contract is specified) expires without being renewed under the same contract.[1]

[1]   Employees can no longer contract out of their right to claim unfair dismissal on expiry of a fixed-term contract – Employment Relations Act 1999, s 18.

E6.2.6   Where the employee is employed to perform a particular task, or the contract is stated to be terminable on an uncertain event, there is no fixed-term contract, because there is no 'defined end' to the duration or term.

C   CONSTRUCTIVE DISMISSAL

E6.2.7   Constructive dismissal[1] arises where the employee terminates the employment contract (either with or without notice) in circumstances in which he is entitled to do so without notice by reason of the employer's conduct.

Example

Employer, without notice or any contractual right to do so, requires employee to relocate immediately from London to Scotland. Employee resigns in disgust in response to employer's conduct.

---

[1]   ERA 1996, s 95(1)(c).

E6.2.8   There must be a fundamental breach of the employment contract by the employer that the employee accepts by resigning. This fundamental breach may be a significant breach of an express term of the contract (such as to pay the employee a particular sum each month by way of wages)[1] or a breach of an implied term eg the duty to maintain mutual trust and confidence. Not every breach will entitle the employee to terminate without notice.[2] Unreasonable behaviour may not suffice.

Examples of implied terms
* to provide a proper and safe working environment
* to enable the employee to properly perform his duties
* to act in a manner consistent with mutual trust and confidence
* to afford employees access to a grievance procedure

---

[1]   *Cantor Fitzgerald International v Callaghan* [1999] IRLR 234.
[2]   *Western Excavating (ECC) Ltd v Sharp* [1978] ICR 2211, CA.

E6.2.9   The employee must also accept, by words or conduct, the employer's repudiation as terminating the employment contract.[1] Without acceptance, there is a risk that the employee will be deemed to have waived the right to claim constructive dismissal. Timing of acceptance can be crucial. If the employee resigns too soon, the employer may argue that the employee left before the breach was even put into effect or could be put right. If he waits too long before resigning it may be argued that he has accepted the breach. It may in certain circumstances be possible for an employee to accept the repudiation as terminating the employment contract, yet remain in employment under a new contract.

Example

In *Alcan Extrusions v Yates*,[2] the employee suffered a unilateral variation in his terms and conditions, which he accepted as a repudiatory breach. He continued to work on the basis of the new terms and conditions. It was held that the employee had not by his subsequent conduct in continuing to work for the employer under the new contract affirmed the original contract, and he was therefore able to bring a claim for constructive dismissal. The circumstances in which this scenario will arise are likely to be rare.[3]

---

[1]   *Thomas Marshall (Exports) Ltd v Guinle* [1978] ICR 905; *Gunton v Richmond-upon-Thames London Borough Council* [1980] ICR 755, CA; *Boyo v Lambeth London Borough Council* [1995] IRLR 50, CA.
[2]   [1996] IRLR 327, EAT.
[3]   See also *WE Cox Toner (International) Ltd v Crook* [1981] ICR 823, EAT.

E6.2.10   The constructive dismissal of an employee does not necessarily mean that he has been unfairly dismissed. Once a tribunal has determined that the employee was constructively dismissed, it must then consider, in the usual way, whether the employee was dismissed for a potentially fair reason and whether the employer acted reasonably in the circumstances.

Acts which do not amount to a dismissal:

- **frustration**: where the future performance of the contract has become impossible by reason of some supervening event, such as death or permanent disablement of the employee;
- **termination by mutual agreement**: where the parties agree to end the employment contract consensually;
- **Resignation by the employee**: in circumstances other than constructive dismissal.

D   THE EFFECTIVE DATE OF TERMINATION (EDT)

E6.2.11   The EDT is particularly important in assessing the employee's period of service (eg in calculating whether there is sufficient service to claim unfair dismissal) and for calculating compensation. The EDT will also determine the time limit within which certain claims must be brought.

E6.2.12   The EDT is determined as follows:

- where the employment contract is terminated by notice, it is the date on which the notice expires;
- where the employment contract is terminated without notice, it is the date on which the termination takes effect; and
- where a fixed-term contract expires without being renewed under the same contract it is the date on which the term expires.

Examples

- Where the employee does not receive the minimum statutory notice to which he is entitled, the EDT is taken to be the date on which statutory minimum notice would have expired.[1]
- Where an employee gives counter-notice expiring on an earlier date than the date on which the employer's initial notice would have expired, the EDT is the earlier date.
- Where an employee is summarily dismissed by his employer, appeals against that decision pursuant to a disciplinary procedure and the appeal is unsuccessful, the EDT will usually be the date of the original decision to dismiss.
- Where an employer, pursuant to a term in the employment contract, gives notice of termination but requires the employee to remain away from work (a 'garden leave' provision), the EDT is the date on which the relevant notice expires.
- Where the employer exercises a right under the contract to terminate the employee's contract without giving notice but by making a payment in lieu of notice, the EDT is the date on which the employee stops work.

---

[1]   ERA 1996, s 97(2).

6.3   Fairness of Dismissal

E6.3.1   The ERA 1996, s 98 establishes a two-stage test in determining whether an employee has been fairly dismissed:

- the employer must show the principal reason for dismissal was a 'potentially fair' one;
- the tribunal must then consider whether in the circumstances the employer acted reasonably or unreasonably in treating that reason as sufficient justification for cause to dismissing the employee.

E6.3.2   Potentially fair reasons for dismissal are:[1]

- capability or qualifications;
- conduct;
- redundancy;
- the employee's inability to continue working in that position without contravening a duty or restriction imposed by or under an enactment;
- some other substantial reason of a kind such as to justify the dismissal of an employee holding the employee's position.

[1]   ERA 1996, ss 98(2) and 98(1)(b).

E6.3.3   The burden of proof in establishing a fair reason is on the employer. Where there is more than one reason for dismissal, the employer must show what the principal reason was.

A   CAPABILITY AND QUALIFICATIONS

E6.3.4   'Capability' is defined as 'capability assessed by reference to skill, aptitude, health or any other physical or mental quality', and 'qualifications' is defined as 'any degree, diploma or other academic, technical or professional qualification relevant to the position' held by the employee. This definition encompasses incompetence or poor performance, or where it is discovered that the employee does not have the necessary qualifications. It is for the employer to show that he reasonably believed in the employee's lack of capability after making reasonable enquiry.

E6.3.5   Capability may also be determined by reference to the employee's health eg where the employee's illness makes it impossible for him to perform his duties.[1]

Long term absence
- medical opinions vital (prognosis etc)
- full consultation
- personal contact
- consideration of alternative employment
- consider protection under Disability Discrimination Act 1995

Short term absence

- consider nature of illness
- likely length/recurrence of illness
- need for employee to do job
- impact on other staff
- review record
- consult
- warn of failure to improve
- medical opinion advisable

---

[1]   Compare absenteeism for other reasons which may be an issue of conduct rather than capability.

E6.3.6   In the case of intermittent absences, the employer must consider carefully whether the issue is one of capability or more accurately one of conduct.

B   CONDUCT

E6.3.7   An employer may seek to rely on an employee's conduct (or misconduct) to justify a dismissal. A warning is the usual sanction for a first act of misconduct unless it is sufficiently serious to warrant instant dismissal. Examples of misconduct include dishonesty, harassment of fellow employees, absenteeism, and failure to obey lawful and reasonable orders. The employer must show the employee was dismissed by reason of the misconduct and that his belief in that reason was genuine. The employer's decision to dismiss must be based on reasonable grounds after reasonable investigation.

E6.3.8   The employer will usually seek to rely on misconduct occurring during working hours. It may be possible to rely on misconduct occurring outside working hours where the employee's behaviour affects the performance of his duties or brings the employer into disrepute.

C   REDUNDANCY

E6.3.9   Redundancy of the employee is a potentially fair reason for dismissal (see paras **E6.5.1–E6.6.9**).

D   CONTRAVENTION OF ANY ENACTMENT

E6.3.10   This situation may arise for example where an employee who is employed solely as a chauffeur is disqualified from driving and loses his licence.

E   SOME OTHER SUBSTANTIAL REASON

E6.3.11   An employer may seek to rely on 'some other substantial reason' as justifying a dismissal where his reason does not fall strictly within one of the above four categories but is based on sound commercial reasons.[1]

Example

A business reorganisation has led to a need on the part of the employer to amend the employees' terms and conditions with the result that they are less favourable to the employees. If only one employee out of a number refuses to accept the new terms, the employer may dismiss him and seek to rely on 'some other substantial reason' as the potentially fair reason. The tribunal will however then go on to consider the fairness of the dismissal.[2]

---

[1] *RS Components v Irwin* [1973] ICR 535, NIRC; *Hollister v National Farmers' Union* [1979] ICR 542, CA.

[2] Care should however be taken by the employer in relying on 'some other substantial reason'. It is not a 'catch all' justification for dismissal where the employer fails to meet the criteria specified in the other potentially fair reasons.

E6.3.12 Other examples could include customer pressure to dismiss a particular employee, or a breakdown in the relationship between two employees such that they could no longer work together.

Written reasons for dismissal

E6.3.13 An employee who has attained one year's continuity of employment as at the EDT is entitled to request and to receive a written statement of reasons for dismissal, which must be provided by the employer within 14 days of the request. Written reasons for dismissal are required without any qualifying period or request on the part of the employee where she is dismissed while pregnant or where dismissal ends her maternity leave period.

E6.3.14 Unreasonable failure to provide the statement, or an inaccurate or incomplete statement, may be used in evidence against the employer in any proceedings, and a tribunal may make an award to the employee of two weeks' pay: ERA 1996, s 93.

Fairness of dismissal

E6.3.15 Once the employer has shown that the reason for dismissal was *potentially* fair, the tribunal must consider whether the dismissal is fair or unfair. The burden of proof as to this issue is neutral as between employer and employee.

Fairness

ERA 1996, s 98(4) provides that:

'. . . the determination of the question whether the dismissal is fair or unfair (having regard to the reasons shown by the employer) –

(a) depends on whether in the circumstances (including the size and administrative resources of the employer's undertaking) the employer acted reasonably or unreasonably in treating it as a sufficient reason for dismissing the employee, and

(b) shall be determined in accordance with equity and the substantial merits of the case.'

E6.3.16 The following points should be noted:

- The tribunal is specifically directed to consider the size and administrative resources of the employer's undertaking. Where the employer has a significant number of employees and has substantial resources at its disposal, it is likely to be expected to achieve a higher standard of fairness than a very much smaller operation.

- The tribunal has a significant degree of discretion in considering the fairness of the dismissal. The tribunal will consider how a reasonable employer would react to the circumstances. The tribunal will consider what is reasonable 'in equity and the substantial merits of the case', but is not permitted to substitute its own decision for the decision made by the employer, provided the employer's decision was a reasonable one. In other words, it is open to the tribunal to decide that it might have come to a different decision to that made by the employer – the so-called 'range of reasonable responses' test.[1]
- The tribunal may consider whether the employer has acted consistently in other similar cases in deciding whether a dismissal was fair.

[1] *British Home Stores Ltd v Burchell* [1978] IRLR 379, EAT; see also *Foley v Post Office* and *HSBC Bank plc v Madden* [2000] IRLR 827, CA.

Procedural fairness

E6.3.17   Disciplinary hearings should be conducted fairly and conform with the principles of natural justice.[1]

[1] In *Khanum v Mid-Glamorgan Area Health Authority* [1979] ICR 40, EAT stated the employee should be given an opportunity to put his case, the employee should know the nature of the allegations against him and the disciplinary panel should act in good faith.

E6.3.18   A tribunal will examine carefully whether the employer followed a fair procedure in dismissal. In particular, the tribunal will have regard to the ACAS Code of Practice on Disciplinary and Grievance Procedures in Employment (revised version in force with effect from September 2000) ('the Code').[1]

A disciplinary procedure should:
- be in writing;
- specify to whom it applies;
- be non-discriminatory;
- provide for matters to be dealt with without undue delay;
- provide for the proceedings, witness statements and records to be kept confidential;
- indicate the disciplinary actions which may be taken;
- specify the levels of management which have the authority to take the various forms of disciplinary action;
- provide for individuals to be informed of the complaints against them and where possible all of the relevant evidence before any hearing;
- provide for individuals to be given an opportunity to state their case before decisions are reached;
- give individuals the right to be accompanied by a trade union representative or a fellow employee of their choice;
- ensure that, except for gross misconduct, no employee is dismissed for a first breach of discipline;
- ensure that disciplinary action is not taken until the case has been carefully investigated;
- ensure that individuals are given an explanation for any penalty imposed; and
- provide a right of appeal, normally to a more senior manager, and specify the procedure to be followed.

---

[1] *Lock v Cardiff Railway Co Ltd* [1998] IRLR 358, EAT.

E6.3.19 The Code advises that where an employee commits a minor infringement of established standards of conduct, an informal oral warning is likely to be appropriate. It suggests that the employer should follow a system of giving formal oral warnings, or where the offence is more serious, written warnings. These should set out the nature of the offence and the likely consequences of further offences. Further misconduct might warrant a final written warning which should advise the employee that any reoccurrence might lead to suspension, demotion or dismissal. The Code suggests alternatives to dismissal such as disciplinary transfer or disciplinary suspension without pay if these are contractually agreed.

E6.3.20 There should be a right of appeal against disciplinary action. Failure to provide an appeal procedure may result not only in a finding of unfairness, but may also deny the employer the opportunity of correcting any procedural defects in the initial disciplinary hearing. An appeal that corrects a defect may be sufficient to save the employer from a finding of procedural unfairness. Compensation may also be adjusted to reflect the availability (or non-availability) of an internal appeals procedure.

E6.3.21 A worker[1] has the right to be accompanied to a disciplinary or grievance hearing by a trade union official or work colleague. Failure to allow this will result in a financial penalty of two weeks' pay (subject to the statutory limit, currently £240). Such an official or colleague may address those present at the hearing but not answer questions on the worker's behalf. Both the worker and his companion are protected against detriment by the employer on the ground that they sought to exercise this right. Dismissal on such ground would constitute an automatically unfair dismissal.[2]

[1] 'Worker' includes home worker, agency staff, Crown employees and staff of the Houses of Parliament.
[2] ERA 1999, s 12.

E6.3.22 The Code is most appropriate in relation to dismissal on the grounds of conduct. Where dismissal takes place on the grounds of capability, the employer should, however, note the provisions regarding the fairness of any hearing and the rules of natural justice. The employee should therefore be informed of his failings, and given an opportunity to explain his position and to improve. The consequence of failure to improve to the specified standard within the set time-frame, such as dismissal, should always be made clear. The Code suggests a separate procedure for dealing with issues of capability/performance.

The effect of procedural unfairness

E6.3.23 The employer's conduct must be examined in assessing whether he has acted fairly.

E6.3.24 The employer can only rely on facts known to him at the time of dismissal.[1] This contrasts with the position in relation to a claim for wrongful dismissal.[2] Discovery of such facts after dismissal may, however, affect the compensation payable to an employee who wins his unfair dismissal claim.

[1] *W Devis & Sons Ltd v Atkins* [1977] ICR 662, HL.
[2] *Boston Deep Sea Fishing and Ice Co v Ansell* (1888) 39 Ch D 339.

E6.3.25   If an employer has failed to comply with a proper procedure, he cannot argue that if he had acted entirely in accordance with fair procedure, he would still have dismissed the employee. This rule is subject to a very limited exception where the offence is very grave (ie it would be utterly useless/futile to go through a full procedure) and the facts entirely undisputed.[1]

[1]   *Polkey v A E Dayton Services Ltd* [1988] ICR 142, HL; see also *Raspin v United News Shops Ltd* [1999] IRLR 9 re loss of opportunity to claim unfair dismissal following failure to observe disciplinary procedure.

6.4   Remedies

E6.4.1   Once unfair dismissal has been established, a tribunal may order compensation, re-instatement *or* re-engagement.

Remedies
- compensation – basic award + £51,700 maximum compensation
- reinstatement – same employer, same job
- re-engagement – same employer, different job

A   REINSTATEMENT/RE-ENGAGEMENT

E6.4.2   In considering these remedies, the tribunal will have regard to the employee's wishes, whether it is practicable to reinstate/re-engage and whether it would be just to make the order. These are discretionary remedies and a tribunal will take into account the disruption that might be caused by re-introducing the employee into the workforce. Failure to comply with a reinstatement or re-engagement order may result in an additional award of compensation against the employer.

B   COMPENSATION

E6.4.3   The tribunal may make an award of compensation comprising a basic award (calculated in almost the same way as a statutory redundancy payment) and a compensatory award with a statutory maximum in almost all cases, set annually (currently £51,700 with effect from 1 February 2001 The compensatory award is calculated on the basis of loss of net earnings, from the date of dismissal to the date of hearing, and future loss. There may be additional elements such as compensation for loss of statutory rights. Principles of mitigation also apply, both actual and prospective. The employee's own contributory fault may reduce the award to him by so much as is just and equitable having regard to the degree of fault.

E6.4.4   The tribunal may adjust the compensation awarded to a successful employee, by either adding or deducting up to two weeks' pay from the award, depending on the availability (or non-availability) of an internal appeals procedure. A week's pay is set at the statutory maximum of £240 for this purpose.[1]

[1]   ERA 1996, s 127A.

REDUNDANCY AND COLLECTIVE DISMISSALS

6.5 Background

E6.5.1 Redundancy is defined exhaustively[1] as follows:

'... an employee who is dismissed shall be taken to be dismissed by reason of redundancy if the dismissal is wholly or mainly attributable to:

(a) the fact that his employer has ceased, or intends to cease –
  (i) to carry on the business for the purposes of which the employee was employed by him, or
  (ii) to carry on that business in the place where the employee was so employed, or;
(b) the fact that the requirements of that business –
  (i) for employees to carry out work of a particular kind, or
  (ii) for employees to carry out work of a particular kind in the place where the employee was employed by the employer,

have ceased or diminished or are expected to cease or diminish.'

[1] ERA 1996, s 139.

E6.5.2 The dismissal must be wholly or mainly attributable to these situations. This is particularly relevant in unfair dismissal claims where an employee may allege that the real reason was not redundancy, but some other reason.

Types of redundancy

- place of work redundancy
- type of work redundancy
- closure of part/whole of business

E6.5.3 Redundancy situations will cover eg reorganisation, the closure of a business (including temporary stoppages), the closure of the employee's workplace or a diminishing need for the employee to do work of a particular kind.

E6.5.4 In *Safeway Stores plc v Burrell*[1] a three stage test was devised:
(a) was the employee dismissed?
(b) if so, had the requirements of the employer's business for the employee to carry out work of a particular kind diminished, or was this likely to be so?
(c) if so, was the dismissal caused by the diminution?

[1] [1997] IRLR 200; See also *High Table Ltd v Horst* [1997] IRLR 513, CA; *Murray v Foyle Meats Ltd* [1999] IRLR 562, HL. In *Safeway Stores* the contract test was rejected ie it is irrelevant that the contract provides for mobility of workplace if in reality the employee only actually worked at one workplace.

E6.5.5 'Bumping' may occur where a dismissed employee is replaced by another employee who is surplus to requirements elsewhere within the employer's business. The dismissed employee is traditionally regarded as dismissed for redundancy even though his job still exists. If the bumped employee does not do work of a similar kind to the employee who takes his job, the dismissal will not be by reason of redundancy.[1]

[1]   *Church v West Lancashire NHS Trust* [1998] IRLR 4, EAT which questioned the validity of bumping dismissals.

A   COMMON LAW RIGHTS

E6.5.6   A dismissed employee is entitled to receive notice of his dismissal. This will depend upon the contractual notice period subject to statutory minima.[1] If an employer fails to give any or gives inadequate notice, the employee may be entitled to a payment in lieu of the wages and other contractual benefits he would otherwise have received. Sometimes, the contract may provide only for salary to be paid. The aim is to put the employee in the position he would have been in if the contract had been properly performed. If the contract is silent as to notice, 'reasonable' notice is implied subject to statutory minima. All the factual circumstances (including pay, position and length of service) are relevant in determining what is reasonable.

[1]   ERA 1996, s 86.

B   STATUTORY RIGHTS

E6.5.7   An employee[1] who is dismissed by reason of redundancy may be entitled to receive a statutory redundancy payment subject to satisfying certain criteria.

[1]   Not self-employed persons eg independent contractors.

E6.5.8   The employee must first prove that he has been dismissed.[1] A volunteer for redundancy will still fall within the statutory definition.[2] A mere warning of redundancy will not suffice.[3] The expiry and non-renewal of a fixed-term contract will constitute a dismissal. The employee must have been continuously employed (full or part-time) for two years at the effective date of termination (when the notice period expires, the fixed term ends or the relationship effectively ends). The employment must be within Great Britain (the test is where the employee 'ordinarily works'[4]).

[1]   ERA 1996, s 136(1).
[2]   *Burton, Allton & Johnson Ltd v RRV Peck* [1975] IRLR 87; *Scott v Coalite Fuels & Chemicals Ltd* [1988] IRLR 131, EAT.
[3]   *Secretary of State for Employment v Greenfield* (22 March 1990, EAT 147/89).
[4]   ERA 1996, s 196(6).

E6.5.9   For the purpose of calculating statutory redundancy payment, an employee's time in service before the age of 18 is excluded. An employee who has reached the normal retiring age for the position (ie the reasonable expectation of the employee in that particular job) or 65 years (if there is no such age) is not entitled to any payment. The payment is tapered between 64 and 65 by one-twelfth for each complete month of employment.

E6.5.10   The amount of the statutory redundancy payment depends on age, length of service and pay. The employee is entitled to:

- one and a half weeks' pay for each complete year of service after reaching the age of 41;
- one week's pay for each complete year of service between the ages of 22 and 40 inclusive; and
- half a week's pay for each complete year of service between the ages of 18 and 21 inclusive.

E6.5.11   There is a statutory maximum on the amount of gross pay[1] for one week for these purposes (presently £240) and this amount is reviewed annually. No more than 20 years' service counts for calculating entitlement.

Example

An employee earning £350 per week aged 52 years after 30 years' service is made redundant. Eleven years of service count at one and a half weeks' pay. Nine years count at one week's pay. He is entitled to 25½ weeks' pay × £240 = £6,120.

---

[1]   This includes any amount for commission but excludes tips, a car, benefits and expenses.

E6.5.12   Statutory redundancy pay is paid tax-free. If the employer fails to pay a statutory redundancy payment, the employee can pursue a claim in a tribunal within six months of the date of termination of employment.[1]

[1]   ERA 1996, s 164.

E6.5.13   The employee will lose his right to a redundancy payment if he is guilty of gross misconduct, has committed a repudiatory breach of contract[1] or if he unreasonably refuses a suitable offer to renew employment or re-engage on new terms. The onus is on the employer to prove that the offer of new employment was objectively suitable with regard to pay, hours, workplace, status and the nature of the job. He must also prove that the refusal was unreasonable. The test is subjective ie did the employee genuinely find it unacceptable to take up the job for personal reasons.

[1]   ERA 1996, s 140(1), (3), (4); *Bonner v H Gilbert Ltd* [1989] IRLR 475, EAT.

E6.5.14   A tribunal looks at the factors relating to the nature of the job on offer as they affect the particular employee and if it considers that the job is suitable (eg job content and status are comparable to the old job, pay and fringe benefits are at the same level, hours of work are not changed to the employee's detriment) it will go on to decide if the employee's refusal is unreasonable. It will take into account the employee's personal circumstances such as health, travel difficulties, housing and domestic problems, with the effect that what is a suitable alternative for one employee may not be suitable for another.

E6.5.15   The employee has a statutory four-week trial period *in the new job*.[1] If there is a constructive dismissal situation where, for example, the employer changes the terms of employment in fundamental breach of contract, the employee also has a right to a reasonable period after the terms are changed to decide whether to leave or stay.[2] An employee may still claim unfair dismissal (see below) where he is re-engaged subject to these statutory provisions.[3]

Example 1

Mrs Jones works as a cleaner at her employer company's offices in South London. The company decides to relocate to North London. Mrs Jones lives in Kent but decides to move with the company. After two weeks, she realises that the travelling is too much for her and resigns. She will be deemed to have been dismissed by reason of redundancy when the original job ended (ERA 1996, s 138(4)) and, as her refusal to take the new job is probably reasonable, she is entitled to a redundancy payment.

Example 2

Mr Smith is a messenger at an office in Aldersgate Street. The building has subsidence and the company decides to move to the building next door. Mr Smith is unhappy with his job and takes the opportunity to refuse the same position in the building next door. There is a redundancy situation but he will probably have unreasonably refused suitable alternative employment, disentitling him from a redundancy payment.

---

[1]   ERA 1996, s 138.
[2]   *Air Canada v Lee* [1978] IRLR 392.
[3]   *Trafalgar House Services Ltd v Carder* (2 December 1996, EAT 306/96); *Jones v Governing Body of Burdett Coutts School* [1997] ICR 390, EAT.

E6.5.16   An employee cannot contract out of his right to a redundancy payment.[1] The only exception to this general rule is where the employee has a fixed-term contract of two years or more[2] and the employee agrees in writing to the contracting out before the dismissal. The dismissal must be the expiry of the fixed term and not for any other reason.

[1]   ERA 1996, s 203.
[2]   ERA 1996, s 197; *Bhatt v Chelsea and Westminster Health Care NHS Trust* [1997] IRLR 660, EAT; *British Broadcasting Corpn v Kelly-Phillips* [1998] IRLR 294, CA.

C   ENHANCED REDUNDANCY PAYMENTS

E6.5.17   An employee may have enhanced redundancy rights[1] (often contained in collective agreements with unions). An agreement with the employee to pay more than the statutory maximum will normally be enforceable. If the terms of the contractual redundancy scheme meet the approved necessary criteria, payment may be tax-free up to an overall maximum of £30,000, and includes any non-contractual pay in lieu of notice, statutory redundancy pay and any other ex gratia sums. Payment of severance pay does not break continuity of employment and does not qualify as statutory redundancy pay unless it is specifically stated to include it.[2]

[1]   See *Pellowe v Pendragon plc* EAT 804/98, as to whether a scheme constitutes a contractual entitlement or merely a policy (which will not be enforceable).

[2]   *Ross v Delrosa Caterers* [1981] ICR 393; see also *Lassman v Secretary of State for Trade and Industry* [1999] IRLR 413 where EAT held that 'redundancy payments' made by the Secretary of State to employees of an insolvent company did not break continuity.

D   UNFAIR DISMISSAL

E6.5.18   Whilst redundancy is prima facie a fair ground for dismissal, an employee with the necessary one year's qualifying service who is made redundant may bring an unfair dismissal application to an employment tribunal. The dismissal may be automatically unfair due to a statutory reason (see para **E6.5.20**) or unfair for other reasons. An employer must show that it acted reasonably in effecting the redundancy. In practice, this involves demonstrating that the employee was warned of the approaching redundancies as soon as practicable, that he was consulted about the proposed redundancies and, if available, suitable alternative employment was offered to him. The employee must also be selected fairly in accordance with objective criteria.

Selection criteria[1]

- are they chosen objectively and applied fairly?
- what is the 'pool' of employees for selection?
- are there established methods of selection?

Examples of criteria:

- last in first out;
- performance and ability;
- poor attendance;
- disciplinary record.

---

[1]   *Williams v Compair Maxam Ltd* [1982] IRLR 83, EAT.

E6.5.19   The claim for unfair dismissal must be brought by an employee with one year's continuous employment who has been dismissed below the normal retiring age (or 65 if there is none). The employee must prove eligibility and dismissal and show that the only or principal reason was redundancy. Once the fact of dismissal is established, dismissal is presumed to be by reason of redundancy (to claim a statutory redundancy payment if this right applies) unless the contrary is proved.[1]

[1]   ERA 1996, s 163(2).

E6.5.20   In certain circumstances, a dismissal will be automatically unfair (no qualifying period of service is necessary) without the need to consider the 'reasonableness' test.

Automatically unfair reasons for selection for dismissal include:
- belonging to/taking part in trade union activities;
- refusing to belong to a trade union;
- pregnancy or maternity-related reasons;
- assertion of a relevant statutory right;
- whistleblowing;
- participating in an election for employee representatives.

E6.5.21 A redundancy dismissal may be unfair if it was unreasonable eg because the procedure was flawed or the selection criteria were biased. A tribunal decides whether, having regard to the reason for the dismissal and the circumstances (including size and administrative resources), the employer acted reasonably.[1] It will consider whether the dismissal lay within the range of conduct which a reasonable employer could have adopted and whether the procedure followed was fair.

[1]   ERA 1996, s 98(4).

E6.5.22 Consultation with an employee has been defined as the communication of a genuine invitation, extended with a receptive mind, to give advice. There must be a two-way process in which the employee who may be made redundant is involved in the decision and his views are taken into account. It follows that if he is merely 'consulted about' a decision that has already been taken, the obligation to consult will not have been satisfied.

E6.5.23 In a small workplace, fewer formalities may suffice. Only where it would be 'utterly useless' or 'futile' to consult will a dismissal in these circumstances be found to be fair.

E6.5.24 The basic award for unfair dismissal is calculated in largely the same way as the statutory redundancy payment and one award wipes out the other. The compensatory award for unfair dismissal of up to £51,700 (calculated by reference to the employee's loss) may be awarded in addition to the basic award.

E6.5.25 Tribunals calculate the compensatory award by working out the employee's net loss of wages and contractual benefits during the period he is likely to be unemployed. A sum is added to the figure in respect of pension loss if the employee was a member of a company pension scheme.

Good Practice

Employers should:
- give as much warning to staff as possible;
- consider introducing a formal policy;
- establish numbers to be made redundant and consider the 'pool';
- apply proper selection procedure;
- consult on a one-to-one basis;
- assist employees in job search and allow reasonable time off to attend interviews.

6.6 Consultation

E6.6.1   Where an employer proposes to dismiss as redundant at least 20 employees at one establishment over a period of 90 days or less, the employer must consult workers' representatives in good time with a view to reaching an agreement.[1] This consultation should run concurrently with individual consultation. These representatives are either representatives of an independent trade union recognised in respect of that group of employees or elected representatives of the employees. Where a union is recognised, an employer must consult with representatives of the union.

[1]   Trade Union and Labour Relations (Consolidation) Act 1992, s 188. For consideration of 'proposal to dismiss' see *Scotch Premier Meat Ltd v Burns* [2000] IRLR 639, EAT.

E6.6.2   Sufficient elected representatives to represent the affected employees must be elected (by secret elections[1]) in good time for consultation to be undertaken. Representatives should be afforded certain rights and protections to enable them to carry out their functions properly.

[1]   If representatives are to be specifically elected, elections must be held in accordance with the requirements of TULR(C)A 1992, s 188(A).

E6.6.3   Consultation should begin 'in good time' and in any event:

(a) where the employer is proposing to make 100 or more employees redundant, at least 90 days; and

(b) otherwise, at least 30 days,

before the first of the dismissals takes effect.[1]

[1]   TULR(C)A 1992, s 188(1A).

E6.6.4   An employer must disclose certain information in writing, namely reasons for the proposals; numbers and descriptions of employees it is proposing to dismiss as redundant; the total number of employees of any such description employed at the establishment; the proposed method of selection; the proposed method of carrying out the dismissal; and the proposed method of calculating any redundancy payments other than statutory payments.[1]

[1]   *MSF v GEC Ferranti (Defence Systems) Ltd (No 2)* [1994] IRLR 113.

E6.6.5   Consultation must include ways of avoiding the redundancies, reducing the numbers involved and mitigating the effect of the redundancies. It is not necessary that the parties should reach agreement but the employer should consult in good faith with a view to reaching agreement.[1]

[1]   *R v British Coal Corpn and Secretary of State for Trade and Industry, ex p Price* [1994] IRLR 72.

E6.6.6   An employer has a special circumstances defence where it is not reasonably practicable to meet the minimum consultation periods.[1]

[1]   *AEEU v Thorn (UK) Ltd* (23 June 1997, unreported), EAT.

E6.6.7   Failure to consult may entitle representatives or an affected employee to complain to an employment tribunal within three months of the date of the last of the dismissals. If a tribunal decides in the employee's favour, it must make a declaration to that effect and may make a protective award (an employee's normal week's pay) for a protected period. The maximum length of the protected period will be 90 days.

E6.6.8   Where an employer proposes to dismiss 20+ employees for redundancy at the same establishment within a 30 day period or 100+ within a 90 day period, the employer must notify the Department of Trade and Industry and send a copy of form HR1 to the appropriate representatives. Notification must take place:

- at least 30 days before the first dismissal takes effect if between 20 and 99 employees are to be made redundant within a period of 90 days;
- at least 90 days before the first dismissal takes effect if 100+ employees are to be made redundant.

E6.6.9   The employer can be fined for breach of this requirement.

7   YOUNG WORKERS

7.1   General Obligations

E7.1.1   The regulation of work involving children and young persons is covered in England and Wales by the Children and Young Persons Act 1933 (CYPA 1933) and, more recently, the Health and Safety (Young Persons) Regulations 1997 and the Children (Protection at Work) Regulations 1998.

E7.1.2   In general terms, English law deals with the protection of children and young persons as a health and safety issue, influenced by the European Community.

A   THE CHILDREN AND YOUNG PERSONS ACT 1933

E7.1.3   The 1933 Act has recently been amended to implement partially the provisions of European Council Directive 94/33/EC on protection of young people at work.

B   EUROPEAN COUNCIL DIRECTIVE 94/33/EC

E7.1.4   Directive 94/33/EC provides that both children and adolescents should be considered specific risk groups and that measures should be taken by member states with regard to their safety and health. This directive, which is applicable to persons aged under 18, allows member states to exclude 'occasional work or short-time work' involving domestic service in a private household or work regarded as not being harmful, damaging or dangerous to young people in a family undertaking.[1] Directive 94/33/EC allows national law to determine whether children of at least 14 years of age may participate in combined work/training schemes or work experience schemes or light work.

[1]   For the purposes of Directive 94/33/EC, a young person is any person under 18 and a child is a young person of less than 15 years of age or who is still subject to compulsory full-time schooling under national law. An adolescent is any young person of at least 15 years of age but less than 18 who is now no longer subject to compulsory full-time schooling under national law.

E7.1.5   Directive 94/33/EC also introduces an obligation on employers to perform an assessment (and monitoring, if appropriate) in relation to specific risks to young people at work. The employer is further obliged to inform young people (or in the case of children, their 'legal representatives') of possible risks and of all measures adopted concerning their health and safety. Directive 94/33/EC makes further provision in relation to working time, night-work, rest periods, annual rest and breaks.

E7.1.6   Directive 94/33/EC was implemented in England and Wales by the Health and Safety (Young Persons) Regulations 1997, SI 1997/135 (the 1997 Regulations) which came into force with effect from 3 March 1997. The 1997 Regulations provide for two categories of persons who are to be protected, namely children[1] and young persons.[2] The 1997 Regulations introduce both the assessment and the information requirements under the Directive. An employer may not employ a young person unless it has first made or reviewed an assessment of that person's ability to work, taking into account: the inexperience, lack of awareness of risks and immaturity of young persons; the fitting-out and layout of the workplace or the workstation; the nature, degree and duration of exposure to physical, biological and chemical agents; the form, range and use of work equipment and the way in which it is handled; the organisation of processes and activities; the extent of the health and safety training provided or to be provided to young persons; and any special dangers from particular forms of risk such as biological or chemical agents. There is however no requirement to perform such an assessment in the case of occasional work or short-term work involving domestic service in a private household or work regarded as not being harmful, damaging or dangerous to young people in a family undertaking.

[1]   Any young person who is not over compulsory school age.
[2]   Persons who have not yet attained the age of 18.

E7.1.7   The 1997 Regulations include a general obligation on the part of an employer to provide comprehensible and relevant information on risks to health and safety and preventive and protective measures.

E7.1.8   The 1997 Regulations expressly provide that employers shall ensure that young persons employed are protected at work from risks to their health and safety arising from their lack of experience or immaturity.

C   CHILDREN (PROTECTION AT WORK) REGULATIONS 1998

E7.1.9   There was further partial implementation of Directive 94/33/EC with the Children (Protection at Work) Regulations 1998 ('the 1998 Regulations'). The 1998 Regulations amend the 1933 Act to provide that no child under the age of 14 may do any work, subject to very limited exceptions and subject to the power of any local authority to make bye-laws which may contain provisions authorising children aged 13 years or over to perform certain categories of 'light work' as defined below. No child (ie a person who is not over compulsory school age) is permitted:

*   to perform any work other than 'light work';[1]

- to work for more than eight hours, or if under 15 years of age, for more than five hours in any day on which he is not required to attend school and which is not a Sunday; or
- to work for more than 35 hours, or if under 15 years of age for more than 25 hours in any week in which he is not required to attend school; or
- to work for more than four hours in any day without a rest break of one hour; or
- to work at any time of year unless he has had or could still have at least two consecutive weeks without employment whilst not required to attend school.

[1]   Work not likely to be harmful to the safety, health or development of children or their attendance at school or their participation in work experience.

D   THE WORKING TIME REGULATIONS 1998

E7.1.10   The Working Time Regulations 1998 which came into force on 1 October 1998 contain special provisions in relation to 'young workers', who are for the purposes of those Regulations workers generally aged 16 and 17 years old. Young workers are entitled to free health assessments when they are required to work between 22:00 and 6:00; a rest period of at least 12 consecutive hours in each 24-hour period; a rest period of at least 48 hours in each seven-day period and a rest break of at least 30 minutes if they work more than 4.5 hours per day. There are limited exceptions to the rest break provisions in the event of unusual and unforeseeable circumstances beyond the employer's control, but it is clear that these are designed to deal with exceptional and temporary circumstances.

E7.1.11   The Health and Safety Executive will enforce certain working time provisions through criminal sanctions and an employer may incur civil liability by breach of the provisions. Employers should also note that a 'worker' within the definition of the Working Time Regulations 1998 includes any person receiving training otherwise than under a contract of employment.

E7.1.12   Where an employer is in breach of any restriction under the 1933 Act, as amended, he commits a criminal offence and is liable to a fine.

E7.1.13   The Department of Trade and Industry has recently announced the intention fully to implement Directive 94/33/EC in relation to young workers. It is not yet clear what specific measures will be introduced (a consultation period on implementation ended on 30 March 2001), but there are three areas in which changes will be required in order to ensure compliance with the Directive:

- the first area is that of working time. The Directive limits the working time allowed for young workers to 8 hours a day/40 hours a week, with no averaging over a reference period, and no individual opt-out permitted;
- the second area is that of night work between midnight and 4:00. This is generally prohibited under the Directive subject to very limited exceptions;
- the third area is that of night work between 22:00 and 6:00 or between 23:00 and 7:00. The Directive requires that work during either the one or the other of these periods must be prohibited.

8 MATERNITY AND PARENTAL RIGHTS

8.1 Background

E8.1.1 Pregnant women are entitled to different levels of maternity benefit and leave rights according to length of service (see below). These rights include the right not to be unfairly dismissed, to paid time off for antenatal care and to paid and unpaid maternity leave. Certain women are excluded from these rights eg women who are not employees, who ordinarily work outside Britain or who are employed in share fishing or the police service.

E8.1.2 Employees' maternity rights are now largely to be found in ERA 1996, Part VIII (as amended) by the Employment Relations Act 1999 (ERA 1999) and the Maternity and Parental Leave Regulations 1999, SI 1999/3312 (the 1999 Regulations). Other important legislation in this area includes the Social Security Contributions and Benefits Act 1992, the Maternity Allowance and Statutory Maternity Pay Regulations 1994 and the Social Security Maternity Benefits and Statutory Sick Pay (Amendment) Regulations 1994. Unless otherwise expressly stated, the references below refer to ERA 1996.[1]

[1]   The Government Green Paper 'Work and Parents: Competitiveness and Choice' was under consultation until 7 March 2001. Proposals include increasing the period of paid maternity leave to six months, allowing mothers to stay at home for a year before returning to work, giving fathers two weeks' paid paternity leave and giving both parents the right to return to work part-time. Giving fathers paid leave has received overwhelming support from parents and employers and will be implemented. Such leave will be funded by the Government and will not be a cost borne by employers.

8.2 General Rights

E8.2.1   All employed women, regardless of length of service and hours of work and size of employer, are entitled to take paid time off work for antenatal care. The right is not to be *unreasonably* refused paid time off. There may be circumstances in which an employer may reasonably refuse time off.

E8.2.2   An employee is entitled to be paid at her appropriate hourly rate for the period of absence. If her employer unreasonably refuses time off (or does not pay for it) the employee may bring a complaint to an industrial tribunal within three months.

E8.2.3   It is also automatically unfair to dismiss a woman or to select her for redundancy because she has insisted on her right to time off.

A   ORDINARY MATERNITY LEAVE

E8.2.4   All employed women, regardless of length of service, hours of work and size of employer, are entitled to 18 weeks' ordinary maternity leave (OML) and have the right to return to work subject to complying with a number of notice requirements. There is a compulsory leave period of two weeks *from childbirth*. During the OML period a woman is entitled to receive her normal contractual terms and conditions of employment, apart from remuneration (cash or cash-based payments) as if she were still at work. For example, holiday entitlement will accrue during this time and she will retain certain benefits.

OML – what benefits?
- 18 weeks statutory maternity pay (SMP)
- company car – yes
- club membership – yes
- holiday – yes
- subscriptions to publications – yes
- pension contributions – yes
- luncheon vouchers – probably
- salary – no
- commission – no
- bonus – no

E8.2.5   The period of OML counts towards continuity of service and is taken into account in calculating entitlement to pension and other benefits.

B   ADDITIONAL MATERNITY LEAVE

E8.2.6   Women who have completed one or more years' continuous service with the same employer by the beginning of the 11th week before the expected date of childbirth (EWC) retain the right to return to work up to 29 weeks after the birth. This additional period is known as additional maternity leave ('additional leave' or 'AML'). The employee retains the right to return at the end of any extended period.

E8.2.7   There is no statutory right to receive normal terms and conditions during the additional period of leave, although some employers will provide more generous contractual schemes that provide additional benefits or incentives to return. The 1999 Regulations, reg 17, provides that an employee's contract of employment continues to exist and the employee benefits from her employer's implied obligation to her of trust and confidence, and any terms and conditions relating to:
- notice of termination;
- compensation in the event of redundancy; and
- disciplinary/grievance procedures.

E8.2.8   Conversely, the employee is bound by her implied obligation to her employer of good faith and any terms and conditions of employment relating to:
- notice of termination;
- disclosure of confidential information;
- acceptance of gifts/other benefits; and
- participation in any other business.

C   COMMENCEMENT AND END OF MATERNITY LEAVE

E8.2.9   The day that the employee notifies her employer as being the date on which she wishes her maternity leave to begin will usually be the commencement of her OML. Maternity leave cannot commence before the eleventh week before the EWC and the latest it may begin is the day of childbirth itself. There are certain exceptions in the case of pregnancy-related sickness.

E8.2.10   Maternity leave will commence automatically if childbirth occurs. However, a woman may work up to the date of birth of her child if she so wishes. The commencement of maternity leave is triggered automatically on the first day of absence if the employee 'is absent from work wholly or partly because of pregnancy' after the beginning of the sixth week before the EWC. The employee should give her employer notice (in writing if requested) of the reason for her absence as soon as is reasonably practicable. Interpreting the provision strictly, a single day's illness that related to pregnancy could trigger the maternity leave period during this time.

E8.2.11   OML usually ends 18 weeks after the day on which it began or two weeks after the birth of the child, if later.[1]

E8.2.12   If an employee is dismissed after the commencement of her maternity leave period but before her leave would otherwise have ended, her maternity leave ends at the time of dismissal.

[1]   It may last until a later date if the woman is prevented by any statutory requirement from working for any period following the end of her maternity leave.

D   NOTICE REQUIREMENTS

E8.2.13   In order for a woman to exercise her right to OML and to receive SMP, she must, at least 21 days before she begins her leave (or as soon as is reasonably practicable), inform her employer in writing that she is pregnant, and state her EWC, which should be confirmed with a medical certificate if requested by the employer (see para **E8.2.13**). If she has already given birth, she should give the date of birth instead of the EWC.

E8.2.14   If the employer requests it, the employee must provide a certificate from a registered medical practitioner or registered midwife stating the EWC.

E8.2.15   If an employee intends to return to work earlier than the end of her maternity leave, she must give her employer at least 21 days' notice of the date on which she intends to return.

E8.2.16   The employee may, however, decide to resign whilst on leave, and will then need to notify the employer of this, giving proper notice.

E   ADDITIONAL REQUIREMENTS FOR ADDITIONAL LEAVE

E8.2.17   Women who have one or more years' continuous employment at the beginning of the eleventh week before the EWC may extend their maternity leave for up to 29 weeks from the beginning of the week in which their baby is born. This period of additional leave lasts from the end of the OML period and counts towards continuity of service for employment protection rights.

E8.2.18   Where an employee has not contacted her employer to notify the date of birth, the employer may request confirmation of the date of birth and intention to return. The employer's request must be made no earlier than 21 days before the end of OML.

E8.2.19   The employer's request must be in writing and be accompanied by a written statement warning the employee of the consequences of failing to respond within 21 days eg disciplinary action. The employer must confirm the last possible date by which the employee must return.

Notice requirements for additional leave:

- employer's request for confirmation of intention to return in writing with 'warning' statement;
- such request to be made no earlier than 21 days before end of OML;
- employee must advise employer in writing within 21 days of request that she intends to return to work.

8.3   Protection from Dismissal

E8.3.1   It is automatically unfair[1] to dismiss, or select for redundancy in preference to other comparable employees, any woman because of her pregnancy or a reason connected with pregnancy or childbirth, regardless of her hours of work or length of service. This protection applies from the beginning of her pregnancy to the end of the statutory maternity leave period (including any extension).

[1]   ERA 1996, s 99.

E8.3.2   Once an employee has shown that the reason or principal reason for her dismissal was one of the prohibited reasons, she will be deemed to have been automatically unfairly dismissed. It follows that if an employee fails to meet the notice requirements for OML she may bring a complaint of unfair dismissal if she is dismissed after she leaves work to have her baby.[1]

[1]   *Hilton International Hotels (UK) Ltd v Kaissi* [1994] IRLR 270, EAT; *Crouch v Kidsons Impey* [1996] IRLR 79, EAT.

E8.3.3   Any employee who has been dismissed or selected for redundancy in these circumstances may claim unfair dismissal before an employment tribunal within three months of the effective date of termination.

A   EMPLOYEE NOT PERMITTED TO RETURN

E8.3.4   If an employee is entitled to AML and has given the requisite 21 days' notice of her intention to return to work but her employer does not allow her to return to her old job or offers her a job on less favourable terms and conditions, she will be treated as if she had been dismissed with effect from her notified date of return for the reason for which she was not permitted to return. Whether or not the dismissal is fair is to be decided on the facts. An employer would have to show that she was fairly dismissed (ie not permitted to return) for a fair reason falling within the ERA 1996, s 98 (ie capability, conduct, redundancy, statutory restriction, or some other substantial reason).

E8.3.5   The employer would then have to show that he acted reasonably in treating this reason as a sufficient one for dismissing the employee.

B   REFUSING AN EMPLOYEE'S RETURN

E8.3.6   If an employee is unfit to return, her contract will continue unless the parties have agreed otherwise. An employer will be expected to act reasonably in accordance with the general test in the ERA 1996, s 98(4), and to investigate the nature of the employee's illness and prognosis as to possible return to work.

Justification for refusing employee's return

Five employees:

Where the total number of employees in the organisation (and any associated employer) did not exceed five immediately before the end of the woman's maternity leave the employer may refuse the employee's return. The employer must also show that it is not reasonably practicable for him to permit the woman to return to her original job or to offer her suitable alternative work on terms and conditions which are not substantially less favourable than those of her original job.

C   WRITTEN REASONS

E8.3.7   An employer must also furnish an employee (irrespective of length of service or hours of work) who is dismissed during her pregnancy or statutory maternity leave, with written reasons for her dismissal.

D   SALARY INCREASES

E8.3.8   An employee who returns to work after OML or additional leave is not only entitled to retain her old terms and conditions but to benefit from any increases in salary which may have been awarded during her absence.[1]

[1]   *Gillespie v Northern Ireland Health and Social Services Board and Others (No 2)* [1997] IRLR 410, NICA.

E   REDUNDANCY

Alternative employment

E8.3.9   An employer must offer any suitable available vacancy with itself, its successors or any associated employer to an employee on maternity leave if her post becomes redundant during this time. The new contract should take effect immediately on termination of the old one and must provide work which is both suitable in relation to the employee and appropriate for her to do in the circumstances. The provisions as to capacity and place of employment and other terms and conditions must not be substantially less favourable.

Example

Mrs K, a legal secretary took maternity leave. Two secretarial posts (including Mrs K's) were made redundant. Later, work increased and a new secretary was recruited. EAT held Mrs K was unfairly dismissed – she had a right to be offered alternative employment if a suitable vacancy arose.[1]

---

[1]   *Philip Hodges & Co v Kell* [1994] IRLR 568, EAT.

Selection for redundancy

E8.3.10   The above requirement does not prevent an employer from making a woman on maternity leave redundant, provided she is not selected for dismissal by reason of her pregnancy or any reason connected with maternity and provided she is offered any suitable alternative work which is available in the usual way.

Unfair dismissal

E8.3.11   If an employer fails to offer a woman on maternity leave suitable and appropriate alternative work (as stated in para **E8.3.9**), her dismissal will be automatically unfair, regardless of hours of work or length of service.

Additional leave

E8.3.12   A woman who is made redundant during her additional leave still has the right to exercise her right to return to work if she repays any redundancy payment on request.

8.4   Health and Safety

A   PREGNANT WORKERS DIRECTIVE

E8.4.1   The EU Pregnant Workers Directive 92/85/EEC ('Pregnant Workers Directive') requires employers to assess health and safety risks to pregnant workers, workers who have recently given birth and those who are breast-feeding. This has now been implemented into UK law alongside existing duties of care owed by an employer to its staff.

E8.4.2   An employer is under statutory and common law duties to protect, as far as reasonably practicable, its employees' (including pregnant women or new mothers) health, safety and welfare at work. Implied terms will be incorporated into contracts of employment to the effect that an employer must look after the health and safety of its employees and an employer cannot contract out of its duties to safeguard the health and safety of its staff. Any contractual term which purports to do so will be void.

E8.4.3   The employer should decide what measures should be taken to avoid exposing a pregnant employee to risk and should consider adjusting working hours and conditions or giving the employee leave. The Pregnant Workers Directive sets out a non-exhaustive list of places and working conditions which are regarded as being potential risks.

B   MANAGEMENT REGULATIONS

E8.4.4   The Management of Health and Safety at Work (Amendment) Regulations 1994, SI 1994/2865 implement the Pregnant Workers Directive by amending the Management of Health and Safety at Work Regulations 1992, SI 1992/2051 (the 'Management Regulations 1992') which provide that an employer must assess the health and safety risks to its employees in order to identify any protective and preventive measures it may need to take to comply with legislation.

C   ASSESSING RISKS

E8.4.5   The Management Regulations 1992 provide that employers have to address specifically the health and safety of new or expectant mothers (ie women who are pregnant, breast-feeding or who have given birth within the past six months). This involves assessing the risks to health and safety to which employees could be exposed and taking preventive or protective measures where appropriate. If risks are identified following an assessment, all new or expectant mothers should be given information about them.

D   PROTECTING EMPLOYEES

E8.4.6   Employees should try to remove the risk or prevent or minimise exposure to it. If all appropriate measures would not avoid the risk, then the employer must alter the woman's working conditions or hours of work. If it is not reasonable to carry out any of the above measures, or if doing so would not avoid the risk, an employer must offer the woman suitable alternative work. If no suitable alternative work is available, then the woman must be suspended from work for as long as is necessary to avoid the risk.

E8.4.7   During any period of suspension, an employee is entitled to receive her normal remuneration unless she has unreasonably refused to perform suitable alternative work that has been offered to her. She continues to be employed throughout this period and retains continuity of employment.

E   SUITABLE ALTERNATIVE WORK

E8.4.8   The new or expectant mother is entitled to be offered any suitable alternative work available, before being suspended if altering working conditions or hours of work would not avoid the risk.

8.5   Maternity Pay[1]

E8.5.1   There are two levels of statutory maternity benefits which new and expectant mothers can claim. SMP is payable by employers to its qualifying employees for a period of 18 weeks. Maternity Allowance is payable by the Benefits Agency where the employee does not qualify for SMP (depending on the employee's National Insurance contributions) for a period of 18 weeks at the lower rate of SMP (see below).

[1]   The provisions relating to payment of statutory maternity pay are contained in Part XII of the Social Security Contributions and Benefits Act 1992 (SSCBA 1992) and in various sets of regulations, most importantly the Statutory Maternity Pay (General) Regulations 1986 (SI 1986/1960) (SMP Regulations 1986) as amended by the Statutory Maternity Pay (General) (Amendment) Regulations 1988 and 1990 (SI 1988/532 and SI 1990/622). The Maternity Allowance and Statutory Maternity Pay Regulations 1994 (SI 1994/1230) and the Social Security Maternity Benefits and Statutory Sick Pay (Amendment) Regulations 1994 (SI 1994/1367) have been introduced to implement the Pregnant Workers Directive.

A   MATERNITY ALLOWANCE

E8.5.2   Maternity allowance is payable to women who have been employed or self-employed for at least 26 weeks in the 66 weeks ending with the week before the EWC and who have paid 26 weeks' National Insurance contributions. An employee otherwise unable to claim SMP may be entitled to claim a maximum of 18 weeks' maternity allowance from the Benefits Agency if she has become pregnant and has reached the start of the 11th week before the EWC.

E8.5.3   Maternity allowance is payable when a woman is absent from work. There are two rates – the higher £60.20 and the lower £52.25. Unlike SMP, maternity allowance is tax free and not subject to NIC deduction.

B   SMP

Entitlement requirements

E8.5.4   A new or expectant mother is entitled to 18 weeks' SMP provided she satisfies certain qualifying conditions. A woman must have completed 26 weeks' continuous service at her qualifying week (QW) ie the fifteenth week before the EWC. It is not necessary for her to actually work until that time provided her contract subsists. Her average weekly earnings in the eight weeks up to and including the QW must be equal to or above the lower earnings limit for National Insurance contributions. She must have ceased to work for her employer wholly or partly because of pregnancy or confinement and she must have complied with certain notification requirements:

Notice requirements for SMP

(a) She must give her employer 21 days' notice of her intended absence or, if not reasonably practicable, she should do this as soon as is reasonably practicable thereafter;

(b) such notification does not have to be in writing unless the employer so requests;

(c) the employee does not have to tell her employer whether she intends to return to work in order to claim SMP;

(d) an employee does not have to give notice if she leaves her employment for a reason unconnected with her pregnancy after the beginning of the fifteenth week before the EWC;

(e) where a woman has given notice but gives birth before the date stated in that notice, she will be entitled to SMP only if she gives a further notice to her employer specifying the date on which the absence from work on account of pregnancy or confinement began; and

(f) where a woman gives birth before the beginning of the fourteenth week before the EWC, she is only entitled to SMP if she gives her employer notice stating that her absence from work is wholly because of her confinement.

Amount of SMP

E8.5.5 SMP is payable for a period of 18 weeks to all employed women who satisfy the qualifying conditions. The first six weeks of SMP are paid at 90% of normal weekly earnings and this is subject to tax and NI deductions as if it were pay. 'Earnings' means gross earnings and include any remuneration or profit derived from a woman's employment. SMP will also be subject to deductions such as pension contributions under an employee's contract. The remaining 12 weeks are paid at the SMP flat rate (presently £60.20).

Backdated pay rise

E8.5.6 Employers must now look carefully at the calculations of a woman's normal weekly earnings if any backdated pay rise is awarded which affects payments made in the relevant period. The ECJ has ruled[1] that in calculating maternity pay, women are entitled to receive the benefit of any pay rise which would have fallen due to them had they been at work.

[1] *Gillespie v Northern Health and Social Services Board* [1996] IRLR 214, ECJ. Further, in *GUS Home Shopping Ltd v Green and McLaughlin* [2001] IRLR 75, EAT held that it was automatic sex discrimination where two women were denied bonus payments whilst on maternity leave.

Employee not returning to work

E8.5.7 An employee who satisfies the qualifying conditions is entitled to SMP even if she does not intend to return to work after her baby is born. SMP becomes payable only when she is absent from work.

Statutory sick pay

E8.5.8   A woman who is receiving SMP will be disqualified from receiving statutory sick pay (SSP) throughout the whole of her 18-week period of entitlement to SMP or maternity allowance, even if she resumes work during the 18 week period and falls ill before the end of that period. If this should happen, she may receive SMP or maternity allowance but not SSP until her maternity pay period has expired.

Summary of rights

• antenatal care	no qualifying service
• OML (18 weeks)	no qualifying service
• AML	one year's service by 11th week before EWC
• automatically unfair to dismiss/select for redundancy	no qualifying service
• written reasons for dismissal	no qualifying service
• maternity allowance	employed/self-employed for 26 weeks in the 66 weeks before EWC
• SMP	26 weeks' continuous employment by fifteenth week before EWC

8.6   Additional Rights to Time Off

A   PARENTAL LEAVE

E8.6.1   The Maternity and Parental Leave etc Regulations 1999 (implementing Council Directive 96/34/EC) gives employees with at least one year's continuous service the right to take three months' unpaid parental leave (where the employee has or expects to have responsibility for a child) in order to care for the child.

E8.6.2   The employee must be:

(a) the parents of the child born on or after 15 December 1999 who is under five years old; or

(b) the parents/a parent who has adopted on or after 15 December 1999 a child under 18 (in this case the right applies for five years following the placement or until the child is 18, whichever is earlier); or

(c) a parent who has acquired parental responsibility (see the Childrens' Act 1989) or Children (Scotland) Act 1995) for a child under five years born on or after 15 December 1999.

E8.6.3   Qualifying employees can take up to 13 weeks' leave per child (pro rata for part-timers). Parents of disabled children can exercise this right up until the child's 18th birthday.

E8.6.4 There are no record keeping requirements and employers and employees are encouraged to put their own schemes into place by way of workforce or collective agreements. If no such agreement is in place, a default scheme will apply.

E8.6.5 Employers and employees can enter into individual agreements at the terms of the scheme but if a default scheme is more favourable to an employee, he or she may take advantage of more favourable terms.

Default Scheme

- Leave can only be taken in blocks or multiples of one week.
- Employees must give at least 21 days' notice of taking leave.
- Maximum of four weeks leave each year.
- Employer can postpone leave for up to six months where there may be a disruption to business.

E8.6.6 Parental leave is unpaid, a controversial point.

E8.6.7 If an employer prevents or attempts to prevent an employee from taking parental leave, the employee may complain to an employment tribunal within three months of the refusal.

B   TIME OFF FOR DEPENDANTS

E8.6.8 An employee can take a 'reasonable' amount of time off during working hours to care for dependants.[1]

Dependant – definition:

- spouse;
- child;
- parent;
- someone living with the employee but who is not his employee, tenant, lodger or boarder.

[1]   ERA 1999, s 8 and Sch 4, Part II, which inserted ss 57A and 57B into ERA 1996.

E8.6.9 Time off can be taken:

- to provide assistance when a dependant falls ill, gives birth, suffers injury or assault;
- to deal with an unexpected incident involving the employee's child at school;
- following the death of a dependant;
- to care for an ill/injured dependant;
- when care arrangements for a dependant break down.

E8.6.10 The time off must be for necessary action and the employee must tell the employer of the need for time off, why and for how long as soon as possible. There is no right to payment for time off – the contract will determine whether payment is due.

E8.6.11   Failure to allow time off will entitle an employee to complain to a tribunal which may award such compensation as is just and equitable having regard to the employer's fault and employee's loss.

9   BUSINESS TRANSFERS

9.1   Background

E9.1.1   The previously weak position of employees in the context of a sale of a business was substantially changed as a result of legislation introduced to comply with the EC Acquired Rights Directive 77/187/EEC which sought to 'provide for the protection of employees in the event of a change of employer' (see also Directive 98/50/EC which amends Directive 77/187/EEC).[1]

[1]   The amendment to Directive 77/187/EEC provides a new definition of 'transfer' (to apply 'minimum organisational frameworks'), confirms that TUPE 1981 applies to public and private undertakings engaged in economic activities (whether or not for gain) and introduces the option for member states to transfer occupational pension schemes. The UK has until July 2001 to implement Directive 98/50/EEC.

E9.1.2   The Transfer of Undertakings (Protection of Employment) Regulations 1981 (TUPE 1981) were passed to implement Directive 77/187/EEC and apply when there is a transfer of a business or a part thereof.

E9.1.3   Directive 77/187/EEC was amended in 1998 and member states are obliged to incorporate those changes into national law by 17 July 2001. The Government was expected to publish new Transfer Regulations last year but these are still awaited at the date of publication.[1] The Regulations do not apply to the transfer of shares in a company.

The Directive enshrines three principles that are adopted by the TUPE 1981:

- automatic transfers of employment together with the terms and conditions and collective agreements of those employees transferred (art 3) – TUPE 1981, regs 5, 6, 7, 9;
- special protection against dismissal in connection with the business transfer (art 4) – TUPE 1981, reg 8;
- informing and consulting workers' representatives about the transfer (art 6) – TUPE 1981, regs 10, 11.

---

[1]   However, the DTI press release states that the amendments will: (a) make clear that the Directive applies to subcontracting operations; (b) clarify that it applies to transfers from the public to the private sector; (c) enable member states to apply the Directive to pension rights; (d) spell out requirements for consultation; and (e) give employee representatives the power to negotiate to save jobs when an insolvent business is transferred.

E9.1.4   Since the TUPE 1981 have been implemented to comply with Directive 77/187/EEC, employment tribunals and courts are required to give them a purposive construction/interpretation that fully complies with their parent directive. Thus, European cases will shape the decisions of UK courts.

Influence of European law
*   where UK legislation is ambiguous
*   purposive interpretation
*   where EC legislation is directly effective[1]

---

[1] Where a Directive is sufficiently clear and unconditional it may be relied on in UK courts – see *Defrenne v SABENA* 43/75 [1976] ECR 455, ECJ.

E9.1.5 The supremacy of EC law above that of member states was emphasised in the case of *Marleasing SA v La Commercial Internacional de Alimentacion SA.*[1]

[1] [1990] ECR I–4135, ECJ. See also *Francovich v Italian Republic* [1992] IRLR 84, ECJ.

9.2   Identifying a Relevant Transfer

E9.2.1   UK courts will keep pace with EC judgments to define what may constitute a relevant transfer. The crucial question is whether, having taken a realistic view of the activities in which the employees are involved, there exists a stable[1] (ie not short term or one-off) economic entity which retains its identity, despite changes.[2] An economic entity may consist of activities, assets and employees, although the transferee cannot refuse to take on employees as a means of circumventing the TUPE 1981. In certain labour intensive sectors an organised group of workers engaged together on a permanent basis may constitute an economic entity.[3]

Ayse Suzen v Zehnacher Gebandereinigung GmbH Krankenhausservice [1997] IRLR 255

'An entity cannot be reduced to the activity entrusted to it. An identity also emerges from other factors such as its workforce, its management staff, the way in which its work is organised, its operating methods or indeed . . . the operational resources available to it.'

---

[1] *Rygard v Sto Molle Akustik A/S* C–48/94 [1996] IRLR 51, ECJ.
[2] *Spijkers v Gebroeders Benedik Abbatoir CV* 24/85 [1986] ECR 1119, ECJ.
[3] *Ayse Suzen*; see also *Vidal* C–127/96 [1999] IRLR 132 and *Sánchez Hidalgo* C–173/96 [1999] IRLR 136. The extent to which UK courts are bound by the decisions in *Suzen* was considered in *RCO Support Services and Aintree Hospital Trust v UNISON* [2000] IRLR 624, EAT and *Argyll Training Ltd v (1) Sinclair and (2) Argyll and Islands Enterprise Ltd* [2000] IRLR 630. EAT stated that *Suzen* did not overrule previous ECJ case law and that all factors should be taken into consideration. See also *Cheesman v R Brewer Contracts Ltd* [2001] IRLR 144, EAT.

E9.2.2   The economic entity does not have to be exactly the same before and after the transfer – the crucial question is whether the 'economic entity'[1] has 'retained its identity' even if the business is not precisely the same.

[1]   See *Collino and Chiappero v Telecom Italia SpA* [2000] IRLR 788, ECJ and *Whitewater Leisure Management Ltd v Barnes* [2000] ICR 1049, EAT.

E9.2.3   Directive 77/187/EC applies where, following a legal transfer or merger, there is a change in the natural or legal person responsible for carrying on the business and who, by virtue of that fact, incurs the obligations of an employer vis-à-vis the employees of the undertaking, regardless of whether ownership of the undertaking is transferred.

E9.2.4   Following *Ayse Suzen*, it was thought that if tangible or intangible assets (which might include most of the relevant workforce) did not transfer, there would be no relevant transfer. In *Vidal* and *Sanchez Hidalgo,* the European Court of Justice (ECJ) clarified the position by stating the aim of Directive 77/187/EEC was to 'ensure continuity of employment relationship within an economic entity, irrespective of a change of ownership'.

E9.2.5   It is important to identify an economic entity which *retains its identity*, a matter which will largely be a question of fact and degree for a tribunal to determine (and, therefore, often very difficult to appeal). A business that changes in fundamental respects after transfer, may not be deemed to have retained its identity.[1]

[1]   See *Convy v Saltire Press Ltd* EAT 1269/99.

E9.2.6   Employees in sectors such as cleaning or surveillance where there is a substantial workforce but few other assets would not necessarily be excluded from protection under Directive 77/187/EEC where there was a change in service provider.

Example
A hospital shop sells flowers, newspapers and sweets. It is taken over by WH Smith Ltd which expands its operations, selling books, cards, gifts and toiletries. It has so changed in its essential character that it has not 'retained its identity'.

E9.2.7   There may be a series of transactions – will these amount to one relevant transfer or a succession of relevant transfers? This will be a question of fact – is the transfer effected by one or more of the transactions?[1]

Examples of possible TUPE transfers
- licences/franchises
- inter-group transfers
- mergers/acquisitions/joint ventures
- property transactions

---

[1]   *Longden v Ferrari Ltd* [1994] IRLR 157, EAT.

9.3 Affected Employees

E9.3.1 The TUPE 1981 protect 'employees' ie 'any individual who works for another person whether under a contract of service or apprenticeship or otherwise but does not include anyone who provides services under a contract for services' (TUPE 1981, reg 2(1)). The contract of employment is 'any agreement between an employee and his [or her] employer determining the terms and conditions of his [or her] employment.'

E9.3.2 The ECJ has determined that it is for domestic courts and tribunals to decide who is an employee. The extended definition in the TUPE 1981, reg 2(1), may cover workers supplied to an employer through an employment agency under a contract which is not exactly a contract of employment but is not a contract for services. Care needs to be taken in deciding whether or not individuals who are presumed not to be employees are, indeed, employees for the purposes of the TUPE 1981.

E9.3.3 The employee must be employed by the transferor in order for TUPE 1981, reg 5 (which transfers employees and their rights and entitlements) to apply. Clearly, where only part of a business is being transferred this may be a problem. The test is whether, as a question of fact and degree, that employee can be said to be 'assigned' to the part being transferred. Tribunals will be quick to see through devices such as service companies or complicated group structures that conceal the true position. Tribunals must keep in mind the purpose of the TUPE 1981and Directive 77/187/EEC and the need to prevent complicated corporate structures from getting in the way of a result which gives effect to that purpose, namely to protect employees.

E9.3.4 In *Botzen v Rotterdamsche Droogdok Maatshappij BV*[1] the ECJ ruled that the court should ask whether there is a transfer of part of the undertaking to which employees 'were assigned and which formed the organisation or framework within which their employment relationship took effect'. The fact that the employee also provides services to other parts of the business is not necessarily fatal.[2] The ECJ said that an employment relationship is 'essentially characterised by the link existing between the employee and the part of the undertaking or business to which he or she is assigned to carry out his or her duties'. In order to decide whether Directive 77/187/EEC and TUPE 1981, reg 5 applies 'it is sufficient to establish to which part of the undertaking or business the employee was assigned'.

Example

In *Botzen* the ECJ considered employees employed in certain general departments of an undertaking including personnel, portering services, general maintenance and administration, which were not themselves transferred. The ECJ held that such employees would not be transferred even if they performed duties involving the use of assets assigned to the part transferred or carried out duties for the benefit of that part.

---

[1]   [1985] ECR 519, ECJ.
[2]   *Duncan Webb Offset (Maidstone) Ltd v Cooper* [1995] IRLR 633; *Buchanan-Smith v Schleicher & Co International Ltd* [1996] ICR 613, EAT.

E9.3.5   One practical problem may be how much importance to attach to the terms of the employment contract in determining an employee's assignment and, in particular, the impact of broad job descriptions and express or implied mobility clauses.[1]

[1]   See *Securicor Guarding Ltd v Fraser Security Services Ltd* [1996] IRLR 552, EAT.

E9.3.6   The question of assignment is essentially one of fact for tribunals. A number of factors need to be considered including:

* the amount of time which an employee spends on one part of the business or on others;
* the amount of value given to each part by the employee;
* the terms of the contract of employment showing what the employee could be required to do; and
* how the cost to the employer of the employee's services is allocated between the different parts of the business.

9.4   Effects of the Transfer

E9.4.1   The main effect of TUPE 1981, reg 5 is to transfer outstanding liabilities, rights, duties and obligations (ie all existing contract terms, express and implied, and statutory rights) in respect of employees in the undertaking from the transferor to the transferee. Thus, for example, any outstanding wages or holiday pay due to the employee are transferred and will be recoverable by him from the transferee even though he was not its employee at the time the liability was incurred. In addition, his personnel record and all commitments made by the transferor are transferred. In effect the transferee 'steps into the shoes' of the transferor. Only civil liabilities[1] are subject to transfer; criminal liabilities remain with the transferor as do third party liabilities eg to the Inland Revenue. There is a further exception in respect of occupational pension schemes (TUPE 1981, reg 7), the liability for which does not automatically pass to the transferee under the TUPE 1981.[2] All collective agreements with any recognised trade union, and recognition itself, will also transfer to the transferee.

What can transfer?

Examples:

* all rights under and in connection with the contract of employment;
* health and safety claims;
* discrimination claims arising from acts before transfer;
* promises given by transferor;
* claims for (constructive or actual) unfair dismissal;
* disciplinary proceedings.

---

¹   See *Bernadone v Pall Mall Services Group Ltd* [1999] IRLR 617 – liability to pay
     personal injuries claim passed to transferee together with right of transfer of an
     indemnity from insurers. See also (1) *Martin v Lancashire County Council; (2)
     Bernadone v Pall Mall Services Group* [2000] IRLR 487.
²   Note, however, that the 1998 Directive provides that member states may provide
     for pension rights to transfer. The TUPE 1981 is to be amended and the UK is
     likely to allow a transferee to make comparable rather than identical pension
     arrangements.

E9.4.2   Once TUPE 1981, reg 5(2) has operated to transfer rights and
duties to a transferee, it is not possible for a transferring employee to bring
a claim against the transferor in respect of a liability transferred. Equally, a
transferor will no longer be able to assert any right transferred to the
transferee in respect of the transferred employees.

E9.4.3   There are problem areas, for example stock options[1] (which may
form part of a collateral contract), restrictive covenants[2] and profit share
schemes. These may need to be reconsidered in the context of the
transferee's business. In one case, it was held that liability to pay employees
under a group profit-related pay scheme passed to the transferee even
though the scheme related to the group from which the undertaking
transferred.[3]

¹   *Chapman and Elkin v CPS Computer Group plc* [1987] IRLR 462; *Thompson v
     ASDA-MFI Group plc* [1988] 2 All ER 722.
²   See *Morris Angel & Son Ltd v Hollande* [1993] IRLR 169, CA.
³   *Unicorn Consultancy Services Ltd v Westbrook* [2000] IRLR 80, EAT.

E9.4.4   Regulation 5 of TUPE 1981 does not apply where the employee is
retained by the transferor in another part of the organisation or has ceased
to be employed by the transferor prior to 'immediately before the transfer'.

E9.4.5   The words 'immediately before' should be widely read to mean
'immediately before the transfer or would have been so employed if he had
not been unfairly dismissed . . . by Regulation 8(1)'. Regulation 8(1) deals
with the circumstances where a dismissal is automatically unfair if it is in
connection with a relevant transfer and does not fall within an exception
expressly provided for (see para **E9.5.1**).

E9.4.6   Therefore, where there are dismissals connected with the transfer
that cannot be justified, the transferee will be the person primarily liable for
the employees' compensation which may include money in lieu of notice,
statutory redundancy payments and compensation for unfair dismissal
(since the dismissal will be automatically unfair).

E9.4.7   An employee has the somewhat limited right to object to a transfer
(TUPE 1981, regs 4A, 4B) – in essence, the employee's employment
terminates but he has no right to claim dismissal by the transferor.
However, in *University of Oxford v Humphries*,[1] Mr Humphries resigned
and objected to a transfer on the grounds that the new employer would
significantly alter his terms and conditions to his detriment. On transfer, Mr
Humphries brought a claim against his old employer for damages for
wrongful dismissal on the grounds that the proposed transfer was a
constructive dismissal. His claim was upheld by the Court of Appeal.

> The main effects of the TUPE 1981 include:
> - the transfer of the employment of all employees (TUPE 1981, reg 2(1), provides a definition of 'employee' for this purpose of the Regulations) in the economic entity from the transferor to the transferee (TUPE 1981, reg 5(1));
> - the transfer of all of the rights, duties, liabilities and obligations of those employees under their employment contracts from the transferor to the transferee (with the current exception of pensions);
> - anything done by the transferor in connection with the transfer is treated as having been done by the transferee.

---

[1]   [2000] 1 All ER 996. See also *Euro-Die (UK) Ltd v (1) Skidmore (2) Genesis Diesinking Ltd* EAT 1158/98.

Liability for redundancy pay

E9.4.8   The TUPE 1981 do not affect the entitlement of dismissed employees to redundancy pay provided that those employees qualify for redundancy pay in the normal way. Those employees who are transferred automatically by the TUPE 1981 have no right to claim redundancy pay against their old employer, the transferor.

E9.4.9   If the employees are dismissed before the transfer for a reason not connected with the transfer, they may claim redundancy pay in the normal way against the transferor. However, where the dismissal takes effect on or immediately before and is connected with the transfer, the obligation for redundancy pay passes to the transferee.

9.5   Dismissal of Employees

> **TUPE 1981, reg 8(1)**
> 'Where either before or after a relevant transfer, any employee of the transferor or transferee is dismissed, that employee shall be treated ... as unfairly dismissed if the transfer or a reason connected with it is the reason or principal reason for the dismissal.'

E9.5.1   The TUPE 1981, reg 8, provides that if the reason or principal reason for an employee's dismissal is connected with[1] the transfer, his dismissal is automatically unfair. This applies to dismissals that take place both before and after the transfer unless the employer can establish:[2]
- the reason was an economic, technical or organisational (ETO) one (TUPE 1981, reg 8(2));[3] and
- it entailed changes in the workforce of either the transferor or the transferee.[4]

Examples
- an 'economic' reason might be where demand for the company's product has fallen to such an extent that the company's profitability will no longer allow staff to be employed and the staff have to be dismissed.
- a 'technical' reason might be where a company has been employing staff on manually-operated machines and the new owners wish to use only computerised machinery, with the result that the employees of the transferor company might not have the technical skills necessary to be employed by the transferee.
- an 'organisational' reason might be where a company at one location is taken over by a purchaser at a distant location. In such a case, it might be appropriate to dismiss the staff on the grounds that it is not practical to relocate them.

---

[1] There is no recognised 'cut off' point when sufficient time has elapsed after which a dismissal is not regarded as being in connection with the transfer – it is a question of fact and degree. See *Taylor v Connex South Eastern Ltd* EAT 1243/99.

[2] TUPE 1981, reg 8(2).

[3] See *Collins v John Ansell & Partners Ltd* EAT 124/99 which clarifies that an employer is entitled to put in an ETO defence even if the dismissal is in connection with the transfer.

[4] *Delabole Slate Ltd v Berriman* [1985] IRLR 305, CA; *Crawford v Swinton Insurance Brokers Ltd* [1990] IRLR 42, EAT.

E9.5.2 Any argument that an employee has been dismissed for an ETO reason will not usually be sustainable where the employee (having been re-engaged by the transferee) continues to work for the transferee.

E9.5.3 Even if a dismissal does satisfy the above criteria, the employer must still act reasonably in all the circumstances in dismissing the relevant employees.

'Acting reasonably' will involve showing that:
- as much advance warning as is reasonably practicable has been given of an impending redundancy;
- the dismissed employee has been consulted;
- the possibility of alternative employment has been investigated and offered to him; and
- objective and fair selection criteria have been adopted and fairly applied.

E9.5.4 Where dismissals are effected prior to or on completion, such dismissals will not satisfy the requirements of the TUPE 1981, reg 8, unless there are exceptional circumstances. Where a transferor is required to dismiss employees prior to the transfer, so that the transferee can offer re-employment to all or some of them on changed terms and conditions of employment, this will not be regarded as necessary for the running of the business. It will be regarded as automatically unfair, with liability for the unfair dismissal passing to the transferee.

E9.5.5   The second requirement of the TUPE 1981, reg 8(2), ie entailing a change in the workforce, also needs to be satisfied. This means changes in the overall numbers or functions of the workforce. The unilateral imposition of new terms and conditions does not amount to 'changes in the workforce' while the overall numbers and functions of the employees remain unchanged.[1] Dismissals or resignations resulting from an employee's refusal to accept changes in terms and conditions offered by the transferor will be automatically unfair.

[1]   *Servicepoint Ltd v Clynes* EAT 154/88.

9.6   Variation of Contract

E9.6.1   The ECJ has stated that Directive 77/187/EEC provides protection for employees that must be considered to be 'mandatory'. It is not therefore possible to derogate from the rules in a way that is unfavourable to employees. Employees are not entitled to waive the rights conferred upon them even with their consent. This applies even if detrimental changes are balanced against changes to their advantage so that the employee is not left in a worse position overall. The parties cannot vary the terms of the contract by agreement and/or affirmation.

E9.6.2   If an employer dismisses an employee], after the transfer, for failure to agree to changes of employment terms and conditions, this may only be fair if the employer can show an ETO reason entailing changes in the workforce (see para **E9.5.1**). If this cannot be shown, the dismissal is effective but will be unfair.

E9.6.3   If the employee negotiates with the new employer and agrees to changes to his or her terms and conditions, this will only be valid if the changes are unconnected with the transfer or the employer can show an ETO reason entailing a change in the workforce.

E9.6.4   If such a change to terms and conditions is in connection with the transfer (and no ETO reason can be shown) the variation is ineffective and cannot be relied upon by the employer.[1]

Example
Company A has recently purchased Company B. Company A wishes to harmonise terms and conditions so that both workforces have the same terms. It imposes new contracts on all staff; some terms are more beneficial to staff of old Company B but company cars are taken away. An employee of Company B complains. The variation is in connection with the transfer, is not for an ETO reason and he is entitled to bring a claim to a tribunal saying the variation is ineffective and he is entitled to his previous terms and his car back.

[1] *Wilson v St Helens Borough Council; British Fuels Ltd v Meade and Baxendale*
[1998] IRLR 706, HL; *Credit Suisse First Boston (Europe) Ltd v Lister* [1998]
IRLR 700, CA. In *Ministry of Defence v Clutterbuck* EAT 322/97 held that new
contracts awarded to transferring employees were effective where employees had
been dismissed and re-engaged.

9.7   Duty to Inform and Consult

E9.7.1   The Collective Redundancies and Transfer of Undertakings
(Protection of Employment) (Amendment) Regulations 1999, SI 1999/1925
(the 1999 Regulations) came into effect on 1 November 1999. The 1999
Regulations set out the obligation to inform and consult representatives
where there is a relevant transfer.

E9.7.2   The main provisions of the 1999 Regulations are:
*   where redundancies or a business transfer is proposed, employees will
    have to consult with a recognised union or, if there is none, with
    employee representatives (who themselves must be employees);
*   employers do not have to set up standing arrangements for employee
    representatives until such time as they are needed. They can be
    designated on an ad hoc basis but there are specific rules for election;
*   both the transferor and transferee of a business are required to give
    certain information to any recognised union or elected employee
    representatives for any employee of theirs affected by a TUPE transfer
    (including those who do not actually transfer).[1]

Information to be given to appropriate representatives
*   the fact of the transfer, when it is to take place and reasons for it
*   the legal, economic and social implications of the transfer for the affected
    employees
*   measures which the employer envisages it will take in relation to those
    employees
*   measures which the transferee envisages it will take in relation to the
    affected employees who will become its employees after the transfer
*   where no such measures are to be taken by the transferor or transferee,
    that fact should also be stated

---

[1] Where there is no recognised union and where affected employees fail to elect
representatives (having had a genuine opportunity to do so), the employer may
(and should) fulfil its obligations by providing relevant information to those
employees direct.

E9.7.3   There is only an obligation to *consult* (as opposed to 'inform' as set
out above) if either the transferor or transferee intend to take any measures
in relation to affected employees. The TUPE 1981 define consultation as
listening to representatives' representations, considering them and replying
to them (with reasons). The obligation is to consult 'with a view to seeking
agreement' on those measures. There is no 'numbers' threshold for the

requirement to consult where there is a TUPE transfer (contrast consultation for collective redundancies), and so consultation must take place even if only one employee is affected.

E9.7.4 Failure to inform or consult entitles a union, employee representative or affected person or persons to make a complaint to a tribunal within three months of the completion of the transfer. If a complaint is established the tribunal must make a declaration and may order the employer to pay 'appropriate compensation' to the affected employees, but this is subject to a maximum of 13 weeks' pay (gross) per employee.[1]

[1]   There is no provision for offset of compensation for failure to consult in the case of collective redundancies and TUPE transfers.

E9.7.5   In *Kerry Foods Ltd v Creber*, the EAT[1] construed those liabilities that pass to the transferee under the TUPE 1981, reg 5 (ie under or 'in connection with' a contract of employment) as including the obligation to provide information and to consult. In this case, the transferee was held liable for the protective award payable because the transferor had failed to consult.[2]

[1]   [2000] IRLR 10.
[2]   This reverses the previous line of thinking in *Angus Jowett & Co Ltd v National Union of Tailors and Garment Workers* [1985] IRLR 326, EAT.

10   COLLECTIVE RIGHTS AND BARGAINING

10.1 Background

E10.1.1   There is no Labour Code, or other fundamental source of labour law, in the UK. Trade union law derives from a wide variety of sources, including statute, the common law and codes of practice. Trade unions have a number of rights and duties that do not apply to other associations.[1] In order to take advantage of various statutory rights, a trade union must be independent[2] and recognised by the employer for the purposes of collective bargaining on behalf of its workers[3] in one or more of the following areas:

(a) terms and conditions of employment (including physical conditions of work);
(b) engagement or non-engagement, or termination or suspension of employment of worker(s);
(c) allocation of work or duties between workers;
(d) disciplinary issues;
(e) a worker's membership or non-membership of the union;
(f) facilities for union officials;
(g) machinery for negotiation and consultation.[4]

[1]   The definition of a trade union is contained in the Trade Union Law Reform (Consolidation) Act 1992 (TULR(C)A 1992), s 1(a) as an organisation which consists wholly or mainly of workers of one or more descriptions and whose principal purposes include the regulation of relations between workers of that description(s) and employers or employers' associations.

2   Ie not under the domination or control of an employer or group of employers
and is not liable to interference by an employer.
3   TULR(C)A 1992, ss 295, 297.
4   TULR(C)A 1992, s 178(2).

E10.1.2   If an employer agrees to recognise a union as being authorised to
bargain on behalf of its workers on these issues, it will normally agree with
the union a procedure for conducting collective bargaining. Any agreements
reached between the employer and the union on areas (such as pay) are
known as 'collective agreements' which will normally be directly
enforceable by workers against their employer. However, prior to the
implementation of the ERA 1999, a union could not compel an employer to
recognise it for collective bargaining, and existing recognition agreements
could be abandoned at will. The ERA 1999 introduces a procedure to
enable a union to compel an employer to recognise it for collective
bargaining on pay, hours and holiday for the relevant workers.
Consequently many employers are now voluntarily agreeing to recognise
unions in order to avoid a compulsory recognised agreement which cannot
be abandoned at will.

10.2 Compulsory Recognition of Unions

E10.2.1   The ERA 1999's provisions are designed to encourage employers
voluntarily to recognise unions for collective bargaining on their employee's
terms and conditions of employment. If an employer refuses voluntarily to
agree recognition, a union can apply to the Central Arbitration Committee
(CAC) to invoke the compulsory recognition procedure provided the
following conditions are satisfied:

(a) the union is independent;
(b) the employer or group to which it belongs employs at least 21 workers;
(c) there is not already in force a collective agreement under which a union
     is recognised to conduct collective bargaining;
(d) at least 10% of relevant workers are members of the union and the
     union appears to have the support of a majority of the workers to be
     covered by the proposed collective bargaining (known as the
     'bargaining unit');
(e) there are no competing applications for recognition by other unions
     unless all the unions can show that they will co-operate and act together
     if granted recognition;
(f) that no unsuccessful application to the CAC for recognition has been
     made within three years in respect of the same group of workers.

E10.2.2   Whilst an employer and a union can voluntarily agree collective
bargaining on a wide range of issues, if the union compels an employer to
recognise it for collective bargaining under this procedure then the only
issues which must be covered by that process will be employees' pay, hours
and holidays.

A   THE RECOGNITION PROCESS

E10.2.3   Strict time-scales govern the compulsory recognition process. An
employer has only 10 days to agree in principle to a request for recognition.

If within at least a further 20 days (or longer if the parties agree) the bargaining unit is agreed then the CAC will not be involved.

E10.2.4   A failure to agree the principle or scope of recognition or the bargaining unit will trigger intervention by the CAC at the behest of the union, provided the conditions set out in para **E10.2.1** are met.

B   THE BARGAINING UNIT

E10.2.5   An independent union seeking recognition must define the extent of the group or groups of workers ('the bargaining unit') on behalf of which it intends to conduct collective bargaining. If the scope of the bargaining unit cannot be agreed it must be determined by the CAC in accordance with specified criteria, the most important being compatibility with effective management. In essence, groups of workers who are managed separately are likely to constitute separate bargaining units.

C   THE NEED FOR A BALLOT

E10.2.6   If the CAC is satisfied that a majority of the workers in the bargaining unit are members of the union, it *must* issue a declaration that the union is recognised as entitled to conduct collective bargaining on behalf of the workers in the bargaining unit, unless one of the following three situations exist:

- a ballot should be held in the interests of good industrial relations;
- a significant number of union members state they do not want the union to conduct collective bargaining on their behalf;
- there is evidence to show doubt whether a significant number of union members want the union to conduct bargaining on their behalf,

in which case a secret ballot must be held.

E10.2.7   Strict rules and a Code of Practice govern the conduct of such a ballot, the cost of which is shared equally between the union and the employer. Further, the employer must allow the union access to its premises to inform employees about the ballot and to canvass for support. To win the ballot, a majority of those voting and at least 40% of the total workforce in the bargaining unit must vote in favour of compulsory recognition.

E10.2.8   If there is evidence that a majority of workers in the bargaining unit are members of the union (or have voted in favour of recognition in a ballot) the employer and the union will have 30 days in which to agree a method for conducting collective bargaining. If no agreement is reached they can refer the question to the CAC which will allow a further 20-day period of negotiations to secure agreement. If agreement proves impossible the CAC will impose a method of conducting collective bargaining.[1]

[1]   Unless agreed by the parties to the contrary in writing, the method of collective bargaining imposed by the CAC will 'have effect as if it were contained in a legally enforceable contract made by the parties'.

D   ENFORCING RECOGNITION

E10.2.9   Any recognition agreement reached without recourse to the CAC will be wholly voluntary and, unless stated to the contrary in writing, will not be legally enforceable between the employer and the union and may be abandoned at will. However, as soon as a union has applied to the CAC for recognition, any subsequent 'voluntary' recognition agreement negotiated with the employer must remain in force for at least three years, as will recognition agreements imposed by the CAC, which may also contain a legally enforceable method of collective bargaining.

E10.2.10 Interestingly, the ERA 1999 does not specify how a declaration by the CAC that a union must be recognised should be enforced, although it is likely that the High Court would intervene, if requested, to compel an employer to grant recognition. If the CAC imposes a method of collective bargaining then this method will be enforceable in the High Court. Consequently, if the method imposed a procedure for resolving disputes before the union could call for industrial action, the employer could compel the union to follow that procedure before organising industrial action. There is no prescribed avenue for either an employer or union to appeal against a CAC decision.

E10.2.11 If an employer and a union have already established collective bargaining, either may apply to the CAC for help in determining the method of conducting collective bargaining.

E   DERECOGNITION

E10.2.12 A trade union that is recognised voluntarily outside the compulsory recognition process can be derecognised by an employer with relative ease – collective agreements are not generally legally enforceable. However, the position is more complicated in the case of compulsorily recognised unions. If a union makes a valid application for recognition that is agreed by the employer prior to the CAC making a declaration that the union is entitled to conduct collective bargaining, then, whilst the union may terminate that recognition agreement at any time, the employer may not terminate it for at least three years. If, having reached a voluntary agreement, the parties fail to agree a method for conducting collective bargaining then the CAC may intervene and impose a method that will also subsist for three years.

E10.2.13 If subsequently the collective bargaining unit changes because of:

• a change in the business organisation structure; or
• a change in the business activities; or
• a substantial change in the number of workers employed in the bargaining unit,

then either party can apply to the CAC to decide what should be the appropriate bargaining unit. An employer may also apply on these grounds to bring the collective bargaining arrangements to an end if it believes that the original bargaining unit has ceased to exist.

E10.2.14 An employer may apply to derecognise the union if at any time the number of its employees fall below the threshold. An employer may also request the union to agree to end the bargaining arrangements and, provided no similar application has been made within the previous three years, the CAC may agree to hold a secret ballot to determine this issue. The

CAC must be satisfied that at least 10% of the workers in the bargaining unit favour the end of bargaining arrangements and the majority of the workers appear likely to favour an end of the bargaining arrangements.

E10.2.15   One of the preconditions to triggering the compulsory recognition process is that no collective agreements already exist for any part of the bargaining unit. This condition is designed to prevent unions upsetting existing recognition arrangements with independent unions. If, however, an employer has recognised a non-independent union (typically a 'tame' in-house union) then an independent union – or the employer's workers – can apply to the CAC to have that union derecognised as a precursor to bringing about the recognition of an independent union. The CAC will only intervene if the same conditions as specified in para **E10.2.14** apply. The subsequent ballot for derecognition must be supported by a majority of those voting and at least 40% of the entire workforce covered by the existing collective bargaining arrangements with the non-independent union.

10.3 The Consequences of Recognition

A   PROTECTION FOR INDIVIDUAL WORKERS

E10.3.1   Protection is given to workers from suffering any detriment (by any act or deliberate failure to act) on the grounds that the worker took action to obtain or prevent recognition or collective bargaining, provided always that the worker's actions do not constitute 'an unreasonable act or omission'.

E10.3.2   A worker bringing a successful claim will be entitled to potentially unlimited compensation assessed on a 'just and equitable' basis. If a worker's contract is terminated, he will be entitled to compensation as if he had been fairly dismissed. If the worker is an employee, the dismissal will be deemed to be *automatically unfair*. There is no qualifying period for these purposes.

E10.3.3   There are certain other statutory rights including:
*   protection for individual employees against detrimental treatment or dismissal if they refuse to enter into contracts containing terms which differ from those negotiated collectively;
*   the right for trade union officials to have reasonable paid time off work to carry out their duties and to undergo training;
*   the right to reasonable unpaid time off for trade union members to participate in union activities.

B   RIGHT TO INFORMATION AND CONSULTATION

E10.3.4   In addition to the right to conduct collective bargaining, recognition carries with it a number of general statutory rights including:
*   the right to receive relevant information prior to conducting collective bargaining;
*   the right to information and consultation on redundancies;
*   the right to information and consultation on business transfers;
*   the right to information and consultation on health and safety issues.

C   LEGAL STATUS OF COLLECTIVE AGREEMENTS

E10.3.5   Collective agreements generally fall into two categories; first, agreements on the method(s) of conducting collective bargaining; and secondly, agreements about employees' terms and conditions of employment reached as a consequence of collective bargaining.

E10.3.6   The first type of agreement, on the method of conducting collective bargaining, will not be legally enforceable between an employer and a union unless they have either agreed in writing that it should be binding or the method has been imposed by the CAC as a consequence of compulsory recognition.

E10.3.7   The second type of agreement, directly affecting employees' terms and conditions, such as altering pay rates or introducing a new redundancy procedure, will normally be legally enforceable by (and against) those employees. All employees in the grades for which the union is recognised to conduct collective bargaining will be bound by these agreements, including those who are not union members or are opposed to the agreement. These employees will continue to enjoy the benefit of those agreements even if the union is subsequently derecognised. However, the union itself cannot enforce these agreements against the employer unless both parties have agreed that they should be legally enforceable.

10.4 Collective Bargaining and Collective Representation

E10.4.1   An employer must consult with appropriate 'representatives' when it proposes to dismiss as redundant 20 or more employees at one establishment within a period of 90 days or less.

E10.4.2   By contrast, consultation on transfers need only take place if measures are envisaged in relation to employees affected by the transfer. There is, however, always a duty to inform representatives of affected employees about the transfer.

E10.4.3   Employers are required to consult and/or inform a union recognised for collective bargaining purposes in respect of any of the affected employees. It will not matter for these purposes whether or not any of the affected employees are themselves union members provided they belong to the grade in respect of which the union is recognised. Only if no union is recognised in respect of affected employees may the employer chose to consult or inform either existing employee representatives with appropriate authority or employee representatives elected for these purposes.

E10.4.4   Rules have been introduced to regulate the conduct of elections for employee representatives, obliging the employer to make 'reasonably practicable' arrangements for the election to ensure that it is fair and to allow the necessary consultations to take place in good time once elected representatives have been appointed. Those representatives must be members of the affected work force[1] and there must be enough of them to be able to properly represent all relevant employees. All affected workers must be entitled to vote in secret and the votes must be fairly and accurately counted.

[1]   'Affected' employees include employees who may be directly or indirectly affected by any redundancies or a transfer eg any employees whose terms and conditions are changed as a result of redundancies.

E10.4.5   If the employees fail to take up the opportunity to elect representatives, the employer may discharge its obligations to inform and consult by giving individual employees the information that would have been given to their representatives.[1]

[1]   The Collective Redundancies and Transfer of Undertakings (Protection of Employment) (Amendment) Regulations 1999.

E10.4.6   In the event of any complaint of a failure to inform or consult, the burden of proof will be on the employer to show that any employee representatives with which it consulted had the authority to represent the affected employees and/or that the election requirements set out above were satisfied.

E10.4.7   Both trade union and employee representatives will have the right to time off to undergo training to perform their functions in these situations. Employees and their representatives will have the right not to be subjected to any detriment by any act or any deliberate failure to act by their employer in consequence of their participation in an election of employee representatives. It will become automatically unfair to dismiss any employee on the grounds that they took part in an election of employee representatives for these purposes.

10.5 Industrial Action

E10.5.1   Unlike many countries, English law does not give workers a positive right to organise or participate in industrial action.

E10.5.2   Any employee participating in industrial action will usually (but not always) be in breach of contract and consequently subject to disciplinary proceedings including dismissal. If the employer has evidence that the union has authorised or endorsed the employee's participation in industrial action, the union may be liable to the employer for the unlawful act (tort) of inducing the employee to breach his contractual duty to work normally, and consequently for any losses arising from that breach. Depending upon the circumstances, the employer may also be able to obtain an injunction to restrain the union's continued inducement of employees to breach their contracts of employment.

E10.5.3   However, a union may be protected from specified liabilities (including inducement of employees to breach their contracts) provided it ensures that any industrial action it endorses arises out of a legitimate 'trade dispute' and that the industrial action is lawful by complying with detailed balloting and notification requirements.

E10.5.4 If an employer has evidence that a union has tacitly authorised or endorsed its members to take industrial action without going through the balloting and notification requirements, it can demand that the union repudiate the industrial action. If the union refuses to do so, the employer can issue proceedings against it for an injunction and/or damages.

E10.5.5 A union will not be liable for any acts (such as encouraging its members to take industrial action) unless they were authorised or endorsed by one of the following:

- a person empowered by the union rules to do, authorise or endorse the industrial action;
- the Executive Committee, President or General Secretary;
- any other committee of the union and any other official whether or not employed by the union.[1]

[1] TULR(C)A 1992, s 20.

E10.5.6 A union can escape liability for wrongly encouraging its members to take industrial action by repudiating any call by its officials (but not, for example, its Executive Committee) to take industrial action, provided the repudiation:

- involves 'an open disavowal and disowning of the acts of the officials concerned';
- is given in writing 'without delay' to the relevant official; and
- is followed up by the union doing 'its best' to give every member whom it has reason to believe might take part in the industrial action written notice of the repudiation.

A   LAWFUL INDUSTRIAL ACTION

E10.5.7 In order for industrial action to be lawful (thereby giving the union immunity from liability for any losses incurred by an employer as a result of the industrial action) the union must establish that:

- there is statutory protection for its intended actions;[1] and
- the intended actions must be done in contemplation or furtherance of a 'trade dispute'.[2]

[1] TULR(C)A 1992, s 219(1).
[2] TULR(C)A 1992, s 244.

B   WHICH ACTS ATTRACT STATUTORY PROTECTION?

E10.5.8 The most common actions of a union encouraging its members to take industrial action will normally constitute unlawful acts (torts) such as:

- inducing breach of contract;
- interfering with the performance of a contract;
- intimidation; and
- conspiracy.

These are covered by the TULR(C)A 1992, s 219, which provides the union with immunity from liability to these torts subject to its complying with a number of conditions. The conditions include the rules governing the conduct of a ballot of members to authorise the industrial action and an obligation to notify employers prior to calling any industrial action. If the union is in breach of these conditions, any industrial action will be 'unlawful' and therefore the union will be legally liable unless it is in a position to 'repudiate' the action.

The following actions are excluded from statutory immunity under the TULR(C)A 1992, s 219, and consequently a union encouraging its members to participate in these actions will always be liable for any damages suffered by an employer as a consequence of them:

- action which constitutes unlawful picketing;
- action to enforce trade union membership;
- action in response to the dismissal of participants in unlawful industrial action;
- action which constitutes secondary action;
- action to enforce union recognition by third parties;
- industrial action not supported by a ballot or due notice to employers.

C   THE MEANING OF A 'TRADE DISPUTE'

E10.5.9   The TULR(C)A 1992, s 224(1) defines a trade dispute as:

'a dispute between workers and their employer which relates wholly or mainly to one or more of a number of specified matters.'

E10.5.10   The specified matters include terms and conditions of employment, union membership, discipline or allocation of work. In assessing whether the subject matter of the dispute relates *wholly or mainly* to one of the specified matters the court will take into account the 'predominate purpose' of the dispute to ascertain if the union is using the dispute to advance an improper purpose.[1]

[1]   The courts apply a subjective test when assessing the union's actions.

D   THE REQUIREMENT TO HOLD A BALLOT

E10.5.11   To be lawful, all industrial action organised by a union must be authorised by a ballot of relevant members. A new Code of Practice gives guidance on the conduct of the ballot.

E10.5.12   The union must allow all members whom it reasonably believes 'at the time of the ballot' will be called upon to take part in the industrial action to vote. No others may vote.

E10.5.13   If the members whom the union believes will be induced to take part in the industrial action have different places of work, there must normally be a separate ballot for each work place and a separate majority must be obtained in each work place for the industrial action to be lawful.

E   CONDUCTING THE BALLOT

E10.5.14   The ballot must be postal and so far as is 'reasonably practicable' every member entitled to vote must be sent a ballot paper. Strict rules govern the content of the ballot paper.

E10.5.15   Members must be able to vote in secret without interference or constraint by the union, although it is free to campaign openly for a 'yes' vote.

E10.5.16   A majority in number of those voting must support the relevant industrial action for it to be lawful.

F   THE REQUIREMENT TO GIVE NOTICE OF INDUSTRIAL ACTION

E10.5.17   To be protected the union must ensure that the employer of members to be called out on industrial action is given:

- notice of the ballot and a sample voting paper;
- notice of the result of the ballot;
- notice of the intended industrial action.[1]

---

[1]   The legal consequences of failing to provide the requisite notice vary depending upon the notification; failure to notify an employer of the ballot result exposes the union to liability to any employer suffering loss as a consequence of the industrial action; failure to provide information prior to conducting the ballot or proper notice of industrial action will only remove protection in relation to the unnotified employer.

G   DISTINGUISHING 'OFFICIAL' FROM 'UNOFFICIAL' AND 'LAWFUL' FROM 'UNLAWFUL' INDUSTRIAL ACTION

E10.5.18   Industrial action will be official if it is authorised by a union. Industrial action will be lawful if it concerns a legitimate 'trade dispute' and the union complies with a series of statutory requirements, including those on balloting and notification. As this involves the union authorising industrial action by its members, it follows that all lawful industrial action will also be official.

E10.5.19   If industrial action is lawful, the union will be immune from liability to the employer for any losses arising from the industrial action and consequently free from the threat of an injunction to restrain the industrial action or claims for damages. Participating employees will be protected from dismissal under the new provisions introduced by the ERA 1999 making their dismissal automatically unfair in most circumstances.

E10.5.20   If the union has failed to comply with the balloting and notification requirements, or if the dispute does not constitute a 'trade dispute', the industrial action will be unlawful. If in these circumstances the union is deemed to have authorised or endorsed the unlawful industrial action, making it 'official', this will protect participating employees from selective dismissal, but will leave the union vulnerable to employers seeking injunctive relief and/or damages, arising from any losses they incur as a result of the industrial action. The union's liability for these losses is capped by the TULR(C)A 1992.

E10.5.21   If the union has not authorised or endorsed the industrial action it will be unofficial and participating employees will forfeit their right to complain of unfair dismissal. Employers can therefore 'cherry pick' any participants for dismissal with impunity as they will not have any right to complain of unfair dismissal.

H   THE IMPACT OF THE ERA 1999 ON DISMISSING EMPLOYEES TAKING INDUSTRIAL ACTION

E10.5.22   The ERA 1999 has fundamentally changed the position of employees participating in official industrial action whilst leaving the position of participants in unofficial industrial action unchanged. They remain deprived of their right to claim unfair dismissal.

E10.5.23   The ERA 1999 provides that an employee will be automatically unfairly dismissed in certain circumstances if the reason (or if more than one, the principal reason) for his dismissal is that he took 'protected industrial action'. Put simply, this means refusing to work normally following a call by his union to participate in official industrial action.

E10.5.24   The protection provided by the ERA 1999 will only apply in the following circumstances:

- if a dismissal takes place within eight weeks beginning with the day on which the employee started to take 'protected industrial action';
- if the employee is dismissed after the expiry of the eight-week period but had stopped taking protected industrial action before the end of that period; or
- if the employee continues to take industrial action after the expiry of that eight-week period and is subsequently dismissed in circumstances where 'the employer had not taken such procedural steps as would have been reasonable for the purposes of resolving the dispute to which the protected industrial action relates'.

E10.5.25   No prudent employer is likely to wish to test its ability to defend a large number of claims from dismissed employees by persuading a tribunal that it has taken reasonable steps to resolve a dispute. Consequently employees taking 'protected industrial action' are relatively immune from dismissal, both within and beyond the initial eight-week period.

E10.5.26   If the industrial action is official but unlawful, it will not be 'protected' and, consequently, participating employees who are dismissed will only have the protection of the old law. This means that they can only complain of unfair dismissal if, on the day of their dismissal, not all of the participating employees at their 'establishment' were dismissed or if any other dismissed employees are reinstated within three months. Employers in these circumstances have previously been careful to ensure that they dismiss all participants on the same day and either reinstate none or all of them. Provided an employer meets this requirement none of the dismissed employees can claim unfair dismissal.

10.6 European Works Councils

> The European Works Council Directive applies to:
> - an 'undertaking' or 'groups of undertaking'
> - employing 1,000 within the European Economic Area (EEA)
> - and employing 150 in each of two EEA member states.

E10.6.1   The Transnational Information and Consultation of Employees Regulations 1999, SI 1999/3323 came into force on 15 January 2000.[1] These Regulations implement the EU European Works Council Directive (the EWC Directive).

[1]   Jurisdiction to hear certain breaches of these Regulations has been conferred on the Employment Appeal Tribunal.

E10.6.2   The EWC Directive establishes mechanisms for informing and consulting employees at a European level; a separate Directive is under consideration for establishing mechanisms for informing and consulting employees at national level.

E10.6.3   The EWC Directive has been implemented in other EU states for some time (since 1996) and, in consequence, approximately 120 UK based companies have already had to take steps to comply with the EWC Directive as they employed significant numbers in two or more EEA states already covered by the EWC Directive.

E10.6.4   Only an 'undertaking' (defined as 'public or private entities carrying out an economic activity whether or not for gain' or 'groups of undertakings' employing 1,000 persons throughout the EEA and at least 150 in each of two separate EEA member states will be affected.

E10.6.5   It should be noted that voluntary agreements negotiated prior to 15 December 1999 (known as 'article 12 Agreements') circumvent the obligation to establish an EWC.

E10.6.6   If a UK-based undertaking or group of undertakings triggers this threshold by virtue of the inclusion of its UK workforce following the implementation of the EWC Directive then it may:
- do nothing and hope that its employees or their representatives will not request the formation of an EWC;
- agree the creation of a 'special negotiating body' (SNB) to oversee the creation of 'an information and consultation procedure' which may act as an alternative to the creation of an EWC; or
- respond to a petition by employees to form a EWC. ·

E10.6.7   A petition of 100 or more employees or their representatives can request the establishment of a SNB to oversee the creation of an EWC. Any failure by management to begin negotiating within six months of the creation of the SNB will lead to a statutory EWC being set up. Disputes about whether an undertaking employs above the threshold or other factors governing the validity of a request for an SNB to be established will be determined by the CAC.

E10.6.8   There are detailed rules on the number of seats to be allocated for the SNB and on the selection of its members; the government proposes to establish guidelines for the election of representatives and to place responsibility for the funding those elections on the undertaking.

E10.6.9   Once the SNB has been established, the parties are obliged to negotiate 'in the spirit of co-operation with a view to reaching an agreement' on the detailed arrangements for the information and consultation of employees. The employee representatives may seek assistance from experts, one of which must be funded by management. The SNB may decide by two-thirds majority not to open negotiations with management or to terminate those negotiations, in which case, no new request may be made to convene the SNB for two years.

E10.6.10   If no agreement is reached within three years and there is no prospect that one may be concluded soon, the EWC Directive provides for the adoption of a statutory EWC. If negotiations are successful on the establishment of an EWC (or indeed a more informal 'information and consultation procedure') it will form a binding 'article 6' agreement which must satisfy certain requirements, including the specification of:
- the undertakings or establishments covered;
- the composition of the EWC, the number of members, the allocation of seats and term of office;
- the functions and procedure for information and consultation;
- the venue, frequency and duration of meetings;
- the financial and material resources to be allocated to the EWC; and
- the duration of the agreement and the procedure for its renegotiation.

A   THE OBLIGATION TO INFORM AND CONSULT

E10.6.11   A refusal to negotiate or agree will lead to the imposition of a statutory EWC. This will have the right to meet central management annually to be informed and consulted by reference to a management report on the undertaking's prospects. This must include 'substantial changes concerning organisation, new working methods or production processes, transfers of production, mergers, cutbacks or closures of businesses, establishments and collective redundancies'. Further, in 'exceptional circumstances' the EWC has the right to be informed and to meet with management and to be consulted on 'measures significantly affecting employees interests'.

E10.6.12   There is a limited right for management to withhold information from an EWC if 'according to objective criteria it would seriously harm the functioning of the undertaking or be prejudicial to it'. If information is withheld, the SNB/EWC representatives can appeal to the CAC for it to be disclosed. It should be noted that these provisions do not apply to art 12 agreements. Disclosure of confidential information by a member of an SNB/EWC is likely to constitute a criminal offence.

B   ENFORCEMENT

E10.6.13   The procedure for enforcing the establishment of an EWC will largely be overseen by the CAC which may issue declarations requiring an undertaking to move to the next stage in the negotiation process, which if ignored will constitute a contempt of court. Intentional failure to comply with any obligation could give rise to penalties of up to £75,000 with additional fines on a daily basis for continuing non-compliance with a court order. Again, failure to comply with any declaration would be treated as a contempt of court

11   EMPLOYMENT DISPUTES

11.1 Background

E11.1.1   Disputes between employer and employee are usually resolved:

- at work (either informally or in a formal context by using the company's grievance or disciplinary procedure);
- in court – County Court or High Court usually for contractual issues eg restraint of trade, breach of contract, injunctions etc;
- in employment tribunals – these were set up to deal with statutory employment claims eg discrimination and unfair dismissal. They have *limited* jurisdiction to hear breach of contract claims up to the value of £25,000.

E11.1.2   Appeals from a tribunal may be made to the Employment Appeals Tribunal (EAT) on very limited grounds. An appeal from the EAT may be made to the Court of Appeal and thereafter to the House of Lords. Where there is a question concerning the interpretation of EU law, the tribunal or court may request the European Court of Justice to give a ruling.

E11.1.3   An employee may wish to bring proceedings in the civil courts (eg for a substantial wrongful dismissal claim) and in the employment tribunal (eg for unfair dismissal or discrimination). Whilst both sets of proceedings may be commenced at the same time, it is common to stay the tribunal proceedings pending the resolution of the court proceedings.[1] However, findings of fact in a tribunal will bind a court (the principle of res judicata) and on occasion it may be advantageous to have these findings in advance of the court hearing.[2]

[1]   *First Castle Electronics Ltd v West* [1989] ICR 72, EAT.
[2]   *Munir v Jang Publications Ltd* [1989] ICR 1, CA.

11.2 Labour Courts/Tribunals

E11.2.1   Employment tribunals were established in 1964 as 'industrial' tribunals to address workplace disputes between employer and employee. Since then, their jurisdiction has increased greatly and their proceedings have become more formalised.

E11.2.2   Employment tribunals comprise a panel of three: a legally qualified chairperson (appointed by the Lord Chancellor) and two lay members representing both sides of industry (eg the CBI and the TUC). The

President of Employment Tribunals for England and Wales presides over the tribunal system which is divided into twelve regions.

E11.2.3   Full hearings are held before a full panel of three members, although a chairperson may sit with one lay member if the parties agree. Some proceedings must be heard by a chairperson alone – these include determination of jurisdictional issues.

E11.2.4   Tribunals are relatively informal and, in contrast to a formal court proceedings, have relaxed rules on evidence and procedure. Formal rules of procedure do, however, govern the conduct of proceedings.

Examples of claims which may be heard by an employment tribunal

- unfair dismissal
- breach of contract (up to £25,000)
- miscellaneous claims pursuant to the ERA 1996 eg deduction from wages; redundancy payments; maternity leave issues; request for written particulars of employment or reasons for dismissal
- discrimination (race, sex, marital status, disability)
- breach of National Minimum Wage Act 1998
- breach of Working Time Regulations 1998
- breach of Public Interest Disclosure Act 1998
- dismissal for trade union reasons – other protection for trade unions
- equal pay

11.3 Settlements

E11.3.1   As a general rule it is not possible for an employee to 'opt-out' of his employment rights under English law, either by agreeing that the rights in question do not apply to his employment or by agreeing not to enforce those rights by application to an employment tribunal. An exception exists where the employee enters into a valid severance or compromise agreement that complies with various statutory requirements.[1]

[1]   Depending on the particular complaint to be compromised: ERA 1996, s 203; SDA 1975, s 77; RRA 1976, s 72; DDA 1995, s 9.

E11.3.2   The statutory requirements are inter alia that the employee in question has received independent advice from a 'relevant adviser', who may be a qualified lawyer or alternatively an adviser from a voluntary body subject to certain additional conditions.[1] It is also a requirement that the advice given must be covered by a contract of insurance or an indemnity provided for members of a profession or professional body. There is no requirement that the employer should pay for the employee's independent advice, although this is arguably customary. The agreement should specify exactly what claims the parties are seeking to exclude, since statute provides that the agreement must relate to the 'particular complaint' at issue.[2] The

245

compromise agreement procedure also has the advantage of allowing the employer to include additional clauses in the agreement relating to the termination of the employment relationship, such as provisions relating to confidentiality and employee references.

1   ERA 1996, s 203(3)(c), (d), (e) as amended by the Employment Rights (Dispute Resolution) Act 1998, ss 9, 10.
2   ERA 1996, s 203(3)(b) – see also *Lunt v Merseyside TEC Ltd* [1999] IRLR 458.

E11.3.3   It is also possible for an employee to refrain from instituting or continuing with an employment claim where a conciliation officer of the Advisory, Conciliation and Arbitration Service (ACAS) has taken action in relation to the claim (in practice, this will mean that the parties have concluded what is commonly known as a 'COT3 agreement', settling their dispute with the assistance and involvement of an ACAS officer).[1]

1   ERA 1996, s 203(2)(e).

12   WHISTLEBLOWING/DATA PROTECTION

12.1 Whistleblowing

A   BACKGROUND

E12.1.1   At common law, if an employee discloses (or threatens to disclose) confidential information, he will be in breach of his duties of fidelity and confidentiality to his employer. The employer may discipline and/or: dismiss him; sue for damages; apply for an injunction to prevent disclosure. An employee's defence would be to show that the disclosure was made 'in the public interest'. The Public Interest Disclosure Act 1998 (PIDA 1998) supplemented by The Public Interest Disclosure (Compensation) Regulations 1999 (SI 1999/1548) and The Public Interest Disclosure (Prescribed Persons) Order 1999 (SI 1999/1549) encourages the disclosure of malpractice at work by setting up a statutory framework for protection of employees who 'blow the whistle'. The PIDA 1998 inserts new provisions into the ERA 1996. References to sections below are references to the amended ERA 1996.

B   THE PIDA 1998

E12.1.2   The PIDA 1998 protects workers[1] (a wider definition than employees including certain agency workers) who disclose certain types of information. To be a 'qualifying disclosure' the information must, in the reasonable belief of the worker,[2] tend to show that one of the following matters has happened, is happening or is likely to happen:[3]

*   the commission of a criminal offence;
*   the failure to comply with a legal obligation;
*   a miscarriage of justice;
*   endangerment to health and safety;
*   damage to the environment;
*   concealment of any of the above.

1   Inserted by the PIDA 1998, s 1.
2   What is 'reasonable belief' will be for the courts or tribunals to decide.
3   ERA 1996, s 43B.

E12.1.3   The extent to which a qualifying disclosure is protected depends on the motives and belief of the worker and the status of the recipient. The more 'public' the recipient the higher the standards of probity.

E12.1.4   There are six different ways in which a worker can make a 'protected disclosure'.[1] These are:
- internal disclosures in good faith to an employer or another person responsible for that matter;
- disclosures to a legal advisor in the course of obtaining legal advice;
- disclosures in good faith to a minister of the Crown;
- disclosures in good faith to (a) prescribed person(s);[2]
- external disclosures (eg to the media) in good faith where the worker reasonably believes the information disclosed is substantially true. The worker must not make the disclosure for personal gain and it must be reasonable in all the circumstances to make the disclosure. The worker must also satisfy one of the following conditions:
  - (a) he reasonably believes he will be subjected to a detriment;
  - (b) the worker reasonably believes that it is likely that evidence will be concealed or destroyed; or
  - (c) the worker has previously made a disclosure of substantially the same information to his employer (ERA 1996, s 43G);
- exceptionally serious failures in good faith where the worker reasonably believes the information disclosed is substantially true. The failure should be of an exceptionally serious nature, the worker should not make the disclosure for personal gain and should ensure that, in all the circumstances of the case, it is reasonable to make the disclosure (ERA 1996, s 43H).

[1]   ERA 1996, ss 43C–43H.
[2]   A prescribed person is a person or body prescribed by the Secretary of State for the purpose of receiving disclosures about the matter concerned – Public Interest Disclosure (Prescribed Persons) Order 1999.

E12.1.5   Before any disclosure to the media can be justified, a worker must have raised his concerns about alleged malpractice with his employer or with a prescribed regulator.

Confidentiality clauses

E12.1.6   Any clause or term in an agreement between a worker and employer that tries to prevent the worker from making a protected disclosure will be void.[1] This includes an agreement to refrain from instituting or commencing any proceedings under the ERA 1996 or any proceedings for breach of contract; care needs to be taken when agreeing the terms of compromise agreements or ACAS conciliated settlements.

[1]   ERA 1996, s 43J.

Remedies

E12.1.7   The PIDA 1998 protects employees from dismissal and action short of dismissal and protects other workers from any detriment or victimisation (including the termination of contracts).

E12.1.8   Compensation for dismissed workers or those who have suffered a detriment is unlimited.[1] A tribunal may also award reinstatement or re-engagement to a dismissed employee. If an employee is dismissed for the sole or principal reason that he made a protected disclosure then such dismissal will be deemed to be automatically unfair.

[1]   Such as the tribunal considers to be 'just and equitable' in all the circumstances taking into account the worker's duty to mitigate his loss.

E12.1.9   Applications for unfair dismissal or for having suffered a detriment must be made within three months of the date of termination or the date on which the detriment was suffered.

12.2 Data Protection

E12.2.1   The provisions of the Data Protection Act 1998, which came into force on 1 March 2000, should be noted where employers hold 'personal data' in relation to employees. This is defined under the Data Protection Act 1998 as any data from which a living individual is identifiable, whether contained on computer or in a filing system; hard copies of personal data such as personnel files kept in relation to employees are therefore covered. The general aim is to ensure that information held in relation to employees is adequate, relevant, and not excessive and that employees are able to review the contents of any files held on them.

E12.2.2   Subject to limited transitional relief for employers that had a system in place for keeping employee records as at 24 October 1998, as a general principle the Data Protection Act 1998 allows for access to information by employees. The data to which an employee will have access includes statements of opinion or intention (such as appraisals), legal and other advice, and medical reports and records. There are also provisions in the Data Protection Act 1998 restricting the processing of 'sensitive data', including data relating to racial or ethnic origin, political or religious beliefs, trade union membership, and health, sexual, and criminal matters. Transferring data outside the European Economic Area (the fifteen member states of the European Union plus Norway, Iceland and Liechtenstein) is not permitted without the employee's consent unless the recipient jurisdiction has an adequate level of data protection.

E12.2.3   The Regulation of Investigatory Powers Act 2000 aims to ensure that investigatory powers do not breach human rights. It is now unlawful to intercept, without lawful authority or consent, communications that are transmitted by way of a public or private telecommunications system.

E12.2.4   In response to pressure from business, the Telecommunications (Lawful Business Practice) (Interception of Communications) Regulations 2000, SI 2000/2699 were introduced to entitle employers to record and monitor employees' emails and telephone calls without consent in certain prescribed circumstances.

13   HUMAN RIGHTS

13.1 Rights and Obligations

E13.1.1   The Human Rights Act 1998 (HRA 1998) set out to enforce the rights contained in the European Convention on Human Rights (ECHR) in British Courts. The HRA 1998 incorporates the operative parts of the ECHR into UK domestic law. It is unlawful for any public authority to act in a way that is incompatible with the ECHR (HRA 1998, s 6(1)). When applying legislation, UK courts and tribunals must interpret it as far as possible to be compatible with ECHR rights. To this extent the HRA 1998 and the ECHR will be relevant in the context of employment law.[1]

Public authority
Public authority includes any court or tribunal or 'any person certain of whose functions are functions of a public nature' (HRA 1998, s 6(3)) eg:
- publicly funded educational bodies
- police force
- immigration officers
- bodies carrying out public functions of local or central government
- prison service
- privatised utilities
  but not either House of Parliament or a person exercising functions in connection with proceedings in Parliament

---

[1]   HRA 1998, s 2, requires courts and tribunals to have regard to the case law of the ECHR. See also the not legally-binding EC Charter of Fundamental Rights (with provisions relating to information and consultation, freedom of association and the right to strike).

Private organisations

E13.1.2   The HRA 1998 only applies to activities of public authorities and so employees of private entities will have no direct rights under the ECHR or the HRA 1998 (although it will affect the way in which courts and tribunals apply existing common law and statutory rights).

E13.1.3   The HRA 1998 does not incorporate the Convention for the Protection of Human Rights and Fundamental Freedoms, art 13, which provides that there shall be an effective remedy before a national authority for anyone (arguably including workers of a private entity) whose rights and freedoms have been violated.

E13.1.4   The articles considered to be most relevant to employment law will be arts 8–11 and 14:
- article 8: respect for private and family life, home and correspondence;
- article 9: freedom of thought, conscience and religion;
- article 10: freedom of expression;

- article 11: freedom of peaceful assembly, freedom of association;
- article 14: no discrimination on grounds of sex, race, language, religion, opinion or status.

Article 8

E13.1.5 This right, which ensures respect for an individual's privacy, is subject to an exception permitting a public authority to interfere with the right if interference is:

- in accordance with the law; and
- necessary in a democratic society in the interests of national security, public safety or the economic well-being of the country;
- for the prevention of disorder or crime;
- for the protection of health or morals; or
- for the protection of the rights and freedom of others.

E13.1.6 This right includes the right to respect for personal identity (eg sexual, moral or physical).[1]

[1] See *Lustig-Prean v United Kingdom* (1999) 29 EHRR 548, ECtHR.

Article 9

E13.1.7 There is an absolute right to hold religious beliefs and a qualified right to manifest religious beliefs in worship,[1] teaching, practice and observance. The latter qualified right is subject to limitations prescribed by law that are:

- necessary in a democratic society in the interests of public safety;
- for the protection of public order, health or morals; or
- for the protection of the rights and freedom of others.

[1] See eg *Stedman v United Kingdom* (1997) 23 EHRR CD 168.

Article 10

E13.1.8 Under art 10 an individual has the right to hold opinions and to receive/impart information and ideas.[1] Interference with this right may be justified if it is:

- prescribed by law; and
- necessary in a democratic society:
- for the protection of the reputation or rights of others;
- for preventing the disclosure of information received in confidence; or
- for maintaining the authority and impartiality of the judiciary.

[1] For a definition of 'expression' see *Stevens v United Kingdom* (1986) 46 DR 245.

E13.1.9 There may be a new right of action for whistleblowers under art 10 (in cases where claims are brought against public authorities).

Article 11

E13.1.10 The rights under art 11 include the right to freedom of peaceful assembly and to freedom of association with others which includes the right to form and join trade unions to protect an individual's interests. Interference with this right is permitted where it is:

• prescribed by law; and
• necessary in a democratic society in the interests of national security or public safety:
   (a) or the prevention of disorder or crime;
   (b) for the protection of health or morals; or
   (c) for the protection of the rights and freedom of others.

Article 14

E13.1.11   This article secures ECHR rights without discrimination on any ground such as sex, race, colour, language, religion, political or other opinion, national or social origin, association with a national minority, property, birth or other status. However this is not a free standing right and can only be exercised with another ECHR right.

Enforcement

E13.1.12   All employees may be able to indirectly enforce the HRA 1998 against their employers in tribunals or courts which are obliged to give effect to the fundamental rights contained in the ECHR. UK law must be construed in accordance with the ECHR and decisions must be based on human rights principles. Further, under art 6, a litigant has the right to a fair trial. This right only applies to civil rights and obligations that probably include employment rights. It may therefore be possible to use art 6 to judge the fairness of court or tribunal procedures.

Examples of possible situations giving rise to claims under the HRA 1998

• compulsory psychometric/drug testing
• working arrangements conflicting with religious observance
• victimisation for whistleblowing
• intrusive interest by employers in employees private life
• legislation re industrial action (including picketing)

---

[1]   For a definition of 'expression' see *Stevens v UK* (1986) D&R 245.

14   UK IMMIGRATION LAW

14.1 Introduction

A   WHO REQUIRES PERMISSION TO WORK IN THE UK?

E14.1.1   British citizens, Commonwealth citizens with the right of abode in the UK and Irish citizens are not subject to UK immigration control. This means that they do not require permission to enter or remain in the UK.

E14.1.2   Nationals of the European Economic Area (EEA) countries (ie nationals of European Union countries and Iceland, Liechtenstein and Norway) are generally free to come to the UK to reside and work without any prior formalities. The current members of the European Union are Austria, Belgium, Denmark, Finland, France, Germany, Greece, Ireland, Italy, Luxembourg, the Netherlands, Portugal, Spain, Sweden and the UK. The family members of an EEA national (who are not themselves EEA nationals) require an EEA Family Permit, which is obtained from a British diplomatic post outside the UK, to accompany or join an EEA national who is exercising his or her treaty rights to reside in the UK.

E14.1.3   In theory, all other nationals require permission to work in the UK. However, individuals may have an immigration status or potential status that allows them to work in the UK and their background and connections must be examined carefully. For example, they may be married to a British citizen or are a commonwealth national with UK ancestry.

B   OVERVIEW OF THE MAIN IMMIGRATION CATEGORIES

E14.1.4   There are five main immigration categories for individuals who are seeking to work in the UK on a long-term basis. These are work permit holder, businessperson, innovator, sole representative and investor. After four years in one of these categories an individual may apply for indefinite leave to remain, colloquially known as 'permanent residence'. One year later the individual may be eligible to naturalise as a British citizen.

C   VISA NATIONALS AND DEPENDANTS

E14.1.5   In addition to satisfying the requirements of a particular immigration category, nationals of certain countries must obtain a visa from a British diplomatic post overseas before entering the UK in any capacity. In effect this imposes an additional hurdle to their entry to the UK. The list of visa nationals is amended from time to time.

E14.1.6   Spouses and dependent children up to the age of 18 can apply to accompany or to join individuals who are seeking entry to the UK in an established immigration category. There is also a provision for unmarried and same sex partners where certain conditions are met. In all cases, family members are required to obtain entry clearance from a British diplomatic post overseas before travelling to the UK.

D   EMPLOYER SANCTIONS

E14.1.7   Individuals who work in the UK in breach of their immigration permission are committing a criminal offence and are liable to be removed from the UK. In addition, it is a criminal offence to employ a person who does not have current and valid permission to live and work in the UK. Managers could face prosecution and a fine if the offence was committed with their consent or as a result of their failing to take reasonable care to ensure that checking procedures to prevent illegal working were in place.

14.2 Visitors

E14.2.1   An individual is permitted to enter the UK as a visitor for a period of up to six months and can transact business directly linked to their employment or business abroad (although visa nationals are required to obtain a visa beforehand: see paras **E14.1.1–E14.1.7**). However, as a business visitor, the individual must not carry out productive work or any work that would constitute employment.

E14.2.2   It is irrelevant that the work being carried out in the UK is unpaid or that the individual is being paid by an overseas company. It is also irrelevant if the individual only intends to stay in the UK a short time. A person can be in breach of the Immigration Rules if they are carrying out productive work in the UK for only one day.

14.3 Work Permit Applications

E14.3.1   Applications for work permits are made by UK employers or their representatives to the Department for Education and Employment (DfEE) which is based in Sheffield, England. Applications cannot be made by individuals who are the subject of the work permit but only the employing organisation. It follows that there must be an established business in the UK before a work permit application can be made.

There are various types of work permits but they principally fall into two categories – main work permits and Training and Work Experience Scheme (TWES) permits. The first type of work permit may be issued for a period of up to 60 months, and can lead to an employee being granted permission to stay in the UK indefinitely. The TWES permit requires the employee to leave the UK at the end of their training and work experience.

A   MAIN WORK PERMIT SCHEME

E14.3.2   The following criteria must normally be satisfied to obtain a main work permit, although the DfEE frequently exercises its discretion if one or more of the requirements cannot be satisfied:

* there must be a genuine vacancy for an employee in the UK;
* the job must normally require a degree or three years' specialist work experience;
* the individual must possess the qualifications and experience required for the position; and
* the employer must show that there are no suitably qualified and experienced 'resident workers'[1] available. This requirement is normally satisfied by advertising the position, providing details of an alternative recruitment method used or explaining why a search is not appropriate. It is not necessary to advertise intra-company transfers where the individual has at least six months' experience with the company overseas. In addition, board-level positions and positions which the DfEE designate as a 'skills shortage' need not be advertised. The current skills shortage list includes IT Managers and therefore these positions need not be advertised.

[1]   Resident workers are nationals of EEA countries and individuals who have indefinite leave to remain in the UK.

Training and Work Experience Scheme

E14.3.3   The Training and Work Experience Scheme is split into two categories. As with the main work permit scheme, applications are made by

UK employers or their representatives to the DfEE. Permits can be issued to enable individuals to train for a professional or specialist qualification (eg accountancy) or undertake a period of work experience. Applications should only be submitted under the Training and Work Experience Scheme where the person is additional to the employer's normal staffing requirements.

Procedure for obtaining work permits

E14.3.4 Visitors (see paras **E14.2.1–E14.2.2**) must always leave the UK before submission of the work permit application to the DfEE. While the application is being considered, which could take up to four weeks, the individual should remain outside the UK, unless they are genuinely visiting the UK. Where an individual is required urgently, and there are business reasons to support this, it is possible to expedite the application and have it dealt with much more quickly. To activate the work permit, the individual must enter the UK with the permit. Visa nationals (see paras **E14.1.5–E14.1.7**) are required to obtain a visa before travelling to the UK.

14.4 Investors

E14.4.1 Where individuals intend to seek entry to the UK as an investor, they must intend to bring funds under their control and disposable in the UK amounting to not less than £1m. The individual must intend to invest not less than £750,000 of the capital by way of UK Government bonds, share capital or loan capital in active and trading UK registered companies (other than those principally engaged in property investment and excluding investment by way of deposits with a bank, building society or other enterprise whose normal course of business includes the acceptance of deposits). The individual must be able to maintain and accommodate himself or herself and any dependants without recourse to public funds or taking employment, although self-employed business activities are permitted. A person seeking admission for the purpose of investing in the UK must obtain prior entry clearance from a British diplomatic post overseas.

14.5 Persons Intending to Establish Themselves in Business

E14.5.1 There are three types of business activity permitted under this category: acting as a sole trader, participation in a partnership and ownership of a company registered in the UK. Individuals intending to enter the UK under this category must meet a number of detailed requirements. The businesspersons must invest a minimum of £200,000 of money of their own and applicants must have additional funds to support themselves and their dependants in the UK until the new business provides an adequate income. The business must create at least two new full-time jobs for persons already settled in the UK. The businessperson and his/her family must obtain entry clearance from a British diplomatic post prior to arrival in the UK.

E14.5.2 The UK government is likely to introduce a new immigration category for innovators by the end of the year 2000.

14.6 Innovators

E14.6.1   The innovator category is aimed at entrepreneurs who wish to set up a business in the UK. The category was introduced in September 2000 as a pilot scheme and will initially run until September 2002. It differs from the main businessperson category in several ways, the main difference being that the individual is not required to invest his or her own money in the business. The application is submitted in the same way as a business person application and is assessed using a points system which covers three areas: the individual's skills and experience; the viability of the business plan; and the potential economic benefits to the UK, particularly in the areas of science and technology, including e-commerce.

14.7 Representatives of Overseas Firms which have no Branch, Subsidiary or Other Representative in the UK[1]

E14.7.1   Individuals intending to enter the UK as sole representatives of an overseas company with no representative in the UK may come to the UK to set up a registered branch or wholly-owned subsidiary of the overseas company, which must remain based overseas. The representative must be a senior employee, recruited overseas, with full authority to take operational decisions and must apply for entry clearance at a British diplomatic post overseas before travelling to the UK.

[1]   Sole representatives.

14.8 Indefinite Leave to Remain

E14.8.1   Individuals who have been admitted to the UK as work permit holders, investors, persons intending to establish themselves in business and sole representatives may be eligible to apply for indefinite leave to remain in the UK, along with their spouse and dependent children who have been granted leave in line. They must have been continuously resident in the UK for four years or more and continue to meet the conditions of their immigration category. It is not generally possible to amalgamate periods of time spent in the UK in different immigration categories.

14.9 Naturalisation on the Basis of Residence

E14.9.1   Individuals may apply to naturalise as British citizens if they satisfy various requirements. These include the five year residence requirements, which will be met if the individual: was in the UK on the date five years before the application; has not been outside the UK for more than 450 days during the five year period; has not been outside the UK for more than 90 days in the last 12 months; has held indefinite leave to remain for at least 12 months; and has not been in breach of the immigration laws at any time during the five-year period. In addition, the individual must normally intend to live in the UK if he or she is naturalised.

USEFUL WEBSITES

Europa – European legislation, the Official Journal, treaties etc:

• europa.eu.int/eur-lex/en/index.html

Employment Appeal Tribunal – official guidance on how to appeal to an EAT, cause lists and full text of judgments:
*   www.employmentappeals.gov.uk

Department of Trade and Industry:
*   www.dti.gov.uk

DTI Employment relations:
*   www.dti.gov.uk/ER/empcont.htm

Department for Education and Employment:
*   www.dfee.gov.uk

Employment Service:
*   www.employmentservice.gov.uk/english/home

Equal Opportunities Commission:
*   www.eoc.org.uk/index.html

Advisory, Conciliation and Arbitration Service (ACAS):
*   www.acas.org.uk

Court Service:
*   www.courtservice.gov.uk

Employment Lawyers Association:
*   www.elaweb.org.uk

Butterworths Links Library:
*   www.butterworths.com/cgi-bin/linkscgi.exe

F   Northern Ireland

Chris Ritchie

Chris Ritchie is an insurance-related litigation solicitor and practices in areas which include issues related to discrimination in employment at Kennedys, Belfast. He qualified as a solicitor in September 1995. He obtained an MA in Administration and Legal Studies from Ulster in December 1993.

Kennedys, Belfast

Phone: +44(0)28 9024 0067
Fax: +44(0)28 9031 5557
Email: c.ritchie@kennedys-law.com
Website: www.kennedys-law.com

NORTHERN IRELAND

Rights	Yes/No	Explanatory Notes
CONTRACTS OF EMPLOYMENT		
Minimum notice	YES	See England and Wales
Terms:		See England and Wales
Express	YES	See England and Wales
Implied	YES	See England and Wales
Incorporated by statute	YES	See England and Wales
REMUNERATION		
Minimum wage regulation	YES	See England and Wales
Further rights and obligations:		
Right to paid holiday	YES	See England and Wales
Right to sick pay	YES	See England and Wales
WORKING TIME		
Regulation of hours per day/ working week	YES	See England and Wales
Regulation of night work	YES	See England and Wales
Right to paid holiday		See England and Wales
Right to rest periods	YES	See England and Wales
EQUAL OPPORTUNITIES		
Discrimination protection:		
Sex	YES	See England and Wales
Race	YES	See England and Wales
Marital status	YES	See England and Wales
Disability	YES	See England and Wales
Religion	YES	differ from England and Wales
Political belief	YES	differ from England and Wales
Age	NO*	*(but see text) See England and Wales
Sexual orientation	NO*	*(but see text) See England and Wales
Gender reassignment	YES	See England and Wales
Equal pay legislation	YES	See England and Wales
TERMINATION OF EMPLOYMENT		
Right not to be dismissed in breach of contract	YES	See England and Wales
Statutory rights on termination	YES	(unfair dismissal) See England and Wales
REDUNDANCY		
Statutory definition	YES	See England and Wales
Right to payment on redundancy	YES	(statutory payment and/or additional contractual payment) See England and Wales

258

Right to consultation:

Individual	YES	See England and Wales
Collective	YES	See England and Wales

YOUNG WORKERS

Protection of children and young persons at work	YES	See England and Wales

MATERNITY RIGHTS

Right to time off – ante natal care	YES	See England and Wales
Right to maternity leave	YES	See England and Wales
Notice requirements		See England and Wales
Maternity pay (during leave)	YES/NO	(maternity allowance, statutory maternity pay, etc) See England and Wales
Protection from dismissal	YES	(statutory protection – unfair dismissal/sex discrimination) See England and Wales
Health and safety protection	YES	See England and Wales
Right to parental leave	YES	See England and Wales

TRANSFERS OF BUSINESSES

Right to protection on transfer	YES	See England and Wales
Transfer of employment obligations	YES	See England and Wales
Right to information and consultation	YES	See England and Wales
Right not to be dismissed	YES	See England and Wales

COLLECTIVE RIGHTS

Compulsory recognition of trades unions	YES	See England and Wales
European works council	?	See England and Wales
Right to take industrial action		See England and Wales

EMPLOYMENT DISPUTES

Civil court jurisdiction	YES	See England and Wales
Statutory body	YES	(Employment Tribunals) See England and Wales

WHISTLEBLOWING

Protection from dismissal/ detriment	YES	See England and Wales

DATA PROTECTION

Protection	YES	See England and Wales

HUMAN RIGHTS

Statutory protection of human rights		See England and Wales
Public authority	YES	See England and Wales
Private organisations	NO	See England and Wales

1   GENERAL

1.1   Background

F1.1.1   To a large extent (and with one significant exception), the employment law of Northern Ireland is very similar to that in England and Wales. Some English Acts of Parliament apply directly, whilst many others find a direct parallel in equivalent legislation. Prior to 1972, this took the form of Acts of the Northern Ireland Parliament. When that institution was suspended and 'direct rule' (ie government from Westminster) commenced, legislation was enacted by way of Order in Council. With one brief interlude in 1974, this was the usual method of enacting legislation from 1972 onwards. The Disability Discrimination Act 1995 provides a good example of an English Act applying directly to Northern Ireland. In most cases, however, a similarly named Order is enacted, eg the Employment Rights Act 1996 finds expression in the Employment Rights (Northern Ireland) Order 1996.

F1.1.2   Of course, the bulk of legislation will now be enacted by the new Northern Ireland Assembly, which was established as part of the 1998 Belfast Agreement. Under the Agreement, the Assembly has legislative powers in respect of those matters previously within the remit of the Northern Ireland government departments dealing with agriculture, economic development, the environment, finance and personnel and health and social services.

F1.1.3   The most significant difference between the employment law in the two jurisdictions is found in the legislation in Northern Ireland dealing with discrimination on the grounds of religious and political belief (otherwise known as the Fair Employment legislation). A section dealing with this legislation is incorporated into the chapter on Equal Opportunities.

How to read this chapter

F1.1.4   The following notes cross refer to the England and Wales chapter (in which paragraph numbers have the prefix 'E'), and set out the differences that do exist together with the relevant legislation. To avoid over-repetition, the table below sets out some of the primary English legislation with its equivalent in Northern Ireland.

ENGLISH LEGISLATION	NORTHERN IRISH LEGISLATION
Equal Pay Act 1970	Equal Pay Act (Northern Ireland) 1970
Health and Safety at Work Act 1974	Health and Safety at Work (Northern Ireland) Order 1978
Sex Discrimination Act 1975 (SDA)	Sex Discrimination (Northern Ireland) Order 1976 (SDO)
Race Relations Act 1976 (RRA)	Race Relations (Northern Ireland) Order 1997 (RRO)
Trade Union and Labour Relations (Consolidation) Act 1992	Industrial Relations (Northern Ireland) Order 1993

ENGLISH LEGISLATION	NORTHERN IRISH LEGISLATION
Disability Discrimination Act 1995 (DDA)	Applies directly to Northern Ireland
Employment Rights Act 1996 (ERA)	Employment Rights (Northern Ireland) Order 1996 (ERO)
Working Time Regulations 1998	Working Time Regulations (Northern Ireland) 1998
Human Rights Act 1998	Applies directly to Northern Ireland
National Minimum Wage Regulations 1999	Apply directly to Northern Ireland
Employment Relations Act 1999	Employment Relations (Northern Ireland) Order 1999

F1.1.5 The provisions in Northern Ireland are not always identical to the English ones, and the 'mirror' legislation does not always follow swiftly (as can be seen from the 21-year delay in the enactment of race relations legislation). The numbering of the legislation also differs, the section number in the Act not necessarily finding its match in the corresponding article number in the Order.

Case law

F1.1.6 The English law reports are used as a matter of course where equivalent or analogous legislation applies. Naturally, local reports are also referred to (the Northern Ireland Law Reports, Judgments Bulletin and the Bulletin of Northern Ireland law).

2 THE EMPLOYMENT RELATIONSHIP

2.1 Contract of Service

F2.1.1 See para **E1.2.1**.

Note 1 Articles 326 and 9(2) of the Companies (Northern Ireland) Order 1986.

F2.1.2 See para **E1.2.2**.

Note 1 Articles 33–39 of the Employment Rights (Northern Ireland) Order 1996 (ERO).
Note 2 Article 118 ERO.

F2.1.3 See para **E1.2.7**. The Labour Relations Agency is the equivalent of ACAS.

F2.1.4 See para **E1.2.9**.

Note 1 Article 33 ERO.

F2.1.5 See para **E1.2.26**.

Note 6 Health and Safety at Work Order (Northern Ireland) Order 1978.

F2.1.6 See para **E1.2.28**.

Note 1 Section 1 of the Equal Pay Act (Northern Ireland) 1970 as amended.
Note 5 RO; art 77 SDO; art 68 RRO.

3 REMUNERATION

3.1 Background
F3.1.1 See para **E2.1.1**. Both the National Minimum Wage Act 1998 and the Regulations (SI 1999/584) apply directly to Northern Ireland.

4 FURTHER RIGHTS AND OBLIGATIONS

4.1 Background
F4.1.1 See para **E3.2.1**.

Note 1 Social Security Contributions and Benefits (Northern Ireland) Act 1992.

5 WORKING TIME

5.1 Background
F5.1.1 See para **E4.1.1**.

Working Time Regulations (Northern Ireland) 1998.

6 EQUAL OPPORTUNITIES

6.1 Background
F6.1.1 The law in Northern Ireland is the same as in England and Wales except that it also prohibits discrimination on the grounds of religious and political belief (see para **F6.2.1**). The corresponding legislation is the Sex Discrimination (Northern Ireland) Order 1976, the Equal Pay Act (Northern Ireland) 1970 and the Race Relations (Northern Ireland) Order 1997. The Disability Discrimination Act 1995 applies directly to Northern Ireland. The Fair Employment and Treatment (Northern Ireland) Order 1998 deals with discrimination on grounds of religious and political belief. Note that under the Northern Ireland Act 1998, the separate equality bodies in Northern Ireland (the Equal Opportunities Commission, the Fair Employment Commission, the Northern Ireland Disability Council and the Commission for Racial Equality (Northern Ireland)) have merged to form a new Equality Commission dealing with all aspects of equal opportunities.

6.2 Unlawful Discrimination
F6.2.1 Unlike the position in England and Wales, discrimination on the grounds of religious and political belief is unlawful in Northern Ireland. The relevant legislation is the Fair Employment and Treatment Order 1998. As with other forms of discrimination, any attempts to contract out of the legislation are (with certain exceptions) void. Note, however, that the legislation does not protect political views which support the use of violence for political ends connected with Northern Ireland.

F6.2.2 For the purposes of discrimination on the grounds of religious or political belief, a claim may be founded on the basis of either direct or indirect discrimination.

A DIRECT DISCRIMINATION

F6.2.3 Article 3(2) of the Fair Employment and Treatment (Northern Ireland) Order 1998 provides that:

> 'A person discriminates against another person on the ground of religious belief or political opinion ... if ... on either of those grounds he treats that other less favourably than he treats or would treat other persons ...'

B INDIRECT DISCRIMINATION

F6.2.4 Indirect discrimination occurs where an employer applies a requirement or condition to all employees which has a disproportionate impact on members of one religious or political group.

F6.2.5 Individual complaints of discrimination are dealt with by the Fair Employment Tribunal, which has the following powers. It may:
- make an order declaring the rights of the parties;
- make an order requiring the employer to pay the complainant compensation;
- make a recommendation that the employer take action to mitigate the effects of the discrimination.

F6.2.6 If the claim is 'mixed' eg it involves allegations of unfair dismissal or gender discrimination as well as religious/political discrimination, the Fair Employment Tribunal has all the powers of an employment tribunal to deal with these aspects as well.

F6.2.7 Proceedings must be commenced by the end of a period of three months from when the individual had actual or constructive knowledge of the discrimination or at the end of six months beginning with the day on which the discrimination occurred, whichever is the earlier.

F6.2.8 The principles that apply to religious and political discrimination are similar to (and can readily be extrapolated from) the principles dealing with gender and race discrimination set out in the England and Wales chapter. Note, however, that there is no defence of genuine occupational qualification. However, the employer may attempt to justify indirect discrimination on the basis that the discriminatory criterion is important for the job in question, using similar principles to those used in gender/race cases.

F6.2.9 Certain types of employment are exempted from the provisions of the legislation eg school teachers, members of the clergy and employment in a private household. In addition, the provisions also do not apply in relation to permitted instances of affirmative action (see paras **F6.2.13–F6.2.15**).

F6.2.10 As with gender, disability and racial discrimination, victimisation may also arise in relation to a complaint. This consists of treating a person less favourably than others are or would be treated in the same circumstances because that person has done, or intends to do, or is suspected of having done, something by reference to the Fair Employment legislation eg made a complaint of discrimination or given evidence as a witness for a complainant in the proceedings.

F6.2.11   In addition, art 19(b)(iii) of the Fair Employment and Treatment Order provides that it is unlawful for an employer to discriminate against a person in relation to employment in Northern Ireland 'by subjecting him to any other detriment'. This provision has found particular use in combating sectarian harassment eg displays of flags, symbols etc in the workplace.

F6.2.12   The aim of the Fair Employment legislation is to achieve a situation where there is proportionate representation of Protestants and Catholics in all types and levels of employment in Northern Ireland. Until recently, the body charged with promoting this aim was the Fair Employment Commission. Under the Northern Ireland Act 1998, this Commission is now the Fair Employment Directorate of the Equality Commission for Northern Ireland (FED).

F6.2.13   The FED has three main duties under the legislation:
- promoting equality of opportunity in employment between persons of different religious beliefs;
- working for the elimination of religious and political discrimination in employment;
- promoting affirmative action. Affirmative action is defined in art 4 of the 1998 Order as:

  'action designed to secure fair participation in employment by members of the Protestant, or members of the Roman Catholic, community in Northern Ireland by means including the adoption of practices encouraging such participation, and the modification or abandonment of practices that have or may have the effect of restricting or discouraging such participation'.

F6.2.14   To achieve these ends it imposes duties on employers registered with the FED. These duties are best expressed in the FED Code of Practice. Whilst this Code does not have the force of law, the 1998 Order provides that:

  'if any provision of the code appears to the Tribunal to be relevant to any question arising in the proceedings it shall be taken into account in determining that question.'

F6.2.15   Employers with more than 10 employees must register with the FED and monitor the religious composition of their workforce. Public sector employers are automatically registered. Registered employers must also review their workforce composition and employment practices at least once every three years in order to:
- determine whether members of each community are enjoying, and are likely to continue to enjoy, fair participation in employment;
- ensure, where this does not appear to be the case, that the employer determines reasonable and appropriate affirmative action and, where practicable, set goals and timetables.

F6.2.16   All employers with over 250 employees must also monitor all applications for employment. Details must then be submitted to the FED on an annual basis to enable it to consider whether the employer is complying with its duties under the Code.

F6.2.17   Since 1995, the upper limit on the damages that can be awarded for religious and political discrimination has been removed. In one of the largest settlements since, a Catholic prison officer received £60,000 in settlement of the case, which he had brought against the Northern Ireland Office following his dismissal. He alleged that he had been treated less favourably, in being dismissed, than a number of Protestant prison officers who had not been dismissed or adequately disciplined for matters more serious than those alleged against him.

F6.2.18   See para **E5.1.4**.

Note 1   Positive discrimination is also generally unlawful in Northern Ireland. However, as mentioned (see paras **F6.2.13–F6.2.15**, 'affirmative action' is actively encouraged in the context of religious and political discrimination. In relation to sex discrimination, there is a limited exemption for 'positive action' which allows employers to train women, or men, for work which has previously been wholly or mainly done by the other sex, but they may not discriminate in the selection for recruitment or promotion to such work. See the erstwhile Equal Opportunity Commission's publications 'Removing sex bias from recruitment and selection: A Code of Practice (1995)' and 'Equal pay: A Code of Practice (1998)'.

6.3   Unlawful Discrimination

F6.3.1   See para **E5.2.2**. Article 6 SDO. Substitute Northern Ireland for the reference to Great Britain.

Note 2   Article 5(1) of the RRO.

F6.3.2   See para **E5.2.3**. RRO.

F6.3.3   See para **E5.2.5**. SDO and RRO.

F6.3.4   See para **E5.2.17**. SDO and RRO.

F6.3.5   See para **E5.2.29**.

Note 1   Article 30 RRO; art 40 SDO.
Note 2   Article 3 RRO; art 41 SDO.

F6.3.6   See para **E5.2.30**.

Note 1   Article 4 RRO; art 6 SDO.

6.4   Equal Pay

F6.4.1   See para **E5.5.1**. Equal Pay Act (Northern Ireland) 1970.

F6.4.2   See para **E5.5.6**.

Note 1   Article 77(3) SDO.

F6.4.3   See para **E5.5.6**.

Note 1   Section 1(1) Equal Pay Act (Northern Ireland) 1970.

F6.4.4   See para **E5.5.12**.

Note 1   Section 1(4) Equal Pay Act (Northern Ireland) 1970.
Note 2   Section 1(2)(b) Equal Pay Act (Northern Ireland) 1970.
Note 3   Equal Pay (Amendment) Regulations (Northern Ireland) 1984.

F6.4.5   See para **E5.5.13**.

Note 1   Section 1(3) Equal Pay Act (Northern Ireland) 1970.

7   TERMINATION OF EMPLOYMENT

7.1   Background

F7.1.1   See para **E6.1.3**.
Northern Ireland should be substituted for the reference to Great Britain.

Note 1   Article 239 ERO.

7.2   Nature of Claims

F7.2.1   See para **E6.2.1**.

Note 1   Article 127(1) ERO.
Note 2   Article 127(1) ERO.

F7.2.2   See para **E6.2.7**.

Note 1   Article 127(1)(c) ERO.

F7.2.3   See para **E6.2.12**.

Note 1   Article 129(2) ERO.

7.3   Fairness of Dismissal

F7.3.1   See para **E6.3.1**. Article 130 ERO.

F7.3.2   See para **E6.3.2**.

Note 1   Article 130(2) and 130(1)(b) ERO.

F7.3.3   See para **E6.3.14**.

Note 1   Article 125 of ERO.

F7.3.4   See para **E6.3.15**. Article 130(4) ERO.

F7.3.5   See para **E6.3.17**. LRA Code of Practice on Disciplinary Practice and Procedures in Employment.

7.4   Remedies

F7.4.1   See para **E6.4.3**. The figure is £50,000 pursuant to art 33 of the Employment Relations (Northern Ireland) Order 1999.

7.5   Redundancy and Collective Dismissals

F7.5.1   See para **E6.5.1**. Article 174 ERO.

F7.5.2   See para **E6.5.6.**

Note 1   Article 118 ERO.

F7.5.3–F7.5.4   See para **E6.5.8.**

Substitute Northern Ireland of the reference to Great Britain.
Note 1   Article 171(1) ERO.
Note 4   Article 239(6) ERO.

F7.5.5   See para **E6.5.12.**

Note 1   Article 199 ERO.

F7.5.6   See para **E6.5.13.**

Note 1   Article 175(1), (3) and (4) ERO.

F7.5.7   See para **E6.5.15.**

Note 1   Article 173 ERO.

F7.5.8   See para **E6.5.16.**

Note 1   Article 245 ERO.
Note 2   Article 240 ERO.

F7.5.9   See para **E6.5.19.**

Note 1   Article 198(2) ERO.

F7.5.10   See para **E6.5.21.**

Note 1   Article 130(4) ERO.

F7.5.11   See para **E6.6.1.**

Note 1   Collective Redundancies and Transfer of Undertakings (Amendment)
Regulations (Northern Ireland) 1995. See also the Transfer of Undertakings
(Protection of Employment) Regulations 1981 (as amended) and art 216 ERO.

8   YOUNG WORKERS

8.1   General Obligations

F8.1.1   See para **E7.1.1.** The relevant legislation is the Children and Young
Persons Act (Northern Ireland) 1968 and Pt XII of the Children (Northern
Ireland) Order 1995. As a result of the latter, the law on most areas of child
protection is the same as that in England and Wales. The Health and Safety
(Young Persons) Regulations (Northern Ireland) 1997 follow the similarly
named English regulations. There is no direct equivalent of the 1998
regulations because the import of these had largely been dealt with already
in the Children Order.

F8.1.2   The Health and Safety (Young Persons) Regulations (Northern
Ireland) 1997 came into force on 1 October 1997 and perform the same
function in Northern Ireland as the English regulations ie to comply with
Directive 94/33/EC.

F8.1.3   The Children (Northern Ireland) Order 1995 protects children as follows:

- children cannot be employed at all if under 13;
- children cannot be employed before the close of the school day or for more than two hours a day on a day on which they are required to attend school (or before 7:00 or after 19:00);
- children cannot be employed in any occupation likely to be injurious to their life, limb, health or education (taking into account their physical condition);
- children cannot be employed in street trading;
- children cannot take part in a performance which would endanger their life or limbs;
- children under 12 cannot be trained to take part in dangerous performances.

Certain exceptions are permitted via a system of licences. For the purposes of this part of the Order, a child means a person below school leaving age.

F8.1.4   The Working Time Regulations (Northern Ireland) 1998 apply to young workers only, the provisions of the Directive in relation to children having been implemented in the Children Order.

9   MATERNITY AND PARENTAL RIGHTS

9.1   Background
F9.1.1   See para E8.2.1.

9.2   Protection from Dismissal
F9.2.1   See para E8.3.1.

Note 1   Article 131 ERO.

9.3   Health and Safety
F9.3.1   See para **E8.4.4**. Management of Health and Safety at Work (Amendment) Regulations (Northern Ireland) 1994 amending the Management of Health and Safety at Work Regulations (Northern Ireland) 1992.

F9.3.2   See para **E8.4.5**. The Management of Health and Safety at Work Regulations (Northern Ireland) 1992.

9.4   Maternity Pay
F9.4.1   See para **E8.5.1**. The equivalent legislation in Northern Ireland is the Social Security Contributions and Benefits (Northern Ireland) Act 1992, the Statutory Maternity Pay (General) Regulations (Northern Ireland) 1987 (as amended by the Statutory Maternity Pay (General) Regulations (Northern Ireland) 1988 and 1990). The Social Security Maternity Benefits and Statutory Sick Pay (Amendment) Regulations (Northern Ireland) 1994 implemented the pregnant workers' directive.

9.5 Additional Rights to Time Off

F9.5.1 See para **E8.6.1**. Maternity and Parental Leave Etc Regulations (NI) 1999. In Northern Ireland, parental responsibility is defined in art 6 of the Children (Northern Ireland) Order 1995.

F9.5.2 See para **E8.6.8**. Article 9 and Pt 11 of Sch 4 Employment Relations (Northern Ireland) 1999 inserting arts 85A and 85B into ERO.

10   BUSINESS TRANSFERS

10.1 Background

F10.1.1   See para **E9.1.2**. TUPE apply directly to Northern Ireland.

10.2 Duty to Inform and Consult

F10.2.1 See para **E9.7.1**. The equivalent rules are Collective Redundancies and Transfer of Undertakings (Amendment) Regulations (Northern Ireland) 1995.

11   COLLECTIVE RIGHTS

11.1 Background

F11.1.1   For many years, trade union law in Northern Ireland followed a different format and terminology from that applying in Great Britain. This has largely been remedied by the enactment of the Trade Union and Labour Relations (Northern Ireland) Order 1995. Whilst the Industrial Relations (Northern Ireland) Order is still in force, it has been significantly amended and repealed by the 1995 Order in order to bring Northern Irish law into line with that in Great Britain.

See para **E10.1.1**.

Note 1   Defined in similar terms by art 3(1) of the Industrial Relations (Northern Ireland) Order 1992.

11.2 Compulsory Recognition of Unions

F11.2.1   See para **E10.2.1**. In Northern Ireland, the Labour Relations Agency performs a roughly analogous function although on a less formalised basis. See art 97 of the Trade Union and Labour Relations (Northern Ireland) Order 1995 and art 127 of the Trade Union and Labour Relations (Northern Ireland) Order 1995.

11.3 European Works Councils

F11.3.1 See para **E10.6.1**. The Transnational Information and Consultation of Employees Regulations 1999 apply to Northern Ireland.

12   EMPLOYMENT DISPUTES

12.1 Background

F12.1.1 See paras **E11.1–E11.1.3**. There is no Employment Appeal Tribunal (EAT) in Northern Ireland. Appeals are made by way of case stated to the Northern Ireland Court of Appeal.

12.2 Labour Courts/Tribunals

F12.2.1 See paras **E11.2.1–E11.2.4**. Despite initial intentions, the Industrial Tribunal in Northern Ireland cannot be described as informal. Procedural rules are adhered to strictly, even to a greater extent than in the Courts proper.

13   WHISTLEBLOWING/DATA PROTECTION

13.1 Whistleblowing

F13.1.1 See para **E12.1.1**. The corresponding legislation is the Public Interest Disclosure (Northern Ireland) Order 1998.

F13.1.2 See para **E12.1.4**.

Note 1   Public Interest Disclosure (Northern Ireland) Order 1998, arts s 67C–67H.

13.2 Data Protection

F13.2.1 See para **E12.2.1**. The Data Protection Act 1998 extends to Northern Ireland.

14   HUMAN RIGHTS

14.1 Rights and Obligations

F14.1.1 See para **E13.1.1**. As in England and Wales, the Human Rights Act 1998 came into force in Northern Ireland in October 2000.

F14.1.2 See para **E13.1.2**. In addition to the protection afforded by the new Act, Northern Ireland has a Human Rights Commission (instituted by the Northern Ireland Act 1998) which is required (inter alia) to advise the Secretary of State on the enshrinement of rights supplemental to the European Convention on Human Rights that might be considered necessary in the context of the particular circumstances that apply in Northern Ireland. The Commission has interpreted this duty as requiring the implementation of a Bill of Rights for Northern Ireland. The development of this bill is still at a consultative stage but it is expected to be presented to the Secretary of State for implementation purposes towards the end of 2001. For the purposes of this chapter, it should be noted that the Commission has issued a pamphlet on Social and Economic Rights and it must be anticipated, therefore, that additional employment rights could find their way into the legislation.

USEFUL WEBSITES

The website www.legal-island.com is a particularly useful resource. Legislation and even some case law can be accessed via this site. It also includes links to other sites of interest, for example, the Directorates for Equal and Fair Employment (www.eocni.org.uk, www.fec-ni.org). The Northern Ireland Assembly's site can be found at www.ni-assembly.gov.uk.

G   Finland

Jan Kuhlefelt

Jan Kuhlefelt is a Partner at Castrén & Snellman, Helsinki. He has work experience as a judge at the District Court of Raasepori 1986. He is a member of various professional organisations: Finnish Bar Association, Union of Finnish Lawyers and the Juridiska Föreningen i Finland.

Castrén & Snellman, Helsinki

Phone: +358-9-228 58 338
Fax: +358 9 228 58 371
Email: jan.kuhlefelt@castren.fi
Website: www.castren.fi

FINLAND

Rights	Yes/No	Explanatory Notes
CONTRACTS OF EMPLOYMENT		
Minimum notice	YES	Between 14 days and six months (employer's notice)
Terms:		
Express	YES	
Implied	YES	Although relationship is essentially a contractual one
Incorporated by statute	YES	Although relationship is essentially a contractual one
REMUNERATION		
Minimum wage regulation	NO	
Further rights and obligations:		
Right to paid holiday	YES	2–2½ days paid holiday per month
Right to sick pay	YES	Paid sick leave for seven days of illness
WORKING TIME		
Regulation of hours per day/ working week	YES	Maximum 40 hours per week
Regulation of night work	YES	Notification of night work (between 23:00 and 06:00) necessary
Right to rest periods	YES	One hour rest in every six hour working period
EQUAL OPPORTUNITIES		
Discrimination protection:		
Sex	YES	
Race/origin/colour	YES	
Marital status	YES	
Disability	YES	
Political/trade union activity	YES	
Religion	YES	
Age	YES	
Sexual orientation	YES	
Equal pay legislation	YES	
TERMINATION OF EMPLOYMENT		
Right not to be dismissed in breach of contract	YES	Unless breach is serious
Statutory rights on termination	YES	Unfair dismissal

REDUNDANCY/ COLLECTIVE DISMISSALS

Statutory definition	YES	Collective dismissals are regulated by statute
Right to payment on redundancy	NO	

Right to consultation:

Collective	YES	

YOUNG WORKERS

Protection of children and young persons at work	YES	

MATERNITY RIGHTS

Right to maternity leave	YES	105 days' paid leave
Maternity pay (during leave)	YES	Social security benefit
Protection from dismissal	YES	Statutory protection – unfair dismissal/sex discrimination
Health and safety protection	YES	
Right to parental leave	YES	32 weeks – can be shared by parents
Right to paternity leave	YES	18 days
Right to time off for dependants	YES	

TRANSFERS OF BUSINESSES

Right to protection on transfer	YES
Transfer of employment obligations	YES
Right to information and consultation	YES
Right not to be dismissed	YES

COLLECTIVE RIGHTS

Recognition of trade unions	YES	
European works councils	YES	
Right to take industrial action	YES	But strictly regulated

EMPLOYMENT DISPUTES

Civil court jurisdiction	YES	
Statutory Body	YES	The Labour Courts for matters connected with collective agreements

WHISTLEBLOWING

Protection from dismissal/ detriment	NO

DATA PROTECTION

Protection	YES

HUMAN RIGHTS ACT

Statutory protection of human rights

Public authority	YES
Private organisations	NO

1   THE EMPLOYMENT RELATIONSHIP

1.1   Background

G1.1.1   The Finnish legal system is based on statute law. However, the law has not properly been codified in the Continental sense of the term. There is no Civil Code in Finland, but there are numerous independent laws adopted by the Parliament and based on a Government Bill. The precedents of the highest courts (Supreme Court and Supreme Administrative Court) have no binding effect. However they are followed quite closely. In some unregulated areas and issues customary law may have binding effect.

G1.1.2   In the beginning of the last century the industrialisation and the emerging political power of employees provided a basis on which to review the legislation concerning individual employment contracts. After difficult preparation, an Employment Contracts Act was enacted in 1922, replacing the Servant's Act 1865 and the provisions on employment contracts of the Trades Act 1879. The Employment Contracts Act was replaced in 1970 by an Act with the same name (ie Employment Contracts Act 320/1970 introducing several new principles, such as non-discrimination and job security.

G1.1.3   One of the main principles of Finnish labour legislation has been to provide protection to the weaker party in an employment relationship ie the employee. A clear expression of this policy is the mandatory legal requirements for the protection of employees; the main body of Finnish labour law is of general application, avoiding unnecessary categorisation. An important policy has also been to avoid rights that could be regarded as privileges to a certain category of employees. However, the rule of general applicability is not a rule without exceptions. Certain groups of employees have been regarded as needing special protection. The essence of the Finnish labour relationship is contractual, although it is evident that the modern employment relationship is governed more and more by statute. The provisions in legislation generally set minimum conditions to be freely exceeded, at least for the benefit of the employee, by contract between the employer and the employee.

THE NEW ACT

G1.1.4   The Finnish Parliament has enacted a new Employment Contracts Act (55/2001), which will come into force on 1 June 2001 and will replace the old Employment Contracts Act (320/1970) as amended). The new Act has amended the wording of many sections of the old Act and also the structure of the Act (ie the order of the sections) in order to make the act easier to understand. However, there are few major changes in the actual content of the legislation.

G1.1.5   The new Act is divided into Chapters. The titles of the Chapters are as follows:
1   General Provisions;
2   The Obligations of the Employer;

1.2   Contract of Service

A   CONTRACT AND ITS WRITTEN PARTICULARS

G1.2.1   Every person who has reached the age of 15 may enter into an employment contract as an employee. The employer may be either a physical or a legal entity. Employment contract is defined in the Employment Contracts Act (320/1970 as amended), s 1, as a contract whereby one party, the employee, undertakes to perform work for the other party, the employer, under his direction and supervision in return for wages or other remuneration. This definition includes the central parts of Finnish labour law, the employer, the employee and the employment relationship (the legal relationship between the employer and the employee).

Thus, the employment relationship according to Finnish labour legislation includes four central characteristics:

- the employment relationship must be based on a contract, which means that, for example, military servicemen, prisoners etc remain outside the scope of labour law;
- the aim of the employment contract must be that one of the contract parties performs work for the other party. Thus, a contract that aims to perform work for a third party is not an employment contract;
- the work shall be performed in return for wages or other remuneration, which means that charity and work otherwise performed for free does not constitute an employment relationship. However, it should be taken into account that the remuneration need not be money. It can, for instance, consist of work performed in return for work. It is expressly stated in the new Employment Contracts Act (55/2001) that a relationship is regarded as an employment relationship, although the parties have not agreed the terms of remuneration, if it is evident from the facts that the parties have not intended the work to be done without remuneration;
- The party who is performing the work does so under the direction and supervision of the party for whom the work is to be done.

G1.2.2 However, the contract of employment need not expressly contain any of the above mentioned characteristics, so that in cases where it is unclear whether an employment relationship exists, one must weigh up several factors. For example, the existence and the form of supervision and direction of the one party over the other and the type of remuneration that is given in return for the work performed. The definition of an employee in Finnish law is broad. Work done at home and work done with the employee's machines may constitute an employment relationship.

G1.2.3 Whereas only the conditions that have been agreed upon by the employer and the employee are covered by the employment contract, different types of norms (eg mandatory rules of law, a generally applicable collective agreement (see paras **G1.2.12–G1.2.14**)) may come into effect in an employment relationship.

G1.2.4 'Employment contract' is defined in the new Employment Contracts Act (55/2001), s 1, as 'a contract whereby an employee undertakes personally to perform work for an employer under his direction and supervision in return for wages or other remuneration'. Even though the wording has been very slightly amended, the content of the definition remains the same as under the present Act.

B TERMS OF THE CONTRACT

G1.2.5 According to the Employment Contracts Act (320/1970 as amended), a contract of employment may be in any form, orally or in writing, or it may even be based on a conclusion of fact. In the case of an oral agreement, each party shall, upon request of the other party, provide a written certificate stating the contractual conditions.

G1.2.6 The new Employment Contracts Act (55/2001) states that an employment contract may be concluded orally, in writing or electronically. An employer must provide to an employee, who is employed for a period longer than one month, a written statement containing the essential terms of the employment relationship, unless such terms are included in a written employment contract.

G1.2.7 An employment contract may be for a specified period, or for an indefinite period with the possibility of termination by giving notice. According to the Employment Contracts Act (320/1970 as amended), s 2, a contract of employment may only be for a specified period set by the employer if:

(a) the nature of the work so requires;
(b) the person is engaged as a substitute only;
(c) it is an apprenticeship or equivalent;
(d) the employer has any other justified reason for the conclusion of a contract of employment; or a specified period, which relates to the operations of the business or to the work to be performed.

An employment contract for a specified period that conflicts with these limitations is deemed valid for an indefinite period of time.

G1.2.8 An employment contract for a specified period in excess of one year should be in writing. A contract of employment that is not in writing becomes a contract for an indefinite period, one year from the date when the contract began. The provisions of the Employment Contracts Act (320/1970 as amended) are in parts mandatory so that exceptions can only be made for the benefit of the employee. For some parts, exceptions can be made only by a collective agreement, but in most cases the employer and the employee can make exceptions to the provisions of Employment Contracts Act (320/1970 as amended) for the benefit of the employee.

G1.2.9 It is now enacted in Chapter 1, section 3[1] of the Employment Contracts Act (55/2001) that an employment contract is for an indefinite period unless it has been made due to a justified reason for a definite period. If an employment contract has been made for a definite period without a justified reason and this is due to the employer's (not employee's) suggestion, the contract will be regarded as made for an indefinite period. The same applies where the parties have, without a justified reason, entered into successive contracts for a definite period. In contrast to the Employment Contracts Act (320/1970 as amended) the new Employment Contracts Act (55/2001) does not list the only justifiable reasons for a definite period. In addition, it will no longer be mandatory to do a contract for a specific period exceeding one year, in writing.

[1]   Chapter 1, section 3 is the new equivalent to the Employment Contracts Act (320/1970 as amended), s 2. The new Employment Contracts Act (55/2001) is divided into Chapters and these Chapters are divided into sections, each Chapter starting from section 1. When references are made to the sections of the new Act, it is always necessary to indicate the relevant Chapter as well. In Finnish legal literature the typical method of indication is, for instance, 1:3 (ie Chapter 1, section 3).

C   EXPRESS TERMS

G1.2.10   Although a contract of employment does not have to follow any specific form it should expressly include provisions concerning at least the following matters:

(a) the parties;
(b) the first date of work;
(c) the specified period of the work (when necessary);
(d) the place where the work shall be performed;
(e) the content of the work;
(f) the remuneration;
(g) the period of payment;
(h) working time;
(i) annual holiday and the holiday bonus;
(j) sick pay;
(k) notice.

G1.2.11   It can also be useful to include provisions concerning the following matters (when considered necessary):

(a) increase in the remuneration;
(b) training organised by the employer;
(c) travel expenses;
(d) permission to have a secondary occupation.

D   IMPLIED AND INCORPORATED TERMS

G1.2.12   Although the individual employment relationship is basically a contractual one and contains terms agreed in the individual contract of employment, the Employment Contracts Act (320/1970 as amended extends the scope of certain collective agreements beyond the limits set in them. According the Employment Contracts Act, s 17:

> 'in the contract of employment or otherwise in the employment relationship the employer shall comply with at least such wage and other conditions as are prescribed for the work concerned or the activity most closely comparable thereto in the national collective agreement which may be deemed to be general practice in the branch concerned.'

Thus, if a national collective agreement can be regarded as effective in the field concerned its terms shall be applied as minimum conditions by all employers in this field. The notions 'national', 'deemed to be general' and 'the branch concerned' have not been defined in the provisions in question. A collective agreement concluded by national associations on both sides will usually be a national agreement, as may an agreement concluded by a national association of employees and the leading employer or the leading employers in the branch concerned. The 'field concerned' is either the industry or the craft in question.

G1.2.13   It is important to note that national general collective agreements generally contain obligations for the employer and rights for the benefit of the employee. It is legally irrelevant whether the employer or the employee is contractually bound by the agreement. The collective agreement contains obligations for the employee and rights for the employer only when the employer and the employee are bound by the agreement according to the Collective Agreements Act.

G1.2.14   The Employment Contracts Act (320/1970 as amended), s 17, has become the new Employment Contracts Act (55/2001), Ch 2, s 7. The wording of the section has been amended but the content of the section remains the same. According to section 7, the employer shall comply with at least the same terms and conditions as are prescribed in the national collective agreement which may be deemed to be general practice in the branch concerned or the activity most closely comparable thereto. This does not, however, concern the employer who is bound to a collective agreement (other than the general practice) with a national employment union.

E   STATUTE

G1.2.15   The employment relationships according to Finnish labour law provisions are in principle based on contracts, although it appears that the modern employment relationship is governed more and more by a statute. The provisions in legislation generally set minimum conditions to be freely exceeded, at least for the benefit of the employee, by contract between the employer and the employee. There are numerous statutory provisions setting minimum conditions to a contract of employment and all of them cannot be dealt with here. However, in cases concerning conflicts of norms

281

in the individual employment relationship the normal order of priority in the field of diverse Finnish labour regulation is as follows:

---

(1) the absolute rules of law;
(2) the norms in a collective agreement which are generally applicable;
(3) the norms in a collective agreement which bind the parties;
(4) the absolute statutes from which one can deviate through a collective agreement;
(5) the provisions in an employment contract;
(6) the conditions in a collective agreement from which one can deviate in an employment contract.

1.3 Variation of Contract

G1.3.1 The employment relationship is based on an employment contract. This contract is legally binding and cannot be altered unilaterally. After the beginning of an employment relationship it is only possible for a party to withdraw from the employment contract by observing the term of notice. Furthermore, the employer must have a reason for the termination provided by the Employment Contracts Act (320/1970 as amended).

G1.3.2 During the course of an employment relationship the terms of the employment contract may be altered only by mutual consent or, if terminated unilaterally, the existing contract can be terminated by giving notice and offering employment under a new contract of employment with new terms.

G1.3.3 As mentioned at para **G1.3.1** if the employer wants to introduce changes, which the employee does not accept, the employer must first have legal grounds for termination. If such legal grounds exist, the changes to the contract become valid on expiry of notice.

G1.3.4 Unless the employee accepts a unilateral change to the agreement, he may stop working after the expiry of notice and claim compensation for illegal serving of such notice. If a change to the contract is made without an employee's express consent and he continues working without objection, it is arguable that he has relinquished his right to object to the changes in question.

1.4 Remedies

G1.4.1 The main remedies for breaches of duties in the employment relationship are the right to terminate the employment contract and the right to damages. A punishment (fine or imprisonment) is also possible in certain cases. Termination by the way of cancelling the contract of employment is governed by the Employment Contracts Act (320/1970 as amended), s 43, and the provisions concerning liabilities in damages for breach of contract are for the most part in s 51. These issues are treated in detail later at paras **G6.1.1–G6.6.5**.

G1.4.2   Termination by way of cancelling the contract of employment is governed by the new Employment Contracts Act (55/2001), Ch 8. Damages as remedies are dealt with under the Employment Contracts Act (55/2001), Ch 12.

2   REMUNERATION

2.1   Background

G2.1.1   In an employment relationship, the main obligation of the employer is remuneration. It is the counterpart of work performed by the employee. The provisions concerning remuneration are in the Employment Contracts Act (320/1970 as amended), ss 18–31.

G2.1.2   The provisions concerning remuneration can be found in the new Employment Contracts Act (55/2001) Ch 2, ss 10–17.

2.2   Legal Regulation of Remuneration

G2.2.1   In Finland there is no general minimum wage system and in principle, the terms of remuneration can be freely agreed between the parties. The Employment Contracts Act on the other hand does contain general provisions on the different kinds of wages; the basis for fixing the wage, the time and the place, and manner of payment, as well as the employee's right to a wage during the time he has been unable to work on account of causes brought about by the employer, or on account of unavoidable or comparable hindrances (eg fire or an exceptional natural event) or on account of the employee's illness. However, the relevant collective agreement must be taken into consideration and for most employees the collective agreement has the essential effect of a minimum wage system. According to the Employment Contract Act (320/1970 as amended), s 17:[1]

> 'the employer shall comply with at least such wage and other conditions as are prescribed for the work concerned or the activity most closely comparable thereto in the national collective agreement which may be deemed to be general practice in the branch concerned'.

[1]   The equivalent provision in the new Employment Contracts Act (55/2001) can be found at Ch 2, s 7.

G2.2.2   The wages must be paid in legal tender according to the Employment Contract Act (320/1970 as amended), s 18.[1] However, an agreement between the parties may be made for the employee to receive goods or other benefits in kind (such as a right to a residence, car or food) as part of his remuneration, or in addition to his pay, or for other remuneration the value of which can be assessed in monetary terms.

[1]   The equivalent provision in the new Employment Contracts Act (55/2001) is at Ch 2, s 16.

G2.2.3 Remuneration may be based on the time spent on the work or on results or on any other agreed criteria. Wages in money shall be paid in respect of each pay period. The remuneration shall be paid on the last workday of each month, unless otherwise agreed (Saturdays excluded). Where an agreement provides for the remuneration to be paid into the employee's bank account, any expenses entailed shall be borne by the employer. Unless otherwise agreed, the remittance or the transfer order must be sent in such time that the remuneration may be presumed to be at the disposal of the employee on the due date. Upon the employee's request, the employer shall give the employee a certificate stating the amount of the wages paid to him.

G2.2.4 If an employee who has been employed for at least one month is prevented from performing his work by an illness or accident, neither caused by him wilfully nor by his gross negligence, he is entitled to receive his wages during the period of disability up to the end of the seventh working day following the day on which the disability began.

G2.2.5 If the employer is entitled to give notice to terminate a contract of employment or to cancel it (these issues are dealt with at paras G3.3.1–G3.38), he has the right to lay off the employee at 14 days notice and to suspend the work and the payment of wages until further notice or for a specified period. The employee may be laid off like this for no more than 90 days where the amount of work has temporarily diminished and the employer cannot reasonably arrange for other work or training relevant to his needs.

2.3 Deductions from Wages

G2.3.1 In Finland there is no special provision concerning deductions from wages in general. However, the principles of set-off are, with certain limitations, applied to deductions. Some deductions are also made compulsory for the employer by laws or collective agreements.

G2.3.2 The requirement for set-off is that the employer has an undisputed due claim, specified as a sum of money, from the employee. The absolute maximum amount an employer can deduct from an employee's wages is set out in the Execution Act, Ch 4, ss 6–8. According to the Execution Act, no more than one-third of the wages may be taken in execution or deductions. The employer may never make deductions that would leave the employee with less money than minimum income. A special minimum income limit has been set at Fmk 97 per day per employee. This is increased by Fmk 35 per every person (child, wife etc) dependant on the employee's support. The employer may not deduct more than three-quarters of the wages that exceed the minimum income. When counting the deductions the net income is used and all kinds of remuneration are considered. An agreement enabling larger deductions is void.

Lawful deductions
The following are lawful deductions:
• withholding of tax;

- compulsory social insurance ie retirement pension, unemployment, accident and group life insurance as well as social security;
- recovery of a debt by a court's enforcement order;
- deduction because of the worker's participation in a strike or other industrial action;
- employer's lockout;
- deduction by reason of an overpayment;
- trade union membership fee;
- agreement-based deductions.

G2.3.3 Withholding of income taxes is compulsory for all employers, as is the deduction of compulsory social insurance and the recovery of debt by a court's enforcement order. These deductions must follow the rules set out in statutes. Deduction by reason of the worker's participation in a strike is based on the negligence of the employee's main contractual duty. The employer's right not to pay wages during a lockout is based on a Supreme Court precedent (KKO 1993:39). Deduction by reason of an overpayment is possible based on the principles of unjust enrichment and set-off (described at para **G2.3.2**). In some cases the employer's right to make this deduction can be adjusted in the favour of an employee. Trade union membership fee deduction is based on collective agreements, in most of which this deduction has been declared compulsory.

G2.3.4 Deductions based on agreement are valid as long as the limits set out in the Execution Act, Ch 4, ss 6–8, are not exceeded and the agreements do not conflict with other binding provisions. Voluntary insurance falls into this category. In an employment contract an employee may be made liable, for instance, for cash deficit and accordingly such a deduction is possible. Disciplinary deductions may also be made on agreement bases.

2.4   Itemised Pay Statement

G2.4.1 There is no provision concerning itemised pay statements in Finnish law. However, such a provision is in most of the collective agreements. This means that most Finnish workers are entitled to receive an itemised pay statement once in a month.

G2.4.2 According to the new Employment Contracts Act (55/2001), Ch 2, s 16, the employer must give to the employee an itemised pay statement when the payment of the salary is made.

3   FURTHER RIGHTS AND OBLIGATIONS

3.1   Holiday Entitlement

G3.1.1 The Annual Holidays Act (272/1973) shall be applied to the employer and employee as specified in the Employment Contracts Act (320/1970 as amended). The Annual Holidays Act shall not in any business, establishment or undertaking be applied to members of the employer's family unless the business regularly employs other employees. In addition, the Act shall not apply to any person whose remuneration consists solely of a share in the profits. The annual holidays of seafarers are the subject of special provisions.

G3.1.2 According to the Annual Holidays Act (272/1973), s 3, an employee is entitled to two weekdays of paid holiday for each full holiday credit month. A full holiday credit month is defined as a calendar month that is part of the holiday credit year and during which an employee has been working for the employer at least 14 days. An employee whose employment has lasted for at least one year, without interruption, by the end of the holiday credit year immediately preceding the holiday season, shall be entitled to two and a half weekdays of holiday for each full holiday credit month. The holiday credit year begins on 1 April and ends on the last day of March in the next year.

G3.1.3 A full holiday credit month is defined as a calendar month of the holiday credit year (ending on the last day of March preceding the holiday period), if the employee has worked for the employer on at least 14 days during the said calendar month. If, according to the employee's contract, employment comprises so few working days that he would not be at work for 14 days in any one month, or if for the same reason only some of the calendar months include at least 14 working days, then a holiday credit month shall be defined as being a calendar month during which the employee has worked at least 35 hours for the employer.

G3.1.4 According to the Annual Holidays Act (272/1973), s 4, the holiday season is the period between 2 May and 30 September inclusive. Annual holiday shall be granted as a summer holiday within this period at a time determined by the employer. That part of the holiday which exceeds 24 days shall, however, be granted as a winter holiday at a time determined by the employer, after the holiday season and before the beginning of the holiday season of the following year. Before determining the holiday dates, the employer shall provide the employee or his representative with an opportunity to express an opinion concerning when the holiday should take place. If the granting of annual holiday within the periods defined in s 4 hinders the operations of a business due to the seasonal nature of the work, holiday may be granted during the calendar year in which the holiday credit year in question ends.

G3.1.5 The workers who, due to the ending of a working relationship or too few working days/hours, do not have the right to an annual paid leave, have the right to holiday remuneration from the employer. This remuneration, in cases where the employee due to too few working days/hours does not qualify for the annual leave, is 8.5% of the employee's wages during the holiday credit year. When leave is compensated with money because of the ending of the employment relationship, the basis for calculating the remuneration is the length of the leave the employee has earned during the holiday credit year. The remuneration is the amount of the wages to which the employee would earn if he would work that time. The provisions concerning this matter are in the Annual holidays Act (272/1973), ss 7–10.

3.2 Sick Pay

G3.2.1 According to the Employment Contracts Act (320/1970 as amended), s 28, para 1,[1] if an employee who has been employed for at least one month is prevented from performing his work by illness or an accident neither caused by him wilfully nor by his gross negligence, he shall be entitled, while his employment continues, to receive his wages during the period of the said disability up to the end of the seventh working day following the day on which it commenced. In cases where a collective agreement is applied the period can be even longer.

[1] The equivalent provision in the Employment Contracts Act (55/2001) is at Ch 2, s 11.

G3.2.2 In cases where the employee has been employed for a shorter period than one month when the said disability commences, he is entitled to receive 50% of his wages during the period of disability. If the employee becomes entitled to daily sickness benefit under the Sickness Insurance Act (1963/364) at an earlier date, the time during which his wages are paid shall be reduced accordingly.

G3.2.3 According to the Employment Contracts Act (320/1970 as amended), s 28, para 2,[1] an employee's rights under the preceding paragraph may not be restricted except by collective agreement. Such provision in a collective agreement may be applied by an employer who is a party to it, even if the relevant employee is not bound by the agreement, where the conditions of employment are otherwise governed by the agreement. Employees are bound by a collective agreement when they are members of an association that is bound by the agreement. If the contract of employment so provides, any provision in the collective agreement may continue to be applied after the expiry of the relevant agreement until a new collective agreement takes effect. This is on condition that the said provision would have applied to the employment relationship if the original collective agreement had remained in force.

[1] The equivalent provision in the Employment Contracts Act (55/2001) is at Ch 13, s 7.

G3.2.4 Except for the Employment Contracts Act (320/1970 as amended), s 26,[1] which covers the employer's right of set-off, any amount paid to the employee by way of daily cash benefit or similar compensation from compulsory accident insurance or another insurance wholly or partly financed by the employer may be deducted from the wages payable under paragraph 1 of Section 28.[2]

[1] The equivalent provision in the Employment Contracts Act (55/2001) is at Ch 2, s 17.
[2] This is stated in the new Employment Contracts Act (55/2001) at Ch 2, s 11, para 3.

3.3 Miscellaneous Domestic Rights and Obligations

G3.3.1 Labour law legislation is guided by the policy of trying to provide legal protection to the weaker party in an employment relationship ie the employee. A clear expression of this policy can be seen in the legislation establishing mandatory legal minimum protection for employees. The principle of protection is relevant as a principle of interpretation in labour law. There is a principle of advantage in Finnish case law, which constitutes a special application of the principle of protection. The principle of advantage means that the normal treatment that is the most advantageous to the employee is to be applied in cases where there are a variety of possible options.

G3.3.2 In Finnish legal practice there is an established custom concerning the employer's right to interpret conditions of the employment relationship. According to custom the employees concerned are obliged to respect the employer's interpretation until the matter has been properly solved. The employer's right to interpret conditions of employment is not based on any specific law or conditions of collective agreements.

G3.3.3 The principle of reasonableness has as its goal the balance of rights and obligations of the employer and employee concerned. According to the Employment Contracts Act (320/1970 as amended), s 48, para 3,[1] if the application of any term in the contract of employment not related to wages manifestly breaches good practice or is otherwise unreasonable, such provision may be modified or disregarded.

[1] This is replaced in the new Employment Contracts Act (55/2001) by Ch 10, s 2: 'If the application of a provision in an employment contract is in breach of good practice or is otherwise unreasonable, such provision may be modified or discarded'. In contrast to the Employment Contracts Act (320/1970 as amended), the new section does not mention anything about provisions related to salary.

G3.3.4 Based on many international agreements to which Finland is a party, there is a section in the Employment Contracts Act (320/1970 as amended) which states that the employer shall treat his employees impartially without any unwarranted discrimination on the basis of origin, religion, age, political or trade union activity or any other comparable circumstance. This provision includes both the requirement of equality and prohibition against discrimination. Provisions on the prohibition of discrimination on the basis of sex are included in the Act on Equality between Women and Men. This Act includes general provisions forbidding discrimination in all areas of social life that have not been expressly excluded from its area of application.

G3.3.5 According to the Employment Contracts Act (320/1970 as amended), s 32,[1] the employer shall ensure safety at work and take all precautions that are reasonably necessary in view of the nature of the work, the working conditions and the employee's age, sex, skill and other qualifications, in order to protect him against employment accidents and health hazards arising out of the work. According to the Employment Contracts Act, s 32, para 2, in the event that a chemical substance, radiation or contagious disease connected with the work of a pregnant employee or with the circumstances of her workplace is considered to endanger the development of the foetus or the pregnancy, and it has not been possible to eliminate the hazard from the work or the circumstances of the workplace, the woman shall be transferred, if possible, to other tasks suitable in regard to her skills and experience, until the beginning of her maternity leave.[2] The Employment Contracts Act, para 3, states that the employer and the employee shall co-operate at the workplace to ensure and promote occupational safety and health.

1   The Employment Contracts Act, s 32, is replaced by the Employment Contracts Act (55/2001), Ch 2, s 3, according to which the employer shall ensure safety at work to protect employees against accidents and health hazards arising out of the work as laid down by the Protection of Labour Act.

2   The rights of a pregnant employee are enacted in the new Employment Contracts Act (55/2000), Ch 2, s 3 and have not altered significantly.

G3.3.6 A most important item of legislation in the field of employee protection is the Protection of Labour Act. It is a general law for an employee's protection. Under this act the employer has the duty to continually monitor the work environment and to immediately deal with shortcomings in order to avoid dangers. The basic principle gives the employer primary responsibility to organise the work, the work conditions and the work environment so that there is no damage or risk to health. This should already be covered in the planning of work conditions. In the final instance, an employee has the right to refuse to carry out a task which may bring about serious danger to the employee's or another employee's life or health. The labour protection representative has the right to stop work that may result in immediate or serious danger to the life or health of an employee. The labour protection representative is the employee's statutory representative in questions involving labour protection. If at least ten employees are working regularly at a working place they are obliged to elect from among them a labour protection representative for two calendar years.

G3.3.7 The employer or the employer's representative is responsible for ensuring that the Protection of Labour Act is followed. Employee protection is enforced by industrial inspectors. Industrial inspectors are civil servants who ensure that the legislation in the field of employee protection is followed. The Labour Council grants exceptions from provisions concerning employee protection. The Labour Council is an organ which has at least nine members. Three members, including the chairman, are impartial and the other members are-representatives of both employers and employees in equal numbers. Breach of the law is punishable by criminal procedure. Responsibility for breaches of the Protection of Labour Act may rest with producers, importers and sellers as well as with those who breach the law, remove a safety or warning installation or sign. The duties of combating health hazards connected with employment are covered in the Work Health Care Act 1978.

G3.3.8 Employment contracts concluded individually between employers and employees are regulated by the Employment Contracts Act (320/1970 as amended). Most of the Act's provisions are applicable unless otherwise agreed, but a number of provisions are mandatory.

A   EMPLOYEE'S OBLIGATIONS

G3.3.9 An employee shall, according to the Employment Contracts Act (320/1970 as amended), s 13,[1] perform the tasks assigned to him with care and in accordance with the instructions given by the employer within its authority as to the manner in which the work is to be performed, the nature and extent of the work and the time and place for its performance. He shall refrain from doing anything that is contrary to what may reasonably be expected from an employee in his position and might be liable to cause prejudice to the employer. According to the Employment Contracts Act (320/1970 as amended), s 14,[2] the employee shall observe the precautions required by safety at work and shall inform the employer of any faults and deficiencies in machinery, plant, tools or safety devices in his use or custody which may constitute a safety or health hazard.

[1] The equivalent provision in the Employment Contracts Act (55/2001) is at Ch 3, s 1.

[2] The equivalent provision in the Employment Contracts Act (55/2001) is at Ch 3, s 2.

G3.3.10 For the duration of the contractual relationship, the employee shall not, according to the Employment Contracts Act (320/1970 as amended), s 15,[1] para 1, exploit for his own use or divulge to a third party any of his employer's business or trade secrets that have been entrusted to him or otherwise come to his knowledge. Liability for damages shall rest not only with the employee who divulges a secret but also with the person for whose benefit the secret is divulged, if the latter person knew or should have known that the employee acted in breach of his duties. An employee shall not accept, stipulate or demand a gift or any other advantage in return or as a reward for favouring another in any business activity.

[1] The equivalent provision in the Employment Contracts Act (55/2001) is at Ch 3, s 4.

G3.3.11 Except with his employer's consent, an employer shall not, according to the Employment Contracts Act (320/1970 as amended), s 16,[1] para 1, carry out such work for another person or otherwise exercise such activity as would cause manifest prejudice to the employer as a competing activity contrary to fair employment practices. The employer shall be deemed to have given his consent, if at the time the contract of employment is made he is aware of the competing activity and no explicit agreement is made that it is to be discontinued.

[1] The equivalent provision in the Employment Contracts Act (55/2001) is at Ch 3, s 3.

G3.3.12 A court of law may, on the employer's application, cancel a contract of employment concluded in breach of the preceding paragraph and require the employee to refrain from exercising the competing activity. Anyone who engages a person whom he knows to be debarred from accepting such work, under these provisions or otherwise, on account of an earlier contract of employment, shall be liable jointly and severally with the employee for any damage thereby caused to the employer.

G3.3.13 For a particularly serious reason connected with the employment relationship, an agreement (restraint of trade agreement) can[1] limit the employee's right to:

- conclude an employment contract, after the employment has ceased, with someone who engages in a certain kind of business, profession or other operations competing with the employer; or
- engage by himself in such operations.

[1] The Employment Contracts Act (320/1970 as amended), s 16, para 1.

G3.3.14 In assessing the particularly serious reason referred to in the Employment Contracts Act (320/1970 as amended), s 16, para 1, the following, among other things, shall according to s 16a,[1] para 2, be taken into account:

- the nature of the employer's operations and the need for protection that arises from the preservation of a business or a professional secret or from special training organised by the employer for the employee; and
- the position and duties of the employee.

[1] The equivalent provision in the Employment Contracts Act (55/2001) is at Ch 3, s 5.

G3.3.15 The restraint of trade agreement may limit the employee's right to conclude a new employment contract or to engage in a trade for six months at most. The period of restraint may be, at most, a year if the employee can be considered to have received reasonable compensation for the disadvantage caused by the restraint. A contractual penalty linked with the restraint of trade agreement may not exceed the salary received by the employee during the six months prior to the termination of the employment. If no penalty has been agreed on, the provisions in the Employment Contracts Act, s 51, para 3,[1] shall apply to the employee's liability to indemnify damages incurred from the breach of such contract. The restraint of trade agreement does not bind the employee if the employment has been terminated because of the employer's breach.

[1] The equivalent provision in the Employment Contracts Act (55/2001) is at Ch 12, s 1, para 3.

G3.3.16 Any employee who fails to discharge his obligations under the Employment Contracts Act (320/1970 as amended) or his contract of employment wilfully or through negligence, or who through his wilful act or negligence affords grounds for the employer to cancel the contract under s 43, shall compensate the employer in accordance with the principles laid down in the Compensation for Damages Act 1412/1974, Ch 4, s 1, for any loss so caused.[1] The same principles shall apply to compensation for loss that a employee causes to his employer in the course of his work.

[1] Employment Contracts Act (320/1970 as amended), s 51, para 3.

B EMPLOYER'S OBLIGATIONS

G3.3.17 In the contract of employment or otherwise in the employment relationship, the employer shall, according to the Employment Contracts Act (320/1970 as amended), s 17, para 1, comply with at least such wage and other conditions as are prescribed for the work concerned or the activity most closely comparable thereto in the national collective agreement, which may be deemed to represent general practice in the business concerned. Paragraph 2 states that any part of the contract of employment that is contrary to the preceding paragraph shall be invalid and superseded by the corresponding provisions of the applicable collective agreement.

G3.3.18 The employer shall treat his employees impartially without any unwarranted discrimination on the basis of origin, religion, age, political or trade union activity or any other comparable circumstance. Equal treatment principles shall also apply when the employer engages personnel. Provisions on the prohibition of discrimination on the basis of sex are included in the Act on Equality between Women and Men (609/1986).

G3.3.19 The employer shall ensure safety at work and take all precautions that are reasonably necessary in view of the nature of the work and the working conditions as well as the employee's age, sex, skill and other qualifications in order to protect him against employment accidents and health hazards arising out of the work.[1]

[1] Employment Contracts Act (320/1970 as amended), s 32.

G3.3.20 The work shall, according to the Employment Contracts Act (320/1970 as amended), s 33, be arranged so as to give the employee sufficient time for rest, recreation and personal development as well as for the performance of his civic duties. Unless otherwise agreed or in accordance with prevailing practices in the business concerned, the employer shall supply tools and working materials.

G3.3.21 The principle of the general applicability of collective agreements is of central importance to the minimum obligations of an employer. The principle of general applicability means that even employers who are not members of an employer organisation and are not a party to any collective agreement are nevertheless obliged in certain cases to follow the terms of the relevant collective agreement. The duty to follow the general binding stipulations of the collective agreement applies only to the employer. Usually, binding collective agreements do not impose any duties on an employee but instead give the employee the right to demand that the employer apply the stipulations that are more advantageous to the employee than those in other provisions (eg labour contracts or law) dealing with similar matters.

G3.3.22 The employer's other duties eg the right to maternity, paternity and parental leave as well as child-care leave, are based on separate statutes in the Employment Contracts Act (320/1970 as amended). The Annual Holidays Act (272/1973) which guarantees the right to an annual holiday, the Hours of Work Act, the Protection of Labour Act, and other Acts impose a number of legal duties on the employer and grant a number of rights to the employee.

4 WORKING TIME

4.1 Background

G4.1.1 The new Working Hours Act (605/1996) became effective in 1996. During the enactment process the object was to enable the use of more flexible practices concerning working hours. The new Working Hours Act extended the possibilities to depart from its rules by means of negotiation. The leading principle of the Act is that the more equal the contracting parties are, the greater is the possibility of departure from its rules. On the other hand, contract terms that reduce employees rights guaranteed by the Act are null and void unless they are expressly permitted by the Act.

G4.1.2   The Working Hours Act gives detailed rules on the regulation of working time. Regular working hours shall not exceed eight hours a day or 40 hours a week. The regular weekly working hours can also be arranged in such a way that the average is 40 hours over a period of no more than 52 weeks. For certain kinds of work the normal working time can also be organised as periodic work with a maximum of 128 hours over three weeks or a maximum of 88 hours over two weeks. Some, mainly minor, provisions concerning the working hours have been taken to collective agreements.

4.2   Legislative Control

G4.2.1   The Working Hours Act (605/1996) shall apply to all work performed under an employment contract as referred to in the Employment Contracts Act (320/1970 as amended), s 1, para 1, or within a civil service employment relationship, unless otherwise provided. In addition, the Act on Young Employees (993/1993) applies to work performed by persons under the age of 18.

The Working Hours Act does not apply:

- to work that must be considered management of an undertaking, corporation or foundation or an independent part thereof by virtue of the relevant duties or of the employee's position or otherwise, or independent work directly comparable to such management;
- to employees who perform religious functions in the Evangelical-Lutheran Church, Orthodox Church or some other religious community;
- to work performed by an employee at home or otherwise in conditions where it cannot be considered a duty of the employer to monitor arrangement of the time spent on the work;
- to forest, forest improvement and timber-floating work or to related work, excluding mechanical forest and forest improvement work and short-distance timber transport performed off-road;
- to children's day-care in the home of the employee as referred to in the Children's Day-Care Act;
- to work performed by members of the employer's family;
- to reindeer husbandry;
- to fishing and processing of the catch immediately connected therewith;
- to work where the working hours have been separately prescribed or which has been exempted from working hour restrictions under some other Act concerning working hours; or
- to work performed by civil servants or by civil servants of the Frontier Guards covered by the Act on the Working Hours of Defence Force Civil Servants, unless otherwise prescribed by decree.

G4.2.2   Time spent on work and the time an employee is required to be present at a place of work at the employer's disposal are considered working hours.[1] Daily periods of rest as referred to in the Working Hours Act (605/1996), s 28, or based on agreement are not included in working hours if

293

the employee is free to leave the place of work during these times. Travel time is not included in working hours if it does not constitute work performance.

¹   Working Hours Act, Ch 2, s 4.

G4.2.3   Regular working hours shall not exceed eight hours a day or 40 hours a week.¹ The regular weekly working hours can also be arranged in such a way that the average is 40 hours over a period of no more than 52 weeks.

¹   Working Hours Act, Ch 3, s 6.

G4.2.4   Employers must always obtain the specific consent of the employee each time overtime is required.¹ Employees can, however, give their consent for short periods if the nature of the work arrangements so requires. The maximum amount of overtime during a four-month period is 138 hours, though 250 hours must not be exceeded in a calendar year.

¹   Working Hours Act, Ch 4, s 18.

4.3   Opting Out and Deviations from Working Time Regulations

G4.3.1   The working time regulations are binding. The situations where deviations from the working hours regulations are possible are described in the Working Hours Act, ss 20–21.

G4.3.2   The Working Hours Act, s 20, is entitled 'commencement and ending works'. It provides that deviations from the working hours regulations are possible in three cases which are:
*   A situation where some tasks must be done immediately before the start or after the end of regular working hours in order to enable the other workers (a majority of them) to work days of full length and keep the production rolling.
*   Corresponding executive work. Here the requirement of necessity is not as strict as it is for the work done by the blue-collar workers.
*   Exchange of information between the shifts.

G4.3.3   The commencement and ending work can be agreed upon in the employment agreement or otherwise.

G4.3.4   The Working Hours Act, s 21, is entitled 'emergency work'. It allows work to be done despite the working time regulations in emergency situations. The emergency requirement is fulfilled when there is a concrete and immediate risk of production interruption or a threat to someone's life, health or property. The emergency must be unexpected. The maximum length of emergency work is two weeks. Emergency work is not compulsory for the employee, so it must be agreed upon.

4.4   Night Employees

G4.4.1   Work carried out between 23:00 and 06:00 is considered night work.¹ An employer must notify the labour protection authorities of regular night work, when the said authorities so request. Labour protection authorities are eg local labour protection districts.

Night work is allowed by the Working Hours Act (605/1996):

- in period based work;[2]
- in work which has been divided into three or more shifts;
- in work which has been divided into two shifts, but only until 01.00;
- in the maintenance and cleaning of public roads, streets and airfields;
- in pharmacies;
- at newspapers and magazines, news and photographic agencies and in other media work, and in the delivery of newspapers;
- in service and repair work in undertakings, corporations or foundations which is necessary to allow work to proceed regularly, or in work which cannot be carried out simultaneously with the regular work of the workplace concerned or which is necessary in order to prevent or confine losses:
- at peat sites during the peat extraction season;
- at sawmill drying houses;
- in heating work at greenhouses and hot-air plants;
- with the employee's consent, in urgent sowing and harvesting, in work directly related to parturient farm animals or to the treatment of ill farm animals and in other such farm work which cannot be postponed due to its nature;
- with the employee's consent in bakeries; between 05:00 and 06:00 such consent is not, however, required;
- in work which is carried out almost completely at night due to its nature;
- with permission from and under conditions set by the exemption section of the labour protection board of the labour protection district, in work where the technical nature or other specific reasons so require.

---

[1]   Working Hours Act (605/1996), Ch 5, s 26.
[2]   Period based work means that regular working hours may in certain circumstances be arranged in such a way that it shall not exceed 120 hours over a period of three weeks or 80 hours over a period of two weeks.

G4.4.2   In particularly dangerous or physically/mentally highly stressful work laid down by decree or agreed upon by collective agreement,[1] working hours during a 24-hour period may not exceed eight hours if the work is carried out at night.

[1]   Working Hours Act (605/1996), s 40, para 1.

4.5   Rest Period

G4.5.1   If the working hours in a 24-hour required period exceed six, and an employee's presence at the workplace is not required, the employee must be granted a regular rest period of at least one hour within the shift, during which he is free to leave the workplace.[1] An employer and an employee can agree on a shorter rest period, but this may not be less than half an hour.

The rest period cannot be placed immediately at the beginning or the end of a work day. If working hours in a 24-hour period exceed ten, employees are entitled to a rest period of up to half an hour following eight hours of work.

[1]   Working Hours Act, Ch 6, s 28.

G4.5.2 If working hours in shift or period-based work exceed six, employees must be allowed a rest period of at least half an hour or an opportunity to eat while they are working. Motor vehicle drivers must be given a minimum of 30 minutes' rest in one or two periods for each work period of five hours and 30 minutes.

G4.5.3 Working hours must be organised to allow employees at least 35 hours of uninterrupted free time each week, preferably around Sunday.[1] The weekly free time can be arranged so that it averages 35 hours within a 14-day period. Weekly free time must, however, total at least 24 hours. Employees can be required to work on a Sunday or church holiday only when the work concerned is regularly carried out on the said days due to its nature, or when agreed upon in the employment contract or with the separate consent of the employees.

[1]   Working Hours Act (605/1996), Ch 6, s 31.

4.6 Remedies

G4.6.1 A defined period within which an action must be brought for remuneration, as referred to in the Working Hours Act (605/1996), is exceptional. While an employment relationship is in force, the entitlement to remuneration shall lapse if it is not claimed within two years from the end of the calendar year in which the entitlement arose.[1] Once an employment relationship ends, the claim concerning remuneration, must be filed no later than two years after the employment contract ends.

[1]   Working Hours Act, Ch 8, s 38, para 1.
[2]   Employment Contracts Act (320/1970 as amended), s 47c.

G4.6.2 An employer or an employer's representative who deliberately or out of carelessness breaches the Working Hours Act (605/1996) or rules and regulations issued under it (other than those concerning duty to pay, agreement, the form of a legal act, the working hour register or display) shall be fined for breach of the working hours regulations.

G4.6.3 Compliance with the Working Hours Act (605/1996) shall be supervised by the labour protection authorities such as the local labour protection district.

5   EQUAL OPPORTUNITIES

5.1 Background

G5.1.1 In Finland the non-discrimination rules and practices have their basis in the Constitution. There has been a provision in the Finnish constitution since its enactment in 1919, according to which 'all Finnish citizens are equal before the law'. However this provision has not always been considered to be directly applicable in the courts and used only to bind the legislator.

G5.1.2   This provision has grown in importance. In 1995 the provision adopted its present form, which is much wider than the old one. At present, the provision concerns not only Finnish citizens, but all the people. In the amendment of 1995, three whole new paragraphs were also added. The new second paragraph states that 'no one shall, without an acceptable reason, be treated differently from other persons on the ground of sex, age, origin, language, religion, conviction, opinion, health, disability or other reason that concerns his or her person'. The third paragraph promotes the rights and special protection of children. In the last paragraph, it is required that equality of men and women is to be promoted in the society, particularly in working life, and especially when it comes to wages and other conditions of employment. In 1999, this Form of Government, s 5, was transferred to the whole new Constitution of Finland (731/1999) and became s 6. The new constitution came into force on 1 March 2000.

G5.1.3   The provisions of the constitution mainly oblige the government officials, courts and even the Parliament, but it is argued in the Finnish legal literature, that these provisions may also have a direct horizontal effect on relations between private individuals or bodies. However in the area of labour law, this question does not have that much importance. That is due to the fact that today discrimination in working life is well covered by special laws. The provisions of the constitution have mainly an indirect effect as they regulate the competence of the Parliament to enact laws. In addition, the provisions of the constitution also affect the interpretation of the laws. The laws are to be interpreted so that decisions are in line with the principles found in the constitution.

G5.1.4   Laws that contain regulations concerning discrimination in working life are the Employment Contracts Act (320/1970 as amended), the laws of state and communal civil servants and the Act on Equality between Men and Women. In the Penal Code, the offences against all four of these laws are made punishable to a very large extent.

G5.1.5   Finland has ratified the European Convention for the Protection of Human Rights and Fundamental Freedoms as well as the United Nations' International Covenant on Civil and Political Rights. Therefore the provisions of these treaties which protect the equality of the people are also directly applicable in Finland, even though their direct effect is very limited due to the covering national laws.

5.2   Unlawful Discrimination

G5.2.1   The ILO Convention Concerning Discrimination in Respect of Employment and Occupation No 111, was taken into consideration when the Finnish non-discrimination statutes were enacted and all the requirements of this treaty have been met. In some respects Finnish law is even stricter (eg age discrimination, discrimination based on trade union membership).

G5.2.2 The Employment Contracts Act (320/1970 as amended), s 17, paras 3, 4,[1] states that:

> 'The employer shall treat his employees impartially without any unwarranted discrimination on the basis of origin, religion, age, political or trade union activity or any other comparable circumstance.'

> 'What has been laid down on equal treatment of employees in paragraph 3 shall apply also when the employer engages personnel.'

[1] The equivalent provision in the Employment Contracts Act (55/2001) is at Ch 2, s 2. According to this section, the employer shall not without a justified reason treat employees in a different way due to the 'employee's age, health, origin, sexual preferences, language, religion, opinion, family relations, trade union or political activity or any other comparable reason'. In addition, the employer shall otherwise treat the employees impartially unless there exists a justified reason [not to,] based on the employee's duties and position. The non-discrimination provision applies also when the employer engages personnel.

G5.2.3 This provision does not concern discrimination based on sex. There is a special law for the equality of men and women. This law does not apply to civil servants either, and they do form a major group of employees in Finland. However, there are similar non-discrimination provisions in the laws concerning civil servants as well. Despite some differences in the detail of these provisions they are interpreted just like the provisions in the Employment Contract Act (320/1970 as amended).

G5.2.4 The requirement of impartial treatment and prohibition of unwarranted discrimination means that all the employees in a similar situation are to be handled the same or equivalent way unless there is an objective reason to treat them differently. The employer does not only have to abstain from directly discriminating on the grounds set out in the relevant provisions, but he also has a general obligation to act so that the result is an equal treatment of all the employees. However, equal treatment does not mean that everybody should be handled exactly the same way. On the contrary, all the relevant differences must affect the decisions.

G5.2.5 To decide if an act discriminates or not, some kind of comparison is required. However the requirements for the comparison are not very strict. The treatment of the employee may, for example, be compared to the treatment of former employees of the company, to the treatment of other employees in the same branch or even quite abstractly to a presumed due treatment. Here the Finnish law differs again from the ILO standards.

G5.2.6 Warranted reasons for discrimination may be based on the real requirements of the work. For example, in Finland a civil servant or a telephone sales person has to be able to speak Finnish. To require that is not a discriminatory act. The law also allows positive discrimination. This is not explicitly stated in the statutes except when it comes to the equality of men and women, but affirmative action may always be taken to ensure the rights of those who are in a disadvantaged position based on their religion, age, etc. This right to reverse discrimination illustrates the aspiration to not only formal but to factual equality. To be lawful, this kind of action has to be consistent and systematic.

A   DIRECT AND INDIRECT DISCRIMINATION

G5.2.7   Finnish law does not make any distinction between direct and indirect discrimination. What matters is the outcome. If a practice or an act leads to factual inequality for an unwarranted reason, it is discriminatory and therefore prohibited irrespective of the factors upon which the employer nominally based his actions or what his intentions were.

B   VICARIOUS LIABILITY

G5.2.8   The term 'employer' in the non-discrimination provisions does not usually restrict the applicability of the rule. An act is considered to be committed by the employer if the person who carried it out had the competence to decide on things like that or he acted under the directions of his superior. In these cases, the person has acted on behalf of the employer and thus all the non-discrimination rules are applicable. This is also the case if the employer later approves the act either explicitly or implicitly.

C   OTHER DISCRIMINATION GROUNDS AND SITUATIONS

G5.2.9   In the Employment Contracts Act (320/1970 as amended), s 17, 'origin' can mean eg race, colour of the skin, national or ethnic origin. It is worth noticing that age and trade union activity are also among the prohibited segregation grounds. It is not permissible to let age affect decisions unless the nature of the task really requires that to be taken into consideration. In the courts, discrimination based on trade union membership is by far the most usual case.

G5.2.10   'Other comparable circumstances' mean eg language, disability, health condition, family status, opinion and sexual orientation. Even though these things are not mentioned in the Employment Contracts Act (320/1970 as amended) it is evident that they are among the prohibited grounds. They are either personal qualities which a person cannot change, or they fall into the category of his personal freedoms guaranteed under international conventions and in the Finnish constitution. Such factors cannot be discriminated against and are also referred to in the Penal Code, s 47, concerning discrimination at work.

G5.2.11   The Employment Contracts Act (320/1970 as amended), as well as the civil servant laws, prohibits discrimination in engaging personnel. However, because of the problems related to acquiring information concerning applicants, this provision has only a limited effect at best in the courts.

G5.2.12   The Employment Contracts Act (320/1970 as amended), s 37, concerns the termination of employment contracts. In the second paragraph of this section, certain matters are excluded from the permitted reasons for termination of an employment contract. These excluded matters include illness, provided that it has not resulted in a substantial and permanent reduction of the employees work capacity, participation in a legal strike, an employee's political, religious and other views and participation in public activities. The termination may be illegal if it discriminates in some other respect. Here it is worth noticing that freedom of association and freedom of speech are very well protected. Even if a person is an activist in an organisation that criticises the company very harshly, that activity may not be a ground for termination as long as the employee does his job well. A private person may also, for example, publicly express his concerns for the company's environmental plan as long as he sticks to facts.

D   EQUALITY BETWEEN SEXES

G5.2.13   The Act on Equality between Men and Women came into force in 1987 and has ever since played a very important role in making the sexes more equal. Before 1987, the non-discrimination rules of the Employment Contracts Act (320/1970 as amended) applied to discrimination between men and women.

G5.2.14   The non-discrimination provisions of the Act on Equality between Men and Women resemble the ones in the Employment Contracts Act (320/1970 as amended). However, there are several extra provisions. Many of these extra provisions require active measures. The aim of this law is clearly the material, and not only the superficial, equality of men and women. This aim is typical of a Nordic welfare state like Finland. Even though many of the goals of this law have been achieved, at least to a great extent, it remains a fact that there is a clear statistical difference in the wages of men and women, even within the same businesses.

G5.2.15   Finland has ratified the Convention on the Elimination of all forms of Discrimination against Women, and this convention is therefore directly applicable in Finland. However, because of the existence of the Act on Equality between Men and Women the treaty hardly has a direct effect.

G5.2.16   Although the central aim of the law is to improve the position of women in working life, this does not mean that it will not give any protection to men. The non-discrimination rules of this law apply equally to both sexes, but there are also provisions that directly promote women. This law applies to public employers as well as private employees. Public servants enjoy the same protection as other employees. The law is also not restricted to working life, but is applied in all areas of social life unless expressly excluded. The exceptions are family life and the practice of a religion. This means that whereas, for example, political organisations may not discriminate against men or women in choosing people to undertake tasks, congregations have the right to consider gender as a deciding factor in issues concerning the practising of their religion. Naturally, the law does not affect unofficial relations between private persons.

Non-discrimination rules

G5.2.17   The basic non-discrimination provision is in the Act on Equality between Men and Women, s 7. It covers all gender-based practices that directly or indirectly result in inequality between men and women. It expressly states that all discrimination based on pregnancy or giving birth, as well as discrimination based on motherhood and even fatherhood is considered to be based on gender and therefore illegal.

G5.2.18   In the Act on Equality between Men and Women, s 37, para 5, there is a presumption according to which termination of an employment contract is considered to be discriminatory if the terminated person is pregnant. In these cases, to avoid liability the employer has to show that the pregnancy was not the reason for the termination, and that he had a proper, not gender-related, reason for the termination. Similar presumptions are found in s 8, which specifies what is considered to be discriminatory in working life.

G5.2.19   One of the presumptions concerns recruitment. If a person with less education or experience is hired instead of a more educated and/or experienced person, and these persons are of different gender, the employer has to show that he had good objectively-justified reasons for his conduct. This provision protects both genders equally.

G5.2.20   Two other presumptions concern situations where a direct comparison to other employees in the same firm may be made, and as a result of this comparison it seems that gender could have been the reason for certain practices carried out there. One of these two presumptions requires equal pay for men and women for the same or equivalent jobs. Here the actual tasks are the deciding factors, not the title. The payment is to be interpreted widely, covering all kinds of remuneration from the work.

G5.2.21   An employer may never terminate an employee's contract during the employee's special maternity, maternity, paternity, parental or child-care leave. This rule is non-negotiable and applies to all situations, so the person on such leave has an extremely strong protection against termination. This rule is in the Employment Contracts Act (320/1970 as amended), s 37, para 5. After this kind of leave, the person has a right to return to his/her previous position at work or to equivalent tasks.

G5.2.22   In the Act on Equality between Men and Women, s 14, there is a ban on the discriminatory advertisement of jobs. A job must be offered to representatives of both sexes, unless there is a reason based on the nature of the work which means it can only be done by either men or women.

Acts that are to be held non-discriminatory

G5.2.23   In the Act on Equality between Men and Women, s 9, some actions are specially declared as non-discriminatory. Special protection given to women on the basis of pregnancy or giving birth is thus always considered non-discriminatory. Actions which seek the equality of men and women and are based on a plan are not considered discriminatory. This includes so-called positive discrimination: affirmative action is allowed in order to provide the representatives of one sex an opportunity to obtain a balance with members of the opposite sex. For example, a plan that gives special advantages to disabled persons would not be held to be discriminatory.

Sexual harassment and active promotion of equality

G5.2.24   In the Act on Equality Between Men and Women, s 6a, a special equality action plan is made compulsory to all employers with at least 30 employees. This plan has to be reviewed yearly. Employers have other active duties too. Section 7 states that every employer has to promote equality in a systematic way. This especially includes hiring both men and women and distributing the task evenly. An employer has to create equal advancement opportunities to everyone and make the working conditions suitable for both genders. The employer also has an obligation to prevent sexual harassment from happening in the workplace.

5.3   Disability Discrimination

G5.3.1   Finnish labour law does not specifically deal with disability discrimination. It is not mentioned as a ground for discrimination. However, it is unquestionably covered by the expression 'other comparable circumstances' in the general non-discrimination provision of the Employment Contracts Act (320/1970 as amended). It is a personal quality which a person cannot change. The general non-discrimination rules apply to disability discrimination. A person's condition of health is mentioned in the Penal Code, s 47, concerning discrimination at work and as the list is not exhaustive, discrimination based on disability may also be a ground for criminal liability.

5.4   Enforcement and Remedies in Discrimination Cases

A   CASES UNDER THE EMPLOYMENT CONTRACTS ACT

G5.4.1   Any term of an employment contract which is contrary to the statutory provisions which protect the equality of the employees is null and void. However, this does not affect the validity of the remainder of the contract.[1]

[1]   Employment Contracts Act (320/1970 as amended), s 50.

G5.4.2   The employer is liable to the employee for every loss caused by the employer's intentional or negligent breach of this law or the employment contract.[1] The wording of this provision is very wide, so it secures compensation for all kind of losses. However the level of restitution has stayed very reasonable. The idea is to cover the real losses, not to let the employee financially benefit from the fact that he has been discriminated against.

[1]   Employment Contracts Act (320/1970 as amended), s 51.

G5.4.3   All the acts committed, against the non-discrimination provisions of the Employment Contracts Act (320/1970 as amended), may also be a basis for criminal liability. The Penal Code, Ch 47, concerns labour offences and s 3 regulates discrimination crimes. Section 3 covers all kind of discrimination based on unfair reasons and also applies to recruitment situations. It does not require a breach of the material rules, but in practise that is always the case because the laws cover the same actions. The widest list of reasons held discriminatory in the Finnish law are to be found in this provision. It includes race, national or ethnic origin, colour of skin, language, sex, age, family status, sexual orientation, health, religion, social opinion, political or trade union activity. However the list is still not exclusive. The punishment is either a fine or imprisonment up to six months. There is no corporate criminal liability, but the employer or the representative of the employer may be responsible for the actions of subordinates where the employer or representative has neglected his/her duties to supervise. When judging who is to be punished for the discrimination, the persons' responsibilities, their position in the corporation, duties and authorities are to be considered.

G5.4.4 It is difficult in all discrimination cases to get sufficient information from the employer. There is no special provision in the Employment Contracts Act (320/1970 as amended) that provides a right for the person who believes that he has been discriminated against to obtain information concerning eg other employees' wages and other terms of their employment from the employer. This has a big impact because the burden of proof is on the employee. He has to show that it is likely that the employer has breached the non-discrimination rules. If he succeeds in this, the employer then has to show a due reason for his actions to avoid liability. The right to hypothetical comparisons may ease the burden of proof.

B   CASES UNDER THE ACT ON EQUALITY BETWEEN MEN AND WOMEN

G5.4.5 Liability to compensate follows every breach of the non-discrimination rules. There is a special provision of this liability in the Act of Equality between Men and Women, s 11. The compensation does not directly depend on loss, and therefore it is called compensation, not damages. There are fixed limits for this compensation. Since 1998, the minimum compensation has been Fmk 15,600 and the maximum Fmk 51,900. This special provision does not affect the applicability of the provisions in the Damages Act. As a result, an employee may have the right to both compensation and damages simultaneously. The Damages Act requires wilfulness or negligence and is based on actual losses. The compensation paid under the Act on Equality between Men and Women is taken into consideration when deciding the amount of damages to award.

G5.4.6   In addition, if the employer neglects his duty to prevent sexual harassment in the workplace, that counts as a breach of the non-discrimination requirement and may lead to a liability to pay compensation. This liability is not attached to any other of the affirmative action regulations.

G5.4.7   Contrary to the Employment Contracts Act (320/1970 as amended), there is a special rule in the Act on Equality between Men and Women which gives the employee an extended right to get information from the employer in order to find out if he or she has been discriminated against. This means that the employee has the right to receive information concerning eg other employees' wages and other terms of their employment.

G5.4.8   A special monitoring and enforcement system has been created for the Act on Equality between Men and Women and provides for an the Equality Ombudsman and Council for Equality. The Equality Ombudsman monitors the observance of the Act on Equality between Men and Women and, in addition, advises and informally influences cases concerning equality between men and women. The Ombudsman, who has an office with staff, arbitrates, initiates actions, gives pieces of advice and instructions, and also prepares statements for cases in contravention of the Act. The Office of the Equality Ombudsman is a unit within the Ministry of Social Affairs and Health, which funds its operation. The services of the Ombudsman are free of charge. The actions of the Ombudsman are initiated by himself or by private people as well as organisations. The Ombudsman has the right to gain all the necessary information from companies and authorities to be able to control the equality practices of them. He may conduct inspections in workplaces, prohibit actions under threat of a fine and bring discrimination cases as well as discriminatory job advertisement cases before the Council for Equality.

G5.4.9   The Council for Equality's function is to promote social equality between men and women and to prepare reforms increasing equality. It does this by undertaking and co-ordinating research in the field of equality, by preparing and making legislative motions and by monitoring and promoting the implementation of the legislation. It may prohibit certain conduct in a particular case under the threat of a fine. It may also impose these fines and fines set by the Equality Ombudsman.

G5.4.10   Suspected breaches of the Act on Equality between Men and Women may also be submitted to a general lower court of justice. In addition to compensation and damages claims, an employee may claim eg that a term in the employment contract is to be held null and void. Thus he could also claim that he should be paid better wages. This right has however proved to be rather theoretical.

G5.4.11   Criminal liability is based on the same provision as in the case of the Employment Contracts Act (320/1970 as amended) violations (ie the Penal Code, s 47). All the breaches of the non-discrimination rules are covered, but neglecting the positive discrimination provisions does not lead to criminal liability.

5.5   Equal Pay

G5.5.1   Equal pay is covered by the general non-discrimination rules. However, because of the contractual nature of the remuneration, there always has to be another employee within the company with whom to compare the wages. Hypothetical comparison or comparators in other companies is not allowed. There is only one provision in the Act on Equality between Men and Women that explicitly concerns equal pay. It is in the form of a presumption: when a person has lower wages than a person of the opposite sex in the same or an equivalent job within the company, the difference in wages is presumed to depend on the sex and therefore held to be discriminatory. The actual tasks, not the titles, are the deciding factors. Wages are to be interpreted widely. The term covers all kinds of remuneration from the work.

6   TERMINATION OF EMPLOYMENT

6.1   Background

G6.1.1   An employment contract made for an unspecified period is normally terminated with notice given by one of the contracting parties to the other. It is possible for the term of notice to be fixed by an individual or by a collective agreement, but it may not exceed six months and must not be longer for the employee than the employer. If no express term of notice has been stipulated, according to the Employment Contracts Act (55/2001), Ch 6, s 3, the period to be observed by the employer is 14 days to six months depending on the length of the employment relationship in question.

G6.1.2   An employment contract lawfully concluded for a specified period comes automatically to an end when the agreed period ends or when the agreed-upon work has been completed.[1] There is no job security beyond the agreed period and neither of the parties may extend the contract against the will of the other party. However, the parties may renew the contract for a specified or indefinite period.

[1]   Employment Contracts Act (55/2001), Ch 6, s 1.

G6.1.3   The employment relationship may always be ended by mutual agreement. This means that if one of the parties wants to terminate the relationship, the other party may relieve him of the duty to observe the term of notice.

G6.1.4   In the case of a valid agreement for a trial period, either of the parties may terminate the employment relationship with immediate effect. Thus, during the trial period, no period of notice needs to be observed. Termination on discriminatory or other unfair grounds is unlawful but the employer need not show the unsuitability of the employee for the job.

G6.1.5   If serious grounds exist a contract of employment may be cancelled in accordance with the provisions of the Employment Contracts Act (320/1970 as amended).

6.2   Conditions and Choice of Law

G6.2.1   In Finland there are no special conditions concerning the employee, the length of the employment etc for bringing a case before a court.

G6.2.2   On 1 April 1999, the Rome Convention on the Choice of Law and Contractual Relationships came into force in Finland. At the same time, Finland bound itself to the EC regulations and the rulings of the European Court of Justice concerning these matters. The Employment Contracts Act (55/2001) Ch 11, s 1, refers to this convention. According to this convention, the applicable law is the one agreed upon by the parties. In the absence of an explicit agreement, the applicable law is the law of the country to which the contract has the closest connection.

6.3   Nature of Claims

A   TERMINATION IN BREACH OF CONTRACT

G6.3.1   Irrespective of the agreed period or term of notice, a contract of employment may be terminated/'cancelled' if serious grounds exist.[1] Such grounds may be considered as existing if the employee breaches or omits his duties under the employment contract or law so gravely that the employer cannot reasonably be expected to continue the employment relationship even for the period of notice. The employee may cancel a contract of employment irrespective of the agreed period or term of notice, if the employer breaches or omits his essential duties under the employment contract or law so gravely that the employee cannot reasonably be expected to continue the employment relationship even for the period of notice.

[1]   Employment Contracts Act (55/2001), Ch 8, s 1.

G6.3.2   According to the list, both the employer and the employee may terminate/'cancel' an employment contract if:
- one of the parties has misled the other in any important respect when agreeing the contract; or
- one of the parties through his carelessness, jeopardises safety at the workplace, assaults the other party or grossly insults him.

G6.3.3   According to the list an employer may terminate/'cancel' an employment contract if an employee:
- is unable to perform his duties for a permanent reason;
- wilfully or through gross negligence fails to fulfil his obligation to work – in spite of being warned of such conduct;
- is guilty of a serious breach of the Employment Contracts Act's provisions concerning business secrets and competing contracts of employment;
- comes to work in a state of intoxication or (in spite of rules prohibiting their use) uses intoxicants (alcohol, drugs etc) at the workplace.

G6.3.4   The employee is entitled to cancel the employment contract if:
- his remuneration is not paid according to the contract;
- he is not given a sufficient amount of work;
- the employee's reputation or morals (which are judged by generally accepted criteria) are jeopardised by the employment relationship.

B   UNFAIR DISMISSAL

G6.3.5   The grounds for termination by notice are provided in the Employment Contracts Act. The Act contains rules on individual grounds for termination, ie grounds that are related to the employee's person or behaviour and collective grounds concerned with reduction of work on account of economic reasons or causes related to production. These two categories of grounds play an important role in the Finnish termination procedure, especially in the cases concerning compensation for unjustified termination. It must be noted, however, that because of the broad definition, the grounds are not always easy to distinguish in practice.

6.4   Fairness of Dismissal

G6.4.1   The rules governing the fairness of dismissal are laid down in the Employment Contracts Act (55/2001), Ch 7. Chapter 7, section 1 states that an employer may terminate an employment contract made for an indefinite period only for a just and serious reason. In addition, the employer must comply with either s 2 (grounds related to the employee) or s 3 (economic and production grounds).

G6.4.2   A breach or omission of a duty that is based on law or the employment contract and has an essential effect on the employment relationship can be considered a just and serious reason. There must be essential changes in the employee's capacity to work so that the employee becomes incapable of performing his/her work.

G6.4.3   The employer shall not give notice to terminate a contract of employment for a reason due to the employee, unless that reason is particularly serious. The following reasons may not be considered as just and serious:

- illness or accident, unless the employee's capacity to work has diminished substantially and for such a long time that one cannot reasonably expect the employer to continue the employment relationship;
- the employee's participation in a strike; or
- the employee's political, religious or other opinions, his/her participation in public activities or any association;
- the employee relying on protection granted to him/her by law.

G6.4.4   In addition, the employer's right to give notice may be restricted by agreement, to the specified grounds. The employer must not terminate the contract of employment because of the employee's pregnancy. When the employer terminates the contract of a pregnant employee, the termination is deemed to be motivated by the employee's pregnancy, unless the employer shows another reason.

G6.4.5   The Employment Contracts Act does not give examples of an employee's person or behaviour which may be considered to constitute sufficient grounds for termination. According to legal practice, grounds such as failure to follow instructions which fall within the area of competence of the employer, gross negligence, dishonesty or absence without reason constitute sufficient grounds. When considering the reasons for the termination, the nature of the work, the position of the employee in the undertaking, the specific characteristics of the work as well as the result of the neglect or mistake on the employer or other employees, must be taken into account.

G6.4.6   The employer may terminate the employment contract if the amount of work has diminished due to reasons related to economy or production or the reorganisation of the business of the employer and the diminishing is substantial and permanent.

G6.4.7 The employer does not have the right to terminate if the employer can provide the employee with other work or the employee can be trained for other work. Neither of the following grounds constitute the right to terminate:

- termination is preceded or followed by the engagement of a new employee on similar duties, and no changes have occurred in the employer's circumstances during the corresponding period;
- the reorganisation of tasks put forward as the grounds for the termination does not in fact reduce the amount of work the employer can make available, or change the nature of the tasks.

Written reasons for dismissal

G6.4.8 Notice of termination of an employment contract must be forwarded to the employer or his representative or to the employee in person.[1] If this is not possible, the notice may be sent by mail to a postal address given by the employee or to a known address. When requested, the employer must also, without delay, inform the employee of the main grounds[2] for the notice or the cancellation as well as the date of termination of the employment contract.

[1]   Employment Contracts Act (55/2001), Ch 9, s 4.
[2]   Employment Contracts Act (55/2001), Ch 9, s 5.

6.5   Remedies

A   REINSTATEMENT/RE-ENGAGEMENT

G6.5.1 According to the Employment Contracts Act (55/2001), Ch 6, s 6, when the employer has terminated a contract of employment for reasons not personal to the employee, and he needs labour for the same or similar dates within nine months of the expiry of the period of notice, he must ask the local manpower authority if any of his former employees have registered there as job-seekers, and if that is the case, give first priority to these job-seekers.

B   COMPENSATION

G6.5.2 An employer who fails to observe the period of notice is liable to pay the employee's remuneration in full for the period of notice according to the Employment Contracts Act (55/2001), Ch 6, s 4. The employee is equally liable to pay the employer a sum corresponding to the pay for the period of notice, in full compensation for non-observance when resigning without observing the period of notice.

G6.5.3 The provisions concerning compensation for termination of a contract of employment without grounds are in the Employment Contracts Act (55/2001), Ch 12, s 2. If the employer has terminated an indefinite employment contract contrary to the grounds laid down in the Act, the employer must pay compensation of an amount equivalent to the pay for at least three and at most 24 months. On determining the amount of compensation, the following factors must be taken into account as either reducing or increasing the compensation:

- estimated time without employment;
- estimated loss of earnings;
- length of the employment relationship;
- employee's age and chances of later finding employment corresponding to his/her vocation or education;
- the employer's notice procedure;
- any reason for termination due to the employee;
- the general circumstances of the employee and the employer;
- other comparable matters.

G6.5.4   According to the Employment Contracts Act (55/2001), Ch 12, s 1, any employer who wilfully or negligently fails to discharge his obligations (under the Employment Contracts Act or under a contract of employment) is liable to compensate the employee for the prejudice he has thereby sustained. In addition, when a contract of employment is terminated on account of the employer's wilful act or negligence, he is liable to compensate the employee for unlawful termination of the contract. The compensation is an amount equivalent to pay for at least three and at most 24 months (as at para **G6.5.3**).

6.6   Collective Dismissals – Consultation

G6.6.1   In addition to the provisions of the Employment Contracts Act and binding provisions of a collective agreement regarding termination of an employment contract, the provisions of the Co-operation Within Undertakings Act (which came into force in 1979 and has since been amended numerous times) must be taken into account. The Co-operation Within Undertakings Act has a substantial impact on collective terminations within undertakings. It provides regulations which aim to increase the opportunities for staff to exercise an influence on those matters being considered, which relate to their work and workplace, and to increase co-operation within the firm. This has been established by obliging the employer to negotiate with staff groups eg in cases concerning collective terminations, and requiring information to be given to staff about important matters.

G6.6.2   According to the Co-operation Within Undertakings Act, s 2, the provisions apply to undertakings normally employing at least thirty persons. However, where the employer considers the termination of at least ten employees, the Act also applies to undertakings with at least twenty employees.

G6.6.3   Before the employer may take a decision on a collective termination, he shall provide the concerned workers and their representatives with all necessary information regarding the matter, and negotiate the reasons for the proposed action, its effects and possible alternatives, with the wage earners or salaried employees concerned or their representatives. The Co-operation Within Undertakings Act sets precise conditions and time-limits for the negotiations and notices of terminations are not allowed to be given until the conditions have been properly fulfilled.

When the provisions are not observed, the employee will be entitled to receive pay for a maximum of 20 months as indemnification from the employer.

G6.6.4 Usually the consultations take place between a single representative of the employer and a representative of staff. However, if it is considered necessary, a special consultation organ, a consultative committee, is to be founded. At least 50% of the members of this committee should always be staff representatives.

G6.6.5 A negotiating proposal shall be given by the employer at least five days before the intended beginning of the negotiations. The notices of termination may be given after an agreement between the negotiating parties has been reached, or when the negotiations have continued for at least seven days, which ever comes first. However, if the intended redundancy leads to a termination of more than ten employment contracts or to a lay-off of the same number of workers for more than 90 days, the negotiations, if an agreement is not reached, must go on for at least six weeks, before the notices may be given. Deviations from these rules are possible on the grounds of unforeseeable and particularly weighty economic reasons.

7 YOUNG WORKERS

7.1 General Obligations

The regulations concerning young workers may be divided into three groups:
- the rules regulating the young peoples' right to work and conclude employment contracts as well as the employers right to employ;
- the working hours regulations;
- protection at work.

G7.1.1 Most of these rules are written in the Young Employees Act and in the Statute on Protection of Young Employees, but some are found in the Employment Contracts Act as well as in other laws.

G7.1.2 All the provisions concerning young employees are mandatory. In addition to the special Young Employees Protection Rules, all the regulations that protect adult employees apply to minors as well. Minors have the right to decide on the use of the money and other remuneration they receive from the job, as well as the assets that derive from these wages. This rule is set out in the Guardianship Act.

A RIGHT TO WORK AND CONCLUDE AN EMPLOYMENT CONTRACT

G7.1.3 A young employee is a person, who has not yet attained the age of 18. The right to employ minors is based on the Young Employees Act. According to this law, a person who has attained the age of 15 and has completed compulsory education may be employed. A 14 year old, or a person who will turn 14 during the same calendar year, may be employed only for light jobs, which do not harm his health or development or cause inconvenience to his schoolwork. A person under 13 may not be employed.

G7.1.4 Fifteen year olds have an independent right to conclude an employment contract on their own behalf, as well as withdraw from it. This is regulated in the Young Employees Act, s 3. The same provision also provides that the legal guardian of the minor has a right to dissolve these contracts if it is necessary in view of the minor's education, development or health.

G7.1.5 To enter into an employment contract, the 13 and 14 year olds need a permit from the person who is responsible for their care and custody. These persons may also enter an agreement on behalf of a minor, provided it has the approval of the child. The right to cancel the contract is the same as in the case of the 15–17 year olds.

B   HOURS OF WORKING

G7.1.6 In the Young Employees Act there are several working-hour regulations. These rules can be divided into three groups, which are:
the rules concerning the maximum working hours;
the placing of the working hours; and
rest periods.

G7.1.7 Fifteen year olds may regularly work up to 40 hours a week, like adults, but unlike adults they have a very restricted right to exceed this limit. The absolute maximum weekly working hours for 15 year olds is 48 hours. Young employees under the age of 15 may only work two hours on those days they are at school and seven hours on all the other days. The maximum weekly working hours for them is 12 hours. During the holidays, however, weekly hours of work may rise to 35. Thirteen and fourteen year olds are not allowed to do any additional work. Young employees have a right to annual holidays on the same basis as other employees.

G7.1.8 Children may not work at nights. Those under 15 years old may only work until 20:00 and 15–17 year olds until 22:00.

G7.1.9 The minimum uninterrupted daily rest period for those under 15 is 14 hours. For other young employees it is 12 hours. A 38-hour uninterrupted weekly period of rest is the right of all minors. There are rules about breaks during the working time too.

G7.1.10 The employer has an obligation to ensure that the job of a young employee is not harmful to his mental or physical development, and that it does not require more effort or include more responsibility than what is reasonable considering the young employee's age and capabilities.

G7.1.11 The Statute on Protection of Young Employees lists jobs forbidden for young employees. This list includes: the slaughter of animals; treating mentally ill people; handling of corpses; and jobs where the employee is exposed to poisonous or carcinogenic substances or harmful radiation. It is also forbidden to let a minor do a risky job without supervision. When judging what a young employee may and may not do, extra attention must be paid to his personal capabilities.

G7.1.12 The Ministry of Labour has also created a list of jobs that are found to be dangerous for young employees. Young employees may not do these jobs unless tight security standards are met. A special factory inspector must be notified before a minor may take up this kind of dangerous task. Young employees under 16 may not do these jobs under any circumstances.

G7.1.13 The employer has to provide young employees with proper training, instructions and guidance. The employer has to supervise the employee so that he does not cause any danger to himself or other people. There are also rules concerning health inspections of minors.

G7.1.14 Special health and safety inspectors monitor how the Young Employees Act is followed. Safety regulation breaches are made criminal under the Penal Code, Ch 47. Infringements of working hour rules are penalised in Ch 47. The punishment is up to one year's imprisonment. Those breaches of the Young Employees Act that are not covered by the Penal Code are punishable under the Young Employees Act itself. The penalty for these offences is a fine.

8 MATERNITY AND PARENTAL RIGHTS

8.1 Background

G8.1.1 Since the enactment of the Employment Contracts Act (320/1970) there has been a provision which guarantees the right to leave for mothers giving birth to a child. However, this is not just a right but also an obligation. Mothers are not allowed to do jobs that may harm the baby and employers are not allowed to let mothers do these jobs, or indeed jobs that may harm the mother herself.

G8.1.2 In 1982, a new provision was added to the Employment Contracts Act (320/1970) and this introduced a right to leave for fathers as well. The right to leave has expanded since and today the various leaves are divided into maternity, special maternity, paternity, parental and child care leaves.

G8.1.3 A right to leave has never been the only parental right in working life. There are also provisions that protect pregnant women and the babies they carry from dangers at work. In addition, parents have the right to several different social benefits.

G8.1.4 Parental rights also have a close connection to equality rules. In the Act on Equality between Men and Women conduct causing disadvantage to a pregnant woman or parents is considered to be discriminatory and thus illegal.

312

8.2   General Rights

G8.2.1   The Employment Contracts Act (55/2001), Ch 4, covers family leaves, which include maternity, special maternity, paternity, parental and child-care leave. These rights to leave depend for the most part on the right to receive social benefits on the grounds of parenthood. These rights to a family allowance are regulated in the Sickness Insurance Act, ss 21–23g. The allowances are monetary benefits paid by the state. The right to maternity, paternity and parental allowances require that the person has resided in Finland for at least 180 days immediately before the birth of the child. However, this does not mean, that the child would have had to be born in Finland. The definition of 'residing' is the fulfilling of formal criteria set out in the Act on the Application of the Residence-Based Social Security Legislation. There is no limit for the length of the employment before the leave. Therefore in theory even one day is enough. The family leave provisions are mandatory: an employee cannot renounce his right to leave.

A   MATERNITY LEAVE

G8.2.2   An employee whose pregnancy has lasted at least 154 days has the right to a maternity allowance and therefore also to maternity leave. The right to maternity leave usually begins 30–50 days before the expected time of the childbirth, however, at the latest, at the time of the birth. The employee is also entitled to start the leave earlier if it is necessary on the grounds of the child's or mother's state of health.

G8.2.3   The maternity allowance and leave last 105 working days and they do not depend on the number of children born.

G8.2.4   The mother does not have to have the whole 105 days off work. She may work during the maternity allowance term, except during a period of two weeks before the expected time of birth and two weeks after giving birth. Nevertheless, during the rest of the maternity allowance term she may only perform work that does not pose a risk to her or the unborn or newly born child. Both the employee and the employer have the right to discontinue the work at any time during the maternity allowance. The employee cannot renounce her right to this.

G8.2.5   The employer has no general obligation to pay wages during maternity leave. However, an obligation to pay wages follows from many collective agreements. It can also be based on the employment contract.

B   PARENTAL LEAVE

G8.2.6   Parental leave starts right after maternity leave. Parental leave is intended for both mothers and fathers. The length of parental leave is the length of the parental allowance, which at its maximum is 158 working days (circa 32 weeks). The right to parental leave ends 263 working days from the beginning of the maternity allowance. The allowance and leave is granted to one parent at a time. Both parents are entitled to take parental leave in one or two periods during the 158 working days. That means, that the parents may share the leave and have it in four periods. The periods must be at least 12 working days each. If there is more than one baby born at the same time to one family, the leave is extended by 60 working days per every additional baby. Parents are not obliged to take parental leave.

G8.2.7 For fathers there is a special requirement. To have the right to parental leave the father must permanently live with the mother or be the person primarily responsible for taking care of the child.

G8.2.8 As for maternity leave, the employer has no general obligation to pay wages.

C PATERNITY LEAVE

G8.2.9 In addition to parental leave, the fathers have the right to paternity leave, which depends on the right to paternity allowance. This means that the grounds upon which a claim to paternity leave are based are the same as the grounds to paternity allowance as regulated in the Sickness Insurance Act. This leave does not affect the right to maternity or parental leave. That means, among other things, that both parents may be on family leave at the same time and receive support for this from the state. Fathers are not obliged to take paternity leave.

G8.2.10 As in the case of parental leave, the right to take paternity leave depends on the father permanently living with the mother or being the person primarily responsible for taking care of the child.

G8.2.11 Paternity leave is divided into two parts: the first part usually takes place in conjunction with childbirth or at least during the maternity allowance period. The second part may take place either during the maternity or parental allowance term. Both leaves may also be taken in immediate succession.

G8.2.12 The first allowance term and leave is six to twelve working days. The minimum requirement of six days means that if a father only wants to take, for example, two days off work, the employer does not have to comply with this request. The father does not have a protected right to take this leave in shorter periods. The second allowance term and leave is fixed at six working days.

G8.2.13 Altogether, a father may receive paternity allowance and be on a leave for 18 working days.

G8.2.14 As for maternity and parental leave, the employer has no general obligation to pay wages during paternity leave. However, an obligation to pay salary follows from many collective bargains. It may also be based on the employment contract.

D CHILD-CARE LEAVE

G8.2.15 The right to child-care leave does not depend on the right to receive a family benefit. All the requirements for this leave are in the Employment Contracts Act (55/2001), Ch 4, s 3. Both men and women are entitled to this leave in order to take care of their own child or some other child living permanently in their household until the child reaches the age of three. It is worth noticing that the child need not be the son or daughter of the one who is taking the leave.

G8.2.16   Employees taking this leave have the right to decide how much leave they have and when they take the time off. However, this right is not totally without restrictions. The leave must not be taken in more than two separate periods and these periods must always be of at least one month long. However, the employee and employer may agree on longer and/or shorter periods.

G8.2.17   Only one person having the care and custody of a child is entitled to child-care leave at a time. Nonetheless, during maternity or parental leave, the other parent or person having the care and custody may be on child-care leave. During a child-care leave the person is entitled to child home-care allowance.

E   PARTIAL CHILD-CARE LEAVE

G8.2.18   In addition, an employee who has been employed by the same employer for at least one year during the last two years is entitled to partial child-care leave. This means that an employee has the right to reduced working hours till the end of the year during which the child living in the same household begins comprehensive school, which in Finland happens at the age of six or seven.

G8.2.19   The basis is that the employee and the employer agree on the reduction of the work. However, if they cannot reach an agreement, the partial leave must be granted for one unlimited period in every year during which the daily hours of work will be reduced to six. The duration and timing of this period will be according to the employee's proposal.

G8.2.20   The right to partial child-care leave is not absolute. The employer may refuse to grant this leave if it would cause serious inconvenience to the functions of the firm that can not be avoided through reasonable arrangements.

F   LEAVES IN CONJUNCTION WITH ADOPTION

G8.2.21   A person who has adopted or is about to adopt a child has the right to parental allowance and parental leave. The adoptive father also has the right to paternity allowance and leave for six working days, but the mother does not have the right to maternity allowance and leave. This is so because the adoptive mother is the one who is most likely to take parental leave.

G8.2.22   These adoption benefits are available only when the adopted child is under seven years of age. The parental leave lasts 180 working days from the adoption or 234 working days from the birth of the child, whichever is longer. This means that the parents who adopt a newly born child have the right to a longer leave than other adoption parents.

G8.2.23   The adoption parents and other members of a household have the right to take child-care leave on the same grounds as other parents and household members.

G COMMENCEMENT AND END OF LEAVE

G8.2.24 In order to claim maternity, paternity parental and child-care leave there is no other procedural requirement other than to give notice to the employer within a certain time before the intended start of the leave. The employer must comply with the notice. In some sudden situations the leave can be started right away without any notice. (See paras **G8.4.1–G8.4.2.**)

G8.2.25 Maternity, paternity, parental and child-care leaves end automatically when the allowance terms end. Unless another allowance term begins immediately, the employee must then return to his or her work. If he fails to return to work, it constitutes a breach of his duties as an employee. The general rules concerning employee's breaches are applied to this breach.

G8.2.26 An employee has no right to return to work whenever he chooses. He has to comply with the terms he has given to the employer in advance. However the employer and employee may together agree not to stick to the intended terms. A mother may never start working before two weeks from the birth of a child.

G8.2.27 Partial child-care leave ends when agreed on and the temporary child-care leave when the requirements for it are not met anymore, or at the latest on the fifth day after it began.

G8.2.28 When any of the leaves mentioned in paras **G8.2.1–G8.2.31** ends, the employee has the right first and foremost to return to his or her former duties. However, if this is not possible, the person must be offered equivalent work or if even that is not possible, other work, in accordance with the employment contract. The impossibility requirement is to be interpreted quite strictly.

H NOTICE REQUIREMENTS

G8.2.29 The employee must notify the employer of the leave in advance. The usual notice period is two months before the start of the leave. When there is a justified reason, an employee may change the term and duration of the leave by notifying the employer at least one month before the change is due to take place. The notice must cover the intended length of the leave. If the leave is taken in more than one period, the employer must be notified of all these periods according to these same rules.

G8.2.30 There are also situations, where no notice beforehand can be required. This is the situation where the need for the leave is so sudden that there is no time for an advance notice. This could be, for instance, because of the sudden birth of a child. When this happens, the maternity leave begins automatically and the father has the right to immediately begin the first part of his paternity leave. These leaves may also be started without any notice in advance if the mother's, child's or father's state of health requires it to do so. The employer must be notified as soon as possible of these sudden changes in the timing of leaves. The temporary child-care leave is also such in nature that notice in advance is impossible and therefore not required. In these cases, the employer must be notified as soon as possible.

G8.2.31   In the case of adoption, the employer must be notified at least two months before the leave starts. However, for a justified reason, the adoptive parents may change this term by notifying the employer at the earliest possible date.

8.3   Protection from Dismissal

G8.3.1   According to the Employment Contracts Act (55/2001), Ch 7, s 9, an employer may only terminate the employee's contract during that person's special maternity, maternity, paternity, parental or child-care leave on economic and production grounds.

8.4   Health and Safety

SPECIAL MATERNITY LEAVE

G8.4.1   If a pregnant woman at work is exposed to radiation, toxic substances or contagious diseases such that it may cause danger to the development of the foetus or the pregnancy, the mother has a right to special maternity allowance and leave. A mother may be on this leave right from the beginning of the pregnancy, if it is necessary to protect the baby. An additional precondition for this leave is that the employee cannot be transferred to other tasks suitable for her with regard to her skills and experience.

G8.4.2   Dangerous substances, diseases and radiation are defined in the Sickness Insurance Statute.

8.5   Maternity Pay and Family Benefits

G8.5.1   The right to almost every family leave is dependent on the right to receive social benefit from the state. These benefits are maternity, special maternity, paternity, parental and child home-care allowances. The amount of these allowances depend on the incomes: the larger the income the larger the allowance. This is to encourage those who earn more to take leave. On the contrary to the other allowances, maternity and parental allowances are also paid when the persons entitled to them do not take the leave or a part of it. In these cases, however, only the minimum amount of the allowance is paid. This minimum is FIM 60 (circa € 10) per day.

G8.5.2   In addition to monetary benefits, the mothers receive a baby package, which contains all kinds of things necessary and useful for the well-being of a baby. There is also a free child health and welfare system, which starts to function during the pregnancy and a municipal child-care system. The municipalities are obliged to arrange day-care for every child who does not yet go to school.

8.6   Additional Rights to Time Off

A   TEMPORARY CHILD-CARE LEAVE

G8.6.1   In the event of the sudden illness of a child, the persons responsible for him or her have the right to stay home and take care of the child for up to four working days at a time. The child must be under ten years of age. Only one person may take this leave at a time.

B   ABSENCE FOR COMPELLING FAMILY REASONS

G8.6.2   Close to the provision of temporary child-care leave is the provision concerning absence for compelling family reasons. In this case, the reason for absence has to be even more sudden and compelling, however the illness or accident does not have to concern a child, but any family member.

9   BUSINESS TRANSFERS

9.1   Background

G9.1.1   Legislation to comply with the EC Acquired Rights Directive 77/187/EEC, which sought to 'provide for the protection of employees in the event of a change of employer' was introduced in 1993. Directive 98/50/EC, amending Directive 77/187/EEC on the Approximation of the Laws of Member States relating to the Safeguarding of Employee's Rights in the event of Transfers of Undertakings, Businesses or parts of Businesses, was implemented by the new Employment Contracts Act (55/2001) and the Act on Co-operation within Undertakings.

G9.1.2   The Employment Contracts Act (55/2001) is applied when there is a transfer of an undertaking or of an economic entity which continues its activity without long interruption. It is not applied to the transfer of shares in a company.

The Directive (77/187/EC as amended) enshrines three principles that are adopted by the Employment Contracts Act (55/2001) and the Act on Co-operation within Undertakings:

- automatic transfers of employment together with the rights and liabilities. The same principle also covers rights derived from a collective agreement;
- special protection against dismissal in connection with the transfer of business;
- informing and consulting workers' representatives about certain matters related to the transfer.

G9.1.3
Since the Employment Contracts Act (55/2001) and the Act on Co-operation within Undertakings have been implemented to comply with Directive 77/187/EC (as amended) courts are required to give them a purposive interpretation that fully complies with their parent directive.

Influence of European law
- where Finnish legislation is ambiguous
- purposive interpretation
- where EC legislation is directly effective

9.2 Identifying a Relevant Transfer

G9.2.1 The Employment Contracts Act (55/2001), Ch 1, s 10, defines a 'business transfer'. The transfer of an undertaking, a business, a society or a functional part of any of these to another employer will be a 'business transfer' if the transferred undertaking or the part transferred remains the same or similar after the transfer.

G9.2.2 There is a relevant transfer where there is a transfer of an undertaking or of an economic entity which continues its activity without long interruption. This means that a transfer that only includes shares is not regarded as a relevant transfer, because the company stays the same. The target of the relevant transfer has to be a functional entity ie it constitutes an individual business of its own. When the employer transfers his undertaking to another person, the employer's rights and duties also have to be transferred. The concept of a relevant transfer requires that there is some kind of a legal relationship between the transferor and the transferee. This is the case, for instance, when a bankrupt's estate sells or rents out certain fixed capital assets or current assets to a company which begins to carry on a same kind of production activity within the same premises.

G9.2.3 Identifying a relevant transfer requires a matching of domestic and EC legislation. Unlike in Finland, the Court of Justice of the European Communities emphasises in its practise, the importance of an economic entity retaining its identity.

9.3 Affected Employees

G9.3.1 According to the Employment Contracts Act (55/2001), Ch 1, s 7, para 1, no rights derived from a contract of employment shall be transferred to a third party by either the employee or the employer without the other party's consent, except for claims that have fallen due for payment.

G9.3.2 The essential question concerning affected employees when transferring a business is whether their employment relationship continues or is discontinued. The continuation of the relationship guarantees that those of the employees' benefits that are dependent upon the duration of employment are preserved.

9.4 Effects of the Transfer

G9.4.1 The former employer's rights and liabilities based on the contract of employment, that are in force at the time of the transfer, shall pass directly to the new owner or possessor.[1] The Employment Contracts Act (55/2001) is based on the principle of maintaining the status quo concerning rights and liabilities in the case of a change in ownership of the undertaking. The same principle also covers rights derived from a collective agreement.[2] Employment is not regarded as terminated on account of a change in ownership of the undertaking.[3]

[1] Employment Contracts Act (55/2001), Ch 1, s 10.
[2] Collective Agreements Act, s 5.
[3] Annual Holidays Act, s 6.

G9.4.2 The transferor and the transferee shall be jointly and severally liable for the employee's wages or other claims arising out of the employment relationship that have fallen due before the transfer.[1] In such a circumstance, the transferor shall, unless otherwise agreed, be responsible to the transferee for any claim of the employee that has fallen due before the transfer. The right to give notice of termination in connection with a transfer of an undertaking shall be governed by the Employment Contracts Act (55/2001), Ch 7, s 5.

[1] Employment Contracts Act (55/2001), Ch 1, s 10.

G9.4.3 Where an undertaking is transferred by a bankrupt's estate, the transferee shall not be responsible for an employee's pay or other claims arising out of the employment relationship that have fallen due before the transfer, except if the decisive power in both the undertaking declared bankrupt and in the transferee undertaking, belongs, or has belonged, to the same persons on the basis of ownership, agreement or other arrangement.

[1] Employment Contracts Act (55/2001), Ch 1, s 10, para 3.

9.5   Dismissal of Employees

G9.5.1 The transferee must not terminate an employee's contract solely because of the transfer. A termination will only be justified if it is for a ground related to the employee's person or for collective grounds.

[1] Employment Contracts Act (55/2001), Ch 7, s 5.

G9.5.2 The employee may, in the event that the employer transfers his undertaking to another person in a way defined in the Employment Contracts Act (55/2001), Ch 1, s 10, without regard to the period of notice or the duration of the contract, terminate such contract as of the date of the transfer of the undertaking, or if he has been notified of the transfer later than one month before the date of transfer, as of a later date, but no later than within one month of the date of notification.[1]

[1] Employment Contracts Act (55/2001), Ch 7, s 5.

9.6   Duty of Information and Consultation

G9.6.1 The purpose of the Act on Co-operation within Undertakings is (according to its s 1, para 1) to increase opportunities for the wage-earners and salaried employees concerned to exercise influence in the handling of matters relating to their work and to their workplaces with the object of developing the operations of an undertaking, improving its working conditions and furthering co-operation between the employer and the staff and among members of the staff.

G9.6.2 The purpose of co-operation to be observed within a business group (group co-operation) is to promote interaction between the group management and the staff and among members of the staff. The Act on Personnel Representation in Company Administration covers the right of staff to participate in the administration of companies.

G9.6.3 The Act on Co-operation within Undertakings shall apply to undertakings normally employing at least thirty persons as parties to an employment relationship. When the employer considers the termination of the contracts of at least ten employees due to production and financial reasons, the Act on Co-operation within Undertakings shall also apply to undertakings employing not more than thirty but at least twenty people. The Act shall not apply to government offices or public services or state-owned businesses, or to the offices and public services of a municipality. The Act shall apply to a state-owned company if it has so decided on the basis of the Act on State-owned Companies (1987/627), s 18. According to provisions agreed upon by decree, it shall apply to the businesses and industrial plants of municipalities or public corporations other than the Government.

G9.6.4 The parties to the co-operation referred to in the Act on Co-operation within Undertakings, s 3, para 1, shall be the employer and the staff of the undertaking. The co-operation shall take place between the wage-earners or salaried employees concerned and their superiors or between the employer and the staff representatives. In a matter concerning the effects of a business transfer or merger, the transferee or the receiving undertaking may also be a party to the co-operation referred to in the Act on Co-operation within Undertakings.

G9.6.5 Where there is reason to do so, having regard to the circumstances and the number of staff representatives, the employer and the staff representatives may (according to the Act on Co-operation within Undertakings, s 4) agree that the co-operation (referred to in the Act) within the undertaking or any part of the undertaking is to be arranged in the form of a committee as a joint body for the employer and the staff representatives. The representatives of each of the staff groups falling within the committee's jurisdiction shall elect the members of the committee from among their own number for one year at a time, the number of members elected corresponding to the size of the staff groups. Agreement shall be reached at the same time on the issues with which the committee is to deal. According to the Act on Co-operation within Undertakings, s 4, para 2, the number of persons representing the employer on the committee shall not exceed one-half of the total number of persons representing the staff.

G9.6.6 The matters covered by the co-operation procedure are listed in the Act on Co-operation within Undertakings, s 6. They are as follows:

- any major changes in duties, working methods or the arrangement of work that affect the position of the staff and any transfers from one job to another;

- any major acquisitions of machinery and equipment, in so far as they affect the staff, and any major rearrangements of the working premises and changes in the range of goods and services provided, affecting the position of the staff;
- the closure of the undertaking or any part of the undertaking, its transfer to another place or any major expansion or reduction of its activities;
- after the business transfer or merger, any ensuing reduction of contracts of employment into part-time contracts, layoffs and termination of contracts, and the related arrangements for training and reassignments;
- reducing contracts of employment into part-time contracts, layoffs and termination of contracts, due to productional and financial reasons, and the related arrangements for training and reassignments, including staff arrangements in connection with the procedure of reorganising the undertaking;
- periodical rationalisation schemes, plans regarding staff and training, and any relevant changes to be made to them during the period the plans cover, the action programme for labour protection and any measures to promote the attainment of equality between women and men in workplaces to be included in the plans regarding staff and training or in the action programme for labour protection;
- any arrangements required for the purposes of the Act on Co-operation within Undertakings, s 6, sub-paras 1–4, if they affect the size of the staff employed on different duties;
- the times for the beginning and end of normal hours of work and the times for breaks for rest or meals;
- the principles governing recourse to labour from outside the undertaking; otherwise recourse to outside labour shall be dealt with as laid down in the Act on Co-operation within Undertakings, s 9;
- the principles governing recruitment, the procedure to be followed and the information to be obtained, the information to be given to new recruits and the arrangements to be made for their familiarisation with the work;
- matters connected with internal information services (broadsheets, notice boards and the arrangement of information meetings);
- the working rules of the undertaking, comparable rules of order, and rules for suggestion schemes;
- budget estimates for training in co-operation and vocational training;
- the organisation of training in co-operation;
- the general principles to be followed in the allocation of accommodation provided by the employer, and the determination of the shares to be enjoyed by the different groups of staff, but not in so far as such accommodation is allocated to members of the management; and
- within the limits of the funds earmarked by the undertaking for various welfare purposes, the arrangements of works canteens and child-care facilities, the use and planning of welfare premises, recreational and holiday activities, the grant of subsidies and donations to the staff and, subject to the principles referred to in the Act on Co-operation within Undertakings, s 6, sub-para 13, the fixing of grounds for the allocation of service-related accommodation and the allocation of such accommodation in accordance with those grounds.

G9.6.7   Following a business transfer or merger, it shall (according to the Act on Co-operation within Undertakings, s 6a) be determined through a co-operation procedure whether the transfer or merger brings consequences that fall within the obligation to negotiate.

G9.6.8   Before the employer takes a decision on any matter covered by the Act on Co-operation within Undertakings, s 6, he shall, according to s 7, discuss the reasons for the action envisaged, its effects and possible alternatives, with the wage-earners or salaried employees concerned, or with their representatives.

G9.6.9   According to the Act on Co-operation within Undertakings, s 7, para 2, the employer shall provide the wage-earners or salaried employees concerned and the relevant staff representatives with any information necessary for dealing with the matter before initiating the co-operation procedure. Whenever the employer is considering terminating the contract of, or laying-off for a minimum of 90 days, at least ten wage-earners and/or salaried employees, or reducing their contracts of employment to part-time contracts, the said information, including information on the grounds for the planned reduction of personnel, an estimation of the number of wage-earners and salaried employees in each group affected by the reduction. an estimate of the time during which the planned reductions are to be carried out, and information on the principles according to which the employees affected by the reduction will be determined, shall be given in writing.

G9.6.10   Any matter affecting a particular wage-earner or salaried employee shall, according to the Act on Co-operation within Undertakings, s 7, para 3, in the first instance be discussed between the employer and the person concerned. Where the employer or the wage-earner or salaried employee concerned so requests, the matter shall also be discussed between the employer and the relevant staff representative.

G9.6.11   Unless otherwise agreed, a proposal for negotiations on a matter referred to in the Act on Co-operation within Undertakings, s 6, sub-paras 1–5, shall (according to s 7, para 1) be submitted in writing at least three days before the negotiations begin. This period shall, however, be extended to five days if a measure to be negotiated under s 6, sub-paras 1–5 is likely to lead to the laying-off or termination of contract of one or more wage-earners or salaried employees, or the reduction of their contracts of employment to part-time contracts. The proposal shall indicate the time and location at which negotiations will begin and the issues to be dealt with in the negotiations. The information required under s 7, para 2, shall be either appended to the proposal for negotiations or submitted separately before the negotiations begin.

G9.6.12   When a representative of staff requests that a co-operation procedure be started in a matter referred to in the Act on Co-operation within Undertakings, s 6, sub-paras 1–5, the employer shall make the proposal for negotiations or a written communication indicating the grounds on which the co-operation procedure is not considered necessary. A proposal for negotiations on a matter referred to in s 6 shall be submitted within a week of the transfer or merger, provided that negotiations have not been entered into previously. The provisions of s 7a, para 1 (see para **G9.6.11**) shall apply to the submission of proposals and the commencement of negotiations.

G9.6.13 When the proposal for negotiations referred to in the Act on Co-operation within Undertakings, s 7a, includes measures for the reduction of personnel, the proposal or its material contents shall, according to s 7b, be brought in writing to the knowledge of the employment authorities at the beginning of the negotiations, provided that corresponding information has not been provided previously in some other context. If the relevant material accumulated during the negotiations differs essentially from any delivered earlier, the employer shall deliver this material also to the manpower authorities.

G9.6.14 The employer shall be deemed to have fulfilled his obligation to negotiate, as referred to in the Act on Co-operation within Undertakings, s 7, if the matter has been dealt with in the co-operation procedure with the wage-earners or salaried employees concerned, or with their representatives or within the committee referred to in s 4. However, in some cases the fulfilment of the obligation to negotiate involves certain time limits.

G9.6.15 If a measure subject to negotiation under the Act on Co-operation within Undertakings, s 6, sub-paras 1–5, is likely to result in the reduction of contracts of employment to part-time contracts, in layoffs or in the termination of contracts, affecting one or more wage-earners or salaried employees, the employer shall be deemed not to have fulfilled his obligation to negotiate.

G9.6.16 On the other hand, the employer shall be deemed to have fulfilled the obligation to negotiate if in an effort to reach agreement, negotiations have been held first on the causes and effects of the measure, and subsequently on ways to limit the number of people affected by reductions and to alleviate the consequences of the reductions, and at least seven days have elapsed since the beginning of the negotiations.

G9.6.17 If the measure is likely to result in the reduction of contracts to part-time ones, termination of contracts or lay-offs for more than 90 days affecting at least ten employees, the period specified shall be at least six weeks from the beginning of the negotiations. In this case, the discussion of alternatives shall not begin until seven days have elapsed from the time of the negotiation of causes and effects, unless otherwise agreed.

G9.6.18 If the co-operation procedure has been initiated before a transfer or merger, the negotiation period for the transferee and the receiving undertaking shall, according to the Act on Co-operation within Undertakings, s 8, para 4, be deemed to include the time they have been parties to negotiation.

G9.6.19 Where particularly important and unforeseeable circumstances that are detrimental to the undertaking's production or business constitute an obstacle to the co-operation procedure, the employer may (Act on Co-operation within Undertakings, s 10, para 1) take a decision in a matter covered by s 6 without a prior co-operation procedure. Any matter covered by s 10, para 1, shall be discussed without delay in the manner prescribed as soon as there is no longer any reason to depart from the normal procedure. The employer shall at the same time explain the circumstances requiring the change to the normal procedure.

G9.6.20 According to the Act on Co-operation within Undertakings, the transferor and transferee of the undertaking shall inform the staff representatives of:

> - the reasons for the transfer;
> - the legal, financial and social consequences for the employees caused by the transfer; and
> - the planned measures concerning employees.

G9.6.21 The transferor shall provide the staff representatives with the information referred to in good time before the transfer occurs. In bilingual municipalities the employer shall supply the information and documents referred to in both the national languages, where there are at least ten persons in the language minority and the number of such persons represents more than ten per cent of the staff.

G9.6.22 When the wage-earners or salaried employees or staff representatives in an undertaking become acquainted with information relating to the employer's business or trade secrets and the dissemination of such information would probably be prejudicial to the undertaking (or to any business relation of or contracting party to the undertaking) and the fact has been indicated by the employer, such information shall be discussed only by the wage-earners or salaried employees or staff representatives concerned in the matter and the information shall not be revealed to any other person. Information relating to a private person's financial situation or state of health or concerning him/her personally in any other way must also be kept secret if the person's permission to reveal the information has not been obtained.

10   COLLECTIVE RIGHTS

10.1 Background

G10.1.1 During the last decades of the 19th century, employers and employees in industry started to organise themselves. In the beginning of the 20th century these organisations developed into labour associations and local unions and this led to the first modern strikes and lockouts. The first collective agreements were concluded in the 1940s when the employers' and employees' central organisations first recognised each other and in the agreement of 1944 agreed on the first fundamental provisions to be observed by industry-wide organisations and their members.

G10.1.2 From 1946, when the Collective Agreements Act was amended, the Finnish collective agreement system has been characterised by a high degree of centralisation with the system being built through central labour market agreements and the directives of the central organisations. In addition, the state has played an important role in the field of collective labour relations through the structure of incomes policy agreements (see paras **G10.2.1–G10.2.2**).

G10.1.3 The modern collective labour relations system in Finland consists of two different parts: a collective agreements system and a 'participation system'. The collective agreements system regulates the forming of collective agreements and regulates conflicts concerning these agreements. The system creates the conditions to collectively agree on the essential terms concerning labour relations and, in a case of conflict, aids its resolution.

G10.1.4 During the last decade 'the participation system' has markedly developed. The system consists of regulation, which makes it possible for the employees to get information concerning the employer and, to a certain extent, influence the actual decisions and policies to be concluded by the employer (as an example, see paras **G9.5.1–G9.5.2**).

Structure of the Finnish collective agreement system

G10.1.5 The Finnish labour market system consists of different levels. At the highest level the employers' and employees' central organisations enter into incomes policy agreements and general agreements. The incomes policy agreement consists of a wide range of agreements concerning wages, tax policy and questions concerning economic policy. The labour market organisations, some other interest organisations and the Government of Finland are involved. Since the provisions of law do not regulate this type of collective agreement involving the central organisations and the state, the incomes policy agreement can best be characterised as an informal agreement even though it is often concluded in writing using legal terminology. The central labour market agreements and the incomes policy agreements establish the basis and guidelines for the collective agreements to be concluded by each labour association and have no direct legal effect on the parties to a collective agreement. In practise, the general agreements have often been implemented by the acceptance of the parties to a collective agreement.

G10.1.6 Nowadays, the most important level in the regulation of work conditions within the various branches is the level of collective agreements that are concluded by the nationwide industrial labour associations. These agreements are described and regulated in the Collective Agreements Act(see paras **G10.2.1–G10.2.2, G10.3.1–G10.3.5**).

G10.1.7 Concluding collective agreements at a local workplace has for a long time occurred only within a few larger companies. However, during recent years both the interest and the need for more local solutions has increased. It is likely that the role of local workplace agreements will increase as it becomes more difficult to find the right solutions at the higher association level. Whether the local workplace agreements will become the rule rather than the exception remains to be seen. These agreements are also described and regulated in the Collective Agreements Act.

G10.1.8   Finally, it is always possible to agree on conditions in an individual employment contract, which, to the advantage of the employee, exceed the conditions provided in the applicable collective agreement (see para **G1.2.1–G1.2.15**).

10.2 Collective Agreements

Content and parties

G10.2.1   According to the Collective Agreements Act a collective agreement is an agreement concerning conditions to be observed in employment contracts or in employment relationships generally. A collective agreement must meet certain requirements in order to have legal effect. A collective agreement must be written and may be concluded on the employer side by one or more employers (company agreement) or one or more employers' associations. On the employee side, one or more employees' associations (trade unions) may only conclude a collective agreement. In order to be able to conclude a collective agreement, an employers' association or a trade union must be a registered association under the Associations Act, having as one of its essential objects the furtherance of employers' or employees' interests.

G10.2.2   A collective agreement must contain conditions to be observed in employment relationships between an employer and at least some of his employees. If the agreement does not contain such provisions it is not a collective agreement.

10.3 Legal Effects of a Collective Agreement

G10.3.1   According to the Collective Agreements Act a collective agreement shall be binding on:
- the employers and associations who concluded the collective agreement or subsequently accede to the agreement in writing and with the consent of the parties;
- registered associations which are subordinated directly or through one or more intermediaries to the associations mentioned in the preceding point;
- employers and employees who are, or during the period of the agreement were, members of an association bound by the agreement; and the said employers and employees shall be required to observe the provisions of the collective agreement in all contracts of employment concluded between them.

G10.3.2   An employer bound by the agreement may not conclude, within the area covered by the collective agreement, any contract of employment, containing conditions which are at variance with the collective agreement, with an employee who, though not bound by the collective agreement performs work covered by the agreement.

G10.3.3 If an employment contract term is at variance with an applicable collective agreement, such term shall be invalid and superseded by the corresponding provisions of the collective agreement.[1]

[1] Collective Agreements Act, s 6.

G10.3.4 In addition to this, the Employment Contracts Act (55/2001) extends the scope of certain collective agreements beyond the limits set in the Collective Agreements Act. If a collective agreement can be regarded as general in the field concerned, all employers in the field must observe its terms in employment relationships as minimum conditions (see para **G1.2.12–G1.2.14**).

G10.3.5 A collective agreement fills two functions: firstly, it guarantees minimum standards for employment contracts; secondly, its objective is to guarantee industrial peace during an agreement period. According to the Collective Agreements Act, s 8, those bound by the agreement must refrain from any hostile action directed against the collective agreement as a whole or against any of its particular provisions. The duty of industrial peace ceases with the expiry of the period of the collective agreement.

10.4 Collective Bargaining and Collective Representation

G10.4.1 There are both statutory and non-statutory systems institutionalising the employer-employee relationship at the enterprise level. In the statutory systems, the trade unions have no formal role but it should be noticed that in practice their influence may be considerable. The non-statutory system, in turn, is based on the relations between the employer and the trade union. In paras **G10.4.2–G10.4.6** the major systems are briefly described.

G10.4.2 One of the most important statutory regulations institutionalising employer-employee relations, set out in The Co-operation Within Undertakings Act 1978, is aimed at developing the operations of an undertaking and improving its working conditions and furthering co-operation between the employer and the staff. The Act is applicable to private workplaces that normally have at least 30 employees. In addition, the provisions on collective terminations (see also paras **G6.6.1–G6.6.5, G9.6.1–G9.6.22**) are applicable to private workplaces with at least 20 employees provided that the termination is intended to comprise at least 10 employees.

G10.4.3 The matters subject to co-operation are listed in the Act. The list includes a variety of matters which materially influence the position of staff and the functioning of the enterprise eg major changes in duties and working methods, the closure of the undertaking, reducing contracts of employment into part-time contracts and lay-offs and terminations of contracts due to productional and financial reasons (this has been dealt with in greater detail in paras **G6.6.1–G6.6.5, G9.6.1–G9.6.22**).

G10.4.4 The non-statutory system of shop stewards is based on agreements and practice. The present system was constituted in the General

Agreement of 1997 and it in general consists of a chief steward for the establishment, a shop steward for every department and a substitute for the chief shop steward. The shop steward is the representative of the local trade union in the workplace and his task is, on one hand, to see that the employer fulfils his obligations towards the union and its members, and on the other hand, to see that the union members honour their obligations towards the employer. The General Agreement states that shop stewards shall be elected by the local trade union concerned. The union is entitled to organise the elections at the workplace. The personal employment relationship of the shop steward shall not be altered because of his election.

G10.4.5   According to the Act on Labour Protection Supervision etc the employer and the employee shall co-operate in labour protection matters. The employer shall appoint a labour protection supervisor for each workplace. At any workplace where at least ten employees are regularly employed, the employees shall elect a labour protection representative and two substitutes for him to represent them in labour protection matters and to co-operate with the labour protection authorities. At a workplace where at least 20 employees are regularly employed, a labour protection committee shall be appointed to further the safety and healthiness of work.

G10.4.6   The Act on the Representation of the Personnel in the Administration of Enterprises applies to Finnish corporate employers that regularly employ at least 150 persons in Finland. The Act states that the purpose of the participation is to develop the activities of the enterprise, to intensify the co-operation between the enterprise and the staff and to enhance the influence of the staff. The representation can be arranged by agreement between the employer and the employees or, in absence of such agreement and if required by the personnel, the personnel is entitled to elect its representatives to the administration of the enterprise. The employers may in this case choose whether the representatives will be elected to the board of directors, to the council of administration or to management groups covering the activities of the whole corporation. The number of representatives shall be one-quarter of other members of the organ in question, but at least one and at most four.

10.5 Industrial Action

G10.5.1   According to the Collective Agreements Act those bound by the agreement must, firstly, refrain from any hostile action directed against the collective agreement as a whole or against any of its particular provisions. Secondly, the associations which are bound by the agreement are required to ensure that the associations, employers and employees subordinated to them and covered by the agreement refrain from any such hostile action and that they do not contravene the provisions of the collective agreement in any other matter.

G10.5.2   For an action to be forbidden under the peace obligation two prerequisites must be met: firstly, it must be an industrial action and it must be directed against the collective agreement as a whole or a provision in it. Neither of these definitions have statutory definitions. However, a forbidden industrial action is obvious when the action is used in order to compel the opposite party to modify the current collective agreement in force. It should also be noted that strikes and lockouts are not the only forms of industrial actions, the notion of industrial action also covers actions such as blockades, go-slows and overtime bans.

G10.5.3   According to Collective Agreements Act the most important remedy is a compensatory fine to be paid by the violator to the wronged party. When a compensatory fine is imposed, all the facts that have emerged, such as the extent of the damage, the degree of guilt, any cause given by the other party to the violation, and the size of the association or undertaking, shall be taken into account. A collective agreement can also be rescinded if the agreement has been violated to such a degree that those bound by the agreement on the opposite side cannot reasonably be required to continue to be bound.

10.6 European Works Councils

G10.6.1   The European Works Council Directive (EWC Directive) has been implemented in Finland since 1996 through the amendments in the Act on Co-operation Within Undertakings. The regulation in the Act on Co-operation Within Undertakings concerning European Work Councils applies to a Finnish Group with at least 1000 workers in the European Economic Area and at least 150 workers in at least two member states. This regulation aims at reaching an agreement on international group co-operation between the group management and the Special Negotiating Body. The Special Negotiating Body is established for this negotiating purpose and it includes one representative elected by the staff from each of the European Economic Area member states in which the group has an undertaking or business.

G10.6.2   If agreement between the group management and the special negotiation body is not reached, international group co-operation shall be arranged as provided in the Act on Cooperation Within Undertakings. The provisions of the Act concerning statutory group co-operation in an international group comprise detailed regulation on matters such as the information that must be given to the Works Council and the number of representatives of staff in the Special Negotiating Body and in the Works Council. The number of representatives in the Works Council shall be at least 3 and at most 30. The representatives are elected from the European Economic Area member states in which the group has an undertaking or business.

G10.6.3   In order to examine this regulation thoroughly, a closer look at the European Works Council Directive is recommended.

11   EMPLOYMENT DISPUTES

11.1 Background

G11.1.1   Depending on the nature of the dispute in question, employment disputes are decided by several official organs. To a certain extent, such procedures are agreed by the parties, either by the parties to the dispute, or by parties to a collective agreement that binds the parties to the dispute. However, disputes over rights in labour questions are in principle settled by the parties themselves.

11.2 Labour Courts/Tribunals

G11.2.1   All labour law disputes not belonging to the competence of other organs, are heard and tried by the regular courts. Finland has a three-tier system of regular courts. The following matters lie within the jurisdiction of regular courts:

(a) disputes concerning the interpretation of individual employment contracts;
(b) disputes concerning other claims based on individual employment contracts;
(c) disputes concerning individual claims based on collective agreements as far as such claims are not to be tried by the Labour Court;
(d) disputes concerning claims for overtime compensation, holiday pay etc; and
(e) prosecutions for breaches of labour legislation (on safety, health etc) and claims for damages because of such breaches.

G11.2.2   The Labour Court is a single specialised court for matters connected with collective agreements and it is composed of four neutral members (which include the president and the vice-chairman), four employers' members, four employee's members and four additional members for cases concerning public officials. The posts of the president and the vice-chairman are full- time. The plaintiff and the defendant before the Labour Court are, in general, employers' and employees' associations that are party to a collective agreement.

G11.2.3   The disputes tried by the Labour Court are of three principal kinds: breaches of duties based on the contents or existence of collective agreements; the interpretation of collective agreements; and sanctions regarding the breaches. This means that the Labour Court can try individual as well as collective disputes over rights. If the settlement of an individual claim depends on the interpretation of a collective agreement, the Labour Court can confine its judgment to the interpretation issue and direct the parties of the individual dispute to institute proceedings at the competent regular court. The regular court then settles the individual claim in accordance with the decision of the Labour Court on the interpretation issue and may also ask the Labour Court for an advisory opinion in a single case, but this advisory opinion is not binding.

G11.2.4   Labour Courts decisions are final ie its decisions may not be appealed.

G11.2.5   The collective bargaining system is based on freedom of negotiation and freedom to contract. According to the Mediation in Labour Disputes Act a work stoppage ie a strike or a lockout, may not take place over a labour dispute without a minimum two-week written notification of the work stoppage been given to a conciliator. The Ministry of Labour may in certain exceptional cases of public interest delay the time for the commencement of the work stoppage. This is possible when, due to the branch in question or the scope of the work stoppage, the action is considered to be directed against vital functions of society or to cause considerable damage to the public interest.

G11.2.6 For the promotion of relations between employers and employees and for the mediation of labour disputes, the state administration includes two National Mediators appointed by the President of the Republic. However, depending on the situation in the labour field, one of the posts may be left vacant and indeed is vacant at present. The term of a National Conciliator is four years. The statutory functions of the National Mediator consist of three different groups. As a preventive function, the National Mediator promotes relations between employees and employers and their organisations. Secondly, the National Mediator has an actual conciliation function in a labour dispute. Thirdly, the National Conciliator has administrative duties relating to conciliation administration. As part of the conciliation function, the National Conciliator begins negotiations between the parties after the referred written notification of the work stoppage has been given. During the minimum two-week period the conciliator has the opportunity to negotiate with the parties in order to resolve the dispute. However, a settlement is not compulsory according to Finnish labour law, although it is obligatory to take part in the negotiating process.

11.3 Settlements

G11.3.1 In Finland, an employee may not opt-out of his employment rights unless otherwise provided for in law. The employee may naturally choose not to bring action against the employer, but it is not possible for him to bind himself to that in advance. In addition, employment crimes fall under the authorisation of the public prosecutor ie the public prosecutor may bring charges against a violator even without the employee's consent.

12 WHISTLEBLOWING/DATA PROTECTION

12.1 Whistleblowing

G12.1.1 Whistleblowing is not a concept familiar to Finnish law. The disclosure of confidential information is prohibited by the Employment Contracts Act (55/2001), Ch 3, s 4, and by the Unfair Business Activities Act, s 4, but there is no statute dealing with the employee's right to disclose an employer's business or trade secrets in certain situations. The Employment Contracts Act (55/2001) states: 'For the duration of the relationship the worker shall not exploit for his own use or divulge to others any of the employer's business or trade secrets'. If the information has come to the worker's knowledge wrongfully, this prohibition continues after the termination of the employment relationship.

G12.1.2 The parties to an employment relationship also have the right to enter into agreements that add to the employee's duty not to disclose confidential information. Prohibition of competition clauses, which restrict the employee's right to make use of the former employer's business secrets are allowed for up to six months from the end of the employment relationship. Deviations from the basic rule of non-disclosure can be made by the courts on a case-by-case basis.

G12.1.3   In the Act on Publicity of the Actions of the Public Authorities, s 24, there is a provision which gives protection to employers whose business or trade secrets have been disclosed to public authorities. According to this provision documents containing information on business or trade secrets shall be kept confidential. This provision also covers corresponding matters if the disclosure of such information would cause financial losses to the employer.

12.2 Data Protection

G12.2.1   Statutes concerning this matter are found in Personal Data File Act (523/1999) which came into force on 1 June 1999 and is based on Directive 95/46/EC. Following the directive, this law applies whenever an employer stores 'personal data' concerning an employee (or other persons) in a register. Both 'register' and 'personal data' are interpreted widely. All information from which a living person is identifiable is personal data, whereas 'register' covers all kind of systems, which allows the information to be browsed.

G12.2.2   The information that is stored must fulfil the requirements of relevance and validity (Personal Data File Act, s 9). The relevance requirement means that an employee may not, for example, store information concerning facts that are to be held discriminatory (eg race, religion, sexual orientation etc) or any other information not relevant to the employment relationship. The relevance of pieces of information is considered in relation to the purpose of the database.

G12.2.3   The second requirement for the registration of information, is the consent of the person concerned ([Personal Data File Act, s 8). Such consent may be given implicitly and in employment relationships that is often the case. However, when it comes to sensitive pieces of information (eg information concerning the health of a worker) the consent must be explicit (s 11).

G12.2.4   The employer may not use the stored data for any purpose unconnected with the aim of the register. He shall also secure the safety of the register, so that the information in it can not be misused or altered or destroyed (Personal Data File Act, s 32). In addition, the employee shall have access to the data concerning him (s 26). This right recognises the requirements of valid and relevant information, as well as the employee's right to self-determination. Apart from some rare exceptions, transferring data outside the European Economic Area is not permitted without the employee's consent, unless the recipient jurisdiction has an adequate level of data protection.

13   HUMAN RIGHTS

13.1 Rights and Obligations

G13.1.1   Finland is a member of the Council of Europe and has ratified the European Convention for the Protection of Human Rights and Fundamental Freedoms as well as the United Nations' International Covenant on Civil and Political Rights. The provisions of these treaties are directly applicable in Finland. However their direct effect is very limited due to the underlying national laws, mainly the Constitution of Finland and more precisely its second Chapter. Due to the European Court of Human Rights, human rights are to a large extent interpreted the same way as in the rest of Europe.

G13.1.2   The human rights conventions or the Finnish Constitution mainly governs the legislator and other officials. However, the requirements of the constitution and the conventions are included in other laws. The human rights and fundamental freedoms are also taken into consideration when laws are being interpreted.

G13.1.3   Section 6 of the Finnish Constitution provides for the equal treatment of all people as follows.

Section 6 – Equality

'Everyone is equal before the law.

No one shall, without an acceptable reason, be treated differently from other persons on the ground of sex, age, origin, language, religion, conviction, opinion, health, disability or other reason that concerns his or her person.

Children shall be treated equally and as individuals and they shall be allowed to influence matters pertaining to themselves to a degree corresponding to their level of development.

Equality of the sexes is promoted in social activity and working life, especially in the determination of pay and the other terms of employment.'

For the interpretation and meaning of this provision see paras G5.1.1–G5.5.1.

There is also a special provision in the Finnish Constitution concerning work:

Section 18 – The right to work and the freedom to engage in commercial activity:

'Everyone has the right, to earn his or her livelihood by the employment, occupation or commercial activity of his or her choice. The public authorities shall take responsibility for the protection of the labour force.

The public authorities shall promote employment and work towards guaranteeing everyone the right to work. Provisions on the right to receive training that promotes employability are laid down by statute.

No one shall be dismissed from employment without a lawful reason'.

G13.1.4   The last sentence emphasises the importance of following the rules of dismissal in a very straightforward way. It is unarguable that the rules of dismissal have to be interpreted strictly.

G13.1.5   Other fundamental rights named in the Finnish Constitution worth mentioning in connection with labour issues are: the right to privacy (s 10); the freedom of religion and conscience (s 11); the freedom of expression and right of access to information (s 12); the freedom of assembly and association (s 13); as well as the protection of property (s 15). All these rights are secured by other, regular laws. The provisions of the constitution emphasise the importance of these rights. In connection with labour law, the protection of property statute gives protection, among other things, to earned pensions rights and prevents legislative encroachments upon earlier agreements in the labour market.

BIBLIOGRAPHY

Suviranta Antti *Labour Law in Finland* (2000)
Suviranta Antti *Labour Law and Industrial Relations in Finland* (2nd edn, 1997)
Suviranta Antti *Finnish National Report to the Fourteenth Congress of the International Academy of Comparative Law* (1994)

USEFUL WEBSITES

Parliament of Finland (Finnish, Swedish, English, French):
• http://www.eduskunta.fi
Council of State (Finnish, Swedish, English):
• http://www.vn.fi/
Ministry of Labour (Finnish, Swedish, English):
• http://www.mol.fi
Ministry of Justice (Finnish, Swedish, English):
• http://www.om.fi
Office of the Ombudsman for Equality (Finnish, Swedish, English, French):
• http://www.tasa-arvo.fi
Employment and Economic Development Centre (Finnish, Swedish, English):
• http://www.te-keskus.fi
The Social Insurance Institution of Finland (Finnish, Swedish, English):
• http://www.kela.fi
Electronic Finnish statute collection, statue translations and precedents of the highest courts of justice (Finnish, Swedish):
• http://finlex.edita.fi
Finnish Competition Authority (Finnish, English):
• http://www.kilpailuvirasto.fi
Finnish Tax Administration (Finnish, Swedish, English):
• http://www.vero.fi
The Finnish Work Environment Fund (Finnish, Swedish, English):
• http://www.tsr.fi

H France

Pascale Lagesse and Hubert Flichy

Pascale Lagesse is admitted as Avocat to the Paris Bar. She joined Freshfields Bruckhaus Deringer in 2000 to head the labour law group in Paris. Before joining the firm, she spent ten years (from 1989 to 1999) in one of the largest French law firms, Gide Loyrette Nouel, as an employment lawyer.

In February 1999, she co-founded the niche firm Flichy Lagesse Montanier Ayache, which specialises in employment law. She studied law at the University of Paris–II (Maîtrise Carrières Judiciaires) and Paris–I (DEA de droit privé). She has advised a significant number of industrial and commercial groups as well as financial institutions in the context of national and cross-border transactions on labour law, pensions, employment law and share schemes.

Freshfields Bruckhaus Deringer, Paris

Phone: +33 1 44 56 44 56°
Fax: +33 1 44 56 44 00/01/02/03
Email: pascale.lagesse@freshfields.com
Website: www.freshfields.com

Hubert Flichy, one of the country's most senior labour lawyers, was a partner at the Paris firm of Gide Loyrette Nouel from 1974 to 1999, where he headed the Labour Law Department. In February 1999, he founded his own labour-law practice, now called Flichy & Associés.

He has specialised in advice and litigation on labour law and social security matters for major private and public companies, as well as employers' associations. His expertise has been applied both to large-scale restructuring operations, redundancy schemes, industrial disputes, and to pension and contingency schemes. He has been co-Chairman of the Paris Bar's Labour Law commission, and is a past member of the Bar Council. Author of many books and publications, including a monthly column in *Capital*, Hubert Flichy has frequently been interviewed on radio and television.

Flichy & Associés

Phone: +33 1 56 62 30 00
Fax: +33 1 56 62 30 01
Email: hubertflichy@flichy-associes.com

FRANCE

Rights	Yes/No	Explanatory Notes
THE EMPLOYMENT RELATIONSHIP		
Minimum notice	YES	Minimum periods set by statute or agreement
Terms:		
Express	YES	Certain contracts/provisions must be in writing
Implied/ incorporated YES	YES	By statute or collective bargaining agreements or custom
REMUNERATION		
Minimum wage regulation	YES	42.02 FF (€ 6.41) per hour as at 1 July 2000
Further rights and obligations:		
Right to paid holiday	YES	Standard leave: 2.5 days per month worked, up to 30 days per annum (more may be agreed)
Right to sick pay	YES/NO	There may be entitlement depending on collective bargaining agreements or the *accord de mensualisation*
WORKING TIME		
Regulation of hours per day/ working week	YES	35 or 39 hours per week, depending on size of employer; some additional hours may be worked but these must be compensated as overtime and are subject to maximum limits
Regulation of night work	YES	Compulsory rest periods; employees under 18 may not work at night
Right to rest periods	YES	Daily/weekly/Sunday rest
EQUAL OPPORTUNITIES		
Discrimination protection:		
Sex	YES	Employees are protected by the provisions of the Labour Code
Race	YES	Employees are protected by the provisions of the Labour Code
Nationality	YES	Employees are protected by the provisions of the Labour Code
Marital status	YES	Employees are protected by the provisions of the Labour Code
Disability	YES	Employees are protected by the provisions of the Labour Code

Religion	YES	Employees are protected by the provisions of the Labour Code
Sexual orientation	YES	Employees are protected by the provisions of the Labour Code
Equal pay legislation	YES	Employees are protected by the provisions of the Labour Code

TERMINATION OF EMPLOYMENT

Right not to be dismissed in breach of contract	YES	
Statutory rights on termination	YES	If the employer does not follow the correct procedure or does not have proper grounds for dismissal, the dismissal may be irregular or unfair

REDUNDANCY

Statutory definition	YES	
Right to payment on redundancy	YES	There may be special payments other than usual dismissal indemnity

Right to consultation:

Individual	YES	Employer is obliged to consult and to offer a retraining agreement
Collective	YES	Less than 10 employees: consultation with works council. Ten or more employees: employer must consult works council and notify local labour authorities, as well as drawing up a Social Plan

YOUNG WORKERS

Protection of children and young persons at work	YES	Protection for school-age children/limitation of working hours and activities for children under the age of 18

MATERNITY RIGHTS

Rights during pregnancy	YES	Right to a lighter workload during the initial period of pregnancy
Right to maternity leave	YES	Between 16 and 46 weeks' leave depending on size of family and other factors
Notice requirements	YES	
Maternity pay (during leave)	YES/NO	No statutory right to salary during leave, although collective bargaining agreements or custom may provide otherwise
Protection from dismissal	YES	Employee may not be dimissed during pregnancy/on leave, and for four weeks after return, save in limited circumstances

339

Health and safety protection	YES	Employee may not work for two weeks before and six weeks after confinement
Right to parental leave	YES	Applies to both male and female employees with one year's service

BUSINESS TRANSFER

Right to protection on transfer	YES	Applies to all employment and apprenticeship contracts in force as at the date of transfer
Transfer of employment obligations	YES	Transferee may only change terms and conditions with the employee's consent
Right to information and consultation	YES	Consultation must take place with the works council
Right not to be dismissed	YES	Unlawful for the transferor to dismiss employees with the intent of avoiding the transfer; this prohibition does not apply to the transferee

COLLECTIVE RIGHTS AND BARGAINING

Compulsory recognition of trade unions	YES	Provided that the union can prove itself to be 'representative' in accordance with statutory criteria
Other forms of staff representation	YES	Staff delegates, the works council, Health and Safety Committee, and staff representatives on the Board of Directors
European works councils	YES	EU Directive on European Works Councils incorporated into the French Labour Code
Right to take industrial action	YES	Right guaranteed by the French Constitution

EMPLOYMENT DISPUTES

Civil court jurisdiction	YES	Only in relation to collective labour disputes and occupational accidents
Statutory body	YES	Industrial Tribunal has jurisdiction over disputes between employer and individual employees

WHISTLEBLOWING

Protection from dismissal/ detriment	YES	Employees protected by general right to freedom of expression, provided the right is not abused

DATA PROTECTION

Protection	YES	Statutory protection in relation to automated processing and non-automated files; additional protection under the Labour Code

HUMAN RIGHTS

Statutory protection	YES	Human rights protected by European Convention on Human Rights and domestic law, including the French Constitution

1 THE EMPLOYMENT RELATIONSHIP

1.1 Background

H1.1.1 There is no definition of an employment contract in French law. However, legal writers and caselaw indicate that the employment contract is an agreement by one party to work for another under the latter's supervision, in exchange for remuneration.

H1.1.2 There are thus three elements to an employment contract:
- services rendered;
- payment of remuneration in exchange for those services; and
- subordination, from a legal standpoint.

H1.1.3 The third element is the most important. Caselaw indicates that this involves carrying out work of whatever nature, under the authority of an employer who issues orders and guidelines, supervises, and imposes sanctions for shortcomings on the employee's part.

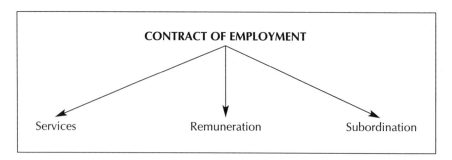

H1.1.4 An individual in service under an employment contract is considered to be an employee, which status will afford him French labour law's safeguards. It is therefore important to distinguish an employment contract from other forms of service contracts:
- *contrat de mandat* – a contract pursuant to which one party empowers another to act in his name. The contract differs from an employment contract, as the *mandataire* or agent enjoys a far greater degree of freedom than an employee in carrying out the purpose of the contract;
- *contrat d'entreprise* – an agreement pursuant to which one, independent party undertakes to carry out a certain task for another to whom he is in no way a subordinate, in exchange for remuneration;
- *contrat de société* – a contract pursuant to which several people agree to mutually undertake a project, and share any resulting profits. None of the contracting parties can be considered a subordinate.

H1.1.5 The courts will not be bound by any actual title or definition the parties may have given their contract, but will examine all of the facts in assessing the nature of their legal relationship.

H1.1.6 It is a basic principle of French law that an employment contract is always entered into for an indefinite term, although there are a few, restrictively defined instances where fixed-term contracts may be permissible, to carry out a specific, temporary task. Permanent jobs related to the company's usual activity may not be filled by employees on fixed-term contracts, save on a one-off basis.

H1.1.7 Employees may be hired under fixed-term contracts to:
- stand in for an employee who is away on leave, eg sick leave or maternity leave;
- deal with a temporary upswing in activity, for example, due to a major client order;
- carry out seasonal tasks eg at harvest time, or for a country fair.

H1.1.8 Employees may also be hired under certain special, fixed-term contracts pursuant to statute or ministerial edicts intended to deal with a shortfall in the labour pool.

H1.1.9 It is strictly forbidden to hire anyone under a fixed-term contract to:
- replace an employee whose contract has been suspended owing to a labour dispute;
- undertake particularly dangerous tasks;
- fill the position of someone who has just been made redundant, on the basis that there has been a temporary upswing in activity;
- take over from another employee who was himself hired under a fixed-term contract, save under certain specific conditions.

H1.1.10 To hire someone under a fixed-term contract which does not fit one of the exceptions described in para **H1.1.7** is a criminal offence, and fixed-term contracts must be carefully distinguished from indefinite-term contracts. Moreover, the employee may petition to have the courts redefine his contract as an indefinite-term contract.

1.2 Contract of Service

H1.2.1 An employment contract is subject to the common law of contract, and to four essential conditions: consent on the part of the individual entering into service, legal capacity, definite purpose, and lawful purpose.
- Consent – this must be personal, mutual, and relate to the contract's essential terms. Although contracts are normally signed, tacit or verbal consent will suffice. Consent must not have been obtained by error, false representation or force.
- Capacity – both parties must have legal capacity.
- Definite and lawful purpose – although the parties are free to define the precise nature of the services to be rendered, the employment contract will be null and void if those services are themselves illegal or immoral, nor may a party lawfully enter the service of a company whose activity is itself unlawful.

H1.2.2 Where one of the above basic conditions is lacking, the contract will be null and void, and cannot be enforced as to any future effects it may have. The courts have, however, acknowledged the past effects of such contracts.

H1.2.3 Where an indefinite-term contract is concerned, the Labour Code, ie the compilation of current French law and regulations, does not require that its terms be set down in writing, although most collective bargaining agreements (see paras **H10.2.1–H10.2.11**) do. Under the ordinary rules of law a mere tacit or verbal agreement will suffice.

H1.2.4 However, French law requires that the employer must file what is known as a *Déclaration préalable à l'embauche*[1] with the authorities, and thereafter give the new recruit:

* a document setting out the information the employer has filed with the Social Security authorities;
* an official receipt for the *Déclaration préalable à l'embauche,* which refers to the information which has been filed.

[1] A form which must be completed and forwarded to the authorities before a recruit enters his new employer's service.

H1.2.5 A European Directive dated 14 October 1991 imposes a duty on all employers to set down in writing the basic terms of the working relationship, whether in an employment contract, a letter of engagement or otherwise. Since in France employers must give each member of their workforce a payslip on which the relevant information appears, no legislation has been enacted to that effect.

H1.2.6 In the following instances, inter alia, the Labour Code does require a written contract:

* fixed-term contracts;
* part-time contracts;
* contracts where the employer is a temporary employment agency ('temping');
* apprenticeships;
* *contrat d'insertion en alternance* (a special, fixed-term contract pursuant to statute or edict);
* the agreement between an employer and a medical officer;[1]
* contracts between an individual, and a group of employers.

[1] In France, the *médecin du travail* is the equivalent of an occupational health officer, or factory doctor.

H1.2.7 Where a written contract is signed in France, it must be drafted in the French language, whether or not the contract is intended to be performed there. Foreign workers may demand a translation.

H1.2.8 Apart from the two central terms, namely services rendered against remuneration, the trend is towards ever more detailed contractual terms which impose specific duties on both employer and employee. Although such terms will normally be express, the courts may imply them.

A   EXPRESS TERMS

H1.2.9 The parties are free to include in their contract any lawful terms save those which either are against public policy (such as terms forbidding trade union membership), or contravene regulations or any relevant collective bargaining agreement. The courts will also not uphold clauses which impose constraints on either party which are not called for by the nature of the tasks or the contract's intended purpose.

H1.2.10   In practice, virtually all written employment contracts contain the same general clauses: nature of the contract, services to be rendered, date of engagement, qualifications and remuneration, as well as whatever terms the relevant collective bargaining agreement may dictate (eg trial period, working hours).

Examples of express terms

Exclusivity undertaking

H1.2.11   Undertakings as to exclusivity are designed to prevent the employee from entering anyone else's employ whilst in his current employer's service.

Mobility clause

H1.2.12   The employee may agree to undertake business trips, or to change his place of work.

Clause de conscience

H1.2.13   A *clause de conscience* allows for rescission of the contract by the employee, in the event of a marked variation in the company's activities or business philosophy.

Restrictive covenants

H1.2.14   A restrictive covenant restrains the employee from competing with the employer after termination of the contract. Such clauses may appear in the original contract, take the form of a supplemental contract, or be agreed upon termination. Compensation in exchange for the clause is not required for the clause to be binding.

H1.2.15   As these are in fact clauses in restraint of trade, the courts will uphold them only where they are strictly required to protect a legitimate interest on the employer's part, and where they allow the employee to continue to exercise his trade.

Clause de dédit formation

H1.2.16   Under a *clause de dédit formation*, the employer pays for occupational training, while in exchange the recruit undertakes to remain in the company's service for a certain length of time, failing which he will be bound to refund any training costs incurred by the employer.

H1.2.17   Provided they do not represent an absolute bar on resignation, such clauses are enforceable, as the recruit's undertaking represents consideration for the employer's promise to invest in training at a cost above and beyond that which he would have been obliged to incur by law or under the collective bargaining agreement.

Guaranteed employment clauses

H1.2.18   With a guaranteed employment clause, the employer undertakes not to terminate the contract for a certain specified period. Such clauses are enforceable provided that the parties remain free to terminate the contract by mutual agreement, and that the employer retains the right to dismiss an employee who is guilty of serious misconduct.

Quota or performance clauses

H1.2.19   In a quota or performance clause, the employee undertakes to reach a certain target or quota, failing which, under certain, strictly defined circumstances, the employer may dismiss him.

Secrecy clause

H1.2.20   The employee undertakes not to disclose trade or other company secrets.

H1.2.21   Most of the clauses above will be enforceable only if the employee has signed a written employment contract.

B   IMPLIED TERMS

H1.2.22   The courts may find that a contract contains certain implied terms, on the basis of section 1134 para 3 of the Civil Code, which states that enforceable agreements must be performed in good faith, and section 1135, which states that:

> '... contracts bind the parties [to achieve] not only what is explicitly stated, but all those results which fairness (*équité*), custom or the law would call for, in the light of the contract's nature.'

H1.2.23   One example of such terms is the typical exclusivity clause, pursuant to which the employee undertakes not to work for any third party whilst in his current employer's service.

1.3   Variation of Contract

H1.3.1   An employment contract, whether for a fixed or for an indefinite term, may need to be adapted to suit the company's, or the employee's, changing circumstances. The fact that contracts can be so adapted ensures that they remain enforceable over time. However, certain changes may be proposed to the employee which he does not care to agree to, and which may lead to termination of the contract.

H1.3.2   In French law, a clear distinction has been drawn by the courts between variation of the contract (*modification*) as such, and a change to working conditions. Different legal rules apply in each instance.

H1.3.3   Where the employment contract itself is to be varied, no matter how slightly, the principle that it is binding on the parties means that both parties' consent will be required.

H1.3.4   On the other hand, where the change involves working conditions only, the employee must comply with the change, failing which the employer will be entitled to impose disciplinary measures. For example, if the contract includes a mobility clause, and an employee refuses to transfer, this may, under certain circumstances, constitute grounds for dismissal.

A   VARIATION OF THE EMPLOYMENT CONTRACT

Definition of the notion of variation

H1.3.5   In principle, the distinction outlined in paras **H1.3.2–H1.3.4** would appear to be perfectly clear. In practice, however, the scope of the contract itself will have to be carefully defined.

- *Where there is a written employment contract*, the parties' respective rights and obligations have been made explicit, and one need only consult the contract. Any change to its clauses qualifies as a variation.
- *Where there is no written employment contract*, it will be far more difficult to ascertain what, precisely, is contractual in scope. The courts will normally examine the parties' intention at the point the contract was first entered into.

H1.3.6   Until recently, there was no schedule of what the courts would deem basic contractual terms; however the *Cour de Cassation* (French Supreme Court) has recently given some guidance where variation is concerned.

H1.3.7   In a series of cases, the *Cour de Cassation* has held that neither remuneration nor the number of working hours may be varied without the employee's consent. It has also found that adding a clause in restraint of trade to an employment contract which initially included no such clause, or cutting back the contractually-agreed notice period, were variations which the employee was entitled to reject.

H1.3.8   On the other hand, a mere proposal or scheme will not represent variation, as the employer may yet withdraw them.

H1.3.9   Similarly, the employee will not be allowed to claim that his contract has been varied where such variation has been specifically provided for by the contract itself or by the collective bargaining agreement.

H1.3.10   Thus, where an employee is transferred in accordance with a geographical mobility clause, transfer will be deemed a mere change to working conditions, which the employer is within his rights in imposing.

Legal effects

H1.3.11   Where a change is made to an employee's contract for economic reasons, the works council must be consulted, and a statutory dismissal procedure must be complied with (see paras **H6.2.1–H6.3.16**). In other cases, before any variation is made to his employment contract, the employee's consent must be obtained.

The employee agrees to the variation

H1.3.12   Once the employee has agreed to the change, variation of the contract is deemed to have taken place. Neither party may subsequently require that the initial terms remain in force.

H1.3.13   The burden of proof as to consent rests with the employer, save where variation has been imposed for economic reasons, or where the employee has been given a deadline within which to accept or reject the change, silence implying tacit consent. Tacit consent will be binding on the employee if his subsequent behaviour has made his intention plain.

The employee rejects the variation

H1.3.14   If the employee rejects a substantial variation to the contract, the employer must either restore the contract's initial terms, or take the initiative of terminating the contract.

H1.3.15   An employee who refuses a change put to him by his employer may thus carry on working as before. If the employer really intends not to be bound by the initial contractual terms, he will have to dismiss the employee.

H1.3.16   However, if the employer has tried to impose a change to the contract unilaterally, the employee's options are not restricted to reporting for work while expressing dissatisfaction with the change. He is in fact entitled to resign, as under these circumstances, resignation will be deemed to constitute dismissal, and he will be entitled to claim a remedy for dismissal.

B   CHANGES IN WORKING CONDITIONS

H1.3.17   The employer has the power to alter working conditions unilaterally, other than those stipulated by contract, without the workforce's consent.

H1.3.18   The courts have found that if an employee refuses to carry on working after such a change to his working conditions, he may be guilty of serious misconduct, and the employer is within his rights in dismissing him.

1.4   Remedies

H1.4.1   Individual disputes between employer and employee arising from the employment contract may be referred to an Industrial Tribunal (*Conseil de Prud'hommes*) notably with respect to wages, dismissal indemnities, and so forth. The Industrial Tribunal may also hear unfair dismissal claims, and order reinstatement or damages corresponding sometimes to at least six months' wages. Such disputes may also be heard by courts other than the Industrial Tribunal.

H1.4.2   The employer may impose disciplinary sanctions on a sliding scale, which may take the form, inter alia, of a warning, suspension, transfer for disciplinary reasons, demotion or dismissal.

H1.4.3 The employer may refer an individual dispute arising from an employee's employment contract, eg a dispute over a clause in restraint of trade, to the Industrial Tribunal.

H1.4.4 Such disputes may also be heard by other courts.

2 REMUNERATION

2.1 Background

H2.1.1 In exchange for his services, the employee is paid remuneration, which, depending on the trade in question, may have various names, such as wages, salary or fees, and which may take various forms. Thus an employee may be paid by the hour, by quantity or results, by assignment, or relative to turnover.

H2.1.2 In principle, the parties are free to set whatever salary they please, subject to the statutory minimum wage, or the minimum wage set by collective bargaining agreement or other collective agreements. The employer must also comply with anti-discrimination regulations.

H2.1.3 In companies where trade unions are represented, there must be annual wage negotiations (see Collective Rights and Bargaining, paras **H10.1.1–H10.4.35**).

A   AMOUNT AND TYPE OF REMUNERATION

Basic salary

H2.1.4 Basic salary is the fixed remuneration which the employer must pay the employee for his services. The parties decide in advance how it will be assessed and paid.

H2.1.5 The following additional items may also be included:

- *Benefits in kind and perquisites*: these could include items such as food, lodging, heating or clothing. The employment contract or collective bargaining agreement may also provide for a company car. All of these constitute part of salary.
- *Business expenses*: in many trades, the employee will be entitled to refunds for business expenses, intended to compensate the employee for costs he incurs in the course of his activities, or for the conditions under which he performs them. It should be borne in mind that where a lump sum refund is provided to the employee, which is not intended to cover real and concrete expenses incurred, the lump sum payment will qualify as salary.
- *Tips*: tips may either be the employee's only source of income (in certain trades), or they may be paid as well as fixed wages.
- *Bonuses*: these may take a variety of forms, ranging from bonuses paid for insalubrious or dangerous tasks, or for being on call at certain times, to end-of-year bonuses, performance bonuses, holiday bonuses, and so forth.

Bonuses fall into two categories. Where the employer has complete discretion as to whether or not to pay the bonuses, they are known as *bénévole*.

Where it has been the employer's practice to pay bonuses, where it is stipulated by contract, or where the employer has undertaken on his own initiative to pay it, the bonus is deemed to be part of salary and must be paid.

- *Length of service bonus*: imposed by ministerial edicts, such bonuses are generally fixed by collective bargaining agreements or by custom.
- *Public transport bonus*: in the Ile de France area, the employer must refund half the employee's commuting costs.

Forms of remuneration
- *Hourly pay*: the employee's wages will depend on how many hours he puts in. In principle, and subject to certain exceptions, he need not be paid if he is away from work.
- *Pay by results*: the principle is that there is a basic standard for each type of work, corresponding to a basic salary. The moment the standard is exceeded, the employee's wages rise, and the greater the overshot the more they rise.
- *Case-by-case*: to encourage the workforce, companies may tailor salary to the individual's results, through a bonus, an individual pay rise, wages on merit etc.
- *Tips*: remuneration by means of tips occurs only in establishments in contact with the public, and is paid by the client, not by the employer. Depending on the circumstances, tips may be either the entire wage, or a wage item.
- *Commission on turnover*: this is a percentage of the turnover achieved by the employee, team or workforce. It may be applied to the entire salary, or as a perk over and above basic salary.
- *Accord de mensualisation* (monthly wage packet): this involves paying a monthly salary to employees who had previously been paid by the hour, no matter how many days there are in the month, and affording them the benefits to which only employees paid by the month are normally entitled. Since a 1977 agreement known as the *accord de mensualisation*, extended to cover virtually the entire French workforce by an Act dated 19 January 1978, employers are, as a rule, under a duty to pay wages on a monthly basis.

2.2 Legal Regulation of Remuneration

H2.2.1 Since an Act dated 11 February 1950, the parties have been free to negotiate wage levels, either contractually, or through collective bargaining (or other) bgreements. There are however restrictions to the principle of freely negotiated wage levels:
- collective bargaining and other agreements will often establish categories within each trade, and lay down a minimum wage for each category, which the employer must respect;
- the employer may not discriminate when fixing wage levels, and must apply the rule 'same work, same pay';

- the employer must comply with the terms of the *Salaire Minimum National Interprofessionel de Croissance*, or SMIC (statutory minimum wage).

STATUTORY MINIMUM WAGE (SALAIRE MINIMUM NATIONAL INTERPROFESSIONEL DE CROISSANCE – SMIC)

H2.2.2   The purpose behind the SMIC is to allow the workforce to profit from overall economic expansion, on the basis that 'the tide lifts all boats'.

H2.2.3   To that end, the SMIC is reviewed as follows:
- as soon as prices have risen by 2% or more, the SMIC is raised accordingly, by edict;
- the SMIC is reviewed annually by edict, in the light of general economic trends;
- the Government has the power to raise the SMIC at any time during the fiscal year.

H2.2.4   The SMIC applies nationwide to all trades to which a collective bargaining agreement may apply. It is guaranteed to all able-bodied workers aged 18 and over, no matter how their wages are paid.

H2.2.5   The SMIC is stated as an hourly minimum wage. For the purposes of assessing the SMIC, an hour is understood as an hour's actual work.

H2.2.6   As at 1 July 2000, the SMIC stood at 42.02 FF/hour (€ 6.41).

2.3   Deductions from Wages

H2.3.1   In principle, the Labour Code prohibits the practice of docking, ie a set-off between outstanding salary, on the one hand, and debts the employee may owe to his employer in respect of his employment on the other hand.

H2.3.2   However, nothing in the Labour Code prohibits an employer from docking from sums which the employee may owe him, particular items which do not qualify as salary, such as the dismissal indemnity. Nevertheless the employee's written agreement should be obtained before doing so.

H2.3.3   In practice, since the conditions under which docking is permissible are fixed by statute, employment contracts need not contain any such clauses. Indeed, such clauses should be left out altogether, because if they do not comply with any of the principles laid down by the Labour Code, the employee may claim repayment of any sums unduly docked, as well as damages for any prejudice he may have incurred.

2.4   Itemised Pay Statement

H2.4.1   French law requires that the employer provides employees with an itemised payslip, which includes the amount of both gross and net salary, as well as all national insurance payments and other levies for which the employee is liable (also called *précompte*).

3   FURTHER RIGHTS AND OBLIGATIONS

3.1   Holiday Entitlement

H3.1.1   All individuals in salaried employment, no matter what their trade, are entitled to paid holidays, and the employer is under a legal duty to grant them.

H3.1.2   The Labour Code stipulates that once an employee has been in a given employer's service for a number of days corresponding to one month's actual work at any time between 1 June of the previous year and 31 May of the current year,[1] the employer must allow him paid leave.

[1]   This is known as the Reference Year (période de référence).

H3.1.3   Working periods equivalent to four weeks or 24 working days, as well as the previous year's paid leave, maternity leave, sick leave owing to occupational illness or accident, military service including extended service, will all count towards one month's actual work.

H3.1.4   Since a Governmental Order (*Ordonnance*)[1] dated 16 January 1982, employees are entitled to 2.5 days' paid leave for each month actually worked, up to a ceiling of 30 working days' leave a year, although the employment contract, custom or collective bargaining or other agreements may allow for additional leave.

[1]   The term *Ordonnance* refers to law enacted directly by the Government, by delegation of Parliament's powers, in areas normally within the latter's sole remit.

Holidays

- Holiday entitlement period: 1 June–31 May
- 2.5 days entitlement per month worked
- Maximum statutory entitlement: 30 days per year
- Additional holiday may be granted by agreement

H3.1.5   Employees must take their paid holidays every year, and, save for statutory exceptions, neither the employer nor the employee may require that all or part of the holiday is put off to the following year. The parties may nevertheless come to an express agreement to do so, just as they may agree to allow the employee to take holiday in anticipation of his entitlement (*congés par anticipation*).

H3.1.6   The workforce takes paid holidays at dates (which must necessarily include the period between 1 May and 31 October each year) set either by the collective bargaining agreement, where relevant, or by the employer, in accordance with custom, and after consulting the staff delegates and works council.

H3.1.7   After consulting the staff delegates, the employer is responsible for fixing the dates for each employee's leave, unless a schedule for leave has been laid down by the collective bargaining agreement. The works council must also be consulted on the schedule for leave.

H3.1.8   The employer may either implement staggered leave, allowing him to keep the business running non-stop, or otherwise close down the business entirely in the quiet season, in which case the entire workforce will be compelled to take their holiday at that time.

H3.1.9   Both employer and employee must comply with the leave schedule, and with the dates fixed by the employer. Any change must be notified at least one month before the planned date of departure, save in exceptional circumstances.

H3.1.10   Exceptions may be allowed in the case of employees working overseas, but as a general rule, employees may not take over 24 working days' leave in a single stretch.

H3.1.11   Where the employee has acquired rights to a main holiday (between 12 and 24 days), the employer may ask him to stagger his leave over more than one period, but only if the employee so consents. Under certain circumstances, this may entitle the employee to extra leave.

HOLIDAY PAID IN LIEU

- *This falls due at the end of the period of paid leave*, replaces salary, and as such appears on the employee's payslip. It corresponds to one-tenth of total remuneration received by the employee during the reference period, but may not be less than the remuneration the employee would have received had he worked instead of taking holiday. Of the two methods of calculation, the one most to the employee's advantage must be applied. In terms of payment, the rules which apply to salary will also apply to holiday pay.
- *When an employment contract has been terminated* during the Reference Year, and holiday leave remains outstanding, the employee must receive an indemnity to compensate for those days, no matter which party took the initiative of terminating the contract. The indemnity is calculated on the same basis as paid holiday. However, an employee dismissed on grounds of gross misconduct (*faute lourde*) is barred from claiming the indemnity.

H3.1.12   Other forms of leave include leave granted for family events eg parental leave, leave granted in order to attend occupational or trade union training courses, leave to set up one's own firm (*création d'entreprise*), sabbatical leave, retraining leave, and *congés de solidarité internationale*.[1]

[1]   This is a form of statutory leave, to allow an employee to do volunteer work for recognised overseas charities.

H3.1.13 Unlike standard holiday leave, these other forms of leave require the employer's permission, and must be taken for very precise reasons. Such leave is financed in different ways, beyond the scope of the present discussion.

3.2 Sick Pay

H3.2.1 In principle, the contract of an employee who is away on sick leave, even if it is due to occupational illness or accident, will be suspended, which means that the employer is under no obligation to pay his wages. However, under certain conditions laid down by collective bargaining agreements, or by a 1977 agreement known as the *accord de mensualisation* (see paras **H2.1.1–H2.4.1**), the employer may find himself under a duty to pay all or part of wages during sick leave.

H3.2.2 The indemnities paid to an employee on sick leave may either represent the difference between Social Security sickness benefit and salary, or be paid in addition to Social Security sickness benefit. Alternatively, the employer may pay the employee's full wage, in which case, the Social Security system will pay sickness benefit directly to the employer.

H3.2.3 In case of sickness or accident, the *accord de mensualisation* stipulates that the employee will be entitled to full pay provided that:

• he has over three years' service with the employer as at the first day of sick leave, *and*
• he produces a medical certificate within 48 hours, *and*
• he has social insurance, *and*
• he obtains medical treatment in France or in an EU member state.

H3.2.4 Under the *accord de mensualisation*, sick pay is payable from the first day of sick leave if caused by an occupational illness or accident, and from the 11th day of leave in all other cases. From that day onwards, and for the 30 succeeding days, the employee receives 90% of the gross remuneration he would have been paid had he continued to report for work. During the following 30-day period, he receives two-thirds of his pay.

H3.2.5 Beyond three years' service with the employer, and for each tranche of five years' service, the employee is entitled to an extra 10 days' pay. In other words, an employee with 15 years' service will be entitled to 60 days' sick leave at 90% of pay, 60 days at two-thirds' pay and so on, while an employee with 30 years' service is entitled to 90 days' sick leave at 90% of pay, 90 days at two-thirds' pay etc. The ceiling for each such period is 90 days.

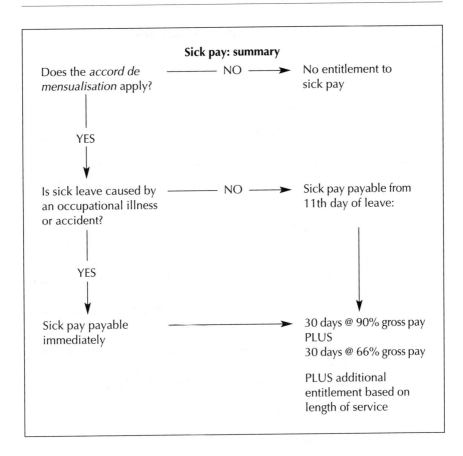

Sick pay: summary

Does the *accord de mensualisation* apply? —————— NO ————▶ No entitlement to sick pay

YES

Is sick leave caused by an occupational illness or accident? —————— NO ————▶ Sick pay payable from 11th day of leave:

YES

Sick pay payable immediately —————————————————▶ 30 days @ 90% gross pay
PLUS
30 days @ 66% gross pay

PLUS additional entitlement based on length of service

H3.2.6 Any sick pay paid over and above Social Security sickness benefit is subject to social security contributions.

H3.2.7 The *Cour de Cassation* has held that although the employee is entitled to a guaranteed *income* while on sick leave, this does not guarantee his continued employment. If his absence disrupts the company's operations, he may be replaced.[1]

[1]   Cass Soc, 4 June 1982, Bull V p 279.

H3.2.8 Collective bargaining agreements will often stipulate that employers are entitled to demand a second medical opinion where an employee has been granted sick leave. In such cases, if the employee refuse to submit to a second examination, he may be barred from claiming any payment beyond Social Security sickness benefit.

3.3 Miscellaneous

H3.3.1 Employees are deemed to enjoy certain basic rights within the company, such as freedom to belong to a trade union, freedom of speech, of expression, of belief, and the right to respect for private life.

H3.3.2 There are a number of important legal sources for these rights, notably:

- the 1958 Constitution of France;
- the Universal Human Rights Declaration of 1789;
- the Preamble to the 1946 Constitution;
- the European Human Rights Convention.

H3.3.3 Section 120–2 of the Labour Code provides that 'no-one may infringe upon individual and collective rights and liberties, save as may be justified by the nature of the tasks, and proportionate to the purpose at hand'.

4 WORKING TIME

4.1 Background

H4.1.1 L 212–4 of the Labour Code states that actual working hours (*durée du travail effectif*) are defined as those hours during which the employee is at his employer's disposal, must comply with his employer's instructions, and may not attend to his own affairs.

H4.1.2 Over the last 80 years, the statutory working week has fallen by 13 hours, the equivalent of one-and-a-half working days:

- 1840–1900 – legislation on women and children's working hours;
- 23 April 1919: the 48-hour week;
- 21 June 1936: the 40-hour week;
- 16 January 1982: the 39-hour week;
- 13 June 1998: the 35-hour week.

H4.1.3 A governmental Order (*Ordonnance*) dated 16 January 1982 fixed the statutory working week at 39 hours. This has now been lowered to 35 hours by an Act dated 13 June 1998, which came into force on 1 January 2000 for companies with more than 20 employees, and which will enter into force on 1 January 2002 for smaller companies. A further Act dated 19 January 2000, which entered into force on 1 February 2000, has now defined the final version of the 35-hour working week.

4.2 Legislative Control

A   THE STATUTORY WORKING WEEK

H4.2.1 As of 1 January 2000 on, the statutory working week was cut back to 35 hours in companies employing more than 20 employees.

H4.2.2 The 39-hour working week will remain in force up to 31 December 2001 for companies with a workforce of 20 or fewer employees.

H4.2.3 The statutory working week, whether 39 or 35 hours, is based on a calendar week. It applies to all trades and businesses whatever their activity, in each and every one of their establishments, and whether these businesses are public or private. It also applies to civil servants, and to employees of partnerships, trade unions and associations, and of family-run businesses. It applies to apprentices and *cadres*, but it does not apply to *cadres dirigeants* (upper-echelon management).

H4.2.4   There are certain trades, nonetheless,[1] to which the statutory working week does not apply.

[1]   These exceptions include agriculture, underground mining operations, the Merchant Marine, certain nationalised companies with a special status, and public hospitals.

H4.2.5   Ministerial Decree deals with how the statutory working week is to be applied in practice.

H4.2.6   Actual working hours (*durée du travail effectif*) are defined as those hours during which the employee is at his employer's disposal and must comply with his instructions, without being free to attend to his own affairs. Breaks and mealtimes must be considered in the light of this definition, and each situation must be examined on a case-by-case basis. If, during the break, the employee remains at his employer's disposal and must be on call to comply with his instructions, the break will count as actual working time.

H4.2.7   The new Act also deals with the time needed for dressing and undressing where working clothing is required. Although this does not count as actual working time, either monetary compensation or extra rest must be granted in exchange for such time.

H4.2.8   There are also trades or professions where the employee, although bound to remain on company premises, has slack periods during the day with nothing to do. In such trades, pursuant to regulations or to the applicable collective bargaining agreement, employees may be bound to remain on the premises beyond the statutory working week, which time will be deemed to correspond to a certain number of actual working hours. For example, in hospitals or clinics, 41 hours and 55 minutes will be deemed to correspond to a 39-hour working week, and 37 hours and 37 minutes, to a 35-hour working week.

H4.2.9   Decrees applicable to certain defined trades or professions may also provide specific temporary, or permanent exceptions to the statutory working week. These exceptions will as a rule fall into the category of paid overtime, rather than into the sort of scheme for hospitals which is described in para **H4.2.8**.

B   SCHEDULING

The collective work schedule

H4.2.10   The statutory working week must be seen in the context of the overall work schedule which involves all or part of an establishment's workforce.

H4.2.11   There are also specific schedules such as:

- *relay shifts* – where the workforce is divided into shifts, and employees report for work at different times during the working day. The relays may overlap, or they may alternate;
- *rotation* – the employees involved do not all work the same days, neither do their days off fall on the same day of the week.

H4.2.12

- *alternating shifts* – one shift succeeds another, without overlap, so that the business may run round the clock.

H4.2.13   These schedules may be authorised either by Decree, by collective agreements extended to every business or establishment in that branch of industry by Decree, or by a company-wide agreement.

Flexitime (horaires de travail individualisés)

H4.2.14   There may be exceptions to the collective work schedule where flexitime systems or standing shifts are established: see paras **H4.2.15–H4.2.17**.

Flexitime

H4.2.15   Management establishes a core schedule, during which the entire workforce must be present. Outside the core schedule, flexitime may be implemented as each employee chooses.

H4.2.16   The preconditions for implementing flexitime are:

- a request for flexitime from the workforce;
- notification to the Labour Inspector;
- approval from the works council or staff representatives.

Standing shifts

H4.2.17

Since 1982, industry has been authorised to establish standing shifts, so that plant and machinery may run non-stop whilst the rest of the workforce take their days off. This practice is subject either to approval from the Labour Inspector, or to specific provisions in the relevant collective bargaining agreement.

Changes to a collective work schedule

H4.2.18   Statutory working hours are, as a rule, assessed on a weekly basis. However, exceptions may be granted to enable employers to deal with sharp fluctuations in workload.

- The French term *modulation* refers to an annual accounting system for working hours. This system is designed to enable employers to avoid having either to put their workforce on short-time, when business is slow, or to pay overtime when it is exceptionally busy.

- The French term *cycle* refers to a system designed to take into account regular, predictable variations in the workload.
- The Act dated 13 June 1998 and the Act dated 19 January 2000 allow companies which intend to shorten the collective working week to do so by granting the workforce extra days off.

4.3   Overtime

H4.3.1   Overtime and mandatory rest to recuperate from overtime (*repos compensateur*) are among the major issues dealt with by the new Acts on the statutory working week.

A   DEFINITION

H4.3.2   Overtime is defined as hours worked beyond the statutory working week, or beyond a number of hours deemed to correspond to the statutory working week. Overtime will as a rule be assessed per calendar week.

H4.3.3   The purpose of these Acts is *not* to make the 35-hour working week compulsory, nor has the shorter working week become a *right* from the standpoint of the workforce. The point is that overtime will henceforth be calculated as of the thirty-fifth, rather than the thirty-ninth, hour of work. The employer is quite within his rights to require that employees work over 35 hours a week, provided he pays overtime in respect of any additional hours.

H4.3.4   However, no employee may, in principle, work beyond 10 hours a day, 48 hours a week, or 44 hours a week on average (or 46 hours where there is an agreement extended to every business or establishment in that branch of industry), over a single 12-week period.

B   IMPLEMENTATION

H4.3.5   Although application of the new statutory working week in 2000 or 2002 will directly affect the issue of overtime, under the Act dated 19 January 2000, there will be a one-year transitional period, not only insofar as overtime rates are concerned, but also with regard to the assessment of overtime.

C   GENERAL PRINCIPLES

Overtime bonus granted as time off (bonification)

H4.3.6   In principle, and unless there is a collective agreement to the contrary, where the law refers to *bonification* for overtime, this will be covered by mandatory rest rather than by salary.

H4.3.7   For example, if an employee works 37 hours, two of which represent overtime, he will be entitled to time-and-a-quarter in the form of half an hour's mandatory rest ($2 \times 25\%$).

H4.3.8   The two hours will count towards the annual ceiling (*contingent annuel*) on overtime.

H4.3.9 The employee may choose to take this time off by the day, or by the half-day, except for a period (likely to be between 1 July and 31 August 31) which will be established by Regulations. The employee may decide whether he wants to take a half-day or full day off, but he may not stipulate a precise date. In principle, the employee must take his mandatory rest within two months of having become entitled to the same.

Annual ceiling on overtime

H4.3.10 The annual ceiling on overtime remains at 130 hours per employee, but will gradually accrue from the thirty-sixth hour onwards.

H4.3.11 By law, and unless the Labour Inspector has specifically so authorised, no employee may perform more than 130 hours overtime a year, unless the relevant collective bargaining agreement provides for an arrangement which is more advantageous to the workforce.

H4.3.12 Overtime must be reported to the Labour Inspector and to staff representatives.

H4.3.13 Where a company is faced with an unusually heavy workload, the works council may approve overtime above and beyond the 130-hour cut-off point, provided the Labour Inspector gives his approval to this.

H4.3.14 If the company applies a significant *accord de modulation* (agreement relating to the annual accounting system for working hours), pursuant to a Decree dated 31 January 2000, the annual ceiling on overtime mentioned in para **H4.3.10** is not 130 hours per employee but 90 hours. However, this annual ceiling will not be cut back to 90 hours and will remain at 130 hours where *modulation* is slight ie:

- where a collective agreement provides for a spread ranging from 31 hours in slack periods, and 39 hours in busy periods; or
- where a collective agreement provides for an annual number of 70 hours beyond the statutory 35-hour working week.

Mandatory rest

H4.3.15 Mandatory rest (*repos compensateur obligatoire*) applies in addition to the rest of overtime legislation. Arrangements will differ, depending on whether the company's workforce exceeds ten people or not.

H4.3.16 In companies with more than 10 employees, overtime entitles the employee to mandatory rest at the following rate:

- 50% of all hours worked beyond the 41st hour, below a ceiling of 130 hours per annum;
- Once the employee has overshot the 130-hour ceiling, 100% for every hour beyond:
- 35 hours in companies with a workforce exceeding 20 employees;
- 39 hours up to 31 December 2001, and 35 hours from 1 January 2002, in companies with a workforce of between 11 and 20 employees.

H4.3.17 In other words, if an employee has overshot the 130-hour ceiling by one hour, the employer must not only pay one hour's overtime, or allow him one hour off in lieu of pay, but must also allow him a further full hour's mandatory rest.

H4.3.18 In companies with up to 10 employees, only overtime beyond the statutory 130-hour (or 90-hour in case of *modulation*) ceiling entitles the employee to mandatory rest at a rate of 50% of all hours worked beyond the 40th hour.

H4.3.19 However, in all cases the employee must have earned the right to at least eight hours of mandatory rest, before he may take it.

H4.3.20 Furthermore, where the employer requires the workforce to work beyond 39 hours a week, to make up for hours lost either through inventory, or through work stoppage caused by *force majeure* or accidental factors such as bad weather, those extra hours worked will not count as overtime

D   TRANSITIONAL SCHEME: 2000 OR 2002[1]

H4.3.21 In any given week, compensation for the first four hours' overtime (from the 36th to the 39th hour) will be a 10% overtime bonus (this refers to *bonification* as defined above), either in the form of time off (six minutes per hour) or in the form of overtime pay where a collective agreement so provides. Failing such an agreement, only time off can be granted.

[1]   Up to 2000 for companies with workforces over 20, to 2002 for companies with workforces 20 or less.

H4.3.22 Between the 40th and 43rd hour of overtime, the employee will be entitled to time-and-a-quarter, and beyond 43 hours, to time-and-a-half.

H4.3.23 Companies whose workforce is under 20 will continue to apply the scheme currently in force (time-and-a-quarter between the 40th and 47th hour, and time-and-a-half beyond that) up to 31 December 2001.

E   DEFINITIVE SCHEME: 1 JANUARY 2001 OR 1 JANUARY 2003

H4.3.24 Once the transitional period ends, the final overtime arrangement will be as follows.

H4.3.25 Between the 36th and 39th hour, compensation will be a 25%, rather than a 10% overtime bonus (this refers to *bonification* as defined above), which in principle will take the form of rest (15 minutes per hour). Where a collective agreement so provides, either time off, or overtime pay (time plus 25%) will be granted.

H4.3.26 For overtime beyond 39 hours, the rules will remain the same as during the transitional period. In this case, as an exception to the general rule, under certain conditions it may be permissible not to pay overtime, but rather to grant time off in lieu.

H4.3.27 Over and above overtime pay, or time off in lieu for overtime, the employer must also grant mandatory rest.

4.4 The Shorter Working Week in the Form of Days Off

H4.4.1 Section 9 of the Act dated 19 January 2000 refers to this option, which already appeared in the Act dated 13 June 1998. Extra days or half-days off may be taken either by periods of four consecutive weeks, or annually.

H4.4.2 Where extra days or half-days off are taken by periods of four consecutive weeks, the employer schedules this in advance. If he wishes to change that schedule, he must notify the employee concerned seven days in advance. The employer may set up such an arrangement without there being a collective agreement, but in that case, he will not be entitled in principle to the national insurance rebates otherwise granted under the June 1998 and January 2000 Acts.

H4.4.3 Where days or half-days off are to accrue on an annual basis, there must be a collective agreement to that effect. The choice of days off is made partly by the employee, and partly by the employer. Therefore, in companies where a 39-hour working week remains in force, the employer may grant staff 22 or 23 extra days off to arrive at a 35-hour working week on average.

H4.4.4 Where a collective agreement so provides, the transition to a 35-hour working week may combine both a shorter working week, and extra days off. For example, an agreement may call for cutting the working week back to an average of 37 hours, combined with 10 or 11 extra days off.

H4.4.5 In the latter case, all hours worked beyond the weekly ceiling of 39 hours (or beyond the weekly ceiling provided by the collective agreement, ie 37 hours in the example mentioned above in para 4.4.4) will count as overtime. At the end of the year, if the employee has worked over 1600 hours, those extra hours – less any overtime hours which have already been paid – will count as overtime as well.

Working time

The working week:

- Employer has more than 20 ————————▶ 35 hour 'working week'
  employees
- Employer has 20 or fewer ————————▶ 39 hour 'working week'
  employees

Maximum hours to be worked each week:

- 10 hours per day/48 hours per week

OR

- 44 hours per week over a 12 week period
- Any work in excess of 35/39 hour working week = *overtime*

Maximum overtime to be worked:

- 130 hours per year

Overtime compensation:

- Overtime pay

PLUS

- Mandatory rest

4.5   Cadres[1]

A   PARTICULAR STATUS

H4.5.1   Until the current legislation appeared, no distinction had been drawn between *cadres* and other categories of workers, with respect to working hours.

[1]   *Cadres* is a blanket term which cannot be translated directly into English. It refers to very diverse categories of upper-echelon white-collar workers, such as engineers, foremen, managers and executives, and in some cases, even executive assistants or secretaries.

H4.5.2   A long line of case law had previously established that upper-echelon management constituted an exception, in terms of the statutory working week, based on the argument that their duties and level of responsibility meant they could not adhere to any specific schedule.[1]

[1]   Cass Soc, 15 December 1971, Chaulet c/ Buda.

H4.5.3   Now, and for the first time, the Act dated 19 January 2000 deals with the particular status of *cadres*.

H4.5.4   The 19 January 2000 Act establishes three categories of *cadres*: *cadres dirigeants* (upper-echelon management), *cadres intégrés dans une unité de travail* (*cadres* working as part of a team), and a middle category.

B   DEFINITIONS

Upper-echelon management

H4.5.5   Under the new L 212–15–1, this term is defined as:

'... *cadres* entrusted with responsibilities of such importance, that they require a considerable degree of freedom in organising their schedule, and who habitually take decisions quite independently, their remuneration being at the highest level relative to the various remuneration systems in their company or establishment'.

H4.5.6   These three criteria, taken together, ie weight of responsibilities, freedom in terms of organising one's schedule, and wage level, narrow considerably the number of employees likely to fall into this category.

Cadres working as part of a team

H4.5.7   Cadres working as part of a team refers to the notion of *cadres* as defined by branch collective bargaining agreements, ie as persons who comply with a work schedule applied to their particular workshop, department or team overall, and whose hours can be defined in advance.

Cadres middle category

H4.5.8   This refers to *cadres*, as the notion is defined by branch collective bargaining agreements, who fall outside the two categories as stated at paras **H4.5.5–H4.5.7**.

C   RULES APPLICABLE TO EACH CATEGORY OF CADRES

Upper-echelon management

H4.5.9   The statutory working week does not apply, but they are entitled to paid holidays.

Cadres working as part of a team

H4.5.10   The statutory working week applies, as it does to the rest of the workforce.

H4.5.11   Therefore, from 1 January 2000, if their working week regularly exceeds 35 hours, a lump sum may be agreed to cover a certain number of hours.

H4.5.12   Case law indicates that the minimum for such lump sum wage agreements must correspond to the minimum wage stipulated by the relevant collective bargaining agreement, taking into account a certain amount of overtime, plus overtime pay, plus the *bonifications*.

Middle category

H4.5.13   Under the 19 January 2000 Act, working hours for other *cadres* are to be reduced. This may take the form of individual agreements stipulating a specific number of hours or days, on a weekly, monthly, or annual basis.

H4.5.14   Annual agreements are the subject of particular rules, namely there must be a collective branch agreement, a company or establishment-wide agreement allowing annual agreements, defining the categories of *cadres* involved, and setting out the agreement's main terms.

H4.5.15   Individual agreements may be reached stipulating a specific number of hours per week or per month without a collective agreement having first been signed to that effect.

H4.5.16   Where the annual agreement is expressed in a specific number of days (*forfait annuel en jours*), the collective agreement may define exactly how many days may be worked, the ceiling being 217. Where it is intended to be expressed in hours (*forfait annuel en heures*), the collective agreement must specify the exact number of hours per annum on which the agreement is based.

H4.5.17   All such agreements must first define the categories of employee concerned, and how a day's, and a half-day's, work (and a day's, and a half-day's, time off) are to be counted. Secondly, the agreements must be specific as to how implementation is to be monitored, and a system for checking the schedule and exact number of hours worked must be set up.

H4.5.18   There must also be a system for monitoring *cadres'* workload, as those subject to an agreement stipulating a specific number of days a year, are concerned neither by the 35-hour working week, nor by rules restricting their working hours on a daily or weekly basis, save for the fact that they are entitled to 11 consecutive hours rest per day, and 24 hours consecutive rest once a week. They may not work more than six days a week.

H4.5.19   Collective agreements must lay down precise guidelines as to how these provisions are to be applied. They may also create what is known as a *compte épargne-temps,* ie a virtual 'savings-account' into which employees 'deposit' time off which they do not intend to take immediately.

H4.5.20   In case of dispute, the employer must provide the court with proof as to how many hours the employee actually put in, which proof must also be made available to the Labour Inspector.

H4.5.21   The minimum for such lump sum wage agreements must correspond to the minimum wage stipulated by the relevant collective bargaining agreement, taking into account a specific amount of overtime, plus overtime pay, plus the *bonifications.*

H4.5.22   The Act thus reflects case law, which indicates that the practice of lump sum remuneration will be allowed provided that the employee's wage packet corresponds to whatever he would have been entitled to by law, plus overtime and bonuses.

H4.5.23   Thus, for a lump sum agreement to be valid, a comparison must be drawn between the agreement and the minimum wage stipulated by the relevant collective bargaining agreement, plus overtime and bonuses.

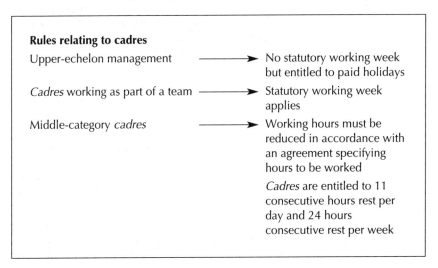

Rules relating to cadres

Upper-echelon management ⟶ No statutory working week but entitled to paid holidays

Cadres working as part of a team ⟶ Statutory working week applies

Middle-category *cadres* ⟶ Working hours must be reduced in accordance with an agreement specifying hours to be worked

Cadres are entitled to 11 consecutive hours rest per day and 24 hours consecutive rest per week

4.6   Guaranteed Minimum Wage

A   THE MINIMUM WAGE IN FRANCE

H4.6.1   The minimum wage in France is an hourly rate, known as the SMIC or *Salaire Minimum Interprofessionnel de Croissance* (see paras

H2.2.2–H2.2.6). Therefore, employees whose working week is cut back to 35 hours may not be paid less than the minimum hourly wage multiplied by the number of hours which applied before the new statutory working week was implemented.

B   SAFEGUARDING MONTHLY WAGE LEVELS IN THE TRANSITION TO THE 35-HOUR WORKING WEEK

H4.6.2   The Act dated 19 January 2000 contains a particular arrangement, the purpose of which is to safeguard the monthly wage level of workers who receive the SMIC, notwithstanding the shorter working week.

H4.6.3   Employees who earn the SMIC will be guaranteed the same wage level. This guarantee may take the form of an allowance known as *complément différentiel de salaire*. Paid by the employer, it represents the difference between the wage the employee would have received for a 39-hour working week, and the hourly SMIC multiplied by the number of hours which corresponds to the new 35-hour working week.

H4.6.4   The *complément différentiel de salaire* will be cut back as the hourly SMIC is raised, and will be eliminated in 2005. In other words, each time the SMIC rises, the subsidy will fall correspondingly.

H4.6.5   In the case of those workers whose working week is cut back to between 36 and 38 hours, the guaranteed minimum wage will apply in a similar fashion, so as to subsidise their wage up to the same level as a monthly, 39-hour a week SMIC. The *complément différentiel de salaire* will thus be smaller.

H4.6.6   In practice, 87% of company-wide agreements entered into to date have maintained current wage levels.

H4.6.7   However, many of these agreements still modify the remuneration structure. Current wage levels are maintained by paying a bonus to compensate for the difference between a salary for a 39-hour working week, and that for a 35-hour working week. Such arrangements do not change the employees' hourly rate of pay.

H4.6.8   Other agreements simply maintain the current monthly wage as it is, which of course amounts to increasing the hourly rate as compared to the 39-hour working week.

4.7   Night Work

H4.7.1–2   By statute, employees under the age of 18 may not work at night. Aside from this, the law provides compensation for night work, in the form of mandatory rest, a surcharge on standard wages, or both. The details are fixed either by collective bargaining or other collective agreements, or company or establishment-wide agreements.

H4.7.3   Neither workers, nor apprentices under the age of 18, may work between 22:00 and 6:00. This applies to all businesses no matter what their activity, in each of their establishments, and whether these business are public or private. It also applies to civil servants, and to employees of partnerships, trade unions and associations.[1]

[1]   Sections L 213–7 to L 213–10 of the Labour Code.

H4.7.4   Moreover, workers under the age of 18 must be granted at least 12 consecutive hours' rest per day.

H4.7.5   A Labour Inspector may, however, allow exceptions for the theatre and show business, and for the retail trade. The restaurant and hotel trade, as well as bakeries, may also be granted exceptions, under conditions fixed by Decree.

H4.7.6   Lastly, in order to prevent impending accidents or to deal with the effects of an accident which has already arisen, young men over the age of 16 may be summoned to work at night.

4.8   Rest Period

H4.8.1   By statute,[1] all employees are entitled to at least 11 hours' consecutive rest per day. There are exceptions however, in the following instances:

- *for certain specific activities*: where the safety of persons or property is at stake, or where a certain service or operation cannot be interrupted. These exceptions are fixed by collective agreements extended to every business or establishment in that branch of industry;
- *to deal with a sudden, heavy workload*: by collective agreements extended to every business or establishment in that branch of industry, by a company or establishment-wide agreement, or, after consultation with staff representatives, with the Labour Inspector's permission;
- *in emergencies*, to deal with an impending accident or the effects of an accident which has already arisen, to rescue persons or property, or, under exceptional, pressing circumstances, to ensure there is no breakdown in operations. The employer must take an unilateral decision, and then inform the Labour Inspector.

[1]   Section L 220–1 of the Labour Code.

H4.8.2   No employee may work over six hours at a stretch, without taking at least 20 minutes off. No pay need be granted, however, for the break, unless a collective agreement provides otherwise.

H4.8.3   Two principles are enshrined in the Labour Code:
(1) weekly rest;
(2) Sunday rest.

A PRINCIPLE OF WEEKLY REST

H4.8.4 No employee may work over six days a week, and the weekly rest period must correspond to at least 35 consecutive hours (one 24-hour period plus 11 consecutive hours of daily rest).

H4.8.5 There are exceptions to this principle.

*   *permanent, automatic exceptions*: no specific permission need be granted by the authorities, as the specific categories of employees concerned (watchmen, caretakers, maintenance staff assigned to monitor equipment, etc) are granted mandatory rest periods.
*   *temporary exceptions*: the weekly day of rest may be disregarded in emergencies, in trades where activity is seasonal, where perishables must be handled, where there is a sudden, extraordinarily heavy workload, where goods must be loaded or unloaded, and in establishments attached to the Defence Ministry.[1]

[1] Sections L 221–12 and –14, sections L 221–20 to –22 of the Labour Code.

B PRINCIPLE OF SUNDAY REST

H4.8.6 The weekly rest day must, in principle, be Sunday, from midnight on the Saturday to midnight on the Sunday. Furthermore, the employer must allow the entire workforce, as a body, to take the weekly day of rest.

H4.8.7 There are exceptions to this principle:

*   *permanent, automatic exceptions*: no specific permission need be granted by the authorities, as the establishments concerned cannot close down for one full day a week, either owing to technical reasons, or to the public's requirements.[1]
*   *individual exceptions*: permission from the authorities is required. The employer must be in a position to demonstrate either that the establishment's operations would be disrupted, or that the public might incur prejudice, were the entire workforce to be off work on Sundays. The authorities may allow the rest day to be taken other than on Sundays, either year-round, or at certain times in the year.

    It is the Prefect of the *département* where the establishment's head office is located who defines for how long the exception shall remain in force.[2]
*   *occasional exceptions*: by municipal order, retail establishments may occasionally be granted an exception.[3]
*   *exceptions pursuant to collective agreements*.

[1] For the list of these establishments, see sections L 221–9 and –10 of the Labour Code.
[2] Cf sections L 221–6 and L 221–8–1 of the Labour Code.
[3] Section L 221–19.

4.9 Sanctions

H4.9.1 The authorities have at their disposal a wide range of measures to monitor compliance with statutory working hours, failing which the employer may incur criminal liability.

A   WORKING HOURS

H4.9.2   Under section D 212–21 of the Labour Code, where, in a single establishment, no single overall schedule prevails, the employer must clock each employee's working hours on a daily basis.

H4.9.3   The burden rests with the employer to show how many hours the employee actually spends at his job.

H4.9.4   Failure to keep such a schedule is an offence known as a *contravention de 3ème classe,* punishable by fines of up to 3,000 FF (€ 457). A repeat offence becomes a *contravention de 4ème classe.* The fine may be imposed for each fresh offence.

H4.9.5   Failure to comply with section D 212–22 of the Labour Code (duty to inform the workforce of their rights to mandatory rest) is also a *contravention de 3ème classe.*

H4.9.6   Lastly, failure to comply with L 212–5 of the Labour Code (overtime and mandatory rest) is an offence, punishable by fines (*contraventions de 4ème classe*).

B   FAILURE TO DISCLOSE GAINFUL EMPLOYMENT

H4.9.7   The Act dated 11 March 1997 instituted a new offence known as *délit de travail dissimulé* (failure to disclose work performed). Thus, under L 324–10 of the Labour Code, where fewer hours appear on the payslip than those actually performed, this will constitute the offence of 'failure to disclose gainful employment'.

H4.9.8   This is a criminal offence, punishable with a sentence of imprisonment of up to two years, and fines of up to 200,000 FF (€ 30,490).

H4.9.9   It has become common practice for employers to record 169 hours a month, year in year out, on the payslip of *cadres* who habitually work over 39 hours a week. Where no agreement has been reached as to the exact number of hours or days *cadres* are to work in exchange for a certain specified lump sum, this practice results in a monthly pay cheque which bears little relation to the actual number of hours the *cadres* may be spending on the job.

H4.9.10   On 21 June 1999, the High Court at Versailles imposed a fine of 50,000 FF (€ 7,622) on the former President of Thomson RCM for 'failure to disclose gainful employment'.

H4.9.11   On the same day, the Magistrates court at Strasbourg imposed fines of 451,000 FF (€ 68,755) on the Personnel Manager of a bank, SOGENAL, for failure to fully remunerate overtime.

H4.9.12   In March 1999, Renault was fined for failure to clock the workforce's hours, while the following month, several managers at *Carrefour* supermarkets were ordered to pay fines of 25,000 FF (€ 3,811) each, for refusing to allow Labour Inspectors to monitor the working hours of their *cadres.*

H4.9.13 Thus, an employer may very well incur liability for *'failure to disclose gainful employment'*, and the new Act on the 35-hour working week will doubtless increase this risk. There is already a notable difference between the hours many *cadres* put in, and the 39-hour working week, which will increase once the 35-hour week becomes the norm.

H4.9.14 Furthermore, *cadres* are often called upon to travel extensively, attend outside meetings, commute long distances, and/or remain on stand-by. This may lead to a marked divergence between the way employers may have chosen to assess actual working hours, and the systems applied by the authorities.

H4.9.15 The employer may be liable for fines arising from failure to comply with statutory working hours, imposed for each fresh offence. He may also incur criminal liability for failing to disclose gainful employment and obstructing a Labour Inspector in the course of his duty.

H4.9.16 In terms of the employer's civil liability, within the five-year statute of limitations, any employee may sue to obtain payment of overtime and any mandatory rest that the employer may have failed to grant him.

H4.9.17 The current flurry of litigation in this respect may increase substantially as the Act on the 35-hour working week is implemented.

H4.9.18 Finally, failure to comply with this legislation may also lead to various forms of retaliation by the authorities, such as levying national insurance contributions from which an employer might otherwise be excused.

Failure to disclose gainful employment: penalties
- Criminal liability
- years' imprisonment
- Fine up to 200,000 FF (€ 30,490)
- Action for compensation (overtime/mandatory rest) by employee

---

5   EQUAL OPPORTUNITIES

5.1   Background

H5.1.1 The French term *discrimination* is used to describe prejudiced behaviour, ie treating individuals differently in accordance with private rather than professional criteria, such as their race, gender, origin, state of health or opinions or other private matters. Such prejudice necessarily contradicts the fundamental principle of equality enshrined, inter alia, in the Universal Human Rights Declaration (26 August 1789).

H5.1.2 Accordingly, French law expressly prohibits all forms of discrimination in labour law, and this is enforced by way of various penalties.

H5.1.3 Equal treatment is required, not only as regards recruitment, but in all aspects of working relationships, such as salary, promotion and disciplinary sanctions. The principle of equality does not mean that the employer is barred from exercising all personal discretion; he is perfectly entitled to distinguish between one employee and the next, provided that in doing so he does not unlawfully discriminate.

5.2 Unlawful Discrimination

H5.2.1 Under the general principles laid down by section L 122–45 of the Labour Code no-one may be:

- excluded from a recruitment process; or
- penalised or dismissed;

on the grounds of origin, sex, mores, marital status, nationality or racial group.

H5.2.2 There are further, more specific provisions of the Labour Code:

- neither gender nor family situation may be taken into account during the recruitment process (section L 123–1);
- pregnancy does not constitute legitimate grounds for firing, transferring, or refusing to hire someone (section L 122–25);
- no-one may be penalised or dismissed for having been subjected to sexual harassment, or for having refused to be so subjected, or for having witnessed or reported incidents of sexual harassment perpetrated by the employer or by his representative (section L 122–46);
- nothing in company rules and regulations may cause an employee to incur prejudice in his career, or his daily tasks, owing to his gender, mores, family situation or origin (section L 122–35 para 2);
- under section L 122–45 of the Labour Code, refusing to hire, penalising, or firing someone because of their sexual mores is an offence. Thus, on 17 April 1991, the *Cour de Cassation* found that a sexton fired by a religious association on the grounds of his homosexuality had been unfairly dismissed, as the association's activities had in no way been disrupted, and the sole ground adduced for dismissal was his sexuality.

H5.2.3 Although the general principle prohibiting such discrimination is intended to be very broadly applied, such discriminatory practices are difficult to prevent and to prove.

5.3 Disability Discrimination

H5.3.1 Under section L 122–45 of the Labour Code, refusing to hire, penalising, or firing someone owing to their state of health or a disability is an offence, unless the factory doctor (*médecin du travail*)[1] finds that the employee can no longer properly discharge his tasks.[2]

[1] The *médecin du travail* or factory doctor (occupational health officer) is an employee.

[2] If, in the factory doctor's opinion, a given employee will no longer be able to discharge his duties, he may be dismissed. Whereas, if the disability is only partial or temporary, the employer will be under a duty to find him another position.

H5.3.2 However, an employer may nevertheless be entitled to dismiss an employee on the grounds of ill-health, as section L 122–45 is not intended to establish an 'across the board' guarantee of continued employment for sick or disabled employees.[1] Where performance of the employment contract has become impossible, the ordinary rules of law will continue to apply, while the courts will decide, on a case by case basis, whether or not dismissal actually involved a disguised, but prohibited, form of discrimination.[2]

[1] An employee suffering from an occupational accident or illness may not be dismissed while away on sick leave.

[2] Cass Soc, 16 July 1998, RJS 1200, confirmed by a decision handed down by the Labour Law Division on 10 November 1998, RJS 12/98.

5.4   Enforcement and Remedies in Discrimination Cases

H5.4.1   Section L 122–45 provides that any measure or provision which contradicts the principle prohibiting discrimination shall be automatically null and void.

H5.4.2   Although section L 122–45 does not invalidate the selection or non-selection of a candidate for a position on discriminatory grounds, the unsuccessful candidate may nevertheless proceed in law on the basis of art 1382 of the Civil Code, and demand compensation for prejudice, defined as the loss of a chance to take up the desired position. He may also claim exemplary damages for mental distress (*préjudice moral*). The unsuccessful candidate may also choose to lodge a criminal complaint.[1]

[1] Under section 225–2 of the New Criminal Code (NCP), discriminating against a candidate during the recruitment process is an offence punishable by a sentence of up to two years' imprisonment, and fines of up to 200,000 FF (€ 30,490). There are also specific sanctions under the Labour Code.

H5.4.3   Section L 122–45 provides that disciplinary measures imposed on discriminatory grounds are automatically null and void. The employee may lodge a court claim to confirm the nullity, and he may also instigate criminal proceedings.[1]

[1] Under section 225–2 of the New Criminal Code (NCP), imposing disciplinary sanctions motivated by discrimination is an offence punishable by a sentence of up to two years' imprisonment, and fines of up to 200,000 FF (€ 30,490). There are also specific sanctions under the Labour Code.

H5.4.4   Section L 122–45 provides that dismissal on discriminatory grounds is automatically null and void. The employee concerned may lodge a court claim to confirm the nullity.

H5.4.5   The employment contract will be deemed to have remained in force throughout, while the employee must be reinstated in his former position and paid all arrears of salary for the period during which he was unable to report for work owing to his employer's decision. The court may impose fines until such time as the employer complies with its direction.

H5.4.6   The employee may prefer nevertheless not to be reinstated, and sue for wage arrears and damages alone. He may also instigate criminal proceedings.[1]

[1] Under sections 225–1 to 225–3 of the Criminal Code, dismissal motivated by discrimination is an offence punishable by a sentence of up to two years' imprisonment, and fines of up to 200,000 FF (€ 30,490).

5.5   Equal Pay for Equal Work

H5.5.1   A specific application of the general principle of 'equal pay for equal work' is found in section L 140–2 of the Labour Code, which requires all employers to pay women the same wages as men, where they are engaged in the same, or equivalent, tasks.

H5.5.2   The various items making up the wage packet must be identical for both sexes, as must job description, career levels, assessment criteria, and so forth.

H5.5.3   Where the employment contract, a decision on the employer's part, or the Collective Bargaining or other agreement contradicts these requirements, the relevant provisions are automatically null and void, and the employee may demand the higher wage level as of right.

H5.5.4   The Labour Inspectors are empowered to apply the above provisions, and to report any offences. They may also conduct investigations at establishments where women are employed.

H5.5.5   Where an employee believes that he or she is being paid less by reason of gender, he or she may proceed in law to demand equal treatment, and may not be dismissed. Where there is a dispute, the burden of proof is on the employer to demonstrate that he had good grounds for not paying equal wages. The court may order further investigation, while the employee will be given the benefit of any doubt.

H5.5.6   The trade unions may also lodge an equal pay claim on behalf of the employee.[1]

[1] Section L 123–6.

H5.5.7   An employer who disregards the principle of equal pay is guilty of an offence which falls into the category of *contraventions de 5ème classe*. The offence will be deemed to have been committed as many times as there are workers concerned[1].

[1] Section R 154–0.

6   TERMINATION OF EMPLOYMENT

6.1   Background and Procedure

H6.1.1   A fixed-term contract may be discharged only at term, save by mutual agreement, or in the event of serious misconduct or *force majeure*.

H6.1.2 Indefinite-term contracts may be discharged in the following ways:

(a) resignation;
(b) dismissal;
(c) termination of the contract by amicable settlement;
(d) retirement, or forced retirement;
(e) death of the employee;
(f) judicial rescission;
(g) force majeure.

A   RESIGNATION

H6.1.3   The employee informs his employer that he intends to end the contract. To be valid, resignation must be the expression of the employee's own free will, and his intention must be serious and free of ambiguity. The employee does not need to give any reason for resigning, nor need he comply with any particular formality. The notice period will begin to run from the date the employer is first notified of the resignation.

B   DISMISSAL

H6.1.4   Dismissal may either be on economic grounds (redundancy), or on personal grounds (see paras **H6.2.1** ff).

C   TERMINATION OF THE CONTRACT BY AMICABLE SETTLEMENT

H6.1.5   Except for those employees who enjoy special status (eg works council members), the parties may negotiate the employee's departure. Initially, the courts only recognised settlement on personal grounds, whereas they will now also uphold settlements entered into on economic grounds. In general, the employee will be paid a specific indemnity payment (in consideration for his agreement).

D   RETIREMENT, OR FORCED RETIREMENT

H6.1.6   After complying with the contractual notice period, an employee may choose to retire of his own free will, in order to draw his pension (*départ volontaire à la retraite*).

H6.1.7   An employer may force an employee to retire (*mise à la retraite*) only where the latter is entitled to a full old-age pension, and where he has reached the age at which a state pension will be paid to him. In principle, this will be the age of 60, although collective bargaining agreements may provide for an age limit higher than statute. Otherwise, the employee will be deemed to have been dismissed.

E   DEATH OF THE EMPLOYEE

F   JUDICIAL RESCISSION

H6.1.8   Where one party – whether employer or employee – is in breach of an important contractual term, the other may petition the Industrial Tribunal to have the employment contract rescinded. Where the employer is the respondent to such a claim, and the Industrial Tribunal finds for the employee, the legal effects will be similar to those flowing from an unfair dismissal.

G   FORCE MAJEURE

H6.1.9   This occurs when an unforeseeable, outside, irresistible event makes performance of the contract impossible, and leads to the employment contract being either suspended, or terminated, depending on whether the event is temporary or final in nature. Termination of the contract owing to *force majeure* does not constitute dismissal.

6.2   Dismissal

H6.2.1   The rules governing redundancy (dismissal on economic grounds, or *licenciement économique*) are quite distinct from those governing dismissal on personal grounds, the latter arising from reasons inherent to the employee as an individual.

A   DISMISSAL ON PERSONAL GROUNDS

Real and serious cause

H6.2.2   Although the law recognises the principle that either party may take the initiative of terminating the contract, the employer must have 'real and serious grounds' (*cause réelle et sérieuse*) for doing so.

H6.2.3   The grounds must be objective and concrete (*existant*), ie they must be precise and tangible, and not a figment of the employer's imagination.

H6.2.4   *Cause réelle et sérieuse* does not necessarily imply misconduct on the employee's part, nor is there an absolute requirement that the employer has suffered particular risk or prejudice.

H6.2.5   The courts must try the issue of whether or not the grounds adduced were indeed 'real and serious', with the employee being given the benefit of any doubt.

Grounds related to the employee as an individual

H6.2.6   The facts which led to dismissal must have arisen from the employee's own actions, and must have occurred in the course of performing the employment contract.

Where the employee is not guilty of misconduct

H6.2.7   The employee's behaviour may significantly disrupt operations, and may make dismissal legitimate. Incompetence (without misconduct), physical inaptitude, repeated absence owing to sickness, personal disagreements, refusal to work as a team, or personality clashes are among the motives frequently adduced for dismissal.

Where the employee is guilty of misconduct

H6.2.8   Misconduct in principle involves an act, or a refusal to act, on the employee's part. The effects will depend on how serious the event is. When the employee dismissed has committed neither serious misconduct (*faute grave*) nor gross misconduct (*faute lourde*) he has the right to outstanding wages, together with his notice period, or an indemnity payment in lieu of notice, an indemnity payment for outstanding holiday leave, and, if he has more than two years' service, the right to a dismissal indemnity payment.

Serious misconduct (faute grave)

H6.2.9   The courts have consistently held that serious misconduct arises where the employee has, in person, perpetrated acts which, taken as a whole, constitute a breach of his contractual duties, or a disruption to the working relationship, such that the employee cannot be kept on even during the notice period.

H6.2.10   Serious misconduct may entitle the employer to dismiss the offender without notice or an indemnity payment in lieu of notice and without the right to a dismissal indemnity payment. However, the employee would still have the right to outstanding wages and an indemnity payment for outstanding holiday leave.

Examples of serious misconduct

- a night watchman sleeps whilst on duty
- a shop steward leavs his work station for two hours leading to a breakdown in production
- an employee disrupts operations owing to persistent lateness and unjustified absence
- an employee racially insults a colleague

Gross misconduct (faute lourde)

H6.2.11   Gross misconduct arises where the employee actually intended to harm the employer or the company.

H6.2.12   Gross misconduct entitles the employer to dismiss the employee without any compensation whatsoever save his outstanding wages.

Examples of gross misconduct

- a lorry driver is drunk and speeding whilst on duty
- a pilot takes risks with passengers' lives
- a salesman pockets cash on the pretext that there were errors on his own payslips
- an employee leaves on holiday before the appointed date where the employer had reconfirmed those dates by registered post.

B   DISMISSAL PROCEDURE

H6.2.13   The main steps of the dismissal procedure are as follows (however, other specific rules must be followed in relation to the dismissal of staff representatives, which must also be authorised by the labour authorities, even where gross misconduct has occurred).

Preliminary meeting

H6.2.14   The employee must be sent a letter by certified post or by hand delivery summoning him to a meeting prior to dismissal. The letter must indicate that he is entitled to be assisted at the meeting by another employee or, in companies without staff representatives, by an external counsellor whose name appears on a list drawn up to this effect, which can be consulted at the Labour Inspectorate or at the Town Hall.

H6.2.15   Where there are no staff representatives, the law provides that at least five working days must be allowed to elapse after presentation of this letter to the employee. In all other cases, a reasonable delay must be allowed before the meeting.

H6.2.16   At the meeting, the employer must give the employee the reasons for dismissal and ask the employee to provide his explanation.

Dismissal letter

H6.2.17   The employee must be notified of dismissal by registered post. The letter must set out the precise grounds for dismissal.

H6.2.18   Failure to specify these grounds will allow the employee to claim that he has been unfairly dismissed. The employer will not be able to tell the courts that the employee had been properly informed of the grievances against him.

H6.2.19   This letter may not be sent on the same day as the preliminary meeting is held. At least one clear day must elapse between the meeting and posting the notification letter.

H6.2.20   If the notification letter fails to set out the ground for termination or is too vague, dismissal will automatically be held to be unfair, and the employee may claim damages.

	Dismissal
'Real and serious cause'	• no misconduct
	• misconduct
	• serious misconduct
	• gross misconduct
Dismissal procedure	• Preliminary letter + 5 working days
	• Meeting + 1 clear day
	• dismissal letter: grounds for dismissal

6.3 Redundancy and Collective Dismissals (*licenciement économique*, ie dismissal on economic grounds)

A   NOTION OF REDUNDANCY IN FRENCH LAW

H6.3.1   Under section L 321–1 of the Labour Code, dismissal on economic grounds

> '. . . may not rest on one or more reasons inherent to the employee's person, but on the fact that the employee's position is to be eliminated or transformed, or that substantial changes are to be made to his employment contract, owing in particular to financial difficulties or technological changes'.

H6.3.2   The rules governing dismissal on economic grounds will depend on whether the number of employees to be dismissed over a single 30-day period is less than ten, or ten or over.

H6.3.3   In all cases, the employer must attempt to redeploy the employees concerned in other positions before dismissing them, failing which dismissal will be deemed unfair.

H6.3.4   Where at least two employees are liable to be dismissed, the employer must apply objective criteria to determine the order of dismissal, such as the number of dependants, length of service, and any disability which might make redeployment especially difficult.

B   DISMISSAL OF ONE EMPLOYEE (LICENCIEMENT INDIVIDUEL) ON ECONOMIC GROUNDS

H6.3.5   An individual employee must be summoned to a preliminary meeting at which, in theory at least, an attempt must be made by both parties to find an alternative to dismissal. The employee is given official documents relating to what is known as a *convention de conversion*, or retraining agreement[1]. The employee has 21 days from the date of the meeting to decide whether or not to accept the retraining offer. Under certain precise conditions, the dismissed employee will have priority when it comes to filling any new positions which might become available in the company over the course of the following year.

[1]   A retraining agreement is a state scheme affording the employee special status for six months, including a retraining allowance and a form of outplacement. Once the employee has agreed to enter the scheme, his employment contract will be deemed terminated at the end of the 21-day reflection period, and the dismissal procedure will end.

C   COLLECTIVE DISMISSAL OF LESS THAN 10 EMPLOYEES (LICENCIEMENT COLLECTIF) ON ECONOMIC GROUNDS

H6.3.6   In collective dismissals of less than 10 employees, the first step is for the employer to consult the works council, or where there is none, the staff representatives. He must then summon each employee individually to a preliminary meeting, and notify the local labour authorities (*Direction départementale du travail et de l'emploi* – DDTE)[1] of his decisions. Under certain precise conditions, the dismissed employees will have priority when it comes to filling any new positions which might become available in the company over the course of the following year.

[1]   Civil servants reporting to the Labour Ministry.

D   COLLECTIVE DISMISSAL OF 10 OR MORE EMPLOYEES (LICENCIEMENT COLLECTIF) ON ECONOMIC GROUNDS

H6.3.7   Where collective dismissal of 10 or more employees is envisaged, the employer is under a duty to keep the redundancies down to a minimum, and to make every effort to redeploy those employees whose dismissal is unavoidable.

H6.3.8   Where the size of the workforce is at least 50, the employer must draw up a Social Plan, including retraining agreements, and other specific, concrete measures.[1]

[1]   The Labour Inspector may find the Social Plan unsatisfactory, and draw up a report to that effect.

H6.3.9   Before taking any concrete steps, the employer must also consult the works council or staff representatives, study and reply to their suggestions, and forward all of this information to the labour authorities (DDTE, see para **H6.3.6**).

H6.3.10   Where the relevant collective bargaining agreement has not defined an order for dismissal, the employer must establish it, after consulting the works council or staff representatives.[1] After informing the authorities, he may proceed to send formal dismissal notices to the employees concerned. No preliminary meeting with each employee individually needs to be held, except where the employee being dismissed is an employee representative.

[1]   The criteria for defining the order of dismissal include number of dependants, length of service, and any disability which might make redeployment especially difficult.

H6.3.11   Where the redundancies arise from bankruptcy or liquidation of a business, the procedure will be similar to that for collective dismissal of 10 or more employees on economic grounds over a single 30-day period.

H6.3.12   In any event, the dismissal letter should, in addition to setting out the grounds for dismissal, state that the employee will enjoy precedence over other candidates should any suitable position within the company become available, and that if he wishes to exercise that right, he must so inform his former employer in writing within four months of termination of the contract.[1]

[1]   Section L 122–14–2 of the Labour Code.

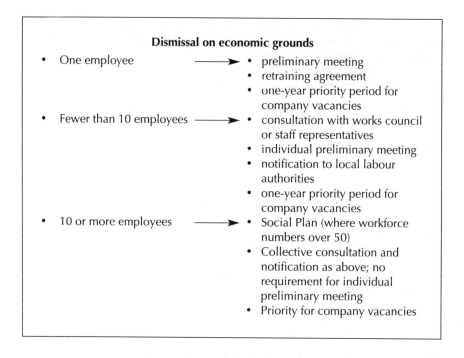

Dismissal on economic grounds

- One employee ⟶
  - preliminary meeting
  - retraining agreement
  - one-year priority period for company vacancies

- Fewer than 10 employees ⟶
  - consultation with works council or staff representatives
  - individual preliminary meeting
  - notification to local labour authorities
  - one-year priority period for company vacancies

- 10 or more employees ⟶
  - Social Plan (where workforce numbers over 50)
  - Collective consultation and notification as above; no requirement for individual preliminary meeting
  - Priority for company vacancies

E   REAL AND SERIOUS CAUSE – JUDICIAL REVIEW

H6.3.13   As stated in paras **H6.3.5–H6.3.12**, the authorities will monitor redundancy measures at various stages of the procedure. Moreover, the courts are also empowered to review the issue of whether the employer had real and serious cause for dismissal.

H6.3.14   The lower courts will inquire into both:
- the veracity of the facts alleged by the employer; and
- whether there is a causal link between those facts and the dismissal.

H6.3.15   The *Cour de Cassation* has applied section L 321–1 of the Labour Code. The fact that a position is to be eliminated or transformed, or that the contract is to be substantially altered, will not in and of itself suffice to constitute economic grounds in the eyes of the courts; the driving force behind the elimination, transformation etc must itself be economic.

H6.3.16   There is thus a double causal link, the existence of which must be demonstrated to the courts' satisfaction.

6.4   Remedies

H6.4.1   Failure to comply with the formal dismissal procedure, or implementing dismissal without real and serious grounds, is a breach of the provisions of the Labour Code. The sanctions will depend on the employee's length of service, and on the size of the workforce.

A   WHERE THE EMPLOYEE HAS OVER TWO YEARS' SERVICE AND THE COMPANY HAS AT LEAST 11 EMPLOYEES[1]

Dismissal was fair, but due procedure was disregarded

H6.4.2   The courts will order the employer to comply with the required procedure, and award the employee an indemnity payment of up to one month's wages.

[1]   Section L 122–14–4 of the Labour Code.

Unfair dismissal

H6.4.3   The courts may propose reinstatement of the employee, on his former terms and conditions. If either party rejects the proposal, or the courts choose not to order reinstatement, the employee will be awarded an indemnity payment of at least six months' wages. The courts may also order the employer to refund the state unemployment scheme (ASSEDIC) in respect of any unemployment benefit the employee may have drawn, up to a ceiling of six months' benefit. These sanctions apply whether or not the employer complied, from a formal standpoint, with the dismissal procedure.

B   WHERE THE EMPLOYEE HAS LESS THAN TWO YEARS' SERVICE OR THE COMPANY HAS LESS THAN 11 EMPLOYEES

H6.4.4   The courts will assess actual prejudice incurred by the employee, if any, and make an award accordingly.[1]

[1]   Section L 122–14–4 of the Labour Code.

C   INSTANCES WHERE DISMISSAL IS AUTOMATICALLY DEEMED NULL AND VOID[1]

H6.4.5   If the employer disregards the Labour Code and dismisses the employee anyway, the employee may petition the courts for reinstatement, or claim damages.

[1]   Express prohibition under the Labour Code – cf sections L 122–45, L 123–1, L 123–46 Discrimination.

D   DISMISSAL ON ECONOMIC GROUNDS – SANCTIONS FOR NON-COMPLIANCE

Failure to consult/notify

H6.4.6   The courts will award the employees concerned damages for the employer's failure to consult the works council or staff representatives or to notify the labour authorities, according to the prejudice actually suffered.

H6.4.7   Moreover, pursuant to section L 483.1 and section L 482.1 of the Labour Code, disregard for staff representatives' prerogatives may lead to an employer incurring penal sanctions, a sentence of imprisonment of up to one year, and fines of up to 25,000 FF (€ 3,811).

Unfair dismissal, procedural irregularities

H6.4.8   The penalties laid down by sections L 122–14–4 and –5 of the Labour Code will apply.

H6.4.9   Litigation relating to economic grounds for dismissal where one of the parties is a works council or trade union will normally be referred to the High Court rather than to an Industrial Tribunal.

Social Plan

H6.4.10   The employer is under a duty to establish, in collaboration with the works council and/or trade unions, what is known as a Social Plan (*Plan Social*). This is a compendium of pecuniary and other measures, the purpose of which is to keep redundancies down to a minimum, and to assist those employees whose dismissal is unavoidable.

H6.4.11   In 1997, the *Cour de Cassation* held in the *Samaritaine* case[1] that where a Social Plan has been held to be null and void, the workforce made redundant must either be reinstated or paid the wages they would have earned since the dismissal date. As several years may elapse between dismissal and a ruling by the Cour de Cassation, the arrears may be considerable. Subsequently, this principle has been applied by the courts on a number of occasions.

[1]   Cass Soc, 13 February 1997, 1299.

7   YOUNG WORKERS

7.1   General Obligations

H7.1.1   Although a variety of apprenticeship and other special contracts have been set up over the last few years to help combat youth unemployment, there remains considerable statutory protection for minors under the age of 16. Pursuant to section R 261–1 of the Labour Code, fines of up to 10,000 FF (€ 1,524) (up to 20,000 FF (€ 3,049) where there are repeat offences within a single year) may be imposed for non-compliance.

H7.1.2   As a general principle, school-age children may not work.

H7.1.3   Pursuant to section L 211–1 of the Labour Code, children may not work in any capacity whatsoever in any establishment until they have reached school-leaving age. In France, this is 16 years of age.

H7.1.4   Section L 200–1 of the Labour Code defines establishments as trades and businesses of any kind, workshops of any kind, whether public or private, including Church property. No exception is made for teaching or charitable institutions, state or ministerial offices or agencies, professionals' offices, partnerships, or trade unions and associations.

H7.1.5   An exception is made for family establishments run by the minor's mother, father or tutor, including open-air activities such as street vending or market stalls.

A   EXCEPTIONS

H7.1.6   The Labour Code provides for five types of exception:
*   light work during the school holidays;
*   pupils whose studies include periods of internship with a trade or business;
*   apprentices aged 15 or over;
*   children in the theatre or show business;
*   child models in the fashion industry.

H7.1.7   Even under these circumstances, however, recruitment and working conditions are strictly regulated.

B   MINORS' WORKING HOURS

H7.1.8   Those under the age of 18 may not work more than 8 hours a day and 39 hours a week. The Labour Inspector may nonetheless allow exceptions of up to an additional five hours a week, with the approval of the factory doctor (*médecin du travail*, the occupational health officer) in the establishment where the minor works. No minor may work for over four and a half hours without a break, and under no circumstances may a minor work longer hours than those habitually put in by the adults employed in the same establishment. Minors may not be employed on relay or rotating shifts.

C   FORBIDDEN ACTIVITIES AND EMPLOYER'S DUTIES

H7.1.9   Night work (between 20:00 and 6:00) is prohibited for minors. The Labour Inspector may, however, allow exceptions for certain trades, in the theatre and show business. Specific exceptions have been laid down by the *Conseil d'Etat* to this effect and for the hotel and restaurant trade and bakeries.

H7.1.10   Minors may not be employed in establishments serving alcoholic beverages (although exceptions may be made for establishments run by members of the minor's family).

H7.1.11   Minors may not be employed in the clothing industry and in heavy manual labour.

H7.1.12   Minors may not perform certain dangerous tasks, a list of which is established by Decree.

H7.1.13   Minors may not be employed in certain unhygienic or dangerous trades.

H7.1.14   In addition to the above, the head of a business must discharge a number of general duties in relation to minors, and notably must ensure that:
*   there is a climate of propriety and decency in the establishment, failing which he may incur penal sanctions;
*   legislation restricting the amount of weight which may be carried by minors is complied with;
*   legislation restricting the use of minors to hawk wares on the street (*étalages extérieurs*) is complied with.

383

8   MATERNITY AND PARENTAL RIGHTS

8.1   Background

H8.1.1   Pregnant women are afforded statutory protection throughout the employment relationship. They are protected against discrimination not only during the recruitment process but also during performance of the employment contract.

H8.1.2   The Labour Code allows both parents to adapt their employment contract on the birth of a child, eg to take parental leave (*congé parental d'éducation*), or to work part-time.

H8.1.3   Provisions regarding pregnant women and parental rights should not be taken lightly, as failure to comply on the employer's part may lead not only to liability for damages, but to penal sanctions (fines of up to 50,000 FF (€ 7,622) for natural persons, and up to 100,000 FF (€ 15,245) for legal entities).

8.2   General Rights

H8.2.1   As soon as the employee has notified her employer that she is pregnant, she is entitled to various statutory safeguards. According to the Labour Code, she must either give the employer a medical certificate to that effect, or send it by registered post with acknowledgement of receipt.

H8.2.2   The medical certificate must state that the employee is pregnant, and give the date on which she is expected to give birth, or the effective date on which confinement is to take place if known, and, in the event of a medical condition requiring maternity leave to be extended, the expected duration of such extension. However, the courts have found that this particular formality is not a strict legal requirement, and that once an employer has been informed of the pregnancy, no matter how he learned of it, the employee concerned is entitled to statutory safeguards.

A   LIGHTER WORKLOAD

H8.2.3   The employee may be excused from performing part of her usual tasks.

H8.2.4   This may take the form of a shorter working week, or a temporary change in duties where the employee's state of health so requires, whether at her own request or as proposed by her employer.

H8.2.5   Where an employee is excused from performing part of her usual tasks, the employer is not permitted to dock her pay in proportion to the tasks which she no longer performs.

B   MATERNITY LEAVE

H8.2.6   A pregnant woman need not take maternity leave, save for the period during which there is a statutory prohibition against pregnant women working (see para **H8.4.1**). If she does intend to take maternity leave, she must inform the employer (by registered post with acknowledgement of receipt) of her pregnancy and the date on which she plans to return to work. No particular deadline is specified for sending the letter.

Position during maternity leave

H8.2.7   Six weeks before the expected date of confinement, the employee is entitled to demand that her employment contract is suspended and need no longer report for work. During this period, the employee receives maternity benefit from the Social Security authorities.

H8.2.8   There is no statutory right to salary during leave, although collective bargaining agreements or company custom may provide otherwise.

H8.2.9   For the purposes of calculating paid holiday rights and length of service, maternity leave qualifies as actual working time (*période de travail effectif*).

H8.2.10   When the employee returns to work, she is entitled to return to the same or a similar post, at a salary at least equal to that which she was paid before taking maternity leave.

H8.2.11   In principle, a pregnant woman may not be dismissed.

	Maternity			**Adoption**
Family situation	*Before confinement (in weeks)*	*After confinement (in weeks)*	*Total[1] (in weeks)*	*After the child enters the home (in weeks)*
Single birth or adoption size of family becomes				
• 1 or 2	6	10	16	10
• 3 or more[2]	8[3]	18[3]	26	18
Multiple birth or adoption				
• twins	12[4]	22	34	22
• triplets etc	24	22	46	22
Medical complications (employee)	2 extra weeks	4 extra weeks		

Duration of statutory maternity leave

[1]   In case of premature birth, post-natal leave is extended up to the permissible total, ie up to 16, 26, 34 or 36 weeks. If birth is delayed, post-natal leave will not be reduced, as it is counted from the actual day of confinement.

[2]   The employee or household has at least two dependent children, or the employee has already given birth to two viable babies.

[3]   The mother may choose to go on maternity leave up to two weeks earlier, which will shorten post-natal leave accordingly.

[4]   The mother may choose to go on maternity leave up to four weeks earlier, which will shorten post-natal leave accordingly.

8.3   Protection from Dismissal

H8.3.1   Under the Labour Code, pregnant women, women away on maternity leave and women in the course of adopting a child may not be dismissed.

H8.3.2   The employee may not be dismissed in the interval between the date the medical certificate confirming pregnancy was issued, and the date four weeks after the date on which the suspended employment contract comes back into force.

H8.3.3   However, an employer may dismiss a pregnant woman if:

* *she is guilty of serious misconduct, unrelated to her state of pregnancy*: examples of such misconduct include violent or insulting behaviour[1] serious professional misconduct, dishonesty or embezzlement. Caution must nevertheless be exercised, as the courts may find the employee's pregnancy to have been a factor in mitigation of her misconduct; or
* *where the employer is unable, for reasons unrelated to the pregnancy, confinement or adoption, to maintain the employment relationship*: thus, dismissal will be permitted where the employee's position is to be eliminated as a result, for example, of the establishment being closed down owing to economic hardship, or as a result of a restructuring operation in the department.[2] Even in such cases, dismissal may neither be notified nor implemented during that period.

[1]   Cass Soc, 21 January 1987.
[2]   However, the mere fact that there are economic grounds for dismissal will not suffice to make it fair (Cass Soc, 19 November 1997).

H8.3.4   Save for the exceptions referred to above, dismissal of a pregnant woman is null and void.

H8.3.5   Nullity will lead to:

* reinstatement, if the employer offers to reinstate the employee, or if the courts so order, although the employee need not accept the offer; or
* payment of wage arrears for the period during which dismissal was a nullity, ie the interval between the date the woman was compelled to stop working owing to dismissal and the date four weeks after the date on which maternity leave expired. This applies even where the employee began to work for another employer upon dismissal; and
* payment of dismissal and notice indemnity payments; and
* damages, to compensate for prejudice suffered owing to unfair dismissal.

8.4   Health and Safety

H8.4.1   There is a total period of eight weeks before and after confinement during which the woman may not work at all. Six weeks must have elapsed from the time of confinement before she may report back for work.

H8.4.2   Throughout the year following the date of their confinement, mothers may take off one hour a day during working hours to breast-feed, and they may do so on company premises.

8.5   Maternity Pay/Social Security

H8.5.1   The employee herself, or the wife of an insured employee as well as their dependent children, may claim certain benefits. These include 100% refunds of all medical and hospital expenses arising from pregnancy, confinement and its aftermath. The insured person incurs no cost at all.

H8.5.2   Cash benefits include a daily allowance corresponding to basic daily salary, evaluated on the same basis as sickness benefit, less the employee's share of social insurance levies and CSG (*contribution sociale généralisée*). There is both a ceiling and a floor on such allowances.

H8.5.3   To be entitled to the daily allowance, the mother, if insured herself, must:

* be able to show that she has been insured for at least 10 months by the expected date of confinement, and that she has been in gainful employment for a certain length of time;
* cease reporting for work for at least eight weeks during the period in which benefit is paid;
* have notified the national health service *(Caisse Primaire d'Assurance Maladie)* that she is pregnant, within the first fourteen weeks;
* have undergone compulsory medical examinations both before and after confinement.

H8.5.4   In relation to salary entitlement during leave, see para **H8.2.8**.

8.6   Additional Rights to Time Off

PARENTAL LEAVE

H8.6.1   Both male and female employees with at least one year's service at the time their child is born, or at the time an adopted child under 16 enters their home, may request parental leave or a working week at least one-fifth shorter than the general rule in the establishment. However, the working week may not be less than 16 hours.

H8.6.2   The employer must be notified, by registered post with acknowledgement of receipt, of the beginning and end of the period during which the employee wishes to take advantage of these provisions. Notice must be given at least two months before the parental leave or part-time work is due to begin. When parental leave is to follow immediately after maternity leave, as often happens, the employee must notify her employer by registered post with acknowledgement of receipt at least one month before the maternity leave period is due to end.

H8.6.3   Parental leave and part-time work are initially granted for one year at most, but may be extended twice. At the latest, this privilege comes to an end on the child's third birthday, or, where a child of less than three years of age has been adopted, once three years have elapsed from the date the adopted child entered the employee's home.

H8.6.4   Parental leave must be taken in one go. It cannot be taken in several separate periods of leave.

H8.6.5 During parental leave, the employment contract is deemed suspended, and the employee's salary need not be paid unless the collective bargaining agreement so provides.

H8.6.6 An employee afforded the benefit of these provisions may not enter another employer's service, save as a child-minder.

H8.6.7 When an employee's length of service is calculated in order to assess his or her length of service benefits, only half of the employee's time spent on parental leave will count towards the total length of service.

H8.6.8 Once the parental leave or part-time work ends, the employee returns to his or her initial or similar position, at a wage level at least equal to that he or she had previously been afforded.

9 BUSINESS TRANSFERS

9.1 Background

H9.1.1 As early as 1928, the French National Assembly was concerned to prevent changes in corporate structure and control from leading to unnecessary redundancies, and accordingly established the principle that the workforce is to be maintained, even where, from a strictly legal standpoint, there is a change of employer.

H9.1.2 Thus, according to section L 122–12, para 2 of the Labour Code:

'Where there is a change in the legal situation of the employer, owing notably to succession, sale, merger, change in the stock-in-trade or establishment of a company, all employment contracts in force as of the day the change remain in force between the new employer and the company's workforce'.

H9.1.3 The same principle was enshrined by Directive 77/187/EEC (the Acquired Rights Directive).

H9.1.4 Over the years, decisions handed down by the *Cour de Cassation* (French Supreme Court) have come to emphasise and even reinforce the importance of these provisions.

9.2 Identifying a relevant transfer

H9.2.1 Section L 122–12 para 2 lists transactions which amount to a change in employer. The fact that Parliament has qualified the list by using the expression '*notamment*' (notably), indicates that it is not intended to be exhaustive.

H9.2.2 The courts have further refined the notion of change in employer (*modification de la situation juridique de l'employeur*) in the light of Directive 77/187/EEC.

H9.2.3 Until 1990, French courts tended to apply section L 122–12 narrowly, requiring a contractual relationship of some kind between the successive employers. A number of transactions thus remained outside the scope of the Directive. However, on 10 February 1988, the European Court of Justice held that the principle should apply even where there was no privity between successive employers.

H9.2.4 On 16 March 1990, the *Cour de Cassation* handed down three decisions relating to the same principle, finding that section L 122–12 applies:

> '... to any transfer involving an economic entity which retains its identity and whose activity carries ... over, even where there is no privity between successive employers'.[1]

As a contractual relationship is no longer required, the decisive issue has thus become whether both the company's identity and activity carry over to the new employer, that is whether an independent economic entity (*entité economique autonome*) is transferred.

[1] Case 311, *pourvoi* 86–40–686, Case 312, *pourvoi* 89–45–730, Case 313, *pourvoi* 86–40–155.

H9.2.5 The *Cour de Cassation* has recently defined an *entité économique autonome* as:

> '... [an] organised unit of persons and tangible and intangible property such as allow it to carry out an economic activity, which unit pursues a defined purpose.'[1]

[1] Cass Soc, 7 July 1998.

H9.2.6 The courts have, for example, found the following to constitute an independent economic entity for the purposes of transfer:
- a butcher's concession within a supermarket;[1]
- a carpenter's shop within a company which produced and sold seeds;[2]
- the client portfolio of a real estate agency.[3]

[1] Cass Soc, 26 September 1990.
[2] Cass Soc, 12 December 1990.
[3] Cass Soc, 23 September 1992.

H9.2.7 For the purposes of section L 122–12, the transferred entity must retain its own identity, and its activity must be carried over.[1] Previously,[2] the *Cour de Cassation* had already stressed the requirement that:

> '... despite formal changes, the same activity had been carried over, with the same workforce, clientele and equipment.'

[1] Cass Soc, 19 December 1990.
[2] Cass Soc, 12 June 1986.

H9.2.8 The courts will examine whether the positions which staff members had previously held carry over to the new company, no matter where these positions may be found within the new company.

H9.2.9 The identical activity must carry over to the new employer, which means that the economic entity must continue to operate both before, and after, the transfer, except for whatever interruption organising the launch of the new entity may call for.

9.3 Affected Employees

H9.3.1 As these terms of section L 122–12 concern public policy, no contractual or other exclusions are permissible.

H9.3.2 All contracts in force as at the day the activity is transferred are carried over to the new employer. This applies to apprenticeship and suspended contracts, as well as to contracts of secondment, provided that the employees concerned were, at the time of transfer, still in the employ of the original company.

H9.3.3 The new employer replaces the old, automatically and as of right. This is binding on both employer and employee, and the latter need not be formally notified of the same.[1] Again, as these terms of section L 122–12 concern public policy, no contractual or other exclusions are permissible.

[1]   Cass Soc, 23 October 1968.

9.4 Variation and termination of contract

H9.4.1 The principle is that all employment contracts remain in force, under the terms and conditions prevailing at the time of transfer.

H9.4.2 The *Cour de Cassation* has nevertheless held that although under section L 122–12, employment contracts do transfer, the same does not automatically apply to all acquired benefits or perquisites, whether these terms are essential to the contract or not.[1]

H9.4.3 The new employer is therefore entitled to propose changes to the employee's contract, or novation of the contract, subject to the following conditions:

- the purpose of the changes may not be to avoid the purpose of section L 122–12;
- the employer must obtain the employee's consent to any change to the contract (as opposed to mere changes to working conditions, see paras H1.3.1 ff), otherwise termination of the contract will be deemed to have been at the employer's initiative.

[1]   Cass Soc, 19 October 1983; 2 June 1992; 20 October 1994.

H9.4.4 The new employer may not put an ultimatum to the employee, such as that the employee must agree to a new contract including clauses which would tend to avoid the purposes of section L 122–12. Such clauses will be null and void.[1]

[1]   Cass Soc, 7 March 1979.

9.5 Dismissal of Employees

H9.5.1 It is unlawful to dismiss employees prior to a transfer with the intent of avoiding the effect of section L 122–12.

H9.5.2 Even where there is no clear evidence of such intent, the original employer will be required to show the court that he had no alternative but to dismiss the employees concerned before the transfer. The *Cour de Cassation* has thus held[1] that dismissal must have been a matter of the company's survival, or essential, in order for its activity to be pursued.

[1]   Cass Soc, 4 July and 21 March 1990.

H9.5.3   The courts have consistently found that a new employer is entitled to terminate the contracts of transferred employees, and, in the course of exercising its managerial powers, to undertake restructuring measures.

H9.5.4   A new employer may also rely on events which occurred whilst the employee was in the service of his former employer, to justify dismissing him.[1]

[1]   Cass Soc, 29 May 1990.

H9.5.5   The dismissal indemnity payment will then be assessed so as to include length of service acquired with the former employer.[1]

H9.5.6   Where dismissal is on economic grounds (redundancy), the new employer must comply with the order of dismissal, taking into account the workforce as a whole and not just those employees who have been transferred.

[1]   Cass Soc, 4 October 1995.

9.6   Duty to Inform and Consult

H9.6.1   Section L 432–1 of the Labour Code expressly refers to transfers as falling within the scope of the requirement to inform and consult the works council, as emphatically confirmed by recent decisions handed down by the *Cour de Cassation*.

H9.6.2   From now on, a change in business or restructuring of an operation likely to lead to the dismissal of at least ten employees calls for two works council consultations:
*   pursuant to section L 432–1 of the Labour Code; and
*   pursuant to sections L 321–1 ff of the Labour Code.

10   COLLECTIVE RIGHTS AND BARGAINING

10.1 Background

H10.1.1   French labour law devotes considerable attention to collective relations. Since the so-called 'Auroux' Acts in 1982, collective bargaining has been greatly encouraged, both at company and industry level. Over the last 20 years, the number of collective bargaining and other collective agreements has greatly increased. These agreements carry considerable weight in terms of the hierarchy of French labour law.

H10.1.2   Collective relations may be seen from the following three standpoints:
*   the collective bargaining system as set out by law;

- the parties to collective bargaining: employers on the one side, trade unions on the other;
- elected staff representatives: staff delegates, the works council and the Health and Safety Committee.

10.2 The Collective Bargaining System

A   PUBLIC POLICY

H10.2.1 It is a fundamental principle of French labour law that no exceptions will be allowed to the Labour Code, unless the terms in question – whether they are contained in a collective bargaining agreement, or in an employment contract – are more advantageous to the workforce.

B   RANK OF COLLECTIVE BARGAINING AGREEMENTS

H10.2.2 In terms of the hierarchy of law, collective bargaining agreements lie between the law ie the Labour Code, and employment contracts. Collective bargaining agreements must comply with law and public policy considerations, and employment contracts must comply with the terms of the relevant collective bargaining agreement.

H10.2.3 There are two levels of agreements: industry-wide collective bargaining agreements (*accords de branche*) and company-wide agreements. In general, the term 'collective bargaining agreement' refers only to industry-wide agreements. Company-wide agreements must be consistent with industry-wide collective bargaining agreements, to which there may be no exceptions unless they are more advantageous to the employee.

H10.2.4 The company's economic activity defines which branch of industry it belongs to, and consequently the applicable collective bargaining agreement.

C   NEGOTIATING A COLLECTIVE BARGAINING OR OTHER
     COLLECTIVE AGREEMENT

H10.2.5 At industry-wide level, a collective bargaining agreement is negotiated between the employers' unions in the branch on the one hand, and the recognised trade unions on the other (see below as to recognised trade unions).

H10.2.6 At company level, the agreement is negotiated between the head of the company, on the one hand, and the trade union delegates on the other. The latter are chosen by each recognised trade union, amongst the members of trade union sections in companies with a workforce of at least 50, or among staff delegates, in companies with a workforce of less than 50 (section L 412–11 of the Labour Code).

D   OUTCOME OF NEGOTIATIONS

H10.2.7 An agreement may be implemented once it has been signed by at least one party on each side. A minority trade union may be a party. All employees are covered by the collective bargaining agreement, whether or not they belong to one of the trade unions which signed it. On the other hand, the employer is, in principle, bound by an industry-wide collective bargaining agreement only if he belongs to an employers' union which is a party to it.

E   EXTENSION PROCEDURE FOR COLLECTIVE BARGAINING AGREEMENTS

H10.2.8   In order to avoid competing firms being subject to rules which may differ according to which employers' union the head of the company belongs to, the Labour Minister may issue a Decree, pursuant to which a given collective bargaining agreement is extended to apply to every company in that given branch of industry, whether or not the relevant head of the company belongs to one of the employers' unions party to the agreement. Such Decrees are common in French labour law.

F   NOTICE OF TERMINATION OF A COLLECTIVE BARGAINING AGREEMENT

H10.2.9   One or more of the organisations party to a collective bargaining agreement may give notice of termination (section L 132–8 of the Labour Code), provided at least three months' notice is given.

H10.2.10   From the moment all of the employers' unions or all trade unions party to the collective bargaining agreement have announced their intention to give notice of termination, the agreement continues to remain in force for one year from the date notice of withdrawal was given. Once that year has elapsed, the employees retain only the individual advantages they acquired under the collective bargaining agreement.

H10.2.11   If one of the parties so demands, fresh negotiations with a view to a new agreement must be opened within three months of termination of a collective bargaining agreement. For example, in the autumn of 1998, the Medef (*Mouvement des Entreprises de France*) gave notice that it intended to terminate the collective bargaining agreement for the banking sector, which covered over 300,000 employees. On 10 January 2000, a new collective bargaining agreement was signed, with retroactive effect as of 1 January 2000.

10.3 Recognised Trade Unions

H10.3.1   The principle of trade union freedom is enshrined in the Preamble to the 1946 Constitution and in various sections of the Labour Code. Thus, section L 411–2 states that there shall be no hindrance on the establishment of trade unions, while section L 412–21 states that the exercise of trade union rights in accordance with the provisions of the law may not be restricted, whether by internal memorandum, or by a unilateral decision on the employer's part.

A   NATIONAL LEVEL

Employers' unions

*Medef (*Mouvement des Entreprises de France*)*

H10.3.2   Thc Medef is the main institution which represents French employers as a body.

Other employers' unions

H10.3.3   There are also bodies which represent certain categories of employers, such as the CGPME (*Confédération Générale des Petites et Moyennes Entreprises*) for small and medium-sized businesses. Some employers' organisations represent only a single branch of industry, such as the *Association Française des Banques* (AFB) for the banking sector.

Trade union organisations

The five major federations

H10.3.4   Five trade union federations are presumed to be representative nationwide, no matter what the area of activity:

*   CGT (*confédération générale du travail* – General Confederation of Labour);
*   CGT–FO (*confédération générale du travail force ouvrière* – Workers' General Confederation of Labour);
*   CFDT (*confédération Française démocratique du travail* – Democratic French Confederation of Labour);
*   CFTC (*confédération Française des travailleurs chrétiens* – French Confederation of Christian Workers);
*   CFE–CGC (*confédération générale des cadres* – General Confederation of Executives ('cadres')).

H10.3.5   These five organisations need not prove that they are representative, and may accordingly take part in collective bargaining without further proof, both at company level, and industry-wide.

Other trade union organisations

H10.3.6   Other trade union organisations must prove that they are representative. According to section L 133–2 of the Labour Code there are five criteria for recognising a trade union as representative:

*   size;
*   independence;
*   paid-up membership;
*   experience and seniority of the union;
*   patriotic stand during the German Occupation (in practice, the final requirement is no longer very significant).

H10.3.7   In practice, the courts also examine the union's electoral results.

H10.3.8   A trade union may be recognised either in relation to a particular branch of industry, or in relation to a single company.

B   COMPANY LEVEL

Trade union sections

H10.3.9   Pursuant to its trade union mandate, a union section represents the interests, both material and moral, of its members.

H10.3.10   Each representative trade union may set up a section in any company, without any particular formalities being required.

H10.3.11   A trade union has the following rights:
- it has premises: if the size of the workforce is between 200 and 1,000, the premises will be used by all trade union sections. Where the workforce is over 1,000, each section must be afforded separate premises by the employer;
- it is afforded a notice board, separate from that used by the works council and staff delegates;
- it may collect dues from employee members on company premises;
- it may circulate publications and leaflets on company premises as staff members clock in or out;
- outside working hours, it may set up two types of meeting: a monthly members' meeting, and occasional meetings to invite outside persons, with the company manager's approval.

Trade union delegates

Appointment

H10.3.12   In principle, trade union delegates may be appointed only in companies with a workforce of at least 50. However, in companies with a workforce of less than 50, by law, staff delegates may be appointed as trade union delegates.

H10.3.13   The number of trade union delegates to be appointed per company depends on the size of the workforce.

Number of trade union delegates	
Number of employees	*Number of delegates*
Between 50 and 999 employees	1 delegate
Between 1,000 and 1,999 employees	2 delegates
Between 2,000 and 3,999 employees	3 delegates
Between 4,000 and 9,999 employees	4 delegates

H10.3.14   Delegates must be at least 18 years of age, have been in the company's service for at least one year, and have the right to vote in political elections. No employee who, in the light of the powers he holds, would qualify as a manager of the company, may be elected as a delegate.

H10.3.15   No term is set for their mandate; it ends either when the trade union, or the delegate himself, puts an end to it, or when the delegate leaves the company.

Characteristics

H10.3.16   The role of trade union delegates is to represent their trade union in dealings with the company's manager. In principle, they take part in collective negotiations within the company (see para **H10.2.6**).

H10.3.17   The employer must allow trade union delegates to take time off to discharge their duties (*crédit d'heures*), between 10 and 20 hours per month in principle, depending on the company's size. These hours, known as *heures de délégation*, are paid as of right, as though they are working hours.

10.4 Elected Company Staff Representatives

A   STAFF DELEGATES (DÉLÉGUÉS DU PERSONNEL)

H10.4.1   Staff delegates must be elected in all establishments where the workforce comprises more than 11 people. They are elected every two years by the workforce, and may stand for election more than once.

Prerogatives

H10.4.2   Staff delegates present the employer with collective or individual demands concerning:
* the workforce;
* application of the Labour Code and other laws and regulations relating to social benefits and health and safety;
* application of collective bargaining and other collective agreements.

H10.4.3   The employer must hold a monthly meeting with the staff delegates in order to take note of their demands.

H10.4.4   Staff representatives are allowed time off, between 10 and 20 hours per month, during which hours they may circulate freely throughout the company. They are also authorised to post up staff notices, and may hand out fliers.

H10.4.5   Staff delegates carry out duties, or receive information, in the following areas:
* paid holidays;
* safeguarding individual rights and freedoms in the company;
* appointing members of the Health, Safety and Working Conditions Committee (*Comité d'hygiène, de sécurité et des conditions de travail –* CHSCT);
* collective redundancy, in companies with under 50 employees;
* (re)deploying an employee after an occupational accident;
* *repos compensateur* (rest to compensate for overtime);
* Collective bargaining and other collective agreements;

- Staff Register (the register containing the names of all employees and other information relating to them, for example nationality, date of birth, sex, qualifications, and start date);
- documents relating to working hours;
- contracts for temporary staff seconded to the company;
- liaison between the various staff representative bodies.

Additional prerogatives

H10.4.6   Staff delegates stand in for the works council and the CHSCT in companies with at least 50 employees, where no such bodies have been set up (eg where no candidate stood for election).

B   WORKS COUNCIL

H10.4.7   A works council must be set up in companies with at least 50 employees. Works council members are elected every two years, and may stand for re-election.

H10.4.8   Where a company has several establishments with at least 50 employees in each, a works council must be set up in each such establishment. A *Comité Central d'Entreprise* (Central Works Council) must also be set up. The Central Works Council is made up of the head of the company, an elected delegation made up of works councils from the various establishments and optional representation from trade union organisations. A Group Works Council must also be set up at Group level.

Modus operandi

H10.4.9   The works councils are legal entities, which can own and manage property. They are chaired by the employer, and made up of elected members and of trade union representatives. The works council must meet at least once a month.

H10.4.10   The works council must be given suitable office space. Its members are entitled to take time off (20 hours a month) during which they may circulate freely both on and off company premises. Its operating subsidy, paid by the employer, must correspond to at least 0.2% of gross payroll.

Prerogatives

Economic prerogatives

H10.4.11   The works council's role is to ensure that the workforce has a collective voice, and that its views are taken into account on an ongoing basis.

H10.4.12   The works council is informed:
- within a month of its being elected, as to the company's structure and overall situation;
- quarterly, as to general trends in production, orders, and the financial situation.

H10.4.13   It is also given:

- the company's annual report;
- accountancy data;
- *bilan social* (an overview of all issues of concern to the workforce, such as occupational accidents etc), which must be drafted every year in all companies with over 300 employees.

H10.4.14   The works council may be assisted by a chartered accountant, who must, in some cases, be paid by the company.

H10.4.15–16   Finally, in the following instances the works council must be *consulted*:

(a) as to decisions affecting the company's structure, notably:

- any major change in production structures, or to the company's economic or legal structure (section L 432–1 of the Labour Code);
- in case of merger, transfer or sale of the company itself, or where subsidiaries are purchased or sold (section L 432–1 of the Labour Code);

(b) as to decisions relating to the company's general operations, notably:

- company research and development policy (section L 432–2 of the Labour Code);
- any plans to borrow funds, or issue new equity;
- personnel policy (including recruitment and training);
- *participation* (profit-sharing);
- working hours (section L 432–3, para 4 of the Labour Code);
- company rules and regulations.

In all cases where the works council must be consulted, it must also be provided with all necessary information prior to its meeting. Consultation must give rise to a debate, following which the works council issues an opinion on the topic under discussion. The opinion is not however binding on the employer. A new Act was passed 2 May 2001 providing for specific provisions regarding, notably, the expanding role of the works council.

Social and cultural prerogatives

H10.4.17   The works council manages or oversees all social and cultural activities which take place in the company for the benefit of the workforce or their families (section L 432–8 of the Labour Code).

H10.4.18   This covers:

- staff provident and contingency funds;
- measures to promote the well-being of the workforce and their families;
- occupational or educational agencies linked to the company;
- company social services;
- medical services;
- leisure and sports activities.

H10.4.19   The works council has a budget to this effect, to which the employer contributes.

C   DÉLÉGATION UNIQUE DU PERSONNEL (SOLE STAFF
    REPRESENTATIVE BODY)

H10.4.20   In companies with fewer than 200 employees, the head of the company may decide that the staff delegates should also represent staff on the works council (section L 431–1–1 of the Labour Code). The same elected officials will thus act both as works council members, and as staff representatives.

D   HEALTH AND SAFETY COMMITTEE (COMITÉ D'HYGIÈNE, DE
    SÉCURITÉ ET DES CONDITIONS DE TRAVAIL – CHSCT)

Setting up the CHSCT

H10.4.21   A CHSCT must be set up in all companies or establishments where the workforce numbers more than 50. It includes the head of the company or establishment, elected representatives, and consultants notably the Labour Inspector, and the factory doctor (*médecin du travail*, the occupational health officer).

H10.4.22   The elected representatives are appointed by elected Central Works Council or Establishment Works Council members, and by the staff delegates. The sole requirement for standing for CHSCT elections is that the candidate must be employed in the company or establishment.

Procedures

H10.4.23   The CHSCT meets at least once a quarter at the invitation of the head of the company or establishment, but may meet more frequently if required. It will also meet following any serious accident. Two of its members may also demand a meeting if they have proper grounds for so doing.

H10.4.24   The CHSCT may rely upon expert advice, at the company's expense, if a project intended to change health and safety or working conditions is to be implemented.

H10.4.25   The CHSCT is *informed* by the head of the company, who must present it with an annual written report, and a prevention scheme. The CHSCT gives an opinion on both of these documents.

H10.4.26   The CHSCT must be *consulted* in the following cases:
- health, safety and working arrangements (changes to shifts, production rates, new security equipment, canteen arrangements for the workforce);
- recruiting disabled persons;
- giving an opinion on documents relating to company rules and regulations, and security training programmes.

H10.4.28   Finally, the CHSCT may be assigned to monitoring and analysis, for example analysing workplace hazards, inspections and enquiries and considering preventive measures.

H10.4.29
Like all staff representatives, CHSCT members are entitled to a certain amount of time off (*crédit d'heures*), depending on the company's size. This time off is paid at the same rate as normal working hours.

Staff delegates	• where the workforce numbers at least 11 • elected every two years • must meet monthly with employer • deal with terms of employment, collective agreements, working hours, liaison between representative bodies
Works council	• where the workforce numbers at least 50 • elected every two years • elected members and trade union representatives • subsidised by employer • significant rights to company information and consultation
Health and Safety Committee (CHSCT)	• where the workforce numbers more than 50 • elected representatives, the Labour Inspector, and occupational health officer • must meet at least once a quarter • rights to information and consultation on health and safety issues • monitoring and inspection rights

E   OTHER FORMS OF STAFF REPRESENTATION

Staff representatives on the Board of Directors or Advisory Board (Conseil d'administration ou de surveillance)

H10.4.29A   In *sociétés anonymes*, the works council must be represented at Board of Directors or Advisory Board meetings.[1] The number of representatives varies depending on the number of electoral colleges in the company. French law requires that the workforce is broken down into two or three electoral colleges, each electing its own president. The electoral colleges are as follows:

• white and blue-collar workers;
• engineers, department heads, technicians, foremen and similar categories;
• where the number of engineers, department heads, technicians, foremen and similar categories amounts to at least 25, the company will have a third electoral college.

[1]   In France, a *société anonyme* (SA, a limited company) may take one of two forms: SA with a Board of Directors (*conseil d'administration*), or SA with a *directoire* and Advisory Board (*conseil de surveillance*).

H10.4.30   Therefore, if the company has two electoral colleges, the works council will appoint two members to be its representatives at Board of Directors or Advisory Board meetings. If the company has three electoral colleges there will be four members on the delegation.

H10.4.31   These persons take part in all Board of Directors or Advisory Board meetings, and have a consultative role. They may present demands formulated by the works council to these bodies, to which demands a detailed reply must be given.

European Works Council

H10.4.32   By an Act dated 12 November 1996, the European Directive relating to European Works Councils was incorporated into the French Labour Code.

H10.4.33   A European Works Council must be set up in companies which have an EU dimension, ie companies which have a total workforce of at least 1,000, and which have at least one establishment with a workforce of at least 150 in at least two different member states.

H10.4.34   Staff representative institutions play a significant role, and the employer must accordingly pay due regard to their rights and powers.

H10.4.35   Any infringement, or attempt to infringe, upon the workforce's right to freely appoint a staff representative, or to hinder a staff representative in the exercise of his duties, is a criminal offence known as *délit d'entrave* (obstruction) punishable by a sentence of imprisonment of up to one year, and/or by fines of up to 25,000 FF (€ 3,811).

11   EMPLOYMENT DISPUTES

11.1 Background

H11.1.1   The Industrial Tribunal (*Conseil de Prud'hommes*) has sole jurisdiction over disputes between an employer and individual employees. Members are elected: see paras **H11.2.1** ff.

H11.1.2   The Industrial Tribunal also has jurisdiction over apprenticeship contracts, dismissal on economic grounds (redundancy), and over work-related disputes between employees, and deals with wage claims in the event of bankruptcy (insolvency).

H11.1.3   Collective labour disputes (other than those relating to the grounds for dismissal) and occupational accidents are dealt with by other courts, as are disputes relating to civil servants, unless the latter's terms of employment are governed by private law.

H11.1.4   Both the Tribunal itself, and the applicable procedure, are quite distinct from those of other courts.

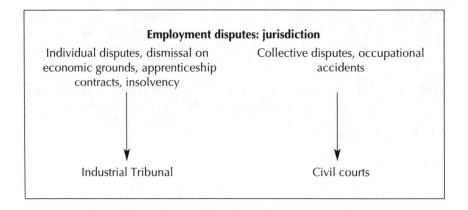

Employment disputes: jurisdiction

Individual disputes, dismissal on economic grounds, apprenticeship contracts, insolvency

Collective disputes, occupational accidents

Industrial Tribunal

Civil courts

11.2 Industrial Tribunals

A   ELECTIONS

Electorate

H11.2.1   Electors must be aged 16 or over, and be active in a trade or business. Apprentices and the unemployed are nonetheless entitled to vote.

Candidate eligibility

H11.2.2   The prerequisites are the same as for the electorate, save that candidates must be aged 21 or over. They must be entered on the electoral lists of the city in which they pursue their trade.

Elections

H11.2.3   Elections for Industrial Tribunal members are held every five years, on the level of the *Commune,* a territorial division headed by a Mayor. Magistrates may stand for re-election. The next round of elections will take place in December 2002.

H11.2.4   Elections are held during working hours, either at the Town Hall, or on premises, fixed by the local Prefect's Order, close to the elector's workplace. Postal voting is allowed.

Président and Vice Président

H11.2.5   Employees and employers chair the panel alternately.

Privileges

H11.2.6   While in office and for a six-month period thereafter, magistrates who are employees may not be dismissed, unless the Labour Inspector so authorises. Candidates to the office of magistrate enjoy the same privilege for a three-month period.

B   ORGANISATION

H11.2.7   Each Industrial Tribunal is divided into five separate sections, each of which is empowered to grant emergency relief:

- *encadrement* (employees who fall into the category of *cadre*);[1]
- industry;
- sales and related activities;
- agriculture;
- miscellaneous (professionals, trade unions).

[1]   *Cadre* is a blanket term which cannot be translated directly into English. It refers to very diverse categories of upper-echelon white-collar workers, such as engineers, foremen, managers and executives, and in some cases, even executive assistants or secretaries.

H11.2.8   Save for the *encadrement* section, which may try all disputes relating to *cadres*, it is the employer's real and principal activity which determines which section shall have jurisdiction.

C   THREE DIVISIONS

Bureau de conciliation *(Conciliation Division)*

H11.2.9   The *Bureau de conciliation* has two magistrates, one of whom is an employer, while the other is an employee. They chair the division alternately. The magistrates assigned to this division attempt to have the parties reach an amicable solution.

Bureau de jugement *(Trial Division)*

H11.2.10   The *Bureau de jugement* stage follows where no amicable solution has been found. There are four magistrates, two of whom are employers and two employees. Decisions are by absolute majority.

Référé prud'homal

H11.2.11–13   The *Référé prud'homal* deals with emergency proceedings. One magistrate is an employer, the other an employee.

If the tribunal fails to reach a decision by absolute majority, the case must be retried by the same magistrates in the relevant division. On this occasion, however, the tribunal will be chaired by a professional magistrate, ie a High Court judge.

This type of hearing is then known as an *audience de départage,* during which the entire case is retried from the beginning.

D   TERRITORIAL JURISDICTION

H11.2.14   In principle, the tribunal of the place where the establishment employing the individual concerned is located will have jurisdiction.

H11.2.15 However, if the work is habitually performed outside any particular establishment, or if the employee works from home, the tribunal of the place where the employee resides will have jurisdiction.

H11.2.16 Finally, the employee may choose to refer the matter to the tribunal of the place where he was initially hired, or where the employer is established.

H11.2.17 Any contractual term contradicting these provisions will be automatically null and void.

E   USUAL PROCEDURE

H11.2.18 To commence proceedings, the employee need only make an oral request, or send a letter by registered post, to the Secretary of the Industrial Tribunal. The request must set out the name, profession and address of the parties, and the matter of the dispute. The Secretariat will then send the petitioner a receipt.

H11.2.19 In principle, the parties must appear in person. They may appoint a proxy, or rely for example on the assistance of a trade union delegate, a spouse or a lawyer. The Industrial Tribunal may nevertheless decide that the parties must appear in person.

H11.2.20 The petitioner, having entered his suit, receives written notice of the time, place and hour of the conciliation hearing, to which he is asked to bring any relevant documents.

H11.2.21 The conciliation hearing is then held before a panel of magistrates. Even if the respondent does not appear, the magistrates may order that an investigation takes place, or that protective measures are taken (eg handing over payslips or a Work Certificate), or payment of a deposit.

H11.2.22 Following the conciliation hearing, there are three possible avenues:
- the matter may be sent before *conseillers rapporteurs*. These magistrates, whose role is important, will thoroughly review the matter and may, for example, hear the parties, or order an investigation and/or production of various documents;
- the matter may be sent to the *bureau de jugement* for trial;
- the magistrates may hand down an *ordonnance de conciliation*. This is a court order arising from a hearing during which an amicable settlement was reached.

H11.2.23 The parties are summoned to appear before the *bureau de jugement* either orally, or by registered post with acknowledgement of receipt.

F   EMERGENCY REMEDIES

H11.2.24 Under sections R 516–30 ff of the Labour Code, the magistrates may hear petitions for an injunction when the matter is urgent. Within the limits placed on the Industrial Tribunal's jurisdiction, the magistrates may take any and all measures where the merits of the case are not at issue, or which may be called for by the nature of the dispute.

H11.2.25   Even in instances where the merits of the case are at issue, the magistrates may grant an injunction for protective or other measures to prevent imminent harm or unlawful disorder.

H11.2.26   Finally, where there is a clear duty on one of the parties, the magistrates may order that a deposit is given to the creditor, or grant a remedy corresponding more or less to specific performance (*obligation de faire*). In practice, a petition is often entered for an injunction, as emergency relief can readily be obtained.

H11.2.27   The petitioner is free to refer the matter to this division, either by process served by a bailiff (*assignation*), by oral request, or by a letter sent by registered post.

H11.2.28   The Industrial Tribunal must try cases at least once a week.

G   APPEAL

H11.2.29   The parties have one month to appeal against a decision handed down by the *bureau de conciliation* or the *bureau du jugement*, from the date on which it was formally notified.

H11.2.30   Where injunctive relief has been granted, the appeal must be lodged within a fortnight.

H11.2.31   No appeal may be lodged unless the main claim exceeds 22,500 FF (€ 3,430). However, if the claim is of a lower value, the parties have two months from the date of the Industrial Tribunal's decision to appeal to the *Cour de Cassation* (French Supreme Court).

H11.2.32   An appeal to the *Cour de Cassation* is the only avenue open for appeal against a decision relating to demands for production of a Work Certificate, payslips, or other documents which the employer is under a duty to issue to the employee.

12   WHISTLEBLOWING/DATA PROTECTION

12.1 Whistleblowing

A   DUTY OF DISCRETION

H12.1.1   In French law, if an employee discloses information which he has obtained at work and which is potentially harmful to the company, he will be in breach of his duty of discretion (*obligation de discrétion*) to his employer. Such disclosure will also constitute a breach of the employee's general duties of loyalty and good faith under his employment contract. In French law this duty of discretion is twofold:

- an obligation not to disclose such information to external third parties (competitors or clients); and
- an obligation not to disclose confidential information to other employees in the company.

H12.1.2 Employees who are members of the company's works council (*comité d'entreprise*) and employees who are trade union delegates in the company are subject to a special duty of discretion.

H12.1.3 Depending on the circumstances of the case, including taking into account the functions and responsibilities of the employee in the company, breach of the duty of discretion may constitute serious or gross misconduct (*faute grave* or *lourde*) and can lead to dismissal, and in the case of *faute lourde*, to the employee being held liable to the employer for damages. With respect to the duty of discretion regarding other employees of the company, this obligation is imposed particularly strictly on employees having a managerial function in the company, and especially where the employee discloses information regarding the company's financial difficulties.

H12.1.4 Where the circumstances of the employee are such that there is a risk that the employee will disclose information in breach of his duty of discretion, the employer may be justified in dismissing the employee on the grounds of loss of confidence (*perte de confiance*). Whether or not the employer is justified in doing so depends on the circumstances of the case.

H12.1.5 The duty of discretion cannot prevent an employee disclosing embezzlement of funds which he is aware of to the managers of the company, nor can it provide a defence to an employee who obeys wrongful orders or who participates in the fraudulent actions of his superiors.

B   EMPLOYEES' RIGHTS OF EXPRESSION

The right to freedom of expression

H12.1.6 An employee will have a defence to having 'blown the whistle' if he shows that the disclosure was made in pursuance of the employee's general right to freedom of expression as contained in arts 10 and 11 of the 1789 *Déclaration des droits de l'homme et du citoyen* (Universal Human Rights Declaration) and art 10 of the European Convention on Human Rights.

H12.1.7 The right to freedom of expression is an individual right allowing each employee to express himself outside the company on matters concerning the company which he knows by reason of his employment there. The employee is justified in disclosing the information because a more important interest is at stake, for example public health.[1] The *Cour de Cassation* has also recently affirmed that this right to freedom of expression is a fundamental right and is only limited by the condition that the exercise of the right must not be abused by an employee.[2]

[1] Cass Soc, 4 February 1997, RJS 3/97.
[2] Cass Soc, 4 February 1997, RJS 3/97.

H12.1.8 An abuse of the right to freedom of expression is committed by an employee where, for example, he:

- intends to harm his employer;
- acts patently in bad faith;
- is guilty of gross misconduct;
- exercises the right imprudently or negligently.

H12.1.9 It is also necessary that the employee's conduct has caused the employer damage.

Other rights of expression

H12.1.10 The right to freedom of expression is to be distinguished from the various rights which exist in French law for employees to express themselves within the company. In particular it should be distinguished from the right of employees to express themselves collectively and directly to their employer concerning the content, the conditions of exercise, and organisation of their work, as well as the quality of production (*le droit d'expression direct et collectif*).[1]

[1] Section L 461–1 of the Labour Code.

H12.1.11 It should also be distinguished from the *droit d'alerte*, that is the right of the works council to inform managers of the company of facts affecting the financial health of the company, or the right of employees or members of the *Comité d'hygiène, de sécurité et des conditions de travail* (the Committee of Hygiene, Security and Conditions of Work) to inform the employer immediately of any serious and impending danger.[1]

[1] Sections L 231–9; R 236–9; L 432–5 and R 432–17 et seq of the Labour Code.

Confidentiality clauses

H12.1.13 An employer may ask an employee to sign a confidentiality agreement (*serment de confidentialité*) or have a clause in his contract (*clause de secret professionnel*) by which the employee agrees not to divulge either within or outside of the company information of any kind which he has obtained as a result of his employment. However, in light of the affirmation by the *Cour de Cassation* that the only limit on the employee's freedom of expression is if the employee exercises the right in an abusive manner,[1] it seems that even with such a clause or agreement the employee is free to exercise his freedom of expression and disclose the relevant information so long as he does not abuse this right.[2]

[1] Cass Soc, 4 February 1997, RJS 3/97.
[2] Antoine Mazeaud *Droit du Travail* para 443, page 262.

12.2 Data Protection

A   THE 1978 ACT RELATING TO DATA PROCESSING AND INDIVIDUAL LIBERTIES

H12.2.1 The provisions of the Act concerning data processing and individual liberties (loi 78–17 '*loi informatique et libertés*') dated 6 January 1978 (the 1978 Act), should be noted where employers hold data relating to employees. The aim of the 1978 Act is to balance the competing demands between respect for an individual's private life and safeguarding the public interest. Under the 1978 Act data processing must not infringe an individual's identity, his human rights, his private life or his individual or public freedoms. A National Commission has been set up under the 1978 Act to ensure compliance with the law and to take initiatives in this area (the *Commission nationale de l'informatique et des libertés* – the CNIL).

H12.2.2 The 1978 Act covers both:

- information, in whatever form, which allows, directly or indirectly, the identification of an individual (*les informations nominatives*); and
- the automated processing (*traitement automatisé*) of this data, that is all operations carried out by automatic means pertaining to the collection, recording, elaboration, modification, conservation and destruction of the data. It also includes all operations of a similar nature pertaining to the use of the files or databases.

H12.2.3 Many of the provisions of the Act also apply to non-automated files with the exception of those files which are strictly personal, for example a personal diary.[1]

[1] *Loi* 78–17, articles 1, 4, 5, 45.

H12.2.4 Under the 1978 Act the following principles must be adhered to:

- the collection of the information must not be operated by a fraudulent, disloyal or illicit method;
- it is forbidden to record or store data pertaining to a person's racial origins, political, philosophical or religious opinions, trade union membership or lifestyle;
- every person has the right to know and, if necessary, contest the data concerning him which is subject to automated processing under the Act, there being therefore a right both to access to and rectification of the data. Individuals providing information must therefore be informed whether it is mandatory or optional for them to respond to the questions, the consequences of not responding, who the recipients of the information are, and the right to access to and rectification of the information;
- no decision of an administrative nature affecting an individual can be based on information subjected to automated processing aimed at giving an indication of the profile or the personality of the individual;
- the data must not be kept beyond the normal duration of use of the information (the *droit à l'oubli*);
- there are severe sanctions for breach of the principles, the severity of the sanction being relative to the importance given to the information in question;
- under art 16 of the 1978 Act, the automated processing of *informations nominatives* on behalf of a private organisation must be preceded by a declaration to the CNIL.[1] Article 19 of the 1978 Act sets out the information which must be contained in the declaration, the automated processing of the data only being allowed to be such as is necessary in order to achieve the objective pursued. This requirement is strictly controlled by the CNIL.

[1] The employer can only put into operation the automated processing intended after he has received a receipt from the CNIL that it has received the declaration. Breach of the obligation constitutes a criminal offence punishable by up to three years' imprisonment and/or a fine of up to 300,000 FF (€45,735) (section 226–16 of the Criminal Code.) Employees can receive reparation from the employer for breach of this obligation (even if the employer later regularises the situation.)

H12.2.5 It should be noted that there are exceptions to some of the provisions in the Act based on the need to protect the public interest.[1]

[1] For example the prohibition on keeping data relating to an individual's opinions, origins or allegiances can be lifted for reasons of public interest. For example religious organisations, philosophical and political organisations and trade unions are authorised to keep a register on their members.

B   PROTECTION OF THE PRIVATE LIFE AND LIBERTIES OF JOB APPLICANTS AND EMPLOYEES

H12.2.6 In addition to the protection afforded by the 1978 Act, the Act of 31 December 1992 on employment, part-time work and unemployment, (*loi sur l'emploi, le temps partiel et le chômage*), introduced into the Labour Code the general principle of protection of the private life and individual liberties of job applicants and employees. As a result of this legislation, the only restrictions which can infringe a job candidate's or employee's rights and individual and collective liberties are those which are not justified by the nature of the task to accomplish nor proportional to the objective pursued.[1] Not only is the employer bound by this law, but so also is any other company employee and any outside intermediary intervening in the event that there is a recruitment procedure.

[1] Section L 120–2 of the Labour Code.

H12.2.7 Section L 121–6 of the Labour Code provides that:

'... information, in whatever form, which may be requested from a candidate or an employee, may only be aimed at assessing the candidate's/employee's ability to fulfil the position advertised or his professional aptitude. Such information must be directly related and necessary to the proposed job or to the evaluation of professional aptitude'.

H12.2.8 In assessing whether an employer has complied with section L 121–6, the courts will examine all the circumstances to ascertain whether the information was indispensable to evaluate the candidate's/employee's suitability/professional aptitude. The provision therefore allows a candidate/employee to refuse to give information unless the information is directly related to the position on offer. Where a candidate/employee can show that he has incurred prejudice, he may sue for damages.[1]

[1] Employers should note that this protection extends to, for example, trainees/apprentices.

H12.2.9 If a staff representative notes that there may be a breach of an individual's rights and liberties within the company which cannot be justified by the nature of the task to be accomplished nor proportional to the aim sought, he can immediately notify the employer.[1]

[1] Section L 422–1 of the Labour Code.

H12.2.10 Under section L 121–7 of the Labour Code, an employee or candidate must be previously informed of the methods and techniques used to evaluate or recruit him before their implementation, and the results of the evaluation or recruitment must stay confidential. Such techniques must be relevant to the objective being pursued.

H12.2.11 The works council must be informed of methods or techniques of recruitment before they are put into operation, and must be informed beforehand of any modification to them (section L 432–2–1 of the Labour Code).

H12.2.12 Section L 121–8 of the Labour Code states that no data concerning an employee personally can be collected by a device or technique which has not been brought to his knowledge beforehand.[1]

[1] The CNIL has also issued principles concerning the collection of information and methods of recruitment. These principles follow the same lines as the provisions included in the Labour Code.

H12.2.13 According to a deliberation of the CNIL, the use of automated processing for the management of personnel (the *traitements automatisés de gestion du personnel*), for example regarding employees' salary and social charges, career development and absences, is allowed, so long as it is in conformity with the principles that the use is justified by the objective being pursued; that each user only has access to that data which is strictly necessary in order for him to fulfil his task; and that the information is not used for the compilation of professional profiles.[1] Employers must be careful to respect all the deliberations of the CNIL in this area.[2] The works council must be informed in advance of all automated processing regarding the management of personnel before such processing is put into operation, as well as of any modification to it (section L 432–2–1).

[1] Deliberation 89–48 of 30 May 1989.
[2] In particular employers should be careful to abide by provisions in the Labour Code and CNIL deliberations relating to sensitive information, for example information relating to an employee/candidate's disability, and provisions relating to the automated processing of salary or information relating to salary.

H12.2.14 In order to enact Directive 95/46/EC concerning the protection of personal information and the free circulation of this information, a new law on the protection of personal information should reinforce the protection afforded to employees and the powers of the CNIL. Although, at the time of writing, France has not yet passed such a law, employers should be aware of the provisions of the Directive.

13 HUMAN RIGHTS

13.1 The European Convention on Human Rights

H13.1.1 France ratified the European Convention on Human Rights (the ECHR) in 1974, and allowed the right of individual petition in 1981. By ratifying the ECHR, by virtue of art 55 of the French constitution, France incorporated the ECHR and accorded it priority over domestic law. As a result judges in France are able to rely on the ECHR when deciding cases and over recent years in several cases Industrial Tribunal judges have made reference to the ECHR.[1]

¹   For example, Industrial Tribunal judges have referred to art 6(1) of the ECHR, the right to an impartial tribunal (Cass Soc, 8 January 1997, Dr soc 1997). Other relevant provisions of the ECHR for the purposes of employment law include arts 8–11 and art 14. For example, under art 8 of the ECHR, every person has the right to respect for his private and family and home life. The employee's freedom of choice with respect to his personal and family home is one of the attributes of this right. A restriction on this liberty by the employer by application of a mobility clause in the employment contract is only valid to the extent it is indispensable to the protection of the legitimate rights of the company, and proportional, taking into account the job occupied and the work expected, to the objective pursued (Cass Soc, 12 January 1999).

13.2 Human Rights Protection within Domestic Law

H13.2.1   In addition to the protection given to human rights by the ECHR, French law itself contains numerous safeguards of employees' human rights. Some examples of provisions of particular relevance to the employment relationship are set out below.

A   THE FRENCH CONSTITUTION

H13.2.2   The Preamble to the 1946 Constitution, incorporated by reference into the 1958 Constitution, asserts a person's right to work, to join a trade union, to strike and to participate in the running of a business. It also states that no person may be discriminated against in his/her job or trade owing to his origins, opinions or beliefs.

B   THE RIGHT TO PRIVACY

H13.2.3   In addition, a general right to privacy is enshrined in French law. Section 9 of the Civil Code states that everyone has the right to respect for his private life. In addition sections 226–1 ff of the Criminal Code provides criminal sanctions for infringement of this right.

H13.2.4   The Labour Code also contains specific provisions to protect the right to privacy. Thus, section L 120–2 of the Labour Code states:

> 'No infringement on an employee's individual or collective liberties may be made, except where justified by the nature of the task involved and to the extent such infringement is proportionate to the objective sought.'¹

¹   Inserted by *loi* 31–12–92 into the Labour Code (see para **H12.2.6.**) See also para **H12.2.9**, section L 422–1 regarding the staff representative's right to notify the employer of a potential breach of the obligation contained in section L 120–2).

H13.2.5   The employer must strictly adhere to these principles when drawing up the *règlement intérieur* (ie the rules relating to security and discipline in the company, see section L 122–35 of the Labour Code). The potential scope of section L 120–2 is wide. For example whilst professional telephone calls made to and from employees' mobile telephones may be justified if they are proportional to the needs of the company, any abuse by the employer concerning the number and timing of these calls could fall within the ambit of section L 120–2 and constitute an infringement of the privacy of employees, criminally sanctioned under section L 226–1 of the Criminal Code.

H13.2.6 The general provision contained in section L 120–2 is further elaborated by texts pertaining to the type of information an employer may request from an employee or from a candidate during the recruitment process. According to these provisions,[1] the information an employer may request from a potential recruit or an employee must necessarily be directed at assessing the individual's ability to hold the position, or his professional skills, and must stand in direct and necessary relation to the position on offer or which he holds.[2]

[1]   Paras **H12.2.6** ff.
[2]   Section L 121–6 of the Labour Code; paras **H12.2.7** ff.

H13.2.7 To ensure compliance with this right to privacy, employers should also be careful to comply with the provisions of the 1978 Act regarding computer data processing[1] and legal provisions regarding the use of computers for the management of personnel.[2]

[1]   *Loi* dated 78–17 '*Loi informatique et libertés*'; see para **H12.2.1**.
[2]   See para **H12.2.13**.

C   THE SURVEILLANCE OF EMPLOYEES

H13.2.8 The monitoring of employees' activities directly challenges employees' human rights, particularly their right to privacy. French law provides significant protection to employees in this regard.

H13.2.9 Under a general condition of openness and loyalty, an employer can monitor the activities of his employees. In order to fulfil this condition, an employer who envisages putting in place a device for control and monitoring of employees must comply with an obligation of openness to the *Commission Nationale de l'Iinformatique et des Libertés* (the CNIL), the works council and the employees.[1]

[1]   The CNIL is the body established under *Loi* dated 78–17 '*Loi informatique et libertés*' to ensure compliance with that Act, and to take initiatives in this area of law; paras **H12.2.1** and **H12.2.13**.

Obligation to the CNIL

H13.2.10 Under art 16 of the Act of 1 January 1978, the automated processing on behalf of a private organisation, of information, in whatever form, which allows, directly or indirectly, the identification of an individual (*les informations nominatives*), must be preceded by a declaration to the CNIL.[1]

[1]   See paras **H12.2.1** ff. Failure by the employer to make the necessary declaration constitutes a criminal offence punishable by a sentence of up to three years' imprisonment and/or by a fine of up to 300,000 FF (€45,735) (section 226–16 of the Criminal Code). The failure also constitutes a fault by the employer enabling the employees to obtain reparation from the employer, even if the situation has subsequently been regularised (Cass Soc, June 1995).

Obligation to the works council

H13.2.11 According to section L 432–2–1 of the Labour Code, the works council must be informed of all automated processing used for the management of personnel before it is put into operation, as well as any modification to it.[1] Under this provision the works council must also be informed and consulted as to the methods and techniques allowing the surveillance of the activity of employees before the decision to implement such techniques is made.[2] If the employer fails to fulfil his obligation under section L 432–2–1, the works council can institute a criminal claim on the basis that the employer was obstructing the proper functioning of the works council (*délit d'entrave*). The works council may also simply request the intervention of the CNIL.

[1]   Para **H12.2.13**.
[2]   This provision provides significant protection to employees, but it should be noted that such protection is limited to automated processing of the relevant information. Therefore if the employer uses more traditional methods to process the information, under this provision the works council will not need to be informed beforehand. For example, a professional diary does not constitute automated processing of data, but can constitute a form of monitoring of an employee's activity.

Obligation to the employees

H13.2.12   Section L 121–7 of the Labour Code stipulates that employees are to be informed of methods and techniques of professional evaluation put into operation concerning them. These methods must be directly related to the objective being pursued.[1] In the same way, section L 121–8 states that no information concerning an employee personally can be collected by a technique which has not previously been notified to him.[2]

Example

In French law, an employer is authorised to install a listening device on telephone lines which are exclusively reserved for professional use so long as the employer has informed the employees beforehand that he will be doing so. However, where telephone lines are not exclusively without their consent reserved for professional use, listening to the telephone conversations of employees constitutes a criminal offence under section 226–1 of the Criminal Code.

---

[1]   Para **H12.2.10**.
[2]   Para **H12.2.12**.

H13.2.13   With regard to the practice of video surveillance, a topic of increasing pertinence today, video surveillance is permitted in French law if such surveillance takes place in accordance with the following conditions:[1]

• in places open to the public which are particularly exposed to the risk of aggression or theft;
• with the sole aim of protecting the security of persons and property; and

- the techniques of video surveillance having been submitted to the prior authorisation of the *Préfet*.

[1] Statute of 21 January 1995; Deliberation 94–56 of 21-6-94; Circular of 22 November 1996.

H13.2.14 The law covers the simple transmission of images, as well as the transmission and recording of images. Therefore, for example, no authorisation is required for a system involving neither recording nor transmission of images. If the images recorded are intended to be used to create a data file which allows, directly or indirectly, the identification of an individual (a *fichier nominatif*), the CNIL will also have competence. In every case of video surveillance, the employees and works council must be informed of the implementation of such a system of control.[1]

[1] Where an employer discovers reprehensible conduct by an employee as a result of his illicit surveillance of the employee and his recording of the relevant information, a different approach is taken by the Social Chamber of the *Cour de Cassation* on the one hand and the Criminal Chamber of the *Cour de Cassation* on the other hand, as to whether such evidence may be produced in court by an employer in support of his case.

H13.2.15 In addition, employers should be aware of the potential penal sanctions for breach of the employee's right to privacy and respect for his private life.

H13.2.16 According to section 226–1 of the Criminal Code:

'. . . any deliberate infringement, by whatever means, of an individual's privacy by:

- listening in on, recording or transmitting, without the consent of their author, words spoken in a private or confidential capacity; and
- observing, recording or transmitting, without the person's consent, the image of that person when in a private place;

is punishable by a sentence of up to one year's imprisonment and/or a fine of up to 300,000 FF [€ 45,735].'

H13.2.17 Therefore, in application of the principles of this section, an employer concealing a voice-activated listening device in the false ceiling of an office occupied by two employees constitutes an infringement of their right to privacy, in the event that:

- the employees have not given their consent to this surveillance system being installed;
- the office is a private place;
- the permanent functioning of the system shows a deliberate intent on the employer's part to listen to the employees (Cass Crim, 24 January 1995).

H13.2.18 However, filming employees in a public area of the workplace in order to discover criminal acts perpetrated against the employer is not considered an infringement of the employee's privacy (Cass Crim 23 July 1992).

H13.2.19   Similarly, with regard to the inviolability of employee correspondence, section 226–15 of the Criminal Code states that:

> '... where, in bad faith, a third party's correspondence is opened, destroyed, delayed, or diverted, whether or not it had already been delivered, or where knowledge of its contents has been fraudulently acquired, this shall constitute an offence, punishable by a sentence of up to one year's imprisonment and/or a fine of up to 300,000 FF [€ 45,735].'

Paragraph two of this section also covers correspondence conveyed by telecommunications as well as the use of interception devices.

H13.2.20   Therefore under this provision, an employer cannot in bad faith monitor the correspondence of its employees in one of the ways set out in the section, and, by virtue of para 2 of the section, this prohibition appears to also include e-mail.[1]

[1]   Employers should be careful to respect the human rights issues raised by surveillance of employees' e-mail and use of the internet, there being various domestic and European provisions bearing on these sensitive topics. For example, in addition to section 226–15 of the Criminal Code, employers should note the obligation to inform and consult the works council on techniques allowing the surveillance of employees' activities (section L 432–2–1 of the Labour Code, see para **H13.2.11**); as well as the fact that an organisation's Intranet network (including, *inter alia*, e-mail and web-site access) is made up partly by information on employees which may or may not constitute information of a personal character (*les informations nominatives*) under the *loi informatique et libertés*' dated 6 January 1978 (see paras **H12.2.1** ff) as well as under Directive 95/46/EC (see para **H12.2.14**). Employers should therefore be aware of the relevant obligations contained in these legal provisions.

D   THE RIGHT NOT TO BE DISCRIMINATED AGAINST

H13.2.21   With regard to the employee's right not to be discriminated against, excluding potential candidates from employment or recruitment on discriminatory grounds is penalised under both the Labour Code and under criminal law.

H13.2.22   Section L 122–45 of the Labour Code states that:

> 'No person may be excluded from a recruitment process, nor may an employee be dismissed or penalised on the basis of his origins, sex, lifestyle, domestic situation, race, nationality, ethnic origin, political opinions, trade union membership, religion or (unless the *médecin du travail* [factory doctor/occupational health officer] has declared him unfit to work) on the basis of his state of health or handicap.'

H13.2.23   Any decision which contradicts this provision will qualify as discrimination. The courts may declare the disputed decision null and void, and grant the potential recruit/employee damages. With the aim of preventing discrimination, the Labour Code includes several provisions regarding transparency of recruitment procedures and evaluation of employees (paras **H12.2.6** ff; and see paras **H5.1.1–H5.5.7** regarding equal opportunities and unlawful discrimination.).

H13.2.24 Falling within the ambit of section L 122.45 is the delicate question of whether an employer may put questions to a candidate or employee concerning their state of health.

H13.2.25 Under French law, no questions may be put to a candidate or employee concerning their state of health. The rationale is that to the extent that there are no visible, pathological signs of illness, and the illness has no impact on the employee or potential recruit's work, it is not the employer's business. Only under exceptional circumstances, where the position that the employee holds or is being offered is such as to make this a legitimate concern, may the employer do so. This principle applies, for example, to the testing of employees for alcoholism,[1] narcotics addiction[2] and AIDS.[3]

[1] Regarding testing for alcohol consumption, only in certain restrictively defined cases would a test be considered justified. Therefore, company rules and regulations may stipulate that people who handle dangerous substances or operate potentially dangerous machinery may be 'breathalysed'. A Government Directive dated 15 March 1983 states that an employee may be requested to take a breath test to assess the alcohol level in his blood where the employee handles dangerous products, is in charge of dangerous machinery or transports passengers in his vehicle. In other cases, however, testing would not appear to be justified.

[2] On 9 July 1990, the Higher Council for Preventing Occupational Hazards (*Conseil supérieur de la prévention des risques professionnels*) issued a Note stating that there were no grounds for systematically testing all potential recruits to a certain position, or the entire workforce of a company, for narcotics addiction. Under exceptional circumstances, where there is a relation between narcotics use and aptitude for a position proposed, or held, the *médecin du travail* may be empowered to carry out drug tests. According to the National Consultative Committee on Ethics (*Comité Consultatif National d'Ethique*), only where narcotics use is likely to represent a danger to the user, to other employees or to third parties, should testing be justified. There is no pre-defined list of positions or activities which would allow for systematic testing.

[3] In 1988, the serious nature of AIDS led the *Conseil supérieur de la prévention des risques professionnels* to make a number of recommendations. Save under exceptional circumstances, where there is a direct and necessary link between the information requested and the position on offer, there are no grounds for enquiring into the employee's state of health, and in particular whether or not he is infected with the AIDS virus. Deeming the risk that one employee might infect another under normal working conditions to be very slight, the Council also considers that testing for AIDS is not justified. Only the *médecin du travail* may take the initiative of testing, and take the decision as to whether an AIDS-infected employee is in a position to work.

H13.2.26 Regarding discrimination against employees on grounds of their religious convictions, art L 122–45 clearly prohibits an employer from dismissing or punishing an employee because of his religious beliefs. However, in spite of this principle, employees exercising teaching functions in a private establishment must respect the establishment's particular character (Statute 77–1285 of 25 November 1977). On the other hand, the practice of a religion may affect the employment relationship because of the absences from work it can lead to. In the same way as with every non-authorised absence from work, an employee's unauthorised absence from work in order to practice his religion may justify a dismissal.

H13.2.27   With regard to criminal sanctions in respect of discrimination, employers should note the provisions of sections 225–1 and 225–2 of the Criminal Code.[1]

[1]   Pursuant to these provisions, a discriminatory act may be punishable by a fine of up to 200,000 FF (€ 30,490), and/or by a sentence of up to two years' imprisonment. The burden of proof lies on the person claiming to have been discriminated against.

E   THE RIGHT TO FREEDOM OF EXPRESSION

H13.2.28   Employees enjoy the right to freedom of expression, having both rights to expression within and outside the company.[1] The right to freedom of expression could constitute a defence to an employee who has 'blown the whistle'.

[1]   See paras **H12.1.6** ff.

F   THE RIGHT TO JOIN A TRADE UNION AND THE RIGHT TO STRIKE

H13.2.29   Recognised as one of the rights guaranteed by the French Constitution, the right of employees to join a trade union must be respected by all companies.[1] The right consists of three principles:

(1) the employee's freedom to join a trade union;
(2) the obligation of the employer to remain neutral with respect to trade union membership within the company; and
(3) a prohibition on the employer from taking any measures of a discriminatory nature against an employee because of the employee's trade union membership or activity.

[1]   See also section L 412–1 of the Labour Code.

H13.2.30   In addition each employee has the right to strike, this right being recognised in the Preamble to the 1946 Constitution.

1 Germany

Marion Keunster, Dr Ante-Kathrin Uhl and Astrid Wellhöner

Marion Kuenster is a Partner of CMS Hasche Sigle Eschenlohr Peltzer, Berlin. She was admitted to the German Bar in 1995. She is a lecturer at the University of Potsdam on employment law. She is author of various articles and texts.

Dr Ante-Kathrin Uhl is a Partner of CMS Hasche Sigle Eschenlohr Peltzer Schäfer, Stuttgart. She is a participant of the CMS Labour Law Practice Group.

Astrid Wellhöner is a lawyer at CMS Hasche Sigle Eschenlohr Peltzer Shäfer, Stuttgart.

CMS Hasche Sigle Eschenlohr Peltzer Shäfer, Berlin

Phone: +(49–30) 203 600
Fax: +(49–30) 201 60 290
Email: marion.kuenster@cmslegal.de
Website: www.cmslegal.de

CMS Hasche Sigle Eschenlohr Peltzer Schäfer, Stuttgart

Phone +49(0)711/9764–0
Fax: +49(0)711/9764–900
Email: Kathrin.uhl@cmslegal.de; Astrid.wellhoener@cmslegal.de
Website: www.cmslegal.de

SUMMARY TABLE

GERMANY

Rights	Yes/No	Explanatory Notes
THE EMPLOYMENT RELATIONSHIP		
Written contract required	NO	Generally, certain particulars must always be provided by written statements
Minimum notice	YES	Minimum period set by statute, depending on length of service
Terms:		
Express	YES	May be written or oral, but are subject to mandatory provisions of statute/collective agreement
Implied	YES	Apply to both employer and employee, based on the principles of loyalty and good faith
Incorporated	YES	By works rules, works agreements, collective bargaining agreements; also by protective statutes
REMUNERATION		
Minimum wage regulation	NO	Although may be determined by collective bargaining agreement
Further rights and obligations:		
Right to paid holiday	YES	Four weeks/24 working days per annum (including Saturdays)
Right to sick pay	YES	Full salary for six weeks (after four weeks' qualifying service)
WORKING TIME		
Regulation of hours per day/ working week	YES	Eight hours per day/48 hours per week, although employer may introduce flexible working time
Regulation of night work	YES	Usual limit eight hours per night
Right to paid holiday	YES	See above
Right to rest periods	YES	Eleven hours per day plus daily rest breaks. Work on Sundays or public holidays generally forbidden
EQUAL OPPORTUNITIES		
Discrimination protection:		
Sex	YES	Employees are protected by the Basic Law/Civil Code
Race	YES	Employees are protected by the Basic Law/Civil Code

420

Marital status	YES	Employees are protected by the Basic Law/Civil Code
Disability	YES	Employees are protected by the Basic Law/Civil Code
Part-time and fixed-term work	YES	Employees are protected by the Basic Law/Civil Code and the Act on Part-time Employment and Fixed-term Employment Contracts
Religion	YES	Employees are protected by the Basic Law/Civil Code, and the Act on the Promotion of Employment
Age	NO	Employees are protected by the Basic Law/Civil Code, and the Act on the Promotion of Employment
Equal pay legislation	YES	Employees are protected by the Basic Law/Civil Code, and the Act on the Promotion of Employment

TERMINATION OF EMPLOYMENT

| Right not to be dismissed in breach of contract | YES | In order for dismissal to be effective, the employer must comply with notice periods and any statutory procedures |
| Statutory rights on termination | YES | The employee may be a 'protected employee' (eg disabled) or the Protection against Dismissal Act may apply; special rules apply to summary termination |

REDUNDANCY

Statutory definition	NO	But may relate to place/type of work, or total or partial closure of business
Right to additional payment	NO	No additional payment required unless provided for by collective bargaining agreement/works agreement
Right to collective consultation	YES	Consultation/negotiations with works council/Department of Employment required

YOUNG WORKERS

| Protection of children and young persons at work | YES | Restrictions on nature of work/ working hours |

MATERNITY RIGHTS

| Right to time off antenatal care | YES | |
| Right to maternity leave | YES | Generally six weeks before and eight weeks after the birth |

421

Notice requirements	NO	But if the employer is not notified of pregnancy the employee may lose her right to protection from dismissal
Maternity pay	YES	Employee receives all benefits excluding salary; maternity benefit paid by health insurance company
Protection from dismissal	YES	Protected period runs during pregnancy to four months after childbirth. Also applies in relation to parental leave
Health and safety protection	YES	During pregnancy, and following childbirth/during breastfeeding
Right to parental leave	YES	Applies to both parents; usually up to three years' leave. Right to return to same job and same terms and conditions of employment, and right to request part-time employment during the parental leave

BUSINESS TRANSFERS

Right to protection on transfer	YES	Employees are protected by the Civil Code
Transfer of employment obligations	YES	All terms and conditions including collective rights are transferred
Right to information and consultation	NO	No right unless there is a works council, and, changes in operations are proposed
Right not to be dismissed	YES	Dismissal by transferor or transferee is invalid if the transfer is the principle reason for dismissal

COLLECTIVE RIGHTS AND BARGAINING

Right to join a trade union or employer's association	YES	Union or association has right to advertise, distribute literature, and access to employees even where no employees are members in the workplace
Collective bargaining agreements	YES	Very common, regulating working time, pay, holiday, notice periods and other matters
Works councils	YES	Works council has the right to information and notification in relation to social, staff and commercial matters
European works councils	YES	Directive 94/95/EC implemented by the European Works Council Act

EMPLOYMENT DISPUTES

Special jurisdiction	YES	All employment disputes are heard by special employment courts

WHISTLEBLOWING

Protection from dismissal/detriment	NO	No specific statutory protection, subject to very limited possible exceptions justified by law

DATA PROTECTION

Protection	YES	Personal data is protected, although there is no specific statutory protection for employees

HUMAN RIGHTS

Statutory protection of human rights	YES	Fundamental human rights are contained in the Basic Law (applying only to the legislature, executive and judiciary, not private employers).

1.   THE EMPLOYMENT RELATIONSHIP

1.1   Background

I1.1.1   As in English law, the essence of the relationship between employer and employee is contractual. However, this relationship is crucially governed by statute and – often – by collective bargaining agreements. As distinct from English law, there are no formal disciplinary or grievance procedures which should be followed.

1.2   Contract of Service

A   CONTRACT AND ITS WRITTEN PARTICULARS

I1.2.1   An employment contract consists of a legally binding offer and an acceptance. In general, it can be oral and/or in writing. However, there is a statutory obligation to provide written particulars of employment. In any event it is preferable to confirm the terms of agreement (and any subsequent amendments or arrangements) in writing.

I1.2.2   Certain written particulars[1] must be provided to an employee (except those employed on an occasional basis) not later than one month from the agreed date of commencement of employment.

(a)   the name and the address of the employer and the employee;
(b)   the date on which the employment began;
(c)   in the case of fixed-term contracts: the intended length of employment;
(d)   the place of work, or where the employee is required to work at various places, a clause allowing for such flexibility;
(e)   a short description of the work which the employee is recruited to carry out;
(f)*   the composition and amount of remuneration including supplementary payments, bonuses and other parts of remuneration and the intervals at which remuneration is paid;
(g)*   hours of work;
(h)*   holiday entitlement;
(i)*   length of notice periods to terminate the contract of employment;
(j)   a general reference to applicable collective bargaining agreements and/or works agreements;
(k)   where the employee is required to work outside Germany for a period of more than one month the employer must provide certain specified details:
  (i)   the period of work outside Germany;
  (ii)* the currency in which payment will be made, while working outside Germany;
  (iii)* additional pay and benefits to be provided by reason of the work being carried out outside Germany; and
  (iv)   any terms and conditions relating to the employee's return to Germany.

[1]   Section 2 of the Evidence Act (*Nachweisgesetz*), which came into force in July 1995, incorporating EU Directive 91/533 (OJ 1991 L288/32).

I1.2.3   As to certain specified particulars (those marked with an asterisk* in para **I9.2.2**) the contract of employment can refer the employee to another agreement, for example to applicable collective bargaining agreements, works agreements or other similar agreements.

I1.2.4   The employer must inform the employee in writing of any change in any of the particulars specified in para **I1.2.2** as soon as possible and, in any event, no later than one month after the change.

I1.2.5   An employee who has been employed for more than one month may make a reference to an employment court if he has not been provided with a written statement (or if he has been provided with one but it is incomplete or inaccurate). The employment court then can order the employer to provide the applicant with a written statement or to complete an existing statement setting out all the relevant terms and conditions.

I1.2.6   There is a crucial difference in the nature of the relationship between an employer and an employee (a 'contract of service') and that between an employer and a self-employed consultant/freelancer etc (a 'contract for services'). The main difference under German employment law is that the latter is not governed by protective statutory employment provisions.

EMPLOYED → governed by statute and contract

SELF EMPLOYED → governed by contract

B   TERMS OF THE CONTRACT

I1.2.7   Contracts of employment are made up of terms and conditions which are not necessarily set out only in a written statement. They may be in writing, oral and be implied or incorporated.

Sources of contract terms

Express   •   oral
                 •   written

Implied
Incorporated

C   EXPRESS TERMS

I1.2.8   Express terms (oral and/or written) set out the agreement reached between employer and employee. Under German employment law, the parties must at least agree upon the fundamental obligations (*Hauptpflichten*). These are – on the one hand – the employee's duty to work and – on the other hand – the employer's obligation to pay remuneration. In addition, the parties

425

usually agree on additional points, eg confidentiality, notice periods, annual holiday entitlement etc. However, any such term will be overridden if it is contrary to a mandatory statute or an applicable collective agreement which is more favourable to the employee in question. Moreover, each term should be clear and unambiguous. In the event of ambiguity a term must be interpreted from the point of view of an 'officious bystander'.

Examples of express terms

Summary dismissal

I1.2.9 Employers sometimes set out a non-exhaustive list of examples of what type of behaviour is considered by the company to be gross misconduct, eg being under the influence of alcohol or drugs whilst at work. Without express provision, an employer may still terminate the contract in the event of the employee's fundamental breach, but there may be circumstances where it is unclear whether the employee's behaviour constitutes gross misconduct.

Intellectual property protection

I1.2.10 The employee's rights in relation to his intellectual property are governed by statute, namely the Copyright Act. The parties can agree, however, that the employee grants a right of use of a copyright.

Confidentiality

I1.2.11 It is an implied term that an employee must not breach the confidentiality of his employer, even after termination of the employment contract. Nevertheless, the parties may emphasise this duty by setting it out in an express clause or they can set out examples of what the employer considers to be confidential information (this list should be non-exhaustive).

Restrictive covenants

I1.2.12 The parties can, if they wish, agree on a post-termination restrictive covenant which limits competition after the termination of employment. This agreement must be expressly included and is only valid if certain statutory requirements are fulfilled.[1] One of the conditions which must be met is the employer's obligation to pay monthly compensation for the duration of the prohibition in the amount of at least 50% of the average income earned by the employee immediately prior to his or her employment ending. Moreover, the parties can only agree on a restrictive time period up to two years, and the covenant must be reasonable in the interests of the contracting parties; the prohibition must serve to protect the legitimate business interest of the former employer and it may not unreasonably hinder the employee from making a living.

[1] Sections 74–75d of the Commercial Code (*Handelsgesetzbuch*).

Choice of law

I1.2.13 In principle, the parties are free to choose the law governing the contract of employment.[1] In the absence of an express choice the contract of employment will be governed by:

- the law of the country in which the employee habitually carries out his work in performance of that contract, even if he temporarily works in another country; or
- if the employee does not habitually carry out his work in any one country, by the law of the country in which the registered office of the employer is situated or in which currency he is paid.[2] However, if from the circumstances as a whole it appears that the contract is more closely connected with another country the law of that country may apply.

[1]   Section 27(1) of the Introductory Act to the Civil Code (*Einfuehrungsgesetz zum Buergerlichen Gesetzbuch* – EGBGB).
[2]   Section 30(2) of the EGBGB.

I1.2.14   Articles 30(1) and 34 of the Introductory Act to the Civil Code (*Einfuehrungsgesetz* – EGBGB) limit the freedom of the parties to choose the law applicable to a contract of employment. A choice of law must not deprive the employee of the protection afforded to him by the mandatory rules of the law which would apply in the absence of choice.

I1.2.15   So far as statutory employment rights are concerned, it is not possible to exclude the jurisdiction of employment courts. Any clause attempting to do so will be void.

D   IMPLIED TERMS

I1.2.16   Under German law, both parties to an employment contract have additional duties apart from their central contractual obligations to work and to pay remuneration. These so-called implied obligations (*Nebenpflichten*) are based on the principles of loyalty and good faith, which are considered as the basis of each contractual relationship. They exist regardless of whether the parties agree on them expressly or not.

Examples of implied terms

Employee's duties

(i)   Reasonable care in performing duties
(ii) Fidelity, loyalty and good faith
(iii) Confidentiality
(iv) Duty to care about the employer's property

Employer's duties

(i)   To provide work
(ii) To care about the employees' health and safety
(iii) Trust, good faith and reasonableness

E   INCORPORATED TERMS

I1.2.17   The parties can incorporate terms from other sources into a contract of employment eg works rules, collective bargaining agreements or works agreements. Incorporation should be express.

> **Examples of incorporated terms**
> - works rules
> - collective agreements (collective bargaining agreements and/or works agreements)
> - pension schemes

F   PROTECTIVE LAWS

I1.2.18   The contractual freedom is restricted by numerous protective laws, by collective agreements and by the decisions of the Federal Employment Court (BAG). Where there are two or more alternative regulations regarding one subject, eg within a federal law and a collective bargaining agreement, the regulation which is most favourable to the employee will apply.

Statutory provisions

I1.2.19   The most significant protective laws, which stipulate the minimum requirements, are:

Protection against Dismissal Act (see paras **I6.3.1** ff);
Sick Pay and Paid Holiday Act (see paras **I3.2.1** ff);
Working Time Act (see section 4);
Disability Act;
Maternity and childcare provisions (see section 8);
Protection against Dismissal Act;
Enhancement of Company Pension Schemes Act.

Protection against Dismissal Act

I1.2.20   The Protection against Dismissal Act[1] applies if the employee has been employed for more than six months and the company regularly employs more than five employees, excluding trainees. It allows termination (with notice) only by reason of a 'social justification'.

[1]   *Kuendigungsschutzgesetz* – KSchG.

Paid holidays

I1.2.21   The statutory minimum annual vacation is four weeks per year (24 working days, but the working week includes Saturdays), although in practice five to six weeks are common. The law also provides paid time off work on public holidays.[1]

[1]   Sections 2 and 3 of the Sick Pay and Paid Holiday Act (*Gesetz ueber die Zahlung des Arbeitsengelts an Feiertagen und im Krankheitsfall – Entgeltfortzahlungsgesetz*).

Sick Pay and Paid Holiday Act

I1.2.22   The Sick Pay and Paid Holiday Act[1] governs the conditions under which an employee continues to receive salary from his employer in cases of sickness or a public holiday and the duration of such payment.

[1]   *Entgeltfortzahlungsgesetz.*

Regulation of Working Hours Act

I1.2.23   The Regulation of Working Hours Act[1] contains the most important principles regulating working hours. The daily maximum number of working hours is basically (with some exceptions) eight hours based on a six-day working week. The daily maximum working time can be extended to 10 hours a day.

[1]   *Arbeitszeitgesetz – ArbZG.*

I1.2.24   Work on Sundays and public holidays is generally forbidden although it is possible in restricted circumstances to be granted a special licence, eg for restaurants, hospitals etc.

Disability Act

I1.2.25   The Disability Act[1] regulates an employer's obligation to contract with a certain percentage of disabled persons if he employs more than 20 employees. If an employer does not comply, he has to pay a monthly penalty per disabled person who is not under contract.

[1]   *Gesetz zur Sicherung der Eingliederung Schwerbehinderter in Arbeit, Beruf und Gesellschaft (Schwerbehindertengesetz – SchwbG).*

I1.2.26   Furthermore, disabled persons have additional holiday entitlement and are protected against termination with and even without notice. In exceptional cases, a termination might be justified, but the employer has to ask the relevant authority's permission in advance (see paras **I6.4.1** ff).

Maternity and childcare provisions

I1.2.27   Pregnant women and persons who take long-term childcare leave enjoy special protection under the provisions of the Maternity Leave Act[1] and the Child Care Leave Act.[2] An employed woman is entitled to take six weeks paid time off work before the birth and eight weeks paid time off work after the birth of the child. There are also special prohibitions on certain activities for pregnant women, particularly immediately before and after the birth. In addition, a mother and a father of a young child is entitled to parental leave (without a qualifying period) up to a period of three years without being paid.

[1]   *Gesetz zum Schutze der erwerbstaetigen Mutter (Mutterschutzgesetz – MuSchG).*
[2]   *Gesetz ueber die Gewaehrung von Erziehungsgeld und Erziehungsurlaub (Bundeserziehungsgeldgesetz – BErzGG).*

Enhancement of Company Pension Schemes Act

I1.2.28   Under the Enhancement of Company Pension Schemes Act,[1] the employer and the employee can agree on a pension scheme either in the employment contract itself or in the form of a collective promise to all or to a certain category of the employees. Another legal basis of a pension scheme can be a works council agreement or – especially in the public sector – a collective bargaining agreement.

[1]   *Gesetz zur Verbesserung der betrieblichen Altersversorgung – BetrAVG.*

I1.2.29 There are different types of pension schemes. A pension scheme can take the form of, for example, a promise of the employer to pay a certain sum during retirement. It can also take the form of a special insurance, where the employer contracts with an insurance company to insure the employee's life. In addition, the pension can consist of the membership of the employee in a pension trust (*Pensionskasse*) or in a support trust (*Unterstuetzungskasse*).

I1.2.30 Which pension scheme applies depends on the agreement of the parties. They can, for example, also agree that the employer pays money on top of the employee's contribution or they can agree that a certain amount of the regular salary is used to fund it.

I1.2.31 If the employer has agreed with an employee to make payments to a company pension scheme but the employment ends before the employee reaches pensionable age, the right to the future benefits is preserved under certain conditions. That is usually the case if the employment contract has lasted longer than ten years and the employee is at least 35 years old. The law also provides for insolvency insurance.

Collective agreements

I1.2.32 Further provisions, which always stipulate the minimum requirements, are *collective agreements,* insofar as they contain rights of the individual employee. The provisions of collective agreements have the same effect as the above laws.

Collective bargaining agreements

I1.2.33 A collective bargaining agreement is a contract between one or more trade unions and an employers' association or an individual employer that regulates the working conditions of the employees. The Collective Bargaining Agreements Act[1] regulates the provisions and the operation of such agreements (see paras I10.1.1 ff).

[1]   *Tarifvertragsgesetz* – TVG.

Works agreements

I1.2.34 If the workforce of a company has elected a works council as its representative, the works council can reach an agreement with the employer upon any matter that requires co-determination under the Works Council Constitution Act[1] and which stipulates minimum working conditions. The Works Council Constitution Act regulates the appointment, the organisation and the rights and duties of the works council and the requirements of a valid works agreement (see paras 10.2.1 ff).

[1]   *Betriebsverfassungsgesetz* – BetrVG.

Law based on the decisions of the Federal Court of Employment (Bundesarbeitsgericht – BAG)

I1.2.35 Finally, the employment relationship will also be determined by law based on BAG decisions.

I1.2.36 As an example, the BAG has decided that company practice can shape the legal basis for an employee's claim to additional remuneration. An employer's action becomes company practice when such action is repeated to the extent that the employee concludes that the employer will continue to act in such a way in the future and the employee may rely on this.[1] This can be the case, for example, if an employer paid an extra month's salary per year over three years in succession. Although the employment contract does not provide for this payment, the employee will have a legal right to this payment in future. However, the employee will not be entitled to claim such remuneration if the employer makes it clear to the employee that he will pay on a voluntary basis only and that it remains in his sole discretion whether he will make additional payments in the future.

Examples of protective laws

Principle of equality[2]	The employment relationship is determined by the principle of equal treatment of all employees.
Patents[3]	The employer is entitled to take over an invention created by an employee within the scope of his work or his contractual duties. If he does so, he is obliged to pay the employee adequate and reasonable compensation.
Copyright[4]	Where a literary, dramatic, musical or artistic work is created by an employee in the course of his employment, the employer is entitled to claim for the transfer of the copyright obtained, provided a main purpose of the employment is to create works for which a copyright may be obtained.
Working time[5]	48 hour working week is implied by statute

---

[1] BAG, *Der Betrieb* (DB) 1994, 2034.
[2] See part 5, especially paras **I5.1.1–I5.1.5**.
[3] Section 4 of the Patents Act (*Patentgesetz* – PatG).
[4] Sections 31(5) and 43 of the Copyright Act (*Urhebergesetz* – UrhG).
[5] Working Time Act (*Arbeitszeitgesetz* – ArbZG), see paras **I4.1.1** ff.

1.3 Variation of Contract

I1.3.1 A contract is legally binding and cannot be altered unilaterally. Throughout the course of an employment relationship terms will, of course, change eg salary, and there may be a need for other employment terms to alter. Usually, this can be achieved by mutual consent. However, if the employer wishes to introduce a change which the employee does not accept the employer has to rely on other means of variation. One way of changing the conditions is for the contract to include a right to vary. Such an agreement is, however, only valid in limited circumstances. A contractual mobility clause may, for example, allow an employer to move an employee from one workplace to another. Individual terms and conditions of employment may also be varied by a collective bargaining agreement which is binding on individual employees. However, such changes can only be altered to the detriment of an employee if the employment contract does not provide a corresponding provision which is more favourable to the employee.

I1.3.2 Another way of varying an employment contract is for the employer to give notice to terminate, pending a change of contract. This consists of notice of termination combined with a binding offer of an employment agreement containing all conditions of the former employment contract and the changes (for further details see paras **I6.3.19–I6.3.20**).

Variation of contract

- by consent
- contractual right to vary
- collective agreement
- termination pending a change of contract

1.4 Remedies

A   EMPLOYEE'S REMEDIES

Fulfilment of contractual duties

I1.4.1 If the employer does not fulfil his contractual duties, the employee concerned can seek to have the contract enforced by taking legal action.

Damages

I1.4.2 If the employer does not fulfil his contractual duties properly, the employee concerned can sue for damages. Damages are aimed at putting the employee in a position he would have been in had the breach not occurred.

I1.4.3 German employment law does not recognise anything similar to 'constructive dismissal' as exists in English law. Thus an employee dismissed in breach of contract is not entitled to accept the employer's repudiatory breach and claim damages. In the case of an employee's dismissal in breach of contract, the employee will claim continuous employment and sue for damages, eg loss of salary which the employer did not pay in breach of contract.

Withholding work

I1.4.4 Withholding of work is a possible remedy where an employer is refusing to fulfil his contractual duties, especially the duty to pay remuneration.

Dismissal/resignation

I1.4.5 If an employer's breach is serious enough, the employee may be entitled to terminate the contract without notice and to sue the employer and claim damages.

Injunctive relief

I1.4.6   Under certain circumstances, an employee may apply for an interlocutory injunction, eg to enforce his holiday entitlement.

B   EMPLOYER'S REMEDIES

Fulfilment of contractual duties

I1.4.7   If the employee does not fulfil his contractual duties, the employer in question can also take legal action. The judicial decision would not be enforceable,[1] but it is necessary to be able to claim equivalent compensation for further inaction under s 61(2) of the Employment Court Act (*Arbeitsgerichtsgesetz* – ArbGG).

[1]   Section 62 Abs 2 of the Employment Court Act (*Arbeitsgerichtsgesetz*), 888 Abs 2 of the Code of Civil Procedure (*Zivilprozessordnung*, ZPO).

Damages

I1.4.8   If an employee does not fulfil his contractual obligations properly, an employer can sue the employee in damages for breach of contract. This happens only rarely, principally because an employer's loss is harder to quantify.

Withholding wages

I1.4.9   Withholding of wages is a possible remedy where an employee is refusing to work normally.

Dismissal

I1.4.10   If an employee's breach is sufficiently serious, the employer may be entitled to terminate the contract either with notice or with immediate effect (see paras **I6.2.1–I6.3.20**).

Injunctive relief

I1.4.11   An employer may apply for an interlocutory injunction to restrain the disclosure of confidential information or to enforce a restrictive covenant.

2   REMUNERATION

2.1   Background

I2.1.1   As distinct from English employment law, there is no general law on minimum wages in Germany. Employer and employee are basically free to agree on the amount and type of remuneration. This is not the case, however, where a collective bargaining agreement applies, which contains minimum wage provisions. In that case, an agreement between the employer and the employee for lower salary would be unenforceable.

2.2 Legal Regulation of Remuneration

I2.2.1 Subject to the application of collective bargaining agreements, the parties are free to decide on the type of remuneration and the method of pay. Commonly, salaries are paid on a monthly basis. Instead of a fixed sum the parties can, for example, agree on a lower basic salary combined with a commission. Alternatively, they can base their agreement to a great extent on performance-related pay. It is quite common to agree on a '13th month' salary payment, or bonus. However, employers are increasingly paying this 13th month salary as a discretionary bonus.

I2.2.2 By statute, salary is payable at the end of each calendar month, although the parties can agree on another due date.

2.3 Deductions from Wages

I2.3.1 The employer must deduct income tax from earnings, and is also obliged to deduct social security contributions and even church tax if the employee is a member of the Catholic or Protestant Church or of another religious group which has the rights of a public law corporation.

I2.3.2 In all other respects the employer is not entitled to unilaterally reduce earnings. An agreement between the parties to the employment contract under which the employer is entitled to unilaterally reduce earnings is invalid as, if valid, such an agreement would deprive the employee of statutory protection against notice of termination pending a change of contract (see paras **I1.3.2** and **I2.3.3**).[1] If the employee carries out poor work this does not entitle the employer to reduce earnings either, for the employee is only under obligation to work, not under obligation to be successful in a specific way. In such cases the employer can only set off any claim for damages against the employee's right to earnings.

[1]   BAG, Federal Employment Court, decision dated 12 December1984, Betriebs-Berater 1985, 731.

I2.3.3 Reduction in earnings is only possible if there is an appropriate agreement between employer and employee regarding the specific amount of the reduction or if there has been a notice of termination pending a change of contract (*Änderungskündigung*) in accordance with s 2 of the Protection against Dismissal Act (*Kündigungsschutzgesetz* – KSchG). Notice of termination pending a change of contract must be socially justified. The requirements of case law on social justification are very stringent. A reduction in earnings would be socially justified if the employer can illustrate that if it continues to pay the original remuneration the economic existence of the business would be threatened or the workplace jeopardised, and that economic survival would be secured by reduction in remuneration.

2.4 Itemised Pay Statement

I2.4.1 There is no explicit duty set out in statute to provide a written statement regarding earnings. As a rule it is regarded as an ancillary duty arising from the working relationship. Section 82(2) of the Works Council Constitution Act (*Betriebsverfassungsgesetz* – BetrVG) establishes the right of all employees to have the calculation and completion of their earnings explained. The employer undertakes to provide the employee with written proof of completion and the amount of earnings including bonuses, allowances, premiums and special payments and other components of earnings on the date on which it is due, one month at the latest after commencing work (s 2(1) of the No 6 Evidence Act (*Nachweisgesetz*).

3 FURTHER RIGHTS AND OBLIGATIONS

3.1 Holiday Entitlement

I3.1.1 The statutory minimum holiday entitlement is four weeks per year, ie at least 24 working days based on a six-day working week including Saturdays.[1] However, in practice five to six weeks are common. Moreover, existing collective bargaining agreements often provide special regulations regarding holiday entitlement, its extent and a holiday bonus calculated with reference to the employee's income.

[1] Section 3(1) of the Paid Holiday Act (*Bundesturlaubsgesetz fuer Arbeitnehmer – Bundesurlaubsgesetz – BUrlG*).

I3.1.2 Under the Paid Holiday Act (*Bundesurlaubsgesetz*), full holiday entitlement arises after six months of employment. If the employee leaves the company earlier, he can claim his holiday entitlement on a pro-rata basis. In principal, the employee must take his vacation days during the calendar year. However, an employee is allowed to carry over vacation days to the next year which he could not take during the current calendar year, provided that this is based on urgent personal or business reasons. Carried-over days must be taken before 31 March of the following calendar year. Otherwise, the employee will lose the holiday entitlement.

I3.1.3 If an employee leaves a company and did not take his vacation days, he can claim pay in lieu of his accrued holiday entitlement.

3.2 Sick Pay

I3.2.1 The Sick Pay and Paid Public Holidays Act[1] governs the conditions under which an employee continues to receive salary from his employer in the event of sickness, and the duration of such payment. The entitlement arises after the fourth week of the employment relationship. Then, the employee is entitled to claim sick pay in the event of sickness for a period of six weeks in the amount of 100% of his regular pay, excluding payments for overtime. However, in exceptional cases he may lose his entitlement, eg if he caused the sickness intentionally or by his gross negligence.

[1] Sick Pay and Paid Public Holidays Act (*Gesetz ueber die Zahlung des Arbeitsentgelts an Feiertagen und im Krankheitsfall – Entgeltfortzahlungsgesetz*).

I3.2.2 In principle, the employer is not obliged to continue paying sick pay if the illness lasts longer than six weeks. As employees are required to have health insurance, the employee then receives an insurance payment from his health insurance company of 70% of his monthly salary.

I3.2.3 The regulations also cover the employee's duty to notify his employer in the event of illness as soon as possible; furthermore, he or she has to present a medical certificate, if the illness lasts longer than three calendar days, although the employer can claim such certificate at an earlier date.[1] While the employee fails to comply with these legal obligations, the employer may withhold sick pay.

[1] Section 5 of the Sick Pay and Paid Public Holidays Act (*Entgeltfortzahlungsgesetz*).

3.3   Part-time Employment

I3.3.1 The employment relationship may be concluded as a part-time employment relationship from the outset. It is also possible to reduce the working hours specified in the employment contract in the course of the term of the existing employment relationship.

I3.3.2 The Act on Part-time and Fixed-term Employment Contracts (*Teilzeit- und Befristungsgesetz* – TzBfG) came into force on 1 January 2001. It implements the frame agreements of the European social partners which form the basis of Directives 97/81/EC and 99/70/EC on fixed-term employment relationships, and supersedes the Promotion of Employment Act (*Beschäftigungsförderungsgestez*). The most striking aspect of the new Act is that it grants employees, including key employees, a right to claim part-time employment.

I3.3.3 Employees are entitled to demand a reduction in their working hours from their employer *TzBfG*, s 8(1)). This applies to all employees in the private sector and the German civil service (*öffentlicher Dienst*), including key employees in the private sector and senior civil servants, employees with fixed-term contracts and part-time staff. In order to qualify for part-time employment the following conditions must be satisfied:

• the employer generally employs more than 15 employees. In calculating the number of employees, each member of staff counts regardless of the number of hours worked (per capita principle); and
• the employee concerned has been employed with the current employer for a minimum of six months (minimum period of employment).

I3.3.4 The employer may refuse the desired reduction in the working week for operational reasons only. Of the existence of operational reasons is contested, the burden of presentation and proof lies with the employer. Under *TzBfG*, s 8(4) operational reasons are deemed to exist in particular if the reduction in working time would substantially impair the organisation, operational procedures or safety at work, or if it would cause the employer unreasonable costs. In practice it will be up to case law to define more closely the rather loose term 'operational reasons'.

I3.3.5 In addition, the employer is obliged in principle to advertise any position which he advertises publicly or internally as a part-time position.

4   WORKING TIME

4.1   Background

I4.1.1   The obligations under the Working Time Act, which came into force in 1994, are aimed at safeguarding the health and safety of workers and improving the conditions for flexible working hours.

Summary of obligations

- In general, working time may not exceed eight hours per working day (48 hours per week).
- However, the employer is allowed to introduce flexible working time.
- There are special regulations and exceptions for night work, work on Sundays and public holidays and in particular industries.
- Under certain circumstances, the employer has to establish and maintain records.
- Generally, workers are entitled to 11 hours uninterrupted rest per day and 24 hours uninterrupted rest per week, and a rest break of 30–45 minutes when working 6–9 hours or more per day.

4.2   Legislative Control

I4.2.1   The Working Time Act (*Arbeitszeitgesetz* – ArbZG) protects employees, trainees and other individuals who personally undertake work for others (eg temporary workers). It does not cover self-employed contractors who are genuinely pursuing a business activity on their own account. The law also provides exclusions for workers in certain sectors (eg doctors) and for employees in senior positions. Moreover, there are specified categories of workers to whom the limits on night work and the limits on Sundays or public holidays do not apply.

I4.2.2   Working time is the period of time from the beginning of the work until its end without any rests. Under s 3 of the Working Time Act (ArbZG), the daily working time of an employee may not exceed eight hours per working day, including Mondays to Saturdays. It is, however, permissible to prolong the daily working time up to ten hours per working day, if the average working time of eight hours per working day will not be exceeded within a time period of six calendar months or 24 weeks. This equalisation period can be considerably increased if a collective bargaining agreement is applicable, eg to 12 months. Thus, the Working Time Act offers a certain amount of flexibility to adapt the individual working time of the employees to the work required.

I4.2.3   Employers are under a duty to display a copy of the statutory provisions of the Working Time Act (ArbZG) and any supplementary working time regulations, including applicable collective bargaining agreements. Furthermore, an employer is obliged to record the daily working time of any employees, if it exceeds the permissible working time of eight hours per working day. The employer is obliged to maintain these records for a period of two years.

4.3 Opting Out

I4.3.1 Unlike in English employment law, employers may not secure employees' agreement to opt out of the 48-hour week. The employer can, however, introduce flexible working hours as described above (see para I4.2.2).

4.4 Night Workers

I4.4.1 Night time is a period of seven hours covering the period between 23:00 and 6:00. A night worker for the purpose of the Working Time Act (ArbZG) is one who regularly works at least two hours a night during night time or on at least 48 working days of the calendar year.

I4.4.2 Normal hours of work may not exceed an average of eight hours a night. This working time can only be increased up to ten hours a night in limited circumstances. Night workers are also entitled to free health checks to assess whether they night worker are fit to work at night.

4.5 Rest Period

I4.5.1 In general, employees are entitled to 11 hours consecutive rest each day. Work on Sundays and public holidays is generally forbidden. However, the Working Time Act provides a wide range of exceptions, eg working in hospitals, restaurants, in public markets etc.

I4.5.2 Workers are entitled to a rest break of at least 30 minutes[1] away from the work station if the worker works in excess of six hours, and to a break of at least 45 minutes if he or she works in excess of nine hours.

[1]   The Working Time Act does not answer the question of whether rest breaks need to be paid or not.

4.6 Remedies

I4.6.1 The Supervising Authorities are the bodies responsible for supervising the observance of the Working Time Act. In the case of an infringement against the statutory provisions of the Working Time Act, the Supervising Authority has the power to impose an administrative fine upon the employer. Intentional infringement which results in health risks for the employees is considered a criminal offence.

I4.6.2 An employee can also bring a claim before the employment courts for breach of his rights under the Working Time Act, for example if the employer dismisses him because he refuses to work longer than the prescribed limits.

5   EQUAL OPPORTUNITIES

5.1 Background

I5.1.1 German law guarantees equal opportunities in two ways. Firstly, it states the principle of equal treatment of comparable employees, which is one of the basic pillars of German employment law. The principle of equal opportunities is based on art 3(1) of the Basic Law (*Grundgesetz* – GG), which the Federal Court of Employment (*Bundesarbeitsgericht* – BAG) transferred into employment law as a general rule regarding employment regulations with a collective dimension. The principle protects employees – as individuals or as a group – from different treatment compared to the treatment of others in a comparable situation, unless the employer can show a justifiable reason for it.

I5.1.2 Secondly, German law prohibits discrimination based on various aspects, eg on grounds of sex, race or origin, religion and disability and, in addition, on grounds of part-time work compared to full-time employees. Discrimination can be either direct or indirect. It may be positive, eg where members of a certain sex are promoted favourably to equalise previously unlawful discrimination on grounds of their sex.

I5.1.3 Although German law provides a large range of statutory rules against discrimination, court cases concerning breach of the prohibition on discrimination have not been of great significance. Particularly questions of sex discrimination, eg regarding equal pay, might be of relevance to practice. In addition, the number of complaints from employees regarding bullying in the workplace has increased.

I5.1.4 The main statutory provisions are:
- principle of equality (art 3(1) and (2) of the Basic Law (*Grundgesetz* – GG) and based on the decisions of the Federal Court of Employment (*Bundesarbeitsgericht* – BAG);
- prohibition of discrimination against an employee due to race, religion etc (art 3(3) of the Basic Law;
- the principle of equal pay for equal work regardless of sex (art 141 – previously art 119 – of the Contract of Foundation of the European Community (*Vertrag zur Gruendung der Europaeischen Gemeinschaft* – EGV) and s 612(3) of the Civil Code;
- prohibition of discrimination against part-timers and fixed-term employees due to their working time (s 4 of the Act on Part-time Employment and Fixed-term Employment Contracts (*Teilzeit- und Befristungsgesezt* – TzBfG));
- principle of equal treatment regardless of sex, especially in relation to job applications and any measures or agreements regarding the employment contract (s 611a and 611b of the Civil Code.

I5.1.5 There is currently no legislation outlawing age discrimination in Germany.

5.2 Unlawful Discrimination: Sex, Race and Marital Status

I5.2.1 Discrimination on the grounds of sex is prohibited by several provisions of the Civil Code, particularly by s 611a and 611b. In contrast to this, discrimination on the grounds of race and marital status is not of great significance in Germany. Apart from the abovementioned principle (see para I5.1.4) which is set up in the Basic Law, these modes of discrimination are not prohibited by special statutory provisions.

Sections 611 a and 611 b of the Civil Code provide that it is unlawful to discriminate against a person on the grounds of sex:

(i)   in advertising for employment, or

(ii) in offering employment, or

(iii) by refusing or omitting to offer employment.

Furthermore, it is unlawful for an employer to discriminate against a person on the grounds of sex:

(iv) in the way he affords access to opportunities for promotion or training, or

(v) in any measure or agreement regarding the employment relationship, or

(vi) by dismissing him.

I5.2.2 Unequal treatment on the ground of sex is permissible if the particular sex of the person in question is a requirement for that employment. The legislation does not provide an exhaustive list of such circumstances. Unequal treatment can be justified, for example, where an actress is needed for a particular theatre performance or where a model is required to present female fashions during a fashion show.

I5.2.3 If an applicant or an employee can show probable cause, which justifies the presumption that he or she has suffered less favourable treatment on the ground of his or her sex, the burden of proof rests on the employer to show that there was a legitimate explanation for the treatment in question.

I5.2.4 The complainant can claim reasonable compensation for an unjustified sex discrimination. The maximum compensation awarded amounts to three months' salary.

A   DIRECT DISCRIMINATION

I5.2.5 Discrimination may be direct or indirect. Direct discrimination occurs where the employer treats the complainant less favourably than another employee (the comparator) and the unequal treatment refers directly to a specific reason, eg sex or part-time work. For the purposes of sex discrimination, the comparator must be a person of the opposite sex. For the purposes of part-time discrimination, the comparator must be a full-time employee.

Example

An employer has to make a choice on redundancy between dismissing a man or a woman, both of whom are married with children. He decides to dismiss the woman, on the basis of a preconception that her husband is likely to be the family's main source of income. Although he may have had no conscious desire to discriminate against the woman on the basis of her sex, he has done so. Having subjected her to the detriment of dismissal, he has therefore unlawfully discriminated against her on the grounds of her sex.

B   INDIRECT DISCRIMINATION

I5.2.6 Indirect discrimination prohibits discrimination which occurs where an employer applies a requirement or condition to all employees which has a disproportionate impact on members of a special group, eg on members of one sex. As distinct from direct discrimination, the employer does not differentiate on these grounds, either expressly or impliedly.

I5.2.7 The complainant must show that although the requirement or condition is applied equally to the complainant and the comparator, that requirement or condition has a considerably bigger impact on the complainant's group. Discrimination on the ground of sex will then be presumed and the employer has to prove its justification. He must show not only that the requirement is justifiable irrespective of sex, but also that the means chosen correspond to a real need and are appropriate and necessary to that end.

> **Example**
> An employer introduces a pension scheme. He decides to exclude part-timers from the pension entitlement, on the basis of his wish to promote full engagement for the company. Although he may have had no intention to discriminate against the woman on the basis of her sex, he has done so, if a major proportion of the part-time workers are female.

C   HARASSMENT

I5.2.8 The Protection against Sexual Harassment at the Place of Employment Act (*Gesetz zum Schutz der Beschaeftigten vor sexueller Belaestigung am Arbeitsplatz – Beschaeftigtenschutzgesetz*) aims to protect men and women from sexual harassment at their place of work. It covers all employees in the private and in the public sector, including trainees and other individuals who personally undertake work for others. Sexual harassment includes every intentional behaviour on the ground of sex which offends the person's dignity, regardless of whether it is a criminal offence or not. The Act provides extensive protection against such treatment. Apart from preventive measures which must be taken by the employer, sexual harassment is considered to be a breach of contract. The employer is obliged to take all reasonable steps which are appropriate in the individual circumstances. This can result in a warning, but also in termination of the employment agreement either with or without notice.

D   VICTIMISATION

I5.2.9 German law provides legal protection for those who complain of unlawful discrimination. Section 612a of the Civil Code provides that the employer is not allowed to treat an employee less favourably than he treats or would treat other persons if he or she has exercised his rights legally.

5.3 Disability Discrimination

I5.3.1 Disability discrimination is forbidden by the Basic Law. However, there is no special disability discrimination law (cf the one that exists as to sex discrimination, for example).

5.4 Enforcement and Remedies in Discrimination Cases

I5.4.1 As mentioned above, compensation for sex discrimination under s 611a(2) and (3) of the Civil Code is limited to three months' pay of the applicant or employee concerned. It must be claimed within a period of two to six months from the discriminatory act, in writing, depending on the time limits set out in the employment agreement or in an applicable collective agreement.

I5.4.2 If the applicant claims equal pay in a case of sex discrimination and is successful, the employment court will award the difference in pay between the complainant and the comparator. There is no limit on the amount of compensation that may be awarded. Subject to a contractual time limit *(Ausschlussfrist)* or an applicable collective bargaining agreement, which may also provide a cut-off period, there is no statutory obligation to make an application within a certain period of time.

5.5 Equal Pay

I5.5.1 The principle of equal pay regardless of sex is set out in s 612(3) of the Civil Code and art 141 – formerly art 119 – of the Contract of Foundation of the European Community (*Vertrag zur Gruendung der Europaeischen Gemeinschaft* – EGV).

I5.5.2 Pay is the ordinary, basic or minimum wage or salary plus any other consideration whether in cash or in kind, eg a car, including supplementary payments, bonuses or pensions, which the worker receives, directly or indirectly, in respect of his employment from his employer.

I5.5.3 The law provides that the employer is obliged to agree on equal remuneration for the same work or for work to which equal value has been attributed, regardless of the sex of the employee concerned. An agreement on a lower remuneration level cannot be justified either, where there are protective laws which provide a prohibition or restrictions for employment relating to a particular sex.[1]

[1] Section 612(3) of the Civil Code (*Buergerliches Gesetzbuch* – BGB).

I5.5.4 First, the complainant must show that he or she is employed on like or broadly similar work to the work of the comparator. This depends on the job characteristics and on the value of the work in question. Furthermore, he or she must show that the remuneration for the work of the comparator, who is of the opposite sex, is considerably higher than the complainant's own remuneration.

I5.5.5 The employer concerned must then prove that the difference between the complainant's remuneration and that in the comparator's contract is genuinely due to a material factor which is not the difference of sex. If he fails, the complainant is entitled to the higher remuneration.

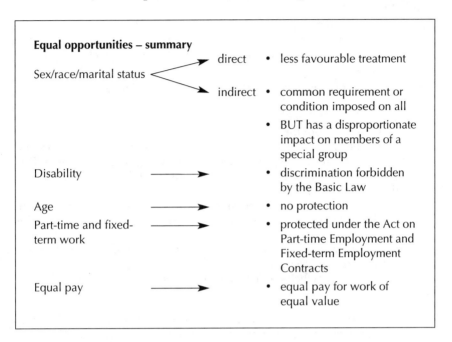

Equal opportunities – summary

Sex/race/marital status
- direct → • less favourable treatment
- indirect → • common requirement or condition imposed on all
  - • BUT has a disproportionate impact on members of a special group

Disability → • discrimination forbidden by the Basic Law

Age → • no protection

Part-time and fixed-term work → • protected under the Act on Part-time Employment and Fixed-term Employment Contracts

Equal pay → • equal pay for work of equal value

6   TERMINATION OF EMPLOYMENT

6.1   Background

MODES OF TERMINATION

I6.1.1   A contract of employment can be terminated either mutually or unilaterally. The most important ways of terminating an employment contract are by:

(i) termination by agreement;
(ii) expiry of a fixed-term contract;
(iii) notice of termination (either with or without period of notice).

A   TERMINATION BY AGREEMENT

I6.1.2   In principle, the parties are free to agree upon the termination of an employment contract at any time. The advantage of such an agreement is that those statutory provisions which protect against dismissal or which state further requirements allowing notice of termination do not apply. In addition, the employer is able to calculate precisely the economic effects of such an agreement, whereas it might be more difficult to estimate the financial risk of a notice of termination, which is subject to legal proceedings. However, the employee must be aware of possible disadvantages in terms of social benefits in the case of unemployment.

I6.1.3 With effect from 1 May 2000 s 623 was added to the Civil Code. This stipulates that termination agreements must be in writing. This means that there must be:

(i) a uniform document;
(ii) signed by both parties to the agreement; and
(iii) one original of the signed document must be sent to each party to the agreement.

Thus, a termination agreement can no longer be concluded by fax.

I6.1.4 A termination agreement usually covers:

(i) final date of employment;
(ii) the amount of a severance payment, which is tax-free up to an amount of DM 16,000 for an employee who is younger than 50 years (up to DM 24,000 depending on the age of the employee and the time he worked with the company);
(iii) agreement upon a paid suspension of the employee requiring him to take the remainder of his annual holiday entitlement during his suspension;
(iv) confidentiality (although this is a legal duty even if the employment contract is terminated);
(v) return of property belonging to the employer;
(vi) any reference.

I6.1.5 The parties can, of course, agree on other or on additional conditions eg regarding a company car, restrictive covenants etc. However, the most important point will normally be the amount of the payment the employer agrees to pay on top of regular salary. The amount of the severance payment is a result of free negotiations between the parties. German employment law does not stipulate any specific payment in the case of dismissal. There are no legally binding formulae for calculation of severance payments. There is only a non-binding basis for the calculation of redundancy payments, which is based on the employment courts' practice and which might be considered as a guideline: in the event of termination on the grounds of essential business reasons, the employment court regularly suggests a settlement payment in the amount of half a month's salary per year of the working time the employee has spent with the company.

B   EXPIRY OF A FIXED TERM CONTRACT

I6.1.6 If the parties agree upon a fixed-term employment contract, the employment relationship ends at the time of expiry, provided that the agreement as to the time-limit is valid. The fixed-term contract then ends without the necessity of dismissing the employee. A valid fixed-term contract may be agreed in one of the following ways:

(a) Fixed-term contract under the Act on Part-time Employment and Fixed-term Employment Contracts (*Teilzeit- und Befristungsgesezt* – TzBfG)

   The Act allows fixed-term contracts with new employees for a period of up to two years without any special reason. Within these 24 months, the employer is able to extend the contract three times. When the applicant is over 58 years old, the parties can agree on a fixed-term contract without these restrictions (see TzBfG, s 14(2)).

(b) Fixed term contract based on objective grounds

The fixed term contract based on objective grounds is always permissible if there is a reason which can be justified on objective grounds. By analogy with established case law of the Federal Employment Court (*Bundesarbeitsgericht* – BAG), the Act on Part-time and Fixed-term Employment Contracts (TzBfG) contains a list of typical reasons justifying a fixed-term contract (eg temporary requirement for additional manpower, substitution of another employee, fixed-term during probationary period, fixed term following training or study) which apply without the term being explicitly stated.[1] There are also other reasons which would justify the conclusion of fixed-term contracts which are not mentioned in the Act.

[1]   Act on Part-time and Fixed-term Employment Contracts (TzBfG), s 14(1).

I6.1.7   If the employer is unable to prove one of the above-mentioned reasons for fixing the term of an employment contract, such a contract is deemed to continue for an indefinite term.

C   NOTICE OF TERMINATION

I6.1.8   In contrast to termination by agreement or by expiry of a fixed-term contract, notice of termination arises where the employer issues written termination to the employee. Since 1 May 2000 termination must be made in writing (see Civil Code (BGB), s 623).[1] It is desirable for notice of termination to be handed to the employee in person or to be transmitted to him by courier. The date of handing over the written termination is of great significance with regard to the period of notice of termination and deadline for appealing.

[1]   Act for Simplification and Acceleration of Labour Court Proceedings (*Gesetz zur Vereinfachung und Beschleunigung des arbeitsgerichtlichen Verfahrens*) also referred to as the Labour Court Acceleration Act (*Arbeitsgerichtsbeschleunigungsgesetz*), as a result of which s 623 was inserted into the German Civil Code.

I6.1.9   In relation to the conditions and the effects of a valid notice of termination under German employment law, there is a crucial difference between termination without notice, which is covered by s 626 of the Civil Code and termination with notice. Referring to the latter, the freedom to terminate a contract of employment by observing the notice period only is restricted by the Protection against Dismissal Act (*Kuendigungsschutzgesetz* – KSchG) provided that its provisions apply. In that case the employer must have special ('social') reasons for dismissing an employee (see paras **I6.3.1–I6.3.20**).

I6.1.10   If the Protection against Dismissal Act does not apply, the employer is free to terminate the employment in compliance with the notice period, but without any special reasons. However, it should be pointed out that the employer is not allowed to make a payment in lieu of notice; he is only permitted to suspend the employee from his work while paying him during the regular notice period.

I6.1.11   Regardless of whether the Protection against Dismissal Act applies or not, termination by notice is also governed by s 102 of the Works

Constitution Act (*Betriebsverfassungsgesetz* – BetrVG), provided that a works council was elected by the employees of a company (see paras **I10.2.4–I10.2.5**).

6.2 Summary Termination

I6.2.1 Like an employee, an employer may be entitled to terminate the contract of employment unilaterally with immediate effect (s 626 of the Civil Code). Under s 623 of the Civil Code termination must be in writing. Law requires good cause, which makes it unreasonable to expect the terminating party to continue the employment relationship until expiry of the regular notice period or, in the case of a fixed-term contract, the expiry date of the contract.

I6.2.2 Section 626 of the Civil Code establishes a two-stage test in determining whether the terminating party has a good cause for dismissal:

• the terminating party must show the principal reason for dismissal was a good one;
• the employment court must then consider whether in the circumstances the terminating party had a sufficient reason for terminating the contract with immediate effect.

I6.2.3 In addition, the relevant notice must be given within two weeks of the terminating party becoming aware of the good cause – termination without notice is not permissible after expiry of this period. Thus, a termination without notice will be valid in exceptional cases only.

I6.2.4 The person who is dismissed with immediate effect is entitled to request and to receive a written statement of reasons for dismissal, which must be provided as soon as possible. Failure to provide the statement, or an inaccurate or incomplete statement, may entitle the dismissed person to claim damages resulting from the failure.

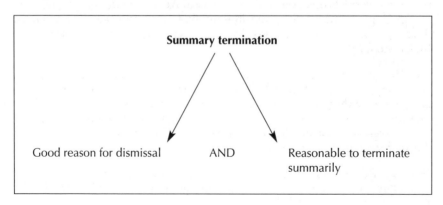

Summary termination

Good reason for dismissal   AND   Reasonable to terminate summarily

A   SUMMARY TERMINATION BY THE EMPLOYER

I6.2.5   The employer may be entitled to terminate the employment contract without giving notice under the requirements of s 626 of the Civil Code (see para **I6.2.7**). This right might arise in the following situations:

- persistent refusal to comply with the employer's lawful instructions;
- gross breach of the contractual obligation of loyalty, eg where an employee pretends to be ill;
- criminal acts to the detriment of the employer, eg a theft of objects belonging to the employer;
- serious violation of a competition restriction or secrecy clause to the detriment of the employer.

B   SUMMARY TERMINATION BY THE EMPLOYEE

I6.2.6   If an employee wishes to terminate the employment contract without notice, he is only allowed to do so in compliance with the requirements of s 626 of the Civil Code as described above.

I6.2.7   In particular, there must be a good reason. In most cases, the employee will be entitled to terminate the employment contract immediately by reason of the employer's conduct, for example a grave breach of the employment contract. This breach may be a significant breach of an express term of the contract (such as to pay the employee's salary) or a breach of an implied term (such as to provide a safe working environment). Not every breach will entitle the employee to terminate without notice. Unreasonable behaviour may not suffice.

6.3   Termination with Notice – Social Justification

A   CONDITIONS

I6.3.1   If the employer cannot terminate the employment contract without notice, either because he cannot prove good cause or he has, for example, missed the two-week period, or if he just intends to terminate the employment agreement with notice, the legal requirements depend on whether the Protection against Dismissal Act (*Kuendigungsschutzgesetz –* KSchG) applies.

I6.3.2   The Protection against Dismissal Act applies if:

(a) the employee has been employed for more than six months, and
(b) the company regularly employs more than five employees excluding trainees.

I6.3.3   An employee is not protected by the Protection against Dismissal Act where, under the contract of employment, he or she ordinarily works outside Germany. In addition, there are certain exclusions, eg members of a companies' board or a managing director of a limited company. However, employees over normal retirement age (65) may bring an unfair dismissal claim.

Qualifying conditions: Protection against Dismissal Act

- six months' service
- more than five employees
- ordinarily employed in Germany
- is not in an excluded class
- if notice was given

B   REASONS FOR DISMISSAL

I6.3.4   If the Protection against Dismissal Act applies, termination of any employment agreement requires social justification. In particular, the employer must have a valid reason. Moreover, the right to dismiss an employee is governed by the principle of proportionality. Therefore, the employer must consider in advance whether he can take alternative steps, eg if a warning would suffice or if there are job vacancies which could be offered to the employee in question.[1]

[1]   Section 1(2) of the Protection against Dismissal Act (*Kuendigungsschutzgesetz –* KSchG).

I6.3.5   Potentially, there are three different types of reasons for dismissal.[1] These are as follows:

- reasons relating to the person of the employee (eg illness, capability or qualifications);
- reasons relating to the conduct of an employee (eg breach of contract);
- important business reasons (redundancy).

[1]   Section 1(2) of the Protection against Dismissal Act.

I6.3.6   The burden of proof in establishing a fair reason is on the employer. Where there is more than one reason for dismissing, the employer can theoretically show all of them and argue that the reasons as a whole justify the dismissal. However, the legal requirements of a valid dismissal will remain the same. In principle, an employment court will examine the individual reasons for compliance with the legal requirements to justify the dismissal.

Reasons relating to the person of an employee

I6.3.7   A reason relating to the person of an employee can be, for example, the long-term illness of an employee. The Federal Court of Employment (*Bundesarbeitsgericht* – BAG) has held that a termination by reason of long-term illness may be justified, if it lasts at least 18 months and if it is unpredictable whether the illness will end in the near future.

Termination for reasons relating to the person can also be valid in cases of short-term illnesses. If the employee's short-term illnesses last considerably longer than six weeks per calendar year for at least three subsequent calendar years, termination with notice can be justified.

The employee can, however, argue that the illnesses are cured and that his future short-term illnesses will not exceed an average level (which is up to six weeks per calendar year). In this case, the employer must obtain a medical opinion to prove that the reason for dismissal was a fair one.

I6.3.8   Another reason relating to the person of the employee can be a lack of capability assessed by reference to skill, aptitude, health or any other physical or mental quality. It is for the employer to show and to prove the lack of capability and that the employee is not able to perform his contractual duties as a result.

I6.3.9   Finally, a situation may arise, for example, where an employee who is employed solely as a chauffeur is disqualified from driving and therefore loses his licence. This can justify a dismissal relating to the person of the employee, especially if the employer is not able to offer alternative employment to the employee concerned.

Reasons relating to the conduct of an employee

I6.3.10   An employer may seek to rely on an employee's conduct (or misconduct) to justify a dismissal. Examples of misconduct include dishonesty, harassment of fellow employees, inexcusable absenteeism, failure to obey lawful and reasonable orders, persistent and intentional refusal to work or to work properly, embezzlement and working for a competitor.

I6.3.11   The less fundamental a breach of a contract is, the more important is its repetition to justify notice of termination. In general, it is necessary that the employer documents a history of attempts to secure the proper fulfilment by the employee of his contractual duties. In general he has to give him at least one warning to document a former breach of contract combined with a reminder that termination of employment will be considered unless the employee changes his behaviour and properly fulfils his contractual duties.

I6.3.12   The employer will usually seek to rely on misconduct occurring during working hours, although it may sometimes be possible to rely on misconduct occurring outside working hours where the employee's behaviour may affect the performance of his duties or brings the employer into disrepute.

Important business reasons/redundancy

I6.3.13   A further potential reason for dismissal which is socially justified is an essential business reason including redundancy of the employee. As distinct from English law, German law does not provide a legal definition of redundancy.

I6.3.14   Redundancy situations will cover, for example, a corporate reorganisation in order to cut overheads and employment costs, the closure of a business, the closure of the employee's workplace or a diminishing need for the employee to do work of a particular kind, eg because of a shortage of orders.

I6.3.15 In principle, the question to be answered is whether the requirements of the employer's business for the employee to carry out work of a particular kind have diminished, or will they diminish by the expiry date of the notice given by the employer.

Types of redundancy
- place of work redundancy
- type of work redundancy
- closure of part/whole of business

I6.3.16 The employer must allege and prove the essential business reason making termination unavoidable in detail. He is obliged to show and to prove:

(i) the company's decision in question (the person who made it, when and where it was made);
(ii) if intended, the restructuring of the company or the plant including its reason; and
(iii) how the company's decision will be realised (instructions to other employees, termination of contracts with suppliers etc) and what the consequences are with regard to the quantity of work.

I6.3.17 In addition, the employer must select the employees to be made redundant.[1] Termination is socially unjustified if the employer, during the selection process, has not, or has not sufficiently, considered social factors. The most important social criteria are seniority, the age of an employee and the number of dependent persons. But there are other factors which can be relevant if the employer knows them, such as incapacity, wealth of an employee or labour market conditions.

[1] Section 1(3) of the Protection against Dismissal Act (*Kuendigungsschutzgesetz –* KSchG).

I6.3.18 In general, the employee who is dismissed by reason of redundancy is not entitled to receive a statutory redundancy payment. An exception to this general rule is where the employee is entitled to compensation on the basis of a collective agreement, which can be either an applicable collective bargaining agreement or a works agreement (social plan) with the works council of the company concerned.

	Examples	
Valid reasons for dismissal		
Personal	• illness	• long-term
		• short-term
	• capability	
	• other	
Conduct	• dishonesty	
	• harassment	
	• absenteeism	
	• failure to obey lawful and reasonable orders	
	• competition	
Business reasons/redundancy	• place of work	
	• type of work	
	• closure of whole/part	

C   NOTICE OF TERMINATION PENDING A CHANGE OF CONTRACT

I6.3.19   If the employer wishes to amend or change any terms of the employment contract and he cannot agree them with the employee, he must give notice to terminate pending a change of contract (*Aenderungskuendigung*, see s 2 of the Protection against Dismissal Act. This consists of a notice of termination combined with a binding offer of an employment agreement, which normally contains all conditions of the former employment contract including the intended changes.

I6.3.20   If the Protection against Dismissal Act is applicable, the requirements for termination pending a change of contract are the same as for standard termination by notice (see paras **I6.3.4–I6.3.18**). The employee has three options:

(i)   he can accept the notice of termination pending a change of contract, in which case, the contract of employment continues with the changed conditions after expiry of the notice period;

(ii) he can accept the notice of termination pending a change of contract subject to an examination by the employment court; or

(iii) he can repudiate it.

Depending on the employee's reaction, the terms of the new offer or – if the employee refuses it unreservedly within three weeks after delivery – the notice of termination must be socially justified. In addition, the period of notice must be complied with.

6.4   Protected Employees

I6.4.1   In certain circumstances, termination – whether with or without notice – is only permissible in extraordinary cases and is often only permissible with the prior consent of the relevant public authority. Lack of permission will automatically result in an invalid termination. The most important examples are:

(a) pregnancy, maternity, parental leave;
(b) membership of the works council or a youth assembly;
(c) disabled employees;
(d) apprentices;
(e) collective bargaining agreements.

(a) Pregnancy, maternity, parental leave

16.4.2 An employer cannot terminate the employment contract of a pregnant woman from the time the employer becomes aware of the employee's pregnancy until the expiry of the fourth month after the child's birth. Termination is only permissible in exceptional cases, ie if there is a good cause in the meaning of s 626 of the Civil Code which is not connected with the pregnancy or maternity. In addition, the employer must obtain written consent from the relevant authority in advance.[1]

[1] Section 9 of the Maternity Leave Act (*Mutterschutzgesetz* – MuSchG).

16.4.3 The law also provides protection against dismissal during parental leave, unless there are exceptional reasons for it. Where there are such exceptional circumstances, the employer again needs to obtain the authority's prior consent.[1]

[1] Section 18 of the Parental Leave Act (*Bundeserziehungsgeldgesetz* – BErzGG).

16.4.4 For complaints of this special protection during pregnancy, maternity and parental leave, no qualifying period of service is necessary.

(b) Membership of the works council or a youth assembly

16.4.5 Members of the works council or a youth assembly will be protected against termination of employment for the duration of their membership and for a period of one year after termination of membership[1] without any qualifying period. Termination without notice is only permissible with the prior consent of the works council.[2]

[1] Section 15(1) of the Protection against Dismissal Act (*Kuendigungsschutzgesetz* – KSchG).

[2] Section 103 of the Works Constitution Act (*Betriebsverfassungsgesetz* – BetrVG).

(c) Disabled employees

16.4.6 Employees who fall under the Disability Act (*Schwerbehindertengesetz* – SchwbG) can only be given notice of termination – whether with or without notice – with prior approval of the Principal Social Security Office (*Hauptfuersorgestelle*) if they have been employed for at least six months.[1] The Principal Social Security Office (*Hauptfuersorgestelle*) must ask the opinion of the Labour Office, the works council – if there is one – and the parties involved.[2] Where the company closes down, the Principal Social Security Office is obliged to give its approval to the termination of employment. Where part of the company is closing down, approval will only be granted if the employee cannot be transferred elsewhere in the company.[3]

[1]   Section 15 and 20 of the Disability Act (*Schwerbehindertengesetz* – SchwbG).
[2]   Section 17(2) of the Disability Act.
[3]   Section 19 of the Disability Act.

I6.4.7   Decisions of the Principal Social Security Office (*Hauptfuersorgestelle*) can be appealed to the Administrative Court.

(d)   Apprentices

I6.4.8   Persons employed under an apprenticeship contract cannot have their contracts of employment terminated, as they are usually employed for a fixed-term period of two to three years.[1] However, an apprenticeship contract may be terminated during the probationary period (which can be up to three months long), without any reason. After its expiry, the apprenticeship contract can only be terminated by written notice in exceptional cases.[2]

[1]   Section 14(1) of the Vocational Training Law (*Berufsbildungsgesetz* – BBiG).
[2]   Section 15 of the Vocational Training Law.

(e)   Collective bargaining agreements

I6.4.9   In some collective bargaining agreements (eg in the metal industry), old-age protection is provided for employees who reach a certain minimum age (eg 53 years), and have a minimum length of service (eg three years).

6.5   Notice Periods

I6.5.1   The law specifies the minimum notice which must be given in all cases.[1] The length of the minimum notice period depends on the employee's length of service with the employer beginning from his 25th birthday.

[1]   Section 622 of the Civil Code (*Buergerliches Gesetzbuch*).

I6.5.2   The statutory minimum periods can only be shortened if a collective bargaining agreement applies or if the employee will be employed on a temporary basis for a very short period of time. The statutory minimum periods do not apply where the employer is entitled to dismiss the employee summarily. The contract can of course provide for a longer period of notice or for a certain expiry date which is more favourable to the employee.

The minimum notice periods under the statute are as follows:

To be given by the employer

Length of service	*Notice period and expiry date*
Probationary period (up to six months if agreed):	Fourteen days to expire any day
Less than two years' continuous employment:	Four weeks' notice to expire on the fifteenth or on the end of a calendar month.
Between two and less than five years' continuous employment:	One months' notice to the end of a calendar month.
Between five and less than eight years' continuous employment:	Two months' notice to the end of a calendar month.
Between eight and less than ten years' continuous employment:	Three months' notice to the end of a calendar month.
Between ten and less than twelve years' continuous employment:	Four months' notice to the end of a calendar month.
Between twelve and less than fifteen years' continuous employment:	Five months' notice to the end of a calendar month.
Between fifteen and less than twenty years' continuous employment:	Six months' notice to the end of a calendar month.
Twenty and more years' continuous employment:	Seven months' notice to the end of a calendar month.

To be given by the employee:

Length of service	*Notice period*
Probationary period (up to six months if agreed):	Fourteen days' notice to expire any day.
Any employee regardless of length of service:	Four weeks' notice to expire on the fifteenth or on the end of a calendar month.

I6.5.3   The failure of a prescribed period of notice does not result in the invalidity of notice. The employment relationship will, however, be terminated at the correct termination date.

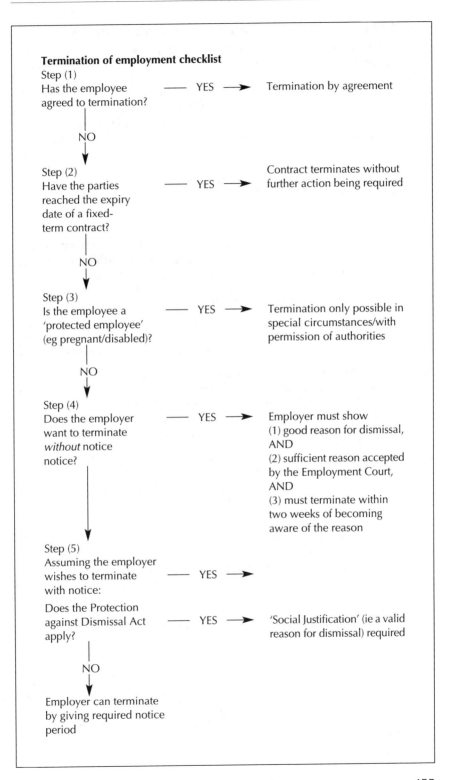

Termination of employment checklist

Step (1)
Has the employee   —— YES ——▶   Termination by agreement
agreed to termination?

│
NO
▼

Step (2)   Contract terminates without
Have the parties   —— YES ——▶   further action being required
reached the expiry
date of a fixed-
term contract?

│
NO
▼

Step (3)
Is the employee a   —— YES ——▶   Termination only possible in
'protected employee'   special circumstances/with
(eg pregnant/disabled)?   permission of authorities

│
NO
▼

Step (4)
Does the employer   —— YES ——▶   Employer must show
want to terminate   (1) good reason for dismissal,
without notice   AND
notice?   (2) sufficient reason accepted
                                                  by the Employment Court,
                                                  AND
                                                  (3) must terminate within
                                                  two weeks of becoming
                                                  aware of the reason

│
▼

Step (5)
Assuming the employer
wishes to terminate   —— YES ——▶
with notice:

Does the Protection
against Dismissal Act —— YES ——▶   'Social Justification' (ie a valid
apply?   reason for dismissal) required

│
NO
▼

Employer can terminate
by giving required notice
period

6.6 Collective Termination including Redundancies

I6.6.1 Where an employer proposes to dismiss at least five employees at one establishment over a period of 30 calendar days or less, the employer is obliged to notify the Department of Employment, if the company regularly employs more than 20 and fewer than 60 employees (see s 17 of the Protection against Dismissal Act (*Kuendigungsschutzgesetz* – KSchG). A similar obligation exists where an employer, who regularly employs more than sixty and fewer than 500 employees, proposes to dismiss at least 10% of the employees or at least 25 employees at the same establishment. Finally, an employer has the duty to inform the Department of Employment if he regularly employs more than 500 employees and intends to dismiss at least 30 of them at the same establishment.

I6.6.2 Section 18 of the Protection against Dismissal Act provides a minimum period for notification which should begin within at least one month before dismissals take effect. However, the Department of Employment has the power to determine that dismissals will not take effect before expiry of two months after notification.

I6.6.3 An employer must disclose certain information in writing, namely:
- the reasons for the intended dismissals;
- numbers and descriptions of employees it is proposed to dismiss;
- the total number and descriptions of employees employed at the establishment;
- the proposed period of time during which the dismissals are proposed to be carried out;
- the proposed social criteria for the selection of the employees concerned; and
- the proposed method of calculating any redundancy payments.

I6.6.4 Where there is a works council, the employer must notify the representative in writing as described in para **I6.6.3** and send a copy of the notification to the Department of Employment. The consultation between the employer and the works council must include ways of avoiding dismissal, of reducing the numbers involved and mitigating the effect of the dismissals. It is not necessary that the parties reach agreement but the employer should consult in good faith with a view to reaching agreement.

I6.6.5 Failure to notify may entitle an affected employee to bring a complaint to an employment court. Such a complaint need not be brought within a special period of time. If an employment court decides that information was not provided, or not properly, it will hold that dismissal was invalid.

Collective dismissals

Protection against Dismissal Act

Employees dismissed within 30 days:

• 21–59 employees	dismissal of at least five employees
• 60–499 employees	dismissal of at least 10%, or at least 25 employees
• more than 500 employees	dismissal of at least 30 employees

Information to be disclosed:

• Reasons for dismissal
• Number/descriptions of employees
• Number/descriptions of employees at establishment
• Proposed period of time
• Proposed social criteria
• Proposed calculation method for redundancy pay

Notification requirements:

• Works council
• Department of Employment

6.7   Remedies for Dismissal

I6.7.1   Under the Protection against Dismissal Act the employee has to file an action with the Employment Court within three weeks of receiving notice of termination, regardless of whether it is termination with or without notice. If he does not file an action within that period, the termination will deemed to be socially justified, which means it will become binding even if the dismissal did not comply with the above-mentioned legal requirements under the Protection against Dismissal Act. However, the employee can file an action against the dismissal for other reasons, eg alleging that the period of notice was not procedurally correct or the required works council hearing did not take place.

I6.7.2   Once an invalid dismissal has been established, an employment court may suggest a compromise agreement including compensation or, if the parties do not reach agreement, can require the employee to be reinstated. In exceptional cases only the employment court will terminate the employment relationship by judgment and assess compensation.

Remedies

Compromise agreement including compensation – no statutory rules
Judgment (reinstatement) – same employer, same job
Judgment (termination plus compensation – maximum of 18 month's salary)

A   COMPROMISE AGREEMENT

I6.7.3 A considerable number of legal proceedings are settled by an agreement between the parties. They usually agree on the termination of the employment contract and an additional severance payment.

I6.7.4 In principle, the amount of the severance payment is a result of free negotiations between the parties. Although German law does not provide legally binding rules for its amount, most employment courts suggest a payment calculated by applying a non-binding rule based on the employment courts' practice. In the event of termination on the ground of essential business reasons, the employment courts regularly suggest a payment in the amount of a half month's salary per year of service. However, this rule can only be considered as a guideline. The exact amount depends on the circumstances and will often be influenced by the possible validity of the notice in question, the economic conditions of the employing company etc.

B   REINSTATEMENT/RE-ENGAGEMENT

I6.7.5 If an employment court holds that dismissal was invalid, judgment automatically results in reinstatement. The employer must pay the employee's salary from the intended end of the employment contract until the present time. Thus, the financial risk for the employer increases with the length of a court trial, which can last up to one year in the first instance. In addition, as a matter of law the employment relationship will continue with the same conditions as before for an indefinite period of time, so that the employer must continue to pay the employee and to provide him or her with work.

I6.7.6 Re-engagement occurs in exceptional cases only. An employee can claim re-engagement if a reason for dismissal, which existed at the time notice was given, does not remain constant until the effective date of termination of the employment relationship. In the case of termination by reason of redundancy an employer can, for example, claim re-engagement if he can show that, contrary to the employer's original belief, work became available during the notice period and that therefore the employer's need for the employee to work did not diminish.[1]

[1]   BAG, 26 June 2000, *Der Betreib* (DB) 2000, p 1413.

C   COMPENSATION

I6.7.7 If the employment court holds that termination of employment was not socially justified and that therefore the employment relationship continues, the court may, in exceptional cases only, terminate the contract of employment on the application of either party. The court has the power to do so if it holds that it is impossible for the applicant or the respondent or for both parties to continue the employment relationship. With certain employees, the employer can claim termination without having to specify any reasons. The employment court then dissolves the employment contract by judgment and will award compensation in lieu thereof.[1]

[1]   Section 9 of the Protection against Dismissal Act (*Kuendigungsschutzgesetz* – KSchG).

I6.7.8 Usually, compensation will be calculated in the same way as a redundancy payment (see paras **I6.7.3–I6.7.4**). The employment court can also consider further circumstances, for example the reasons for termination, the economic situation of the employer, loss of earnings from the date of dismissal to the date of hearing, and the loss of the employee's statutory protection.

I6.7.9 The law provides a statutory maximum payment of 12 months' gross salary, which includes all other remuneration. This maximum payment is increased to 15 months' salary for employees who are at least 50 years old and with a minimum of 15 years service, and to 18 months' salary for employees aged 55 years or more with at least 20 years' service.

7 YOUNG WORKERS

7.1 General Obligations

I7.1.1 The regulation of work involving children and young persons is covered mainly by the Young Persons Protection at Work Act,[1] which came into force with effect from 12 April 1976. The Young Persons Protection at Work Act is supplemented by a directive determining which kinds of work may be carried out by children of at least 14 years of age.[2]

[1] Gesetz zum Schutze der arbeitenden Jugend (*Jugendarbeitsschutzgesetz* – JArbSchG).
[2] Verordnung ueber den Kinderarbeitsschutz (*Kinderarbeitsschutzverordnung* – KindArbSchV).

I7.1.2 In general terms, German law deals with the protection of children and young persons as a health and safety issue.

I7.1.3 For the purposes of the Young Persons Protection at Work Act, a young person is any person aged from 15 but under 18, and a child is a young person under 15 years of age. The statutory provisions regarding children are also applicable to a young person who is still subject to compulsory full-time schooling under national law.[1]

[1] Section 2 of the Young Persons Protection at Work Act (*Jugendarbeits-schutzgesetz* – JArbSchG).

I7.1.4 Section 5(1) of the Young Persons Protection at Work Act constitutes a general prohibition on work by children, subject to very limited exceptions. For example, children are allowed to participate in combined work/training schemes. If they are at least 14 years old, they are allowed to do certain light work.[1]

[1] Section 5 of the Young Persons Protection at Work Act.

I7.1.5 In addition, s 22 of the Young Persons Protection at Work Act provides a general prohibition on dangerous work for young persons. Moreover, young persons are not allowed to work more than eight hours a day and 40 hours a week.[1] Further restrictions are made for trainees, and in relation to working time, night work, rest periods, annual leave and breaks.

[1] Section 8 of the Young Persons Protection at Work Act.

459

I7.1.6 The Young Persons Protection at Work Act also introduces an obligation on employers to perform an assessment in relation to specific risks to young people at work.[1] An employer must also ensure that a doctor examines the young person's ability to work regularly, taking into account his state of health and development and any special dangers or risks from particular forms of work.[2] There is, however, no such requirement in the case of occasional work or short-term work or work regarded as not being harmful, damaging or dangerous to young people.

[1] Section 28a of the Young Persons Protection at Work Act.
[2] Sections 32–38 of the Young Persons Protection at Work Act.

I7.1.7 The law expressly provides that employers must ensure that young persons employed are protected at work from risks to their health and safety arising from their lack of experience or immaturity.[1] The employer is further obliged to inform young people of possible risks and of all the measures adopted concerning their health and safety.[2]

[1] Section 28 of the Young Persons Protection at Work Act.
[2] Section 29 of the Young Persons Protection at Work Act.

I7.1.8 Some of the working time provisions can be enforced by the Health and Safety Executive by means of administrative fines or even criminal sanctions.[1]

[1] Sections 58–60 of the Young Persons Protection at Work Act.

8   MATERNITY AND PARENTAL RIGHTS

8.1   Background

I8.1.1 Pregnant women are entitled to a variety of maternity benefits and leave rights. These rights include the right to be protected from dismissal, to paid time off for ante-natal care and to paid maternity leave after the child's birth. In addition, parents and adoptive parents are entitled to unpaid parental leave, regardless of their sex.

I8.1.2 Protection for women during pregnancy and after the child's birth is provided by the Maternity Leave Act (*Gesetz zum Schutze der erwerbstaetigen Mutter (Mutterschutzgesetz* – MuSchG). Employees' parental rights are to be found in the Parental Leave Act (*Gesetz ueber die Gewaehrung von Erziehungsgeld und Erziehungsurlaub (Bundeserziehungsgeldgesetz* – BErzGG).

I8.1.3 Certain persons are excluded from these rights, eg persons who are not employees or who ordinarily work outside Germany.

8.2   General Rights

I8.2.1   All employed women, regardless of length of service and hours of work and size of employer, are entitled to take paid time off work. Usually, they can claim six weeks on full pay before the expected birth date.[1]

[1]   Section 3(2) of the Maternity Leave Act (Gesetz zum Schutze der erwerbstaetigen Mutter (*Mutterschutzgesetz* – MuSchG).

I8.2.2   After a child's birth, all employed women, regardless of length of service, hours of work and size of employer, are entitled to eight weeks' maternity leave and have the right to return to work.[1]

[1]   Section 6(1) of the Maternity Leave Act (Gesetz zum Schutze der erwerbstaetigen Mutter (*Mutterschutzgesetz* – MuSchG).

I8.2.3   During this period of time a woman is entitled to receive her normal contractual terms and conditions of employment apart from regular salary. For example, holiday entitlement will accrue during this time and she will retain certain benefits. Regarding remuneration, a woman is entitled to a maternity benefit payable by her health insurance company with a contribution from either her employer or the Federal Government, so that she receives the average amount of her salary during the last 13 weeks before her pregnancy.[1]

Pregnancy and maternity – what benefits?

- company car – yes
- holiday – yes
- pension contributions – yes
- salary – no (receives a maternity payment including contribution from the employer)
- bonuses – yes, if the parties did not agree that the bonus would be reduced on a pro-rata-basis for time off work.

---

[1]   Section 11 of the Maternity Leave Act (Gesetz zum Schutze der erwerbstaetigen Mutter (*Mutterschutzgesetz* – MuSchG).

I8.2.4   The period of maternity leave counts towards continuity of service and is taken into account in calculating entitlement to pension and other benefits.

A   COMMENCEMENT AND END OF MATERNITY LEAVE

I8.2.5   As mentioned in para **I8.2.1**, maternity leave normally begins six weeks before the expected date of childbirth. There are certain exceptions in the case of pregnancy-related sickness. Maternity leave will commence automatically if childbirth occurs.

I8.2.6   Leave usually ends eight weeks after the child's birth.[1] However, the protection period will amount to 12 weeks in exceptional circumstances.

[1]   Section 6(1) of the Maternity Leave Act (Gesetz zum Schutze der erwerbstaetigen Mutter (*Mutterschutzgesetz* – MuSchG).

B   NOTICE REQUIREMENTS

I8.2.7   Once a woman is aware of her pregnancy, she should – but is not obliged to – notify her employer (see s 8 of the Maternity Leave Act (*Mutterschutzgesetz* – MuSchG). In order for a woman to ensure that she cannot be lawfully dismissed during pregnancy she must inform the employer of her pregnancy within two weeks of any attempt to dismiss her.

I8.2.8   If the employer requests, the employee must provide a certificate from a registered medical practitioner.

I8.2.9   An employee who fails to give the proper notification at the right time may lose her protection against dismissal.

I8.2.10   The employee may, however, decide to resign during her pregnancy.

Notice requirements for maternity
- tell employer that she is pregnant (only if the employer attempts to dismiss her)
- provide certificate on request

8.3   Protection from Dismissal

I8.3.1   In general, it is not permissible to dismiss a woman during her pregnancy and within four months after childbirth, regardless of her hours of work or length of service. This protection applies from the beginning of her pregnancy. However, in order to benefit from protection, the law requires that the employer is either aware of the employee's pregnancy or that he is notified within two weeks of any attempt to dismiss her.[1]

[1]   See s 9 of the Maternity Leave Act (*Mutterschutzgesetz* – MuSchG).

I8.3.2   In exceptional cases only, dismissal can be valid if the notice of termination is not connected with the woman's condition and the employer obtains the authority's permission in advance.[1] Notice of termination must be given in writing; furthermore, the document must contain the reason for dismissal.

[1]   Section 9(3) of the Maternity Leave Act (*Mutterschutzgesetz* – MuSchG).

I8.3.3   In addition, a mother or father is protected against dismissal during parental leave. The protection period begins with the date on which he or she notifies the employer that he or she wishes the parental leave to begin, but no earlier than six weeks before parental leave begins. It automatically ends with the termination of parental leave. Again, dismissal might be valid in limited circumstances if the employer obtains the special permission of the authority in advance.[1]

[1]   Section 18 of the Parental Leave Act (*Bundeserziehungsgeldgesetz* – BErzGG).

8.4   Health and Safety

I8.4.1   The Maternity Leave Act and a EU Directive regarding the protection of pregnant employees and mothers at their workplace[1] require employers to assess health and safety risks to pregnant workers, workers who have recently given birth and those who are breastfeeding. The Directive, which came into force on 15 April 1997, provides that an employer must assess the health and safety risks to its employees in order to identify any protective and preventive measures it may need to take to comply with legislation. Furthermore, the employer is obliged to inform its female employees and – if it exists – the company's works council accordingly (section 2 of the Directive).

[1]   *Verordnung zum Schutze der Muetter am Arbeitsplatz.*

I8.4.2   An employer is under statutory duties to protect, as far as reasonably practicable, its employees' (including pregnant women or new mothers) health, safety and welfare at work. An employer cannot contract out of its duties to safeguard the health and safety of its staff.

I8.4.3   There are also special prohibitions on certain activities for pregnant women, particularly immediately before and after the birth.[1] The new or expectant mother is entitled to be offered any suitable alternative work which is available or to be suspended on full pay if changing working conditions or hours of work would not avoid the risk. However, she does not lose her entitlement to her usual remuneration.

[1]   Sections 3(1), 4 and 6(3) of the Maternity Leave Act (*Mutterschutzgesetz –* MuSchG) and section 5 of the Directive (*Verordnung zum Schutze der Muetter am Arbeitsplatz*).

8.5   Additional Rights to Time Off

I8.5.1   The Parental Leave Act[1] allows a mother and a father of a child to take unpaid parental leave (*Elternzeit*) of up to three years simultaneously in order to care for the child, and to return afterwards to the same job. Subject to the consent of the employer, it is possible for one year of the parental leave to be taken between the child's third and eighth birthdays, eg during the first year at school (Parental Leave Act, s 15(2)). During the leave period the employer is not entitled to receive his or her normal contractual terms and conditions of employment, as these are suspended. However, the implied terms (*Nebenpflichten*) of the contract of employment, in particular the mutual obligations of loyalty and good faith, still continue. During the first 18 months of leave, he or she is entitled to a special payment from the state in the amount of DM 900 (approximately £300) per month, if the annual income of both parents does not exceed a certain amount.[2]

[1]   Gesetz ueber die Gewaehrung von Erziehungsgeld und für Elternzeit (*Bundeserziehungsgeldgesetz –* BErzGG).
[2]   Sections 1–14 of the Parental Leave Act (*Bundeserziehungsgeldgesetz –* BErzGG).

I8.5.2   The Parental Leave Act (*Bundeserziehungsgeldgesetz –* BErzGG) covers protection of employees and trainees regardless of their sex and their length of service. The employee has to have or expect to have responsibility for a child. This includes natural mothers and fathers as well as adoptive parents.

I8.5.3 An amendment of the Federal Parental Allowance Act (*Bundeserziehungsgeldgesetz – BerzGG*) came into force on 1 January 2001: both parents may now take parental leave (*Elternzeit* – new term now used) simultaneously (Parental Leave Act, s 15(3)).

I8.5.4 Since 1 January 2001, the employee is entitled to request part-time employment during the three-year parental leave period, provided the employer generally employs 15 people and the employee concerned has been continuously employed with the company for at least six months. The employer may refuse the request for part-time work only for urgent operational reasons. The maximum weekly part-time employment is 30 hours for each parent (Parental Leave Act, s 15(4)–(7)). Provided that the employer agrees, the employee is entitled to work with another employer during parental leave. If the employee wishes to work part-time for another company, the original employer can only refuse his consent in writing within four weeks if he can rely on business reasons.[1]

[1]   Section 15(4) of the Parental Leave Act (*Bundeserziehungsgeldgesetz* – BErzGG).

A   COMMENCEMENT AND END OF PARENTAL LEAVE

I8.5.5 Parental leave is limited to three years in total. It can be separated into four parts.[1] Two years of parental leave must be taken during the first two years of the child's life. The third year of parental leave can be taken either during the third year of the child's life or between the child's third and eighth birthdays. The employee must determine the date and the individual length of these time periods in advance. This declaration is legally binding in the sense that the employee is not allowed to shorten, to prolong or to postpone the intended parental leave periods unilaterally. However, such modification will be valid if the employer agrees.[2]

[1]   Section 16 of the Parental Leave Act (*Bundeserziehungsgeldgesetz* – BErzGG).
[2]   Section 16(3) of the Parental Leave Act (*Bundeserziehungsgeldgesetz* – BErzGG).

I8.5.6 An employee exercising the right to parental leave must be allowed to return to his old job and the same conditions as before, including the extent of the working time. Consequently, he or she is not in general entitled to claim part-time work, if he or she worked full-time before. As of the introduction of the Part-time and Fixed-term Employment Act (*Teilzeit- und Befristungsgesetz*) on 1 January 2001 employees are entitled to demand a reduction in their working hours from their employer (see paras I3.3.1–I3.3.5).

B   NOTICE REQUIREMENTS

I8.5.7 If an employee aims to exercise the right to parental leave, he or she must, at least six weeks before the leave, claim the right to take leave and notify the employer of the start date and the intended length of parental leave. If the employee wishes to divide the parental leave into parts, he or she has to notify the employer at the same time of the exact periods of time, namely the respective start and end dates.

The Parental Leave Act

- mother and father
- natural or adoptive parents
- up to three years' leave (unpaid)
- before the child's third birthday or third year between third and eighth birthdays
- employee may request part-time work *during* leave period
- right to return to same job/terms and conditions after leave

---

9 BUSINESS TRANSFERS

9.1 Background

I9.1.1   The legal position of employees in the context of a transfer of a business is covered by s 613a of the Civil Code (*Buergerliches Gesetzbuch* – BGB), which was primarily introduced in the Civil Code in 1972. Although the original version of s 613a of the Civil Code did comply with the EC Acquired Rights Directive 77/187/EC in major parts, it had to be adapted to the Directive in certain points:

The Directive enshrines various principles, which were adopted by s 613a of the Civil Code:

- automatic transfers of employment regarding collective agreements of the employees transferred (art 3) – s 613a(1) of the Civil Code;
- special protection against dismissal in connection with a business transfer (art 4) – s 613a(4) of the Civil Code.

I9.1.2   A new Directive (98/50/EC) has now been introduced as a result of the extensive jurisdiction of the European Court of Justice (ECJ) regarding the question of a relevant transfer of a business or a part of it on the basis of Directive 77/187/EC. It makes clear that the right of transfer does not apply where a transfer of certain activities only occurs (without the transfer of significant staff or assets).

I9.1.3   Employment courts are required to give a purposive construction/ interpretation to s 613a of the Civil Code, which fully complies with European law (which is directly binding). Directive 77/187/EC was implemented into German law several years ago. However, Directive 98/50/EC has not been implemented into national law yet, and so it is not yet effective in Germany. Only its principles are directly binding. Nevertheless, German employment courts are allowed to consider its requirements regarding the interpretation of s 613a of the Civil Code and the courts make use of these. The influence of Directive 98/50/EC can already be perceived in the current jurisdiction of the employment courts and even the Federal Court of Employment (*Bundesarbeitsgericht* – BAG).

465

Influence of European Directives

- Once an EU Directive comes into force, it is directly binding in the member state as to its principles, but it is in the member's discretion how the Directive will be implemented into national law.
- However, its provisions can be taken into account regarding the interpretation of existing national law.
- Once a Directive is implemented into national law, the courts are obliged to give a purposive interpretation to the (implemented) provisions of national law.

9.2   Identifying a Relevant Transfer

I9.2.1   Section 613a of the Civil Code applies when there is a transfer of a business or a part thereof. Having taken Directive 98/50/EC into consideration, the crucial question of what may constitute a relevant transfer in the meaning of s 613a(1) of the Civil Code is currently whether there exists a stable (ie not short term or one-off) economic entity which retains its identity.

I9.2.2   An economic entity may consist of activities, assets and employees although the transferee cannot refuse to take on employees as a means of circumventing the law. In certain *labour intensive sectors* an *organised* group of workers engaged together on a permanent basis may constitute an economic entity. The Federal Court of Employment has held, for example, that the transfer of more than 85% of the workforce can induce the application of s 613a(1) of the Civil Code.[1] Much also depends on the qualifications of the employees concerned. Even if a significant percentage of the employees transfer (57% and even 75%), s 613a(1) of the Civil Code may not apply if the employees are unskilled and only do simple work.[2]

[1]   BAG, *Neue Zeitschrift fuer Arbeitsrecht* (NZA) 1998, 534.
[2]   BAG, *Neue Zeitschrift fuer Arbeitsrecht* (NZA) 1999, 1884, and LAG Koeln, *Arbeitsrechtliche Praxis* (AP) No 144 refering to s 613a(1) of the Civil Code (*Buergerliches Gesetzbuch* – BGB).

I9.2.3   However, an economic entity cannot be reduced to certain activities only.

Ayse Süzen [1997] IRLR 255, ECJ

'An entity cannot be reduced to the activity entrusted to it. As identity also emerges from other factors such as its workforce, its management staff, the way in which its work is organised, and its operating methods . . .'

I9.2.4   Following *Ayse Süzen*, it was thought that if tangible or intangible assets (which might include most of the relevant workforce) did not transfer there would be no relevant transfer. In *Vidal* and *Sanchez Hidalgo*[1] the ECJ clarified the position by stating that the aim of Directive 77/187/EC was to 'ensure continuity of the employment relationship within an economic entity, irrespective of a change of ownership'. Employees in sectors such as cleaning or surveillance would not necessarily be excluded from protection under Directive 77/187/EC where there was a change in service provider.

¹   *Vidal* [1999] IRLR 132, ECJ and *Sánchez Hidalgo* [1999] IRLR 136, ECJ.

I9.2.5   The economic entity need not be the same before and after the transfer – the pivotal question is whether the 'economic entity' has 'retained its identity', which may occur notwithstanding that the business is not precisely the same. Therefore, it is important to identify an economic entity which *retains its identity*, a matter which will largely be a question of fact and degree for an employment court to determine. A business which changes in fundamental respects after transfer may not be deemed to have retained its identity.

Example

A restaurant sells German food. It is taken over by a company which converts the restaurant fundamentally, renovates the kitchen including the cold-storage house and other installations and then reopens offering Thai food. The business has so changed in its essential character that it has not 'retained its identity'.[1]

---

¹   BAG, *Neue Zeitschrift fuer Arbeitsrecht* (NZA) 1998, 31.

I9.2.6   There may be a series of transactions. In principle, this will amount to a succession of relevant transfers.

I9.2.7   Finally, s 613a of the Civil Code applies where, following a legal transfer or merger, there is a change in the natural or legal person responsible for carrying on the business, who, by virtue of that fact, incurs the obligations of an employer vis-à-vis the employees of the undertaking, regardless of whether ownership of the undertaking is transferred. This provision does not apply to the transfer of shares in a company.

9.3   Affected Employees

I9.3.1   Section 613a of the Civil Code protects 'employees', ie any individual who works for another person whether under a contract of service or apprenticeship or otherwise, but does not include anyone who provides services under a contract for services.

I9.3.2   The employee must be employed by the transferor. This might be a problem where only part of a business is being transferred. The test is whether, as a question of fact and degree, that employee can be said to be 'assigned' to the part being transferred.

I9.3.3   In *Botzen v Rotterdamsche Droogdok Maatshappij BV* [1985] ECR 519 the ECJ ruled that the court should ask whether there is a transfer of part of the undertaking to which employees 'were assigned and which formed the organisation or framework within which their employment relationship took effect'. The fact that the employee also provides services to other parts of the business is not necessarily fatal. The ECJ said that an employment relationship is 'essentially characterised by the link existing between the employee and the part of the undertaking or business to which he or she is assigned to carry out his or her duties'. In order to decide whether the law of transfers applies 'it is sufficient to establish to which part of the undertaking or business the employee was assigned'.[1]

Example

In *Botzen*, the ECJ considered employees employed in certain general departments of an undertaking including personnel, portering services, general maintenance and administration, which were not themselves transferred. The ECJ held that such employees would not be transferred even if they performed duties involving the use of assets assigned to the part transferred or carried out duties for the benefit of that part.

---

[1]   BAG, *Neue Zeitschrift für Arbeitsrecht* (NZA) 1998, 249.

I9.3.4   One practical problem may be how much importance is to be attached to the terms of the employment contract in determining an employee's assignment and, in particular, the impact of broad job descriptions and contractual mobility clauses.

I9.3.5   The question of assignment is essentially one of fact for employment courts. A number of factors need to be considered including:

*   the amount of time which an employee spends on one part of the business or on others;
*   the terms of the contract of employment showing what the employee could be required to do; and
*   how the cost to the employer of the employee's services is allocated between the different parts of the business.

9.4   Effects of the Transfer

I9.4.1   The main effect of s 613a(1) and (2) of the Civil Code is to transfer outstanding liabilities, rights, duties and obligations (ie all existing contract terms, express and implied, and statutory rights) in respect of employees in the undertaking from the transferor to the transferee. Thus, for example, any outstanding wages or holiday pay due to the employee are transferred and will be recoverable by him from the transferee even though he was not its employee at the time the liability was incurred. In addition his personnel records and all commitments made by the transferor are transferred. In effect the transferee 'steps into the shoes' of the transferor.

I9.4.2   All collective agreements, including applicable collective bargaining agreements with a trade union and existing works agreements, will also transfer to the transferee. Referring to this, s 613a(1) of the Civil Code provides that these collective rights cannot be modified to the detriment of the employees for at least one year after the transfer, unless there are corresponding collective agreements in the transferee's business (see para I9.5.5).

I9.4.3   Only civil liabilities are subject to transfer; criminal liabilities remain with the transferor as do third party liabilities. There is a further exception in respect of entitlements based on pension schemes, the liability for which does not pass to the transferee under s 613a of the Civil Code.

What can transfer?

Examples:

- all rights and obligations under and in connection with the contract of employment, including applicable collective agreements
- health and safety claims
- promises given by transferor
- claims for invalid dismissal

I9.4.4   Although the contractual rights and duties will be transferred to the transferee, it may be possible for a transferring employee to bring a claim against the transferor in respect of a liability transferred. A transferor remains responsible for such claims which arose before the transfer until the date of transfer, even if they become due within one year after. The transferor is responsible for such claims up to one year after transfer. Nevertheless, the transferee is also jointly liable for such claims.

I9.4.5   There are problem areas, for example restrictive covenants. These may need to be reconsidered in the context of the transferee's business.

I9.4.6   In summary, some of the main effects of s 613a(1) and (2) of the Civil Code include:

- the transfer of the employment of all employees of the business or the part of the business in question;
- the transfer of all of the rights, duties, liabilities and obligations of those employees under their employment contracts from the transferor to the transferee, including collective rights (with the exception of pensions) – however, new collective rights will be adopted where there are corresponding collective agreements which are applicable for the transferee;
- anything done by the transferor in connection with the transfer is treated as having been done by the transferee.

9.5   Variation and Termination of Contract

Section 613a(4) of the Civil Code:

'Any notice of termination of an employment contract by the transferor or transferee either before or after a relevant transfer is invalid, if the transfer of the business or a part of it is the reason or principal reason for the dismissal.'

I9.5.1   Section 613a(4) of the Civil Code provides that if the reason or principal reason for an employee's dismissal is connected with the transfer, his dismissal is automatically invalid, regardless of whether the Protection against Dismissal Act (*Kuendigungsschutzgesetz* – KSchG) is applicable or not. The provision applies to dismissals which take place both before and after the transfer, both by the transferor and by the transferee. Furthermore, the Federal Court of Employment (*Bundesarbeitsgericht* – BAG) has held that the statutory provision also prohibits termination agreements which are connected with the transfer,[1] if the parties do not intend to terminate the employment relationship definitively.

[1]   BAG, *Neue Zeitschrift fuer Arbeitsrecht* (NZA) 1999, 262.

I9.5.2   However, a dismissal can be valid in the case of a transfer of a business, if the employer can establish that the dismissal was based on another valid reason, eg an essential business reason within the meaning of s 1 of the Protection against Dismissal Act. In that case, the dismissal must comply with all statutory obligations referred to above (see paras **I6.1.1– I6.7.9**).

I9.5.3   Section 613a of the Civil Code provides protection for employees which must be considered to be 'mandatory'. It is not therefore possible to derogate from the rules in a way which is unfavourable to employees. Employees are not entitled to waive the rights conferred upon them even with their consent. This applies even if detrimental changes are balanced against changes to their advantage so that the employee is not left in a worse position overall. The parties cannot vary the terms of the contract by agreement and/or affirmation.

I9.5.4   If the employee negotiates with the new employer and agrees to changes to his terms and conditions this will only be valid if the changes are unconnected with the transfer. If such a change to terms and conditions is in connection with the transfer, the variation is ineffective and cannot be relied upon by the employer.

Example

Company A has recently purchased Company B. Company A wishes to harmonise terms and conditions so that both workforces have the same terms. It imposes new contracts on all staff; some terms are more beneficial to the staff of Company B, but their company cars are taken away. An employee of Company B complains. If the complainant can show that the variation is in connection with the transfer, the change of conditions may be ineffective, and he can claim his car back.

I9.5.5   As a consequence of Directive 77/187/EC, s 613a(1) of the Civil Code provides special protection regarding the collective agreements of the employees transferred. Those rights and obligations which form part of an applicable collective bargaining agreement or a works agreement will automatically transfer and cannot be changed to the detriment of the employees concerned for one year after the transfer. However, if these rights and obligations are subject to collective agreements which apply to the new employer's company, the latter apply, even if the new regulations contain changes to the disadvantage of the employees transferred.

I9.5.6   If an employer dismisses an employee post-transfer, for failing to agree to changes to his terms and conditions, the dismissal may be ineffective under s 613a(4) of the Civil Code (see para **I9.5.1**).

9.6   Duty to Inform and Consult

I9.6.1   There is no provision that a trade union or an employee representative must be informed or consulted about the transfer unless there is a works council. It may be, however, that the transfer of business includes a change of the operations and that the works council has additional rights under the Works Council Constitution Act (especially under s 111 of the Works Council Constitution Act (*Betriebsverfassungsgesetz* – BetrVG), see paras **I10.3.10–I10.3.14**.

10   COLLECTIVE RIGHTS AND BARGAINING

10.1 Background

I10.1.1   German employment law consists of two different parts: individual employment law, which deals with the relationship between the employer and the employee, and collective employment law, which itself is separated in two different parts. One is the collective bargaining agreement law, which regulates the provisions and the operation of a collective bargaining agreement (Collective Bargaining Agreement Act (*Tarifvertrags-gesetz* – TVG); the other part consists of the rights of the works council vis-à-vis the employer (Works Council Constitution Act.

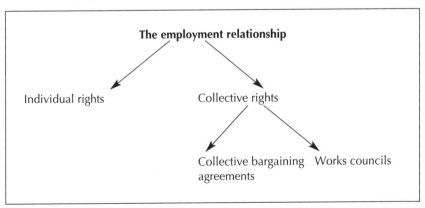

10.2 Collective Bargaining Agreements

A   BACKGROUND

I10.2.1   A collective bargaining agreement is an agreement that governs the rights and duties of the parties to the agreement (unions and employers' associations) and the determination of legal standards, in particular with regard to the entering into of employment contracts, the contract terms and the termination of working relationships.

I10.2.2 There are, on a rough estimate, about 51,500 current collective bargaining agreements in Germany. As a rule, collective bargaining agreements exist for a geographical area of a particular branch of industry (territorial agreements). For example, a company which is in the metal-working industry and is situated in Baden-Wuerttemberg will be subject to a different agreement from that for a similar company situated in Saxony. Any branches, offices or outlets of the Baden-Wuerttemberg company that are located in a different federal state will be subject to a different agreement.

I10.2.3 Approximately 13 million employees are members of a trade union. This represents an average membership of 39% of all employees (this does, however, include civil servants who have an above-average membership).

B   FREEDOM OF ASSOCIATION

I10.2.4 Each individual is guaranteed the right to join and be an active member of an association (a trade union or an employers' association) under art 9(3) of the Basic Law (*Grundgesetz* – GG). This basic right is strictly applied.

Example

A applies to employer B for employment. B wishes to employ as few union members as possible in his business. He therefore offers A DM 1,000 to leave the union. This agreement in invalid because it is a breach of art 9(3) of the Basic Law.

I10.2.5 If no employee in the office or plant is active in the relevant trade union, that union still has the right under art 9(3) of the Basic Law to advertise in the office or plant. It may use the bulletin board for this purpose.[1] It may also distribute election literature before the election of the works council. Furthermore, it has guaranteed access to the workplace (s 2(1) and (2) of the Works Council Constitution Act (*Betriebsverfassungsgesetz* – BetrVG). The employer cannot prevent the trade union from visiting the workplace.

[1]   BAG, *Neue Zeitschrift fuer Arbeitsrecht* (NZA) 1997, 164.

C   THE APPLICATION OF A COLLECTIVE BARGAINING AGREEMENT AND ITS EFFECTS

I10.2.6 A collective bargaining agreement is a contract between a trade union as an employee's representative, on the one hand, and either the employer or an employers' association, on the other (s 2(1) of the Collective Bargaining Agreements Act (*Tarifvertragsgesetz* – TVG). Both the employees as well as the employers are organised according to their branch of industry.

I10.2.7   The relevant collective agreement is only applied to an individual working relationship when:

- both parties (the individual employer and the individual employee) are members of the relevant organisations, or the employee is a member and the employer has not concluded a collective bargaining agreement with the relevant trade union himself;[1] or
- the collective agreement involved has been declared by the appropriate employment ministry to be generally binding – on account of its fundamental importance – on all companies in the geographical area in question and/or involved in such commercial activity;[2]
- the parties (employer and employee) have agreed upon the application of a particular collective agreement; or
- a particular collective bargaining agreement applies in the company by way of company practice or by way of the principle of equal treatment.

[1]   Section 3(1) of the Collective Bargaining Agreements Act.
[2]   Section 5 of the Collective Bargaining Agreements Act.

I10.2.8   Once a collective bargaining agreement is applicable on the basis of s 3(1) of the Collective Bargaining Agreements Act, especially in the case of a membership of both parties in the relevant organisations, all its provisions are mandatory. An employee who is a trade union member cannot validly waive collective rights by a separate agreement with the employer.[1]

[1]   Section 4(1)–(4) of the Collective Bargaining Agreements Act.

I10.2.9   Further, the employer is not free to terminate the application of a collective bargaining agreement unilaterally, eg by resigning from the employers' association. Sections 3(3) and 4(5) of the Collective Bargaining Agreements Act contain provisions governing the post-termination application of the relevant collective agreements, even if they are terminated by notice or on expiry of a fixed term.

I10.2.10   It is not possible to derogate from the rules in a way which is unfavourable to the employee, if a collective bargaining agreement is generally applicable.

I10.2.11   However, detrimental changes are possible in certain circumstances: if the application of the collective bargaining agreement is based on an individual agreement between the employer and the employee or on company practice, the employer and the employee are allowed to agree on modifications even to the detriment of the employee in question. Detrimental modifications between the employer and his employees are also valid, if the employer resigns his association membership, as soon as the collective bargaining agreement itself is terminated, eg by notice of termination of the trade union or the employers' association involved.

D   TYPES AND CONTENTS OF COLLECTIVE BARGAINING AGREEMENTS

I10.2.12   Collective bargaining agreements are, as a rule, divided into two types:

- outline collective bargaining agreements, and

- special collective bargaining agreements – in particular, on grading of employees, other wage components, details on holiday entitlement and additional holiday pay.

I10.2.13   The outline collective bargaining agreement covers general, but very important regulations, for example:

- the length of the working week and payment for overtime;
- the periods of notice and additional restrictions or prohibitions on termination; and
- exclusion clauses.

10.3 The Works Council Constitution Act

I10.3.1   The Works Council Constitution Act (*Betriebsverfassungsgesetz –* BetrVG) deals with co-operation between the employer and the works council in respect of the workplace (*Betrieb*). A fundamental reform to the Works Council Constitution Act is planned and should come into force in the course of 2001. The ministerial draft bill was published on 15 December 2000. The purpose of the reform is to strengthen the work of the works council and to adapt the Works Council Constitution Act to the changing requirements of today's working environment (ie teleworking). A works council is a standing employee representative, elected by the employees of a company. It can be formed at any time if the enterprise generally employs at least five employees, and if the employees decide to do so. Otherwise, there is no obligation for the employer to establish a works council.

A   THE WORKS COUNCIL

I10.3.2   A works council is a body that represents the employees in a particular company vis-à-vis their employer. Sections 1–73 of the Works Council Constitution Act regulate the election, the term of office, the control of business and organisation of the works council as well as the rights of representation of young persons and apprentices. The elections for a works council generally take place every four years between 1 March and 31 May. However, if the employees wish to establish a works council, the election can take place at any time.

B   RIGHTS OF A WORKS COUNCIL

I10.3.3   The Works Council Constitution Act also governs participation by the employees and co-determination by the works council. The rights to participate and to co-determine exists particularly in relation to:

(i)   social matters;
(ii)   the layout of the workplace and organisation of work;
(iii)   staff matters; and
(iv)   commercial matters.

I10.3.4   The basic principle of co-operation grants the works council the right to notification and comprehensive information from the employer. The works council, for example, has to be informed in a timely and comprehensive fashion in order to be able to fulfil its duties under the Works Council Constitution Act.[1]

---

[1]   Sections 74 and 80(2) of the Works Council Constitution Act.

I10.3.5   In several cases the works council has the right to be consulted. The most important right to be heard is the obligation imposed on the employer, pursuant to s 102 of the Works Council Constitution Act, to consult the works council before any notice of termination of employment. The employer is obliged to inform the works council about all the facts and circumstances that justify the intended notice of termination. If the works council is not properly involved in accordance with both this statute and the relevant decisions of the Federal Court of Employment, termination of employment will be ineffective.

I10.3.6   In addition, the employer must obtain the consent of the works council in relation to all individual staff measures, eg the hiring and transfer of staff. The works council may only refuse to give its consent for specific reasons, as set out in s 99(2) of the Works Council Constitution Act. If it refuses to give consent (even if it alleges specific reasons), the employer must apply to an employment court for the necessary consent. Without that consent the employer is not allowed to effect the intended staff measures.

I10.3.7   Finally, there are mandatory requirements for co-determination in respect of social matters. The employer can only act in respect of the matters listed in s 87 of the Works Council Constitution Act if it has previously reached agreement with the works council. If the employer acts without the consent of the works council, then the measure is unlawful and ineffective. If they do not reach agreement, the employer has to apply to a conciliation committee *(Einigungsstelle)* which consists of a chairperson (generally a judge of an employment court) and an equal number of participants from both sides. The conciliation committee reaches a decision that is binding on both parties.

I10.3.8   It is not only the employer who can initiate social matters, but the works council also has the right to require the employer to commence talks at any time on social matters.

I10.3.9   Social matters of particular importance include:

• the beginning and the end of the working day, including breaks, as well as the allocation of the time worked on each day of the week (but not the length of the working day);
• the temporary reduction or extension of regular working hours (overtime, extra shifts and short-time);
• the establishment of general holiday regulations;
• the introduction and application of mechanised supervision of the behaviour and performance of employees (eg video cameras at the workplace);
• questions regarding the workplace's wage structure, in particular the establishment of principles of remuneration; and
• the introduction and application of new methods of payment of salaries or any changes to such methods (this is not to be confused with the fixing of salaries and wages pursuant to the collective bargaining agreement under s 77(3) of the Works Council Constitution Act.

C   SPECIAL RIGHTS WHERE THERE IS A CHANGE IN THE OPERATIONS

I10.3.10   If the employer wishes to carry out a change in operations such as:

- closure of a whole plant or office or a major part thereof;
- mass redundancy (the actual number of employees required for a mass redundancy depends on the total number of employees);
- relocation;
- modernisation of production;

he is obliged to involve the works council (s 111 of the Works Council Constitution Act. The employer must negotiate a 'reconciliation of interests' *(Interessenausgleich)* and a social plan with the works council. Both the reconciliation of interests and the social plan are agreements between the employer and the works council. The parties – in particular the employer – are therefore obliged to fulfil the agreements.

I10.3.11   The reconciliation of interests *(Interessenausgleich)* regulates individual measures in the context of the change in operations and its execution. In other words, it is concerned with the reasons for the change and the method for realising such change.

I10.3.12   The social plan regulates the reconciliation of the possible disadvantages to which the employees could be subjected as a result of the change in operations. In particular, the social plan will regulate compensation payments (and the basis on which to calculate them) to employees who are to be dismissed or who are seriously disadvantaged.

I10.3.13   If an employer does not meet his obligation to negotiate the reconciliation of interests and a social plan, the affected employees can claim compensation (s 113 of the Works Council Constitution Act). These amounts are always higher than the amounts that an employer would agree to pay under a negotiated settlement. They can be up to 12 and – depending on the age of the employee and his length of service with the company – 15 or even 18 months' salary.

I10.3.14   If a works council is active, it can significantly delay the negotiations concerning the reconciliation of interests and the social plan. It can even cause a breakdown in the negotiations and demand that a conciliation committee *(Einigungsstelle)* is appointed to mediate.[1] This body will then determine the severance payments at its own discretion. The decision of the conciliation committee is binding on the parties. Severance payments determined by a conciliation committee are generally higher than those negotiated between the parties.

[1]   Section 112(2)–(5) of the Works Council Constitution Act *(Betriebsverfassungsgesetz* – BetrVG).

10.4 European Works Councils

I10.4.1   The European Works Council Act dated 28 October 1996 *(Europäisches Betriebsräte-Gesetz* – EBRG)[1] came into effect on 1 November 1996. The Act implemented Directive 94/95/EC regarding the establishment of a European Works Council or the creation of a process to inform and consult with employees in companies and company groups operating EU-wide.

1   Federal Gazette (*Bundesgesetzblatt*) 1996 I 1548.

I10.4.2   The European Works Council Act covers companies with their domicile in Germany which operate EU-wide and company groups which operate EU-wide, whose dominant company is in Germany (EBRG, s 2(1)). A company is deemed to operate EU-wide if it employs a minimum total 1,000 employees in the member States, and of which at least 150 employees are employed in at least two member States (EBRG, s 3(1)). A company group operates EU-wide if it also employs at least 1,000 employees in the member States, and has at least two companies with their domicile in various member States which for their part have at least 150 employees in those member States (EBRG, s 3(2)).

I10.4.3   The primary purpose of the EBRG is that the cross-border co-operation of employees should principally be guaranteed by an agreement between central company management and a special negotiating body for the employees' side. Only if such an agreement has not been reached voluntarily is a European works council established by virtue of law (EBRG, ss 22 and 23).

I10.4.4   The special negotiating body (EBRG, ss 8 ff) leads negotiations and is partner to the agreements regarding cross-border information and consultation for the employees' side. It is formed on the initiative of central management or on written application from at least 100 employees from at least two different member States (EBRG, s 9). The application must be sent to central management. If this application is effective it triggers the start of certain time periods, on the expiry of which a European works council is established by virtue of law (see EBRG, s 21(1)). Central management undertakes to inform the applicants, the local plant or company management and those employee representative bodies whether a separate negotiating body is to be formed and how many seats each member State gains (EBRG, s 9(3)).

I10.4.5   One employee representative from each member State in which the company or the company group operates is sent to the special negotiating body (the 'principle of representation'). A member State with at least 25% of the employees may send one, a member state with at least 50% two, and a member state with at least 75% may send three additional representatives to the special negotiating body (the 'principle of pro-portionality'). The appointment of German members to the special negotiating body is made in a company operating EU-wide by the central works council or, if such a body does not exist, by the works council and in company groups operating EU-wide by the groups' works council (EBRG, s 11).

I10.4.6   It is the task of the special negotiating body to negotiate and conclude with central management, on a confidential basis, an agreement regarding a cross-border informing process and hearings (EBRG, s 8(1)).

The central management and the special negotiating body are completely free to structure the cross-border information process and hearing of employees (EBRG, s 17). They can make provision for the establishment of a European Works Council or can also agree to a decentralised information and hearing process. The agreement must be recorded in writing. The strongest form of trans-national co-operation is the hearing. A hearing is defined as 'an exchange of opinion and the establishment of dialogue between employee representatives and central management' (EBRG, s 1(4)) and is therefore to be regarded as more comprehensive and intensive than the concept of hearing in the Works Council Constitution Act.

I10.4.7 If a solution is not reached, a European works council is formed by virtue of law. This is the case if central management refuses to enter into negotiations within six months of the application, when agreement has not been reached within three years of application, if central management or the special negotiating body prior to this declare that negotiations have failed (EBRG, s 21(1)). The European Works Council is a permanent establishment without any fixed period of office. Membership of the European Works Council is restricted to four years.

I10.4.8 The competence of the European Works Council is restricted to matters which have cross-border effect (EBRG, s 31). In particular, this includes economic matters if they affect the company or the company group as a whole, or at least two plants or companies in various member States.

I10.4.9 Central management must inform the European Works Council in accordance with EBRG, s 32 once per calendar year regarding the development of the business and the perspectives of the company or company group operating EU-wide, and must give the European Works Council a hearing in these matters. In addition to the right to be informed and listened to on a regular basis, the European Works Council is granted further co-operation rights by virtue of law if extraordinary circumstances, such as transfer or shutdown of companies and mass dismissals, occur which have a considerable effect on the interests of employees. If such extraordinary circumstances occur, management must inform the European Works Council without undue delay, providing them with the necessary documents and giving them an audience on request, in principle giving enough time so that its proposals and concerns can be taken into consideration.

11 EMPLOYMENT DISPUTES

11.1 Background

I11.1.1 All disputes between employer and employee are resolved in special employment courts, regardless of the value of the dispute.[1]

[1] Sections 2 and 2a of the Employment Court Proceedings Act (*Arbeitsgerichtsgesetz* – ArbGG).

I11.1.2 Appeals from an employment court may be made to the Regional Employment Court (*Landesarbeitsgericht*) on a point of fact or on a point of law, if the value exceeds DM 1,200 (as of 1 January 2002: € 600), or if the appeal is expressly permitted by the employment court.

I11.1.3   An appeal from the Regional Employment Court (*Landesarbeits-gericht*) may be made to the Federal Employment Court (*Bundesarbeits-gericht*) in Erfurt, if the appeal on a point of law is specifically permitted by the Regional Employment Court or was compelled in particular proceedings by the Federal Employment Court itself.

11.2 Employment Courts

I11.2.1   Employment courts comprise a panel of three: a legally qualified chairperson and two wing members representing both sides of industry.

I11.2.2   There are usually at least two hearings. The first hearing is held before the chairperson only, and the subsequent hearings are held before a full panel of three members. The first hearing is relatively informal and, in contrast to the later proceedings, has relaxed rules on evidence and procedure. The main target of this first hearing is to reach a compromise agreement. If the negotiations fail, formal rules of procedure will, however, govern the conduct of proceedings.

I11.2.3   The composition of the employment courts, their jurisdiction and the rules of procedure are regulated in the Employment Court Proceedings Act (*Arbeitsgerichtsgesetz* – ArbGG).

12   WHISTLEBLOWING/DATA PROTECTION

12.1 Whistleblowing

I12.1.1   The employee's obligation to observe secrecy with regard to internal company matters may be governed by the law of an employment contract, or it may be covered by the implied terms of the employment contract. The duty to observe confidentiality may be enforced by means of an injunction to cease and desist. If the employee deliberately infringes contractual or statutory obligations to observe secrecy, he may be liable to pay compensation. Termination of an employee's contract on the grounds of conduct and, in the event of serious infringements termination without notice, may still be justified.

I12.1.2   Unlike at Common Caw, there is no German law which permits whistleblowing under certain specific circumstances. Under German case law, the view which is generally held is that an employee is not entitled to take public matters into his own hands and take action against an employer who is acting in breach of the law. Bringing action or initiating other official proceedings (eg with the tax authorities, supervisory bodies etc) is in breach of contract in principle and may constitute grounds for termination. An exception to this is made only for serious offences or if the offence is directed against the employee himself. Occasionally the employee is regarded as being entitled to file a report with the relevant authority if the circumstances or offences in question affect the public and if they cannot be effectively remedied through internal procedures.

12.2 Object of Confidentiality

I12.2.1 Business and trade secrets are generally recognised as being confidential in the context of an employment contract without any express agreement to this effect. Such secrets comprise all facts connected with business operations which are only known to a limited group of people, and which are not therefore common knowledge, and which are kept secret in accordance with the will of the employer on the grounds of justified economic interest.

I12.2.2 The general obligation to observe secrecy can be extended to individual employment contracts. It is, for example, permissible to extend the general obligation to observe secrecy to facts which are expressly designated as confidential by the employer. This includes the duty to observe confidentiality with regard to wage and salary data, except where the employee is required to disclose his income to public authorities.

I12.2.3 The duty to observe confidentiality commences in principle when the employment contract is agreed and continues beyond the end of the employment relationship even in the absence of any express agreement to this effect.

12.3 Confidentiality Clauses

I12.3.1 It is in principle possible to extend the obligation to observe secrecy by contract. However, so-called 'all-clauses', whereby the employee undertakes to observe secrecy with regard to all company and business facts of which he gains knowledge, are disproportionate because they impose excessive contractual commitments on the employee and the clauses concerned are therefore void under s 138 I Civil Code. A clause of this breadth is not covered by the justified interests of the employer, although inclusion of a confidentiality clause in an employment contract is still common practice.

12.4 Data Protection

I12.4.1 Under German law there is not at present any special statutory regulation regarding data protection for the employee. The EC Data Protection Directive[1] was not implemented by the Federal Government within the prescribed period (by October 1998). An infringement procedure in the EU is therefore likely.

[1] EU Directive 95/46, OJ 1995 L281/31.

I12.4.2 The Federal Data Protection Act (*Bundesdatenschutzgesetz*) applies to the collection, processing and use of personal data by public and non-public agencies, in as far as they process or use data in or from files for business, professional or commercial purposes. The Federal Data Protection Act embodies in statute a series of rights for employees affected by data processing. An employee must, for example, be notified when personal data is to be saved for the first time or when it is transmitted to third parties for the first time. The employee is entitled to receive information on all personal data which has been saved. He is also entitled to inspect the file kept on him by the employer at any time.[1]

[1]   See s 83 I Works Council Constitution Act (*Betriebsverfassungsgesetz* – BetrVG)).

I12.4.3   Under the Federal Data Protection Act the employer is obliged to take a series of precautionary organisational measures to prevent unlawful saving, use or transmission of data. The employer must, for example, ensure that any persons doing data processing in the context of their work submit themselves to data secrecy. If at least five persons are employed in automatic data processing, a data protection officer must be appointed. A comprehensive right of codetermination is conferred on the works council with regard to saving, use and processing of employees' personal data.

13   HUMAN RIGHTS

13.1 Background

I13.1.1   As distinct from Common Law, under German law there is no special law requiring the application of the ECHR through German courts.

I13.1.2   The human rights and basic liberties which are enshrined in the European Convention on Human Rights (ECHR) and which appear relevant with regard to employment law are reproduced in the English chapter. The European Commission on Human Rights decides whether there has been an infringement of the European Convention on Human Rights in response to an application from a member state or, in particular, a complaint from an individual citizen, a non-state organisation or group of persons. If it considers that there has been an infringement, it generally refers the case to the European Court of Human Rights. The type of case most frequently referred to the European Court of Human Rights deals with the interpretation of **art 11(1)** (freedom of association).

I13.1.3   In practice, in the field of employment law the European Convention on Human Rights plays only a very limited role in Germany. Fundamental human rights are already contained in the catalogue of basic rights in the Basic Law (*Grundgesetz*). Legislature, executive and judiciary are bound by the basic rights. These basic rights do not apply directly between private individuals (employer, employees) but apply to contractual relationships in an indirect manner via general clauses (principle of good faith, public morality).

I13.1.4   The provisions dealing with fundamental rights in the Basic Law which are of particular relevance to employment law are:

Article 3: equality before the law, particularly of men and women;

Article 5: freedom of expression;

Article 9: freedom of association;

Article 11: freedom of movement;

Article 12: the right to freely choose an occupation, place of work and place of training;

Article 12 II, III: prohibition of forced labour.

I13.1.5   The basic rights prevail over all other legal sources in employment law, including legislation. The principle of the state order, as enshrined in art 20 of the Basic Law, establishes a guideline for the legislator to organise employment law in such a way that it meets contemporary social requirements.

BIBLIOGRAPHY

Münchener Handbuch Arbeitsrecht Vol I 2000, Vol II 2000, Vol III 2000

Günther Schaub *Arbeitsrechtshandbuch* (9th edn, 2000)

Erfurter Kommentar zum Arbeitsrecht (2nd edn, 2000)

USEFUL WEBSITES

Homepage of the Federal Ministry for Labour and Social Affairs (*Bundesministerium für Arbeit und Sozialordnung*):

* www.bma.de

Homepage of the Federal Labour Court (*Bundesarbeitsgericht*) with press releases on EU rulings:

* www.bundesarbeitsgericht.de

J   Ireland

James Trueick and Jennifer Cashman

James Trueick is a Partner in the firm of A & L Goodbody, Solicitors. He is a director of the firms employment unit, the largest unit of its kind in Ireland.

Jennifer Cashman is an associate solicitor in the firm of A & L Goodbody, Solicitors.

A & L Goodbody, Dublin

Phone: +353 1 649 2000
Fax: +353 1 649 2649
Email: jtrueick@algoodbody.ie; jcashman@algoodbody.ie
Website: www.algoodbody.ie

SUMMARY TABLE

IRELAND

Rights	Yes/No	Explanatory Notes
CONTRACTS OF EMPLOYMENT		
Minimum notice	YES	
Terms:		
Express	YES	
Implied	YES	
Incorporated by statute	YES	
REMUNERATION		
Minimum wage regulation	YES	IR £4.40 per hour
Further rights and obligations:		
Right to paid holiday	YES	Four weeks paid holiday and nine paid public holidays
Right to sick pay	YES	State disablement benefit
WORKING TIME		
Regulation of hours per day/working week	YES	Maximum 48 hour working week
Regulation of night work	YES	Maximum 48 hour night work per week
Right to rest periods	YES	11 hour rest period in every 24 hours; 30 minute break every 6 hours/15 minute break every 4½ hours
EQUAL OPPORTUNITIES		
Discrimination protection:		
Sex	YES	
Race/origin/colour	YES	
Marital and family status	YES	
Disability	YES	
Religion	YES	
Age	YES	
Sexual orientation	YES	
Equal pay legislation	YES	
Membership of travelling community	YES	
TERMINATION OF EMPLOYMENT		
Right not to be dismissed in breach of contract	YES	
Statutory rights on termination	YES	Unfair dismissal

REDUNDANCY

Statutory definition	YES	
Right to payment on redundancy	YES	Statutory redundancy payment

Right to consultation:

Individual	YES	
Collective	YES	5–30 employees to be made redundant in period of 30 days depending on size of organisation

YOUNG WORKERS

Protection of children and young persons at work	YES	

MATERNITY RIGHTS

Right to time off-ante natal care	YES	
Right to maternity leave	YES	18 paid weeks, at least 4 weeks prior and 4 weeks after birth and additional 8 unpaid weeks
Notice requirements	YES	For additional eight weeks and return to work as well as triggering entitlement to leave
Maternity pay (during leave)	YES	State maternity benefit
Protection from dismissal	YES	Such a dismissal is unlawful
Health and safety protection	YES	
Right to parental leave	YES	14 weeks unpaid leave in respect of child under age of five
Right to time off for dependants	YES	'Force majeure' leave in event of injury/illness of close relative. Paid leave up to three days per annum

TRANSFERS OF BUSINESSES

Right to protection on transfer	YES	
Transfer of employment obligations	YES	
Right to information and consultation	YES	
Right not to be dismissed	YES	

COLLECTIVE RIGHTS

Compulsory recognition of trade unions	NO	(Expected in 2001)
Recognition of trade unions	YES	
European works councils (EWCs)	YES	
Right to take industrial action	NO	

EMPLOYMENT DISPUTES

Civil court jurisdiction	YES	
Statutory Body	YES	Employment tribunals

WHISTLEBLOWING

Protection from dismissal/ detriment	NO	(Expected in July 2001)

DATA PROTECTION

Protection	YES

HUMAN RIGHTS ACT

Protection of human rights	YES	Fundamental rights protected by Constitution
Public authority	NO	Although legislation following UK model expected to be introduced
Private organisations	NO	

1   THE EMPLOYMENT RELATIONSHIP

1.1   Background

J1.1.1   An individual who is under a contract of service to another person, called the employer, under which the employer has the right to direct the individual, not only as to what is to be done but also as to how it is to be done, is an employee, and employees generally have access to employment protection legislation.[1]

[1]   Terms of Employment (Information) Act 1994.

J1.1.2   Industrial Relations Act 1990, s 23, states that a contract of employment may be 'expressed or implied, oral or in writing'. Many of the terms of a contract of employment may emerge from the common law, statutes and/or collective agreements or may be derived from custom and practice.

J1.1.3   Employees who work under a contract of service must be distinguished from independent contractors who operate under a contract for services and are not subject to the control of the person for whom the contract is completed.

1.2   Contract of Service

J1.2.1   There is a statutory obligation to provide written particulars of employment (see paras **J1.2.2–J1.2.6**). Employers often use staff manuals, hand books or supplementary documentation which contain details of standard terms and conditions applicable to all employees. These will form part of the contract of employment if expressly or impliedly incorporated.

A   CONTRACT AND ITS WRITTEN PARTICULARS

J1.2.2   There is no legal requirement for a contract of employment to be in writing (except for apprentices and merchant seamen). However, the Terms of Employment (Information) Act 1994 imposes an obligation on employers to furnish their employees with a written statement containing the following details:
- full names of the employer and employee;
- address of the employer;
- place of work or where there is no fixed or main place, a statement that the employee is required or permitted to work at various locations;
- job description;
- commencement date of the employee's contract of employment;
- duration of a temporary contract or the date on which a fixed-term contract is due to expire;
- rate or method of calculation of the employee's remuneration;
- payment intervals eg weekly, monthly etc;
- hours of work (including overtime);
- holiday and other paid leave;
- sick leave arrangements and pension scheme provisions (only if applicable);

- notice to be given by the employer and employee;

The Minimum Notice and Terms of Employment Acts 1973–1991 provide that employees are entitled to the following notice:

Length of service	*Minimum notice entitlement*
13 weeks to 2 years	1 week
2–5 years	2 weeks
5–10 years	4 weeks
10–15 years	6 weeks
15 years +	8 weeks

- reference to any collective agreements;
- details of rest periods and breaks;
- terms implied by a collective agreement.

J1.2.3 The written statement must be provided within two months of the employee commencing employment. When an existing employee so requests, he/she must be given a written statement within two months of the request.[1]

[1] Terms of Employment (Information) Act 1994.

J1.2.4 Employers must also give new employees a written summary of the procedures that would be used should it become necessary to invoke disciplinary action. This must be furnished within 28 days of the commencement of employment.

J1.2.5 It is these terms and conditions that are often referred to as the employment contract, although they are in reality only a statement of what the employer believes the main terms to be.

J1.2.6 Apart from the statutory rights of employees, the law does not specify what the detail of a contract should be. Subject to the statutory rights, employers are free to impose on employees whatever arrangements they wish and the other person is free to accept whatever terms they choose.

B   TERMS OF THE CONTRACT

J1.2.7 Contracts of employment are made up of terms and conditions that are not necessarily all contained in the written statement or handbook. Terms and conditions may be in writing or oral and may be implied or incorporated.

C   EXPRESS TERMS

J1.2.8 These are contractual terms that are spelt out orally or in writing. Each term must be clear and unambiguous and can only be overridden if contrary to public policy or statute. Examples of express terms including those dealing with intellectual property rights, confidentiality, restrictive covenants and summary dismissal: see paras **J1.2.9–J1.2.12**.

Intellectual property rights

J1.2.9   The Copyright Act 1963, s 10(4), provides that works of an employee prepared in the course of either his or her employment belong to the employer. If the employee has to write and prepare materials in the course of his/her employment, the contract should contain an express term that the copyright vests in the employer. It would also be advisable to include a specific clause governing ownership of inventions in the contract of employment as, under Irish law, the invention of an employee referable to his or her work belongs to the employer, unless otherwise agreed between the employer and the employee.[1]

[1]   The Competition Acts 1991–1996.

Confidentiality

J1.2.10   It is an implied term that an employee must not breach the confidentiality of his employer and it is prudent to include a clause to this effect by stating that the employee shall not disclose to any third party details of the employer's business without the employer's prior written consent. In some cases, an employer may have a separate agreement containing clauses relating to restraint of trade, secrecy, confidentiality and competition. These are referred to as confidentiality agreements.

Restrictive covenants

J1.2.11   Such covenants concern the right of a former employee to compete with their former employer after they have left their employment. It is important that such clauses do not distort competition in the market. General common law provisions apply to restraint of trade clauses in employment contracts. Therefore, the restraint must be reasonable in terms of the conduct sought to be restricted, the duration and the geographical extent and the employer must have a legitimate interest to protect. If the proposed restraint clause is found to be unreasonable, it is completely unenforceable and, although the jurisprudence is not settled on this matter, it is likely that the court will not rewrite the clause to make it enforceable. It is advisable, therefore, to include a provision in the contract to state that the restraint of trade clause is severable from the remainder of the contract and that if that particular clause should be found to be unenforceable, it can be severed from the contract in order that the remainder of the contract remains enforceable.

Summary dismissal

J1.2.12   It is advisable for employers to clearly state the grounds for summary dismissal, eg insubordination; theft; violence; being under the influence of alcohol or drugs whilst at work. Without such an express clause, an employer may still terminate the contract of employment for fundamental breach. However, there may be circumstances where it is unclear whether the misconduct entitles the employer to summarily dismiss.

D   IMPLIED TERMS

J1.2.13   Implied terms are those which are not spelt out because they are too obvious to be recorded, or because they are common practice in the business or industry concerned or because the parties to the contract have shown by their behaviour that they accept such terms. It is a question of law whether particular terms can be implied in a contract. There are various provisions that should be included in an employment contract to ensure compliance with the many pieces of protective employment legislation. If, for example, there is no express term in the contract allowing for maternity leave in compliance with the legislation in this area, such a term will automatically be implied into the contract.

Examples of implied terms
- custom and practice
- the employer's duty to take care of the employee's safety and to act fairly
- the employee's duties of skill and care, obedience, fidelity and confidentiality
- the mutual duty of respect
- terms implied by the Irish Constitution eg the right to natural justice
- like pay for like work

E   INCORPORATED TERMS

J1.2.14   These are terms that may be incorporated into an individual contract of employment through collective agreements or work rules.

Examples of incorporated terms
- work rules
- collective agreements
- disciplinary policy
- sexual harassment policy

F   STATUTORY PROVISIONS

J1.2.15   There are a number of statutory rights that apply when an employment contract is entered into, although a number of these are dependent on length of employment. Employees have the right:
- not to be discriminated against on grounds of gender, marital status, family status, sexual orientation, religious belief, age, disability, race colour, nationality, ethnicity or national origins, or membership of the travelling community;
- to equal pay for equal work, (ie for work of equal value or work regarded as equivalent);

- to an itemised pay statement;
- to maternity benefits;
- to notice of termination of employment;[1]
- to redundancy pay;[2]
- to a safe system of work;
- to time off for jury duty and to look for work if declared redundant with at least two years service;
- to belong or not belong to a trade union and to take part in trade union activities outside work time or during times permitted by the employer;
- to protected employment rights when the business is transferred to a new employer;
- not to be unfairly dismissed;[3]
- to written reasons for dismissal upon request;
- to a written statement of particulars of employment;
- to paternity leave, but only in very restricted circumstances (ie when the mother dies during her maternity leave);
- to rest periods, rest breaks and maximum working time;
- to holiday entitlements;
- to payment of certain entitlements where an employer becomes insolvent;
- to holiday pay;
- to adoptive leave;
- to parental leave.

[1]   Thirteen weeks.
[2]   Two years.
[3]   One year's qualifying service is necessary.

1.3   Variation of Contract

J1.3.1   Once the terms and conditions have been agreed, an employer may not, generally speaking, vary them unilaterally, unless the circumstances are exceptional. Changes to terms and conditions must have the consent of the employee.

J1.3.2   The most frequent change, an increase of salary after review, is, of course, normally agreed by the employee. However, other changes such as an attempt to reduce hours and holidays could well be resisted by an employee. Where an employer attempts to force such changes through, the employee may be able to sue for damages for breach of contract and/or claim constructive dismissal, on the basis that the employee was forced to resign by the actions of the employer, which amounted to a clear indication that the employer did not intend to hold itself bound by the terms of the contract.

J1.3.3   There are certain situations in which the employer may be able to make changes without the employee's consent. Probably the clearest and most common situation in which the employer has the right to unilaterally vary the contract of employment is when the contract contains flexibility and mobility clauses. These are clauses by which the employer reserves the right to require the employee to carry out his/her duties at a different location or to change those duties. It should be noted, however, that merely relying on such a flexibility clause to dismiss an employee who refuses to comply with any changes made, or against an employee who resigns and claims constructive dismissal, may not be a sufficient defence against a claim for unfair dismissal. The employer also has to take account of other commitments of the employee that might make compliance with the flexibility provision difficult or impossible.

Variation of the contract
- either orally or in writing
- through collective bargaining
- where the employee works in accordance with the new arrangements without objecting to the changes
- through a term which provides for variation of the contract eg where a change of location may be envisaged

---

J1.3.4 It is also the case that a mobility clause cannot be used to avoid a claim for redundancy following the change of an employee's location.

J1.3.5 An employer has an implied right to alter the contract of employment, provided that:
- the amendments are so obvious that it would go without saying that the parties would have agreed to them;
- they are necessary to give business efficacy to the contract.

Variation of the contract
- by agreement
- between employer and employee
- with trade unions
- reliance on flexibility clause
- statute: statutory instrument or EU Directive
- collective agreement work rules
- custom and practice
- dismissal and re-employment

1.4 Remedies

A   EMPLOYEE'S REMEDIES

J1.4.1 On dismissal by an employer, an employee may have rights under the Unfair Dismissal Acts 1977–1993 with the right of access to a Rights Commissioner, the Labour Court or Employment Appeals Tribunal (paras **J6.5.1, J11.2.1–J11.2.5**).

Damages

J1.4.2   An employee can bring a case for wrongful dismissal before the courts and seek damages against the employer. Employees can claim that they were constructively dismissed and seek damages for loss of salary and contractual benefits throughout the notice period.

Injunctive relief

J1.4.3   Normally, a court will not enforce a contract of employment once it has been breached. However, the courts will grant an employee an injunction to restrain the employer from taking action to breach the contract eg to prevent an employer from dismissing the employee and to ensure that all stages of a contractual disciplinary procedure are fully complied with where trust and confidence still exists.

B   EMPLOYER'S REMEDIES

Damages

J1.4.4   An employer can sue an employee in damages for breach of contract eg where an employee leaves without working a full notice period. This happens very rarely as an employer's loss is hard to quantify and usually any judgment would be hard to enforce. However, such a claim may be useful where an employee has set up in business or is employed by a competitor in breach of restrictive covenants.

Summary dismissal

J1.4.5   If an employee's breach of contract is a fundamental breach the employer may accept that breach and terminate the contract with immediate effect.

Injunctive relief

J1.4.6   An employer may apply for an interlocutory injunction to restrain the disclosure of confidential information or to enforce restrictive covenants.

2   REMUNERATION

2.1   Background

J2.1.1   Employers have an obligation to pay an employee for his services. Under the Payment of Wages Act 1991, 'employee' means the person who has entered into or works under a contract of employment, or has worked under such a contract in the past. Legally, references to an employee, in relation to an employer, should be construed as references to an employee employed by that employer. An employer in relation to an employee means the person with whom the employee has entered into, or for whom the employee works under, a contract of employment or, where the employment has ceased, entered into or worked under such a contract.

J2.1.2 Where employees are hired through an employment agency, the general rule is that they are employees of the person paying their salary or wages, whether that is the organisation where they are working or the employment agency.

2.2   Legal Regulation of Remuneration

J2.2.1 A contract of employment should state the salary or the rate of pay per week/hour. The timing of the payment should be stated and the method of payment should also be agreed. If there are bonus payments or commission paid, the method of calculation and when paid should be clearly spelt out. Any deductions from wages or salary (other than income tax or Pay Related Social Insurance) must be clearly stated in the employment contract, giving authorisation to the employer to deduct such monies. For the purposes of the Payment of Wages Act 1991, the term 'wages' in relation to the employee, means any sums payable to the employee by the employer in connection with his or her employment, including:

- any fee, bonus or commission, or any holiday, sick or maternity pay, or any other emolument, referable to his or her employment, whether payable under his or her contract of employment or otherwise; and
- any sum payable to the employee upon termination by the employer of his or her contract of employment without the appropriate prior notice, being a sum paid in lieu of the giving of such notice.

J2.2.2 The following payments are not regarded as wages:

- any payment in respect of expenses incurred by the employee in carrying out his or her employment;
- any payment by way of a pension, allowance or gratuity in connection with the death, retirement or resignation of the employee or compensation for loss of office;
- any payment referable to the employee's redundancy;
- any payment to the employee otherwise than in his or her capacity as an employee;
- any payment in kind or benefit in kind.

2.3   Deductions from Wages

J2.3.1 Under the Payment of Wages Act 1991, s 5, an employer is not permitted to make any deduction (or receive any payment) from the wages or salary of an employee unless one of the following conditions is satisfied:

- the deduction is authorised by law (eg PAYE/PRSI);
- the deduction (or payment) is required or authorised to be made by virtue of a term of the employee's contract of employment included in the contract before, and in force at the time of, the deduction or payment;
- in the case of a deduction, the employee has given his or her prior consent in writing.

J2.3.2 An employer cannot deduct money from an employee for something that the employee has done or failed to do, nor can the employer deduct money unless the deduction is authorised by a term of the contract. The employee must have been referred to a copy of the term or a note in writing declaring the term's existence and its effect, and the deduction must be fair and reasonable with regard to all the circumstances. These conditions do not apply to:

- any overpayment of wages or expenses, provided the deduction does not exceed the amount of the overpayment. If the amount of the overpayment is considerable, the employer should make it possible for the employee to repay by way of instalments;
- a deduction made in consequence of disciplinary proceedings held by virtue of a statutory provision ie where an employer is entitled by statute to bring proceedings;
- requirements imposed upon the employer to deduct and pay to a Government Minister, the Revenue Commissioners or a local authority the amounts due from the employee;
- deductions made pursuant to a strike or any other industrial action by the employee, or deductions made by the employer following an Attachment of Earnings Order.

2.4   Itemised Pay Statement

J2.4.1   Under the Terms of Employment (Information) Act 1994, all employees have a statutory right to receive an itemised pay statement when or before they are paid or, if paid by credit transfer, as soon as possible after the transfer has been effected. This must include:

- the gross amount of the wages or salary;
- the amounts of any fixed deductions and the purpose for which they are made (eg voluntary deductions such as trade unions subscriptions, additional voluntary pension contributions etc);
- the amounts of any variable deduction and the purposes for which they are made ie Pay As You Earn (PAYE), Pay Related Social Insurance (PRSI).

3   FURTHER RIGHTS AND OBLIGATIONS

3.1   Holiday Entitlement

J3.1.1   The Organisation of Working Time Act 1997 sets out the statutory rights for employees in respect of rest, maximum working time and holidays. This Act repeals the Holidays (Employees) Act 1973, and the Worker Protection (Regular Part Time Employees) Act 1991, s 4. The Organisation of Working Time Act 1997 now provides minimum legally enforceable entitlements for all employees to holidays and public holidays. These provisions came into effect on 30 September 1997.

J3.1.2   The Organisation of Working Time Act 1997 applies to any person:

- working under a contract of employment or apprenticeship;
- employed through an employment agency;

- in the service of the state (excluding members of the police force and the defence force but including Civil Servants and employees of any local authority, Health Board, Harbour Authority or a Vocational Education Committee).

J3.1.3 There is no qualifying period for holidays and all employees, regardless of status or service, qualify for paid holidays. All time worked qualifies for paid holiday time. From 1 April 1999, depending on time worked, employees' holiday entitlements should be calculated by one of the following methods below.

Calculation of holiday entitlements
- four working weeks in a leave year in which the employee works at least 1,365 hours (unless it is a leave year in which he/she changes employment)
- one-third of a working week per calendar month that the employee works at least 117 hours
- eight per cent of the hours an employee works in a leave year (but subject to a maximum of four working weeks)

J3.1.4 Annual leave must be granted within the leave year unless the employee consents to the leave being granted within six months of the following year. If an employee on annual leave is medically certified as ill, the period of leave shall not be counted as annual leave. In calculating how many days holiday to which an employee may be entitled, an employer should include all hours worked including overtime, time spent on maternity or adoptive leave as well as holidays and public holidays taken during the calculation period.

3.2 Sick Pay

J3.2.1 There is no common law or statutory obligation in Irish law for employers to pay employees whilst they are sick. However, many employers do operate sick pay schemes and if this is the case, the employer must give the employee written details of same. Sick pay schemes will usually provide that an employee will be paid a certain amount of sick leave eg six weeks. Thereafter, employees have to rely on state disability benefit, which is now subject to income tax. Some employers may provide that the sick pay scheme will pay an employee for the first twenty-six weeks of illness and that an employee then moves on to an income continuance plan, if one exists. This is invariably linked to a pension scheme and is underwritten by an insurance company.

4 WORKING TIME

4.1 Background

J4.1.1 The Working Time Directive (Directive 93/104/EC) was implemented in Ireland by the Organisation of Working Time Act 1997.

The Act sets out the statutory rights of employees in relation to maximum working hours, minimum rest periods, holidays, night work, Sunday work and 'zero hour contracts' and replaces the myriad of legislation that had previously existed in this area.[1] The Organisation of Working Time Act 1997 applies to all employees working under a contract of employment. This includes all state employees and agency workers but does not apply to members of the police force or members of the defence forces.

[1] The Organisation of Working Time Act 1997 repeals the Conditions of Employment Acts 1936 and 1944, the Night Work (Bakeries) Acts 1936 and 1981, the Shops (Conditions of Employment) Acts 1938 and 1942, the Holidays (Employees) Acts 1973–1991 and the Worker Protection (Regular Part-time Employees) Act 1991, s 4 (which provided for annual leave and public holiday benefits for regular part-time employees).

4.2 Legislative Control

J4.2.1 The Organisation of Working Time Act 1997, s 15, provides that an employer shall not permit an employee to work more than an average of 48 hours in each seven-day period. In most cases, compliance with this is calculated over a reference period that does not exceed four months. However, in the case of employees whose place of work is distant from their own residence, or their work involves security and surveillance activities requiring a permanent presence, or it is subject to seasonality or foreseeable surges in activity, then a six month reference period may be used. In cases where a collective agreement has been entered into *and* approved by the Labour Court, it may be possible to use a maximum reference period of twelve months. The reference period cannot include statutory annual leave, sick leave, maternity or adoptive leave. However, it may include any leave that the employee is entitled to over and above the minimum statutory requirements.

J4.2.2 The 48-hour maximum working week came into effect on 1 March 1998. The maximum working hour provisions do not apply to certain categories of workers. These include junior hospital doctors, workers at sea, family employees working on a farm or in a private house (where the employee is employed by a relative and is a member of that relative's household). It also includes employees who determine the duration of their working time (other than any minimum period of time that is stipulated by their employer), whether or not provision enabling the employee to determine his/her own hours is made by the contract of employment.

4.3 Opting Out

J4.3.1 There is no right under Irish law for employees to opt out of the provisions of the Organisation of Working Time Act 1997.

4.4 Night-workers

J4.4.1 The Organisation of Working Time Act 1997, s 16, provides that 'night-time' means the period between midnight and 7:00 on the following day. 'Night-workers' are employees who normally work at least three hours of their daily working time during night time *and* whose annual number of hours worked at night equals or exceeds 50% of their annual working time. The maximum night-working time for night-workers generally is 48 hours per week, which is to be averaged over two months. However, this averaging period may be extended if specified in a collective agreement that is approved by the Labour Court. In general, night-workers are not permitted to work more than an average of eight hours per night over a two-month period but this may also be extended by a Labour Relations Commission approved collective agreement. 'Special category' night-workers are night-workers in relation to whom an assessment has been carried out pursuant to the Safety, Health & Welfare at Work Act 1989, s 28(1), which has indicated that their work involves special hazards or a heavy physical or mental strain. Such employees are not permitted to work in excess of eight hours night-work in any 24-hour period.

4.5 Rest Periods

J4.5.1 An employee should be entitled to a rest period of not less than 11 consecutive hours in each period of 24 hours during which they work for their employer. Employees are entitled to a rest of 15 minutes for every 4½ hours worked and are entitled to a 30-minute break for every six hours worked. Breaks at the end of the working day are not sufficient to comply with these provisions. Specific regulations may be made in respect of certain classes of employee eg shop workers.

J4.5.2 Employees must be granted a weekly rest period of 24 consecutive hours in addition to their daily rest period entitlements. Alternatively, an employer may decide to grant its employee two rest periods of 24 consecutive hours over a 14-day period. The weekly rest period must include a Sunday, unless the employee's contract of employment makes express provision for this. Therefore, if an employer requires an employee to work on a Sunday, they must put this in the contract of employment.

4.6 Paid Annual Leave

J4.6.1 The Organisation of Working Time Act 1997 removed the length of service qualification period that previously existed for holiday leave. The position is now that all employees whether full-time, part-time, temporary or casual, earn their holiday entitlements on a pro rata basis from the time that work is commenced. Most employees are entitled to four weeks annual holiday during each leave year. If an employee is ill during his/her annual leave, such days are not regarded as part of the holiday entitlement provided he/she furnishes the employer with a medical certificate. Where an employee has worked at least eight months in the year he/she is entitled to at least two weeks' unbroken holiday.

J4.6.2 It is important to note that the employer determines the timing of holidays. In doing so the employer can take into account work requirements, but they must also consider the need for the employee to reconcile work and any family responsibilities and the opportunities that are available to the employee for rest and recreation. The timing of holiday is also subject to the employer consulting with the employee or his trade union. Payment for holiday must be made in advance and should be calculated at the normal weekly rate (or, as the case may be, at a rate which is proportionate to the normal weekly rate). It is the employer's responsibility to ensure that the employee takes his full statutory leave allocation within the appropriate period. It is only possible for an employer to pay an employee wages in lieu of holidays if the employment relationship is terminated.

A   PUBLIC HOLIDAYS

J4.6.3   The Organisation of Working Time Act 1997 also provides for nine public holidays which are as follows: Christmas Day; St. Stephen's Day; St. Patrick's Day; Easter Monday; the first Mondays in May, June and August; the last Monday in October; and 1 January.

The Organisation of Working Time Act 1997, s 21, provides that in respect of each public holiday, an employee is entitled to:

(a) a paid day off on that day;
(b) a paid day off within a month of that day;
(c) an additional day of annual leave; or
(d) an additional day's pay.

J4.6.4   It is up to the employer to decide which of these, or combination of these, will be given to the employee. While there is no service requirement in respect of public holidays for full-time employees, other categories of employees are required to have worked at least 40 hours during the previous five weeks (ending on the day before the public holiday) in order to qualify for that public holiday. If the employment relationship is terminated during the week ending on the day before a public holiday, employees who have worked for the four preceding weeks are entitled to be paid for that public holiday. Church holidays, including Good Friday, are *not* public holidays and therefore employees do not have any entitlements by statute in relation to these days. An employer is required to retain whatever records are necessary to show that the Organisation of Working Time Act 1997 has been complied with for three years.

B   SUNDAY WORK

J4.6.5   The Organisation of Working Time Act 1997, s 14, provides that an employee who is required to work on a Sunday is entitled to an extra allowance, or an increased rate of pay, or paid time off work, or a combination of these based on whatever is reasonable having regard to all the circumstances.

C   ZERO-HOUR CONTRACTS

J4.6.6   Employees who are required to be available for work but where no work is guaranteed to them are entitled to be paid for 25% of the time for which they are required to be available for, or for 15 hours work, whichever is the lesser amount (Organisation of Working Time Act 1997, s 18). This provision effectively makes it economically unattractive for an employer not to give such an employee a minimum amount of work, as they will be paying them in any event. It should be noted that s 18 does not apply where the employee is not required to work due to lay off, or where the employee is being kept on short time for that week, or where it was due to exceptional circumstances or an emergency, or in cases where the employee would not have been available to work for the employer in that week due to illness or for any other reason. The Organisation of Working Time Act 1997, s 18(5), provides that being available on call for an emergency is not a 'zero hours' situation as it does not mean that the employee is available for work.

D   INFORMATION

J4.6.7   The Organisation of Working Time Act 1997, s 17, is particularly relevant to factory and shift workers as it provides that an employer must inform their employees at least 24 hours before the beginning of the week of their starting and finishing times for that week, including overtime requirements. This only applies in cases where no such information has been provided to the employee either in their contract or in a collective agreement. However, sub-s (4) makes provision for changes in the times or requiring the employee to work additional hours where circumstances which could not reasonably have been foreseen arise. It is sufficient notification if the information concerned is posted on a notice in a conspicuous position in the workplace.

5   EQUAL OPPORTUNITIES

5.1   Background

J5.1.1   The Irish Constitution, art 40.1, provides that all citizens, as human beings, shall be held equal before the law. In *Murtagh Properties Ltd v Cleary* [1972] IR 330 it was held that there was a constitutional right to earn a livelihood and that this applies equally to both men and women. However, it was not until Ireland joined the European Economic Community (the 'EEC'; now the European Union, the 'EU') and enacted the Anti-Discrimination (Pay) Act 1974 that the right to equal pay was established. On 1 October 1999, the Employment Equality Act 1998 came into effect.

J5.1.2   The Employment Equality Act 1998 repealed both the Anti Discrimination (Pay) Act 1974 and the Employment Equality Act 1977. The Employment Equality Act 1998, Part III, re-enacts into Irish law, Ireland's obligations under the Directives on Equal Pay (75/117) and Equal Treatment (76/207) as they apply to gender-based discrimination.

J5.1.3   The Employment Equality Act 1998, s 6, outlaws discrimination on the basis of gender, marital status, family status, sexual orientation, religion, age, disability, race and membership of the travelling community. This is taken to occur where, on any one of these grounds, a person is treated less favourably than another is, has been or would have been treated. Seven of these nine grounds for discrimination are new to Irish law, as previously only discrimination based either on gender or on martial status was actionable.

> **Example**
>
> *Medical Council v Barrington* (EE13/1988) concerned questions relating to sex or marital status which were allegedly put to a female applicant for a job during her interview. The Equality Officer found that, in the circumstances, the questions constituted discrimination in relation to access to employment (contrary to the Employment Equality Act 1977, s 3, which was in force at the time). The conclusion to be drawn from the Recommendation of the Equality Officer is that if, for pension-related purposes, an employer requires information on marriage or children, such information should only be requested from candidates who have received a job offer.

J5.1.4 The Employment Equality Act 1998, s 19, provides than men and women shall be entitled to the same rate of remuneration for 'like work' if they are employed by the same or an associated employer. The Employment Equality Act 1998, Part IV, carries the principle of equal pay for like work through to the non-gender categories.

J5.1.5 Although the Employment Equality Act 1998 alters the equality legislation that previously existed in Ireland, the changes in relation to gender discrimination reflect the provisions of the Treaty of Rome, the equal pay and equal treatment directives and the relevant case law from the European Court of Justice (ECJ). Relevant Irish case law under the Anti Discrimination (Pay) Act 1974 and the Employment Equality Act 1977, is cited where it is still applicable under the new Employment Equality Act 1998.

5.2 Unlawful Discrimination

A   DIRECT DISCRIMINATION

J5.2.1 The Employment Equality Act 1998, s 6(1), provides that discrimination occurs where 'one person is treated less favourably than another is, has been or would be treated'. This opens up more possibilities than the definition in the Employment Equality Act 1977, which confined the definition to the present tense, namely, where 'a person *is* treated less favourably' (emphasis added).

J5.2.2 The Employment Equality Act 1998 (EEA 1998) prohibits discrimination in relation to access to employment, conditions of employment, training or experience for or in relation to employment, promotion or re-grading, or classification of posts in relation to employees, prospective employees and agency workers (EEA 1998, s 8). Discrimination is also specifically prohibited in collective agreements in relation to the above and also in relation to equal pay for like work (EEA 19981998, s 9). Advertising relating to employment that indicates or might reasonably be understood to indicate an intention to discriminate is also prohibited (EEA 1998, s 10), as is discrimination by employment agencies against any person seeking their services or guidance (EEA 1998, s 11). The EEA 1998, s 12, prohibits discrimination in vocational training but it allows an exemption in relation to the training of nurses and primary school teachers only in relation to maintaining the religious ethos of the vocational training bodies. Discrimination by professional or trade organisations is also prohibited (EEA 1998, s 13).

Exception

J5.2.3   It should be noted that the Employment Equality Act 1998, s 25, permits discrimination where the sex of the employee amounts to an 'occupational qualification' for the post in question.

Positive discrimination

J5.2.4   The Employment Equality Act 1998, s 24(1), allows an employer to put in place positive action measures to promote equal opportunities, particularly those geared to remove existing inequalities that affect women's opportunities in access to employment, vocational training and promotion and working conditions. This provision is therefore a significant improvement on the Employment Equality Act 1977, which confined positive action measures to training.

J5.2.5   The Employment Equality Act 1998, s 33 provides that nothing in Part II (the general provisions in relation to discrimination) or in Part IV (specific provisions as to equality between other categories of persons) shall prevent measures which are intended to reduce or eliminate the effects of discrimination against persons who are or have attained the age of 50 years, or measures concerning persons with a disability or members of the travelling community to facilitate these persons either generally or in particular areas of the workplace.

J5.2.6   The Employment Equality Act 1998, s 33(3), allows the minister to provide training or work experience for a disadvantaged group of persons if he certifies that, in the absence of the provision in question, it is unlikely that that disadvantaged group would receive similar training or work experience.

B   INDIRECT DISCRIMINATION

J5.2.7   The Employment Equality Act 1998 defines indirect discrimination for the first time in Irish legislation. The Employment Equality Act 1998, s 22, defines it in relation to pay on the gender ground. Indirect discrimination occurs where a provision which applies to both sexes operates in such a way as to unfairly prejudice one sex over the other, and where such provision cannot be justified on objective grounds other than gender. Any such provision is prohibited in so far as it relates to equal treatment in employment, vocational training, employment by an agency, a professional body or a trade union.

J5.2.8   The Employment Equality Act 1998, s 31, prohibits indirect discrimination in relation to marital status, family status, sexual orientation, religion, age, disability, race and membership of the travelling community (the 'non-gender grounds').

C   VICARIOUS LIABILITY OF EMPLOYERS

J5.2.9   The Employment Equality Act 1998, s 15(1) provides that:

'Anything done by a person in the course of his or her employment shall, in any proceedings brought under this Act, be treated for the purposes of this Act as done also by that person's employer, whether or not it was done with the employer's knowledge or approval.'

J5.2.10   Any acts done by agents, who have either express or implied authority (whether precedent or subsequent) from another person, are to be treated as if the acts were also done by the principal (EEA 1998, s 15(2)). However, the EEA 1998, s 15(3), provides that it shall be a defence for the employer to prove that he or she took such steps as were reasonably practicable to prevent the employee from doing that act or, from doing the act in the course of his or her employment.

Example

In *Health Board v BC and the Labour Court* [1994] ELR 27 (High Court) the court held that the test of vicarious liability in this case was whether the employees were acting within the scope of their employment when they sexually harassed and assaulted a female employee. The Judge decided that, as he could not envisage any employment in which the employees were engaged in respect of which a sexual assault could be regarded as so connected with it as to amount to an act within its scope, that the employer could not be vicariously liable.

J5.2.11   It is also a defence for an employer if it can prove that it took such steps as were reasonably practicable to prevent the claimant from being treated differently in the workplace and to reverse the effects of it and to prevent the different treatment. An employer may of course be held liable in cases where it is guilty of discrimination. It is important to note that an employer may also be held liable for anything done by an employee, a client, customer or other business contact of the employer in cases where the employer ought reasonably to have taken steps to prevent it.

J5.2.12   For example, it constitutes discrimination by an employer on the gender ground in relation to the employee's conditions of employment if B sexually harasses A (the employee) at the workplace or otherwise in the course of A's employment and either:

(a) A and B are both employed at that place or by the same employer;
(b) B is A's employer; or
(c) B is a client, customer or other business contact of A's employer and the circumstances of the harassment are such that A's employer ought reasonably to have taken steps to prevent it (Employment Equality Act 1998, s 23(1)).

J5.2.13 The Employment Equality Act 1998, s 23(2), (without prejudice to the generality of sub-s (1)) provides that sexual harassment will constitute discrimination by the employer if:

- it sexually harasses the employee (whether or not in the workplace or in the course of employment); *and*
- the employee is treated differently in the workplace (or otherwise in the course of their employment) by reason of their reaction to the sexual harassment, or it could reasonably be anticipated that the employee would be so treated.

See also paras J5.2.25–J5.2.26 and para J5.2.30.

D   SEXUAL HARASSMENT

Definition of sexual harassment

J5.2.14 Sexual harassment is defined for the first time in Irish legislation in the Employment Equality Act 1998. It is outlawed in the workplace and in the course of employment whether it is carried out by an employer, another employee, or by clients, customers or business contacts.

The Employment Equality Act 1998, s 23(3), which defines sexual harassment, provides as follows:

'*For the purposes of this Act:*

(a) *any act of physical intimacy by B towards A;*

(b) *any request by B for sexual favours from A; or*

(c) *any other act or conduct of B (including, without prejudice to the generality, spoken words, gestures or production, display or circulation of written words, pictures or other material),*

shall constitute sexual harassment of A by B if the act, request or conduct is unwelcome to A and *could reasonably be regarded as* sexually, or otherwise on the gender ground, offensive, humiliating or intimidating to A' (emphasis added).

J5.2.15 The reasonable test definition adopted by the legislation is at odds with the previous case law on sexual harassment that had previously built up under the Employment Equality Act 1977 (which was repealed by the Employment Equality Act 1998). The old test ignored the intention of the alleged harasser and applied the subjective test of whether the claimant regarded the behaviour as sexually offensive, humiliating or intimidating. This new test looks instead to what a *reasonable* person would regard as sexual harassment.

J5.2.16 Most of the case law on sexual harassment relates either to working conditions or dismissal. The cases fall into two categories, namely 'quid pro quo' sexual harassment (which occurs where employment decisions affecting an employee are contingent on compliance with sexual demands) and 'hostile environment' sexual harassment (which occurs where offensive sex-based behaviour results in an abusive or demeaning work environment).

J5.2.17   The European Commission published its Code of Practice on the Dignity of Women and Men at Work in 1991 and the Irish Code, which was published in 1994, closely follows this. In both the European and Irish Codes, sexual harassment is broadly defined as:

> 'unwanted conduct of a sexual nature or other conduct based on sex affecting the dignity of women and men at work'.

J5.2.18   The Employment Equality Agency (the Agency), which is now the Equality Authority, made representations to the Irish Government prior to the Employment Equality Bill being signed into law. The Agency proposed the following alternative wording for the definition of sexual harassment:

> 'any act of physical intimacy by B towards A, *which A could reasonably consider* to be sexually offensive, humiliating or intimidating' (emphasis added).

J5.2.19   However, this wording of the definition was not accepted and instead the 'reasonable person' test was signed into law. A further request by the Agency to include same sex harassment (which is to be differentiated from harassment on the grounds of sexual orientation), which is covered in the Employment Equality Act 1998, s 32, was also rejected.

Common law duty of care

J5.2.20   At common law, an employer owes a general duty of care to his/her employees to take reasonable care for the employees' safety. The duty of care is discharged if the employer does what a reasonable and prudent employer would have done in the circumstances. In the case of sexual harassment, a victim may make a claim for personal injury based on alleged negligence or breach of duty of the employer which leads to stress, anxiety or other related problems. Such a claim must be brought within three years from the date of the cause of injury.

Safety, Health And Welfare At Work Act 1989

J5.2.21   The Safety, Health and Welfare at Work Act 1989, s 6(1), states that:

> 'It should be the duty of every employer to ensure, so far as is reasonably practicable, to provide for the safety, health and welfare at work of all his employees.'

J5.2.22   The Safety, Health and Welfare at Work (General Application) Regulations 1993 provide that:

> 'It should be the duty of every employer to ensure that:
> (a) In taking measures necessary for the safety and health protection of employees these measures take account of changing circumstances and the general principles specified in the First Schedule.'

J5.2.23   These Regulations provide, under General Principles of Prevention, Part (g), that:

> 'The development of adequate prevention policy in relation to safety, health and welfare which takes account of technology, organisation of work, working conditions, social factors and the influence of factors related to the working environment.'

J5.2.24 Therefore, there is an obligation on every employer to put in place a prevention policy to ensure that the health and well-being of employees within the workplace is protected. An employer who allows sexual harassment to take place could be regarded as not doing everything possible to protect the health, safety and well-being of his/her employees. It is clear therefore that employers have a duty to provide a safe working environment that extends to the emotional and mental well-being of their employees.

Policy on prevention of sexual harassment

J5.2.25

It is important that employers, employment agencies and vocational training bodies take such steps as are reasonably practicable to ensure a harassment free work environment. It is essential therefore to set down clearly defined procedures to deal with sexual harassment in the workplace, and the best way to do this is by setting out an unambiguous policy on prevention of sexual harassment. Employers who take a pro-active and vocal stance on sexual harassment will place themselves in a much stronger position with regard to defending any claims.

A policy should contain the following elements:

(1) The existence of the policy itself ought to be well publicised throughout the workplace so that it is clear that sexual harassment is unacceptable and will not be tolerated;

(2) Sexual harassment should be clearly and broadly defined;

(3) The policy should state the company's commitment to the prevention of sexual harassment and a willingness to resolve existing sexual harassment problems;

(4) Procedures should be developed for reporting and noting all incidents of sexual harassment, these should be user friendly and informal in the first instance and prompt and confidential investigation should be assured;

(5) A formal procedure for dealing with persistent and serious sexual harassment ought to be established which should provide for a written complaint procedure and a full and immediate investigation;

(6) A programme of support including counselling and advice should be available to those affected, this should include help for the victims and rehabilitative measures should also be undertaken for those engaged in sexual harassment in order to minimise the likelihood of it occurring again;

(7) The disciplinary procedures should be clearly set out and any such procedure should make it obvious that sexual harassment is a serious issue that can ultimately lead to dismissal;

(8) The principles of natural justice should be followed in dealing with any complaint and it should also be noted that any frivolous or vexatious allegations will also be treated as a disciplinary issue and that fair procedures will be followed in all instances;

(9) The effectiveness of the programme in preventing sexual harassment should be reviewed on a regular basis.

J5.2.26 The policy on prevention of sexual harassment should be included in the company's Safety Statement.

Importance of following natural justice and of informing employees of sexual harassment policy

> **Examples**
>
> In *Maurice O'Regan v Killarney Hotels Ltd* (UD786/93), an assistant head waiter who was accused of sexual harassment of a female member of staff, was awarded more than IR£11,000 (€13,967) when the Employment Appeals Tribunal found that he was unfairly dismissed. The Tribunal held that the hotel had failed to comply with the requirements of natural justice by not informing Mr O'Regan of the case against him or providing him with an opportunity to be heard in his own defence. The Tribunal also found that there was no evidence to show that following the incident the company put in place a programme to inform and educate its employees about sexual harassment so as to ensure a stress-free work environment for them. The Tribunal held that Mr O'Regan's dismissal was unfair. However, they deducted one-third of his compensation in respect of his own contribution to his dismissal.
>
> In January 1995, the Tribunal held in *Allen v Dunnes Stores Ltd* (5M7UD/94) that there is an onus on an employer to inform, educate and instruct its employees on sexual harassment and that the respondent's failure to do so was fatal to their case.
>
> In this case the claimant, James Allen, was employed as a security manager by Dunnes Stores Limited. Following a complaint made by one of the shop assistants that he commented on the perfume she was wearing and attempted to kiss her, the claimant was first suspended with pay and ultimately dismissed. The Tribunal held that sexual harassment is a broad category of offence and that there should therefore be a similarly broad range of penalties commensurate with the seriousness of the offence, that can be imposed in any particular instance. In this case, the dismissal was disproportionate to the behaviour complained of and therefore the Tribunal found that Dunnes Stores had unfairly dismissed Mr Allen.

Sexual harassment by e-mail

J5.2.27 As the definition of sexual harassment includes '*production, display or circulation of written words, pictures or other material*' and due to the increasing availability of e-mail in the workplace, it is possible that Irish case law will follow the trend established in America in relation to e-mail sexual harassment.

Sexual harassment by women

J5.2.28 In what is believed to be the first case in which a male employee was found to be sexually harassed by a female superior (contrary to the

Employment Equality Act 1977, s 3(4)) the Labour Court awarded IR£ 1,000 (€1,270) compensation to an apprentice graphic reproducer who was dismissed in March 1991. The company claimed that the employee had been dismissed due to poor work performance. However, he claimed that a female company director had sexually harassed him and that he was subjected to offensive comments of a sexual nature.

E   BULLYING IN THE WORKPLACE

Definition of bullying

J5.2.29   Bullying or harassment in the workplace is repeated aggression, verbal, psychological or physical, conducted by an individual or group against another person or persons. Isolated incidents of aggressive behaviour, while to be condemned, should not be described as bullying. Harassment is increasingly perceived as a problem in the workplace, with repercussions both for employers and employees.

Examples of bullying could include the following:

(a) publicly insulting a colleague;

(b) setting impossible work targets or objectives;

(c) dealing with a colleague through a third party so as to isolate them;

(d) taking credit for another persons work;

(e) undermining someone's authority in the workplace;

(f) subjecting an individual to unreasonable scrutiny; or

(g) excessive or unfair criticism about minor matters.

Anti-bullying policy

J5.2.30   All employers should have a policy to prevent and deal with harassment at work and management should be trained to deal with bullying complaints. If an employer does not have an anti-bullying policy they leave themselves vulnerable to claims against them, even in cases where the employer has no knowledge of the harassment until the claim is actually made. Employers should implement an anti-bullying policy along the same lines as a sexual harassment policy (see para **J5.2.25**). The penalties imposed must be proportionate to the bullying behaviour.[1]

[1]   See *Timmons v Oglesby & Butler Ltd* [1999] ELR 119, EAT.

Bullying guidelines

J5.2.31   The Health and Safety Authority introduced bullying guidelines in October 1998. They list the key areas to look out for in workplace bullying, vulnerable groups, characteristics of bullying and how to put an effective anti-bullying policy in place. They also state that this anti-bullying policy must be included in a company's safety statement and explain that, when examining safety statements, the Authority's Inspectors will have regard to this anti-bullying policy.

5.3 Disability Discrimination

J5.3.1 Disability discrimination is covered by the Employment Equality Act 1998 (see paras **J5.1.1–J5.2.8**).

5.4 Enforcement and Remedies

J5.4.1 An employee who feels that his dismissal has resulted from discrimination may appeal under the Employment Equality Act 1998 or the Unfair Dismissals Acts 1977–1993. An appeal under the 1998 Act may be of particular use where the employee has less than the qualifying period of service required by the Unfair Dismissals Acts 1977–1993 (one year's continuous service is required) and the dismissal is not pregnancy-related (such cases will automatically qualify). This is because there is no qualifying period of service under the Employment Equality Act 1998.

A DIRECTOR OF EQUALITY INVESTIGATION, THE LABOUR COURT AND THE CIRCUIT COURT

J5.4.2 The Employment Equality Act 1998 established the office of Director of Equality Investigation. The Director is effectively the first port of call for most claimants and is assisted by Equality Officers and Equality Mediation Officers. The Director is given extensive powers under the Employment Equality Act 1998, which include the ability to summon witnesses to answer questions and to issue warrants and enter premises to obtain information.

J5.4.3 Under the Employment Equality Act 1998, s 77, any person who claims that they have been discriminated against, that they are not receiving equal pay (or benefits) for equal work, or that they are being victimised, may seek redress by referring the case to the Director.

J5.4.4 If a person claims that they have been dismissed in circumstances that amount to discrimination or victimisation then they should apply directly to the Labour Court.

J5.4.5 If the claim relates to anything in the Employment Equality Act 1998, Part III, (specific provisions as to equality between woman and men) or in relation to any other circumstances where the Equal Pay Directive or the Equal Treatment Directive are relevant, then the case should be referred to the Circuit Court.

J5.4.6 In all cases outlined above, the claimant has six months from the date of the occurrence, or the most recent occurrence of the act of discrimination or victimisation to which the case relates, to refer the claim. However, if the Director, Labour Court or Circuit Court (as the case may be) is satisfied that exceptional circumstances prevented the case from being referred within the time, the time may be extended to a maximum of twelve months. Separate provisions apply to the defence forces, the police force and civil servants.

J5.4.7 If an employer or any other person, bound by the terms of either a final decision of the Director or a final determination of the Labour Court, fails to comply with the terms of the decision or determination, an application can be made under the Employment Equality Act 1998, s 91, to the Circuit Court (in certain circumstances) to have that decision enforced.

Redress

J5.4.8 The Employment Equality Act 1998, s 82, sets out (inter alia) the types of redress that the Director may order in cases of discrimination. These include an order for compensation in the form of arrears of remuneration or equal remuneration up to a maximum of three years. In other cases, the maximum amount which may be ordered by the Director or the Labour Court by way of compensation in relation to equal treatment is up to two years' pay, or up to IR£10,000 (€ 12,697) where the claimant is not an employee. The decision of the Director may be appealed to the Labour Court (within 42 days), which can offer the same types of redress and can also order the Director to investigate the claim further.

J5.4.9 In a dismissal case that is held before the Labour Court, an order for re-instatement or re-engagement may be made with or without compensation of up to two years' remuneration.

J5.4.10 The Employment Equality Act 1998, s 82(3), provides that similar orders of redress can be made in claims regarding gender, by bypassing the normal system and going straight to the Circuit Court. In such circumstances, the Circuit Court can award up to six years in arrears of remuneration and it is not subject to its normal jurisdictional limit of IR£30,000 (€38,092). An appeal then lies to the high court on a point of law (Employment Equality Act 1998, s 90(2)).

B   THE EQUALITY AUTHORITY

J5.4.11 The Employment Equality Act 1998, s 38, provides that the Employment Equality Agency[1] shall continue as a body and shall be known as the Equality Authority ('the Authority'). The aim of the Authority is to facilitate the enforcement of the Employment Equality Act 1998 by implementing strategic plans to achieve its key objectives.

[1]   The Employment Equality Agency was established by the Employment Equality Act 1977, s 34.

J5.4.12 The Authority's brief has been widened to include new powers to prepare legally recognised codes of practice (subject to approval by the minister) and to undertake equality reviews and action plans for businesses. The Authority may also serve non-discrimination notices and the Employment Equality Act 1998 makes it an offence not to comply with such notices.

Offences

J5.4.13 It is an offence to dismiss an employee in circumstances amounting to victimisation. It is sufficient in such circumstances to prove that the employee was dismissed and that the employee was victimised (as defined in paragraphs (a) to (d) of s 74(2)). On conviction of an offence under this section the court may, if it thinks fit, make an order for the re-instatement or re-engagement of the employee. The court may also decide to fine the employer (a maximum of IR£25,000 (€ 31,743) and/or 2 years imprisonment, if convicted on indictment) and can order the employer to pay the employee compensation.

C   RIGHT TO INFORMATION

J5.4.14   Section 76 of the 1998 Act provides for a right to information with a view to assisting a person who considers that another person may have discriminated against them or where they believe that there was victimisation. However, an employer is not required to furnish any reference or report relating to the character or the suitability for employment of any person (including the claimant) or to disclose the contents of such a reference or report. If information is denied to the person then the Director, Labour Court or Circuit Court may, in proceedings before them, make appropriate inferences from such a denial. There are specific arrangements covering the provision of information in the case of the Civil Service and Local Appointments Commission, the Garda Siochana and the Defence Forces.

J5.4.15   The Data Protection Bill, which is due to be published in mid 1999, will give effect to Directive 95/46/EC by extending the protection given to data subjects under the Data Protection Act 1988. While the 1988 Act only covers computer held files, the new Bill will cover all means of holding personal data (including manual files) and it will relate to all of a company's files on, inter alia, employees, former employees and interviewees.

5.5   Equal Pay

A   EQUAL PAY FOR LIKE WORK FOR MEN AND WOMEN

J5.5.1   The Treaty of Rome, art 119, requires each member state to maintain the application of the principle that men and women should receive equal pay for equal work. As discussed in at para **J5.1.4**, the Employment Equality Act 1998, s 19, provides that men and women shall be entitled to the same rate of remuneration for like work if they are employed by the same or an associated employer. The Employment Equality Act 1998, s 7(1), defines 'like work':

> '. . . another person shall be regarded as employed to do like work, if:

> (a) both perform the same work under the same or similar conditions, or each is interchangeable with the other in relation to the work;

> (b) the work performed by one is of similar nature to that performed by the other and the differences between the work performed are of small importance in relation to the work as a whole or occur with irregularity [so] as not to be significant to the work as a whole; or

511

(c) the work performed by one is equal in value to the work performed by the other, having regard to such matters as skill, physical or mental requirements, responsibility and working conditions.'

J5.5.2 The Employment Equality Act 1998, s 7(2), provides that the work which an agency worker is employed to do may only be compared with that of another agency worker and not with the work of a non-agency worker.

Example 1

In *Murphy v An Bord Telecom Eireann* [1988] ECR 673, the ECJ held that the fact that women employees did work of higher value than a male colleague who was paid more than the female employees should not prevent them claiming the same wages under equal pay legislation. This was incorporated into the Employment Equality Act 1998, s 7(3). This provides that if an employee is receiving less pay that a comparator, even though the work being performed by them is of greater value than that of the comparator, then the claimant's work should be regarded as being equal in value to the comparator's work. This therefore allows the employee to make a claim for equal pay for like work in such situations. Like work can be shown by making a comparison between the person claiming discrimination (the claimant) and another employee (a comparator) of the same or of an associated employer. However, the comparator must be employed at the same time as, or at any time within three years before or after, the claimant (Employment Equality Act 1998, s 19(2)).

Example 2

In *C & D Food Ltd v Cunnion* (High Court, Barron J, 30 July 1996) it was held that employers could still be in breach of the legislation where they face a claim from female workers for equal pay for like work even where other female workers are employed for the same remuneration as the male comparators. The High Court went on to hold that 'even where the employer genuinely believes that the value of the work being carried out by employees in one occupation is higher than the value of work being carried out by employees in another occupation, he cannot avail of that belief because ultimately what is like work is a matter not for the employer but for an Equality Officer or the Labour Court on appeal'.

Defence

J5.5.3 A good defence to a claim for equal pay for like work for men and women, would be to prove that the discrimination is based on grounds other than gender.[1]

[1] See eg *Flynn v Primark/Penneys* [1999] ILR 89, [1997] ELR 218, High Court.

Implied term

J5.5.4   The Employment Equality Act 1998, s 20, provides that where an employment contract does not include a term regarding equal pay for like work, such a term will be implied into the contract and it shall also override any express term which conflicts with this implied term. This follows on from the Anti-Discrimination (Pay) Act 1974, which provided that where an agreement contained a provision in which differences in rates of remuneration were based on, or related to, the sex of employees, such a provision was null and void (note that this proviso applied both to collective agreements and to orders made under other legislation).[1]

[1]   See Supreme Court case of *PMPA Insurance Co Ltd v Keenan* [1985] ILRM 173.

B   EQUAL PAY FOR LIKE WORK FOR THE NON-GENDER GROUNDS

J5.5.5   The Employment Equality Act 1998, s 29, extends the entitlement to equal pay for like work to the non-gender grounds (which are marital status, family status, sexual orientation, religious belief, age, disability, race and membership of the travelling community) where the comparator is employed by the same or an associated employer. The Employment Equality Act 1998, s 28, explains how the comparators are to be found in relation to these non-gender grounds.

Defence

J5.5.6   In the same way as with the gender issue, it is a good defence for an employer to show that the difference in pay is not based on any of the discriminatory grounds. There are certain exemptions provided for in the legislation, such as discrimination by religious, educational and medical institutions run by religious bodies. Requirements as to residency, citizenship or proficiency in the Irish language and some general exemptions in relation to age, family and disability are also given special treatment. Prior to the enactment of the Employment Equality Act 1998, a previous attempt to reform the law was struck down as being unconstitutional in part because it would have required employers to expend sums of money on employment premises to make them 'disability friendly'. Under the Employment Equality Act 1998 it is only necessary for an employer to do all that is *reasonable* to accommodate the needs of a person who has a disability. There is no need to provide special treatment or facilities if this would entail anything more than a 'nominal cost' to the employer. Anything more than this was thought to impinge on the constitutional property rights of the employer.

Implied term

J5.5.7   The Employment Equality Act 1998, s 30, provides that:

> 'If and so far as the terms of a contract of employment do not include (expressly or by reference to a collective agreement or otherwise) a non-discriminatory equality clause they shall be taken to include one'.

Example

In *Grant v South-West Trains Ltd* [1998] ECR I-621, the ECJ ruled that the refusal by an employer to allow travel concessions to persons of the same sex with whom a worker has a stable relationship, where such concessions were allowed to a worker's spouse or to a person of the opposite sex with whom a worker has a stable relationship outside marriage, does *not* constitute discrimination as prohibited by the EC Treaty, art 119, or the Equal Pay Directive (75/117/EEC). This is because it applies in the same way to female and male workers, since the concessions would be refused to a male worker who was living with a man, and they would also be refused to a female worker who was living with a woman.

J5.5.8   The current state of EU law is that stable relationships between two persons of the same sex are not regarded as equivalent to marriages or stable relationships outside marriage between persons of the opposite sex. However, the Employment Equality Act 1998 goes further than EU law in that it *(inter alia)* outlaws discrimination on the grounds of sexual orientation.

6   TERMINATION OF EMPLOYMENT

6.1   Background

J6.1.1   Most cases of termination concern a claim that an employee was unfairly or wrongfully dismissed. Providing that the employee has the requisite service, the former action will come before the Employment Appeals Tribunal (EAT) and the later action will come before the civil courts, principally the circuit or high courts with a final appeal to the Supreme Court.

6.2   Conditions

J6.2.1   Prior to the enactment of the unfair dismissals legislation, an employee who considered that they were wrongfully dismissed could only pursue an action to the courts for wrongful dismissal. This is a more lengthy and expensive process than an appeal before the EAT. The employee in a wrongful dismissal action is technically only entitled to damages in respect of his notice as provided under the contract of employment, if he did not receive that notice. An employee may also be entitled to other damages (eg relocation expenses) although proceedings are generally drafted to seek many and various forms of damage. In the UK case of *Malik v Bank of Credit and Commerce International SA (In Compulsory Liquidation)* [1997] IRLR 462, the plaintiff successfully obtained an award for 'stigma' damages.

J6.2.2   The majority of applications to the civil courts are taken by senior employees. This is a fact principally driven by costs. Actions may also be taken by employees who have less than the required service under the unfair dismissals legislation, but such cases are relatively infrequent. The civil courts have, however, become more frequently used in recent times by employees seeking to restrain the decision to dismiss.

6.3   Nature of Claims

J6.3.1   The Unfair Dismissals Act 1977 came into force on 15 April 1977. This Act allowed for the first time, an employee claiming unfair dismissal to be entitled to a statutory remedy of reinstatement or re-engagement or a maximum of 104 weeks' remuneration. This Act was amended in 1993 and applies to all dismissals on or after 1 October of that year.

J6.3.2   The substantive part of the Unfair Dismissals Act 1977 provides that all dismissals are deemed 'unfair' unless there were substantial grounds justifying the dismissal. A dismissal is automatically deemed unfair if it relates to any of the following:
- membership of a trade union or involvement in trade union activities;
- religious or political views;
- race, colour or sexual orientation;
- age;
- membership of the travelling community;
- dismissal arising out of pregnancy, maternity, adoptive leave and parental leave.

6.4   Fairness of Dismissal

J6.4.1   There is a presumption under the Unfair Dismissals Act 1977 that all dismissals are deemed unfair except: (i) where the dismissal is not in dispute (eg where the claimant has resigned and is claiming constructive dismissal); and (ii) where there are jurisdictional points at issue (eg the employees continuity of service or time limits). In cases where the employee proves that neither of the above applies, the burden of proof shifts onto the employer to prove that the dismissal was fair.

J6.4.2   In practically all situations of employment, an employer must be able to demonstrate that a fair procedure was applied. This means that an employee whose employment is in jeopardy must be made aware of all the evidence against him and be given reasonable opportunity to respond to any allegations.

J6.4.3   The Unfair Dismissals Act 1977, s 6, provides a number of grounds that may constitute a fair dismissal.

'(4) Without prejudice to the generality of sub-section 1(1) of this Section, the dismissal of an employee shall be deemed, for the purpose of this Act, not to be an unfair dismissal, if it results wholly or mainly from one or more of the following:

(a) the capability, competence or qualification of the employee for performing work of a kind which he was employed by the employer to do;

(b) the conduct of the employee;

(c) the redundancy of the employee, and the employee being unable to work or continue to work in a position which he held without contravention (by him or his employer) of a duty or restriction imposed by or under any statute or instrument made under statute.'

A   CAPABILITY

J6.4.4   The decided cases on capability or incapability invariably deal with the issue of illness and the unavailability of the employee to present himself for work.

J6.4.5   In the case of *Bolger v Showerings (Ireland) Ltd*[1] the key requirements to be met by an employer in order for a dismissal to be considered fair were set out, namely:
- it was the ill health which was the reason for the dismissal;
- that this was a substantial reason;
- that the employee receive fair notice that the question of his dismissal for incapacity was being considered;
- the employee was afforded the opportunity of being heard.

[1]   [1990] ELR 184.

B   COMPETENCE

J6.4.6   In the case of *Richardson v H Williams & Co Ltd*[1] the claimant was dismissed because the company had been dissatisfied with his work performance over a period. In this case, the Tribunal noted that the claimant was not given an opportunity to defend himself and applied the following the principles.

(a) When an employee has been given a justified warning that, unless his work improved in a specific area, his job would be in jeopardy, then it follows that such an employee must be given:
- a reasonable time within which to effect such an improvement;
- a reasonable work situation within which to concentrate on such defects.

(b) If an employee improves in the complained of area to the reasonable satisfaction of the employer, and the defect is not repeated, then such a warning cannot be solely relied on in relation to dismissal for other reasons.

[1]   UD17/1979.

J6.4.7   In the case of *O'Neill v Bus Eireann*[1] Judge O'Malley in the Circuit Court adopted the statement of Lord Denning in *Alidair Ltd v Taylor*[2] but with some reservations.

[1]   [1990] ELR 35.
[2]   [1978] ICR 445, CA.

J6.4.8   'Whenever a man is dismissed for incapacity or incompetence, it is sufficient that the employer honestly believes on reasonable grounds that the man is incapable or incompetent. It is not necessary for the employer to prove that he is in fact, incapable or incompetent.'

C   QUALIFICATIONS

J6.4.9   An employee may be fairly dismissed if he does not have the requisite qualifications for performing the work for which he was employed. In the case of *Ryder and Byrne v Comrs of Lights* (16 April 1980, unreported), High Court, Costello J, the employer had a requirement for two of its staff to obtain higher technical qualifications within a reasonable time. They failed to comply with the requirement and it was considered a fair dismissal.

D   CONDUCT

J6.4.10   An employee may be dismissed by reasons of their conduct or 'misconduct', although the term 'misconduct' is not contained in the Unfair Dismissals Act 1977. Misconduct is a very broad term and may include the following:
- abuse of sick pay schemes;
- clocking offence;
- conflict of interest;
- theft/irregularities;
- refusal to obey instructions;
- violence.

E   REDUNDANCY

J6.4.11   The redundancy of an employee may be a good defence to an unfair dismissals claim. Redundancy is defined as meaning one of the grounds of statutory redundancy in the Redundancy Payments Act 1967, s 7(2)(as amended by the Redundancy Payments Act 1971, s 4). See summary in para **J6.4.12**.

J6.4.12   An employee is dismissed by reasons of redundancy if dismissal is attributable wholly or mainly to:
- the fact that the employer has ceased or intends to cease to carry on a business for the purposes of which the employee was employed by it;
- the fact that the requirements of that business for employees to carry out work of a particular kind in the place where the employee was so employed has ceased or diminished;
- the fact that the employer has decided to carry on the business with fewer or no employees;
- the fact that the employer had decided that the work for which the employee had been employed should henceforth be done in a different manner for which the employee is not sufficiently qualified;
- the fact that the employer has decided that the work for which the employee has been employed should henceforth be done by a person who is capable of doing other work for which the employee is not sufficiently qualified or trained.

6.5   Remedies

J6.5.1   An employee who is unfairly dismissed is entitled to redress consisting of whatever the Rights Commissioner, the Employment Appeals Tribunal or the courts consider appropriate 'having regard to all the circumstances'. Such redress may be reinstatement, re-engagement or compensation. The Unfair Dismissals Act provides that where redress is being awarded, the Rights Commissioner, the Tribunal or the court has to give reasons in writing as to why either of the other two forms of redress was not awarded to the employee.

A   RE-EMPLOYMENT

J6.5.2   Re-employment orders by the EAT are given although they are not that frequent. A re-employment order is more likely to be applied to unskilled, semi-skilled or skilled workers in larger organisations than members of management or to those working for small businesses. This takes into account the obvious difficulties of the parties working together after one party has taken a case against the other.

B   REINSTATEMENT

J6.5.3   The Unfair Dismissals Act, s 7(1)(a), defines reinstatement as follows:

'Reinstatement by the employer of the employee in the position which he held immediately before his dismissal on the terms and conditions on which he was employed immediately before his dismissal together with a term that the reinstatement shall be deemed to have commenced on the day of the dismissal.'

In effect, reinstatement means that an employee who has been unfairly dismissed is awarded his/her old position back immediately as if he/she had never been dismissed. It is usually awarded where there is no blame attributable to the employee. This means that loss of earnings must also be paid to the former employee. This would also include loss of pension contributions, if appropriate.

REDUNDANCY AND COLLECTIVE DISMISSALS

6.6   Background

J6.6.1   The statutory definition of redundancy is referred to at paras **J6.4.11–J6.4.12**. The Protection of Employment Act 1977 (as amended by the Protection of Employment Order 1996 (SI 1996/370)) provides for the procedural requirements when collective redundancies occur. Collective redundancies mean dismissals arising from redundancy during any period of 30 consecutive days where the employees to be made redundant are:

- 5 employees in an establishment employing 21 to 49 employees;
- 10 employees in an establishment normally employing 50 to 99 employees;
- 10% of employees in an establishment normally employing 100 to 299 employees;
- 30 employees in an establishment normally employing 300 or more employees.

A   STATUTORY RIGHTS

J6.6.2   An employee with 104 consecutive weeks' service with his employer who is advised of his redundancy, is entitled to statutory redundancy payments as follows:

- half a week's normal weekly remuneration for each year of continuous service between 16 years and their 41st birthday; plus
- one week's normal weekly remuneration for each year of continuous service between 41 and 66 years; plus
- the equivalent of one week's normal weekly remuneration.

J6.6.3   Statutory redundancy payments are tax-free in the hands of the employee. Providing the employer has given appropriate notice to his employees and, in a collective redundancy situation, to the Minister for Enterprise, the employer may be entitled to a rebate of up to 60% of the statutory redundancy payments paid to his employees.

B   EX GRATIA PAYMENTS

J6.6.4   In redundancy situations it is not unusual that payments in addition to the minimum statutory sums are also made to employees. This ex gratia sum is fully paid for by the employer, there is no rebate from the state. Depending on the size of the ex gratia payment, it may be taxable in the hands of the employee. The Taxes (Conciliation) Act 1997 (as amended) provides for certain further allowances (in addition to the statutory redundancy payments) for employees on termination of employment. The first IR£8,000.00 of a termination payment together with IR£600.00 for each complete year of service, may be paid tax-free. There is a further potential allowance of IR £4,000.00 provided that the employee has never claimed that extra relief before, giving a total of IR£12,000.00 tax-free.

6.7   Consultation

J6.7.1   The Protection of Employment Act 1977 provides that an employer proposing to create collective redundancies must initiate consultations with 'employees' representatives' with a view to reaching an agreement. 'Employees' representative(s)' means a trade union or staff association where the person or persons chosen by the employees is likely to be affected by the redundancies to represent them.

J6.7.2   The consultation should take place at the earliest opportunity and at least 30 days before the first dismissal takes effect. The subject matter of the consultation includes the possibility of avoiding the proposed redundancies by reducing the number of employees to be dismissed or the re-employment or retraining of employees to be made redundant. The employer is obliged to provide the employees' representatives with all information in writing in relation to the proposed redundancies including: the reason, the number and description of categories of employees; the period in which it is proposed to effect the redundancies; the criteria proposed for the selection of workers to be made redundant; and the method for calculating redundancy payments other than the method set out in the Redundancy Payments Act 1967–1991, or if an ex gratia payment is to be made, the basis of calculation must be given. An employer who does not comply with this consultation process is guilty of an offence and is liable to a fine of up to IR£500.00.

J6.7.3 There is also an obligation on the employer to notify the Minister for Enterprise, Trade and Employment of the proposed redundancies at the earliest opportunity, but at least 30 days before the first dismissal takes effect. An employer who breaches this requirement may be guilty of an offence and liable to a fine of up to IR£500.00. As the employer is required to give the employees information, he is also required to give certain particulars to the Minister including: the name and address of the employer; the total number of persons to be made redundant; the reasons for the collective redundancies; names and addresses of any trade union or staff associations; the date on which consultation with each trade union or staff association commenced; and the progress achieved in those consultations to the date of notification.

7 YOUNG WORKERS

7.1 General Obligations

J7.1.1 The Protection of Young Persons (Employment) Act 1996 came into effect on 2 January 1997. This gave effect to Directive 94/33/EC on the protection of young people at work. The 1996 Act repeals and replaces the protection of Young Persons' (Employment) Act 1977.

J7.1.2 The Protection of Young Persons (Employment) Act 1996 increases the minimum legal full-time working age from 15 to 16 and sets out the rules regarding hours, rest breaks and the duties of employers. The legislation forbids children and young persons from being employed for night-work except in certain limited circumstances. There is a prohibition on double employment, unless the total hours worked do not exceed the maximum allowed under the Protection of Young Persons (Employment) Act 1996. Every employer is required to display a prescribed abstract of the 1996 Act at the principle entrance to the premises where persons under 18 are employed.

A YOUNG PERSONS

J7.1.3 The Protection of Young Persons (Employment) Act 1996 provides that 'young persons' (those who have reached 16 years or the school leaving age, but are less than 18 years of age) may not work more than 40 hours per week or 8 hours per day. They are not permitted to work between 22:00 and 6:00, unless there is no school the next day, in which case they can work until 23:00 (but not before 1:00 the following morning). In all cases, they must be given a minimum rest period of 12 hours each day, a minimum break of 30 minutes after every four-and-a-half hours of work and have a two-day rest period each week. These times do not apply to the fishing or shipping industries.[1]

[1] The Protection of Young Persons (Employment) (exclusion of workers in the fishing and shipping sectors) Regulations, 1997 (SI 1997/1).

B CHILDREN

J7.1.4 The Protection of Young Persons (Employment) Act 1996 also provides that, except in certain circumstances, children (persons under 16 years of age or of school leaving age, whichever is the higher) may not work. However, it is possible, if specific provisions are complied with, to employ a child who is over 14 years of age to do night-work outside the school term. A child over 15 may also do such work for up to eight hours a week during the school term.

C   EMPLOYERS' DUTIES

J7.1.5   An employer who wishes to employ a child or young person must first obtain:

1.
    (a)   a copy of their birth certificate; or
    (b)   other satisfactory evidence of age; *and*
2.   written permission from their parent or guardian.

J7.1.6   The employer must maintain a register containing, in relation to each child or young person, the details of time worked, rates of pay and total pay. This register must be retained for at least three years in order to show compliance with the Protection of Young Persons (Employment) Act 1996.

D   EXCLUSIONS

J7.1.7   Persons who employ close relatives do not have to comply with the provisions in relation to prohibition of employment of children, the duties of an employer to obtain details in relation to date of birth, minimum hours and inclusion of time on vocational training as working time. The defence forces do not have to comply with the hours of work and night-work provisions in certain circumstances (the minimum age for recruitment is 17).

J7.1.8   The Minister for State and the Department of Enterprise, Trade and Employment may authorise by a licence and by regulation the employment of children in cultural, artistic, sport and advertising activities in cases where these are not harmful to the safety, health or normal development of the children and where they are not likely to interfere with attendance at school, vocational guidance or training programmes.

E   COMPLAINTS

J7.1.9   The Protection of Young Persons (Employment) Act 1996 allows the parent or guardian of a child or young person to present a written complaint to a Rights Commissioner within six months[1] where the employer has penalised a child or young person for not allowing the employer to breach the 1996 Act, or where the employer has used the commencement of the 1996 Act to reduce the terms and conditions of employment. The Rights Commissioner's recommendation may be appealed to the Employment Appeals Tribunal. If the Rights Commissioner's recommendation is not carried out and the time limit for appeal has expired, the case can still be referred to the Tribunal who will issue a determination in the same terms as the Rights Commissioner's recommendation. In such circumstances, the

Tribunal will not hear evidence from the employer except that regarding the non-implementation of the Rights Commissioner's recommendation.

¹ This time limit can be extended by the Rights Commissioner for a further six months in exceptional circumstances.

F   OFFENCES

J7.1.10   If a person is guilty of an offence under the Protection of Young Persons (Employment) Act 1996, they shall be liable, on summary conviction, to a fine not exceeding IR£1,500.00 (€1,800.00). If there is a continuation of the offence, the offender shall be liable to a fine of IR£250.00 (€300.00) per day for every day that the offence continues.

G   SAFETY, HEALTH AND WELFARE AT WORK

J7.1.11   The Safety, Health and Welfare at Work (General Application) Regulations 1993,¹ reg 10, which came into effect on 18 February 1993, provides that every employer must have a written assessment of the risks to safety, health and must provide for protective measures, in the preparation of the safety statement.

¹ SI 1993/44.

J7.1.12   The Protection of Young Persons (Employment) Act 1996 provides that an employer must carry out a risk assessment before employing any children or young persons and at any stage where there is a change in conditions.¹ The risk assessment should relate to the child/young person's lack of maturity or experience as regards exposure to physical, biological and/or chemical agents or work processes.

¹ See the Safety, Health and Welfare (Children and Young Persons) Regulations 1998 (SI 1998/504).

J7.1.13   If the finding is that the work is beyond the child/young person's capacity or involves certain risks, then he/she should not be employed. If there is a risk, but the child is being employed, the child and his/her parent or guardian must be informed of this and the child's health must be monitored. In cases where any night-work is being undertaken by a child or young person, they must be given a free assessment of their health prior to the commencement of any such work. The results of the test must be given to the employee and his/her parent or guardian.

8   MATERNITY AND PARENTAL RIGHTS

8.1   Background

J8.1.1   The Maternity Protection Act 1994 repealed the Maternity Protection of Employees Acts 1981-1991. The 1994 Act was intended, along with the Safety, Health and Welfare at Work (Pregnant Employees) Regulations 1994 and the EC (Social Welfare) Regulations 1994, to give effect to the Pregnant Workers Directive (92/85/EEC) of 19 October 1992.

J8.1.2   The Maternity Protection Act 1994 came into effect on 30 January 1995. The 1994 Act aims to provide protection for all pregnant employees, employees who have recently given birth and employees who are breast-feeding. It also covers fathers (where the mother has died) for the balance of the maternity leave or additional maternity leave. The rights provided under the Maternity Protection Act 1994 are available to all female employees who have notified their employer of their condition. They are available equally to part-time and full-time employees, employees on agency contracts or on fixed-term contracts and to apprentices. They are available to all civil servants, members of the police force and the defence forces and there is no length of service requirement.

8.2   General Rights

J8.2.1   The Maternity Protection Act 1994 provides the right not to be dismissed because of pregnancy (see also paras **J8.3.1–J8.3.2**) and the right to be reinstated in the same job or suitable alternative work at the end of protective leave (Maternity Protection Act 1994, ss 26–27). The 1994 Act also provides for a minimum period of maternity leave of 14 consecutive weeks (Maternity Protection Act 1994, s 8). At least four weeks of the maternity leave must be taken prior to the end of the expected week of confinement and at least four weeks is to be taken after the end of the expected week of confinement (Maternity Protection Act 1994, s 10). If the baby arrives late and the employee is left with less than four weeks at the end of maternity leave, then the leave can be extended up to a maximum of four weeks.

J8.2.2   Maternity Protection Act 1994, s 14, provides for an additional maternity leave of four weeks (after the 14-week period). This is not subsidised by the state. This additional maternity leave is subject to notification in writing when giving the initial notice of intention to take maternity leave or, not later than four weeks before the date on which the employee would have been expected to return to work, had she not taken the additional maternity leave.

J8.2.3   The period of employment prior to maternity leave is regarded as continuous with post-maternity leave employment. Therefore, it is taken into account when calculating a period of continuous employment under the Minimum Notice and Terms of Employment Acts 1973–1991, the Unfair Dismissal Acts 1977–1993 and the Redundancy Payments Acts 1967–1991. The employees' holiday entitlement is not affected by a period of maternity leave, as there is no break in continuity.

A   PATERNITY LEAVE

J8.2.4   An extremely limited form of paternity leave is provided under the Maternity Protection Act 1994, s 16. Employed fathers are entitled to the remainder of the mother's leave if the mother dies before the tenth week of confinement or, if she dies after the tenth week, the father can obtain leave ending on the fourteenth week following the week of her confinement. This entitlement is subject to written notification of the mother's death, the birth of the child and of the length of leave to which he believes he is entitled, being furnished to the employer as soon as the father intends to take leave. Copies of the death certificate of the mother and the birth certificate of the child should be provided to the employer as soon as possible. The father may be entitled to a further four weeks' leave where he commences the leave before the tenth week following confinement. He must notify his employer of his intention to take such additional leave at least four weeks prior to his expected date of return to work (see also paras **J8.6.1–J8.6.13**).

B   ANTENATAL AND POSTNATAL CARE

J8.2.5   Since 30 January 1995, pregnant employees have been entitled to paid time off work during normal working time for antenatal medical or related appointments. This is subject to an employee giving written notice of the date and time of the appointment to her employer at least two weeks beforehand. However, in cases where the appointment is urgent, the employee should advise her employer within one week after the appointment and should explain the circumstances for the non-compliance. The paid time-off for postnatal care applies for up to fourteen weeks following the birth of the baby. The employer may require the employee to produce an appointment card stating the time and date of the appointment and confirming the pregnancy or specifying the expected week of confinement.

C   RIGHT TO RETURN TO WORK AFTER MATERNITY LEAVE

J8.2.6   It is important to note that there is no automatic right to return to work after pregnancy. The right to return to work only exists if the employee exercises it. In order to exercise the right, the employee must give her employer prior notice in writing of the intention to return to work, not later than four weeks before the date on which she expects to return.[1] This four-week time limit may be extended by a Rights Commissioner or the Employment Appeals Tribunal if there are reasonable grounds to do so (Maternity Protection Act 1994, s 28(2)). In the absence of reasonable grounds, the failure to give the required notification may be taken into account if the employee is dismissed and there is a claim for unfair dismissal.

[1]   Maternity Protection Act 1994, s 28.

D   NOTICE REQUIREMENTS

J8.2.7   It is primarily the rather complex sections of the Maternity Protection Act 1994 which deal with the giving of notice and the manner in which notice has to be given by the employee that have given rise to appeals before the Employment Appeals Tribunal. In *Ivory v Ski-Line Ltd* [1989] ILRM 433, the High Court confirmed that the requirement in the Maternity Protection Act 1981, s 22(1) (which was replaced by the Maternity Protection Act 1994, s 27) is mandatory and a condition precedent to an entitlement to return to work.

8.3   Protection from Dismissal

J8.3.1   The Maternity Protection Act 1994 provides the right not to be dismissed because of pregnancy (see para **J8.2.1**).

J8.3.2   Any purported termination of the employment contract while the employee is absent from work on maternity leave, additional maternity leave, paternity leave or health and safety leave under the Maternity Protection Act 1994, s 18, or leave during natal care, is void (Maternity Protection Act 1994, s 23). For such notice to be effective, the employer must serve a new notice of termination on the employee on his/her return to work. If an employee is employed under a fixed-term contract that is due to expire during the maternity or health and safety leave period, protection under the Maternity Protection Act 1994 also expires on that date.

8.4   Health and Safety

J8.4.1   The Maternity Protection Act 1994, s 18, provides for health and safety leave where there is a risk to a pregnant employee, to one who has recently given birth (ie has given birth not more than 14 weeks earlier) or to one who is breast-feeding (ie has given birth at least 26 weeks earlier and is breast-feeding). In all cases, it is necessary for the employee to have informed her employer of her condition.

A   RISK ASSESSMENT

J8.4.2   Employers have a duty under the Safety, Health and Welfare at Work (General Application) Regulations 1993, reg 10, to carry out a risk assessment of the risks to safety and health and must provide for protective measures in the preparation of a safety statement. In addition to this, employers must carry out a risk assessment in relation to the health and safety of employees who are pregnant, have recently given birth or are breast-feeding.

J8.4.3   The employer must assess the risk resulting from any activity at the employee's place of work which is likely to involve the risk of exposure to a potentially harmful agent, process or to hazardous working conditions. The employer must then take preventative and protective measures to ensure the health and safety of pregnant and breast-feeding employees and employees who have recently given birth.

J8.4.4   Where the risk assessment reveals a risk to the employee's safety or health, and protective or preventative measures are not practicable, then the working conditions or hours of the employee should be adjusted so that the exposure to such risk is avoided. Where that is not possible, the employee should be provided with other work.

B   ENTITLEMENT TO HEALTH AND SAFETY LEAVE

J8.4.5   An employee (who is pregnant, has recently given birth or is still breast-feeding) is entitled to health and safety leave where:
(1) The employer is required to move an employee from her normal work as a result of a risk assessment or because the employee can not be required to perform night work; *and*
(2) (a)   it is not technically or objectively feasible for the employer to move the employee as required by the regulations; *or*

(b)   such a move cannot reasonably be required on duly substantiated grounds; *or*

(c)   other work to which the employer proposes to move the employee is not suitable for her (this is a subjective test).

J8.4.6   Where an employee is granted health and safety leave under the Maternity Protection Act 1994, s 18, she is entitled to request a certificate from her employer stating that she has been granted leave and specifying the date on which leave began and its expected duration.

J8.4.7   The employer must *pay* the employee for the first 21 days of health and safety leave and the employee is entitled to a social welfare payment in respect of the balance of time on which she is on this leave. The employee must, as soon as is reasonably practicable, notify the employer when she is no longer vulnerable to the risk. The employer shall then notify the employee in writing that she can resume work in her job and the leave shall end within seven days (or earlier) of such notification.

C   NIGHT-WORK

J8.4.8   'Night-work' is where at least three hours of an employee's work is usually between 23:00 and 6:00 the following morning, or where at least 25% of the employee's monthly working time is during these hours. Employers must transfer an employee to day work if she obtains a doctor's certificate stating that she should not perform night-work during pregnancy or within 14 weeks of the birth. If this is not possible she must be granted leave or extended maternity leave. The Workplace Regulations 1993,[1] Sch 4, provides that pregnant women and nursing mothers shall be able to rest in appropriate conditions.

[1]   SI 1993/44.

8.5   Maternity Pay

J8.5.1   There is no obligation on an employer to pay an employee during maternity leave. An employee will be entitled to state maternity benefit under the social welfare legislation if she has 39 weeks' contributions in the twelve months immediately proceeding the first day of maternity leave[1] (or if she has at least 39 weeks' contributions since starting work and has at least 39 weeks paid or credited in the relevant tax year before maternity leave commences). In such cases, the state will pay the employee 70% of her gross weekly earnings, subject to a minimum of IR£86.70 (€110.09) and a maximum of IR£162.80 (€206.71) (based on earnings of up to IR£12,094.00 per annum).

[1]   Social Welfare (Consolidation) Act 1981, s 25, as amended by the Social Welfare Act 1987, s 8.

J8.5.2   Since 9 June 1997, self-employed persons who have 52 paid contributions in either of the two complete contribution years preceding the beginning of the benefit year in which the confinement begins, are entitled to 14 weeks maternity benefit.[1]

[1]   Social Welfare Act 1997.

8.6   Additional Rights to Time Off

J8.6.1   The Parental Leave Act 1998, which was intended to implement the Directive on parental leave (96/34/EEC), came into operation on 3 December 1998. The two main purposes of the 1998 Act are as follows:

(i)   to entitle male and female employees to avail themselves of unpaid leave from employment to enable them to take care of their young children; and

(ii) to provide for a limited paid force majeure leave to enable employees to deal with family emergencies resulting from the injury or illness of a family member.

A   PARENTAL LEAVE

J8.6.2   The law currently provides that an employee who has completed one year's continuous employment is entitled to 14 weeks' unpaid leave in respect of each child under the age of five years who was born or adopted on or after 3 June 1996.[1] The purpose of this leave is to enable the employee to take care of the child and if the employer has reasonable grounds for believing that the leave is being abused it is possible to terminate the leave by giving the requisite notice. The 14 weeks' leave may be taken in one continuous period or the employee may agree with the employer to take the leave in the form of days or hours of work. Employees who have not yet completed one year's continuous service, but who have completed three months employment, are entitled to one week's leave for each month of continuous employment completed. An employee is not entitled to take more than 14 weeks' parental leave in any 12-month period. While each parent has a separate entitlement to parental leave from their job, the leave is not transferable (either in whole or in part) between parents. Any public holidays that fall during the period of parental leave are added to the end of parental leave. An employee may not take more than 14 weeks' parental leave in any period of 12 months, unless the employer agrees to waive this restriction. In the case of children of a multiple birth, this restriction does not apply. While parental leave is unpaid, the employee retains their other employment rights (other than the right to remuneration and superannuation benefits).

[1]   Officials from the employment and social affairs section of the European Commission have recently issued a 'Reasoned Opinion' (April 2000) which noted that 'by restricting the rights to parental leave to employees with children born on or after 3 June 1996' Ireland had not fully complied with the obligations in D96/34/EC (Parental Leave Directive). The Irish Department of Justice is now examining the 'Reasoned Opinion' with a view to identifying the measures required to be put in place in order to conform.

B   PROCEDURAL REQUIREMENTS

J8.6.3   An employee must give his/her employer six weeks' written notice prior to taking leave to enable the employer to make alternative arrangements for the performance of the employee's job. This notice must specify the date the employee intends to commence parental leave, the duration of the leave and the manner in which the employee proposes to take the leave.

J8.6.4 The employer must sign a Confirmation Document, confirming agreement to the parental leave, not less than four weeks before the leave begins. The employer is entitled to postpone parental leave if it would have a substantial adverse effect on the business concerned. The postponement may be to an agreed date not later than six months from the intended start of parental leave. The employer may only postpone it once unless the reason for the postponement is 'seasonal variations in the volume of work', in which case it can be postponed twice.

J8.6.5 Where an adopted child is three or more years old but is less than eight years old at the time of the adoption, the parental leave must be taken within two years of the date of the adoption order. In the case of an adopted child who is under three years of age at the time of adoption, the parental leave must be taken before the child is five.[1]

[1] This requirement will have to change as a result of the European Commissions 'Reasoned Opinion'. When the Irish government gives effect to the finding, parents of all children up to the age of seven will be entitled to avail themselves of parental leave as the measure is retrospectively applied to children born after 1993.

C   RETURNING TO WORK AFTER PARENTAL LEAVE

J8.6.6 Parental Leave Act 1998, s 14, provides that an employee on parental leave is to be regarded as still working and that none of the employee's rights relating to employment are to be effected by the leave (other than the right to remuneration and superannuation benefits).

D   FORCE MAJEURE LEAVE

J8.6.7 Force majeure leave is available when the injury or illness of specified close relatives requires the immediate presence of the employee. This is a paid leave for up to three days in any period of twelve months, or for up to five days in any period of 36 months. While there is no requirement to produce a medical certificate in relation to the leave, the employee must confirm to his/her employer that they have taken force majeure leave and set out the facts entitling them to the leave as soon as reasonably practicable.

E   DISPUTES AND APPEALS

J8.6.8 Claims in relation to any disputes regarding either parental or force majeure leave must be brought within six months and are, in general, dealt with by a Rights Commissioner. The Rights Commissioner is empowered to hear the parties to the dispute and to receive any relevant evidence tendered.

J8.6.9 Where either party is dissatisfied with the decision of the Rights Commissioner, they may appeal to the Employment Appeals Tribunal within four weeks of the date of the recommendation. A determination of the Tribunal may be appealed to the High Court on a point of law. In relation to parental leave, the award may be in the form of parental leave or monitory compensation, up to a maximum of 20 weeks pay, or both.

F   ADOPTIVE LEAVE

J8.6.10   The Adoptive Leave Act 1995 came into force on 20 March 1995. Prior to this, there was no statutory requirement to provide parents who were adopting children with any leave from work. The 1995 Act includes several similar provisions to those contained in the Maternity Protection Act 1994, thus going some way to address the inequality that had hitherto existed between the treatment of natural mothers and adopting mothers.

J8.6.11   Adopting mothers are, however, only entitled to ten consecutive weeks' leave from work rather than the 14 weeks' leave which are afforded to natural mothers. The justification for this is that the first four weeks of the natural mothers' leave (which are to be taken prior to the date of confinement) are intended to be for medical purposes. The adoptive mother is entitled to a social welfare allowance during her leave, based on the Social Welfare Act 1995, s 11.

J8.6.12   A further period of four weeks' unpaid leave is provided for under the Adoptive Leave Act 1995, s 8. The special circumstances of foreign adoptions are recognised by s 8(5), which allows some or all of this additional leave to be taken prior to the date of placement of the child.

J8.6.13   Adoptive fathers are only entitled to adoptive leave where the adopting mother has died either before or during the adoptive leave. The Adoptive Leave Act 1995, s 6, provides that the sole male adopter is then treated in the same way as an adopting mother.

9   BUSINESS TRANSFERS

9.1   Background

J9.1.1   The European Communities (Safeguarding of Employees' Rights on Transfer of Undertakings) Regulations 1980 implement the Transfer of Undertakings Directive 77/187/EEC and came into force on 3 November 1980.

J9.1.2   The European Communities (Safeguarding of Employees' Rights on Transfer of Undertakings) Regulations 1980, reg 5, states that:

> 'The transfer of an undertaking, business or part of a business shall not in itself constitute grounds for dismissal by the transferor or the transferee.'

J9.1.3   However, if a dismissal can be proven to be as a result of *'economic, technical or organisational reasons'*, then the dismissal will be treated as a redundancy.

9.2   Identifying a relevant transfer

J9.2.1   Although the case law in this area is still evolving, the test as to whether a transfer falls within the ambit of the European Communities

(Safeguarding of Employees' Rights on Transfer of Undertakings) Regulations 1980 is:

(a) has there been a change in the entity/person who is responsible for running the business?; or
(b) is the business being transferred as a going concern?; or
(c) has the business retained its identity?[1]

[1] It was held in the case of *Francisco Hernandez Vidal SA v Gómez Pérez* [1999] IRLR 132, ECJ that 'the decisive criterion for establishing if a transfer of undertaking' had occurred was 'whether the entity in question retains its identity'.

J9.2.2 In this jurisdiction, recent case law suggests that it is sufficient that only one of these tests need be met for the Transfer of Undertakings Directive 77/187/EEC to apply.[1]

[1] In the case of *Mary Cannon v Noonan Cleaning Ltd and CPS Cleaning Services Ltd* [1988] ELR 153, there was no transfer of physical assets, no transfer of goodwill, but the undertaking was deemed to have retained its identity and came within the Transfer of Undertakings Directive 77/187/EEC.

J9.2.3 As well as determining whether the undertaking has retained its identity and is being transferred as a going concern, the following aspects of the transferring business should be considered:

(a) are the actual assets being transferred?[1]
(b) are the customers being transferred?
(c) is the goodwill being transferred?

[1] *JMA Spijkers v Gerbroeders Benedict Abbatoir CV* [1986] ECR 1119, ECJ, where it was held that the transferring of physical assets gave a strong indication that the transfer fell within the ambit of the Transfer of Undertakings Directive 77/187/EEC. In *Christel Schmidt v Spar-und Leihkasseder Fruheren Amter Bordesholm, Kiel and Cronshagen* [1994] IRLR 302, ECJ, it was held that the lack of physical assets transferring did not prevent the transfer coming within the 1977 Directive. See also the case of *Merchx and Nevhuys* [1996] IRLR 467, ECJ.

J9.2.4 A transfer of one of these entities on their own may be insufficient to come within the ambit of the European Communities (Safeguarding of Employees' Rights on Transfer of Undertakings) Regulations 1980.

SERVICE PROVIDERS

J9.2.5 The European Court of Justice (ECJ) in two recent decisions *(Hernandez I* and the double-case of *Sánchez Hildago v Asociación de Servicios Aser and Sociedad Cooperativa Minerva* [1999] IRLR 136, ECJ) confirmed that the transfer of services between sub-contractors fell within the scope of the Transfer of Undertakings Directive 77/187/EEC on the basis that there was a transfer of an economic entity.

The EJC held that 'an economic entity refers to an organised grouping of persons and assets enabling the economic activity which pursues a specific objective to be exercised. Whilst such an entity must be sufficiently structured and autonomous it will not necessarily have significant tangible or intangible assets. In certain sectors such as cleaning and surveillance, the activity is essentially based on manpower. Thus, an organised grouping of wage earners who are specifically and permanently assigned to a common task may in the absence of other factors of production, amount to an economic entity.'

9.3 Affected Employees

J9.3.1 The Acquired Rights Directive 98/50/EC (which became operative on 29 June 1998) defines '*an employee*' as any person who is protected as an employee under the national law of the member state.

J9.3.2 The European Communities (Safeguarding of Employees' Rights on Transfer of Undertakings) Regulations 1980 were put in place to preclude a transferee of a business from dismissing employees as a result of the transfer.

J9.3.3 The Unfair Dismissals (Amendment) Act 1993, s 15, provides that a transfer of a business will not break an employee's continuity of service unless the employee receives and accepts a redundancy payment from the transferor '*at the time of and by reason of the transfer*'. The transferor will usually insist on the employee signing a discharge in these circumstances.

9.4 Effects of the Transfer

J9.4.1 The European Communities (Safeguarding of Employees' Rights on Transfer of Undertakings) Regulations 1980, reg 3, provides 'the rights and obligations of the transferor arising from a contract of employment or from an employment relationship existing on the date of a transfer shall by reason of such transfer be transferred to the transferee'.

J9.4.2 However, the European Communities (Safeguarding of Employees' Rights on Transfer of Undertakings) Regulations 1980, reg 3, was not intended to ignore the commercial realities facing employers, and in the case of *Foreningen af Arbejdsledere i Danmark v Daddy's Dance Hall AISS* [1988] IRLR 315, the ECJ held:

> 'Directive 77/187 does not preclude an alteration in the employment relationship agreed with the new proprietor of the undertaking in so far as such an alteration is permitted by the applicable national law in cases other than the transfer of undertakings'.

J9.4.3 What rights and obligations can transfer?:
- all rights under the contract of employment;[1]
- discrimination/sexual harassment/personal injury claims arising prior to the transfers;[2]
- disciplinary proceedings (ie previous warnings whether written or verbal will remain 'on file' for as long as they would have done under the employment of the transferor).

[1] See *Rask and Christensen v ISS Kantinerservice A/S* [1993] IRLR 133. The ECJ held 'that on the transfer the terms of the contract of employment . . . relating to salary, and in particular to its date of payment and composition, may not be varied, notwithstanding that the total amount remains unchanged'.

[2] *DJM International Ltd v Nicholas* [1996] IRLR 76, EAT.

J9.4.4
The new Acquired Rights Directive 98/50/EC, art 3(4) sets out the position
with regard to the employees' pension entitlement:

'(a) Unless Member States provide otherwise, paragraphs 1 and 3 shall
not apply in relation to employees' rights to old-age, invalidity or
survivors' benefits under supplementary company or inter-
company pensions schemes outside the statutory social security
schemes in Member States.

(b) Even where they do not provide in accordance with sub paragraph
(a) that paragraphs 1 and 2 apply in relation to such rights,
Member States shall adopt the measures necessary to protect the
interests of employees and of persons no longer employed in the
transferor's business at the time of the transfer in respect of rights
conferring on them immediate or prospective entitlement to old-
age benefits, including survivors' benefits under supplementary
schemes referred to in sub paragraph (a)'.

LIABILITY OF TRANSFEREE

J9.4.5   Ireland has not included the second part of art 3(1) from the
original Transfer of Undertakings Directive 77/187/EEC in its European
Communities (Safeguarding of Employees' Rights on Transfer of
Undertakings) Regulations 1980, which states:

'Member States may provide that, after the date of transfer, the
transferor and the transferee shall be jointly and severally liable in
respect of obligations which arose before the date of transfer from a
contract of employment or an employment relationship existing on the
date of transfer'.

J9.4.6   Despite the issue of joint liability being reviewed in this
jurisdiction[1] a subsequent ECJ decision[2] clarified the position, so that a
transferee should expect that the liability flowing from the transfer at the
date of transfer shall rest with him.

[1]   *Mythen v Employment Appeals Tribunal, Butterkrust Ltd and Joseph Downes
and Sons Ltd* [1990] ELR.
[2]   *Rotsart de Hertaing v J Benoidt SA (in liquidation)* [1997] IRLR 127.

9.5   Dismissal of Employees
J9.5.1   See paras J9.6.1–J9.6.5.

9.6   Variation of Contract
J9.6.1   An employee cannot contract out of his rights under the European
Communities (Safeguarding of Employees' Rights on Transfer of
Undertakings) Regulations 1980. These provisions are mandatory and even
with an employee's consent, such rights cannot be waived. Accordingly, the
contract of employment or 'employment relationship' is protected in this
regard.

J9.6.2   In the case of *Rask*, the ECJ stated:

'The Directive does not however preclude a variation of the employment relationship with a new employer insofar as national law allows the employment relationship to be altered in a manner unfavourable to employees in situations other than the transfer of an undertaking provided that the transfer of the undertaking itself is not the reason for the alteration'.

J9.6.3   If an employee feels they have been pressurised into signing less favourable terms and conditions with the transferee (ie under duress), a claim may be brought under unfair dismissals legislation.

J9.6.4   A dismissal of an employee for failure by that employee to accept amended terms and conditions to his/her contract, following the transfer of an undertaking, will be automatically unfair unless the transferee can show that the implementation of these terms and conditions was for 'economical, technical or organisational reasons'.

J9.6.5   If there are to be redundancies as a result of the transfer, it is important that a fair selection is made having regard to both employees of the transferor and the transferee.

9.7   Duty to Inform and Consult

J9.7.1   The Transfer of Undertakings Directive 77/187/EEC, art 6, and the European Communities (Safeguarding of Employees' Rights on Transfer of Undertakings) Regulations 1980, reg 7, deal with the duties and obligations of both transferor and transferee to inform and consult affected employees. The new Acquired Rights Directive 98/55/EC, art 6, incorporates these original provisions and adds further criteria to be adhered to by both transferor and transferee.

J9.7.2   The requirements are as follows:
- the obligation to inform rests with both the transferor and the transferee;
- if no employee representative(s) exist, employees must be informed directly;
- the announcement of the transfer must be made '*in good time*' *prior* to the transfer, and in particular, prior to any of the employees' terms and conditions being altered. '*In good time*' is not defined.
- the information to be given to the appropriate employee representatives or directly to the employees should include:
  (a)   the fact of the transfer;
  (b)   when it is to take place;
  (c)   the reasons for the transfer;
  (d)   the legal, social and economic effect the transfer will have on all employees;
  (e)   the proposed new terms and conditions of the affected employees.

J9.7.3 However, employers are not specifically obliged to inform employees whether or not there will be redundancies but rather they must explain what 'measures' are envisaged.

- This information must be provided by both the transferor and the transferee.
- Consultation is only applicable when employee representatives exist and *'whether the transferor or transferee envisages measures in relation to his employees'* in which case the consultation shall be *'in good time and on such measures with a view to reaching an agreement'*.

10   COLLECTIVE RIGHTS AND BARGAINING

10.1 Background

J10.1.1 Prior to the Transnational Information and Consultation of Employees Act 1996, there was no legislation in Ireland dealing with worker participation other than in respect of certain state bodies.

J10.1.2 The Transnational Information and Consultation of Employees Act 1996 implements Directive 94/95/EC and came into force in this jurisdiction on 22 September 1996. The Act is aimed at encouraging the exchange of information by way of consultation between 'central management' and the workforce by the establishment of a European Works Council (EWC) as a forum at group level.

J10.1.3 These are agreements by or on behalf of an employer, on the one hand, and by or on behalf of an authorised trade union representing the employee to whom the agreement relates, on the other hand. Collective agreements may be incorporated into contracts of employment. The enforceability of such an agreement may depend on whether or not it was intended to create legal relations. Pursuant to the Industrial Relations Act 1946, collective agreements may be registered with the Labour Court, making them legally binding upon the parties. Before such agreements can be registered, the Labour Court must be satisfied that the parties to the agreement are substantially representative of such workers and employers.

10.2 Works Councils

J10.2.1 The Transnational Information and Consultation of Employees Act 1996 applies to community-scale undertakings where the number of employees within the member states is at least 1000 *and* where there are at least 150 employees in two member states. It also applies to *group* undertakings with the same employee-number threshold. *'Community'* is defined as all EU member states together with Norway, Iceland and Liechtenstein, but excluding the United Kingdom.

- The Transnational Information and Consultation of Employees Act 1996, s 4, stipulates that to calculate the relevant number of employees, it is necessary to determine the average number of employees (including part-time employees) over the two years prior to the request/decision to set up a Special Negotiating Body ('SNB').

- Central management is obliged to create '*the conditions and means necessary*' for the setting up of an EWC but it only becomes compulsory for an employer to commence the implementation of the process on the written request of at least 100 employees spread over two undertakings in two member states. However, central management may begin the process on its own initiative, without such a request.
- Central management and the SNB may decide to create a 'European Employees' Forum'.

J10.2.2   The negotiations to establish the form and functions of an EWC take place between central management and the SNB. If the parties fail to conclude an agreement, then three years after the initial request, the EWC will be established via the '*subsidiary requirements*' as set out in the Transnational Information and Consultation of Employees Act 1996, Sch 2.

- The Transnational Information and Consultation of Employees Act 1996, Sch 2, para 5, stipulates the areas of discussion that should be dealt with at the EWC meetings:
  (1)   the structure of the company/group of companies;
  (2)   the economic and financial situation;
  (3)   the probable development of the business;
  (4)   the probable development of production and sales;
  (5)   the probable trend of employment;
  (6)   the probable trend of investments;
  (7)   the substantial changes concerning the organisation;
  (8)   the introduction of new working methods or production processes;
  (9)   the transfer of productions;
  (10) mergers, cut-backs or closures of undertakings; and
  (11) collective redundancies.
- The EWC shall have between 3 and 30 employee members.
- The cost of the meetings, travel and reasonable expenses shall be borne by central management. The employee members are also entitled to the cost of an expert attending the meetings.

J10.2.3   The Transnational Information and Consultation of Employees Act, s 15, offers protection to employers by way of providing that central management may withhold material which it feels is commercially sensitive subject to proving that the disclosure would be likely to 'prejudice significantly and adversely the economic or financial position' of the undertaking.

11   EMPLOYMENT DISPUTES

11.1 Background

J11.1.1   A claim may be brought by an employee for breach of contract at common law (ie wrongful dismissal) before any of the civil courts. A right of appeal exists.

11.2 Labour Courts/Employment Appeals Tribunals

A   RIGHTS COMMISSIONERS

J11.2.1   A Rights Commissioner can hear individual grievances/disputes under the Industrial Relations Act 1969, the Payment of Wages Act 1991, the Unfair Dismissals Acts 1977–1993, the Maternity Protection Act 1994, the Terms of Employment (Information) Act 1994, the Adoptive Leave Act 1995, the Protection of Young Persons (Employment) Act 1996, the Organisation of Working Time Act 1997, and the Parental Leave Act 1998. The role of the Rights Commissioner is principally that of mediator between the employer and employee. If there is no settlement of the dispute, the Rights Commissioner's recommendation may be appealed to the Labour Court.

B   LABOUR COURT

J11.2.2   Where a decision of a Rights Commissioner has not been carried out in accordance with its terms and the time period for bringing an appeal (six weeks) has expired and no appeal has been brought, the employee may bring the complaint, in writing, to the Labour Court. The court shall only hear evidence about the non-implementation of the Rights Commissioner's recommendation and shall make a determination in the same terms as the Rights Commissioner's decision. The court does not hear any evidence on behalf of the employer. If an employer fails to implement a Labour Court determination within six weeks of the date of communication to the parties, application may be made to the Circuit Court and the court has the discretion to award interest under the Courts Act 1981, in respect of compensation for a period dating from six weeks from the date of the determination of the Labour Court.

C   EMPLOYMENT APPEALS TRIBUNAL

J11.2.3   The Tribunal hears claims and appeals under the following acts:
* The Redundancy Payments Acts 1967–1991;
* Minimum Notice and Terms of Employment Acts 1973–1991;
* Unfair Dismissals Acts 1977–1993;
* Protection of Employees (Employer's Insolvency) Acts 1984, 1991;
* Worker Protection (Regular Part-Time Employees) Act 1991;
* Payment of Wages Act 1991;
* Terms of Employment (Information) Act 1994;
* Maternity Protection Act 1994;
* Adoptive Leave Act 1995;
* Protection of Young Persons (Employment) Act 1996;
* Organisation of Working Time Act 1997;
* Parental Leave Act 1998;
* Protection for Persons Supporting Child Abuse Act 1998.

J11.2.4   With a number of small exceptions (eg maternity), an employee is required to have a requisite period of continuous employment with his employer before he is entitled to access to the Employment Appeals Tribunal. He must be in a position to demonstrate twelve months continuous service.

J11.2.5   A claim must be brought within six months from the date of dismissal/termination of employment, although in 'exceptional circumstances' this time limit may be extended to twelve months. The costs of an Employment Appeals Tribunal action are borne by each side; the Employment Appeals Tribunal only have the ability to award witness expenses if they feel a claim is vexatious. The employee applicant elects for the relief he wishes to obtain: reinstatement, re-engagement or compensation up to a maximum of two years remuneration. A decision of the Employment Appeals Tribunal can be appealed on a point of law to the Circuit Court. Costs in the civil courts are almost invariably borne by the unsuccessful party. If an employer fails to carry out the terms of a determination by the Tribunal, the Minister for Enterprise, Trade and Employment may, if he thinks it appropriate, institute proceedings in the Circuit Court against an employer on behalf of an employee.

11.3 Settlements

J11.3.1   The Industrial Relations Act 1990 established the Labour Relations Commission which formally came into operation on 21 January 1991. The Commission has general responsibility for promoting the improvement of industrial relations and resolving trade disputes through conciliation without reference to the Labour Court. Part of its functions is to prepare codes of practice relevant to industrial relations and to nominate persons for appointment as Rights Commissioners.

12   WHISTLEBLOWING/DATA PROTECTION

12.1 Whistleblowing

J12.1.1   The Whistleblowers Protection Bill 1999 has not yet been enacted in Ireland but is expected to be enacted before the end of July this year. The purpose of the Bill is to provide protection from civil liability to employees who make certain disclosures 'reasonably and in good faith' to their employer or to somebody other than their employer in relation to the conduct of the business and affairs of their employers. The type of information covered by the Bill includes, for example, such information as amounts to or relates to or supports an allegation that a criminal offence has been, is being, or is likely to be committed and the health and safety of an individual is being endangered, to information concerning a failure to comply with legal obligations. The Bill provides protection against unfair dismissal for the employee concerned. The chief regulatory authorities of the state to whom disclosures may be made under the Bill would be the Garda Siochana, Health and Safety Authority and the Central Bank.

12.2 Data Protection

J12.2.1   Pursuant to the Data Protection Act 1988, employees have a right of access to personal data kept on computer or word processor and this protection has been extended by the Data Protection Bill 1999 which provides for protection in respect of all means of holding personal data, including manual files. This Bill is expected to be enacted in this jurisdiction before the end of the year. The Bill relates to all company files in relation to employees, former employees, interviewees, customer base, and health records in the case of the medical profession. The processing of this personal data under the Bill is only permitted where the subject has unambiguously given his/her consent. Some exceptions are provided for by the Bill eg where the performance of a contract to which the data subject is a party requires the processing of data without consent, or where processing without consent is required for compliance with a legal obligation to which the controller is subject.

13   HUMAN RIGHTS

13.1 Rights and Obligations

J13.1.1   Currently, Ireland does not have an equivalent of the UK Human Rights Act 1998. However, legislation is expected in this jurisdiction in respect of the European Convention for the Protection of Human Rights and Fundamental Freedoms. It is likely that the UK will be used as a model for the legislation to be introduced in this jurisdiction.

[1]   The Competition Acts 1991–1996.

K   Italy

Franco Toffoletto

Franco Toffoletto is a Partner at Toffoletto & Soci, Milan. He was admitted in 1982 and admitted to the Supreme Court in 1996. He has written various articles and texts.

Toffoletto & Soci, Milan

Phone: +39 (0)2 541 641
Fax: +39 (0)2 541 64 500
Email: f.toffoletto@toffoletto.it
Website: www.toffoletto.it

SUMMARY TABLE

ITALY

Rights	Yes/No	Explanatory Notes
CONTRACTS OF EMPLOYMENT		
Minimum notice	YES	For indefinite term contracts: contained in contract or CBA
Terms		
Express	YES	In contract of employment
CBA	YES	CBAs are common in Italy
Statutory requirement	YES	Particulars must be provided within 30 days
REMUNERATION		
Minimum wage regulation	NO	Salaries provided by CBA are considered minimum wage by the judge
Further rights and obligations:		
Right to paid holiday	YES	Length of holiday usually determined by CBAs
Right to sick pay and statutory job protection	YES	
WORKING TIME		
Regulation of hours per day/ working week	YES	8 hours a day or 48 hours a week
Regulation of night-work	YES	No more than 8 hours in 24 hours
Right to rest periods	YES	One day a week
Remedies for breach	YES	Damages
EQUAL OPPORTUNITIES		
Discrimination protection:		
Sex, race, language, religion, political opinion and personal and social conditions	YES	Contained in the Italian Constitution and statute
Marital status	YES	Dismissal because of marital status null and void
Disability	YES	Quota obligation
Equal pay legislation	YES	Contained in the Italian Constitution and statute
TERMINATION OF EMPLOYMENT		
Right not to be dismissed in breach of contract	YES	
Statutory rights on termination	YES	Dismissal must be for just cause or justifiable reason
Disciplinary dismissal	YES	Strict procedure must be followed

COLLECTIVE DISMISSALS

Statutory definition	YES	Minimum five dismissals
Procedure	YES	
Right to consultation:		
Collective	YES	

YOUNG WORKERS

Protection of children and young persons at work	YES	

MATERNITY RIGHTS

Compulsory maternity leave	YES	Two weeks before childbirth and three months after birth
Maternity pay (during leave)	YES	80% of normal salary during compulsory maternity leave – payable by Social Security. CBAs often oblige employer to top up to 100%
Protection from dismissal	YES	No dismissal from beginning of pregnancy until one year after childbirth – dismissal null and void
Health and safety protection	YES	Must be offered other work on same salary
Right to parental leave	YES	For either parent six months in first eight years of child's life

TRANSFERS OF BUSINESSES

Right to protection on transfer	YES	Italian Civil Code and Statute implement EC Directive
Transfer of employment obligations	YES	
Right to information and consultation	YES	Works Council or trade union must be consulted
Right not to be dismissed	YES	Automatically unfair unless justified

COLLECTIVE RIGHTS

Compulsory recognition of trades unions	YES	
European works councils	NO	Italy in default of EC Directive – currently without regulation. A CBA has implemented the Directive for industrial companies

EMPLOYMENT DISPUTES

Civil court jurisdiction	YES	Special sections of civil courts deal with employment disputes
Statutory Body	YES	Commissions of Conciliation of the Provincial Labour Office

541

WHISTLEBLOWING

Protection from dismissal/ detriment	NO	Such a dismissal will be 'abusive' and unfair

DATA PROTECTION

Protection	YES	Incorporates European Directive

HUMAN RIGHTS ACT

Statutory protection of human rights	YES	European Convention incorporated into domestic law

1   INDIVIDUAL EMPLOYMENT REGULATIONS

1.1   Background

K1.1.1   The sources of Italian law are as follows:

- statutes (constitutional and those of ordinary status; 'ordinary' statutes are promulgated primarily by Parliament and by the regions subject to certain limits – the Civil Code is an ordinary statute);
- regulations;
- corporate statutes; and
- custom and practice.

K1.1.2   Corporate collective agreements, as corporate statutes, had the force of law until 1943. After the abrogation of the fascist corporate system, collective agreements became private contracts and are now effective and binding only for employers who are members of an association which stipulates them and those who, although still not members of a union, choose to refer to the collective agreement in their individual contract. Therefore, a company which is not a member of an employers' association can choose not to apply a collective agreement. See paras **K10.4.4, K10.4.5, K10.4.11** and **K10.4.12**.

A collective agreement (*contratto collettivo di lavoro*) in Italy is an agreement concluded (usually every three or four years) between a trade union organisation and an employer or an employers' association, with the aim of regulating the content of individual employment contracts and relationships between the parties. Each sector of industry has its own collective bargaining agreement, and there are typically two agreements for each sector, one for employees and one for executives (*dirigenti*, see paras **K1.5.1–K1.5.5**).

1.2   Contract of Service

A   INDEFINITE TERM EMPLOYMENT CONTRACTS

Who is an 'employee'

K1.2.1   Italian employment law applies solely to 'employment' (known as 'subordinate' employment), while self-employment is generally regulated by civil law.

[1]   See para **K1.2.30**.

K1.2.2   In Italy, there are four important definitions to be taken into account when determining who is an employee.

K1.2.3   The first is the definition provided by the Civil Code, art 2094:

'*Employment contract.* A [subordinate] employee is a person who binds himself, for remuneration, to co-operate in the enterprise by contributing his intellectual or manual work in the employment and under the management of the enterprise.'

K1.2.4   The second is the corresponding definition of a self-employment contract, as established by the Civil Code, art 2222:

'*Self-employment contract.* When a person binds himself to perform a piece of work or render a service for compensation, primarily by his own effort and without a relationship of subordination to the principal, the provisions of this chapter apply unless the relationship is subject to particular rules in Book IV.'

K1.2.5   There are then two further important definitions to be considered. The Civil Procedure Code, art 409, states that the court (special section for employment disputes) has jurisdiction not only for disputes between employee and employer but also for a dispute between a commercial agent or another person (not a company) who has a contract with an employer, the object of which is a collaboration, not characterised by a *subordinate link*, but by a continuous and co-ordinated one.

K1.2.6   Lastly Statute 877 (18 December 1973), art 1, gives a definition of people working from home, stating that despite the definition provided by the Civil Code, art 2094, they must be considered to be employees when they use materials or equipment owned by them or by the employer, even if they are delivered by a third party, and when they are obliged to follow an employer's instructions with regard to the way in which they perform their duties.

K1.2.7   The basic point here is that the services rendered by a self-employed consultant might be considered by the courts or by the Social Security Institutes as services rendered in the context of an employment relationship.

K1.2.8   The first consequence is that the consultant could be protected by guarantees under Italian law and national collective agreements for employees (eg the right to an indemnity for termination of the contract (the TFR – see para **K6.5.2**) and limits on the right to dismiss). As a further consequence, social security contributions would have to be paid by the employer on the compensation paid to the self-employed consultant.

K1.2.9   In order to determine whether the self-employed consultant is in effect an employee, the courts first analyse the parties' intentions when entering into the contract and then analyse their behaviour during the performance of the contract in order to ascertain whether what happened, from a factual point of view, was consistent with what the parties had provided in the contract itself. In the event of disagreement, aspects such as the way in which and the place in which this activity is carried out, the adherence to working time (if this exists), who owns the materials used by the consultant, the reimbursement of expenses and other factors, are taken into account.

K1.2.10   However, this is an issue that is frequently debated in the courts. It often occurs that, after having worked under a contract defined as one of 'independent collaboration', a self-employed consultant may claim that the relationship actually had the characteristics of employment. Court decisions have occasionally recorded conflicts relating to the weight that should be given to the willingness expressed by the parties in the contract. In *Decision 61* (13 February 1999), for instance, the *Corte di Cassazione* (the supreme judge in Italy who is responsible for the interpretation of rules) supported the guidelines which negate the importance of the parties' stated intentions in favour of the actual content of the employment relationship.

K1.2.11   In the case mentioned in para **K1.2.10**, a worker provided services to a company under a contract in which he demonstrated his willingness to establish a relationship of 'independent collaboration'. At a later stage, he asked the court to establish that, in effect, he had worked as an employee and to order the company to pay him the sums due in an employment relationship. The company argued that a consultancy contract between the parties could not be considered as an employment relationship. The judge both in the first instance (the Tribunal) and in the second instance (the Court of Appeal) upheld the claim, maintaining that the parties, despite having acknowledged their desire to establish an independent consultancy, had in fact entered into an employment relationship. The characteristics of this relationship were the employee's subjection to the rules and regulations of the employer, monthly remuneration, the inclusion of the worker into the staff body and the obligation to observe daily working hours.

K1.2.12 The court pointed out that the difference between the *nomen juris* and the true nature of the relationship may occur in three cases:

(a) when the parties in the contract formally refer to a relationship of self-employment/consultancy in order to avoid the major costs deriving from an employment relationship;

(b) when the terms of the contract have misrepresented the true intentions of the parties;

(c) when the parties, despite wanting to establish an independent consultancy relationship when agreeing the contract, demonstrate, based on the facts, that they have changed their intentions and instead have transformed the relationship into an employment one.

EMPLOYED:

- governed by statute, collective agreement if applied (see para **K1.1.2**), and individual contract

SELF-EMPLOYED:

- governed by civil law and individual contract

General rules

K1.2.13 The general contractual rules that govern an employment contract do not differ in principle from the general rules of the Italian Civil Code on contracts. For example, according to the general civil law rules, an employment contract needs the agreement of both parties. Moreover, the object of the contract must be capable of being fulfilled, not contrary to mandatory rules of law, public order or morality, and be determined or determinable under sanction of nullity. It should be noted that in practice, cases of nullity for violation of these requirements are rare.

K1.2.14 Mistake, duress and deceit relating to the essential elements of the contract may lead to the annulment of the contract. An error in the identity or in the essential qualities of the employee can only be relevant when it relates to the professional capabilities of the employee. The relevance of other personal characteristics is indirectly excluded by Statute 300 (20 May 1970), art 8 (the Workers' Statute) which prohibits any inquiry by the employer into matters which do not affect the professional capability of the employee.

K1.2.15 An important exception to the civil law principles is provided by the Civil Code, art 2126, which states that, in the case of nullity or annulment of an employment contract, the effects of the contract remain in force for the duration of the employment relationship, in spite of the nullity or annulment of the contract.

The requirements of an employment contract

K1.2.16 In compliance with the Legislative Decree 152 (26 May 1997) (the Legislative Decree which implemented EEC Directive 91/533), art 1, public or private employers must communicate the following written particulars to an employee within 30 days of hiring him or her (certain written particulars – marked with an asterisk below – must not be given if a collective agreement applies):

(a) the name of the employer and the name of the employee;
(b) the place of work or if the employee is required to work at various places, an indication that this is the case and details of the main address of the employer;
(c) the date on which the employment relationship began;
(d) the duration of the employment relationship, specifying the nature of the contract (fixed-term or open-ended);
(e) *the length of the trial period, if provided;
(f) the job title of the employee, or a short description of the work which the employee is recruited to carry out;
(g) *the employee's starting remuneration and the intervals at which remuneration is paid;
(h) the amount of paid holiday to which the employee is entitled;
(i) *working hours;
(j) *the length of notice period required in the event of dismissal or resignation.

K1.2.17 However, if the duration of the employment contract is less than 30 days and the working hours are less than eight per week, the employer does not have to comply with the requirements set out in para **K1.2.16**.

K1.2.18 According to the Legislative Decree, art 3, the employer must inform the employee in writing of any change (not deriving from the law or collective bargaining) in any of the particulars specified in para **K1.2.16** no later than one month after the change.

Terms of the contract

K1.2.19 Contracts of employment are made up of terms and conditions setting out the agreement reached between employer and employee. In light of the Italian sources of law system, these terms must comply with the provisions of the collective agreements if applied. Only in cases where the collective agreements do not apply are the parties allowed to regulate the employment contract within the limits of the Italian law (and the erga omnes[1] collective agreements). Examples of contract terms follow.

[1]   Erga omnes is a Latin expression that means, literally, 'effective for everyone'. This expression identifies some collective agreements which have been included in a 1959 statute. See paras **K10.4.7–K10.4.8**.

Duties and place of work

K1.2.20   The duties of the employee and the place of work must be set out in the contract. Employers often reserve the right to change the duties and to send the employee to other workplaces. However, any change should be made in compliance with the Italian Civil Code, art 2103. This means that an employee may only be moved to a job equivalent to that for which he has been hired, or to a higher job. Moreover, an employer can transfer an employee from one place of work to another only when the transfer is justified by organisational, technical or economic reasons.

Trial period

K1.2.21   The probationary, or trial period, is aimed at assessing the working relationship before the engagement becomes definite. During the trial period either party can terminate the employment relationship without giving any notice, stating any reasons or being obliged to pay any indemnity.

K1.2.22   If the parties agree to a trial period it must be set out in writing in the contract. The duration of the trial period must also be specified in writing; as a general rule, trial periods cannot exceed six months after which the normal regulations concerning termination and dismissal come into effect.

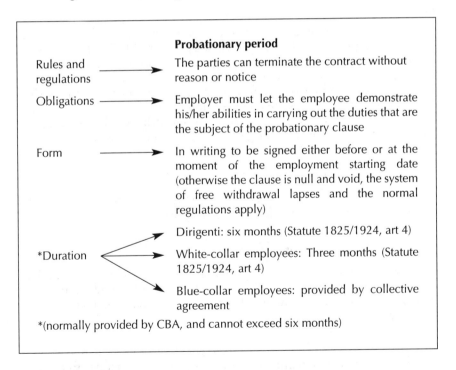

Probationary period

Rules and regulations → The parties can terminate the contract without reason or notice

Obligations → Employer must let the employee demonstrate his/her abilities in carrying out the duties that are the subject of the probationary clause

Form → In writing to be signed either before or at the moment of the employment starting date (otherwise the clause is null and void, the system of free withdrawal lapses and the normal regulations apply)

*Duration →
- Dirigenti: six months (Statute 1825/1924, art 4)
- White-collar employees: Three months (Statute 1825/1924, art 4)
- Blue-collar employees: provided by collective agreement

*(normally provided by CBA, and cannot exceed six months)

Exclusivity of services

K1.2.23   The employee can be prohibited from entering into any other employment relationship involving work of any form (employment, self-employment, collaboration, participation) even if it is not in competition with the employer's business, without the prior and express consent of the employer.

K1.2.24 The employer may also stipulate that the violation of this obligation is a just cause for terminating the employment relationship without the need to give notice (or pay in lieu).

Confidentiality

K1.2.25 According to the Italian Civil Code, art 2105, an employee must not breach the confidentiality of his employer. However, an express clause can set out examples of what the employer considers to be confidential information. For instance, an agreement can provide that the employee shall not, during his employment or at any time after the termination, disclose to any person, firm or company any secret or confidential information, knowledge or data which may come to his knowledge during his employment and which relates to the business, finances, affairs or customers of the employer.

Inventions

K1.2.26 There are certain rights in relation to inventions of the employee during his employment. This is governed by Statute 1127 (29 June 1939). However, an express clause can regulate employers' and employees' obligations more fully. For example, an agreement can state that any invention made during the performance of the employment duties shall belong to the employer, as the remuneration has been agreed by the parties taking into account any possible inventions which may be made by the employee, for which he has no right to further compensation.

Minimum duration guaranteed

K1.2.27 The employer and the employee may undertake not to terminate the contract before a certain date (except for just cause).

Non-competition covenant

K1.2.28 In order to enforce a non-competition covenant, the conditions provided by the Italian Civil Code, art 2125, must be met under sanction of nullity. Particular attention is required in drafting a non-competition covenant.

K1.2.29 By way of example, an agreement to restrain the activities of an employee after the termination of the employment contract has to be made in writing and should contain the following:

(a) a limit on competitive activities (eg which prohibits the employee from working for a competitor who produces, markets or sells products in competition with those of the employer);

(b) a time limit (maximum duration of five years for the executives – '*dirigenti*', see paras **K1.5.1–K1.5.2** – or three years for any other employee);
(c) a geographic limit;
(d) in addition to normal remuneration, further compensation must be granted to the employee as compensation for entering into the undertaking.

B   DIFFERENT TYPES OF EMPLOYMENT

Introduction

K1.2.30   The most common type of employment contract under Italian employment law is the full-time indefinite term employment contract. For years, up until the second half of the 1980s, the law considered different kinds of contracts, such as part-time and fixed-term contracts, as contracts which should be highly restricted. All the statutes in the early 1960s and 1970s went in this direction: the hiring of employees was a state monopoly (1970); any kind of intermediation or temporary work through a third party was prohibited (1960); the Civil Code, art 2097, was modified to restrict the possibility of employers agreeing fixed-term contracts to certain specific and exceptional cases (1962); individual dismissal is possible only under specific circumstances (1966, 1970); part-time contracts were not allowed by law.

K1.2.31   The situation changed between the mid-1980s and today. It became easier to agree fixed-term contracts (1978, 1979, 1983, 1987, 1991); part-time contracts have been fully allowed by law (1984); temporary work is no longer prohibited (1997). However, these contracts require a number of formalities in order to be fully valid. In fact, it is possible for judges to declare the invalidity of a contract and to substitute it with an indefinite term contract. Moreover, it should not be forgotten that these 'atypical' employees are entitled to the same rights as those provided in an indefinite contract for full-time employees. In respect of employment conditions 'atypical' employees are treated in a no less favourable manner than comparable permanent workers solely because they have a fixed-term or part-time contract etc. The general principle set out in the Framework Agreement on Fixed-Term Work and signed by the European Social Partners on 14 January 1999 in order to remove discrimination against fixed-term employees and prevent the abuse of fixed-term contracts, already exists in the rather strict and protective provisions of the Italian employment legal system.

C   FIXED-TERM CONTRACT

K1.2.32   A fixed-term contract is a contract which lasts for a definite period of time and terminates automatically without requiring a notice period for termination. The contract must be in writing, signed by both parties before the work commences and only be drawn up under specific circumstances provided by law. Otherwise the contract will be considered as an open-ended one.

K1.2.33   Below are the cases in which a fixed-term contract can be entered into:

(a) when it is required by the seasonal nature of the activity (seasonal activities are indicated by Statute 1525 of 7 October 1973);

(b) in order to replace an employee who is temporarily absent from work and whose position is protected by law (military service, work accidents, illness, maternity, other protected reasons for leave of absence); for this purpose it is necessary to note the name of the absent worker and the reason for the substitution in the contract. This kind of substitution is, however, not possible if the worker's absence has to be considered a 'normal' one eg in the case of holidays;

(c) when the worker is engaged for a specific job, predetermined in duration, and having an extraordinary or occasional nature (extraordinary meaning that it must not even be recurrent within the enterprise);

(d) for work which is complementary to the main activity and of an occasional nature, that creates a need for employees having skills which are different to those normally employed within the enterprise;

(e) when hiring technical and artistic employees for specific TV or radio programmes;

(f) for executives (*dirigenti*) the law allows a fixed-term contract to be agreed in any circumstances, the only limitation being that of time: not more than five years. After three years, however, the executive can resign giving notice under the general rules.

K1.2.34 In 1978, the use of fixed-term contracts was expanded to encompass the tourism and commercial sectors. Employers can resort to such contracts if in certain periods of the year there is a huge increase of work that cannot be met by the existing number of regular employees. This provision has been extended to all sectors of the economy by Statute 79 (25 May 1983), art 8-bis.

K1.2.35 A major change in legislation has been established by Statute 56 (28 February 1987), art 23, which provides the possibility to foresee in collective agreements different hypotheses for agreeing fixed-term contracts, and this provides the maximum percentage of fixed-term contracts in relation to open-ended contracts in a company. Since then, all collective agreements have rules regarding this.

K1.2.36 A fixed-term contract can be terminated before the expiry date only if there is a just cause.[1] Otherwise, both parties are obliged to pay damages for breach of contract. In the event of dismissal, damages are normally determined by the salary from the date of the termination until the end of the contract, if the employer cannot prove that the employee has received other remuneration during that period. The contract's expiry date cannot be extended more than once, provided that consent has been given by the employee, the extension does not exceed the duration of the first contract, and it is due to unforeseeable events. If these conditions are not met, the fixed-term contract will be considered as an open-ended one.

[1] Ie a cause which does not allow the continuation of employment even on a provisional basis without the notice period: the Civil Code, art 2119.

K1.2.37   Finally, an employment contract for a fixed term must be distinguished from an employment contract with a clause guaranteeing a minimum duration. In this case, an employer is bound not to dismiss an employee for a specified period of time.

D   PART-TIME CONTRACT

K1.2.38   Statute 863 (19 December 1984) sets out rules governing part-time workers and defines them as 'workers who agree to perform an activity with working hours shorter than the normal period of work provided by collective agreements or for predetermined periods during the week, month or year'. It also states that this type of contract must be set out in writing with a specific job description and the distribution of working hours in the day, week, month or year. The employer must send a copy of the written contract to the Labour Inspectorate.

K1.2.39   It is common to refer to two forms of part-time work:
- the '*horizontal*' type of part-time contract, where the employee works during the whole week, but for less hours than the normal working hours (ie four hours per day, five days per week, all year around); and
- the '*vertical*' form, where the employee works for the normal daily working hours, but only on special weeks or months (ie eight hours per day, two months per year).

K1.2.40   Collective agreements define the maximum percentage of employees who may be hired for part-time work in relation to the workers being employed full-time in a company, the tasks and kind of job for which part-time work is possible and the means of performing the job.

K1.2.41   The employee is not allowed to work for more hours than are set out in the contract, but collective agreements may introduce rules for hypothetical circumstances in which extra work could be allowed.

K1.2.42   There are special provisions regarding the payment of social security contributions.

K1.2.43   A written agreement is necessary for the transformation of a full-time contract into a part-time contract but the transformation from a part-time contract into a full-time contract need not be in any specific form.

K1.2.44   Finally, all the rules governing work under a full-time contract are also applicable to part-time contracts.

E   WORK-TRAINING CONTRACT (CONTRATTO DI FORMAZIONE E LAVORO)

K1.2.45   Another atypical form of employment agreement is the work-training contract[1] whereby it is agreed that the employer must provide for the worker's training.

[1]   Statute 863 (19 December 1924) continuously amended until Statute 451 (19 July 1994) and Statute 196 (24 June 1997).

K1.2.46 The legislator has provided for two types of such a contract, neither of which are renewable:

(a) a training contract to an intermediate or high professional level with a maximum duration of 24 months;
(b) a training contract with a maximum duration of 12 months in order to facilitate the entrance of young workers into work.

K1.2.47 The contract must be set out in writing. Only workers between 16 and 32 years of age can enter into this type of contract. A copy of the contract has to be given to the employee stating the training project and the contract's duration. The lack of a written contract transforms the work-training contract into an open-ended one.

K1.2.48 One of the advantages of this contract is the reduction of social security contributions. The reduction has been differentiated according to areas of the country in order to favour mainly the depressed southern areas and according to the type of enterprise.

K1.2.49 In cases where the training project has not been properly performed, the employee could, after termination, seek an order from the court for the termination to be declared invalid and for the contract to be converted into an open-ended one. In this event, the employer would forfeit the reduction of the amount of social security contributions to be paid with respect to the work-training employee.

F   APPRENTICESHIP

K1.2.50 The contract of apprenticeship is a special contract whereby a business undertakes to teach (or provide instruction for) an apprentice in order for him to acquire the technical capability to become a skilled worker, and the apprentice agrees to work under the employer's direction.

K1.2.51 The young person's training includes both periods of practical instruction, intended to provide the apprentice with the skills required for the work, and periods of theoretical tuition, designed to provide an organised framework for the knowledge acquired through the practical work experience.

K1.2.52 Statute 196 (24 June 1997), art 16, only provides apprenticeship contracts for persons no younger than 16 years and no older than 24 years. Moreover, the duration of the apprenticeship cannot be less than 18 months or more than four years.

G   STAGE

K1.2.53 The contract of '*stage*'[1] is intended to match requests and offers of work by means of the introduction of young workers to work. Under the terms of Statute 196 (24 June 1997), the '*stage*' does not create an employment relationship (and therefore, for example, the *stagiaire* is not entitled to any remuneration unless otherwise stated in the agreement).

Bodies entitled to promote *'stages'* are universities, local education authorities, state schools, ministerial labour local offices, regional employment agencies and social co-operatives. Statute 196 provides that the onus of insurance for accidents at work falls upon the promoters.

[1] See the definition laid down by Statute 196 (24 June 1997).

K1.2.54 Employers must designate a person who will be responsible for the traineeship.

K1.2.55 The duration of the *'stage'* cannot be more than 12 months, except in cases of *'stages'* regarding disabled people, which cannot last longer than 24 months.

H   TEMPORARY WORK

K1.2.56 Italy (unlike other European countries) traditionally prohibited temporary work until Statute 196 (24 June 1997) was passed.

K1.2.57 Under this law, the agency places the workers in an enterprise (hiring company), that uses their services to satisfy temporary demands. Only companies that fulfil the criteria determined by Statute 196 (24 June 1997), art 2, and which have received special authorisation may supply workers.

K1.2.58 The temporary contract (*contratto per prestazioni di lavoro temporaneo*) is the contract by which the agency hires the employee with:
(a) a fixed-term contract; or
(b) an open-ended contract, where the agency has to pay a certain amount of compensation to the worker for the periods when he does not work.

K1.2.59 Temporary contracts can be entered into only in the following cases: those provided by a collective agreement; when a worker is hired to substitute an absent worker, except in the cases provided by Statute 196 (24 June 1997), art 4, (ie to substitute a worker on strike); and for the temporary use of employees with skills other than those found in the enterprise.

K1.2.60 The number of hired temporary workers cannot exceed a certain percentage (fixed by collective agreements) of the number of open-ended employees of the hiring company.

K1.2.61 The agency has to pay social security contributions and work accident insurance.

K1.2.62 In the event of a hiring which is against the law, temporary workers can apply to court for the contract to be judged to be an open-ended one.

'Normal' individual employment contract • indefinite term **'Atypical' employment contracts** • fixed-term • part-time • work-training • apprenticeship • *stage* • temporary work

1.3   Variation of Contract

K1.3.1   In general, the employment contract, like any other contract, is legally binding and cannot be altered unilaterally. Therefore, any variation needs the employee's consent. This means that if the employer varies the contract unilaterally, this is a breach of contract. However, in certain cases employers may vary the contract without the employee's consent. For example, an employer can move an employee from one workplace to another, provided that the transfer is justified by organisational, technical or production reasons(Civil Code, art 2103). Moreover, the employer may change the employee's contractual duties but art 2103 must be respected: it states that an employee may only be moved to a job equivalent to that for which he has been hired, or to a higher job.

K1.3.2   In the event that a national collective agreement applies (see para **K1.1.2**), individual contracts may also be varied by these agreements that are binding on individual employees. Finally, if a change is introduced without an employee's express consent and he continues working without objection, it is arguable that he has waived his right to object. However, waivers relating to mandatory rules of law may be challenged by the employee within six months from the date of termination of employment.

1.4   Remedies

K1.4.1   Under Italian law (Civil Code, art 2103) the employer cannot reduce the employee's salary unilaterally. Only if the employee's salary is above the minimum wage fixed by the collective agreements, the parties may agree by mutual consent to reduce the pay, provided that the salary does not fall below the mentioned minima provided by the collective agreements.[1] If the employer reduces the salary without the employee's consent, the reduction is not effective.

[1]   See *Case 6083* (5 July 1997), the *Corte di Cassazione* confirming what it had said in *Case 3145* (8 November 1971).

K1.4.2   If the employee refuses to work properly or at all, the employer can apply sanctions or dismiss him.

1.5   The *Dirigenti*

Background

K1.5.1   Italian law lists different categories of employees, each governed by special rules. The list includes the *dirigenti* (executives), the *quadri* (a function which is half-way between a *dirigente* and a normal employee) and employees and blue-collar workers.

K1.5.2   Generally speaking, *dirigenti* are at the top of the hierarchical structure of an enterprise; they perform high skill and professional tasks with independent initiative powers and are entitled to issue directions to other employees either of the whole or part of the enterprise.

K1.5.3   The *quadri* are employees who, although not being managers, hold important positions in the business and are charged with the development and carrying out of the business objectives. These employees are one step lower in the hierarchy of the enterprise than the *dirigenti*; the *quadri* perform the most varied functions but this never includes manual work.

K1.5.4   Finally, blue-collar workers are considered to be all those manual workers who do not fit into any of the other categories.

Definition of *dirigente*

K1.5.5   A *dirigente* is part of the organisational structure of the enterprise. He is designated to carry out the general orders of the employer and to exercise decision-making power at his discretion with regard to the aims of the enterprise. In particular, the relationship existing between the *dirigente* and the employer must be one of immediate collaboration, with full autonomy and full freedom of decision-making for the *dirigente*, who is not required to ask for or await instructions and agreement for every single action he takes. However, a *dirigente* is an employee. This means that even a *dirigente* is subject to the management of the business, which can exercise disciplinary power and authority over him. There are no specific qualifications necessary in order to be registered as a *dirigente*. It depends rather on the job performed by the employee as described in paras **K1.5.1–K1.5.4**.

Registration as a *dirigente*

K1.5.6   If a company does not register an employee as a *dirigente* when he carries out the relevant duties he can apply to be registered as one. The risk in not registering an employee as a *dirigente* is that employees who are not registered can demand to be. If the employee receives a salary less than that established in the collective agreement for *dirigenti* he could request and obtain the difference and for the extent that this difference has occurred to be taken into account on the payment for termination of the contract. Generally, it can be said being registered as a *dirigente* is preferable from an economic point of view *(for the dirigente* – the minimum treatment provided for *dirigenti* in collective agreements is higher than that for the other employees) and in terms of status. But *dirigenti* are excluded from many protections such as regulation of working time, termination, fixed-term contracts and others.

Dismissal

K1.5.7 Whether or not a collective agreement is applied, *dirigenti* are excluded from statutory protection in the event of dismissal provided for other employees. Dismissal of a *dirigente* is always valid (except dismissal because of marriage, maternity and pregnancy or discrimination based on religion, political opinion etc), and statute does not require any reason to be specified.

Rights of *dirigenti*

K1.5.8 The rights of *dirigenti* vary enormously depending on whether or not a collective agreement applies. In fact, the application of a collective agreement gives the *dirigente* the following advantages (for example): longer holidays; a longer job preservation period in the event of illness and accident; a longer notice period; compensation in the event of travel and transfer; civil and criminal liabilities are taken on by the employer; complementary pension funds etc. Moreover, if an employer applies a collective agreement, the *dirigente* is entitled to know the reason for the dismissal and therefore he can claim for a supplementary compensation (*indennità supplementare*) if the dismissal is unjustified. For way of example, for *dirigenti* of the industrial sector this compensation varies between a minimum payment equal to the notice period compensation (from 8 to 12 months depending on seniority), plus two months' salary, and a maximum of 22 months' salary. Further, the compensation is automatically increased in proportion to the age of the *dirigente*. On the other hand, the *dirigente*'s statutory rights include only the right to receive TFR (see para **K6.5.2**), and a notice period (shorter) according to the provisions of erga omnes depending on the seniority of the employee: no reason need be given for dismissal and therefore no supplementary compensation is due to the *dirigente*.

Directors and *dirigenti*

K1.5.9 A director of a company who is a member of the board of directors may or may not also be an employee (usually a *dirigente*). A mere director can never be considered an employee, but it is possible to have a director, who is also an employee, having two relationships with the company: an employment contract and the position of director.

2 REMUNERATION

2.1 Background

K2.1.1 Remuneration is the employer's essential obligation to the employee, which characterises the employment contract as a bilateral one: remuneration is the counterpart of the work performed. According to the Italian Constitution, art 36, the employee has the right to fair remuneration for his work. More precisely, this article entitles the employee to receive a wage 'proportionate to the quality and quantity of his work and in any case sufficient to guarantee a free and decent life to him and to his family'.

2.2   Legal Regulation of Remuneration

K2.2.1   The general provision of the Civil Code, art 2099, does not give a definition of remuneration. In fact the article states that the remuneration can be determined in different forms (payment according to time, at piece rate, profit sharing or product sharing, commission earnings, payment in cash and in kind) paid on the customary terms and conditions.

K2.2.2   As a consequence, a uniform legal definition of remuneration does not exist. Many disputes have arisen in the courts about this, particularly with respect to the various fringe or additional benefits established either by law or by collective agreements in addition to basic pay, eg overtime pay, bonuses, housing, indemnities for special hard or hazardous jobs, benefits deriving from stock option plans, family allowances, luncheon vouchers. The trend is to consider these payments to be remuneration in order to include all payments made by an employer to an employee that arise in the employment relationship.

K2.2.3   A wide definition of remuneration is used to determine the remuneration on which social security contributions must be paid, with the aim of taxing as many benefits as possible. More restrictive definitions of remuneration are adopted for other purposes. For example, the Italian Civil Code, art 2121, provides that in order to calculate the payment in lieu of notice, only the sums paid as regular remuneration can be taken into account, which excludes sums of an occasional character payable as remuneration for overtime pay, night shift pay etc. Further, the Civil Code, art 2120, states that unless otherwise provided by collective agreements, the annual remuneration for the purpose of calculating TFR (payment for termination of employment – see para **K6.5.2**) includes all sums, including the equivalent of compensation in kind, paid in connection with the employment on a basis other than an occasional one and excluding payment by way of an expenses refund.

K2.2.4   Italy does not have minimum wage legislation. However, the Italian Constitution, art 36, entitles the employee to receive, regardless of agreement to the contrary by the parties, a wage 'in proportion to the quality and quantity of his work'. One of the most discussed issues in Italian employment law literature and precedents concerns the application of art 36. Established judicial opinion indirectly grants any employee the right to a minimum wage as determined by the courts. This wage is usually determined by the judge, taking into account the current relevant national collective bargaining agreements.

K2.2.5   The minimum wage depends on the applicable collective agreement. Each sector has a national labour contract stipulating a minimum wage and salary scale and, in particular, fixing the minimum monthly gross salary which must be paid to each employee according to his professional category.

2.3   Deductions from Wages

K2.3.1   Special provisions apply to deductions and seizure. The law particularly protects an employee against excessive deductions of his wage in various ways. Statute 300 (1970), art 7, fixes a maximum level of deductions by an employer for fines (four hours) and disciplinary suspension (ten days). A maximum of one-fifth can be seized for distraint by creditors.

2.4 Itemised Pay Statement

K2.4.1 Statute 4 (5 January 1953) binds the employer to give to employees – except for *dirigenti* – an itemised pay statement (so-called *busta paga*) in which the name, surname, and professional qualification of the employee should be stated, as well as: the period to which the remuneration refers; family allowances and all other payments or benefits that, in any manner, make up the remuneration; and the individual deductions. This pay statement should bear the signature, initials or stamp of the employer or whoever takes his place. The pay statement should be sent to the employee at the same time as the remuneration is paid.

3 FURTHER RIGHTS AND OBLIGATIONS

3.1 Holiday Entitlement

K3.1.1 The employees' right to an annual holiday is recognised by the Constitution, art 36, and by the Civil Code, art 2109. During holiday, employees are entitled to receive their regular pay from the employer.

K3.1.2 The length of the holiday is determined usually by collective agreements. Most collective agreements generally provide for four weeks paid vacation, with longer periods for more senior employees. If a collective agreement is not applicable, the minimum holiday entitlement is as follows:

- three weeks each year as provided by the OIL[1] Convention of 24 June 1970, implemented by Statute 157 (10 April 1981); the EC Directive no 104 of 23 November 1993 states that employees are entitled to paid holiday of at least four weeks, but Italy has so far failed to introduce legislation that properly and fully implements the Directive;
- 30 days for employees of 25 years plus service as provided by Statute 1825 (13 November 1924), art 7;
- as far as *dirigenti* are concerned, it depends on the erga omnes provisions eg *dirigenti* of trade companies (*dirigenti di aziende commerciali*) are entitled to 30 days paid holiday irrespective of seniority as provided by the corresponding erga omnes.

[1] *Organizzazione Internazionale del Lavoro* – International Labour Organisation.

K3.1.3 The Civil Code, art 2109, provides that a holiday must be continuous, fixed by the employer taking into account both the needs of the business and the employee.

K3.1.4 Under the Italian Constitution, art 36, an employee cannot relinquish his holiday entitlement. If, on the termination of the employment relationship, the employee has outstanding holiday entitlement, the employee is entitled to a payment in lieu of this entitlement.

3.2   Sick Pay

K3.2.1   Under the terms of the Italian Civil Code, art 2110, and Statute 1825 (13 November 1924) employees are entitled to leave of absence in the event of sickness and injury.

K3.2.2   If work is interrupted due to illness or injury at work, the employee is entitled to a statutory job protection for the following periods:
- three months for a length of service shorter than or equal to ten years;
- six months for a length of service longer than ten years.

K3.2.3   Moreover, the employee is entitled to receive the following amounts from the company:
- in the case of length of service shorter than or equal to ten years: normal remuneration during the first month; 50% of the normal remuneration during the second and the third month;
- in case of length of service longer than ten years: normal remuneration during the first two months; 50% of the normal remuneration during the last four months.

K3.2.4   During these periods employees can be dismissed only in extreme cases where a just cause is proven.

K3.2.5   Employees' rights have been greatly increased by collective bargaining, both with regard to the length of the period during which the employee cannot be dismissed and the amount of remuneration.

K3.2.6   Collective agreements also impose a specific duty on an employee to inform the employer about sickness and accidents, usually within two days in the case of sickness and immediately in the case of work accidents; if this is not done (without a justified reason) the absence will be considered as unjustified. The employee must forward a medical certificate that confirms the illness within three days. A duty to be at the company's disposal for medical checks, during certain hours, is also imposed by law.

3.3   The 'Workers' Statute' (Statute 300 of 20 May 1970)

K3.3.1   Statute 300 (20 May 1970) is one of the most important laws in the employment field. The purpose of the Workers' Statute is to grant a number of rights and guarantees to the employees. In particular, the Workers' Statute lays down the following rights:
- article 1 guarantees freedom of thought in the workplace;
- article 2 and 3 imposes strict regulations for using private police in the workplace;
- article 4 expressly forbids the employer from installing audio-visual devices or other equipment for the purpose of remote surveillance of employee activity. The second section of this article states that monitoring devices whose use is for organisational reasons, productivity, or security may be installed only upon consent of the union representatives or, in lieu of such, consent of the internal committee;
- article 7 regulates the procedure for applying disciplinary sanctions against an employee;

- article 8 prohibits any inquiry by the employer into matters which do not affect the professional capacity of the employee;
- article 9 entitles the employees to verify compliance with the regulations concerning health and safety in the workplace;
- article 10 entitles student employees attending regular courses to a working schedule which favours attending courses and the preparation of examinations;
- article 14 reaffirms the right for all workers to form trade unions, to join them and to take part in the union activity;
- article 15 declares null any act intended to dismiss a worker, discriminate against him in the assignment of jobs, or in job classifications, in transfer, in disciplinary sanctions or to otherwise prejudice him because of his union affiliation or activity or his participation in a strike;
- article 18 provides specific regulations in case of dismissal (see individual termination at para **K6.3.1**);
- article 19 provides that trade union plant delegations may be established on the initiative of the workers at each production unit within the framework of labour associations that are signatories of nationwide or province-level collective bargaining agreements that apply to the production unit involved. In enterprises with more than one production unit, the trade union delegations may establish co-ordination bodies;
- article 28 provides that in the event of an employer taking actions that limit trade union freedom or union activities or the right to strike, the courts may order the employer to cease those actions immediately. This may occur in cases where the unions bring an action against the employer for anti-union behaviour (when it has been ascertained that violations have taken place). The employer may file an appeal against the order. Employers who fail to obey the order in the decision will be liable to prosecution under the Penal Code, art 650. Judicial authorities may order that the penal decision be published pursuant to the Penal Code, art 36.

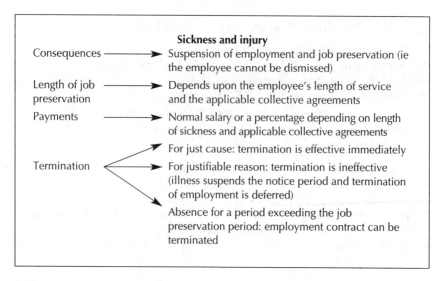

Sickness and injury

Consequences ⟶ Suspension of employment and job preservation (ie the employee cannot be dismissed)

Length of job preservation ⟶ Depends upon the employee's length of service and the applicable collective agreements

Payments ⟶ Normal salary or a percentage depending on length of sickness and applicable collective agreements

Termination ⟶ For just cause: termination is effective immediately

⟶ For justifiable reason: termination is ineffective (illness suspends the notice period and termination of employment is deferred)

Absence for a period exceeding the job preservation period: employment contract can be terminated

3.4   Marriage Leave

K3.4.1   In the event of marriage, an employee is entitled to special paid leave of 15 days, as provided by Statute 2387 (23 December 1937).

3.5   Posted Workers Rights

K3.5.1   By a recent law (Legislative Decree 72 of February 2000) Italy implemented Directive 96/71/EC of 16 December 1996 concerning the posting of workers in the framework of the provision of services. A brief summary of this Decree follows.

K3.5.2   Decree 72, art 1, states that the Decree shall apply to undertakings established in a member state of the European Union other than Italy which, in the framework of the transnational provision of services, post workers to Italy.

K3.5.3   Decree 72, art 2, states that for the purposes of the Decree, a posted worker means a worker who, for a limited period, carries out his work in Italy and not in the state in which he normally works. The second paragraph of art 2 further clarifies that this limited period must be either determined or determinable from the beginning of the posting by means of reference to a future and certain event.

K3.5.4   Decree 72, art 3 requires workers who are posted to Italy to be guaranteed the same terms and conditions of employment as those laid down by law, regulation or administrative provision and collective agreements in the place where the work is carried out. This means that the employment relationship of workers who are posted to Italy is governed by Italian employment regulations.

K3.5.5   According to Decree 72, art 6, in order to enforce the right to the same terms and conditions of employment guaranteed in art 3, legal proceedings may be instituted either in Italy or in a state with whom an international convention or jurisdiction on employment relationships exists. It is expressly provided that should the posted worker decide to file a claim in Italy, the provisions of the Italian Civil Procedure Code, art 410, shall not apply (in accordance with art 410 it is mandatory for the parties to try to reach a conciliation in front of the Provincial Labour Office before a complaint is presented to an employment court).

4   WORKING TIME

4.1   Background

K4.1.1   Statute 692 (15 March 1923), art 1, states that the maximum normal duration of working time for employees of industrial or commercial firms of any type cannot exceed eight hours a day or forty-eight hours a week. Statute 692 (15 March 1923), art 5, states that it is possible to perform additional working time within the limit of two hours per day or twelve hours per week.

4.2   Legislative Control

K4.2.1   Two recent laws (Statute 196 of 24 June 24 1997; Statute 409 of 27 November 1998) have partially amended Statute 692 (15 March 1923): the normal working time is now 40 hours per week. Any work in excess of 40 hours per week (within the limit of 250 hours per year or 80 hours every three months) shall be considered as overtime.

Directive personnel

K4.2.2   Statute 692 (15 March 1923) excludes from the limit on working hours, employees in a position with powers of direction (*directive personnel*). The Working Hours Regulations 1955 (10 September 1923), art 1, gives a specific definition of *directive personnel*:

K4.2.3   *Directive personnel* are considered to be those responsible for the administrative or technical management of the company or of one of its departments having immediate responsibility for the performance of work ie:

- agents charged to manage a business (*institori*);
- managing agents (*gerenti*);
- technical   or   administrative   managers   (*direttori   tecnici   o amministrativi*);
- office managers (*capi ufficio*);
- heads of department who only rarely participate in manual work (*capi reparto*).

K4.2.4   The definition of *directive personnel* does not include shop assistants and other employees of ordinary rank.

K4.2.5   Statute gives no further definitions with respect to employees in a senior executive position and their identity. However, employees in the categories listed at para **K4.2.3** are excluded from the limits on working hours in so far as they are effectively granted powers of direction by employers. More precisely, jurisprudence (eg *Corte di Cassazione Case 3914* of 30 March 1992) points out that in order to determine whether an employee is to be included or not in the *directive personnel* category it is necessary to analyse the duties performed and their correspondence to the definition provided by the Working Hours Regulations 1955 (10 September 1923), art 3. The mere and formal qualification of an employee as a *directive* does not mean that the employee is excluded from the working hours limitations.

K4.2.6   Finally, it must be emphasised that the working activity carried out by the *directive personnel* must not exceed the limit of (as it is referred to in Italian jurisprudence) 'reasonableness'.[1] The *Corte di Cassazione* states that the determination of the limit of 'reasonableness' is delegated to a case-by-case analysis by the judges, who may fix the limit at their discretion with regard to the kind of activity performed by the employee.[2] Some decisions have stated that senior employees performing their jobs beyond the limit of reasonableness are entitled to further remuneration, in accordance with the principle of proportional correspondence between working, activity and remuneration laid down by the Italian Constitution, art 36.[3]

[1]   See eg *Corte di Cassazione Case 2374* (5 April 1986); *Case 6145* (6 December 1985); *Case 5618* (6 November 6 1984); *Case 4042* (19 June 1981).
[2]   See eg *Corte di Cassazione Case 2393* (18 May 1989).
[3]   See eg *Corte di Cassazione Case 2070* (19 February 1992); *Case 1321* (17 February 1987); *Case 117* (12 January 1987) and the 'Labour Judge of Milano' (4 February 1994) Lav Giur Review, 621.

Non-regular work

K4.2.7   The maximum hours limit fixed by Royal Decree 692 of 1923 and now by Statute 196 of 1997 does not apply to non-regular work and custodian[1] activities (caretakers, guardians, etc) nor to workers who work in a family.

[1]   Indicated in a list attached to the Royal Decree 2657 of 1923.

Working time and collective bargaining

K4.2.8   Collective agreements can determine the normal weekly working time within statutory limits. Collective agreements often provide more favourable conditions to employees (since 1970 collective bargaining has reduced normal working time to 40 hours or less).

Example: the banking sector

In the banking sector, the working week for full-time employees who are not excluded from the limits on working hours is considered to be:

- 37.5 hours in the case of termination of the normal working day before 18:30;
- 37 hours in the case of termination after 18:30;
- 36.5 in the case of termination between 19:00 and 19:15;
- 36 hours in the case of termination either beyond 19:15 or in the case of a working week of six days (six hours each day) or four days (nine hours each day).

Overtime

K4.2.9   Overtime was defined in Royal Decree 692 of 1923, art 1, as working time which exceeds 48 hours per week or 8 hours per day. After recent legislative modifications the limit of 48 hours has been reduced to 40. A distinction has to be made between overtime, which is the time worked beyond the legal maximum length, and supplementary time, which is time worked beyond the maximum length provided by the collective agreement, in which case the collective agreement has to be complied with. Non-occasional recourse to overtime in industrial companies was forbidden by Royal Decree 692 of 1923, art 5-bis, para 1. This stated that recourse to overtime was allowed only in exceptional circumstances that were impossible to deal with by using normal manpower or by hiring new employees.

K4.2.10   Statute 409 of November 1998 has introduced a new art 5-bis, which establishes in para 2 that overtime is allowed within the limits provided by the national collective agreement. It also states that, when there are no national collective agreements, overtime is allowed, provided the employee agrees, up to a limit of 250 hours per year and 80 hours quarterly. This agreement can be a collective one signed, for instance, by the company. The law provides that the internal collective agreements have to respect the limits fixed by the national ones.

K4.2.11   Statute 409 (27 November 1998), art 5-bis, para 3, provides that overtime is allowed over the set limits and in the absence of any provision by collective agreements, in exceptional circumstances eg: technical and production requirements that are impossible to meet by hiring new employees; in circumstances outside one's control; where abiding by the normal working hours would represent a danger; and finally, in cases of fairs and exhibitions. These cases are exceptional and are not subject to fixed periods.[1] There are, however, limits established by any applicable collective agreement, and by the duty to protect the employee's health and safety.

[1]   Circ Min Lav 10 of 1999.

K4.2.12   Statute 409 (27 November 1998), art 5-bis also provides that when the limit of 45 hours per week is exceeded, the employer has to inform the *Direzione Provinciale del Lavoro* (Labour Office) within 24 hours. The employer also has to inform the unions when overtime is due to technical and production requirements that are impossible to face by hiring new employees, or to circumstances outside one's control.

K4.2.13   The law provides that the employer has to pay a minimum premium salary of ten per cent for hours worked over the legal maximum. This percentage is normally increased by collective agreements.

4.3   Opting Out/Additional Hours

K4.3.1   The legal requirements on working time cannot be derogated: the employer cannot ask employees to do so nor can the employer and the employee be allowed to agree to waive any legal maxima or other requirements relating to working hours. *Directive personnel* (those in a chief position with directive powers), sales people, workers who work in a family and those who perform activities of mere custody (caretakers, guardians etc) are excluded from the limits on working time.[1]

[1]   A list of other particular cases where the limits on working time do not apply is provided by: Royal Decree 1957 (10 September 1923); Royal Decree 2657 (6 December 1923).

4.4   Night Work

K4.4.1   Statute 532 (26 November 1999) regulates night work; this law defines night work as activity carried out for at least seven consecutive hours and including the hours between midnight and 5:00. Night workers cannot work more than eight hours within the 24 hours (art 4) unless otherwise stated by applicable collective agreements and provided that, on the average of a determined period of time, the eight hours limit is respected.

4.5   Rest Period

K4.5.1   All employees have the right to rest one day a week (Italian Constitution, art 36), usually on Sunday (Civil Code, art 2109). Workers employed on Sundays are generally paid a premium wage rate (eg: for metalworkers 50%). Workers employed on Sundays are entitled to a compensatory rest.

4.6   Paid Annual Leave

K4.6.1   See paras **K3.1.1–K3.5.5**.

4.7   Remedies

K4.7.1   An employee who is forced to work over the limits of the legal maximum overtime (ie more than 2 hours per day or 12 hours per week over the legal maximum length of 40 hours per week) may sue the employer for damages. The employee may also seek an order that the employer is subject to the sanctions provided by the relevant laws. For example: in the event of breach of the regulations governing the maxima for normal working hours and overtime fixed by Statute 692/1923 the employer is subject to financial penalties of between Itl 50.000 and Itl 300.000 (€ 26–155); in the event of breach of the regulation regarding night-work established by Statute 532/1999, penalties of between Itl 100.000 and Itl 300.000 (€ 52–155) apply for every day and every employee carrying out night-work beyond the maximum limits (Statute 532/1999, art 12D); in the case of violation of the regulations concerning working hours of minors established by Statute 977 (17 October 1967) the sanction may be imprisonment not exceeding six months or a fine of up to L10.000.000 (€ 5,165).

5   EQUAL OPPORTUNITIES

5.1   Background

K5.1.1   There are some positive measures against discrimination in Italy, however no systematic policy has yet been implemented aimed at promoting equal opportunities for disadvantaged groups.

5.2   Unlawful Discrimination

K5.2.1   The Italian Constitution prohibits discrimination based on grounds of sex, race, language, religion, political opinion and personal and social conditions (Italian Constitution, art 3).

K5.2.2   Statute 125 (10 April 1991) has expressly recognised and promoted positive action against discrimination. The definition of these actions is similar to those developed in other European countries and in particular to those adopted by the EEC recommendation of 13 December 1984: all initiatives to remove the obstacles which hinder equal opportunities are included.

Dismissal because of marriage

K5.2.3   Statute 7 (9 January 1963), art 1, states that dismissals for reason of marriage and all agreements providing that marriage is a reason for terminating the employment contract are null and void. Any dismissal decided between the publishing of the banns of marriage and the year after the marriage is presumed to be in violation of this Statute; so is the resignation by the woman during the same period, unless personally confirmed before the Labour Office. The nullity implies that the woman must be paid the normal wage by the employer from the date of termination until reinstatement.

5.3   Disability Discrimination

Disabled persons placement regulation

K5.3.1   Statute 482 (2 April 1968) required private employing entities to employ 15% of their work force from people in these categories: war invalids; war civil invalids; work invalids; war orphans and widows; civil invalids; blind or deaf-mute people.

K5.3.2   Statute 68 (12 March 1999) has substituted Statute 482 (2 April 1968) and its subsequent modifications and addition. It has, however, confirmed the general philosophy of the former Statute, which is based on the obligation to employ a minimum percentage of disabled persons (under the new Statute: 7% in the case of a workforce exceeding 50 individuals; two disabled persons in the case of a workforce between 36 and 50 individuals; one disabled person in the case of a workforce between 15 and 35 individuals). It has moreover extended to public bodies the obligations originally aimed at private companies with more than 35 employees.

Area covered by the law: public and private employers	Compulsory quota of disabled workers
From 1–14 employees	0
From 15–35 employees	1
From 36–50 employees	2
More than 50 employees	*75% of the workforce*

The following are not included when determining the number of employees:

(a) disabled employees;
(b) executives;
(c) apprentices;
(d) workers with a training contract;
(e) temporary workers;
(f) home-workers;
(g) employees with a fixed-term contract of no more than nine months;
(h) part-time workers are included only in proportion to the hours worked.

5.4 Enforcement and Remedies

K5.4.1 Statute 903 (9 December 1977), art 13, declares null and void all acts and agreements that discriminate on grounds of sex, race, language. Article 15 grants the employee who has been discriminated against the right to bring a claim for an order that the discriminatory behaviour be ceased and its effects cancelled. Moreover, if the employer discriminates, the employee can sue him for damages. Statute 157 (11 May 1990), art 3, states that if the discrimination is the reason for the dismissal, the dismissal is null and void. The Workers' Statute, art 18, applies (see paras **K6.3.1–K6.3.3**) irrespective of how many workers are employed. This rule also applies to *dirigenti*.

5.5 Equal Pay

K5.5.1 The Italian Constitution, art 37, provides that women workers have the same rights as men workers and must be paid equal remuneration for equal work.

K5.5.2 Statute 903 (9 December 1977) has confirmed the principle of equal treatment for male and female workers as regards hiring, wages, job classification, career possibilities and, in general, all terms of employment.

6 TERMINATION OF EMPLOYMENT

6.1 Background

K6.1.1 Italian laws try to grant all employees a certain degree of security on issues such as disciplinary measures and protection against unfair or arbitrary dismissal. This is mainly achieved by providing a set of strict mandatory rules on the circumstances that may lead to dismissal.

6.2 Conditions

K6.2.1 Whilst a worker can decide to resign at any time, the only limit being that he has to observe the notice period set by law or by the applicable national collective employment contract, an employer does not have this freedom.

6.3 Nature of Claims

Individual dismissals

K6.3.1 There are two ways in which the employment contract can be terminated:

(a) for a just cause, consisting of a cause which does not allow the continuation of the employment relationship even on a provisional basis, with immediate effect (Civil Code, art 2119). Therefore, the existence of just cause (eg gross insubordination, rioting, wilfully damaging materials) may entail termination without notice; or

(b) for a justifiable reason (Statute 604 of 15 July 1966, art 3), which may be:

- 'subjective', consisting of a serious breach of the employee's contractual obligations (the seriousness of the breach is to be assessed by the *judge* – examples of justifiable reason are: repeated and unjustified absences from work; serious damage to the employer's property; working without permission for third persons; insubordination); or

- 'objective', justified by economic reasons inherent in the production activity, the organisation of work and its proper functioning, with a notice period (the courts have underlined the principle that the termination of employment contracts due to the liquidation of an enterprise constitutes termination for an 'objective' justifiable reason[1]).

[1] See eg *Corte di Cassazione Case 9147* (15 September 1997).

Disciplinary dismissal

K6.3.2 If the dismissal is caused by a failure of the employee to observe his legal duties or contractual obligations, a special procedure is necessary in order to dismiss (ie the 'disciplinary dismissal'). The employer must:

- immediately send a letter to the employee, before the dismissal, setting out the employee's breaches, and describing the facts on which the dismissal will be based (facts known to the employer months ago cannot be used as a just cause because the response must be immediate, whether that immediacy relates to the date of the event occurred or the date on which the employer discovered the fact);
- wait for a reply from the employee within five days;
- send the employee the dismissal letter, explaining why the employer did not accept his justification.

K6.3.3 Failure to comply with this procedure will result in the nullity of the dismissal.

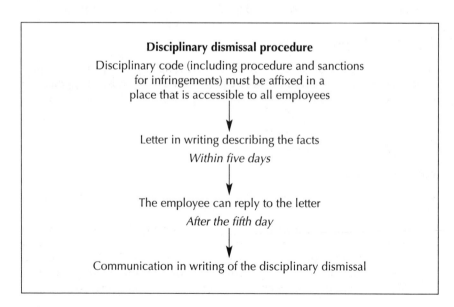

Disciplinary dismissal procedure

Disciplinary code (including procedure and sanctions for infringements) must be affixed in a place that is accessible to all employees

Letter in writing describing the facts
Within five days

The employee can reply to the letter
After the fifth day

Communication in writing of the disciplinary dismissal

6.4   Fairness of Dismissal

K6.4.1   For 'just cause' see para **K6.3.1**.

6.5   Remedies

K6.5.1   The consequences of an unfair dismissal depend on the number of people employed by the enterprise, as follows:

- if there are no more than 60 employees in total on Italian territory, or less than 16 in a single work unit, the employer has a choice between making a new contract or paying damages. Damages may vary between two-and-a-half and six months' pay;
- in all other cases, the employee can obtain reinstatement and damages which cover the period between the invalid dismissal and the reinstatement order, with a minimum of five months' salary. The employee can elect, after the reinstatement order, to obtain, instead of the reinstatement itself, a sum of money equal to 15 months' salary plus the damages (Workers' Statute, art 18).

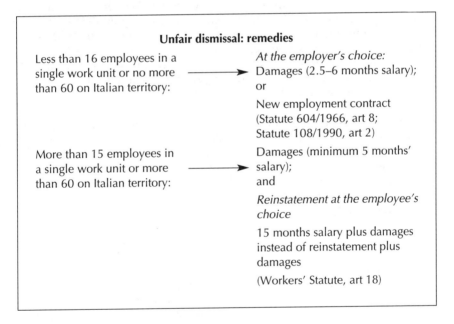

Unfair dismissal: remedies	
Less than 16 employees in a single work unit or no more than 60 on Italian territory:	*At the employer's choice:* Damages (2.5–6 months salary); or
	New employment contract (Statute 604/1966, art 8; Statute 108/1990, art 2)
More than 15 employees in a single work unit or more than 60 on Italian territory:	Damages (minimum 5 months' salary); and
	Reinstatement at the employee's choice
	15 months salary plus damages instead of reinstatement plus damages (Workers' Statute, art 18)

Indemnity for the termination of the employment relationship (Trattamento di fine rapporto – TFR)

K6.5.2   Pursuant to the Italian Civil Code, art 2120, in any termination of the employment relationship employers have to pay TFR, even if there is just cause. This is equal to the sum of the employee's annual salary divided by 13.5. *Trattamento di fine rapporto* has to be paid on termination of the contract (although the employer and the employee can come to an agreement that it will be paid every month or every year during the performance of the contract) but it must accrue every year in the balance sheet. No social security contributions have to be paid on it.

K6.5.3 Under the terms of this article, unless otherwise provided by collective agreements, the annual remuneration for the purpose of calculating TFR includes all sums, including the equivalent of compensation in kind, paid in connection with the employment on a basis other than an occasional one but excluding that paid by way of refunding expenses. Therefore, only expenses and payments made for reasons unrelated to the employment relationship (eg unforeseeable or chance events) are excluded when determining the TFR. In fact, every payment made by the employer to the employee has to be considered as salary even if it is not specifically related to the employee's contractual obligation.

Notice period and payment in lieu

K6.5.4 If there is no just cause for the dismissal, the employee is entitled to his notice period. The employee may be paid in lieu of notice, provided that he agrees to cease work immediately and does not work out his notice.

K6.5.5 Most judicial opinion takes the view that the notice period cannot be converted by the employer to the payment in lieu of it without the consent of the employee. This means that where the employee does not give his consent, the employment relationship will continue until the end of the notice period. As a consequence, those events that can suspend the notice period (such as illness) will defer the course of the notice period and, therefore, the termination of the employment relationship (with any relevant consequence such as the payment of salary).

K6.5.6 The length of the notice period depends upon the number of years the employee has worked–and also upon the job classification, level and qualifications of the employee. According to the Civil Code, art 2121, the payment in lieu of notice shall be calculated by computing the commissions, bonuses, share of profits and any other compensation of a regular nature, excluding reimbursement of expenses. Social security contributions must be paid by the employer on the payment in lieu of notice.

6.6 Redundancy and Collective Dismissals: Background

K6.6.1 Implementing EEC directive of 17 February 1975, Statute 223 (23 July 1991) has greatly modified collective terminations in Italy. Statute 223 (23 July 1991), s 24, defines collective dismissals (redundancy) as a consequence of a reduction or change in activities or labour. The definition of collective dismissal requires a minimum of five dismissals.

K6.6.2 The law applies to all the terminations that occur within the same period – provided as 120 days – and in the same territorial jurisdiction, that are in any way connected to the same reasons for redundancy. The law also states that the company must employ at least 15 workers.

K6.6.3 In other cases, terminations will always be considered to be individual, even if they are multiple. Dismissals can be effective only at the end of a three-month procedure that starts with the notification of a social plan to the unions. Workers to be dismissed must be chosen according to criteria determined by law or collective agreements.

K6.6.4   Another case for which a special regulation is provided – which is not technically-speaking a collective dismissal but is treated as redundancy – is the 'lay-off on CIGS' (*Cassa Integrazione Guadagni Straordinaria*) – Wages Guarantee Fund. This kind of dismissal,[1] takes place if, while the CIGS programme is going on, the company decides it cannot reinstate all the workers who have been suspended and it cannot resort to any alternative measures. In this case, the consequences would be the same as those for collective terminations, but there is no limit on numbers.

[1]   Provided by Statute 223 (23 July 1991), s 4(1).

6.7   Consultation

K6.7.1   The employer must give written notice (containing specific information prescribed by law) to the representatives of the labour union at the company[1] and to the relevant labour associations. If there are no such representatives, notice should be given to the labour associations that belong to the labour confederations with larger representatives on a national scale. Such notice must be given together with a copy of the receipt of payment to INPS (National Agency for Social Security) of a sum equal to (for the year 2001) Itl 1.447.709 (€ 760) Itl 3,182,908 (€ 1644) (for those earning more, the sum is Itl 1,768,238 (€ 913) gross), multiplied by the number of affected employees. This sum is paid as an advance on the contribution to the mobility programme: in fact, for each dismissed employee, the business must pay a sum equal to nine times these sums. This sum may be reduced to one-third if an agreement with the unions is reached.

[1]   As prescribed in the Workers' Statute, s 19.

K6.7.2   Within seven days from the date of receipt of the notice, at the request of the union's representatives and the relevant labour associations, the parties must meet to discuss and analyse the possibility of employing all or part of the 'redundant' work force in different ways within the company, including the implementation of flexible working. Such procedures must be completed within 45 days (23 if the number of workers involved is less than ten). The company must give written notice to the Labour Office about the results of the negotiations and specify the reasons in the event of a negative outcome. If a trade union agreement is reached, pursuant to Statute 223 (23 July 1991), art 5, the procedure will be complete and the employees may be dismissed and placed onto the mobility list. Where the parties do not agree, the Director of the Labour Office must summon them for a last negotiation. This period may not last longer than thirty days (15 days if the number of workers involved is less than ten).

K6.7.3   Whether the parties reach an agreement or not, the company is entitled to dismiss the 'redundant' workforce by giving written notice of termination. The selection of the employees to be dismissed must be carried out taking into account each employee's age, family situation (ie if married and how many children), length of service (last in, first out), technical, production and organisational demands. Non-compliance with either the procedure outlined in paras **K6.6.1–K6.7.2** or the selection criteria will render the dismissals null and void. As a consequence, the provisions set out in the Workers' Statute, art 18, apply (reinstatement and an indemnity for damages).

K6.7.4 Finally, *dirigenti* are excluded from the collective termination provisions – in their case, the employer is entitled to terminate the contract on notice.

K6.7.5 The law states that failure to give written notice and non-compliance with the procedure will render the lay-off ineffective. The lay-off is, however, void only if the selection criteria are breached. Consequently, the provisions set out in the Workers' Statute, art 18, apply, making it possible for the worker to be reinstated in his old job.

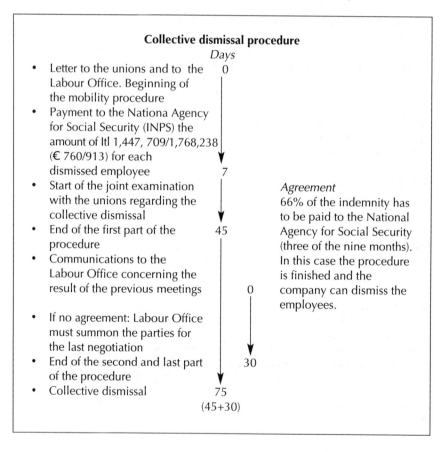

Collective dismissal procedure
Days

- Letter to the unions and to the Labour Office. Beginning of the mobility procedure — 0
- Payment to the Nationa Agency for Social Security (INPS) the amount of Itl 1,447, 709/1,768,238 (€ 760/913) for each dismissed employee — 7
- Start of the joint examination with the unions regarding the collective dismissal
- End of the first part of the procedure — 45
- Communications to the Labour Office concerning the result of the previous meetings — 0
- If no agreement: Labour Office must summon the parties for the last negotiation
- End of the second and last part of the procedure — 30
- Collective dismissal — 75 (45+30)

Agreement 66% of the indemnity has to be paid to the National Agency for Social Security (three of the nine months). In this case the procedure is finished and the company can dismiss the employees.

7 YOUNG WORKERS

7.1 General Obligations

K7.1.1 Statute 977 (17 October 1967) has recently been amended by Statute 345 (4 August 1999) to implement the provision of European Council Directive 94/33/EC on the protection of young people at work.

Prohibited employment for minors under 15 years

K7.1.2   Under Statute 977 (17 October 1967), art 3, as amended by Statute 345 (4 August 1999), art 5, minors under the age of 15 are expressly prohibited from employment.

K7.1.3   However, minors between the ages of 15 and 18 (*adolescenti*) may be employed in some occupations (subject to a medical visit paid for by the employer) but are forbidden to work in other specified job occupations. The majority of forbidden occupations involve working in a hazardous environment.

K7.1.4   The employer is obliged to inform young people and their legal guardians of possible risks and of all measures adopted concerning their health and safety.

Limit on hours of work

K7.1.5   Minors may not work more than eight hours in any one day, nor more than five consecutive days in any one week. Minors may not work before 6:00 or after 23:00.

K7.1.6   Presently, no minor may work for more than a four-and-a-half hour period without one interval of at least one hour.

Remuneration

K7.1.7   Minors are entitled to the same rate of remuneration as for adult employees.

Penalties

K7.1.8   Any person who violates the provisions of these statutes will be fined not less than one million Lire (€ 516) , not more than ten million Lire (€ 5164), and/or imprisoned for not more than six months.

8   MATERNITY AND PARENTAL RIGHTS

8.1   Background

K8.1.1   Under Statute 1204 (30 December 1971) as amended by Statute 53 (8 March 2000) female employees enjoy special protection in the case of pregnancy and maternity. There is no minimum period of employment for the enjoyment of the following rights.

8.2   General Rights

Compulsory maternity leave

K8.2.1   The woman shall not work, or be permitted by the employer to work, for a period commencing two months before the expected date of childbirth. The compulsory abstention from working continues for three months after the birth.

Maternity and parental leave

K8.2.2   The mother and father of a child can take leave from work for a period of six months for each parent beyond the compulsory period of rest. This further period must be used within the first eight years of the child's life for a total period (for both parents jointly, not individually) of a maximum of ten months (eleven months if the father uses three months), as provided by Statute 1204 of 1971, art 7, as modified by Statute 53 of 2000. During this further period of absence, the parents have the right to a payment equal to 30% of their remuneration until the child reaches three years of age, and for a maximum period of six months.

K8.2.3   Both parents have the right, alternatively, to time off during the illness of a child of less than eight years of age, with no limits if the child is of less than three years of age; if the child is of between three and eight years of age, the parents can benefit from this leave for five days per year for each parent. The periods of absence for illness count for the purposes of calculating length of service but not for holidays or the thirteenth month salary.

K8.2.4   The mother has the right, during the first year of the child's life to two periods of paid rest (lasting one hour each), in the day. The father has the right to this period of rest only:
* instead of the mother, if she does not make use of it;
* when the father has sole custody of the child;
* when the mother is not an employee and therefore does not have this leave.

In the event of multiple birth, the rest periods are doubled.

Rights of the father

K8.2.5   Some rights reserved to the mother by Statute 1204/1971 have been granted to the father by Statute 903 (9 December 1977) and recently by Statute 53/2000.

K8.2.6   In addition to the rights set out in paras **K8.2.2–K8.2.4**, a father also has the following entitlements:
* in the event of the mother's death or serious illness or where the father has exclusive custody, Statute 53/2000, art 6-bis, also recognises the father's right to be absent from work for the first three months following the birth of the child;

- both father and mother, following absence from work, have the right to be given the same or equivalent duties as those they carried out prior to leave, to return to the same business unit where they previously worked (or to another business unit in the same locality) and to stay there until the child has reached one year of age.

8.3   Protection from Dismissal

K8.3.1   A woman cannot be dismissed from the beginning of her pregnancy until one year after the child's birth, and in this period a woman who resigns has the right to payment in lieu of notice as if she was dismissed.

K8.3.2   A woman will automatically be held to be unfairly dismissed in any dismissal during this period. The dismissal is null and void.[1]

[1]   See *Decision 61* (8 February 1990) of the *Corte Costituzionale* (Constitutional Court).

K8.3.3   The employment contract can be terminated only:

- when a just cause exists;
- where the company terminates its activity;
- on the expiry of the specific work for which the woman has been hired;
- on the expiry of the term of the contract.

8.4   Health and Safety

K8.4.1   In case of unhealthy working conditions, a pregnant woman must be offered suitable alternative work on the same salary.

8.5   Maternity Pay

K8.5.1   During compulsory maternity leave, the woman is entitled to 80% of her normal salary from social security and the period is considered to be actual work with respect to seniority, holiday entitlement, and thirteenth month (ie the supplementary monthly payment). Collective agreements usually oblige employers to pay the difference up to full normal salary.

Compulsory absence

- two months before the child's birth until three months after

Maternity absence

- six months after the compulsory absence

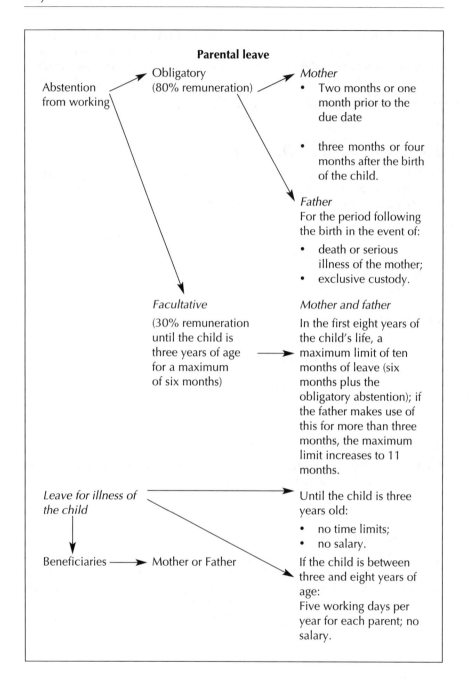

Parental leave

Abstention from working → Obligatory (80% remuneration)

Mother
- Two months or one month prior to the due date
- three months or four months after the birth of the child.

Father
For the period following the birth in the event of:
- death or serious illness of the mother;
- exclusive custody.

Facultative
(30% remuneration until the child is three years of age for a maximum of six months)

Mother and father
In the first eight years of the child's life, a maximum limit of ten months of leave (six months plus the obligatory abstention); if the father makes use of this for more than three months, the maximum limit increases to 11 months.

Leave for illness of the child

Until the child is three years old:
- no time limits;
- no salary.

Beneficiaries → Mother or Father

If the child is between three and eight years of age:
Five working days per year for each parent; no salary.

8.6   Additional Rights to Time Off

Parental Leave

K8.6.1   For parental leave and father's rights see paras **K8.2.1–K8.2.6**.

9 BUSINESS TRANSFERS

9.1 Background

K9.1.1 Far-reaching rules for the protection of employees' rights on the transfer of an undertaking are contained in the Italian Civil Code, art 2112, as amended by Statute 428 of 29 December 1990 (which implemented the EU Business Transfer Directive 77/187, recently amended by EU Directive 98/50) which a new law, Statute 18 (2 February 2001), has partially changed.

K9.1.2 Italian Civil Code, art 2112, lays down that in a transfer of an undertaking, the contract of employment continues with the transferee, and the employees retain all the rights which derive from it. The transferee is jointly liable with the transferor for all existing employment claims at the time of the transfer. Subject to complying with the procedures set out by the Code of Civil Procedure, arts 410–411, the employee may agree to release the transferor from the obligations arising from the employment. The transferee is obliged to apply the existing collective agreements (ie those applied by the transferor) until the date they expire unless they are substituted by the collective agreements applied by the transferee. The provisions of this article also apply in the case of a lease of the undertaking.

9.2 Identifying a Relevant Transfer

K9.2.1 An undertaking for the purposes of the Italian Civil Code, art 2112, is defined by the Italian judiciary as a commercial venture in the nature of an organised body that includes individuals and assets which consent to the carrying out of an economic activity. Such a definition concurs with that of the European Court of Justice.[1]

[1] See eg C-13/95, *Ayse Süzen v Zehnacker Gebäudereinigung GmbH* [1997] ECR I–1259.

K9.2.2 The Civil Code, art 2112, covers the transfer of part of an undertaking. The judiciary takes the view that a part of an undertaking means a unit that is to some extent autonomous from the remainder of the business.[1] Moreover, article 2112 applies only to the transfer of an undertaking or a part of an undertaking from one legal person to another and does not apply to the transfer of shares.[2]

[1] See eg the *Corte di Cassazione* in *Case 5492* (12 May 1995) and *Case 5971* (1 August 1924).
[2] *Corte di Cassazione Case 10068* (26 November 1994) and *Case 10829* (15 October 1991).

9.3 Affected Employees

K9.3.1 Employees who are employed by the vendor immediately before the transfer automatically become the employees of the purchaser from the time of the transfer on the terms and conditions of employment they previously held with the former employer.

9.4 Effects of the Transfer

K9.4.1 Employees transfer to the new owner of the business and retain accrued employment rights (eg with full continuity of service).

K9.4.2 If an employee is unable to obtain his entitlement to a payment for an existing debt from the new employer, he may claim such payment from the former employer as the transferor is jointly liable with the transferee for such debts. However, the transferor may be released from the obligations arising from the employment by virtue of the settlement procedures set out by the Code of Civil Procedure, arts 410–411.

K9.4.3 The transferee is obliged to pay TFR (see paras **K6.5.2–K6.5.3**) to those employees whose employment relationship comes to an end after the transfer in respect of the whole period of employment[1] unless the parties agree otherwise.

[1] See eg *Corte di Cassazione Case 9189* (27 August 1991).

9.5 Dismissal of Employees

K9.5.1 If the transfer or a reason connected with it is the principal reason for the dismissal of an employee or employees, the resulting dismissal will be unfair unless it is expressly justified pursuant to the principles laid down by statute.[1] Should a dispute arise, the burden of proof shifts to the employer to prove on balance that the alleged reasons for dismissal were true.

[1] *Corte di Cassazione Case 9642* (9 September 1991).

9.6 Variation of Contract

K9.6.1 According to the Italian Civil Code, art 2112, employees who are employed by the seller immediately before the transfer automatically become the employees of the purchaser from the time of the transfer on the terms and conditions of employment they previously held with the former employer.

K9.6.2 Only in the event of a change of the applicable national collective agreements, the transferred employees' employment relationship will be governed by the new agreement, even if this provides for less favourable conditions than they previously enjoyed under the old one.[1]

[1] *Corte di Cassazione Case 12751* (28 December 1992); Employment Court of Appeal of Milan (24 January 1996).

9.7 Duty to Inform and Consult

K9.7.1 A brief outline of the procedures to be used, follows:
- first, in the case of a transfer involving a firm which employs more than 15 workers, Statute 428 (29 December 1990), art 47, states that the vendor and the purchaser must give written notice, at least 25 days before the transfer, either to the respective work council set up (in accordance with the Workers' Statute, art 19) in the affected unit, or, if

representatives are absent in the unit, to the trade union associations of a category which are affiliated to the most representative unions on a national level.
- second, the notice must include the following: reasons for the transfer, its legal, economic and social consequences in respect of the affected employees and the prospective measures that will be taken, if any. Within seven days of receipt of the notice, the unions can request a meeting to examine the matter. The vendor and the purchaser are obliged to commence a joint examination within seven days of receipt of the request.
- third, the Workers' Statute, art 28, provides that failure to comply with the procedural requirements may result in the trade unions applying to the courts for anti-union behaviour.

K9.7.2   If, after ten days from the commencement, the parties do not reach an agreement, the procedure is to be considered completed.

10   COLLECTIVE RIGHTS AND BARGAINING

10.1 Background

K10.1.1   All employees have the right, guaranteed in the Workers' Statute, art 14, to form union associations, to belong to them and to carry out union activities within the workplace; particular rights are recognised for the union bodies formed in the workplace in accordance with the provisions of the Workers' Statute, art 19.

10.2 Compulsory Recognition of Unions

K10.2.1   The internal union (works council) formed in accordance with the Workers' Statute, art 19, is called *rappresentanza sindacale aziendale* (plant-level union, 'RSA'). This is the most important union body in the Italian system because it is the only form of union representation provided by law in Italy. At the initiative of the employees, a plant-level union structure can be formed within every work/production unit with more than 15 employees for each of the trade unions that are signatories to collective agreements applied in the unit.

10.3 The Consequences of Recognition

K10.3.1   The law recognises specific rights (provided in the Workers' Statute, Title III) for the trade union activity of RSA only, ranging from the right to convene meetings and conduct secret ballots among employees (art 20, s 21), and the right to paid or unpaid time off for carrying out trade union duties (art 23, s 24), to the provision of a room for their activities (art 27) and space to display notices (art 25).

K10.3.2   Since 1994, Italian industrial relations have been implementing the National Multi-Industry Agreement *(Accordo Interconfederale)* of 1 December 1993 which deals with the constitution of the RSU *(rappresentanze unitarie aziendali)*. This is a plant-level single representative body that has in some companies already substituted the RSA provided by the Workers' Statute, art 19, and it will very soon be the employer's counterpart at company-level industrial relations. The agreement extends all the rights and prerogatives of which the RSA already benefits, to the new RSU.

10.4 Collective Bargaining and Collective Representation

K10.4.1   Collective bargaining has different levels of agreements:

- *Accordo interconfederal* – National Multi-Industry Agreement;
- *Contratto collettivo nazionale di lavoro* (CCNI) – National collective agreements (Industry wide);
- *Contratto collectivo aziendale* – Company collective agreement.

K10.4.2   At the moment collective bargaining is mostly carried out at two levels: national and company. Within a collective agreement there are two distinct parts: a 'substantive part' and an 'obligatory part'. The substantive part fixes the general terms and conditions of employment, which must then be applied to the various individual employment contracts. The obligatory part lays down rights and obligations for the signatory associations (eg no strike clauses, institutional clauses, clauses concerning the administration of the agreement, disclosure of information/rights to inform).

K10.4.3   The *Protocollo* of 23 July 1993 outlined a precise arrangement of collective bargaining: a national collective agreement for the various employers' categories (first level) of four years duration for the normative part and of two years duration for the retributive part; and a second level of collective bargaining, at company level or alternatively territorial. The second level contract also lasts for four years and relates to matters other than those negotiated at the first level. A collective agreement (*contratto collettivo di lavoro*) in Italy is an agreement concluded (usually every three or four years) between a trade union organisation and an employer or an employers' association, with the aim of regulating the content of individual employment contracts and relationships between the parties. Each sector of industry has its own collective bargaining agreement, and there are typically two agreements for each sector, one for employees and one for executives (*dirigenti*).

Different types of collective agreement in Italy

K10.4.4   In the collective bargaining system there are many different collective agreements as there are four possible legal models:

(a) the corporate collective agreement (fascist period);
(b) the collective agreement provided by the Italian Constitution, art 39;
(c) the collective agreement incorporated in a Decree under the terms of Statute 741 of 14 July 1959 (erga omnes);
(d) the current collective agreement concluded in accordance with the principles of law of contract (private collective agreements).

Only the last of these agreements (d) is fully operative.

K10.4.5   The corporate collective agreement was an agreement concluded under the terms of Statute 563 of 3 April 1926 (instituting the Fascist corporate regime) and the Italian Civil Code, arts 2067–2077, by the only unions then legally recognised (one for employers and one for employees in each industrial category). From 1926 onwards, such an agreement was binding on all employers and employees within the industrial category in question and could not be modified to be less binding by the individual employment contract.

K10.4.6   With the issuing of the Civil Code of 1942, the collective agreement became one of the sources of law, hierarchically subordinate to laws and regulations. After the corporate system had been abolished by Decree-Law 386 of 23 November 1944, the corporate collective agreements were kept in force to guarantee minimum protection for employees. They have now, however, been almost entirely superseded by subsequent collective agreements and, in the case of workers not covered by these agreements, by the collective agreements given erga omnes force by Statute 741 (14 July 1959).

K10.4.7   Political reasons, chiefly the representative powers of trade unions (there is government control on their internal structure and a registration system), prevented art 39 of the Constitution, issued in 1948, from being implemented.[1] Therefore, none of the collective agreements provided for by art 39, which apply to all workers in a certain bargaining sector or industry regardless of whether or not they belong to a union or whether or not that union is registered, have ever been signed. In order to make the application of certain collective bargaining agreements mandatory for all employees, the Italian Parliament in 1959, by Statute 741, directed the Government to issue, within one year, decrees incorporating all existing, collective agreements, which would apply to all employees.

[1]   The Italian Constitution, art 39, stipulates that: 'the organisation of trade unions is free. No obligation shall be imposed on trade unions except that of registering at local or central offices according to the provisions of the law. Trade unions shall only be registered on condition that their by-laws shall establish internal organisations based on democratic principles. Registered trade unions shall be legal persons. Being represented in proportion to the number of their registered members, they may jointly enter into collective labour contracts which shall be mandatory for all those who belong to the industry to which the said contracts refer.'

K10.4.8   In this way, the Italian bargaining system achieved, almost through the back door, the aims of art 39 of the Constitution. After these powers of incorporation had been renewed by Statute 1027 (October 1960), the Constitutional Court blocked the institutionalisation of such a mechanism; it kept Statute 741/59 in force by virtue of its transitory nature, while declaring the renewal of Statute 1027/60 to be unconstitutional since it implied the permanence of a procedure for extending the applicability of collective agreements contrary to the provisions of the Constitution.

K10.4.9   The Decrees, incorporating the contents of the collective agreements, issued under Statute 741/59, are erga omnes collective agreements. At the moment they still apply to cases where no collective agreement applies to the employment relationship, giving minimum protection to employees.

K10.4.10 The private collective agreement signed according to and governed by the civil law (*contratto collettivo di diritto comune*) between trade unions and employers' associations, is now the only type of agreement that exists in the collective bargaining system.

Collective agreements erga omnes
applied where
Collective agreements *di diritto comune* are not applicable

K10.4.11 The collective bargaining that developed after the fall of the corporate system (1944) is regulated by private law. A collective contract in Italy is in fact nothing more than a 'normal' contract under private law that is binding, like any other private contract, on the two contracting parties. The two parties are the associations of employers, or the individual employer in the case of a company-level contract,[1] on one hand, and the trade union associations of workers on the other, both of which are unrecognised associations (Civil Code, art 36 – ie devoid of public law significance or at least of recognition by public law). As such, the collective contract is an atypical contract, which is not specifically regulated by the law, but is the outcome of the contractual independence accorded to all private parties (Civil Code, art 1322).

[1] In Italy, collective bargaining is based on two levels: at industry wide level (resulting in national collective agreements) and at company level. Bargaining at company-level is not compulsory and usually relates to matters other than those negotiated at industry bargaining level.

K10.4.12 This means that the collective contract is not generally binding except for those parties (employers or employees) who belong to union associations, or who have referred to the collective agreement in the individual contract or by custom and practice. Employers are not obliged to be members of a union association, and therefore have the option of not applying the collective agreements. As a result, only where the collective agreements are not in force are employers allowed to regulate employment contracts with their employees within the limits of the Italian law (and the erga omnes contracts). In the event that the collective agreements apply, the employment relationship must observe the strict provisions of the collective agreements (these are binding unless more favourable conditions for the employee are agreed upon in individual employment contracts).

Collective agreements
Effective and binding only for:
- employers who are members of an association which concludes the agreements;
- employers who, although not members of a union, choose to refer to the collective agreement in the individual employment contract.

A company that is not a member of an employers' association can choose not to apply a collective agreement.

10.5 European Works Council

K10.5.1   Particular procedures concerning information and consultation must be complied with in certain cases such as collective dismissals[1] or transfers of an undertaking.[2] In general, certain additional obligations of consultation and information of the internal unions may be provided by the collective agreements. These obligations are triggered according to the number of employees.

[1]   Statute 223 (23 July 1991).
[2]   Statute 428 (29 December 1990).

K10.5.2   A further important obligation relating to the informing and consulting of employees relates to the undertakings of *'dimensioni comunitarie'* ('community dimension'). This obligation however, is not based on the Italian system, rather on the European Directive 94/45/EC that has not yet been acknowledged in Italy. The requested requirements involved in the application of the EC Directive 94/45 'the Directive' are to reach and pass over both of the two general thresholds in order to define the *community-scale undertaking* ('at least 1000 employees within the Member States and at least 150 employees in each of at least two Member States') or the other definitions concerning the *group of undertakings* and the *community-scale group of undertaking*.

K10.5.3   Parliament[1] has delegated power to the Italian Government in order to issue the legal decrees necessary for the application of the Directive, but once again Italy's default has lead to the bringing of a case for breach of community obligations by the European Commission, leaving the situation entirely without regulation at present. Consequently, in the absence of a legislative regulatory text there is no juridical obligation for employers of *'dimensioni comunitarie'* (community dimension) in Italy relating to the formation of a special delegation for negotiation.

[1]   See Statute 128 (24 April 1998).

K10.5.4   Independently of the Directive, the only other obligation under Italian law to establish a European Works Council (EWC) is the National Multi-Industry Agreement[1] signed on 27 November 1996 by the *Confindustria ed Assicredito* (employers' association) and the unions, with the objective of anticipating the implementation of the Directive. This agreement, which is in effect without any legislative force, can only be effective towards members of the stipulated union organisations (and therefore members of the *Confindustria ed Assicredito* if employers) or in relation to those employment relationships in which express reference to the agreement is made in the contract.

[1]   Interconfederal agreement for the acknowledgement of the Directive 94/45/EC.

11   EMPLOYMENT DISPUTES

11.1 Background

K11.1.1   Disputes between employer and employee are usually resolved:

- before the Commission of Conciliation of the Provincial Labour Office (*Direzione Provinciale del Lavoro*);
- in special sections of the courts for employment disputes.

11.2 Labour Courts and Tribunals

Commissions of Conciliation of the Provincial Labour Office

K11.2.1 These were established by Statute 533 (11 August 1973) in order to attempt the settlement of extra-judicial employment disputes. The Commissions comprise a panel of three members: a representative of each of the Labour Office, the employees and the employer. Any conciliation reached before the Commissions (as well as those reached before the special sections of the courts for employment disputes) cannot be challenged notwithstanding the general principle of the Italian Civil Code, art 2113, which states that waivers and compromise settlements relating to the rights of employees arising from mandatory provisions of the law and collective agreements are not valid.

K11.2.2 Statute 80 (31 March 1998) states that a mandatory attempt at conciliation must be made before the Commission before a claim is brought to the special sections of the courts for employment disputes. If this attempt has not been made or the claim has been filed by the applicant without waiting 60 days after the attempt has been requested, the tribunal is obliged to suspend the claim and provide for a period of 60 days during which the attempt at conciliation must be made.

Special sections of the courts for employment disputes

K11.2.3 These special sections (established in 1973) are first instance, single-judge courts. The judge (once called *Pretore* and now *Giudice Unico* after the latest reform – Statute 51 of 19 February 1998) handles all disputes concerning work-related relationships. The proceedings before these courts bear significant differences from ordinary civil proceedings, being streamlined in order to increase the speed. The main differences to ordinary proceedings are: restrictions from the start (eg the list of witnesses and the facts on which their evidence is based must be specified by the applicant and the respondent before the beginning of the first hearing ie in the applicant's starting claim – the *ricorso* – and in the respondent's starting defence – the *memoria*); concentration of hearings (ie the judge must be able to consider the case and announce his decision after the end of the first hearing: in practice, this happens very rarely, and only in cases where no evidence needs to be given); and greater examining powers.

K11.2.4 The second stage is the appeal, before the Court of Appeal (Employment Section), which is composed of three judges. The appeal against the decision to the court of second instance must be lodged either within 30 days from the notification of the sentence by the winning party or within one year from the publication in the event of the absence of notification. The appeal must contain a brief summary of the facts and the specific reasons for appealing ie the mistakes made by the judge in the first sentence. In the appeal judgment, the proposal of new requests, new pleas and new evidence is forbidden except in specific circumstances. The appeal sentence completely replaces the first sentence, which may be confirmed or re-formulated.

K11.2.5   The third and last stage of judgment takes place before the Supreme Court, the *Corte di Cassazione*. The *Corte di Cassazione* may only examine and determine questions of law on appeal from an appellate decision and cannot amend the facts as already determined. The Supreme Court can:

• decide the case with a definitive decision;
• decide, for a series of reasons, not to pronounce on the case and to return it to a previous stage (ie to a judge equal to the one that gave the contested decision). A new examination on the merits by a new judge may take place. In his judgment, the new judge is bound by the legal principles expounded by the Supreme Court in its decision.

Examples of claims which may be heard by the special sections of the courts for employment disputes:

• individual dismissal;
• collective dismissals;
• anti-union behaviour;
• wage differences;
• discrimination;
• social security issues;
• enforcement of non-competition clause;
• job classification;
• maternity leave issues;
• safety at work and work accidents.

11.3 Settlements

K11.3.1   Under the terms of the Italian Civil Code, art 2113, waivers and compromise settlements concerning all the statutory mandatory employment rights of the employee can be challenged by the employee. Such a challenge must be made within six months from the date of the termination of employment or from the date of the waiver or compromise settlement, if this occurred after the termination. The waiver or compromise settlement may be challenged by the employee with any written document that makes his intention known.

K11.3.2   This invalidity limits the individual employee's capacity to dispose of certain basic rights, on the assumption that the individual is in a position of weakness during the employment relationship which prevents him from handling and settling properly the disputes arising out of the relationship.

K11.3.3 The sanction of invalidity does not apply when the settlement of disputes occurs through the Commissions of Conciliation of the Provincial Labour Office or the courts.

12 WHISTLEBLOWING/DATA PROTECTION

12.1 Whistleblowing

K12.1.1 According to the Italian Civil Code, art 2105, if an employee discloses confidential information, he will be in breach of his duties of fidelity and confidentiality to his employer. An express clause can set out examples of what the employer considers to be confidential information (see eg para **K1.2.25** – Terms of the contract – Confidentiality). Should the employee breach these duties, the employer may discipline and/or dismiss him/her and sue for damages.

K12.1.2 In certain cases, the disclosure of confidential information may lead to criminal prosecution. For example, as provided by the Penal Code, art 622, the disclosure of professional secrets (ie secrets that have come to the employee's knowledge during the course and by virtue of his employment) may be punishable by imprisonment for up to one year if the disclosure is made without a just cause or for personal gain. Moreover, the disclosure of industrial or scientific secrets that have come to the employee's knowledge in the discharge of his duties is punished by the Penal Code, art 623, by imprisonment for up to two years. Finally, according to Statute 58 (24 February 1998), art 180 (unlawful use or disclosure of inside privileged information on securities), the employee who trades or recommends the trading of securities by using inside privileged information may be punished with imprisonment for up to two years and fines up to 300.000 Euro. For the purposes of Statute 58/1998, information is 'inside privileged information' if it:

(a) is in respect of securities;
(b) has not been publicly disclosed; and
(c) had it been disclosed, then it would have been likely to have a material effect on the share price of the company to which it relates.

K12.1.3 In Italy there is no body of law that encourages the disclosure of malpractice at work by setting up a statutory framework for protection of employees who 'blow the whistle' (such as the Public Interest Disclosure Act 1998 – PIDA 1998 – in England). The possible defence of the employee who disclosed confidential information will be based on the specific circumstances of the case (eg if the disclosure was made to public prosecutors and concerned the commission of a criminal offence, the disclosure of a professional secret would be made for just cause).

12.2 Data Protection

K12.2.1 In recent years in Italy, an increasing amount of attention has been paid to a legislation protecting an employee's right of privacy. The Italian Data Protection Act (Statute 675 of 31 December 1996) deals with the protection of privacy taking account of guidelines already included in the European Directive of 1995. The level of protection ensured by the Italian Act is considerable. This applies to the *processing* of *personal data* and *sensitive data* carried out by any person whomsoever on the state's territory (Statute 675 (31 December 1996), art 2). The Act does not apply to 'anonymous data' (any data which in origin, or by its having been processed, cannot be associated with any identified or identifiable data subject).

K12.2.2   *Processing* means any operation, or set of operations, carried out with or without the help of electronic or automated means, concerning the collection, recording, organisation, keeping, elaboration, modification, selection, comparison, utilisation, interconnection, communication, dissemination, erasure and destruction of data (Statute 675 (31 December 1996), art 1).

K12.2.3   *Personal data* means any information relating to natural or legal persons, bodies or associations that are or can be identified, even indirectly, by reference to any other information including a personal identification number (Statute 675 (31 December 1996), art 1).

K12.2.4   *Sensitive data* means any information allowing the disclosure of racial or ethnic origin, religious, philosophical or other beliefs, political opinions, membership of parties, unions, associations or organisations of a religious, philosophical, political or trade-union character, as well as of health conditions and sex life (Statute 675 (31 December 1996), art 22).

K12.2.5   According to the Data Protection Act,Statute 675 (31 December 1996), art 5, (processing carried out without electronic means), the processing of personal data carried out without electronic or, at all events, automated means shall be governed by the same provisions applying to the processing carried out by these means.

K12.2.6   Processing of personal data shall be deemed lawful only if the data subject gives his express consent (Statute 675 (31 December 1996), art 11). Sensitive data may be processed only if the data subject gives his consent in writing, subject to authorisation by the *Garante* (the Supervisory Authority – Statute 675 (31 December 1996), art 22). More precisely, the following procedure must be observed when processing and transmitting to third parties information relating to persons that are or can be identified (personal data).

K12.2.7   A just cause of disclosure exists when the consequence of the disclosure is 'just' in the sense of 'protected by the law'.[1]
(a) In accordance with Statute 675 (31 December 1996), art 7, notification shall have to be given to the *Garante*. The notification shall specify:
   • the name, denomination or trade name, the domicile, residence or registered office of the controller;
   • the purposes and methods of the processing;
   • the nature of the data, the place where it is kept and the categories of data subjects to which it refers;

- the communication and dissemination sphere of the data;
- any proposed transfer of the data either to countries not belonging to the European Union or, where such transfer concerns sensitive data, outside national borders;
- a general description allowing assessment of the adequacy of technical and organisational safeguards adopted for data security;
- the data bank(s) to which the processing refers and any link with other processing operations' data banks, including those outside the state's territory;
- the name, denomination or trade name, the domicile, residence or registered office of the processor – in default of such data, the person giving the notification shall be regarded as the processor;
- the qualification and title of the person giving said notification.

No notification is required if the processing is necessary to comply with obligations laid down by laws, regulations or Community legislation or is carried out exclusively in order to comply with specific obligations concerning accounting, salaries, social security, benefits and fiscal issues.

(b) According to Statute 675 (31 December 1996), art 10, the data subject shall first be informed as to: the purposes and method of the processing for which the data is intended; the obligatory or voluntary nature of providing the requested data; the consequences if he/she fails to reply; the subjects or the categories of subjects to whom the data can be communicated; and the area within which the data may be disseminated.

(c) The data subject must give his express consent (arts 11, 20). The data subject's consent shall be deemed to be effective only if it has been given freely, in a specific form and in writing, and if the data subject was provided with the information as per art 10.

The data subject's consent is not required if the processing concerns data collected and kept in compliance with an obligation imposed by law regulations or Community legislation.

(d) With particular reference to the sensitive data, information may be processed and transmitted only if the data subject gives his consent in writing, subject to authorisation by the *Garante*. If the processing is necessary to comply with obligations laid down by law, regulations, collective agreements or Community legislation or is carried out exclusively in order to comply with specific obligations concerning accounting, salaries, social security, health and safety at work, benefits and fiscal issues, a specific authorisation is not necessary. This has been provided by the *Garante* in general authorisation 1 of 1999 (processing of sensitive data in employment relationships).

(e) Personal data undergoing processing must be kept and controlled (also in consideration of technological innovations, of their nature and the specific characteristics of the processing) in such a way as to limit to the very minimum, by means of suitable security measures, the risk of their destruction or loss, even if accidental, of unauthorised access to the data or of their being processed unlawfully or in a way that is not consistent with the purposes for which they have been collected (art 15, data security).

(f) Communication of personal data to third parties shall be allowed with the data subject's express consent (art 20). Where the processing consists in transferring personal data across national borders, art 28 shall apply. Under art 28, cross-border transfer of personal data undergoing processing, temporarily or not, in any form and by any means whatsoever, shall have to be notified in advance to the *Garante* if the country of destination is not a member state of the European Union or the transfer concerns sensitive data.

[1]   *Corte di Cassazione Case 542* (15 December 1961).

K12.2.8   According to a decision of the *Garante* of 17 June 1999, the employees are entitled to have access on request to any evaluation made by the employer of their professional ability.

K12.2.9   Finally, whoever fails to comply with the provisions of the Data Protection Act may be punished by imprisonment for between three months and three years.

13   HUMAN RIGHTS

13.1 Rights and Obligations

K13.1.1   Statute 848 (4 August 1995) enforced in Italy the rights set out under the European Convention on Human Rights. More precisely, it incorporates the Convention for the Protection of Human Rights and Fundamental Freedoms into domestic law. Therefore, as a consequence of such incorporation, it is unlawful to act in a way that is incompatible with the Convention.

K13.1.2   However, it should not be forgotten that in Italy the relevant provisions of the Convention already existed in the Italian Constitution of 1947 and were also confirmed by other subsequent laws.

K13.1.3   For example, the right to form and to join trade unions (Convention, art 11) had been already provided by the Constitution, art 39, and was confirmed by the Workers' Statute (1970), art 19.

K13.1.4   Other examples are the following:
- respect for private and family life, home and correspondence (Convention, art 8) had been already guaranteed by the Constitution, arts 14–15; moreover, it is a criminal offence to violate the domicile or correspondence, as provided by the Penal Code, arts 614, 616.
- freedom of thought, conscience and religion, and freedom of expression (Convention, arts 9–10) had been already guaranteed by the Constitution, arts 19, 21; with particular reference to the exercise of this freedom in the workplace, they are confirmed by the Workers' Statute, arts 1, 8;
- freedom of peaceful assembly, freedom of association (Convention, art 11) had been already guaranteed by the Constitution, arts 17–18; in the workplace it is confirmed by the Workers' Statute, art 14;
- no discrimination on grounds of sex, race, language, religion, opinion or status (Convention, art 14) had already been provided by the Constitution, art 3; this principle is confirmed by the Workers' Statute, arts 1, 8, 15.

USEFUL WEBSITES

Website of the Ministry of Employment (*Ministero del Lavoro*), providing legislation, regulations, researches, useful addresses and links on employment and pensions:

* http://www.minlavoro.it

Website of the National Social Security Agency for old age pensions and invalidity (*Istituto Nazionale della Previdenza Sociale*), providing information on the Agency and its services:

* http://www.inps.it

Website of the National Social Security Agency for insurance on accidents at work (*Istituto Nazionale Assicurazione Infortuni sul Lavoro*), providing information on the Agency and its services, legislation, regulations and updated news on employers' obligations regarding employees' compulsory insurance:

* http://www.inail.it

Website of the National Social Security agency for *dirigenti* of industrial companies (*Istituto Nazionale di Previdenza per i Dirigenti di Aziende Industriali*), providing legislation, regulations, forms, updated news and links regarding these category of *dirigenti*:

* http://www.inpdai.it

Website of the National Social Security Agency for commercial agents (*Ente Nazionale Assistenza Agenti e Rappresentanti di Commercio*):

* http://www.enasarco.it

Website of the Italian Banking Association (*Associazione Bancaria Italiana*), providing laws, documentation, text of the banking collective agreement, comments, calendar of meetings and seminars:

* http://www.abi.it

Website of the labour law journal published by the University of Bologna, providing legislation, case law, articles, updates and opinions on employment law:

* http://www.labourlawjournal.it

Website of the labour law journal *Rivista Critica di Diritto del Lavoro*, providing legislation, case law, articles, updates and opinions on employment law:

* http://www.di-elle.it

Website of the labour law journal *Lavoro e Previdenza Oggi*, providing legislation, case law, articles, updates and opinions on employment law:

* http://www.lpo.it

Website of labour and employment law journal, providing case law and links on employment law:

* http://www.legge-e-giustizia.it/fattoediritto.htm

Website of the Italian Association of Labour Law and Social Security (*Associazione Italiana di Diritto del Lavoro e della Sicurezza Sociale*), providing information on national and international congresses and conferences on employment law and links:

*   http://www.univr.it/AIDLASS

Website of the authority for privacy protection, providing full text of Statute 675 (31 December 1996) – also in English; FAQ, forms, decisions and general authorisations of the *Garante* and newsletters on the Data Protection Act:

*   http://www.privacy.it

Website of the city of Milan Bar Association (*Ordine degli Avvocati di Milane*), providing information, legislation, case law archives, calendar of congresses and conferences, and links:

*   http://www.avvocati.milano.it

Website of Toffoletto law firm providing information, case law, and updates on employment law – also in English and French:

*   http://www.toffoletto.it

L   LUXEMBOURG

Guy Arendt and Anne Morel

Bonn & Schmitt & Steichen

Phone: +352 45 58 58–1
Fax: +352 45 58 59
Email: garendt@bsslaw.lu; amorel@bsslaw.lu

SUMMARY TABLE

LUXEMBOURG

Rights	Yes/No	Explanatory Notes
THE EMPLOYMENT RELATIONSHIP		
Written contract required	YES	Minimum term set out by statute
Minimum notice	YES	Between 2–6 months depending on length of service
Terms:		
Express	YES	See above – CBAs common
Implied	YES	
Statutory	YES	
REMUNERATION		
Minimum wage regulation	YES	Statutory minimum depends on whether employee is 'skilled' or 'unskilled'; may also be determined by CBAs
Further rights and obligations:		
Right to paid holiday	YES	Twenty-five days per calendar year. 'Special' leave (eg educational leave) also set by statute
Right to sick pay	YES	Paid by employer but may be refunded from social security funds
WORKING TIME		
Regulation of hours per day/ working week	YES	Eight hours per day/40 hours per week
Regulation of night work	YES	
Right to paid holiday	YES	See above
Right to rest periods	YES	Sunday working prohibited in principle – general right to 44-hour uninterrupted weekly rest period
EQUAL OPPORTUNITIES		
Discrimination protection:		
Sex	YES	Protection against discrimination, victimisation and harassment
Race	NO	
Marital status	YES	
Disability	YES	Non-discrimination measures; also obligation to employ a quota of disabled persons
Equal pay legislation	YES	Guaranteed by statute
TERMINATION OF EMPLOYMENT		
Right not to be dismissed in breach of contract	YES	Right to minimum notice plus severance payment set by statute (1–12 months pay)
Statutory rights on termination	YES	Right not to be unfairly dismissed

594

COLLECTIVE TERMINATION/ REDUNDANCY

Statutory definition	YES	Applies to dismissals of seven within 30 days or 15 within 90 days
Right to payment	YES	Right to notice and severance pay as set out above. Additional payments are usually provided for by Social Plan

Right to consultation:

Individual	YES	
Collective	YES	'Social Plan' must be prepared with staff representative; advance notification to authorities required. Dismissals ineffective if the correct procedure is not followed

YOUNG WORKERS

Protection of children and young persons at work	YES	Employment of children under 15 generally prohibited

MATERNITY RIGHTS

Right to maternity leave	YES	Pre-natal leave: eight weeks plus post-natal leave: up to 12 weeks
Notice requirements	YES	Certification of pregnancy required
Maternity pay (during leave)	YES	Maternity allowance paid for duration of leave
Protection from dismissal	YES	Employee may not be dismissed during pregnancy or for 12 weeks after birth
Health and safety protection	YES	
Right to parental leave	YES	'First parental leave' taken at end of maternity leave; 'second parental leave' before child reaches five years
Right to time off for dependants	NO	(but there are special holiday leave provisions)

TRANSFERS OF BUSINESSES

Right to protection on transfer	YES	All contracts remain in force between the transferee and the employees of the business
Transfer of employment obligations	YES	
Right to information and consultation	YES	Information and consultation of the works council and staff representative committee
Right not to be dismissed	YES	Dismissal in relation to transfer is unfair

COLLECTIVE RIGHTS

Right to join a trade union	YES	Guaranteed by the Luxembourg Constitution
Staff representative committee	YES	Applies to all businesses employing at least 15 employees

595

Works councils	YES	All businesses employing at least 150 employees must have a works council
Employee participation in company management	YES	Applies to public limited companies employing at least 1,000 employees

WHISTLEBLOWING

Protection from dismissal/ detriment	NO	

DATA PROTECTION

Protection	YES	Relates to personal data subject to automatic processing

HUMAN RIGHTS ACT

Constitutional rights	YES	Certain freedoms provided by the Luxembourg Constitution
European Convention on Human Rights	YES	Approved in Luxembourg by statute

1   THE EMPLOYMENT RELATIONSHIP

1.1   Background

L1.1.1 The respective rights and responsibilities of employers and employees are primarily governed by arts 1779 et seq of the Luxembourg Civil Code and by statutory law.

L1.1.2 Various laws have been gradually introduced to regulate every aspect of the relationships between employers and employees.

L1.1.3 Under Luxembourg law, the legislation distinguishes between 'private' employees and manual workers, although the rules for the contract of employment provided for in the Law of 24 May 1989[1] (hereafter the 'the 1989 Law') apply to both private employees and manual workers.

[1]   Mémorial 1989, p 611.

L1.1.4 The distinction between manual workers and private employees is defined by art 3 of a general law dated 5 December 1989. A private employee is an employee who:

- performs work for someone else – the work in question must be wholly or mainly intellectual – for an indefinite period of time, or continuously;
- in exchange for remuneration.

L1.1.5 Private employees include those working in the following fields:

- management;
- supervision and control involving responsibility from a technical and economic point of view (eg a foreman);
- office work;
- sales;
- performing artists;
- medical/dental workers;
- education and social workers.

L1.1.6 Public officers do not fall within the scope of the 1989 Law, but a Law dated 16 April 1979 regulates their status.

1.2   Contract of Service

L1.2.1 A contract of service can be defined as an agreement pursuant to which a person agrees to perform an activity for another person in exchange for remuneration.[1]

[1]   *Jean Wenzel and Chalotte Majerus v SA Texaco Luxembourg*, decision dated 2 February 1989.

L1.2.2 There are therefore three elements to this definition:

(i)   the performance of work;
(ii) the payment of remuneration or salary; and
(iii) the submission of the employee to the authority of the employer.

L1.2.3 Contracts of employment are normally concluded for an indefinite period of time.

L1.2.4   A fixed-term contract (for a definite period of time) is permitted in certain circumstances and may only be used when all the conditions laid down by the law are met. Article 5 of the 1989 Law provides that such contracts may only be concluded in respect of a specific and temporary task such as replacement of a sick employee, for seasonal jobs, for specific tasks which do not form part of the normal activities of the undertaking, or when there is a temporary increase in the activity of the undertaking.

L1.2.5   Such contracts may not be renewed more than twice, or be renewed for a total period of more than 24 months.

L1.2.6   A fixed-term contract must be drawn up individually for each employee no later than the day on which he or she commences work. Two copies of the contract must be produced, one for each of the employer and the employee.

L1.2.7   Fixed term contracts must be in writing and must contain certain statutory particulars.

L1.2.8   According to the Law dated 26 February 1993[1] as amended, the employee may also agree to perform his duties part-time. A contract of employment for part-time employees must provide for fewer than 40 hours a week, and must contain the following details:
- the weekly duration of work agreed upon between the employer and the employee;
- the distribution of work as between the days of the week;
- if appropriate, the limits, conditions and terms of any overtime.

[1]   Mémorial 1993, p 272.

L1.2.9   The laws on contracts of service provide only minimum safeguards for the employee, but apply to all employer/employee relationships which are subject to Luxembourg law. Specific industries and business sectors have special features, which are beyond the scope of this chapter.

A   COLLECTIVE BARGAINING AGREEMENTS (CBAs)

L1.2.10   The Law dated 12 June 1965 provides for the conclusion of CBAs, which are defined as contracts covering reciprocal relationships and general conditions of employment concluded between one or more trade union organisations on the one hand, and one or more employers' organisations, or a single business or group of businesses in the same business sector, or all the businesses in the same trade or industry, on the other.

L1.2.11   Such CBAs may be declared generally binding on all employees and employers in the trade, industry or sector for which they have been concluded. CBAs are common in Luxembourg.

B   STATUTORY PROVISIONS

L1.2.12   An employment contract must be in writing, and a copy must be given to the employee by the time he starts work. It must, as a minimum, state the following specific information:[1]
- the identity of the parties;

- the effective date of employment;
- the place of employment, or, in the absence of a determined place of work, the employee may be employed in various locations and/or, more specifically, abroad or at the employer's private residence;
- the nature of the employment with, if appropriate, a description of the employee's tasks or functions at the time of employment, without prejudice to any subsequent appointment;
- the employee's normal working day or week;
- the employee's normal working hours;
- the basic salary or wage to be paid, plus any additional payments, together with the frequency with which the employee's remuneration is to be paid;
- the length of paid holiday leave to which the employee is entitled; or, if this is not possible to state at the outset of the contract, the method of calculation and determination of such holiday;
- the length of any trial period;
- the length of the notice period to be observed by the employer and the employee;
- a reference to any applicable collective bargaining agreement, any derogation from the general law, where permitted, and any additional terms that the parties have agreed upon;
- a reference to the existence and nature of any pension scheme, whether it is mandatory or optional, description of the rights to benefits, as well as a reference to personal contributions.

[1]   Article 4 of the 1989 Law.

L1.2.13   A fixed-term contract must also state the following information:

- a definition of its object;
- the expiry date where the contract is concluded for a definite period;
- the minimum duration where the contract cannot provide for an expiry date;
- when the contract is concluded on account of the absence of another employee, the name of the absent employee;
- the duration of any trial period;
- any renewal clause.

L1.2.14   As the relationship between employer and employee is in principle individual, the employer must enter into a written contract with each of his employees.

L1.2.15   The 1989 Law lays down the minimum rights and responsibilities of each party. Therefore, the contract may simply refer to these statutory provisions, or may set out further conditions that are more favourable to the employee. In any case, the contract may not provide for exceptions to the minimum statutory requirements which would disadvantage the employee.

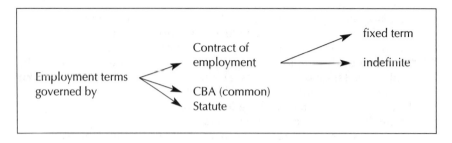

C   OPTIONAL PROVISIONS

Trial periods

L1.2.16   Trial periods may vary between two weeks and a maximum of 12 months, depending on the employee's qualifications and salary, and are not renewable. Trial periods provide a mechanism for both parties to terminate the contract by shorter notice and without providing a reason. If neither party has given notice of termination within the trial period, the contract is deemed to be effective as of the first day of the trial period.

Exclusivity clause

L1.2.17   The contract of service may further provide that throughout the performance of the contract, the employee agrees to devote substantially all of his time, attention and energies to the business of the employer and shall act at all times in accordance with his orders and for the exclusive benefit of the employer. Pursuant to such a clause, the employee may not exercise any other professional activities, either directly or indirectly, without the prior written consent of the employer.

Non-competition clause

L1.2.18   The employee may agree in the contract that in the event of termination of his contract with the employer for whatever reason, he will not be employed in any capacity with a competitor of the employer, or in any of the markets in which the employer or any of the companies of the group for which the employee may have worked. The restriction may not apply to an area outside the Grand Duchy of Luxembourg, and may not apply for a period more than 12 months from the termination date.

Confidentiality and secrecy clause

L1.2.19   A typical confidentiality and secrecy clause would provide that the employee may not, at any time during the term of the contract nor at any time subsequent to its termination (whatever the reason for termination) disclose to any person or entity, or use for personal gain, any confidential information of or pertaining to the employer or the group, or their services, products, trade or clients, which was disclosed to or obtained by the employee during the term of the contract.

L1.2.20   The contract may provide that any violation of this obligation will be treated by the employer as an act of gross misconduct justifying dismissal without notice, notwithstanding any other criminal or civil proceedings which the employer may be entitled to take against the employee as a matter of law.

L1.2.21   Within the framework of such a clause, the parties may further agree that any documents, copies of documents, credit cards, books, records, tapes, photographs, correspondence, data, know-how documentation and any other working materials of whatsoever nature that the employee may receive or use while performing his services remain the property of the employer, and must be returned by the employee to the employer at his request or at the expiry or termination of the contract for any reason.

Inventions and copyright

L1.2.22   The contract of service may also provide that all inventions, devices or concepts, as well as the results of any research, or any original creation or programme, related to the field of activity of the employer and made or developed by the employee in the course of his employment relationship with the employer and for a period of one year after termination of such relationship for whatsoever reason, belong exclusively to the employer, in accordance with the relevant provisions of patent and copyright law applicable in Luxembourg.

Governing law and jurisdiction

L1.2.23   The contract may provide that it will be governed by and construed in accordance with the laws of the Grand Duchy of Luxembourg. Matters not expressly provided for in the contract will be governed by applicable Luxembourg laws and regulations, and in particular by the 1989 Law.

L1.2.24   The contract is likely to provide that any dispute arising out of the performance, interpretation or termination of the contract is to be submitted to the exclusive jurisdiction of the courts of Luxembourg, unless the employee's principal place of work is not Luxembourg, in which case jurisdiction will lie with such principal place of work.

L1.2.25   The contract may also refer to statutory provisions, regulations, administrative rules, staff rules or CBAs providing for other rules regarding working conditions.

1.3   Variation of the Contract

L1.3.1   Any amendment to the employment contract which is unfavourable to the employee and which concerns an essential clause of the contract must, be notified to the employee in the form prescribed for an individual dismissal, and must state the date at which the amendment will be effective. Amendments which are not so notified are invalid. The employee is entitled to request that the employer justifies the proposed amendment.[1]

[1]   Article 37 of the 1989 Law.

L1.3.2   Termination of the employment contract as a result of the employee's refusal to accept a substantial amendment is considered to be a dismissal, entitling the employee to bring an action for unfair dismissal.

1.4 Remedies

L1.4.1 If there is no written contract as required by law, only the employee may give evidence of the contract's existence and of its content by any means, notwithstanding the value of the litigation.[1]

[1] Article 4(5) of the 1989 Law.

L1.4.2 If any of the parties refuses to sign a written contract, the other party may terminate the contract without giving any period of notice and without payment of compensation. Such action may, however, only be taken no earlier than three days after making a request for a signed contract and no later than 30 days after the commencement of employment.

2 REMUNERATION

2.1 Background

L2.1.1 The description 'remuneration' covers:

- compensation for the work performed;
- gratuities;
- profit share;
- discounts;
- bonuses;
- free housing and any other services of a similar nature.

L2.1.2 Bonuses are in principle not considered to be part of the employee's remuneration, unless they are expressly provided for in the contract of service or CBA or unless the payment of such bonuses is the result of an employer's customary salary procedure.

L2.1.3 The employer's customary salary procedure is characterised by three elements:

- persistence of payments: the payment of such bonuses must regularly and invariably occur at a certain period of time (for example any bonus that the employer may decide to pay at the end of each year);
- calculation of the amount: the various bonus amounts must always be calculated using the same method, which cannot be altered by the employer;
- majority of employees: such bonuses must be paid to all employees or to one or several categories of employees.

L2.1.4 Moreover, the employer must be aware that the payment is mandatory and does not constitute an exercise of his discretion, and the employee must be aware that the bonus is an addition to his usual salary.

2.2 Legal Regulation of Remuneration

L2.2.1 Luxembourg has adopted legislative measures providing for the guarantee of a statutory minimum wage to all employees. These measures are considered to be a matter of public interest. The Law of 12 March 1973 (as amended) provides for a minimum statutory wage for all employees, but states a distinction between skilled and non-skilled employees.

L2.2.2 As of 1 April 2001 the gross minimum statutory wage (index 590.84) is LUF 62,457 (€ 1,548.27) per month for skilled employees and LUF 52,047 (€ 1,290.22) per month for unskilled employees.

L2.2.3 An employee is deemed to be skilled:

- when he has a CATP (*certificat d'aptitude technique et professionnelle*), its equivalent, or a higher qualification; or
- when he has a CCM (*certificat de capacité manuelle*) plus two years' practical experience in the trade in question; or
- when he has a CITP (*certificat d'initiation technique et professionnelle*) plus five years' practical experience in the trade in question; or
- when he has ten years' experience in the business in question.

L2.2.4 Apart from the statutory minimum wage scale, wages are determined by reference to collective bargaining agreements negotiated at work or industry level, or to individual agreements negotiated between employer and employee. Moreover, wages and salaries automatically increase with the cost of living.

L2.2.5 The employer is required to give to each employee at the end of each month a detailed statement of his remuneration indicating the method of calculation, the working period, the total number of working hours, the rate, and any other payments or benefits in cash or in kind.[1]

[1] Article 40 of the 1989 Law relating to employment contracts.

L2.2.6 In the event of termination of the employment contract, this statement, as well as any remuneration still owed, must be given to the employee at the time at which the contract terminates or within five days thereafter.

L2.2.7 Non-compliance with these provisions constitutes an offence punishable by a fine of between LUF 2,501 and 50,000 (between € 61.99 and 1239.46).

A   PAYMENT OF SALARY OF MANUAL WORKERS

L2.2.8 The remuneration of manual workers (except agricultural workers and servants) is regulated by the Law dated 12th July 1895 as amended. Manual workers must receive their salary in two payments at intervals of no more than 16 days. However, in practice payment is made once a month at the end of each month.

B   PAYMENT OF SALARY OF PRIVATE EMPLOYEES

L2.2.9 The Law of 5 December 1989 regulates the payment of salary to private employees.

L2.2.10 Remuneration must be paid every month, on the last day of the month at the latest. However, a private employee may obtain a pre-payment of salary corresponding to the work performed in the event of particular, justified and urgent need.

L2.2.11 Payment of additional elements of salary such as bonuses or gratuities must be made within two months following the end of the working year, ie the employer's accounting period/year.

603

L2.2.12   Save as set out above in relation to the minimum wage, remuneration may be freely determined between the employer and the employee.

3   FURTHER RIGHTS AND OBLIGATIONS

3.1   Holiday Entitlement

A   ANNUAL HOLIDAY

L3.1.1   The Law of 22 April 1966 as amended provides for holiday entitlement both for private employees and for manual workers. Article 4 sets the holiday period at 25 working days per year irrespective of the employee's age.

L3.1.2   The right to such holiday begins on the completion of three months' uninterrupted service with the same employer.

L3.1.3   An employer may refuse to grant holiday if the employee has been absent without valid reason for more than 10% of the time when he should have been at work during the previous year. Absence authorised by the employer, on account of sickness or injury, and during a public holiday or a lawful strike all constitute valid reasons for absence.

L3.1.4   The 25 days' leave must usually be taken during the calendar year but can be taken up until 31 March of the following year in the case of operating needs or the legitimate wishes of other employees.

L3.1.5   The employee is entitled to a holiday indemnity payment for each day of paid holiday, which is calculated on the basis of the average remuneration of the employee within the last three months.

L3.1.6   If the employment terminates during the course of the calendar year, the employee is entitled to one twelfth of the annual holiday not yet taken for each full month worked.

B   ADDITIONAL HOLIDAY

L3.1.7   Additional holiday of six days is granted to disabled workers, three days to mine workers and one day for each period of eight working weeks to employees whose work does not allow them to take an uninterrupted rest period of at least 44 hours per week.

L3.1.8   Various forms of special leave also exist under the law:
* educational leave: women at the end of their maternity leave (see para **3.1.8**) may take educational leave and require the employer to re-employ them within a period of one year after the expiry of the term of educational leave;
* training leave;
* cultural leave;
* leave for sporting purposes;

- political leave;
- leave allowing the performance of civic rights and duties;
- leave allowing the performance of a mandate as member of a professional chamber;
- leave allowing the performance of the duty as assessor at the Labour Court;
- leave for volunteers in charge of fire, assistance and rescue services;
- leave to seek a job: this leave may be taken during the notice period by employees who have been dismissed and may not exceed six days. The employer must pay the employee for the leave, provided that the employee is registered as a job applicant and is able to prove an offer of employment. If he does not receive any offers, he is not entitled to be paid for his leave;
- maternity leave;
- sick leave;
- leave in case of adoption (specific additional leave of eight weeks);
- extraordinary leave for personal reasons: the employee is entitled to one day's additional leave in case of death of a relative or a relative by marriage at second degree; two days' leave for the birth of a child, the wedding of a child or moving home; three days' leave on the death of a spouse or of a relative or relative by marriage at the first degree; six days' leave for the wedding of the employee; two days' leave in case of adoption of a child (under 16 years old) unless special adoption leave has already been granted.

C   PUBLIC HOLIDAYS

L3.1.9 Pursuant to a Law dated 10 April 1976 governing public holiday, all private sector employees with an employment contract or an apprenticeship contract are entitled to 10 public holidays per year:

- New Year's Day;
- Easter Monday;
- 1 May;
- Ascension Day;
- Whit Monday;
- National holiday (23 June);
- Assumption of the Virgin Mary (15 May);
- All Saints' Day (1 November);
- Christmas Day (25 December);
- Boxing Day (26 December).

L3.1.10 If a public holiday falls on a Sunday, a replacement day off must be granted within three months of the date of the relevant public holiday. Only three public holidays over a calendar year may be replaced.

L3.1.11 When special conditions of an employee's employment do not allow for the observance of a statutory public holiday, an employee working on such a day will receive in addition to his usual remuneration double his usual hourly remuneration, or double his average hourly remuneration in the event of monthly pay.

Holiday: summary
- 25 working days holiday
- unauthorised absence may justify withholding holiday
- additional holiday for special workers eg disabled
- 10 public holidays pa

3.2 Sick Pay

L3.2.1 Manual workers are entitled to benefits from the first day of incapacity up to a maximum of 52 weeks. These benefits are paid by the employer, who receives a refund from Social Security Funds (*Caisse Nationale d'Assurance Maladie des Ouvriers*).

L3.2.2 Private employees are entitled to similar benefits paid by the employer. However, the Social Security Authority (*Caisse de Maladie des Employés Privés*).only provides benefits from the first day of the fourth month of absence.

L3.2.3 Self-employed workers are entitled to sickness benefit, proportionate to the basis of their contributions at the onset of the incapacity but no more than five times the statutory minimum wage, from the first day of the fourth month following that in which the sickness was notified to the insurance scheme (ie the mandatory public social security scheme).

4 WORKING TIME

4.1 Background

A MANUAL WORKERS

L4.1.1 The statutory provisions governing working time of manual workers[1] apply to manual workers in the private and public sector as well as to manual workers on apprenticeships.

[1] Law dated 9 December 1970.

L4.1.2 The provisions do not, however, apply to family businesses (as defined by the law), to river transport and to travelling showmen, or to work performed at home.

L4.1.3 The following employees are also not subject to the statutory provisions on working time:
- domestic employees;
- agricultural, wine-producing and horticultural family businesses;
- employees of hotels, restaurants, bars and other establishments serving beverages;
- employees working in hospitals;
- employees working in road transport.

L4.1.4 Certain of these sectors may however be governed by CBAs in relation to working time.

B   PRIVATE EMPLOYEES

L4.1.5   The statutory provisions governing working time apply to all persons falling within the legal definition of 'private employees'.

L4.1.6   These provisions do not however apply to:
- employees occupied in family businesses;
- commercial travellers and representatives working away from the business premises;
- senior managers whose presence at the business is essential for operating and supervisory reasons.

L4.1.7   The performance of overtime work requires authorisation from the Labour Minister.

L4.1.8   The Law of 26 February 1993 on voluntary part-time working provides that the employee and employer may conclude a part-time employment contract for less than 40 hours a week.

4.2   Legislative Control

L4.2.1   Working time is limited to eight hours a day and 40 hours a week both for manual workers[1] and for private employees.[2]

[1]   Law dated 9 December 1970, art 4(1) as amended by a Law dated 12 February 1999.
[2]   Co-ordinated Law dated 5 December 1989, art 6(1) as amended by the Law dated 12 February 1999.

L4.2.2   Private employees may be requested to work more than 8 hours a day and 40 hours a week, on condition that the average weekly working time, calculated over a four-week period, does not exceed 40 hours a week. Every employer must draw up an Organisation Plan with respect to the working time of his employees over the next four weeks.

L4.2.3   The absolute maximum time which may be spent at work (for either manual workers or private employees) is 10 hours a day and 48 hours a week.

Example

An employee could work 40 hours in week 1, 48 hours in week 2, 40 hours in week 3 and 32 hours in week 4. His average weekly working time over the four weeks is 40 hours.

L4.2.4   Working time is defined by the law as the period of time during which the employee is at the service of his employer or employers.

Remuneration

L4.2.5   The performance of work can continue beyond the normal working day or week provided that the employee is granted time off equivalent to the excess hours worked.

607

L4.2.6   A manual worker is entitled either to time off in lieu of overtime worked, or to a supplementary payment of 25% per hour.

L4.2.7   A private employee is entitled either to time off in lieu of overtime worked, or to a supplementary payment of 50% per hour.

L4.2.8   Offences relating to the rules governing working time are punishable by a fine of between LUF 25,000 and 150,000 (between € 619.73 and 3,718.40), as well as a possible term of imprisonment of between eight days and one month.

4.3   Night Workers

L4.3.1   Work at night is generally permitted, except in certain cases.

L4.3.2   A Law dated 28 October 1969 prohibits in principle night work for adolescents (ie persons aged under 18) during a period of 12 consecutive hours which must cover at least the period between 20:00 and 05:00 (for example, from 19:00 to 07:00 or from 20:00 to 08:00).

L4.3.3   A Law dated 3 July 1975 prohibits night work for pregnant women and women following confinement provided they produce a medical certificate which confirms that they breastfeed their child.

L4.3.4   Special rules cover night work in bakeries.

4.4   Rest Period

L4.4.1   Sunday work is in principle prohibited by the Law of 1 August 1988 concerning the weekly rest period of private employees and manual workers.

L4.4.2   Private employees are entitled to an uninterrupted weekly rest period of 44 hours. As far as possible this rest period must be include Sunday.

L4.4.3   In the event that the operating needs of the business do not allow for a weekly rest period of 44 hours, a private employee will be entitled to additional annual leave of six days.

L4.4.4   Moreover, the Law dated 22 April 1966 relating to the annual leave of employees in the private sector grants both private employees and manual workers the right to additional leave of 6 days a year when the employee is not able to rest for 44 hours per week.

L4.4.5   The Law of 1 August 1988 recognises four exceptions as to Sunday work/rest periods. The categories can be summarised as:
(i)   certain employees;
(ii)   specified businesses;
(iii)   certain occupations;
(iv)   adolescents.

EXCEPTION: CERTAIN EMPLOYEES

L4.4.6 The prohibition on Sunday working does not apply to:
- employees with an effective management position;
- senior managers whose presence at the business is essential for operational and supervisory reasons;
- commercial travellers and representatives working away from the business premises.

EXCEPTION: BUSINESSES

L4.4.7 The prohibition on Sunday working does not apply to the following businesses:
- family businesses in which the only employees are the employer's first degree relatives in the ascending or descending line (parents, children, brothers or sisters, parents-in-law, son-in-law, daughter-in-law, brother-in-law or sister-in-law);
- hotels, restaurants, canteens, bars and other establishments serving beverages;
- pharmacies, drugstores and retailers of medical and surgical appliances;
- travelling showmen;
- farms and vineyards;
- places of public entertainment;
- gas, electricity and water undertakings;
- transport firms;
- hospitals and establishments for the sick, the disabled, the homeless and the mentally disturbed, dispensaries, children's homes, children's holiday homes, retirement homes, orphanages, boarding schools;
- businesses authorised to organise work on a team basis for round-the-clock work, on the grounds that the work cannot be interrupted or delayed for technical reasons;
- domestic employees.

EXCEPTION: OCCUPATIONS

L4.4.8 The prohibition on Sunday work is also lifted for certain occupations, regardless of the nature of the business. These include:
- surveillance of the business's premises;
- cleaning, repair and maintenance required for sustained operations;
- non-productive work on which the following day's resumption of work is dependent;
- work required to prevent the deterioration of raw materials or products;
- urgent work, which must be accomplished immediately: eg salvage work, or work to prevent a threatened accident or to repair accidental damage to the firm's plant, equipment or premises.

L4.4.9 The abovementioned tasks may be performed on Sundays insofar as the normal running of the business does not allow the performance of these tasks on another day.

L4.4.10 In order to take advantage of any of these exceptions, the employer must inform the Director of the Labour and Mines Inspectorate (*Directeur de l'Inspection du Travail et des Mines*) as well as the staff representatives, in advance. Every industrial, commercial or craft business in the private sector regularly employing 15 or more paid employees must have staff representatives, who are elected for a term of five years. The representatives committee is designed to defend the interests of the employees as to issues of working conditions, job security and social legislation.

L4.4.11 The law also permits up to four hours' Sunday work in retail shops, provided that the establishment is authorised to open on Sundays under the law on opening hours.

L4.4.12 Firms may be exempted from the prohibition on Sunday work by Grand-Ducal regulation permitting them to operate on a Sunday activities:

(i) which are not carried on all year round; or
(ii) which operate more intensively at certain times of the year; or
(iii) meeting a public need principally on a Sunday, or equally every day of the week; or
(iv) which are in the public interest.

EXCEPTION: ADOLESCENTS

L4.4.13 As far as adolescents (ie persons aged between 15 and 18) are concerned, work on Sundays is possible under two conditions.

L4.4.14 Firstly, employers may ask adolescents to work on Sunday in the event of force majeure or if the existence or security of the business so requires, and only in order to prevent a serious impediment to the normal functioning of the business. The Director of the Labour and Mines Inspectorate must immediately be informed of the reasons.

L4.4.15 Secondly, the Director of the Labour and Mines Inspectorate may grant extended authorisation to employ young persons on every second Sunday in:

• hotels, restaurants, cafés and tea rooms; or
• clinics and children's homes.

L4.4.16 Adolescents may work every Sunday during July and August.

L4.4.17 If time off is taken in lieu of Sunday work, a supplementary payment of 70% is due. Otherwise for Sunday work, the rate is 170% of the normal rate and 200% for adolescents.

4.5 Remedies

L4.5.1 See para L4.2.8.

Working time: summary of procedure

- maximum 8 hours a day; 40 hours per week
- extra hours may be worked by private employees
  but ⟶ average weekly working time must not exceed 40 hours
  per week over four weeks
  ⟶ absolute maximum = 10 hours a day; 48 hours per week
- overtime = time off in lieu or 25%/50% supplementary pay
- no Sunday working (certain exceptions
- weekly rest period of 44 hours

---

5   EQUAL OPPORTUNITIES

5.1   Background

L5.1.1   The universal declaration of human rights confirms the principle of non-discrimination, that all humans are born free and equal and may exercise any rights and freedoms regardless of their sex. Discrimination is not therefore permitted with respect to access to employment nor regarding conditions of remuneration.

L5.1.2   The principle of equal opportunities between men and women applies to access to employment, promotion, orientation, training and access to a liberal profession and terms of employment.[1] Moreover, equal opportunities also apply in relation to social security.[2]

[1]   Law of 8 December 1981, Mémorial 1981, p 2194.
[2]   Law of 15 December 1986, Mémorial 1986, p 2343.

L5.1.3   Furthermore, Luxembourg has ratified the Convention signed in New York on 18 December 1979[1] abolishing any form of discrimination against women.

[1]   Mémorial 1988, p 1276.

5.2   Discrimination: Sex, Race and Marital Status

A   POSITIVE ACTION

L5.2.1   In January 1995 a Ministry of Female Promotion (*Ministère de la Promotion Féminine*) was created in order to establish structures and to develop appropriate strategies to modify the behaviours and aspirations of women or men, allowing both sexes to assume their responsibilities in their private and public lives.

L5.2.2   On 26 March 1997, the Council of the Government (*Conseil de Gouvernement*) adopted a national action programme to implement the declaration and action programme adopted by the fourth world-wide conference relating to women organised by the United Nations in Peking: Action Programme 2000.

L5.2.3 A Grand-Ducal regulation dated 31 March 1996 created an interdepartmental committee investigating all questions relating to equal opportunities for men and women.

B   EQUAL TREATMENT BETWEEN MEN AND WOMEN

Employment access and criteria for professional aptitude tests

L5.2.4   The Law dated 8 December 1981 (as amended) provides for equal treatment between men and women as far as access to employment, professional training and promotion, and labour conditions is concerned. It requires equal treatment as regards conditions of access to employment positions.

L5.2.5   The law prohibits any direct or indirect references to the sex of the employee in employment offers or notices and in criteria for professional aptitude tests.

L5.2.6   Any employer or person publishing an offer or notice in violation of this legal requirement incurs a fine.

L5.2.7   Further, an employer may not refuse or impede access to a position on account of expressed or implied reasons based on the sex of the applicant/employee.

L5.2.8   Any legal or contractual provision violating the principle of equal treatment is deemed to be null and void.

C   CELIBACY CLAUSES

L5.2.9   Celibacy clauses are null and void, as are clauses providing that a woman's contract of service may be terminated, or that a female employee may be dismissed, on account of her marriage.

D   RECENT LEGISLATION

L5.2.10   The following provisions have recently been introduced:

- Law dated 7 July 1998 regarding the appointment of a delegate in charge of equal treatment in private sector corporations. The delegate is entrusted with equal treatment between male and female employees of the corporation as far as access to employment, professional training and promotion, salary, and working conditions are concerned;
- Law dated 7 July 1998 regarding the protection of pregnant women at work;
- Law dated 12 February 1999 regarding the implementation of a national action programme in favour of employment. This law establishes a legal basis for positive discrimination in the private sector, allowing concrete measures providing for specific advantages to facilitate the performance of professional activity by the under-represented sex, or to anticipate or compensate for career disadvantages.

E   VICTIMISATION AND HARASSMENT

L5.2.11   On 26 May 2000 the Luxembourg Parliament adopted a law[1] relating to protection against sexual harassment in working relationships.

Sexual harassment is defined as being any sexual behaviour or any other behaviour based on sex which knowingly hurts the dignity of a person in the work place, where:

- the behaviour is inopportune, abusive and hurtful; and
- the fact that one person refuses or accepts such behaviour from the employer, another employee, a client or supplier is explicitly or implicitly used to affect the rights of this person in matters of professional training, employment, continuance of employment, professional promotion, remuneration or any other decision relating to employment; and
- such behaviour creates a feeling of intimidation, hostility or humiliation for the victim.

[1]   Published in the official gazette (*Mémorial*) on 30 June 2000.

L5.2.12   The employer must do whatever is necessary to put an end to any act of sexual harassment as soon as he is advised of it. If he fails to do so, the President of the Labour Court (*Président du Tribunal du Travail*) may require him to do so.

L5.2.13   This law also introduces a new ground of termination of the employment contract, namely resignation based on sexual harassment. The victim is entitled to terminate the employment contract with immediate effect, and the employer may have to pay damages to the employee if the court considers her (or his) resignation was justified.

5.3   Disability Discrimination

A   OBLIGATORY EMPLOYMENT OF DISABLED EMPLOYEES

L5.3.1   Public sector businesses are required[1] for 5% of their total staff to be full-time disabled employees, provided that disabled employees comply with the requirements of education and of legal access to employment.

[1]   Law dated 12 November 1991 relating to disabled employees.

L5.3.2   The following are considered public sector businesses:

- the State;
- the cities;
- the Luxembourg national railway company;
- certain public establishments.

L5.3.3   Private sector businesses are required to employ full-time disabled employees in the following proportions:

- one disabled employee in businesses with at least 25 employees;
- 2% of total staff for businesses with at least 50 employees;
- 4% of total staff for businesses with at least 300 employees.

B   WORKING CONDITIONS

L5.3.4   A disabled employee may not be discriminated against in terms of remuneration.

L5.3.5   Disabled employees are granted additional paid leave of six days per year.

L5.3.6   Under certain circumstances professional training and vocational guidance measures should be offered to disabled employees.

5.4   Enforcement and Remedies

L5.4.1   Any legal or contractual provision violating the principle of equal treatment between men and women is deemed to be null and void.

L5.4.2   In the event of refusal by a private sector employer to employ disabled employees as prescribed by law, a compensation tax equal to 50% of the minimum statutory wage must be paid each month by the employer to the Treasury.

L5.4.3   This tax is due for as long as the employer refuses to comply with these legal requirements and in respect of each non-employed disabled individual.

L5.4.4   However, in the event that a disabled employee refuses to be employed according to his professional skills or to be submitted to training and vocational guidance measures he loses his right to a position reserved for disabled employees.

5.5   Equal Pay

L5.5.1   All employers must ensure equal remuneration between men and women for similar work or work of equal value.[1]

[1]   Grand-Ducal Regulation dated 10 July 1974 (based on art 119 of the Treaty of Rome – now art 141 Treaty of Amsterdam – and of the provisions of Convention No 100 of the International Labour Organisation.

L5.5.2   Any collective bargaining agreement must also comply with these requirements.

L5.5.3   The minimum statutory wage is legally assured to any employed person irrespective of his or her sex.

6   TERMINATION OF EMPLOYMENT

6.1   Modes of Termination

A   TERMINATION BY THE EMPLOYER: DISMISSAL

Dismissal with notice

L6.1.1   Termination with notice is possible only in the case of a contract concluded for an indefinite period of time.

L6.1.2   If the employer wishes to dismiss the employee, notice of dismissal must be sent by registered letter, under penalty of invalidity. The employee's countersignature on the letter of dismissal is proof of receipt.

L6.1.3   Notice by the employer must be given as follows:

Length of service	Notice required
Less than 5 years	2 months
5 to 10 years	4 months
over 10 years	6 months

L6.1.4   Notice takes effect only on the first or the fifteenth of the month. Thus notice given before the fifteenth of the month takes effect on the fifteenth; notice given after the fourteenth takes effect on the first of the following month.

Examples
1. The employee receives a dismissal letter on 11 July 2000. His notice period starts on 15 July 2000.
2. The employee receives a dismissal letter on 18 July 2000. His notice period starts on 1 August 2000.

L6.1.5   The employer must state his reasons for dismissal. The employee may request communication of the detailed reasons, although such request must be made of the employer by registered letter within one month of the date of the notification of dismissal. The employer must then state his reasons in detail within a further month by registered letter.

L6.1.6   Reasons for dismissal must be supported by demonstrable and explicit facts connected with the employee's aptitude, the employee's conduct or the operating needs of the business, establishment or department.

Length of service (years)	Severance pay (months' pay)
5 and less than 10	One
10 and less than 15	Two
15 and less than 20	Three
20 and less than 25	three (manual workers)
	six (private employees)
25 and less than 30	three (manual workers)
	nine (private employees)
30 and over	three (manual workers)
	twelve (private employees)

Dismissal as a consequence of gross misconduct

L6.1.7   The employer may terminate the contract without notice in the case of a contract concluded for an indefinite period of time, and before the end of its term in the case of a fixed-term contract, in the event of gross misconduct by the employee.

L6.1.8   The employer must notify the dismissal according to the same rules set out above (as to the date from which the dismissal is effective and the means of communicating the dismissal to the employee). The employer must, however, immediately state in the dismissal letter the explicit and detailed reasons for the dismissal.

Special statutory protection against dismissal

L6.1.9   An employee who is unable to attend work as a result of sickness or accident must, on the first day of incapacity, advise the employer either personally or via a third person.[1] Notification may be given orally or in writing, or by telegram, telex or fax.

[1]   Article 35 of the 1989 Law.

L6.1.10   On the third day of absence at the latest, the employee must supply the employer with a doctor's certificate confirming that he is unfit for work, and stating the likely duration of his incapacity.

L6.1.11   An employer who has been duly notified of his employee's incapacity to work within the proper time, or who has received the medical certificate in due form within the proper time, is prohibited from terminating the employee's contract or summoning him to an interview prior to dismissal (an employer who employs more than 150 people must interview an employee he intends to dismiss prior to dismissal: see paras **L6.1.21–L6.1.24**).

L6.1.12   The employer's right to dismiss is thus suspended, even in cases of gross misconduct which occurred before the employee's incapacity.

L6.1.13   The suspension period (and therefore protection from dismissal) lasts for a minimum of 26 weeks following the date of incapacity for manual workers, and for the remainder of the month following the date of incapacity and the next three months for private employees.

L6.1.14   Employees remain entitled throughout this period to their remuneration and to any other benefits accruing during their absence.

L6.1.15   An employer may not dismiss a female employee during her pregnancy or during the 12-week period following her confinement.[1]

[1]   Article 10 of the Law dated 3 July 1975 (as amended) relating to the protection of maternity.

L6.1.16   An employer may not dismiss an employee during parental leave.

L6.1.17   For the 'first parental leave' (as defined hereinafter at para **L8.6.2**), protection starts from the last day preceding the beginning of maternity leave.

L6.1.18   For the 'second parental leave' (as defined hereinafter at para **8.6.2**), protection starts from the fourth month preceding the beginning of parental leave.

L6.1.19   Staff representatives and their alternates are protected from dismissal throughout their term of office. Any dismissal is deemed to be null and void, whatever the reason. There is a specific procedure enabling suspension and termination of staff representatives for their gross misconduct: see paras **L6.1.34–L6.1.38**.

L6.1.20   This protection is extended to former staff representatives for the six months following the end of their term of office, and to candidates for election to such office for a period of three months following the announcement of their candidacy.[1]

[1]   Article 34 of the Law dated 18 May 1979 (as amended) relating to staff representatives.

Procedure

L6.1.21   An employer with 150 employees or more who contemplates dismissing any employee must, before reaching any decision, interview the employee concerned.

L6.1.22   Notice of such interview must be given in writing by registered letter or by hand duly acknowledged as received. The letter must give an indication of the purpose of the interview and its date, time and place.

L6.1.23   Dismissal, whether with notice or for gross misconduct, must be notified:

- no earlier than the day following the interview;
- no more than one week later.

L6.1.24   If, having being summoned to an interview, the employee does not attend, the dismissal may be notified:

- no earlier than the day following the day set for the interview;
- no more than one week later.

Reasons for dismissal

L6.1.25   Reasons for dismissal must be supported by demonstrable and explicit facts. Such facts may include:

- reasons connected with the employee's aptitude;
- reasons connected with the employee's conduct;
- reasons arising from the operating needs of the business, establishment or department.

Dismissal: summary
- right to dismiss without notice
  in case of gross misconduct
- special treatment of sick ⟶ 1. employee notifies employer
  employee   of sickness
                                   2. employer's right to dismiss
                                      is suspended
                                   3. three months or 26 weeks
                                      paid suspension

- large employer must interview
  employee prior to decision making
- reason for dismissal must be fair
  and objective
- right to claim unfair dismissal eg
  invalid grounds

B   TERMINATION BY THE EMPLOYEE: RESIGNATION

L6.1.26 An employee willing to terminate the contract of service must send the employer a registered letter.[1] The employer's countersignature on the resignation letter is proof of receipt. Unless the contract of service is terminated on account of gross misconduct on the part of employer, the employee must give notice. The notice period required on resignation by the employee is half that required in the case of dismissal by the employer.

[1]   Article 21 of the 1989 Law.

C   TERMINATION BY MUTUAL AGREEMENT

L6.1.27 A contract of service (either fixed-term or indefinite) may be terminated by the parties by mutual agreement.[1]

[1]   Article 33 of the 1989 Law.

L6.1.28 The parties' common consent must be stated in writing in duplicate and signed by the employer and the employee, under penalty of invalidity.

D   TERMINATION PURSUANT TO ART 30 OF THE 1989 LAW
RELATING TO THE CONTRACT OF SERVICE

L6.1.29 Employment is terminated with immediate effect in the event of cessation of business due to the death or physical disability of the employer or bankruptcy.

L6.1.30 If the business is not taken over by a successor or by the administrator of the bankruptcy, the employees are entitled to receive:
- the remuneration relating to the month in which the event occurred and the remuneration of the subsequent month; and
- compensation equal to 50% of the monthly payments corresponding to the notice period to which the employees would have been entitled.

L6.1.31 The contract of service is automatically terminated when the employee dies.

L6.1.32 The family of a private employee is entitled to the deceased's remuneration for the month in which the death occurred and for the following three months.

E   TERMINATION ON ACCOUNT OF A BREACH OF CONTRACT

L6.1.33 One party may terminate the contract under common law and the Civil Code on account of a breach of a contractual obligation by the other party.

L6.1.34 Although staff representatives and their alternates are on the one hand legally protected against dismissal (see paras **L6.1.19–L6.1.20**) Luxembourg law provides a specific procedure for termination.[1]

[1]   Law dated 18 May 1979 relating to staff representatives.

L6.1.35 This procedure applies to staff representatives in office, their alternates, former representatives for the six months following the end of their term of office and candidates for election to such office for a period of three months following the announcement of their candidacy.

L6.1.36 The employer is entitled in the event of gross misconduct by a staff representative or by alternates and former representatives within six months of their holding office to pronounce a temporary suspension.[1] During the suspension the staff representative will not be entitled to remuneration, unless he makes a request to the Labour Court. The employer must immediately refer the matter to the Labour Court which will decide whether the employment contract should be terminated for breach of contract.

[1]   Article 34(2) of the Law dated 18 May 1979.

L6.1.37 In the event that the Labour Court decides that the gross misconduct justifies the termination of the employment contract, termination takes effect from the first day of suspension. If the employee had obtained the right to remuneration during the period of suspension, the employer may request that the wages paid during the suspension be refunded.

L6.1.38 If the Labour Court decides that the alleged gross misconduct does not terminate the employment contract, the suspension is cancelled and the employee must be reinstated.

6.2 Statutory Claims – Unfair Dismissal

L6.2.1 Dismissal is regarded as unfair and contrary to social and economic reason, if it takes place for unlawful reasons, or if it is not well-founded on valid grounds related to the employee's aptitude or conduct, or arising from the operating needs of the business, establishment or department.

L6.2.2 If the employee challenges the reasons given by the employer in support of the dismissal, the onus is on the employer to prove not only the facts but their validity and seriousness. The employer is entitled to bring before the court new evidence additional to that set out in the letter of dismissal, but may not refer to new reasons.

L6.2.3 The employee may bring an action for unfair dismissal and damages before the court within a period of three months from the letter of dismissal (where dismissal was for gross misconduct) or the letter of justification (where dismissal with notice took place).

L6.2.4 If the employee has made a written claim to the employer within three months, an action for unfair dismissal may still be commenced within one year from the date of the written claim.[1]

[1] Article 28 of the 1989 Law.

6.3 Collective Terminations Including Redundancies

L6.3.1 The statutory procedure regarding collective dismissals must be followed as soon as an employer proposes to dismiss at least seven employees within a period of 30 days or to dismiss 15 employees within a period of 90 days.[1]

[1] Chapter III of the Law dated 23 July 1993 relating to measures in favour of employment.

A   PROCEDURE ON COLLECTIVE DISMISSALS

L6.3.2 The employer must enter into negotiations with staff representatives *before* proceeding with collective dismissals, in order to come to an agreement relating to the establishment of a Social Plan (*Plan Social*).[1] A Social Plan is a written agreement signed by both parties (the employer and the representatives) which contains the results of the negotiations. The employees' representatives are either the staff representatives, the joint works council (composed of an equal number of management and employees' representatives) or the trade unions if a collective bargaining agreement applies to the employer/employee relationship.

[1] Article 7(1) of the Law dated 23 July 1993.

L6.3.3 Before the negotiations begin, and at the latest at the beginning of the negotiations, the employer must inform each employee in writing of the proposed collective dismissal and must provide the employees with the following information:[1]

* reasons for the proposed dismissals;
* number and description of employees affected;
* number and description of employees usually employed;
* period of time within which the dismissals are proposed;
* method of selecting employees to be dismissed (unless all employees are to be dismissed);
* proposed method of calculating the amount of any redundancy payment.

[1] Article 8(1) of the Law dated 23 July 1993.

L6.3.4 Written notification of the proposed redundancies should be sent to the Employment Administration (*Administration de l'Emploi*) by the employer, together with a copy of the notification to the employees, before the negotiations start.[1]

[1] Article 8(2) and 9(1) of the Law dated 23 July 1993.

L6.3.5 The notification is forwarded by the Employment Administration to the Labour and Mines Inspectorate *(Inspection du Travail et des Mines)*.

L6.3.6 The employer and the individual employees then enter into negotiations. They must, within a period of 15 days from the beginning of the negotiations, come to an agreement relating to the establishment of a Social Plan.[1]

[1] Article 7(5) of the Law dated 23 July 1993.

L6.3.7 At this stage, if the parties have reached agreement, they must sign a Social Plan. After the signature of the Social Plan, the employer is entitled to notify the dismissal to each employee on an individual basis.[1] Any dismissal notified to the employees before the signature by the parties of the Social Plan is null and void.

[1] Article 10(1) of the Law dated 23 July 1993.

L6.3.8 If the parties have not reached agreement within the 15-day period referred to above, the minutes of the negotiations stating the goodwill and motivation of the parties regarding the negotiated issues is signed and immediately forwarded to the Employment Administration (*Administration de l'Emploi*).[1] Both parties must jointly refer the matter to the National Arbitration Committee (*Office National de Conciliation*) within three days of signature of the minutes, under penalty of invalidity of the whole procedure.[2]

[1] Article 7(6) of the Law dated 23 July 1993.
[2] Article 7(7) of the Law dated 23 July 1993.

L6.3.9 Within two days the President of the *Office National de Conciliation* will appoint the members of a committee (*Commission Paritaire*) to consider the issues. Within three days of the convening notice, the *Commission Paritaire* will hold a meeting.[1]

[1] Article 7(7) paragraph 4 of the Law dated 23 July 1993.

L6.3.10 The *Commission Paritaire* will consider the matter within a maximum of 15 days from the date of the first meeting. The minutes of the deliberations are forwarded to the Employment Administration and to the Labour and Mines Inspectorate.[1]

[1] Article 7(7) paragraph 5 of the Law dated 23 July 1993.

L6.3.11 After the signature of the minutes by the *Office National de Conciliation*, the employer is entitled to notify each employee of dismissal on an individual basis.[1] Any dismissal notified to the employees before the signature of the minutes is null and void.

[1] Article 10(1) of the Law dated 23 July 1993.

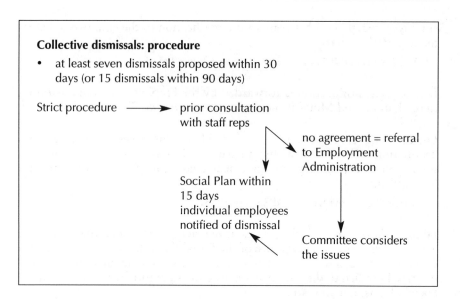

Collective dismissals: procedure

- at least seven dismissals proposed within 30 days (or 15 dismissals within 90 days)

Strict procedure ⟶ prior consultation with staff reps

no agreement = referral to Employment Administration

Social Plan within 15 days individual employees notified of dismissal

Committee considers the issues

B   STATUTORY RIGHTS

L6.3.12   Collectively dismissed employees have the same rights as employees dismissed on an individual basis.[1] They are therefore entitled to notice and to severance pay calculated according to their length of service (see paras **L6.1.3** and **L6.1.6**).

[1]   According to a court decision dated 24 March 1994 (*Associated Metal Powders SA c/ Almeida Da Silva*), the redundant employee has the same rights as the employee dismissed on an individual basis.

L6.3.13   The dismissals come into effect after a period of 75 days without prejudice to any other longer period of notice provided by law.

[1]   Article 11(1).

L6.3.14   Moreover the Labour Minister can extend the notice period up to a maximum of 90 days upon request by either of the parties, if the problems raised by the collective dismissals will not be resolved within the initial notice period.

L6.3.15   The employer as well as the employees must be informed of the extension and the reasons for it by the fifteenth day before the expiry of the initial notice period at the latest.

Length of uninterrupted service	Notice required or payment in lieu	Severance pay
Less than 5 years	75 days (or 90 days in case of extension – see above)	0
5–10 years	4 months	1 month
10–15 years	6 months	2 months
15–20 years	6 months	3 months

L6.3.16   Notice can only begin on the first or the fifteen of the month. Notice given before the fifteen of the month takes effect on the fifteenth; notice given after the fourteenth takes effect on the first of the following month.

L6.3.17   Depending on business circumstances or in the event of the earlier closure of the business, the employees may be asked not to work any of the notice period, in which case they will receive pay in lieu of notice based on their current salary.

L6.3.18   If so requested by the employee, the employer must give reasons for dismissal. The request must be made by registered letter within one month of the date of notification of dismissal (according to the postmark).

L6.3.19   The employer must give reasons in detail within a further month (again, counting from the postmark on the employee's request). The statement of reasons must be sent by registered letter.

L6.3.20   Reasons for dismissal must be supported by demonstrable and explicit facts relating to the operating needs of the business.

L6.3.21   Employees will also be entitled (as they would on an individual dismissal) either to take their remaining holiday as earned on a pro-rata basis for the year, or to receive payment in lieu of holiday (again, on a pro-rata basis).

C   ADDITIONAL PAYMENT

L6.3.22   In addition to the notice period and severance pay referred to above, the Social Plan may take into consideration further payments:

- *redundancy payment* for an amount usually varying between one to five months' salary, taking into account the age, length of service, and family situation of each employee;
- *loyalty incentive* for employees working during their notice period, usually varying from one to five months' pay depending on the length of the notice period;
- *additional bonus* for employees who have not been re-employed by the end of the notice period. Such payments usually amount to between one to five months' salary depending on the employee's age and family situation;

L6.3.23   The Social Plan must also contain provisions regarding:

- alternative employment opportunities, re-grading and re-deployment measures for all employees or for certain employees chosen on the basis of non-discriminatory criteria;
- outplacement assistance; and
- an undertaking to give former employees priority in the event of future recruitment.

6.4   Remedies

A   INVALIDITY OF THE DISMISSAL NOTICE

L6.4.1   Failure to comply with the requirements set out above in relation to the Social Plan and the minutes of the *Office National de Conciliation* renders any dismissal notice void.

L6.4.2 The employees may refer the matter to the President of the Labour Court within 15 days of the dismissal, requesting an order declaring the dismissal void and ordering the continuance of the employment contract.

B   UNFAIR DISMISSAL

L6.4.3 If the employees fail to commence Court proceedings for invalidity of the dismissal notice (see paras **L6.4.1–L6.4.2**) within 15 days of dismissal, they can commence proceedings for unfair dismissal and claim an award of compensation. Compensation is based on the effective damage suffered and may be unlimited.

7   YOUNG WORKERS

7.1   General Obligations

L7.1.1 According to a Law dated 28 October 1969 the employment of children under the age of 15 years old is prohibited, except:

- to work in technical and professional schools on condition that the work has essentially an educational character, that commercial profit is not its purpose, and finally that it is approved and supervised by public authorities;
- housekeeping assistance given by children of the family.

L7.1.2 The employment of young children in public shows is permitted subject to authorisation under the following conditions:

- the participation of the child in the show does not harm his health and morality, or his education;
- the child must be at least six years old;
- the child may not participate in the show after 23:00;
- the child must rest for at least 14 hours between shows.

L7.1.3 Circus activities, variety shows and cabarets will not be granted authorisation.

L7.1.4 Authorisation is granted by the Minister of National Education after having sought the advice of the Labour and Mines Inspectorate. The parents or the legal representatives of the child must also give their written authorisation.

L7.1.5 Finally, the law does not allow the employment of adolescents under the age of 18 years old to perform certain tasks which:

- do not correspond to the degree of development of the adolescent; or
- require disproportionate efforts from the adolescent; or
- may be harmful to the physical or mental health of the adolescent.

8   MATERNITY AND PARENTAL RIGHTS

8.1   Background

L8.1.1 Maternity leave is governed by the Law dated 3 July 1975. It does not interrupt the contract of service, but merely suspends it throughout the period of enforced absence. The contract comes back into effect when the reason for its suspension ceases to exist.

8.2   General Rights

A   MATERNITY LEAVE

L8.2.1   Maternity leave is in two stages:
*   antenatal leave consisting of eight weeks preceding the expected date of confinement, extending if necessary up to the actual date of confinement;
*   postnatal leave of eight weeks, extended to 12 weeks in the case of premature birth, in the case of a multiple confinement, and in the case of a mother breast-feeding her child.

B   NOTICE REQUIREMENTS

L8.2.2   The employee must supply the employer with a medical certificate certifying the pregnancy and the expected date of confinement. The employee is also required to send the employer (by registered letter) a medical certificate concerning her breast-feeding within seven weeks of her confinement.

8.3   Protection from Dismissal

L8.3.1   An employer may not dismiss a female employee during her pregnancy, or during the 12 weeks following her confinement.[1]

[1]   Article 10 of the Law dated 3 July 1975 (as amended).

L8.3.2   This provision does not, however, prevent the termination of a contract concluded for a definite period of time on its completion; neither does it give the employee immunity from dismissal for gross misconduct.

L8.3.3   Any dismissal notified in contravention of this rule is null and void.

8.4   Health and Safety

L8.4.1   Pregnant or breast-feeding women may not be employed between 22:00 and 06:00. Moreover it is prohibited to assign physically arduous tasks to pregnant women or to women following confinement (for a period of three months after confinement or seven months if breast-feeding), or to expose her to harmful materials, radiation, dust, gas, heat, cold, humidity, shocks or vibration.

8.5   Maternity Pay

L8.5.1   Maternity benefit is payable to female employees throughout the statutory maternity period.

L8.5.2   Self-employed women are entitled to maternity benefit determined on the same basis as (but not in addition to) sickness benefit. Women who are not employed at all are entitled to a maternity allowance for 16 weeks following the eighth week before the expected date of confinement.

8.6 Parental Leave

L8.6.1 Parental leave and leave for family reasons was introduced in Luxembourg by a Law dated 12 February 1999.

L8.6.2 Each parent under certain conditions is entitled to parental leave at the time of birth or adoption of a child. One parent must take parental leave directly at the end of the maternity leave period ('first parental leave'). The other parent can take parental leave at any time until the child reaches five years of age ('second parental leave').

L8.6.3 The duration of parental leave is six months, or 12 months in the event the employee wishes to keep working at least half-time.

L8.6.4 In the case of multiple births, the duration of parental leave is eight months, or 16 months half-time.

L8.6.5 The employer may under certain conditions require the postponement of 'second parental leave' up to two months, or up to six months if the employer employs fewer than 15 employees.

L8.6.6 At the end of the parental leave period, the employee is entitled to be restored to his position. If he is not restored to his position, the employee may commence proceedings for unfair dismissal or to claim that the employment contract has been amended to his disadvantage (see para **6.2.3**).

9   BUSINESS TRANSFERS

9.1   Identifying a Relevant Transfer

L9.1.1 Article 36 of the 1989 Law relating to contracts of service provides that, in the event of a modification of the situation of the employer, especially by inheritance, sale, merger, business transformation, or incorporation, all contracts of employment existing at the time of the modification will remain in force between the new employer and the employees of the business.

L9.1.2 The transfer of a business, in particular due to a contractual transfer or to a merger, does not constitute in itself a justification either for the transferor or for the transferee to dismiss the employees working in the transferred business.

L9.1.3 These provisions derive from the implementation of Directive 77/187 (the acquired rights Directive) in Luxembourg's domestic legislation.[1]

[1]   Law dated 18 March 1981.

A   DEFINITION GIVEN BY THE EUROPEAN COURT OF JUSTICE

L9.1.4 It is useful to refer to the decisions taken by the European Court of Justice (ECJ), in order to define the notion of 'transfer of a business' and in particular the notion of 'business' in Luxembourg law.

L9.1.5 Indeed, in *Spijkers*,[1] the ECJ considered that a 'transfer of a business' refers to any economic entity that keeps its identity after its transfer to other management.

[1]   24/85: *Spijkers Gebroeders Benedik Abbatoir CV* [1986] ECR 1119, ECJ.

L9.1.6 Moreover, the ECJ will consider the existence of a transfer of a business in the light of the actual circumstances under which the operation has been carried out.

L9.1.7 The ECJ requires that the same business is carried on or taken over by the new employer with identical economic activities or similar activities.

L9.1.8 The transfer must also concern a stable economic entity and its activities should not be limited to the performance of one defined form of work, following the ECJ's decision in *Rygaard*.[1]

[1]   C–48/94: *Rygaard* [1995] ECR I–2745, ECJ.

L9.1.9 According to the *Süzen* case[1] the notion of an 'entity' refers to persons and elements organised as a whole allowing the performance of an economic activity with its own purpose. The entity must correspond to a self- governing and independent structure.

[1]   C–13/95: *Süzen* [1997] ECR I–1259, ECJ.

L9.1.10 The *Süzen* decision indicated that the identity of the economic entity is characterised by the staff, supporting measures, work organisation, methods of exploitation or available means of exploitation.

L9.1.11 The fact that a similar activity is performed one moment by the transferor and the next by the transferee does not of itself allow the conclusion that an entity has been transferred, according to three recent decisions.[1]

[1]   Dated 10 December 1998: C–127/96, C–229/96, C–74/97, *Francisco Hernández Vidal SA v Prudencia Gómez Perez, Maria Gomez Perez, Contratas y Limpiezas Sl, Friedrich Santner v Hoechst AG, Mercedes Gomez Montaña v Claro Sol SA, Red Nacional de Ferrocarriles Espanoles* [1998] ECR I–8179.

B   DEFINITION GIVEN BY THE LUXEMBOURG COURTS

L9.1.12 The decisions of the national courts of Luxembourg[1] refer also to the continuation of a corporate purpose taking into consideration the continuation and permanence of the business, which is a condition to the application of art 36 of the 1989 Law.

[1]   CSJ 22 January 1969, *Jean Hoffman v Société de Produits Chimiques SA.*

L9.1.13 Thus the activities performed by the employees must be carried out after the transfer in the same location with a view to achieving the same purpose. Article 36 requires the continuation of the existence of the business but not of its legal structure.[1]

[1]   CSJ 1 July 1981, *Alice Kaempf v Edmond Schmit.*

L9.1.14 To fall within the scope of art 36 of the Law the transfer must concern an economic entity as a whole which has, as far as the human and technical sphere is concerned, enough consistency to qualify as an establishment or a centre of activity.[1]

[1]   CSJ 1 January 1998, *Steinmetz v Steinmetz*.

9.2   Effects of the Transfer

L9.2.1   Article 36 operates as an automatic transfer of the contracts of employment which binds the transferor, the transferee, and the employees.[1]

[1]   Decision of the European Court of Justice dated 25 July 1991, C–362/89: *D'Urso v Ercole Marelli Elettromeccanica Generale SpA* [1991] ECR I–4105 and CSJ 12 March 1992, *Pia Esterman v Nicolas Reding, Alice Schneider et Shopping Alzette Sàrl*.

L9.2.2   The employer (transferor or transferee) may not opt out of the transfer. If an employee is dismissed in relation to the transfer, the dismissal is unfair and the employee may commence proceedings against either the transferor or the transferee.

L9.2.3   It is however possible at any time for the employment contract to be terminated by the mutual consent of both parties (ie the transferor or transferee, and the employee).

10   COLLECTIVE RIGHTS AND BARGAINING

10.1 Trade Unions

L10.1.1   Article 11 of the Luxembourg Constitution guarantees freedom to join a trade union. Luxembourg workers and private employees, as well as employers are organised on a voluntary basis into a number of trade unions, respectively trade and professional federations, whose principle action is to negotiate collective bargaining agreements.

10.2 Staff Representative Committee

L10.2.1   Every industrial, commercial or craft business regularly employing at least 15 employees must have staff representatives.[1] Staff representatives are elected in a secret ballot by proportional representation. The term of office is the same for all businesses and is set at five years. Elections may be held less than five years after the previous ones in businesses which reach the threshold of 15 employees, where the number of representatives in office cannot be made up and elected alternates are not available to occupy the vacant posts. Staff representatives may be re-elected.

[1]   Law of 18 May 1979.

L10.2.2   The staff representative committee defends the interests of the employees in matters of working conditions, job security and social legislation insofar as these tasks do not fall within the scope of the works council's tasks.

L10.2.3   Staff representatives must be given the time off needed to carry out their duties.

10.3 Works Councils

L10.3.1   In addition to the staff representative committee, every business employing at least 150 employees over a three-year reference period must have a works council.[1] The number of members depends on the size of the business. Work councils are composed of an equal number of employer and employee representatives.

[1]   Law of 6 May 1974.

L10.3.2   The employer representatives are chosen by the head of the employer's management, and the employee representatives are elected by proportional representation in a secret ballot of the staff representatives.

L10.3.3   The works council is essentially an advisory body. The head of management must inform and advise the works council prior to any major decision relating to any modification brought to manufacturing processes or management processes, equipment or work methods. The works council must be informed and advised of existing and foreseeable needs relating to personnel and training measures at least once a year. The head of management must also inform and consult the works council in writing at least twice a year as to the economic and financial situation of the business.

10.4 Employee Participation in Company Management

L10.4.1   The Law of 6 May 1974 provides, under certain conditions, for employee representation on the employer's board of management and board of auditors. The Law only applies to public limited companies employing at least 1,000 employees over a three-year reference period.

L10.4.2   As an exception to the rule that directors are appointed by the general meeting of the shareholders, the Law confers on staff representatives the right to appoint directors representing the staff, by a ballot carried out under proportional representation rules.

11   EMPLOYMENT DISPUTES

11.1 The Labour Court

L11.1.1   The Labour Court *(Tribunal du Travail)* is competent to hear disputes relating to employment contracts and contracts of apprenticeship arising between employers and employees, even after termination of the contract. The jurisdiction of the Labour Court depends on the place of performance of the work. The Labour Court is composed of a professional magistrate and two assessors.

L11.1.2   The action is brought by way of a written brief indicating the name, profession, and domicile of the parties, as well as the object of the action and a concise account of the points of dispute. Failure to provide these details makes the request invalid.

L11.1.3   The court summons the parties to a hearing to examine the case, after which it pronounces judgment. The Labour Court usually orders compensation but may order reinstatement of the employee at the employee's request, if the continuation of the contract of service is possible.

L11.1.4 Either party may file an appeal against the judgment within 40 days from the date of notification of the judgment to the parties. The appeal is brought before the Labour Court of Appeal *(Cour d'Appel)* by way of an appeal request served by a bailiff. The Appeal Court pronounces a judgment on appeal *(arrêt)*.

L11.1.5 Under certain circumstances, the matter may be referred to the *Cour de Cassation* (the Supreme Court) only on strict legal grounds.

L11.1.6 Provisions have been introduced[1] regarding summary proceedings in the field of labour law, with cases being dealt with by the President of the Labour Court. The action is brought in the same way as for the Labour Court. The judge pronounces an interim order. Either party may file an appeal against the order within 15 days from the notification of the order to the parties.

[1] Law dated 6 December 1989.

12   WHISTLEBLOWING/DATA PROTECTION

12.1 Whistleblowing

L12.1.1 Whistleblowing is not regulated under Luxembourg law.

L12.1.2 Employers and employees may, however, provide in contracts of service for a confidentiality and secrecy clause as described under para 1.2.19.

12.2 Data Protection

L12.2.1 The employer may collect personal data concerning his employees in a manual register without any express authorisation from a governmental authority. However, if the relevant data is to be stored on an electronic register, the employer must apply for express authorisation by the competent authority, ie the Luxembourg State Minister.[1]

[1] Grand Ducal Regulation of 11 August 1999.

L12.2.2 As a general principle, only personal data subject to automatic processing is protected under Luxembourg law. Indeed the Law of 31March 1979 on the protection of personal data provides the general framework under which a person is protected against the abusive use of personal data with regard to automatic processing.

L12.2.3 The Law applies to:
- any database that is either implemented or used in Luxembourg;
- any database established in Luxembourg, even if it is only used abroad;
- any database established abroad, but made available in Luxembourg by means of a server.

L12.2.4   Legal protection is triggered in the following cases:

- when the data is collected in order to be processed automatically;
- when registration of the data takes place;
- during the automatic processing of the data;
- on the transmission of the data to third parties.

L12.2.5   According to Luxembourg law, the owner[1] as well as the manager[2] of a personal data processing[3] operation must ask for prior authorisation[4] to be issued by the domestic authorities.[5]

[1]   The owner is the person on behalf of whom the data processing takes place: Law of 1979, art 2.
[2]   The manager is the person who effectively operates the data processing: Law of 1979, art 2.
[3]   Assuming that the data processing is aimed at private use.
[4]   The Law of 1979 provides for criminal sanctions (imprisonment of eight days to six months and/or a fine of LUF 10,001 to 500,000 (€ 247.91 to 12,394.67), if a database is used without prior ministerial authorisation.
[5]   If a foreign database is used in Luxembourg, the local user must ask for such authorisation.

L12.2.6   Personal data is defined as all information relating to a determined person or a person who can be determined. A database is a collection of data processed by a software system.[1]

[1]   Law of 31 March 1979, art 1 and 2.

L12.2.7   Article 18 of the Law provides that the persons from whom information is collected in order to be processed must be automatically informed as to the following issues:

- the aim of the automatic processing of their data;
- the compulsory or optional character of their responses;
- the consequences of their failure to respond;
- the third parties to whom the information is to be sent;
- the existence of a right to access and rectification of the information.

L12.2.8   Furthermore, the Law expressly specifies[1] that where ministerial authorisation is required the application letter must contain the following information:

- the name, object of the company, and address of the owner and user of the database;
- name of the database;
- detailed description of the aim of the database;
- nature and origin of the data accessible in the database as well as the pertinence of the data to the aim pursued by the database;
- where the transfer of the data to third parties is envisaged, the nature of the data and the results to be transmitted as well as the identification of the third parties.

[1]   Law of 31 March 1979, art 5(2).

L12.2.9   Persons who intervene in the collection, processing and transmission of personal data have a duty of confidentiality.[1] The owners and managers of a database must keep the database updated ie they must correct errors in the data or delete information which is outdated or obtained by fraud.[2]

[1]   Law of 31 March 1979, art 25.
[2]   Law of 31 March 1979, art 26.

L12.2.10   More specifically, the persons operating the database must guarantee the safekeeping of the data ie they must avoid the information being distorted, damaged, or transmitted to unauthorised third parties. Therefore, adequate software programmes must be installed for the automatic and regular processing of the data.

L12.2.11   The collection of data is strictly regulated. It is prohibited to collect and store personal data relating to the political, philosophical or religious activities or opinions of a person, or data concerning the racial origin or private life of a person.

L12.2.12   Insofar as the specific issue of the transmission of personal data to third parties is concerned, the Law mentions transmission of data to third parties without expressly regulating this issue. The Law does, however, implicitly legalise the transfer of personal data to third parties who are expressly covered by the ministerial authorisation. The transfer of the data to third parties will only be authorised where the third parties concerned can be clearly identified and where the nature of the data justifies such transfer. As expressly provided by art 6 of the Law of 1979, authorisation is generally granted either where there is no reason to fear any abuse of the personal data or where there is no risk of breach of any of the Law's provisions.

L12.2.13   Directive 95/46 of 24 October 1995 on the protection of individuals with regard to the processing of personal data and on the free communication of such data has not been yet implemented into Luxembourg domestic legislation. The Directive provides for more stringent provisions, especially with respect to the processing of personal data and its transmission for the purposes of direct marketing.

13   HUMAN RIGHTS

13.1 Luxembourg Constitution

L13.1.1   Article 11 of the Luxembourg Constitution protects all citizens in respect of their rights under Luxembourg labour law, in relation to social security, protection of workers' health and rest, and freedom to join a trade union.

L13.1.2   The right to strike is not explicitly provided for in the Constitution or in any other Luxembourg law. This right however derives from a broad interpretation of the freedom to join a trade union, pursuant to art 11 of the Constitution. The Supreme Court has decided[1] that the participation of an employee in a professional and lawful strike constitutes the exercise of a right implicitly declared by art 11 of the Constitution.

[1]   Cour de Cassation, 24 July 1952, *B v C* the participation of an employee in a professional and lawful strike constitutes the exercise of a right implicitly declared by art 11, n 5 of the Luxembourg Constitution. The employment contract is suspended during the participation to such strike, which constitutes a justified reason of absence.

L13.1.3   Moreover, freedom of association is guaranteed by art 26 of the Constitution.

13.2 The European Convention on Human Rights

L13.2.1   The European Convention on Human Rights ('ECHR') was approved in Luxembourg by a Law dated 29 August 1953 (as amended).

L13.2.2   No Law was specifically implemented to enforce the rights contained in the ECHR in the Luxembourg Courts and to incorporate its provisions into domestic law. The Supreme Court had decided that judges should take arts 8 to 14 of the ECHR into consideration in the framework of disputes brought before their courts, because they produce a direct effect in domestic law and grant to each individual personal rights which domestic courts must protect.[1] However the position as to enforcement of ECHR rights remains unclear.[2]

[1]   Cour de Cassation, January 17, 1985, *Engel and Schlosser v Consorts Engel*.
[2]   Cour d'Appel, chambre des mises en accusations, 12 February 1982; and Cour de Cassation, 31 May 1991, *Schreiner v Ministère Public*.

BIBLIOGRAPHY

* *Droit du Travail* Romain Schintgen (January 1996) Service Information et Presse du Gouvernement Luxembourg
* *Droit du Travail: Guide Pratique* Marc Feyereisen, Editions Promo-culture
* *Droit du Travail: Jurisprudence* Marc Feyereisen, Editions Promo-culture

USEFUL ADDRESSES

* Chamber of Commerce of the Grand Duchy of Luxembourg (*Chambre de Commerce du Grand-Duché de Luxembourg*)
  7, rue Alcide de Gasperi
  Luxembourg
  Tel (352) 42 39 39-1 Fax (352) 40 61 40
  E-mail chamcom@cc.lu
* Employment Administration (*Administration de l'Emploi*)
  10, Rue Bender BP 2208
  L-1022 Luxembourg
  Tel (352) 487-5300   Fax (352) 40 44 81
* Joint Social Security Centre (*Centre Commun de la Sécurité Sociale*)
  125, Route d'Esch
  L-1471 Luxembourg
  Tel (352) 40 14 11   Fax (352) 40 44 81
* Ministry of Labour (*Ministère du Travail*)
  26, Rue Zithe
  L-2763 Luxembourg
  Tel (352) 478-1   Fax (352) 478-6325

M   The Netherlands

Jos W M Poshof

Jos Pothof is a Partner at CMS Derks Star Busmann Hanotiau, Utrecht.

CMS Derks Star Busmann Hanotiau, Utrecht

Phone: +31 30 212 1645
Fax: +31 30 212 1165
Email: j.pothof@cmsderks.nl
Website: www.derks.nl

THE NETHERLANDS

Rights	Yes/No	Explanatory Notes
CONTRACTS OF EMPLOYMENT		
Minimum notice	YES	
Terms:		
Express	YES	Freedom of contract may be restricted by: • mandatory rules of law • ¾ mandatory law (deviation only possible by CBA) • semi-imperative law • regulatory law
REMUNERATION		
Minimum wage regulation	YES	
Further rights and obligations:		
Right to paid holiday	YES	4 × working days each week for 52 weeks – up to 70% of wages
Right to sick pay	YES	
WORKING TIME		
Regulation of hours per day/ working week	YES	Breaches treated seriously. 40 hour maximum averaged over 13 week period
Regulation of night work	YES	
Right to rest periods	YES	
EQUAL OPPORTUNITIES		
Discrimination protection:		
Sex	YES	
Race	YES	
Marital status	YES	
Disability	YES	But limited
Religion	YES	
Age	NO	
Sexual orientation	YES	
Equal pay legislation	YES	
Immigrant	YES	Proportional representation
TERMINATION OF EMPLOYMENT		
Right not to be dismissed in breach of contract	YES	
Statutory rights on termination	YES	Unfair dismissal. But unusual as strict procedure and permission from local authority required before dismissal

REDUNDANCY

Statutory definition	YES	
Right to payment on redundancy	NO	But if sub-district court allows dissolution of employment contract based on change in circumstances a payment based on formula may be made
Right to consultation:		
Collective	YES	Where 20+ employees to be dismissed

YOUNG WORKERS

Protection of children and young persons at work	YES	

MATERNITY RIGHTS

Right to maternity leave	YES	16 weeks' paid leave
Maternity pay (during leave)	YES	
Protection from dismissal	YES	During pregnancy /maternity leave and pregnancy/childbirth related illness
Health and safety protection	YES	
Right to parental leave	YES	
Right to time off for dependants	YES	

TRANSFERS OF BUSINESSES

Right to protection on transfer	YES	
Transfer of employment obligations	YES	
Right to information and consultation	YES/NO	Works council must be consulted.
Right not to be dismissed	YES	Application to regional employment office for permission to dismiss will be rejected

COLLECTIVE RIGHTS

Union recognition	YES	Freedom of organisation
Right to take industrial action	YES	But collective consultation culture tends to result in agreement

EMPLOYMENT DISPUTES

Civil court jurisdiction	YES	
Statutory body	NO	

WHISTLEBLOWING

Protection from dismissal/   NO
detriment

DATA PROTECTION

Protection   YES

HUMAN RIGHTS ACT

Statutory protection of human
rights
Public authority   YES
Private organisations   NO

1   THE EMPLOYMENT RELATIONSHIP

1.1   Background

A   SOURCES OF LAW

M1.1.1   Provisions regarding the individual employment contract are to be found in the Dutch Civil Code (*Burgerlijk Wetboek* – BW), arts 7:610 et seq.

M1.1.2   In part these provisions are imposed by the European Community, the main aim being to secure the free movement of goods and services, including labour, between the member countries of the EC.

M1.1.3   To reach this goal the Council of Ministers and the Commission of the EC often give rulings to harmonise or otherwise develop legal provisions within the EC.

M1.1.4   Other sources of law are jurisprudence and the writings of acknowledged authorities on this part of law.

B   CONTRACTS

M1.1.5   The Dutch Civil Code provides for three types of contract under which work may be carried out:
- the employment contract;
- the fixed-price contract;
- the commission contract.

Employment contract

M1.1.6   The employment contract is the most usual form of contract. Sections 7:610 to 7:690 of the Dutch Civil Code form the legal basis for the employment contract.

M1.1.7   The employment contract, consisting of the following four elements, is defined by s 7:610 of the Civil Code as follows:
- work must be performed by the individual concerned;
- wages must be paid;
- there must be a relationship of authority (see para **M1.1.15**);
- the contract must last for a certain period of time.

Fixed-price contract

M1.1.8   The law[1] defines a fixed-price contract as one where one party, referred to as the contractor, undertakes with the other party, the contracting party, to render certain work of a tangible nature on payment of a specific price. The distinctive feature of this relationship is the rendering of specific tangible work, there being neither a relationship of authority between the parties nor any obligation on the part of the contractor to carry out the work personally.

[1]   Section 7a:163 of the Civil Code.

Commission contract

M1.1.9   The commission contract is defined[1] as where one party, the commissioned party, undertakes to carry out work for the commissioning party without the existence of an employment relationship. It consists of something other than the carrying out of tangible work, the custody of goods, the allocation of work or the transport or arranging the transport of people or goods.

[1]   Section 7:400 of the Civil Code.

M1.1.10   As indicated, the employment contract has four characteristic elements which must be present if an employment contract is to exist, even if the contracting parties do not realise that these four elements are present.

M1.1.11   There is a legal presumption[1] that an employment contract exists. If work has been performed personally and remuneration has been paid for a period of three months, on a weekly basis, or for at least 20 hours a month, then it is presumed that an employment contract has come into force between the parties. This legal presumption may be rebutted on provision of sufficient proof.

[1]   Section 7:610a of the Civil Code.

M1.1.12   An employer is legally obliged to provide certain information to an employee about the employment contract. For example, the employer must provide the most relevant details of the employment contract in writing to the employee, such as:
- the identities of the parties;
- place of the employment;
- job duties;
- date of commencement;
- duration; applicable notice periods;
- wages;
- holiday or weekly working hours;
- pension schemes; and
- whether a Collective Bargaining Agreement (CBA) applies.[1]

[1]   Section 7:655 of the Civil Code.

M1.1.13   Work must be carried out personally by the employee. This therefore excludes the possibility of a person other than the employee carrying out the work.

M1.1.14   Work is understood to mean the performance of any duties of a physical or 'intellectual' nature by the employee for the employer.

M1.1.15   The relationship of authority (see para **M1.1.7**), which implies the subordination of the employee, means that the employee is obliged to follow the employer's orders or instructions. In practice, this is not always easy to distinguish clearly. In determining whether a relationship of authority exists, it is important to know whether the employer is contractually entitled to give orders or instructions. Whether the employer actually exercises this authority is not conclusive. It is not necessary that the employer exercises this relationship of authority himself; the employer may transfer this authority to a third party.

M1.1.16   The term 'certain period of time' (see para **M1.1.7**) indicates that the employee is obliged to make himself available to the employer during a specific period of time to carry out work. The availability of the employee is more important than actually carrying out the work.

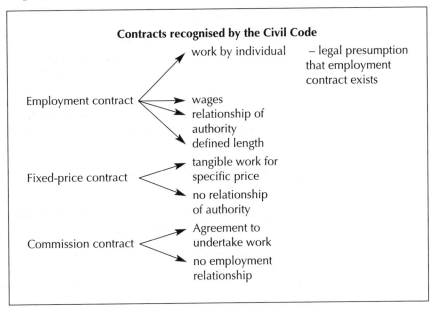

1.2   The Contract of Service

M1.2.1   As long as the definition of an employment contract as set out above is met, the agreement need not be in writing. However, certain details of the employment contract must by law be recorded in writing.[1]

[1]   Section 7:655 of the Civil Code.

M1.2.2   A written contract may also be required for certain agreements between the parties and for deviations from the law. A CBA may also prescribe that the employment contract shall be in writing.

M1.2.3   Freedom of contract between the parties can be restricted in four ways:

- Mandatory rules of law might apply, in which case it is not possible to deviate from the statutory provisions.
- Three-quarters mandatory law: only a CBA can deviate from such statutory provisions. A simple written contract will not suffice.
- Semi-imperative law: the statutory provisions may only be deviated from by a written employment contract.
- Directory law or regulatory law: such provisions can be deviated from, either verbally or in writing, but will apply unless the parties have agreed otherwise.

M1.2.4 The contents of the employment contract should be provided to the employee within one month of starting employment. This should include: the term; any probationary period; wages; job description; working hours; holidays and notice. It is also advisable to agree on clauses such as confidentiality and non-competition and any fringe benefits such as expense allowances, the use of company cars, telephones, PCs, and so on.

A   FIXED-TERM/INDEFINITE CONTRACTS

M1.2.5 Employment contracts may be for an indefinite or a fixed term. In the Netherlands an enormous increase has been noticed in employment contracts for an indefinite period of time, since the recent introduction of amendments to the law.

M1.2.6 In contrast to a fixed-term employment contract, an employment contract for an indefinite period of time has to be terminated by giving notice.

M1.2.7 A contract for a fixed term ends by operation of law, without requiring any action by either party.

M1.2.8 A number of CBAs contain restrictions on concluding employment contracts for a limited period of time.

M1.2.9 At the end of an employment contract for a fixed period, an employee cannot argue that the employer must give notice or that he has unreasonably given notice of termination.

M1.2.10 A fixed-term employment contract can be entered into for:
- a specific number of months or years with an expiry date;
- for a specific project or piece of work (the moment at which the employment contract ends being clearly apparent);
- or for a specific situation, for example to replace another employee in the case of illness or holiday leave.

M1.2.11 Employment contracts for a fixed term end by law unless there is a fourth employment contract for a definite period of time[1] where the intervals between the various employment contracts do not exceed three months or the employment relationship has lasted for longer than 36 months (intervals of less than three months counting when calculating this period of 36 months).

[1]   Section 7:668a of the Civil Code.

M1.2.12 If a fourth employment contract is entered into or the employment relationship between the parties has lasted for 36 months or longer, the employment contract is deemed by law to be for an indefinite period of time.

M1.2.13 If an employment contract for a fixed period is extended without any further agreement(s), the employment relationship is considered to be continued for the same period as the fixed term.

M1.2.14   An employment contract for a fixed period of more than three years can be renewed once for a maximum period of three months. This renewed employment contract also ends by operation of law.

M1.2.15   Employment contracts entered into for longer than five years can always be terminated by the employee giving six months' notice after the expiry of five years.

M1.2.16   Fixed-term employment contracts can also be terminated prematurely by a competent court. It is becoming increasingly evident in case law that sub-district courts will take account of the agreed period of an employment contract in deciding compensation for terminating the employment contract.

M1.2.17   Entering into a fixed-term employment contract does not prevent premature notice of termination from being given, provided that this has been agreed upon between the parties.[1] Risks are attached to such a termination clause.

[1]   Section 7:667 of the Civil Code.

M1.2.18   In practice, arrangements of this kind, which are considered to be termination clauses, are included and are meant to serve as warning clauses. These clauses do not in fact mean any more than that employers will inform employees in good time whether they want to renew the contract after termination by operation of law.

M1.2.19   An employment contract can also be concluded on condition; in other words, the employment contract ends by law on the occurrence of a particular contingency. This contingency must not, however, be within the power of the employer.

Termination of contract

Term	Termination	*Warning*
Definite	Expiry of operation of law (unless exceeds four renewals or 36 months)	CBAs may contain restrictions
Indefinite	Terminates on notice	Bans on giving notice apply (see paras **M6.3.1–M6.3.4**)

B   NON-COMPETITION CLAUSES

M1.2.20   The law[1] defines a non-competition clause as one in which the employee's freedom to be employed is restricted on termination of the employment. The law sets out two requirements:

*   the clause must be entered into with an employee who has reached his majority; and
*   the clause must be agreed upon in writing with the employee directly.

[1]   Section 7:653 of the Civil Code.

643

M1.2.21   The need for a non-competition clause to be agreed directly with the employee to be valid means that reference cannot be made to, for example, a CBA.

M1.2.22   A valid non-competition clause will remain in force on termination of the employment contract during any probationary period.

M1.2.23   A non-competition clause also remains in force by operation of law after the termination of an employment contract for a definite period of time.

M1.2.24   If, in the course of the term of the employment contract, a substantial change occurs in the nature of the employee's job, the original non-competition clause will not always remain valid. In the event of a substantial change in the nature of the job, a new non-competition clause must be agreed upon by the parties.

M1.2.25   If the employer has to pay compensation to the employee because of the way in which the employment contract has been terminated, the employer will not be entitled to derive any rights from the non-competition clause agreed upon by the parties. Compensation is payable when the employer does not observe the prescribed notice period for terminating the employment contract or where the employer's voluntary decision or negligence has given the employee urgent reason for the employment contract to be terminated with immediate effect.[1]

[1]   See sections 7:653.3 and 7:677 of the Civil Code.

M1.2.26   The Civil Code[1] sets out reasons which can restrict a non-competition clause. The court can cancel the non-competition clause totally or partially after assessing whether it is reasonable, ie whether the employee's interests would be unreasonably harmed if he had to comply with the clause. The court can enforce the restriction in respect of the nature of the activities, the period and/or the region agreed between the parties for which the non-competition clause is valid.

[1]   Section 7:653 of the Civil Code.

M1.2.27   An employee who by virtue of the non-competition clause is impeded to a considerable degree from being employed other than by his (former) employer can ask the court to order the employer to pay him compensation for the duration of the clause. In this case the non-competition clause remains in full force, but the employee's financial demands are met.

M1.2.28   Such compensation for the employee is determined in accordance with standards of reasonableness and fairness.

M1.2.29   There can be no such compensation if the employee was obliged to pay compensation to the employer because of the way in which he terminated the employment contract. This is the case if the employee did not observe the prescribed notice period applying to the termination of the employment contract or the employee gave the employer cause to dismiss him/her instantly.

M1.2.30 An employee with whom a non-competition clause was not agreed is not limited in his freedom of action, which could result in problems for his old employer. However, the former employee may act contrary to what could be demanded of an employee acting reasonably[1] and/or commit an unlawful act with respect to his former employer.[2]

1   Section 7:611 of the Civil Code.
2   Section 6:162 of the Civil Code.

M1.2.31 In the latter case, the employer must prove that he has suffered a loss and/or damage due to the employee's behaviour. It can be concluded from case law that not every action against the interests of the old employer will be unlawful behaviour. There must also be proof of breach eg systematically approaching the old employer's customers, misusing personal information and/or knowledge, etc.

M1.2.32 An employee who does not comply with a non-competition clause applying to him will in general be liable to pay a penalty or be forced to pay compensation and/or damages. In addition, it is possible in interim injunction proceedings to demand the cessation of certain activities. Such legal action could also be instigated against the employee's new employer if the new employer profits from the breach of contract committed by the old employee.

Non competition clauses
- covenant in CBA not enforceable
- must be agreed in writing with employee change in job function may render covenant invalid
- court may order compensation be paid to employee whose work prospects are impeded → compensation 'fair and reasonable'
- absence of covenant = employee free to do as he wishes

1.3   Variation of Contract

M1.3.1 The content of an employment contract is binding on the parties. It is common to have a clause which entitles the employer to unilaterally change the terms and conditions of employment. However, the law[1] stipulates that this authority must be balanced against the interests of the employer and the employee. The employer's interests must outweigh the employee's interests. In addition, terms which fundamentally affect the employee's position will not be easy to change.

1   Section 7:613 of the Civil Code.

1.4   Remedies

M1.4.1 Remedies for breach of the employment contract or for early termination are set out at paras **M1.2.16–M1.2.18**.

M1.4.2 An employee can compel an employer to respect his legal/contractual obligations by bringing interlocutory proceedings before the President of the District Court or the sub-district court.

M1.4.3 If there is a serious breach, an employee can immediately terminate his employment and sue for damages/loss.

M1.4.4 The same principles apply if the employee breaches his obligations, express or implied, under the terms of his employment contract.

2 REMUNERATION

2.1 Background

M2.1.1 Wages are the consideration paid by the employer in return for work carried out by the employee. Wages need not be in the form of money, nor must they be a fixed amount.

2.2 Legal Regulation of Remuneration

2.2.1 Wages and wage levels are subject to the Minimum Wage and Minimum Holiday Allowance Act (WML) 1968. Wage levels are also determined by the Equal Opportunities Act 1980.

M2.2.2 As the name indicates, the WML obliges the employer to pay the employee a minimum wage. An expense allowance, the object of which is to cover costs actually incurred, is not considered to be wages. In practice, however, it is often not the (whole) purpose of the expense allowance to reimburse costs incurred by the employee; in these circumstances, the allowance is referred to as hidden wages.

M2.2.3 An employee is entitled to such wages as are customary or reasonable at that time for similar work.[1] In order to determine what is customary, the CBA in the relevant industry can serve as a reference point.

[1] Section 7:618 of the Civil Code.

M2.2.4 The WML applies to employees from 23 to 64 years of age, employees younger than 23 being entitled to a certain percentage of the applicable minimum wage.

M2.2.5 The WML defines wages as pecuniary income for the employee, with certain exceptions such as overtime and holiday allowance. The minimum wage must be paid in money, although any remuneration over and above the statutory minimum need not be paid in money.

M2.2.6 If an employer does not pay the applicable minimum wage, the employee has the right to an increase of 5% of wages for every day commencing from the fourth working day up to and including the eighth working day and for every day more 1% up to a maximum of 50% of the total amount due. In such cases, the court has the power to moderate pay only in exceptional circumstances. This statutory increase deviates from the general provisions in the law[1] and refers only to the minimum wage payable by law.

[1]   Section 7:625 of the Civil Code.

M2.2.7   There are different types of wages and the Civil Code[1] provides a comprehensive list. Besides money, wages may, to a certain degree, be paid in kind, for example by providing food, clothing, instruction, board and lodging. Wages may also be paid in securities, and in the form of a company car or childcare.

[1]   Section 7:617 of the Civil Code.

M2.2.8   The law[1] prohibits any rule that wages must be spent in a way to be determined by the employer, unless this involves participation in funds, life insurance or a savings scheme, whereby statutory provisions are fulfilled, such as for example the Pension and Savings Fund Act.

[1]   Section 7:631 of the Civil Code.

M2.2.9   Terms such as profit-share, profit-share bonus, bonus or commission are not used in Dutch law. However, these payments relate to amounts of money and are admissible types of wages.

M2.2.10   An exception to the basic rule of 'no work, no wages' is where the employee does not carry out his work because he has to comply with an obligation imposed by law or by the government or in very special circumstances such as the death of other members of the household or close relatives.

M2.2.11   The employee also retains his entitlement to wages if he has not carried out the agreed work because of the employer's actions or omissions; for example, where the employer's illness hinders the employee carrying out his duties or where the business closes down because of holidays. In addition, not having a work permit is in principle at the expense and risk of the employer.

M2.2.12   The employee also has a right to wages if he has won a case for wrongful dismissal. In such a case, the court can moderate the claim for wages to the wages that would have been owed in the event of termination by the applicable notice period. The moderation can, however, never amount to more than three months' wages. The court only has the power to moderate the wages claimed if it has been established that the full payment of wages would have unacceptable consequences for the employer. In practice, wages are often moderated (sometimes even to a considerable extent) by the courts.

M2.2.13   Wages must normally be paid in legal Dutch tender or by means of funds transfer. Payment in foreign currency is permitted but the employee is still entitled to ask to receive payment in Dutch currency.

M2.2.14   The employer is obliged to pay the employee his wages on a certain date, although the parties have considerable freedom to make their own arrangements. The parties can decide to set the wages according to a period of time or to set specific payment dates.

M2.2.15 If the employer pays the wages to the employee late, then the employee is entitled to an increase of between 5% to 50% of arrears. In practice, this claim is often moderated by the court, usually to 10% or 15% of the total wage claim, for which grounds of 'fairness' have to be put forward and accepted by the court. A right to action to recover back wages lapses after five years.[1]

[1] Section 3:308 of the Civil Code.

2.3 Deductions from Wages

M2.3.1 A wage payment to an employee can only be set off to a very limited degree against a debt owed by the employee to the employer (and cannot be permitted on termination of employment).

M2.3.2 In addition, the normal statutory requirements for setting off must be complied with. The types of claims capable of being set off are comprehensively detailed.[1] This means that compensation, penalties, payment of rent for housing, and wages paid in excess qualify for setting off.

[1] Section 7.631 of the Civil Code.

M2.3.3 The Civil Code[1] contains a provision which prohibits an employer from making any deduction from wages unless the employee has given his authorisation in writing for a deduction to be made. Such authorisation may be revoked at any time.

[1] Section 7.631 of the Civil Code.

M2.3.4 Exceptions include payments to which the Pensions and Savings Funds Act apply.

M2.3.5 An employer can never deduct the total amount of wages – an employee must be allowed to keep 90% of the national assistance benefit level as minimum income.

2.4 Itemised Pay Statement

M2.4.1 If wages depend on the employer's financial records, according to the law the employee has a right to check that the wages have been determined correctly. The employer is therefore obliged to provide the employee with relevant documentary evidence of wages paid to him.

M2.4.2 The employer is obliged to provide a written statement to the employee about any change in the amount of wages to be paid in money.

3 FURTHER RIGHTS AND OBLIGATIONS

3.1 Holiday Entitlement

M3.1.1 The law provides that an employee retains his entitlement to wages for the length of the holiday period; this is an obligatory statutory provision. Unpaid leave is therefore an exception.

M3.1.2   The law provides for 'special leave', for example where an employee has to fulfil a statutory obligation, or in certain family circumstances.[1]

[1]   Section 7:629 of the Civil Code.

M3.1.3   An employee has an annual entitlement[1] to at least four times the stipulated number of days worked in a week, which in the case of a five-day working week amounts to 20 days' holiday. In practice, 25 days is the generally recognised holiday allowance per year. This entitlement can be increased by agreement between the parties or by virtue of a CBA.

[1]   Section 7:634 of the Civil Code.

M3.1.4   Holiday leave is recognised as important by the law; leave cannot be replaced by money during any period of employment. Only at the end of the employment can holiday leave which has not been taken be paid in lieu. Even then, the employee in principle retains his entitlement to holiday leave with respect to his new subsequent employer, but the new employer is not obliged to pay the wages owing for this period.

M3.1.5   Part-time employees are entitled to a proportionate number of days' holiday per year.

M3.1.6   If the employment relationship between the parties has not lasted for a full year, then the holiday entitlement applies proportionately.

M3.1.7   The number of days' holiday is usually determined by the number of days worked on a yearly basis, but in a number of situations, holiday also accrues even if the employee has not carried out any work. Holiday leave therefore accrues where the employee completes military service, is involuntarily unemployed (strikes, suspension), pregnant or giving birth, and in the case of compulsory education for young people, illness and accidents.

Holiday

Entitlement	*Principal features*
4 × days worked per week	• cannot be compensated in lieu (except on termination)
	• can be carried forward to new employer
	• part timers get pro rata

A   HOLIDAY DATES

M3.1.8   The law provides that holiday is to be fixed by the employer after consulting the employee. The employee does not therefore have the freedom to fix the date(s) of his holiday. The employer has to take into account his obligation to make sure that the employee has at least two consecutive weeks of holiday a year.

M3.1.9   In addition, the holiday period must so far as possible be between 1 May and 1 October of each year.

M3.1.10 The employer's right to set the dates of holiday also means that the employer can subsequently change a holiday already approved. Any loss suffered by the employee as a result must be paid for by the employer.

B   TERMINATION OF EMPLOYMENT

M3.1.11 As already indicated in para **M3.1.4**, only at the end of the employment contract is it possible to make payment in lieu of entitlement to leave. Frequently, an employee is released from the obligation to carry out work and the employer then requires the employee to use this period to take the balance of his holiday entitlement.

M3.1.12 The employer is permitted to do this, but must take into account the period referred to above or the holiday period customary for the employee. Such unilateral arrangements cannot be made afterwards, as there can have been no consultation between the parties.

M3.1.13 Alternatively, the employer may provide the employee with a statement of the number of days' holiday he is owed on termination. The employee can still take his leave from his subsequent employer, although the subsequent employer is not then required to make any payment in lieu.

C   HOLIDAY PAY

M3.1.14 Holiday pay is the common term for holiday allowance, as set out in the WML. Holiday pay must amount to at least 8% of the employee's wages. Deviation can only be made in a CBA. It is usually paid in May or June each year.

M3.1.15 The parties may also agree in writing that holiday pay can be paid at other times, for example monthly.

M3.1.16 Claims with respect to holiday entitlement lapse after two years, calculated from the last day of the calendar year in which the entitlement arose.[1] Claims with respect to compensation or payment in lieu of leave lapse after five years. In this case the general limitation period as referred to in s 3:307 of the Civil Code applies. Illness of the employee does not suspend the limitation periods.

[1]   Section 7:642 of the Civil Code.

M3.1.17 The law provides that claims for holiday allowance lapse after two years commencing from the date on which the payment should have been made.

3.2   Sick Pay

M3.2.1 As a basic rule, no wages are payable for any time that the employee has not carried out the agreed work. There are important exceptions to this basic rule.[1] The first exception (ie holiday) is set out in paras **M3.1.1–M3.1.17**.

[1]   Section 7:627 of the Civil Code.

M3.2.2 The second exception is where the employee is ill or has had an accident as a result of which he is prevented from carrying out his work. In this case, the employer is obliged to continue paying wages unless the illness or accident has been caused intentionally by the employee.

M3.2.3 In the event of the illness or accident of the employee, the employer is obliged to pay his wages for 52 weeks and at least 70% of his wages. The employee is entitled to the minimum wages according to WML.

M3.2.4 This rule cannot be deviated from. It may be agreed that the first two days of sick leave are borne by the employee; however, such an arrangement must be agreed in writing or in the relevant CBA.

M3.2.5 An employer has authority to give reasonable instructions concerning information about his health to be given by the employee and to do all that which is conducive to, and to refrain from doing all that which is not conducive to, a rapid recovery. In addition, under certain circumstances the employer can instruct the employee to do other suitable work, even for another employer.

M3.2.6 If the parties disagree whether the employee is ill or unfit for work, a second opinion can be requested from a doctor employed by the benefit agency under the Sickness Benefits Act 1913. A second opinion is obligatory if the employee wants to bring an action against the employer to recover back wages if the employer has not continued to pay wages.

M3.2.7 The period of illness, with interruptions of less than four weeks, should be related to the same cause of illness. When breaks in sick leave are longer than four weeks, a new illness is considered to have arisen.

M3.2.8 An employee who has made holiday plans should consult his employer.

M3.2.9 An employee who receives sickness benefit via a social security administrative agency can go on holiday in the Netherlands while retaining this benefit, although permission must be obtained for a holiday abroad.

M3.2.10 An employee who becomes ill while on holiday is not considered to have used any holiday entitlement from the day he falls ill unless the parties have agreed otherwise in writing. This reduction cannot exceed the minimum number of days' holiday stipulated by law to which the employee is still entitled.[1]

[1] Section 7:634 of the Civil Code.

M3.2.11 If an employee is completely unfit to work for a prolonged period of time, then his entitlement to holiday is limited to the holiday calculated over the last half year of his period of illness. In the case of partial incapacity for work, the same rules apply as those in force for part-time employees.

M3.2.12 If an employee terminates the employment contract on his/her initiative when ill, the employee is not entitled to claim payment in money for any holiday not taken during the last half year during which the employee has built up sick leave.

> **Sick pay: summary**
> * employer must pay up to 70% of employee's wages for 52 weeks
> * second opinion may be requested of benefit agency doctor
> * illness on holiday = holiday entitlement preserved

4   WORKING TIME

4.1   Background

M4.1.1   The Netherlands has strict rules limiting working time, breaches of which will be treated seriously and, in some cases, as a criminal offence.

4.2   Legislative Control

M4.2.1   The number of hours an employee (aged 18 or more) has to work must be organised in such a way that he has an uninterrupted rest period of at least 36 hours in every consecutive period of 7 x 24 hours or a rest period of at least 60 hours in every consecutive period of 9 x 24 hours. This rest period may be reduced to 32 hours once in every period of five consecutive weeks.

M4.2.2   In addition, work for an adult employee must be organised in such a way that the employee has an uninterrupted rest period of at least 11 hours in every period of 24 consecutive hours. This rest period may be reduced to a minimum of eight hours in every period of two consecutive weeks.

M4.2.3   Finally, an employee who is older than 18 may not work any more than 9 hours in each duty period, 45 hours a week and an average of 40 hours a week in every period of 13 consecutive weeks.

M4.2.4   On 1 July 2000 a new Act came into effect: the Working Hours Amendment Act (*Wet Aanpassing Arbeidsduur* – WAA)). This Act gives employees the right to submit a request to their employer to work more or fewer hours.

M4.2.5   The WAA applies not only to employees within the meaning of employment law, but also to civil servants, who have their own laws and regulations. The WAA attempts to create a better combination of work and care, arising from the desires of women to work more in order to achieve economic independence and of men to work less so that they can care for their children. This objective is not, however, specifically mentioned contained in any provisions of the WAA itself.

M4.2.6   The most important provision of the WAA is that the employee is entitled to submit a written request to the employer for adjustment of his or her working hours. The adjustment may entail fewer as well as more hours.

M4.2.7 The employer must honour that request, unless he can indicate that urgent company interests stand in the way of permission. Urgent company interests mean, for example, the serious problems for the business operations in relation to re-staffing of the free hours, safety, scheduling problems or financial or organisational problems. If the employee wants an increase in his or her working hours, a serious problem leading to refusal of the request may only be that not enough work is available and/or the fixed number of full time employees or the personnel budget is insufficient to allow for this.

4.3 Opting Out

M4.3.1 The provisions outlined in paras **M4.2.2–M4.2.7** can only be deviated from in a CBA.

4.4 Night Work

M4.4.1 Night work may amount to a maximum of eight hours per night. Work carried out at night must be followed by an uninterrupted rest period of at least 14 hours. Depending on the length of time in which night work has to be carried out, other longer periods of rest apply.

M4.4.2 This regulation may also only be deviated from in a CBA. Stringent rules apply, however, concerning the amount of night work and compulsory rest periods.

4.5 Rest Period

M4.5.1 Rest periods are also provided for by the Working Hours Act 1995 which, together with the Working Conditions Act 1999 and Working Conditions Regulations 1999, provides for these aspects and other matters concerning work, rest periods, Sunday work, night work and so on.

4.6 Paid Annual Leave

4.6.1 This subject is fully covered in paras **M3.1.1–M3.1.17**.

4.7 Remedies

M4.7.1 Compliance with these rules is monitored by public servants employed by the Health and Safety Inspectorate who are authorised to carry out an inspection. For this purpose they can enter company premises, request information and ask to inspect documents. Everybody is obliged to give any assistance required within the framework of the inspection.

M4.7.2 A Health and Safety Inspectorate officer has the authority, in the case of serious breaches, to order that work be stopped.

M4.7.3 Violations of the Working Hours Act are offences which can be prosecuted by the criminal court.

M4.7.4 It is therefore advisable for employers to notify the Health and Safety Inspectorate if violations are discovered. In addition, employers can submit any relevant matter to a competent court.

Working time: summary
- 40-hour working week (averaged over 13 weeks)
- breaches treated seriously
- uninterrupted rest period of 36 hours each week
- employees can request longer or shorter hours
- maximum eight hours night work to be followed by rest period of 14 hours

---

5   EQUAL OPPORTUNITIES

5.1   Background

M5.1.1 Section 1 of the Dutch Constitution provides that every person who is in the Netherlands must be treated equally in similar cases. Discrimination on the grounds of religion, belief, political opinion, race, sex or on any grounds whatsoever is not permitted.

M5.1.2 Dutch legislation is based on a number of Conventions governed by European law and EC law, such as the International Convention on the Elimination of All Forms of Racial Discrimination and the International Covenant on Civil and Political Rights. The International Labour Organisation also has conventions (on non-discrimination and equal opportunities for men and women).

5.2   Unlawful Discrimination

M5.2.1 Section 1 of the Dutch Constitution formed the basis of the Equal Treatment of Men and Women Act 1980, and, later, the Equal Opportunities Act in the Netherlands.

M5.2.2 With respect to employment law discrimination on the grounds of sex, race, marital status, religion, political belief or sexual orientation is prohibited. Thus the employer may not make any discriminatory distinction on these grounds in the case of recruitment and selection, entering into an employment contract, terms of employment, training programmes, career development and the right to terminate employment.

M5.2.3 Policies and procedures contrary to the Equal Treatment Act are null and void.

M5.2.4 In the case of apparent breaches not only the individual employee may take action, but a group action is also possible. The Equal Treatment

Commission is a commission set up under the Act for this purpose. It can investigate and make decisions on alleged breaches of the Equal Treatment Act.

M5.2.5 In addition, the Equal Opportunities Act (*Wet Gelijke Behandeling van Mannen en Vrouwen* – WGB) is a more detailed statute elaborating the principles in the Constitution and EC law.

M5.2.6 Sections 7:646 and 647 of the Civil Code specifically provide that the employer may not make any distinction between men and women with respect to entering into and giving notice of termination of employment contracts, providing training and in general with respect to terms of employment. In addition, the career development of men and women must not differ.

M5.2.7 There are, however, three exceptions. The first is where the sex of the employee is decisive according to objective criteria, for example, the clergy, actors, models and so on.

M5.2.8 A second exception concerns the specific protection of women, especially in connection with pregnancy and motherhood.

M5.2.9 The third exception concerns positive discrimination, for example to remove inequalities.

M5.2.10 Acts, rules or policies which conflict with statutory provisions are null and void.

M5.2.11 An employee who has been discriminated against can claim unlimited compensation, although historically awards are not large.

Unlawful discrimination

- sex and sexual orientation
- race
- marital status
- religion
- political belief

5.3   Disability and Immigrant Discrimination

M5.3.1 In the Netherlands there is also specific legislation, in particular for immigrants and disabled/handicapped people. The Employment of Minorities (Promotion) Act 1994 applies to immigrants. This Act obliges the employer to aim at having a proportional representation of immigrants within the company.

M5.3.2 The Employment of Minorities (Promotion) Act 1994 (EM(P)A) applies to companies with more than 35 employees.

M5.3.3 The obligation under the EM(P)A is to perform to the best of an employee's abilities and does not therefore imply a result where ratios are concerned. No results are to be guaranteed.

M5.3.4 In this context, an employer is obliged to draw up and publish an annual report concerning the representation of immigrants within the company and the measures taken to achieve more proportional representation.

M5.3.5 In addition, the employer must keep up to date a separate personnel register of the immigrants employed. They can, however, refuse to allow their personal details to be recorded in these separate records.

M5.3.6 With respect to disabled/handicapped people, the Disability Reintegration Act (*Wet op de Reïntegratie van Gehandicapten*) has been introduced recently. This Act contains provisions to enable disabled people to be employed. Moreover, a provision is included which gives a disabled employee the same entitlement to wages as a non-disabled employee in a similar job. There is no other specific legislation dealing with disabled employees/job applicants.

5.4 Equal Pay

M5.4.1 The Equal Opportunities Act provides that an employee is entitled to wages equal to the wages that an employee of the other sex usually receives for carrying out work of equal value.

6 TERMINATION OF EMPLOYMENT

6.1 Background

M6.1.1 Action by one of the parties is generally required to end an employment contract. Such action may be unilateral or bilateral. An example of a unilateral legal act is sending notice of termination of the employment contract to the other party, while a mutually-agreed termination is a bilateral legal act. However, where the employment contract is terminated by operation of law (eg at the end of a fixed-term employment contract) no explicit action by the parties is required.

M6.1.2 The methods of terminating employment contracts are dealt with in paras **M6.1.3–M6.1.11**.

A   NOTICE OF TERMINATION (INDEFINITE TERM CONTRACTS)

M6.1.3 Notice of termination of an employment contract is a unilateral act. There are no procedural requirements; notice can be given orally or in writing. Notice is only effective if it has been received by the other party.

M6.1.4 If the party who has been given notice of termination requests reasons for termination, these reasons must be given in writing.

M6.1.5 The law provides that either of the parties can terminate the employment contract at all times by giving notice. If the agreed notice period is not complied with, the employment contract may still be terminated: however, the party who does not comply with the notice period becomes liable to pay compensation.

M6.1.6 In addition to complying with the applicable notice period, notice of termination must also be given on the correct date.

M6.1.7 The date for giving notice of termination is prescribed by law. As a basic rule, it must be given as from the end of a calendar month.[1] The parties can, however, agree in writing or in a CBA not to observe this rule.

[1] Section 7:672 of the Civil Code.

B   NOTICE PERIOD

M6.1.8 In law, the length of the notice period depends on the term of the employment contract.

Duration of contract	Notice period
Employer's notice periods	
Less than 5 years	1 month
5 years but less than 10 years	2 months
10 years but less than 15 years	3 months
15 years or more	4 months
Employee's notice periods	One month

M6.1.9 The statutory notice period can be extended and this extension must always be made in writing or in a CBA.

M6.1.10 The notice period which applies to the employee can therefore be extended, but never for longer than a maximum of six months. In addition, it must also be agreed that the employer's notice period must always be twice as long as that which applies to the employee: but see para **M6.1.11**.

M6.1.11 The employer's notice to employee can also be shortened, but only in a CBA and with the additional stipulation that the notice period applying at the time to the employer will not be any shorter than that which applies to the employee.

6.2   Nature of Claims

M6.2.1 If the employer gives no or inadequate notice, the employee can claim compensation[1] equal to the wages which would have been paid earned if the correct notice period had been complied with. Compensation can also be claimed from the employee if he does not comply with the notice period applying to him.

[1] Sections 7:677 and 680 of the Civil Code.

M6.2.2   It is possible for an employee to claim unfair dismissal, but this is unusual as dismissal needs to be authorised by the local employment authority in advance (see para **M6.3.5**). A dismissal effected without the requisite authority is rendered null and void. A dismissal effected with such authority can still be challenged by the employee as being unfair. No qualifying service period is necessary to claim unfair dismissal.

M6.2.3   Full compensation can also be claimed for any additional losses on dismissal. In this case, the full extent of the loss will have to be proved and can be an issue if, for example, the employee is customarily paid tips.

M6.2.4   The court[1] can also order reinstatement of the employee. If this claim is allowed by the court, the employee can 'buy' the remedy off. The amount of this lump sum payment is determined by the court in accordance with the requirements of reasonableness and fairness.

[1]   Sub-district and District Court (sections 1:116 and 1:289 respectively of the civil proceedings rules and regulations).

Notice of termination (indefinite term contracts)

Mode of notice	Procedure	Non-compliance
• oral	correct notice on correct	compensation = wages +
• in writing	date	additional losses

6.3   Fairness of Dismissal

A   BANS ON GIVING NOTICE

M6.3.1   Prohibitions ('bans') on giving notice of termination are set out in the Civil Code, s 7:670. This means that a dismissal will not be allowed in certain cases.

Examples of bans on notice
- when employee is ill (for period less than two years)
- during employee's pregnancy or where it involves sex or race discrimination or victimisation
- during employee's military service
- if employee is member of a works council, trade union or takes part in trade union activities (unless carried out during working hours without employer's permission)
- during parental leave

M6.3.2   In addition, the law provides that prior permission is required from the sub-district court to give notice of termination[1] if the notice of termination is for an employee who:

(1) is on the list of candidates for a works council, or

(2) has been a member of the works council within the last two years; or

(3) is a member of a preparatory committee of the works council; or
(4) has been a member of an employment committee within the last two
    years; or
(5) has been employed as a mentor or expert employee within the meaning
    of the Working Conditions Act. The term 'works council' should be
    regarded in the widest sense.

¹   Section 7:670a of the Civil Code.

M6.3.3   The bans on giving notice of termination are important if a party
wants to terminate the employment contract without notice. In such cases
the sub-district court will have to ascertain whether the request is connected
to a ban on giving notice and, if the dissolution of an employment contract
with a sick employee is involved (see paras **M6.5.1–M6.5.1**), the employer
will have to submit a reintegration plan to be considered by the National
Institute for Social Insurance.

M6.3.4   The bans on giving notice do not apply if notice of termination is
given during a probationary period; in the case of instant dismissal given
with good reason; termination by operation of law; mutually-agreed
termination and the dissolution of the employment contract by the sub-
district court.

B   THE DISMISSAL PROCEDURE

M6.3.5   Because all dismissals (other than summary dismissals) must be
authorised by the Regional Employment Office, claims for unfair dismissal
are not common. The dismissal procedure has no formal rules, although the
procedure is in principle a written one.¹ The parties can nevertheless express
a wish to be heard, and this request must be acceded to.

¹   Section 6 Labour Relations Decree.

M6.3.6   It is assumed that the procedure will take between four and six
weeks, but in fact it usually takes eight weeks. An employment relationship
must be terminated on notice with the permission of the Director of the
Regional Employment Office. This means that permission has to be
obtained before valid notice of termination can be given. It is not, however,
necessary to ask for permission to give notice during any probationary
period and in the case of notice of termination for an urgent reason (ie
summary dismissal).

M6.3.7   Authority for a request to give notice is given by the Director of
the Regional Employment Office of the area in which the work is usually
carried out or where the employee is based or where the employer's
registered office is located if the work extends over the area of more than
one Regional Employment Office.

M6.3.8   A request to terminate employment by giving notice must contain
the personal details of both parties as well as the reasons for the dismissal.

M6.3.9   In essence, a dismissal must be for commercial or organisational
reasons, or reasons which are personal to the employee.

Commercial or organisational reasons

M6.3.10   Sufficient financial information must be provided, including an annual report drawn up by an external accountant as well as the most recent balance sheets and profit and loss accounts. Internal figures are usually not adequate.

M6.3.11   In addition, the employer will also have to state that he has considered other measures to prevent dismissal or other alternatives. Finally, when the employer selects the employees to be dismissed selection must be based on the principles of seniority and consideration of the jobs and ages of the employees.

M6.3.12   The principle of seniority means – in short – that those employees who have been employed longer are protected in preference to those who have been employed for a shorter period of time.

M6.3.13   This principle of seniority only applies to similar, equivalent jobs. It is possible to deviate from this principle and reasons must be given for so doing.

M6.3.14   If more than 20 employees are to be dismissed, the principle of considering the jobs and ages of the employees applies: a proportion of the employees in each age group and age category will have to be affected by the dismissal.

Personal

M6.3.15   If the reason for the dismissal is personal, this may or may not be connected to the employee's illness. An illness can be unlawful, long-term or repeated. Illness is unlawful when it cannot be confirmed by a medical doctor. Repeated illness must put a disproportionate burden on the company's organisation, and termination of the employment contract must be shown to be justified.

M6.3.16   An important ground for dismissals for personal reasons is that the employment relationship has broken down. This will, however, be subject to a critical investigation by the Regional Employment Office.

C   INSTANT (SUMMARY) DISMISSAL

M6.3.17   Permission need not be requested from the Regional Employment Office for summary dismissal, nor does a notice period have to be given. Dismissal can be immediate. However, strict conditions must be fulfilled:

* there must be a serious and urgent reason, both in the objective and the subjective sense; and
* the other party must be informed immediately of the reason for the dismissal, and the dismissal must be immediate as soon as the presumption arises that an urgent reason is involved.

M6.3.18   The law provides examples of what may be considered to be an urgent reason.[1] However, the statutory provisions only set out examples and it is therefore possible to have an urgent reason in other cases.

[1]   Sections 7:678 and 7:679 of the Civil Code.

M6.3.19   An objective urgent reason means that in similar circumstances every employer/employee would consider the circumstances to be urgent. This means that the court, which has to consider the urgency, will also have the same opinion.

M6.3.20   A subjective urgent reason means that the reason for termination in these circumstances is urgent for the employer.

M6.3.21   Since the law only gives examples and several stringent conditions are involved for an instant dismissal to be justified, the case law gives a very varied picture of what can be considered to be an urgent reason.

M6.3.22   The most frequent types of cases involve the persistent refusal to comply with the employer's reasonable orders or instructions and the employee's disregard for his duty as a good employee.

Example

An employee asserts that he/she is ill, while in the employer's opinion this is not the case. The onus of proof in such a case is on the employer.

In addition, cases occur in practice in which the employee is repeatedly late for work, takes a day off without consultation, etc.

M6.3.23   An employee can also terminate the employment contract with immediate effect by sending notice of termination to the employer's address.[1]

[1]   See sections 7:678 (employers) and 7:679 (employees) of the Civil Code for examples of reasons.

M6.3.24   It is evident from the examples and the stringent conditions that the employer or the employee must act quickly, and without delay. As soon as the facts which provide the urgent reason have arisen, notice of termination must follow immediately.

Example

An employee is suspected of stealing. The employer must decide whether an urgent reason both in the subjective and objective sense is involved as soon as it is noticed and if so the employer must then terminate the employment contract without delay and with immediate effect.

M6.3.25 In practice, there is often a suspicion that an urgent reason exists, but some investigation will be necessary to substantiate this suspicion.

M6.3.26 Case law allows such an investigation, provided that the investigation does not take too long and is carried out adequately. Depending on the circumstances, the summary dismissal can then be delayed for up to 10 to 14 days.

M6.3.27 In the cases, a line of argument has developed that it is possible to notify an employee in advance that he will be dismissed instantly if and as soon as there is any question of refusal to work. In such a case, the prospect of instant dismissal can put to the employee, provided it does not lie too far in the future.

6.4   Remedies

M6.4.1 See nature of claims (paras **M6.2.1–M6.2.4**) for details of compensation for non-compliance with notice periods.

M6.4.2 If an employer terminates employment without obtaining the required permission (see paras **M6.3.1–M6.3.16**), then the employee can request nullification of this notice of termination within six months in accordance with s 9 of the Labour Relations Decree 1945. The period of six months commences from the moment that notice of termination is given. A request for nullity does not need to be in any prescribed form and does not have to be in writing.

M6.4.3 The consequence of nullity is that the employment contract continues in full force and the employee will be able to commence an action to claim back wages.

M6.4.4 In cases where the employer doubts whether it is necessary to get permission for a notice of termination, permission can be requested as far as required by law. This can be relevant if, for example, the employer has doubts about the legal validity of a case of instant dismissal.

M6.4.5 It is not possible to appeal against the decision of the Director of the Regional Employment Office.

M6.4.6 It follows from case law that summary dismissal is not always without risk. The employer must be sure of his case, as otherwise the employee will be able to have the dismissal declared the null, for example, the permission of the Regional Employment Office to allow the employment contract to be terminated has not been requested. The result of this is that the employment contract continues unimpaired and the employee will retain his entitlement to wages.

M6.4.7 In addition, an employee can also decide to claim compensation because the employer has not given him the proper notice period.

M6.4.8 In cases of summary dismissal it is therefore recommended that as far as is still required, proceedings be instituted with the Regional

Employment Office or sub-district court to effect the termination of the employment contract. In this case permission is requested to terminate or dissolve the employment contract if the employment contract has not yet been terminated by giving notice of termination for an urgent reason.

MANIFESTLY UNREASONABLE DISMISSAL

M6.4.9 See paras **M6.2.1–M6.2.4**. An employee whose employment contract is coming to an end by the employer giving notice of termination can apply to the court and request compensation or reinstatement in his old job.

M6.4.10 For such compensation or reinstatement to be awarded, the competent court must judge the dismissal to be manifestly unreasonable. Manifestly unreasonable is understood to mean that the party who gives notice of termination could not have made this decision in all reasonableness. This is a limited review by the court.

Examples of manifestly unreasonable dismissals

The court will judge as manifestly unreasonable any dismissal where the employer fails to give reasons or gives a false reason.

The court could also hold a dismissal to be manifestly unreasonable if the consequences for the employee are serious compared with the employer's interest in dismissing the employee.

M6.4.11 The law[1] distinguishes five cases in which dismissal by the employer must be judged to be manifestly unreasonable.

[1] Section 7:681 of the Civil Code.

M6.4.12 It appears, therefore, that the court not only judges the dismissal in itself but can also include in its deliberations an examination of the consequences of this termination for the employee.

M6.4.13 The employee can claim reasonable compensation from the employer which will (partially) compensate him for the consequences of the termination of the employment contract.

M6.4.14 Apart from the court's ability to award reasonable compensation it can also decide to reinstate the employment contract. If reinstatement proves impossible, financial compensation may be awarded.

M6.4.15 The right to claim that a dismissal is manifestly unreasonable lapses after six months, calculated from the end of the employment contract.

6.5 Redundancy and Other Dismissals

See also paras **M6.3.10–M6.3.14** which detail dismissals for commercial and organisational reasons (ie including redundancy, both individual and collective).

DISSOLUTION OF THE EMPLOYMENT CONTRACT

M6.5.1 The law provides for a special means of dissolving the employment contract.[1] Either party is entitled at any time to apply to the sub-district court to request that the employment contract be dissolved for a serious reason. The employment contract cannot limit or exclude this right.

[1] Section 7:685 of the Civil Code.

M6.5.2 A serious reason can be an urgent reason, namely instant dismissal or a change in circumstances such that the dissolution of the employment contract must be the reasonable consequence.

M6.5.3 In the case of an instant dismissal the employer does not terminate the employment contract immediately but applies to the sub-district court to dissolve the employment contract.

M6.5.4 If the employment contract is to be dissolved for an urgent reason, the employee is liable to pay compensation if he has given the employer an urgent reason for dissolution because of his negligence or intent.

M6.5.5 Most proceedings in which the court is requested to dissolve the employment contract are, however, based on a change in circumstances. This change can be due to economic reasons, frequent or long-term absence of the employee due to illness, etc.

M6.5.6 If the sub-district court allows the dissolution of the employment contract by virtue of a change in circumstances, it is authorised to award reasonable and fair compensation to one party at the expense of the other. The sub-district court does not have this option if the employment contract is dissolved for an urgent reason.

M6.5.7 The reasonable compensation to be awarded by the sub-district court is based on the so-called sub-district court formula. This formula takes into account the number of years of service, the wages applying to the employee and an adjustment factor.

M6.5.8 The age of the employee is an important factor when determining the number of years of service, in that the years of service which the employee has worked before he reaches the age of 40 count once; years between the age of 40 and 50 count 1.5 times and years of service above 50 years of age count twice.

M6.5.9 Years of service of six months or more are rounded up to a full year and the reference date for the age of the employee is the presumed date of dissolution of the employment contract.

M6.5.10   The employee's gross monthly salary is used as the basis on which the employee's wages are calculated, plus any fixed and agreed wage components such as holiday allowance, overtime pay and other fixed allowances. Fringe benefits such as a company car, bonuses and profit-sharing schemes are not included in the calculation.

Adjustment factor

M6.5.11   Finally, the sub-district court determines the 'adjustment factor' which is fixed at one (1) if neither party is to blame for the dissolution of the employment contract. An example is a neutral circumstance, such as a reorganisation which the company considers necessary.

M6.5.12   This adjustment factor can be varied upwards or downwards depending on the behaviour of the employer or the employee and also on specific circumstances such as the applicability or otherwise of a non-competition clause and other circumstances. This is irrespective of whether the application to dissolve the employment contract is requested by the employer or the employee.

M6.5.13   Apart from the application of, say, a non-competition clause, determining the level of compensation can also depend on whether there is a Social Plan or whether the employee has, for example, been offered outplacement counselling.

M6.5.14   Although the compensation is determined according to a basic formula, the final result depends on numerous circumstances, reasonableness and fairness.

M6.5.15   To have the employment contract dissolved by the subdistrict court, the employer must submit a reintegration plan with his application. This is considered by the National Institute for Social Insurance. Failure to submit such a reintegration plan will result in the application to dissolve the employment contract being rejected outright. The proceedings to get an employment contract dissolved by the subdistrict court take about two months.

M6.5.16   Any reasonable compensation which the sub-district court may award has an effect on the date on which the employee is able to receive benefits under the Unemployment Act. The benefits agency concerned will take into account the notice period applying to the employee; and this also applies in cases where the employment contract is dissolved by the subdistrict court. This notional notice period is at least one month, during which the employee will not receive any benefits under the Unemployment Act. The employee must use any reasonable compensation as a source of income during this period.[1]

[1]   Unemployment Act, s 16(3).

M6.5.17   If the sub-district court dissolves the employment contract, there is no question of observing notice periods. Since there is no question of notice of termination being given, it is not possible for the employee to instigate legal proceedings based on alleged manifestly unreasonable dismissal.

M6.5.18 No appeal is possible against the decision of the sub-district court. Only in exceptional cases, for example if elementary rules governing the legal proceedings are contravened, is an appeal possible. No appeal lies with respect to the grounds stated by the sub-district court in its decision.

Summary of types of termination

On notice
- permission required from sub-district court
- must satisfy one of following reasons:
  (1) commercial or organisational; or
  (2) personal

Instant
- permission not necessary
- must be for urgent reason, both objective and subjective
- other party must be informed of reason for dismissal

Dissolution
- application to sub-district court for dissolution
- must be for serious reason eg change in circumstances
- reasonable compensation according to sub-district formula

6.6   Consultation

M6.6.1 Collective redundancy arises where an employer intends to dismiss 20 or more employees within a period of three months.[1]

[1]   Notification of Redundancy Act 1976.

M6.6.2 If the dismissal of 20 or more employees is requested, the employer will first have to notify the trade unions and the Director of the District Employment Services Authority about these redundancies in good time (ie giving trade unions the opportunity to discuss the decision to terminate) and in writing.

M6.6.3 The trade unions must also be invited for consultation in good time. The aim of this consultation must be to try to prevent the mass redundancies and to reduce the consequences.

M6.6.4 In addition, data on each employee will have to be provided to the trade unions and the Director of the Employment Services Authority. This information must also include the date when the works council was contacted about the proposed redundancies.

M6.6.5 One month after the notification (as outlined in para **M6.6.2**) has been made, the dismissal procedure can be commenced. At this stage the collective redundancies are the same as any other individual dismissals applied for.

M6.6.6 An important matter for consideration is the way in which an employer intends to terminate the employment contracts. This can be done by submitting the case to the Director of the District Employment Services Authority or bringing it before the sub-district court. Both the Director of the District Employment Services Authority and the trade unions will ask for a social plan, the conditions of which are to be discussed with the unions. If done, the social plan is binding on all employees to be made redundant.

7   YOUNG WORKERS

7.1   General Obligations

M7.1.1   Under Dutch law, minors are those who have not yet reached the age of 18, and are not or have not been married.

M7.1.2   However, employment law provides that a minor aged 16 or older may enter into a contract of employment independently. A minor who has not yet reached 16 may also conclude a contract of employment, with the consent of his or her legal representative. If consent is not given in advance, it is deemed to have been given if a minor has performed work for four weeks without objection from that legal representative.[1]

[1]   Section 7:612 Dutch Civil Code.

M7.1.3   A contract of employment concluded with a minor is little different from a contract of employment entered into with an adult and, for example, the same notice periods and notice provisions apply to a minor employee.

M7.1.4   There are a few differences: no competition clause may be concluded,[1] and the minimum wage applies to employees up to 23 years of age (see para **M2.2.2**). There is also a difference in the sense that the years worked prior to majority do not count in calculating the notice period.[2]

[1]   Section 7:653 Civil Code.
[2]   Section 7.671 Civil Code.

A   TRAINING AND EDUCATION OF YOUNG PEOPLE

M7.1.5   The Working Hours Act (*Arbeidstijdenwet*) provides that the work of a young employee must be organised so that he or she can receive the relevant education. That training time counts as working hours.[1]

[1]   Section 4.4 Working Hours Act.

M7.1.6   In addition, the Compulsory Education Act (*Leerplichtwet*) provides that young employees remain subject to partial compulsory education for two years. A young person may be exempted from partial compulsory education if he or she is not suitable physically or psychologically to attend school; if there are strong objections to the type of education at all schools within a reasonable distance from the home; or if a school in a foreign country is attended regularly. Requests for such exemptions must be submitted to the Health and Safety Inspectorate.

B   WORKING HOURS

M7.1.7   The Working Hours Act also regulates the work and rest times for young employees. The maximum duration of the work per day is nine hours, with a maximum of 45 hours a week and an average of 40 hours a week in each consecutive four-week period.

M7.1.8   Work for young people must be organised in such a way that they have an uninterrupted rest time of at least 36 hours in each continuous period of one week. Every 24 consecutive hours, there must be an unbroken rest period of at least 12 hours, and that rest period must cover the hours between 23:00 and 6:00. A break must always follow after 4.5 hours of work.

M7.1.9   Agreements concerning the work and training of young people are frequently made in collective employment contracts.

8   MATERNITY AND PARENTAL RIGHTS

8.1   Background

LEGISLATIVE CONTROL

M8.1.1   The Working Hours Amendment Act is the first in a planned series of new Acts in the context of employment and care. A second Act will follow, setting out a statutory right to maternity leave and adoption leave. A further Act will deal with a special right to short-term care leave and will be a comprehensive set of the currently existing leave regulations. Finally, yet another Act will cover the right to longer-term, paid care leave.

M8.1.2   The law already includes parental leave, without retention of wages.[1]

[1]   Section 7:644 Civil Code.

8.2   General Rights

M8.2.1   Maternity leave is included in the legislation among the provisions pertaining to sickness. A pregnant employee is entitled to 16 weeks' paid maternity leave (at full rate subject to a statutory maximum).[1] Maternity leave can be taken flexibly, in the sense that the pregnancy leave can start four to six weeks before the expected date of giving birth.

[1]   Sickness Benefits Act 1913.

M8.2.2   An employee is entitled to her old job if she goes back to work after maternity leave expires.

M8.2.3   An employee can request specific performance of the employment contract if she is refused her old job back.

8.3   Protection from Dismissal

M8.3.1   An employer is prohibited from giving notice to terminate an employment contract during the pregnancy of an employee.

M8.3.2   This prohibition applies during the term of the pregnancy and for a period of six weeks after expiry of the maternity leave.

M8.3.3   In principle, the burden of proof that the woman was pregnant at the time of the notice of termination rests with the employee. The employer can request that the employee obtains a certificate from a doctor or a midwife.

8.4   Maternity Pay

M8.4.1   An employee who is prevented by illness from carrying out work due to pregnancy or giving birth is entitled to continued payment of wages for a period of 52 weeks, subject to a statutory maximum.[1] This is payable by the employer who recoups the money from the state. Where no such illness is involved, maternity pay is payable up to a maximum of 16 weeks after giving birth.

[1]   Section 7:69 of the Civil Code.

8.5   Additional Rights to Time Off

M8.5.1   The law[1] provides for 'parental leave' under which an employee who is the parent of or looks after a child and resides at the same address as the child is entitled under certain circumstances to special leave. The child must not be more than eight years old and the employment contract has to have been in effect for at least one year.

[1]   Section 7:644 of the Civil Code.

M8.5.2   Parental leave can be no longer than six months, unless the employee requests that it be prolonged. The leave may be taken flexibly, but at least half the working hours per week must still be worked. The employee may make a request to extend the period of leave or to increase the number of hours' leave per week. This request must be honoured by the employer unless there is urgent cause not to do so.

M8.5.3   The request to take parental leave must also be made in good time and the leave can be terminated prematurely.

M8.5.4   The Career Break (Funding) Act (*Wet Financiering Loopba-anonder-breking*) gives employees the opportunity to interrupt their career temporarily, completely or partially. An employee must have completed one year's service and he may then partially interrupt his career for at least two months for care (see para **M8.5.6**) or study.

M8.5.5   The employee is entitled to a limited gross monthly amount for a maximum of six months. This amount is paid by the National Institute for Social Insurance (LISV). If an employee wants to make such a claim for payment, he must be replaced by an unemployed or disabled person.

M8.5.6   If an employee indicates that the career break will be used to care for a terminally-ill person in his care, the requirements for the minimal duration of employment and minimum leave will not apply. In addition, the requirement as to the employee's replacement (see para **M8.5.5**) does not apply.

669

Maternity leave and other rights to time off: summary
- sixteen weeks paid maternity leave
- right to return to old job
- employee who is ill through pregnancy or childbirth entitled to wages for 52 weeks
- six months parental leave for child up to age eight
- two months career break for care or study

---

9   BUSINESS TRANSFERS

9.1   Background

M9.1.1   The law set out in the Acquired Rights Directive 77/187/EEC concerning the retention of employees' rights upon the transfer of businesses is contained in s 7:662–666 of the Civil Code.

9.2   Identifying a Relevant Transfer

M9.2.1   Directive 77/187/EEC defines the transfer of a business as the transfer of an economic unit which retains its identity, with a view to continuing an already existing economic activity whether or not this is a core activity, which is understood to include the totality of the organised resources. This is reflected in the Civil Code.

9.3   Affected Employees

M9.3.1   An employee is defined as any person in a member state who by virtue of the national labour law enjoys protection as an employee. An employee employed in the part of the business being transferred will be transferred automatically.

9.4   Effects of the Transfer

M9.4.1   The main consequence of the transfer of a business is that the transferor's rights and obligations arising under the employment contract are transferred by operation of law to the purchaser.

M9.4.2   For the employees involved, this transfer by operation of law means that all the rights and duties arising from employment contracts not yet terminated will be transferred to the purchaser. These rights and duties include non-competition clauses, employees' continuity of service, and the employer's obligations such as compensation to be paid in the case of a manifestly unreasonable dismissal or an employee's rights arising from notice of dismissal.

M9.4.3   The employer transferring business activities remains jointly and severally liable with the purchaser for a period of one year after the transfer with respect to the fulfilment of obligations under the employment contract which existed before the date of the transfer. Specific examples are arrears of wages and National Insurance contributions.

9.5   Dismissal of Employees

M9.5.1   An intended transfer of a business cannot be used as a reason to effect notice of termination of the employment contract. Thus, an application for permission to terminate an employment contract based on this ground will be rejected by the Director of the Regional Employment Office.

M9.5.2   If the old employer, ie the transferring party, has obtained permission to give notice of termination, he can transfer the rights ensuing from the notice of dismissal to the new employer.

9.6   Variation of Contract

M9.6.1   An employee who, because of the transfer of the business, is faced with a change of circumstances to his disadvantage may demand that the employment contract be dissolved by the sub-district court. The court can award the employee reasonable compensation at the expense of the new employer. In cases where the employee takes the initiative to effect the dissolution of the employment contract, he will nevertheless be deemed as involuntarily unemployed, and thus can qualify for benefit under the Unemployment Act.

9.7   Duty to Inform and Consult

M9.7.1   The Works Councils Act 1971[1] provides that the works council must be given the opportunity, in good time, by the business to advise about the takeover or selling off of a company.

[1]   Works Councils Act 1971, s 25.

M9.7.2   This Act also provides that a summary of the proposed decision must be submitted to the works council in writing and that the works council's advice must be requested on such a date that it could have a real effect on the decision to be taken. The summary must include the grounds for the decision as well as the consequences for the people employed at the company and the measures to be taken in this respect.

10   COLLECTIVE RIGHTS AND BARGAINING

10.1 Background

M10.1.1   The formation of trade unions is not governed by any special rules in the Netherlands, so the general rules of the law of association govern the formation and organisation of trade unions. The formation of a trade union does not require the prior permission of the Government and nor does the Government supervise the formation and organisation of a trade union. Therefore a considerable amount of freedom exists for trade unions.

10.2 Compulsory Recognition of Unions

M10.2.1 To operate as such, a trade union must have full legal competence to enter into a collective bargaining agreement. This legal competence will exist if the trade union is formed by notarial deed. The deed must contain the charter of the trade union, which must include:

- the name of the trade union;
- the registered office;
- the object and a description of the obligations of the members; and
- the way in which the general meeting of the members is convened and the way in which officers are appointed and dismissed.

M10.2.2 In addition to the requirement that trade unions must be of full legal personality, ie the trade union must be considered to be representative, ie the group of employees which is said to be represented by the trade union must be of sufficient significance to be able to take part in negotiations with other parties in the CBA.

10.3 Recognised Unions

M10.3.1 About 30% of the Dutch workforce is unionised. There are three large federations of trade unions on the employee's side, namely the *Federatie Nederlandse Vakbeweging* – FNV (Federation of Netherlands Trade Unions), the *Christelijk Nationaal Vakverbond* – CNV (National Federation of Christian Trade Unions) and the *Unie mhp, middengroepen en hoger personeel* (Trade Union Federation for Middle and Senior Management).

M10.3.2 On the employer's side, there is the *Vereniging VNO-NCW* (Confederation of Netherlands Industry and Employers), originating from the *Verbond van Nederlandse Ondernemingen* (Confederation of Netherlands Industry) and the *Nederlands Christelijk Werkgeversverbond* (Dutch Christian Federation of Employers).

M10.3.3 Small and medium-sized enterprises (MKB) have their own central organisation, the *Koninklijke Vereniging MKB–Nederland* (Royal Association of Small and Medium-sized Enterprises in the Netherlands).

M10.3.4 The agricultural, horticultural and livestock farming sector has its own organisation in the form of the *Vereniging LTO-Nederland* (Dutch Organisation for Agriculture and Horticulture).

10.4 Collective Bargaining and Collective Representation

M10.4.1 Collective bargaining between collective industrial organisations is based on freedom of contract, under which the contracting parties are completely free to determine the content of a CBA themselves. In addition, freedom of contract means that a collective industrial organisation is free to determine with whom it would like to enter into a CBA.

M10.4.2 It is possible to effect a CBA at industry level as well as at individual company level. There are about 1,000 CBAs in the Netherlands,

80% of which have been entered into at industry level and 20% at individual company level.

M10.4.3   Collective bargaining agreements are concerned with employees' terms of employment. The terms of employment can range from quite restricted to very comprehensive terms. They usually deal with primary elements of remuneration but also frequently cover fringe benefits.

10.5 Industrial Action

M10.5.1   There is a collective consultation culture specific to the Netherlands, called the Polder model. Its main purposes are to aim for harmony and coalition. As a result, Dutch society is not often affected by strikes and if they do occur, strikes never last very long. Legal precedent with respect to strikes is therefore not very extensive in the Netherlands. It is usually the case that the court sends the parties to the negotiating table with a view to resolving the conflict.

M10.5.2   In the event of a strike, organised by trade unions and used as a way of strengthening demands with respect to the terms and conditions of employment, striking employees are in principle not entitled to wages. The strikers have no entitlement to wages since they are not prepared to carry out their work.

M10.5.3   With respect to other strikes, not organised by trade unions, it depends on the circumstances of each case whether employees who do not carry out their work are nevertheless entitled to wages.

M10.5.4   Situations where the employee is dependent on a supplying company whose employees are on strike, or where an employee cannot carry out the work because he cannot enter the company on strike, are in principle at the expense and risk of the employer and the employee retains his entitlement to continued payment of wages.

11   EMPLOYMENT DISPUTES

11.1 Background

M11.1.1   Industrial relations in the Netherlands are characterised by openness between the parties. Employment law disputes are usually easily and calmly discussed between the employer on the one hand and the individual works council or trade union on the other hand. The harmony model mentioned above also applies to individual employment relationships.

11.2 Labour Courts/Tribunals

M11.2.1   If a dispute between an employer and an employee cannot be solved by mutual consultation, with or without the assistance of third parties, the case can be brought before the sub-district court (see exception as to managing directors: para **M11.2.3**). The sub-district court is the court of first instance before which cases pertaining to employment law are brought.

M11.2.2 Decisions taken by the sub-district court can be appealed to the District Court. Finally, an appeal pertaining to employment law can be brought before the Supreme Court.

M11.2.3 However managing directors under the articles of association must take their employment law disputes to the District Court in the first instance.[1] The District Court decisions can be appealed to the Court of Appeal and from there to the Supreme Court.

[1] Dutch company law and the articles of association provide that a managing director must be appointed, suspended and dismissed by a decision of the meeting of the company shareholders.

M11.2.4 The District Court is a single-judge court, whereas the other judicial bodies always have several judges. This means that these other courts have three or five judges.

12 WHISTLEBLOWING/DATA PROTECTION

12.1 Whistleblowing

M12.1.1 Employees do not have any specific protection under Dutch employment law if they are dismissed on the grounds that they have disclosed abuses in the employer's company. It will depend on the specific circumstances whether a dismissal made on this ground is sustainable or not.

M12.1.2 So, for example, the chairman of a works council, who by virtue of his position was bound to a specific confidentiality clause, was rightly dismissed when he violated this confidentiality, although he felt forced to do so. The judge decided that the obligation to secrecy in the man's position as chairman must weigh more heavily and that he therefore was not entitled to make certain matters public.[1]

[1] Supreme Court decision 20 April 1990, NJ 1990, 702.

12.2 Data Protection

M12.2.1 The Data Protection Act provides that personal details may only be used for the purpose for which they have been given.

M12.2.2 The employer is therefore not at liberty to make the personal details of an employee known to third parties.

[1] Data Protection Act, s 7:655.

M12.2.3 An employer is obliged to provide to the employee a written statement[1] which contains at least:
- the names and addresses of the parties concerned;
- the place where the work is (to be) carried out;
- the employee's job or the nature of his/her work;
- the commencement date of employment;
- the term of the employment contract; and
- the entitlement to holiday or the way of calculating this entitlement to holiday.

[1] See para **M1.1.12**.

M12.2.4 The following details also need to be made known to the employee:

- the length of the notice period to be given by the parties;
- the wages and the payment period;
- the customary working hours per day or per week;
- a pension scheme if applicable and the applicability of a CBA.

M12.2.5 In addition, section 7:655 of the Data Protection Act provides that the employer who refuses to provide such statement, or includes incorrect information on it, is liable with respect to the employee for the damage/loss caused as a result.

M12.2.6 This statutory provision is mandatory and the parties cannot opt out.

13 HUMAN RIGHTS

13.1 Rights and Obligations

M13.1.1 Dutch labour legislation is also based on European legislation, for example the European Convention on Human Rights. It is therefore generally accepted, for example, that legal proceedings must be conducted in a reasonable period of time and that the courts must give a ruling within a reasonable period of time.

BIBLIOGRAPHY

WCL van der Grinten *Arbeidsovereenkomstenrecht* (law of employment agreements)
HL Bakels en L Opheikens *Schets van het Nederlandse Arbeidsrecht* (Outlines of Dutch Labour law)
Kluwer: *Arbeidsovereenkomst* (Handbook: employment agreements)

USEFUL ADDRESSES

Employers' organisations
Vereniging VNO-NCW (Confederation of Netherlands Industry and Employers)
Postbus 93002
2509 A Den Haag
Koninklijke Vereniging MKB-Nederland (Royal Association of Small and Medium-sized Enterprises in the Netherlands)
Postbus 5096
2600 GB Delft

Land- en Tuinbouw Organisatie Nederland (LTO – Dutch Organisation for Agriculture and Horticulture)
AgriCentrum
Postbus 29773
2502 LT Den Haag

Employees' organisations

FNV (*Federatie Nederlandse Vakbeweging* – Federation of Netherlands Trade Unions)
Postbus 8456
1005 AL Amsterdam

CNV (*Christelijk Nationaal Vakverbond* – National Federation of Christian Trade Unions)
Postbus 2475
3500 GL Utrecht

Vakcentrale MHP (Trade union for middle and higher personnel)
Postbus 400
3990 DK Houten

De Unie
Postbus 200
3990 DE Houten

Ministerie van Sociale Zaken en Werkgelegenheid, afd arbeidsinspectie (Ministry of Social Affairs and Work)
Postbus 90801
22509 BJ's-Gravenhage

Association of Chambers of Commerce
Vereniging van Kamer van Koophandel
Postbus 265
3440 AG Woerden

N   Norway

Jan Tormod Dege and Erik Aas

Jan Tormod Dege is a Partner at Brækhus Dege, Oslo. He was awarded his PhD in 1998 for his books on Employment law. He has a MBA obtained from Arhus School of Economics in 1964 and has also published books on European philosophy.

Eric Aas has been an Associate with Braekhus Dege since 1999.

Brækhus Dege, Oslo

Phone: +47 23 23 90 90
Fax: +47 22 83 60 60
Email: dege@brakhusdege.no; aas@brakhusdege.no
Website: www.brakhusdege.no

SUMMARY TABLE

NORWAY

Rights	Yes/No	Explanatory Notes
CONTRACTS OF EMPLOYMENT		
Minimum notice	YES	
Terms:		
Express	YES	
Implied	YES	
Incorporated by statute	YES	Eg collective agreements or work rules
REMUNERATION		
Minimum wage regulation	NO	But see collective agreements
Further rights and obligations:		
Right to paid holiday	YES	Minimum 25 days pa. Holiday payment payable every summer
Right to sick pay	YES	248 days payable over three years
WORKING TIME		
Regulation of hours per day/ working week	YES	Maximum 40 hour working week
Regulation of night work	YES	Prohibited with limited exceptions
Right to rest periods	YES	One rest break when working hours exceed 5½ hours per day
EQUAL OPPORTUNITIES		
Discrimination protection:		
Sex	YES	
Race	YES	
Marital status	YES	
Disability	YES	Limited. Harassment prohibited
Religion	NO*	*(but see text)
Sexual orientation	YES	Discrimination prohibited in respect of recruitment and harassment
Gender reassignment	YES	Discrimination prohibited in respect of recruitment and harassment
Equal pay legislation	YES	
TERMINATION OF EMPLOYMENT		
Right not to be dismissed in breach of contract	YES	
Statutory rights on termination	YES	(Unfair dismissal)

REDUNDANCY

Statutory definition	YES	In respect of collective redundancies
Right to payment on redundancy	NO	

Right to consultation:

Collective	YES	In respect of at least ten employees being made redundant in 30 days

YOUNG WORKERS

Protection of children and young persons at work	YES	

MATERNITY RIGHTS

Right to time off – ante natal care	YES	
Right to maternity leave	YES	42–52 weeks' maternity leave
Maternity pay (during leave)	YES	Maternity benefits paid by Government
Protection from dismissal	YES	Presumption that dismissal is unfair unless the employer proves otherwise
Health and safety protection	YES	
Right to parental leave	YES	Ten days per annum until child aged 12 (20 days if parent has sole responsibility). This is a general rule which applies for both parents as a parental right, not connected to maternity

TRANSFERS OF BUSINESSES

Right to protection on transfer	YES
Transfer of employment obligations	YES
Right to information and consultation	YES
Right not to be dismissed	YES

COLLECTIVE RIGHTS

Right to organisation	YES	
European works council	YES	
Right to take industrial action	YES	If lawful

EMPLOYMENT DISPUTES

Civil court jurisdiction	YES	Central Labour Court deals only with disputes concerning collective agreements

WHISTLEBLOWING

Protection from dismissal/ detriment	NO	No specific legislation protecting 'whistleblowers'

DATA PROTECTION
Protection   YES

HUMAN RIGHTS ACT
Statutory protection of human
rights
Public authority   YES
Private organisations   NO

1   THE EMPLOYMENT RELATIONSHIP

1.1   Background

N1.1.1   The basis for the relationship between an employee and an employer is contractual. In Norway there will always be an individual contract, which as a general rule will be in writing. About 50% of Norwegian employees have the terms in their individual contract linked to a collective agreement negotiated by trade unions. We will revert to this in section 10 (see paras **N10.1.1** ff).

N1.1.2   The parties are, however, not free to insert any kind of contractual terms in the individual contract. The employee as the supposed weaker part in the relationship is protected by statute. Norway was one of the first countries in Europe to introduce regulations for protection from unfair dismissal (1936).

N1.1.3   The main law governing the relationship between the employer and the employee in the private and public sectors (which are not directly under the supervision of the Government) is Act No 4 of the Norwegian Parliament (*Stortinget*) of February 4 1977 relating to Worker Protection and the Working Environmental Act (WEA). The 1936 law was revised in 1956 and 1977, while the 1977 law was revised in 1995.

N1.1.4   Much of the 1995 amendment was based on implementing EEA Directives eg 77/187/EEC (Transfer of business enterprises), 75/129/EEC (Information with major redundancies) and 71/533/EEC (Contents of employment agreements). On these issues, Norwegian courts are basically obliged to follow EU court rulings.

N1.1.5   It follows from the WEA, s 5, that provisions of the WEA may not be set aside by agreement unless this is expressed in the law. An employee cannot contractually waive any rights he/she may have in the law.

N1.1.6   If the parties agree, for example, that the employee is entitled to 12 months salary on termination of employment only, the employee and not the employer may rely on this. An employee cannot in advance waive his/her rights in the WEA. If the employee and the employer in connection with a termination agree on other terms than those in the WEA (eg a shorter termination period etc) that is legal.

N1.1.7   The following sectors are exempted from the WEA: shipping, hunting and fishing, and military aviation. The public sectors, which are under the supervision of the Government, are also exempted from the WEA. Public servants have had such protection since 1918. The present Act regulating the protection of public servants is from 1983. These sectors will not be covered in this chapter.

1.2 Contract of Service

N1.2.1 There are three basic kinds of employment relationship:

• When a person is employed he or she must usually go through a trial period which cannot exceed six months. The period can be extended because of absence due to sickness etc if agreed in the employment contract. If the trial period is successful, the employee will have a permanent position until termination. During the trial period, protection against dismissal is slightly weaker for the employee than when permanently employed.
• A person may also be employed on a temporary basis.
• Finally, the employee may be employed on a permanent basis.

N1.2.2 The WEA regulates all three kinds of employment relationships.

N1.2.3 In Norway, every employee is entitled to a contract of employment.[1]

All employment relationships shall be subject to a written contract of employment. In the case of employment relationships lasting at least one month, the contract shall be entered into as soon as possible and not later than one month after commencement of employment.

In the case of employment contracts relating to employment relationships of less than one month or agency workers, a written contract of employment shall be entered into immediately.

---

[1] WEA, s 55B.

Employment relationship

• Trial period ⟶ Six months maximum

• Temporary employee

• Permanent employee

All must have contract of employment

Terms set by agreement between employer/ employee
  • statute
  • CBAs
  • implied terms

A   CONTRACT AND ITS WRITTEN PARTICULARS

N1.2.4 Every employee is entitled to a written employment contract. WEA, s 55 sets out minimum terms, which must be part of the written contract:

The employment contract shall at least contain the following:

(a) the identities of the parties;

(b) the place of work; where there is no fixed or main place of work, the employment contract shall state that the employee is employed at various locations, and shall set out the registered place of business or, where appropriate, the domicile of the employer;

(c) a description of the work or the employee's title, position or category of work;

(d) the date of commencement of the employment relationship;

(e) in the case of a temporary employment relationship, the expected duration thereof;

(f) the amount of holiday and holiday pay to which the employee is entitled, and the rules governing the determination of dates for holidays;

(g) the periods of notice of termination applicable to the employee and the employer;

(h) the wage applicable or agreed at the commencement of the employment relationship, any additional payments and other remuneration not included in the wage, eg pension payments and meals/accommodation allowances, and wage payment dates;

(i) the normal daily or weekly hours of work;

(j) where appropriate, provisions relating to a trial period of employment;

(k) information concerning any wage agreements governing the employment relationship. If parties outside the enterprise have concluded the agreements, the contract shall contain information regarding the names of the parties to the wage agreements.

The information referred to in the first paragraph, (f), (g), (h) and (i) above may be given in the form of a reference to the Acts, Regulations and/or wage agreements regulating these matters.

B   TERMS OF THE CONTRACT

N1.2.5 The terms of the contract are usually express. All written terms are considered to be express. Some terms may also be implied. These are unwritten terms, which can be implied from the written terms of the contract or other factors outside the contract. There may also be incorporated terms, which are normally set out in legislation concerning certain categories of work.

C   EXPRESS TERMS

N1.2.6 The express terms may be written in the contract or expressed orally.

D IMPLIED TERMS

N1.2.7 One common implied term is the term of loyalty between the employee and the employer. This term is usually an implied term. However, the contract may include examples of what is considered to be breach of loyalty.

Other implied terms can include how the employee is expected to conduct himself or to wear appropriate clothes.

E INCORPORATED TERMS

N1.2.8 These are terms from other sources than the contract. Examples are collective agreements, legislation or work rules in the company.

Statutory provisions

N1.2.9 A number of terms must form part of the written agreement. There are restrictions concerning terms that prevent the employee seeking work with competitor employers after his dismissal.[1] If the restrictions are considered unreasonable, they may be declared null and void.

[1] Act No 4 of 31 May 1918 relating to the Closing of Agreements Act, s 38.

N1.2.10 Other terms may be declared null and void through the Closing of Agreement Act, s 36. The main condition is that the term is unreasonable. The courts have interpreted this condition strictly. It is more difficult to get a term nullified through s 36, than to nullify a term relating to competitive employment through s 38.

1.3 Variation of Contract

N1.3.1 The employer is not free to make many changes in an individual's contract. Basic terms cannot be changed without consent. If that is done, the employee may consider this a termination of the contract. For such a change, the employer must have a valid reason. However, within the boundaries of the managerial prerogatives, the employer has certain rights to change some of the conditions, but not those that involve an important issue (eg terms of payment).

N1.3.2 The employer has to some extent the right to change an employee's duties. The right to change duties must be based on an interpretation of the contract, its purposes and how it has been practised. If the changes are within the boundaries of the contract, the employee must accept the changes.

N1.3.3 If the change of duties or terms results in the employee feeling degraded or the work is of another kind, the employee does not necessarily have to accept it, as it may be deemed to amount to a termination of employment.

N1.3.4 Every individual contract may be subject to re-negotiation. The parties are free to do so within the boundaries of the law and wage agreements.

1.4 Remedies

N1.4.1 Conflicts concerning the content of individual agreements may be brought in the common courts (see section 11, paras **N11.1.1** ff for more details). Conflicts regarding the interpretation of collective agreements may be brought before the Labour Court in Oslo (see section 10, paras **N10.1.1** ff).

2 REMUNERATION

2.1 Background

N2.1.1 There is no legislation which secures employees minimum wages in Norway. About 50% of all employees are affected by different collective agreements. The collective agreements have regulations concerning minimum wages, and every employer who is a member of an organisation is obliged to follow the regulations set out in the relevant agreement.

2.2 Legal Regulation of Remuneration

Amount

N2.2.1 The amount of remuneration may depend on individual agreements between the employer and the employee.

N2.2.2 If the employer or employee is a member of an organisation, which has made a collective agreement, the collective agreement is the basis for the remuneration.

Type of remuneration

N2.2.3 There are different kinds of remuneration. The most common kind is ordinary wages paid to the employee every two weeks or every month. The payment from the employer may also include fringe benefits such as cheap loans, free phone, company car or presents. Examples of additional benefits are Christmas presents or a special recognition if an employee has done a good job or has worked for a long period of time for the company.

N2.2.4 Some companies give their employees an annual bonus if the year has been profitable.

N2.2.5 Besides fixed wages based on an agreement between the employer and employee, there are also agreements which contain clauses about piece-work. The employee then receives his remuneration when the agreed work is finished partially or completely.

2.3 Deductions from Wages

N2.3.1 There is a general prohibition on any deduction from a worker's wages.[1] The exemptions from this rule are:

(a) deductions authorised by law;
(b) regulation payments to pension or medical schemes;

(c) deductions stipulated in advance by written agreement;

(d) deductions stipulated by wage agreements concerning the withholding of trade union dues, including the collective home insurance premium or contributions to information and development funds, or to low-income funds;

(e) compensation for damage or loss suffered by the business and caused wilfully or by gross negligence on the part of the employee in connection with the work, when the employee has acknowledged his liability in writing or it has been established by court decision, or when the employee illegally leaves his job;

(f) when, owing to prevailing routines for calculation and disbursement of wages, it has in practice been impossible to take account of absence due to work stoppages or lockouts during the accounting period.

[1] WEA, s 55.

N2.3.2 Deductions in wages or holiday pay pursuant to (e) and (f) above are limited to that part of the claim which exceeds the amount reasonably needed by the employee to support himself and his household.

N2.3.3 Before making deductions in accordance with (e) above, the employer must consult the elected union representatives or two representatives elected by the employees concerning the basis for and the amount of deduction.

2.4   Itemised Pay Statement

N2.4.1 An employee is entitled to a written itemised pay statement.
At the time of payment or immediately thereafter, the employee shall receive a written statement of the method used for calculating the pay, the basis on which the holiday allowance is calculated, and any deductions made.

Remuneration – summary

- no minimum wage
- terms often regulated by CBAs
- regulation on deductions from wages

---

3   FURTHER RIGHTS AND OBLIGATIONS

3.1   Holiday Entitlement

N3.1.1 Act No 21 of 29 April 1988 relating to Holidays (HA) contains regulations relating to holiday entitlement.

N3.1.2 The length of the holiday is regulated in the HA, s 5:

Section 5 – Length of holidays

(1) Normal annual leave in connection with holidays
Employers shall ensure that employees have 25 workdays' leave in connection with holidays each holiday year.

(2) Extra holidays for employees over the age of 60
Employees who reach the age of 60 before 1 September in a holiday year shall be given six workdays' extra holiday.

N3.1.3 The time of holiday is regulated in the HA, s 7:

Section 7 – Holiday periods

(1) Main holiday
An employee may demand to have his main holiday, comprising 18 workdays, during the main holiday period, 1 June–30 September. This does not apply, however, to an employee who takes up his post after 15 August in the holiday year.

(2) Remaining holiday
An employee may demand to take the remaining holidays (seven working days) together within the holiday year.

(3) Departure
The rules in this section governing holiday periods within the holiday year may be departed from in a collective agreement or other agreement. Written agreements may also be entered into concerning the taking of holidays in advance and the transfer of holidays of up to 12 workdays to the following holiday year. Transfers of holidays beyond that limit cannot be agreed.*

*Even if the parties agree to this, such an agreement is not legal.

Holiday payment

N3.1.4 Every employee is entitled to receive a holiday payment every summer. The holiday payment is calculated as 10.2% of last year's income. The employee receives the holiday payment normally in June instead of the regular salary he or she would receive in June.

3.2 Sick Pay

N3.2.1 The regulation concerning sick pay entitlement is found in Act No 19 of 28 February 1997 relating to social security (SSA) at Chapter 8.

Requirements

N3.2.2 To be entitled to receive sick pay, the worker must have been employed for at least two weeks immediately before he became sick.

N3.2.3 In Norway there is a national health care system. The state or the community owns most of the hospitals. As part of the tax system, each employee pays 7.8%, which is deducted from salary as part of the tax. Part of this (5.3%) covers pension, while the rest (2.8%) covers healthcare.

N3.2.4 If a person is working in Norway, but living abroad, he or she is still obliged in principle to contribute in this way.

Basis of calculation

N3.2.5 The basis of calculation of sick pay is the salary received by the employee. If he or she receives payment per hour, the basis of calculation is the salary received over the past four weeks. If the employer receives a fixed salary for each month, the basis for calculation is the salary received for the previous month. If the employment has lasted less than four weeks, the actual time of employment is the basis of calculation.

Period of entitlement

N3.2.6 The total period an employee may receive sick pay is limited to 248 days over a total period of three years. To be entitled to receive further sick pay, he or she must be able to work for at least 26 weeks before a new period of entitlement commences.

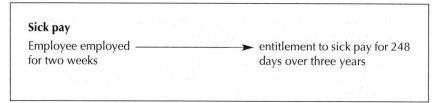

Sick pay
Employee employed ⟶ entitlement to sick pay for 248
for two weeks days over three years

3.3 Legislation and Health and Safety Measures

N3.3.1 The Working Environmental Act, s 12 sets out regulations concerning the organisation of work:

> **Section 12 – Planning the work**
>
> (1) General requirements
> Technology, organisation of work, execution of work, working hours and wage systems shall be arranged so that employees are not exposed to adverse physical or mental effects, and their possibilities of exercising caution and observing safety considerations are not impaired. Necessary means to prevent adverse physical effects shall be placed at the disposal of the employees. Employees shall not be subjected to harassment or other improper conduct.
> Conditions shall be arranged so that employees are afforded reasonable opportunity for professional and personal development through their work.

(2) Arrangement of work

The individual employee's opportunity for self-determination and professional responsibility shall be taken into consideration when planning and arranging work.

Efforts shall be made to avoid undiversified, repetitive work and work that is governed by machine or conveyor belt in such a manner that the employees themselves are prevented from varying the speed of the work. Otherwise efforts shall be made to arrange the work so as to provide possibilities for variation and for contact with others, for connection between individual job assignments, and for employees to keep informed about production requirements and results.

The work must be arranged so as not to offend the dignity of the employee.

(3) Control and planning systems

The employees and their elected union representatives shall be kept informed about the systems employed for planning and effecting the work and about planned changes in such systems. They shall be given the training necessary to enable them to learn these systems, and they shall take part in designing them.

(4) Work involving safety hazards

(a) Performance premium wage systems shall not be employed for work where this may materially affect safety.

(b) If work is to be carried out in the enterprise that may involve particular hazard to life and health, a special directive shall be issued prescribing how the work is to be done and the safety precautions to be observed, including any particular instruction and supervision.

(c) When the work is of such a nature that it involves danger of a disaster or disastrous accident, plans shall be drawn up for first aid, escape routes and rescue measures, registration of employees present at the workplace and so on.

(d) Employees shall be informed of the regulations and safety rules etc relating to the area concerned and of the plans and measures mentioned under (c).

(e) When satisfactory precautions to protect life and health cannot be achieved by other means, employees shall be provided with suitable personal protective equipment. Employees shall be trained in the use of such equipment and if necessary shall be ordered to use it.

'The King', which in practice usually means the Norwegian Government, can issue further rules.

Obligations

N3.3.2   The Working Environmental Act contains regulations concerning obligations for both employer and employees:

(a)   Employers' obligations

Section 14 – Duties of employer

The employer shall ensure that the enterprise is arranged and maintained, and that the work is planned, organised and performed in accordance with the provisions stipulated in or by virtue of this Act.

To ensure that the safety, health and welfare of the employees is taken into consideration at all levels throughout the enterprise, the employer shall:

(i)   when planning new workplaces, alteration of workplaces or production methods, procurement of technical appliances and equipment etc, study and evaluate whether the working environment will be in compliance with the requirements of this Act and effect the measures necessary;

(ii)   arrange continuous charting of the existing working environment in the enterprise as regards risks, health hazards and welfare, and effect the measures necessary;

(iii)   arrange continuous checks of the working environment and the health of employees when there may be a risk of health injuries caused by long-term effects from influences in the working environment;

(iv)   arrange for expert assistance and for testing and measuring equipment when this is necessary in order to comply with the requirements of the Act;

(v)   organise and arrange the work giving due consideration to the age, proficiency, working ability and other capabilities of the individual employees;

(vi)   ensure the systematic promotion of safety within the enterprise and that employees charged with directing or supervising other employees have the necessary understanding of safety matters to see that the work is performed in a proper manner as regards safety and health;

(vii)   ensure compliance with the provisions of the Act relating to systematic promotion of safety;

(viii) ensure that employees are informed of any accident risks and health hazards that may be connected with the work and that they receive the necessary training, practice and instruction.

(b)   Employees' obligations

Section 16 – Duties of employees

(1) Employees shall take part in the creation of a sound, safe working environment by carrying out the prescribed measures and participating in the organised safety and environmental work of the enterprise.

Employees shall perform their work in conformity with orders and instructions from superiors or from the Labour Inspectorate. They shall use the prescribed protective equipment, exercise caution and otherwise co-operate to prevent accidents and injury to health.

If employees become aware of faults or defects that may involve a hazard to life or health and they themselves are unable to remedy the fault or defect, they shall immediately notify the employer or his authorised representative, the safety delegate and, to the extent necessary, the other employees.

An employee who finds that the work cannot continue without danger to life or health shall cease his work.

Employees who suffer injury at work or who contract disease, which they believe result from the work or conditions at the workplace, shall report this to the employer or his representative.

(2) Employees whose duty it is to lead or supervise other employees shall ensure that safety and health are taken into consideration when work that comes under their areas of responsibility is being planned and carried out.

4   WORKING TIME

4.1   Background

N4.1.1   The Working Environmental Act covers the regulations considering working time. It is the employer's responsibility to make sure that the requirements concerning working time are met.

4.2   Legislative Control

N4.2.1   The main regulations governing working time are set out in the WEA, s 46:

Section 46 – Length of ordinary working hours

(1) Definition of working hours and off-duty time
Working hours means time when the employee is at the disposal of the employer.
Off-duty time means time when the employee is not at the disposal of the employer.
Rest breaks shall be regarded as working time when the employee is not free to leave the workplace during the break.

(2) 40-hour working week
In the case of work not covered by subss 3 and 4 below, ordinary working hours shall not exceed 9 hours per day and 40 hours per week.

(3) 38-hour working week
Ordinary working hours shall not exceed 9 hours per day and 38 hours per week in the case of:

(a) discontinuous shift work and other comparable work by rotation;
(b) work on two shifts which are regularly operated on Sundays and public holidays;
(c) work which necessitates that an individual employee work every third Sunday;
(d) work principally performed at night.

Disputes concerning the length of ordinary working hours shall be settled by the Labour Inspectorate.

---

(4) 36-hour working week

Ordinary working hours shall not exceed 9 hours per day and 36 hours per week in the case of:

(a) continuous shift work and comparable work by rotation;

(b) work below ground in mines. The 'walking time' (the time which passes from meeting at the gate of the mine, to the working place below ground and back to the entrance gate at the end of the working day) shall also be counted as working time;

(c) tunnelling and blasting subterranean rooms when the distance between tunnel openings is at least 50 meters, or the subterranean room is at least 25 meters deep, measured from the opening. This includes all work at such workplaces until the tunnel or room has been permanently secured.

Disputes concerning the length of ordinary working hours shall be settled by the Labour Inspectorate.

(5) Extended working hours for standby duties etc

In cases where the work wholly or mainly consists of the worker having to stay at the workplace to perform duties if required, working hours may be extended by up to one half of the waiting periods, but not by more than 2 hours per day and 10 hours per week.

(6) Extended working hours for passive duties

In the case of work where, except for short or occasional intermittent periods, the employee is exempted from work and the duty of attentiveness, the Labour Inspectorate may consent to the daily and weekly working hours being extended beyond those stipulated in subs 5.

(7) Extended working hours for preparatory and finishing work

When the normal operation of an enterprise cannot be ensured unless certain employees begin their work before or finish their work after the other employees, the ordinary working hours of such employees may be extended by up to half an hour per day.

(8) Work periods, which extend beyond the dividing point between two full days

If a work period extends into the following day it shall be regarded as one work period and must not exceed the limits on working hours permitted in a single day.

(9) Standby at home

In cases where the employee is required to stay in his home in order to perform work if required, at least 20% of such standby period shall as a general rule be included in the ordinary working hours.

At enterprises where employees are bound by wage agreements, the employer and the elected union representatives may conclude an agreement to the effect that the working hours shall include a lesser share of the standby period at home, or that such standby duties shall not be included.

(10) Exceptions from rules regarding the length of working hours in certain cases

The Labour Inspectorate may make exceptions from the rules for employees who voluntarily undertake work of a social nature in addition to their ordinary work for the same employer.

4.3   Opting Out

N4.3.1   As a main rule all employers are affected by the WEA regulations regarding the employees working time. This is regulated in the WEA, s 50:

Section 50 – Length of overtime work

(1) General provisions
The employer shall seek to distribute overtime so as to avoid placing too great a strain upon an individual employee.
Overtime work must not together with the ordinary working hours result in any employee working for more than a total of 14 hours in any 24-hour period. Overtime shall not exceed 10 hours in any one week, and shall not exceed 25 hours during four consecutive weeks, or 200 hours per calendar year. In the case of an excessive volume of work within agriculture, an agreement may be made to extend weekly overtime, though not in excess of 15 hours per week.

(2) Extended overtime by agreement with elected union representatives
In enterprises bound by a wage agreement, the employer and the employees' elected representatives may conclude a written agreement applicable to a period of up to three months and stipulating overtime work for up to 15 hours per week, provided however that the total overtime worked does not exceed 40 hours in the course of four consecutive weeks. Total working hours must not exceed 16 hours in any 24-hour period. No employee shall work more than 300 hours of overtime per calendar year. If the agreement is binding upon a majority of the employees, the employer may make it applicable to all employees in the enterprise that performs work of the type covered by the agreement.
Extended overtime by agreement with the elected representatives may only be imposed on employees who in each individual case have agreed to such work.

(3) Extended overtime by permission of the Labour Inspectorate
In special cases the Labour Inspectorate may permit overtime for up to 20 hours per week, and overtime amounting to more than 200 hours per calendar year.
Before permission is granted, the question of working overtime in excess of the general framework of this Act shall be discussed with the employees' elected representatives. Records of the discussions shall accompany the application. If the enterprise submits an application for overtime within the limits prescribed in sub-s 2 of this section, the reason why the matter has not been settled by means of an agreement with the elected representatives shall always be stated. When making its decision, the Labour Inspectorate shall attach particular importance to the health and welfare of the employees.

Working time
- limit of 40 hours per week (36 and 38 hours in certain cases)
- no opt out unless in specified circumstances including:
  - agricultural work
  - by agreement with elected union representatives
  - with permission of the Labour Inspection
- specified rest periods (at least one rest break in 5½-hour day)

4.4 Night Workers

N4.4.1 Night work is basically prohibited. However, there are a few exceptions stated in the WEA, s 42:

Section 42 – Night work

Work between the hours of 2100 and 0600 is night work and must not be performed in cases other than those mentioned in this and the following section. The employer shall consult the employees' elected representatives in advance concerning the necessity of night work.

Permissible night work is:

(a) work that cannot be performed unless other work at the workplace is interrupted, and which must be performed at night owing to the operating hours at the workplace;

(b) maintenance and repair work that must be performed at night to ensure normal operation of the enterprise. When important reasons so necessitate, such work may also be performed at night to ensure normal operation of other enterprises;

(c) work that is necessary to prevent damage to the plant, machinery, raw materials or products;

(d) watchmen's and doormen's work;

(e) supervision and care of animals;

(f) permanently organised transport activities and necessary loading, unloading and storage connected therewith, and the despatching of mail, telegrams and telephone calls. Work that must be performed at night to ensure the operation of means of transport or to meet the needs of passengers, shall be considered equivalent to transport activities;

(g) work in two shifts that fall between the hours of 0600 and 2400;

(h) work in institutions providing medical care and nursing, and in boarding accommodations attached to schools, children's homes, kindergartens, etc;

(i) work necessary to provide services for guests in hostelry and catering establishments;

(j) work by police, fire service, customs service, prison service, church officials, work at rescue operation centres and in broadcasting services, newspapers, telegram and news service agencies;

(k) work at theatres and other shows and performances;

(l) work at sales outlets;

(m) salvage and diving work when conditions necessitate night work;

(n) work that for technical reasons cannot be interrupted;

(o) agricultural work when there is an excessively great volume of work;

(p) supervision and care of live plants;

(q) necessary work in connection with production of bakery goods.

Disputes as to whether the work is permissible night work shall be settled by the Labour Inspectorate.

4.5 Rest Period

N4.5.1 The rest period is regulated in the WEA, s 51:

Section 51 – Breaks and time off

(1) Breaks

When working hours exceed 5½ hours per day, there shall be at least one rest break during work. The break shall be stipulated by written agreement between the employer and the employees or their elected union representatives, provided, however, that the breaks total at least half an hour when working hours are eight hours or more per day. If the parties fail to reach agreement, the matter shall be settled by the Labour Inspectorate. When necessary to protect the health of employees, the Labour Inspectorate may order a system different from that agreed upon between the parties.

Unless operations within the facilities (the working place) stop completely during breaks, employees shall not remain in the workrooms. When conditions so necessitate, the break may be postponed, but shall then be taken at the first opportunity.

When the nature of the enterprise renders this necessary, instead of breaks as mentioned in the first paragraph above, the employer may allow employees to take their meals during breaks while work is in progress, the employees being required to stay at the workplace the entire time if necessary. In such cases, and in cases where no satisfactory canteen or restroom is provided, the break shall be regarded as part of the working hours.

Disputes concerning the employer's right to apply the provisions of the preceding paragraph shall be settled by the Labour Inspectorate.

When an employee is required to work overtime for more than two hours after ordinary working hours, he shall first be allowed a break of at least half an hour which is to be included in the working hours. When circumstances render this necessary, this break may be shortened or postponed. Breaks which come after the end of ordinary working hours shall be subject to remuneration as overtime but shall not be included in the number of hours it is permitted to work overtime. If the break comes before the end of ordinary working hours, it is to be regarded as part of ordinary working hours.

(2) Daily off-duty time

Working hours must be arranged so that employees have a continuous off-duty period of at least ten hours between two working periods. Nevertheless, it may be verbally agreed with the individual employee that works assignments of short duration may be performed during the off-duty period when a risk of serious disruptions in operations suddenly arises.

At a company bound by a wage agreement, the employer and the employees' elected representatives may conclude a written agreement that overtime work may be performed during the off-duty period when this is necessary to avoid serious operational disruptions and employees having to be on call when off-duty. At enterprises which are not bound by a wage agreement, the employer and the employee representatives may conclude a written agreement on the same terms to the effect that overtime may be worked during the off-duty period. At agricultural enterprises, which are not bound by a wage agreement, such an agreement may be made orally, provided that none of the parties demand a written agreement.

If it is necessary in order to ensure that the work is completed in a suitable manner, and the enterprise is bound by wage agreement, the employer and the employees' elected representatives may conclude a written agreement that the off-duty period between two working periods shall be reduced to under ten hours, but not to less than eight hours.

Shorter off-duty periods may be permitted by the Labour Inspectorate in special cases.

(3) Weekly off-duty time

Ordinary working hours for employees shall be arranged so that each week they have a continuous off-duty period of at least 36 hours which always includes one full 24-hour day. Whenever possible the off-duty time shall be on a Sunday or public holiday and shall be granted at the same time to all employees at the enterprise.

At businesses companies which are bound by a wage agreement, the employer and the employees' elected representatives may agree that this off-duty period shall on average be 36 hours, but never shorter than 28 hours in any single week. The period for which off-duty time is calculated shall correspond to the average period of working hours calculated according to the WEA.

At businesses not bound by a wage agreement, the Labour Inspectorate may permit a corresponding calculation of average off-duty time as in the previous paragraph. Before permission is given, the organisation of off-duty time shall be discussed with the employees' representatives. A record of the discussions shall accompany the application. In its decision the Labour Inspectorate shall pay due regard to the employees' health and welfare.

An employee who has worked on a Sunday or public holiday shall be off-duty on the following Sunday or public holiday in conformity with the requirement of the first paragraph of the WEA, s 44. When circumstances render it particularly necessary, the Labour Inspectorate may permit modifications of this rule. If there are two or more successive Sundays and public holidays following each other successively, 10 pm shall be considered the dividing point between these days.

At businesses bound by a wage agreement, the employer and the employees' elected representatives may, for a period of up to six months, agree on an arrangement of working hours which ensures that the employees will be off-duty on average every other Sunday and public holiday. This is on condition that the weekly 24-hour off-duty period falls on a Sunday or public holiday at least every third week.

In the case of work in hotel and catering establishments or work performed without interruption throughout the week, the work schedule may stipulate a different distribution of off-duty days from that prescribed. However, the weekly 24-hour off-duty period must fall on a Sunday or public holiday at least every third week.

4.6   Paid Annual Leave

N4.6.1   Full-time workers are entitled to at least four weeks paid leave each year. Part-time workers are entitled to a pro rata holiday. The calculation of the payment is set out in the HA, s 10:

Calculation of holiday pay

(1) Basis for calculating holiday pay

Holiday pay from an employer is calculated on the basis of wages paid in the qualifying year. Wages do not include payments to cover expenses for car travel, board, lodging and the like.

The following payments are not included in the basis for calculating holiday pay:

(a) holiday pay according to the Act, paid during the qualifying year;
(b) shares of net profits;
(c) regular payments earned and paid irrespective of absence of holiday; or
(d) the value of goods, services or other benefits other than payments in money.

The value of full or partial board received as part of payment for work shall, however, be included in the basis for calculating holiday pay.

The basis on which holiday pay is calculated shall be shown in the salary and deduction statement for the qualifying year.

(2) The general percentage rate

An employee is entitled to holiday pay from his employer amounting to 10.2% of the basis on which holiday pay is calculated.

(3) (Higher rate for employees over the age of 60)

For employees who are over 60 years of age and entitled to extra holidays, the rate rises by 2.3 percentage points.

4.7 Remedies

N4.7.1 Disputes in relation to working time may be settled by the Labour Inspectorate. Both employer and employee are bound by the decisions made by the Labour Inspectorate.

5 EQUAL OPPORTUNITIES

5.1 Background

N5.1.1 The law in Norway prohibits discrimination on the basis of sex, race and marital status. The relevant regulations are to be found in Act No 45 of 9 June 1978 on Equality Between Sexes and Act No 4 of 4 February 1977 relating to Worker Protection and the Working Environment.

5.2 Unlawful Discrimination based on Sex, Race and Marital Status

Direct discrimination

N5.2.1 Direct discrimination occurs when the employer treats an employee less favourably than another employee. The comparator is a person of the opposite sex in relation to sex discrimination. The comparator is an unmarried person of the same sex in relation to marital status discrimination. The comparator in racial discrimination cases is a person from a different racial group to that of the employee discriminated against.

N5.2.2 Proving direct discrimination can be very difficult for the employee. It is usually not a problem for the employer to find acceptable reasons to treat two employees differently.

Indirect discrimination

N5.2.3 Indirect discrimination occurs when an employer applies a requirement or condition to all employees, which has a disproportionate impact on members of one sex, marital status or racial group.

Vicarious liability

N5.2.4 The employer may be responsible for discrimination carried out by an employee in the course of his employment. The person who has been exposed to the discrimination can bring a claim against both the discriminator and the employer. The employer may be responsible even though he is unaware of the discrimination. This was stated in a verdict of the Norwegian Supreme Court in 1997. The verdict states that if the harassment is carried out in connection with the employee's working situation, the employer can be held liable for the harassment even though he does not know about the situation. This form of liability for the employer only applies if the harassment is severe. The employer will usually not be responsible for minor forms of harassment which do not cause any great physical or mental damage to the employee.

Harassment and victimisation

N5.2.5   Employees may be exposed to harassment from their employer or other fellow employees. The Working Environmental Act, s 12, specifically prohibits any form of harassment or other improper conduct. This prohibits direct discrimination in the form of harassment concerning sex, race and marital status. It is the employers' responsibility to make sure that any form of harassment does not occur in the place of work.

Same sex, transsexuals and sexual orientation

Recruitment

N5.2.6   In the Working Environmental Act, s 55A, there are prohibitions against demanding certain information when advertising vacant posts. Such information includes political, religious or cultural views. The same applies for information regarding sexual orientation. The employer therefore cannot in any way ask for this kind of information during the recruitment process. He is also prohibited from seeking this information in other ways.

N5.2.7   The employer is furthermore prohibited from discriminating against people on the basis of sexual orientation, race, skin colour or national or ethnic origin in the employment process.

The place of work

N5.2.8   The Working Environmental Act, s 12, prohibits harassment on the basis of same sex, transsexuality or sexual orientation.

5.3   Disability Discrimination

Requirements

N5.3.1   The only legislation considering disability discrimination at present is found in the WEA, s 12. This states that if the discrimination is considered harassment, it is prohibited.

N5.3.2   When a person applies for a vacant post in the Government or another public office, the employer may not use irrelevant reasons when deciding which applicant gets the job. Disability can in some cases be an irrelevant reason.

N5.3.3   When advertising a vacant post in a private business, the applicant has no cause of action against the employer if the employer refuses to hire a disabled person because of his disability.

Different kinds of discrimination

N5.3.4   Disability discrimination can be justified or unjustified.

N5.3.5   An employer has discriminated against the disabled person if he treats him less favourably than other employees and the disability is not a justified reason for the discrimination. This is unjustified discrimination.

N5.3.6   Disability discrimination may appear in different situations:

- The employer can in some cases discriminate against the disabled employee if his disability may disqualify him from certain kinds of work. If the disability makes it very difficult or impossible to work it is justified discrimination if the employer gives the employee different work which he is able to handle.
- As mentioned above, the disabled person has no protection from discrimination in the recruitment process. If the employer chooses one person instead of the disabled person, and the reason for the choice is the disabled person's disability, the employer is not liable for the discrimination.
- The disabled person may also be exposed to discrimination in social activities, for instance if he or she is not invited to parties arranged by the business because of the disability.
- If the disabled person receives lower pay than his fellow employees because of his disability, there will be discrimination.
- Discrimination is also possible if a disabled person is dismissed because of his disability.

Justification

N5.3.7   Since there is no particular legislation considering disability discrimination, the employer does not have to justify any discrimination against a disabled person. However, if the employer has no justified reason for the discrimination, it can easily be considered to be harassment.

Victimisation and harassment

N5.3.8   The Working Environmental Act, s 12, prohibits any victimisation and harassment at the place of work. This general prohibition includes harassment because of someone's disability.

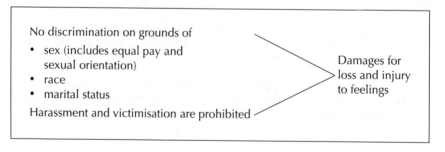

No discrimination on grounds of
- sex (includes equal pay and sexual orientation)
- race
- marital status

Harassment and victimisation are prohibited

Damages for loss and injury to feelings

5.4   Enforcement and Remedies in Discrimination Cases

N5.4.1   If an employee has been subjected to harassment or victimisation by the employer or another employee he may issue proceedings against the employer or employee.

N5.4.2   The employee may claim compensation for the losses that he has already suffered. This can be loss due to absence as a result of the harassment, loss of future earnings and for injury to feelings.

Remedies

N5.4.3–4   If it is proven that there is unequal pay between men and women, and they work in the same business doing work of the same value, the 'underpaid sex' may go to court to obtain equal pay.

5.5   Equal Pay

Requirements

N5.5.1   The Equality Between Sexes Act, s 5 states that women and men working in the same business are entitled to equal pay for work of similar value. The salaries are to be fixed on the same basis for both women and men. If it can be proven that there is a difference in treatment between men and women in their salaries, and they do work of the same value in the same business, the employer must make it clear that the reason for the discrimination is not due to the employees' sex.

Remedies

N5.5.2   If proven that there is unequal pay between men and women, and they work in the same business doing work of the same value, the lower paid employee may claim equal pay.

Example

In a case before the Labour Court in 1990, male engineers and female bio-engineers working at the same hospital laboratories were paid under an agreement with the county council. The main agreement had been made between the county council and its employees.. The agreement regulated the salaries for the people working in the county council.

After the local salary negotiations, the men and the women received partially unequal pay. The industrial tribunal found that the lower pay for the bio-engineers was not in accordance with the Equality Between Sexes Act, s 5. The tariff decisions in which the bio-engineers were given a lower salary were also null and void. There was no decisive difference concerning work and responsibility, or concerning qualifications and skill. The assessment must be based on the actual situation where the work was performed. The deciding point had to be if the standards for the salary negotiations were the same and not necessarily whether a similar payment resulted.

---

6 TERMINATION OF EMPLOYMENT

6.1 Background

N6.1.1 Each party can terminate the employment relationship. The employer must have a valid reason to do so.

N6.1.2 There are three basic types of termination: individual termination of employment with notice, mass lay-offs and summary dismissal.

N6.1.3 Termination of employment is bound by the regulations in the WEA. There are many similarities between English and Scandinavian employment law as regards the reasons which must be given for terminating the employment relationship.

N6.1.4 If an employee challenges the employer's decision to terminate the employment relationship before the court, he/she, as a general rule, is entitled to remain in his/her position until the court has decided whether the termination was fair or not. This does not apply to summary dismissal and termination during the probationary period.

Research on reasons for dismissal

Based on research Dege has done on Norwegian court rulings for the period prior to 1988, he found that in cases of summary dismissal, there were no cases where redundancy was the reason. Where gross misconduct was the reason, the employees were successful in 61.7% of all cases where the employees sued the employers claiming that the summary dismissal was invalid. Therefore the employers were successful in only 38.3% of the cases brought before the courts.

Of all the rulings regarding termination of contract with notice, where the employee had sued the employer stating that the reason for termination was not valid (fair) and redundancy was stated as the reason, the courts ruled in favour of employers in 54% of all cases, while the employee was successful in 46% of the cases.

If the reason for termination was not redundancy, but alleged misconduct, the employees won in 56.4% of the cases and the employer lost therefore in 43.6%.

Furthermore Dege found that for the period 1992–1995, 75% of all cases brought before the court were reconciled without any judgement by the court. This is similar to the UK, as out of 134,000 cases brought before the Advisory, Conciliation and Arbitration Service (ACAS) in the period 1988–1991, only 20% were ultimately taken to court.

N6.1.5 In Norway there is no similar institution to ACAS for labour disputes.

N6.1.6 There are specific requirements for information in connection with mass lay-offs. The definition of a mass lay-off is when at least ten employees are being laid-off within a period of not more than 30 days.

N6.1.7   Summary dismissal of an employee is when an employee is dismissed with immediate effect due to alleged gross misconduct in relation to the employee's duties as determined by his/her working agreement. This is the main rule. However, it could also be that an employee's actions away from the workplace, although not specifically linked to work, may show that he is unsuitable for the job. In such circumstances summary dismissal may be appropriate. Examples could be if a policeman commits a crime, a teacher sells narcotics etc.

N6.1.8   Summary dismissal is regulated in the WEA, s 66.

N6.1.9   Termination in breach of contract constitutes a dismissal.

Termination by the employer

N6.1.10   If an employer makes it clear to the employee, orally or in writing, that he wishes the employment to terminate, this could be considered to be a termination of the employment contract. The reasons for such termination may be fair or unfair.

N6.1.11   Before deciding to give notice of termination, the employer shall, to the extent that is practically possible, discuss the matter with the employee and the employee's elected representatives, unless the employee does not wish this.

N6.1.12   The employee has the right to stay in his position during the notice period. This right does not apply if the employee is summarily dismissed due to alleged gross misconduct. In these cases, the employee must go to court to resume the right to stay in his position during the notice period. The same applies to termination during trial period.

N6.1.13   The termination must be written and delivered to the employee personally or sent as registered letter.

N6.1.14   The written termination shall inform the employee of his right to demand negotiations and to institute legal proceedings and his right to remain in his post, and shall inform the employee of the time limits applicable for demanding negotiations, instituting legal proceedings and remaining in his post. If the employee has been given notice owing to lack of work, the notice shall also inform him of his preferential claim to new employment. The notice shall also state the name of the employer and the appropriate defendant in the event of legal proceedings.

N6.1.15   Temporary employment contracts shall terminate when the agreed period of time expires, or when the given work is completed, unless otherwise agreed in writing or stipulated by a wage agreement.

N6.1.16   If the temporary engagement has lasted for at least one year, the employee is entitled to written notice at least one month prior to the termination of the engagement.

Termination by the employee

N6.1.17   If an employee makes it clear to the employer that he does not wish to continue his employment, this is considered to be a termination of the contract by the employee.

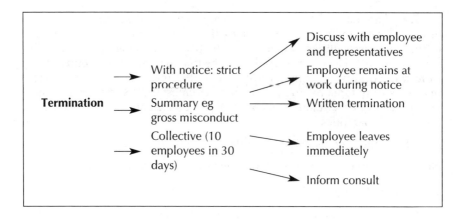

6.2   Statutory Claims – Unfair Dismissal

Background

N6.2.1   Most employment disputes in Norway occur where employment has been terminated and the employee claims that this was unfair. The regulation concerning protection from unfair termination is stated in the WEA, s 60, while summary dismissals are regulated by the WEA, s 66, as stated above.

Reasons for dismissal

Fairness

N6.2.2   There is no statutory provision for 'fair' reasons for dismissal.

N6.2.3   What is fair may vary from case to case and is related to the duties of the employee. There are several examples of what are considered unfair reasons:

Section 60 – Protection against unwarranted notice to leave

(a) Employees may not be given notice unless this is warranted by circumstances connected with the enterprise, the employer or the employee.
(b) Notice to leave due to curtailed operations or rationalisation measures are not warranted if the employer has other suitable work to offer the employee in the enterprise. When deciding whether curtailed operations or rationalisation measures warrant any lay-offs, the needs of the enterprise shall be weighed against the inconvenience such lay-offs involve for the individual employee.

Notice of termination owing to an employer's actual or planned contracting out of the enterprise's ordinary operations to a third party shall not be warranted unless it is absolutely essential in order to maintain the continued operations of the enterprise.
(c) Notice to leave before becoming 70 years of age due solely to the fact that the employee has reached retirement age under the National Insurance

---

Act, shall not be deemed to be warranted. After the employee reaches 66 years of age, but not later than six months before he reaches retirement age, the employer may inquire in writing whether the employee wishes to retire from his post upon reaching retirement age. A reply to this inquiry must be returned in writing not less than three months before the employee reaches retirement age.

Provided that this is expressly stated in the inquiry, protection against notice to leave under the preceding paragraph lapses if no reply is received within the time limit stated.

[1]   WEA, s 60.

Capability and qualifications

N6.2.4   An employer must expect that the employee will carry out his work in a satisfactory way in accordance with the guidelines given by the employer, and at a speed comparable to other employees doing the same type of work. When the capability and qualifications of the employee prevent him from doing this, there may be a fair reason for dismissal.

Conduct

N6.2.5   There are no direct regulations in the Working Environmental Act considering employees' conduct, except the prohibitions against harassment.

N6.2.6   Conduct by the employee, which may justify a dismissal, can be threats and violence towards the employer or other employees. The same applies for any kind of sexual harassment or any other improper behaviour. Misconduct in dealings with the firm's customers may be an acceptable reason to dismiss an employee.

Redundancy

N6.2.7   If an employee is being dismissed because of redundancy, he has priority for any other vacant position in the company. This is set out in the WEA, s 67(1):

Section 67 – Preferential claim to employment
(1) Employees who have been given notice owing to lack of work shall have a preferential claim to new employment in the same business, unless the vacant post is one for which the employee is not suited. This shall also apply in respect of employees who were engaged for a limited period of time, and whose engagement is terminated owing to lack of work, as well as employees who have accepted an offer of reduced employment in lieu of notice.

However, this shall not apply to employees engaged as temporary replacements.

The preferential claim shall apply only to employees who have been employed by the enterprise for a total of at least 12 months during the past two years.

Contravention of any enactment

N6.2.8   Contravention of law in the course of business may be a fair reason for dismissal. However, the enactment must be in accordance with the regulations stated in the WEA. If not, the dismissal may be considered unfair. For instance, a lawyer commits a felony, which results in his licence to practice law being revoked. If he loses his job at the law firm where he is working, it is unlikely that the dismissal will be considered unfair.

Some other substantial reason

N6.2.9   Examples of some other substantial reason may be direct or indirect disobedience towards the employer. If the employee was found to be intoxicated at work, this would be a substantial reason for dismissal. The same applies if the employee steals from his employer or fellow employees.

Written reasons for dismissal

N6.2.10   The notice of termination shall be given in writing. This written notice does not have to include the reasons for the dismissal, but the employee is entitled to receive this information if he or she demands it.

6.3   Collective Terminations including Redundancies

Background

N6.3.1   Collective terminations may occur due to different reasons. The most common reasons are the closure of the business or the rationalisation of the business, leading to redundancies.

Contractual rights, statutory rights and consultation

N6.3.2   Section 56A contains the regulations concerning collective terminations. This is based on EEA Directive 75/129:

Section 56A – Information in the case of collective redundancies

(1) The term 'collective redundancies' shall mean notice of termination given to at least ten employees within a period of 30 days, without being caused by reasons related to the individual employees. Other forms of termination of employment contracts, which are not caused by reasons related to the individual employee, shall be included in the calculation, provided that at least five persons are made redundant.

(2) An employer contemplating collective redundancies shall at the earliest opportunity enter into consultations with the employees' elected representatives with a view to reaching an agreement to avoid collective redundancies or to reduce the number of persons made redundant. If redundancies cannot be avoided, efforts shall be made to mitigate their adverse effects. The consultations shall cover possible social welfare measures aimed, inter alia, at providing aid for redeploying or retraining workers made redundant. The employees' representatives shall have the right to receive expert assistance.

---

(3) Employers shall be obliged to give the employees' elected representatives all relevant information, including written notification of the grounds for the projected redundancies, the number of employees who may be made redundant, the categories of workers to which they belong, the number of employees normally employed, the categories of employees normally employed, and the period of time during which such redundancies may be effected. The written notification shall also include criteria for selection of those who may be made redundant and the criteria for calculation of additional severance pay, if appropriate. Such notification shall be given at the earliest opportunity, not later than at the same time as the employer calls a consultation meeting.

(4) Copy of the notification pursuant to sub-s 3 shall be sent to the Employment Service, (which is the local authority's official body responsible for employment matters).

(5) The employees' elected representatives may give any comments they may have regarding the notification directly to the Employment Service.

(6) Projected collective redundancies shall not come into effect earlier than 30 days after the Employment Service has been notified. If necessary in order to reach an agreement, the Employment Service may extend the period by up to 30 days. If the Employment Service alters this period, written notification of such alteration shall be given to the employer. The period may not be extended when the activities of an enterprise are terminated as the result of a judicial decision.

(7) The Employment Service shall make use of the period pursuant to sub-s 6 above to find solutions to the problems caused by the projected redundancies. The Ministry may issue further rules as to how the right to postpone redundancies shall be exercised and the role of the Employment Service in the event of postponement. The employer shall have an obligation to enter into consultation, even if someone other than the employer causes the projected redundancies and has superior authority over the employer, such as the management of a group of companies.

6.4 Summary Dismissal

N6.4.1 An employer may dismiss an employee with immediate effect if the employee is guilty of a gross breach of duty or other serious breach of the employment contract.

N6.4.2 In the event of a dispute concerning the legality of summary dismissal, the employee shall not be entitled to remain at work while the case is continuing unless a court decides otherwise.

N6.4.3 If the dismissal is not valid, the employee may claim compensation. Compensation shall be set at the amount the court considers reasonable in view of the financial loss, the circumstances of the employer and employee, and other facts of the case. The employee can also claim to be reinstated in his/her former position.

6.5 Remedies

N6.5.1 If an employee has been unlawfully dismissed, he may bring a claim against the employer. This can result in reinstatement/re-engagement and/or compensation.

N6.5.2 If the termination is considered to be unfair by a court, it may be declared null and void (if the employee specifically claims this).

N6.5.3 In special cases, however, if claimed by the employer, the court may decide that employment shall be terminated when, after weighing the interests of the parties, the court finds it clearly unreasonable that employment should continue.

N6.5.4 If the termination is unfair, the employee can require compensation.

N6.5.5 If the notice is invalid, the employee may claim compensation. Compensation shall be stipulated in the amount the court deems reasonable in view of the financial loss, the circumstances of the employer and employee and other circumstances.

N6.5.6 If the court finds that a temporary engagement dismissal is declared null and void, the court shall at the request of the employee pass judgement that the employment relationship exists. In special cases, the court may however, in response to a request from the employer, decide that the employment relationship shall terminate if, after weighing up the interests of the respective parties, the court finds that a continuation of the employment relationship would be clearly unreasonable. If a temporary engagement dismissal is declared null and void, the employee may claim compensation. If legal proceedings are instituted more than one year after the completion of negotiations, or more than one year after the date on which the employee leaves his post, judgement may only be passed for compensation.

7   YOUNG WORKERS

7.1   General Obligations

N7.1.1 The main rule for workers under the age of 18 is that they need their parents' consent to work.

N7.1.2 There is one exception to this rule. If the young worker is over the age of 15, but under the age of 18, he has the right to enter into a working agreement if he has previously been working and supporting himself with his salary.

N7.1.3 The main rule concerning children under the age of 15 is that they are not allowed to work.

N7.1.4 Set out below are the exemptions in the WEA, s 35:

- Children over the age of 15 who are required to attend school

  Persons aged 15 or more that are still undergoing compulsory schooling may be employed for work if their health, development and schooling will not suffer.

  Acceptable work is normally part-time work on Saturdays or after school.

- Children over the age of 14

  Persons aged 14 or more may be employed for work as part of their schooling or practical vocational guidance if the work is not detrimental to their health or development. The training programme involving such work shall be approved by the educational authorities. Conditions for allowing school pupils to perform work under this provision may be stipulated by the Directorate of Labour Inspection.

- Children over the age of 13

  Persons aged 13 or more may be employed for light work if their health, development and schooling will not suffer. The Directorate of Labour Inspection shall determine the types of work permitted under this provision, and in so doing may issue rules concerning the length of working hours and the conditions for such work.

  The main difference between these sections is that children at the age of 13 are not allowed to do heavier work irrespective of whether it will have a detrimental effect on their health, development or schooling.

- Children under the age of 15

  Regardless of their age, children may be allowed to work in certain cases. Subject to the consent of the Labour Inspectorate, persons under the age of 15 and persons undergoing compulsory schooling may be employed in commercial films, theatre performances and other performances that will not be detrimental to their health, safety, development or schooling.

  In each case the child's parents must apply to the Labour Inspectorate for consent to their child working. The Labour Inspectorate decides if the requirements are met before consent is granted.

Prohibition against night work

N7.1.5 The main rule is that young workers are not allowed to work at night. Employees under the age of 18 shall have an off-duty period of at least 12 hours between two working periods. The off-duty period shall always include the period from 21:00 to 07:00 hours in the case of employees under the age of 16 and the period from 23:00 to 06:00 hours in the case of employees from 16 to 18 years of age.

N7.1.6 The Directorate of Labour Inspection may, when necessary for the vocational training of the employee, consent to persons aged 16 or more being employed for work between the hours of 2300 and 0600. The permit shall stipulate the conditions considered necessary for the safety, health, and development of the employee, including the condition that the off-duty period between two working periods shall be at least 13 hours.

Working hours

N7.1.7 The Working Environmental Act, s 38, contains specific regulations concerning working hours for children and young people. The working hours should not prevent school attendance necessary for their education or prevent the children from benefiting from their tuition.

N7.1.8 The working hours for employees under the age of 18 must not exceed an average of 9 hours per day or 48 hours per week, without special permission from the Directorate of Labour Inspection.

N7.1.9 Employees under the age of 18 must not be employed for overtime work.

Annual holiday for school pupils

N7.1.10 Persons under the age of 18 who attend school shall have at least four weeks' holiday per year. Furthermore, at least two weeks must be taken during the summer holiday.

8 MATERNITY AND PARENTAL RIGHTS

8.1 Background

N8.1.1 Pregnant women are entitled to different levels of benefits and maternity leave rights. These benefits and rights include the right to be paid maternity leave before and after the birth and not to be unfairly dismissed during maternity leave. Fathers are also entitled to some benefits, though not to the same extent as mothers.

N8.1.2 In adoption cases women have basically the same maternity benefits.

N8.1.3 Employees' maternity rights are regulated in the WEA, and Act No 19 of 28 February 1997 on National Security.

8.2 General Rights

General maternity leave

N8.2.1 Every pregnant woman is now entitled to a total of 42 weeks maternity leave. They receive full maternity benefits during this period. They can also choose to extend the maternity leave to 52 weeks by reducing the maternity benefits to 80% during the maternity leave period.

N8.2.2 When adopting a child, the mother is entitled to adoption leave for 37 weeks with full maternity benefits, and 46 weeks with 80% maternity benefits.

N8.2.3 From the time the woman starts her maternity leave, which is three weeks before the expected birth, she immediately starts receiving her maternity benefits. For the first six weeks after the birth the mother is obliged to have maternity leave. After this period, the father of the child can choose to stay home instead of the mother.

Fathers' parental rights

N8.2.4 The father of the child is entitled to two weeks unpaid leave of absence in relation to the birth if he is living with the mother, and the father uses the two weeks to take care of his family and home. Under certain circumstances, the father gets benefits from the community. The father does not have the right to maternity benefits during this period and therefore the leave of absence is unpaid during these two weeks. Four weeks of the maternity leave period after the birth is reserved for the father, which means that the mother's maternity leave period is shortened by four weeks.

Antenatal care

N8.2.5 An employee has the right to a one-hour reduction in her daily working hours in relation to antenatal care, or she can leave work for half an hour two times a day for antenatal care.

Maternity clinic check-up

N8.2.6 A pregnant employee is entitled to leave of absence without salary reduction in relation to the maternity clinic check-up. One condition for this right is that the check-up cannot be performed after working hours.

Adopted and foster children

N8.2.7 The regulations concerning adoption and foster children are basically in accordance with the regulations concerning pregnancy and birth. In other words, the foster parents have the same rights when adopting a child as the biological parents have when the child is born. This does however not apply if a stepchild is being adopted.

Time account – right to reduced working hours

N8.2.8 The parents can choose a more flexible arrangement concerning their maternity leave period. This is called time account arrangement, and it makes it possible to spread the maternity benefit over a longer period. The mother (or father) then resumes her (or his) work with reduced hours before the end of the regular 42 or 52 weeks. He or she can then use the remaining maternity benefit to have reduced working hours after he or she resumes his or her work.

N8.2.9 A maximum of 29 weeks with full maternity benefits can be spread over a period of minimum 12 weeks and not more than two years.

Commencement and end of leave

N8.2.10 An employee can start her maternity leave 12 weeks before the birth. The maternity leave period commences when the employee decides. The employer must be notified.

N8.2.11 Maternity leave starts automatically when the birth occurs.

N8.2.12   Before the employee starts her maternity leave she must notify the Social Security Office if she wishes to have the 42 weeks with full maternity benefits or the 52 weeks with 80% maternity benefits. The maternity leave ends when the 42 or 52 weeks have expired.

Notice requirements

N8.2.13   An employee must notify her employer as soon as possible and not later than one week in advance before leave of absence where the leave of absence shall last at least two weeks.

N8.2.14   If the father wants to exercise his right to leave of absence in connection with the birth, he must notify the employer as soon as possible.

N8.2.15   If the leave will exceed 12 weeks after the birth, the employer must be notified by the employee as soon as possible, and no later than four weeks before the commencement of the leave.

N8.2.16   If the employee wishes to use the time account system with reduced hours he or she must notify the employer as soon as possible and at least four weeks in advance. The consequence for the mother, if she chooses to use the time account system, is that the employer must be notified at least seven weeks before the birth, since the mother has the right to maternity benefits for three weeks before the birth.

8.3   Protection From Dismissal

N8.3.1   Pregnant women are protected against notice of termination during their pregnancy if the reason for the dismissal is their pregnancy. If the employer cannot give any fair reason for the dismissal, the pregnancy is presumed to be the real reason for termination of employment during the pregnancy. A pregnant employee can consequently be dismissed eg because of redundancy, if it can be proved that there is no link between the fact that the employee is pregnant and the employer's needs to reduce the staff.

N8.3.2   Employees who are absent from work in accordance with their general maternity leave are protected against dismissal which becomes effective during their period of absence. If notice is given before the commencement of the absence, the termination period will be prolonged with the maternity leave period.

8.4   Health and Safety

N8.4.1   An employer is, according to the WEA, obliged to protect his employees' health, safety and welfare at work.

N8.4.2
It is the employer's responsibility to make sure that the workplace is arranged so that the working environment is fully satisfactory regarding the safety, health and welfare of the employees. This is something the employer must particularly consider if he has pregnant or new mothers among his employees.

8.5   Maternity Pay

N8.5.1   All pregnant women and new mothers are entitled to statutory maternity pay (SMP) when the maternity leave period commences. The SMP is maternity benefits paid by the Government. This is regulated in the National Security Act, Chapter 14. In relation to the birth, the mother receives SMP if she has been working for a minimum six of the past ten months (s 14–4). The same applies if the mother has been receiving a daily allowance due to unemployment, sickness benefit or child's illness benefit.

N8.5.2   Maternity pay is payable for a period of 42 weeks. The mother then receives the full amount of benefits. She can also choose to receive maternity pay for 52 weeks. She then receives only 80% of the full amount of benefits during the period. The amount is calculated on the basis of each of the parents' income. The maternity pay limit is six times the National Security's 'Basic Amount'. This presently approximates NOK 272.220.

N8.5.3   The parents decide which of them will remain at home with the child for the first six weeks after the birth. The father may receive maternity pay if the mother returns to work after the first six weeks following the birth. The same applies if the mother starts or resumes education. If the mother is seriously ill during her maternity leave period and is dependent on the father being at home, the father is also entitled to maternity pay. If the mother is in hospital or other health care institution, the father has the right to maternity pay for the remaining maternity leave period.

Maternity rights

antenatal care and right to clinic
check ups not to be unfairly
dismissed
maternity leave
- 42 weeks to all pregnant women
- maternity and benefits for whole period
- extension to 52 weeks on 80% benefits

father entitled to two weeks'
unpaid leave on birth
'time accounting' ie resumption
of work on flexi basis prior to
expiry of maternity leave
maternity pay
- after six months' employment
- calculated according to employee's income
- limit: 6 × National Security basic amount
- father can receive maternity pay if mother returns to work

8.6 Additional Rights to Time Off

PARENTAL LEAVE

N8.6.1 Parents have the right to leave of absence in the event of a child's or childminder's illness.[1] This right applies up to and including the calendar year for the child's twelfth birthday. If the child is chronically ill or disabled the right to leave of absence applies up to and including the calendar year of the child's sixteenth birthday.

[1] WEA, s 33A.

N8.6.2 If the person responsible for the daily supervision of the child is ill, the employee is entitled to leave of absence when necessary to attend the child.

N8.6.3 Leave of absence is limited to a total of ten days per calendar year per employee. If the employee has more than two children in his or her care the limit is 15 days. If the child is chronically ill or disabled, the limit is 20 days per calendar year.

N8.6.4 If the employee has the sole responsibility for the child, he or she is entitled to 20 days per calendar year or 30 days if he or she has more than two children in her or his care. If the child is chronically ill or disabled, he or she is entitled to up to 40 days' leave of absence per calendar year.

N8.6.5 If a child is suffering from a terminal or other extremely serious illness or injury, the employee is entitled to leave of absence if the employee must, out of regard for the child, stay at the health institution while the child is hospitalised there.

N8.6.6 The National Security Act, Chapter 9 gives the parents full benefits during their leave of absence. The benefits are calculated on the same basis as the SMP, and therefore limited to six times the National Security's Basic Amount (total NOK 272.220). The parent receives the benefits for the entire leave of absence period he or she is entitled to in accordance with the WEA, s 33A.

9   BUSINESS TRANSFERS

9.1 Background

N9.1.1 Regulation regarding the rights of employees in the event of change of ownership of enterprises is found in the WEA, Chapter 12A. The TUPE regulations in Norway follow EU court rulings based on EEA Directive 77/187.

N9.1.2 Formerly in the Working Environment Act, it was Norwegian law to protect workers in the same way as the present law when there was transfer from one owner to another. The scope of protection has been extended by the new Directive.

9.2 Identifying a Relevant Transfer

N9.2.1 A transfer of a business may occur in several ways, most commonly by mutual agreement between two parties (eg purchase of one company by another).

N9.2.2 Relevant transfers include the transfer of employees between two companies within a concern if a business identity is being transferred from one owner to another through a leasing contract or a business is transferred through a gift or inheritance.

N9.2.3 Another common way to transfer business is merger between two or more companies. Other forms of transfers of business are transfers from a general partnership to one of the partners, transfers from a joint ownership to one of the owners and transfer from a limited partnership to one of the partners.

9.3 Affected Employees

N9.3.1 The regulations in Chapter 12A apply to the employees attached to the transferred business. If only a part of the business is being transferred, the regulations only apply to the employees attached to the transferred part.

9.4 Effects of the Transfer

N9.4.1 When a transfer of business is occurring, the obligations and rights of the affected employees are regulated by ss 73B–73D:

Section 73B – Wage and working conditions

(1) Rights pursuant to the employment contract
  The rights and obligations of the previous owner pursuant to an employment contract or an employment relationship in force at the time of transfer of ownership, shall be transferred to the new owner. Claims pursuant to the first paragraph may still be raised against the previous owner.

(2) Rights pursuant to the collective wage agreement
  When a change of ownership has taken place, the new owner shall maintain the individual working conditions pursuant to the collective wage agreement applicable to the previous owner, until the collective wage agreement expires or is replaced by another collective wage agreement.

(3) Pensions
  Subsections 1 and 2 shall not apply to employees' rights to benefits in connection with old age and invalidity or benefits payable to surviving relatives in accordance with pension schemes.

Section 73C – Protection against dismissal

(1) Transfer of ownership to another owner shall not in itself constitute grounds for dismissal.

(2) If the contract of employment or the employment relationship is terminated because a transfer of ownership entails significant changes in working conditions to the detriment of the employee, the termination shall be deemed the result of circumstances related to the employer.

Section 73D – Protection of elected union representatives

(1) In cases where the enterprise preserves its autonomy, the elected union representatives affected by transfer shall retain their legal status and junction.

(2) The provision in subs 1 shall not apply if the transfer entails that the basis for the employees' representation ceases to exist. In such cases the elected representatives shall continue to be protected in accordance with the agreements protecting the elected representatives in this area.

N9.4.2 In Norway only those employees' representatives recognised in collective agreements are covered by this section. If this is not the case, such representatives are to be dealt with as other employees and they have no special protection against dismissals.

9.5 Variation of Contract

N9.5.1 The mere fact of a transfer of business is not a fair reason to terminate an employment contract.

9.6 Duty to Inform and Consult

N9.6.1 Employees are entitled to sufficient information and consultation when a business is being transferred to a new owner:[1]

The previous and new owner are obliged to discuss the transfer with the elected representatives as early as possible. In particular, information shall be given concerning:
(a) the reason for the transfer;
(b) the legal, economic and social implications of the transfer for the employees;
(c) measures planned in relation to the employees. If the previous or new owner is planning measures in relation to their respective employees, they shall consult with the elected representatives as early as possible on the measures with a view to reaching agreement.

---

[1] Section 73E.

10   COLLECTIVE RIGHTS

10.1 Background

N10.1.1   The rules governing collective agreements and the relations between the parties are dealt with in collective labour law. The fundamental source in the private sector is a 1927 statute – *Arbeidstvistloven*.

N10.1.2   The basic premise is the principle of liberalism without state intervention. The parties representing the employers and the workers are considered to be equal in strength and wages and working conditions can be freely negotiated without the interference of the government or other public offices.

N10.1.3   In Norway there is a free right to organise in unions. This is a principle which is more than one hundred years old. Collective agreements may be entered into with any employer who has employees.

N10.1.4   The main agreements will often have regulations about co-operation between the parties concerned and how to solve disputes. The first main agreement between the Employer's Association and the leading labour union (LO) was entered into in 1935.

Establishing a collective agreement

N10.1.5   If an employer does not want to enter into a collective agreement with a union, there is no statute which can force the employer to do so in the private sector. In such a case, the union can terminate the employment relationship with two weeks notice in order to force the employer to enter into such an agreement.

[1]   WEA, s 56; *Arbeidstvistloven*, s 29.

Formalities

N10.1.6   Unlike an individual contract, a collective agreement must be in writing to be valid.

The parties to a collective agreement

N10.1.7   One of the parties to a collective agreement must be a union. A union must have at least one member among the employees of the employer. A union can also have purposes other than negotiating salary and working conditions. Although not directly set down/required by statute, it is assumed that a union must be independent from the employer.

N10.1.8   The employer can either be a single company or an association of employers taking care of the employer's interests in relation to the employees of the company.

N10.1.9   In one of the key agreements a protocol states that there can be no industrial action demanding a collective agreement if there is only a minority demanding this. Often there is a requirement that at least 50% of the employees are members of the union.

N10.1.10 Collective agreements are as a general rule made only between the parties to the contract and its members and other parties (employers and union) which in their own terms of association state that they are bound by such agreements.

The terms of a collective agreement

N10.1.11 The terms of an ordinary collective agreement can be divided into two parts:

• terms concerning wages, working time etc which are considered part of the individual contract.

• collective terms which cannot be said to be a part of the individual contract but are strictly between the contractual parties eg the rights and duties of the employee as union official, how to resolve disputes etc.

Changing terms of the collective agreement

N10.1.12 The terms of a collective agreement cannot be altered without mutual consent as long as the agreement is valid.

N10.1.13 If there is an individual employment agreement with terms other than those in the collective agreement, the terms of the collective agreement will be valid and take precedence over those terms in the individual agreement, irrespective of whether the collective agreement terms are better or worse.

Non-industrial action while there is a collective agreement

N10.1.14 There are two types of conflict in the field of collective labour law. One relates to the interpretation and understanding of a collective agreement. Such disputes can be brought before the Labour Court in Oslo (*Arbeidsretten*). The other area for conflict is the material contents of the agreement where wages are often the most important issue.

N10.1.15 The statute from 1927 (*Arbeidstvistloven*) is based on the principle that there shall be no industrial action to resolve any conflict during the duration of an agreement, whilst industrial action can take place in connection with the termination of one agreement and the establishment of a new one.

N10.1.16 As the principle against industrial action relates only to the terms of the collective agreement, industrial actions which have another purpose, eg political action, action of sympathy, are allowed.

Negotiations for a new collective agreement

N10.1.17 The parties to a collective agreement are free to decide on the period for which the agreement shall be valid. If no agreement is made, statute provides that the agreement shall be valid for three years. If none of the parties to the agreement has given notice at the time of expiry, the agreement is prolonged for another year. If nothing else is agreed upon, a notice for termination must be given in writing three months prior to the expiry of the agreement.

N10.1.18

If the parties are negotiating, and no industrial action has taken place, the terms of the expired agreement are still in force.

Termination of collective agreement

N10.1.19   If the parties do not agree on the terms for a new agreement, either party can terminate the agreement. If nothing else is agreed upon, the termination period is 14 days. At the same time, a report about the termination shall be given to a central mediator in Oslo (*Riksmeglings-mannen*). Even if there has been a termination of a collective agreement, the parties can continue to negotiate.

Mediation

N10.1.20   There is one primary mediator for the country (*Riksmeglingsmannen*). He has several other mediators in his staff.

N10.1.21   The mediator can forbid industrial action to take place until he has tried to resolve the conflict. The mediator has a rather short period (ten days) to find a solution. In Norway there are few industrial actions as the parties usually reach an agreement.

N10.1.22   If no agreement is made, the parties can refer the conflict to another central body in Oslo (*Rikslønnsnemnda*). This forum consists of seven members. Each party has two members and the other three are neutral. In a specific case, the employer and the union each have one member. The forum will then consist of five persons. The decision of *Rikslønnsnemnda* has the same effect as a collective agreement.

Lawful industrial action

N10.1.23   If no agreement is made, both parties have the right to initiate industrial action. Usually this starts with the union member or some of the members. In Norway lockouts are rare, but they do occasionally happen.

N10.1.24   If nothing else is agreed upon, the effect of the industrial action is that the individual contracts for the members who are affected and do not meet turn up for work, are terminated. It is however common that when a new agreement is made, the workers who have been out of work are taken back in their former positions.

N10.1.25   During industrial action all rights to salary, sick pay etc from the employer are suspended for those participating in the action. As long as the industrial action lasts for those not in conflict, the terms of the former collective agreement remain in force.

The central labour court

N10.1.26   The Labour Court in Oslo (*Arbeidsretten*) is a special court, which decides on conflicts with regard to the understanding of a collective agreement. There are seven judges out of whom three are neutral, two are representatives for the Employers Association and two represent the union.

The judges are appointed for a period of three years. This court's decision may for all practical purposes be considered as final.

10.2 European Works Council

N10.2.1   EU Directive 94/95 was implemented in Norway in 1996. This means that multinational organisations in Norway must set up European Works Councils if they employ at least 1,000 employees with at least 150 employees in at least two member states.

11   EMPLOYMENT DISPUTES

11.1 Background

N11.1.1   Individual employment disputes are settled by regular courts, and not in the central Labour Court in Oslo which only deals with disputes regarding collective agreements.

N11.1.2   In Norway there are about 90 regular courts. In each county one of these ordinary courts deals with labour disputes. In some counties, like Akershus, there are two courts. In the northern part of Norway there are often more than one in a county because of the long distance.

N11.1.3   A decision by the lower court may be appealed to a High Court. There are six High Courts in Norway, each having its local area. Some cases are even decided by the Supreme Court, which is the highest court in Norway. The Supreme Court seldom decides a labour law case. Recently, however, there have been several rulings on the interpretation of TUPE-related issues and more are expected.

N11.1.4   An employee who wants to challenge the employer's decision, and wants to negotiate the issue, must give notice within two weeks to the employer and ask for negotiations. Usually such negotiations are held. If no request is made or no negotiation takes place, this has no legal consequence as regards the fairness of the termination. If the employee however instigates legal proceedings or notifies that legal proceedings will be started without negotiations having been conducted, the employer may demand negotiations with the employee. Such demand must be made within two weeks. Court proceedings will then be postponed until such negotiations have been completed (s 61A). If no agreement is made, the employee must, if he/she wants to remain in office and continue to work until the court has decided about the fairness of the dismissal, within eight weeks from the date of ending the negotiations and within the expiry of the notice period, either send a writ to the court, or inform the employer within the same period that this will be done. If there has been no negotiation, the eight weeks period starts upon receipt of the notice of termination.

N11.1.5   If the employee does not want to remain in office, the writ does not have to be within the notice period. If only compensation is sought, the period will be within six months.

N11.1.6   If an employee is summarily dismissed, he/she does not have the right to remain in his position unless the court decides this. The same applies in the probation period.

Results of a court decision

N11.1.7   If the court finds the notice unwarranted, and the employee so wishes, the notice will be declared invalid. This means that the employee will have the right to continue his work.

12   WHISTLEBLOWING/DATA PROTECTION

12.1 Whistleblowing

N12.1.1   One of the basic duties in an employment relationship is that of loyalty and the concept that the employee shall take care of the interests of the employer. As part of this duty the employee is obliged not to disclose any information to any third party concerning the employer's business. This basic confidentiality principle may in some cases be broken without the employee being in breach of contract.

N12.1.2   Unlike in the UK, Norway does not have an act similar to the Public Interest Disclosure Act, neither are there regulations similar to art 5(c) in the ILO Convention 158 stating as a general principle that there is not a valid reason for termination of employment because of:

> 'the filing of a complaint or the participation in proceedings against an employer involving alleged violation of laws or regulations or recourse to competent administrative authorities.'

N12.1.3   In Norway an employee cannot cover himself behind this article without first trying to solve the problem internally – if possible. The employee must make efforts to correct the matter internally. This relates especially to matters regarding damage to the environment, danger to health and safety etc. The employee shall not be forced to remain silent about matters that he has good reasons to criticise. The employee must have a valid reason to 'blow the whistle' and disclose internal matters. Furthermore the whistleblowing must not be motivated by a desire to damage the employer or the management.

N12.1.4   However if, for example, there is a serious tax fraud internally, the principle of loyalty does mean that the employee must not damage the employer more than is necessary. Thereby the report should only be sent to the relevant tax authorities, and not for instance to the press, as generally a publication in the press will lead to greater damage than is necessary to rectify the matter.

12.2 Data Protection

N12.2.1   Norway has a general act, the Personal Register Act, dating from 1978, which regulates the right to create and update registers that contain personal information.

N12.2.2   Personal information is defined as information and evaluations, which directly or indirectly can be connected to an identifiable person.

N12.2.3   A personal register is defined as a register, notes and so on, where information on people is systematically stored so that information on a person is retrievable (s 1).

N12.2.4   The main condition for collecting and storing personal data is that the gathering of the information must have an objective reason. In a business, the employer must therefore prove that the information is necessary to the business and the administration (s 6).

N12.2.5   Unless it is considered to be necessary the employer is not allowed to register:
- information of race, religious or political belief;
- information of a person's criminal record;
- information of a person's medical history or history of drug or alcohol abuse;
- information of sexual relationships;
- other information of family relations except information of family status, revenue arrangements between spouses and support burden.

N12.2.6   Everyone has the right to read his or her own file, which is stored on computers. However this does not apply for registers whose purposes are only to provide statistics, research or general planning purposes.

N12.2.7   The Data Authority is appointed by the government to make sure that the regulations in the Personal Register Act are not being violated.

13   HUMAN RIGHTS

13.1 Rights and Obligations

N13.1.1   The Convention for the Protection of Human Rights and Fundamental Freedoms was entirely incorporated into Norwegian domestic law with the Human Rights Act (the Human Rights Act, s 2). This means that Norwegian courts must interpret Norwegian legislation in accordance with the Human Rights Convention. If any Norwegian legislation is in conflict with the Convention of Human Rights, the Norwegian legislation must yield to the Convention of Human Rights (the Human Rights Act, s 3).

N13.1.2   The articles in the Convention of Human Rights considered to be most relevant to Norwegian employment law are:
- article 8: respect for private and family life, home and correspondence;
- article 9: freedom of thought, conscience and religion;
- article 10: freedom of expression;
- article 11: freedom of peaceful assembly, freedom of association;
- article 13: rights to effective remedy;
- article 14: no discrimination on grounds of sex, race, language, religion, opinion or status.

N13.1.3 The Norwegian employment legislation is considered to be in accordance with the Convention of Human Rights. Thus the Human Rights Act probably will not have much impact on Norwegian employment legislation. However, since the Human Rights Act is a recent amendment to Norwegian legislation, the boundaries of the Act and the Convention of Human Rights have so far not been tested much by Norwegian courts. One can therefore not exclude the possibility that the incorporation of the Convention of Human Rights may result in changes to the Norwegian employment legislation.

BIBLIOGRAPHY

P Berg *Arbeidsrett* (1930)
JT Dege *Arbeidsgivers styringsrett. Ytre rammevilkår og arbeidsavtalen* Bind I(1995)
JT Dege *Arbeidsgivers styringsrett, Oppsigelse og avskjed. Den alminnelige del* Bind II (1997)
JT Dege *Arbeidsgivers styringsrett, Oppsigelse og avskjed. Den spesielle del* Bind III (1997)
A Fanebust *Oppsigelse i arbeidsforhold* (3 utg) Oslo 1995
A Fanebust *Innføring i arbeidsrett. Den individuelle del* (1997)
J Fougner Fougner, Arbeidsavtalen–utvalgte emner (1999)
O Friberg, J Fougner og L Holo *Arbeidsmiljøloven med kommentarer* (7 utg) (1998)
T Gjone og EC Aagaard *Bedriftens personalhåndbok. Rett og plikt i arbeidsforhold* (5 utg) (1998)
H Jakhelln *Oversikt over arbeidsretten* (2 utg), (1996)
Storeng, Bech og Due Lund *Praktisk arbeidsrett* (1995)

O Portugal

Carlos Costa e Silva

Carlos Costa e Silva is an associate lawyer at Barrocas & Alves Pereira, Lisbon and was admitted to the bar in 1998. He was educated at the University of Lisbon Law School. He specialises in labour law and general contract law.

Barrocas & Alves Pereira, Lisbon

Phone: +351 21 384 33 00
Fax: +351 21 387 02 65
Email: Bap-lis@mail.telepac.pt; costaesilva@bap.pt

SUMMARY TABLE

PORTUGAL

Rights	Yes/no	Explanatory Notes
CONTRACTS OF EMPLOYMENT		
Minimum notice (indefinite term)	NO	Notice only applies to fixed contracts, not indefinite term
Probationary period	YES	60 or 90 days
Indefinite term		
• formalities	NO	
Fixed term		
• formalities	YES	Must be in writing (otherwise it becomes indefinite term
REMUNERATION		
Minimum wage regulation	YES	Established annually by the *Conselho de Concertacao Social*
Further rights and obligations:		
Right to paid holiday	YES	22 days a year
Right to sick pay	YES/NO	No right to receive salary from employer but receives 60% of salary from Social Security
WORKING TIME		
Regulation of hours per day/ working week	YES	See collective agreements. Maximum 40 hours per week for industry; 37.5 hours for administrative staff
Regulation of night work	YES	Between 7 and 11 hours long. See collective agreements
Right to rest periods	YES	Daily period of work cannot exceed five consecutive hours. One hour's rest each day
EQUAL OPPORTUNITIES		
Discrimination protection:		
Sex	YES	
Race	YES	
Social conditions	YES	
Working conditions	YES	
Disability	NO	But covered generally by the Portuguese Constitution
Equal pay legislation	YES	
TERMINATION OF EMPLOYMENT		
Right not to be dismissed in breach of contract		
Indefinite term	NO	No notice obligation – but must be fair reason and proper procedure
Fixed term	YES	Dismissal must be for 'just cause'. If incorrect procedure or unfair reason, dismissal is null and void

REDUNDANCY

Procedure	YES	
Right to payment on redundancy	YES	Compensation according to length of service
Right to consultation:		
Collective	YES	With works council or workers representatives

YOUNG WORKERS

Protection of children and young persons at work	YES	

MATERNITY RIGHTS

Right to time off – ante-natal care	YES	
Right to maternity leave	YES	
Maternity pay (during leave)	YES	Statutory maternity pay
Protection from dismissal	YES	Dismissal during pregnancy and first year after childbirth is null and void
Health and safety protection	YES	
Right to parental leave	YES	Subsidy payable if qualifying conditions are met

TRANSFERS OF BUSINESSES

Right to protection on transfer	YES	Statute partly implements EC Directive
Transfer of employment obligations	YES	Purchaser and seller jointly and severally liable
Right to information and consultation	YES/NO	Public announcement but no duty to inform and consult except for ETO reason
Right not to be dismissed	YES	

COLLECTIVE RIGHTS

Compulsory recognition of trades unions	YES	
European works councils	YES	

EMPLOYMENT DISPUTES

Civil court jurisdiction	YES	
Statutory body	NO	

WHISTLEBLOWING

Protection from dismissal/detriment	YES	Such a dismissal will be 'abusive' and unfair

DATA PROTECTION

Protection	YES	

HUMAN RIGHTS ACT

Statutory protection of human rights	YES	

1 THE EMPLOYMENT RELATIONSHIP

1.1 Background

O1.1.1   Labour law in Portugal is based on statute, which is similar to that in most industrialised countries. Casclaw assists in its interpretation. Generally speaking, it protects the worker on termination of the employment contract. Sources of Portuguese labour law are the Constitution of the Portuguese Republic, statute and collective bargaining agreements. Statute includes laws passed by the Portuguese Parliament (*lei*), the Council of Ministers (*decreto-lei* or decree law) and the Minister of Labour (*portaria*).

O1.1.2   The relationship between employer and employee is fundamentally contractual although Portuguese law prescribes statutory minimum rights which cannot be derogated from.

O1.1.3   In practice, when employer and employee enter into an employment contract both parties know that a complex mix of statute and caselaw will apply to the contract.

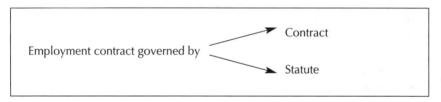

1.2 Contract of Service

O1.2.1   No formalities are required for a contract of an indefinite (permanent) period and no notice is required to terminate the agreement. There must, however, be a fair reason for dismissal and a proper procedure must be followed (see paras **O6.1.1–O6.5.9**). This is the most common contract and can be agreed in writing, orally or by a combination of both.

O1.2.2   A fixed-term employment contract (a contract that terminates at the end of an agreed period or any extension) must always be in writing. If it is not, an established employment relationship is considered to be an indefinite term contract. Written employment contracts are often very brief since most terms are imposed by law and collective agreements. A contract is only required to be set out in writing when the work is complex or when a fixed term is agreed. In all other cases, it will be considered to be an indefinite term contract.

A   TYPES OF EMPLOYMENT CONTRACT

O1.2.3   There are two main types of employment contract: 'indefinite term' and 'fixed term' contracts of employment. An outline of the formalities required to establish such contracts and of the procedure for their termination has been set out above. The rights and duties of the contracting parties are the same for indefinite term, fixed term, and 'part-time' contracts.

Main employment contracts
- indefinite – no definite term → no formalities required
- fixed-term – terminates at end of period → in writing
- part-time – can be either indefinite or fixed term → rights and duties are the same
- *contrato de comissão de serviço* – for senior management → terminable on 30–60 days notice

---

Contrato de comissão de serviço

O1.2.4 A special employment agreement, the *contrato de comissão de serviço*, exists for staff occupying management positions on the boards of companies or senior managers directly responsible to the Board of Directors, as well as the private secretaries of those holding these positions. A *comissão de serviço* may be concluded either with existing employees of the company or with persons from outside the company. However, there are restrictions in section 398 of the Company Code to this kind of contract in connection with public limited companies (*Sociedades anónimas*). It is advisable to get advice from a specialist about this matter.

O1.2.5 A *contrato de comissão de serviço* may be terminated at any time without the need to invoke a 'just cause'[1] reason, provided that prior notice of 30 or 60 days (depending on whether the contract has lasted less or more than two years) is given to the employee.[2] If he is also an employee of the company he keeps his original employment agreement. In any case, the termination of the *comissão de serviço* entitles the employee to receive compensation equal to one month for each year the contract lasts, if the termination of *contracto de comissão de serviço* implies the termination of the employment contract which was in existence before the *contrato de comissão de serviço* was entered into. This will be the case whenever a pre-existing employee is hired to perform managerial functions under a *contrato de comissão de serviço*. Another alternative is where a non pre-existing employee has been hired under a contract of that kind to perform managerial functions only and terminates the employment relationship as soon as the *contrato de comissão de serviço* terminates. In both cases, an indemnity is due to the employee.

[1] For definition of 'just cause' see para **O6.2.2**.
[2] Section 4(2) of Decree-law 404/91, dated 16 October.

B   PROBATIONARY PERIOD

O1.2.6 The law provides for a trial period of 60 or 90 days,[1] within which period either the employer or the employee can terminate the contract without giving notice, payment in lieu or a fair reason for dismissal. Where it is difficult to assess the aptitude of the employee within 60 days due to the complexity of the job or the high degree of responsibility involved, a longer probationary period may be agreed, either through a collective agreement or by written agreement between the parties, but this longer probationary period cannot exceed eight months.

[1] Generally, it is 60 days. If the employer employs 20 or less workers – 90 days.

C   CONFIDENTIALITY

O1.2.7   During the performance of an employment agreement, the employee must keep confidential under the statutory duty of loyalty all confidential information belonging to the employer which he may have acquired as a result of his employment.

O1.2.8   A post-termination duty to keep confidential privileged information must be agreed between the employer and the employee either in the employment agreement or in an agreement which expressly addresses this issue. Of course, if a former employee infringes any right which is protected by intellectual property law, then it is subject to the same sanctions as any other third party.

1.3   Variation of Contract

O1.3.1   Portuguese law allows unilateral variation of contract by the employer in two different situations:
(1) the so-called 'functional' reason; and
(2) the '*jus variandi*'.
Both are set out in the Employment Contract Act, s 22.[1]

[1]   Decree law 49408, dated 24 November 1969.

O1.3.2   In the case of variation under the functional regime, if the employee is qualified and is able to perform any function or duty other than the one for which he was hired, the employer may unilaterally require him to perform such ancillary activities, provided that these ancillary activities are related to or have a functional link with his normal activity.

O1.3.3   The performance of ancillary activities must not cause any detriment to working conditions, including remuneration. In addition, the employee's main or normal activity must be the same. If the ancillary activities are usually more highly paid than the employee's usual job, then the employee is entitled to the higher salary. After six months of performing the additional activities (for which a higher salary is due), the employee is entitled, if he wishes, to be re classified as carrying out the new functions and to obtain the appropriate professional category.

O1.3.4   Under the *jus variandi*, the employer is entitled to unilaterally require an employee to perform, on a transitional basis, functions which are not included in the job description for which he was hired, provided that such variation does not entail a decrease in the employee's salary or a substantial modification of his position in the hierarchy or structure of the employer's organisation.

O1.3.5   Whenever the new functions give rise to better labour conditions, including salary, the employee is entitled to those better conditions.

O1.3.6   In the case of variation due to functional reasons, the performance of the additional functions is not transitional and may only be implemented if the above conditions are met.

O1.3.7   In the case of *jus variandi*, new functions are given on a strictly transitional basis. They are not dependant upon these conditions and are essentially connected to an emergency situation where it is necessary to ensure the proper development of the employer's activity.

Unilateral variation

Functional • strict conditions require employee → re-classification after
to do ancillary functions six months, if wished

Jus variandi • additional functions on a → no detriment
transitional basis to employee
• no conditions; just 'emergency'

---

2   REMUNERATION

2.1   Background

O2.1.1   The standard approved each year by the representatives of the
industrial, trade and agricultural sectors and the unions within the *Conselho
de Concertação Social*[1] establish the parameters of the annual salary policy.

[1]   The *Conselho de Concertação Social* is a body comprised of representatives of the
Government (usually the Minster of Economy), the Employers Association and
Central Unions who discuss national salary policies to be implemented each year.

2.2   Legal Regulation of Remuneration

O2.2.1   There is a minimum national monthly salary.[1] Traditionally, it is
the practice to pay additional remuneration in the form of Christmas and
holiday bonuses (as a rule each equal to one month's average wage),
allowances for shift work, length of service premiums and productivity
premiums. Christmas and holiday bonuses are obligatory and are paid to
most of the working population: other additional payments are optional
and only some are set out in collective agreements.

[1]   Decree Law 69–A/87, dated 9 February 1987.

O2.2.2   Portuguese law does not consider any sum paid by the employer as
a reward or bonus for the employee's good performance to be
remuneration. Only regular payments made by the employer to the
employee are considered remuneration.

O2.2.3   Payment for a thirteenth and fourteenth month each year is
obligatory[1] (as mentioned above – Christmas and holiday bonuses). These
additional salary payments are calculated on basic salary which does not
include any additional remuneration or other payments based on uncertain
factors (eg, volume of sales or productivity).

[1]   Christmas bonus – Decree law 88/96 dated 3rd July 1996. Holiday bonus –
Section 6(2) Decree-law 874/76, dated 28 December.

O2.2.4   There are many different types of salary: fixed salary, variable
salary (depending on the productivity of the employee) or a mixture of both.
Completely variable salaries, without a fixed basic sum, do not exist in
practice.

WAGE CONTROL BY GOVERNMENT

O2.2.5   In past periods of economic recession, the Government declared maximum limits to annual pay rises. During more favourable economic times this has not occurred, but the Government encourages the fixing of maximum percentage increases for salaries. In particular, wholly State owned corporations are an important reference point when it comes to annual salaries, because these salaries cannot be fixed without Government authorisation. Mandatory provisions also exist which forbid the payment of additional amounts of more than 50% of the basic salary. To calculate this percentage, Christmas and holiday bonuses are not considered to be additional payments and neither are special payments, such as productivity premiums, length of service premiums or payments for work in revolving shifts, etc.

2.3   Deductions from Wages

O2.3.1   The employer and the employee are not allowed to come to any agreement under which the employer pays taxes and other deductions which are strictly due from the employee.

O2.3.2   The payroll deductions for social contributions are:
* employer – 23.75%;
* employee – 11%.

O2.3.3   Both deductions are calculated on all remuneration and allowances paid by the employer. All employees as well as members of the Board of Directors are required to pay Social Security contributions. However, foreigners who are temporarily working for a branch or subsidiary in Portugal need not make contributions provided they can prove that they are subject to obligatory payments in their country of origin. However, they can opt to be covered by both Social Security schemes.

2.4   Itemised Pay Statement

O2.4.1   It is general practice for an employee to sign a discharge statement (a receipt) where each payment by way of remuneration received (eg salary, fringe benefits etc) is set out. This is of use, not only to prove the actual payment made, but also for tax purposes.

O2.4.2   The employer must deduct and retain at source Social Security and income tax charges on the account of the employees and remit them, on the employee's behalf, to the respective authorities.

3   FURTHER RIGHTS AND OBLIGATIONS

3.1   Holiday Entitlement

O3.1.1   There is a legal obligation to provide 22 paid working days holiday a year[1] although collective agreements may provide for longer entitlement. Employees are also entitled to public holidays (there are around

12–14 each year). The right to holiday accrues according to work carried out the previous year and the entitlement is calculated on 1st January of the following year. This means that the right to take holiday arises only after the employee has worked for the relevant period. The employer may, if he so wishes, suspend totally or partially the activity of the company and provide holiday to all employees at the same time.

Examples

Employee 1 commences work on 8 October 1999. His entitlement to holiday arises from 1 January 2000 for the pro-rata period worked.

Employee 2 commences work on 1 April 1999. As work has started in the first half of the relevant year, he is entitled to 8 days holiday after completing 60 days work in 1999.

---

[1] Decree law 874/76 dated 28 December 1976.

O3.1.2 'Closure time' (ie closure of the business for a 'holiday' period) is allowed for a period of 15 days between 1 May and 31 October. Closure for a period in excess of 15 days or in a period different from this is allowed if provided for in collective bargaining agreements or agreed with the unions representing the workers.

O3.1.3 Suspension of business for holiday purposes does not prevent the employee from taking a longer holiday period which he has not yet utilised before closure. Employees hired for a fixed term not in excess of one year (that is, for a pre-agreed term in order to carry out a specific job) are entitled to have two working days for each full month of work.

O3.1.4 In any case (that is, either in the case of an indefinite term contract or a fixed term contract), the employee is entitled to receive the salary which is due when he is on duty and a holiday allowance of the same amount of the salary due during the holiday period.

O3.1.5 An employee is entitled to holidays even if he has been absent from work during the relevant year except where the contract has been suspended for a long period due to the employee's extended absence (eg suspension for military service).

O3.1.6 Entitlement to holiday may not be replaced by compensation, except on termination. If business reasons mean that an employer cannot allow his employee to take all his holiday, the employee is entitled to 3 times his daily rate of pay for each day lost and to holiday in lieu of the lost holiday in the next year.

O3.1.7 Employer and employee should agree on when the employee will take his holiday. If they cannot agree, the employer may unilaterally fix the holiday period provided this falls in the 'closure time' ie between 1 May and 31 October (see para **O3.1.2**).

O3.1.8   Holiday pay is at the normal rate of pay plus a fringe benefit called *subsídô de férias* equal to one month's basic salary.

Summary of holiday entitlement

- 22 paid working days holiday per annum – fixed term less than 1 year = 2 days per month
- entitlement calculated on 1 January each year
- 'closure for 15 days between 1 May–31 October
- employee receives salary and holiday allowance
- no payment in lieu of holiday

3.2   Sick Pay

O3.2.1   If an employee is ill he has no right to receive salary from his employer for days of illness since he will benefit from Social Security payments. Social security provides him with 60% of his salary after the third day of illness. Some collective agreements state, however, that the employer is obliged to pay the difference between the 60% payment from the Social Security and his full salary[1]. Such provision is more common in wholly State-owned corporations. In any case a maximum period during which this supplementary pay is payable is often set out in collective agreements. It is not common for private employers to 'top up' sick pay for their staff.

[1]   Eg in wholly or ex-wholly state owned companies.

3.3   Compulsory Profit Sharing and Pension Schemes

A   NON-EXISTENCE OF COMPULSORY PROFIT SHARING

O3.3.1   In Portugal there are no compulsory profit sharing schemes: instead such schemes are dependent upon provisions established in collective agreements or on the decision of the general meeting of shareholders or the management board. Cases of employee profit sharing are rare at present. Many social benefits are provided by larger companies (canteens, crèches, etc).

B   CATEGORIES OF PENSIONS

O3.3.2   There are three types of pensions provided by Portuguese law:[1] retirement pensions, incapacity pensions and pensions for widowed spouses. The legal retirement age is 65 years for men and women. A contract terminates at retirement age unless the employee is retained by the employer with the agreement of the employee after the age of 65. The contract is then converted by operation of law into a fixed-term contract for an initial period of six months, renewable indefinitely for successive periods of six months. Either party is entitled to terminate in writing the employment contract up to eight days before the end of each term.

[1]   Decree-law 329/93 dated 25 September 1993; Decree 7/94 dated 11 March 1994 and Order (*Potaria*) 883/94 dated 17 September 1994.

O3.3.3   Retirement as a result of incapacity occurs when a worker is considered totally or partly unable to carry out normal work.

O3.3.4   In either case of retirement the employment contract is automatically terminated, except in cases of partial incapacity or if the business, in accordance with any collective agreement, is obliged to re-employ the worker in another suitable function.

O3.3.5   Pensions are paid to the spouse of a deceased worker. These pensions are provided by Social Security, and the amount which a worker or his spouse receives depends on the contributions paid by the employer and employee during the period of employment.

C   COMPLEMENTARY PENSIONS

O3.3.6   By voluntary decision the employer can agree to pay his employees a supplementary pension over and above the pension received from social security, in order to give them an income close to the salary they received when working. Recently, however, for senior staff there has been a general tendency to favour pensions guaranteed by life insurance companies. The Ministry of Labour only allows the creation of an internal supplementary pension fund (which requires employee contributions) by companies which it recognises as having sufficient financial capacity. If no agreement with the employee representatives exists, companies are free to create their own funds in favour of their employees without employees' obligatory contributions.

D   OTHER PENSIONS AND SOCIAL SECURITY FACILITIES

O3.3.7   Pensions due to accidents at work are not paid by social security, but by an insurance company. Medical assistance and medicines for accidents at work are also paid for by the insurance company as well as normal consultations that are now required by law. However, industrial diseases (such as silicosis etc) are covered by social security. The employee's monthly contributions mean that the employee can receive the following benefits from social security:

- unemployment benefit;
- sickness benefit and other medical treatments;
- marriage benefit;
- childbirth benefit;
- funeral benefit;
- medical and hospital assistance, and medicines for disabled workers and family;
- family benefit for each child.

O3.3.8   Members of the board of directors of each company are obliged to pay contributions towards social security, with the exception of foreigners who can prove that they are only temporarily in Portugal and that they pay Social Security contributions in their country of origin. This also applies to foreign employees working temporarily in Portugal. However, they can opt to participate in both systems.

E   PENSION SCHEMES FOR PROFESSIONALS

O3.3.9   Professionals either benefit from personal Social Security schemes organised by their professional societies (lawyers, doctors, etc), or join the general Social Security scheme on a voluntary basis.

3.4   Residence and Work Permits for Aliens

A   INTRODUCTORY NOTE

O3.4.1   Foreigners resident in Portugal benefit from practically the same rights as Portuguese citizens except when it comes to political rights and some rights of the Constitution of the Portuguese Republic which are reserved for nationals. Foreign citizens are allowed free access into Portuguese territory. Exceptions apply to those who have no means of subsistence or who have no entry visas (in cases where these are necessary) or to those who come from foreign countries that do not have diplomatic relations with Portugal. Since Portugal is a member of the European Union a distinction has been made between EU nationals and others in regard to residence and work permits. As a general rule, foreigners (EU nationals or non-EU nationals) who do not intend to reside in Portugal can stay for three months, whether or not they have a visa for entry. If this stay is for longer than three months they are obliged to get a residence permit.

B   EU NATIONALS

O3.4.2   Community treaties and legislation provide for the freedom of movement of EU nationals and the right to establish and develop an economic activity in any EU country.

O3.4.3   As a result of these provisions, EU nationals may enter into and reside in Portugal if they wish to:
(a) perform a specific job working for a third party under an employment contract; or
(b) exercise the right to establish an economic activity or provide services.

O3.4.4   However, EU nationals who wish to enter Portugal for leisure or similar activities enjoy no special advantage vis-à-vis non-EU nationals. Therefore, unless a bilateral treaty applies, a tourist from an EU country must also have a valid passport (or other national identity card). In these circumstances, both EU and non-EU nationals may stay in Portugal for up to 90 days.

C   NON-EU NATIONALS

O3.4.5   Foreigners wishing to take up residence in Portugal must apply to the *Serviço de Estrangeiros* (Immigration Office) before coming to Portugal. The application should be presented in a Portuguese consulate abroad before entering the country. Residence permits depend on the activity exercised in Portugal or on retirement, or similar. If the individual is engaged in a professional activity, the contracts signed with a local registered company must be registered at the Ministry of Labour, and only after this procedure is completed can permission for work and a residence permit be issued through the Consulate.

4   WORKING TIME

4.1   Background

Collective agreements set out the maximum amount of working time per week for each business sector.

4.2   Legislative Control

O4.2.1   Directive 93/104/EC has now been implemented in Portugal. However, in general terms, practically all provisions of the Directive are less favourable to the worker than under Portuguese domestic law.

O4.2.2   The maximum weekly total for industry personnel is 40 hours, and for administrative personnel 37.5 hours.

O4.2.3   The law[1] only allows overtime where there is increased workload, emergency or other exceptional cases with certain limits, eg up to two hours a day. Overtime[2] is paid at a minimum hourly rate of 1½ times salary for the first hour and 1¾ times salary for the subsequent hours. Work carried out during weekends or public holidays attracts a special rate of remuneration (this depends on each collective agreement, but it is normally equal to double the salary per day) as well as the right to a rest day on another working day.

[1]   Section 4 of Decree-law 421/83, dated 2 December.
[2]   Overtime is paid for all levels of staff except those with no daily working time limits – this requires the prior agreement of the worker and implies special remuneration established in collective bargaining agreements for the particular sector of business. If there is no collective bargaining agreement, that special remuneration must be, at least, equal to one hour of overtime work each day (ie one hour of normal work plus 50%).

4.3   Opting Out

O4.3.1   Opting out from the regulations on working time is not, in general, allowed. Each employee is subject to a weekly maximum working time pre-defined by agreement with the employee and within the limits established by collective bargaining agreements. If there are no such agreements, the law does not allow any working time in excess of 8 hours a day and 44 hours a week. In the case of clerical employees those limits are 7 hours and 42 hours under the law, but there is a regulation[1] which establishes a maximum weekly period of 37 hours for clerical employees.

[1]   *Portaria de regulamentação do trabalho.*

O4.3.2   An opt-out regime exists, however, for some jobs which entail the exercise of managerial functions or those which require a strong link of trust between the employer and the employee as well as those which entail a supervisory nature. In addition, jobs which are ancillary to a main activity of the employer and which can be performed only before or after the main employer's activity is carried out may have an opt-out clause.

O4.3.3   Finally, jobs which are substantially performed outside the employer's premises and without immediate physical control may be performed without any time limit.

O4.3.4   Due to the exceptional nature of these opt-out regimes, an employer wishing to implement any of the exemptions above must apply for permission from the labour authorities (IDICT) and obtain the consent of the employee.

O4.3.5   An employee working in such conditions is entitled to special remuneration, in addition to his basic salary, which cannot be less than one hour's extra pay per day, unless the collective bargaining agreement establishes a higher amount. Employees exercising managerial functions may agree to forego that special remuneration.

4.4   Night Work

O4.4.1   The minimum duration of night work is of seven hours and the maximum is 11 hours. Collective bargaining agreements may establish night work limits. If not established by collective bargaining agreements, the period between 20:00 and 7:00 of the following day is deemed the night working period.

O4.4.2   Salary during the night period is equal to the daily work rate plus 25%.

4.5   Rest Period

O4.5.1   The daily period of work cannot be more than five consecutive hours. There must be at least one hour's continuous period of rest during a working day.

O4.5.2   The law requires one day of weekly rest and that should be on a Sunday except in special cases.

4.6   Paid Annual Leave

O4.6.1   Paid annual leave is dealt with in paras O3.1.1–O3.1.8.

4.7   Remedies

O4.7.1   Employees may be obliged to work overtime in exceptional circumstances. Overtime may be required by the employer from an employee when the employer faces any occasional increase in the need for manpower which does not justify taking on a new employee, or in cases of force majeure, or when it is necessary to prevent serious damage or to remedy serious damage to the employer.

O4.7.2   Overtime may not exceed an aggregate of 200 hours a year or two hours a day or the normal maximum daily working time if it occurs during the weekly rest days (usually Saturday and Sunday).

O4.7.3 An employee is, therefore, entitled to refuse to work beyond those limits. If he is dismissed for such refusal, he is entitled to be reinstated, or if he prefers, to receive double the normal indemnity for unfair dismissal.

O4.7.4 An employee working overtime is, in addition, entitled to receive special remuneration which is equal to 50% of the salary for the first hour of overtime and 75% for the following hours.

Working time: summary
- administrative staff – 37.5 hours maximum
- industry staff – 40 hours maximum
- overtime only in certain specified cases at minimum rate of × 1½ for first hour; × 1¾ subsequent hours
- no opt out except for 'managers' and 'supervisors'
- no time limit for jobs performed outside work premises
- night work length between 7 hours–11 hours (between 20:00–7:00) at daily rate + 25%
- daily work period = 5 hours; 1 hour's rest in working day;
- one day weekly rest
- maximum overtime 200 hours per annum or 2 hours a day

---

5   EQUAL OPPORTUNITIES

5.1   Unlawful Discrimination

O5.1.1 Discrimination[1] is unlawful if it is:
- in relation to sex, race, language, political/ideological convictions, origin, education, status or social condition;
- in relation to working conditions.

[1]   See art 7 of the Human Rights Universal Declaration, the European Convention on Human Rights and art 13 of the Portuguese Constitution.

O5.1.2 Discrimination is forbidden under the Portuguese Constitution, which provides that all Portuguese citizens are equal. Labour law entitles the discriminated worker to enjoy the more favourable conditions of the comparator worker. Discrimination at work should be seen on the basis of the principle of equal treatment which requires that work and working conditions must be equal.

O5.1.3 The equal opportunities regime essentially means equal access to employment, equal remuneration for the same job (art 59 of the Portuguese Constitution) and equal working conditions.

O5.1.4 Sex discrimination is specifically prohibited by Law 105/97 and Decree Law 392/79 dated 20 September 1979. Direct and indirect sex discrimination is against the law. A register must be kept of all employees recruited in the last five years. Any breach of the discrimination legislation makes the employer liable to a fine.

5.2 Disability Discrimination

O5.2.1 There is no specific legislation dealing separately with disability discrimination. However, the Portuguese Constitution is understood to cover discrimination on disability grounds so that a disabled worker who carries out the same work with the same capacity to work, productivity, etc as a non-disabled worker may not be discriminated against in comparison with the non-disabled worker who provides the same kind of work.

O5.2.2 Decree Law 40/83 dated 25 January 1983 sets out specific duties for employers of disabled persons, including (for example) the provision of medical and other support and the duty not to discriminate.

5.3 Enforcement (and Remedies)

O5.3.1 A worker who has been discriminated against is entitled to the salary and other benefits which he was denied during the discrimination period. The burden of proof is on the employer to show that he has not treated the employee less favourably. An employee who has been discriminated against is also entitled to compensation for any further damage he has suffered, including injury to feelings.

O5.3.2 An order for compensation etc may be made through the Labour Courts either during or after the employment agreement is terminated. If employment has ended, the action must be commenced before the end of the year starting on the date of the termination of the employment contract.

5.4 Equal Pay

O5.4.1 The Portuguese Constitution[1] applies the principle of equal treatment for men and women in all aspects of employment, including equal pay for equal work. There is no other legislation dealing with this principle, other than the sex discrimination legislation.

[1] Constitution of Portuguese Republic, art 59(1).

6 TERMINATION OF EMPLOYMENT

6.1 Background

O6.1.1 There was a long and intense dispute between employers and trade unions some years ago concerning the issue of dismissal. Employers, economists and liberal politicians maintained that the freedom to dismiss is an essential condition for economic development and growth. Trade unions opposed this line of thinking. The recent low unemployment rate (of around 5% of the working population) has moderated this discussion to some degree.

O6.1.2 Certain categories of employee (such as pregnant women) are presumed to have been unfairly dismissed unless the employer proves otherwise and are entitled to additional compensation if their claim is upheld.[1]

1 Law 100/97 dated 13 September and Decree Law 143/99 dated 30 April.

6.2 Nature of Claims

O6.2.1 In fact, contracts made for an indefinite term cannot be terminated, in principle, by the employer even when notice is given to the

740

employee. An employer can only terminate the contract by following a proper written disciplinary procedure showing that 'just cause' (*justa causa*) exists for the dismissal.

O6.2.2   The legal definition of just cause for dismissal is: a fault on the part of the employee, which due to its seriousness, impedes the continuation of work because it breaks the link of trust.[1] The employer must send a written 'note of blame'[2] to the employee as well as an independent written statement of dismissal to the worker who may answer it in writing within a certain pre-determined time (at least five working days).

1   Section 9(i) of Decree-law 64 – A/89 dated 27 February.
2   A 'note of blame' is a description of the facts. If, at the outset, the employer believes the conduct sufficiently serious to warrant dismissal, it must state its intention to dismiss the employee in the note.

O6.2.3   Documented proof and evidence should be included in the disciplinary procedure, and the works council, if any, must be heard before a final decision is made by the employer.

TEMPORARY DURATION CONTRACTS

O6.2.4   Because it is difficult for an employer to dismiss an employee contracted for an indefinite term, the temporary duration contract (*contrato a prazo*) became common in Portugal. However, because these contracts had been used abusively in non-temporary situations, the rules on dismissing an employee contracted for an indefinite term have been relaxed and the temporary duration contract is now confined strictly to temporary work.

O6.2.5   Contracts for a temporary duration of six months or less can be entered into if the nature of the work is considered temporary, ie special and transitional work, such as seasonal jobs, and where a company starts its business or launches a new business activity of uncertain duration.

O6.2.6   A temporary duration contract can be successively renewed for equal periods of time (as a rule every six months) up to a maximum of three years from the starting date or to a maximum of two renewals. Such a contract can be terminated as long as the employee is given written notice of at least eight days by the employer stating that his contract will not be renewed at the end of the fixed period. If before, all remunerations until the end of the fixed period are due. However, a temporary contract may also be entered into on a non-fixed basis, but to perform a certain temporary task. In such a case, the contract will terminate when the task is performed. Any employment contract, other than a temporary duration contract, can be terminated at any time by agreement between the employer and the employee.

O6.2.7   All contracts can be terminated when it is impossible for the employment to continue (due to unforeseeable reasons such as force majeure, winding-up of the company, bankruptcy, etc) or for the employee to attend work (for instance due to an incurable illness). However, the employee can always terminate an indefinite term contract by giving two months' notice[1] (or one month if the contract has been in existence for less than two years). If notice is not given or is less than the legal minimum the employer can demand compensation from the employee for the value of the number of days by which the notice he has given falls short of the full notice period.

[1] Section 38 of Decree-law 64–A/89 dated 27 February.

O6.2.8 In the case of a temporary duration employment contract, the employee can end the contract by giving eight days' notice (like the employer's notice) before the end of the initial term or extension. If neither party gives such notice then the contract is automatically renewed for the same term, and if it goes over the agreed periods, the contract automatically becomes a contract for an indefinite term.

Dismissal

Indefinite term	• must show just cause → employee's fault
	• procedure must be followed
	• if procedure is inadequate or reason is unfair, dismissed is null and void = salary + reinstatement or compensation
	• employee must give one/two months' notice (or compensation in lieu)
Temporary duration (certain or uncertain duration)	• for temporary work only
	• can be renewed up to three years
	• terminable on giving eight days' notice (if term is certain, and notice to be given up until eight days before term ends)
	• employee can terminate on eight days' notice (if term is certain)

6.3 Fairness of Dismissal

O6.3.1 Reasons that are considered fair grounds for dismissal are specified by law[1] including, amongst others, redundancy, misconduct by disobeying orders, non co-operation, drunkenness, violence and swearing, dishonesty, incompetence, lack of qualifications, poor time keeping, poor performance, etc.

[1] Section 9(2)(b) of Decree-law 64–A/89 dated 27 February 1989.

O6.3.2 The employment agreement may be also terminated, not for disciplinary reasons, but because of the employee's inability to discharge his contractual obligations. The formalities required to terminate the agreement are similar to those applicable to termination for disciplinary reasons.[1]

[1] Decree-law 400/91 dated 16 October 1991.

O6.3.3 Dismissal during illness is in principle not permissible because the employment contract is suspended during that period of time unless there is any just disciplinary cause. After three years of illness, however, the contract can be terminated (and the employee can be considered as retired or in a state of pre-retirement due to illness) and is recognised as such by Social Security.

6.4   Remedies

O6.4.1   If the employer dismisses an employee without having followed the correct disciplinary procedure or having considered the employee's case in writing or if the dismissal is unfair, the employee may bring a claim for unfair dismissal before the Labour Court (*Tribunal do Trabalho*). If successful, the dismissal may be considered null and void. As a result, the employee has the right to receive all the salary that he would receive in normal circumstances and to ask for reinstatement in the undertaking. Alternatively, he may ask for compensation for his dismissal, a minimum of one month's salary for every year that he has worked for the employer (with a minimum of three months). There is no compensation for future loss. Most employees choose compensation rather than reinstatement.

O6.4.2   The employee also has the right to apply to the Labour Court[1] (within five days of the dismissal date) for interim relief.[2]

[1]   Alleging any of the following grounds under s 39 of the Labour Procedure *Code* (*Codigo de Processo do Trabalho*):

(1) there were no fair disciplinary proceedings before dismissal;
(2) it is evident there is no fair reason or just cause to dismiss the employee;
(3) that the employer has failed to present the disciplinary proceedings to the court within the time specified by the court; or
(4) if the 60-day period to institute disciplinary proceedings has elapsed under s 31(1) of Decree-law 49408 dated 24 November 1969; or the one-year period within which to reach a conclusion once disciplinary proceedings have commenced has elapsed, with no conclusion.

[2]   The court may suspend dismissal.

6.5   Redundancy and Collective Dismissals: Background

O6.5.1   The law permits some or all workers to be made redundant through a process of negotiation with the works council (*comissão de trabalhadores*), if any of the company or other workers' representatives under the supervision of the Ministry of Labour (*Ministério do Trabalho*). This is deemed to be a just cause dismissal. Redundancy can occur due to the closure of the company, or the closure of one or a number of its production or service departments; or because of the need to reduce staff for restructuring, technical or market reasons, or for a combination of these reasons. Redundancy can be collective or individual.

O6.5.2   If the contracts of two or more workers are terminated within a three-month period by a company which employs up to 50 workers, or if the contracts of more than five workers are terminated by a company employing more than 50 workers, the reason is deemed to be redundancy and adherence to a strict procedure is required. Compensation (redundancy payment) equal to one month per year worked (with a minimum of three months) must be paid to each dismissed worker.

Procedure for collective redundancies

(1) Notice of intention of redundancy in each case to works council, trade union or each employee affected.

(2) Exchange of information (for at least 15 days) between employer and employees' committees/works council (if any) to try to agree ways of minimising the impact of redundancy or avoiding it and/or negotiating compensation. The *Ministério do Trabalho* must be informed of outcome, with full details.

(3) If negotiations fail, the employer must write to each redundant employee terminating employment.

(4) Each dismissed employee is entitled to compensation equal to one month's salary for each year of work with a minimum of three months' salary.

O6.5.3 If the requirements set out at (1) and (4) above are not met or negotiations (2) do not take place, the redundancy is null and void and the employee is entitled to re-instatement and to receive his salary as if he had continued working.

O6.5.4 After negotiations have ended without solution, the employer may only dismiss the employees after a 60-day period has elapsed from the date of the decision having been made.

Procedure for individual redundancy

(1) Notice must be given to affected employee, giving reasons and details.

(2) A copy of the notice must be given to the *Ministério do Trabalho*.

(3) Negotiations for 15 days.

(4) After 15-day negotiation period, notice may be served to terminate employment.

(5) Dismissal cannot take place until period of 60 days from final decision.

A   LAY-OFFS

O6.5.5 Lay-offs follow more or less the same procedure as redundancy. Lay-offs can only occur when justified by market economic or technical reasons or by other factors which seriously affect the normal business of the company.

O6.5.6 A lay-off may consist of a temporary suspension of work or of the interruption of work for one or more normal work shifts or in the reduction of the normal number of working hours.

O6.5.7   While the lay-off lasts the worker has the right to receive a salary equal to the national minimum monthly salary plus a compensation which, together with the amount of the minimum salary, should be equal to two-thirds of his normal salary. The amount corresponding to the national minimum monthly salary is paid by the employer. The additional compensation required to meet the equivalent sum of two-thirds of his normal salary is paid equally by the employer and Social Security.

O6.5.8   A period of lay-off may not last for longer than six months, or one year if it has been due to circumstances which seriously affect the normal activity of the company. A period of lay-off is renewable for one additional period of six months.

Redundancy
- closure or business or part
- need to reduce staff
- compensation of one month per year worked per worker

Lay-off
- temporary suspension/interruption of work
- reduction in normal working hours
- only when justified by market, economic or technical reasons
- worker receives national minimum monthly salary and compensation up to two-thirds of salary.

B   PLACE OF WORK REDUNDANCY

O6.5.9   An employer may wish to transfer the employee to another location. This is permitted in two situations:

(a) if the worker is not seriously prejudiced by the move; or

(b) if it occurs as a result of the total or partial move of the company or of the premises where the worker has worked. The company must pay the employee's expenses[1] incurred as a direct result of the move.

[1] Compensation must be agreed directly with the worker but will include any expenses which he would not have suffered if the move had not occurred eg removal costs, increased travel expenses, increase in salary to compensate for higher living costs).

7   YOUNG WORKERS

O7.1.1   Juvenile work is allowed from the age of sixteen.[1]

[1] Section 125 of Decree-law 49/408 dated 24 November 1969.

O7.1.2   Certain types of work are forbidden and a special scheme exists for student workers.

8 MATERNITY AND PARENTAL RIGHTS

8.1 General Rights

O8.1.1 Rights relating to leave due to pregnancy or confinement are also prescribed by law.[1] Both men and women are allowed by law to take time off work to assist their families in certain limited situations without loss of salary. For example both men and women may reduce their weekly working time without loss of pay to assist a disabled child until the child has reached the age of one. Men and women are entitled to have their contracts of employment suspended (without pay) for up to six months to look after children up to the age of three (or twelve, in the case of handicapped children).

[1] Law 4/84 dated 5 April 1984 as amended by Decree Law 142/99 dated 3 August and Decree Law 70/2000 dated 4 May.

O8.1.2 Women are entitled to paid time off work to attend antenatal appointments. A man is entitled to be absent from work without loss of pay for up to five working days on the birth of his child.[1] A woman is entitled to 120 working days' maternity leave (being entitled only to Social Security benefits) on the birth of the child. A father may take this leave if the mother cannot look after the child. Up to 30 days' maternity leave can be taken prior to the expected date of childbirth.

1 Decree Law 142/99 dated 3 August 1999.

8.2 Protection from Dismissal

O8.2.1 During pregnancy and during the first year after childbirth, a dismissal is considered null and void.[1] Prior approval to dismiss a pregnant employee (or one who is breast-feeding) must be obtained from the *Ministério do Trabalho* and from Social Security. Failure to do so will result in reinstatement or compensation, which can be substantial. Further, any dismissal which infringes the principle of equality between men and women will be seen as unfair.

[1] Section 18–A of law 4/84, dated 5 April 1984, as amended.

O8.2.2 An employee on maternity leave is entitled to return to her old job after maternity leave and may not be dismissed without just cause for one year after childbirth.

8.3 Health and Safety

O8.3.1 A woman is not allowed to work at night for 112 days before and after the birth as well as during breast-feeding.

O8.3.2 Pregnant women or women with children under the age of 10 cannot be obliged to work overtime.

O8.3.3 Heavy work may not be carried out by women.[1]

[1] Work at night and under medical advice. Work at night by women in industrial premises can only be authorised in cases of force majeure, which affects the normal work activity or when the composition of materials or materials in use in the production process may alter or change rapidly and work at night is indispensable to avoid loss of the materials.

8.4   Maternity Pay

O8.4.1   An employee on maternity leave only receives Social Security subsidies if she has been in paid employment for six months. She does not receive any salary from her employer unless that employer has set up a specific scheme to complement Social Security payments. The Social Security payments are a little less than the employee's full salary and are paid for up to 120 days. A lower rate of subsidy is paid in circumstances where a parent has to take time off work to care for a sick child under the age of 10 or for a disabled child.

9   BUSINESS TRANSFERS

9.1   Identifying a Relevant Transfer

O9.1.1   An employer is entitled to sell all or part of the 'establishment' which constitutes the basis where his company or business activity is developed. This is governed by Decree-Law 49408. Establishment means the premises, the stock (if any), the goodwill, etc of the enterprise. Where the enterprise retains its identity after the transfer, a relevant transfer will have taken place.

9.2   Affected Employees

O9.2.1   If there is a sale of an establishment, the employees assigned to that part or whole are included in the establishment and their jobs and employment contracts and all rights thereunder are transferred to the new owner of the establishment, the purchaser. Continuity of employment is preserved. There is no statutory right to object to transfer.

9.3   Effects of the Transfer

O9.3.1   The purchaser is jointly and severally liable with the seller for the employment obligations (other than criminal liability) which have crystallised during the six months prior to the transfer date.[1] After transfer, the purchaser is solely liable for any such obligations.

[1]   Article 37(2) of Decree-law 49408 dated 24 November 1969.

O9.3.2   The seller may previously agree with some or all of the employees that their employment contracts will not transfer to the purchaser. If they transfer, employees keep all the rights and seniority they enjoyed with the former owner of the establishment. Their rights are not affected at all by reason of the transfer. If any employee decides to leave the employer's business, he may do so under the usual terms of termination of an employment agreement.

9.4   Duty to Inform and Consult

O9.4.1   The seller must make a public announcement (affixed to the premises during the 15-day period before the transfer) informing the

747

employees that they are entitled to claim from the purchaser any employment rights which they may have against the seller after the transfer. If this notice is not given, the seller will be jointly liable with the purchaser for all liabilities. There are no other obligations to inform and consult, other than with any works council who will have general rights of information, but not consultation.

9.5 Dismissal of Employees

O9.5.1   Any termination of an employment contract in the context of a business transfer is unfair.[1] However, economic, technical or organisational reasons may justify a dismissal.

[1]   Employment Contract Act, s 24.

9.6 Variation of Contract

O9.6.1   An employer can transfer an employee to another location if the employee agrees; if the transfer does not cause 'serious damage' to the employee, or if the transfer is as a result of the total or partial change of the workplace. The concept of 'serious damage' is determined on a case-by-case basis taking into consideration the employee's living conditions (eg if he is married, has children studying locally etc). However, the purchaser cannot otherwise change the terms and conditions of employees who transfer.

10   COLLECTIVE RIGHTS AND BARGAINING

10.1 Background

O10.1.1   Portuguese law[1] regulates the creation and activities of trade unions and provides that a worker has the right to participate in promoting and defending his socio-professional interests if he so chooses. Incorporation of a trade union depends simply upon a decision being taken by a constitutive[2] meeting, the union's articles of association being registered at the Ministry of Labour and their publication in the official gazette.

[1]   Decree-law 215–B/75 dated 30 April 1975.
[2]   Ie a meeting in which a number (no minimum) of workers pass a resolution to set up a union.

10.2 Compulsory Recognition of Unions

O10.2.1   All workers are free to join a trade union and these are usually organised around industrial, commercial and service activities including metallurgy, transport, civil construction, office workers, electrical and electronic industries, textile industries and public enterprise workers. Trade unions can join federations and the latter can become members of confederations. There are two large confederations: UGT (*União Geral de Trabalhadores* – General Workers' Union) and the CGTP – INTERSINDICAL (*Confederação Geral de Trabalhadores Portugueses – Intersindical* – General Confederation of Portuguese Workers).

10.3 Consequences of Recognition

O10.3.1   Members of a works council and representatives of trade unions in a company are entitled to work only a certain number of hours per month and can therefore attend to the duties of their office without loss of salary.[1] Night shifts are allowed provided the shifts revolve every nine hours (between 20:00 of one day to 7:00 of the following day). This kind of work normally attracts a 25% increase in the average salary.[2]

[1]   Section 20 of Law 46/79 dated 12 September.
[2]   Section 30 of Decree-law 215–B/75 dated 30 April 1975.

O10.3.2   Activities may take place through union delegations or union committees. The following principles[1] apply at the workplace:

- workers have the right to meet during working hours (up to a maximum limit of 15 hours per year) with no loss of salary;
- union representatives are entitled to have a room set aside for trade union activities and have the right to display information in an agreed place.

The dismissal of a union representative in office or within five years of losing office or of candidates for elections to a union post is presumed unfair (*juris tantum*). If a dismissal has taken place without fair reason or otherwise than in accordance with legal requirements, the dismissed worker has the right to be reinstated and to receive compensation equal to double the wages for each year of work he has rendered to the employer (with a minimum of 12 months' pay).

Union members' rights

- to meet during working hours
- facilities set aside for meetings
- to display information
- presumption of unfair dismissal (with a right to reinstatement and compensation)

---

[1]   Section 25 of Decree-law 215–B/75 dated 30 April 1975.

10.4 Collective Bargaining

O10.4.1   The employment conditions of a large part of the working population are governed by collective agreements. The aims, limits and rules of proceedings for negotiations which can be laid down in the agreements are regulated by law. A collective agreement can only be established between one or more trade unions (or one or more union federations) and one or more employers or one or more associations of employers.

O10.4.2   A trade union wishing to start negotiations with an employer should submit a collective agreement proposal to the employer (an employer may also submit proposals to the trade union – there is a 30-day notice period for acceptance or rejection, or for a counterproposal to be made). Negotiations should be started within 15 days of any counter proposal. If agreement is not possible, either party can request the intervention of the Ministry of Labour to attempt a conciliation. If there is no agreement, the Ministry of Labour may decide upon the terms of the collective agreement through governmental act (*portaria*), or the parties may agree to submit the dispute to mediation or arbitration. If neither of these take place there is no other way of negotiating a resolution to the legal conflict.

O10.4.3 Collective agreements are in force for an obligatory minimum period of one year. They are only valid and binding after they have been published in the monthly labour gazette, unless the employer or the employees covered by the agreement decide to implement some or all of the provisions already agreed upon before the publication of the collective agreements.

10.5 Industrial Action

O10.5.1 In Portugal, unlike in many other European countries, the right to strike is governed by statute. However, the law does not require strike action to be taken only to achieve specified purposes or to serve specified interests. The law only provides for the basic requirements of strike proceedings, such as notice of strike (48 hours as a general rule and five days for services connected with the public interest), picketing, duties of the strikers during the period of strike, prohibition on employers against the substitution of strikers by non-union workers, etc. Generally, only trade unions can call a strike, but workers who are not represented by a trade union can also do so if the majority of workers in the business are not represented by a trade union and if certain other conditions[1] are satisfied.

[1] Ie if at least 20% of the workers of a company or at least 200 workers meet in assembly and pass a resolution to go on strike.

O10.5.2 Lock-outs are forbidden by the Constitution of the Portuguese Republic and any person in violation is liable to criminal sanctions. If there are certain essential or strategic economic sectors of public interest or if it is in the national economic interest, the Government can send the strikers back to work, failing which they may be dismissed and/or suffer criminal sanctions.

10.6 European Works Council

O10.6.1 The organisation and activity of a works council is regulated by law.[1] The Constitution of the Portuguese Republic sets out the right of every worker to organise and participate in a works council, in order to further their labour interests. These councils are not be confused with union representation in the company. They are quite distinct in their nature, origin and respective rights, and sometimes their interests may not be the same.

[1] Law 46/79 dated 12 September 1979 and Law 40/99 dated 9 June 1999.

A   ORGANISATION

O10.6.2   The law lays down a maximum number of members for the works council (*comissão de trabalhadores* or CT) as the following table shows:

companies with less than 201 workers	3 members
companies with 201–500 workers	3 to 5 members
companies with 501–1,000 workers	5 to 7 members
companies with over 1,000 workers	7 to 11 members
companies with less than 10 workers, where the volume of annual sales does not exceed P Esc 30 million	2 members

O10.6.3   If a company has several premises in different geographical locations, sub-works councils can be formed, and these also have a limit to the number of members. The works councils of various companies, whether or not they belong to the same economic group, can form an association of works councils,[1] which exist for the purpose of dealing with matters relating to a particular regional or national economic sector. The powers of the CT, the sub-CT or the association of CTs are not defined by law because it has been understood that they should not be determined by statute. The establishment of associations between union representatives[2] in a particular company, and the respective works council is possible, although they are not legally defined. Such an association is normally called an ORT.[3] Technically speaking, a works council (or a sub-works council) is an executive body of the workers in a particular company.

[1]   *Comissões coordenadoras* (co-ordinating committees).
[2]   *Delegações sindicais, comissão sindical* or *comissão intersindical*.
[3]   *Organição Representativa de Trabalhadores*, ie, representative organisation of workers.

B   POWERS

O10.6.4   The law sets out the rights of CTs and these generally comprise the right of access to information and the right to consult management.

The rights of a CT

- to receive all necessary information for carrying out its activities;
- to exercise control over management in the respective companies;
- to intervene in:
  (a) the reorganisation of the company's production or
  (b) restructuring of the respective regional and national economic productive sectors;
- to manage or participate in the management of canteens, crèches, etc in the company;

- to participate, through the works council organisations, in the development of labour legislation and the socio-economic plans for respective sectors;
- to convene a meeting periodically (at least monthly) with the company's management bodies (the sub-CTs can meet, under the same conditions, with the management body of the respective local enterprise);
- to use the premises and the equipment available in the enterprise for meetings and also for the distribution of information related to the interest of the workers. They have the right to receive information on matters such as:

  (a) general plans of company activity and budgeting;
  (b) internal rules and regulations;
  (c) organisation of production and corresponding levels of required labour;
  (d) forecast, volume and management of sales;
  (e) personnel management (including total amount of annual salaries and extras, social benefits, minimum levels of production, absenteeism);
  (f) accounts position of the company;
  (g) ways of financing the company;
  (h) company's position vis-à-vis the tax authorities;
  (i) projects for alteration of the share capital.

O10.6.5 Members of the works council are bound to secrecy in respect of this information, at the risk of criminal and disciplinary sanctions.[1] The business must provide the required information within ten days, or within 30 days in more complex cases.

Obligatory consultation

The following matters must be subject to consultation in writing before being decided by the business:

- finalising contracts in order to make a company which is in economic or financial difficulty solvent;
- finalising contracts with the Government or with financial institutions for similar purposes;
- winding-up the enterprise on bankruptcy;
- the closure of sections or production lines of the company;
- any measures that lead to substantial reduction in the number of workers or the deterioration of working conditions;
- alterations to the working timetable;
- alteration of the essential criteria for professional ranking or promotion of the workers;
- the change of location of the company or some of its departments.

A response must be given by the CT within 15 days unless more time is allowed by the business. Management control is exercised by the CT and this right cannot be delegated in favour of third parties. Management control objectives are:

- to analyse and offer opinions on the company's budgets and plans;
- to ensure that the company makes adequate use of its technical, human and financial resources;

- to initiate, together with the managing board, measures that contribute towards improved production;
- to ensure the fulfilment of the legal provisions and the statutes of the company and of the National Economic Plan[2] established by the Government concerning the links of the company with the economic sector with which it is integrated;
- to make suggestions, proposals or criticisms on matters such as professional training and to help to maintain high standards of safety and hygiene in the company and a high standard of living for the workers. These suggestions should be directed towards the respective competent departments of the company;
- to inform the authorities, or the company supervisory Board and auditors of contraventions of the company statutes or the law.

[1]   Law 40/99 dated 9 June 1999 provides that a member in breach may be dismissed with fair cause. Other sanctions include a variable fine with a cap of £10,000 and an obligation to compensate the company for any tort.
[2]   The National Economic Plan is the annual list of governmental political-economic-financial and social objectives

O10.6.6   In wholly state-owned companies, the works council has the right to appoint one member of the supervisory board. In companies in the private sector the participation of any worker on the board of a company is governed by the company's articles of association.

O10.6.7   If a business does not permit the CT to exercise the rights outlined in paras **O10.6.4** and **O10.6.5** it will be fined. Members of the board of directors are jointly liable with the company. On the other hand, if the CT members abuse such rights they will be subject to civil, criminal and disciplinary sanctions.[1] If the company or members of the works council do not perform their duties they can be sued. Members of the CT are granted a certain number of hours per month to carry out their activities without any loss of salary. Dismissal of members of the CT is subject to the same special regime which applies to trade union representatives in the company.

[1]   Section 37 of Law 46/79 dated 12 September 1979.

O10.6.8   A works council does not have the right to make decisions, unless allowed by collective agreement or by the provisions in the company articles.

11   EMPLOYMENT DISPUTES

11.1 Background

O11.1.1   Labour disputes are settled in Portugal by Labour Courts. Arbitration is not available since some employees' rights are not waivable and so the Labour Courts have a special role in controlling the fulfilment of law on this matter. This control is not given to arbitration tribunals. In addition, labour law has a special nature which is not entirely definable as a pure private law body of rules, but as social law in which the satisfaction of the rights of the employees and the workers in general are supervised by the judge of the Labour Courts. Such a function cannot be attributed to arbitrators.

11.2 Labour Courts

O11.2.1 There are three levels of judgment/appeal. A first instance court hears all cases. Judgments adjudicated by these courts can be appealed to the Court of Appeal (*Tribunal da Relação*) if the claim is higher than a certain amount (€ 3,700). From the judgment of this court an appeal may be made to the Supreme Court of Justice if the claim is for more than € 15,000 and on matters of law only.

O11.2.2 Portuguese courts may hear a case with an international connection (eg issues as to the domicile of the parties, residence, head office located outside Portugal, the overseas place where the employment contract was executed) if the facts (in full or partially) on which the cause of action is based occurred in the Portuguese territory as well as whenever one or both of the parties are domiciled or resident in Portugal.

12 WHISTLEBLOWING/DATA PROTECTION

12.1 Whistleblowing

O12.1.1 No employee can be dismissed for properly exercising his rights. If he is dismissed improperly for such a reason, it is considered to be an unfair and 'abusive' dismissal entitling the employee to double the normal compensation for unfair dismissal or, alternatively, to reinstatement.

O12.1.2 In addition, an employee must alert his employer to any malpractice at work, in accordance the employee's duty of loyalty to his employer.

12.2 Data Protection

O12.2.1 An employee is entitled to access to information about him kept by the employer and to ensure that this information is not given to any third party without his consent.

13 HUMAN RIGHTS

13.1 General

O13.1.1 Portugal is a party to the European Convention on Human Rights. The Convention was ratified by Portugal and is incorporated into domestic law in Portugal as a result. In addition, the Portuguese Constitution provides that the Convention is directly applicable in Portugal.

USEFUL ADDRESSES

• Ministry of Labour (*Ministério do Trabalho e da Solidariedade Social*)
Praca de Londres, 2
1250 Lisbon
Tel: (351) 21 844 1700
Fax: (351) 21 840 0189
Email: mts@mts.gov.pt

- Lisbon Labour Court

Av Almirante Reis, 130
1150 Lisbon
Tel: (351) 21 811 4000
Fax: (351) 21 815 1826
Email: trib.trab.lisbona@mail.telepac.pt

- IDICT – Instituto do Desenvolvimento e Inspecção da Condições do Trabalho (Inspection of Work Conditions Institute)

Praça de Alvalade, 1
1700 Lisbon
Tel: (351) 21 792 4500
Fax: (351) 21 793 71 49
Email: idict@idict.gov.pt

- UGT – União Geral de Trabelhadores

Rua Buenos Aires, 11
1200 Lisbon
Tel: (351) 21 393 1200
Fax: (351) 21 397 4612
Email: ugtp@mail.telepac.pt

- CGTP – INTERSINDICAL (*Confederação Geral de Trabalhadores Portugueses – Intersindical* – General Confederation of Portuguese Workers)

Rua Vítor Cordon, 1–2nd Floor
1200 Lisbon
Tel: (351) 21 323 6500
Fax: (351) 21 323 6695

P   Scotland

Alexander M S Green

Alexander M S Green is a Partner at CMS Cameron McKenna, Aberdeen. He has a M Theol, LLB, LLM, is qualified as an Advocate in Aberdeen, Solicitor and Notary Public, and is admitted to practice in Scotland and England and Wales.

CMS Cameron McKenna, Aberdeen

Phone: +44(0)1224 622 002
Fax: +44(0)1224 622 066
Email: asg@cmck.com
Website: www.cmck.com

SUMMARY TABLE

SUMMARY TABLE

SCOTLAND

Rights	Yes/No	Explanatory Notes
THE EMPLOYMENT RELATIONSHIP		
Minimum notice	YES	As for England and Wales
Terms:		
Express	YES	As for England and Wales
Implied	YES	As for England and Wales
Incorporated by statute	YES	As for England and Wales
REMUNERATION		
Minimum wage regulation	YES	As for England and Wales
Further rights and obligations:		As for England and Wales
Right to paid holiday	YES	
Right to sick pay	YES	As for England and Wales
WORKING TIME		
Regulation of hours per day/ working week	YES	As for England and Wales, save that the provisions as to Sunday trading do not apply in Scotland
Regulation of night work	YES	
Right to paid holiday	YES	As for England and Wales
Right to rest periods	YES	As for England and Wales
EQUAL OPPORTUNITIES		
Discrimination protection:		
Sex	YES	As for England and Wales
Race	YES	As for England and Wales
Marital status	YES	
Disability	YES	As for England and Wales
Religion	NO	As for England and Wales
Age	NO	
Sexual orientation	NO	As for England and Wales
Gender reassignment	YES	As for England and Wales
Part-time workers	YES	As for England and Wales
Equal pay legislation	YES	As for England and Wales
TERMINATION OF EMPLOYMENT		
Right not to be dismissed in breach of contract	YES	As for England and Wales
Statutory rights on termination	YES	As for England and Wales
REDUNDANCY		
Statutory definition	YES	
Right to payment on redundancy	YES	As for England and Wales
Right to consultation:		
Individual	YES	As for England and Wales
Collective	YES	As for England and Wales

YOUNG WORKERS

Protection of children and young persons at work	YES	Directive 94/33/EC implemented in Scotland; specific amendments introduced for Scotland

MATERNITY RIGHTS

Right to time off ante-natal care	YES	As for England and Wales
Right to maternity leave	YES	As for England and Wales
Notice requirements	YES	
Maternity pay (during leave)	YES	As for England and Wales
Protection from dismissal	YES	As for England and Wales
Health and safety protection	YES	As for England and Wales
Right to parental leave	YES	As for England and Wales
Right to time off for dependants	YES	As for England and Wales

BUSINESS TRANSFERS

Right to protection on transfer	YES	As for England and Wales
Transfer of employment obligations	YES	As for England and Wales
Right to information and consultation	YES	As for England and Wales
Right not to be dismissed	YES	As for England and Wales

COLLECTIVE RIGHTS

Compulsory recognition of trade union	YES	As for England and Wales
European works councils	YES	As for England and Wales
Right to take industrial action	NO	As for England and Wales

EMPLOYMENT DISPUTES

Civil court jurisdiction	YES	
Statutory body	YES	Scottish system of employment tribunals similar to, but separate from, employment tribunals in England and Wales with their own separate rules of procedure

WHISTLEBLOWING

Protection from dismissal/ detriment	YES	As for England and Wales

DATA PROTECTION

Protection	YES	As for England and Wales

HUMAN RIGHTS ACT

Statutory protection of human rights:

Public authority	YES	As for England and Wales
Private organisations	NO	As for England and Wales

1   INTRODUCTION

1.1   Background

P1.1.1   Employment law in Scotland is a combination of common law and statutory regulation. Statutory regulation has played an increasingly important role in the development of employment law, especially in the years since the introduction of statutory redundancy payments (1965), unfair dismissal protection (1971) and the United Kingdom's entry to the European Union (1973).

P1.1.2   This chapter contains the principal differences between employment law in Scotland compared to England and Wales. In many areas, the law is same as that of England and Wales, and considerable weight is given to English authorities by the Scottish courts and tribunals. Decisions of the Employment Appeal Tribunal sitting in England, the Court of Appeal and the House of Lords can be cited as binding authority in Scots law to the extent that they are concerned with the interpretation of statutory provisions common to both jurisdictions. Since the Human Rights Act 1998 entered into force on 2 October 2000, Scots courts and tribunals have been obliged, like the English ones, to interpret all primary and secondary legislation in accordance with the provisions of the European Convention of Human Rights and its associated jurisprudence. It remains to be seen what precise effect this will have in the employment field.

P1.1.3   It should be noted that whilst the legislation is United Kingdom based, separate provisions relate to the constitution and operation of the courts and tribunals in Scotland.

2   THE EMPLOYMENT RELATIONSHIP

2.1   Background

P2.1.1   As in the rest of the United Kingdom and Northern Ireland, the primary mechanism for governing the relationship of the employer and the employee is the contract of employment.

P2.1.2   The general rules of offer and acceptance, certainty and other aspects of Scots contract law apply equally to contracts of employment. Generally speaking, a contract of employment does not need to be in a particular form. It may be oral or in writing and it may be of any duration as the parties choose. The terms of the contract can be express or implied.

P2.1.3   Since the passing of the Requirements for Writing (Scotland) Act 1995 (the 1995 Act), the law relating to formal validity of contracts of employment has been simplified. Contracts for more than one year that were entered into before the 1995 Act came into force were termed *obligationes literis*. This meant that to be formally constituted, the contract had to be both in writing and probative. This rule did not, however, apply to contracts of employment of indefinite duration terminable by notice.[1] Contracts of employment for more than one year entered into after the 1995 Act came into force (ie, on or after 1 August 1995) are not required to be constituted in writing to be formally valid.[2] However, as in England, s 1(2) of the Employment Rights Act 1996 states that an employee must be given a written statement of particulars of employment within two months of beginning employment.

1   *Walker v Greenock and District Combination Hospital Board* 1951 SC 464.
2   Requirements of Writing (Scotland) Act 1995, s 1.

P2.1.4   Unlike English law, there is no requirement for a contract to supported by consideration.

2.2   Contract of Service

A   TERMS OF THE CONTRACT

P2.2.1   As in English law, a contract of employment that is governed by Scots law may be made up of terms and conditions of employment that are not necessarily set out in a written statement or handbook. They may be written or oral and be implied or express or incorporated.

B   EXAMPLES OF EXPRESS TERMS

Restrictive covenants

P2.2.2   As in England, general contractual rules apply to post-termination restrictive covenants which limit competition after termination of employment. Any term which limits the employee's freedom to pursue a trade or take up employment if the contract is terminated will be *pactum illicitum* (an unlawful and unenforceable agreement) if the restriction is wider than necessary to protect the employer's legitimate interests.[1]

1   *Scottish Farmers' Dairy Co (Glasgow) Ltd v McGhee* 1933 SC 148.

Implied terms

P2.2.3   At common law it is presumed that the employee gives his services in return for payment. This presumption can be rebutted depending on the circumstances and the relationship of the parties.[1] If there is neither an express nor an implied term as to the level of wages payable, the employee will be entitled to payment[2] calculated on the basis of *quantum meruit.*[3]

1   *Thomson v Thomson's Trustee* (1889) 16 R 333.
2   *Sinclair v Erskine* (1831) 9 S 487.
3   Literally 'as much as he deserves'.

2.3   Employee's Remedies

A   DAMAGES

P2.3.1–2   In order to claim damages, the employee must have suffered a breach of contract. Scots law recognises two species of breach of contract: material breach and minor breach. If there has been a material breach of contract (ie a breach that goes to the root of the contract), the employee may rescind the contract and sue for damages. If there has been a minor breach of contract, the employee may not rescind but can claim damages. Under Scots law, the right to claim damages prescribes five years from the date of the loss, injury or damage.[1] If the employee is dismissed and is paid his wages and other contractual entitlements in lieu of notice, he will have no competent right of action as no breach has occurred.[2]

[1] Prescription and Limitation (Scotland) Act 1973, s 11.
[2] *Graham v Thomson* (1822) 1 S 309.

B   DECLARATOR

P2.3.3   As an alternative to rescission, the employee may raise an action of declarator. Pending the decision, the contract will be maintained. The object of a declaratory action is:

> '... either that the court should declare in the pursuer's favour that some right exists, or that the court should declare to be non-existent what appears to be an existent right. It is incompetent to bring an action to have a fact declared which has no legal consequences for the pursuer, or to seek a judicial opinion on an abstract question of law'.[1]

[1] I D Macphail *Sheriff Court Practice* (2nd edn, 1998), p 649.

P2.3.4   The employee must have a live, practical issue which is sufficiently real and pressing before the court will grant declarator.

C   INTERDICT

P2.3.5   An interdict is the Scottish equivalent of the injunction. Because a contract of employment is a contract of *delectus personae* (ie it is of a personal nature requiring the performance of the particular employee), the courts will generally be reluctant to grant interdict if the effect of the interdict would be to compel the continuation of the employment relationship.[1] Unlike in England, an interdict will not be granted to prevent dismissal of an employee.

[1] *Murray v Dumbarton County Council* 1935 SN 47.

2.4   Employer's Remedies

A   DAMAGES

P2.4.1   If an employee leaves his employment and in doing so acts in breach of contract, the employer will be able to claim damages from the employee. The normal rules of assessing the measure of damages will apply.[1] Under these circumstances, the employer could claim damages for the cost of hiring a replacement, assuming of course that he could prove that the loss was as a direct result of the employee's breach or that it was at least contemplated by the parties when they entered the employment contract.[2]

[1] *Hadley v Baxendale* (1854) 9 Exch 341.
[2] *Strathclyde Regional Council v Neil* 1983 SLT (Sh Ct) 89.

B   INTERDICT

P2.4.2   The employer may apply for an interim interdict to restrain the employee. Typically, interdict will be sought to restrain disclosure of confidential information or to prevent infringement of a restrictive covenant. This remedy is discretionary and will not be granted if a restrictive covenant is unreasonable.[1] The Scottish courts will generally insist that the employer must not just show that there has been a breach of a restrictive covenant (which has been drafted in reasonable terms) but also that the perceived actual or potential harm is real and not fanciful and would justify an interim interdict to avoid such harm being inflicted.[2] Where there are several separate covenants in one contract, and one is unreasonable, the court will, when it is satisfied that it is appropriate so to do, 'sever' the latter and enforce the others.[3]

[1]   *Reed Stenhouse (UK) Ltd v Brodie* 1986 SLT 354.
[2]   *Jack Allen (Sales & Service) Ltd v Smith* [1999] IRLR 19, Ct of Sess.
[3]   See the discussion in *Rentokil Ltd v Hampton* 1982 SLT 442.

3   WORKING TIME

3.1   Remedies

P3.1.1   The Health and Safety Executive or the relevant council for the local government area are the bodies responsible for enforcing record keeping.[1]

[1]   Health and Safety (Enforcing Authority) Regulations 1998, SI 1998/494.

3.2   Sunday Working

P3.2.1   Sections 36–42 of the Employment Rights Act 1996, which relate to the protection of shop and betting workers, do not apply to Scotland. Shops in Scotland tended to open on Sundays before the Sunday Trading Act 1994 was passed in England, hence the protection was not extended north of the border. Thus Sunday working in Scotland is a matter of contract between the employer and the employee.

P3.2.2   One result of this is that it is not an automatically unfair dismissal, in Scotland, to dismiss an employee who refuses to work on Sundays.

4   YOUNG WORKERS

4.1   Children and Young Persons (Scotland) Act 1937

P4.1.1   The Children and Young Persons (Scotland) Act 1937 has recently been amended to implement the provisions of European Council Directive 94/33/EC on the protection of young people at work.

4.2   Directive 94/33/EC

P4.2.1   Directive 94/33/EC was implemented in Scotland by the Health and Safety (Young Persons) Regulations 1997, SI 1997/135 (the 1997 Regulations). The Regulations are UK-wide, with specific amendments for Scotland. For Scotland, a young person means a person who is not over school age, construed in accordance with s 31 of the Education (Scotland) Act 1980 ie school age being between five and sixteen years.

5   EMPLOYMENT DISPUTES

5.1   Jurisdiction

P5.1.1   Disputes between employer and employee are usually resolved:
*   at work (in a formal context by using the company's grievance or disciplinary procedure);

- in court – the relevant sheriff court or more usually for valuable or complex contractual issues the Court of Session (eg restraint of trade, breach of contract, interdicts etc);
- in employment tribunals – these were set up to deal with statutory employment claims (eg discrimination and unfair dismissal). They have jurisdiction to hear breach of contract claims up to the value of £25,000.

P5.1.2 Appeals from an employment tribunal may be made to the Employment Appeals Tribunal (EAT) on very limited grounds.[1] The EAT comprises at least one judge of the Court of Session nominated by the Lord President of the Court of Session. The EAT tends to sit permanently in Glasgow.

[1] Ie that the employment tribunal misdirected themselves in law, entertained the wrong issue, proceeded on a misapprehension or misconstruction of evidence, took irrelevant matters into account, or reached a decision which no reasonable employment tribunal, properly directing themselves in law could have arrived at.

P5.1.3 An appeal from the EAT may be made to the Inner House of the Court of Session and thereafter to the House of Lords. Where there is a question of interpreting EU law, the tribunal or court may request that the ECJ give a ruling.

5.2 Employment Tribunals

P5.2.1 In Scotland, employment tribunals comprise a panel of three: a legally qualified chairperson (selected from a panel of persons being advocates or solicitors of at least seven years' standing appointed by the Lord President of the Court of Session[1]) and two wing members representing both sides of industry, appointed by the Secretary of State. Neither the Chairman nor the lay members are given security of tenure by the Regulations, which state that they shall hold and vacate office in accordance with the terms of the instrument under which they were appointed.[2] The lack of tenure and the involvement of the Secretary of State lead one to question whether an Employment Tribunal as currently constituted can be said to be an independent and impartial tribunal for the purposes of art 6 of the convention.[3]

[1] Employment Tribunals (Constitution and Rules of Procedure)(Scotland) Regulations 1993, SI 1993/2688, Employment Tribunals (Constitution and Rules of Procedure) (Scotland) (Amendment) Regulations 1994, SI 1994/538, Employment Tribunals (Constitution and Rules of Procedure) (Scotland) (Amendment) Regulations 1996, SI 1996/1758.
[2] See SI 1993/2688, reg 5(2).
[3] See *Starrs v Ruxton* 2000 SLT 42; *Clancy v Caird* 2000 SLT 546.

P5.2.2 The President for the Employment Tribunals for Scotland presides over the tribunal system. In Scotland, there is a Central Office of Employment Tribunals which is based in Glasgow. There are three additional tribunal offices; however due to the centralisation of the organisation all applications must be sent to and registered at the Central Office. The three other tribunal offices do not have the same degree of autonomy as tribunal offices in England and Wales.

A   TERRITORIAL JURISDICTION

P5.2.3   If an applicant wishes to raise an action in the employment tribunal in Scotland one of the following conditions must be satisfied:

(a) the respondent or one of the respondents must reside or carry on business in Scotland; or

(b) the proceedings must relate to a contract of employment, the place of execution or performance of which is in Scotland; or

(c) the proceedings are to determine a question which has been referred to the tribunal by a sheriff in Scotland.

1   Employment (Constitution and Rules of Procedure) (Scotland) Regulations, SI 1993/2688, reg 8(3).

B   PREPARATION OF DOCUMENTS

P5.2.4   Unlike in England and Wales, there is no President's note governing preparation and disclosure of documents. However, in practice the chairman of the tribunal will consider each case and may order submission of documents in advance of the hearing.

C   EXCHANGE OF WITNESS STATEMENTS (PRECOGNITIONS)

P5.2.5   Unlike England and Wales, it is not customary for the parties to exchange witness statements or indeed witness details in advance of the hearing.

D   TRANSFER OF PROCEEDINGS

P5.2.6   The Scottish rules of procedure permit transfer of proceedings to an English employment tribunal. An application can be made by any party or by the President on his own motion or the chairman. The consent of the President of the Employment Tribunals (England and Wales) is required. Consent will be granted if it appears to him that the proceedings could be, or would be, more conveniently determined in an employment tribunal in England and Wales.[1] Notice of transfer must be given to all parties concerned who must be given an opportunity to show cause why the proceedings should not be transferred.

1   Employment Tribunals (Constitution and Rules of Procedure)(Scotland) Regulations 1993, SI 1993/2688, reg 19.

P5.2.7   The Trade Union and Labour Relations Act, s 212A, yet to be brought into force, will provide a basis for arbitrating employment disputes. In Scotland, unlike in England and Wales, it will be possible to refer a preliminary point of law to the Court of Session or to an Employment Appeal Tribunal.

5.3   Employment Appeal Tribunals

P5.3.1   Employment Appeal Tribunals are essentially identical to those in England and Wales, the few differences being procedural.

P5.3.2   Scottish employment tribunals are bound by the decisions of EATs in England and Wales, and English and Welsh Tribunals are bound by decisions of the Scottish EAT.

P5.3.3   The procedure for the listing of the appeals themselves in Scotland is simpler than in England and Wales. In Scotland, once the respondent's answer is received, a copy is served on the appellant. The appeal must be ready for hearing within six weeks. The parties are notified of the date three to four weeks in advance and formal notice is given 14 days prior to the hearing. Once the date is set, it can only be vacated by the tribunal, and only if due cause is shown.

P5.3.4   Unlike in England and Wales, there is no procedure in Scotland for making an application for the production of the Chairman's notes of evidence – however, in practice an order will be made on such an application, where cause is shown.

P5.3.5   Scottish EAT awards are enforced by extract registered decree pronounced by the Sheriff Court (with a warrant for execution attached).

Q   Spain

Lourdes Martin, Marina Mengotti Gonzalez and Juan Reyes Herreros

Lourdes Martin is a lawyer at Uria & Menéndez, Madrid. She was admitted in 1987. Her practice area is labour and social security law. She is editor of *Justicia Laboral*. She is a member of the Spanish Association of Labour and Social Security Law. She is author of many articles for journals and chapters in employment law publications including 'Spain' in ABA, Section of Employment Law.

Marina Mengotti is a lawyer at Uria & Menéndez, Madrid. She was admitted in 1996. Her practice area is labour and social security law. She is a contributor to *Justicia Laboral* and is a monthly contributor to *New Law Journal*, and contributor to the up-dated version of 'Spain' in ABA, Section of Employment Law.

Juan Reyes Herreros is a lawyer at Uria & Menéndez. His practice area is labour and social security law.

Uria & Menéndez, Madrid

Phone: + 34 91 586 03 34
Fax: + 34 915 860 403
Email: Lourdes at lmf@uria.com; Marina at mme@uria.com; Juan at jrh@uria.com
Website: www.uria.com

SPAIN

Rights	Yes/No	Explanatory Notes
CONTRACTS OF EMPLOYMENT		
Minimum notice	YES	Damages payable for failure to give notice
Terms:		
Express	YES	
Implied	YES	
Incorporated by statute	YES	
REMUNERATION		
Minimum wage regulation	YES	Established annually by central government. Also prescribed by CBA
Further rights and obligations:		
Right to paid holiday	YES	30 days paid holiday: no right to pay in lieu
WORKING TIME		
Regulation of hours per day/ working week	YES	Maximum 40 hours per week. See contracts and CBAs
Regulation of night work	YES	No more than eight hours night work a day
Right to rest periods	YES	One and a half days per week
EQUAL OPPORTUNITIES		
Discrimination protection: Sex, race, political or religious beliefs or other personal or social condition	YES	Contained in the Spanish Constitution
Sex, origin, marital status, race, social status, religious or political ideas, membership of a trade union (this includes disability)	YES	Statute
Equal pay legislation	YES	Statute
TERMINATION OF EMPLOYMENT		
Right not to be dismissed in breach of contract	YES	
Statutory rights on termination	YES	
COLLECTIVE DISMISSALS		
Statutory definition	YES	
Right to payment on termination	YES	Negotiated sum or 20 days' salary per year of service (maximum 12 months' salary)
Right to consultation:		
Collective	YES	And approval of Labour Authorities

YOUNG WORKERS

Protection of children and young persons at work	YES	

MATERNITY RIGHTS

Right to time off – ante natal care	YES	Reasonable time off
Right to maternity leave	YES	16 weeks maternity leave; compulsory six weeks leave after birth
Maternity pay (during leave)	YES	Statutory maternity pay paid by Social Security – see also CBAs and employment contracts
Protection from dismissal	YES	Dismissal of pregnant woman/woman on maternity leave is null and void
Health and safety protection	YES	
Right to parental leave	YES	Unpaid absence to both parents up to three years to care for a child

TRANSFERS OF BUSINESSES

Right to protection on transfer	YES	Implements Directive 77/181/EC
Transfer of employment obligations	YES	
Right to information and consultation	YES	Breach renders employer liable to fine
Right not to be dismissed	YES	

COLLECTIVE RIGHTS

Compulsory recognition of trades unions	YES	
European works councils	YES	

EMPLOYMENT DISPUTES

Civil court jurisdiction	YES	
Statutory body	NO	

WHISTLEBLOWING

Protection from dismissal/ detriment	NO	No specific legislation

DATA PROTECTION

Protection	YES	

HUMAN RIGHTS ACT

Statutory protection of human rights	NO/YES	Covered in some legislation but EC convention has not specifically been incorporated

1 THE EMPLOYMENT RELATIONSHIP

1.1 Background

Q1.1.1   Spanish labour law is generally protective of employees' rights. The Spanish system is constructed on the principle of security of employment as well as the *pro-operario* principle, which means that in the case of doubt, the applicable law must be interpreted in the employee's favour.

Main sources of Spanish law

Spanish Constitution

Q1.1.2   The Spanish Constitution of 27 December 1978 is the principal piece of legislation of the Spanish legal system. It is composed of 169 articles which provide the structure of the legal system. As a consequence, fundamental rights, the guidelines for political action and the main powers of the public authorities are established in the Spanish Constitution.

Civil Code

Q1.1.3   The Civil Code of 29 May 1889 follows the Latin tradition incorporated in the Civil Code of Napoleon of 1804. Article one establishes that the law, use and rules of law are the sources of the Spanish legal system. Nevertheless, the basic characteristics are that the Code contains the fundamental regulation of private relationships, that is to say, personal statute (birth, marriage, paternity, affiliation, disability, age etc), property, obligations and contracts.

Penal Code

Q1.1.4   The Penal Code of 23 November 1995 establishes the conduct which is punishable by law and legal remedies for criminal acts.

Commercial Code

Q1.1.5   The Commercial Code of 22 August 1885, with the Civil Code, also regulates private relationships. In particular, commercial practice and the regulation of different types of companies is covered.

Statute of Workers

Q1.1.6   The Statute of Workers of 24 March 1995 is the framework which contains the fundamental rights and obligations that establish the employment relationships, that is the basic aspects of the relationship existing between the employee and the employer.

Law on the Legal Regime of the Public Administrations and Administrative Procedure

Q1.1.7   The Law on the Legal Regime of the Public Administrations and Administrative Procedure of 26 November 1992, establishes the following: principles of administrative action, structure of the Administration, administrative procedure, effects of administrative acts and appeals against administrative acts.

Q1.1.8   Spanish labour relationships are mainly regulated by the Statute of Workers (SW), originally enacted by Act 8/1980 of 10 March, amended on several occasions and replaced by a consolidated version passed by Royal Legislative Decree 1/1995 of 24 March, which has been since modified, mainly in those aspects regarding the types of employment contracts and the rules governing them. The regulation of standard labour relationships is also contained in other local rules, international treaties and collective bargaining agreements (CBAs), which have recently become increasingly important.

Q1.1.9   In addition, certain employment relationships are governed by special regulations, which must respect basic rights established in the Constitution.[1] The special employment relationships are the following:

(i)   senior executives;
(ii)   commercial representatives;
(iii)   artists;
(iv)   professional sportsmen;
(v)   domestic workers;
(vi)   disabled employees who render services at Special Employment Centres;[2]
(vii)   prisoners; and
(viii) stevedores.

[1]   Spanish Constitution of 27 December 1978.
[2]   Special Employment Centres are public or private centres, whether or not they are profit-making, with the dual purpose of carrying out productive work and employing disabled people. These centres must have a minimum of 70% of disabled employees.

1.2   Contract of Service

Q1.2.1   An employment contract is defined as an agreement by which one individual (employee) voluntarily renders remunerated services for an individual or legal entity (employer) under its management, organisation and control.

A   CONTRACT TERMS

Q1.2.2   The object of the employment contract is to set out the specific duties performed by an individual for a third party under its management, control and organisation in exchange for agreed remuneration. As a general rule, the parties to the contract are free to agree on the content of the employment contract, with two exceptions:

(i)   the contract may not have a clause prohibited by law or contrary to public policy; and
(ii)   the employment contract may not include terms and conditions considered to be either less favourable than those established in the applicable labour legislation or less favourable than those set out in the applicable CBA.

Q1.2.3   The parties may agree to include a trial period in the employment contract, during which both the employee and the employer can freely terminate the employment relationship, the former not being obliged to give prior notice, nor the latter to pay a severance payment. CBAs may establish the trial period that applies to employees. If the applicable CBA does not regulate the duration of trial periods, it will be as follows:

(i) up to six months in the case of qualified employees;[1] and

(ii) up to two months in the case of unqualified employees.[2]

In companies with less than 25 employees, the trial period could be up to three months in the case of unqualified employees.

Trial period

The CBA usually establishes the duration of a trial period. In its absence, the duration will be as follows:

- qualified employees – up to six months
- unqualified employees – up to two months (or three months in small companies)

---

[1] Qualified employees are those employees who hold a university or technical degree.

[2] Unqualified employees are those employees who do not hold a university or technical degree.

B TYPES OF CONTRACTS

Q1.2.4 The SW establishes that employment contracts may be of an indefinite or temporary duration. Indefinite employment relationships are the general rule in Spanish labour law, whilst employment contracts executed on a temporary basis are the exception, since they may only be entered into subject to certain conditions.

Types of temporary employment contracts

- Training contracts[1]
- Learning contracts[2]
- Contracts for the creation of employment for handicapped employees[3]
- Contracts for the completion of a specific work or service[4]
- Contracts for production needs[5]
- Interim contracts[6]
- Relief contracts[7]

---

[1] Contracts with holders of academic degrees entered into during the four years following the termination of their studies that legally qualify them for a profession. The period may be increased to six years if the employee is handicapped. Employees may be hired under this type of contract either in the same or different company for a minimum period of six months and a maximum of two years.

[2] Contracts for the training of an employee between 16 and 21 years of age who does not have the academic qualifications required for a training contract. The age limit is not applicable if the employee is handicapped. The minimum duration cannot be less than six months and the maximum duration cannot exceed two years.

3 The duration of this contract cannot be less than one year nor greater than three years. Upon termination of this contract, the employee is entitled to a severance payment equivalent to 12 months of salary per year of service.

4 Contract for the completion of a specific work or the rendering of a specific service with proper autonomy within the activity of the company, limited in time although of uncertain duration. The contract will expire when the work or services are completed.

5 Contracts intended to meet urgent and circumstantial production needs due to a growth in demand or accumulation of tasks, even if the needs result from the normal activity of the employer. The maximum duration of these contracts is six months within a period of 12 months. CBAs may increase their maximum duration up to 13.5 months within a period of 18 months.

6 Contracts for the replacement of employees who are entitled to maintain their positions while their employment contracts are suspended or to cover a specific position whilst a selection process is taking place.

7 Employment contracts for the replacement of an employee who has requested a partial early retirement pension from the Social Security System by an applicant who is registered at the National Institute of Employment (INEM) office.

Q1.2.5 Should a temporary employment contract not meet the legal requirements, eg, it is not for a proper reason or does not meet the necessary formalities, it is presumed to be executed on a permanent basis. In such a case, if the contract is terminated at the end of the term, the employee may bring a claim for unfair dismissal, and the employer has the burden of proving why it was a temporary contract. If the dismissal is deemed unfair, the employer has a choice (unless the employee is an employee or trade union representative, in which case the option is his/hers) of either reinstating the employee to his/her former job position or paying a severance payment equivalent to 45 days of salary per year of service with a maximum limit of 42 months' salary (see paras **Q6.4.1–Q6.4.5**).

Q1.2.6 The Spanish government is promoting the indefinite hiring of employees (in preference to fixed-term contracts). Royal Decree – Law 5/2001 of 2 March[1] establishes a specific type of permanent employment contract for the conversion of temporary employment contracts into indefinite contracts and the indefinite hiring of unemployed persons belonging to the following groups:

(i) persons between 16 and 30 years of age;
(ii) persons older than 45 years of age;
(iii) handicapped persons;
(iv) unemployed persons registered with the Spanish Employment Office (INEM) for at least six months; and
(vi) unemployed women hired to perform services in jobs where female unemployment is higher than the male level.

1 Royal Decree-Law 5/2001 of 2 March, concerning urgent measures for improving the labour market and promoting the employment and quality of employment. This legislation has extended and improved what was provided in Law 63/1997 of 26 December, concerning urgent measures for improving the labour market and promoting the permanent hiring of employees, which was limited to 16 May 2001.

Q1.2.7   If the dismissal, for objective reasons, of employees hired under this type of contract is declared unfair by the labour courts, the severance payment will be equivalent to 33 days' salary per year of service with a maximum limit of 24 months' salary, instead of the usual 45 days of salary per year of service, with the maximum limit of 42 months (see para **Q6.4.2**). In addition, the Spanish government annually establishes different reductions[1] in the employer's contributions to the Social Security system in order to encourage the indefinite hiring of unemployed people.

[1]   This reduction consists of different percentages applicable to the usual rates. This reduction does not have any unfavourable effects on the employees' benefits.

Q1.2.8   It is also possible to enter into part-time employment contracts under Spanish labour law. This kind of employment contract may be of definite or indefinite duration. The employee is employed for a certain number of hours per day, week, month or year which must be less than the full-time working hours of an equivalent employee, or, in the absence of such an employee, of the full-time working hours stated in the applicable CBA, or of the legal maximum working hours generally established by law. Overtime is forbidden for part-time employees. Special rules will apply with respect to Social Security contributions.[1]

[1]   The Social Security provisions regulating part time contracts are multiple and complex. However, the most important point is a reduction in the contribution base in accordance with the hours effectively worked. In addition, there are special regulations for calculating the part-time employees' benefits in order to place these employees on the same level as full-time employees.

C   FORM OF THE CONTRACT

Q1.2.9   Employment contracts may be executed either orally or in writing. An employment contract is considered to exist between an individual rendering services for another within its organisational scope and direction (an employee) and the person who receives such services by paying remuneration (employer).

Q1.2.10   Should a written employment contract not be agreed in an employment relationship lasting more than four weeks, the employer must inform the employee about the essential elements of his/her employment contract and the conditions[1] of employment. This information must be provided in writing during the term of two months from the date on which the employment contract has commenced.

[1]   The employer is obliged to inform the employee about the labour conditions that will regulate his/her labour relationship, such as the duration of the labour relationship, the date of effectiveness, the professional category in which the employee will be included, the amount of the salary, the holidays and the applicable CBA.

Q1.2.11   However, there are certain employment contracts that must be executed in writing or follow a special form, as follows:

Employment contracts that must be executed in writing

Temporary contracts	*Special form*
• Training contracts	Yes
• Learning contracts	Yes
• Contracts for the completion of a specific work or service	No
• Contracts for production needs	No
• Interim contracts	No
• Relief contract	Yes
• Contract for the employment of disabled employees	Yes
Other contracts	
• Contracts for promoting the permanent hiring of employees	Yes
• Part-time contracts	Yes

Q1.2.12   Should the abovementioned employment contracts not be executed in writing, there is a legal presumption that they are full-time indefinite contracts.

D   SPECIAL AGREEMENTS

Q1.2.13   An employee may not be employed by more than one employer nor be a self-employed worker if this would be considered unfair competition or if it has been expressly agreed by the parties through the payment of compensation. In the latter case, the employee may resign his agreement and regain his/her freedom to either render services for another company or work as a self-employed worker by giving 30 days' prior notice, giving up his/her right to compensation by working exclusively for the employer.

Q1.2.14   If an employee receives special training from an employer in order to carry out a specific project or perform a certain job, a 'permanence agreement' (*pacto de permanencia*) may be entered into by the parties for a period not exceeding two years. By virtue of this agreement, the employee is obliged to render services for the company during the agreed period. Such an agreement must be executed in writing. Should the employee leave the company before the agreed term, the employer would be entitled to claim damages. Such damages are usually established in the contract.

Example

'Company A' intends to sell a new product in a difficult market. The management of Company A believes that one of its employees, 'Mr B', has the professional qualification to prepare a marketing plan in connection with such product, although he has no experience in this activity. For this reason, Company A bears the cost of a Masters Program in Marketing for Mr B in order that this employee prepares a specific marketing plan for the sale of the mentioned product. In exchange for this, Mr B is obliged to continue working for Company A for a period of two years. Should Mr B leave Company A before such period of time, he must reimburse Company A for all its costs in connection with the Masters in Marketing as it has been agreed by both parties in the employment contract.

Q1.2.15   Non-competition covenants after the termination of employment may be expressly agreed by the parties, with the following requirements:
(i)   the duration of the non-competition obligation cannot exceed two years for technicians[1] and six months for other employees;
(ii) the employer should have an actual business or commercial interest; and
(iii) the employee should receive an adequate payment for the covenants, which should be expressed in the employment contract or in the document in which the non-competition agreement is set out.

[1]   Technicians are those employees holding a university or technical degree.

Statutory provisions

Q1.2.16   The SW regulates employment rights and obligations relating to the execution of work. It establishes the minimum terms and conditions that the employment contract must include, regardless of whether the parties have agreed to them. However, either CBAs or individual employment contracts may improve these minimum statutory provisions. In other cases, SW nullifies certain provisions agreed by the parties.

Examples of terms implied by SW

Equal pay	The contract must establish the principle of equal pay for equal work.
Extra payment	The employee is entitled to receive two extra payments per year, one payable at Christmas and the other in the month established in the CBA. The amount of these extra payments is also established in the CBA.
Working time	At least 12 hours must elapse between the end of one working day and the beginning of the next.

Examples of terms considered null and void by SW

Race, sex, religion, origin or ideology[1] discrimination	All rules, provisions of CBAs, specific individual agreements and policies containing any kind of discrimination shall be considered null and void.
Trial period	Any contractual provision establishing a trial period when the employee has previously rendered the same services for the same company shall be null and void. Taxes and Social Security contributions All taxes and Social Security contributions corresponding to employees will be paid by the employees, and any agreement establishing the contrary shall be null and void.

[1]   Ie religious and/or political beliefs.

1.3   Variation of Contract

Q1.3.1   Pursuant to art 1256 of the Civil Code,[1] the validity and performance of a contract cannot be left to the discretion of one of the parties. However, this provision is not strictly applied in the case of employment contracts. The content of an employment contract might be modified by a change of law or an applicable CBA. In other cases, employment contracts may be modified by a unilateral decision of the employer, provided that certain circumstances exist. For example, 'functional mobility' may be distinguished from 'material changes in the employment conditions' (see paras **Q1.3.2–Q1.3.7**).

[1]   The Civil Code is the basic Spanish provision regulating private relationships, which is considered to be supplementary in the absence of other private rules, which was enacted by Royal Decree of 24 July 1889.

A   FUNCTIONAL MOBILITY

Q1.3.2   The employer may unilaterally oblige the employee to perform tasks other than those previously agreed by the parties, provided that these new duties are considered to be appropriate for the employee's professional category.

Example

'Employee A' holds a professional degree in secretarial skills, and performs the duties of the secretary of the Commercial Deputy Manager. Due to a temporary accumulation of tasks in the production department, Employee A is obliged to perform other administrative tasks in such department.

Q1.3.3 Functional mobility for the discharge of duties of a non-equivalent[1] professional group or category will only be possible if there are technical or organisational reasons to justify it, and will only be possible for the time absolutely necessary to carry out these duties. If duties of a lower status are given to the employee, this should be justified by urgent or unforeseen needs of the business.[2] In cases of functional mobility, the employee is entitled to remuneration corresponding to the duties he/she actually discharges, unless duties of a lower status are given to him, in which case he/she shall retain his original remuneration.

[1] Pursuant to the SW, art 22.3, one professional category shall be deemed equivalent to another when the necessary professional capabilities to perform the duties pertaining to the former permits the performance of the basic professional services of the latter, after the employee undergoes simple training or adaptation processes, if necessary.

[2] This is a legal concept that may be defined as those extraordinary and unforeseen business situations which require a certain employee to perform duties of a lower professional category.

B   MATERIAL CHANGES IN THE EMPLOYMENT CONDITIONS

Q1.3.4 An employer may modify the employment conditions of employees on the grounds of economic, technical, organisational or production reasons.[1] Such reasons exist when the measures adopted contribute to the improvement of the employer's business by means of a reorganisation of its resources that either improves its competitive edge or provides a better response to the market's demands.

[1] Economic reasons exist when there is an economic situation within the company, as well as a negative balance-sheet which, taking into account the financial, production and commercial aspects, endangers the company's viability. Technical reasons exist when the company's production equipment has been renewed and, as a consequence a certain percentage of the workforce has become unnecessary. Organisational or production reasons require persuasive argument since these reasons are often considered to be too vague; they usually relate? to the introduction of new working methods and outsourcings, with the subsequent necessary organisational readjustment. Thus, in practice, organisation or production reasons are strongly linked to economic reasons.

Q1.3.5 If an employer intends to unilaterally and essentially change the employment conditions (either the workplace or the working day, working time, working shifts, remuneration system, work and productivity systems or duties) the following procedures must be followed, depending on whether the modification is considered individual or collective.

Changes to individual employment conditions

Q1.3.6 Changes to an individual employee's employment conditions must be notified to him and his legal representatives, giving prior notice of 30 calendar days.[1] It is not necessary to consult in advance either the affected employee(s) or their legal representatives. After this period of time, the employer's decision will be effective notwithstanding the right of the affected employees to challenge the decision (see para **Q1.4.2**).

[1] SW, art 41.3.

Collective changes

Q1.3.7   In the event of collective changes in employment conditions, the procedure consists of a consultation period of 15 calendar days with the employees' legal representatives. Once the negotiation period has finished, whether an agreement has been reached or not, the employer must provide the affected employees with 30 calendar days' notice of the changes. The SW only allows the essential modification of working conditions established in a CBA relating to working time, working shifts, remuneration system as well as work and performance system by means of an agreement between the employer and the employees' legal representatives.

1.4   Remedies

A   EMPLOYEES' REMEDIES

Q1.4.1   An employee may request the termination of his/her employment contract without having to bring a claim before the labour courts on the grounds of unilateral change to terms and conditions of work when:

- the conditions of the working day, working time or working shifts have been essentially altered by the employer (see paras **Q1.3.1–Q1.3.7**). If the employee disagrees with such changes and such modifications mean a detriment for him/her, the employee may terminate his/her employment contract and is entitled to a severance payment equivalent to 20 days' salary per year of service with a maximum limit of nine months' salary; or
- the change of location of the employee's workplace requires the employee to move home, unless the employee had been employed to render services in several work centres or movable centres. In this case, the employee is entitled to terminate the employment contract and to receive a severance payment of 20 days' salary per year of services with a maximum limit of 12 months' salary.

Q1.4.2   In both cases, an employee who does not wish to terminate his/her employment contract but disagrees with the employer's decision may file a claim before the labour courts (*Juzgados de lo Social*) to be reinstated in his/her former employment conditions. The labour courts will determine whether the employer's decision is fair or unfair. If unfair, the employer must reinstate the employee with his previous terms and conditions; otherwise, the labour courts will make a declaration that the employment relationship has terminated and the employee is entitled to a severance payment corresponding to unfair dismissal: 45 days of salary per year of service with a maximum limit of 42 months' salary (see para **Q6.4.2**).

Termination of the contract – dismissal

Q1.4.3   Regarding the employee's remedies in the event of dismissal, see paras **Q6.4.1–Q6.4.9**.

Damages

Q1.4.4   When a severance payment or damages are awarded or agreed upon by the parties, no other compensation is payable. However, there are certain circumstances in which the employee may bring a claim based on a serious breach by the employer which damages the employee's rights eg in the event that the employer does not reinstate the employee after enjoying a voluntary leave of absence when there is a genuine vacancy in the company.[1] In this case, the court may order the employer to cease the behaviour complained of and to pay the damages caused by such conduct. There are no legal guidelines to determine the amount of the damages to be paid. This sum is entirely at the court's discretion.

[1] Civil Code, art 1101 states that 'those who, in the performance of their obligations, incur fraud, negligence or delay, and those who act in contravention of the fulfilment of the obligation, are liable for the resulting damages'.

B   EMPLOYER'S REMEDIES

Q1.4.5   In principle, if the employee causes damage to the employer by his failure to fulfil his obligations under the employment contract, the employer is entitled to claim damages, which are determined at the court's discretion. However, this happens only rarely. The cases in which the employee pays damages to the employer are generally related to the breach of special agreements of exclusivity, permanence and non-competition after the termination of the employment as set out in paras **Q1.2.13–Q1.2.15**.

Example

Mr Garcia participated in a Masters Programme in Marketing paid for by his employer. In exchange, Mr Garcia undertook to work for his employer for two years to do a specific marketing project. As Mr Garcia resigned his employment before the two year period, the Labour Court declared that Mr Garcia must pay his employer damages equivalent to the value of the Masters Program paid by the company.

Q1.4.6   The failure to comply with the obligation to give notice in the event of voluntary resignation, if applicable, may also result in damages for the employer, usually equivalent to the salary for the period of notice which was not fulfilled.

2   REMUNERATION

2.1   Background

Q2.1.1   There is a presumption that all the sums received by an employee as a consequence of employment are considered to be salary.

Q2.1.2   Remuneration in cash or in kind received by employees is subject to Social Security contributions. All remuneration (eg including salary in kind, in cash, commissions and bonuses) must be taken into account to calculate any severance payment in the event of termination of employment.

2.2 Legal Regulation of Remuneration

Q2.2.1 The amount of salary is agreed upon by the employer and the employee. However, this agreement must respect the legal minimum wage established every year by the central government, considering the next year's forecasts for these indices: retail price index, average national productivity, increase of the labour contribution in the Gross National Product and the general economic situation.[1] Likewise, the agreed salary cannot be lower than that established in the applicable CBA for the corresponding professional category.

[1] The minimum legal wage established for is Ptas 2,404 (€ 14.45) per day or Ptas 72,120 (€ 433.45) per month: ie Ptas 1,009,680 (€ 6,068.30) per annum.

Q2.2.2 In addition, a specific prohibition against discrimination on the grounds of sex is established in the SW, which also states that equal pay must be granted for equal work (see para **Q5.5.1**).

Q2.2.3 Salary is usually fixed annually, although it is payable monthly in arrears. Employees are entitled to receive at least two extra payments, usually payable in December and in the summer months (June or July).[1] The amounts of these extra payments are usually established in the CBAs. In addition, CBAs usually provide for fringe benefits relating to the specific work performed or the personal conditions of employees, such as shift bonuses or bonuses for night work, and seniority or language bonuses, respectively.

[1] SW, art 31.

Q2.2.4 Salary, up to certain limits established by the SW, enjoys preferential status so that employees receive their salary before other employers' creditors. In addition, employees are entitled to exercise their rights of preference in bankruptcy proceedings or in separate enforcement proceedings *(ejecucion separada)*.

2.3 Deductions from Wages

Q2.3.1 An employer can make a deduction from an employee's wages to recover any debt owed to it by the employee.[1]

[1] Civil Code, art 1196.

2.4 Itemised Pay Statement

Q2.4.1 Payment of salary must be punctual and at the time and place agreed upon by the parties or in accordance with usual practice. The employer must deliver to the employee a document explaining the salary payments. This document must be executed in official form, although certain exceptions are permitted.

3 FURTHER RIGHTS AND OBLIGATIONS

3.1 Background

Q3.1.1 The SW sets out employees' primary rights and obligations. Such rights and obligations imply correlating obligations and rights for the employer and, in fact, constitute the principles on which employment relations are based. In addition, there are other secondary rights and obligations that will be referred to in the relevant section.

3.2 Holiday Entitlement

Q3.2.1 Holiday entitlement is covered at paras **Q4.6.1–Q4.6.4**.

3.3 Special Leaves of Absence

Q3.3.1 Without prejudice to particular provisions set out in the applicable CBAs, and provided that prior notice and proper justification is given, all employees are entitled to the following paid leave:

* 15 calendar days in the event of marriage;
* two calendar days in the case of birth of children, severe accident or illness, hospitalisation or death of a close relative;
* one day for change of residence/home;
* reasonable time off to comply with a personal and unavoidable political or personal duty, including voting;
* time off (as agreed by law) to carry out trade union activities or representation of employees;
* reasonable time off to attend ante-natal appointments.

3.4 Additional Entitlements

Non-discrimination

Q3.4.1 The Spanish Constitution and the SW prohibit any kind of discrimination on the basis of sex, marital status, age, race, social status, religious or political beliefs, membership of a trade union or language. Disabled persons may not be discriminated against provided such individuals are able to perform the relevant activity or position.

Health and safety and in the workplace

Q3.4.2 Employees have the right to be kept physically healthy and to work in a safe environment. Employers are obliged to implement preventive measures aimed at protecting employees from workplace risks.[1]

In particular, employers are obliged to:

(i) carry out a risk assessment;
(ii) prepare an emergency plan and a labour risk prevention plan;
(iii) organise a labour risk prevention service; and
(iv) establish a health and safety committee.

In addition, employers must take preventive measures appropriate to the activities performed by their employees.

1   In accordance with Law 31/1995 of 8 November on prevention of labour risks, developed by Royal Decree 39/1997 of 17 January approving the Prevention Services Regulation (*Reglamento de los Servicios de Prevención*).

Actual work

Q3.4.3   Employees are entitled to be given work. Otherwise, they have the right to terminate their employment relationship and receive a severance payment equivalent to 45 days of salary per year of service with a maximum limit of 42 months' salary.[1]

1   For further details in relation with the calculation of the severance payment, see para **Q6.4.2**.

3.5   Employees' Obligations

Q3.5.1   Employees must comply with their employment duties, acting diligently and in good faith.

Q3.5.2   Employees must also observe legitimate orders and instructions given to them by their employer.

Q3.5.3   Employees are obliged to contribute to the productivity of the company.

3.6   Contracting of Services

Q3.6.1   Under Spanish labour law,[1] a company can manage its own business or can delegate the performance of some of its activities to another company (the 'contracting company'), provided that certain requirements are met to guarantee the rights of the contracting company's employees. Case law has established the requirements defining a legal services contract, as follows:

- The contracting company must carry out its own business and must have its own employees, assets, work equipment and machinery, as well as a stable organisation to perform the services.
- The contracting company must actually control and manage the activity to be performed for the main company. The submission of the employees of the contracting company to the internal rules, policies or procedures of the main company is considered to be evidence of illegal subcontracting of services.
- The contracting company must perform an actual economic activity distinct from that of the main company.
- The contracting company must take a real business risk. Spanish labour courts have upheld this principle, considering that if the price of the service is only based on the cost of the salary of the employees executing activities for the main company, the contracting company is not taking the business risk.

1   SW, art 42. Royal Decree – Law 5/2001 of 2 March has amended art 42 SW, increasing the information obligations as regards the employees of the contracting company and the employees of the company for which the contracting company performs services.

Q3.6.2   In the event of legally contracting out a part of their own business, a company has the following responsibilities:

- It is jointly and severally liable for the salary obligations assumed by the contracting company with their employees and Social Security obligations for the term of the agreement.
- It is also jointly and severally liable during the term of the contract for any breach of the obligations of the contracting company under the regulations on prevention of labour risks.

3.7   Social Security

Q3.7.1   Spanish nationals habitually residing in Spain and foreign nationals legally residing in Spain, who work in the Spanish territory, are covered by the Social Security system (*Sistema de Seguridad Social*), provided that they belong to any of the following groups:

- employees working for a third party;
- self-employed workers;
- working partners in production co-operatives;
- students; and
- civil and military servants.

Spanish nationals who do not reside and work in Spain may be covered by the Social Security system under certain circumstances.[1]

[1]   In this regard, the following must be taken into account: EEC Council Regulation 1408/71 (14 June 1971) on the application of social security schemes to employed persons and their families moving within the Community, and EEC Council Regulation 574/72 (21 March 1972) fixing the procedure for implementing EEC Regulation 1408/71 on the application of social security schemes to employed persons and their families moving within the Community, as well as bilateral treaties.

Q3.7.2   The Social Security system consists of a General Regime (*Régimen General*) including employees working for a third party,[1] and some Special Regimes (*Regímenes Especiales*).[2]

[1]   Certain former Special Regimes are now integrated in the General Regime: artists, railway employees, bullfighters and professional football and basketball players.
[2]   Currently existing Special Regimes are the following: (i) agricultural workers; (ii) seamen; (iii) self-employed workers; (iv) domestic employees; (v) civil and military servants; (vi) coal mining workers; and (vii) students.

Q3.7.3   Any person or legal entity who intends to hire employees is obliged to register itself with the Social Security system before commencing its activities, by filing the appropriate official form and certain documents with the competent office of the Social Security General Treasury (*Tesoreria General de la Seguridad Social*).

Q3.7.4   Affiliation with the Social Security system is mandatory for all individuals included in its scope of application. Affiliation takes place once in a lifetime, and applies for the whole Social Security System.

Q3.7.5   Before an employee starts work, employers are obliged to give notice to the Social Security system of the beginning of his/her employment.

Q3.7.6   Employers and employees are obliged to contribute monthly to the Social Security system. Employers are also obliged to withhold contributions due from employees from their monthly salaries.

Social Security contributions are calculated by applying the contribution rates set out below to a monthly amount referred to as the 'contribution base' (*base reguladora*), depending on the employee's salary and professional category. The contribution base is also subject to maximum and minimum limits fixed yearly by the government.

Social Security contributions for permanent employment contracts consist of different items, the rates of which follow:

Contribution item	Employer	Employee	Total
Common contingencies	23.60%	4.70%	28.30%
Unemployment[1]	6.00%	1.55%	7.55%
Salary Guarantee Fund	0.40%	–	0.40%
Professional training	0.60%	0.10%	0.70%
Total	**30.60%**	**6.35%**	**36.95%**

In addition, employers must contribute to the Social Security system for work accident and work-related illness. The contribution rate depends on the type of activity performed by the relevant employee.

[1]   There are different rates for unemployment contributions for full-time and part-time temporary employment contracts.

Q3.7.7   The General Regime provides employees with the following benefits:

- medical assistance in the event of maternity, sickness or accident;
- economic benefits for temporary disability, maternity, risk during pregnancy,[1] and permanent disability;
- coverage of dependants;
- retirement pensions;
- unemployment benefits; and
- death and survivor benefits.

[1]   This benefit was introduced by law 39/1999 of 5 November for promotion of conciliation between work and family life.

3.8   Foreign Employees

Q3.8.1   Foreign citizens from non-EU countries must obtain work and residence permits in order to be allowed to reside and work in Spain.

Q3.8.2   EU citizens only need to be provided with a EU residence card (*Tarjeta de Residencia para nacionales comunitarios*) in order to legally reside and work in Spain.

4 WORKING TIME

4.1 Background

Q4.1.1   The an employee's maximum working time is generally set out by CBAs or individual employment contracts. However, there is a maximum limit of 40 hours of actual work per week, calculated as a yearly average.[1]

[1]   SW, art 34.

4.2 Legislative Control

Q4.2.1   In principle, work actually performed cannot exceed nine hours per day. A 12-hour minimum break must exist between the end of one working day and the beginning of the next. In addition, employees are entitled to a weekly uninterrupted rest period of one and a half days, which, as a general rule, consists of all day Sunday in addition to either Saturday afternoon or Monday morning, unless a different regime is agreed. There are special working time rules for different sectors (seamen, oil drilling, road transportation, hotel trade, etc).

4.3 Opting Out/Additional Hours

Q4.3.1   Employees cannot opt out of the regulation on working time. Therefore all the legal restrictions in respect of maximum working time or periods of rest must be respected.

Q4.3.2   Overtime is considered to be work performed in excess of ordinary working time (see para **Q4.1.1**). Overtime is not mandatory for employees, unless expressly provided by the relevant CBA, or agreed in the employment contract. In any case, overtime cannot exceed 80 hours per year. However, overtime performed to prevent or to deal with accidents or any other urgent and extraordinary events is not included within the 80-hour limit.

Q4.3.3   In accordance with the provisions contained in the SW, overtime can be remunerated either in cash or by equivalent time in lieu, as set out by the CBAs or the individual employment contracts. Failing any express provision, overtime must be compensated for by equivalent time in lieu within four months after its performance. Overtime remunerated in this manner does not count towards the maximum limit mentioned in para **Q4.3.2**. Compensation in cash cannot be lower than that paid for ordinary working time.

4.4 Night Work

Q4.4.1   Work performed between 22:00 and 6:00 qualifies as night work and is remunerated in the manner established in the relevant CBA, unless the remuneration has been established bearing in mind that the work is performed at night or time off in lieu has been agreed. Employees working nights cannot work more than an average of eight hours per day, based on reference periods of two weeks.

4.5   Rest Period

Q4.5.1   Employees are entitled to an uninterrupted weekly rest period of one and a half days (see para Q4.2.1).

4.6   Paid Annual Leave

Q4.6.1   Employees are entitled to a legal minimum of 30 calendar days of paid holidays per year. There is no right to be paid in lieu.

Q4.6.2   Holiday periods are determined by agreement between the employer and the employee, in accordance with the provisions of the relevant CBAs. Any disputes are resolved by the labour courts following a summary procedure.

Q4.6.3   In addition to 30 days' annual leave, employees are also entitled to public holidays, which cannot exceed 14 days per year.

Q4.6.4   Employers must prepare a holiday schedule, so that employees know their holiday periods at least two months in advance.

4.7   Remedies

Q4.7.1   If an employee is required to work excessive hours which are not paid or compensated with periods of rest, he may bring a claim against his employer before the Labour Court.

If the employee proves his claim, the employer will be ordered to compensate the employee in cash or by giving equivalent time off in lieu in accordance with the collective bargaining agreement or individual employment contract.

5   EQUAL OPPORTUNITIES

5.1   Background

Q5.1.1   Article 14 of the Spanish Constitution prohibits any discrimination based on race, sex, political or religious beliefs or any other personal or social condition or circumstance. Moreover, art 35 of the Constitution establishes the right to employment of all Spaniards, also prohibiting discrimination on account of their sex.

Q5.1.2   In addition, art 17 of the SW prohibits any positive or negative discrimination regarding remuneration, working hours and other employment conditions on account of sex, origin, marital status, race, social status, religious or political ideas, membership in a trade union, family link with other employees or language.

Q5.1.3   The prohibition against discrimination refers to:
(i)   access to employment;
(ii) conditions of employment, and
(iii) legitimate prospects.

5.2 Unlawful Discrimination

Q5.2.1 In addition to direct discrimination there are other types of discrimination: indirect discrimination and the 'appearance of protection'.

Indirect discrimination

Q5.2.2 Indirect discrimination consists of adopting apparently neutral measures that cause differential and detrimental treatment of certain employees.

> **Example**
> A lower production bonus is paid to employees assigned to department A than that paid to employees assigned to department B of a certain company. The affected employees of both departments perform different jobs which have a similar value. The employer always assigns male employees to department B and female employees to department A. This situation is considered to be indirect discrimination, since the different remuneration arises from the differences in the employees' sex.[1]

[1]   Judgment of the Superior Court of Justice of Basque Country of 16 June 1993.

Appearance of protection

Q5.2.3 Measures adopted ostensibly to protect one group which, in practice, perpetuate and exacerbate the position of one group, such as disabled people or women, are also discriminatory.

> **Example**
> The provision establishing the right of women to terminate their employment contracts on marriage on receiving a compensation payment was declared discriminatory by the Constitutional Court,[1] since this measure encouraged the termination or interruption of the professional career of women on the grounds of marriage, and was based on the assumption that women are physically inferior to men or have a more significant vocation with respect to domestic duties, a principle which makes no sense in current society.

[1]   Judgment 1994/317 of 28 November 1994.

Q5.2.4 A unilateral decision which has the effect of discriminating in terms of remuneration, working time, training, promotion as well as other employment conditions will have the following consequences:
*   It will be considered null and void.
*   It will be considered a very serious breach and the employer may be penalised by the Labour Authorities (*Autoridades Laborales – Inspección*

de Trabajo y Seguridad Social) with a fine ranging from Ptas 500,001
(€ 3,005.07) to Ptas 15,000,000 (€ 90,151.82).
• It will also be considered a criminal offence. Article 314 of the Criminal
Code[1] provides that an employer which – after having been required to
change its behaviour or fined by the Labour Authorities for serious
discrimination in private or public employment on the basis of ideology,
religion, race, sex or sexual orientation, family circumstances, illness,
disability or any other basis – does not remedy the unequal treatment
and repay the damages suffered, is liable to a prison term or fine.

[1] Law 10/1995 of 23 November.

5.3 Disability Discrimination

5.3.1 Disability discrimination is covered by the Statute of Workers (see
para Q5.1.2).

5.4 Enforcement and Remedies

Q5.4.1 When an issue of sexual discrimination arises in a trial, the labour
court may request a report from the competent public authorities. Such a
report may also be proposed by the parties.

Q5.4.2 When an applicant alleges the existence of discrimination, the
defendant has the burden of proving the existence of an objective and
reasonable justification of the measures adopted and showing that they were
necessary means to an end. The employee must show grounds for unequal
treatment as well as of the existence of discrimination, and the employer
must prove that the unequal treatment was legal.

Example

Employee B filed a claim against his employer, Company A, for
discrimination as a result of his membership in a trade union. He claimed
that the fact that he was the only employee of his department who did not
receive a special annual bonus was related to the fact that he was the only
employee of the corresponding department who belonged to a trade union.
The only evidence of this unequal treatment that the employee provided to
the Labour Court consisted of documents confirming that he was the only
employee of the department who did not receive the annual bonus. As
Company A was not able to show that the mentioned unequal treatment was
justified by legal reasons, the labour court ruled in favour of Employee B.

5.5 Equal Pay

5.5.1 The SW specifically states that employers are obliged to pay equal
pay for equal work, without discrimination on the ground of sex.

6 TERMINATION OF EMPLOYMENT

6.1 Background

Q6.1.1 An employment contract may be terminated for the following reasons:[1]

- mutual agreement;
- 'fair' reasons identified in the employment contract;
- agreed expiry date;
- the employee's resignation;
- death or permanent disability of the employee;
- retirement of the employee;
- death, retirement or permanent disability of the employer;
- *force majeure* making the rendering of services permanently impossible;
- collective dismissal based on economic, technical, organisational or production reasons;
- resignation of the employee following fundamental breach of contract by the employer;
- disciplinary dismissal of the employee; and
- individual dismissal for objective reasons.

[1] SW, art 49.

Q6.1.2 There is an additional reason for termination that is not included in art 49 of the SW: non-fulfilment of the employment requirements during the probationary period (see para **Q1.2.3**).

6.2 Nature of Dismissals

A   DISCIPLINARY DISMISSAL

Q6.2.1 An employee can also be dismissed as a result of serious and wilful non-compliance with his/her duties.[1] Breaches that can cause an employee's dismissal are:
- continued and unjustified absences from the workplace;
- continuous and unjustified lateness;
- lack of discipline or insubordination towards the employer or other employees;
- breach of the covenant of good faith, and abuse of trust;
- continued poor performance; and
- habitual drunkenness or drug addiction that affects work performance.

[1] SW, art 54.

Q6.2.2 The employer must provide the employee with written notice containing a precise description of the breach and the date on which the dismissal becomes effective. A disciplinary dismissal may be effective on the date of the notice. The employees' legal representatives should be notified of the termination by the employer. In order to dismiss an employee who belongs to a trade union, the employer must also previously inform the trade union of the intention to dismiss such an employee.[1]

[1]   When the employee is a legal representative of employees , a different procedure must be followed, in which the employer, prior to dismissing the affected employee, is obliged to hear the reasons of the affected employee as well as other employees' legal representatives in the company.

Q6.2.3   If the employee does not agree with the termination, he/she may bring a claim against the employer before the Labour Court. In fact, the employee is obliged to contest the fairness of the dismissal in order to receive unemployment benefits. The Labour Court will determine whether the dismissal was fair, unfair or null and void (see paras **Q6.4.1–Q6.4.5**).

Example

Mr A has repeatedly failed to attend work without giving any explanation to his employer. Mr A has missed six days of work during the last three months. In addition, Mr A continually arrives at work late without justification. This is considered a very serious breach in accordance with the corresponding CBA, and the employer decides to dismiss him.

B   DISMISSAL FOR OBJECTIVE REASONS

Q6.2.4   Dismissals for objective reasons[1] can be based on any of the following reasons:
- lack of capacity;
- failure to adapt to technical changes relating to the employee's job, as long as such changes are reasonable and more than two months have elapsed since the modifications were introduced;
- non-continuous and justified absences amounting to a total of 20% of the working days in two consecutive months, or 25% of the working days in four discontinuous months within a period of 12 months, provided that in both cases the overall level of absenteeism of employees in that organisation is greater than 5% during the same period.
- employers may reduce the number of jobs due to economic, technical, production, or organisational needs.
- employment contracts entered into to carry out a public program which depends of a public budget.

The criterion which determines whether there should be an individual (as opposed to collective) dismissal due to any of the above reasons is numerical. Dismissals are individual if, within a period of 90 days, the number of employees affected does not reach the following thresholds:
- the whole workforce of the company, if the affected employees are less than five;
- 10 employees in companies of fewer than 100 employees;
- 10% of the work force in companies with between 100 and 300 employees; and
- 30 employees in companies with 300 or more employees.

[1]   SW, art 52.

Q6.2.5 Employees' legal representatives[1] have priority for retention in the company in the event of either collective or individual dismissal based on objective reasons.

[1] See para **Q10.3.1**.

Q6.2.6 A dismissal initiated by the employer must provide the affected employee with 30 calendar days' notice. The notice must include an explanation of the reasons for the dismissal and the offer of a legal severance payment, which consists of 20 days of salary per year of service, with a maximum limit of 12 months of salary.[1] In the event that the 30 calendar days' notice is not respected, the employer must also offer to pay an amount equivalent to the employee's salary for the default period. During the 30 calendar days, the employer must provide the employee with six hours of paid absence per week in order to look for new employment.

[1] This severance payment applies to individual objective dismissals which are considered to be fair as well as to collective dismissals. The severance payment for unfair dismissal amounts to 45 days' salary per year of service with a maximum limit of 42 months of salary (see para **Q6.4.7**).

C   TERMINATION BY THE EMPLOYEE

Q6.2.7 An employee may request the termination of the employment contract by the Labour Courts on the grounds of the employer's substantial breach of contract, such as a serious change to the employment conditions which prejudices the professional training or dignity of the employee, or the failure to pay salary or continued delays in the payment of salary.

Q6.2.8 If an employee requests the termination of the employment relationship before a Labour Courts for any of reasons set out in para **Q6.2.7** and a judgment upholds the termination of such a relationship, the employee is entitled to receive a severance payment equivalent to 45 days' salary per year of service with a maximum limit of 42 months' salary.

6.3   Fairness of Dismissal

Q6.3.1 In any case, the dismissal can be challenged by the employee before the Labour Court, which declares whether the dismissal is fair, unfair or null and void (see paras **Q6.4.6–Q6.4.9**). Employees who decide not to contest the validity of dismissals for objective reasons retain the right to receive unemployment benefits as well as the severance payment (cf para **Q6.2.3** as to disciplinary dismissals).

Example
Certain organisational changes made in Company B, which were necessary to ensure the competitiveness and profitability of the company, caused the duplication of roles in department 'D'. Company B objectively dismissed certain employees of this department based on organisational reasons with the purpose of guaranteeing the company's viability and future level of employment; had the company not made such dismissals, it would have continued to incur highly onerous costs without compensating revenues.

6.4   **Remedies**

A   DISCIPLINARY DISMISSAL

Procedure

Q6.4.1   If an employee argues that the dismissal was unfair, he/she may bring a claim against the employer within the following 20 working days before the Mediation, Arbitration and Conciliation Services (*Servicios de Mediación, Arbitraje y Conciliación* – SMAC). The SMAC will summon both parties to a meeting in which they can reach a settlement (see para **Q6.4.2**).

Q6.4.2   In the event that no agreement is reached before the SMAC, the employee can bring a claim against the employer. If the Labour Court declares that the dismissal is unfair because the alleged reasons have not been proven by the employer or are insufficient, or the legal formalities have not been observed (eg the employee has been orally dismissed), the employer may choose (unless the employee is a legal representative of employees) between:

(i)   reinstating the employee in his/her prior position; or
(ii) paying him/her the legal compensation for unfair disciplinary dismissals, which is 45 days' salary per year of service with a maximum limit of 42 months of salary.

In addition, the employer must pay the employee the salary accrued during the period between the date of the dismissal and the notification of any judgment. However, the payment of such salary may be limited to the salary accrued between the date of dismissal and the meeting before the SMAC. In such a case, the employer must recognise in the meeting that the dismissal is unfair and offer the employee the legal severance payment for unfair dismissal plus all the salary accrued until the meeting before the SMAC, depositing these payments in the Labour Court's bank account at the employee's disposal within 48 hours after such meeting.

Examples

- Mr Garcia was unfairly dismissed on 1 May 1999. As he joined the company on 5 August 1963 and his current daily salary is Ptas 8,913 (€ 53.57), his severance payment amounts to Ptas 11,230,380 (€ 67,495.94), which is the maximum allowed: 42 months' salary.

- Mr Martinez was also unfairly dismissed on 1 May 1999. He joined the company on 7 October 1974 and his current daily salary is Ptas 7,836 (€ 47.1). He is entitled to a severance payment of Ptas 8,650,944 (€ 51,993.22).

Q6.4.3   The dismissal is deemed to be null and void if the employer has infringed the employee's constitutional rights or the dismissal is considered discriminatory.

Q6.4.4 Likewise, the disciplinary dismissal of a pregnant woman or a dismissal made while the corresponding employment contracts are suspended on the grounds of maternity, risks during pregnancy, paid absence for breastfeeding, or leave of absence to care for a child or other family member will be considered null and void, unless it is shown that the dismissal is fair because it is based on reasons unrelated to pregnancy.[1]

[1] Law 39/1999 of 5 November for promoting conciliation between work and family life.

Q6.4.5 When a dismissal is deemed to be null and void the employer must reinstate the employee to his old job. The employee is entitled to receive his salary from the date of the dismissal up to the date of the reinstatement.

B   DISMISSAL FOR OBJECTIVE REASONS

Q6.4.6 If no settlement is reached before the SMAC, an employee may bring a claim against his employer before the Labour Court, as described in paras **Q6.4.1** ff. If the dismissal is held to be fair, the employee will be entitled to the legal severance payment of 20 days' salary per year of service to a maximum of 12 months' salary.

Example

Mr A was objectively dismissed on 30 September 1999. As he joined the company on November 26, 1999 and his daily salary as of 30 September 1999 was Ptas 7,917 (€ 47.59), his severance payment for objective dismissal (20 days' salary per year of service with a maximum limit of 12 months' salary) amounted to Ptas 145,139 (€ 872.3).

Q6.4.7 If the dismissal is held to be unfair by the Labour Court, the employer will be required either to reinstate the employee to his old job or to pay a severance payment of 45 days' salary per year of service, with a maximum limit of 42 months' salary. In the event that an employee has already received the severance payment of 20 days' salary per year of service with a maximum limit of 12 months' salary, he/she will be entitled to the difference between these two amounts.

Example

Mr A filed a claim against his employer for unfair dismissal. The Labour Court declared that the dismissal was unfair. Mr A is entitled to a severance payment of Ptas 326,563 (€ 1,962.68). As he had received Ptas 145,139 (€ 872.3) as a severance payment for objective dismissal, the company is now only obliged to pay Mr A the difference between the two amounts, ie, Ptas 181,424 (€ 1,090.38); (Ptas 326,563 – Ptas 145,139 = Ptas 181,424).

Q6.4.8   Employees whose contracts were made in accordance with Royal Decree – Law 5/2001 of 2 March and Law 63/1997 of 26 December[1] (or Royal Decree Law 8/1997 of 16 May reinstated by Law 63/1997) will be entitled to a lower severance payment in the event of dismissals for objective reasons which are declared unfair. The severance payment will be equivalent to 33 days' salary per year of service, with a maximum limit of 24 months' salary (see para **Q1.2.7**).

[1]   Law 63/1997 of 26 December concerning urgent measures for improving the labour market and promoting the indefinite hiring of employees.

Q6.4.9   A dismissal for objective reasons can be held to be null and void if the employer does not offer the payment of the legal severance payment at the moment of the notification, proceeds with an individual dismissal when a collective dismissal is compulsory (see para **Q6.5.1**) or if a constitutional right is considered to have been violated.

Likewise, the objective dismissal of a pregnant woman or a dismissal made while an employment contract is suspended on the grounds of maternity, risks during pregnancy, paid absence for breast-feeding or leave of absence to care for a child or other family member will be considered to be null and void, unless it is shown that the dismissal is fair because it is based on reasons unrelated to the pregnancy or such other reason for suspension.[1]

If an objective dismissal is declared null and void, the employee must be reinstated to his old job and receive the salary accrued from the date of dismissal up to the date of reinstatement.

[1]   Law 39/1999 of 5 November for promoting conciliation between work and family life.

6.5   Redundancy and Collective Dismissals: Background

Q6.5.1   Collective dismissals occur when, within a period of 90 days, termination of employment contracts based on economic, technical, organisational or production reasons affect at least the thresholds established in para **Q6.2.4** or the whole workforce of the company, if the affected employees are more than five, and the collective dismissal is a consequence of the total cessation of the company's activities.[1]

[1]   SW, art 51.

Reasons for collective dismissals

Q6.5.2   There are two broad categories of reasons for collective dismissals:

- *economic reasons*: when the termination of the employment contracts contributes to overcoming the poor economic situation of the company; and
- *technical, organisational or production reasons*: when termination of the employment contracts contributes to guaranteeing the company's viability and the level of employment within the company in the future, by means of a more effective use of its resources.

6.6   Consultation

Q6.6.1   In either case, the carrying out of a collective dismissal requires the approval of the Labour Authorities. At the same time as making such a request, the employees' legal representatives must be notified and a minimum negotiation period of 30 calendar days (or 15 days in companies with less than 50 employees) between the employer and the employees' legal representatives must follow. After the period of negotiation, the Labour Authorities must decide the case within a period of 15 days.

Q6.6.2   If an agreement is reached between the employer and the employees' legal representatives, the Labour Authorities will simply endorse such an agreement, and will authorise the termination of the employment contracts, unless the Labour Authorities determine that the agreement has been reached on the basis of wilful misconduct, coercion or circumvention of the applicable law. In this event, the Labour Authorities will refer the case to the Labour Court.

Q6.6.3   If no agreement has been reached during the negotiation period, the Labour Authorities have the following alternatives:

- to issue a resolution authorising the termination of the employment contracts (see para **Q6.6.7**);
- to deny the authorisation if the situation of the company does not sufficiently support the termination of the contracts;
- to partially authorise the termination of the employment contracts; or
- not to issue any resolution within a period of 15 calendar days. In this case, it is understood that the termination of the employment contracts is authorised.

Q6.6.4   If no approval is granted, the employer will not be entitled to dismiss the employees. Any collective dismissal will be considered null and void and the reinstatement of the employees will be mandatory.

Q6.6.5   Employees who have their employment contracts terminated in a collective dismissal have the right to receive either the legal severance payment equivalent to 20 days' salary per year of service with a maximum limit of 12 months' salary or the severance agreed during the negotiation period. In addition, the employer has to pay the affected employees the salary accrued during the dismissal proceedings.

Example

Mr A was included in the collective dismissal proceedings initiated by Company B. The competent labour authority authorised the collective dismissal due to the company's very serious economic situation. The application requesting the collective dismissal authorisation was filed on 30 November 1999, and the authorising resolution of the competent labour authority was issued on 11 January 2000. The resolution authorises the employer to terminate the employment contracts of the affected employees in the terms established in the corresponding application, eg on 15 February 2000. The affected employees will also be entitled to receive a severance payment plus all salaries accrued up to such date.

---

7   YOUNG WORKERS

7.1   General obligations

A   CAPACITY

Q7.1.1   Hiring workers under 16 years of age is prohibited. An employment contract executed with a minor of less than 16 years is considered null and void. However, in that event, the minor is entitled to the salary which corresponds to the services rendered. The participation of children under 16 years of age in public entertainment will only be authorised by the Labour Authorities in exceptional cases, provided that the work is not likely to endanger their physical health or their professional and personal development.

Q7.1.2   Individuals older than 16 and younger than 18 years of age may only be employed if:
(i)   they are legally independent or enjoy the majority of age benefit;[1] or
(ii)   their parents or tutors permit the employment.

[1]   The majority of age benefit is granted by a competent judge by application on the part of the affected minor. Article 320 of the Civil Code states that the majority of age benefit can be granted when: (i) the father/mother holding the paternal authority marries or live with someone who is not the mother/father of the minor; (ii) parents are separated; or (iii) in the event of existence of any reason which is seriously against the exercise of the paternal authority.

B   WORKING TIME

Q7.1.3   Employees younger than 18 years of age may not perform:
(i)   night work (see para **Q4.4.1**);
(ii)   overtime; and
(iii) any activity or job which the government declares to be unhealthy, burdensome, noxious or hazardous for their health and for their professional and personal development.

In addition, employees under 18 years of age may not perform more than eight hours of effective work per day, including time devoted to training. When the continuous daily working time exceeds four and a half hours, such employees are entitled to a rest time of 30 minutes.

C   EMPLOYMENT CONTRACTS

Q7.1.4   The SW regulates learning and training contracts in connection with the employment of young workers. Learning contracts are for the training of:

(i)   an employee between 16 and 21 years old who does not have academic qualifications;
(ii)   unemployed disabled;
(iii) foreign employees during the two first years of their work permit;
(iv)   unemployed persons without work for more than three years;
(v)   unemployed persons in situation of social exclusion; and
(vi)   unemployed persons which take part of professional programs.

At least 15% of working time must be dedicated to Occupational Professional Education. Remuneration will be established in the applicable CBA and may not be lower than the minimum legal wage. Training contracts are those entered into with holders of university or occupational training degrees during the four years following the termination of studies that legally qualify them for a profession (see para **Q1.2.4** notes 1 and 2). Remuneration will be established in the corresponding CBA failing which, it cannot be lower than 60 to 75% of the salary stated in the applicable CBA for employees occupying the same job during the first and second year of the contract, respectively.

Q7.1.5   As stated in paras **Q1.2.6** and **Q1.2.7**, Royal Decree – Law 5/2001 establishes a type of permanent employment contract for the promotion of the indefinite hiring of employees belonging to certain groups, including employees between 18 and 29 years old.

8   MATERNITY AND PARENTAL RIGHTS

8.1   Background

Q8.1.1   Spanish law provides special protection for maternity, including the following benefits:
- health assistance;
- maternity leave;
- paid absence for breastfeeding;
- reduction of working time based on legal custody;[1]
- leave of absence to care for a child under three years old; and
- special protection regarding objective and disciplinary dismissal.

[1]   See para **Q8.2.7**.

8.2   General Rights

Health assistance

Q8.2.1   Health assistance during gestation, birth and postnatal period is provided to:
(i)   women registered with the Social Security system;
(ii)   pensioners and women periodically receiving benefits;
(iii) employees' wives; and
(iv) dependants of persons with the right to health assistance.

Q8.2.2   Employed women may be absent from work with the right to remuneration for the time attending birth training courses and attending antenatal classes, and receiving medical assistance during gestation (see para **Q3.3.1**)

Maternity leave[1]
Q8.2.3   All employed women, regardless of their seniority, working hours or type of employment contract are entitled to 16 weeks of maternity leave. In case of multiple births, the maternity leave will be extended by two weeks for each child beginning with the second.

[1]   This right has been recently improved by Law 39/1999, of 5 November for promoting conciliation between work and family life.

Q8.2.4   If both parents work, the mother, at the beginning of the period of maternity leave, may opt for the father to enjoy an uninterrupted part of this leave after the birth,[1] which may be either simultaneous with or consecutive to the period enjoyed by the mother, provided that this does not imply a risk for the mother's health. In any case, the mother must take mandatory leave of at least six weeks after the birth. If the mother dies, the father is entitled to the entire period of maternity leave or, if applicable, the remaining period.

Example

Ms A works for Company B. Her husband, Mr C, works for Company D. Their child was born on 1 March 2000. The mother opted for her husband to enjoy part of the maternity leave simultaneously with her. Thus, Mr C had two weeks of the maternity leave just after the birth of their child. Consequently, Ms A had 14 weeks of leave of absence instead of the total 16 weeks, since her husband used two weeks of the leave at the same time as her.

---

[1]   The total duration of the maternity leave is 16 weeks (in cases of individual child births). The father and the mother benefit from suspension of the employment simultaneously, provided that the total suspension does exceed 16 weeks. The father alone can enjoy up to 10 weeks of maternity leave, since the six weeks immediately after childbirth must be used by the mother.

Q8.2.5   In the event of adoption or fostering, should the child be under six years of age, the period of maternity leave has a maximum duration of 16 weeks. In the event of multiple adoption or fostering, the maternity leave period will be extended by two weeks for each child beginning with the second. In cases of international adoption, the maternity leave may begin four weeks prior to the date of formal adoption, when it is necessary for the parents to stay in the adopted child's country previous to the birth. If both parents work, only one of them may exercise this right, even if they work for different employers.

Paid absence for breastfeeding

Q8.2.6   Employees are entitled to one hour per day of paid absence from work for the breast-feeding/bottle feeding of a child under nine months. The employee may exchange, at his/her option, this hour of absence for a half an hour reduction in his/her working day. Either the mother or the father (but not both) may enjoy this leave of absence if both are employed. The reduction of working time does not mean a salary reduction.

Reduction in working time

Q8.2.7   Employees who have legal custody of a child under six years of age shall be entitled to a reduction in their working time of a minimum of one third to a maximum of one half of their working time and a proportional reduction of their salary. This right may be exercised by the employee until the child reaches six years of age.

Example

Mrs B has a one-year-old child. Pursuant to the CBA, the agreed working time for Mrs B is eight hours of effective work per day. Her remuneration is Ptas 4,000,000. Mrs B decides to reduce her working day by one half in order to care for her child. Consequently, Mrs B's remuneration is proportionally decreased to Ptas 2,000,000.

8.3   Protection from Dismissal

Q8.3.1   Law 39/1999 of 5 November introduced additional protection in the event of either disciplinary or objective dismissals of pregnant women or of employees with suspended contracts on the grounds of maternity, paid absence for breastfeeding or leave of absence to care for a child, by deeming such dismissals null and void (see paras **Q6.4.4** and **Q6.4.5**).

8.4   Health and Safety

Q8.4.1   A pregnant woman is entitled to have a job which does not pose any risk for her or her unborn child's safety.[1]

[1]   Article 26 of Law 31/1995 of 8 November on prevention of labour risks.

Q8.4.2   A new Social Security benefit has also been established.[1] This benefit covers risks during pregnancy ie where the employment contract is suspended because the mother or unborn baby's safety is in danger and it is not possible to change the mother's role at work to avoid the risk.

[1]   Law 39/1999 of 5 November on promotion of conciliation between work and family life.

8.5   Maternity Pay

Q8.5.1   Certain subsidies are provided during maternity leave as long as the employee concerned has contributed to the Social Security system for at least 180 days during the five-year period before the birth. This subsidy will be 100% of the 'regulatory base' (*base reguladora*), which is calculated based on the monthly amount of the 'contribution base' (*base de cotización*) to the Social Security system. The contribution base is calculated taking into account the salary and professional skill of the employee. As the contribution base is also subject to maximum and minimum limits, it may not be equivalent to the total salary paid to the employee.

Q8.5.2   However, in many cases, CBAs or individual employment contracts provide for certain supplements to be paid by companies to make up the total salary of the employee during the maternity leave period.

8.6 Additional Rights to Time Off

Q8.6.1 Employees are entitled to unpaid leave of absence of a maximum of three years to care for a child from the date of birth, adoption or fostering. This right is granted equally to both parents if both are employed. Subsequent births will give rise to fresh leaves of absence which will, if applicable, terminate any existing leave that has not yet ended.

Q8.6.2 The period of this leave of absence is taken into account regarding the employee's seniority in the company, as is the employee being entitled to participate in training courses organised by the company. During the first year of leave of absence, employees are entitled to insist on their jobs being kept open for them. After the first year, the affected employee shall only be entitled to a job position in the same group.

9 BUSINESS TRANSFERS

9.1 Background

Q9.1.1 Under Spanish labour law, transfers of businesses are governed by art 44of the SW, which implements Council Directive 77/187/EEC, on the approximation of the laws of the Member States relating to the safeguarding of employees' rights in the event of transfers of undertakings, businesses or parts of undertakings or businesses.

9.2 Identifying a Relevant Transfer

Q9.2.1 Subrogation[1] by virtue of art 44 of the SW requires two elements, as repeatedly underlined by Spanish case law:
- the transfer of all the essential assets of the undertaking, business or parts of the undertaking or business which may qualify as an autonomous production unit; and
- continuity of the operation of the business or undertaking by the transferee.

[1] Ie transfer of the business so that the transferee takes on all the liabilities and obligations of the transferor in respect of the employees – in other words, the transferee stands in the transferor's shoes.

Q9.2.2 Subrogation occurs not only when transferring an entire company, but also when a single work centre or even an independent production unit is transferred. It includes all business possibilities which involve the continuation of an activity by the new employer, provided that the activity which is transferred forms a productive and economic unit with sufficient autonomy to carry out services and activities, and that the performance of such services and activities is continued from the time at which the transfer becomes effective.

Q9.2.3 Subrogation may extend to all legal business and corporate operations which involve a change in the exercise of the transferred activity, such as the sale or purchase of companies or assets, including leases, mergers, take-overs, spin off etc.

Q9.2.4   However, legal subrogation does not occur where there is a mere transfer of the business premises and not the business itself, nor when the transfer relates to material assets that are not connected with the commercial or business activity; nor does it occur in the event of a mere transfer of shares or when the object of the transfer is the activity itself without any assets to support it.

Q9.2.5   A transfer of undertaking exists when the subject of the transaction is an independent organisational unit made up of material and non-material assets to which several labour relationships are linked and the new employer is able to continue a specific activity.

9.3   Affected Employee

Q9.3.1   Employees affected by the transfer will be those whose employment relationships are linked to the business, undertaking or part of the business or undertaking that is transferred.

Q9.3.2   However, when the part transferred is an independent production unit, the employees affected by the transfer will be those who are mainly or exclusively assigned to the activity which is subject to the change of ownership. A clear identification of these employees is not always possible. Case law has declared that no proportional criteria are applicable in the case of just a part of the business or undertaking.

9.4   Effects of the Transfer

Q9.4.1   By operation of law, the transferee of a business, undertaking or part of a business or undertaking is subrogated in all employment rights and obligations of the former employer (transferor) with respect to the relevant employees. The main effect, therefore, is the maintenance of all rights acquired by the employees. As case law has clearly stated: 'subrogation implies continuity of the former contract in the same conditions.'[1]

[1]   Judgment of the Labour Chamber of the Supreme Court of 20 January 1997.

Q9.4.2   The mere fact of the transfer entitles neither the transferor nor the affected employees to terminate their employment contracts.

Q9.4.3   In the event that the employment relationships of the transferor and transferee are governed by different CBAs, the CBA applicable before the transfer continues to be applicable to the transferred employees until the date on which its period of enforceability ends or until a new CBA becomes applicable.[1] However, if the new employer is subject to a more favourable CBA, it would apply to the employees affected by the transfer.[2]

[1]   Article 3.3 of Directive 77/187/EEC.
[2]   Judgments of the Labour Chamber of the Supreme Court of 5 and 10 December 1992.

Labour and Social Security liabilities arising from the transfer

Q9.4.4   When a business, undertaking or part of a business or undertaking is transferred, both the transferor and the transferee are jointly and severally liable for:

- All employment obligations arising prior to the transfer date that have not been fulfilled. This liability continues for three years from the date of the transfer.
- Payment of all contributions to the Social Security system accrued before the transfer date. This liability has a statutory limitation of five years from the date on which such contributions were due.
- All labour and Social Security obligations arising after the transfer date, provided that such transfer is deemed to constitute a criminal offence (ie a transfer which is made in order to defraud the employees' rights; for instance, a transfer of the business to a known insolvent party).

Q9.4.5   The above liabilities, however, may only arise with respect to those employment relationships (linked to the transferred business) existing at the transfer date[1] and to employment relationships which ended prior to the transfer date but with respect to which there are still amounts due and payable.

[1]   Judgments of the Labour Chamber of the Supreme Court of 15 February, 20 March and 17 May 1993 and 24 July 1994.

9.5   Dismissal

Q9.5.1   The mere fact of transfer does not terminate employment contracts. Therefore any termination of an employment contract must be based on one of the general reasons set out at para **Q6.1.1**.

9.6   Variation of Contract

Q9.6.1   The transferee of a business, undertaking or part of the same is subrogated insofar as all employment rights and obligations of the transferring employees are concerned. If employment conditions are, however, modified by the new employer, the employee is entitled to the remedies set out at paras **Q1.3.1–Q1.3.7**.

9.7   Duty to Inform and Consult

Q9.7.1   The transfer of a business must be notified to the legal representatives of the transferor's employees. Failure to serve that notice does not render the transfer invalid; however, such failure is considered a serious breach which may be fined by the Labour Authorities: fines range from Ptas 50,001 (€ 300.50) to Ptas 500,000 (€ 3,005.06). If no employees' legal representatives have been elected, notice must be given to all the affected employees.

Q9.7.2   Employees' legal representatives have no right of veto nor to place conditions on the transfer of the business.

Q9.7.3   The notification must be made by the transferor or, failing this, by the transferee. Quite frequently, such a notification is made jointly by the transferor and the transferee. The SW does not provide any time period during which the transfer must be notified to the employees' legal representatives. Article 44 of the SW does not require that such notification be served prior to the transfer date, nor within a certain period of time.

Article 6 of Directive 77/187/EEC sets out that the notice must be served in good time before the transfer is carried out. Thus, since Directive 77/187/EEC should be used for interpreting national rules, the notice should be served prior to the transfer.

Q9.7.4 The notification should at least contain the identity of both employers, the employees affected, and the date on which the transfer becomes effective. Moreover, in accordance with Directive 77/187/EEC, the employees' representatives must be informed of the reasons for the transfer. This, however, apparently does not require an exhaustive explanation of the reasons.

Q9.7.5 Further, when the legal structure of the company is altered (for instance, as a result of a merger) and such a change is likely to affect the employment levels, the employees' legal representatives have the right to issue an informative report within a period of 15 days. This report does not bind the employer.

Q9.7.6 In some industrial sectors, subrogation is provided by CBAs in the case of service agreements.

Q9.7.7 In the event of the termination of a service agreement and subsequent execution of another agreement with a different company, some CBAs (eg cleaning, private security, etc) provide for the subrogation of the new contractor in all the employment rights and obligations of the former contractor with respect to the employees assigned to the rendering of such services.

Q9.7.8 Further, the terms and conditions of service agreements executed with government bodies frequently envisage that the service provider must be subrogated in all the employment rights and duties of the previous service provider with respect to its employees.

10   COLLECTIVE RIGHTS AND BARGAINING

10.1 Background

Q10.1.1 Employees are represented by works councils (*comités de empresa*) and employees' delegates (*delegados de personal*), depending on the number of employees of the company or work centre. In principle, works councils and employees' delegates are elected in each work centre if that the company has more than one.

10.2 Compulsory Recognition

Q10.2.1 Employees in companies or work centres with 11 to 49 employees are represented by employees' delegates and in companies or work centres with 50 or more employees by works councils In companies or work centres with six to 10 employees, the employees may appoint one employees' delegate, if the majority so decide.

Q10.2.2   The employees' delegates jointly represent the employees of the relevant work centre or company. In companies or work centres with up to 30 employees, one employees' delegate may be appointed, and in companies with 31 to 49 employees, three employees' delegates may be appointed.

Q10.2.3   A works council is a committee of legal representatives for all of the employees of the work centre for which it was elected. The maximum number of employees' representatives in a works council varies depending on the number of employees of the work centre, as follows:

Number of employees	Number of representatives
From 50 to 100	5
From 101 to 250	9
From 251 to 500	13
From 501 to 750	17
From 751 to 1,001	21

Q10.2.4   From 1,001 employees upwards, there are two additional representatives for each 1,000 employees, up to a maximum number of 75 members.

Q10.2.5   The normal duration of the representatives' term of office is four years. However, there are certain cases in which elections may be called before that term is up such as:

(i)   when the majority of the electorate, summoned to a special assembly by one-third of the electorate, decides by means of secret, personal, free and direct vote to revoke the mandate of the previously elected employees' representatives; or

(ii)   when the prior electoral process has been found null and void by a court.

Q10.2.6   If four years have elapsed and no elections have been called, the mandate of the elected representatives will continue until new elections have been held.

10.3 The Consequences of Recognition

Q10.3.1   The SW grants various rights and powers to the legal employee representatives, whether employees' delegates or members of the works councils, which may be summarised as follows:

- the right to receive quarterly information from the company regarding developments in the relevant economic sector, as well as information regarding production and sales and likely developments in employment;
- the right to receive the basic copies[1] of all contracts that must be executed in writing, as well as copies of extensions and terminations of such contracts;
- the right of access to the employer's balance sheet, profit and loss statement, annual report, and any other documents made available to the shareholders, in the same way that the shareholders receive them;

- the right to produce a report prior to implementation by the company of decisions concerning:
  - (i) staff restructuring and dismissals;
  - (ii) reductions of working time;
  - (iii) relocation in whole or part of the facilities;
  - (iv) programs for professional training;
  - (v) establishment or revision of labour organisation and control systems; and
  - (vi) incentive systems, evaluation of positions, professional classifications, flexible schedules, and work shifts.
- the right to issue a report when the merger, absorption or change of the legal status of the company implies any consequence that may affect the volume of employment;
- the right to be informed as to the types of employment contracts that are being used in the company, as well as to receive information concerning the documents related to termination of such contracts;
- the right to be informed of all sanctions the employer imposes on employees for very serious breaches or violations of workplace rules;
- the right to be informed at least quarterly of the statistics concerning absenteeism, labour accidents, and occupational disease;
- the right to oversee the employer's compliance with
  - (i) labour and Social Security regulations and
  - (ii) rules for occupational safety and health;
- the right to participate in the negotiation of the CBA;
- the right to participate, as determined by the CBA, in the management of social projects established in the company for the benefit of the employees or members of their families;
- the power to co-operate with the company's management to obtain the establishment of measures that may ensure the maintenance and increase the productivity, in accordance with the CBA; and
- the power to keep the employees they represent informed about all the abovementioned matters when they have either direct or indirect consequences for employment relationships.

[1] The basic copy includes the most relevant data of the contract, except for the identity card number, domicile, and any other data that could violate an employee's right of personal privacy.

Q10.3.2 Employees' delegates and members of works councils enjoy the following protections or labour guarantees (*garantías laborales*), without prejudice to any additional protections that may be determined through the CBA:

- priority for retention in the company in the case of collective suspension or dismissal, or in cases of work centre changes;
- the right not to be dismissed or penalised during the performance of their functions or during the year following the expiration of their mandate, if the penalty is based on actions undertaken in the exercise of their representative functions;
- freedom to express their opinion in matters relating to their representative functions; and
- a credit of paid working hours to use for the performance of their functions as employees' legal representatives.

10.4 Collective Bargaining and Collective Representation

Q10.4.1 Collective bargaining agreements are concluded by representatives of the employees and employers, in order to determine labour and productivity terms and conditions, as well as to achieve peaceful labour relationships through mutual obligations.

Q10.4.2 The scope of application of collective bargaining agreements varies greatly; a CBA may apply to a single work site, to a company or a group of companies, to sectors of activity, or on a local, provincial, regional or national basis. By means of CBAs, the employees and the employers establish the terms and conditions for employment which are binding for all employees and employers included within their scopes of application and throughout the entire term they are in effect.

Q10.4.3 CBAs cannot contain working conditions considered to be inferior to those established by the Statute of Workers or other laws or regulations. Therefore, a CBA can only maintain or improve such minimum conditions.

Q10.4.4 The negotiating parties of a CBA are responsible for establishing the duration of the CBA. The CBA succeeding a previous one cancels the previous agreement in its entirety unless otherwise agreed. CBAs shall be renewed on a yearly basis if no express notice of termination is served by any of the parties.

11   EMPLOYMENT DISPUTES

11.1 Background

Q11.1.1 The Labour Jurisdiction (see para **Q11.2.1**) is competent to decide any dispute related to the following matters:
- disputes between employers and employees as a consequence of their employment relationships;
- Social Security matters;
- disputes against the Government, when it is liable in accordance with labour provisions; employers' associations and trade unions; and
- union elections, challenge of collective bargaining agreements and industrial conflicts.

11.2 Labour Courts/Tribunals

Q11.2.1 The Labour Jurisdiction consists of the following judicial bodies:
- Labour Courts (*Juzgados de lo Social*). There can be several such courts in a district, each served by a sole judge. In general terms, these courts are competent to deal with all sorts of individual claims arising out of employment contracts or Social Security issues.
- Labour Chambers of the High Courts of Justice (*Salas de lo Social de los Tribunales Superiores de Justicia*). A High Court of Justice exists in every Autonomous Community (*Comunidad Autónoma*).[1] Such a court can be split into different divisions, each one composed of three judges. These Chambers handle appeals against rulings of the Labour Courts and first

instance cases regarding trade union issues, collective bargaining agreements and industrial conflicts, where the territorial scope does not exceed the geographical limits of the relevant Autonomous Community.

- Labour Chamber of the National Court (*Sala de lo Social de la Audiencia Nacional*). There is only one court of this category, located in Madrid, which is competent for the entire Spanish territory and is composed of three judges. It is the court of the first instance for the same types of cases as the High Court of Justice where the dispute affects the territory of more than Autonomous Community.
- Labour Chamber of the Supreme Court (*Sala de lo Social del Tribunal Supremo*). Again there is only one such court, and it is located in Madrid. It is split into divisions, each of which is composed of five judges. The Social Chamber in the Supreme Court is competent for special appeals (*recursos de casacion*), revision appeals (*recursos de revision*) and resolves conflicts of jurisdiction between Labour Courts which do not have a common higher court.

[1] Autonomous Communities are political and administrative units consisting of one or more provinces having historic, cultural and economic common features. There are 19 Autonomous Communities in Spain. Autonomous Communities have some political power and autonomy.

11.3 Settlements

Q11.3.1 Before filing any court proceedings, certain prerequisites must be fulfilled. Such prerequisites aim to solve individual labour disputes without the intervention of the labour courts.

Q11.3.2 Arbitration before the SMAC (see paras **Q6.4.1** and **Q6.4.2**) or entities created by collective bargaining agreements must take place prior to filing a claim before the labour courts. However, labour conflicts relating to holidays, Social Security, union elections, challenging collective bargaining agreements and others are exempt from this requirement. In addition, arbitration is not required when the prior administrative claim referred to in the following paragraph must be filed. Settlement agreements reached as a result of individual or collective arbitration proceedings have full effect on the parties involved and may be enforced as if they were judicial rulings.

Q11.3.3 Before filing suit against the Government, the Autonomous Communities, municipalities or state agencies on employment matters, a claim with the relevant administrative body (for instance, to attack an Infraction Act of the Labour Inspection) must be filed. Once the administrative body has rejected the claim, or after one month has passed without any express decision having been issued, the court procedure can be initiated.

12 WHISTLEBLOWING/DATA PROTECTION

12.1 Whistleblowing

Q12.1.1 There is no specific legislation on whistleblowing in Spain. However, a general obligation of confidentiality exists in Spanish law. This obligation arises from the duty of good faith that must be respected by the employee. As a consequence, the constitutional right to freedom of information may be limited by the employer to prevent communication by an employee to a third party of information of a privileged nature or information used to voluntarily prejudice the company.

12.2 Data Protection

Q12.2.1   Under Spanish law, the protection of personal data is governed by Law 15/1999 of 13 December on personal data protection. It entered into force on 14 January 2000 and implements Directive 95/46/EC. In general terms, this body of law establishes various provisions to protect individuals with respect to the processing of personal data and to regulate its transfer.

13   HUMAN RIGHTS

13.1 Rights and Obligations

Q13.1.1   Human rights is a subject that generally goes beyond the framework of Spanish employment law. Nevertheless, some labour law provisions specifically aim to protect human rights. For example, under Spanish law the hiring of workers under 16 years of age is prohibited, and any such employment contracts celebrated are absolutely null and void. Likewise, the right of equality is expressly included in employment legislation, and as a consequence, any behaviour based on discriminatory reasons of race, sex, affiliation with a trade union, among others, are prohibited under Spanish law.

USEFUL WEBSITES

Ministry of Labour and Social Issues (*Ministerio de Trabajo y Asuntos Sociales*):
*   http://www.mtas.es

National Institute of Employment (*Instituto Nacional de Empleo* – INEM):
*   http://www.inem.es

International Labour Organisation (*Organización Internacional del Trabajo* – OIT):
*   http://www.ilo.org/public/spanish/index.htm

National Institute of Health and Safety at Work (*Instituto Nacional de Seguridad e Higiene en el Trabajo*):
*   http://mtas.es/insht

Social Security System (*Secretaría de Estado de la Seguridad Social*):
*   http://www.seg-social.es

National Institute of Health (INSALUD):
*   http://www.msc.es/insalud

Migrations and Social Services Institute (*Instituto de Migraciones y Servicios Sociales* – IMSERSO):
*   http://www.seg-social.es/imserso

Economic and Social Council (*Consejo Económico y Social*)
*   http://www.ces.es

R   Sweden

Sven Erfors

Sven Erfors is a Partner at Lindh Stabell Horten KB, Stockholm. He has practised law since 1983. He has considerable experience in labour law. He is a member of the Swedish Bar Association and was admitted to the bar in 1988.

Lindh Stabell Horten KB, Stockholm

Phone: +46 8 701 7800
Fax: +46 8 796 8223
Email: Sven.Efors@lindhs.se
Website: www.lsh-law.com

SWEDEN

Rights	Yes/No	Explanatory Notes
CONTRACTS OF EMPLOYMENT		
Minimum notice	YES	For indefinite term contracts
Terms:		
Express	YES	
Implied	YES	
Incorporated by statute	YES	Statutory obligation to provide written particulars
REMUNERATION		
Minimum wage regulation	NO	
Further rights and obligations:		
Right to paid holiday	YES	Annual working time in Sweden is shortest in the world
Right to sick pay	YES	Employer pays sick pay for 13 days thereafter payable by National Security
WORKING TIME		
Regulation of hours per day/ working week	YES	40 hour weekly limit
Regulation of night work	YES	Free time for nightly rest
Right to rest periods	YES	36 consecutive hours weekly rest
EQUAL OPPORTUNITIES		
Discrimination protection:		
Sex	YES	
Race	YES	
Disability	YES	
Religion	YES	
Age	NO	
Sexual orientation	YES	
Equal pay legislation	YES	
TERMINATION OF EMPLOYMENT		
Right not to be dismissed in breach of contract	YES	
Statutory rights on termination	YES	'Just cause' requirement
REDUNDANCY/COLLECTIVE DISMISSALS		
Right to payment on termination	NO	Other than notice pay
Right to consultation:		
Collective	YES	
Priority ratings	YES	Based on length of service and age

YOUNG WORKERS

Protection of children and young persons at work	YES	

MATERNITY RIGHTS

Right to maternity leave	YES	14 weeks and time off to breastfeed
Maternity pay (during leave)	YES	Statutory maternity pay
Protection from dismissal	YES	
Health and safety protection	YES	
Right to parental leave	YES	

TRANSFERS OF BUSINESSES

Right to protection on transfer	YES	Implements EC Directive 77/181
Transfer of employment obligations	YES	
Right to information and consultation	YES	
Right not to be dismissed	YES	May be justifiable for economic or organisational reasons

COLLECTIVE RIGHTS

Compulsory recognition of trades unions	YES	Sweden is heavily unionised (70% of working population)
Right to take industrial action	YES	Industrial action is lawful

EMPLOYMENT DISPUTES

Civil court jurisdiction	YES	Labour Court (*Arbetsdomstolen*)
Statutory body	NO	

1 THE EMPLOYMENT RELATIONSHIP

1.1 Background

R1.1.1 In Sweden, the traditional employer's freedom to hire at will prevails. Union attempts to impose restrictions on this have met with very little success. The most important statute in this area is the Employment Protection Act[1] (EPA) which contains rules on the duration of employment contracts. A distinction is made between contracts for a limited period and contracts for an indefinite period. Generally speaking, indefinite employment offers the employee considerably better legal protection since the employer has to have 'just cause' (defined below) to end an employment contract for an indefinite period. Since the aim of the EPA is to protect employees it is only natural that it favours indefinite employment by restricting employer freedom to contract for a limited period. Employment agreements for a fixed term period may be entered into in the following cases:

- agreement for a specific period or seasonal job if this is required by the specific nature of the work;
- agreement for a specific period in connection with a temporary stand-in, practical experience or a holiday job;
- agreement for a specific period, subject to a maximum of six months in any two-year period, if this is necessary on account of temporary peak work loads;
- agreement for the period prior to the employee's commencement of national service or other comparable service that will be more than three months in duration;
- agreement for a specific period of employment after retirement, if the employee has reached an age requiring him to leave his employment on pension or, if there is no such obligation to retire, when the employee has reached 67 years of age.

[1] SFS 1982:80.

R1.1.2 Under Swedish law, agreements to perform work fall into two major categories; employment agreements and contract agreements. Labour law is concerned with employment agreements. The distinction between the two is of great importance. Whereas the employment relationship is covered by a vast body of law, there is little legislation concerning contract work. Furthermore, labour law on the whole aims to protect one party to the contract, the employee, which in Sweden is often referred to as the weaker party of the contract. Labour law is binding upon employers, in the sense that provisions in employment contracts which are contrary to the rules in statutes or in collective agreements are void. This applies to important rules in the EPA, for example the employee cannot negotiate shorter terms of notice than those stated.

R1.1.3 The distinction between employment work and contract work is decisive, not only for the purposes of deciding the applicability of relevant employment legislation, but also for legislation in many other areas, such as taxation and social security. Swedish law offers no definition of what an employee is. The concept is broad and is interpreted in accordance with the facts and circumstances in each case.

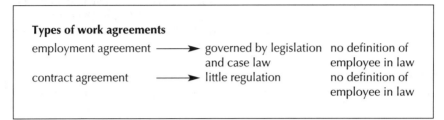

1.2   Contract of Service

R1.2.1   In general, an employee is obliged under the terms of his employment contract to carry out work personally according to the instructions of his employer, at the employer's risk and expense, under the employer's supervision and in the employer's name. In consideration of this duty, the employee receives pay, usually based on time spent on the work.

R1.2.2   Under the EPA, s 6a there is a statutory obligation for the employer to provide written particulars of the terms and conditions applicable to the employment. The information must be provided to the employee no later than one month following the commencement of service. The following information must be included:

- name and address of the employer and employee;
- place where the work should be performed;
- description of the work to be performed or statement of position or job category;
- when the employment commences;
- the expected duration of the employment if it is not for an indefinite period of time;
- the employee's rights as regards payment and holiday;
- termination provisions and notice periods;
- the rate of pay including benefits or other allowances such as pension contributions and payment dates;
- the usual working hours per day or per week;
- specification of any collective agreement covering the employment.

R1.2.3   Any subsequent amendments or arrangements should also be notified to the employee in writing no later than one month following the amendment/arrangement.

OBLIGATIONS OF EMPLOYERS AND EMPLOYEES

R1.2.4   The law on the relationship between employers and employees is based on the principle of freedom of contract. However, in reality there are few contractual provisions, this area being ruled by generally prevailing principles of law with roots in the pre-industrialisation master and servant relationship. That relationship gave rise to an employer's prerogative to direct and distribute work.

R1.2.5 Employee obligations are of a different kind. The most important is what employees can be obliged to do: for example, what work they can legally be assigned. Other aspects are such as where, when and how the work is to be performed. Employees are generally subject to the employer's discretion as to what their duties are (and how to perform them), although discrimination and unfairness are not tolerated.

R1.2.6 Employees have far reaching obligations of loyalty to their employer eg the duty to look after the employer's interests, to perform work in a careful and diligent way, to maintain secrecy regarding confidential information obtained during their employment and to refrain from competing with the employer. Upon termination of employment there is no ban on competition unless there is specific contractual provision, but Swedish law looks on restrictive covenants with a certain amount of suspicion and they can be partially or totally set aside by the courts. Employees may spend their spare time as they see fit, but case law nevertheless imposes several restrictions, in general against anything that could have an injurious effect on the employee's job performance. The fruits of an employee's labour belong to the employer in most instances. This also applies in the intellectual property field, though many statutory and contract provisions exist here, for example, the Act on Employee Inventions.[1]

[1] SFS 1949:345.

R1.2.7 Employers have far-reaching obligations as well. The principal duty is to provide paid work. If no work is provided, employers are still obliged in most instances to pay the employee.

1.3 Variation of Contract

R1.3.1 Far-reaching changes in work assignments can be subject to court review and, in some instances, even employee consent. For example, the employer is not allowed to demote an employee who is hired for white-collar work to a lower level to fulfil less qualified tasks. Apart from these rather exceptional instances, the general rule is that employees can be transferred from one job to another. In other words, job classification does not restrict employer discretion.

2 REMUNERATION

2.1 Background

R2.1.1 There is no legislation governing minimum pay in Sweden. A large number of employees are affected by different collective agreements. Collective agreements and regulations often provide for a minimum wage and every employer who is a member of an organisation is obliged to follow the regulations set out in the relevant collective agreements.

3   FURTHER RIGHTS AND OBLIGATIONS

3.1   Holiday Entitlement

R3.1.1   Employees are entitled to time off for several reasons. In fact the combined effect of all schemes for time off is such that the annual working time in Sweden is among the shortest in the world.

R3.1.2   Leave for child-birth and childcare is the oldest scheme for time off. The present Act on Parental Leave[1] is not confined to mothers and society actively promotes paternal leave. Thirty days of the parental leave is must be used by the male. The parents are not allowed to transfer these 30 days to the mother (this can be done with all the other days).

[1]   SFS 1995:584.

R3.1.3   Leave for annual vacation is the second oldest scheme. The Act on Vacation[1] applies to the entire labour market, private as well as public. It entitles employees to a total of 25 days of paid vacation, Saturday and Sunday not counting as holidays. Payment equals earnings during a corresponding period of work, with a slight over-compensation. Only those who have been employed over a 12-month period prior to the vacation year are entitled to full payment.

[1]   SFS 1977:480.

R3.1.4   Numerous other schemes exist. There are rules on time off to study, and Acts concerning the right to:

(i)   education;[1]
(ii)   education in the Swedish language for immigrants;[2]
(iii)   time off due to family matters;[3]
(iv)   time off to carry out business;
(v)   search for another job;
(vi)   hold elected political office; and
(vii)   do military service.

In addition to statutory schemes, collective agreements often allow leave in other instances, for example for personal or family matters.

Time off

Working time in Sweden is among the shortest in the world.

Rights to time off include

- 25 days of holiday
- parental leave
- time off for education
- time off to learn Swedish
- time off to deal with domestic affairs
- time to carry out business, look for another job, hold elected political office and do military service.

---

[1]   SFS 1974:981.
[2]   SFS 1986:163.
[3]   SFS 1998:209.

3.2 Sick Pay

R3.2.1 Regulation of sick pay entitlement is found in the act concerning sick payment.[1]

[1] SFS 1991:1047.

R3.2.2 An employee is entitled to sick pay from the first day of his employment. If the agreed employment time is shorter than one month the right to sick pay arises only after the employee has been employed for 14 consecutive days.

R3.2.3 The basis for calculation of sick pay is the salary received by the employee.

R3.2.4 There is no compensation for the first day of the sick period. For the following 13 days the employer must pay sick pay. After 14 days of sick pay in a row the responsibility to pay is taken over by the National Security system.

4 WORKING TIME

4.1 Background

R4.1.1 Traditional employer discretion to decide when work is to be performed, working hours, working schedules, is greatly restricted by provisions in the Working Time Act[1] (40-hour weekly limit) and in collective agreements. Generally speaking, an eight-hour day and a Monday to Friday working week prevails. As to where work is to be performed, the law is less clear but it is fair to say that absent contractual provisions to the contrary employees are not obliged to accept transfers which involve significant geographical moves.

[1] 982:673.

4.2 Legislative Control

R4.2.1 The National Board of Occupational Safety and Health and the Labour Inspectorate supervise compliance with the Act and the regulations issued.

4.3 Night Work

R4.3.1 All employees have free time for nightly rest. This free time includes the hours between 24:00 and 5:00. Deviations may be made from the rule where certain types of work need to be continued during the night or otherwise carried on before 5:00 or after midnight on account of their nature, the needs of the general public or other special circumstances.

4.4 Rest Period

R4.4.1 In every period of seven days employees must have not less than 36 consecutive hours free time (weekly rest). This weekly rest shall not be taken to include stand-by hours, when an employee is allowed to stay away from the workplace but must remain at the employer's disposal in order to carry out work should the need arise. Weekly rest shall as far as possible take place at weekends.

R4.4.2 Temporary exceptions may be made if there are special circumstances which the employer could not have foreseen.

5   EQUAL OPPORTUNITIES

5.1   Background

5.1.1   In Swedish labour law equal opportunity means equality between women and men. The Equal Opportunity Act (EQA)[1] dates from 1993, but Sweden introduced its first legislation in this area in 1979. The EQA is drafted to conform with corresponding legislation in the EU. Discrimination on the grounds of sex, colour, religion, sexual orientation,[2] ethnic or national origin is prohibited.

[1]   SFS 1991:433.
[2]   Sexual Preference Discrimination Act 1999. Sexual preferences are defined as homosexual, bisexual and heterosexual.

5.2   Unlawful Discrimination

R5.2.1   The EQA aims at promoting equal rights for women and men with regard to employment, conditions of employment and other conditions of work, as well as opportunities for personal development in employment. Direct and indirect sex discrimination is prohibited. The EQA protects both men and women but it aims primarily at improving women's conditions in working life. The EQA applies to both employees and job seekers. The EQA contains two sets of rules, one setting out active measures to promote equality and one containing prohibitions against discrimination.

R5.2.2   Employers with 10 or more employees must draw up an annual equality plan listing necessary measures, when they are to be executed, and an assessment of the efforts made to reach measures listed in the previous annual plan. Employers failing to comply with their statutory obligation, for example to draw the annual equality plan, can be ordered to do so or pay of a sum of money specified in the order. Such an order is decided by a board for equal opportunity after a request from an ombudsman for equal opportunity.[1]

[1]   *Svenska jamstalldhetsmannen* – Jamo.

R5.2.3   The Act on Actions against Ethnic Discrimination in Working Life (AEDWL)[1] prohibits discrimination due to race, skin colour, religion, national or ethnic origin. Discrimination can be direct or indirect. An employer will have to show, by way of defence to a claim of direct discrimination, that any difference in treatment was due to factors other than race etc. To rebut a claim of indirect discrimination an employer must show objective justification.

[1]   SFS 1999:130.

5.3   Disability (and other) Discrimination

R5.3.1   In Swedish labour law there is also an act[1] against discrimination in the working life of people with physical disabilities and an act against discrimination in the working life of people due to their sexual orientation. Physical disabilities are defined as permanent physical and or learning-disabilities affecting a persons ability to function which is ongoing or is expected to arise.

[1]   *Lag om forbud mot diskriminering i arbetslivet av personer med funktion-shinder,* SFR 1999:132.

5.4   Enforcement and Remedies

R5.4.1   An employee who believes that he or she has been discriminated against can bring a claim in a district court or labour court. If successful, compensation is assessed to cover the employee's loss and to punish the employer, where appropriate. Compensation may be unlimited. Victimisation (ie detrimental treatment because an employee has alleged discrimination) is also unlawful.

5.5   Equal Pay

R5.5.1   There is no specific equal pay legislation, but under the terms of the EQA employees should be paid equal pay for equal work.

6   TERMINATION OF EMPLOYMENT

6.1   Background

R6.1.1   The Employment Protection Act (EPA) is probably the single most important piece of labour legislation in Sweden, at least from the employee's perspective. It completely outlaws dismissal at will and replaces it by a 'just cause' requirement. The EPA has a profound influence on conditions in the workplace and its consequences for personnel policy and personnel management are considerable. It applies to all employees alike, private or public, unionised or not, with only four minor exceptions.

R6.1.2   These exceptions are:
- employees who, taking into consideration their nature of the work and their conditions of employment, can be regarded as holding senior executive or comparable positions (ie managing directors);
- employees who are members of the employer's own family;
- employees who are employed in the employer's household;
- employees who have been assigned to public relief work or protected employment.

Foremost among the exceptions is that for chief executive officers, but it is limited to those holding managerial positions.

6.2   Nature of Claims

R6.2.1   The EPA deals with many closely related yet distinct matters. First comes the section outlining various categories of employment contracts. Second come the most important rules, those on just cause for dismissal including rules concerning procedures and formalities on the termination of employment contracts. Thirdly the EPA contains detailed rules on priority ratings in redundancy dismissal (see para **R7.1.3**).

6.3   Fairness of Dismissal

R6.3.1   The 'just cause' requirement primarily applies to employees hired for an indefinite period. Dismissal may be with or without notice. The distinction is very important since dismissal without notice has a strong stigma and adversely affects the reputation of the employee. Dismissal with notice for disciplinary reasons is also serious but far less so. Consequently dismissal without notice is permitted only in rare situations of truly serious misconduct.

R6.3.2   The most important type of termination is dismissal with notice. The EPA does not define what just cause for dismissal notice means. The legislator wanted to avoid a static and rigid construction that would exclude modifications as attitudes in society and the labour market change. However the EPA states that there is no just cause for dismissal where it is reasonable to the employer to provide the employee with alternative work in his undertaking. The courts have historically held this obligation to be far reaching. If the employer has failed in this respect, there is no just cause for dismissal even though employee misconduct might have justified dismissal if the employer had been unable to find alternative work. Only if no alternative work is available or if the employer cannot reasonably be expected to retain the employee is there just cause for dismissal.

Note

There is no definition of 'just cause' dismissal but it must not be reasonable for employer to find alternative work for employee.

R6.3.3   The EPA distinguishes between two major causes for dismissal with notice, dismissal for reasons relating to the employee personally and dismissal for reason of redundancy. The distinction is crucial since shortage of work always constitutes just cause, whereas protection against dismissal for individual reasons is substantial. Reasons relating to the employee personally are those that take into consideration only the individual employee and his situation at the work place. In most cases dismissal for individual reasons is because of misconduct (disciplinary dismissal), but other circumstances may exceptionally be invoked eg prolonged sickness or chronic alcoholism.

R6.3.4   Under the EPA, employees enjoy considerable protection in respect of dismissal for individual reasons. Employers have a far-reaching duty to try to correct any breaches by pointing them out in advance to the employee, giving the employee a chance to remedy the situation and to assist the employee to that end. Employers have to try to find alternative work for the employee. Generally speaking dismissal is justified only if these attempts fail and provided that the breaches are serious. In many instances employers have to accept conduct that is not exemplary. When reviewing a dismissal the courts make an assessment of all relevant factors such as length of employment, previous conduct, advance warnings, efforts to solve the situation short of dismissal and prospects for a satisfactory employee performance in the future. Dismissal is considered a last resort.

Fairness of dismissal

'Just cause' dismissal with notice

- for personal reasons eg misconduct, sickness
- for redundancy

Personal reasons

- employer must give employee chance to remedy breach
- employer should try to find alternative work
- breach must be serious

Redundancy

- priority ratings apply (see para **R7.1.3**)

TERMINATION OF EMPLOYMENT CONTRACTS

R6.3.5 The EPA contains several rules on termination of contract of employment, covering for example notice, procedures and formal requirements. An employer wishing to discharge or dismiss an employee on the grounds of facts that relate to the employee personally must inform the employee of this fact in advance. If the information relates to a dismissal it must be given at least two weeks in advance, and if it relates to discharge it must given at least one week in advance. If the employee is a member of a trade union, the employer must inform the local trade union organisation to which the employee belongs at the same time.

R6.3.6 The employee and the local trade union organisation to which the employee belongs are entitled to discuss with the employer the action to which the information and notice relate. However, the discussions must be requested no later than one week after the information was given. If discussions have been requested the employer may not effect the dismissal or discharge before discussions have concluded.

Dismissal procedure

Inform employee → inform trade union → discussion between employer and employee and his union

- no dismissal before discussions completed
- correct notice must be given

R6.3.7 One set of rules applies when an employer wants to dismiss a worker and another when the employee voluntarily wishes to leave. The rules are much stricter and more detailed in the former.

R6.3.8 An employee holding a permanent position can be dismissed with or without notice. The EPA spells out notice periods, which range from one month to six months depending on the length of service.

R6.3.9 When an employee wants to leave he is obliged to give a minimum notice period of one month under the EPA, s 11. The employer and the employee have the right to agree on a longer period in the individual employment contract.

R6.3.10 For the employer the notice period starts with one month when the employee has been in service for less than two years, and then increases according to this schedule:

Length of employment	Notice period
Up to 2 years	1 month
2–4 years	2 months
4–6 years	3 months
6–8 years	4 months
8–10 years	5 months
10 years or more	6 months

R6.3.11 Dismissal should be in writing. Oral dismissals are legally effective but render the employer liable to damages. Employees holding fixed-term positions must leave once the agreed-upon period is over but are entitled to notice of formal discharge in many instances. They cannot be dismissed early unless there is truly serious misconduct.

6.4   Remedies

R6.4.1 The most important provision concerning disputes arising out of contested dismissals is one that entitles employees in most instances to continue to work during grievance and disciplinary hearings and court proceedings. An employee's interests not to suffer suspension for any period of time until the dispute has been finally settled prevail over the employer's interests to the contrary, even though the outcome of the dispute might be that there was just cause. Only when the court considers that there are special reasons for suspension or dismissal without notice does the contrary apply.

Note

An employee has the right to continue working throughout grievance and disciplinary hearings and court proceedings.

R6.4.2 Damages, financial and punitive, are the standard sanction for infringements of the many formal, procedural and substantial rules of the EPA. Re-instatement is also a remedy under the Act.

R6.4.3 Dismissal without cause is void. The invalidation order by the court is retroactive in most instances and the employment relationship is considered not to have terminated. Thus there is no need for a re-instatement order in this case, although in some instances an order for re-instatement is needed.

R6.4.4 The EPA anticipates the possibility that an employer will simply refuse to obey an invalidation order or an order to re-instate. The EPA provides that specific enforcement is not possible since there can be no such thing as an enforceable obligation to offer work in employment law. As a consequence the employment relationship is considered to have been terminated but in a costly way. The aggrieved employee is entitled to damages ranging from 16 to 48 months' pay depending on length of service and age. Damages are calculated based on the salary of the employee. Benefits are not normally included in calculating salary loss. Damages are calculated on the basis of the employee's total period of employment with the employer when the employment relationship was terminated and are assessed at an amount corresponding to 16 months' pay in the case of less than five years' employment, 24 months' pay in the case of at least 5 and less than 10 years' employment and 32 months' pay in the case of more than 10 years' employment. If the employee has reached 60 years of age, the amount is increased to correspond to 24, 36 and 48 months, pay respectively.

R6.4.5 However, damages may not be assessed at more months pay than the number of months worked with the employer. If the employee has been employed for less than six months, the amount shall in any case correspond to six months' pay.

7   REDUNDANCY AND COLLECTIVE DISMISSALS

7.1   Background

R7.1.1 'Redundancy' is the common denominator for all other cases of dismissal. The prime example is a true redundancy situation. However, there is no right to a statutory redundancy payment. All cases where the decisive considerations are of a purely business nature belong in this category. Such instances cover a wide spectrum of issues at the core of entrepreneur control which means that management enjoys considerable freedom to dismiss employees for business reasons. Examples include the closing down of a business facility whether or not the business is profitable. Subcontracting also belongs in this category, as does the use of independent contractors or seconded employees. In other words, the EPA does not interfere with employer freedom to manage as it sees fit.

R7.1.2 Employees do not have recourse to the courts since it is not within their remit to assess the merits from a business point of view of changes in the running of business. Employer assessments of the need to undertake a change in the mode of business operations must prevail. The EPA tries to soften the harsh realities of a competitive market in various ways. Dismissal must be with notice. Negotiations in advance with the established unions are mandatory. Priority ratings (see paras **R7.1.3–R7.1.10**) must be made.

PRIORITY RIGHTS

R7.1.3   In redundancy situations the problem arises of whom to dismiss. The EPA contains detailed rules in this regard. Priority rating is based on length of service and age. All employees working in the same production unit and covered by the same collective agreement are rated. The effect of rules in this respect is to widen the group of employees to be rated beyond the immediate focus of redundancy. The rules are based on notions of solidarity among employees and on an assessment of what is best from the point of view of labour market policy generally, rather than business efficiency and employee ability and usefulness to the company.

R7.1.4   This can seem somewhat harsh but is softened by the fact that the employer and the recognised union are allowed to have other solutions according to collective agreements. When negotiations are held between the employer and the recognised union, agreements can also be made that will set the priority rights in the EPA aside.

R7.1.5   An employee's position on the priority list is decided on the basis of each employee's total period of employment with the employer. Employees having long periods of employment are given priority over employees with short periods of employment. In the event of periods of employment of equal length, older employees have priority over younger ones.

R7.1.6   If an employee can only be given continued employment with the employer after transfer, priority in accordance with the priority list is conditional upon the employee having sufficient qualifications for the intended employment (see para **R7.1.9**).

R7.1.7   If the employer operates at several establishments, priority lists are drawn up for each establishment separately.

R7.1.8   If the employer is, or is usually, bound by collective agreements, separate priority lists are drawn up for each regulated area. In such a case, if there are several establishments in the same town, a common priority list within a trade union organisation's area must be drawn up for all the establishments in the town, if the union so requests, no later than during negotiations held between the employer and the organisation.

R7.1.9   Closely related are the rules on priority rights to re-employment. Employees who have been dismissed because of a diminution of work have a prior right to re-employment in the activities where they were previously employed. However, such prior rights are conditional upon the employee having been employed with the employer for a total of more than 12 months during the previous three years (or, in the case of prior rights to a new seasonal employment for previously-employed seasonal employees, for six months during the previous two years) and upon the employee having sufficient qualifications for the new work. The EPA contains rules on

825

payment during the period of notice and during lay-off. In short, prior negotiations are mandatory on all matters governed by the EPA. There are dispute procedure provisions and, finally, rules on sanctions and remedies.

R7.1.10   Employees dismissed for reasons of redundancy enjoy a priority right to re-engagement in the activity where they were previously employed. Several conditions must be met, such as a nine-month limit for re-engagement. Priority rating applies so that re-engagement is in reverse order to dismissal.

8   YOUNG WORKERS

8.1   General Obligations

R8.1.1   The regulations employers must observe when employing minors are to be found in the following:

* the Working Environment Act;[1]
* the Code on the employment of minors issued by the Worker's Protection Body (*Arbetarskyddsstyrelsen*).[2]

[1]   Paragraphs 1–5, Chapter 5 SFS 1977:1160.
[2]   AFS 1996.

R8.1.2   These regulations impose a particular obligation on employers to protect the health and development of young employees. These regulations apply not only to minors employed after they have left full-time education, but also to minors still in full-time education who work for businesses during school holidays and outside school hours.

R8.1.3   'Minor' means an employee who is under 18, ie who has not reached his majority.

A   MINORS UNDER 13 YEARS OLD

R8.1.4   The main prohibition is against work being performed by a person under 13 years old.[1]

[1]   Paragraph 2, Chapter 5 of the Working Environment Act.

R8.1.5   The following types of work are excluded:

* Work involving gardening, the feeding of animals, light manual sowing and planting, fruit picking, clearance of garden plots and smaller cultivated fields together with light farming work where the farm is run by a family member.
* The selling of certain goods for charity, special Christmas newspapers and similar occasional work undertaken as a hobby where the time and place of performance of the work together with its scope is determined by the minor.
* Where the Trades Inspectorate (*Yrkesinspection*) gives permission on a case-by-case basis to a minor to appear as an artist, actor, extra or similar work which is not dangerous and imposes negligible psychological or physical demands on the minor. However, handing out flyers and the sale of goods at performance venues for the employer is not permitted.

B   MINORS BETWEEN 13 AND 15

R8.1.6   This group comprises any minor over 13 years old up to including those whose sixteenth birthday falls in the calendar year in question. This group also includes minors of compulsory school age, the upper limit of which is normally set at the spring term of the calendar year in which the pupil reaches 16 years old.

R8.1.7   The permitted categories of work for this group comprise exclusively light manual and risk-free work ie the minor may not be employed to perform tasks that can have a detrimental effect on his/her health, development or schooling.[1]

[1]   Paragraph 2, Chapter 5 of the Working Environment Act.

R8.1.8   The following are example of the permitted categories:
- office work, eg operating a PC, typing, sorting post, filing and photo-copying;
- commercial work, eg shop assistant (light manual work), check-out worker and price labelling;
- restaurant work, clearing tables (light manual work), serving in restaurants and in coffee shops etc.

C   MINORS BETWEEN 16 AND 17

R8.1.9   This group comprises those minors whose sixteenth birthday falls in the relevant calendar year up to and including those who have not yet reached 18 years old (ie the age of majority). In addition, the minor must not be of compulsory school age.

R8.1.10   Minors within this group may perform normal tasks. The work must not involve physical exertion and shall be performed in a safe environment, preferably during the longer school holidays.

R8.1.11   The minor must not perform work that exposes him to the risk of accident or overexertion or that has a detrimental effect on the minor's health or development.[1] The tasks that a minor is asked to perform must be selected carefully with particular regard to his/her physical or psychological condition. Consequently, tasks that impose a physical, psychological or social strain on the minor shall be avoided, eg those involving heavy manual lifting, movements imposing unequal strain on one area of the body, extremes of climate, noise and vibration, working alone, the risk of attack and similar work tasks.

[1]   Paragraph 3, Chapter 5 of the Working Environment Act.

9   MATERNITY AND PARENTAL RIGHTS

9.1   Background

9.1.1   The rules governing maternity and parental rights are to be found in the general insurance law (SFS 1962:381), predominantly in Chapter 4.

9.1.2 There are various differing types of maternity and parental leave: paid leave, unpaid leave, leave with pregnancy pay and leave with temporary pay.

9.2 General Rights

R9.2.1 There are pre-conditions to all forms of parental leave.

R9.2.2 Women are entitled to 14 weeks' maternity leave, seven weeks before and seven weeks after childbirth. A woman may also have time off to breastfeed.

R9.2.3 To qualify for paid and unpaid maternity and parental leave, the employee must have completed 6 consecutive months of employment or have been employed for 12 months out of the preceding two years at the commencement of the leave.

R9.2.4 As parents, employees have a right to parental leave. The expression 'parent' includes biological parents, adoptive parents, legal guardians who are not the child's parents, employees living in a permanent relationship with someone who is a parent provided they are (or have been) married to each other or have (or have had) children in common, as well as employees who act as foster parents with the intention of adopting the children in their care.

R9.2.5 Paid parental leave can be claimed by both parents together for a period of 450 days in the aggregate. This is funded by State parental insurance. If the parents have more than one child at the same time, paid leave can be claimed for a further 180 days for each additional child. Leave may be taken either before the child is eight years old, or has completed his/her first year at school, or in the case of adoption before the child is 10 years old.

R9.2.6 There is a basic right to unpaid leave which comprises a right to full-time leave until the child is one and a half years old and the right to 25% part-time leave until the child is eight years old, or until the child completes his/her first year at school if that is later. The right to unpaid leave exists independently of and is unaffected by the right to paid leave.

R9.2.7 In relation to the right to leave with pre-confinement maternity pay, female workers with physically demanding work tasks have the right to be transferred to other tasks or to take leave from 60 days before the date of confinement. The right of transfer or leave is also available to women who are expecting a baby, have recently given birth or are breast feeding, subject to the condition that the woman is prohibited from continuing with her normal work in accordance with regulations issued pursuant to the Working Environment Law.

R9.2.8 An employee who wishes to take paid or unpaid parental leave must give notice of this to his/her employer at least two months before commencement of the leave or, if this is not practicable, then as soon as possible. The employee must give notice of the anticipated period of leave at the same time.

R9.2.9   If the leave in question is a result of the illness of the person who ordinarily cares for the child, then no notice is required.

R9.2.10   If the employee cuts short his or her leave, then s/he has the right to return to the same scope of work s/he had before taking leave. The employee must give notice to his/her employer of the intention to return to work as soon as possible. However, the employer is not obliged to allow the employee to return to work earlier than one month after the date of such notice. This does not apply to leave that was intended to last for less than one month.

Maternity rights: summary

- 14 weeks' maternity leave and time off to breastfeed
- qualifying service necessary
- paid parental leave for father and mother – 450 days aggregate (180 days for additional child) – to be taken before child is eight
- *unpaid* leave until child is one and a half, 25% part-time leave until child is eight
- notice for parental leave at least two months in advance
- right to return to same/similar work

9.3   Protection from Dismissal

R9.3.1   An employee must not be given notice or dismissed solely by reason of her/his requesting or demanding the right to maternity/parental leave. An employee's employment benefits or working conditions must not be affected or made worse by reason of a request or demand for such leave. The only change that may occur is change directly related to any actual interruption of work as a result of taking leave. The employee can be transferred if this is necessary as a result of the leave. An employee who shortens his working hours must then continue to perform his work tasks – at least initially. If this is not possible, the employee may be transferred to other duties within the terms of his contract of employment. Various additional payments may be lost as a result of such transfer eg shift pay, extra pay for working unsocial hours. However, the employee may retain such additional pay that is continuously and customarily paid alongside salary. An employee who is transferred during part-time or full-time leave can only return to his old work tasks if they are still there.

9.4   Maternity Pay

R9.4.1   Parental leave payments during the period of leave are made by the Regional Department of Social Security (*Försäkringskassan*) in accordance with the general insurance laws. Parental leave payments are calculated on an annual basis and are paid as follows: 80% of the amount which he/she could expect to receive in state sickness benefit payments for the 300 days which the parents can allocate between themselves, the same amount for the 'mother and father month' which comes to 60 days, and a lower amount is paid for 90 days ie the so-called guaranteed level.

10 BUSINESS TRANSFERS

10.1 Background

R10.1.1 The regulations governing the rights of employees in the event of a transfer of an undertaking are contained in s 6(b) of the Employment Protection Act (ETA).

R10.1.2 The regulations provide that in the event of a transfer of an undertaking or business, or a part thereof, from one employer to another, the rights and liabilities are also transferred ie the contracts of employment and working conditions as exist at the time immediately before the transfer. The old employer is, however, also responsible to the employee for the economic obligations at the time immediately before the transfer. The above regulations do not apply to transfers in insolvency situations.

R10.1.3 An employee can object to his transfer to a new employer.

R10.1.4 The current Swedish regulations are based on Directive 77/187/EEC.

10.2 Identifying a Relevant Transfer

R10.2.1 Merely because all assets are included in the transaction is not of itself sufficient to make it a relevant transfer. There must be a transfer of a going concern. This is particularly important when dealing with a business that is not trading at the date of the transaction. The decisive question is therefore whether the business has retained its identity at the date of the transaction. A business will retain its identity, for example, if the new owner continues or resumes trading carrying out the same or similar economic activities.

R10.2.2 To decide whether the conditions for a relevant transfer are fulfilled, it is necessary to take into account of a number of factors. The most significant factors are:
- the type of undertaking or business;
- whether the undertaking's tangible assets have been transferred;
- the value of intangible assets at the date of transfer;
- whether the majority of the employees are taken over by the new employer;
- whether the customers have been taken over;
- the degree of similarity between activities before and after the transfer; and
- the length of any interruption in the activities.

10.3 Affected Employees/Dismissal

R10.3.1   An employee may not be dismissed solely by reason of the transfer. The seller of the undertaking cannot therefore justify a dismissal solely on the grounds that the undertaking will be sold.

R10.3.2   On the other hand, dismissals not connected with the transfer itself are permitted eg for organisational or economic reasons. The issue of whether someone can be dismissed due to scarcity of work can be a grey area. If the dismissal would have taken place irrespective of the transfer, then such dismissal is permitted by the transferor. In this case, the normal rules about selection for dismissal apply.

R10.3.3   In addition, the transferor may not dismiss employees on behalf of the transferee. Consequently, the transferor and transferee may not come to an arrangement about who shall deal with any potentially surplus workforce. In this situation, all necessary dismissals must be made by the transferee, in which case the rules in the ETA on selection for dismissal apply.

10.4 Effects of the Transfer

R10.4.1   When a relevant transfer of an undertaking or a part of an undertaking takes place, the regulations have the effect of automatically transferring to the transferee the contracts of employment of the relevant employees. As a result, the transferee takes over the rights and liabilities under the contracts of employment in force at the date of the transfer. The transferee is obliged to comply with all terms and conditions in the contract of employment.

10.5 Duty to Inform and Consult

R10.5.1   Employers are obliged to inform established trade unions about matters affecting the business, including any prospective transfer (the Co-determination Act 1976). The transferor must inform and consult unions about any important business decisions which affect members of that union. The obligation is simply to consult rather than to agree, and ultimately the employer can make its own decisions.

R10.5.2   Consultation should take place prior to any firm decision being made and should therefore be early enough to permit meaningful consultation. Failure to comply with the consultation obligations properly or at all may expose the employer to a claim for damages by the union.

11   COLLECTIVE RIGHTS AND BARGAINING

11.1 Background

R11.1.1   The Swedish labour market is heavily organised. The rate of unionisation is around or above 70% of the working population and this rate is not decreasing. Union membership is fairly evenly distributed among the three main sectors of the labour market: private, local government and state. Unions are divided into three main areas, one for blue-collar employees, one for white-collar employees and one for professionals. The blue-collar employees belong to a range of industry-wide unions. These unions have a central organisation, the Swedish Confederation of Trade Unions (*Svenska Landsorganisationen*).

R11.1.2 White-collar employees are strongly unionised as well, mainly belonging to the Central Organisation of Salaried Employees (*Tjänstemännens Centralorganisation*).

R11.1.3 Among professionals, the unionisation rate is somewhat lower in the private sector than in the public service sector, where it often reaches a very high level with over 80% of employees being members of the union. The majority of unionised professionals belong to national craft unions which work together in a central organisation.

R11.1.4 Employers in the private sector are organised in much the same way and to the same extent. Most of them either belong to industry-wide organisations of employers or sign their own collective agreements. The Swedish Employers Federation (SAF) completely dominates the private sector. In the public sector, central government and the local governments represent the state for the purpose of collective bargaining and employment matters in general.

R11.1.5 Strong elements of trust, corporation and mutual understanding between the employer and the employee are further characteristics of the industrial relations system in Sweden. A high degree of acceptance of employee trade unionism on the part of employers and of appreciation of trade union contribution to the day-to-day running of business is coupled with acceptance on the part of the union movement of employer freedom to manage the business and the technological change. In most instances the relationship between an employer and his organisation and the union is firm and long standing.

11.2 Compulsory Recognition of Unions

R11.2.1 Three statutes govern this issue: the Trade Union Representatives Act,[1] the Joint Regulation of Working Life Act[2] ('the Joint Regulation Act') and the Act on Board Representation for Employees in Private Employment.[3] Replacing previous statutes dating from the 1920s and 1930s but adding several rules aiming at introducing employee participation in decision making, the Joint Regulation Act is the focal piece of Swedish labour legislation and covers virtually the entire area of collective bargaining and industrial relations. The Joint Regulation Act introduces a scheme for consultation but final decision-making powers remain firmly in the hands of management and the employer.

[1] SFS 1974:358.
[2] SFS 1976:580.
[3] SFS 1987:1245.

R11.2.2   The Joint Regulation Act does not provide employees with any rights within the domain of joint regulation, nor does it substitute employer freedom to direct and distribute work regarding the direction and distribution of work. Instead the Joint Regulation Act invites recognised unions to participate at their own discretion in a dynamic process of directing and distributing work.

11.3 The Consequences of Recognition

R11.3.1   Employees and employers enjoy full freedom of association both in the private and the public sectors. Four separate rights are specified in the Joint Regulation Act:
- to belong to a labour market organisation;
- to make use of the membership;
- to work for the organisation; and
- to work to establish an organisation.

Any violation renders the wrongdoer liable to damages, financial as well as punitive.

R11.3.2   Strength at the bargaining table does not stem from legal requirements and bargaining behaviour but on the willingness and ability on the part of unions to resort to industrial action. Nevertheless, bargaining in Sweden tends to produce a settlement between the negotiating parties instead of a conflict or, in the worst cases, a strike. A breach of the duty to bargain is sanctioned by damages, which of course are often punitive.

R11.3.3   Every union is entitled to bargain collectively with an employer employing at least one of the union's members. All unions have a corresponding duty to bargain with the employer at the latter's request: in other words, the right and duty to bargain is reciprocal. Bargaining rights extend to all levels of trade union hierarchy and the corresponding hierarchy on the employer side. This generally takes place at two levels, local and central.

R11.3.4   By definition a collective agreement is an agreement in writing between an organisation of employers or an employer and an organisation of employees about conditions of employment or about the relationship between employers and employees. The subject of collective agreements is as wide as possible. On the employees' side, only an association can be a part of a collective agreement, not a group of employees even if acting together.

R11.3.5   A collective agreement is legally binding upon the parties to the agreement since they do not act solely as agents for their members but for themselves as well. Unless otherwise stated in the agreement, it is also binding upon all members of the parties to the agreement. If the agreement is industry-wide, it binds all individual members and member organisation on both sides. Since membership rates are very high and since there is an industry-wide agreement in almost every sector of the economy, it follows that the vast majority of the employees and employers in any particular sector of the labour market are covered by such an agreement.

R11.3.6 Collective agreements are mandatory for the employees and employers covered by them. Unless the collective agreement provides otherwise, they have no authority to agree on terms and conditions inconsistent with the collective agreement.

R11.3.7 Anyone in breach of a collective agreement is liable to damages, both financial and punitive. On the employees' side, both the aggrieved employee and the union are entitled to damages.

R11.3.8 Employers traditionally enjoy far reaching managerial rights. Legislation from the mid-1970s and afterwards has changed this to some extent. The Joint Regulation Act is the focal piece of legislation. On the whole, the Joint Regulation Act does not deprive employers of their traditional rights. The employer retains the right to make unilateral decisions but it is obliged to negotiate with the established union before making a decision. The underlying purpose of the Joint Regulation Act is that negotiations will bring about joint decisions in most instances.

R11.3.9 The most important part of the Joint Regulation Act is a set of rules imposing an obligation on employers to negotiate with the recognised union before making decisions. All decisions at the workplace can be submitted to negotiation but it would serve no useful purpose to impose negotiations on all decisions. The Joint Regulation Act acknowledges that and limits the scope of mandatory negotiations in advance to matters involving an important change to either the employer's activities or work or employment conditions of employees. Other decisions are exempted from negotiation in advance but will be submitted to negotiation at the request of the recognised unions.

R11.3.10 An employer can excuse itself from awaiting the outcome of mandatory negotiations only if there are urgent reasons, and from union-initiated negotiations only for special reasons. Since no managerial exemptions exist, the rules imply a virtually complete ban on unilateral employer decision-making procedures.

A   INFORMATION

R11.3.11 A condition for joint regulation is that the employee representatives are adequately informed about the employer's business. The Joint Regulation Act contains provisions aimed at bridging the gap in knowledge and information. The majority of information is given during the negotiations. In addition the Joint Regulation Act imposes an obligation on employers to keep the established union continuously informed about how its activities are developing economically and in respect of production, and to provide guidelines for personnel policy. The established union also has the right to examine books, accounts and other documents concerning the employer's activities. Rules on confidentiality apply to protect sensitive information.

B   BOARD REPRESENTATION

R11.3.12 The Act on Board Representation for Employees in Private Employment entitles the established unions to elect members to boards in limited companies and co-operative associations. A number of conditions must be met. One is that the association must have at least 25 employees. Unions are entitled to elect two members of the board but employee representatives always remain in the minority. With few exceptions, employee board members may hold the same positions as those members representing the business. They have no power of veto so they cannot stop majority decisions taken against them.

11.4 Industrial Action

R11.4.1 A basic principle in Swedish labour law is that industrial action is lawful. All industrial action that is not specifically prohibited is permissible and legal. No social justification is required.

R11.4.2 Industrial action is firmly in the hands of labour market organisations. Most importantly, no concerted action by groups of employees is ever legal industrial action: the action always has to be decided upon by an organisation. This is regardless of whether or not the employees are members of a union or if there is a collective agreement in force. Only actions authorised by a union are permissible, provided in addition that a decision has been duly taken in accordance with the by-laws of the union. A corresponding principle applies for employers who are members of an employer organisation. Employees of non-organised employers are the only individuals that can legally resort to industrial actions of their own volition without organisational support. Most of the labour market organisations vest the right to make decisions of industrial actions at a high level in the hierarchy. Votes by members are not required by law and rules to that effect are very rare indeed in union rules.

R11.4.3 The Joint Regulation Act provides that a stoppage of work – lockout or strike – blockade, boycott or other comparable industrial actions are permissible. The Joint Regulation Act does not explain what comparable actions are, that is left to the courts to decide. One very common comparable action in Sweden is when the union refuses to work overtime.

12 EMPLOYMENT DISPUTES

12.1 Background

R12.1.1 Disputes over the proper meaning of agreements, collective or individual, can ultimately be settled by the courts. Since a court decision cannot be obtained immediately after a dispute has arisen, the problem is how are the parties to act in the meantime? Historically employees have been under a far-reaching duty to obey orders by employers. This body of law is referred to as the employer's 'priority of interpretation'. That priority was not in accord with generally prevailing principles of contract law. However, in most instances where the priority right is invoked, the decision will be final. It is simply not feasible in practice to contest every decision imposed by means of the priority power.

R12.1.2 In the 1970s a number of statutes shifted the priority of interpretation to the employee. The Joint Regulation Act represents the most important switch. Priority rights refer to matters of contractual interpretation only and not to matters of suitability, where the employer retains sovereignty. Under the Joint Regulation Act the recognised union has priority rights of interpretation in three situations, one of which is of considerable importance: where there is a dispute over a member employee's contractual duty under an agreement to perform work. The duty to perform work under a collective agreement or an individual employment agreement is far reaching and includes a number of only loosely related matters. First and foremost come matters concerning proper job functions but other matters are also covered, such as where and when work is to be performed, aspects concerning how it is to be formed and the duty to obey. Employers can overrule union interpretations only in rare situations.

12.2 Labour Courts/Tribunals

R12.2.1 Illegal practices exist in the labour market, as elsewhere. These are dealt with in a number of ways. The union veto right under the Joint Regulation Act is one. Essentially this represents a delegation of public authority to the unions. The right to veto is concerned with contracts with employers to allow a person to perform certain work on his behalf or in his business without that person thereby being employed by him. In other words, union veto rights are aimed at contracts circumventing labour law in favour of contract work.

R12.2.2 Disputes between employees and employers who are covered by a collective agreement are heard by the Labour Court (*Arbetsdomstolen*). Case law in Sweden is of great importance.

R12.2.3 Disputes between unorganised employers and employees can be heard by the district courts in Sweden.

S Switzerland

Dr Rudolf von Erlach and Cyrill P Rigamonti

Dr Rudolf von Erlach holds two law degrees from the University of Zürich (lic iur and Dr iur, both magna cum laude) and a master's degree from the University of Michigan Law School. He is a member of the Zürich and Swiss Bar Associations as well as of several international associations and committees. He is a partner in the law firm of CMS von Erlach Klainguti Stettler Wille and the author of a book on Swiss taxation and of several articles on legal topics including employment and business immigration law.

Cyrill P Rigamonti graduated magna cum laude from the Univerisity of Zürich Faculty of Law, and holds an LLM degree, with distinction, from Georgetown University Law Center in Washington, DC. Prior to joining CMS von Erlach Klainguti Stettler Wille, he worked for a large law firm and interned in the US Court of Appeals for the Federal Circuit, both in Washington, DC. He is admitted to practice in New York and has authored legal articles on a variety of topics published both in the US and Switzerland.

CMS von Erlach Klainguti Stettler Wille, Zürich

Phone: +41 1 285 11 11
Fax: +41 1 285 11 22
Email: office@vonerlach.ch; r.vonerlach@vonerlach.ch
Website: www.vonerlach.ch

SUMMARY TABLE

SWITZERLAND

Rights	Yes/No	Explanatory Notes
CONTRACTS OF EMPLOYMENT		
Minimum notice	YES	Indefinite term contracts terminable on notice periods between seven days and three months
Terms:		
Express	YES	
Implied	YES	
Incorporated	YES	
REMUNERATION		
Minimum wage regulation	NO	
Further rights and obligations:		
Right to paid holiday	YES	Four weeks paid holiday
Right to sick pay	YES	Salary payable by employer for limited period of time
WORKING TIME		
Regulation of hours per day/ working week	YES	45/50 hours per week depending on type of employment
Regulation of night work	YES	Generally prohibited with limited exceptions
Right to rest periods	YES	Minimum breaks depending on daily working hours
EQUAL OPPORTUNITIES		
Discrimination protection:		
Individuality	YES	Broader anti discrimination law not limited to eg race or gender. Dismissals are considered 'abusive'
TERMINATION OF EMPLOYMENT		
Right not to be dismissed in breach of contract	YES	
Statutory rights on termination	YES	
COLLECTIVE DISMISSALS		
Statutory definition	YES	Between 10–30 employees depending on size of organisation
Right to consultation:		
Collective	YES	A dismissal in breach is considered abusive
YOUNG WORKERS		
Protection of children and young persons at work	YES	Generally no employment of children under age of 15

MATERNITY RIGHTS

Right to maternity leave	YES	Compulsory leave of eight weeks after childbirth (subject to limited exception). Dismissal prohibited for 16 weeks after childbirth
Maternity pay (during leave)	NO	Despite legislative proposals no public maternity insurance at present
Protection from dismissal	YES	No dismissal whilst pregnant and for 16 weeks after childbirth
Health and safety protection	YES	
Right to parental leave	NO	
Right to time off for dependants	NO	

TRANSFERS OF BUSINESSES

Right to protection on transfer	YES	
Transfer of employment obligations	YES	
Right to information and consultation	YES	Employer's representative body must be informed and consulted about transfer
Right not to be dismissed	YES	Dismissal considered abusive unless employer informs and consults

COLLECTIVE RIGHTS

European works councils	YES/NO	No implementation of EC Directive but legislation provides for informing and consulting employees with participation rights for employees
Right to take industrial action	YES	Industrial action is lawful under certain circumstances

EMPLOYMENT DISPUTES

Civil court jurisdiction	YES	
Statutory body	YES	Employment Tribunals in half of the Cantons

WHISTLEBLOWING

Protection from dismissal/ detriment	NO	No specific legislation but general principles of loyalty and confidentiality apply

DATA PROTECTION

Protection	YES

HUMAN RIGHTS ACT

Statutory protection of human rights		
Public authority	YES	European Convention applies
Private organisations	NO	But convention taken into consideration by courts and tribunals

839

1 THE EMPLOYMENT RELATIONSHIP

1.1 Background

S1.1.1 Switzerland follows the continental tradition of distinguishing between public and private law. This fundamental distinction affects, inter alia, the body of law applicable to employment relationships in that there are different legal bases for employment relationships of government personnel and those of private employees.

S1.1.2 While employment relationships with private employers are essentially governed by individual contracts, collective bargaining agreements, and statutory rules contained in the Swiss Code of Obligations[1] (CO), employment relationships of federal, state or local government personnel are subject to the public law of the respective public entity, ie government personnel statutes and individual orders of employment issued by the employing government agencies.

[1] *Bundesgesetz vom 30 März 1911 betreffend die Ergänzung des Schweizerischen Zivilgesetzbuches (Fünfter Teil: Obligationenrecht)* [SR 220].

S1.1.3 Such personnel statutes sometimes incorporate by reference specific provisions of the Swiss Code of Obligations, but generally, there is a tremendous variety of different rules to be considered. This is due to the fact that Switzerland has a federal system consisting of the Swiss Federation and 26 Cantons (similar to states), which are often subdivided into municipalities. Therefore, the following overview is limited to the law governing private employment relationships, which is essentially the law of employment contracts.

1.2 Contract of Service

A NATURE OF A PRIVATE EMPLOYMENT CONTRACT

S1.2.1 Under Swiss law, an employment contract is a contract whereby the employee is obliged to perform work in the employer's service for either a fixed or an indefinite period of time, and the employer is obliged to pay wages based either on time periods (time wage) or on the work performed (piecework wage).[1] It is concluded by a legally binding offer and a corresponding acceptance, ie by mutual agreement.

[1] See art 319 para 1 CO.

S1.2.2 As compared to other contracts involving services, the most distinctive feature of the employment contract is the employee's personal and organisational dependence. This illustrates a relationship in which the employee is legally subordinate, ie the employee is not free to choose the time, place or type of work he will perform. For instance, contracts for legal services concluded between lawyers and their clients typically lack such legal subordination and, accordingly, do not qualify as employment contracts. Consequently, different statutory rules will apply.

B   FORMATION OF A PRIVATE EMPLOYMENT CONTRACT

S1.2.3   As for contracts in general, there is no statutory requirement that an employment contract must be in writing in order to be valid.[1] An employment contract may be concluded orally or even inferred from the parties' behaviour. Therefore, an employment contract is deemed to have been concluded if the employer accepts a person to work in his or her service for a given time, when such work, under the circumstances, is only to be expected for wages.[2] Moreover, if an employee performs work in good faith under an employment contract which subsequently proves to be invalid, both parties are bound to fulfil their duties under the employment relationship in the same manner as if the contract were valid.[3] In conformity with this general rule, there is no statutory obligation to provide written particulars of employment, as there is no requirement that there be any written evidence of the terms of the contract. Nevertheless, in practice, contracts are often in writing.

[1]   See art 320 para 1 CO.
[2]   See art 320 para 2 CO.
[3]   See art 320 para 3 CO.

S1.2.4   Under some circumstances, however, employment contracts and certain clauses within them must be in writing in order to be enforceable. For example, apprenticeship contracts[1] and travelling salesman's contracts[2] must be in writing in order to be valid.[3] Furthermore, while a regular employment contract does not need to be in writing, certain individual provisions within an employment contract must be in writing in order to be enforceable. For example, the parties may stipulate that overtime will not be paid or that the notice periods for termination of the employment contract are shorter than the ones provided by the statutory default rule (but not lower than the statutory minimum), but they can only do so in writing.[4]

[1]   Pursuant to art 344 CO, an apprenticeship contract is a contract whereby the master is obliged to train the apprentice in the required manner for a specific trade and the apprentice is obliged to perform work in the master's service for this purpose.
[2]   Pursuant to art 347 CO, a travelling salesman's contract is a contract whereby a travelling salesman undertakes to act as an intermediary or conclude business of any kind outside the premises of the employer on behalf of the owner of a trading, manufacturing or other business carried on in a commercial manner for a salary.
[3]   See art 344a para 1 CO; art 347a para 1 CO.
[4]   See art 321c para 3 CO; art 335c para 2 CO.

C   SOURCES OF EMPLOYMENT CONTRACT TERMS

Express terms

S1.2.5   As a rule, the content of a private contract may, within the limits of the law, be established at the discretion of the parties,[1] in accordance with the fundamental principle of freedom of contract. Therefore, oral or written express terms are the primary source of contract terms.

[1]   See art 19 para 1 CO.

Examples of express terms

S1.2.6

- *Summary dismissal.* As will be further explained (see paras S6.3.7 ff) the employer has the right to terminate the employment contract summarily for cause, ie for 'valid reasons'. Sometimes, it may be difficult to establish whether specific behaviour qualifies as a valid reason for immediate termination. Therefore, employment contracts sometimes expressly define what type of behaviour is considered a valid reason justifying summary dismissal.

- *Intellectual property rights.* By statute, inventions belong to the employer if the employee was hired to invent.[1] However, if the employee was not hired to invent, but still creates an invention while performing his or her employment activity, the invention does not belong to the employer by statute. Therefore, employment contracts may contain express provisions reserving the employer's right to acquire such inventions.

- *Confidentiality.* It is an implied term that an employee must not breach his duty of confidentiality, but an employment contract may set out express terms defining the subject matter of such confidentiality.

- *Non-competition clauses.* Within their discretion, the parties may agree on a post-termination restrictive covenant prohibiting any competitive activity by the former employee within a certain geographic area during a certain time period.[2] Such a clause is often agreed upon if an employee has access to sensitive data, trade secrets, or business confidential information.

- *Foreign employees.* If a residence or work permit is required with respect to a foreign employee, the employment contract must contain a clause stating that it is concluded only under the express condition that the necessary permits will be granted.

[1]   See art 332 para 1 CO. Note that for industrial designs and models as well as copyrights, other rules apply.
[2]   See art 340 CO.

Statutory default rules (implied terms)

S1.2.7   In the event that the parties to an employment contract do not incorporate an express term on a certain issue, statutory default rules may apply. Because these rules apply to every employment contract in the absence of an express term to the contrary, the statutory default rules are essentially implied terms. For example, the employee has implied duties of loyalty, confidentiality and due care regardless of whether or not these duties are expressly agreed upon in the individual employment contract. The same is true for the employer's implied duties, such as the duty to care for the employee's health and safety.

Standard employment contracts

S1.2.8   'Standard employment contracts' are similar to statutory default rules, but are limited to certain types of employment contracts. They are not collective agreements, but governmental decrees establishing provisions concerning the conclusion, content and termination of individual types of employment relationships.[1] Like statutory default rules, the provisions of standard employment contracts apply directly to the relevant employment relationships, unless the parties have agreed otherwise. In terms of formalities, it should be noted that standard employment contracts may provide that agreements deviating from some of its specific provisions are required to be in writing in order to be valid.[2]

[1]   See art 359 para 1 CO.
[2]   See art 360 CO.

Mandatory statutory rules

S1.2.9   There are certain mandatory statutory terms which automatically apply to every employment contract under the Swiss Code of Obligations. The Code breaks these terms into two categories: those which cannot be altered to the detriment of either party,[1] and those which cannot be altered to the detriment of the employee only.[2]

[1]   See art 361 CO.
[2]   See art 362 CO.

Incorporated terms

S1.2.10   In order to facilitate the administration of the workforce, companies may wish to use standard employment conditions or employee manuals or other pre-formulated terms and conditions. If the employee does not actually sign – ie specifically agree to - these standard agreements, they only apply if they were properly incorporated into the individual contract, which may be done by reference. The mere existence of such employment conditions or manuals is not sufficient to make them legally binding.

S1.2.11   There are instances in which such standard terms and conditions are not binding *despite* the fact that they were incorporated into the individual contract. Aside from the obvious requirement that such standard conditions must be lawful in order to be valid, the parties may agree upon a provision in their contract which contradicts provisions in the standard employment conditions or employee manuals to which their contract refers. In such cases, the contract overrides the standard conditions. Furthermore, if a party did not have the opportunity of reviewing the content of the standard conditions prior to agreeing to a contract which incorporates the standard conditions by reference (as opposed to an incorporation by recitation of provisions), a Swiss court is likely to find that the conditions are not binding. Moreover, the conditions are not binding if they are incorporated by reference and the clause at issue is unusual in that a party did not know about the clause and did not have a reason to expect its inclusion, either because the clause is not typical in such a contract or because the clause was 'hidden' in the fine print of the document.

Judicial amendments

S1.2.12   If the individual employment contract is silent on a certain issue in dispute, and if there is no applicable statutory or customary law, the court may 'amend' the contract based on what the parties would have reasonably agreed upon, had they included an express term governing the dispute. In the case of 'typical' contracts, however, the court may 'amend' the contract based on a rule it would create if it were the legislature, ie based on a rule that is sufficiently broad to be applicable to any 'typical' contract as opposed to just the one at issue.[1]

[1] See art 1 para 2 of the Swiss Civil Code (CC) (*Schweizerisches Zivilgesetzbuch vom 10 Dezember 1907* [SR 210]).

1.3 Variation of Contract

S1.3.1 According to a general principle of the Swiss law of contracts, the terms of a contract may not be changed unilaterally. Alterations to contractual terms require mutual consent, unless a right to modify is provided for in the contract itself within the limits of the law. Therefore, if one party wishes to change the terms of the employment contract, the existing contract must be terminated and the terms of the new contract have to be negotiated anew. If one party nevertheless 'changes' the terms of the contract unilaterally, and the other party does not object to such change, but continues to perform the contract according to the new terms, then that party may be deemed to have consented to the new contract with the new terms.

1.4 Remedies

A   EMPLOYEE'S REMEDIES

S1.4.1 In terms of remedies available to employees, Swiss law distinguishes between a breach of the employer's principal duty to pay the salary and breaches of secondary duties.

> If the employer refuses to pay the salary agreed upon, the employee has three options:
> - the employee may refuse to work and still be entitled to payment for the period during which he or she refused to work in response to the employer's failure to pay the salary for work already performed;[1]
> - the employee may enforce the salary claim by instituting debt collection proceedings or by suing the employer in court for specific performance and damages;
> - in cases of repeated and persistent refusals to pay, the employee may terminate the employment immediately and without notice. This is possible even when the employer's failure to pay is due to insolvency, unless the employee is given security for the salary claim within an adequate period of time.[2]

[1] See art 324 CO by analogy.
[2] See art 337a CO.

S1.4.2 If the employer breaches his duty of assistance rooted in the principle of good faith,[1] which includes, inter alia, the safeguarding of the employee's right of individuality and protection against third party breaches, ie by customers, co-workers and supervisors, the employee has the following options:

- The employee may refuse to work.
- The employee may sue for specific performance and for compensation of monetary damages.[2]
- The employee may terminate the employment contract, but will generally have to comply with the notice period requirements applicable to ordinary termination.
- In the event that the employer discriminates against the employee due to gender, the employee is entitled to further remedies based on the Swiss Gender Equality Act (see paras **S5.2.1** ff).

[1] See art 2 para 1 CC.
[2] See art 97 CO.

B   EMPLOYER'S REMEDIES

S1.4.3   The employee's principal duty is to perform personally the work contractually undertaken, and it is implied that the employee has to do so by observing a certain standard of care. Furthermore, the employee owes the employer the duty to safeguard loyally the employer's legitimate interests. As far as the employer's remedies for breach of any such duty is concerned, Swiss law distinguishes between a breach of the principal duty to work and breaches of secondary duties. In any event, however, the employee is liable, according to the general rules governing contracts, for any damages caused by a breach of any of these duties.

If the employee does not perform his duty to work at all, the employer has the following remedies:

- The employer may refuse to pay the salary agreed upon.[1]
- The employer may sue for specific performance, but he or she may generally not obtain injunctive relief preventing the employee from working for another employer.
- The employer may sue for monetary damages, which may be set off against the employee's salary claim; further, the employer is entitled to a general compensation equal to one quarter of the wage for one month, if the employee, without a valid reason, does not appear at the workplace, or if he or she leaves without notice.[2]
- Regardless of any monetary claims, the employer may terminate the employment relationship without notice.

---

[1] See art 82 CO.
[2] See art 337d para 1 CO.

S1.4.4
If the employee performs work, but breaches the duty of care or the duty of loyalty or any other duties arising out of the employment relationship, the employer may not withhold wages or require the employee to work for free in order to make up for the employee's breach of the duty of care.

However, the employer has the following options:

- The employer may sue for monetary damages caused by the employee. He or she may set off such a damages claim against the employee's salary claim, but only if the employee is at fault, as clauses stipulating liability irrespective of the employee's fault are null and void.[1] It should be noted that the standard of care applied to employees is lower than the general standard of care, because one factor to be considered is the employee's abilities and qualities about which the employer knew or should have known.[2]
- The employer may also terminate the employment contract within the ordinary notice periods. In the absence of intent, a breach of the duty of care is generally no reason for immediate termination without notice. However, the employer may enforce the duty of loyalty by obtaining a court order prohibiting the employee from causing further damage to the employer.
- Under certain circumstances and within specified limits, the employer may also use disciplinary measures, especially warnings.

[1] See art 362 CO.
[2] See art 321e para 2 CO.

2 REMUNERATION

2.1 Background

S2.1.1 The amount of the salary owed to the employee by the employer depends on the individual contract or the applicable collective employment contract, if any.

2.2 Legal Regulation of Remuneration

S2.2.1 Generally, there is no statutory minimum wage in Switzerland. However, because individual contractual provisions may deviate from collective employment contracts, provided that such deviation is in favour of the employee, the wages contained in collective employment contracts may be considered the minimum wage.

2.3 Deductions from Wages

S2.3.1 If an individual employment contract does not provide for a specific salary, the customary salary is owed to the employee.[1] The employer is obliged to deduct social security contributions from the employee's salary. Income taxes are not withheld by the employer, unless the employee is a foreigner, in which case the employer is, under certain conditions, obliged to withhold source taxes.

[1] See art 322 para 1 CO.

2.4   Itemised Pay Statement

S2.4.1   An employee is entitled to receive a written wage statement[1] but the statute does not set out any details about what format the statement must have.

[1]   See art 323b para 1 CO.

2.5   Wage Protection

S2.5.1   Because the monthly salary is often the only source of an employee's income, Swiss law provides rules aimed at protecting the employee to ensure that the employee is free to dispose of his or her salary upon payment. For instance, the employee shall be given a written wage statement, and the salary shall be paid in legal tender, unless otherwise agreed upon or customary.[1] Furthermore, it is only possible for the employer to set off his or her counterclaims against wage claims – if at all – to the extent that any wage claim is subject to attachment in an official debt collection proceeding, ie to the extent the wage is not unconditionally necessary for the employee and his or her family.[2] Moreover, agreements as to the use of wages in the employer's interest are null and void,[3] and so are the assignment and pledge of future wage claims to secure liabilities other than support and alimony obligations arising under family law.[4]

[1]   See art 323b para 1 CO.
[2]   See art 323b para 2 CO; art 93 of the Federal Act on Debt Collection and Bankruptcy (*Bundesgesetz vom 11. April 1889 über Schuldbetreibung und Konkurs* [SR 281.1]); note, however, that the employer may set off claims for *wilful* damages without limit.
[3]   See art 323b para 2 CO.
[4]   See art 325 CO; note, however, that the exception for alimony obligations does not apply to future employee benefits, which may not be assigned or pledged at all before they are due (art 331b CO).

3   FURTHER RIGHTS AND OBLIGATIONS

3.1   Holiday Entitlement

S3.1.1   Employers are obliged to grant to each employee at least four weeks of paid annual leave in each year of service, and at least five weeks in the case of juvenile employees until completion of their twentieth year of age.[1] The employer may generally reduce the holiday by one-twelfth for each full month that the employee is prevented from working if the absence is because of a fault of the employee,[2] eg because the employee was driving while intoxicated and caused a car accident preventing him or her from working. As a rule, at least two weeks of holiday shall be granted consecutively in the course of the respective year of service. The employer determines the time of holiday, taking into consideration the employee's wishes to the extent these are compatible with the interests of the enterprise.[3]

[1]   See art 329a CO.
[2]   See art 329b CO.
[3]   See art 329c CO.

S3.1.2 Because it is paid annual leave, the employer is obliged to pay to the employee the full wages otherwise due. In order not to defeat the purpose of the holidays, the employee may not forfeit his time off and take pay or other benefits instead during the employment relationship. By the same token, the employer may refuse to pay the holiday wage and ask for a refund of any payments already made, if the employee performs work for a third party for payment during his holiday.[1]

[1] See art 329d CO.

S3.1.3 The remedies available to the employee for the enforcement of the holiday claim are the same as for any breach of secondary duties by the employer (see para **S1.4.2**).

3.2 Sick Pay

S3.2.1 If the employee is unable to perform the work contractually undertaken due to illness, the employer generally is still obliged to pay the salary for a limited period of time, provided that the employment relationship has existed for more than three months, or that the agreed upon term was more than three months.[1]

[1] See art 324a CO.

Holiday: summary
- 20 days paid leave per annum
- reduction by 1/12th for each month of absence due to employee's fault
- at least two weeks consecutive leave
- no payment in lieu

---

4 WORKING TIME

4.1 Background

S4.1.1 The Swiss Labour Act[1] (LA) and the corresponding Federal Council Ordinances are the most important source of regulations governing working hours,[2] although they also include rules governing young workers, and provisions on health and safety in the workplace and on the protection of women. Generally, the Swiss Labour Act applies to public and private enterprises; and an 'enterprise' exists whenever an employer permanently or temporarily employs one or more employees. However, there are numerous exemptions. For instance, the federal, state and local governments are generally not subject to the Labour Act,[3] and neither are employees in management or teachers in private schools.[4] Therefore, the applicability of the Labour Act and its provisions has to be determined on a case-by-case basis.

[1] *Bundesgesetz vom 13 März 1964 über die Arbeit in Industrie, Gewerbe und Handel* [SR 822.11].

²   Other sources include the Swiss Working Hours Act (*Bundesgesetz über die Arbeit in Unternehmen des öffentlichen Verkehrs* [SR 822.21]), which regulates the working time of public transportation personnel.
³   See art 2 para 1(a) LA.
⁴   See art 3(d) LA.

4.2   Legislative Control

S4.2.1 As a general rule, the maximum weekly working hours for employees subject to the Swiss Labour Act is 50 hours. However, for employees in industrial enterprises and for office personnel, technical personnel and sales personnel in large retail enterprises, the maximum workweek is 45 hours.[1] There are also limits on daily working hours, in that work may not begin before 5:00 in summer and 6:00 in winter and may not continue past 20:00.[2]

¹   See art 9 LA in connection with the Federal Council Ordinance of 26 November, 1975 (*Verordnung zum Arbeitsgesetz über die Herabsetzung der wöchentlichen Höchstarbeitszeit für einzelne Gruppen von Betrieben und Arbeitnehmern* [SR 822.110]).
²   See art 10 para 1 LA.

S4.2.2 While temporary overtime work is allowed under certain circumstances, it may not exceed two hours a day and a total of 220 hours a year, unless the maximum weekly working time is 45 hours, in which case overtime may not exceed a total of 260 hours a year. A permit is required to order overtime work in excess of 60 hours a year, or 90 hours a year if the weekly maximum working time is 45 hours.[1] In any event, the employer is generally obliged to pay at least 25% extra for overtime work unless it is compensated by extra holiday.[2]

¹   See art 12 LA.
²   See art 13 LA.

4.3   Opting Out

S4.3.1 Whenever the Labour Act applies to a particular employer and the employer is not exempt, the employer may not opt out of the regulations. However, it should be noted that any of the above limits on working hours may be deviated from under certain conditions and upon issuance of an according permit by the competent federal government agency. Furthermore, a Federal Council Ordinance issued based on the Labour Act provides for various exceptions to the rules mentioned above. For instance, the maximum workweek of 50 hours is, inter alia, not applicable to hospitals, pharmacies, small restaurants, and petrol stations.[1]

¹   See Federal Council Ordinance of 14 January 1966 (*Verordnung II zum Bundesgesetz über die Arbeit in Industrie, Gewerbe und Handel* [SR 822.112]).

4.4   Night Workers

S4.4.1 As a general rule, night-time work is prohibited. Night-time is defined as the period between 20:00 and 5:00 in summer, and between 20:00 and 6:00 in winter.[1] However, there are exceptions to this rule.

Temporary night work may be allowed by the competent Cantonal Office, if an urgent need for such work is proven. However, it may not exceed nine hours within 24 hours and must be carried out within 10 consecutive hours, including rest periods. Even if allowed, the employer may only select employees who consent to night work. The employer must increase wages paid by at least 25% for night work.[2]

[1] See art 16 LA.
[2] See art 17 LA.

4.5   Rest Periods

S4.5.1   Under the Swiss Labour Act, employees are entitled to certain minimum breaks, which may not be traded in for monetary compensation or other benefits, except at the end of the employment relationship.[1] The length of the rest periods depends on the total daily working hours.[2]

> **Length of rest periods**
> - If the daily working hours are more than five and a half hours, the minimum rest period is 15 minutes;
> - If the daily working hours are more than seven hours, the minimum rest period is 30 minutes;
> - If the daily working hours are more than nine hours, the minimum rest period is 60 minutes.

[1] See art 22 LA.
[2] See art 15 LA.

S4.5.2   Furthermore, if the working week is spread over more than five days, the employees are entitled to have half a day off per week.[1] Additionally, employees are generally prohibited from working on Sundays,[2] but there are exceptions. Occasional work on Sundays may be allowed by the competent Cantonal Office, if an urgent need for such work is proven. However, even in such cases, the employer may only select employees who consent to work on Sundays. For Sunday work, the employer must increase wages paid by at least 50%.[3]

[1] See art 21 LA.
[2] See art 18 LA.
[3] See art 19 LA.

4.6   Paid Annual Leave

S4.6.1   This subject is covered in paras S3.1.1–S3.1.3.

4.7   Remedies

S4.7.1   As far as the enforcement of the Swiss Labour Act is concerned, there are two different mechanisms:

(a) To the extent that the Labour Act imposes a public law obligation on employers and employees which could be part of an individual employment contract, each party is entitled to enforce such obligation as if the obligation were part of the individual employment contract.[1]

(b) In addition to such private action, the Swiss Labour Act is enforced by the cantonal administrative authorities under the supervision of the Federal Council.[2] These government authorities may use general administrative law measures to achieve compliance with the Labour Act on the part of employers and employees.

Additionally, wilful breaches of certain provisions of the Labour Act may give rise to criminal liability.

[1]   See art 342 para 2 CO.
[2]   See arts 41 and 42 LA.

Working time: summary
- 50 hours maximum working week (45 hours for industry, office, technical and sales personnel in retail)
- no working before 5:00 summer/6:00 winter and after 20:00
- temporary overtime up to 2 hours per day (220 hours per annum)
- overtime paid at 25% extra or holiday in lieu
- no opt-out unless permit obtained
- night-time (20:00–5:00/6:00) working prohibited – unless urgent need
- minimum statutory rest breaks

---

5   EQUAL OPPORTUNITIES

5.1   Background

S5.1.1   Under Swiss law, the principle of equal treatment in employment matters is based on the employer's statutory obligation to respect and protect the employee's individuality.[1] As a prohibition of arbitrary treatment of individual employees, this obligation entails a prohibition of less favourable treatment of a certain employee in relation to other employees in comparable positions, unless such different treatment is specifically agreed upon in the individual employment contract. Furthermore, discriminatory dismissals are generally considered abusive (for consequences of abusive termination by notice, see paras **S6.3.2–S6.3.4**). In comparison to the law of other jurisdictions, Swiss law provides a broader anti-discrimination law, because it is not limited to certain criteria such as race or gender. However, for the same reasons, Swiss law is also less specific than the law of other countries. Swiss law offers very specific statutory rules relating to gender discrimination and, to a lesser extent, the right to equal pay for equal work.

[1]   See art 328 CO.

5.2 Gender Discrimination

A OBJECTIVE

S5.2.1 The Swiss Gender Equality Act[1] (GEA) is based on the constitutional mandate requiring the legislature to ensure both de facto and de jure gender equality.[2] In other words, the legislature is not only required to eliminate laws which unjustifiably discriminate between the genders but also to ensure that the laws are effective in promoting day-to-day equality in real life situations. In line with this objective, the GEA applies to all employment relationships, regardless of whether the employer is the government or a private entity.[3]

[1] *Bundesgesetz vom 24 März 1995 über die Gleichstellung von Frau und Mann* [SR 151].
[2] See art 8 para 3 cl 2 Const; art 1 GEA.
[3] See art 2 GEA.

B PROHIBITION AGAINST GENDER DISCRIMINATION

S5.2.2 Less favourable treatment of employees on account of marital status, family situation, or pregnancy qualifies as gender discrimination and is therefore prohibited.[1] Sexual harassment – which includes but is not limited to threats, the promising of advantages, coercive acts or the exercise of pressure in order to obtain favours of a sexual nature – constitutes gender discrimination.[2] However, employers are expressly allowed to discriminate against employees based on gender, if such discrimination consists of reasonable measures whose objective is to achieve equality in fact.[3]

[1] See art 3 para 1 GEA.
[2] See art 4 GEA.
[3] See art 3 para 3 GEA.

C REMEDIES

S5.2.3 In addition to statutory or contractual claims for damages or emotional distress according to the general rules,[1] victims of unlawful gender discrimination have, at their option, the following additional remedies:[2]

*   application for a court order prohibiting the imminent discriminating actions;
*   application for a court order to eliminate the effects of existing discrimination;
*   application for a declaratory judgment in case of persistence of the negative effects of the discrimination;
*   application for a court order to pay the salary owed to the employee.

These general remedies are modified in the case of sexual harassment and if the discriminatory behaviour relates to hiring or dismissal: see paras S5.2.4–S5.2.5.

[1] See art 5 para 5 GEA.
[2] See art 5 para 1 GEA.

S5.2.4 If the discrimination consists of sexual harassment, the employee has an additional remedy. The judge or the competent administrative agency may oblige the employer to pay an indemnity a maximum amount of six months' salary, provided that the employer fails to prove that it took necessary and reasonable steps to prevent sexual harassment from happening in the first place.[1]

³   See art 5 para 3 GEA.

S5.2.5   If, however, the discriminatory behaviour relates to hiring or dismissal in the context of a private employment contract, the above remedies are replaced by a claim for a payment which will be determined by the judge according to the circumstances based on the potential or actual salary.[1] The maximum amount of such payment is three months' salary for discriminatory hiring, and six months' salary for discriminatory dismissal.[2]

¹   See art 5 para 2 GEA.
²   See art 5 para 4 GEA.

S5.2.6   As far as the employer's vicarious liability is concerned, Swiss law requires the employer to make sure that there will be no sexual harassment at the workplace and that the victims of sexual harassment will not suffer additional inconveniences. A violation of this duty constitutes breach of contract.[1]

¹   See art 328 para 1 CO.

D   PROCEDURAL SIMPLIFICATIONS

S5.2.7   In order to facilitate the enforcement of claims based on gender discrimination, the GEA provides two particular procedural devices:

- first, employees benefit from a presumption of discrimination in the context of distribution of tasks, working conditions, salary structure, continuing education, promotion, and dismissal, if the employee is able to show the probability of such discrimination;[1]
- second, certain organisations may, in their own name, file an action for declaratory judgment that specific discrimination exists, if it can be foreseen that the outcome of such action will affect a large number of employment relationships.[2]

¹   See art 6 GEA.
²   See art 7 GEA.

5.3   Disability Discrimination

S5.3.1   There are no specific statutory rules regarding disability discrimination, so the general rules against discrimination apply (see para S5.1.1). It should be noted, however, that the new Swiss Constitution[1] explicitly calls for legislation aiming at eliminating disadvantages affecting the disabled.[2]

¹   *Schweizerische Bundesverfassung vom 18 April 1999* [SR 101].
²   See art 8 para 4 Const.

5.4 Enforcement and Remedies in Discrimination Cases

S5.4.1 Except for gender discrimination (see paras S5.2.1–S5.2.7), Swiss law does not set out any particular remedies for discrimination cases, so the general rules regarding the employer's breach of contract apply (see paras S5.1.1 and S1.4.1–S1.4.4).

5.5 Equal Pay for Equal Work

S5.5.1 The Swiss Constitution provides for equal protection under the law and specifically emphasises the applicability of this principle between men and women.[1] However, as constitutional rights, they are rights to be asserted against the Government and do not directly apply between private parties. Nevertheless, there is an exception regarding the right to equal pay for equal work for men and women, which is directly applicable in the context of private employment contracts by virtue of constitutional law.[2]

[1] See art 8 Const.
[2] See art 8 para 3 cl 3 Const.

S5.5.2 Similar provisions exist with respect to home workers and foreigners. Home workers, ie industrial workers who perform their work at home, are entitled to equal pay compared to industrial workers who perform their work at the employer's place of business.[1] As far as foreigners are concerned, the competent government agency is required to review the terms of employment between a Swiss employer and a foreign employee prior to issuing a work permit. As a condition precedent for such permit, the foreigner must be granted equal pay compared to that of Swiss employees.[2]

[1] See art 4 para 1 of the Home Workers Act (*Bundesgesetz vom 20 März 1981 über die Heimarbeit* [SR 822.31]).
[2] See art 16 para 2 of the Federal Statute on the Temporary and Permanent Residence of Foreigners (*Bundesgesetz vom 26. März 1931 über Aufenthalt und Niederlassung der Ausländer* [SR 142.20]); art 9 of the Ordinance on the Limitation of Employed Foreigners (*Verordnung über die Begrenzung der Zahl der erwerbstätigen Ausländer* [SR 823.21]).

6 TERMINATION OF EMPLOYMENT

6.1 Background

S6.1.1 Because Switzerland is a civil law country,[1] there is no distinction between statutory and common law protection against unfair dismissal. The law governing the termination of employment contracts encompasses unfair dismissal claims. Therefore, the following overview covers the law of termination in general.

[1] In civil law countries such as Switzerland, the primary source of law are the codes and statutes as opposed to judicial precedent, which Swiss courts are not generally bound to follow as a matter of law, even though they regularly do so as a factual matter. Accordingly, judicial decisions are not viewed as an independent source of law (as in common law countries such as the UK and the USA), but rather as a clarification of what is already contained in the statute. As a result, there is no need to distinguish between statutory law and case law or common law.

6.2   General Methods of Termination

S6.2.1   Employment contracts may be terminated by mutual consent,[1] by expiry of a fixed term,[2] by death of the employee,[3] or by unilateral notice of termination.

[1]   See art 115 CO by analogy.
[2]   See art 334 para 1 CO.
[3]   See art 338 para 1 CO. Note, however, that the death of the employer does not automatically terminate the employment agreement: see art 338a CO.

S6.2.2   Because there are numerous mandatory provisions governing notices of termination which might be circumvented by using other methods of termination, Swiss law provides rules aimed at defeating any such attempts of circumvention. For instance, if a contract is terminated by mutual consent, a mandatory provision prevents the employee from waiving any claims resulting from mandatory statutory rules or from mandatory rules contained in collective employment contracts for one month after termination of the employment relationship.[1] Furthermore, in the event of automatic termination of the contract due to expiry of a fixed term, Swiss courts may read the fixed-term contract as a contract concluded for an indefinite period of time, if there was no genuine reason for using a contract for a fixed term other than the circumvention of mandatory statutory rules governing the termination of indefinite contracts.

[1]   See art 341 para 1 CO.

6.3   Notice of Termination

A   GENERAL PRINCIPLES

S6.3.1   Unless stipulated otherwise, notice of termination need not be in writing and need not state any reasons for termination in order to be effective. However, the reasons for termination must be provided in writing upon request by the other party.[1] Upon receipt, the notice of termination becomes irrevocable. Under Swiss law, notices of termination always cover the entire agreement, ie individual provisions alone may not be terminated. There are two different types of notices of termination: ordinary termination with notice and extraordinary termination for cause without notice.

[1]   See art 335 para 2 CO; art 337 para 1 CO.

B   ORDINARY TERMINATION WITH NOTICE

General rules

S6.3.2   Any employment contract concluded for an indefinite period of time[1] may be unilaterally terminated for any reason by both employer and employee,[2] subject to statutory notice periods ranging from seven days to three months, depending upon the nature and length of service.[3] These notice periods may generally be altered by mutual consent,[4] provided that that they are the same for both employer and employee.[5] Swiss statutory law provides protection from termination by notice for both employer and employee, distinguishing between abusive and untimely notice of termination. Unless the law provides otherwise, it is the employee who has to show that the notice of termination was abusive or untimely.[6]

[1] Note that employment contracts concluded for a definite period of time may not be terminated unilaterally, unless the relationship has lasted for over ten years. If so, each party may terminate the relationship with a mandatory notice period of six months effective at the end of a month: see art 334 para 3 CO.

[2] See art 335 para 1 CO.

[3] See art 335b para 1 CO, art 335c para 1 CO.

[4] However, after expiry of the probationary period, the notice periods may be reduced to less than one month only by collective employment contract and only for the first year of service. See art 335c para 2 CO.

[5] See art 335a para 1 CO.

[6] See art 8 CC.

Protection against abusive termination

S6.3.3 With the exception of the last three reasons, which apply to terminations by employers only, termination of the employment contract by either party is considered abusive if given for one of the following reasons:[1]

- personal characteristics of one party (eg race, creed, sexual orientation, age, criminal record), unless they are relevant to the employment relationship or significantly impair co-operation within the enterprise;
- where the other party exercises a constitutional right, unless the exercise of such right breaches a duty of the employment relationship or significantly impairs co-operation within the enterprise;
- where the sole purpose was to frustrate the formation of claims arising out of the employment relationship;
- where the other party asserts, in good faith, claims arising out of the employment relationship;
- where the other party performs compulsory Swiss military service, civil defence service, military women's service, or Red Cross service, or another compulsory statutory duty (eg jury duty);
- where the employee belongs or does not belong to an employee association, or because of a lawful exercise of union activities;
- during the period the employee is an elected employee representative in a company institution or in an enterprise affiliated with it, and, if the employer cannot prove that he had a justifiable reason for the termination;
- in connection with a collective dismissal without prior consultation with the employees' representative body or, if there is none, the employees.

[1] See art 336 CO.

S6.3.4 The party which abusively terminated the employment relationship is legally bound to pay an indemnity not to exceed the employee's wages for six months,[1] above and beyond any claims for damages based on other legal grounds.[2] In order to preserve the claim for indemnity, the party whose contract was abusively terminated must object to the termination in writing no later than the end of the regular notice period. If such objection was validly made and if the parties cannot agree on a continuation of the employment relationship, the claim for indemnity may be asserted in court within 180 days after the end of the employment relationship, otherwise the claim will be forfeited.[3]

1   Note, that if the termination was in connection with a mass dismissal, the indemnity may not exceed the employee's wages for two months: see art 336a para 3 CO.
2   See art 336a CO.
3   See art 336b CO.

Protection against untimely termination

S6.3.5   Termination of the employment relationship after the expiration of the probationary period, if any, is considered untimely, if it was made by the employer – and under certain conditions also by the employee[1] – during the following periods of time:[2]

• during compulsory Swiss military service, civil defence service, military women's service or Red Cross service lasting more than 11 days, and during four weeks before and after the end of service;
• during the period that the employee is prevented from performing his work fully or partially through no fault of his or her own due to illness or accident for 30 days in the first year of service, for 90 days as of the second year of service until and including the fifth year of service, and for 180 days as of the sixth year of service;
• during pregnancy and 16 weeks after the employee has given birth;
• during foreign aid service in which the employee participates with the employer's consent, and where such service has been ordered by the competent federal authority.

1   See art 336d CO.
2   See art 336c CO; art 336d CO.

S6.3.6   Any untimely notice of termination is null and void. In order not to defeat the purpose of the protective periods, the termination notice must be renewed after the expiry of such periods.[1]

1   See art 336c para 2 CO.

Abusive dismissal – statutory reasons → indemnity up to six months wages and damages
Untimely dismissal – statutory reasons → dismissal null and void.

C   EXTRAORDINARY TERMINATION FOR CAUSE WITHOUT NOTICE

General rules

S6.3.7   Both employer and employee have a right to terminate the employment contract immediately and without notice for cause, no matter whether or not the contract was concluded for an indefinite period of time and regardless of any statutory notice periods which would apply in the case of an ordinary termination. By statute, there is cause if the terminating party cannot reasonably be expected to continue the employment relationship, but ultimately, determination of just cause is left to the court to decide.[1] The consequences of extraordinary termination depend on whether the termination was justified, ie whether or not there was cause.

[1] See art 337 CO.

Consequences of justified extraordinary terminations

S6.3.8 If the extraordinary termination was justified, because it was for cause, the court will determine the financial consequences of such termination, taking into account all relevant circumstances. Only if the cause consisted of a party's breach of contract, is that party required by law to provide full compensation for damages arising from the termination of the employment relationship.[1]

[1] See art 337b CO.

Consequences of unjustified extraordinary terminations

S6.3.9 If the employer dismisses the employee without notice and without cause, the employee is entitled to compensation for the sum which he would have earned if the employment relationship had been terminated in compliance with the applicable notice period or until the expiration of the fixed agreement period.[1] Furthermore, the court, in its discretion and taking into account all circumstances, may oblige the employer to pay an indemnity to the employee, which may not exceed the employee's wage for six months.[2]

[1] See art 337c para 1 CO.
[2] See art 337c para 3 CO.

S6.3.10 Similarly, if the employee terminates the employment relationship without notice and without cause, the employer is entitled to a general compensation equal to one quarter of the wage for one month and compensation for further damages. However, the court may reduce such compensation in its discretion, if no damage was caused, or if the actual damages were less than the general compensation. In order to avoid forfeiture of the claim for compensation, the employer must bring a legal action or institute formal debt collection proceedings within 30 days of the employee's failure to appear at or departure from the workplace.[1]

[1] See art 337d CO.

S6.3.11 In summary, while there may be a claim for an indemnity payment in cases of unjustified termination without notice, the legal relationship between employer and employee remains terminated despite the unlawful termination. In other words, there are no rights to reinstatement or re-engagement as provided for in other countries.

6.4 Redundancy and Collective Dismissals – Background

S6.4.1 Swiss law has special rules regarding collective dismissals. Collective dismissals are deemed to be notices of termination in enterprises given by the employer within 30 days for reasons unrelated to the person of the employee and which affect:[1]

- at least 10 employees in enterprises usually employing more than 20 and less than 100 persons;
- at least 10% of all employees in enterprises usually employing more than 100 and less than 300 persons; or
- at least 30 employees in enterprises usually employing at least 300 employees.

[1]   See art 335d CO.

6.5   Collective Redundancies – Consultation

S6.5.1   An employer planning a collective dismissal must first consult with the employees' representative body or, if there is none, with the employees, and provide them with the opportunity to make suggestions on how to avoid the dismissals or to limit the number of dismissals and to alleviate their consequences. The employer is obliged to provide all pertinent information to the employees' representative body and to the Cantonal Labour Office. In any case, the employer must inform them in writing on the following issues:[1]

- the reasons for the collective dismissal;
- the number of employees to be dismissed;
- the number of persons usually employed;
- the time period within which the notification of the dismissals is to be given.

[1]   See art 335f CO.

6.6   Termination in the Context of Collective Dismissals

S6.6.1   If an employer terminates the employment relationship with an individual employee by notice as part of a collective dismissal, the employment relationship ends 30 days after notification of the planned collective dismissal to the Cantonal Labour Office, unless the termination becomes effective at a later time in accordance with contractual or legal provisions.[1]

[1]   See art 335g CO.

S6.6.2   Individual notices of termination are considered abusive by statute, if such notice was given in the context of a collective dismissal and if the employer breached the consultation obligation (as to which see para S6.5.1).[1]

[1]   See art 336 para 2 lit c CO.

7   YOUNG WORKERS

7.1   General Obligations

S7.1.1   The Swiss Labour Act prohibits the employment of children under the age of 15, but there are certain narrowly-tailored exceptions for children over 13.[1] Young workers, defined as employees who have not yet completed their nineteenth year of age and apprentices who have not yet

859

completed their twentieth year of age,[2] enjoy a right to particular assistance and care by the employer.[3] Furthermore, they benefit from a limitation of the maximum working hours to nine hours a day, and the work has to be performed within a time frame of twelve hours. Young workers may not be selected for night work or Sunday work, and if they are under the age of 16, they are not eligible for overtime work.[4]

[1]   See art 30 LA.
[2]   See art 29 LA.
[3]   See art 32 LA.
[4]   See art 31 LA.

8   MATERNITY AND PARENTAL RIGHTS

8.1   Background

S8.1.1   Presently, there are no paternity rights in employment matters under Swiss law. However, the particular situation of pregnant and breastfeeding women is recognised, even though maternity rights are not neatly organised into one single statute. Instead, to the extent they are available, such rights are incorporated into the general law of employment contracts and may have to be inferred from general principles.

8.2   General Rights

S8.2.1   Pregnant women may only work if they consent to work, and they may not be required to work more than the ordinary period of daily work. They are entitled to leave work or stay home based on a simple notification.[1]

[1]   See art 35 LA.

S8.2.2   Women may not work during the eight weeks after delivery, but the employer may, upon request by the employee, shorten this period by two weeks, if the employee's ability to work is proven by a medical certificate. Even after the expiry of the eight-week period, breastfeeding mothers may only work if they consent to such work.[1]

[1]   See art 35 LA.

S8.2.3   While the employer may be allowed to reduce the employee's holiday entitlement if the employee is prevented through his or her fault from working for more than one month in total, such reduction is not allowed if the employee is prevented from working for up to two months due to her pregnancy.[1]

[1]   See art 329b CO.

8.3   Protection from Dismissal

S8.3.1   An employer's termination of the employment relationship during the pregnancy of the employee or 16 weeks after delivery is considered untimely.[1]

[1]   See art 336c lit c CO.

S8.3.2 Discrimination based on pregnancy is prohibited in all employment relationships, including hiring.[1]

[1]   See art 3 GEA.

8.4   Health and Safety

S8.4.1   As in the case of any other employee, the employer must pay due regard to the pregnant woman's health. The law provides that this includes the taking of measures:

•   necessary according to experience,
•   applicable according to the current state of technology, and
•   adequate according to the circumstances of the enterprise,

to the extent that the employer may reasonably be expected to do so, considering the individual employment relationship and the nature of the work to be performed.[1]

[1]   See art 328 CO.

8.5   Maternity Pay

S8.5.1   If the employee is unable to perform her work due to pregnancy, the employer is still obliged to pay the salary for a limited period of time, provided that the employment relationship has existed for more than three months, or that the agreed-upon term of employment was more than three months.[1]

[1]   See art 324a CO.

S8.5.2   In terms of maternity benefits, it should be noted that despite the fact that the Swiss Constitution[1] contains a provision calling for maternity insurance, ie public insurance covering the loss of wages in case of pregnancy, so far the attempts made by the Swiss legislature to pass such legislation have failed. As a result, there is no public maternity insurance in Switzerland at the time of writing.

[1]   See art 116 para 3 Const.

8.6   Additional Rights to Time Off

S8.6.1   Unlike English law, Swiss law does not contain any statutory basis entitling an employee to take time off to care for dependants, but it may be granted by the employer in practice, particularly in cases of emergency.

Maternity rights: summary
•   pregnant women only work if they consent to do so
•   compulsory maternity leave for eight weeks after birth
•   no dismissal during pregnancy and 16 weeks after birth
•   no parental rights

---

9   BUSINESS TRANSFERS

9.1   Background

S9.1.1   As a general rule, if the employer transfers a business or part thereof to a third party, the employment relationship is transferred to the acquiring party, including all rights and obligations as of the date of transfer, unless the employee declines the transfer. If a collective employment contract applies to the transferred employment relationship, the acquiring party is obliged to comply with it for one year, unless it expires earlier or is terminated by notice. Other than in the context of such a business transfer, the employer is not entitled to transfer individual rights under an employment contract to a third party, unless otherwise agreed upon or evident under the circumstances.[1]

[1]   See art 333 CO.

9.2   Identifying a Relevant Transfer

S9.2.1   Two requirements must be met in order for a transfer of a business to be subject to the rules governing business transfers:

a)   a transfer of a business requires the retention of the 'economic identity' of the business prior to the transfer and the business thereafter; and

b)   the transfer must be based on a contract, not based on a statute.

Therefore, business transfers in connection with mergers, transfer of shares of a company, or change of the legal form of a company do not qualify as transfers of business in the legal sense.

9.3   Effects of the Transfer

S9.3.1   If the employee refuses to transfer his contract, the employment relationship is terminated upon expiry of the *statutory* term of notice, as opposed to a potentially deviating *contractual* term of notice. The acquiring party and the employee are legally bound to perform their contractual duties until that termination date. Furthermore, the previous employer and the acquiring party are jointly and severally liable for an employee's claims which have become due prior to the transfer, and those which later will become due until the date upon which the employment relationship could have validly been terminated by contract, or is terminated at the refusal of the transfer by the employee.[1]

[1]   See art 333 CO.

9.4   Duty to Inform and Consult

S9.4.1   Prior to the transfer, the employees or their representative body must be informed about the reason for the transfer, and about the legal, economic and social consequences of the transfer for the employees. If the transfer will result in measures affecting the employees, the employees' representative body must be consulted in time prior to a decision on these measures.[1] Unless the employer complies with these duties to inform and to consult, any dismissal based on the transfer of business is deemed abusive (see paras S6.3.3–S6.3.4).[2]

1   See art 333a CO.
2   See art 336 para 2 lit c CO.

10   COLLECTIVE RIGHTS

10.1 Collective Bargaining Agreements

S10.1.1   Swiss law provides rules on 'collective employment contracts', which are contracts whereby employers, or associations thereof, and labour unions jointly establish provisions concerning the conclusion, content and termination of the individual employment relationships of the participating employers and employees.[1]

1   See art 356 para 1 CO.

S10.1.2   In terms of the legal effects of collective employment contracts, Swiss law distinguishes between provisions resulting in purely contractual rights between the parties to the contract and provisions which are equivalent to statutory rules despite their contractual origin. The latter are mandatory in that they directly apply to the participating employers and employees and in that they may not be changed to the detriment of the employee, unless otherwise provided for by the collective employment contract itself.[1]

1   See art 357 CO.

S10.1.3   It should be noted that collective employment contracts are limited to participating employers and employees, and are generally not binding on outsiders. However, upon request by all parties to the collective employment contract, the government may, under certain circumstances, extend the applicability of the contract to outsiders within the same industry or profession,[1] thereby providing the contract with the legal authority of a statute.

1   See art 1 of the Federal Act on the Extension of the Applicability of Collective Employment Contracts (*Bundesgesetz vom 28 September 1956 über die Allgemeinverbindlicherklärung von Gesamtarbeitsverträgen* [SR 221.215.311]).

10.2 Works Councils

S10.2.1   Since Switzerland is not a member of the European Union, it is not bound by its Directives such as the European Works Council Directive. Nevertheless, Switzerland has enacted a statute on the information and consultation of employees in enterprises,[1] which provides specific participation rights for employees. Elections for works councils must be held if requested by at least 20% of the employees in the case of enterprises with more than 50 employees, or if requested by 100 employees if the enterprise employs more than 500 employees.

1   *Bundesgesetz vom 17Dezember 1993 über die Information und Mitsprache der Arbeitnehmerinnen und Arbeitnehmer in den Betrieben* [SR 822.14].

S10.2.2   Works councils have the right to be informed by the management about all matters relevant to the fulfilment of their tasks. Furthermore, the works councils have a right of participation in matters regarding health and safety measures, transfers of businesses and mass dismissals.

11   EMPLOYMENT DISPUTES

11.1 Labour Courts/Tribunals

S11.1.1   In Switzerland, a variety of courts may have jurisdiction over employment disputes, depending on the subject matter of the particular dispute. For collective labour disputes, for example, conciliatory agencies and arbitrators have jurisdiction. However, as a matter of federal constitutional law, the organisation of the courts on the cantonal level is subject to cantonal law, which provides for different schemes according to the needs and resources of the particular canton. Approximately half of the cantons have specialised employment tribunals whose three-judge panels generally consist of a chairperson (who is an ordinary judge), and two wing members (representing employers and employees, respectively). The details, however, vary from canton to canton. In Zurich, for instance, the Employment Tribunal has jurisdiction over any disputes between employer and employee arising out of their employment relationship, but its jurisdiction does not extend to disputes between the government and its personnel. Furthermore, after the dispute has arisen, the parties may stipulate in writing that their dispute is subject to the jurisdiction of the ordinary courts instead.[1]

[1]   See s 13 of the Zurich Court Organisation Act (*Gerichtsverfassungsgesetz vom 13 Juni 1976*).

S11.1.2   As for the organisation of the courts in general, it is generally a matter of cantonal law which cases may be appealed to appellate courts and, ultimately, to the Federal Tribunal. In the cantons that have employment tribunals, appeals are generally made to ordinary appellate courts. The only exception is Geneva, where an employment appeals court exists. Afterwards, essentially depending upon the amount of money at issue, the aggrieved party may have the right to appeal to the Federal Tribunal.

11.2 Procedural Particularities

S11.2.1   Despite the fact that the law of civil procedure is generally governed by cantonal law,[1] the federal legislature has enacted provisions essentially harmonising the law of civil procedure as applied to matters of employment law.[2] For instance, the cantons must provide a simple and expeditious procedure for cases that have an amount in dispute of no more than CHF 20,000.[3] and no court fees or court expenses must be charged to the parties for such proceedings, except to those parties bringing frivolous actions. It is for the court ex officio to establish the facts and appraise the evidence at its discretion.

1   It should be noted, however, that the Swiss people recently adopted a new constitutional provision empowering the federal legislature to enact a single uniform law of civil procedure to be used throughout Switzerland: see art 122 Const.
2   See art 343 CO.
3   Note that this restriction does not apply whenever the Gender Equality Act applies (art 12 GEA).

S11.2.2   In addition, the Swiss Gender Equality Act provides for free-of-charge conciliatory proceedings conducted by a cantonal conciliation authority to advise the parties and to attempt to settle the dispute prior to the commencement of formal litigation.[1] The conciliatory proceedings are not mandatory, but the cantons may enact rules pursuant to which formal litigation may not be entered into prior to the end of the conciliatory proceedings. If a party wishes to conduct conciliatory proceedings, it must initiate such proceedings before the claim is barred by the applicable statute of limitations. Collective employment contracts may provide for private conciliatory proceedings, instead of governmental proceedings, for disputes between labour unions and individual employees.

1   See art 11 GEA.

11.3 Forum Selection

S11.3.1   If the subject matter of employment litigation does not have any international aspects, the forum is either the domicile of the defendant or, alternatively, the place of the business where the employee works.[1] This forum is mandatory and may not be changed to the detriment of either party by private forum selection clauses.[2]

1   See art 343 CO.
2   See art 361 CO.

S11.3.2   If the subject matter of the international litigation involves member states of the Lugano Convention on Jurisdiction and the Enforcement of Judgments in Civil and Commercial Matters (Lugano Convention), the general forum is the domicile of the defendant[1] or, alternatively, the place of performance, which is defined as the place where the employee usually works.[2] Forum selection clauses excluding this forum are only valid if they have been agreed upon after the dispute arose.[3]

1   See art 2 Lugano Convention.
2   See art 5 no 1 Lugano Convention.
3   See art 17 para 4 Lugano Convention.

S11.3.3   If the subject matter of international litigation does not involve member states of the Lugano Convention, the Swiss Code of International Private Law[1] (CIPL) applies. According to art 115 CIPL, Swiss courts have jurisdiction in the defendant's domicile or in the place where the employee usually performs his work. Additionally, if the employee is the plaintiff, Swiss courts have jurisdiction at the employee's domicile or residence. These jurisdictional provisions are not mandatory, however, and they may be changed by forum selection clauses if the dispute regards monetary claims.[2]

11.4 Choice of Law

S11.4.1   The law applicable to employment contracts is the law of the country in which the employee usually performs his work. If the employee usually performs his work in several countries, the law applicable to the employment contract will be the law of the country of the employer's business establishment or, if such establishment does not exist, the law of the country of the employer's domicile or residence. The parties may provide for a choice of law clause, but their choice is limited to the law of the countries in which the employee usually resides, in which the employer's business establishment is located, or in which the employer has his domicile or usual residence.[1]

¹   See art 121 CIPL.

12   WHISTLEBLOWING/DATA PROTECTION

12.1 Whistleblowing

S12.1.1   Switzerland does not have a separate statute dealing with the issue of whistleblowing. Instead, the general principles governing employment contracts apply. Because of the employee's duty of loyalty,[1] he or she may not provide any information to third parties such as the news media or even government agencies, if the disclosure of such information might be harmful to the employer's reputation, regardless of whether the employee is able to prove that the information disclosed is true. In rare circumstances, a disclosure of internal information to third parties may be absolutely necessary to protect interests that outweigh the employer's right of confidentiality. But even in such cases, the employee must first raise the issue with the employer prior to releasing any information to outsiders. Otherwise, the employee will be in breach of contract.

¹   See art 321a para 1 CO.

S12.1.2   If the facts to be disclosed encompass manufacturing or trade secrets, additional rules must be considered, because the employee is bound by a statutory obligation not to make any use of or inform others of any such secrets.[1] This obligation continues even after the termination of the employment relationship, to the extent required to safeguard the employer's legitimate interests. It should be noted that the breach of the employee's duty of confidentiality need not be intentional to constitute a breach of contract.[2] However, if the disclosure was made intentionally, criminal liability may attach in addition to liability for breach of contract.[3]

¹   See art 321a para 4 CO.
²   See art 321e para 1 CO.
³   See art 162 of the Swiss Penal Code (*Schweizerisches Strafgesetzbuch vom 21 Dezember 1937* [SR 311.0]).

12.2 Data Protection

S12.2.1 The employer may have a legitimate interest in collecting information about a particular employee in order to assess the employee's performance and ability to perform the duties contractually undertaken. However, the employer may only do so to the extent that the data to be collected relates to the fulfilment of the employment contract.[1]

1   See art 328b CO.

S12.2.2 Further, the employer must comply with the Swiss Data Protection Act[1] (DPA). This means that the employer must disclose to the employee that he or she is collecting data about him or her; otherwise, the employer must register any data collection with the Federal Data Protection Officer.[2] Thus, employees must generally be notified in advance about any monitoring of telephone conversations or use of video surveillance equipment which the employer undertakes.

1   *Bundesgesetz über den Datenschutz vom 19 Juni 1992* [SR 235.1].
2   See art 11 para 3 DPA.

S12.2.3   Any application materials submitted by a potential employee for the purpose of recruitment must be given back to the applicant or destroyed, unless the applicant expressly agrees to the employer keeping the materials on file.[1] to An applicant who is rejected by a potential employer is entitled to a written statement about the data processed in the context of the application, eg the content of letters of reference may then be disclosed to the employee.[2] During the employment relationship, the employer must ensure that the data collected about the employee is and remains accurate[3] and that such data is safe from unauthorised access by third parties.[4]

1   See art 12 para 2 lit b, 13 para 2 lit a, 15 para 1 DPA.
2   See art 8 DPA.
3   See art 5 DPA.
4   See art 7 DPA.

13   HUMAN RIGHTS

S13.1.1   The individual rights granted by the European Convention on Human Rights are directly applicable in Switzerland. However, because individual rights under the ECHR must be asserted against the government, persons employed by private employers may not directly invoke these rights against their employer. Nevertheless, human rights should not be disregarded in the context of private employment, because they are taken into consideration by the courts when interpreting and applying broad rules of employment law to specific sets of facts.

Appendix

European Materials

TREATY ESTABLISHING THE EUROPEAN COMMUNITY (THE TREATY OF ROME)

25 March 1957
as revised by the Treaty of Amsterdam with effect from 1 May 1999 (extracts)

Article 12 (ex Article 6)

Within the scope of application of this Treaty, and without prejudice to any special provisions contained therein, any discrimination on grounds of nationality shall be prohibited.

The Council, acting in accordance with the procedure referred to in Article 251, may adopt rules designed to prohibit such discrimination.

Article 39 (ex Article 48)

1 Freedom of movement for workers shall be secured within the Community.

2 Such freedom of movement shall entail the abolition of any discrimination based on nationality between workers of the Member States as regards employment, remuneration and other conditions of work and employment.

3 It shall entail the right, subject to limitations justified on grounds of public policy, public security or public health:

(a) to accept offers of employment actually made;
(b) to move freely within the territory of Member States for this purpose;
(c) to stay in a Member State for the purpose of employment in accordance with the provisions governing the employment of nationals of that State laid down by law, regulation or administrative action;
(d) to remain in the territory of a Member State after having been employed in that State, subject to conditions which shall be embodied in implementing regulations to be drawn up by the Commission.

4 The provisions of this Article shall not apply to employment in the public service.

Article 94 (ex Article 100)

The Council shall, acting unanimously on a proposal from the Commission and after consulting the European Parliament and the Economic and Social Committee, issue directives for the approximation of such laws, regulations or administrative provisions of the Member States as directly affect the establishment or functioning of the common market.

Article 95 (ex Article 100a)

1 By way of derogation from Article 94 and save where otherwise provided in this Treaty, the following provisions shall apply for the achievement of the objectives set out in Article 14. The Council shall, acting in accordance with the procedure referred to in Article 251 and after consulting the Economic and Social Committee, adopt the measures for the approximation of the provisions laid down by law, regulation or administrative action in Member States which have as their object the establishment and functioning of the internal market.

2 Paragraph 1 shall not apply to fiscal provisions, to those relating to the free movement of persons nor to those relating to the rights and interests of employed persons.

3 The Commission, in its proposals envisaged in paragraph 1 concerning health, safety, environmental protection and consumer protection, will take as a base a high level of protection, taking account in particular of any new development based on scientific facts. Within their respective powers, the European Parliament and the Council will also seek to achieve this objective.

4   If, after the adoption by the Council or by the Commission of a harmonisation measure, a Member State deems it necessary to maintain national provisions on grounds of major needs referred to in Article 30, or relating to the protection of the environment or the working environment, it shall notify the Commission of these provisions as well as the grounds for maintaining them.

5   Moreover, without prejudice to paragraph 4, if, after the adoption by the Council or by the Commission of a harmonisation measure, a Member State deems it necessary to introduce national provisions based on new scientific evidence relating to the protection of the environment or the working environment on grounds of a problem specific to that Member State arising after the adoption of the harmonisation measure, it shall notify the Commission of the envisaged provisions as well as the grounds for introducing them.

6   The Commission shall, within six months of the notifications as referred to in paragraphs 4 and 5, approve or reject the national provisions involved after having verified whether or not they are a means of arbitrary discrimination or a disguised restriction on trade between Member States and whether or not they shall constitute an obstacle to the functioning of the internal market.

In the absence of a decision by the Commission within this period the national provisions referred to in paragraphs 4 and 5 shall be deemed to have been approved.

When justified by the complexity of the matter and in the absence of danger for human health, the Commission may notify the Member State concerned that the period referred to in this paragraph may be extended for a further period of up to six months.

7   When, pursuant to paragraph 6, a Member State is authorised to maintain or introduce national provisions derogating from a harmonisation measure, the Commission shall immediately examine whether to propose an adaptation to that measure.

8   When a Member State raises a specific problem on public health in a field which has been the subject of prior harmonisation measures, it shall bring it to the attention of the Commission which shall immediately examine whether to propose appropriate measures to the Council.

9   By way of derogation from the procedure laid down in Articles 226 and 227, the Commission and any Member State may bring the matter directly before the Court of Justice if it considers that another Member State is making improper use of the powers provided for in this Article.

10   The harmonisation measures referred to above shall, in appropriate cases, include a safeguard clause authorising the Member States to take, for one or more of the non-economic reasons referred to in Article 30, provisional measures subject to a Community control procedure.

Article 136 (ex Article 117)

The Community and the Member States, having in mind fundamental social rights such as those set out in the European Social Charter signed at Turin on 18 October 1961 and in the 1989 Community Charter of the Fundamental Social Rights of Workers, shall have as their objectives the promotion of employment, improved living and working conditions, so as to make possible their harmonisation while the improvement is being maintained, proper social protection, dialogue between management and labour, the development of human resources with a view to lasting high employment and the combating of exclusion.

To this end the Community and the Member States shall implement measures which take account of the diverse forms of national practices, in particular in the field of contractual relations, and the need to maintain the competitiveness of the Community economy.

They believe that such a development will ensue not only from the functioning of the common market, which will favour the harmonisation of social systems, but also from the procedures provided for in this Treaty and from the approximation of provisions laid down by law, regulation or administrative action.

Article 137 (ex Article 118)

1 With a view to achieving the objectives of Article 136, the Community shall support and complement the activities of the Member States in the following fields:

- improvement in particular of the working environment to protect workers' health and safety;
- working conditions;
- the information and consultation of workers;
- the integration of persons excluded from the labour market, without prejudice to Article 150;
- equality between men and women with regard to labour market opportunities and treatment at work.

2 To this end, the Council may adopt, by means of directives, minimum requirements for gradual implementation, having regard to the conditions and technical rules obtaining in each of the Member States. Such directives shall avoid imposing administrative, financial and legal constraints in a way which would hold back the creation and development of small and medium-sized undertakings.

The Council shall act in accordance with the procedure referred to in Article 251 after consulting the Economic and Social Committee and the Committee of the Regions.

The Council, acting in accordance with the same procedure, may adopt measures designed to encourage cooperation between Member States through initiatives aimed at improving knowledge, developing exchanges of information and best practices, promoting innovative approaches and evaluating experiences in order to combat social exclusion.

3 However, the Council shall act unanimously on a proposal from the Commission, after consulting the European Parliament, the Economic and Social Committee and the Committee of the Regions in the following areas:

- social security and social protection of workers;
- protection of workers where their employment contract is terminated;
- representation and collective defence of the interests of workers and employers, including co-determination, subject to paragraph 6;
- conditions of employment for third-country nationals legally residing in Community territory;
- financial contributions for promotion of employment and job-creation, without prejudice to the provisions relating to the Social Fund.

4 A Member State may entrust management and labour, at their joint request, with the implementation of directives adopted pursuant to paragraphs 2 and 3.

In this case, it shall ensure that, no later than the date on which a directive must be transposed in accordance with Article 249, management and labour have introduced the necessary measures by agreement, the Member State concerned being required to take any necessary measure enabling it at any time to be in a position to guarantee the results imposed by that directive.

5 The provisions adopted pursuant to this Article shall not prevent any Member State from maintaining or introducing more stringent protective measures compatible with this Treaty.

6 The provisions of this Article shall not apply to pay, the right of association, the right to strike or the right to impose lock-outs.

Article 138 (ex Article 118a)

1 The Commission shall have the task of promoting the consultation of management and labour at Community level and shall take any relevant measure to facilitate their dialogue by ensuring balanced support for the parties.

2 To this end, before submitting proposals in the social policy field, the Commission shall consult management and labour on the possible direction of Community action.

3 If, after such consultation, the Commission considers Community action advisable, it shall consult management and labour on the content of the envisaged proposal. Management and labour shall forward to the Commission an opinion or, where appropriate, a recommendation.

4 On the occasion of such consultation, management and labour may inform the Commission of their wish to initiate the process provided for in Article 139. The duration of the procedure shall not exceed nine months, unless the management and labour concerned and the Commission decide jointly to extend it.

Article 139 (ex Article 118b)

1 Should management and labour so desire, the dialogue between them at Community level may lead to contractual relations, including agreements.

2 Agreements concluded at Community level shall be implemented either in accordance with the procedures and practices specific to management and labour and the Member States or, in matters covered by Article 137, at the joint request of the signatory parties, by a Council decision on a proposal from the Commission.

The Council shall act by qualified majority, except where the agreement in question contains one or more provisions relating to one of the areas referred to in Article 137(3), in which case it shall act unanimously.

Article 140 (ex Article 118c)

With a view to achieving the objectives of Article 136 and without prejudice to the other provisions of this Treaty, the Commission shall encourage cooperation between the Member States and facilitate the coordination of their action in all social policy fields under this chapter, particularly in matters relating to:

- employment;
- labour law and working conditions;
- basic and advanced vocational training;
- social security;
- prevention of occupational accidents and diseases;
- occupational hygiene;
- the right of association and collective bargaining between employers and workers.

To this end, the Commission shall act in close contact with Member States by making studies, delivering opinions and arranging consultations both on problems arising at national level and on those of concern to international organisations.

Before delivering the opinions provided for in this Article, the Commission shall consult the Economic and Social Committee.

Article 141 (ex Article 119)

1 Each Member State shall ensure that the principle of equal pay for male and female workers for equal work or work of equal value is applied.

2 For the purpose of this Article, 'pay' means the ordinary basic or minimum wage or salary and any other consideration, whether in cash or in kind, which the worker receives directly or indirectly, in respect of his employment, from his employer.

Equal pay without discrimination based on sex means:

    (a) that pay for the same work at piece rates shall be calculated on the basis of the same unit of measurement;

    (b) that pay for work at time rates shall be the same for the same job.

3   The Council, acting in accordance with the procedure referred to in Article 251, and after consulting the Economic and Social Committee, shall adopt measures to ensure the application of the principle of equal opportunities and equal treatment of men and women in matters of employment and occupation, including the principle of equal pay for equal work or work of equal value.

4   With a view to ensuring full equality in practice between men and women in working life, the principle of equal treatment shall not prevent any Member State from maintaining or adopting measures providing for specific advantages in order to make it easier for the under-represented sex to pursue a vocational activity or to prevent or compensate for disadvantages in professional careers.

Article 142 (ex Article 119a)
Member States shall endeavour to maintain the existing equivalence between paid holiday schemes.

Article 143 (ex Article 120)
The Commission shall draw up a report each year on progress in achieving the objectives of Article 136, including the demographic situation in the Community. It shall forward the report to the European Parliament, the Council and the Economic and Social Committee.

The European Parliament may invite the Commission to draw up reports on particular problems concerning the social situation.

Article 144 (ex Article 121)
The Council may, acting unanimously and after consulting the Economic and Social Committee, assign to the Commission tasks in connection with the implementation of common measures, particularly as regards social security for the migrant workers referred to in Articles 39 to 42.

Article 145 (ex Article 122)
The Commission shall include a separate chapter on social developments within the Community in its annual report to the European Parliament.

The European Parliament may invite the Commission to draw up reports on any particular problems concerning social conditions.

Article 226 (ex Article 169)
If the Commission considers that a Member State has failed to fulfil an obligation under this Treaty, it shall deliver a reasoned opinion on the matter after giving the State concerned the opportunity to submit its observations.

If the State concerned does not comply with the opinion within the period laid down by the Commission, the latter may bring the matter before the Court of Justice.

Article 234 (ex Article 177)
The Court of Justice shall have jurisdiction to give preliminary rulings concerning:

    (a) the interpretation of this Treaty;

    (b) the validity and interpretation of acts of the institutions of the Community and of the ECB;

    (c) the interpretation of the statutes of bodies established by an act of the Council, where those statutes so provide.

Where such a question is raised before any court or tribunal of a Member State, that court or tribunal may, if it considers that a decision on the question is necessary to enable it to give judgment, request the Court of Justice to give a ruling thereon.

Where any such question is raised in a case pending before a court or tribunal of a Member State against whose decisions there is no judicial remedy under national law, that court or tribunal shall bring the matter before the Court of Justice.

Article 249 (ex Article 189)
In order to carry out their task and in accordance with the provisions of this Treaty, the European Parliament acting jointly with the Council, the Council and the Commission shall make regulations and issue directives, take decisions, make recommendations or deliver opinions.

A regulation shall have general application. It shall be binding in its entirety and directly applicable in all Member States.

A directive shall be binding, as to the result to be achieved, upon each Member State to which it is addressed, but shall leave to the national authorities the choice of form and methods.

A decision shall be binding in its entirety upon those to whom it is addressed.

Recommendations and opinions shall have no binding force.

Article 308 (ex Article 235)
If action by the Community should prove necessary to attain, in the course of the operation of the common market, one of the objectives of the Community and this Treaty has not provided the necessary powers, the Council shall, acting unanimously on a proposal from the Commission and after consulting the European Parliament, take the appropriate measures.

Select Table of Destinations

Treaty of Rome prior to consolidation	Treaty of Rome as consolidated by the Treaty of Amsterdam
art 6	art 12
art 48	art 39
art 100	art 94
art 100a	art 95
art 117	art 136
art 118	art 137
art 118a	art 138
art 118b	art 139
art 118c	art 140
art 119	art 141
art 119a	art 142
art 120	art 143
art 121	art 144
art 122	art 145
art 169	art 226
art 177	art 234
art 189	art 249
art 235	art 308

COUNCIL DIRECTIVE 76/207/EEC

of February 1976

on the implementation of the principle of equal treatment for men and women as regards access to employment, vocational training and promotion, and working conditions

THE COUNCIL OF THE EUROPEAN COMMUNITIES,

Having regard to the Treaty establishing the European Economic Community, and in particular Article 235 thereof;

Having regard to the proposal from the Commission;

Having regard to the Opinion of the European Parliament;

Having regard to the Opinion of the Economic and Social Committee;

Whereas the Council, in its resolution of 21 January 1971 concerning a social action programme included among the priorities action for the purpose of achieving equality between men and women as regards access to employment and vocational training and promotion and as regards working conditions, including pay;

Whereas, with regard to pay, the Council adopted on 10 February 1975 Directive 75/117/EEC on the approximation of the laws of the Member States relating to the application of the principle of equal pay for men and women;

Whereas Community action to achieve the principle of equal treatment for men and women in respect of access to employment and vocational training and promotion and in respect of other working conditions also appears to be necessary; whereas, equal treatment for male and female workers constitutes one of the objectives of the Community, in so far as the harmonisation of living and working conditions while maintaining their improvement are *inter alia* to be furthered; whereas the Treaty does not confer the necessary specific powers for this purpose;

Whereas the definition and progressive implementation of the principle of equal treatment in matters of social security should be ensured by means of subsequent instruments,

HAS ADOPTED THIS DIRECTIVE:

Article 1

1   The purpose of this Directive is to put into effect in the Member States the principle of equal treatment for men and women as regards access to employment, including promotion, and to vocational training and as regards working conditions and, on the conditions referred to in paragraph 2, social security. This principle is hereinafter referred to as 'the principle of equal treatment'.

2   With a view to ensuring the progressive implementation of the principle of equal treatment in matters of social security, the Council, acting on a proposal from the Commission, will adopt provisions defining its substance, its scope and the arrangements for its application.

Article 2

1   For the purposes of the following provisions, the principle of equal treatment shall mean that there shall be no discrimination whatsoever on grounds of sex either directly or indirectly by reference in particular to marital or family status.

2   This Directive shall be without prejudice to the right of Member States to exclude from its field of application those occupational activities and, where appropriate, the training leading thereto, for which, by reason of their nature or the context in which they are carried out, the sex of the worker constitutes a determining factor.

3   This Directive shall be without prejudice to provisions concerning the protection of women, particularly as regards pregnancy and maternity.

4 This Directive shall be without prejudice to measures to promote equal opportunity for men and women, in particular by removing existing inequalities which affect women's opportunities in the areas referred to in Article 1(1).

Article 3
1 Application of the principle of equal treatment means that there shall be no discrimination whatsoever on grounds of sex in the conditions, including selection criteria, for access to all jobs or posts, whatever the sector or branch of activity, and to all levels of the occupational hierarchy.

2 To this end, Member States shall take the measures necessary to ensure that:

(a) any laws, regulations and administrative provisions contrary to the principle of equal treatment shall be abolished;
(b) any provisions contrary to the principle of equal treatment which are included in collective agreements, individual contracts of employment, internal rules of undertakings, or in rules governing the independent occupations and professions shall be, or may be declared, null and void or may be amended;
(c) those laws, regulations and administrative provisions contrary to the principle of equal treatment when the concern for protection which originally inspired them is no longer well founded shall be revised; and that where similar provisions are included in collective agreements labour and management shall be requested to undertake the desired revision.

Article 4
Application of the principle of equal treatment with regard to access to all types and to all levels, of vocational guidance, vocational training, advanced vocational training and retraining, means that Member States shall take all necessary measures to ensure that:

(a) any laws, regulations and administrative provisions contrary to the principle of equal treatment shall be abolished;
(b) any provisions contrary to the principle of equal treatment which are included in collective agreements, individual contracts of employment, internal rules of undertakings or in rules governing the independent occupations and professions shall be, or may be declared, null and void or may be amended;
(c) without prejudice to the freedom granted in certain Member States to certain private training establishments, vocational guidance, vocational training, advanced training and retraining shall be accessible on the basis of the same criteria and at the same levels without any discrimination on grounds of sex.

Article 5
1 Application of the principle of equal treatment with regard to working conditions, including the conditions governing dismissal, means that men and women shall be guaranteed the same conditions without discrimination on grounds of sex.

2 To this end, Member States shall take the measures necessary to ensure that:

(a) any laws, regulations and administrative provisions contrary to the principle of equal treatment shall be abolished;
(b) any provisions contrary to the principle of equal treatment which are included in collective agreements, individual contracts of employment, internal rules of undertakings or in rules governing the independent occupations and professions shall be, or may be declared, null and void or may be amended;
(c) those laws, regulations and administrative provisions contrary to the principle of equal treatment when the concern for protection which

originally inspired them is no longer well founded shall be revised; and that where similar provisions are included in collective agreements labour and management shall be requested to undertake the desired revision.

Article 6
Member States shall introduce into their national legal systems such measures as are necessary to enable all persons who consider themselves wronged by failure to apply to them the principle of equal treatment within the meaning of Articles 3, 4 and 5 to pursue their claims by judicial process after possible recourse to other competent authorities.

Article 7
Member States shall take the necessary measures to protect employees against dismissal by the employer as a reaction to a complaint within the undertaking or to any legal proceedings aimed at enforcing compliance with the principle of equal treatment.

Article 8
Member States shall take care that the provisions adopted pursuant to this Directive, together with the relevant provisions already in force, are brought to the attention of employees by all appropriate means, for example at their place of employment.

Article 9
1   Member States shall put into force the laws, regulations and administrative provisions necessary in order to comply with this Directive within 30 months of its notification and shall immediately inform the Commission thereof.

However, as regards the first part of Article 3(2)(c) and the first part of Article 5(2)(c), Member States shall carry out a first examination and if necessary a first revision of the laws, regulations and administrative provisions referred to therein within four years of notification of this Directive.

2   Member States shall periodically assess the occupational activities referred to in Article 2(2) in order to decide, in the light of social developments, whether there is justification for maintaining the exclusions concerned. They shall notify the Commission of the results of this assessment.

3   Member States shall also communicate to the Commission the texts of laws, regulations and administrative provisions which they adopt in the field covered by this Directive.

Article 10
Within two years following expiry of the 30–month period laid down in the first subparagraph of Article 9(1), Member States shall forward all necessary information to the Commission to enable it to draw up a report on the application of this Directive for submission to the Council.

Article 11
This Directive is addressed to the Member States.

COUNCIL DIRECTIVE 77/187/EEC

of February 1977

on the approximation of the laws of the Member States relating to the safeguarding of employees' rights in the event of transfers of undertakings, businesses or parts of businesses

(Note: this directive has been amended by Council Directive 98/50/EC of 29 June 1998, also reproduced in this Appendix. Member States are required to implement the changes by 17 July 2001.)

THE COUNCIL OF THE EUROPEAN COMMUNITIES,

Having regard to the Treaty establishing the European Economic Community, and in particular Article 100 thereof,

Having regard to the proposal from the Commission,

Having regard to the opinion of the European Parliament,

Having regard to the opinion of the Economic and Social Committee,

Whereas economic trends are bringing in their wake, at both national and Community level, changes in the structure of undertakings, through transfers of undertakings, businesses or parts of businesses to other employers as a result of legal transfers or mergers;

Whereas it is necessary to provide for the protection of employees in the event of a change of employer, in particular, to ensure that their rights are safeguarded;

Whereas differences still remain in the Member States as regards the extent of the protection of employees in this respect and these differences should be reduced;

Whereas these differences can have a direct effect on the functioning of the common market;

Whereas it is therefore necessary to promote the approximation of laws in this field while maintaining the improvement described in Article 117 of the Treaty,

HAS ADOPTED THIS DIRECTIVE:

SECTION I
SCOPE AND DEFINITIONS

Article 1

1   This Directive shall apply to the transfer of an undertaking, business or part of a business to another employer as a result of a legal transfer or merger.

2   This Directive shall apply where and in so far as the undertaking, business or part of the business to be transferred is situated within the territorial scope of the Treaty.

3   This Directive shall not apply to sea-going vessels

Article 2

For the purposes of this Directive:

    (a) 'transferor' means any natural or legal person who, by reason of a transfer within the meaning of Article 1(1), ceases to be the employer in respect of the undertaking, business or part of the business;

    (b) 'transferee' means any natural or legal person who, by reason of a transfer within the meaning of Article 1(1), becomes the employer in respect of the undertaking, business or part of the business;

    (c) 'representatives of the employees' means the representatives of the employees provided for by the laws or practice of the Member States, with the exception of members of administrative, governing or supervisory bodies of companies who represent employees on such bodies in certain Member States.

SECTION II
SAFEGUARDING OF EMPLOYEES' RIGHTS

Article 3

1   The transferor's rights and obligations arising from a contract of employment or from an employment relationship existing on the date of a transfer within the meaning of Article 1(1) shall, by reason of such transfer, be transferred to the transferee.

Member States may provide that, after the date of transfer within the meaning of Article 1(1) and in addition to the transferee, the transferor shall continue to be liable in respect of obligations which arose from a contract of employment or an employment relationship.

2   Following the transfer within the meaning of Article 1(1), the transferee shall continue to observe the terms and conditions agreed in any collective agreement on the same terms applicable to the transferor under that agreement, until the date of termination or expiry of the collective agreement or the entry into force or application of another collective agreement.

Member States may limit the period for observing such terms and conditions, with the proviso that it shall not be less than one year.

3   Paragraphs 1 and 2 shall not cover employees rights to old-age, invalidity or survivors' benefits under supplementary company or inter-company pension schemes outside the statutory social security schemes in Member States.

Member States shall adopt the measures necessary to protect the interests of employees and of persons no longer employed in the transferor's business at the time of the transfer within the meaning of Article 1(1) in respect of rights conferring on them immediate or prospective entitlement to old-age benefits, including survivors' benefits, under supplementary-schemes referred to in the first subparagraph.

Article 4

1   The transfer of an undertaking, business or part of a business shall not in itself constitute grounds for dismissal by the transferor or the transferee. This provision shall not stand in the way of dismissals that may take place for economic, technical or organisational reasons entailing changes in the workforce.

Member States may provide that the first subparagraph shall not apply to certain specific categories of employees who are not covered by the laws or practice of the Member States in respect of protection against dismissal.

2   If the contract of employment or the employment relationship is terminated because the transfer within the meaning of Article 1(1) involves a substantial change in working conditions to the detriment of the employee, the employer shall be regarded as having been responsible for termination of the contract of employment or of the employment relationship.

Article 5

1   If the business preserves its autonomy, the status and function, as laid down by the laws, regulations or administrative provisions of the Member States, of the representatives or of the representation of the employees affected by the transfer within the meaning of Article 1(1) shall be preserved.

The first subparagraph shall not apply if, under the laws, regulations, administrative provisions or practice of the Member States, the conditions necessary for the re-appointment of the representatives of the employees or for the reconstitution of the representation of the employees are fulfilled.

2   If the term of office of the representatives of the employees affected by a transfer within the meaning of Article 1(1) expires as a result of the transfer, the

representatives shall continue to enjoy the protection provided by the laws, regulations, administrative provisions or practice of the Member States.

SECTION III
INFORMATION AND CONSULTATION

Article 6
1 The transferor and transferee shall be required to inform the representatives of their respective employees affected by a transfer within the meaning of Article 1(1) of the following:

- the reasons for the transfer,
- the legal, economic and social implications of the transfer for the employees,
- measures envisaged in relation to the employees.

The transferor must give such information to the representatives of his employees in good time before the transfer is carried out.

The transferee must give such information to the representatives of his employees in good time, and in any event before his employees are directly affected by the transfer as regards their conditions of work and employment.

2 If the transferor or the transferee envisages measures in relation to his employees, he shall consult his representatives of the employees in good time on such measures with a view to seeking agreement.

3 Member States whose laws, regulations or administrative provisions provide that representatives of the employees may have recourse to an arbitration board to obtain a decision on the measures to be taken in relation to employees may limit the obligations laid down in paragraphs 1 and 2 to cases where the transfer carried out gives rise to a change in the business likely to entail serious disadvantages for a considerable number of the employees.

The information and consultations shall cover at least the measures envisaged in relation to the employees.

The information must be provided and consultations take place in good time before the change in the business as referred to in the first subparagraph is effected.

4 Member States may limit the obligations laid down in paragraphs 1, 2 and 3 to undertakings or businesses which. in respect of the number of employees, fulfil the conditions for the election or designation of a collegiate body representing the employees.

5 Member States may provide that where there are no representatives of the employees in an undertaking or business, the employees concerned must be informed in advance when a transfer within the meaning of Article 1(1) is about to take place.

SECTION IV
FINAL PROVISIONS

Article 7
This Directive shall not affect the right of Member States to apply or introduce laws, regulations or administrative provisions which are more favourable to employees.

Article 8
1 Member States shall bring into force the laws, regulations and administrative provisions needed to comply with this Directive within two years of its notification and shall forthwith inform the Commission thereof.

2 Member States shall communicate to the Commission the texts of the laws, regulations and administrative provisions which they adopt in the field covered by this Directive.

Article 9
Within two years following expiry of the two-year period laid down in Article 8, Member States shall forward all relevant information to the Commission in order to enable it to draw up a report on the application of this Directive for submission to the Council.

Article 10
This Directive is addressed to the Member States.

COUNCIL DIRECTIVE 92/85/EEC

of 19 October 1992

on the introduction of measures to encourage improvements in the safety and health at work of pregnant workers and workers who have recently given birth or are breastfeeding (tenth individual Directive within the meaning of Article 16(1) of Directive 89/391/EEC)

THE COUNCIL OF THE EUROPEAN COMMUNITIES,

Having regard to the Treaty establishing the European Economic Community, and in particular Article 118a thereof,

Having regard to the proposal from the Commission, drawn up after consultation with the Advisory Committee on Safety, Hygiene and Health Protection at work,

In cooperation with the European Parliament,

Having regard to the opinion of the Economic and Social Committee,

Whereas Article 118a of the Treaty provides that the Council shall adopt, by means of directives, minimum requirements for encouraging improvements, especially in the working environment, to protect the safety and health of workers;

Whereas this Directive does not justify any reduction in levels of protection already achieved in individual Member States, the Member States being committed, under the Treaty, to encouraging improvements in conditions in this area and to harmonising conditions while maintaining the improvements made;

Whereas, under the terms of Article 118a of the Treaty, the said directives are to avoid imposing administrative, financial and legal constraints in a way which would hold back the creation and development of small and medium-sized undertakings;

Whereas, pursuant to Decision 74/325/EEC, as last amended by the 1985 Act of Accession, the Advisory Committee on Safety, Hygiene and Health Protection at Work is consulted by the Commission on the drafting of proposals in this field;

Whereas the Community Charter of the fundamental social rights of workers, adopted at the Strasbourg European Council on 9 December 1989 by the Heads of State or Government of 11 Member States, lays down, in paragraph 19 in particular, that:

> 'Every worker must enjoy satisfactory health and safety conditions in his working environment. Appropriate measures must be taken in order to achieve further harmonisation of conditions in this area while maintaining the improvements made';

Whereas the Commission, in its action programme for the implementation of the Community Charter of the fundamental social rights of workers, has included among its aims the adoption by the Council of a Directive on the protection of pregnant women at work;

Whereas Article 15 of Council Directive 89/391/EEC of 12 June 1989 on the introduction of measures to encourage improvements in the safety and health of workers at work provides that particularly sensitive risk groups must be protected against the dangers which specifically affect them;

Whereas pregnant workers, workers who have recently given birth or who are breastfeeding must be considered a specific risk group in many respects, and measures must be taken with regard to their safety and health;

Whereas the protection of the safety and health of pregnant workers, workers who have recently given birth or workers who are breastfeeding should not treat women on the labour market unfavourably nor work to the detriment of directives concerning equal treatment for men and women;

Whereas some types of activities may pose a specific risk, for pregnant workers, workers who have recently given birth or workers who are breastfeeding, of exposure to dangerous agents, processes or working conditions; whereas such risks must therefore be assessed and the result of such assessment communicated to female workers and/or their representatives;

Whereas, further, should the result of this assessment reveal the existence of a risk to the safety or health of the female worker, provision must be made for such worker to be protected;

Whereas pregnant workers and workers who are breastfeeding must not engage in activities which have been assessed as revealing a risk of exposure, jeopardising safety and health, to certain particularly dangerous agents or working conditions;

Whereas provision should be made for pregnant workers, workers who have recently given birth or workers who are breastfeeding not to be required to work at night where such provision is necessary from the point of view of their safety and health;

Whereas the vulnerability of pregnant workers, workers who have recently given birth or who are breastfeeding makes it necessary for them to be granted the right to maternity leave of at least 14 continuous weeks, allocated before and/or after confinement, and renders necessary the compulsory nature of maternity leave of at least two weeks, allocated before and/or after confinement;

Whereas the risk of dismissal for reasons associated with their condition may have harmful effects on the physical and mental state of pregnant workers, workers who have recently given birth or who are breastfeeding; whereas provision should be made for such dismissal to be prohibited;

Whereas measures for the organisation of work concerning the protection of the health of pregnant workers, workers who have recently given birth or workers who are breastfeeding would serve no purpose unless accompanied by the maintenance of rights linked to the employment contract, including maintenance of payment and/or entitlement to an adequate allowance;

Whereas, moreover, provision concerning maternity leave would also serve no purpose unless accompanied by the maintenance of rights linked to the employment contract and or entitlement to an adequate allowance;

Whereas the concept of an adequate allowance in the case of maternity leave must be regarded as a technical point of reference with a view to fixing the minimum level of protection and should in no circumstances be interpreted as suggesting an analogy between pregnancy and illness,

HAS ADOPTED THIS DIRECTIVE:

SECTION I
PURPOSE AND DEFINITIONS

Article 1   Purpose
1   The purpose of this Directive, which is the tenth individual Directive within the meaning of Article 16(1) of Directive 89/391/EEC, is to implement measures to encourage improvements in the safety and health at work of pregnant workers and workers who have recently given birth or who are breastfeeding.

2   The provisions of Directive 89/391/EEC, except for Article 2(2) thereof, shall apply in full to the whole area covered by paragraph 1, without prejudice to any more stringent and/or specific provisions contained in this Directive.

3   This Directive may not have the effect of reducing the level of protection afforded to pregnant workers, workers who have recently given birth or who are breastfeeding as compared with the situation which exists in each Member State on the date on which this Directive is adopted.

Article 2 Definitions

For the purposes of this Directive:

(a) *pregnant worker* shall mean a pregnant worker who informs her employer of her condition, in accordance with national legislation and/or national practice;

(b) *worker who has recently given birth* shall mean a worker who has recently given birth within the meaning of national legislation and/or national practice and who informs her employer of her condition, in accordance with that legislation and/or practice;

(c) *worker who is breastfeeding* shall mean a worker who is breastfeeding within the meaning of national legislation and/or national practice and who informs her employer of her condition, in accordance with that legislation and/or practice.

SECTION II
GENERAL PROVISIONS

Article 3 Guidelines

1 In consultation with the Member States and assisted by the Advisory Committee on Safety, Hygiene and Health Protection at Work, the Commission shall draw up guidelines on the assessment of the chemical, physical and biological agents and industrial processes considered hazardous for the safety or health of workers within the meaning of Article 2.

The guidelines referred to in the first subparagraph shall also cover movements and postures, mental and physical fatigue and other types of physical and mental stress connected with the work done by workers within the meaning of Article 2.

2 The purpose of the guidelines referred to in paragraph 1 is to serve as a basis for the assessment referred to in Article 4(1).

To this end, Member States shall bring these guidelines to the attention of all employers and all female workers and/or their representatives in the respective Member State.

Article 4 Assessment and information

1 For all activities liable to involve a specific risk of exposure to the agents, processes or working conditions of which a non-exhaustive list is given in Annex I, the employer shall assess the nature, degree and duration of exposure, in the undertaking and/or establishment concerned, of workers within the meaning of Article 2, either directly or by way of the protective and preventive services referred to in Article 7 of Directive 89/391/EEC, in order to:

- assess any risks to the safety or health and any possible effect on the pregnancies or breastfeeding of workers within the meaning of Article 2,
- decide what measures should be taken.

2 Without prejudice to Article 10 of Directive 89/391/EEC, workers within the meaning of Article 2 and workers likely to be in one of the situations referred to in Article 2 in the undertaking and/or establishment concerned and/or their representatives shall be informed of the results of the assessment referred to in paragraph 1 and of all measures to be taken concerning health and safety at work.

Article 5 Action further to the results of the assessment

1 Without prejudice to Article 6 of Directive 89/391/EEC, if the results of the assessment referred to in Article 4(1) reveal a risk to the safety or health or an effect on the pregnancy or breastfeeding of a worker within the meaning of Article 2, the

employer shall take the necessary measures to ensure that, by temporarily adjusting the working conditions and/or the working hours of the worker concerned, the exposure of that worker to such risks is avoided.

2 If the adjustment of her working conditions and/or working hours is not technically and/or objectively feasible, or cannot reasonably be required on duly substantiated grounds, the employer shall take the necessary measures to move the worker concerned to another job.

3 If moving her to another job is not technically and/or objectively feasible or cannot reasonably be required on duly substantiated grounds, the worker concerned shall be granted leave in accordance with national legislation and/or national practice for the whole of the period necessary to protect her safety or health.

4 The provisions of this Article shall apply *mutatis mutandis* to the case where a worker pursuing an activity which is forbidden pursuant to Article 6 becomes pregnant or starts breastfeeding and informs her employer thereof.

Article 6 Cases in which exposure is prohibited
In addition to the general provisions concerning the protection of workers, in particular those relating to the limit values for occupational exposure:

1 pregnant workers within the meaning of Article 2(a) may under no circumstances be obliged to perform duties for which the assessment has revealed a risk of exposure, which would jeopardise safety or health, to the agents and working conditions listed in Annex II, Section A;

2 workers who are breastfeeding, within the meaning of Article 2(c), may under no circumstances be obliged to perform duties for which the assessment has revealed a risk of exposure, which would jeopardise safety or health, to the agents and working conditions listed in Annex II, Section B.

Article 7 Night work
1 Member States shall take the necessary measures to ensure that workers referred to in Article 2 are not obliged to perform night work during their pregnancy and for a period following childbirth which shall be determined by the national authority competent for safety and health, subject to submission, in accordance with the procedures laid down by the Member States, of a medical certificate stating that this is necessary for the safety or health of the worker concerned.

2 The measures referred to in paragraph 1 must entail the possibility, in accordance with national legislation and/or national practice, of:
  (a) transfer to daytime work; or
  (b) leave from work or extension of maternity leave where such a transfer is not technically and/or objectively feasible or cannot reasonably be required on duly substantiated grounds.

Article 8 Maternity leave
1 Member States shall take the necessary measures to ensure that workers within the meaning of Article 2 are entitled to a continuous period of maternity leave of at least 14 weeks allocated before and/or after confinement in accordance with national legislation and/or practice.

2 The maternity leave stipulated in paragraph 1 must include compulsory maternity leave of at least two weeks allocated before and/or after confinement in accordance with national legislation and/or practice.

Article 9 Time off for ante-natal examinations
Member States shall take the necessary measures to ensure that pregnant workers within the meaning of Article 2(a) are entitled to, in accordance with national

legislation and/or practice, time off, without loss of pay, in order to attend ante-natal examinations, if such examinations have to take place during working hours.

Article 10   Prohibition of dismissal

In order to guarantee workers, within the meaning of Article 2, the exercise of their health and safety protection rights as recognised under this Article, it shall be provided that:

1   Member States shall take the necessary measures to prohibit the dismissal of workers, within the meaning of Article 2, during the period form the beginning of their pregnancy to the end of the maternity leave referred to in Article 8(1), save in exceptional cases not connected with their condition which are permitted under national legislation and/or practice and, where applicable, provided that the competent authority has given its consent;

2   if a worker, within the meaning of Article 2, is dismissed during the period referred to in point 1, the employer must cite duly substantiated grounds for her dismissal in writing;

3   Member States shall take the necessary measures to protect workers, within the meaning of Article 2, from consequences of dismissal which is unlawful by virtue of point 1.

Article 11   Employment rights

In order to guarantee workers within the meaning of Article 2 the exercise of their health and safety protection rights as recognised in this Article, it shall be provided that:

1   in the cases referred to in Articles 5, 6 and 7, the employment rights relating to the employment contract, including the maintenance of a payment to, and/or entitlement to an adequate allowance for, workers within the meaning of Article 2, must be ensured in accordance with national legislation and/or national practice;

2   in the case referred to in Article 8, the following must be ensured:

   (a)   the rights connected with the employment contract of workers within the meaning of Article 2, other than those referred to in point (b) below;
   (b)   maintenance of a payment to, and/or entitlement to an adequate allowance for, workers within the meaning of Article 2;

3   the allowance referred to in point 2(b) shall be deemed adequate if it guarantees income at least equivalent to that which the worker concerned would receive in the event of a break in her activities on grounds connected with her state of health, subject to any ceiling laid down under national legislation;

4   Member States may make entitlement to pay or the allowance referred to in points 1 and 2(b) conditional upon the worker concerned fulfilling the conditions of eligibility for such benefits laid down under national legislation.

These conditions may under no circumstances provide for periods of previous employment in excess of 12 months immediately prior to the presumed date of confinement.

Article 12   Defence of rights

Member States shall introduce into their national legal systems such measures as are necessary to enable all workers who should feel themselves wronged by failure to comply with the obligations arising from this Directive to pursue their claims by judicial process (and/or, in accordance with national laws and/or practices) by recourse to other competent authorities.

Article 13   Amendments to the Annexes

1   Strictly technical adjustments to Annex I as a result of technical progress, changes in international regulations or specifications and new findings in the area

covered by this Directive shall be adopted in accordance with the procedure laid down in Article 17 of Directive 89/391/EEC.

2   Annex II may be amended only in accordance with the procedure laid down in Article 118a of the Treaty.

Article 14   Final provisions

1   Member States shall bring into force the laws, regulations and administrative provisions necessary to comply with this Directive not later than two years after the adoption thereof or ensure, at the latest two years after adoption of this Directive, that the two sides of industry introduce the requisite provisions by means of collective agreements, with Member States being required to make all the necessary provisions to enable them at all times to guarantee the results laid down by this Directive. They shall forthwith inform the Commission thereof.

2   When Member States adopt the measures referred to in paragraph 1, they shall contain a reference of this Directive or shall be accompanied by such reference on the occasion of their official publication. The methods of making such a reference shall be laid down by the Member States.

3   Member States shall communicate to the Commission the texts of the essential provisions of national law which they have already adopted or adopt in the field governed by this Directive.

4   Member States shall report to the Commission every five years on the practical implementation of the provisions of this Directive, indicating the points of view of the two sides of industry.

However, Member States shall report for the first time to the Commission on the practical implementation of the provisions of this Directive, indicating the points of view of the two sides of industry, four years after its adoption.

The Commission shall inform the European Parliament, the Council, the Economic and Social Committee and the Advisory Committee on Safety, Hygiene and Health Protection at Work.

5   The Commission shall periodically submit to the European Parliament, the Council and the Economic and Social Committee a report on the implementation of this Directive, taking into account paragraphs 1, 2 and 3.

6   The Council will re-examine this Directive, on the basis of an assessment carried out on the basis of the reports referred to in the second subparagraph of paragraph 4 and, should the need arise, of a proposal, to be submitted by the Commission at the latest five years after adoption of the Directive.

Article 15

This Directive is addressed to the Member States.

ANNEX I
NON-EXHAUSTIVE LIST OF AGENTS, PROCESSES AND WORKING CONDITIONS REFERRED TO IN ARTICLE 4(1)

A. Agents

1   *Physical agents*

where these are regarded as agents causing foetal lesions and/or likely to disrupt placental attachment, and in particular:

    (a) shocks, vibration or movement;
    (b) handling of loads entailing risks, particularly of a dorsolumbar nature;
    (c) noise;

(d) ionising radiation;

(e) non-ionising radiation;

(f) extremes of cold or heat;

(g) movements and postures, travelling – either inside or outside the establishment – mental and physical fatigue and other physical burdens connected with the activity of the worker within the meaning of Article 2 of the Directive.

2 *Biological agents*

Biological agents of risk groups 2, 3 and 3 within the meaning of Article 2(d) numbers 2, 3 and 4 of Directive 90/679/EEC, in so far as it is known that these agents or the therapeutic measures necessitated by such agents endanger the health of pregnant women and the unborn child and in so far as they do not yet appear in Annex II.

3 *Chemical agents*

The following chemical agents in so far as it is known that they endanger the health of pregnant women and the unborn child and in so far as they do not yet appear in Annex II:

(a) substances labelled R 40, R 45, R 46, and R 47 under Directive 67/548/EEC in so far as they do not yet appear in Annex II;

(b) chemical agents in Annex I to Directive 90/394/EEC;

(c) mercury and mercury derivatives;

(d) antimitotic drugs;

(e) carbon monoxide;

(f) chemical agents of known and dangerous percutaneous absorption.

B. Processes

Industrial processes listed in Annex 1 to Directive 90/394/EEC.

C. Working conditions

Underground mining work.

ANNEX II
NON-EXHAUSTIVE LIST OF AGENTS AND WORKING CONDITIONS REFERRED TO IN ARTICLE 6

A. Pregnant workers within the meaning of Article 2(a)

1 *Agents*

(a) Physical agents

Work in hyperbaric atmosphere, eg pressurised enclosures and underwater diving.

(b) Biological agents

The following biological agents:

– toxoplasma,
– rubella virus,

unless the pregnant workers are proved to be adequately protected against such agents by immunisation.

(c) Chemical agents

Lead and lead derivatives in so far as these agents are capable of being absorbed by the human organism.

2   *Working conditions*

Underground mining work.

B. Workers who are breastfeeding within the meaning of Article 2(c)

1   *Agents*

(a)   Chemical agents
Lead and lead derivatives in so far as these agents are capable of being absorbed
by the human organism.

2   *Working conditions*

Underground mining work.

Appendix

COMMISSION RECOMMENDATION AND CODE OF PRACTICE 92/131/EEC

of 27 November 1991

on the protection of the dignity of women and men at work

THE COMMISSION OF THE EUROPEAN COMMUNITIES,

Having regard to the Treaty establishing the European Economic Community, and in particular the second indent of Article 155 thereof,

Whereas unwanted conduct of a sexual nature, or other conduct based on sex affecting the dignity of women and men at work, including the conduct of superiors and colleagues, is unacceptable and may, in certain circumstances, be contrary to the principle of equal treatment within the meaning of Articles 3, 4 and 5 of Council Directive 76/207/EEC of 9 February 1976 on the implementation of the principle of equal treatment for men and women as regards access to employment, vocational training and promotion, and working conditions, a view supported by case-law in some Member States;

Whereas, in accordance with the Council recommendation of 13 December 1984 on the promotion of positive action for women, many Member States have carried out a variety of positive action measures and actions having a bearing, inter alia, on respect for the dignity of women at the workplace;

Whereas the European Parliament, in its resolution of 11 June 1986 on violence against women, has called upon national governments, equal opportunities committees and trade unions to carry out concerted information campaigns to create a proper awareness of the individual rights of all members of the labour force;

Whereas the Advisory Committee on Equal Opportunities for Women and Men, in its opinion of 20 June 1988, has unanimously recommended that there should be a recommendation and code of conduct on sexual harassment in the workplace covering harassment of both sexes;

Whereas the Commission in its action programme relating to the implementation of the Community Charter of Basic Social Rights for Workers undertook to examine the protection of workers and their dignity at work, having regard to the reports and recommendations prepared on various aspects of implementation of Community law;

Whereas the Council, in its resolution of 29 May 1990 on the protection of the dignity of women and men at work, affirms that conduct based on sex affecting the dignity of women and men at work, including conduct of superiors and colleagues, constitutes an intolerable violation of the dignity of workers or trainees, and calls on the Member States and the institutions and organs of the European Communities to develop positive measures designed to create a climate at work in which women and men respect one another's human integrity;

Whereas the Commission, in its third action programme on equal opportunities for women and men, 1991 to 1995, and pursuant to paragraph 3(2) of the said Council resolution of 29 May 1990, resolved to draw up a code of conduct on the protection of the dignity of women and men at work, based on experience and best practice in the Member States, to provide guidance on initiating and pursuing positive measures designed to create a climate at work in which women and men respect one another's human integrity;

Whereas the European Parliament, on 22 October 1991, adopted a resolution on the protection of the dignity of women and men at work;

Whereas the Economic and Social Committee, on 30 October 1991, adopted an opinion on the protection of the dignity of women and men at work,

RECOMMENDS AS FOLLOWS:

Article 1

It is recommended that the Member States take action to promote awareness that conduct of a sexual nature, or other conduct based on sex affecting the dignity of women and men at work, including conduct of superiors and colleagues, is unacceptable if:

(a) such conduct is unwanted, unreasonable and offensive to the recipient;

(b) a person's rejection of, or submission to, such conduct on the part of employers or workers (including superiors or colleagues) is used explicitly or implicitly as a basis for a decision which affects that person's access to vocational training, access to employment, continued employment, promotion, salary or any other employment decisions; and/or

(c) such conduct creates an intimidating, hostile or humiliating work environment for the recipient;

and that such conduct may, in certain circumstances, be contrary to the principle of equal treatment within the meaning of Articles 3, 4 and 5 of Directive 76/207/EEC.

Article 2

It is recommended that Member States take action, in the public sector, to implement the Commission's code of practice on the protection of the dignity of women and men at work, annexed hereto. The action of the Member States, in thus initiating and pursuing positive measures designed to create a climate at work in which women and men respect one another's human integrity, should serve as an example to the private sector.

Article 3

It is recommended that Member States encourage employers and employee representatives to develop measures to implement the Commission's code of practice on the protection of the dignity of women and men at work.

Article 4

Member States shall inform the Commission within three years of the date of this recommendation of the measures taken to give effect to it, in order to allow the Commission to draw up a report on all such measures. The Commission shall, within this period, ensure the widest possible circulation of the code of practice. The report should examine the degree of awareness of the Code, its perceived effectiveness, its degree of application and the extent of its use in collective bargaining between the social partners.

Article 5

This recommendation is addressed to the Member States.

Done at Brussels, 27 November 1991.

ANNEX
PROTECTING THE DIGNITY OF WOMEN AND MEN AT WORK
A CODE OF PRACTICE ON MEASURES TO COMBAT SEXUAL HARASSMENT

1. INTRODUCTION

This code of practice is issued in accordance with the resolution of the Council of Ministers on the protection of the dignity of women and men at work, and to accompany the Commission's recommendation on this issue.

Its purpose is to give practical guidance to employers, trade unions, and employees on the protection of the dignity of women and men at work. The code is intended to

893

be applicable in both the public and the private sector and employers are encouraged to follow the recommendations contained in the code in a way which is appropriate to the size and structure of their organisation. It may be particularly relevant for small and medium-sized enterprises to adapt some of the practical steps to their specific needs.

The aim is to ensure that sexual harassment does not occur and, if it does occur, to ensure that adequate procedures are readily available to deal with the problem and prevent its recurrence. The code thus seeks to encourage the development and implementation of policies and practices which establish working environments free of sexual harassment and in which women and men respect one another's human integrity.

The expert report carried out on behalf of the Commission found that sexual harassment is a serious problem for many working women in the European Community and research in Member States has proven beyond doubt that sexual harassment at work is not an isolated phenomenon. On the contrary, it is clear that for millions of women in the European Community, sexual harassment is an unpleasant and unavoidable part of their working lives. Men too may suffer sexual harassment and should, of course, have the same rights as women to the protection of their dignity.

Some specific groups are particularly vulnerable to sexual harassment. Research in several Member States, which documents the link between the risk of sexual harassment and the recipient's perceived vulnerability, suggests that divorced and separated women, young women and new entrants to the labour market and those with irregular or precarious employment contracts, women in non-traditional jobs, women with disabilities, lesbians and women from racial minorities are disproportionately at risk. Gay men and young men are also vulnerable to harassment. It is undeniable that harassment on grounds of sexual orientation undermines the dignity at work of those affected and it is impossible to regard such harassment as appropriate workplace behaviour.

Sexual harassment pollutes the working environment and can have a devastating effect upon the health, confidence, morale and performance of those affected by it. The anxiety and stress produced by sexual harassment commonly leads to those subject to it taking time off work due to sickness, being less efficient at work, or leaving their job to seek work elsewhere. Employees often suffer the adverse consequences of the harassment itself and short- and long-term damage to their employment prospects if they are forced to change jobs. Sexual harassment may also have a damaging impact on employees not themselves the object of unwanted behaviour but who are witness to it or have a knowledge of the unwanted behaviour.

There are also adverse consequences arising from sexual harassment for employers. It has a direct impact on the profitability of the enterprise where staff take sick leave or resign their posts because of sexual harassment, and on the economic efficiency of the enterprise where employees' productivity is reduced by having to work in a climate in which individuals' integrity is not respected.

In general terms, sexual harassment is an obstacle to the proper integration of women into the labour market and the Commission is committed to encouraging the development of comprehensive measures to improve such integration.

2.   DEFINITION

Sexual harassment means unwanted conduct of a sexual nature, or other conduct based on sex affecting the dignity of women and men at work. This can include unwelcome physical, verbal or non-verbal conduct.

Thus, a range of behaviour may be considered to constitute sexual harassment. It is unacceptable if such conduct is unwanted, unreasonable and offensive to the recipient; a person's rejection of or submission to such conduct on the part of employers or workers (including superiors or colleagues) is used explicitly or implicitly as a basis for a decision which affects that person's access to vocational training or to employment, continued employment, promotion, salary or any other employment decisions; and/or such conduct creates an intimidating, hostile or humiliating working environment for the recipient.

The essential characteristic of sexual harassment is that it is unwanted by the recipient, that it is for each individual to determine what behaviour is acceptable to them and what they regard as offensive. Sexual attention becomes sexual harassment if it is persisted in once it has been made clear that it is regarded by the recipient as offensive, although one incident of harassment may constitute sexual harassment if sufficiently serious. It is the unwanted nature of the conduct which distinguishes sexual harassment from friendly behaviour, which is welcome and mutual.

3. THE LAW AND EMPLOYERS' RESPONSIBILITIES

Conduct of a sexual nature or other based on sex affecting the dignity of women and men at work may be contrary to the principle of equal treatment within the meaning of Articles 3, 4 and 5 of Council Directive 76/207/EEC of 9 February 1976 on the implementation of the principle of equal treatment for men and women as regards access to employment, vocational training and promotion, and working conditions. This principle means that there shall be no discrimination whatsoever on grounds of sex either directly or indirectly by reference in particular to marital or family status.

In certain circumstances, and depending upon national law, sexual harassment may also be a criminal offence or may contravene other obligations imposed by the law, such as health and safety duties, or a duty, contractual or otherwise, to be a good employer. Since sexual harassment is a form of employee misconduct, employers have a responsibility to deal with it as they do with any other form of employee misconduct as well as to refrain from harassing employees themselves. Since sexual harassment is a risk to health and safety, employers have a responsibility to take steps to minimise the risk as they do with other hazards. Since sexual harassment often entails an abuse of power, employers may have a responsibility for the misuse of the authority they delegate.

This code, however, focuses on sexual harassment as a problem of sex discrimination. Sexual harassment is sex discrimination because the gender of the recipient is the determining factor in who is harassed. Conduct of a sexual nature or other conduct based on sex affecting the dignity of women and men at work in some Member States already has been found to contravene national equal treatment laws and employers have a responsibility to seek to ensure that the work environment is free from such conduct.

As sexual harassment is often a function of women's status in the employment hierarchy, policies to deal with sexual harassment are likely to be most effective where they are linked to a broader policy to promote equal opportunities and to improve the position of women. Advice on steps which can be taken generally to implement an equal opportunities policy is set out in the Commission's guide to positive action.

Similarly, a procedure to deal with complaints of sexual harassment should be regarded as only one component of a strategy to deal with the problem. The prime objective should be to change behaviour and attitudes, to seek to ensure the prevention of sexual harassment.

4. COLLECTIVE BARGAINING

The majority of the recommendations contained in this code are for action by employers, since employers have clear responsibilities to ensure the protection of the dignity of women and men at work.

Trade unions also have responsibilities to their members and they can and should play an important role in the prevention of sexual harassment in the workplace. It is recommended that the question of including appropriate clauses in agreements be examined in the context of the collective bargaining process, with the aim of achieving a work environment free from unwanted conduct of a sexual nature or other conduct based on sex affecting the dignity of women and men at work and free from victimisation of a complainant or of a person wishing to give, or giving, evidence in the event of a complaint.

5. RECOMMENDATIONS TO EMPLOYERS

The policies and procedures recommended below should be adopted, where appropriate, after consultation or negotiation with trade unions or employee representatives. Experience suggests that strategies to create and maintain a working environment in which the dignity of employees is respected are most likely to be effective where they are jointly agreed.

It should be emphasised that a distinguishing characteristic of sexual harassment is that employees subjected to it often will be reluctant to complain. An absence of complaints about sexual harassment in a particular organisation, therefore, does not necessarily mean an absence of sexual harassment. It may mean that the recipients of sexual harassment think that there is no point in complaining because nothing will be done about it, or because it will be trivialised or the complainant subjected to ridicule, or because they fear reprisals. Implementing the preventative and procedural recommendations outlined below should facilitate the creation of a climate at work in which such concerns have no place.

A. PREVENTION

(i) Policy statements

As a first step in showing senior management's concern and their commitment to dealing with the problem of sexual harassment, employers should issue a policy statement which expressly states that all employees have a right to be treated with dignity, that sexual harassment at work will not be permitted or condoned and that employees have a right to complain about it should it occur.

It is recommended that the policy statement make clear what is considered inappropriate behaviour at work, and explain that such behaviour, in certain circumstances, may be unlawful. It is advisable for the statement to set out a positive duty on managers and supervisors to implement the policy and to take corrective action to ensure compliance with it. It should also place a positive duty on all employees to comply with the policy and to ensure that their colleagues are treated with respect and dignity.

In addition, it is recommended that the statement explain the procedure which should be followed by employees subjected to sexual harassment at work in order to obtain assistance and to whom they should complain; that it contain an undertaking that allegations of sexual harassment will be dealt with seriously, expeditiously and confidentially, and that employees will be protected against victimisation or retaliation for bringing a complaint of sexual harassment. It should also specify that appropriate disciplinary measures will be taken against employees found guilty of sexual harassment.

(ii) Communicating the policy

Once the policy has been developed, it is important to ensure that it is communicated effectively to all employees, so that they are aware that they have a right to complain and to whom they should complain; that their complaint will be dealt with promptly and fairly; and that employees are made aware of the likely consequences of engaging in sexual harassment. Such communication will highlight management's commitment to eliminating sexual harassment, thus enhancing a climate in which it will not occur.

(iii) Responsibility
All employees have a responsibility to help to ensure a working environment in which the dignity of employees is respected and managers (including supervisors) have a particular duty to ensure that sexual harassment does not occur in work areas for which they are responsible. It is recommended that managers explain the organisation's policy to their staff and take steps to positively promote the policy. Managers should also be responsive and supportive to any member of staff who complains about sexual harassment, provide full and clear advice on the procedure to be adopted. maintain confidentiality in any cases of sexual harassment and ensure that there is no further problem of sexual harassment or any victimisation after a complaint has been resolved.

(iv) Training
An important means of ensuring that sexual harassment does not occur and that, if it does occur, the problem is resolved efficiently is through the provision of training for managers and supervisors. Such training should aim to identify the factors which contribute to a working environment free of sexual harassment to familiarise participants with their responsibilities under the employer's policy and any problems they are likely to encounter.

In addition, those playing an official role in any formal complaints procedure in respect of sexual harassment should receive specialist training, such as that outlined above.

It is also good practice to include information as to the organisation's policy on sexual harassment and procedures for dealing with it as part of appropriate induction and training programmes.

B.   PROCEDURES
The development of clear and precise procedures to deal with sexual harassment once it has occurred is of great importance. The procedures should ensure the resolution of problems in an efficient and effective manner. Practical guidance for employees on how to deal with sexual harassment when it occurs and with its aftermath will make it more likely that it will be dealt with at an early stage. Such guidance should of course draw attention to an employee's legal rights and to any time limits within which they must be exercised.

(i) Resolving problems informally
Most recipients of harassment simply want the harassment to stop. Both informal and formal methods of resolving problems should be available.

Employees should be advised that, if possible, they should attempt to resolve the problem informally in the first instance. In some cases, it may be possible and sufficient for the employee to explain clearly to the person engaging in the unwanted conduct that the behaviour in question is not welcome, that it offends them or makes them uncomfortable, and that it interferes with their work.

In circumstances where it is too difficult or embarrassing for an individual to do this on their own behalf, an alternative approach would be to seek support from, or for an initial approach to be made by, a sympathetic friend or confidential counsellor.

If the conduct continues or if it is not appropriate to resolve the problem informally, it should be raised through the formal complaints procedure.

(ii) Advice and assistance
It is recommended that employers designate someone to provide advice and assistance to employees subjected to sexual harassment, where possible with

responsibilities to assist in the resolution of any problems, whether through informal or formal means. It may be helpful if the officer is designated with the agreement of the trade unions or employees, as this is likely to enhance their acceptability. Such officers could be selected from personnel departments or equal opportunities departments for example. In some organisations they are designated as 'confidential counsellors' or 'sympathetic friends'. Often such a role may be played by someone from the employee's trade union or women's support groups.

Whatever the location of this responsibility in the organisation, it is recommended that the designated officer receives appropriate training in the best means of resolving problems and in the detail of the organisation's policy and procedures, so that they can perform their role effectively. It is also important that they are given adequate resources to carry out their function, and protection against victimisation for assisting any recipient of sexual harassment.

(iii) Complaints procedure

It is recommended that, where the complainant regards attempts at informal resolution as inappropriate, where informal attempts at resolution have been refused, or where the outcome has been unsatisfactory, a formal procedure for resolving the complaint be provided. The procedure should give employees confidence that the organisation will take allegations of sexual harassment seriously.

By its nature sexual harassment may make the normal channels of complaint difficult to use because of embarrassment, fears of not being taken seriously, fears of damage to reputation, fears of reprisal or the prospect of damaging the working environment. Therefore, a formal procedure should specify to whom the employee should bring a complaint, and it should also provide an alternative if in the particular circumstances the normal grievance procedure may not be suitable, for example because the alleged harasser is the employee's line manager. It is also advisable to make provision for employees to bring a complaint in the first instance to someone of their own sex, should they so choose.

It is good practice for employers to monitor and review complaints of sexual harassment and how they have been resolved, in order to ensure that their procedures are working effectively.

(iv) Investigations

It is important to ensure that internal investigations of any complaints are handled with sensitivity and with due respect for the rights of both the complainant and the alleged harasser. The investigation should be seen to be independent and objective. Those carrying out the investigation should not be connected with the allegation in any way, and every effort should be made to resolve complaints speedily – grievances should be handled promptly and the procedure should set a time limit within which complaints will be processed, with due regard for any time limits set by national legislation for initiating a complaint through the legal system.

It is recommended as good practice that both the complainant and the alleged harasser have the right to be accompanied and/or represented, perhaps by a representative of their trade union or a friend or colleague; that the alleged harasser be given full details of the nature of the complaint and the opportunity to respond, and that strict confidentiality be maintained throughout any investigation into an allegation. Where it is necessary to interview witnesses, the importance of confidentiality should be emphasised.

It must be recognised that recounting the experience of sexual harassment is difficult and can damage the employee's dignity. Therefore, a complainant should not be required repeatedly to recount the events complained of where this is unnecessary.

The investigation should focus on the facts of the complaint and it is advisable for the employer to keep a complete record of all meetings and investigations.

(v) Disciplinary offence

It is recommended that violations of the organisation's policy protecting the dignity of employees at work should be treated as a disciplinary offence and the disciplinary rules should make clear what is regarded as inappropriate behaviour at work. It is also good practice to ensure that the range of penalties to which offenders will be liable for violating the rule is clearly stated and also to make it clear that it will be considered a disciplinary offence to victimise or retaliate against an employee for bringing a complaint of sexual harassment in good faith.

Where a complaint is upheld and it is determined that it is necessary to relocate or transfer one party, consideration should be given, wherever practicable, to allowing the complaint to choose whether he or she wishes to remain in their post or be transferred to another location. No element of penalty should be seen to attach to a complainant whose complaint is upheld and in addition, where a complaint is upheld, the employer should monitor the situation to ensure that the harassment has stopped.

Even where a complaint is not upheld, for example because the evidence is regarded as inconclusive, consideration should be given to transferring or re-scheduling the work of one of the employees concerned rather than requiring them to continue to work together against the wishes of either party.

6.   RECOMMENDATIONS TO TRADE UNIONS

Sexual harassment is a trade union issue as well as an issue for employers. It is recommended as good practice that trade unions formulate and issue clear policy statements on sexual harassment and take steps to raise awareness of the problem of sexual harassment in the workplace, in order to help create a climate in which it is neither condoned or ignored. For example, trade unions could aim to give all officers and representatives training on equality issues, including dealing with sexual harassment, and include such information in union-sponsored or approved training courses, as well as information on the union's policy. Trade unions should consider declaring that sexual harassment is inappropriate behaviour and educating members and officials about its consequences is recommended as good practice.

Trade unions should also raise the issue of sexual harassment with employers and encourage the adoption of adequate policies and procedures to protect the dignity of women and men at work in the organisation. It is advisable for trade unions to inform members of their right not to be sexually harassed at work and provide members with clear guidance as to what to do if they are sexually harassed, including guidance on any relevant legal rights.

Where complaints arise, it is important for trade unions to treat them seriously and sympathetically and ensure that the complainant has an opportunity of representation if a complaint is to be pursued. It is important to create an environment in which members feel able to raise such complaints knowing they will receive a sympathetic and supportive response from local union representatives. Trade unions could consider designating specially trained officials to advise and counsel members with complaints of sexual harassment and act on their behalf if required. This will provide a focal point for support. It is also a good idea to ensure that there are sufficient female representatives to support women subjected to sexual harassment.

It is recommended too, where the trade union is representing both the complainant and the alleged harasser for the purpose of the complaints procedure, that it be made clear that the union is not condoning offensive behaviour by providing representation. In any event, the same official should not represent both parties.

It is good practice to advise members that keeping a record of incidents by the harassed worker will assist in bringing any formal or informal action to a more effective conclusion, that the union wishes to be informed of any incident of sexual harassment and that such information will be kept confidential. It is also good practice for the union to monitor and review the union's record in responding to complaints and in representing alleged harassers and the harassed, in order to ensure its responses are effective.

7.   EMPLOYEES' RESPONSIBILITIES

Employees have a clear role to play in helping to create a climate at work in which sexual harassment is unacceptable. They can contribute to preventing sexual harassment through an awareness and sensitivity towards the issue and by ensuring that standards of conduct for themselves and for colleagues do not cause offence.

Employees can do much to discourage sexual harassment by making it clear that they find such behaviour unacceptable and by supporting colleagues who suffer such treatment and are considering making a complaint.

Employees who are themselves recipients of harassment should, where practicable, tell the harasser that the behaviour is unwanted and unacceptable. Once the offender understands clearly that the behaviour is unwelcome, this may be enough to put an end to it. If the behaviour is persisted in, employees should inform management and/or their employee representative through the appropriate channels and request assistance in stopping the harassment, whether through informal or formal means.

COUNCIL DIRECTIVE 93/104/EC

of 23 November 1993

concerning certain aspects of the organisation of working time

THE COUNCIL OF THE EUROPEAN UNION,

Having regard to the Treaty establishing the European Community, and in particular Article 118a thereof,

Having regard to the proposal from the Commission,

In cooperation with the European Parliament,

Having regard to the opinion of the Economic and Social Committee,

Whereas Article 118a of the Treaty provides that the Council shall adopt, by means of directives, minimum requirements for encouraging improvements, especially in the working environment, to ensure a better level of protection of the safety and health of workers;

Whereas, under the terms of that Article, those directives are to avoid imposing administrative, financial and legal constraints in a way which would hold back the creation and development of small and medium-sized undertakings:

Whereas the provisions of Council Directive 89/391/EEC of 12 June 1989 on the introduction of measures to encourage improvements in the safety and health of workers at work are fully applicable to the areas covered by this Directive without prejudice to more stringent and/or specific provisions contained therein:

Whereas the Community Charter of the Fundamental Social Rights of Workers, adopted at the meeting of the European Council held at Strasbourg on 9 December 1989 by the Heads of State or of Government of 11 Member States, and in particular points 7, first subparagraph, 8 and 19, first subparagraph, thereof, declared that:

'7 The completion of the internal market must lead to an improvement in the living and working conditions of workers in the European Community. This process must result from an approximation of these conditions while the improvement is being maintained, as regards in particular the duration and organisation of working time and forms of employment other than open-ended contracts, such as fixed-term contracts, part-time working, temporary work and seasonal work.

8 Every worker in the European Community shall have a right to a weekly rest period and to annual paid leave, the duration of which must be progressively harmonised in accordance with national practices.

19 Every worker must enjoy satisfactory health and safety conditions in his working environment. Appropriate measures must be taken in order to achieve further harmonisation of conditions in this area while maintaining the improvements made.';

Whereas the improvement of workers' safety, hygiene and health at work is an objective which should not be subordinated to purely economic considerations;

Whereas this Directive is a practical contribution towards creating the social dimension of the internal market;

Whereas laying down minimum requirements with regard to the organisation of working time is likely to improve the working conditions of workers in the Community;

Whereas, in order to ensure the safety and health of Community workers, the latter must be granted minimum daily, weekly and annual periods of rest and adequate breaks; whereas it is also necessary in this context to place a maximum limit on weekly working hours;

Whereas account should be taken of the principles of the International Labour Organisation with regard to the organisation of working time, including those relating to night work;

Whereas, with respect to the weekly rest period, due account should be taken of the diversity of cultural, ethnic, religious and other factors in the Member States; whereas, in particular, it is ultimately for each Member State to decide whether Sunday should be included in the weekly rest period, and if so to what extent;

Whereas research has shown that the human body is more sensitive at night to environmental disturbances and also to certain burdensome forms of work organisation and that long periods of night work can be detrimental to the health of workers and can endanger safety at the workplace;

Whereas there is a need to limit the duration of periods of night work, including overtime, and to provide for employers who regularly use night workers to bring this information to the attention of the competent authorities if they so request;

Whereas it is important that night workers should be entitled to a free health assessment prior to their assignment and thereafter at regular intervals and that whenever possible they should be transferred to day work for which they are suited if they suffer from health problems;

Whereas the situation of night and shift workers requires that the level of safety and health protection should be adapted to the nature of their work and that the organisation and functioning of protection and prevention services and resources should be efficient;

Whereas specific working conditions may have detrimental effects on the safety and health of workers; whereas the organisation of work according to a certain pattern must take account of the general principle of adapting work to the worker;

Whereas, given the specific nature of the work concerned, it may be necessary to adopt separate measures with regard to the organisation of working time in certain sectors or activities which are excluded from the scope of this Directive;

Whereas, in view of the question likely to be raised by the organisation of working time within an undertaking, it appears desirable to provide for flexibility in the application of certain provisions of this Directive, whilst ensuring compliance with the principles of protecting the safety and health of workers;

Whereas it is necessary to provide that certain provisions may be subject to derogations implemented, according to the case, by the Member States or the two sides of industry; whereas, as a general rule, in the event of a derogation, the workers concerned must be given equivalent compensatory rest periods,

HAS ADOPTED THIS DIRECTIVE:

SECTION I
SCOPE AND DEFINITIONS

Article 1   Purpose and scope
1   This Directive lays down minimum safety and health requirements for the organisation of working time.

2   This Directive applies to:

(a) minimum periods of daily rest, weekly rest and annual leave, to breaks and maximum weekly working time; and
(b) certain aspects of night work, shift work and patterns of work.

3   This Directive shall apply to all sectors of activity, both public and private, within the meaning of Article 2 of Directive 89/391/EEC, without prejudice to Article 17 of this Directive, with the exception of air, rail, road, sea, inland waterway and lake transport, sea fishing, other work at sea and the activities of doctors in training;

4   The provisions of Directive 89/391/EEC are fully applicable to the matters referred to in paragraph 2, without prejudice to more stringent and/or specific provisions contained in this Directive.

Article 2 Definitions

For the purposes of this Directive, the following definitions shall apply:

1 *working time* shall mean any period during which the worker is working, at the employer's disposal and carrying out his activity or duties, in accordance with national law and/or practice;

2 *rest period* shall mean any period which is not working time;

3 night time shall mean any period of not less than seven hours, as defined by national law; and which must include in any case the period between midnight and 5 am;

4 *night worker* shall mean:

  (a) on the one hand, any worker, who, during night time, works at least three hours of his daily working time as a normal course; and
  (b) on the other hand, any worker who is likely during night time to work a certain proportion of his annual working time, as defined at the choice of the Member State concerned:
    (i) by national legislation, following consultation with the two sides of industry; or
    (ii) by collective agreements or agreements concluded between the two sides of industry at national or regional level;

5 *shift work* shall mean any method of organising work in shifts whereby workers succeed each other at the same work stations according to a certain pattern, including a rotating pattern, and which may be continuous or discontinuous, entailing the need for workers to work at different times over a given period of days or weeks;

6 *shift worker* shall mean any worker whose work schedule is part of shift work.

SECTION II
MINIMUM REST PERIODS – OTHER ASPECTS OF THE ORGANISATION OF WORKING TIME

Article 3 Daily rest

Member States shall take the measures necessary to ensure that every worker is entitled to a minimum daily rest period of 11 consecutive hours per 24-hour period.

Article 4 Breaks

Member States shall take the measures necessary to ensure that, where the working day is longer than six hours, every worker is entitled to a rest break, the details of which, including duration and the terms of which it is granted, shall be laid down in collective agreements or agreements between the two sides of industry or, failing that, by national legislation.

Article 5 Weekly rest period

Member States shall take the measures necessary to ensure that, per each seven-day period, every worker is entitled to a minimum uninterrupted rest period of 24 hours plus the 11 hours' daily rest referred to in Article 3.

[The minimum rest period referred to in the first subparagraph shall in principle include Sunday.]

If objective, technical or work organisation conditions so justify, a minimum rest period of 24 hours may be applied.

Notes
The words in square brackets are annulled by the decision of the European Court of Justice in *United Kingdom v EU Council* Case C–84/94 (1996) Times, 21 November.

Article 6   Maximum weekly working time

Member States shall take the measures necessary to ensure that, in keeping with the need to protect the safety and health of workers:

1   the period of weekly working time is limited by means of laws, regulations or administrative provisions or by collective agreements or agreements between the two sides of industry;

2   the average working time for each seven-day period, including overtime, does not exceed 48 hours.

Article 7   Annual leave

1   Member States shall take the measures necessary to ensure that every worker is entitled to paid annual leave of at least four weeks in accordance with the conditions for entitlement to, and granting of, such leave laid down by national legislation and/or practice.

2   The minimum period of paid annual leave may not be replaced by an allowance in lieu, except where the employment relationship is terminated.

SECTION III
NIGHT WORK – SHIFT WORK-PATTERNS OF WORK

Article 8   Length of night work

Member States shall take the measures necessary to ensure that:

1   normal hours of work for night workers do not exceed an average of eight hours in any 24-hour period;

2   night workers whose work involves special hazards or heavy physical or mental strain do not work more than eight hours in any period of 24 hours during which they perform night work.

For the purposes of the aforementioned, work involving special hazards or heavy physical or mental strain shall be defined by national legislation and/or practice or by collective agreements or agreements concluded between the two sides of industry, taking account of the specific effects and hazards of night work.

Article 9   Health assessment and transfer of night workers to day work

1   Member States shall take the measures necessary to ensure that:

     (a)   night workers are entitled to a free health assessment before their assignment and thereafter at regular intervals;

     (b)   night workers suffering from health problems recognised as being connected with the fact that they perform night work are transferred whenever possible to day work to which they are suited.

2   The free health assessment referred to in paragraph 1(a) must comply with medical confidentiality.

3   The free health assessment referred to in paragraph 1(a) may be conducted within the national health system.

Article 10   Guarantees for night-time working

Member States may make the work of certain categories of night workers subject to certain guarantees, under conditions laid down by national legislation and/or practice, in the case of workers who incur risks to their safety or health linked to night-time working.

Article 11   Notification of regular use of night workers

Member States shall take the measures necessary to ensure that an employer who regularly uses night workers brings this information to the attention of the competent authorities if they so request.

Article 12   Safety and health protection
Member States shall take the measures necessary to ensure that:

1   night workers and shift workers have safety and health protection appropriate to the nature of their work;

2   appropriate protection and prevention services or facilities with regard to the safety and health of night workers and shift workers are equivalent to those applicable to other workers and are available at all times.

Article 13   Pattern of work
Member States shall take the measures necessary to ensure that an employer who intends to organise work according to a certain pattern takes account of the general principle of adapting work to the worker, with a view, in particular, to alleviating monotonous work and work at a predetermined work-rate, depending on the type of activity, and of safety and health requirements, especially as regards breaks during working time.

SECTION IV
MISCELLANEOUS PROVISIONS

Article 14   More specific Community provisions
The provisions of this Directive shall not apply where other Community instruments contain more specific requirements concerning certain occupations or occupational activities.

Article 15   More favourable provisions
This Directive shall not affect Member States' right to apply or introduce laws, regulations or administrative provisions more favourable to the protection of the safety and health of workers or to facilities or permit the application of collective agreements or agreements concluded between the two sides of industry which are more favourable to the protection of the safety and health of workers.

Article 16   Reference periods
Member States may lay down:

1   for the application of Article 5 (weekly rest period), a reference period not exceeding 14 days;

2   for the application of Article 6 (maximum weekly working time), a reference period not exceeding four months.

The periods of paid annual leave, granted in accordance with Article 7, and the periods of sick leave shall not be included or shall be neutral in the calculation of the average;

3   for the application of Article 8 (length of night work), a reference period defined after consultation of the two sides of industry or by collective agreements or agreements concluded between the two sides of industry at national or regional level.

If the minimum weekly rest period of 24 hours required by Article 5 falls within that reference period, it shall not be included in the calculation of the average.

Article 17   Derogations
1   With due regard for the general principles of the protection of the safety and health of workers, Member States may derogate from Article 3, 4, 5, 6, 8 or 16 when, on account of the specific characteristics of the activity concerned, the duration of the working time is not measured and/or predetermined or can be determined by the workers themselves, and particularly in the case of:

(a) managing executives or other persons with autonomous decision-taking powers;
(b) family workers; or
(c) workers officiating at religious ceremonies in churches and religious communities.

2 Derogations may be adopted by means of laws, regulations or administrative provisions or by means of collective agreements or agreements between the two sides of industry provided that the workers concerned are afforded equivalent periods of compensatory rest or that, in exceptional cases in which it is not possible, for objective reasons, to grant such equivalent periods of compensatory rest, the workers concerned are afforded appropriate protection:

2.1 from Articles 3, 4, 5, 8 and 16:

(a) in the case of activities where the worker's place of work and his place of residence are distant from one another or where the worker's different places of work are distant from one another;
(b) in the case of security and surveillance activities requiring a permanent presence in order to protect property and persons, particularly security guards and caretakers or security firms;
(c) in the case of activities involving the need for continuity of service or production, particularly:
  (i) services relating to the reception, treatment and/or care provided by hospitals or similar establishments, residential institutions and prisons;
  (ii) dock or airport workers;
  (iii) press, radio, television, cinematographic production, postal and telecommunications services, ambulance, fire and civil protection services;
  (iv) gas, water and electricity production, transmission and distribution, household refuse collection and incineration plants;
  (v) industries in which work cannot be interrupted on technical grounds;
  (vi) research and development activities;
  (vii) agriculture;
(d) where there is a foreseeable surge of activity, particularly in:
  (i) agriculture;
  (ii) tourism;
  (iii) postal services;

2.2 from Articles 3, 4, 5, 8 and 16:

(a) in the circumstances described in Article 5(4) of Directive 89/391/EEC;
(b) in cases of accident or imminent risk of accident;

2.3 from Articles 3 and 5:

(a) in the case of shift work activities, each time the worker changes shift and cannot take daily and/or weekly rest periods between the end of one shift and the start of the next one;
(b) in the case of activities involving periods of work split up over the day, particularly those of cleaning staff.

3 Derogations may be made from Articles 3, 4, 5, 8 and 16 by means of collective agreements or agreements concluded between the two sides of industry at national or regional level or, in conformity with the rules laid down by them, by means of collective agreements or agreements concluded between the two sides of industry at a lower level.

Member States in which there is no statutory system ensuring the conclusion of collective agreements or agreements concluded between the two sides of industry at national or regional level, on the matters covered by this Directive, or those Member

States in which there is a specific legislative framework for this purpose and within the limits thereof, may, in accordance with national legislation and/or practice, allow derogations from Articles 3, 4, 5, 8 and 16 by way of collective agreements or agreements concluded between the two sides of industry at the appropriate collective level.

The derogations provided for in the first and second subparagraph shall be allowed on condition that equivalent compensating rest periods are granted to the workers concerned or, in exceptional cases where it is not possible for objective reasons to grant such periods, the workers concerned are afforded appropriate protection.

Member States may lay down rules:

- for the application of this paragraph by the two sides of industry, and
- for the extension of the provisions of collective agreements or agreements concluded in conformity with this paragraph to other workers in accordance with national legislation and/or practice.

4   The option to derogate from point 2 to Article 16, provided in paragraph 2, points 2.1 and 2.2 and in paragraph 3 of this Article, may not result in the establishment of a reference period exceeding six months.

However, Member States shall have the option, subject to compliance with the general principles relating to the protection of the safety and health of workers, of allowing, for objective or technical reasons or reasons concerning the organisation of work, collective agreements or agreements concluded between the two sides of industry to set reference periods in no event exceeding 12 months.

Before the expiry of a period of seven years from the date referred to in Article 18(1)(a), the Council shall, on the basis of a Commission proposal accompanied by an appraisal report, re-examine the provisions of this paragraph and decide what action to take.

Article 18   Final provisions

1 (a) Member States shall adopt the laws, regulations and administrative provisions necessary to comply with this Directive by 23 November 1996, or shall ensure by that date that the two sides of industry establish the necessary measures by agreement, with Member States being obliged to take any necessary steps to enable them to guarantee at all times that the provisions laid down by this Directive are fulfilled.

(b) (i) However, a Member State shall have the option not to apply Article 6, while respecting the general principles of the protection of the safety and health of workers, and provided it takes the necessary measures to ensure that:
- no employer requires a worker to work more than 48 hours over a seven-day period, calculated as an average for the reference period referred to in point 2 of Article 16, unless he has first obtained the worker's agreement to perform such work,
- no worker is subjected to any detriment by his employer because he is not willing to give his agreement to perform such work,
- the employer keeps up-to-date records of all workers who carry out such work,
- the records are placed at the disposal of the competent authorities, which may, for reasons connected with the safety and/or health of workers, prohibit or restrict the possibility of exceeding the maximum weekly working hours,
- the employer provides the competent authorities at their request with information on cases in which agreement has been given by workers to perform work exceeding 48 hours over a period of seven

days, calculated as an average for the reference period referred to in point 2 of Article 16.

Before the expiry of a period of seven years from the date referred to in (a), the Council shall, on the basis of a Commission proposal accompanied by an appraisal report, re-examine the provisions of this point (i) and decide on what action to take.

(ii) Similarly, Member States shall have the option, as regards the application of Article 7, of making use of a transitional period of not more than three years from the date referred to in (a), provided that during that transitional period:

- every worker receives three weeks' paid annual leave in accordance with the conditions for the entitlement to, and granting of, such leave laid down by national legislation and/or practice, and
- the three-week period of paid annual leave may not be replaced by an allowance in lieu, except where the employment relationship is terminated.

(c) Member states shall forthwith inform the Commission thereof.

2   When Member States adopt the measures referred to in paragraph 1, they shall contain a reference to this Directive or shall be accompanied by such reference on the occasion of their official publication. The methods of making such a reference shall be laid down by the Member states.

3   Without prejudice to the right of Member States to develop, in the light of changing circumstances, different legislative, regulatory or contractual provisions in the field of working time, as long as the minimum requirements provided for in this Directive are complied with, implementation of this Directive shall not constitute valid grounds for reducing the general level of protection afforded to workers.

4   Member States shall communicate to the Commission the texts of the provisions of national law already adopted or being adopted in the field governed by this Directive.

5   Member States shall report to the Commission every five years on the practical implementation of the provisions of this Directive, indicating the viewpoints of the two sides of industry.

The Commission shall inform the European Parliament, the Council, the Economic and Social Committee and the Advisory Committee on Safety, Hygiene and Health Protection at Work thereof.

6   Every five years the Commission shall submit to the European Parliament, the Council and the Economic and Social Committee a report on the application of this Directive taking into account paragraphs 1, 2, 3, 4 and 5.

Article 19
This Directive is addressed to the Member States.

COUNCIL DIRECTIVE 94/33/EC

of 22 June 1994

on the protection of young people at work

THE COUNCIL OF THE EUROPEAN UNION,

Having regard to the Treaty establishing the European Community, and in particular Article 118a thereof,

Having regard to the proposal from the Commission,

Having regard to the opinion of the Economic and Social Committee,

Acting in accordance with the procedure referred to in Article 189c of the Treaty,

Whereas Article 118a of the Treaty provides that the Council shall adopt, by means of directives, minimum requirements to encourage improvements, especially in the working environment, as regards the health and safety of workers;

Whereas, under that Article, such directives must avoid imposing administrative, financial and legal constraints in a way which would hold back the creation and development of small and medium-sized undertakings;

Whereas points 20 and 22 of the Community Charter of the Fundamental Social Rights of Workers, adopted by the European Council in Strasbourg on 9 December 1989, state that:

'20   Without prejudice to such rules as may be more favourable to young people, in particular those ensuring their preparation for work through vocational training, and subject to derogations limited to certain light work, the minimum employment age must not be lower than the minimum school-leaving age and, in any case, not lower than 15 years;

22   Appropriate measures must be taken to adjust labour regulations applicable to young workers so that their specific development and vocational training and access to employment needs are met.

The duration of work must, in particular, be limited – without it being possible to circumvent this limitation through recourse to overtime – and night work prohibited in the case of workers of under eighteen years of age, save in the case of certain jobs laid down in national legislation or regulations.';

Whereas account should be taken of the principles of the International Labour Organisation regarding the protection of young people at work, including those relating to the minimum age for access to employment or work;

Whereas, in this Resolution on child labour, the European Parliament summarised the various aspects of work by young people and stressed its effects on their health, safety and physical and intellectual development, and pointed to the need to adopt a Directive harmonising national legislation in the field;

Whereas Article 15 of Council Directive 89/391/EEC of 12 June 1989 on the introduction of measures to encourage improvements in the safety and health of workers at work provides that particularly sensitive risk groups must be protected against the dangers which specifically affect them;

Whereas children and adolescents must be considered specific risk groups, and measures must be taken with regard to their safety and health;

Whereas the vulnerability of children calls for Member States to prohibit their employment and ensure that the minimum working or employment age is not lower than the minimum age at which compulsory schooling as imposed by national law ends or 15 years in any event; whereas derogations from the prohibition on child labour may be admitted only in special cases and under the conditions stipulated in this Directive; whereas, under no circumstances, may such derogations be detrimental to regular school attendance or prevent children benefiting fully from their education;

Whereas, in view of the nature of the transition from childhood to adult life, work by adolescents should be strictly regulated and protected;

Whereas every employer should guarantee young people working conditions appropriate to their age;

Whereas employers should implement the measures necessary to protect the safety and health of young people on the basis on an assessment of work-related hazards to the young;

Whereas Member States should protect young people against any specific risks arising from their lack of experience, absence of awareness of existing or potential risks, or from their immaturity;

Whereas Member States should therefore prohibit the employment of young people for the work specified by this Directive;

Whereas the adoption of specific minimal requirements in respect of the organisation of working time is likely to improve working conditions for young people;

Whereas the maximum working time of young people should be strictly limited and night work by young people should be prohibited, with the exception of certain jobs specified by national legislation or rules;

Whereas Member States should take the appropriate measures to ensure that the working time of adolescents receiving school education does not adversely affect their ability to benefit from that education;

Whereas time spent on training by young persons working under a theoretical and/or practical combined work/training scheme or an in-plant work-experience should be counted as working time;

Whereas, in order to ensure the safety and health of young people, the latter should be granted minimum daily, weekly and annual periods of rest and adequate breaks;

Whereas, with respect to the weekly rest period, due account should be taken of the diversity of cultural, ethnic, religious and other factors prevailing in the Member States; whereas in particular, it is ultimately for each Member State to decide whether Sunday should be included in the weekly rest period, and if so to what extent;

Whereas appropriate work experience may contribute to the aim of preparing young people for adult working and social life, provided it is ensured that any harm to their safety, health and development is avoided;

Whereas, although derogations from the bans and limitations imposed by this Directive would appear indispensable for certain activities or particular situations, applications thereof must not prejudice the principles underlying the established protection system;

Whereas this Directive constitutes a tangible step towards developing the social dimension of the internal market;

Whereas the application in practice of the system of protection laid down by this Directive will require that Member States implement a system of effective and proportionate measures;

Whereas the implementation of some provisions of this Directive poses particular problems for one Member State with regard to its system of protection for young people at work; whereas that Member State should therefore be allowed to refrain from implementing the relevant provisions for a suitable period,

HAS ADOPTED THIS DIRECTIVE:

SECTION I

Article 1   Purpose
1   Member States shall take the necessary measures to prohibit work by children.

They shall ensure, under the conditions laid down by this Directive, that the minimum working or employment age is not lower than the minimum age at which compulsory full-time schooling as imposed by national law ends or 15 years in any event.

2   Member States ensure that work by adolescents is strictly regulated and protected under the conditions laid down in this Directive.

3   Member States shall ensure in general that employers guarantee that young people have working conditions which suit their age.

They shall ensure that young people are protected against economic exploitation and against any work likely to harm their safety, health or physical, mental, moral or social development or to jeopardise their education.

Article 2   Scope
1   This Directive shall apply to any person under 18 years of age having an employment contract or an employment relationship defined by the law in force in a Member State and/or governed by the law in force in a Member State.

2   Member States may make legislative or regulatory provision for this Directive not to apply, within the limits and under the conditions which they set by legislative or regulatory provision, to occasional work or short-term work involving:

(a) domestic service in a private household, or
(b) work regarded as not being harmful, damaging or dangerous to young people in a family undertaking.

Article 3   Definitions
For the purposes of this Directive:

(a) 'young person' shall mean any person under 18 years of age referred to in Article 2(1);
(b) 'child' shall mean any young person of less than 15 years of age or who is still subject to compulsory full-time schooling under national law;
(c) 'adolescent' shall mean any young person of at least 15 years of age but less than 18 years of age who is no longer subject to compulsory full-time schooling under national law;
(d) 'light work' shall mean all work which, on account of the inherent nature of the tasks which it involves and the particular conditions under which they are performed:
   (i) is not likely to be harmful to the safety, health or development of children, and
   (ii) is not such as to be harmful to their attendance at school, their participation in vocational guidance or training programmes approved by the competent authority or their capacity to benefit from the instruction received;
(e) 'working time' shall mean any period during which the young person is at work, at the employer's disposal and carrying out his activity or duties in accordance with national legislation and/or practice;
(f) 'rest period' shall mean any period which is not working time.

Article 4   Prohibition of work by children
1   Member States shall adopt the measures necessary to prohibit work by children.

2   Taking into account the objectives set out in Article 1, Member States may make legislative or regulatory provision for the prohibition of work by children not to apply to:

(a) children pursuing the activities set out in Article 5;
(b) children of at least 14 years of age working under a combined work/training scheme or an in-plant work-experience scheme, provided that such work is done in accordance with the conditions laid down by the competent authority;
(c) children of at least 14 years of age performing light work other than that covered by Article 5; light work other than that covered by Article 5 may,

however, be performed by children of 13 years of age for a limited number of hours per week in the case of categories of work determined by national legislation.

3   Member States that make use of the opinion referred to in paragraph 2(c) shall determine, subject to the provisions of this Directive, the working conditions relating to the light work in question.

Article 5   Cultural or similar activities
1   The employment of children for the purposes of performance in cultural, artistic, sports or advertising activities shall be subject to prior authorisation to be given by the competent authority in individual cases.

2   Member States shall by legislative or regulatory provision lay down the working conditions for children in the cases referred to in paragraph 1 and the details of the prior authorisation procedure, on condition that the activities:

  (i)   are not likely to be harmful to the safety, health or development of children, and
  (ii) are not such as to be harmful to their attendance at school, their participation in vocational guidance or training programmes approved by the competent authority or their capacity to benefit from the instruction received.

3   By way of derogation from the procedure laid down in paragraph 1, in the case of children of at least 13 years of age, Member States may authorise, by legislative or regulatory provision, in accordance with conditions which they shall determine, the employment of children for the purposes of performance in cultural, artistic, sports or advertising activities.

4   The Member States which have a specific authorisation system for modelling agencies with regard to the activities of children may retain that system.

SECTION II

Article 6   General obligations on employers
1   Without prejudice to Article 4(1), the employer shall adopt the measures necessary to protect the safety and health of young people, taking particular account of the specific risks referred to in Article 7(1).

2   The employer shall implement the measures provided for in paragraph 1 on the basis of an assessment of the hazards to young people in connection with their work.

The assessment must be made before young people begin work and when there is any major change in working conditions and must pay particular attention to the following points:

  (a) the fitting-out and layout of the workplace and the workstation;
  (b) the nature, degree and duration of exposure to physical, biological and chemical agents;
  (c) the form, range and use of work equipment, in particular agents, machines, apparatus and devices, and the way in which they are handled;
  (d) the arrangement of work processes and operations and the way in which these are combined (organisation of work);
  (e) the level of training and instruction given to young people.

Where this assessment shows that there is a risk to the safety, the physical or mental health or development of young people, an appropriate free assessment and monitoring of their health shall be provided at regular intervals without prejudice to Directive 89/391/EEC.

The free health assessment and monitoring may form part of a national health system.

3   The employer shall inform young people of possible risks and of all measures adopted concerning their safety and health.

Furthermore, he shall inform the legal representatives of children of possible risks and of all measures adopted concerning children's safety and health.

4   The employer shall involve the protective and preventive services referred to in Article 7 of Directive 89/391/EEC in the planning, implementation and monitoring of the safety and health conditions applicable to young people.

Article 7   Vulnerability of young people – Prohibition of work
1   Member States shall ensure that young people are protected from any specific risks to their safety, health and development which are a consequence of their lack of experience, of absence of awareness of existing or potential risks or of the fact that young people have not yet fully matured.

2   Without prejudice to Article 4(1), Member States shall to this end prohibit the employment of young people for:

(a) work which is objectively beyond their physical or psychological capacity;
(b) work involving harmful exposure to agents which are toxic, carcinogenic, cause heritable genetic damage, or harm to the unborn child or which in any other way chronically affect human health;
(c) work involving harmful exposure to radiation;
(d) work involving the risk of accidents which it may be assumed cannot be recognised or avoided by young persons owing to their insufficient attention to safety or lack of experience or training; or
(e) work in which there is a risk to health from extreme cold or heat, or from noise or vibration.

Work which is likely to entail specific risks for young people within the meaning of paragraph 1 includes:

–   work involving harmful exposure to the physical, biological and chemical agents referred to in point I of the Annex, and
–   processes and work referred to in point II of the Annex.

3   Member States may, by legislative or regulatory provision, authorise derogations from paragraph 2 in the case of adolescents where such derogations are indispensable for their vocational training, provided that protection of their safety and health is ensured by the fact that the work is performed under the supervision of a competent person within the meaning of Article 7 of Directive 89/391/EEC and provided that the protection afforded by that Directive is guaranteed.

SECTION III

Article 8   Working time
1   Member States which make use of the option in Article 4(2)(b) or (c) shall adopt the measures necessary to limit the working time of children to:

(a) eight hours a day and 40 hours a week for work performed under a combined work/training scheme or an in-plant work-experience scheme;
(b) two hours on a school day and 12 hours a week for work performed in term-time outside the hours fixed for school attendance, provided that this is not prohibited by national legislation and/or practice;

in no circumstances may the daily working time exceed seven hours; this limit may be raised to eight hours in the case of children who have reached the age of 15;

913

(c) seven hours a day and 35 hours a week for work performed during a period of at least a week when school is not operating; these limits may be raised to eight hours a day and 40 hours a week in the case of children who have reached the age of 15;

(d) seven hours a day and 35 hours a week for light work performed by children no longer subject to compulsory full-time schooling under national law.

2   Member States shall adopt the measures necessary to limit the working time of adolescents to eight hours a day and 40 hours a week.

3   The time spent on training by a young person working under a theoretical and/or practical combined work/training scheme or an in-plant work-experience scheme shall be counted as working time.

4   Where a young person is employed by more than one employer, working days and working time shall be cumulative.

5   Member States may, by legislative or regulatory provision, authorise derogations from paragraph 1(a) and paragraph 2 either by way of exception or where there are objective grounds for so doing.

Member States shall, by legislative or regulatory provision, determine the conditions, limits and procedure for implementing such derogations.

Article 9   Night work

1 (a) Member States which make use of the option in Article 4(2)(b) or (c) shall adopt the measures necessary to prohibit work by children between 8pm and 6am.

   (b) Member States shall adopt the measures necessary to prohibit work by adolescents either between 10pm and 6am or between 11pm and 7am.

2 (a) Member States may, by legislative or regulatory provision, authorise work by adolescents in specific areas of activity during the period in which night work is prohibited as referred to in paragraph 1(b).
In that event, Member States shall take appropriate measures to ensure that the adolescent is supervised by an adult where such supervision is necessary for the adolescent's protection.

   (b) If point (a) is applied, work shall continue to be prohibited between midnight and 4am.

However, Member States may, by legislative or regulatory provision, authorise work by adolescents during the period in which night work is prohibited in the following cases, where there are objective grounds for so doing and provided that adolescents are allowed suitable compensatory rest time and that the objectives set out in Article 1 are not called into question:

- work performed in the shipping or fisheries sectors;
- work performed in the context of the armed forces or the police;
- work performed in hospitals or similar establishments;
- cultural, artistic, sports or advertising activities.

3   Prior to any assignment to night work and at regular intervals thereafter, adolescents shall be entitled to a free assessment of their health and capacities, unless the work they do during the period during which work is prohibited is of an exceptional nature.

Article 10   Rest period

1 (a) Member States which make use of the option in Article 4(2)(b) or (c) shall adopt the measures necessary to ensure that, for each 24–hour period, children are entitled to a minimum rest period of 14 consecutive hours.

(b) Member States shall adopt the measures necessary to ensure that, for each 24–hour period, adolescents are entitled to a minimum rest period of 12 consecutive hours.

2   Member States shall adopt the measures necessary to ensure that, for each seven-day period:

- children in respect of whom they have made use of the option in Article 4(2)(b) or (c), and
- adolescents

are entitled to a minimum rest period of two days, which shall be consecutive if possible.

Where justified by technical or organisation reasons, the minimum rest period may be reduced, but may in no circumstances be less than 36 consecutive hours.

The minimum rest period referred to in the first and second subparagraphs shall in principle include Sunday.

3   Member States may, by legislative or regulatory provision, provide for the minimum rest periods referred to in paragraphs 1 and 2 to be interrupted in the case of activities involving periods of work that are split up over the day or are of short duration.

4   Member States may make legislative or regulatory provision for derogations from paragraph 1(b) and paragraph 2 in respect of adolescents in the following cases, where there are objective grounds for so doing and provided that they are granted appropriate compensatory rest time and that the objectives set out in Article 1 are not called into question:

(a) work performed in the shipping or fisheries sectors;
(b) work performed in the context of the armed forces or the police;
(c) work performed in hospitals or similar establishments;
(d) work performed in agriculture;
(e) work performed in the tourism industry or in the hotel, restaurant and café sector;
(f) activities involving periods of work split up over the day.

Article 11   Annual rest
Member States which make use of the option referred to in Article 4(2)(b) or (c) shall see to it that a period free of any work is included, as far as possible, in the school holidays of children subject to compulsory full-time schooling under national law.

Article 12   Breaks
Member States shall adopt the measures necessary to ensure that, where daily working time is more than four and a half hours, young people are entitled to a break of at least 30 minutes, which shall be consecutive if possible.

Article 13   Work by adolescents in the event of *force majeure*
Member States may, by legislative or regulatory provision, authorise derogations from Article 8(2), Article 9(1)(b), Article 10(1)(b) and, in the case of adolescents, Article 12, for work in the circumstances referred to in Article 5(4) of Directive 89/391/EEC, provided that such work is of a temporary nature and must be performed immediately, that adult workers are not available and that the adolescents are allowed equivalent compensatory rest time within the following three weeks.

SECTION IV

Article 14   Measures
Each Member State shall lay down any necessary measures to be applied in the event of failure to comply with the provisions adopted in order to implement this Directive; such measures must be effective and proportionate.

Article 15   Adaptation of the Annex
Adaptations of a strictly technical nature to the Annex in the light of technical progress, changes in international rules or specifications and advances in knowledge in the field covered by this Directive shall be adopted in accordance with the procedure provided for in Article 17 of Directive 89/391/EEC.

Article 16   Non-reducing clause
Without prejudice to the right of Member States to develop, in the light of changing circumstances, different provisions on the protection of young people, as long as the minimum requirements provided for by this Directive are complied with, the implementation of this Directive shall not constitute valid grounds for reducing the general level of protection afforded to young people.

Article 17   Final provisions
1 (a) Member States shall bring into force the laws, regulations and administrative provisions necessary to comply with this Directive not later than 22 June 1996 or ensure, by that date at the latest, that the two sides of industry introduce the requisite provisions by means of collective agreements, with Member States being required to make all the necessary provisions to enable them at all times to guarantee the results laid down by this Directive.

   (b) The United Kingdom may refrain from implementing the first subparagraph of Article 8(1)(b) with regard to the provision relating to the maximum weekly working time, and also Article 8(2) and Article 9(1)(b) and (2) for a period of four years from the date specified in subparagraph (a).

   The Commission shall submit a report on the effects of this provision.

   The Council, acting in accordance with the conditions laid down by the Treaty, shall decide whether this period should be extended.

   (c) Member States shall forthwith inform the Commission thereof.

2 When Member States adopt the measures referred to in paragraph 1, such measures shall contain a reference to this Directive or shall be accompanied by such reference on the occasion of their official publication. The methods of making such reference shall be laid down by Member States.

3 Member States shall communicate to the Commission the texts of the main provisions of national law which they have already adopted or adopt in the field governed by this Directive.

4 Member States shall report to the Commission every five years on the practical implementation of the provisions of this Directive, indicating the viewpoints of the two sides of industry.

The Commission shall inform the European Parliament, the Council and the Economic and Social Committee thereof.

5 The Commission shall periodically submit to the European Parliament, the Council and the Economic and Social Committee a report on the application of this Directive taking into account paragraphs 1, 2, 3 and 4.

Article 18
This Directive is addressed to the Member States.

ANNEX
NON-EXHAUSTIVE LIST OF AGENTS, PROCESSES AND WORK REFERRED TO IN ARTICLE 7(2), SECOND SUBPARAGRAPH, OF THE DIRECTIVE

I   Agents

1   *Physical agents*

(a) Ionising radiation;
(b) Work in a high-pressure atmosphere, eg in pressurised containers, diving.

2   *Biological agents*

(a) Biological agents belonging to groups 3 and 4 within the meaning of Article 2(d) of Council Directive 90/679/EEC of 26 November 1990 on the protection of workers from risks related to exposure to biological agents at work (Seventh individual Directive within the meaning of Article 16(1) of Directive 89/391/EEC).

3   *Chemical agents*

(a) Substances and preparations classified according to Council Directive 67/548/EEC of 27 June 1967 on the approximation of laws, regulations and administrative provisions relating to the classification, packaging and labelling of dangerous substances with amendments and Council Directive 88/379/EEC of 7 June 1988 on the approximation of the laws, regulations and administrative provisions of the Member States relating to the classification, packaging and labelling of dangerous preparations as toxic (T), very toxic (Tx), corrosive (C) or explosive (E);
(b) Substances and preparations classified according to Directives 67/548/EEC and 88/379/EEC as harmful (Xn) and with one or more of the following risk phrases:
    –   danger of very serious irreversible effects (R39),
    –   possible risk of irreversible effects (R40),
    –   may cause sensitisation by inhalation (R42),
    –   may cause sensitisation by skin contact (R43),
    –   may cause cancer (R45),
    –   may cause heritable genetic damage (R46),
    –   danger of serious damage to health by prolonged exposure (R48),
    –   may impair fertility (R60),
    –   may cause harm to the unborn child (R61);
(c) Substances and preparations classified according to Directives 67/548/EEC and 88/379/EEC as irritant (Xi) and with one or more of the following risk phrases:
    –   highly flammable (R12),
    –   may cause sensitisation by inhalation (R42),
    –   may cause sensitisation by skin contact (R43);
(d) Substances and preparations referred to Article 2(c) of Council Directive 90/394/EEC of 28 June 1990 on the protection of workers from the risks related to exposure to carcinogens at work (Sixth individual Directive within the meaning of Article 16(1) of Directive 89/391/EEC);
(e) Lead and compounds thereof, inasmuch as the agents in question are absorbable by the human organism;
(f) Asbestos.

II   Processes and work

1   Processes at work referred to in Annex I to Directive 90/394/EEC.

2 Manufacture and handling of devices, fireworks or other objects containing explosives.
3 Work with fierce or poisonous animals.
4 Animal slaughtering on an industrial scale.
5 Work involving the handling of equipment for the production, storage or application of compressed, liquified or dissolved gases.
6 Work with vats, tanks, reservoirs or carboys containing chemical agents referred to in 1.3.
7 Work involving a risk of structural collapse.
8 Work involving high-voltage electrical hazards.
9 Work the pace of which is determined by machinery and involving payment by results.

COUNCIL DIRECTIVE 94/45/EC

of 22 September 1994

on the establishment of a European Works Council or a procedure in Community-scale undertakings and Community-scale groups of undertakings for the purposes of informing and consulting employees

THE COUNCIL OF THE EUROPEAN UNION,

Having regard to the Agreement on social policy annexed to Protocol 14 on social policy annexed to the Treaty establishing the European Community, and in particular Article 2(2) thereof,

Having regard to the proposal from the Commission,

Having regard to the opinion of the Economic and Social Committee,

Acting in accordance with the procedure referred to in Article 189c of the Treaty,

Whereas, on the basis of the Protocol on Social Policy annexed to the Treaty establishing the European Community, the Kingdom of Belgium, the Kingdom of Denmark, the Federal Republic of Germany, the Hellenic Republic, the Kingdom of Spain, the French Republic, Ireland, the Italian Republic, the Grand Duchy of Luxembourg, the Kingdom of the Netherlands and the Portuguese Republic (hereinafter referred to as 'the Member States'), desirous of implementing the Social Charter of 1989, have adopted an Agreement on Social Policy;

Whereas Article 2(2) of the said Agreement authorises the Council to adopt minimum requirements by means of directives;

Whereas, pursuant to Article 1 of the Agreement, one particular objective of the Community and the Member States is to promote dialogue between management and labour;

Whereas point 17 of the Community Charter of Fundamental Social Rights of Workers provides, *inter alia*, that information, consultation and participation for workers must be developed along appropriate lines, taking account of the practices in force in different Member States; whereas the Charter states that 'this shall apply especially in companies or groups of companies having establishments or companies in two or more Member States';

Whereas the Council, despite the existence of a broad consensus among the majority of Member States, was unable to act on the proposal for a Council Directive on the establishment of a European Works Council in Community-scale undertakings or groups of undertakings for the purposes of informing and consulting employees, as amended on 3 December 1991;

Whereas the Commission, pursuant to Article 3(2) of the Agreement on Social Policy, has consulted management and labour at Community level on the possible direction of Community action on the information and consultation of workers in Community-scale undertakings and Community-scale groups of undertakings;

Whereas the Commission, considering after this consultation that Community action was advisable, has again consulted management and labour on the content of the planned proposal, pursuant to Article 3(3) of the said Agreement, and management and labour have presented their opinions to the Commission;

Whereas, following this second phase of consultation, management and labour have not informed the Commission of their wish to initiate the process which might lead to the conclusion of an agreement, as provided for in Article 4 of the Agreement;

Whereas the functioning of the internal market involves a process of concentrations of undertakings, cross-border mergers, take-overs, joint ventures and, consequently, a transnationlisation of undertakings and groups of undertakings; whereas, if economic activities are to develop in a harmonious fashion, undertakings and group of undertakings operating in two or more Member States must inform and consult the representatives of those of their employees that are affected by their decisions;

Whereas procedures for informing and consulting employees as embodied in legislation or practice in the Member States are often not geared to the transnational structure of the entity which takes the decisions affecting those employees; whereas this may lead to the unequal treatment of employees affected by decisions within one and the same undertaking or group of undertakings;

Whereas appropriate provisions must be adopted to ensure that the employees of Community-scale undertakings are properly informed and consulted when decisions which affect them are taken in a Member State other than that in which they are employed;

Whereas, in order to guarantee that the employees of undertakings or groups of undertakings operating in two or more Member States are properly informed and consulted, it is necessary to set up European Works Councils or to create other suitable procedures for the transnational information and consultation of employees;

Whereas it is accordingly necessary to have a definition of the concept of controlling undertaking relating solely to this Directive and not prejudging definitions of the concepts of group or control which might be adopted in texts to be drafted in the future;

Whereas the mechanisms for informing and consulting employees in such undertakings or groups must encompass all of the establishments or, as the case may be, the group's undertakings located within the Member States, regardless of whether the undertaking or the group's controlling undertaking has its central management inside or outside the territory of the Member States;

Whereas, in accordance with the principle of autonomy of the parties, it is for the representatives of employees and the management of the undertaking or the group's controlling undertaking to determine by agreement the nature, composition, the function, mode of operation, procedures and financial resources of European Works Councils or other information and consultation procedures so as to suit their own particular circumstances;

Whereas, in accordance with the principle of subsidiarity, it is for the Member States to determine who the employees' representatives are and in particular to provide, if they consider appropriate, for a balanced representation of different categories of employees;

Whereas, however, provision should be made for certain subsidiary requirements to apply should the parties so decide or in the event of the central management refusing to initiate negotiations or in the absence of agreement subsequent to such negotiations;

Whereas, moreover, employees' representatives may decide not to seek the setting-up of a European Works Council or the parties concerned may decide on other procedures for the transnational information and consultation of employees;

Whereas, without prejudice to the possibility of the parties deciding otherwise, the European Works Council set up in the absence of agreement between the parties must, in order to fulfil the objective of this Directive, be kept informed and consulted on the activities of the undertaking or group of undertakings so that it may assess the possible impact on employees' interests in at least two different Member States; whereas, to that end, the undertaking or controlling undertaking must be required to communicate to the employees' appointed representatives general information concerning the interests of employees and information relating more specifically to those aspects of the activities of the undertaking or group of undertakings which affect employees' interests; whereas the European Works Council must be able to deliver an opinion at the end of that meeting;

Whereas certain decisions having a significant effect on the interests of employees must be the subject of information and consultation of the employees' appointed representatives as soon as possible;

Whereas provision should be made for the employees' representatives acting within the framework of the Directive to enjoy, when exercising their functions, the same protection and guarantees similar to those provided to employees' representatives by the legislation and/or practice of the country of employment; whereas they must not be subject to any discrimination as a result of the lawful exercise of their activities and must enjoy adequate protection as regards dismissal and other sanctions;

Whereas the information and consultation provisions laid down in this Directive must be implemented in the case of an undertaking or a group's controlling undertaking which has its central management outside the territory of the Member States by its representative agent, or be designated if necessary, in one of the Member States or, in the absence of such an agent, by the establishment or controlled undertaking employing the greatest number of employees in the Member States;

Whereas special treatment should be accorded to Community-scale undertakings and groups of undertakings in which there exists, at the time when this Directive is brought into effect, an agreement, covering the entire workforce, providing for the transnational information and consultation of employees;

Whereas the Member States must take appropriate measures in the event of failure to comply with the obligations laid down in this Directive,
HAS ADOPTED THIS DIRECTIVE:

SECTION I
GENERAL

Article 1   Objective
1   The purpose of this Directive is to improve the right to information and to consultation of employees in Community-scale undertakings and Community-scale groups of undertakings.

2   To that end, a European Works Council or a procedure for informing and consulting employees shall be established in every Community-scale undertaking and every Community-scale group of undertakings, where requested in the manner laid down in Article 5(1), with the purpose of informing and consulting employees under the terms, in the manner and with the effects laid down in this Directive.

3   Notwithstanding paragraph 2, where a Community-scale group of undertakings within the meaning of Article 2(1)(c) comprises one or more undertakings or groups of undertakings which are Community-scale undertakings or Community-scale groups of undertakings within the meaning of Article 2(1)(a) or (c), a European Works Council shall be established at the level of the group unless the agreements referred to in Article 6 provide otherwise.

4   Unless a wider scope is provided for in the agreements referred to in Article 6, the powers and competence of European Works Councils and the scope of information and consultation procedures established to achieve the purpose specified in paragraph 1 shall, in the case of a Community-scale undertaking, cover all the establishments located within the Member States and, in the case of a Community-scale group of undertakings, all group undertakings located within the Member States.

5   Member States may provide that this Directive shall not apply to merchant navy crews.

Article 2   Definitions
1   For the purposes of this Directive:

   (a) 'Community-scale undertaking' means any undertaking with at least 1000 employees within the Member States and at least 150 employees in each of at least two Member States;

921

(b) 'group of undertakings' means a controlling undertaking and its controlled undertakings;

(c) 'Community-scale group of undertakings' means a group of undertakings with the following characteristics:
  – at least 1000 employees within the Member States,
  – at least two group undertakings in different Member States, and
  – at least one group undertaking with at least 150 employees in one Member State and at least one other group undertaking with at least 150 employees in another Member State;

(d) 'employees' representatives' means the employees' representatives provided for by national law and/or practice;

(e) 'central management' means the central management of the Community-scale undertaking or, in the case of a Community-scale group of undertakings, of the controlling undertaking;

(f) 'consultation' means the exchange of views and establishment of dialogue between employees' representatives and central management or any more appropriate level of management;

(g) 'European Works Council' means the council established in accordance with Article 1(2) or the provisions of the Annex, with the purpose of informing and consulting employees;

(h) 'special negotiating body' means the body established in accordance with Article 5(2) to negotiate with the central management regarding the establishment of a European Works Council or a procedure for informing and consulting employees in accordance with Article 1(2).

2 For the purposes of this Directive, the prescribed thresholds for the size of the workforce shall be based on the average number of employees, including part-time employees, employed during the previous two years calculated according to national legislation and/or practice.

Article 3 Definition of 'controlling undertaking'

1 For the purposes of this Directive, 'controlling undertaking' means an undertaking which can exercise a dominant influence over another undertaking ('the controlled undertaking') by virtue, for example, of ownership, financial participation or the rules which govern it.

2 The ability to exercise a dominant influence shall be presumed, without prejudice to proof to the contrary, when, in relation to another undertaking directly or indirectly:

(a) holds a majority of that undertaking's subscribed capital; or

(b) controls a majority of the votes attached to that undertaking's issued share capital; or

(c) can appoint more than half of the members of that undertaking's administrative, management or supervisory body.

3 For the purposes of paragraph 2, a controlling undertaking's rights as regards voting and appointment shall include the rights of any other controlled undertaking and those of any person or body acting in his or its own name but on behalf of the controlling undertaking or of any other controlled undertaking.

4 Notwithstanding paragraphs 1 and 2, an undertaking shall not be deemed to be a 'controlling undertaking' with respect to another undertaking in which it has holdings where the former undertaking is a company referred to in Article 3(5)(a) or (c) of Council Regulation (EEC) No 4064/89 of 21 December 1989 on the control of concentrations between undertakings.

5 A dominant influence shall not be presumed to be exercised solely by virtue of the fact that an office holder is exercising his functions, according to the law of a

Member State relating to liquidation, winding up, insolvency, cessation of payments, compositions or analogous proceedings.

6 The law applicable in order to determine whether an undertaking is a 'controlling undertaking' shall be the law of the Member State which governs that undertaking.

Where the law governing that undertaking is not that of a Member State, the law applicable shall be the law of the Member State within whose territory the representative of the undertaking or, in the absence of such a representative, the central management of the group undertaking which employs the greatest number of employees is situated.

7 Where, in the case of a conflict of laws in the application of paragraph 2, two or more undertakings from a group satisfy one or more of the criteria laid down in that paragraph, the undertaking which satisfies the criterion laid down in point (c) thereof shall be regarded as the controlling undertaking, without prejudice to proof that another undertaking is able to exercise a dominant influence.

SECTION II
ESTABLISHMENT OF A EUROPEAN WORKS COUNCIL OR AN EMPLOYEE INFORMATION AND CONSULTATION PROCEDURE

Article 4   Responsibility for the establishment of a European Works Council or an employee information and consultation procedure

1 The central management shall be responsible for creating the conditions and means necessary for the setting up of a European Works Council or an information and consultation procedure, as provided for in Article 1(2), in a Community-scale undertaking and a Community-scale group of undertakings.

2 Where the central management is not situated in a Member State, the central management's representative agent in a Member State, to be designated if necessary, shall take on the responsibility referred to in paragraph 1.

In the absence of such a representative, the management of the establishment or group undertaking employing the greatest number of employees in any one Member State shall take on the responsibility referred to in paragraph 1.

3 For the purposes of this Directive, the representative or representatives or, in the absence of any such representatives, the management referred to in the second subparagraph of paragraph 2, shall be regarded as the central management.

Article 5   Special negotiating body

1 In order to achieve the objective in Article 1(1), the central management shall initiate negotiations for the establishment of a European Works Council or an information and consultation procedure on its own initiative or at the written request of at least 100 employees or their representatives in at least two undertakings or establishments in at least two different Member States.

2 For this purpose, a special negotiating body shall be established in accordance with the following guidelines:

(a) The Member States shall determine the method to be used for the election or appointment of the members of the special negotiating body who are to be elected or appointed in their territories.

Member States shall provide that employees in undertakings and/or establishments in which there are no employees' representatives through no fault of their own, have the right to elect or appoint members of the special negotiating body.

923

The second subparagraph shall be without prejudice to national legislation and/or practice laying down thresholds for the establishment of employee representation bodies.

(b) The special negotiating body shall have a minimum of three and a maximum of [18] members.

(c) In these elections or appointments, it must be ensured:
  - firstly, that each Member State in which the Community-scale undertaking has one or more establishments or in which the Community-scale group of undertakings has the controlling undertaking or one or more controlled undertakings is represented by one member,
  - secondly, that there are supplementary members in proportion to the number of employees working in the establishments, the controlling undertaking or the controlled undertakings as laid down by the legislation of the Member State within the territory of which the central management is situated.

(d) The central management and local management shall be informed of the composition of the special negotiating body.

3 The special negotiating body shall have the task of determining, with the central management, by written agreement, the scope, composition, functions, and term of office of the European Works Council(s) or the arrangements for implementing a procedure for the information and consultation of employees.

4 With a view to the conclusion of an agreement in accordance with Article 6, the central management shall convene a meeting with the special negotiating body. It shall inform the local managements accordingly.

For the purpose of the negotiations, the special negotiating body may be assisted by experts of its choice.

5 The special negotiating body may decide, by at least two-thirds of the votes, not to open negotiations in accordance with paragraph 4, or to terminate the negotiations already opened.

Such a decision shall stop the procedure to conclude the agreement referred to in Article 6. Where such a decision has been taken, the provisions in the Annex shall not apply.

A new request to convene the special negotiating body may be made at the earliest two years after the abovementioned decision unless the parties concerned lay down a shorter period.

6 Any expenses relating to the negotiations referred to in paragraphs 3 and 4 shall be borne by the central management so as to enable the special negotiating body to carry out its task in an appropriate manner.

In compliance with this principle, Member States may lay down budgetary rules regarding the operation of the special negotiating body. They may in particular limit the funding to cover one expert only.

Amendment The number '18' in art 5(2)(b) is substituted for the original '17' by Council Directive 97/74/EC of 15 December 1997 with effect from 15 December 1999.

Article 6   Content of the agreement
1 The central management and the special negotiating body must negotiate in a spirit of cooperation with a view to reaching an agreement on the detailed arrangements for implementing the information and consultation of employees provided for in Article 1(1).

2   Without prejudice to the autonomy of the parties, the agreement referred to in paragraph 1 between the central management and the special negotiating body shall determine:

(a) the undertakings of the Community-scale group of undertakings or the establishments of the Community-scale undertaking which are covered by the agreement;

(b) the composition of the European Works Council, the number of members, the allocation of seats and the term of office;

(c) the functions and the procedure for information and consultation of the European Works Council;

(d) the venue, frequency and duration of meetings of the European Works Council;

(e) the financial and material resources to be allocated to the European Works Council;

(f) the duration of the agreement and the procedure for its renegotiation.

3   The central management and the special negotiating body may decide, in writing, to establish one or more information and consultation procedures instead of a European Works Council.

The agreement must stipulate by what method the employees' representatives shall have the right to meet to discuss the information conveyed to them.

This information shall relate in particular to transnational questions which significantly affect workers' interests.

4   The agreements referred to in paragraphs 2 and 3 shall not, unless provision is made otherwise therein, be subject to the subsidiary requirements of the Annex.

5   For the purposes of concluding the agreements referred to in paragraphs 2 and 3, the special negotiating body shall act by a majority of its members.

Article 7   Subsidiary requirements
1   In order to achieve the objective in Article 1(1), the subsidiary requirements laid down by the legislation of the Member State in which the central management is situated shall apply:

– where the central management and the special negotiating body so decide, or
– where the central management refuses to commence negotiations within six months of the request referred to in Article 5(1), or
– where, after three years from the date of this request, they are unable to conclude an agreement as laid down in Article 6 and the special negotiating body has not taken the decision provided for in Article 5(5).

2   The subsidiary requirements referred to in paragraph 1 as adopted in the legislation of the Member States must satisfy the provisions set out in the Annex.

SECTION III
MISCELLANEOUS PROVISIONS

Article 8   Confidential information
1   Member States shall provide that members of special negotiating bodies or of European Works Councils and any experts who assist them are not authorised to reveal any information which has expressly been provided to them in confidence.

The same shall apply to employees' representatives in the framework of an information and consultation procedure.

This obligation shall continue to apply, wherever the persons referred to in the first and second subparagraphs are, even after the expiry of their terms of office.

2 Each Member State shall provide, in specific cases and under the conditions and limits laid down by national legislation, that the central management situated in its territory is not obliged to transmit information when its nature is such that, according to objective criteria, it would seriously harm the functioning of the undertakings concerned or would be prejudicial to them.

A Member State may make such dispensation subject to prior administrative or judicial authorisation.

3 Each Member State may lay down particular provisions for the central management of undertakings in its territory which pursue directly and essentially the aim of ideological guidance with respect to information and the expression of opinions, on condition that, at the date of adoption of this Directive such particular provisions already exist in the national legislation.

Article 9   Operation of European Works Council and information and consultation procedure for workers
The central management and the European Works Council shall work in a spirit of cooperation with due regard to their reciprocal rights and obligations.

The same shall apply to cooperation between the central management and employees' representatives in the framework of an information and consultation procedure for workers.

Article 10   Protection of employees' representatives
Members of special negotiating bodies, members of European Works Councils and employees' representatives exercising their functions under the procedure referred to in Article 6(3) shall, in the exercise of their functions, enjoy the same protection and guarantees provided for employees' representatives by the national legislation and/or practice in force in their country of employment.

This shall apply in particular to attendance at meetings of special negotiating bodies or European Works Councils or any other meetings within the framework of the agreement referred to in Article 6(3), and the payment of wages for members who are on the staff of the Community-scale undertaking or the Community-scale group of undertakings for the period of absence necessary for the performance of their duties.

Article 11   Compliance with this Directive
1 Each Member State shall ensure that the management of establishments of a Community-scale undertaking and the management of undertakings which form part of a Community-scale group of undertakings which are situated within its territory and their employees' representatives or, as the case may be, employees abide by the obligations laid down by this Directive, regardless of whether or not the central management is situated within its territory.

2 Member States shall ensure that the information on the number of employees referred to in Article 2(1)(a) and (c) is made available by undertakings at the request of the parties concerned by the application of this Directive.

3 Member States shall provide for appropriate measures in the event of failure to comply with this Directive; in particular, they shall ensure that adequate administrative or judicial procedures are available to enable the obligations deriving from this Directive to be enforced.

4 Where Member States apply Article 8, they shall make provision for administrative or judicial appeal procedures which the employees' representatives may initiate when the central management requires confidentiality or does not give information in accordance with that Article.

Such procedures may include procedures designed to protect the confidentiality of the information in question.

Article 12   Link between this Directive and other provisions
1   This Directive shall apply without prejudice to measures taken pursuant to Council Directive 75/129/EEC of 17 February 1975 on the approximation of the laws of the Member States relating to collective redundancies, and to Council Directive 77/187/EEC of 14 February 1977 on the approximation of the laws of the Member States relating to the safeguarding of employees' rights in the event of transfers of undertakings, business or parts of businesses.

2   This Directive shall be without prejudice to employees' existing rights to information and consultation under national law.

Article 13   Agreements in force
1   Without prejudice to paragraph 2, the obligations arising from this Directive shall not apply to Community-scale undertakings or Community-scale groups of undertakings in which, on the date laid down in Article 14(1) for the implementation of this Directive or the date of its transposition in the Member State in question, where this is earlier than the abovementioned date, there is already an agreement, covering the entire workforce, providing for the transnational information and consultation of employees.

2   When the agreements referred to in paragraph 1 expire, the parties to those agreements may decide jointly to renew them.

Where this is not the case, the provisions of this Directive shall apply.

Article 14   Final provisions
1   Member States shall bring into force the laws, regulations and administrative provisions necessary to comply with this Directive no later than 22 September 1996 or shall ensure by that date at the latest that management and labour introduce the required provisions by way of agreement, the Member States being obliged to take all necessary steps enabling them at all times to guarantee the results imposed by this Directive. They shall forthwith inform the Commission thereof.

2   When Member States adopt these measures, they shall contain a reference to this Directive or shall be accompanied by such reference on the occasion of their official publication. The methods of making such reference shall be laid down by Member States.

Article 15   Review by the Commission
Not later than 22 September 1999, the Commission shall, in consultation with the Member States and with management and labour at European level, review its operation and, in particular examine whether the workforce size thresholds are appropriate with a view to proposing suitable amendments to the Council, where necessary.

Article 16
This Directive is addressed to the Member States.

ANNEX
SUBSIDIARY REQUIREMENTS
REFERRED TO IN ARTICLE 7 OF THE DIRECTIVE

1   In order to achieve the objective in Article 1(1) of the Directive and in the cases provided for in Article 7(1) of the Directive, the establishment, composition and competence of a European Works Council shall be governed by the following rules:

    (a) The competence of the European Works Council shall be limited to infor-mation and consultation on the matters which concern the Community-scale undertaking or Community-scale group of undertakings as a whole or at least two of its establishments or group undertakings situated in different Member States.

In the case of undertakings or groups of undertakings referred to in Article 4(2), the competence of the European Works Council shall be limited to those matters concerning all their establishments or group undertakings situated within the Member States or concerning at least two of their establishments or group undertakings situated in different Member States.

(b) The European Works Council shall be composed of employees of the Community-scale undertaking or Community-scale group of undertakings elected or appointed from their number by the employees' representatives or, in the absence thereof, by the entire body of employees.

   The election or appointment of members of the European Works Council shall be carried out in accordance with national legislation and/or practice.

(c) The European Works Council shall have a minimum of three members and a maximum of 30.

   Where its size so warrants, it shall elect a select committee from among its members, comprising at most three members.

   It shall adopt its own rules of procedure.

(d) In the election or appointment of members of the European Works Council, it must be ensured:
   - firstly, that each Member State in which the Community-scale undertaking has one or more establishments or in which the Community-scale group of undertakings has the controlling undertaking or one or more controlled undertakings is represented by one member,
   - secondly, that there are supplementary members in proportion to the number of employees working in the establishments, the controlling undertaking or the controlled undertakings as laid down by the legislation of the Member State within the territory of which the central management is situated.

(e) The central management and any other more appropriate level of management shall be informed of the composition of the European Works Council.

(f) Four years after the European Works Council is established it shall examine whether to open negotiations for the conclusion of the agreement referred to in Article 6 of the Directive or to continue to apply the subsidiary requirements adopted in accordance with this Annex.

   Articles 6 and 7 of the Directive shall apply, *mutatis mutandis*, if a decision has been taken to negotiate an agreement according to Article 6 of the Directive, in which case 'special negotiating body' shall be replaced by 'European Works Council'.

2 The European Works Council shall have the right to meet with the central management once a year, to be informed and consulted, on the basis of a report drawn up by the central management, on the progress of the business of the Community-scale undertaking or Community-scale group of undertakings and its prospects. The local managements shall be informed accordingly.

The meeting shall relate in particular to the structure, economic and financial situation, the probable development of the business and of production and sales, the situation and probable trend of employment, investments, and substantial changes concerning organisation, introduction of new working methods or production processes, transfers of production, mergers, cut-backs or closures of undertakings, establishments or important parts thereof, and collective redundancies.

3   Where there are exceptional circumstances affecting the employees' interests to a considerable extent, particularly in the event of relocations, the closure of establishments or undertakings or collective redundancies, the select committee or, where no such committee exists, the European Works Council shall have the right to be informed. It shall have the right to meet, at its request, the central management, or any other more appropriate level of management within the Community-scale undertaking or group of undertakings having its own powers of decision, so as to be informed and consulted on measures significantly affecting employees' interests.

Those members of the European Works Council who have been elected or appointed by the establishments and/or undertakings which are directly concerned by the measures in question shall also have the right to participate in the meeting organised with the select committee.

This information and consultation meeting shall take place as soon as possible on the basis of a report drawn up by the central management or any other appropriate level of management of the Community-scale undertaking or group of undertakings, on which an opinion may be delivered at the end of the meeting or within a reasonable time.

This meeting shall not affect the prerogatives of the central management.

4   The Member States may lay down rules on the chairing of information and consultation meetings.

Before any meeting with the central management, the European Works Council or the select committee, where necessary enlarged in accordance with the second paragraph of point 3, shall be entitled to meet without the management concerned being present.

5   Without prejudice to Article 8 of the Directive, the members of the European Works Council shall inform the representatives of the employees of the establishments or of the undertakings of a Community-scale group of undertakings or, in the absence of representatives, the workforce as a whole, of the content and outcome of the information and consultation procedure carried out in accordance with this Annex.

6   The European Works Council or the select committee may be assisted by experts of its choice, in so far as this is necessary for it to carry out its tasks.

7   The operating expenses of the European Works Council shall be borne by the central management.

The central management concerned shall provide the members of the European Works Council with such financial and material resources as enable them to perform their duties in an appropriate manner.

In particular, the cost of organising meetings and arranging for interpretation facilities and the accommodation and travelling expenses of members of the European Works Council and its select committee shall be met by the central management unless otherwise agreed.

In compliance with these principles, the Member States may lay down budgetary rules regarding the operation of the European Works Council. They may in particular limit funding to cover one expert only.

DIRECTIVE 95/46/EC OF THE EUROPEAN PARLIAMENT AND OF THE COUNCIL

of 24 October 1995

on the protection of individuals with regard to the processing of personal data and on the free movement of such data

THE EUROPEAN PARLIAMENT AND THE COUNCIL OF THE EUROPEAN UNION,

Having regard to the Treaty establishing the European Community, and in particular Article 100a thereof,

Having regard to the proposal from the Commission,

Having regard to the opinion of the Economic and Social Committee,

Acting in accordance with the procedure referred to in Article 189b of the Treaty,

(1)   Whereas the objectives of the Community, as laid down in the Treaty, as amended by the Treaty on European Union, include creating an ever closer union among the peoples of Europe, fostering closer relations between the States belonging to the Community, ensuring economic and social progress by common action to eliminate the barriers which divide Europe, encouraging the constant improvement of the living conditions of its peoples, preserving and strengthening peace and liberty and promoting democracy on the basis of the fundamental rights recognized in the constitution and laws of the Member States and in the European Convention for the Protection of Human Rights and Fundamental Freedoms;

(2)   Whereas data-processing systems are designed to serve man; whereas they must, whatever the nationality or residence of natural persons, respect their fundamental rights and freedoms, notably the right to privacy, and contribute to economic and social progress, trade expansion and the well-being of individuals;

(3)   Whereas the establishment and functioning of an internal market in which, in accordance with Article 7a of the Treaty, the free movement of goods, persons, services and capital is ensured require not only that personal data should be able to flow freely from one Member State to another, but also that the fundamental rights of individuals should be safeguarded;

(4)   Whereas increasingly frequent recourse is being had in the Community to the processing of personal data in the various spheres of economic and social activity; whereas the progress made in information technology is making the processing and exchange of such data considerably easier;

(5)   Whereas the economic and social integration resulting from the establishment and functioning of the internal market within the meaning of Article 7a of the Treaty will necessarily lead to a substantial increase in cross-border flows of personal data between all those involved in a private or public capacity in economic and social activity in the Member States; whereas the exchange of personal data between undertakings in different Member States is set to increase; whereas the national authorities in the various Member States are being called upon by virtue of Community law to collaborate and exchange personal data so as to be able to perform their duties or carry out tasks on behalf of an authority in another Member State within the context of the area without internal frontiers as constituted by the internal market;

(6)   Whereas, furthermore, the increase in scientific and technical cooperation and the coordinated introduction of new telecommunications networks in the Community necessitate and facilitate cross-border flows of personal data;

(7)   Whereas the difference in levels of protection of the rights and freedoms of individuals, notably the right to privacy, with regard to the processing of personal data afforded in the Member States may prevent the transmission of such data from the territory of one Member State to that of another Member State; whereas this

difference may therefore constitute an obstacle to the pursuit of a number of economic activities at Community level, distort competition and impede authorities in the discharge of their responsibilities under Community law; whereas this difference in levels of protection is due to the existence of a wide variety of national laws, regulations and administrative provisions;

(8) Whereas, in order to remove the obstacles to flows of personal data, the level of protection of the rights and freedoms of individuals with regard to the processing of such data must be equivalent in all Member States; whereas this objective is vital to the internal market but cannot be achieved by the Member States alone, especially in view of the scale of the divergences which currently exist between the relevant laws in the Member States and the need to coordinate the laws of the Member States so as to ensure that the cross-border flow of personal data is regulated in a consistent manner that is in keeping with the objective of the internal market as provided for in Article 7a of the Treaty; whereas Community action to approximate those laws is therefore needed;

(9) Whereas, given the equivalent protection resulting from the approximation of national laws, the Member States will no longer be able to inhibit the free movement between them of personal data on grounds relating to protection of the rights and freedoms of individuals, and in particular the right to privacy; whereas Member States will be left a margin for manoeuvre, which may, in the context of implementation of the Directive, also be exercised by the business and social partners; whereas Member States will therefore be able to specify in their national law the general conditions governing the lawfulness of data processing; whereas in doing so the Member States shall strive to improve the protection currently provided by their legislation; whereas, within the limits of this margin for manoeuvre and in accordance with Community law, disparities could arise in the implementation of the Directive, and this could have an effect on the movement of data within a Member State as well as within the Community;

(10) Whereas the object of the national laws on the processing of personal data is to protect fundamental rights and freedoms, notably the right to privacy, which is recognized both in Article 8 of the European Convention for the Protection of Human Rights and Fundamental Freedoms and in the general principles of Community law; whereas, for that reason, the approximation of those laws must not result in any lessening of the protection they afford but must, on the contrary, seek to ensure a high level of protection in the Community;

(11) Whereas the principles of the protection of the rights and freedoms of individuals, notably the right to privacy, which are contained in this Directive, give substance to and amplify those contained in the Council of Europe Convention of 28 January 1981 for the Protection of Individuals with regard to Automatic Processing of Personal Data;

(12) Whereas the protection principles must apply to all processing of personal data by any person whose activities are governed by Community law; whereas there should be excluded the processing of data carried out by a natural person in the exercise of activities which are exclusively personal or domestic, such as correspondence and the holding of records of addresses;

(13) Whereas the acitivities referred to in Titles V and VI of the Treaty on European Union regarding public safety, defence, State security or the acitivities of the State in the area of criminal laws fall outside the scope of Community law, without prejudice to the obligations incumbent upon Member States under Article 56 (2), Article 57 or Article 100a of the Treaty establishing the European Community; whereas the processing of personal data that is necessary to safeguard the economic well-being of the State does not fall within the scope of this Directive where such processing relates to State security matters;

(14) Whereas, given the importance of the developments under way, in the framework of the information society, of the techniques used to capture, transmit, manipulate, record, store or communicate sound and image data relating to natural

persons, this Directive should be applicable to processing involving such data;

(15)   Whereas the processing of such data is covered by this Directive only if it is automated or if the data processed are contained or are intended to be contained in a filing system structured according to specific criteria relating to individuals, so as to permit easy access to the personal data in question;

(16)   Whereas the processing of sound and image data, such as in cases of video surveillance, does not come within the scope of this Directive if it is carried out for the purposes of public security, defence, national security or in the course of State activities relating to the area of criminal law or of other activities which do not come within the scope of Community law;

(17)   Whereas, as far as the processing of sound and image data carried out for purposes of journalism or the purposes of literary or artistic expression is concerned, in particular in the audiovisual field, the principles of the Directive are to apply in a restricted manner according to the provisions laid down in Article 9;

(18)   Whereas, in order to ensure that individuals are not deprived of the protection to which they are entitled under this Directive, any processing of personal data in the Community must be carried out in accordance with the law of one of the Member States; whereas, in this connection, processing carried out under the responsibility of a controller who is established in a Member State should be governed by the law of that State;

(19)   Whereas establishment on the territory of a Member State implies the effective and real exercise of activity through stable arrangements; whereas the legal form of such an establishment, whether simply branch or a subsidiary with a legal personality, is not the determining factor in this respect; whereas, when a single controller is established on the territory of several Member States, particularly by means of subsidiaries, he must ensure, in order to avoid any circumvention of national rules, that each of the establishments fulfils the obligations imposed by the national law applicable to its activities;

(20)   Whereas the fact that the processing of data is carried out by a person established in a third country must not stand in the way of the protection of individuals provided for in this Directive; whereas in these cases, the processing should be governed by the law of the Member State in which the means used are located, and there should be guarantees to ensure that the rights and obligations provided for in this Directive are respected in practice;

(21)   Whereas this Directive is without prejudice to the rules of territoriality applicable in criminal matters;

(22)   Whereas Member States shall more precisely define in the laws they enact or when bringing into force the measures taken under this Directive the general circumstances in which processing is lawful; whereas in particular Article 5, in conjunction with Articles 7 and 8, allows Member States, independently of general rules, to provide for special processing conditions for specific sectors and for the various categories of data covered by Article 8;

(23)   Whereas Member States are empowered to ensure the implementation of the protection of individuals both by means of a general law on the protection of individuals as regards the processing of personal data and by sectorial laws such as those relating, for example, to statistical institutes;

(24)   Whereas the legislation concerning the protection of legal persons with regard to the processing data which concerns them is not affected by this Directive;

(25)   Whereas the principles of protection must be reflected, on the one hand, in the obligations imposed on persons, public authorities, enterprises, agencies or other bodies responsible for processing, in particular regarding data quality, technical security, notification to the supervisory authority, and the circumstances under which processing can be carried out, and, on the other hand, in the right conferred on individuals, the data on whom are the subject of processing, to be informed that processing is taking place, to consult the data, to request corrections and even to object to processing in certain circumstances;

(26)   Whereas the principles of protection must apply to any information concerning an identified or identifiable person; whereas, to determine whether a person is identifiable, account should be taken of all the means likely reasonably to be used either by the controller or by any other person to identify the said person; whereas the principles of protection shall not apply to data rendered anonymous in such a way that the data subject is no longer identifiable; whereas codes of conduct within the meaning of Article 27 may be a useful instrument for providing guidance as to the ways in which data may be rendered anonymous and retained in a form in which identification of the data subject is no longer possible;

(27)   Whereas the protection of individuals must apply as much to automatic processing of data as to manual processing; whereas the scope of this protection must not in effect depend on the techniques used, otherwise this would create a serious risk of circumvention; whereas, nonetheless, as regards manual processing, this Directive covers only filing systems, not unstructured files; whereas, in particular, the content of a filing system must be structured according to specific criteria relating to individuals allowing easy access to the personal data; whereas, in line with the definition in Article 2 (c), the different criteria for determining the constituents of a structured set of personal data, and the different criteria governing access to such a set, may be laid down by each Member State; whereas files or sets of files as well as their cover pages, which are not structured according to specific criteria, shall under no circumstances fall within the scope of this Directive;

(28)   Whereas any processing of personal data must be lawful and fair to the individuals concerned; whereas, in particular, the data must be adequate, relevant and not excessive in relation to the purposes for which they are processed; whereas such purposes must be explicit and legitimate and must be determined at the time of collection of the data; whereas the purposes of processing further to collection shall not be incompatible with the purposes as they were originally specified;

(29)   Whereas the further processing of personal data for historical, statistical or scientific purposes is not generally to be considered incompatible with the purposes for which the data have previously been collected provided that Member States furnish suitable safeguards; whereas these safeguards must in particular rule out the use of the data in support of measures or decisions regarding any particular individual;

(30)   Whereas, in order to be lawful, the processing of personal data must in addition be carried out with the consent of the data subject or be necessary for the conclusion or performance of a contract binding on the data subject, or as a legal requirement, or for the performance of a task carried out in the public interest or in the exercise of official authority, or in the legitimate interests of a natural or legal person, provided that the interests or the rights and freedoms of the data subject are not overriding; whereas, in particular, in order to maintain a balance between the interests involved while guaranteeing effective competition, Member States may determine the circumstances in which personal data may be used or disclosed to a third party in the context of the legitimate ordinary business activities of companies and other bodies; whereas Member States may similarly specify the conditions under which personal data may be disclosed to a third party for the purposes of marketing whether carried out commercially or by a charitable organization or by any other association or foundation, of a political nature for example, subject to the provisions allowing a data subject to object to the processing of data regarding him, at no cost and without having to state his reasons;

(31)   Whereas the processing of personal data must equally be regarded as lawful where it is carried out in order to protect an interest which is essential for the data subject's life;

(32)   Whereas it is for national legislation to determine whether the controller performing a task carried out in the public interest or in the exercise of official authority should be a public administration or another natural or legal person governed by public law, or by private law such as a professional association;

(33)   Whereas data which are capable by their nature of infringing fundamental freedoms or privacy should not be processed unless the data subject gives his explicit consent; whereas, however, derogations from this prohibition must be explicitly provided for in respect of specific needs, in particular where the processing of these data is carried out for certain health-related purposes by persons subject to a legal obligation of professional secrecy or in the course of legitimate activities by certain associations or foundations the purpose of which is to permit the exercise of fundamental freedoms;

(34)   Whereas Member States must also be authorized, when justified by grounds of important public interest, to derogate from the prohibition on processing sensitive categories of data where important reasons of public interest so justify in areas such as public health and social protection - especially in order to ensure the quality and cost-effectiveness of the procedures used for settling claims for benefits and services in the health insurance system - scientific research and government statistics; whereas it is incumbent on them, however, to provide specific and suitable safeguards so as to protect the fundamental rights and the privacy of individuals;

(35)   Whereas, moreover, the processing of personal data by official authorities for achieving aims, laid down in constitutional law or international public law, of officially recognized religious associations is carried out on important grounds of public interest;

(36)   Whereas where, in the course of electoral activities, the operation of the democratic system requires in certain Member States that political parties compile data on people's political opinion, the processing of such data may be permitted for reasons of important public interest, provided that appropriate safeguards are established;

(37)   Whereas the processing of personal data for purposes of journalism or for purposes of literary of artistic expression, in particular in the audiovisual field, should qualify for exemption from the requirements of certain provisions of this Directive in so far as this is necessary to reconcile the fundamental rights of individuals with freedom of information and notably the right to receive and impart information, as guaranteed in particular in Article 10 of the European Convention for the Protection of Human Rights and Fundamental Freedoms; whereas Member States should therefore lay down exemptions and derogations necessary for the purpose of balance between fundamental rights as regards general measures on the legitimacy of data processing, measures on the transfer of data to third countries and the power of the supervisory authority; whereas this should not, however, lead Member States to lay down exemptions from the measures to ensure security of processing; whereas at least the supervisory authority responsible for this sector should also be provided with certain ex-post powers, e.g. to publish a regular report or to refer matters to the judicial authorities;

(38)   Whereas, if the processing of data is to be fair, the data subject must be in a position to learn of the existence of a processing operation and, where data are collected from him, must be given accurate and full information, bearing in mind the circumstances of the collection;

(39)   Whereas certain processing operations involve data which the controller has not collected directly from the data subject; whereas, furthermore, data can be legitimately disclosed to a third party, even if the disclosure was not anticipated at the time the data were collected from the data subject; whereas, in all these cases, the data subject should be informed when the data are recorded or at the latest when the data are first disclosed to a third party;

(40)   Whereas, however, it is not necessary to impose this obligation of the data subject already has the information; whereas, moreover, there will be no such obligation if the recording or disclosure are expressly provided for by law or if the provision of information to the data subject proves impossible or would involve disproportionate efforts, which could be the case where processing is for historical, statistical or scientific purposes; whereas, in this regard, the number of data subjects,

the age of the data, and any compensatory measures adopted may be taken into consideration;

(41) Whereas any person must be able to exercise the right of access to data relating to him which are being processed, in order to verify in particular the accuracy of the data and the lawfulness of the processing; whereas, for the same reasons, every data subject must also have the right to know the logic involved in the automatic processing of data concerning him, at least in the case of the automated decisions referred to in Article 15 (1); whereas this right must not adversely affect trade secrets or intellectual property and in particular the copyright protecting the software; whereas these considerations must not, however, result in the data subject being refused all information;

(42) Whereas Member States may, in the interest of the data subject or so as to protect the rights and freedoms of others, restrict rights of access and information; whereas they may, for example, specify that access to medical data may be obtained only through a health professional;

(43) Whereas restrictions on the rights of access and information and on certain obligations of the controller may similarly be imposed by Member States in so far as they are necessary to safeguard, for example, national security, defence, public safety, or important economic or financial interests of a Member State or the Union, as well as criminal investigations and prosecutions and action in respect of breaches of ethics in the regulated professions; whereas the list of exceptions and limitations should include the tasks of monitoring, inspection or regulation necessary in the three last-mentioned areas concerning public security, economic or financial interests and crime prevention; whereas the listing of tasks in these three areas does not affect the legitimacy of exceptions or restrictions for reasons of State security or defence;

(44) Whereas Member States may also be led, by virtue of the provisions of Community law, to derogate from the provisions of this Directive concerning the right of access, the obligation to inform individuals, and the quality of data, in order to secure certain of the purposes referred to above;

(45) Whereas, in cases where data might lawfully be processed on grounds of public interest, official authority or the legitimate interests of a natural or legal person, any data subject should nevertheless be entitled, on legitimate and compelling grounds relating to his particular situation, to object to the processing of any data relating to himself; whereas Member States may nevertheless lay down national provisions to the contrary;

(46) Whereas the protection of the rights and freedoms of data subjects with regard to the processing of personal data requires that appropriate technical and organizational measures be taken, both at the time of the design of the processing system and at the time of the processing itself, particularly in order to maintain security and thereby to prevent any unauthorized processing; whereas it is incumbent on the Member States to ensure that controllers comply with these measures; whereas these measures must ensure an appropriate level of security, taking into account the state of the art and the costs of their implementation in relation to the risks inherent in the processing and the nature of the data to be protected;

(47) Whereas where a message containing personal data is transmitted by means of a telecommunications or electronic mail service, the sole purpose of which is the transmission of such messages, the controller in respect of the personal data contained in the message will normally be considered to be the person from whom the message originates, rather than the person offering the transmission services; whereas, nevertheless, those offering such services will normally be considered controllers in respect of the processing of the additional personal data necessary for the operation of the service;

(48) Whereas the procedures for notifying the supervisory authority are designed to ensure disclosure of the purposes and main features of any processing

operation for the purpose of verification that the operation is in accordance with the national measures taken under this Directive;

(49) Whereas, in order to avoid unsuitable administrative formalities, exemptions from the obligation to notify and simplification of the notification required may be provided for by Member States in cases where processing is unlikely adversely to affect the rights and freedoms of data subjects, provided that it is in accordance with a measure taken by a Member State specifying its limits; whereas exemption or simplification may similarly be provided for by Member States where a person appointed by the controller ensures that the processing carried out is not likely adversely to affect the rights and freedoms of data subjects; whereas such a data protection official, whether or not an employee of the controller, must be in a position to exercise his functions in complete independence;

(50) Whereas exemption or simplification could be provided for in cases of processing operations whose sole purpose is the keeping of a register intended, according to national law, to provide information to the public and open to consultation by the public or by any person demonstrating a legitimate interest;

(51) Whereas, nevertheless, simplification or exemption from the obligation to notify shall not release the controller from any of the other obligations resulting from this Directive;

(52) Whereas, in this context, ex post facto verification by the competent authorities must in general be considered a sufficient measure;

(53) Whereas, however, certain processing operation are likely to pose specific risks to the rights and freedoms of data subjects by virtue of their nature, their scope or their purposes, such as that of excluding individuals from a right, benefit or a contract, or by virtue of the specific use of new technologies; whereas it is for Member States, if they so wish, to specify such risks in their legislation;

(54) Whereas with regard to all the processing undertaken in society, the amount posing such specific risks should be very limited; whereas Member States must provide that the supervisory authority, or the data protection official in cooperation with the authority, check such processing prior to it being carried out; whereas following this prior check, the supervisory authority may, according to its national law, give an opinion or an authorization regarding the processing; whereas such checking may equally take place in the course of the preparation either of a measure of the national parliament or of a measure based on such a legislative measure, which defines the nature of the processing and lays down appropriate safeguards;

(55) Whereas, if the controller fails to respect the rights of data subjects, national legislation must provide for a judicial remedy; whereas any damage which a person may suffer as a result of unlawful processing must be compensated for by the controller, who may be exempted from liability if he proves that he is not responsible for the damage, in particular in cases where he establishes fault on the part of the data subject or in case of force majeure; whereas sanctions must be imposed on any person, whether governed by private of public law, who fails to comply with the national measures taken under this Directive;

(56) Whereas cross-border flows of personal data are necessary to the expansion of international trade; whereas the protection of individuals guaranteed in the Community by this Directive does not stand in the way of transfers of personal data to third countries which ensure an adequate level of protection; whereas the adequacy of the level of protection afforded by a third country must be assessed in the light of all the circumstances surrounding the transfer operation or set of transfer operations;

(57) Whereas, on the other hand, the transfer of personal data to a third country which does not ensure an adequate level of protection must be prohibited;

(58) Whereas provisions should be made for exemptions from this prohibition in certain circumstances where the data subject has given his consent, where the transfer is necessary in relation to a contract or a legal claim, where protection of an important public interest so requires, for example in cases of international transfers

of data between tax or customs administrations or between services competent for social security matters, or where the transfer is made from a register established by law and intended for consultation by the public or persons having a legitimate interest; whereas in this case such a transfer should not involve the entirety of the data or entire categories of the data contained in the register and, when the register is intended for consultation by persons having a legitimate interest, the transfer should be made only at the request of those persons or if they are to be the recipients;

(59) Whereas particular measures may be taken to compensate for the lack of protection in a third country in cases where the controller offers appropriate safeguards; whereas, moreover, provision must be made for procedures for negotiations between the Community and such third countries;

(60) Whereas, in any event, transfers to third countries may be effected only in full compliance with the provisions adopted by the Member States pursuant to this Directive, and in particular Article 8 thereof;

(61) Whereas Member States and the Commission, in their respective spheres of competence, must encourage the trade associations and other representative organizations concerned to draw up codes of conduct so as to facilitate the application of this Directive, taking account of the specific characteristics of the processing carried out in certain sectors, and respecting the national provisions adopted for its implementation;

(62) Whereas the establishment in Member States of supervisory authorities, exercising their functions with complete independence, is an essential component of the protection of individuals with regard to the processing of personal data;

(63) Whereas such authorities must have the necessary means to perform their duties, including powers of investigation and intervention, particularly in cases of complaints from individuals, and powers to engage in legal proceedings; whereas such authorities must help to ensure transparency of processing in the Member States within whose jurisdiction they fall;

(64) Whereas the authorities in the different Member States will need to assist one another in performing their duties so as to ensure that the rules of protection are properly respected throughout the European Union;

(65) Whereas, at Community level, a Working Party on the Protection of Individuals with regard to the Processing of Personal Data must be set up and be completely independent in the performance of its functions; whereas, having regard to its specific nature, it must advise the Commission and, in particular, contribute to the uniform application of the national rules adopted pursuant to this Directive;

(66) Whereas, with regard to the transfer of data to third countries, the application of this Directive calls for the conferment of powers of implementation on the Commission and the establishment of a procedure as laid down in Council Decision 87/373/EEC (1);

(67) Whereas an agreement on a modus vivendi between the European Parliament, the Council and the Commission concerning the implementing measures for acts adopted in accordance with the procedure laid down in Article 189b of the EC Treaty was reached on 20 December 1994;

(68) Whereas the principles set out in this Directive regarding the protection of the rights and freedoms of individuals, notably their right to privacy, with regard to the processing of personal data may be supplemented or clarified, in particular as far as certain sectors are concerned, by specific rules based on those principles;

(69) Whereas Member States should be allowed a period of not more than three years from the entry into force of the national measures transposing this Directive in which to apply such new national rules progressively to all processing operations already under way; whereas, in order to facilitate their cost-effective implementation, a further period expiring 12 years after the date on which this Directive is adopted will be allowed to Member States to ensure the conformity of existing manual filing systems with certain of the Directive's provisions; whereas, where data contained in such filing systems are manually processed during this

extended transition period, those systems must be brought into conformity with these provisions at the time of such processing;

(70)   Whereas it is not necessary for the data subject to give his consent again so as to allow the controller to continue to process, after the national provisions taken pursuant to this Directive enter into force, any sensitive data necessary for the performance of a contract concluded on the basis of free and informed consent before the entry into force of these provisions;

(71)   Whereas this Directive does not stand in the way of a Member State's regulating marketing activities aimed at consumers residing in territory in so far as such regulation does not concern the protection of individuals with regard to the processing of personal data;

(72)   Whereas this Directive allows the principle of public access to official documents to be taken into account when implementing the principles set out in this Directive,

HAVE ADOPTED THIS DIRECTIVE:

CHAPTER I   GENERAL PROVISIONS

Article 1   Object of the Directive

1   In accordance with this Directive, Member States shall protect the fundamental rights and freedoms of natural persons, and in particular their right to privacy with respect to the processing of personal data.

2   Member States shall neither restrict nor prohibit the free flow of personal data between Member States for reasons connected with the protection afforded under paragraph 1.

Article 2   Definitions

For the purposes of this Directive:

  (a) 'personal data' shall mean any information relating to an identified or identifiable natural person ('data subject'); an identifiable person is one who can be identified, directly or indirectly, in particular by reference to an identification number or to one or more factors specific to his physical, physiological, mental, economic, cultural or social identity;
  (b) 'processing of personal data' ('processing') shall mean any operation or set of operations which is performed upon personal data, whether or not by automatic means, such as collection, recording, organization, storage, adaptation or alteration, retrieval, consultation, use, disclosure by transmission, dissemination or otherwise making available, alignment or combination, blocking, erasure or destruction;
  (c) 'personal data filing system' ('filing system') shall mean any structured set of personal data which are accessible according to specific criteria, whether centralized, decentralized or dispersed on a functional or geographical basis;
  (d) 'controller' shall mean the natural or legal person, public authority, agency or any other body which alone or jointly with others determines the purposes and means of the processing of personal data; where the purposes and means of processing are determined by national or Community laws or regulations, the controller or the specific criteria for his nomination may be designated by national or Community law;
  (e) 'processor' shall mean a natural or legal person, public authority, agency or any other body which processes personal data on behalf of the controller;
  (f) 'third party' shall mean any natural or legal person, public authority, agency or any other body other than the data subject, the controller, the processor and the persons who, under the direct authority of the controller or the processor, are authorized to process the data;

(g) 'recipient' shall mean a natural or legal person, public authority, agency or any other body to whom data are disclosed, whether a third party or not; however, authorities which may receive data in the framework of a particular inquiry shall not be regarded as recipients;

(h) 'the data subject's consent' shall mean any freely given specific and informed indication of his wishes by which the data subject signifies his agreement to personal data relating to him being processed.

Article 3 Scope

1 This Directive shall apply to the processing of personal data wholly or partly by automatic means, and to the processing otherwise than by automatic means of personal data which form part of a filing system or are intended to form part of a filing system.

This Directive shall not apply to the processing of personal data:

- in the course of an activity which falls outside the scope of Community law, such as those provided for by Titles V and VI of the Treaty on European Union and in any case to processing operations concerning public security, defence, State security (including the economic well-being of the State when the processing operation relates to State security matters) and the activities of the State in areas of criminal law,
- by a natural person in the course of a purely personal or household activity.

Article 4 National law applicable

1 Each Member State shall apply the national provisions it adopts pursuant to this Directive to the processing of personal data where:

(a) the processing is carried out in the context of the activities of an establishment of the controller on the territory of the Member State; when the same controller is established on the territory of several Member States, he must take the necessary measures to ensure that each of these establishments complies with the obligations laid down by the national law applicable;

(b) the controller is not established on the Member State's territory, but in a place where its national law applies by virtue of international public law;

(c) the controller is not established on Community territory and, for purposes of processing personal data makes use of equipment, automated or otherwise, situated on the territory of the said Member State, unless such equipment is used only for purposes of transit through the territory of the Community.

2 In the circumstances referred to in paragraph 1 (c), the controller must designate a representative established in the territory of that Member State, without prejudice to legal actions which could be initiated against the controller himself.

CHAPTER II
GENERAL RULES ON THE LAWFULNESS OF THE PROCESSING OF PERSONAL DATA

Article 5

Member States shall, within the limits of the provisions of this Chapter, determine more precisely the conditions under which the processing of personal data is lawful.

SECTION I
PRINCIPLES RELATING TO DATA QUALITY

Article 6

1 Member States shall provide that personal data must be:

(a) processed fairly and lawfully;

(b) collected for specified, explicit and legitimate purposes and not further processed in a way incompatible with those purposes. Further processing of data for historical, statistical or scientific purposes shall not be considered as incompatible provided that Member States provide appropriate safeguards;

(c) adequate, relevant and not excessive in relation to the purposes for which they are collected and/or further processed;

(d) accurate and, where necessary, kept up to date; every reasonable step must be taken to ensure that data which are inaccurate or incomplete, having regard to the purposes for which they were collected or for which they are further processed, are erased or rectified;

(e) kept in a form which permits identification of data subjects for no longer than is necessary for the purposes for which the data were collected or for which they are further processed. Member States shall lay down appropriate safeguards for personal data stored for longer periods for historical, statistical or scientific use.

2 It shall be for the controller to ensure that paragraph 1 is complied with.

SECTION II
CRITERIA FOR MAKING DATA PROCESSING LEGITIMATE

Article 7
Member States shall provide that personal data may be processed only if:

(a) the data subject has unambiguously given his consent; or

(b) processing is necessary for the performance of a contract to which the data subject is party or in order to take steps at the request of the data subject prior to entering into a contract; or

(c) processing is necessary for compliance with a legal obligation to which the controller is subject; or

(d) processing is necessary in order to protect the vital interests of the data subject; or

(e) processing is necessary for the performance of a task carried out in the public interest or in the exercise of official authority vested in the controller or in a third party to whom the data are disclosed; or

(f) processing is necessary for the purposes of the legitimate interests pursued by the controller or by the third party or parties to whom the data are disclosed, except where such interests are overridden by the interests for fundamental rights and freedoms of the data subject which require protection under Article 1 (1).

SECTION III
SPECIAL CATEGORIES OF PROCESSING

Article 8 The processing of special categories of data
1 Member States shall prohibit the processing of personal data revealing racial or ethnic origin, political opinions, religious or philosophical beliefs, trade-union membership, and the processing of data concerning health or sex life.

2 Paragraph 1 shall not apply where:

(a) the data subject has given his explicit consent to the processing of those data, except where the laws of the Member State provide that the prohibition referred to in paragraph 1 may not be lifted by the data subject's giving his consent; or

(b) processing is necessary for the purposes of carrying out the obligations and specific rights of the controller in the field of employment law in so far as it is authorized by national law providing for adequate safeguards; or

(c) processing is necessary to protect the vital interests of the data subject or of another person where the data subject is physically or legally incapable of giving his consent; or

(d) processing is carried out in the course of its legitimate activities with appropriate guarantees by a foundation, association or any other non-profit-seeking body with a political, philosophical, religious or trade-union aim and on condition that the processing relates solely to the members of the body or to persons who have regular contact with it in connection with its purposes and that the data are not disclosed to a third party without the consent of the data subjects; or

(e) the processing relates to data which are manifestly made public by the data subject or is necessary for the establishment, exercise or defence of legal claims.

3   Paragraph 1 shall not apply where processing of the data is required for the purposes of preventive medicine, medical diagnosis, the provision of care or treatment or the management of health-care services, and where those data are processed by a health professional subject under national law or rules established by national competent bodies to the obligation of professional secrecy or by another person also subject to an equivalent obligation of secrecy.

4   Subject to the provision of suitable safeguards, Member States may, for reasons of substantial public interest, lay down exemptions in addition to those laid down in paragraph 2 either by national law or by decision of the supervisory authority.

5   Processing of data relating to offences, criminal convictions or security measures may be carried out only under the control of official authority, or if suitable specific safeguards are provided under national law, subject to derogations which may be granted by the Member State under national provisions providing suitable specific safeguards. However, a complete register of criminal convictions may be kept only under the control of official authority.

Member States may provide that data relating to administrative sanctions or judgements in civil cases shall also be processed under the control of official authority.

6   Derogations from paragraph 1 provided for in paragraphs 4 and 5 shall be notified to the Commission.

7   Member States shall determine the conditions under which a national identification number or any other identifier of general application may be processed.

Article 9   Processing of personal data and freedom of expression
Member States shall provide for exemptions or derogations from the provisions of this Chapter, Chapter IV and Chapter VI for the processing of personal data carried out solely for journalistic purposes or the purpose of artistic or literary expression only if they are necessary to reconcile the right to privacy with the rules governing freedom of expression.

SECTION IV
INFORMATION TO BE GIVEN TO THE DATA SUBJECT

Article 10   Information in cases of collection of data from the data subject
Member States shall provide that the controller or his representative must provide a data subject from whom data relating to himself are collected with at least the following information, except where he already has it:

(a) the identity of the controller and of his representative, if any;
(b) the purposes of the processing for which the data are intended;

(c) any further information such as
  - the recipients or categories of recipients of the data,
  - whether replies to the questions are obligatory or voluntary, as well as the possible consequences of failure to reply,
  - the existence of the right of access to and the right to rectify the data concerning him
    in so far as such further information is necessary, having regard to the specific circumstances in which the data are collected, to guarantee fair processing in respect of the data subject.

Article 11   Information where the data have not been obtained from the data subject
1   Where the data have not been obtained from the data subject, Member States shall provide that the controller or his representative must at the time of undertaking the recording of personal data or if a disclosure to a third party is envisaged, no later than the time when the data are first disclosed provide the data subject with at least the following information, except where he already has it:

(a) the identity of the controller and of his representative, if any;
(b) the purposes of the processing;
(c) any further information such as
  - the categories of data concerned,
  - the recipients or categories of recipients,
  - the existence of the right of access to and the right to rectify the data concerning him

in so far as such further information is necessary, having regard to the specific circumstances in which the data are processed, to guarantee fair processing in respect of the data subject.

2   Paragraph 1 shall not apply where, in particular for processing for statistical purposes or for the purposes of historical or scientific research, the provision of such information proves impossible or would involve a disproportionate effort or if recording or disclosure is expressly laid down by law. In these cases Member States shall provide appropriate safeguards.

SECTION V
THE DATA SUBJECT'S RIGHT OF ACCESS TO DATA

Article 12   Right of access
Member States shall guarantee every data subject the right to obtain from the controller:

(a) without constraint at reasonable intervals and without excessive delay or expense:
  - confirmation as to whether or not data relating to him are being processed and information at least as to the purposes of the processing, the categories of data concerned, and the recipients or categories of recipients to whom the data are disclosed,
  - communication to him in an intelligible form of the data undergoing processing and of any available information as to their source,
  - knowledge of the logic involved in any automatic processing of data concerning him at least in the case of the automated decisions referred to in Article 15(1);
(b) as appropriate the rectification, erasure or blocking of data the processing of which does not comply with the provisions of this Directive, in particular because of the incomplete or inaccurate nature of the data;
(c) notification to third parties to whom the data have been disclosed of any rectification, erasure or blocking carried out in compliance with (b), unless this proves impossible or involves a disproportionate effort.

SECTION VI
EXEMPTIONS AND RESTRICTIONS

Article 13 Exemptions and restrictions
1   Member States may adopt legislative measures to restrict the scope of the obligations and rights provided for in Articles 6 (1), 10, 11 (1), 12 and 21 when such a restriction constitutes a necessary measures to safeguard:

(a)   national security;
(b)   defence;
(c)   public security;
(d)   the prevention, investigation, detection and prosecution of criminal offences, or of breaches of ethics for regulated professions;
(e)   an important economic or financial interest of a Member State or of the European Union, including monetary, budgetary and taxation matters;
(f)   a monitoring, inspection or regulatory function connected, even occasionally, with the exercise of official authority in cases referred to in (c), (d) and (e);
(g)   the protection of the data subject or of the rights and freedoms of others.

2   Subject to adequate legal safeguards, in particular that the data are not used for taking measures or decisions regarding any particular individual, Member States may, where there is clearly no risk of breaching the privacy of the data subject, restrict by a legislative measure the rights provided for in Article 12 when data are processed solely for purposes of scientific research or are kept in personal form for a period which does not exceed the period necessary for the sole purpose of creating statistics.

SECTION VII
THE DATA SUBJECT'S RIGHT TO OBJECT

Article 14   The data subject's right to object
Member States shall grant the data subject the right:

(a)   at least in the cases referred to in Article 7 (e) and (f), to object at any time on compelling legitimate grounds relating to his particular situation to the processing of data relating to him, save where otherwise provided by national legislation. Where there is a justified objection, the processing instigated by the controller may no longer involve those data;
(b)   to object, on request and free of charge, to the processing of personal data relating to him which the controller anticipates being processed for the purposes of direct marketing, or to be informed before personal data are disclosed for the first time to third parties or used on their behalf for the purposes of direct marketing, and to be expressly offered the right to object free of charge to such disclosures or uses.

Member States shall take the necessary measures to ensure that data subjects are aware of the existence of the right referred to in the first subparagraph of (b).

Article 15   Automated individual decisions
1   Member States shall grant the right to every person not to be subject to a decision which produces legal effects concerning him or significantly affects him and which is based solely on automated processing of data intended to evaluate certain personal aspects relating to him, such as his performance at work, creditworthiness, reliability, conduct, etc.

2   Subject to the other Articles of this Directive, Member States shall provide that a person may be subjected to a decision of the kind referred to in paragraph 1 if that decision:

(a) is taken in the course of the entering into or performance of a contract, provided the request for the entering into or the performance of the contract, lodged by the data subject, has been satisfied or that there are suitable measures to safeguard his legitimate interests, such as arrangements allowing him to put his point of view; or

(b) is authorized by a law which also lays down measures to safeguard the data subject's legitimate interests.

SECTION VIII
CONFIDENTIALITY AND SECURITY OF PROCESSING

Article 16   Confidentiality of processing
Any person acting under the authority of the controller or of the processor, including the processor himself, who has access to personal data must not process them except on instructions from the controller, unless he is required to do so by law.

Article 17   Security of processing
1   Member States shall provide that the controller must implement appropriate technical and organizational measures to protect personal data against accidental or unlawful destruction or accidental loss, alteration, unauthorized disclosure or access, in particular where the processing involves the transmission of data over a network, and against all other unlawful forms of processing.

Having regard to the state of the art and the cost of their implementation, such measures shall ensure a level of security appropriate to the risks represented by the processing and the nature of the data to be protected.

2   The Member States shall provide that the controller must, where processing is carried out on his behalf, choose a processor providing sufficient guarantees in respect of the technical security measures and organizational measures governing the processing to be carried out, and must ensure compliance with those measures.

3   The carrying out of processing by way of a processor must be governed by a contract or legal act binding the processor to the controller and stipulating in particular that:

– the processor shall act only on instructions from the controller,
– the obligations set out in paragraph 1, as defined by the law of the Member State in which the processor is established, shall also be incumbent on the processor.

4   For the purposes of keeping proof, the parts of the contract or the legal act relating to data protection and the requirements relating to the measures referred to in paragraph 1 shall be in writing or in another equivalent form.

SECTION IX
NOTIFICATION

Article 18   Obligation to notify the supervisory authority
1   Member States shall provide that the controller or his representative, if any, must notify the supervisory authority referred to in Article 28 before carrying out any wholly or partly automatic processing operation or set of such operations intended to serve a single purpose or several related purposes.

2   Member States may provide for the simplification of or exemption from notification only in the following cases and under the following conditions:

– where, for categories of processing operations which are unlikely, taking account of the data to be processed, to affect adversely the rights and freedoms of data subjects, they specify the purposes of the processing, the data or categories of data undergoing processing, the category or categories

944

of data subject, the recipients or categories of recipient to whom the data are to be disclosed and the length of time the data are to be stored, and/or

– where the controller, in compliance with the national law which governs him, appoints a personal data protection official, responsible in particular:

– for ensuring in an independent manner the internal application of the national provisions taken pursuant to this Directive

– for keeping the register of processing operations carried out by the controller, containing the items of information referred to in Article 21 (2),

thereby ensuring that the rights and freedoms of the data subjects are unlikely to be adversely affected by the processing operations.

3 Member States may provide that paragraph 1 does not apply to processing whose sole purpose is the keeping of a register which according to laws or regulations is intended to provide information to the public and which is open to consultation either by the public in general or by any person demonstrating a legitimate interest.

4 Member States may provide for an exemption from the obligation to notify or a simplification of the notification in the case of processing operations referred to in Article 8 (2) (d).

5 Member States may stipulate that certain or all non-automatic processing operations involving personal data shall be notified, or provide for these processing operations to be subject to simplified notification.

Article 19 Contents of notification

1 Member States shall specify the information to be given in the notification. It shall include at least:

(a) the name and address of the controller and of his representative, if any;
(b) the purpose or purposes of the processing;
(c) a description of the category or categories of data subject and of the data or categories of data relating to them;
(d) the recipients or categories of recipient to whom the data might be disclosed;
(e) proposed transfers of data to third countries;
(f) a general description allowing a preliminary assessment to be made of the appropriateness of the measures taken pursuant to Article 17 to ensure security of processing.

2 Member States shall specify the procedures under which any change affecting the information referred to in paragraph 1 must be notified to the supervisory authority.

Article 20 Prior checking

1 Member States shall determine the processing operations likely to present specific risks to the rights and freedoms of data subjects and shall check that these processing operations are examined prior to the start thereof.

2 Such prior checks shall be carried out by the supervisory authority following receipt of a notification from the controller or by the data protection official, who, in cases of doubt, must consult the supervisory authority.

3 Member States may also carry out such checks in the context of preparation either of a measure of the national parliament or of a measure based on such a legislative measure, which define the nature of the processing and lay down appropriate safeguards.

Article 21 Publicizing of processing operations

1 Member States shall take measures to ensure that processing operations are publicized.

2   Member States shall provide that a register of processing operations notified in accordance with Article 18 shall be kept by the supervisory authority.

The register shall contain at least the information listed in Article 19 (1) (a) to (e).

The register may be inspected by any person.

3   Member States shall provide, in relation to processing operations not subject to notification, that controllers or another body appointed by the Member States make available at least the information referred to in Article 19 (1) (a) to (e) in an appropriate form to any person on request.

Member States may provide that this provision does not apply to processing whose sole purpose is the keeping of a register which according to laws or regulations is intended to provide information to the public and which is open to consultation either by the public in general or by any person who can provide proof of a legitimate interest.

CHAPTER III
JUDICIAL REMEDIES, LIABILITY AND SANCTIONS

Article 22   Remedies
Without prejudice to any administrative remedy for which provision may be made, inter alia before the supervisory authority referred to in Article 28, prior to referral to the judicial authority, Member States shall provide for the right of every person to a judicial remedy for any breach of the rights guaranteed him by the national law applicable to the processing in question.

Article 23   Liability
1   Member States shall provide that any person who has suffered damage as a result of an unlawful processing operation or of any act incompatible with the national provisions adopted pursuant to this Directive is entitled to receive compensation from the controller for the damage suffered.

2   The controller may be exempted from this liability, in whole or in part, if he proves that he is not responsible for the event giving rise to the damage.

Article 24   Sanctions
The Member States shall adopt suitable measures to ensure the full implementation of the provisions of this Directive and shall in particular lay down the sanctions to be imposed in case of infringement of the provisions adopted pursuant to this Directive.

CHAPTER IV
TRANSFER OF PERSONAL DATA TO THIRD COUNTRIES

Article 25   Principles
1   The Member States shall provide that the transfer to a third country of personal data which are undergoing processing or are intended for processing after transfer may take place only if, without prejudice to compliance with the national provisions adopted pursuant to the other provisions of this Directive, the third country in question ensures an adequate level of protection.

2   The adequacy of the level of protection afforded by a third country shall be assessed in the light of all the circumstances surrounding a data transfer operation or set of data transfer operations; particular consideration shall be given to the nature of the data, the purpose and duration of the proposed processing operation or

operations, the country of origin and country of final destination, the rules of law, both general and sectoral, in force in the third country in question and the professional rules and security measures which are complied with in that country.

3   The Member States and the Commission shall inform each other of cases where they consider that a third country does not ensure an adequate level of protection within the meaning of paragraph 2.

4   Where the Commission finds, under the procedure provided for in Article 31 (2), that a third country does not ensure an adequate level of protection within the meaning of paragraph 2 of this Article, Member States shall take the measures necessary to prevent any transfer of data of the same type to the third country in question.

5   At the appropriate time, the Commission shall enter into negotiations with a view to remedying the situation resulting from the finding made pursuant to paragraph 4.

6   The Commission may find, in accordance with the procedure referred to in Article 31 (2), that a third country ensures an adequate level of protection within the meaning of paragraph 2 of this Article, by reason of its domestic law or of the international commitments it has entered into, particularly upon conclusion of the negotiations referred to in paragraph 5, for the protection of the private lives and basic freedoms and rights of individuals.

Member States shall take the measures necessary to comply with the Commission's decision.

Article 26   Derogations

1   By way of derogation from Article 25 and save where otherwise provided by domestic law governing particular cases, Member States shall provide that a transfer or a set of transfers of personal data to a third country which does not ensure an adequate level of protection within the meaning of Article 25 (2) may take place on condition that:

(a) the data subject has given his consent unambiguously to the proposed transfer; or

(b) the transfer is necessary for the performance of a contract between the data subject and the controller or the implementation of precontractual measures taken in response to the data subject's request; or

(c) the transfer is necessary for the conclusion or performance of a contract concluded in the interest of the data subject between the controller and a third party; or

(d) the transfer is necessary or legally required on important public interest grounds, or for the establishment, exercise or defence of legal claims; or

(e) the transfer is necessary in order to protect the vital interests of the data subject; or

(f) the transfer is made from a register which according to laws or regulations is intended to provide information to the public and which is open to consultation either by the public in general or by any person who can demonstrate legitimate interest, to the extent that the conditions laid down in law for consultation are fulfilled in the particular case.

2   Without prejudice to paragraph 1, a Member State may authorize a transfer or a set of transfers of personal data to a third country which does not ensure an adequate level of protection within the meaning of Article 25 (2), where the controller adduces adequate safeguards with respect to the protection of the privacy and fundamental rights and freedoms of individuals and as regards the exercise of the corresponding rights; such safeguards may in particular result from appropriate contractual clauses.

3   The Member State shall inform the Commission and the other Member States of the authorizations it grants pursuant to paragraph 2.

If a Member State or the Commission objects on justified grounds involving the protection of the privacy and fundamental rights and freedoms of individuals, the Commission shall take appropriate measures in accordance with the procedure laid down in Article 31 (2).

Member States shall take the necessary measures to comply with the Commission's decision.

4   Where the Commission decides, in accordance with the procedure referred to in Article 31 (2), that certain standard contractual clauses offer sufficient safeguards as required by paragraph 2, Member States shall take the necessary measures to comply with the Commission's decision.

CHAPTER V
CODES OF CONDUCT

Article 27
1   The Member States and the Commission shall encourage the drawing up of codes of conduct intended to contribute to the proper implementation of the national provisions adopted by the Member States pursuant to this Directive, taking account of the specific features of the various sectors.

2   Member States shall make provision for trade associations and other bodies representing other categories of controllers which have drawn up draft national codes or which have the intention of amending or extending existing national codes to be able to submit them to the opinion of the national authority.

Member States shall make provision for this authority to ascertain, among other things, whether the drafts submitted to it are in accordance with the national provisions adopted pursuant to this Directive. If it sees fit, the authority shall seek the views of data subjects or their representatives.

3   Draft Community codes, and amendments or extensions to existing Community codes, may be submitted to the Working Party referred to in Article 29. This Working Party shall determine, among other things, whether the drafts submitted to it are in accordance with the national provisions adopted pursuant to this Directive. If it sees fit, the authority shall seek the views of data subjects or their representatives. The Commission may ensure appropriate publicity for the codes which have been approved by the Working Party.

CHAPTER VI
SUPERVISORY AUTHORITY AND WORKING PARTY ON THE PROTECTION OF INDIVIDUALS WITH REGARD TO THE PROCESSING OF PERSONAL DATA

Article 28   Supervisory authority
1   Each Member State shall provide that one or more public authorities are responsible for monitoring the application within its territory of the provisions adopted by the Member States pursuant to this Directive.

These authorities shall act with complete independence in exercising the functions entrusted to them.

2   Each Member State shall provide that the supervisory authorities are consulted when drawing up administrative measures or regulations relating to the protection of individuals' rights and freedoms with regard to the processing of personal data.

3   Each authority shall in particular be endowed with:

–   investigative powers, such as powers of access to data forming the subject-matter of processing operations and powers to collect all the information necessary for the performance of its supervisory duties,

–   effective powers of intervention, such as, for example, that of delivering opinions before processing operations are carried out, in accordance with Article 20, and ensuring appropriate publication of such opinions, of ordering the blocking, erasure or destruction of data, of imposing a temporary or definitive ban on processing, of warning or admonishing the controller, or that of referring the matter to national parliaments or other political institutions,

–   the power to engage in legal proceedings where the national provisions adopted pursuant to this Directive have been violated or to bring these violations to the attention of the judicial authorities.

Decisions by the supervisory authority which give rise to complaints may be appealed against through the courts.

4   Each supervisory authority shall hear claims lodged by any person, or by an association representing that person, concerning the protection of his rights and freedoms in regard to the processing of personal data. The person concerned shall be informed of the outcome of the claim.

Each supervisory authority shall, in particular, hear claims for checks on the lawfulness of data processing lodged by any person when the national provisions adopted pursuant to Article 13 of this Directive apply. The person shall at any rate be informed that a check has taken place.

5   Each supervisory authority shall draw up a report on its activities at regular intervals. The report shall be made public.

6   Each supervisory authority is competent, whatever the national law applicable to the processing in question, to exercise, on the territory of its own Member State, the powers conferred on it in accordance with paragraph 3. Each authority may be requested to exercise its powers by an authority of another Member State.

The supervisory authorities shall cooperate with one another to the extent necessary for the performance of their duties, in particular by exchanging all useful information.

7   Member States shall provide that the members and staff of the supervisory authority, even after their employment has ended, are to be subject to a duty of professional secrecy with regard to confidential information to which they have access.

Article 29   Working Party on the Protection of Individuals with regard to the Processing of Personal Data

1   A Working Party on the Protection of Individuals with regard to the Processing of Personal Data, hereinafter referred to as 'the Working Party', is hereby set up.

It shall have advisory status and act independently.

2   The Working Party shall be composed of a representative of the supervisory authority or authorities designated by each Member State and of a representative of the authority or authorities established for the Community institutions and bodies, and of a representative of the Commission.

Each member of the Working Party shall be designated by the institution, authority or authorities which he represents. Where a Member State has designated more than one supervisory authority, they shall nominate a joint representative. The same shall apply to the authorities established for Community institutions and bodies.

3   The Working Party shall take decisions by a simple majority of the representatives of the supervisory authorities.

4   The Working Party shall elect its chairman. The chairman's term of office shall be two years. His appointment shall be renewable.

5   The Working Party's secretariat shall be provided by the Commission.

6   The Working Party shall adopt its own rules of procedure.

7   The Working Party shall consider items placed on its agenda by its chairman, either on his own initiative or at the request of a representative of the supervisory authorities or at the Commission's request.

Article 30
1   The Working Party shall:

  (a) examine any question covering the application of the national measures adopted under this Directive in order to contribute to the uniform application of such measures;
  (b) give the Commission an opinion on the level of protection in the Community and in third countries;
  (c) advise the Commission on any proposed amendment of this Directive, on any additional or specific measures to safeguard the rights and freedoms of natural persons with regard to the processing of personal data and on any other proposed Community measures affecting such rights and freedoms;
  (d) give an opinion on codes of conduct drawn up at Community level.

2   If the Working Party finds that divergences likely to affect the equivalence of protection for persons with regard to the processing of personal data in the Community are arising between the laws or practices of Member States, it shall inform the Commission accordingly.

3   The Working Party may, on its own initiative, make recommendations on all matters relating to the protection of persons with regard to the processing of personal data in the Community.

4   The Working Party's opinions and recommendations shall be forwarded to the Commission and to the committee referred to in Article 31.

5   The Commission shall inform the Working Party of the action it has taken in response to its opinions and recommendations. It shall do so in a report which shall also be forwarded to the European Parliament and the Council. The report shall be made public.

6   The Working Party shall draw up an annual report on the situation regarding the protection of natural persons with regard to the processing of personal data in the Community and in third countries, which it shall transmit to the Commission, the European Parliament and the Council. The report shall be made public.

CHAPTER VII
COMMUNITY IMPLEMENTING MEASURES

Article 31   The Committee
1   The Commission shall be assisted by a committee composed of the representatives of the Member States and chaired by the representative of the Commission.

2   The representative of the Commission shall submit to the committee a draft of the measures to be taken. The committee shall deliver its opinion on the draft within a time limit which the chairman may lay down according to the urgency of the matter.

The opinion shall be delivered by the majority laid down in Article 148(2) of the Treaty. The votes of the representatives of the Member States within the committee shall be weighted in the manner set out in that Article. The chairman shall not vote.

The Commission shall adopt measures which shall apply immediately. However, if these measures are not in accordance with the opinion of the committee, they shall be communicated by the Commission to the Council forthwith. It that event:

- the Commission shall defer application of the measures which it has decided for a period of three months from the date of communication,
- the Council, acting by a qualified majority, may take a different decision within the time limit referred to in the first indent.

FINAL PROVISIONS

Article 32
1   Member States shall bring into force the laws, regulations and administrative provisions necessary to comply with this Directive at the latest at the end of a period of three years from the date of its adoption.

When Member States adopt these measures, they shall contain a reference to this Directive or be accompanied by such reference on the occasion of their official publication. The methods of making such reference shall be laid down by the Member States.

2   Member States shall ensure that processing already under way on the date the national provisions adopted pursuant to this Directive enter into force, is brought into conformity with these provisions within three years of this date.

By way of derogation from the preceding subparagraph, Member States may provide that the processing of data already held in manual filing systems on the date of entry into force of the national provisions adopted in implementation of this Directive shall be brought into conformity with Articles 6, 7 and 8 of this Directive within 12 years of the date on which it is adopted. Member States shall, however, grant the data subject the right to obtain, at his request and in particular at the time of exercising his right of access, the rectification, erasure or blocking of data which are incomplete, inaccurate or stored in a way incompatible with the legitimate purposes pursued by the controller.

3   By way of derogation from paragraph 2, Member States may provide, subject to suitable safeguards, that data kept for the sole purpose of historical research need not be brought into conformity with Articles 6, 7 and 8 of this Directive.

4   Member States shall communicate to the Commission the text of the provisions of domestic law which they adopt in the field covered by this Directive.

Article 33
The Commission shall report to the Council and the European Parliament at regular intervals, starting not later than three years after the date referred to in Article 32 (1), on the implementation of this Directive, attaching to its report, if necessary, suitable proposals for amendments. The report shall be made public.

The Commission shall examine, in particular, the application of this Directive to the data processing of sound and image data relating to natural persons and shall submit any appropriate proposals which prove to be necessary, taking account of developments in information technology and in the light of the state of progress in the information society.

Article 34
This Directive is addressed to the Member States.

COUNCIL DIRECTIVE 96/34/EC

of 3 June 1996

on the framework agreement on parental leave concluded by UNICE, CEEP and the ETUC

THE COUNCIL OF THE EUROPEAN UNION,

Having regard to the Agreement on social policy, annexed to the Protocol (No 14) on social policy, annexed to the Treaty establishing the European Community, and in particular Article 4(2) thereof,

Having regard to the proposal from the Commission,

(1) Whereas on the basis of the Protocol on social policy, the Member States, with the exception of the United Kingdom of Great Britain and Northern Ireland, (hereinafter referred to as 'the Member States'), wishing to pursue the course mapped out by the 1989 Social Charter have concluded an Agreement on social policy amongst themselves;

(2) Whereas management and labour may, in accordance with Article 4(2) of the Agreement on social policy, request jointly that agreements at Community level be implemented by a Council decision on a proposal from the Commission;

(3) Whereas paragraph 16 of the Community Charter of the Fundamental Social Rights of Workers on equal treatment for men and women provides, *inter alia*, that 'measures should also be developed enabling men and women to reconcile their occupational and family obligations';

(4) Whereas the Council, despite the existence of a broad consensus, has not been able to act on the proposal for a Directive on parental leave for family reasons, as amended on 15 November 1984;

(5) Whereas the Commission, in accordance with Article 3(2) of the Agreement on social policy, consulted management and labour on the possible direction of Community action with regard to reconciling working and family life;

(6) Whereas the Commission, considering after such consultation that Community action was desirable, once again consulted management and labour on the substance of the envisaged proposal in accordance with Article 3(3) of the said Agreement;

(7) Whereas the general cross-industry organisations (UNICE, CEEP and the ETUC) informed the Commission in their joint letter of 5 July 1995 of their desire to initiate the procedure provided for by Article 4 of the said Agreement;

(8) Whereas the said cross-industry organisations concluded, on 14 December 1995, a framework agreement on parental leave; whereas they have forwarded to the Commission their joint request to implement this framework agreement by a Council Decision on a proposal from the Commission in accordance with Article 4(2) of the said Agreement;

(9) Whereas the Council, in its Resolution of 6 December 1994 on certain aspects for a European Union social policy; a contribution to economic and social convergence in the Union, asked the two sides of industry to make use of the possibilities for concluding agreements, since they are as a rule closer to social reality and to social problems; whereas in Madrid, the members of the European Council from those States which have signed the Agreement on social policy welcomed the conclusion of this framework agreement;

(10) Whereas the signatory parties wanted to conclude a framework agreement setting out minimum requirements on parental leave and time off from work on grounds of *force majeure* and referring back to the Member States and/or management and labour for the definition of the conditions under which parental leave would be implemented, in order to take account of the situation, including the situation with regard to family policy, existing in each Member State, particularly as regards the conditions for granting parental leave and exercise of the right to parental leave;

(11)   Whereas the proper instrument for implementing this framework agreement is a Directive within the meaning of Article 189 of the Treaty; whereas it is therefore binding on the Member States as to the result to be achieved, but leaves them the choice of form and methods;

(12)   Whereas, in keeping with the principle of subsidiarity and the principle of proportionality as set out in Article 3b of the Treaty, the objectives of this Directive cannot be sufficiently achieved by the Member States and can therefore be better achieved by the Community; whereas this Directive is confined to the minimum required to achieve these objectives and does not go beyond what is necessary to achieve that purpose;

(13)   Whereas the Commission has drafted its proposal for a Directive, taking into account the representative status of the signatory parties, their mandate and the legality of the clauses of the framework agreement and compliance with the relevant provisions concerning small and medium-sized undertakings;

(14)   Whereas the Commission, in accordance with its Communication of 14 December 1993 concerning the implementation of the Protocol on social policy, informed the European Parliament by sending it the text of the framework agreement, accompanied by its proposal for a Directive and the explanatory memorandum;

(15)   Whereas the Commission also informed the Economic and Social Committee by sending it the text of the framework agreement, accompanied by its proposal for a Directive and the explanatory memorandum;

(16)   Whereas clause 4 point 2 of the framework agreement states that the implementation of the provisions of this agreement does not constitute valid grounds for reducing the general level of protection afforded to workers in the field of this agreement. This does not prejudice the right of Member States and/or management and labour to develop different legislative, regulatory or contractual provisions, in the light of changing circumstances (including the introduction of non-transferability), as long as the minimum requirements provided for in the present agreement are complied with;

(17)   Whereas the Community Charter of the Fundamental Social Rights of Workers recognises the importance of the fight against all forms of discrimination, especially based on sex, colour, race, opinions and creeds;

(18)   Whereas Article F(2) of the Treaty on European Union provides that the Union shall respect fundamental rights, as guaranteed by the European Convention for the Protection of Human Rights and Fundamental Freedoms signed in Rome on 4 November 1950 and as they result from the constitutional traditions common to the Member States, as general principles of Community law;

(19)   Whereas the Member States can entrust management and labour, at their joint request, with the implementation of this Directive, as long as they take all the necessary steps to ensure that they can at all times guarantee the results imposed by this Directive;

(20)   Whereas the implementation of the framework agreement contributes to achieving the objectives under Article 1 of the Agreement on social policy,
HAS ADOPTED THIS DIRECTIVE:

Article 1   Implementation of the framework agreement
The purpose of this Directive is to put into effect the annexed framework agreement on parental leave concluded on 14 December 1995 between the general cross-industry organisations (UNICE, CEEP and the ETUC).

Article 2   Final provisions
1   The Member States shall bring into force the laws, regulations and administrative provisions necessary to comply with this Directive by 3 June 1998 at the latest or shall ensure by that date at the latest that management and labour have introduced the necessary measures by agreement, the Member States being required

to take any necessary measure enabling them at any time to be in a position to guarantee the results imposed by this Directive. They shall forthwith inform the Commission thereof.

[1a   As regards the United Kingdom of Great Britain and Northern Ireland, the date of 3 June 1998 in paragraph 1 shall be replaced by 15 December 1999.]

2   The Member States may have a maximum additional period of one year, if this is necessary to take account of special difficulties or implementation by a collective agreement.

They must forthwith inform the Commission of such circumstances.

3   When Member States adopt the measures referred to in paragraph 1, they shall contain a reference to this Directive or be accompanied by such reference on the occasion of their official publication. The methods of making such reference shall be laid down by Member States.

Amendment   Article 2(1a) was inserted by Council Directive 97/75/EC of 15 December 1997.

Article 3
This Directive is addressed to the Member States.

ANNEX
FRAMEWORK AGREEMENT ON PARENTAL LEAVE

Preamble
The enclosed framework agreement represents an undertaking by UNICE, CEEP and the ETUC to set out minimum requirements on parental leave and time off from work on grounds of *force majeure*, as an important means of reconciling work and family life and promoting equal opportunities and treatment between men and women.

ETUC, UNICE and CEEP request the Commission to submit this framework agreement to the Council for a Council Decision making these minimum requirements binding in the Member States of the European Community, with the exception of the United Kingdom of Great Britain and Northern Ireland.

I.   GENERAL CONSIDERATIONS
1   Having regard to the Agreement on social policy annexed to the Protocol on social policy, annexed to the Treaty establishing the European Community, and in particular Articles 3(4) and 4(2) thereof;

2   Whereas Article 4(2) of the Agreement on social policy provides that agreements concluded at Community level shall be implemented, at the joint request of the signatory parties, by a Council decision on a proposal from the Commission;

3   Whereas the Commission has announced its intention to propose a Community measure on the reconciliation of work and family life;

4   Whereas the Community Charter of Fundamental Social Rights stipulates at point 16 dealing with equal treatment that measures should be developed to enable men and women to reconcile their occupational and family obligations;

5   Whereas the Council Resolution of 6 December 1994 recognises that an effective policy of equal opportunities presupposes an integrated overall strategy allowing for better organisation of working hours and greater flexibility, and for an easier return to working life, and notes the important role of the two sides of industry in this area and in offering both men and women an opportunity to reconcile their work responsibilities with family obligations;

6   Whereas measures to reconcile work and family life should encourage the introduction of new flexible ways of organising work and time which are better suited to the changing needs of society and which should take the needs of both undertakings and workers into account;

7   Whereas family policy should be looked at in the context of demographic changes, the effects of the ageing population, closing the generation gap and promoting women's participation in the labour force;

8   Whereas men should be encouraged to assume an equal share of family responsibilities, for example they should be encouraged to take parental leave by means such as awareness programmes;

9   Whereas the present agreement is a framework agreement setting out minimum requirements and provisions for parental leave, distinct from maternity leave, and for time off from work on grounds of *force majeure*, and refers back to Member States and social partners for the establishment of the conditions of access and detailed rules of application in order to take account of the situation in each Member State;

10   Whereas Member States should provide for the maintenance of entitlements to benefits in kind under sickness insurance during the minimum period of parental leave;

11   Whereas Member States should also, where appropriate under national conditions and taking into account the budgetary situation, consider the maintenance of entitlements to relevant social security benefits as they stand during the minimum period of parental leave;

12   Whereas this agreement takes into consideration the need to improve social policy requirements, to enhance the competitiveness of the Community economy and to avoid imposing administrative, financial and legal constraints in a way which would impede the creation and development of small and medium-sized undertakings;

13   Whereas management and labour are best placed to find solutions that correspond to the needs of both employers and workers and must therefore have conferred on them a special role in the implementation and application of the present agreement,

THE SIGNATORY PARTIES HAVE AGREED THE FOLLOWING:

II.   CONTENT

Clause 1:   Purpose and scope

1   This agreement lays down minimum requirements designed to facilitate the reconciliation of parental and professional responsibilities for working parents.

2   This agreement applies to all workers, men and women, who have an employment contract or employment relationship as defined by the law, collective agreements or practices in force in each Member State.

Clause 2:   Parental leave

1   This agreement grants, subject to clause 2.2, men and women workers an individual right to parental leave on the grounds of the birth or adoption of a child to enable them to take care of that child, for at least three months, until a given age up to 8 years to be defined by Member States and/or management and labour.

2   To promote equal opportunities and equal treatment between men and women, the parties to this agreement consider that the right to parental leave provided for under clause 2.1 should, in principle, be granted on a non-transferable basis.

3   The conditions of access and detailed rules for applying parental leave shall be defined by law and/or collective agreement in the Member States, as long as the

minimum requirements of this agreement are respected. Member States and/or management and labour may, in particular:

(a) decide whether parental leave is granted on a full-time or part-time basis, in a piecemeal way or in the form of a time-credit system;

(b) make entitlement to parental leave subject to a period of work qualification and/or a length of service qualification which shall not exceed one year;

(c) adjust conditions of access and detailed rules for applying parental leave to the special circumstances of adoption;

(d) establish notice periods to be given by the worker to the employer when exercising the right to parental leave, specifying the beginning and the end of the period of leave;

(e) define the circumstances in which an employer, following consultation in accordance with national law, collective agreements and practices, is allowed to postpone the granting of parental leave for justifiable reasons related to the operation of the undertaking (eg where work is of a seasonal nature, where a replacement cannot be found within the notice period, where a significant proportion of the workforce applies for parental leave at the same time, where a specific function is of strategic importance). Any problem arising from the application of this provision should be dealt with in accordance with national law, collective agreements and practices;

(f) in addition to (e), authorise special arrangements to meet the operational and organisational requirements of small undertakings.

4   In order to ensure that workers can exercise their right to parental leave, Member States and/or management and labour shall take the necessary measures to protect workers against dismissal on the grounds of an application for, or the taking of, parental leave in accordance with national law, collective agreements or practices.

5   At the end of parental leave, workers shall have the right to return to the same job or, if that is not possible, to an equivalent or similar job consistent with their employment contract or employment relationship.

6   Rights acquired or in the process of being acquired by the worker on the date on which parental leave starts shall be maintained as they stand until the end of parental leave. At the end of parental leave, these rights, including any changes arising from national law, collective agreements or practice, shall apply.

7   Member States and/or management and labour shall define the status of the employment contract or employment relationship for the period of parental leave.

8   All matters relating to social security in relation to this agreement are for consideration and determination by Member States according to national law, taking into account the importance of the continuity of the entitlements to social security cover under the different schemes, in particular health care.

Clause 3:   Time off from work on grounds of *force majeure*
1   Member States and/or management and labour shall take the necessary measures to entitle workers to time off from work, in accordance with national legislation, collective agreements and/or practice, on grounds of *force majeure* for urgent family reasons in cases of sickness or accident making the immediate presence of the worker indispensable.

2   Member States and/or management and labour may specify the conditions of access and detailed rules for applying clause 3.1 and limit this entitlement to a certain amount of time per year and/or per case.

Clause 4:   Final provisions
1   Member States may apply or introduce more favourable provisions than those set out in this agreement.

2   Implementation of the provisions of this agreement shall not constitute valid grounds for reducing the general level of protection afforded to workers in the field covered by this agreement. This shall not prejudice the right of Member States and/or management and labour to develop different legislative, regulatory or contractual provisions, in the light of changing circumstances (including the introduction of non-transferability), as long as the minimum requirements provided for in the present agreement are complied with.

3   The present agreement shall not prejudice the right of management and labour to conclude, at the appropriate level including European level, agreements adapting and/or complementing the provisions of this agreement in order to take into account particular circumstances.

4   Member States shall adopt the laws, regulations and administrative provisions necessary to comply with the Council decision within a period of two years from its adoption or shall ensure that management and labour introduce the necessary measures by way of agreement by the end of this period. Member States may, if necessary to take account of particular difficulties or implementation by collective agreement, have up to a maximum of one additional year to comply with this decision.

5   The prevention and settlement of disputes and grievances arising from the application of this agreement shall be dealt with in accordance with national law, collective agreements and practices.

6   Without prejudice to the respective role of the Commission, national courts and the Court of Justice, any matter relating to the interpretation of this agreement at European level should, in the first instance, be referred by the Commission to the signatory parties who will give an opinion.

7   The signatory parties shall review the application of this agreement five years after the date of the Council decision if requested by one of the parties to this agreement.

COUNCIL DIRECTIVE 96/71/EC

of 16 December 1996

concerning the posting of workers in the framework of the provision of services

THE EUROPEAN PARLIAMENT AND THE COUNCIL OF THE EUROPEAN UNION,

Having regard to the Treaty establishing the European Community, and in particular Articles 57(2) and 66 thereof,

Having regard to the proposal from the Commission,

Having regard to the opinion of the Economic and Social Committee,

Acting in accordance with the procedure laid down in Article 189b of the Treaty,

(1) Whereas, pursuant to Article 3(c) of the Treaty, the abolition, as between Member States, of obstacles to the free movement of persons and services constitutes one of the objectives of the Community;

(2) hereas, for the provision of services, any restrictions based on nationality or residence requirements are prohibited under the Treaty with effect from the end of the transitional period;

(3) Whereas the completion of the internal market offers a dynamic environment for the transnational provision of services, prompting a growing number of undertakings to post employees abroad temporarily to perform work in the territory of a Member State other than the State in which they are habitually employed;

(4) Whereas the provision of services may take the form either of performance of work by an undertaking on its account and under its direction, under a contract concluded between that undertaking and the party for whom the services are intended, or of the hiring-out of workers for use by an undertaking in the framework of a public or a private contract;

(5) Whereas any such promotion of the transnational provision of services requires a climate of fair competition and measures guaranteeing respect for the rights of workers;

(6) Whereas the transnationalization of the employment relationship raises problems with regard to the legislation applicable to the employment relationship; whereas it is in the interests of the parties to lay down the terms and conditions governing the employment relationship envisaged;

(7) Whereas the Rome Convention of 19 June 1980 on the law applicable to contractual obligations, signed by 12 Member States, entered into force on 1 April 1991 in the majority of Member States;

(8) Whereas Article 3 of that Convention provides, as a general rule, for the free choice of law made by the parties; whereas, in the absence of choice, the contract is to be governed, according to Article 6(2), by the law of the country, in which the employee habitually carries out his work in performance of the contract, even if he is temporarily employed in another country, or, if the employee does not habitually carry out his work in any one country, by the law of the country in which the place of business through which he was engaged is situated, unless it appears from the circumstances as a whole that the contract is more closely connected with another country, in which case the contract is to be governed by the law of that country;

(9) Whereas, according to Article 6(1) of the said Convention, the choice of law made by the parties is not to have the result of depriving the employee of the protection afforded to him by the mandatory rules of the law which would be applicable under paragraph 2 of that Article in the absence of choice;

(10) Whereas Article 7 of the said Convention lays down, subject to certain conditions, that effect may be given, concurrently with the law declared applicable, to the mandatory rules of the law of another country, in particular the law of the Member State within whose territory the worker is temporarily posted;

(11)   Whereas, according to the principle of precedence of Community law laid down in its Article 20, the said Convention does not affect the application of provisions which, in relation to a particular matter, lay down choice-of-law rules relating to contractual obligations and which are or will be contained in acts of the institutions of the European Communities or in national laws harmonized in implementation of such acts;

(12)   Whereas Community law does not preclude Member States from applying their legislation, or collective agreements entered into by employers and labour, to any person who is employed, even temporarily, within their territory, although his employer is established in another Member State; whereas Community law does not forbid Member States to guarantee the observance of those rules by the appropriate means;

(13)   Whereas the laws of the Member States must be co-ordinated in order to lay down a nucleus of mandatory rules for minimum protection to be observed in the host country by employers who post workers to perform temporary work in the territory of a Member State where the services are provided; whereas such co-ordination can be achieved only by means of Community law;

(14)   Whereas a 'hard core' of clearly defined protective rules should be observed by the provider of the services notwithstanding the duration of the worker's posting;

(15)   Whereas it should be laid down that, in certain clearly defined cases of assembly and/or installation of goods, the provisions on minimum rates of pay and minimum paid annual holidays do not apply;

(16)   Whereas there should also be some flexibility in application of the provisions concerning minimum rates of pay and the minimum length of paid annual holidays; whereas, when the length of the posting is not more than one month, Member States may, under certain conditions, derogate from the provisions concerning minimum rates of pay or provide for the possibility of derogation by means of collective agreements; whereas, where the amount of work to be done is not significant, Member States may derogate from the provisions concerning minimum rates of pay and the minimum length of paid annual holidays;

(17)   Whereas the mandatory rules for minimum protection in force in the host country must not prevent the application of terms and conditions of employment which are more favourable to workers;

(18)   Whereas the principle that undertakings established outside the Community must not receive more favourable treatment than undertakings established in the territory of a Member State should be upheld;

(19)   Whereas, without prejudice to other provisions of Community law, this Directive does not entail the obligation to give legal recognition to the existence of temporary employment undertakings, nor does it prejudice the application by Member States of their laws concerning the hiring-out of workers and temporary employment undertakings to undertakings not established in their territory but operating therein in the framework of the provision of services;

(20)   Whereas this Directive does not affect either the agreements concluded by the Community with third countries or the laws of Member States concerning the access to their territory of third-country providers of services; whereas this Directive is also without prejudice to national laws relating to the entry, residence and access to employment of third-country workers;

(21)   Whereas Council Regulation (EEC) No 1408/71 of 14 June 1971 on the application of social security schemes to employed persons and their families moving within the Community lays down the provisions applicable with regard to social security benefits and contributions;

(22)   Whereas this Directive is without prejudice to the law of the Member States concerning collective action to defend the interests of trades and professions;

(23)   Whereas competent bodies in different Member States must co-operate with each other in the application of this Directive; whereas Member States must

provide for appropriate remedies in the event of failure to comply with this Directive;

(24) Whereas it is necessary to guarantee proper application of this Directive and to that end to make provision for close collaboration between the Commission and the Member States;

(25) Whereas five years after adoption of this Directive at the latest the Commission must review the detailed rules for implementing this Directive with a view to proposing, where appropriate, the necessary amendments,

HAVE ADOPTED THIS DIRECTIVE:

Article 1

Scope

1 This Directive shall apply to undertakings established in a Member State which, in the framework of the transnational provision of services, post workers, in accordance with paragraph 3, to the territory of a Member State.

2 This Directive shall not apply to merchant navy undertakings as regards seagoing personnel.

3 This Directive shall apply to the extent that the undertakings referred to in paragraph 1 take one of the following transnational measures:

(a) post workers to the territory of a Member State on their account and under their direction, under a contract concluded between the undertaking making the posting and the party for whom the services are intended, operating in that Member State, provided there is an employment relationship between the undertaking making the posting and the worker during the period of posting; or

(b) post workers to an establishment or to an undertaking owned by the group in the territory of a Member State, provided there is an employment relationship between the undertaking making the posting and the worker during the period of posting; or

(c) being a temporary employment undertaking or placement agency, hire out a worker to a user undertaking established or operating in the territory of a Member State, provided there is an employment relationship between the temporary employment undertaking or placement agency and the worker during the period of posting.

4 Undertakings established in a non-member State must not be given more favourable treatment than undertakings established in a Member State.

Article 2

Definition

1 For the purposes of this Directive, 'posted worker' means a worker who, for a limited period, carries out his work in the territory of a Member State other than the State in which he normally works.

2 For the purposes of this Directive, the definition of a worker is that which applies in the law of the Member State to whose territory the worker is posted.

Article 3

Terms and conditions of employment

1 Member States shall ensure that, whatever the law applicable to the employment relationship, the undertakings referred to in Article 1(1) guarantee workers posted to their territory the terms and conditions of employment covering the following matters which, in the Member State where the work is carried out, are laid down:

- by law, regulation or administrative provision, and/or
- by collective agreements or arbitration awards which have been declared universally applicable within the meaning of paragraph 8, insofar as they concern the activities referred to in the Annex:
  (a) maximum work periods and minimum rest periods;
  (b) minimum paid annual holidays;
  (c) the minimum rates of pay, including overtime rates; this point does not apply to supplementary occupational retirement pension schemes;
  (d) the conditions of hiring-out of workers, in particular the supply of workers by temporary employment undertakings;
  (e) health, safety and hygiene at work;
  (f) protective measures with regard to the terms and conditions of employment of pregnant women or women who have recently given birth, of children and of young people;
  (g) equality of treatment between men and women and other provisions on non-discrimination.

For the purposes of this Directive, the concept of minimum rates of pay referred to in paragraph 1(c) is defined by the national law and/or practice of the Member State to whose territory the worker is posted.

2 In the case of initial assembly and/or first installation of goods where this is an integral part of a contract for the supply of goods and necessary for taking the goods supplied into use and carried out by the skilled and/or specialist workers of the supplying undertaking, the first subparagraph of paragraph 1(b) and (c) shall not apply, if the period of posting does not exceed eight days.

This provision shall not apply to activities in the field of building work listed in the Annex.

3 Member States may, after consulting employers and labour, in accordance with the traditions and practices of each Member State, decide not to apply the first subparagraph of paragraph 1(c) in the cases referred to in Article 1(3)(a) and (b) when the length of the posting does not exceed one month.

4 Member States may, in accordance with national laws and/or practices, provide that exemptions may be made from the first subparagraph of paragraph 1(c) in the cases referred to in Article 1(3)(a) and (b) and from a decision by a Member State within the meaning of paragraph 3 of this Article, by means of collective agreements within the meaning of paragraph 8 of this Article, concerning one or more sectors of activity, where the length of the posting does not exceed one month.

5 Member States may provide for exemptions to be granted from the first subparagraph of paragraph 1(b) and (c) in the cases referred to in Article 1(3)(a) and (b) on the grounds that the amount of work to be done is not significant.

Member States availing themselves of the option referred to in the first subparagraph shall lay down the criteria which the work to be performed must meet in order to be considered as 'non-significant'.

6 The length of the posting shall be calculated on the basis of a reference period of one year from the beginning of the posting.

For the purpose of such calculations, account shall be taken of any previous periods for which the post has been filled by a posted worker.

7 Paragraphs 1 to 6 shall not prevent application of terms and conditions of employment which are more favourable to workers.

Allowances specific to the posting shall be considered to be part of the minimum wage, unless they are paid in reimbursement of expenditure actually incurred on account of the posting, such as expenditure on travel, board and lodging.

8 'Collective agreements or arbitration awards which have been declared universally applicable' means collective agreements or arbitration awards which must be observed by all undertakings in the geographical area and in the profession or industry concerned.

In the absence of a system for declaring collective agreements or arbitration awards to be of universal application within the meaning of the first subparagraph, Member States may, if they so decide, base themselves on:

- collective agreements or arbitration awards which are generally applicable to all similar undertakings in the geographical area and in the profession or industry concerned, and/or
- collective agreements which have been concluded by the most representative employers' and labour organizations at national level and which are applied throughout national territory,

provided that their application to the undertakings referred to in Article 1(1) ensures equality of treatment on matters listed in the first subparagraph of paragraph 1 of this Article between those undertakings and the other undertakings referred to in this subparagraph which are in a similar position.

Equality of treatment, within the meaning of this Article, shall be deemed to exist where national undertakings in a similar position:

- are subject, in the place in question or in the sector concerned, to the same obligations as posting undertakings as regards the matters listed in the first subparagraph of paragraph 1, and
- are required to fulfil such obligations with the same effects.

9 Member States may provide that the undertakings referred to in Article 1(1) must guarantee workers referred to in Article 1(3)(c) the terms and conditions which apply to temporary workers in the Member State where the work is carried out.

10 This Directive shall not preclude the application by Member States, in compliance with the Treaty, to national undertakings and to the undertakings of other States, on a basis of equality of treatment, of:

- terms and conditions of employment on matters other than those referred to in the first subparagraph of paragraph 1 in the case of public policy provisions,
- terms and conditions of employment laid down in the collective agreements or arbitration awards within the meaning of paragraph 8 and concerning activities other than those referred to in the Annex.

Article 4

Cooperation on information
1 For the purposes of implementing this Directive, Member States shall, in accordance with national legislation and/or practice, designate one or more liaison offices or one or more competent national bodies.

2 Member States shall make provision for co-operation between the public authorities which, in accordance with national legislation, are responsible for monitoring the terms and conditions of employment referred to in Article 3. Such cooperation shall in particular consist in replying to reasoned requests from those authorities for information on the transnational hiring-out of workers, including manifest abuses or possible cases of unlawful transnational activities.

The Commission and the public authorities referred to in the first subparagraph shall co-operate closely in order to examine any difficulties which might arise in the application of Article 3(10).

Mutual administrative assistance shall be provided free of charge.

3   Each Member State shall take the appropriate measures to make the information on the terms and conditions of employment referred to in Article 3 generally available.

4   Each Member State shall notify the other Member States and the Commission of the liaison offices and/or competent bodies referred to in paragraph 1.

Article 5

Measures
Member States shall take appropriate measures in the event of failure to comply with this Directive.

They shall in particular ensure that adequate procedures are available to workers and/or their representatives for the enforcement of obligations under this Directive.

Article 6

Jurisdiction
In order to enforce the right to the terms and conditions of employment guaranteed in Article 3, judicial proceedings may be instituted in the Member State in whose territory the worker is or was posted, without prejudice, where applicable, to the right, under existing international conventions on jurisdiction, to institute proceedings in another State.

Article 7

Implementation
Member States shall adopt the laws, regulations and administrative provisions necessary to comply with this Directive by 16 December 1999 at the latest. They shall forthwith inform the Commission thereof.

When Member States adopt these provisions, they shall contain a reference to this Directive or shall be accompanied by such reference on the occasion of their official publication. The methods of making such reference shall be laid down by Member States.

Article 8

Commission review
By 16 December 2001 at the latest, the Commission shall review the operation of this Directive with a view to proposing the necessary amendments to the Council where appropriate.

Article 9
This Directive is addressed to the Member States.

ANNEX

The activities mentioned in Article 3 (1), second indent, include all building work relating to the construction, repair, upkeep, alteration or demolition of buildings, and in particular the following work:

1   excavation
2   earthmoving
3   actual building work

4   assembly and dismantling of prefabricated elements
5   fitting out or installation
6   alterations
7   renovation
8   repairs
9   dismantling
10 demolition
11 maintenance
12 upkeep, painting and cleaning work
13 improvements.

COUNCIL DIRECTIVE 97/80/EC

of 15 December 1997

on the burden of proof in cases of discrimination based on sex

THE COUNCIL OF THE EUROPEAN UNION,

Having regard to the Agreement on social policy annexed to the Protocol (No 14) on social policy annexed to the Treaty establishing the European Community, and in particular Article 2(2) thereof,

Having regard to the proposal from the Commission,

Having regard to the opinion of the Economic and Social Committee,

Acting, in accordance with the procedure laid down in Article 189c of the Treaty, in cooperation with the European Parliament

(1)   Whereas, on the basis of the Protocol on social policy annexed to the Treaty, the Member States, with the exception of the United Kingdom of Great Britain and Northern Ireland (hereinafter called 'the Member States'), wishing to implement the 1989 Social Charter, have concluded an Agreement on social policy;

(2)   Whereas the Community Charter of the Fundamental Social Rights of Workers recognizes the importance of combating every form of discrimination, including discrimination on grounds of sex, colour, race, opinions and beliefs;

(3)   Whereas paragraph 16 of the Community Charter of the Fundamental Social Rights of Workers on equal treatment for men and women, provides, inter alia, that 'action should be intensified to ensure the implementation of the principle of equality for men and women as regards, in particular, access to employment, remuneration, working conditions, social protection, education, vocational training and career development';

(4)   Whereas, in accordance with Article 3(2) of the Agreement on social policy, the Commission has consulted management and labour at Community level on the possible direction of Community action on the burden of proof in cases of discrimination based on sex;

(5)   Whereas the Commission, considering Community action advisable after such consultation, once again consulted management and labour on the content of the proposal contemplated in accordance with Article 3(3) of the same Agreement; whereas the latter have sent their opinions to the Commission;

(6)   Whereas, after the second round of consultation, neither management nor labour have informed the Commission of their wish to initiate the process–possibly leading to an agreement – provided for in Article 4 of the same Agreement;

(7)   Whereas, in accordance with Article 1 of the Agreement, the Community and the Member States have set themselves the objective, inter alia, of improving living and working conditions; whereas effective implementation of the principle of equal treatment for men and women would contribute to the achievement of that aim;

(8)   Whereas the principle of equal treatment was stated in Article 119 of the Treaty, in Council Directive 75/117/EEC of 10 February 1975 on the approximation of the laws of the Member States relating to the application of the principle of equal pay for men and women and in Council Directive 76/207/EEC of 9 February 1976 on the implementation of the principle of equal treatment for men and women as regards access to employment, vocational training and promotion and working conditions;

(9)   Whereas Council Directive 92/85/EEC of 19 October 1992 on the introduction of measures to encourage improvements in the safety and health at work of pregnant workers and workers who have recently given birth or are breastfeeding also contributes to the effective implementation of the principle of equal treatment for men and women; whereas that Directive should not work to the detriment of the aforementioned Directives on equal treatment; whereas, therefore, female workers covered by that Directive should likewise benefit from the adaptation of the rules on the burden of proof;

(10)   Whereas Council Directive 96/34/EC of 3 June 1996 on the framework agreement on parental leave concluded by UNICE, CEEP and the ETUC, is also based on the principle of equal treatment for men and women;

(11)   Whereas the references to 'judicial process' and 'court' cover mechanisms by means of which disputes may be submitted for examination and decision to independent bodies which may hand down decisions that are binding on the parties to those disputes;

(12)   Whereas the expression 'out-of-court procedures' means in particular procedures such as conciliation and mediation;

(13)   Whereas the appreciation of the facts from which it may be presumed that there has been direct or indirect discrimination is a matter for national judicial or other competent bodies, in accordance with national law or practice;

(14)   Whereas it is for the Member States to introduce, at any appropriate stage of the proceedings, rules of evidence which are more favourable to plaintiffs;

(15)   Whereas it is necessary to take account of the specific features of certain Member States' legal systems, inter alia where an inference of discrimination is drawn if the respondent fails to produce evidence that satisfies the court or other competent authority that there has been no breach of the principle of equal treatment;

(16)   Whereas Member States need not apply the rules on the burden of proof to proceedings in which it is for the court or other competent body to investigate the facts of the case; whereas the procedures thus referred to are those in which the plaintiff is not required to prove the facts, which it is for the court or competent body to investigate;

(17)   Whereas plaintiffs could be deprived of any effective means of enforcing the principle of equal treatment before the national courts if the effect of introducing evidence of an apparent discrimination were not to impose upon the respondent the burden of proving that his practice is not in fact discriminatory;

(18)   Whereas the Court of Justice of the European Communities has therefore held that the rules on the burden of proof must be adapted when there is a prima facie case of discrimination and that, for the principle of equal treatment to be applied effectively, the burden of proof must shift back to the respondent when evidence of such discrimination is brought;

(19)   Whereas it is all the more difficult to prove discrimination when it is indirect; whereas it is therefore important to define indirect discrimination;

(20)   Whereas the aim of adequately adapting the rules on the burden of proof has not been achieved satisfactorily in all Member States and, in accordance with the principle of subsidiarity stated in Article 3b of the Treaty and with that of proportionality, that aim must be attained at Community level; whereas this Directive confines itself to the minimum action required and does not go beyond what is necessary for that purpose,

HAS ADOPTED THIS DIRECTIVE:

Article 1   Aim
The aim of this Directive shall be to ensure that the measures taken by the Member States to implement the principle of equal treatment are made more effective, in order to enable all persons who consider themselves wronged because the principle of equal treatment has not been applied to them to have their rights asserted by judicial process after possible recourse to other competent bodies.

Article 2   Definitions
1   For the purposes of this Directive, the principle of equal treatment shall mean that there shall be no discrimination whatsoever based on sex, either directly or indirectly.

2   For purposes of the principle of equal treatment referred to in paragraph 1, indirect discrimination shall exist where an apparently neutral provision, criterion or practice disadvantages a substantially higher proportion of the members of one sex unless that provision, criterion or practice is appropriate and necessary and can be justified by objective factors unrelated to sex.

Article 3   Scope
1   This Directive shall apply to:

(a) the situations covered by Article 119 of the Treaty and by Directives 75/117/EEC, 76/207/EEC and, insofar as discrimination based on sex is concerned, 92/85/EEC and 96/34/EC;

(b) any civil or administrative procedure concerning the public or private sector which provides for means of redress under national law pursuant to the measures referred to in (a) with the exception of out-of-court procedures of a voluntary nature or provided for in national law.

2   This Directive shall not apply to criminal procedures, unless otherwise provided by the Member States.

Article 4   Burden of proof
1   Member States shall take such measures as are necessary, in accordance with their national judicial systems, to ensure that, when persons who consider themselves wronged because the principle of equal treatment has not been applied to them establish, before a court or other competent authority, facts from which it may be presumed that there has been direct or indirect discrimination, it shall be for the respondent to prove that there has been no breach of the principle of equal treatment.

2   This Directive shall not prevent Member States from introducing rules of evidence which are more favourable to plaintiffs.

3   Member States need not apply paragraph 1 to proceedings in which it is for the court or competent body to investigate the facts of the case.

Article 5   Information
Member States shall ensure that measures taken pursuant to this Directive, together with the provisions already in force, are brought to the attention of all the persons concerned by all appropriate means.

Article 6   Non-regression
Implementation of this Directive shall under no circumstances be sufficient grounds for a reduction in the general level of protection of workers in the areas to which it applies, without prejudice to the Member States' right to respond to changes in the situation by introducing laws, regulations and administrative provisions which differ from those in force on the notification of this Directive, provided that the minimum requirements of this Directive are complied with.

Article 7   Implementation
Member States shall bring into force the laws, regulations and administrative provisions necessary for them to comply with this Directive by 1 January 2001. They shall immediately inform the Commission thereof.

When the Member States adopt those measures they shall contain a reference to this Directive or shall be accompanied by such a reference on the occasion of their official publication. The methods of making such references shall be laid down by the Member States.

The Member States shall communicate to the Commission, within two years of the entry into force of this Directive, all the information necessary for the Commission to draw up a report to the European Parliament and the Council on the application of this Directive.

Article 8
This Directive is addressed to the Member States.

Amendment   The second paragraph of art 1 was inserted by Council Directive 98/52/EC of 13 July 1998.

COUNCIL DIRECTIVE 97/81/EC

of 15 December 1997

concerning the Framework Agreement on part-time work concluded by UNICE, CEEP and the ETUC

THE COUNCIL OF THE EUROPEAN UNION,

Having regard to the Agreement on social policy annexed to the Protocol (No 14) on social policy, annexed to the Treaty establishing the European Community, and in particular Article 4(2) thereof,

Having regard to the proposal from the Commission,

(1)   Whereas on the basis of the Protocol on social policy annexed to the Treaty establishing the European Community, the Member States, with the exception of the United Kingdom of Great Britain and Northern Ireland (hereinafter referred to as 'the Member States'), wishing to continue along the path laid down in the 1989 Social Charter, have concluded an agreement on social policy;

(2)   Whereas management and labour (the social partners) may, in accordance with Article 4(2) of the Agreement on social policy, request jointly that agreements at Community level be implemented by a Council decision on a proposal from the Commission;

(3)   Whereas point 7 of the Community Charter of the Fundamental Social Rights of Workers provides, inter alia, that 'the completion of the internal market must lead to an improvement in the living and working conditions of workers in the European Community. This process must result from an approximation of these conditions while the improvement is being maintained, as regards in particular (...) forms of employment other than open-ended contracts, such as fixed-term contracts, part-time working, temporary work and seasonal work';

(4)   Whereas the Council has not reached a decision on the proposal for a Directive on certain employment relationships with regard to distortions of competition, as amended, nor on the proposal for a Directive on certain employment relationships with regard to working conditions;

(5)   Whereas the conclusions of the Essen European Council stressed the need to take measures to promote employment and equal opportunities for women and men, and called for measures with a view to increasing the employment-intensiveness of growth, in particular by a more flexible organization of work in a way which fulfils both the wishes of employees and the requirements of competition;

(6)   Whereas the Commission, in accordance with Article 3(2) of the Agreement on social policy, has consulted management and labour on the possible direction of Community action with regard to flexible working time and job security;

(7)   Whereas the Commission, considering after such consultation that Community action was desirable, once again consulted management and labour at Community level on the substance of the envisaged proposal in accordance with Article 3(3) of the said Agreement;

(8)   Whereas the general cross-industry organizations, the Union of Industrial and Employers' Confederations of Europe (UNICE), the European Centre of Enterprises with Public Participation (CEEP) and the European Trade Union Confederation (ETUC) informed the Commission in their joint letter of 19 June 1996 of their desire to initiate the procedure provided for in Article 4 of the Agreement on social policy; whereas they asked the Commission, in a joint letter dated 12 March 1997, for a further three months; whereas the Commission complied with this request;

(9)   Whereas the said cross-industry organizations concluded, on 6 June 1997, a Framework Agreement on part-time work; whereas they forwarded to the Commission their joint request to implement this Framework Agreement by a Council decision on a proposal from the Commission, in accordance with Article 4(2) of the said Agreement.

(10)   Whereas the Council, in its Resolution of 6 December 1994 on prospects for a European Union social policy: contribution to economic and social convergence in the Union, asked management and labour to make use of the opportunities for concluding agreements, since they are as a rule closer to social reality and to social problems;

(11)   Whereas the signatory parties wished to conclude a framework agreement on part-time work setting out the general principles and minimum requirements for part-time working; whereas they have demonstrated their desire to establish a general framework for eliminating discrimination against part-time workers and to contribute to developing the potential for part-time work on a basis which is acceptable for employers and workers alike;

(12)   Whereas the social partners wished to give particular attention to part-time work, while at the same time indicating that it was their intention to consider the need for similar agreements for other flexible forms of work;

(13)   Whereas, in the conclusions of the Amsterdam European Council, the Heads of State and Government of the European Union strongly welcomed the agreement concluded by the social partners on part-time work;

(14)   Whereas the proper instrument for implementing the Framework Agreement is a Directive within the meaning of Article 189 of the Treaty; whereas it therefore binds the Member States as to the result to be achieved, whilst leaving national authorities the choice of form and methods;

(15)   Whereas, in accordance with the principles of subsidiarity and proportionality as set out in Article 3(b) of the Treaty, the objectives of this Directive cannot be sufficiently achieved by the Member States and can therefore be better achieved by the Community; wheres this Directive does not go beyond what is necessary for the attainment of those objectives;

(16)   Whereas, with regard to terms used in the Framework Agreement which are not specifically defined therein, this Directive leaves Member States free to define those terms in accordance with national law and practice, as is the case for other social policy Directives using similar terms, providing that the said definitions respect the content of the Framework Agreement;

(17)   Whereas the Commission has drafted its proposal for a Directive, in accordance with its Communication of 14 December 1993 concerning the application of the Protocol (No 14) on social policy and its Communication of 18 September 1996 concerning the development of the social dialogue at Community level, taking into account the representative status of the signatory parties and the legality of each clause of the Framework Agreement;

(18)   Whereas the Commission has drafted its proposal for a Directive in compliance with Article 2(2) of the Agreement on social policy which provides that Directives in the social policy domain `shall avoid imposing administrative, financial and legal constraints in a way which would hold back the creation and development of small and medium-sized undertakings';

(19)   Whereas the Commission, in accordance with its Communication of 14 December 1993 concerning the application of the Protocol (No 14) on social policy, informed the European Parliament by sending it the text of its proposal for a Directive containing the Framework Agreement;

(20)   Whereas the Commission also informed the Economic and Social Committee;

(21)   Whereas Clause 6.1 of the Framework Agreement provides that Member States and/or the social partners may maintain or introduce more favourable provisions;

(22)   Whereas Clause 6.2 of the Framework Agreement provides that implementation of this Directive may not serve to justify any regression in relation to the situation which already exists in each Member State;

(23)   Whereas the Community Charter of the Fundamental Social Rights of Workers recognizes the importance of the fight against all forms of discrimination, especially based on sex, colour, race, opinion and creed;

(24)   Whereas Article F(2) of the Treaty on European Union states that the Union shall respect fundamental rights, as guaranteed by the European Convention for the Protection of Human Rights and Fundamental Freedoms and as they result from the constitutional traditions common to the Member States, as general principles of Community law;

(25)   Whereas the Member States may entrust the social partners, at their joint request, with the implementation of this Directive, provided that the Member States take all the necessary steps to ensure that they can at all times guarantee the results imposed by this Directive;

(26)   Whereas the implementation of the Framework Agreement contributes to achieving the objectives under Article 1 of the Agreement on social policy,

HAS ADOPTED THIS DIRECTIVE:

Article 1

The purpose of this Directive is to implement the Framework Agreement on part-time work concluded on 6 June 1997 between the general cross-industry organizations (UNICE, CEEP and the ETUC) annexed hereto.

Article 2

1   Member States shall bring into force the laws, regulations and administrative provisions necessary to comply with this Directive not later than 20 January 2000, or shall ensure that, by that date at the latest, the social partners have introduced the necessary measures by agreement, the Member States being required to take any necessary measures to enable them at any time to be in a position to guarantee the results imposed by this Directive. They shall forthwith inform the Commission thereof.

Member States may have a maximum of one more year, if necessary, to take account of special difficulties or implementation by a collective agreement.

They shall inform the Commission forthwith in such circumstances.

When Member States adopt the measures referred to in the first subparagraph, they shall contain a reference to this Directive or shall be accompanied by such reference on the occasion of their official publication. The methods of making such a reference shall be laid down by the Member States.

[1a   As regards the United Kingdom of Great Britain and Northern Ireland, the date of 20 January 2000 in paragraph 1 shall be replaced by the date of 7 April 2000.]

2   Member States shall communicate to the Commission the text of the main provisions of domestic law which they have adopted or which they adopted in the field governed by this Directive.

Article 3

This Directive shall enter into force on the day of its publication in the *Official Journal of the European Communities*.

Article 4

This Directive is addressed to the Member States.

ANNEX
FRAMEWORK AGREEMENT ON PART-TIME WORK

Preamble

This Framework Agreement is a contribution to the overall European strategy on employment. Part-time work has had an important impact on employment in recent years. For this reason, the parties to this Agreement have given priority attention to this form of work. It is the intention of the parties to consider the need for similar agreements relating to other forms of flexible work.

Recognizing the diversity of situations in Member States and acknowledging that part-time work is a feature of employment in certain sectors and activities, this Agreement sets out the general principles and minimum requirements relating to part-time work. It illustrates the willingness of the social partners to establish a general framework for the elimination of discrimination against part-time workers and to assist the development of opportunities for part-time working on a basis acceptable to employers and workers.

This Agreement relates to employment conditions of part-time workers recognizing that matters concerning statutory social security are for decision by the Member States. In the context of the principle of non-discrimination, the parties to this Agreement have noted the Employment Declaration of the Dublin European Council of December 1996, wherein the Council inter alia emphasized the need to make social security systems more employment-friendly by 'developing social protection systems capable of adapting to new patterns of work and of providing appropriate protection to people engaged in such work'. The parties to this Agreement consider that effect should be given to this Declaration.

ETUC, UNICE and CEEP request the Commission to submit this Framework Agreement to the Council for a decision making these requirements binding in the Member States which are party to the Agreement on Social Policy annexed to the Protocol (No 14) on Social Policy annexed to the Treaty establishing the European Community.

The parties to this Agreement ask the Commission, in its proposal to implement this Agreement, to request that Member States adopt the laws, regulations and administrative provisions necessary to comply with the Council decision within a period of two years from its adoption or ensure[1] that the social partners establish the necessary measures by way of agreement by the end of this period. Member States may, if necessary to take account of particular difficulties or implementation by collective agreement, have up to a maximum of one additional year to comply with this provision.

Without prejudice to the role of national courts and the Court of Justice, the parties to this Agreement request that any matter relating to the interpretation of this Agreement at European level should, in the first instance, be referred by the Commission to them for an opinion.

[1]   Within the meaning of Article 2(4) of the Agreement on social policy of the Treaty establishing the European Community.

General considerations

1   Having regard to the Agreement on Social Policy annexed to the Protocol (No 14) on Social Policy annexed to the Treaty establishing the European Community, and in particular Articles 3(4) and 4(2) thereof;

2   Whereas Article 4(2) of the Agreement on Social Policy provides that agreements concluded at Community level may be implemented, at the joint request of the signatory parties, by a Council decision on a proposal from the Commission.

3   Whereas, in its second consultation document on flexibility of working time and security for workers, the Commission announced its intention to propose a legally binding Community measure;

4   Whereas the conclusions of the European Council meeting in Essen emphasized the need for measures to promote both employment and equal opportunities for women and men, and called for measures aimed at 'increasing the employment

intensiveness of growth, in particular by more flexible organization of work in a way which fulfils both the wishes of employees and the requirements of competition';

5   Whereas the parties to this Agreement attach importance to measures which would facilitate access to part-time work for men and women in order to prepare for retirement, reconcile professional and family life, and take up education and training opportunities to improve their skills and career opportunities for the mutual benefit of employers and workers and in a manner which would assist the development of enterprises;

6   Whereas this Agreement refers back to Member States and social partners for the arrangements for the application of these general principles, minimum requirements and provisions, in order to take account of the situation in each Member State;

7   Whereas this Agreement takes into consideration the need to improve social policy requirements, to enhance the competitiveness of the Community economy and to avoid imposing administrative, financial and legal constraints in a way which would hold back the creation and development of small and medium-sized undertakings;

8   Whereas the social partners are best placed to find solutions that correspond to the needs of both employers and workers and must therefore be given a special role in the implementation and application of this Agreement.

THE SIGNATORY PARTIES HAVE AGREED THE FOLLOWING:

Clause 1   Purpose
The purpose of this Framework Agreement is:

- (a) to provide for the removal of discrimination against part-time workers and to improve the quality of part-time work;
- (b) to facilitate the development of part-time work on a voluntary basis and to contribute to the flexible organization of working time in a manner which takes into account the needs of employers and workers.

Clause 2   Scope
1   This Agreement applies to part-time workers who have an employment contract or employment relationship as defined by the law, collective agreement or practice in force in each Member State.

2   Member States, after consultation with the social partners in accordance with national law, collective agreements or practice, and/or the social partners at the appropriate level in conformity with national industrial relations practice may, for objective reasons, exclude wholly or partly from the terms of this Agreement part-time workers who work on a casual basis. Such exclusions should be reviewed periodically to establish if the objective reasons for making them remain valid.

Clause 3   Definitions
For the purpose of this Agreement:

1   The term 'part-time worker' refers to an employee whose normal hours of work, calculated on a weekly basis or on average over a period of employment of up to one year, are less than the normal hours of work of a comparable full-time worker.

2   The term 'comparable full-time worker' means a full-time worker in the same establishment having the same type of employment contract or relationship, who is engaged in the same or a similar work/occupation, due regard being given to other considerations which may include seniority and qualification/skills.

Where there is no comparable full-time worker in the same establishment, the comparison shall be made by reference to the applicable collective agreement or, where there is no applicable collective agreement, in accordance with national law, collective agreements or practice.

Clause 4   Principle of non-discrimination
1   In respect of employment conditions, part-time workers shall not be treated in a less favourable manner than comparable full-time workers solely because they work part time unless different treatment is justified on objective grounds.

2   Where appropriate, the principle of *pro rata temporis* shall apply.

3   The arrangements for the application of this clause shall be defined by the Member States and/or social partners, having regard to European legislation, national law, collective agreements and practice.

4   Where justified by objective reasons, Member States after consultation of the social partners in accordance with national law, collective agreements or practice and/or social partners may, where appropriate, make access to particular conditions of employment subject to a period of service, time worked or earnings qualification. Qualifications relating to access by part-time workers to particular conditions of employment should be reviewed periodically having regard to the principle of non-discrimination as expressed in Clause 4.1.

Clause 5   Opportunities for part-time work
1   In the context of Clause 1 of this Agreement and of the principle of non-discrimination between part-time and full-time workers:

  (a) Member States, following consultations with the social partners in accordance with national law or practice, should identify and review obstacles of a legal or administrative nature which may limit the opportunities for part-time work and, where appropriate, eliminate them;
  (b) the social partners, acting within their sphere of competence and through the procedures set out in collective agreements, should identify and review obstacles which may limit opportunities for part-time work and, where appropriate, eliminate them.

2   A worker's refusal to transfer from full-time to part-time work or vice versa should not in itself constitute a valid reason for termination of employment, without prejudice to termination in accordance with national law, collective agreements and practice, for other reasons such as may arise from the operational requirements of the establishment concerned.

3   As far as possible, employers should give consideration to:

  (a) requests by workers to transfer from full-time to part-time work that becomes available in the establishment;
  (b) requests by workers to transfer from part-time to full-time work or to increase their working time should the opportunity arise;
  (c) the provision of timely information on the availability of part-time and full-time positions in the establishment in order to facilitate transfers from full-time to part-time or vice versa;
  (d) measures to facilitate access to part-time work at all levels of the enterprise, including skilled and managerial positions, and where appropriate, to facilitate access by part-time workers to vocational training to enhance career opportunities and occupational mobility;
  (e) the provision of appropriate information to existing bodies representing workers about part-time working in the enterprise.

Clause 6   Provisions on implementation
1   Member States and/or social partners may maintain or introduce more favourable provisions than set out in this agreement.

2 Implementation of the provisions of this Agreement shall not constitute valid grounds for reducing the general level of protection afforded to workers in the field of this agreement. This does not prejudice the right of Member States and/or social partners to develop different legislative, regulatory or contractual provisions, in the light of changing circumstances, and does not prejudice the application of Clause 5.1 as long as the principle of non-discrimination as expressed in Clause 4.1 is complied with.

3 This Agreement does not prejudice the right of the social partners to conclude, at the appropriate level, including European level, agreements adapting and/or complementing the provisions of this Agreement in a manner which will take account of the specific needs of the social partners concerned.

4 This Agreement shall be without prejudice to any more specific Community provisions, and in particular Community provisions concerning equal treatment or opportunities for men and women.

5 The prevention and settlement of disputes and grievances arising from the application of this Agreement shall be dealt with in accordance with national law, collective agreements and practice.

6 The signatory parties shall review this Agreement five years after the date of the Council decision, if requested by one of the parties to this Agreement.

Commencement 20 January 1998.

Amendment Article 2(1a) was inserted by Council Directive 98/23/EC of 7 April 1998.

COUNCIL DIRECTIVE 98/50/EC

of 29 June 1998

amending Directive 77/187/EEC on the approximation of the laws of the Member States relating to the safeguarding of employees' rights in the event of transfers of undertakings, businesses or parts of businesses

THE COUNCIL OF THE EUROPEAN UNION,

Having regard to the Treaty establishing the European Community, and in particular Article 100 thereof,

Having regard to the proposal from the Commission,

Having regard to the opinion of the European Parliament,

Having regard to the opinion of the Economic and Social Committee,

Having regard to the opinion of the Committee of the Regions,

(1) Whereas the Community Charter of the Fundamental Social Rights of Workers adopted on 9 December 1989 ('Social Charter') states, in points 7, 17 and 18 in particular that: 'The completion of the internal market must lead to an improvement in the living and working conditions of workers in the European Community. The improvement must cover, where necessary, the development of certain aspects of employment regulations such as procedures for collective redundancies and those regarding bankruptcies. Information, consultation and participation for workers must be developed along appropriate lines, taking account of the practices in force in the various Member States. Such information, consultation and participation must be implemented in due time, particularly in connection with restructuring operations in undertakings or in cases of mergers having an impact on the employment of workers';

(2) Whereas Directive 77/187/EEC promotes the harmonisation of the relevant national laws ensuring the safeguarding of the rights of employees and requiring transferors and transferees to inform and consult employees' representatives in good time;

(3) Whereas the purpose of this Directive is to amend Directive 77/187/EEC in the light of the impact of the internal market, the legislative tendencies of the Member States with regard to the rescue of undertakings in economic difficulties, the case-law of the Court of Justice of the European Communities, Council Directive 75/129/EEC of 17 February 1975 on the approximation of the laws of the Member States relating to collective redundancies and the legislation already in force in most Member States;

(4) Whereas considerations of legal security and transparency require that the legal concept of transfer be clarified in the light of the case-law of the Court of Justice; whereas such clarification does not alter the scope of Directive 77/187/EEC as interpreted by the Court of Justice;

(5) Whereas those considerations also require an express provision, in the light of the case-law of the Court of Justice, that Directive 77/187/EEC should apply to private and public undertakings carrying out economic activities, whether or not they operate for gain;

(6) Whereas it is necessary to clarify the concept of 'employee' in the light of the case-law of the Court of Justice;

(7) Whereas, with a view to ensuring the survival of insolvent undertakings, Member States should be expressly allowed not to apply Articles 3 and 4 of Directive 77/187/EEC to transfers effected in the framework of liquidation proceedings, and certain derogations from that Directive's general provisions should be permitted in the case of transfers effected in the context of insolvency proceedings;

(8) Whereas such derogations should also be allowed for one Member State which has special procedures to promote the survival of companies declared to be in a state of economic crisis;

(9)   Whereas the circumstances in which the function and status of employee representatives are to be preserved should be clarified;

(10)   Whereas, in order to ensure equal treatment for similar situations, it is necessary to ensure that the information and consultation requirements laid down in Directive 77/187/EEC are complied with irrespective of whether the decision leading to the transfer is taken by the employer or by an undertaking controlling the employer;

(11)   Whereas it is appropriate to clarify that, when Member States adopt measures to ensure that the transferee is informed of all the rights and obligations to be transferred, failure to provide that information is not to affect the transfer of the rights and obligations concerned;

(12)   Whereas it is necessary to clarify the circumstances in which employees must be informed where there are no employee representatives;

(13)   Whereas the Social Charter recognises the importance of the fight against all forms of discrimination, especially based on sex, colour, race, opinion and creed, *HAS ADOPTED THIS DIRECTIVE*:

Article 1
Directive 77/187/EEC is hereby amended as follows:

1   the title shall be replaced by the following:

'Council Directive 77/187/EEC of 14 February 1977 on the approximation of the laws of the Member States relating to the safeguarding of employees' rights in the event of transfers of undertakings, businesses or parts of undertakings or businesses';

2   Articles 1 to 7 shall be replaced by the following:

'SECTION I
SCOPE AND DEFINITIONS

Article 1
1 (a)   This Directive shall apply to any transfer of an undertaking, business, or part of an undertaking or business to another employer as a result of a legal transfer or merger.
   (b)   Subject to subparagraph (a) and the following provisions of this Article, there is a transfer within the meaning of this Directive where there is a transfer of an economic entity which retains its identity, meaning an organised grouping of resources which has the objective of pursuing an economic activity, whether or not that activity is central or ancillary.
   (c)   This Directive shall apply to public and private undertakings engaged in economic activities whether or not they are operating for gain. An administrative reorganisation of public administrative authorities, or the transfer of administrative functions between public administrative authorities, is not a transfer within the meaning of this Directive.

2   This Directive shall apply where and insofar as the undertaking, business or part of the undertaking or business to be transferred is situated within the territorial scope of the Treaty.

3   This Directive shall not apply to sea-going vessels.

Article 2
1   For the purposes of this Directive:

   (a)   'transferor' shall mean any natural or legal person who, by reason of a transfer within the meaning of Article 1(1), ceases to be the employer in respect of the undertaking, business or part of the undertaking or business;

(b) 'transferee' shall mean any natural or legal person who, by reason of a transfer within the meaning of Article 1(1), becomes the employer in respect of the undertaking, business or part of the undertaking or business;

(c) 'representatives of employees' and related expressions shall mean the representatives of the employees provided for by the laws or practices of the Member States;

(d) 'employee' shall mean any person who, in the Member State concerned, is protected as an employee under national employment law.

2   This Directive shall be without prejudice to national law as regards the definition of contract of employment or employment relationship.

However, Member States shall not exclude from the scope of this Directive contracts of employment or employment relationships solely because:

(a) of the number of working hours performed or to be performed,

(b) they are employment relationships governed by a fixed-duration contract of employment within the meaning of Article 1(1) of Council Directive 91/383/EEC of 25 June 1991 supplementing the measures to encourage improvements in the safety and health at work of workers with a fixed-duration employment relationship or a temporary employment relationship, or

(c) they are temporary employment relationships within the meaning of Article 1(2) of Directive 91/383/EEC, and the undertaking, business or part of the undertaking or business transferred is, or is part of, the temporary employment business which is the employer.

SECTION II
SAFEGUARDING OF EMPLOYEES' RIGHTS

Article 3

1   The transferor's rights and obligations arising from a contract of employment or from an employment relationship existing on the date of a transfer shall, by reason of such transfer, be transferred to the transferee.

Member States may provide that, after the date of transfer, the transferor and the transferee shall be jointly and severally liable in respect of obligations which arose before the date of transfer from a contract of employment or an employment relationship existing on the date of the transfer.

2   Member States may adopt appropriate measures to ensure that the transferor notifies the transferee of all the rights and obligations which will be transferred to the transferee under this Article, so far as those rights and obligations are or ought to have been known to the transferor at the time of the transfer. A failure by the transferor to notify the transferee of any such right or obligation shall not affect the transfer of that right or obligation and the rights of any employees against the transferee and/or transferor in respect of that right or obligation.

3   Following the transfer, the transferee shall continue to observe the terms and conditions agreed in any collective agreement on the same terms applicable to the transferor under that agreement, until the date of termination or expiry of the collective agreement or the entry into force or application of another collective agreement.

Member States may limit the period for observing such terms and conditions with the proviso that it shall not be less than one year.

4 (a) Unless Member States provide otherwise, paragraphs 1 and 3 shall not apply in relation to employees' rights to old-age, invalidity or survivors' benefits under supplementary company or inter-company pension schemes outside the statutory social security schemes in Member States.

(b) Even where they do not provide in accordance with subparagraph (a) that paragraphs 1 and 3 apply in relation to such rights, Member States shall adopt the measures necessary to protect the interests of employees and of persons no longer employed in the transferor's business at the time of the transfer in respect of rights conferring on them immediate or prospective entitlement to old age benefits, including survivors' benefits, under supplementary schemes referred to in subparagraph (a).

Article 4

1   The transfer of the undertaking, business or part of the undertaking or business shall not in itself constitute grounds for dismissal by the transferor or the transferee. This provision shall not stand in the way of dismissals that may take place for economic, technical or organisational reasons entailing changes in the workforce.

Member States may provide that the first subparagraph shall not apply to certain specific categories of employees who are not covered by the laws or practice of the Member States in respect of protection against dismissal.

2   If the contract of employment or the employment relationship is terminated because the transfer involves a substantial change in working conditions to the detriment of the employee, the employer shall be regarded as having been responsible for termination of the contract of employment or of the employment relationship.

Article 4a

1   Unless Member States provide otherwise, Articles 3 and 4 shall not apply to any transfer of an undertaking, business or part of an undertaking or business where the transferor is the subject of bankruptcy proceedings or any analogous insolvency proceedings which have been instituted with a view to the liquidation of the assets of the transferor and are under the supervision of a competent public authority (which may be an insolvency practitioner authorised by a competent public authority).

2   Where Articles 3 and 4 apply to a transfer during insolvency proceedings which have been opened in relation to a transferor (whether or not those proceedings have been instituted with a view to the liquidation of the assets of the transferor) and provided that such proceedings are under the supervision of a competent public authority (which may be an insolvency practitioner determined by national law) a Member State may provide that:

(a) notwithstanding Article 3(1), the transferor's debts arising from any contracts of employment or employment relationships and payable before the transfer or before the opening of the insolvency proceedings shall not be transferred to the transferee, provided that such proceedings give rise, under the law of that Member State, to protection at least equivalent to that provided for in situations covered by Council Directive 80/987/EEC of 20 October 1980 on the approximation of the laws of the Member States relating to the protection of employees in the event of the insolvency of their employer;
and, or alternatively, that

(b) the transferee, transferor, or person or persons exercising the transferor's functions, on the one hand, and the representatives of the employees on the other hand may agree alterations, insofar as current law or practice permits, to the employees' terms and conditions of employment designed to safeguard employment opportunities by ensuring the survival of the undertaking, business or part of the undertaking or business.

3   A Member State may apply paragraph 2(b) to any transfers where the transferor is in a situation of serious economic crisis, as defined by national law, provided that

the situation is declared by a competent public authority and open to judicial supervision, on condition that such provisions already exist in national law by 17 July 1998.

The Commission shall present a report on the effects of this provision before 17 July 2003 and shall submit any appropriate proposals to the Council.

4   Member States shall take appropriate measures with a view to preventing misuse of insolvency proceedings in such a way as to deprive employees of the rights provided for in this Directive.

Article 5

1   If the undertaking, business or part of an undertaking or business preserves its autonomy, the status and function of the representatives or of the representation of the employees affected by the transfer shall be preserved on the same terms and subject to the same conditions as existed before the date of the transfer by virtue of law, regulation, administrative provision or agreement, provided that the conditions necessary for the constitution of the employees' representation are fulfilled.

The first subparagraph shall not apply if, under the laws, regulations, administrative provisions or practice in the Member States, or by agreement with the representatives of the employees, the conditions necessary for the reappointment of the representatives of the employees or for the reconstitution of the representation of the employees are fulfilled.

Where the transferor is the subject of bankruptcy proceedings or any analogous insolvency proceedings which have been instituted with a view to the liquidation of the assets of the transferor and are under the supervision of a competent public authority (which may be an insolvency practitioner authorised by a competent public authority), Member States may take the necessary measures to ensure that the transferred employees are properly represented until the new election or designation of representatives of the employees.

If the undertaking, business or part of an undertaking or business does not preserve its autonomy, the Member States shall take the necessary measures to ensure that the employees transferred who were represented before the transfer continue to be properly represented during the period necessary for the reconstitution or reappointment of the representation of employees in accordance with national law or practice.

2   If the term of office of the representatives of the employees affected by the transfer expires as a result of the transfer, the representatives shall continue to enjoy the protection provided by the laws, regulations, administrative provisions or practice of the Member States.

SECTION III
INFORMATION AND CONSULTATION

Article 6

1   The transferor and transferee shall be required to inform the representatives of their respective employees affected by the transfer of the following:

- the date or proposed date of the transfer,
- the reasons for the transfer,
- the legal, economic and social implications of the transfer for the employees,
- any measures envisaged in relation to the employees.

The transferor must give such information to the representatives of his employees in good time before the transfer is carried out.

The transferee must give such information to the representatives of his employees in good time, and in any event before his employees are directly affected by the transfer as regards their conditions of work and employment.

2   Where the transferor or the transferee envisages measures in relation to his employees, he shall consult the representatives of his employees in good time on such measures with a view to reaching an agreement.

3   Member States whose laws, regulations or administrative provisions provide that representatives of the employees may have recourse to an arbitration board to obtain a decision on the measures to be taken in relation to employees may limit the obligations laid down in paragraphs 1 and 2 to cases where the transfer carried out gives rise to a change in the business likely to entail serious disadvantages for a considerable number of the employees.

The information and consultations shall cover at least the measures envisaged in relation to the employees.

The information must be provided and consultations taken place in good time before the change in the business as referred to in the first subparagraph is effected.

4   The obligations laid down in this Article shall apply irrespective of whether the decision resulting in the transfer is taken by the employer or an undertaking controlling the employer.

In considering alleged breaches of the information and consultation requirements laid down by this Directive, the argument that such a breach occurred because the information was not provided by an undertaking controlling the employer shall not be accepted as an excuse.

5   Member States may limit the obligations laid down in paragraphs 1, 2 and 3 to undertakings or businesses which, in terms of the number of employees, meet the conditions of the election or nomination of a collegiate body representing the employees.

6   Member States shall provide that, where there are no representatives of the employees in an undertaking or business through no fault of their own, the employees concerned must be informed in advance of:

-   the date or proposed date of the transfer,
-   the reason for the transfer,
-   the legal, economic and social implications of the transfer for the employees,
-   any measures envisaged in relation to the employees.

SECTION IV
FINAL PROVISIONS

Article 7
This Directive shall not affect the right of Member States to apply or introduce laws, regulations or administrative provisions which are more favourable to employees or to promote or permit collective agreements or agreements between social partners more favourable to employees.

Article 7a
Member States shall introduce into their national legal systems such measures as are necessary to enable all employees and representatives of employees who consider themselves wronged by failure to comply with the obligations arising from this Directive to pursue their claims by judicial process after possible recourse to other competent authorities.

Article 7b

The Commission shall submit to the Council an analysis of the effects of the provisions of this Directive before 17 July 2006. It shall propose any amendment which may seem necessary.'

Article 2

1 Member States shall bring into force the laws, regulations and administrative provisions necessary to comply with this Directive by 17 July 2001 at the latest or shall ensure that, by that date, at the latest, the employers' and employees' representatives have introduced the required provisions by means of agreement, Member States being obliged to take the necessary steps enabling them at all times to guarantee the results imposed by this Directive.

2 When Member States adopt the measures referred to in paragraph 1, they shall contain a reference to this Directive or shall be accompanied by such reference on the occasion on their official publication. The methods of making such reference shall be laid down by Member States.

Member States shall inform the Commission immediately of the measures they take to implement this Directive.

Article 3

This Directive shall enter into force on the day of its publication in the *Official Journal of the European Communities*.

Article 4

This Directive is addressed to the Member States.

Commencement   17 July 1998.

COUNCIL DIRECTIVE 98/59/EC

of 20 July 1998

on the approximation of the laws of the Member States relating to collective redundancies

THE COUNCIL OF THE EUROPEAN UNION,

Having regard to the Treaty establishing the European Community, and in particular Article 100 thereof,

Having regard to the proposal from the Commission,

Having regard to the opinion of the European Parliament,

Having regard to the opinion of the Economic and Social Committee,

(1) Whereas for reasons of clarity and rationality Council Directive 75/129/EEC of 17 February 1975 on the approximation of the laws of the Member States relating to collective redundancies should be consolidated;

(2) Whereas it is important that greater protection should be afforded to workers in the event of collective redundancies while taking into account the need for balanced economic and social development within the Community;

(3) Whereas, despite increasing convergence, differences still remain between the provisions in force in the Member States concerning the practical arrangements and procedures for such redundancies and the measures designed to alleviate the consequences of redundancy for workers;

(4) Whereas these differences can have a direct effect on the functioning of the internal market;

(5) Whereas the Council resolution of 21 January 1974 concerning a social action programme made provision for a directive on the approximation of Member States' legislation on collective redundancies;

(6) Whereas the Community Charter of the fundamental social rights of workers, adopted at the European Council meeting held in Strasbourg on 9 December 1989 by the Heads of State or Government of 11 Member States, states, inter alia, in point 7, first paragraph, first sentence, and second paragraph; in point 17, first paragraph; and in point 18, third indent:

> '7. The completion of the internal market must lead to an improvement in the living and working conditions of workers in the European Community (...).
>
> The improvement must cover, where necessary, the development of certain aspects of employment regulations such as procedures for collective redundancies and those regarding bankruptcies.
>
> (...)
>
> 17. Information, consultation and participation for workers must be developed along appropriate lines, taking account of the practices in force in the various Member States.
>
> (...)
>
> 18. Such information, consultation and participation must be implemented in due time, particularly in the following cases:
>
> (-. ...)
>
> (-...)
>
> – in cases of collective redundancy procedures;
>
> (-. ...)';

(7) Whereas this approximation must therefore be promoted while the improvement is being maintained within the meaning of Article 117 of the Treaty,

(8)   Whereas, in order to calculate the number of redundancies provided for in the definition of collective redundancies within the meaning of this Directive, other forms of termination of employment contracts on the initiative of the employer should be equated to redundancies, provided that there are at least five redundancies;

(9)   Whereas it should be stipulated that this Directive applies in principle also to collective redundancies resulting where the establishment's activities are terminated as a result of a judicial decision;

(10)   Whereas the Member States should be given the option of stipulating that workers' representatives may call on experts on grounds of the technical complexity of the matters which are likely to be the subject of the informing and consulting;

(11)   Whereas it is necessary to ensure that employers' obligations as regards information, consultation and notification apply independently of whether the decision on collective redundancies emanates from the employer or from an undertaking which controls that employer;

(12)   Whereas Member States should ensure that workers' representatives and/or workers have at their disposal administrative and/or judicial procedures in order to ensure that the obligations laid down in this Directive are fulfilled;

(13)   Whereas this Directive must not affect the obligations of the Member States concerning the deadlines for transposition of the Directives set out in Annex I, Part B,

HAS ADOPTED THIS DIRECTIVE:

SECTION I
DEFINITIONS AND SCOPE

Article   1

1   For the purposes of this Directive:

(a)   'collective redundancies' means dismissals effected by an employer for one or more reasons not related to the individual workers concerned where, according to the choice of the Member States, the number of redundancies is:

   (i)   either, over a period of 30 days:
   –   at least 10 in establishments normally employing more than 20 and less than 100 workers,
   –   at least 10% of the number of workers in establishments normally employing at least 100 but less than 300 workers,
   –   at least 30 in establishments normally employing 300 workers or more,
   (ii)   or, over a period of 90 days, at least 20, whatever the number of workers normally employed in the establishments in question;

(b)   'workers' representatives' means the workers' representatives provided for by the laws or practices of the Member States.

For the purpose of calculating the number of redundancies provided for in the first subparagraph of point (a), terminations of an employment contract which occur on the employer's initiative for one or more reasons not related to the individual workers concerned shall be assimilated to redundancies, provided that there are at least five redundancies.

2   This Directive shall not apply to:

   (a)   collective redundancies effected under contracts of employment concluded for limited periods of time or for specific tasks except where such redundancies take place prior to the date of expiry or the completion of such contracts;
   (b)   workers employed by public administrative bodies or by establishments governed by public law (or, in Member States where this concept is unknown, by equivalent bodies);
   (c)   the crews of seagoing vessels.

SECTION II
INFORMATION AND CONSULTATION

Article 2
1   Where an employer is contemplating collective redundancies, he shall begin consultations with the workers' representatives in good time with a view to reaching an agreement.

2   These consultations shall, at least, cover ways and means of avoiding collective redundancies or reducing the number of workers affected, and of mitigating the consequences by recourse to accompanying social measures aimed, inter alia, at aid for redeploying or retraining workers made redundant.

Member States may provide that the workers' representatives may call on the services of experts in accordance with national legislation and/or practice.

3   To enable workers' representatives to make constructive proposals, the employers shall in good time during the course of the consultations:
(a)   supply them with all relevant information and
(b)   in any event notify them in writing of:
  (i)   the reasons for the projected redundancies;
  (ii)   the number of categories of workers to be made redundant;
  (iii)   the number and categories of workers normally employed;
  (iv)   the period over which the projected redundancies are to be effected;
  (v)   the criteria proposed for the selection of the workers to be made redundant in so far as national legislation and/or practice confers the power therefor upon the employer,
  (vi)   the method for calculating any redundancy payments other than those arising out of national legislation and/or practice.

The employer shall forward to the competent public authority a copy of, at least, the elements of the written communication which are provided for in the first subparagraph, point (b), subpoints (i) to (v).

4   The obligations laid down in paragraphs 1, 2 and 3 shall apply irrespective of whether the decision regarding collective redundancies is being taken by the employer or by an undertaking controlling the employer.

In considering alleged breaches of the information, consultation and notification requirements laid down by this Directive, account shall not be taken of any defence on the part of the employer on the ground that the necessary information has not been provided to the employer by the undertaking which took the decision leading to collective redundancies.

SECTION III
PROCEDURE FOR COLLECTIVE REDUNDANCIES

Article 3
1   Employers shall notify the competent public authority in writing of any projected collective redundancies.

However, Member States may provide that in the case of planned collective redundancies arising from termination of the establishment's activities as a result of a judicial decision, the employer shall be obliged to notify the competent public authority in writing only if the latter so requests.

This notification shall contain all relevant information concerning the projected collective redundancies and the consultations with workers' representatives provided for in Article 2, and particularly the reasons for the redundancies, the number of workers to be made redundant, the number of workers normally employed and the period over which the redundancies are to be effected.

2   Employers shall forward to the workers' representatives a copy of the notification provided for in paragraph 1.

The workers' representatives may send any comments they may have to the competent public authority.

Article 4
1   Projected collective redundancies notified to the competent public authority shall take effect not earlier than 30 days after the notification referred to in Article 3(1) without prejudice to any provisions governing individual rights with regard to notice of dismissal.

Member States may grant the competent public authority the power to reduce the period provided for in the preceding subparagraph.

2   The period provided for in paragraph 1 shall be used by the competent public authority to seek solutions to the problems raised by the projected collective redundancies.

3   Where the initial period provided for in paragraph 1 is shorter than 60 days, Member States may grant the competent public authority the power to extend the initial period to 60 days following notification where the problems raised by the projected collective redundancies are not likely to be solved within the initial period.

Member States may grant the competent public authority wider powers of extension.

The employer must be informed of the extension and the grounds for it before expiry of the initial period provided for in paragraph 1.

4   Member States need not apply this Article to collective redundancies arising from termination of the establishment's activities where this is the result of a judicial decision.

SECTION IV
FINAL PROVISIONS

Article 5
This Directive shall not affect the right of Member States to apply or to introduce laws, regulations or administrative provisions which are more favourable to workers or to promote or to allow the application of collective agreements more favourable to workers.

Article 6
Member States shall ensure that judicial and/or administrative procedures for the enforcement of obligations under this Directive are available to the workers' representatives and/or workers.

Article 7
Member States shall forward to the Commission the text of any fundamental provisions of national law already adopted or being adopted in the area governed by this Directive.

Article 8
1   The Directives listed in Annex I, Part A, are hereby repealed without prejudice to the obligations of the Member States concerning the deadlines for transposition of the said Directive set out in Annex I, Part B.

2   References to the repealed Directives shall be construed as references to this Directive and shall be read in accordance with the correlation table in Annex II.

Article 9
This Directive shall enter into force on the 20th day following its publication in the *Official Journal of the European Communities.*

Article 10
This Directive is addressed to the Member States.

Commencement   2 September 1998.

Index

987

998